INVINCIBLE

TRUEMAN'S *Specific* Series®

NTA UGC-NET/SET

For JRF and Eligibility Test for Assistant Professor

(and Ph.D/M.Phil Entrance Exams)

Code No. : 03

PHILOSOPHY

New Syllabus

With

Previous Years' Papers

By

A.M. TRIPATHI

Authentic & Dependable

Produced and Published by
Danika Publishing Company
(Publishers of Trueman's *Specific* Series)
4352/4C, Ansari Road,
Daryaganj, New Delhi - 110002
Ph.: 011-23242482, 41501988
e-mail: danikabooks@yahoo.com

Can be had from
Invincible Publishers
2nd Floor, SAS Tower, Medicity, Sector 38,
Gurugram (Haryana)

ISBN : 9788189301217

New Edition : 2025

Price : Rs. 750/-

Data Processing :
Inhouse

Printed at :
Dhruv Printers
New Delhi.

Subject to New Delhi Jurisdiction only

PUBLISHERS' NOTE

The present work is a humble attempt to satisfy the needs of students appearing for UGC NET/SET Examinations. Syllabus and Guidelines for Paper II have been given in the book. After theory and MCQs, model papers are provided for practice. We have also incorporated questions asked in previous NET examinations. The book in the present form shall serve as a reliable evocative book for those preparing for NET/SET examinations.

Any suggestions for the improvement shall be thankfully acknowledged.

— With Best Wishes

CONTENTS

Guidelines and Syllabus

UNIT 1 Classical Indian: Epistemology and Metaphysics 1

UNIT 2 Classical Western: Ancient, Medieval, and Modern: Epistemology and Metaphysics 129

UNIT 3 Indian Ethics 233

UNIT 4 Western Ethics 255

UNIT 5 Contemporary Indian Philosophy 301

UNIT 6 Recent Western Philosophy 357

UNIT 7 Social and Political Philosophy: Indian 415

UNIT 8 Social and Political Philosophy: Western 467

UNIT 9 Logic 525

UNIT 10 Applied Philosophy 541

Multiple Choice Questions 575

Model Papers 783

Previous Years' Papers 801

UGC-NET NEW SYLLABUS

The Test will consist of two papers as given below:

Paper	Marks	Number of Questions	MCQs	Duration
I	100	50	The questions will be generic in nature, intending to assess the teaching/research aptitude of the candidate. It will primarily be designed to test reasoning ability, comprehension, divergent thinking and general awareness of the candidate.	03 hours All the questions will be compulsory.
II	200	100	This will be based on the subject selected by the candidate.	

The Test will be conducted in Computer Based Test (CBT) mode only.

The candidates who desire to appear in the test may see the detailed **Information Bulletin** for UGC-NET which will be available on the website **www.nta.ac.in** and **www.ntanet.nic.in.**

SYLLABUS

UNIT – 1: CLASSICAL INDIAN: EPISTEMOLOGY AND METAPHYSICS

- **Vedic and Upaniscadic:** *Rta* – the cosmic order, the divine and the human realms; the centrality of the institution of yajna (sacrifice), theories of creation *Atman* – Self (and not – self), *Jagrat, Svapna, Susupti* and *turiya, Brahman*.
- **Carvaka :** *Pratyaksa* as the only *pramana*, critique of *anumana* and *sabda*, Consciousness as epi-phenomenon.
- **Jainism :** Concept of reality – *sat, dravya, guna, paryaya, Jiva, ajiva, anekantavada, syadvada* and *nayavada*; theory of knowledge.
- **Buddhism :** Four Noble Truths, *Astangika Marga*, Distinction between *Brahminic* and *Sraminic* traditions. *Pratityasamutpada, ksanabhahgavada, anatmavada*. Schools of Buddhism : *Vaibhasika, Sautrnatika, Yogacara, Madhyamika* and Tibetan Buddhism.
- **Nyaya :** *Prama* and *aprama*, Theories of *pramana: pratyaksa, anumana, upamana, sabda. Hetvabhasa*. Concept of God. Debate between Buddhism and Nyaya about *Pramana-Vyavastha* and *Pramana Samplava. Anyathakhyati.*
- **Vaisesika :** Concept of *padartha* and its kinds, *Asatkaryavada*, Kinds of *Karana*: *samavayi, asamavayi,* and *nimitta karana, paramanukaranavada*.
- **Samkhya :** *Satkaryavada, prakrti* and its evolutes, arguments for the existence of *prakrti*, nature of *purucsa*, arguments for the existence and plurality of *purucsa,* relationship between *purusa* and *prakrti*, atheism.
- **Yoga :** Patanjali's Theory of *Pramana*, concept of *citta* and *citta – vrtti*, stages of *citt-bhumi*, the role of God in Yoga.
- **Purva – Mimamsa :** *Pramanyavada: Svatah-pramanyavda* and *Paratah-pramanyavada, Sruti* and its importance, classification of *sruti-vakyas, vidhi, niscedha* and *arthavada, dharma, bhavana, sabda-nityavada, Jati, saktivada;* Kumarila and Prabhakara Schools of Mimamsa and their major points of difference, *triputi – samvit, jnatata, abhava and anupalabdhi, anvitadbhidhanavada, abhihitanvayavada,* Theories of error: *Akhyati, Viparitakhyati,* atheism.
- **Vedanta**:
- **Advaita :** *Brahman,* relation between *Brahman* and *Atman*, three grades of *satta, Adhyasa, maya, Jiva, Vivartavada, Anirvachniya-khyati.*
- **Visistadvaita :** *Saguna Brahman,* refutation of *maya, aprthaksiddhi parinamavada, Jiva, bhakti and prapatti, Brahma-Parinamavada, Sat-khyati.*
- **Dvaita** : Rejection of *nirguna brahman* and *maya, bheda* and *saksi, bhakti.*
- **Dvaitavaita**: Concept of *Jnanaswaroop*, kinds of inanimate
- **Sudhadvaita**: Concept of *Avikrta-parinamavada.*

UNIT-2 : CLASSICAL WESTERN: ANCIENT, MEDIEVAL, AND MODERN : EPISTEMOLOGY AND METAPHYSICS

- **Pre-Socratic Philosophers**: Thales, Anaxagoras, Anaximenies, Ionians, Pythagoras, Parmenides, Heraclitus and Democritus
- **The Sophists and Socrates**

- **Plato and Aristotle:**
  - Plato – Theory of knowledge, knowledge and opinion, theory of Ideas, the method of dialectic, soul and God.
  - Aristotle – Classification of the sciences, the theoretical, the practical and the productive, logic as an organon, critique of Plato's theory of Ideas, theory of causation, form and matter, potentiality and actuality, soul and God.
- **Medieval Philosophy:**
  - St. Augustine: Problem of Evil.
  - St. Anselm: Ontological argument.
  - St. Thomas Aquinas: Faith and Reason, Essence and Existence, the Existence of God.
- **Modern Western Philosophy:**
  - **Descartes :** Conception of method , Criteria of truth, doubt and methodological scepticism, *cogito ergo sum*, innate ideas, Cartesian dualism: mind and matter, proofs for the existence of God, interactionism.
  - **Spinoza :** Substance, Attribute and Mode, the concept of 'God or Nature', Intellectual love of God, parallelism, pantheism, three orders of knowing.
  - **Leibnitz :** Monadology, truths of reason and fact, innateness of ideas, proofs for the existence of God, principles of non – contradiction, sufficient reason and identity of indiscernibles, the doctrine of pre -established harmony, problem of freedom.
  - **Locke :** Ideas and their classification, refutation of innate ideas, theory of substance, distinction between primary and secondary qualities, theory of knowledge, three grades of knowledge.
  - **Berkeley :** Rejection of the distinction between primary and secondary qualities, immaterialism, critique of abstract ideas, *esse est percipi*, the problem of solipcism; God and self.
  - **Hume :** Impressions and ideas, knowledge concerning relations of ideas and knowledge concerning matters of fact, induction and causality, the external world and the self, personal identity, rejection of metaphysics, scepticism, reason and the passions.
  - **Kant :** The critical philosophy, classification of judgements, possibility of synthetic a priori judgements, the Copernican revolution, forms of sensibility, categories of understanding, the metaphysical and the transcendental deduction of the categories, phenomenon and noumenon, the Ideas of Reason – soul, God and world as a whole, rejection of speculative metaphysics.
  - **Hegel :** The conception of *Geist* (spirit), the dialectical method, concepts of being, non – being and becoming, absolute idealism, Freedom.

UNIT – 3 : INDIAN ETHICS

- Concept of *Purusartha, Sreyas and Preyas*
- *Varnashrama, Dharma, Sadharana Dharma*
- *Rna and yajna*, Concept of duty
- *Karma-yoga, Sthitprajna, Svadharma, Lokasamgraha*
- Apurva and Adrsta
- Sadhya-Sadhana, Itikartavyata
- Law of *Karma*: ethical implications
- *Zta* and *Satya*
- *Yoga-ksema*
- *Astanga Yoga*
- Jainism: *Samvara-nirjara, Tri-ratna, Panch-vrata.*
- Buddhism: *Upaya-Kaushal, Brahma-vihara: matri, karuna, mudit, upeksha, bodhi-sattva*
- Carvaka's Hedonism

UNIT – 4 : WESTERN ETHICS

- Concepts of Good, right, justice, duty, obligation, cardinal virtues, *Eudaemonism*, Intuition as explained in Teleological and Deontological Theories.
- Egoism, Altruism, Universalism
- Subjectivism, Cultural Relativism, Super-naturalism.
- Ethical realism and Intuitionism,
- Kant's moral theory: Postulates of morality, Good-will, Categorical Imperative, Duty, Mean and ends, Maxims.

- Utilitarianism: principle of utility, problem of sanction and justification of morality, kinds of utilitarianism, Moral theories of Bentham, J.S. Mill, Sidgwick
- Theories of Punishment
- Ethical cognitivism and non-cognitivism: Emotivism, Prescriptivism, Descriptivism

UNIT- 5 : CONTEMPORARY INDIAN PHILOSOPHY

- **Vivekananda**: Practical Vedanta, Universal Religion, Religious Experience, Religious Rituals
- **Sri Aurobindo**: Evolution, mind and supermind, Integral Yoga
- **Iqbal**: Self, God, man and superman, Intellect and Intuition
- **Tagore**: Religion of man, ideas on education, Concept of Nationalism
- **K. C. Bhattacharyya**: *Swaraj* in ideas, Concept of Philosophy, subject as Freedom, the doctrine of *Maya*.
- **Radhakrishnan**: Intellect and intuition, the Idealist view of life, concept of Universal Religion, Hindu view of life.
- **J. Krishnamurti**: Conception of thought, Freedom from the known, analysis of self, Choiceless awareness
- **Gandhi**: Truth, Non-violence, *satyagraha*, *swaraj*, critique of modern civilization.
- **Ambedkar:** Annihilation of caste, philosophy of Hinduism, Neo-Buddhism
- **D.D. Upadhyaya**: Integral Humanism, Advaita Vedanta, Purusartha
- **Narayana Guru:** the spiritual freedom and social equality, one caste, one religion, one God.
- **Tiruvallur**: Tirukkural
- **Jyotiba Phule**: Critical understanding of Caste-system.
- **M.N.Roy**: Radical Humanism, Materialism
- **Maulana Azad**: Humanism

UNIT-6 : RECENT WESTERN PHILOSOPHY

- **Analytic and Continental Philosophy:**

Frege: Sense and Reference

Logical Positivism: Verification theory of meaning, Elimination of metaphysics, concept of Philosophy

Moore: Distinction between Sense and Reference, Refutation of Idealism, Defense of common-sense, Proof of an External World.

Russell: Logical Atomism, Definite Descriptions, Refutation of Idealism

Wittgenstein: Language and Reality, Facts and objects, names and propositions, the picture theory, critique of private language, meaning and use, forms of life, notion of philosophy, Wittgensteinian Fideism, *On Certainty*.

Gilbert Ryle: Systematically misleading expressions, category mistake, concept of mind, critique of Cartesian dualism

A. J. Ayer: The Problem of Knowledge

W.V.O. Quine: Two Dogmas of Empiricism

H.P. Grice and P.F. Strawson: In Defense of a dogma

Phenomenology and Existentialism:

Husserl: Phenomenological Method, Philosophy as a rigorous science, Intentionality, Phenomenological Reduction, Inter-subjectivity

Heidegger: The concept of Being (*Dasein*), Man as being in the world, critique of technological civilization

Kierkegaard: Subjectivity as Truth, Leap of faith

Sartre: Concept of Freedom, Bad-faith, Humanism

Morleau-Ponty: Perception, Embodied Consciousness

Pragmatism:

William James: Pragmatic Theories of Meaning and Truth, Varieties of Religious experience

John Dewey: Concept of Truth, Common-faith, education

Post-Modernism:

Nietzsche: Critique of Enlightenment, Will to Power, Genealogy of Moral

Richard Rorty: Critique of representationalism, Against Epistemological method, Edifying Philosophy

Immanuel Levinas: Ethics as a first philosophy, Philosophy of 'other'

UNIT- 7 : SOCIAL AND POLITICAL PHILOSOPHY: INDIAN

- *Mahabharata*: *Danda-niti*, foundations, *Rajdharma*, Law and Governance, Narada's Questions to King Yudhisthir

- Kautilya: Sovereignty, Seven Pillars of State-craft, State, Society, Social-life, State administration, State economy, law and justice, internal security, welfare and external affairs
- Kamandaki: Social order and State elements
- Constitutional Morality, Secularism and Fundamental Rights
- Constitutionalism, Total revolution, terrorism, *Swadeshi*, Satyagrah, Sarvodaya, Social Democracy, State Socialism, Affirmative Action, Social Justice
- Social Institutions: Family, Marriage, property, education and religion
- Colonialism

UNIT- 8 : SOCIAL AND POLITICAL PHILOSOPHY: WESTERN

- Plato: Ideal State and Justice
- Locke, Hobbes, Rousseau: Social Contract Theory
- Isaiah Berlin: Conceptions of Liberty
- Bernard Williams: Idea of Equality
- Liberalism: Rawls; Distributive justice, Nozick; Justice as Entitlement, Dworkin; Justice as equality; Amartya Sen: Global Justice, Freedom and Capability.
- Marxism: Dialectical Materialism, Alienation, Critique of Capitalism, Doctrine of Class Struggle and Classless Society.
- Communitarianism: Communitarian critique of liberal self, Universalism Vs. Particularism, Theory of Charles Taylor, MacIntyre, Michael Sandel
- Multiculturalism: Charles Taylor; Politics of recognition, Will Kymlicka; conception of Minority Rights
- Feminism: Basic Concepts: Patriarchy, misogyny, Gender, Theories of Feminism; Liberal, Socialist, radical and eco-feminism

UNIT- 9 : LOGIC

- Truth and Validity
- Denotation and Connotation
- Nature of Propositions
- Categorical Syllogism
- Laws of thought
- Classification of Propositions
- Square of Opposition
- Truth-Functions and Propositional Logic
- Quantification and Rules of Quantification
- Symbolic Logic: Use of symbols
- Decision Procedures: Truth Table, Using Truth- Tables for testing the validity of arguments
- Venn Diagram, informal and formal Fallacies
- Proving Validity, Argument and Argument-form
- Axiomatic System, Consistency, Completeness
- Differences between Deductive and Inductive Logic

UNIT- 10 : APPLIED PHILOSOPHY

- What is applied Philosophy?
- Philosophy of Technology; technology, dominance, power and social inequalities
- Democratization of Technology
- Public evaluation of science and technology
- Ethical Implication of information technology, bio-technology, non-technology
- Environmental Ethics: Nature as means or end, Aldo-Leopold; land-ethics, Arne Naess: Deep Ecology, Peter Singer; Animal Rights
- Medical-Ethics: Surrogacy, Doctor-patient relationship, abortion, euthanasia, female-infanticide
- Professional Ethics: Corporate Governance and ethical responsibility
- Media Ethics: ethical issues in Privacy, cyber space, pornography, representation and differences-marginalization
- Legal Ethics: law and morality, Legal Obligation, Authority and Validity of Law
- Philosophical Counseling: Managing everyday problems

❖❖

UNIT 1

CLASSICAL INDIAN: EPISTEMOLOGY AND METAPHYSICS

VEDIC AND UPANISADIC

Vedic and Upaniṣadic world, at first, appears with the conception of an absolute reality (God), and, then, shows the presence of dieties like Indra, Agni, Varuṇa, Mitra, Surya etc. to maintain itself in the way that all the creatures should be in harmony with each other without being mechanical.

ṚTA

The Cosmic Order

In the Vedic religion 'Ṛta' is the principle of natural order which regulates and coordinates the operation of the universe and everything within it. 'Ṛta' is properly joined order, rule and truth. In the hymns of the Vedas 'Rta' is the described as that which is ultimately responsible for the proper functioning of the natural, moral and sacrificial orders. The action of the individual in relation to those ordinances, referred to as 'Karma' - two terms which eventually eclipsed. 'Ṛta' in importance as signifying natural, religious and moral order in later Hinduism. 'Rta' is one of the most important religious conceptions of the 'RigVeda'.

'Ṛta' appears most frequently as representing abstract concepts such as "law", "Commandment", "Order", "sacrifice", "truth" and "regularity", but also occasionally or concrete objects such as the waters, the heavens or the sun as manifestations of the operation of 'Ṛta' in the physical universe, 'Ṛta' is also frequently used to reference to various Vedic deities.

While the concept of Ṛta as an abstract, universal principle generally remained resistant to the anthropomorphic tendencies of the Vedic period, it became increasingly associated with the actions of individuals deities, in particular with those of the god Varuna as the omniscient, all-encompassing sky. The connection of Varuna and Ṛta extended beyond the physical realm and into the sphere of ritual worship, with the sacrificial for itself being landed as that which "harnesses the steeds and holds the reins of Ṛta, becoming Varuna when he strives for 'Ṛta'.

Consequently, Rta finds a conspicuous place in the Mantras (Hymns). Expressions Like, 'guardians of Ṛta' (Rtasyagopa) and 'Practisers of Ṛta' (Rtayu) occur frequently in the description of the gods. This word originally meant uniformly of nature or the ordered course of things such as in indicated by the regular alter nation of day and night, while in Mantras is not only bears this significance but also the additional one of 'moral order'. The Vedic gods are accordingly to by viewed not only as the maintainers of cosmic order but also as upholders of moral law. This equal responsibility of divinity for the maintenance of cosmic as well as moral order is particularly dear in the conception of Varuna. He represents the sky and is the God of heavenly light. He is described as having fixed the laws of the physical universe which no one can violate.

The great importance given to Ṛta in the Vedas can be appreciated from the description of there laws in Rigveda 1-75-5 where it says, "ritam satyam vijnani" which would literally mean knowing of truth, which is Ṛta, is the only true knowledge. There laws are part of Vedic higher knowledge. According to these laws one is only free to do any action if he obeys and follow these commands of the God and without following them no individual can seek Moksha-the state of eternal bliss. It is also the state when one reaches the abode of God and avoid rebirth in the phenomenal world.

Vedic Metaphysicists have found that having created these laws God himself follows them sternly, lest a cosmic disorder or chaos may result in the destruction of the universe.

The Divine and the Human Realms

After the emergence of Ṛta as a cosmic order it is also supposed as the settled will of a supreme god, the law of morality and right eousness as well. Even the gods cannot transgress it. We see in the conception of Ṛta a development from the physical to the divine. Ṛta originally meant the "established route of the world, of the sun, moon and stars, morning and evening, day and night". Gradually it became the path of morality to be followed by man and the law of righteousness observed even by gods. "The dawn follows the path of Ṛta, the right path; as if she knew them before. She never oversteps the regions. The sun follows the path of Ṛta". The whole universe is founded on Ṛta and moves in it. This conception of Ṛta reminds us of words worth's invocation to duty.

What law is in the physical world, that virtue is in the moral world. The Greek conception of the moral life as a harmony or an ordered whole is suggested here. Varuṇa who was first the keeper of the physical order, becomes the custodian of the moral order, *Ṛtasya gōpa* and the punisher of sin. The prayer to the gods is in many cases for keeping us in the right path. "O Indra, lead us on the path of Ṛta, on the right path over all evils."

So soon as the conception of Ṛta was recognised there was a change in the nature of gods. The world is no more a chaos representing the blind fury of chance elements, but is the working of a harmonious purpose. This faith gives us solace and security whenever unbelief tempts us and confidence in ourselves is shattered. Whatever might happen, we feel that there is a law of righteousness in the moral world answering to the beautiful order of nature. As sure as the sun rises tomorrow virtue will triumph. Ṛta can be trusted.

Mitra is the companion of Varuṇa and is generally invoked along with him. He represents sometimes the sun and sometimes the light. He is also an all-seeing, truth-loving god. Mitra and Varuṇa and joint-keepers of the Ṛta and forgivers of sin. Gradually, Mitra comes to be associated with the morning light and Varuṇa with the night-sky. Varuṇa and Mitra are called the Ādityas, or the sons of Aditi, along with Aryaman and Bhaga.

Features of Ṛta

Yajur Veda says that we get true knowledge of these cosmic laws from seven forces of the nature, *i.e.*, the Sun, Moon, Firament, Waters, Clouds, Fire and Earth.

It has been also said that by following these laws, you remain away from misery. These laws are regarded as part of Vedic higher knowledge. The Vedic dharma is entirely based on Rta. An ideal and noble living is based on Ṛta.

The lovers of wisdom is needed for the study of Ṛta. Ṛta is also known as Vratani. Dualist like dvaita Vedantist also advises that human beings should find more and more Ṛta because these cosmic laws will guide the individuals towards of path of material wealth and Moksha.

By following Ṛta, the entire mankind on this Earth can live as friends and even as spiritual brothers and sisters in harmony and unity. Each Vedic Ṛta is regarded as complete in itself. These are for once and ever. If any Rta is different for different periods of history then, it is not regarded as Ṛta.

The ancient seers had created symbolic and innocent mythology for conveying the message of "follow Rta and assist your supreme father as the formless and ineffable Brahma and supreme mother as the divine Prākrit".

Vedas

The Vedas are considered the earliest literary record of Indo-Aryan civilization, and the most sacred books of India. They are the original scriptures of Hindu teachings, and contain spiritual knowledge encompassing all aspects of our life. Vedic literature with its philosophical maxims has stood the test of time and is the highest religious authority for all sections of Hindus in particular and for mankind in general.

"Veda" means wisdom, knowledge or vision, and it manifests the language of the gods in human speech. The laws of the Vedas regulate the social, legal, domestic and religious customs of the Hindus to the present day. All the obligatory duties of the Hindus at birth, marriage, death etc. owe their allegiance to the Vedic ritual. They draw forth the thought of successive generation of thinkers, and so contain within it the different strata of thought.

Origin of the Vedas

The Vedas are probably the earliest documents of the human mind and is indeed difficult to say when the earliest portions of the Vedas came into existence. As the ancient Hindus seldom kept any historical record of their religious, literary and political realization, it is difficult to determine the period of the Vedas with precision. Historians provide us many guesses but none of them is free from ambiguity.

It is believed that humans did not compose the revered compositions of the Vedas, which were handed down through generations by the word of mouth from time immemorial. The Vedas were mainly compiled by Vyasa Krishna Dwaipayana around the time of Lord Krishna (c. 1500 BC)

Classification of the Vedas

The Vedas are four. The Rig-Veda, the Sama Veda, the Yajur Veda and the Atharva Veda, the Rig Veda being the main. The four Vedas are collectively known as "Chathurveda, " of which the first three Vedas viz., Rig Veda, Sama Veda and Yajur Veda agree in form, language and content.

Structure of the Vedas

Each Veda consists of four parts–the Samhitas (hymns), the Brahmanas (rituals), the Aranyakas (theologies) and the Upanishads (philosophies). The collection of mantras or hymns is called the Samhita. The Brahmanas are ritualistic texts and include precepts and religious duties. Each Veda has several Brahmanas attached to it. The Upanishads form the concluding portions of the Veda and therefore called the "Vedanta" or the end of the Veda and contains the essence of Vedic teachings. The Upanishads and the Aranyakas are the concluding portions of the Brahmanas, which discuss philosophical problems. The Aryanyakas (forest texts) intend to serve as objects of meditation for ascetics who live in forests and deal with mysticism and symbolism.

The Four Vedas

The Rig Veda

The Rig Veda is a collection of inspired songs or hymns and is a main source of information on the Rig Vedic civilization. The Rig-Vedic 'samhita' or collection of mantras consists of 1,017 hymns or 'suktas', covering about 10,600 stanzas, divided into eight 'astakas' each having eight 'adhayayas' or chapters, which are sub-divided into various groups. The hymns are the work of many authors or seers called 'rishis'. There are seven primary seers identified: Atri, Kanwa, Vashistha, Vishwamitra, Jamadagni, Gotama and Bharadwaja. The rig Veda accounts in detail the social, religious, political and economic background of the Rig-Vedic civilization.

The Sama Veda

The Sama Veda is purely a liturgical collection of melodies ('saman'). The hymns in the Sama Veda, used as musical notes, were almost completely drawn from the Rig Veda and have no distinctive lessons of their own. Hence, its text is a reduced version of the Rig Veda. As Vedic Scholar David Frawley puts it, if the Rig Veda is the word, Sama Veda is the song or the meaning, if Rig Veda is the knowledge, Sama Veda is its realization, if Rig Veda is the wife, the Sama Veda is her husband.

The Yajur Veda

The Yajur Veda is also a liturgical collection and was made to meet the demands of a ceremonial religion. The Yajur Veda practically served as a guidebook for the priests who execute sacrificial acts muttering simultaneously the prose prayers and the sacrificial formulae ('yajus'). There are no less than six complete recessions of Yajur Veda – Madyandina, Kanva, Taittiriya, Kathaka, Maitrayani and Kapishthala.

The Atharva Veda

The last of the Vedas, this is completely different from the other three Vedas and is next in importance to Rig-Veda with regard to history and sociology. A different spirit pervades this Veda. Its hymns are of a more diverse character than the Rig Veda and are also simpler in language. The Atharva Veda consists of spells and charms prevalent at its time, and portrays a clearer picture of the Vedic society.

Upanishads

Upanishad means the inner or mystic teaching. The term Upanishad is derived from upa (near), ni (down) and s(h)ad (to sit), *i.e.*, sitting down near. Groups of pupils sit near the teacher to learn from him the secret doctrine. In the quietude of the forest hermitages the Upanishad thinkers pondered on the problems of deepest concerns and communicated their knowledge to fit pupils near them. If this determination is accepted, upanishad means Brahma-knowledge by which ignorance is loosened or destroyed. The treatises that deal with Brahma-knowledge are called the Upanishads and so pass for the Vedanta. There is a core of certainty which is essentially incommunicable except by a way of life. It is by a strictly personal effort that one can reach the truth.

The Upanishads more clearly set forth the prime Vedic doctrines like Self-realization, yoga and meditation, karma and reincarnation, which were hidden or kept veiled under the symbols of the older mystery religion. The more recent ones are not. The Upanishads became prevalent some centuries before the time of Krishna and Buddha.

The main figure in the Upanishads, though not present in many of them, is the sage Yajnavalkya. Most of the great teachings of later Hindu and Buddhist philosophy derive from him. Other important Upanishadic sages are Uddalaka Aruni, Shwetaketu, Shandilya, Aitareya, Pippalada, Sanat Kumara. Many earlier Vedic teachers like Manu, Brihaspati, Ayasya and Narada are also found in the Upanishads.

Chronology of the Principle Upanishads

Scholars disagree about the exact dates of the composition of the Upanishads. Different researchers have provided different dates for the Vedic and Upanashic eras.

Ranade criticizes Deussen for assuming that the oldest Upanishads were written in prose, followed by those that were written in verse and the last few again in prose.

DATES AND CHRONOLOGY OF THE PRINCIPAL UPANISHADS

Deussen (1000 or 800 - 500 BC)	Ranade (1200 - 600 BC)	Radhakrishnan (800 - 600 BC)
Ancient prose Upanishads: Brihadaranyaka, Chandogya, Taittiriya, Aitareya, Kaushitaki, Kena **Poetic Upanishads:** Kena, Katha, Isa, Svetasvatara, Mundaka **Later prose:** Prasna, Maitri, Mandukya	**Group I:** Brihadaranyaka, Chandogya **Group II:** Isa, Kena **Group III:** Aitareya, Taittiriya, Kaushitaki **Group IV:** Katha, Mundaka, Svetasvatara **Group V:** Prasna, Mandukya, Maitrayani	**Pre-Buddhist, prose:** Aitareya, Kaushitaki, Taittiriya, Chandogya, Brihadaranyaka, Kena **Transitional phase:** Kena (1-3), Brihadaranyaka (IV 8-21), Katha, Mandukya **Elements of Samkhya and Yoga:** Maitri, Svetasvatara

The Centrality of the Institution of Yajñā (Sacrifice)

Yajna, a mean to save the worldly creatures from natural hazards in vedic period, became a way to attain heavenly position in Brahmanic period.

The emphasis on sacrifice, the observance of caste and the Asrams, the eternity of the Vedas, the supremacy of the priest, all were the central theme of this age.

Prayers come to mean to muttering of Mantras or the utterance of sacred formulas. Loud petitions were thought necessary to rouse God to action. The words became artificial sounds with accult powers. Nobody could understand the mystery of it all, except the priest who claimed for himself the dignity of a god on earth. The one ambition was to become immortal like the Gods, and that status was supposed to be attained only by performing sacrifices. All are subject to the influence of sacrifices. The sacrifices please the Gods and profit men. Through them the gods become the friends of men. The sacrifices were made art a rule for gaining earthly profit and not heavenly bliss. The sacrifices of the Vedic hymns were a superfluous appendage of prayers indicative of true religion but now they occupy the central place. Every act done, every syllable uttered at the ceremony is important.

Meaning of Worship in Yajnas

Yajna also has three-fold meaning of worship of deities, unity and charity. The ritual fire is regarded as the essential element of the sacrifice. Vedic yajnas are performed by four Vedic priests, the hota, adhvaryu, the udgata and the Brahman. In the Vedas, there are four hundred Yajnas, but 21 are regarded as compulsory.

Duties and responsibilities of the Hindu life are regarded as the five great Yajnas. Brahm-Yajna is regarded as the study of scriptures. Deva-Yajna is regarded as the worship of the divinities. Pitri Yajna is regarded as the offering. Manushya-Yajna is regarded as the feeding of fellow humans. Bhuta-Yajna is regarded as the feeding of all living creatures.

Concept of Yajnas

Yajna is a ritual of offerings accompanied by chanting of vedic mantras, derived from the practice in Vedic times. It is called worship or prayer or praise or sacrifice. Yajna is an ancient ritual of offering and sublimating the havana samagri in the fire. The sublime meaning of the word 'yajna' is derived from the sanskrit verb 'yaj', which has a three-fold meaning of worship of deities or devapujana, unity or Saogati karana and charity (dana). An essential element is the ritual fire-the divine Agni-into which oblations are poured, as everything that is offered into the fire is believed to reach God.

Vedic yajnas are typically performed by four Vedic priests :

(i) **The Hota** recites invocations and litanies drawn from the Rigveda. The Verses recited by hota are of three kinds - introductony verses, verses pertaining to yajna and eulogistic verses. The hota is also supposed to contemplate on k and identify with the deity of the speech-fire.

(ii) **The Adhvaryu** is an charge of the physical details of the ritual like measuring the ground, building the altar etc. mentioned in the Yajur-veda. The adhvaryu offers three kinds of obligation those that blaze up, those that make great noise and those that sink. Adhvaryu is supposed to contemplate one and identify with the deity of the eye-sun.

(iii) **The Udgata** is the chanter of hymns set to melodies drawn from the Samveda. Those three types of hymns like hota; (chants the introductony, yajna and eulogistic verses) are identified with the three kinds of vital breath prana, Apana and Vyana in the body and the Udgatra himself contemplates on the Vital breath.

(iv) **The Brahman** is the superintendent of the entire performance and is responsible for correcting mistakes by means of supplementary verses invoking the Visvedevas. Brahman has to identify himself with the deity of the mind-moon.

Types of Yajnas

Four hundred yajnas are described in the Vedas, of which 21 are deemed compulsory. These compulsory yajnas are also called 'Nitya Karmas'. The rest of the yajna are optional and are performed for kamyakarma (particular wishes and benefits). The Aupasana Yajna, though not a part of these 21 is still compulsory.

Out of the 21 Nityakarmas, only the Agnihotra and the Aupasana are to be performed twice daily, at dawn and at dusk. The remaining are performed over the course of the year.

1. First seven yajnas are called **Pakayajnas:** They are astaka, sthalipaka, parvana, sravani, agrahayani, caitri and asviyuji. These involve consecrating cooked items.
2. Second sevens are called **Waviryajnas:** They are agniyadhana, agnihotra, Darsapurnamasa, agrayana, caturmasya, nirudha pasu bandha, Sautramani. These involving offering havis or oblations.
3. Remaining sevens are called **Somayajnas**: They are Agnistoma, Atyagnistoma, Uktya, Shodasi, vajpeya, atiratra and aptoryama. These involve the extraction utility and consumption of soma (an extract of a particular chosen tree.)

There are five Panch Maha Yajnas :

(i) Rishi yajna : honouring Rishis by the study of holy scriptures.

(ii) Deva yajna : Worship of the Celestials by pouring oblations into the sacred fire.

(iii) Pitri-yajna : of fering libations to ancestors or pitrs.

(iv) Manushya-yajna : Charitable of ferings of food to fellow humans.

(v) Bhuta-yajna : feeding animals, especially cows and birds.

Effects of Doing Yajna

Through, bond petitions, we can rouse God to do an action. The words are known as an artificial sounds and these artificial sounds have occult powers. The mystery of, it is not understood by anyone. But the priest are able to understand the mystery of it. The priest referred themselves as the dignity of a God on Earth.

There was only one ambition, which is referred as to become immortal like the Gods. By performing sacrifices, we can become immortal. Without sacrifice, the Sun would not rise. It has been also said that we can depose Indra from his throne in heaven, if we are able to perform a hundred horse-sacrifices. The sacricfies has an essential feature of pleasing the Gods and by doing this men will get the profit.

By performing sacrifices Gods become the friends of men. By performing sacrifices we can gain Earthly profits. The sacrifices has become a rule, which have to be followed. Heavenly bliss is not gained through the sacrifices. The Vedic hymns sacrifices are regarded as a superfluous method of prayers indicate true religion.

Every syllable, which is uttered at the ceremony is regarded as an essential feature of sacrifice. Every act done is also regarded as the essential feature of the sacrifice. The Brahmanas religion includes symbolic subtleties and are also lost in a soulless mechanism of idle rites. Yajna is defined as a ritual of offering, which is accompanied by chanting of Vedic mantras, according to Hinduism.

CONCEPT OF ṚNA

Duty/Obligation

Indian ethics has a special characteristic of Ashram system. Every individual by nature passes through various stages of life.

Indian thinkers correlate the stages of individual to the society. Indian thinkers prescribed duties to every stages of life. The prescribed duties contribute to the social welfare and social stability. Ashram system has four stages. Every individual passes through the stages of a Brahmacharin (a student), a Grihastha (a house holder), a Vanaprastha (retired) and a Sanyasin (a wandering monk.)

The stage of a householder is very important for the stability of the society. The individual enters in to the first unit of society *i.e.*, family, by entering Grihasth ashrama. A householder enjoys the pleasures of life. At the same time, he has many responsibilities. He has to take care of his family, the guests and other society members.

The concept of Ṛna implies obligation and responsibility. Man is a social animal. His development is possible, because many other fellow beings have, in some or other way, contributed to his progress. The individual is under obligation of many members of his society.

The individual is born with 3 Ṛnas namely Rishi Ṛna (debt of sages / teachers), Pitri Ṛna (debt of the ancestors) and Deva Rna (Divine debt)

1. Rishi Ṛna

Rishi Ṛna is also called as Guru Ṛna. The first stage in the life of an individual, *i.e.*, Brahmacharya ashrama (a student) is spent with teacher. In ancient time, the sages, wise people were guide posts of society. The wisdom of the sages was passed from one generation to another generation. The sages played important role in the development of the individual as well as in the social progress. By learning Vedas by giving fees, by showing respect by being grateful, Rishi Rna can be discharged. In Brahmacharya ashrama, an individual becomes free from Rishi Rna.

2. Pitri Ṛna

An individual owes many things including his own existence to his ancestors. It becomes responsibility of the individual to sustain the family by giving birth to next generation. By begetting children the individual becomes free from the debt of his ancestors. Thus in Grihasthashrama, an individual becomes free from Pitri Ṛna.

3. Deva Ṛna

God has created this universe. God is sustainer of this universe. Whatever we receive from nature, is due to the blessings of God. The forces of nature are beyond the control of human beings. To please these forces, men used to perform sacrifices. Performance of sacrifices was a way to show respect to deities. Forces of nature are like supernatural, mighty, powerful agents. A man in such a world is at the mercy of God. By performing sacrifices, man becomes free from the Divine debt. In Grihastha and in Vanaprastha Ashrama, an individual becomes free from Deva Ṛna.

By repaying three Rnas the individual reaches the stage of 'Annrunya' which means freedom from all Rnas. Only after reaching the stage of Annrunya, an individual can prepare himself for the highest purushartha- Moksha

The concept of Rna-traya [3 debts] is a commonly known concept. However, "Shataphath Brahman" refers to fourth debt Viz. Manushya Rna. It is obligation towards humanity. By helping other human beings an individual becomes free from debt towards humanity.

Stages of Aśramas

The Vedic Aryan's life has the four stages or āśramas, as they are called (1) Brāhmacārin or student, when he is expected to study one or more Vedas; (2) the Gṛhastha or the householder, when he has to fulfil the duties mentioned in the scriptures, social and sacrificial; (3) the Vānaprastha or the hermit, when the devotee spends his time in fasting and penance; and (4) the Saṅyāsin or the ascetic, who has no fixed abode. He is without any possessions or property and longs for union with God. The four parts of the Veda, the hymns, the Brāhmaṇas, the Āraṇyakas and the Upaniṣads answer to the four stages of the Vedic Aryan's life. Beneath the formalism of ceremonial worship there was at work a spirit of true religion and morality, from which the heart of man obtained satisfaction. It is this ethical basis which has helped the Brāhmaṇical religion with all its weaknesses to endure so long. Side by side with its insistence on the outer, there was also the emphasis on inner purity. Truth, godliness, honour to parents, kindness to animals, love of man, abstinence from theft, murder and adultery, were inculcated as the essentials of a good life.

Theories of Creation

In their search for the first ground of all changing things, Vedic thinkers, like the ancient Greeks, looked upon water, air, etc. as the ultimate elements out of which the variety of the world is composed. Water is said to develop into the world through the force of time, saṁvatsara or year, desire or kāma, intelligence or puruṣa, warmth or tapas. Sometimes water itself is derived from night or chaos, tamas, or air. In X.72 the world ground is said to be the asat or the non-existent, with which is identified Aditi, the infinite. All that exists is diti, or bounded, while the a-diti, the infinite, is non-existent. From the infinite, cosmic force arises, though the latter is sometimes said to be the source of the infinite itself. These theories, however, soon related themselves to the non-physical, and physics by alliance with religion became metaphysics.

In the pluralistic stage the several gods, Varuṇa, Indra, Agni Viśvakarman, were looked upon as the authors of the universe. The method of creation is differently conceived. Some gods are supposed to build the world as the carpenter builds a house. The question is raised as to how the tree or the wood out of which the work was built was obtained. At a later stage the answer is given that Brāhman is the tree and the wood out of which heaven and earth are made. The conception of organic growth or development is also now and then suggested. Sometimes the gods are said to create the world by the power of sacrifice. This perhaps belongs to a later stage of Vedic thought.

When we get to the monotheistic level the question arises as to whether God created the world out of his own nature without any pre-existent matter or through His power acting on eternally pre-existent matter. The former view takes us to the higher monistic conception, while the latter remains at the lower monotheistic level, and we have both views in the Vedic hymns. Hiraṇyagarbha arose in the beginning from the great water which pervaded the universe. He evolved the beautiful world from the shapeless chaos which was all that existed. But how did it happen, it is asked, that the chaos produced Hiraṇyagarbha? What is that unknown force or law of development which led to his rise? Who is the author of the primeval waters? According to Manu, Harivaṁśa and the Purāṇas, God was the author of chaos. He created it by his will, and deposited a seed in it which became the golden germ in which he himself was born as the Brāhma or the Creator God. "I am Hiranyagarbha, the Supreme Spirit Himself become manifested in the form of Hiraṇyagarbha". Thus the two eternally co-existed substances seem to be the evolution of the one ultimate substratum.

Another theory can be drawn from a later hymn called the Nāsadīya hymn, which is translated by Max Müller. We find in this hymn a representation of the most advanced theory of creation. First of all there was no existent or non-existent. The existent in its manifested aspect was not then. We cannot on that account call it the non-existent, for it is positive being from which the whole existence arrives. The first line brings out the inadequacy of our categories. The absolute reality which is at the back of the whole world cannot be characterised by us as either existent or non-existent. The one breathed breathless by its own power. Other than that there was not anything beyond.First cause of all it is older than the whole world, with the sun, moon, sky and stars. It is beyond time, beyond space, beyond age, beyond death and beyond immortality. We cannot express what it is except that it is. Such is the primal unconditioned groundwork of all being. Within that Absolute Consciousness there is first the fact of affirmation or positing of the primal "I". This corresponds to the logical law of identify, A is A, the validity of which presupposes the original self-positing. Immediately there must be also a non-ego as the correlate of the ego. The I confronts the not-I, which answers to "A is not B". The "I" will be a bare affirmation, a mere abstraction, unless there is another of which it is conscious. If there is no other, there is no ego. The ego implies non-ego as its condition. This opposition of ego and non-ego is the primary antithesis, and the development of this.implication from the Absolute is said to be by tapas. Tapas is just the "rushing forth", the spontaneous "outgrowth", the projection of being into existence, the energising impulse, the innate spiritual fervour of the Absolute. Through this tapas we get being and non-being, the I and the not-I, the active Puruṣa and the passive prakṛti, the formative principle and the chaotic matter. The rest of the evolution follows from the interaction of these two opposed principles. According to the hymn, desire constitutes the secret of the being of the world. Desire or kāma is the sign of self-consciousness, the germ of the mind, manaso retaḥ. It is the ground of all advance, the spur of progress. The self-conscious ego has desires developed in it by the presence of the non-ego. Desire is more than thought. It denotes intellectual stir, the sense of deficiency as well as active effort. It is the bond binding the existent to the non-existent. The unborn, the one, the eternal breaks forth into a self-conscious Brāhma with matter, darkness, non-being, zero, chaos opposed to it. Desire is the essential feature of this self-conscious Puruṣa. The last phrase, "ko veda?" ("who knows?") brings out the mystery of creation which has led later thinkers to call it māyā.

PURUṢA

The other of the two co-present co-eternal realities of Sāmkhya is the Puruṣa, the Principal of pure consciousness. Puruṣa is the soul, the self, the spirit, the subject, the knower. It is neither body nor senses nor brain nor mind (manas) nor ego (ahaṇkāra) nor intellect (buddhi). It is itself pure and trasncendental Consciousness. It is ultimate knower which is the foundation of all knowledge. It is beyond time and space, beyond change and activity. It is selfluminous and self-proved. It is uncaused, eternal and all pervading. It is the indubitable real, the postulate of knowledge, and all doubles and denials pre-suppose its existence. It is called nistraiguṇya, udāsīnā, akartā, kevela, madhyastha, Sāksī, drasṭa, sadāprakāshasvarūpa, and Jñāta.

The Sāmkhya believes in the plurality of the Puruṣas. The selves are all essentially alike; only numerically are they different. Their essence is consciousness.

Proofs for the Existence of Puruṣa

Sāmkhya gives the following Proofs for the existence of the Puruṣa:

1. All compound objects exist for the sake of the Puruṣa. The body, the senses, the mind and the intellect are all means to realize to end of the Puruṣa. The three guṇas, the Prakṛti, the subtle body - all are said to serve the purpose of the self. Evolution is teleological or purposive. Prakṛti evolves itself in order to serve the Puruṣa's end. This proof is teleological (*Saṅghātaparārthatvāt*).
2. All objects are composed of the three guṇas and therefore logically presuppose the existence of the Puruṣa who is the witness of these guṇas and is himself beyond them. The three guṇas imply the conception of a nistraiguṇya - that which is beyond them. This proof is logical (*Triguṇādiviparyayāt*).
3. Non-intelligent Prakṛti cannot experience its products. So there must be and intelligent principle to experience the worldly products of Prakṛti. Prakṛti is the enjoyed (*bhogyā*) and so there must be an enjoyer (*bhoktā*), *i.e.*, Puruṣa (*bhoktṛbhāvāt*).

Proofs for the plurality of Puruṣa

Sāmkhya gives the following three arguments for proving the plurality of the Prurṣas:

1. The souls have different sensory and motor organs and undergo separate births and deaths. Had there been only one Puruṣa, the birth or death of one should have meant the birth or death of all and any particular experience of pleasure, pain or indifference by one should have been equally shared by all. Hence the souls must be many.
2. If the self were one, bondange of the should have meant bondage of all and the liberation of one should have meant the liberation of all.
3. Though the emancipated souls are all like and differ only in number as they are all beyond the three guṇas, yet the bound souls relatively differ in qualities also, since in some sattva predominates, while in others rajas, and in still others tamas.

Bondage and Liberation

The earthly life is full of three kinds of pain. The first kind, called ādhyātmika, is due to intraorganic psychophysical causes and includes, all mental and bodily sufferings. The second, ādhibhautika, is due to extra - organic natural causes like men, bastes, birds, thorns etc. The third, ādhidaivika, is due to supernatural causes like the planets, elemental agencies, ghosts, demons etc. Wherever there are gyuṇas there are pains. Even the so-called pleasures lead to pain. Even the life in heaven is subject to the guṇas. The end of man is to get rid of these kinds of pain and sufferings.

Puruṣa is free and pure consciousness. It is inactive, indifferent and possesses no attributes Really speaking, it is above time and space, merit and demerit, bondage and liberation. It is only when it mistakes its reflection in the buddhi for itself and identifies itself wrongly with the internal organ the intellect, the ego and the mind, that it is said to be bound. It is the ego, and not the Puruṣa, which is bound. When the Puruṣa realizes its own pure nature it gets liberated which in fact it always was. Hence bondage is due to ignorance or non-discrimination between the self and the not-self. Liberation cannot be obtained by means of actions. Karna, good or bad or indifferent, is the function of the guṇas and leads to bondage and not to liberation.

The final and the absolute emancipation, the complete disebodied isolation automatically results after death. Sāmkhya liberation is a state of complete isolation, freedom from all pain, a return of the Puruṣa to its pure nature as consciousness.

Sāmkhya believes that bondage and liberation alike are only phenomenal. The bondage of the Puruṣa is a fiction. It is only the ego, the product of Prakṛti, which is bound. And consequently it is only the ego which is liberated. Puruṣa, in its complete isolation, is untouched by bondage and liberation. If Puruṣa were really bound, it could not have obtained liberation even after hundred births, for real bondage can be destroyed. It is Prarṭi which is bound and Prakṛti which is liberated.

ĀTMAN

Self and Non-self

The individual self is the highest thing we know and it is the nearest approach to the Absolute, though it is not itself the Absolute. In fact the individual self is a mixture of the real and the unreal, a knot of the existent and the non-existent, a coupling of the true and the false. It is a product of Ignorance. But its essence is the light of the Absolute. Its real nature is pure consciousness, self-shining and self-proved and always the same. It is called the ultimate witness or the Sākṣī and as such is one with the Absolute. The senses, the mind, the intellect, feeling and will, the internal organ are all products of Avidyā and they invariably surround the individual self and constitute its 'individuality'. But the self really is above them, being the Absolute.

'Ātman' means that which pervades all; which is the subject and which knows, experiences and illuminates the objects; and which remains immortal and always the same. The eye, the body, the mental states, the presentation continuum, the stream of consciousness—are all mere instruments and objects of the self. The self is the ground of waking, dream and sleep states and yet it transcends them all. The self is universal, immanent as well as transcendent. The whole universe lives and moves and breathes in it. It is immortal, self-luminous, self-proved and beyond doubts and denials, as the very principle which makes all doubts, denials and thoughts possible. It is the ultimate subject which can never become an object and which is to be necessarily presupposed by all knowledge.

The self, surely, cannot be identified with the body, senses or the internal organ, nor can it be regarded as a mere by product of matter. The bodily self or the waking self identifies itself with its contents—body, senses, mind, wife, son, daughter, sister, father, mother, brother, relation, friend. It stretches itself and identifies itself with the objects and feels as if they constitute its being, as if it is incomplete, nay, no more, without them. But in fact that which can be known as an object can never itself be the subject. It cannot be a mere bundle of the qualities. It cannot be the empirical self. Dreams have been selected by Prajāpati because here the objects have to be framed by the mind independently of the body or the senses. In the waking life, the objects are there apart from the outside of the mind which are only known and not created by it. Here the mind is helped by the senses which take the fleeting and scattered manifold of sense-impressions caused by external objects to the mind which arranges them into order and gives meaning and unity to them. But in the dreams, the mind has to function alone and fabricate imaginary objects for itself. It is the state, therefore, of perception without sensation. The self in the waking as well as in the dream state is ever changing and therefore cannot be the real self. The self must persist throughout the changes as their knower. The ego, limited by space and time, by birth and death, is a miserable creature.

In the deep sleep the self becomes a mere abstraction as there are no contents at all. A contentless self in the empirical life is an impossibility. The self, as subject, must oppose itself to an object. But in deep sleep there are no objects at all neither real nor imaginary. Hence in the absence of the objects the self also ceases to exist.

The self in the waking state enjoys gross objects, it has the consciousness of the external world and is called 'Vishvā'. In the dreaming state it enjoys subtle objects, it has the consciousness of the internal world and creates its own imaginary objects and is called 'Taijasa'. In the state of sound sleep there is no object, neither gross nor subtle, and hence no subject; the subject-object duality is transcended and here the self is called 'Prājña'. In sleep we have absence of pain. We have neither desires nor dreams. We have the shadow of the supreme bliss. It is called shadow because we do not enjoy positive bliss. Ignorance persists in its negative aspect of concealment in this state, although its power of projection is arrested. Ignorance and unconsciousness remain in this state and therefore a higher positive state is necessary. This is the fourth state of the self, a state of pure consciousness where, like the deep sleep, there is no subject-object duality, but unlike it there is enjoyment of positive bliss. All ignorance vanishes here. The self shines in its own light as the ultimate subject without reducing itself to a mere abstraction. This is the true self, the foundation of all existence and the presupposition of all knowledge. It cannot be fully described for descriptions are possible only in the empirical state of subject object duality. It can be realised directly and intuitively. It is called 'Turīya', the Fourth, or 'Amātra', the Measureless. It is calm, non-dual, blissful and all-consciousness where all plurality is merged. Aumkāra with its parts A-U-M, the waking, dreaming and sleeping states, is its symbol. This self is the common ground of all these states. It manifests itself in these three states and yet in its own nature it transcends them all. The Katha states that the senses are higher than the objects, the mind is higher than the senses, the intellect is higher than the mind, the subtle reason (mahat) is higher than the intellect, the Unmanifest (avyakta) is higher than the subtle reason, and the Puruṣa (ātman) is higher than the Unmanifest, and there is nothing higher than the Puruṣa which is the ultimate end, the highest reality. Objects, senses, mind, intellect, reason—all exist for the self and serve its purpose. It is the self that is immanent in them and gives them life and meaning. But these cannot be identified with the self, for it transcends them all.

Jagrat Svapna Sushupti and Turitya

There are three states viz., Jagrat (waking), Svapna (dreaming) and Sushupti (deep sleep or dreamless sleep). Avastha means a state. The Vedantic school of thought attaches very great importance to the examination and study of the three Avasthas or conditions of life called waking, dream and dreamless sleep.

Jagrat is that state during which the Jivatma enjoys the gross objects of senses such as sound, etc., through the fourteen organs such as the mind etc., having the sun and the rest as their presiding deities. Svapna is that state during which the Jivatma experiences through the fourteen organs associated with the Vasanas of the waking condition, sound and other objects, which are of the form of the Vasanas created for the time being, even in the absence of gross sound and others.

Virat under the orders of Isvara having entered this microcosmic body, and having Buddhi as his vehicle, reaches the state of Visva. Then he goes by the general names of Vijnanatma, Chidabhasa, Visva, Vyavaharika, the one presiding over the waking gross body and the one generated by Karma. Sutratma (Hiranyagarbha) under the orders of Isvara having entered the microcosmic subtle body, and having Manas (mind) as his vehicle reaches the Taijasa state. Then under the orders of Isvara, he who is coupled with Avyakta, the vehicle of Maya, having entered the microcosmic Karana body, reaches the state of Prajna. He goes then by the names of Prajna, Avicchinna, Aparamatrika and Sushupti-Abhimani (the presider over Sushupti).

In Jagrat state the seat of Jiva is the eye. The Vak is Vaikari. The enjoyment is of a gross character. The Jiva enjoys the gross sensual objects. The Sakti that operates is the Kriya Sakti.

In Svapna state the seat of the Jiva is neck (Hita Nadi). The Vak is Madhyama. The Jiva experiences subtle enjoyment through Vasanas. The Sakti that operates is the Jnana Sakti. The prevailing Guna is Sattvaguna.

The seat of the Jiva during deep sleep sate is the heart. Vak is Pasyanti. The Jiva enjoys the bliss of the Self. The Abhimani or he who identifies with this state is Prajna. The tabular form that is given below will help you to remember the different points quite easily.

Three Avasthas

In Svapna a man becomes a king, enjoys all the pleasures that can be desired for; afterwards, he is defeated by the enemy, he goes to the forest and practises austerities. He dreams that he is bitten by a snake and is dead. He opens his eyes now out of fear, knows that everything is a dream only. Just as when awake, a man does not perceive the things he saw in his dream, so also a sage perceives not the universe when he gets knowledge of Brahman.

As soon as you wake up, the dream becomes unreal. The waking state does not exist in the dream. Both dream and waking state are not present in deep sleep. Deep sleep is not present in dream and waking state. Therefore all the three states are unreal.

Jagrat Avastha, Svapna Avastha, Sushupti Avastha

The Jiva is subject to changes. He cannot be called a witness because he vanishes during deep sleep. He is unreal. He is mere reflection in the mind. When the mind is absorbed in the Mula Ajnana during deep sleep, the self-effulgent Atman is shining. He is witnessing the deep sleep state of all beings. Atman can only be a witness, because He is immutable. Srutis emphatically declare: Atman is witness, pure intelligence, one without a second, one homogeneous essence without attributes. The Jiva says: I am happy now. I am miserable. I feel sleepy. I dreamt last night. I am fully awake now. I am quite indifferent. That intelligent Purusha is Satchidananda Atman or Brahman.

Turiya is that state during which Atman is a witness to the existence of the above-mentioned three states, though it is in itself without (their) existence and non-existence and during which it is one uninterrupted Chaitanya (consciousness) alone.

You know the waking state. You know the absence of waking state in the dreaming and deep sleep states. Therefore, you are not the waking state. It does not belong to you at all. It belongs to the gross body. You are witness of the waking state, just as you are the witness of this table or chair. You are witness of the dreaming state, just as you are the witness of this table and chair. You are entirely distinct from the dreaming state. You know the deep sleep state. You also know the absence of deep sleep state in waking and dreaming state. Therefore, you are not the deep sleep state. It does not belong to you at all. It belongs to the causal body.

Analysis of these Self

The bodily self is able to identify itself with its contents body, senses and relation etc. It identifies itself with the objects. But an object can never become a subject. It is also not regarded as a mere bundle of qualities. It is not regarded as an empirical self.

It is the dream stage, the objects are framed by the mind independently. In this stage, the mind takes the help of the senses for its knowing an object. In the dream stage, mind works alone and also fabricate imaginary objects for itself. In this stage, perception without sensation exist. In both stages of waking and dreaming, the self is regarded as ever changing and thus, cannot become the real self. The self is regarded as the knower.

In the deep sleep stage, the self is regarded as a mere abstraction because there are no contents at all. A contentless self is regarded as an impossibility. The self as a subject is opposed to an object. No real nor imaginary objects are found in deep sleep stage. The self creases to exist in the absence of the objects. In the waking stage, the self enjoys gross objects.

The dreaming state enjoys subtle objects. It also has the consciousness of the internal world, it creates its own imaginary objects and also known as **Taijasa**.

In the deep sleep stage, these is no gross or subtle object and as well as subject also does not exist. The subject-object duality is transcended in the deep sleep stage. This stage is called **Prajna**. The absence of pain is found in sleep stage. No desires or dreams exist in this stage.

A higher positive state is necessary and this higher positive bliss is found in the last stage of deep sleep. No ignorance exist in this stage. Pure consciousness is felt in this stage. Here, the self is not regarded as a mere abstraction. Deep sleep stage is regarded as the true self and the foundation of all existence. This stage is realised through intuition only. It's another name is **'Turiya'**. This stage is regarded as calm and blissful.

Brahman

From the objective side this ultimate reality is called Brahman. The word is derived from the root 'Bṛh' which means to grow or to evolve. Brahman is that which spontaneously bursts forth as nature and soul. It is the ultimate cause of this universe. In the Chāndogya, it is cryptically described as 'Tajjalān'–as that (tat) from which the world arises (ja), into which it returns (la), and by which it is supported and it lives (an). In the Taittirīya, Brahman is defined as that from which all these beings are born, by which they live, and into which they are reabsorbed. The evolution of the elements is given in this order: From Brahman arises ether, from either air, from air fire, from fire water and from water earth. But the real theory of evolution is given in the doctrine of the five sheaths (koṣas) in the Taittirīya. The lowest level is that of matter (annamāyā). Matter is unconscious and dead and cannot account for life. It is purely on the physical plane. Brahman cannot rest content with matter. The purpose of matter is fulfilled only when life is evolved. The highest state of matter is therefore life. Though matter cannot account for life, yet there can be no life without matter. The inorganic matter must be transformed into organic life. Hence the second state of evolution is life (praṇamāyā). Now we are on the biological plane. The vegetable life (oṣadhayah) emerges first. But the vegetable life must lead to the animal life. The vegetable products must be transformed into living animal cells. Life pervades the universe and binds man with the rest of creation. But the destiny of life is fulfilled only when consciousness is evolved. Hence the third state of evolution is mind or perceptual Consciousness (manomāyā). Here we are on the mental or psychological plane. This state is shared by lower animals with men. Mind or consciousness remains in the lower animal life at the level of instinct and reflex action. Human beings have also got instincts and reflex and these play an important part in determining the human life. But brute instinct is mute and rebels against itself.

Hence the fourth state of evolution is self-conscious reason (vijñānamāyā). Here we are on the metaphysical plane. This state is the sole monopoly of human beings. Reason becomes self-conscious only at this state and this fact distinguishes human beings from lower animals. Arts, sciences, aesthetics, morals, poetry, philosophy, religion, all become possibly only at this state. The empirical trinity of knower, knowledge and known has been evolved.

The fifth and the highest state of evolution, therefore, is the non-dual bliss (ānandamāyā). Here we are on the mystic plane. The empirical trinity of knower, known and knowledge has been fused into a transcendental unity. Here philosophy terminates. This Brahman, the supreme Reality, transcends all, yet it underlies all as their background. The lower is not lost or annihilated; it is simply transformed in the higher. Matter is not lost in life; life is not lost in mind; mind is not lost in reason; reason is not lost in bliss. Brahman pervades them all. It is the immanent inner controller of all (antaryāmin) and the self of all (sarva-bhūtāntaratmā). As all spokes are contained in the axle and the wheel, so all beings, all gods, all worlds, all organs are contained in the Universal Self, the Brahman. This is the Brahman, the self-luminous, the immortal, the support of all the worlds, the highest and leaving nothing beyond it. Matter is its body, it is its soul; the individual souls are its body, it is their soul. It holds the self and the not-self together which are equally its own manifestations and yet in its own nature it transcends both.

Theory of Evolution

The inorganic matter is transformed into organic matter. The second state of evolution is referred as life. Life is taken on the biological lane. First comes the vegetable life. The vegetable life also leads to the animal life. The vegetable products are transformed into living animal cells. Life has a habit to pervades the universe. Life also birds man.

The third state of evolution means mind or perceptual consciousness. The lower animal life remains at the level of instinct and reflere action. Instincts and reflere actions are also found in the human beings life. It plays an important role for them. It has been also said that brute instinct rebels against itself.

Self-conscious reason is regarded as the fourth state of evolution. This state is depended on the metaphysical plane. This state is regarded as the monopoly of human beings. Arts, sciences, philosophy are possible because of this state only. The empirical trinity of knower, knowledge and known are very essential. And these are also considered for the evolution.

The non-dual is regarded as the fifth and the highest state of evolution. This state is depended on the mystic plane. The empirical trinity of knower, known and knowledge are fused into a unity, which is regarded as transcendental. No philosophy is possible in this state.

The lower is transformed in the higher. Brahman pervades matter, life, mind and reason also. Brahman is regarded as the inner controller of all. It is also regarded as self of all. All beings, all Gods, all worlds are contained in the universal self. Matter is regarded as Brahman's body. The individual souls are also regarded as its body.

Preyas & Sreyas

Sri Krishna and Arjuna are the eternal companions. This companionship is an objective representation of the relationship between Parmatman (Super Soul) and jivatman (individual soul).

All human endeavours fall under two categories: the preyas and the sreyas. Among the human acquisitions and experiences there is not a single aspect that lies outside the pale of these two.

The Katha Upanishad II (Up. I. 2.& 3.) reads: "The good (Sreyas) is one thing, the pleasant (Preyas) is another. These two having different purposes, bind a man.

Pleasures that are sense-bound and prone to mutation come under the category of preyas. The majority of mankind are seekers of preyas. But there are a rare few who aspire for the transcendental. Scriptures describe this transcendental experience as the sreyas.

All virtues, strength, self-denial, and sublimity are born of sreyas. Yoga and spiritual enlightenment are all contained in this sreyas. A life of triumph and conquest is available to all who tread the path of sreyas.

This is the core of the teaching of the Bhagavad Gita. Each of the subsequent chapters in this book is an elaboration of this theme from a particular angle.

The strong and the virile alone are fit for a life of great consequence. Achievements both here and hereafter are born of competence and manly action. Strength nurtures life. Weakness wears it away. Vitality drives away disease; debility aggravates it. It is the feeble that resort to foul play. Action born in manliness leads to freedom and its opposite to bondage. Strength and sreyas are identical. This is the teaching of the Gita.

The first chapter of the Gita reveals that Arjuna was still under the sway of preyas- things that bring prosperity, pleasure, power and glory to life. This enjoyment has a place in the cosmic plan.

Sooner or later comes a turning point in life when the individual self sees the vanity and emptiness of preyas and hankers after something permanent.

The Gita teaches one to equip oneself for the battle of life. Without self-preparation the battles of life cannot be waged successfully.

Each science has its twin aspects- theory and practice. Intellectual grasp of a subject is theory; its application is practice. Brahma vidya - Self Knowledge - is what touches and transforms life. It is intensely practical. When applied to life, it is called Yoga Shastra. The function of the yoga is to train the body and the mind.

If a wage earner applies the principles of the Gita to his life he will become a better wage earner. A farmer will equip himself better if he only translates the Gita principles into action. A merchant is bound to thrive in his business by putting these tenets to practice. Man becomes well equipped for life by taking to yoga. An efficient man is otherwise called a yogi.

All the eighteen yogas contained in the eighteen chapters of the Gita may be reduced to four -The Karma Yoga (the yoga of action), The Bhakti Yoga (the yoga of devotion), The Raja Yoga (the yoga of meditation) and The Jnana Yoga (the yoga of knowledge).

Arjun (the individual embodied soul) is inside the chariot. This body chariot is driven by the Supreme Lord. The four horses of this body chariot -Action, Emotions, Will and Reason should work in perfect harmony. Integral yoga presents a blend of the four major yogas of the Gita corresponding to the four aspects of the human personality.

This harmony can be achieved by integrating the four major yogas. KARMA Yoga unfolds one's hidden potentials while preparing his psychological being to face and confront life's day to day activities. BHAKTI Yoga cultures the feelings and brings about emotional integration in the personality. RAJA Yoga allows one to develop a strong will and a controlled mind and JNANA Yoga (the yoga of wisdom-knowledge) trains and renders the intellect sharp and subtle.

Karma

The law of karma is the counter-part in the moral world of the physical law of uniformity. It is the law of the conservation of moral energy. The vision of law and order is revealed in the Ṛta of the Ṛg-Veda. According to the principle of karma there is nothing uncertain or capricious in the moral world. We reap what we sow.

Since the sense of individual responsibility is emphasised, there are critics who think that the karma doctrine is inconsistent with social service. It is said that there is no emphasis on the bearing of one another's burdens. As a matter of fact, the Upaniṣads hold that we can be free from karma only by social service. So long as we perform selfish work we are subject to the law of bondage. When we perform disinterested work we reach freedom. "While thus you live there is no way by which karma clings to you". What binds us to the chain of birth and death is not action as such but selfish action. In an age when the individual was ever ready to shirk responsibility for what he did by throwing the burden on providence or stars or some other being than his own self, the doctine of karma urged that a man "fetters himself by himself, like a bird by its nest". What looms over us is no dark fate but our own past. We are not the victims of a driving doom. Suffering is the wages of sin. There is no question that such an idea is a great incentive to good conduct.

Man is not a mere product of nature. He is mightier than his karma. If the law is all, then there is no real freedom possible. Man's life is not the working of merely machanical relations. There are different levels—the mechanical the vital the sentient the intellectual and the spiritual—these currents cross and recross and inter-penetrate each other. The law of karma, which rules the lower nature of man, has nothing to do with the spiritual in him. The infinite in man helps him to transcend the limitations of the finite. The essence of spirit is freedom. By its exercise man can check and control his natural impulses. That is why his life is something more than a succession of mechanically determined states.

Karma has a cosmic as well as a psychological aspect. Every deed must produce its natural effect in the world; at the same time it leaves an impression on or forms a tendency in the mind of man. It is this tendency or saṁskāra or vāsanā that inclines us to repeat the deed we have once done. So all deeds have their fruits in the world and effects on the mind. So far as the former are concerned, we cannot escape them, however, much we may try. But in regard to mental tendencies we can control them. Our future conduct holds all possibilities. By self-discipline we can strengthen the good impulses and weaken the bad ones.

The principle of karma is not inconsistent with the reality of the absolute Brahman. The moral law of karma is the expression of the nature of the absolute. Anthropomorphically we can say a divine power controls the process. Ṛta is the law in the Vedas. Varuṇa is the lord of Ṛta. Karma refers to the unchanging action of the gods. It is an expression of the nature of reality.

There is no doctrine that is so valuable in life and conduct as the karma theory. Whatever happens to us in this life we have to submit in meek resignation, for it is the result of our past doings. Yet the future is in our power, and we can work with hope and confidence. Karma inspires hope for the future and resignation to the past.

Meaning and Definition

Karma is the sum total of the works good, bad and mixed-which an individual perform during his life. It is the collective totality of man's actions. It is these actions that determine his future existence. Etymologically the word Karma is derived from the root Kr, to do, which also generates a multitude of other cognate words that are inextricably related to Karma-Kartha (doer), Karthavya [duty], Karana [cause), Karana [instrument) and so on. When explaining the philosophy of Karma, David Frawely observes, 'as you sow, so shall you reap'.

According to Sankaracharya, Karma is only a means to purify the mind and acquire jñāna. He also holds that mokṣa can be obtained by knowledge combined with the renunciation of Karma. Vivekananda defines Karma very broadly to refer to any kind of action, mental or physical.

Annie Besant's opinion is that Karma is natural law in the full sense of the term; it is universal causation, the law of cause and effect. Karma is universal interrelation and is seen in any universe as the law of causation in consequence of the successive appearance of phenomena in the becoming or coming forth, of the universe.

Karma in Indian Scriptures

The doctrine of Karma has existed in all philosophical literatures of India, viz.; the Vedas, epics and Purāṇās. The various schools of Indian philosophy have discussed this doctrine in detail. So Karma has an important role in Indian systems of thought.

Karma in Vedic Literature

The concept of Karma, also found in primitive Indian beliefs, may be ultimately derived from Pre-Aryan, probably Austric sources. It was first expounded in the Śathapatha Brahmaṇa and now forms one of the basic constituents of the Hindu philosophical system. The Samhithās and Brāhmaṇas use the word Karman, which is the same as Karma. In the Samhithās and Brāhmaṇas Karman meant 'any religious act or rite' (as sacrifice, oblation etc.). Yuvaraj Krishnan says in his work 'The Doctrine of Karma' that the word Karman occurs about forty times in the Ṛg veda and means only work or deed, especially sacrificial acts. In the Brāhmaṇas, the word Karman is used to mean meritorious sacrificial work or Yajña Karma-whereas the term used in the Samhithās for sacrificial works or yajñas is istapūrta. The Vedic ritual of istapūrta which in the Brāhmaṇas is called Yajña Karma, provided the roots from which the classical doctrine of Karma grew. According to Karma, one would, after death, enter the kingdom of light, bliss and delight or a world of darkness, dejection and sorrow.

The Ṛg Veda described the theory of rita or truth. Rita is the controller and preserver of the world; Varuna is the Lord of the rita and he brings the pāpis into the world of darkness and the Satkarmīs in to Swarga or Heaven.

Karma in Schools of Philosophy

Karma is an important principle in all Indian darśanās which are categorized as Āstika and Nāstika. It is only carvaka darśana which is included in the Nāstika category that does not give importance to Karma.

The Nāstika darśanas such as Bauddha and Jaina can be seen vividly describing the concept of Karma. Even though the Cārvākadarśana recognises only perception as the means of knowledge a description of the karmas for attaining pleasures on earth can be seen in it.

According to the doctrine of Buddhism the power that controls the universe is karma, literally action; consisting of kuśala and akuśala or merit and demerit. In Buddhism Karma is one of the five categories of causation, known collectively as niyamadhammas, the first being kamma and other four being utu, bija, citta and dhamma. Utu means physical inorganic order. Eg: seasons and weather. Bija means physical organic order. Eg: heredity and seed. Kammaniyama is the order of act and result, Eg: desirable and undesirable acts produced corresponding good and bad results. Dhamma niyama is the order of the norms.

It can be seen that Jaina darśana is also Karma oriented. It believes that Karman is a form of matter and atomic in its nature. In the Jaina doctrine Karma is classified into eight fundamental types such as-

(a) Jñānavaraṇīya, comprehension- obscuring Karma.
(b) Darśanāvaraṇīya, those which acts as an obstruction to right faith.
(c) Mohanīya, delluding Karma.
(d) Vedanīya, feeling producing Karma.
(e) Āyuhkarman, age determining Karma.
(f) Nama Karman, physique making Karma.
(g) Gotra Karman, status determining Karma.
(h) Antaraya, power obscuring Karma.

According to Jaina school the worldly existence is dependent on these eight types of Karma. It believes in the life that is based on Karma. A detailed description of five Mahāvratās- *Ahimsa, Satyam, Āsteyam, Brahmacaryam* and *Apahgraham* can be seen in Jainism. In Jaina thought Karma is a material entity, it is subtle; when a person acts there is inflow of Karmic matter into the soul. The Nyāya vaisesikas contributed the idea of adrṣta in the development of the doctrine of Karma.

The Nyāya vaisesikas also used the word Karma in a special sense that is motion; they used the term dharma and adharma in its place. Adrṣta is a blending of dharma and adharma. Therefore it functions as the cause of joys and sorrows. Also adrṣta is the cause of evaluation of the atoms. It is because of this that the Nyāya-Vaiśeṣikās tried to see Karma as the action between birth and death. Adrṣta is an instrument like prakṛti. But adrṣta itself is Karmavipāka and Karmaphala. Nyāyavaiśeṣika explains that there is an agent that helps adrṣta to reach the wholeness and it sees the God as this agent. According to Nyāya Vaiśeṣika this is how the creation is made possible. Thus Nyaya Vaisesika becomes a theory and praxis of Karma darśana. Pūrvamīmāmsa of Jaimini categorises Karma as Nitya, Naimittika, Kamya and Niṣiddha. It tells that the fruit of Karma is apūrva.

It can be seen that Uttaramīmāsa or the Vedanta darśana also describes karma. Brahmajijñāsa is the subject of study of Vedanta and karma is necessary to gain access to Brahmajijñāsa. According to Vedanta darśana, Brahmavidyādhikāri (one who deserves to know *Brahmavidya)* is one who observes *Sādhanacatuṣtaya;* and *Sādhanacatuṣtaya* is nothing but karma. The concepts of karma and *punarjanma* can be seen constantly described in the foundational scriptures of Vedanta, *i.e.,* the Brahmasūtra, the Upaniṣads and the Bhagavadgītā. According to Sankara, desire (kāma) is the cause of Karma and he said that liberation is eternal, whereas Karma is short-lived or liable to destruction.

Description of Karma in the Purāṇās

The doctrine of Karma and rebirth can be seen in the Purāṇās which are based on Pancalakṣanās and narrates their theory through stories. The important Purāṇās which describe the Karma theory are *Bhāgavata, Matsya, Garuda,* etc. *Matsya Purāṇa* says that human race, in its multiplicity, is born as the result of the deeds of virtue they do. It has been described by Sankaracharya that it is a difficult thing to be born as a human being and for the devotional poet Pūntānam the human life is a blessing that one gets after several lives of hardship. It is because of the same reason that Karma is the cause of all bonds and bondages. In Vayupurāṇa Karma is described as the root cause of the actions between all beings. Here the word 'beings' includes not only the dynamic but also the static things in the world. The Vayupurāṇa and the Matsyapurāṇa describe the rebirth, the concepts of the other world and reincarnation. The Vayupurāṇa tells that even the people who reign the heaven may be degraded to human life as the result of their Karma. Brahmavaivartapurāṇa establishes Karma as the cause of the origin and termination of life. Moreover Purāṇās consider Karma as the reason of Cāturvarṇya, it may be for directing the society to virtuous deeds (satkarma) that the Purāṇās considered the theory of rebirth as a part of Karma. Besides, the Karma theory that is described in different Paranas looks a like. It can be seven that in the other world the concept of caste (varna) etc. the puranas put forward a similar concept. The possible different may be in the story or the mode of description.

- **Karmacakra.** The fivefold Karmacakra of the Supreme Deity consists of five kinds of merciful works towards the fellow souls called Panchakriyas. They are Sṛṣti, Sthiti, Samhāra, Dhīrabhava and Anugraham
- **Sṛṣti.** Evolving bodies for the soul to live and evolving senses for their use, enjoyment, punishment and purification.
- **Sthiti.** Maintain duty for the welfare of the souls.
- **Samhāra.** Destroying in due time whatever had been evolved for the welfare of the souls.
- **Dhīrabhava.** Dhīrabhavas keep veiled in darkness the things of joy and sorrow which have to be experienced by the soul, as a consequence of its works in previous lives, until the proper time comes for experiencing them face to face.
- **Anugraham.** Granting of blessing or the fruition of cherished wishes according to one's desires. These are known as karmacakra of the Supreme Lord according to Hinduism.

Karma as an Action

All actions are Karma. The consequences of an action are really not a separate thing. It is a part of the action and cannot be divided from it. Breathing, thinking, talking, seeing, hearing etc, are karmas.

Karma as an Effect

All karmas have their own effect. If there is a cause, there will be an effect. Birth is a cause for death, which is an effect.

Karma and Purification of Mind

Karma is a means to the end till there is purification of mind. Still the embodied soul (a human being) cannot absolutely renounce all karma as long as the mortal coil is not shuffled off.

Karma as the Laws and Duties

Sometimes Karma evolves laws and duties. Vijñāneswara, the commentator of Yajñāvalkya smrti, classifies the moral duties into six they are :

1. Varṇa Dharma
2. Āśrama Dharma
3. Varṇāśarma Dharma
4. Guṇa Dharma
5. Nimitta Dharma
6. Sādhāraṇa Dharma.

These Dharmas are also duties or Karma. There are four varṇās namely Brāḥmaṇa, Kṣatriya, vaiśya and sūdra. Visṇupurāṇā describes the following duties of Brāḥmaṇās viz. donation, sacrifice, study, offering, oblation to forefathers, preserving fire for daily scarifies, presiding over ceremonies etc.

The duties of kṣatriyās are the protection of the nation, protection of the life and property of all three varnas, study of the Vedas, teaching, non acceptance, donation etc.

The duties of vaiśya are the cultivation of land, protection of animals, trade, study of the vedas , donation etc.

The duties of śūdrās are, service of the three varṇās, sacrifice without mantra etc. These varṇadharmas are duties or the laws of karma.

Desire and Karma

Man is threefold in his nature. He consists of iccha (desire), Jñāna (knowledge) and kriya (willing). These three fashion his Karma. He knows objects. He feels joy and sorrow. He will do this or not do that. Behind the action, there are desires and thought. A desire for an object arises in the mind. Desire produces karma, karma produces fruits, and man desires this fruits. So desire is the part of karma.

Karma and Rebirth

The doctrine of karma and rebirth is certainly an original contribution of India to the philosophical thought of the world. The law of karma is the application of the law of cause and effect in the mortal world. The theory of rebirth is the necessary counterpart of the law of karma and immortality of the soul.

Guṇa and karma

The scriptures are classifiy Guṇa into three categories : Sātvika, Rājasa and Tāmasa. Guṇa means quality. So the karma generates in accordance with Guṇa. Manu classifies the actions into three with reference to the effect they produce as satva (spiritual and religious acts), rajasa (good worldly acts) and Tamasa (evil acts). The three states of existence are determined by the quality of a person's karmas. Sātvika karmas lead to the birth as a Deva, rājasa karma lead to the birth as a human being, tamasa karma lead to the birth as a beast.

Three Kinds of Karma

Generally Kārma is divided into three king:

(a) Sañchita karma, (b) Āgami karma, (c) Kriyamāṇa karma or prārabdha karma

The Sañchita karma is the vast store of accumulated deeds done in the past, the fruits of which have not yet been reaped. The Āgami karma is the action that will be performed by the individual in the future. The prārabdha karma is the action which has begun to fructify, the fruit of which is being reaped in this life. The prārabdha is a part of the sañchita karma since this also is action done in the past. But the difference between the two is that, where as the saṇchita karma is not yet operative, the prārabdha has already begun to yield fruit. The fruit of all karmas must be reaped by the individual himself. The character and circumstances of his life being determine by his prārabdha karma. The prārabdha karma cannot be avoided any way. The enjoyment of pleasure and pain as a result of prārabdha karma comes into operation in three ways .They are-

1. Anicha prārabdha (enjoyed involuntarily)
2. Pareccha prārabdha (enjoyed through other's will)
3. Sveccha prārabdha (enjoyed through ones own will)

Anicha prārabdha is that enjoyment of pleasure or pain which comes to us accidentally and of its own accord without any volition on our part.

Enjoyment and sufferings which we get through others are classified under parecha prārabdha . Taking pains and bearing hardship in cross-cutting a righteous business, deriving profit from the incurring loss or losing the profit once gained constitute instance of svecha prārabdha .

Four Kinds of Karma or Karmacatuṣṭaya

Karma can be classified into four according to its characteristics, as

(i) **Nitya karma.** Nitya karma is obligatory acts such as sleeping, walking, eating etc. that is, daily chores required for maintaining one's body.

(ii) **Naimittika Karma.** Naimittakarma is a special occational acts, such as; vratas, upavāsās and performance of some rites on important days.

(iii) **Kāmya Karma.** It is the desire- impelled actions performed for wordly gains, like putrakāmesti, jyotiṣtoma etc.

(iv) **Niṣiddha Karma.** Niṣiddha karma is prohibited acts by śāstrās and society that run counter to the established norms. Immoral and ethical acts like stealing, killing, incest etc.

Sadananda the author of Vedantasāra describes six types of karma such as Nitya, Naimittika, Kāmya, Niṣiddha, Upāsana and Prayaschita. Niṣiddhakarma are things forbidden such as the killing of a Brahmin. They are what lead to things undesired such as hell. Upāsana is devotion which consists of mental operations whose object is Braḥman with qualities. Prāyascitta is penances such as the cāndrāyana. They are what cause merely the removal of sin.

Sakāma and Niṣkama Karma

There are two types of karma in Hindu philosophy; Sakāma karma and Niṣkama karma:

Sakāma Karma

Sakāma as the opposite of Niṣkama karma. Some actions are done with a view to gaining or obtaining some results, that is Sakāma karma. Sakāma karma binds a person with worldly affairs. Niṣkama karma is the source of freedom from the same.

Niṣkama Karma

Desireless or motiveless action, done without any wish of result or fruit of that action is called Niṣkama karma.

Thus the Karma theory exists in the Indian mind as a fragmented entity and it can be seen that the Bhagavadgita internaliscs all thcse concepts and rationally evaluates Karma.

Buddhist Karma is Mind Specific

The perceptions of Hinduism and Buddhism about 'karma' are quite similar in their content but the way it is explained is some what different. In Buddhism the law of kamma is the moral law of causation - good actions give good results and vice versa. It is the quality of an act which determines its consequences. But what determines the karmic quality of a deed? In Hinduism it is the correct performance of a person's "duty", especially his caste duties that counts. Early Buddhism, which recognised no caste distinctions, evaluates the karmic quality of an act in terms of moral and ethical criteria. In particular it is the mental factors which accompany the commission of deed that determines its consequences or "fruits" (vipa-ka). The Buddha emphasised that it is the mental factors involved, rather than the deeds themselves, that determine future consequences. Thus the same deed committed with different mental factors will have different consequences.

The theory of kamma presupposes that individuals have "free will". Everything that happens to an individual is not the fruit of some past kamma. In fact the experiences that involve an individual may be of three kinds: some are the result of past action, some are deliberately committed free acts; and the remainder could be due to chance factors operating in the environment. The doctrine of kamma is not a theory of predestination of any kind. One common misunderstanding is not to distinguish between the action and its results - between kamma and vipa-ka. It must also be mentioned that the fruiting of an act may be postponed, and that it is possible to reach enlightenment – the goal of the Buddha's path - before all the previous kammas have yielded their results.

Bhagavadgeetha Prescribes Nishkama Karma to End the Cycle of Rebirths

According to Hinduism 'Karma' refers to a person's deeds. These may be either good or bad. The karma of a person is, hence, responsible for the chain of cause and effects. This philosophy is explained by Lord Krishna in Bhagavad Gita. Moreover it is the 'karma' that determines the rebirth or reincarnation. Hinduism states that rebirth results from a person's desire to enjoy the worldly pleasures. So the immortal soul goes through the process of leaving one body and entering the other. However, after many births the person is tired and it is then that he seeks salvation. If Karma is responsible of cycle of birth - death - rebirth, then how to break this endless cycle of material existence and how to reach the absolute bliss and divinity ?

The Bhagavad Gita or the Lord's Song is one of the world's great literary works. Along with bhakti yoga as a means of liberation, the Gita espouses the doctrine of nishkamya karma or pure action untainted by hankering after the fruits resulting from that action. Gita says " Do the job assigned to you in this birth by destiny and never think of its result.

Bhagavad-Gita is one of the greatest contributions of India to the world, it is considered as eye-opener. Many scholars and religious guru had studied on Bhagavad-Gita. Gita has always been obliging people for years, of all class. It provides "all that is needed to raise the consciousness of man to the highest possible level". The Bhagavad-Gita can be detailed as strong ammunition for transformation of an individual from dejection, despondency to edifice of wisdom, visionary perspective and self-transcendence.

What makes the doctrine of nishkamya karma all the more remarkable is the fact that it was divined intuitively by the ancient sages of India and which, in turn, led to a powerful method of modulating aberrant or addictive behaviour at a purely cognitive level. That moved a modern sage like Aldous Huxley to exclaim: "The Gita is one of the clearest and most comprehensive summaries of the perennial philosophy ever to have been done. Hence its enduring value, not only for Indians, but also for all mankind".

The holy Gita is a universal scripture applicable to people of all class. It is deep in thought. This divine book open new ways for living peaceful and calm life it rescues from utter dejection, sorrow, hopelessness and offers techniques of perfect understanding of grief, clarity, renewed strength and achievement. In other words it can intend to be panacea for life diseases.

Rebirth

Rebirth or Reincarnation is a doctrine that rests on the belief that after the death of the physical body, there is some element left of each person that then goes on to survive bodily death. This element is independent of a person's physical being, and after death goes on to be reborn into another physical body.

Lord Krishna says in the **Bhagvad Gita** (Chapter 15, Verse 8), "Just as the air carries over the smell of one flower into another, the spirit, while leaving a body, carries over the mind and knowledge into another. Buddhism and Jainism too have agreed with this "carry over" concept.

Reincarnation plays a major role in Hinduism, a religion from the East. Within the Hindu religion are some sacred writings known as the Upanishads. The Upanishads state that even if the soul does enter a hell or heaven after death, this will be a temporary arrangement only, because the soul will then return to earth.

Reincarnation is not only a Hindu faith but also a science in India since thousand of years. Many saints such as Aadi Shankara, Shiridi Saibaba, etc are believed to have taken out their Souls from their bodies and entered again back into the the same bodies after completing certain assignments.

That the theory of reincarnation is not a mere theory, but an actual fact is being now established beyond reasonable doubt. Many instances have now come to light where individuals were able to recollect their past lives through a process of regression or by other means.

Vedanta maintains primacy of thought over grosser matter - mind over body. It is the mind with all its desires, to be more exact, mind with all its modifications as desires, reincarnates in (or as) a suitable body. Thought is subtle matter that assumes grosser visible form. The tendencies, desires, and thoughts choose suitable environment, parenthood, and circumstances to express or manifest themselves as 'bodies'. The teachings of Buddhism also offer means of escape from the sufferings of life and the endless reincarnations caused by human desires to an indescribable state of no desires known as Nirvana.)

Hatred (or a baser thought), for instance, may manifest in many individuals, but typically one may quote the name of some representative as an 'embodiment' of such a thought. Here the thought of many people, so to say, has reincarnated in its strongest form. Similarly, base or pure thoughts determine birth of a smuggler (greed), a murderer (jealousy and revenge); or a Buddha or a Christ (compassion and love).

These desires, tendencies, and thoughts compel the individual to get engaged in particular actions - Karma - even against his wishes. De facto he is the personification of those desires; he and the desires are not two separate entities. The desires may make a person a saint or a robber, selfish or selfless, happy or miserable. Lord Buddha said that desires are the cause for all miseries in this world.

When we accept the mind as subtle matter or energy, like light and radiation, we can understand that the mind as 'subatomic particle and wave' phenomenon would exist even after death of an individual.

And after death we will not disappear in 'nothing'. The mental tendencies would continue to live even after the body is cremated or buried. We continue to exist as thought-waves even after death. "We all existed eternally as thought and will go on existing as thought", says Swami Vivekananda.

Even though a thought, a desire, or a tendency remains suppressed for many years, it will not get destroyed, and sooner or later it will find its expression in some body form. Depending upon the nature of desire, the objectified form could be a sub-human species or a human being. It may take the form of a virus or a saint. This objectified form will work out (carry out) that desire and thus the 'law of karma' would be enacted.

In such perplexing predicaments, the solution may be:

(1) Not to have any desires, thoughts, or modifying tendencies of the mind, or one can make conscious attempt to minimize the same (practice of Yoga), or

(2) To have only pure thoughts so that one may get the human body every time and thereby a chance to liberate oneself from this 'cycle' (by leading good moral life and associating with holy persons, etc.),

To find out a method of 'undoing this Karma', **Swami Vivekananda** says:

"We learn that, in the first place, we have been existing eternally; in the second place that we are the makers of our own lives. There is no such thing as fate, which is not made by us. Our lives are the result of our previous actions, our Karma.

Reincarnation is evolutionary process characterised by resolution and dissolution of matter till 'the desire to become many' is once again overcome. The process is hastened by conscious spiritual practice (sadhana).

The spiritual aspirant (sadhaka) may have only one desire – that of realizing his Chosen Ideal - at the exclusion of all other desires. His mind, so to say, temporarily reincarnates as his Chosen Ideal. Later, still further, the aspirant may transcend the limitation of this form also to become Free forever.

Person not engaged in spiritual sadhana (non-concentrated mind) through many thousands of years of painful experiences ("blows" as Swami Vivekananda says) reaches the same stage where freedom from all worldly desires is sought. This is the beginning of renunciation. The mind of such a person now merges in spiritual practice.

Before everything there exists Reality as Absolute Consciousness. The Will to become many is the beginning of manifest universe. This concept of 'One consciousness desiring to become many' may also be taken as the beginning of Maya. But as we are discussing relative truths of this changing world, which we have taken for granted to be real, we have to elaborate the hypothetical rationality of reincarnation and related topics of Indian belief system.

The structural arrangement of "matter combined with energy", for instance our brain-mind complex, determines particular manifestation of consciousness. The structure is determined by the quality and nature of desires one has, or by the impressions of the desires one had in the past. However one need not panic if one finds oneself born with worldly tendencies with little hope to escape from the 'law of karma' and reincarnation.

Dr. Radhakrishnan defended the Hindu theory of karma and the ethics of Vedanta. In his lectures Radhakrishnan answered the many Christian critics of Hinduism by formulating his interpretation of the essence of Hinduism. Hinduism is a way of life rather than a dogmatic creed. Its foundation is spiritual experience.

In the Hindu theory of Karma, punya is merit that accumulates as a result of good deeds, acts or thoughts and that carries over to later in life or to a person's next birth. Similarly, Paap is demerit that follows the same law.

Jeevaatama (Individual Soul) and Paramaatma (Universal Soul) are divine and eternal in their existence and so also their relation. Every kind of birth has its won advantages and disadvantages in achieving God. We must ultimately accept the fact that we take birth in either higher or lower caste in order to experience the fruits of our own karmas. So, it hardly matters, whether an individual takes birth as a brahmin or a sudra. Low caste people also became saints and achieved God.

Buddha Taught His Followers the Truth of Rebirth

Rebirth is a reality although one may not be aware of it. The existence of past lives has been confirmed by those who have developed their minds through meditation. Meditators who has attained powers of concentration have been able to recall their previous lives in great detail. The Buddha and His prominent disciples in many countries and at different times have been able to prove the existence of past lives. The Buddha, on the night of His Enlightenment, developed the ability to see His past lives. He also saw beings dying in one state of existence and being reborn in another, according to their actions. Thus it was from personal experience that the Buddha taught His followers the truth of rebirth.

Rebirth in the Six Realms

There are six realms in which one may be reborn after death. They are the realms of gods, the demigods, human beings, animals, hungry ghosts and the hells. These are just general categories and within each, there exist many sub-categories. The six realms of existence include three relatively happy states, and three relatively miserable states. The realms of the gods, the demigods and human beings are considered more happiness and less suffering. The realms of animals, hungry ghosts and the hells are considered relatively miserable because living beings there suffer more from fear, hunger, thirst, heat ,cold and pain.

In general, wholesome actions like good conduct, charity and mental development, are the cause of rebirth in the happy realms of gods, demigods and human beings. On the other hand, unwholesome actions like immoral conduct, miserliness and cruelty cause rebirth in the unhappy realms of animals, hungry ghosts and the hells.

Of all the six realms, the realm of human beings is considered the most desirable. In the realm of human beings, the conditions for attaining Nirvana are better. In general, in the unhappy realms, the suffering of living beings is so intense and their ignorance so great that they are unable to recognise the Truth and follow the path to attain freedom. Alternatively, living beings in the realms of the gods and demigods experience so much happiness and have so many distractions that they do no think of rebirth until is too late. Then they may be reborn in one of the lower realms of suffering. In the realm of human beings, however, people experience both happiness and suffering, and are intelligent enough to recognise the Truth and follow the path to attain freedom from the cycle of birth and death. Therefore, one is indeed fortunate to be born as a human being, and should remember that the principal cause of birth in this realm is Good Conduct.

Saṃsāra

'Saṃsāra', literally means, "continuous flow", that is the repeating cycle of birth, life, death and rebirth (reincarnation) in Indian philosophy.

According to the view of Indian religions our current life is one of many-stretching back before birth into past existences and reaching forward beyond death into future incarnations. During the course of each life the quality of the actions or karma performed determine the future destiny of each person. The Buddha taught that there is no beginning or end to this cycle. The goal of Indian religions is to escape this process, the achievement of which is called Moksha. In popular use, 'Saṃsāra' may refer to the world in the sense of the various worldly activities which occupy ordinary human beings, the various sufferings thereof ; or the unsettled and agitated mind through which reality is perceived.

Saṃsāra means, "to flow on", to perpentually wander, to pass through states of existence. The historical origins of a concept of a cycle of repeated reincarnation are obscure but the idea appears frequently in the religions and philosophical texts. All discuss the transmigration of beings from one life to another. The concept of 'Saṃsāra' is closely associated with the belief that one continues to be born and reborn in various realms in the form of a human, animal or other being (depending on karma). Jainism maintains that one who performs extremely evil karma can also be reborn as a plant or even as a rock. Similar tendencies can be found in puranas, in Manusmiriti. Nonethelss most philosphics traditions of Hinduism and Buddhism maintain that plant and even more obviously rocks cannot be included in Saṃsāra since they lack the possibility of experience (bhoga) and hence of karma.

'Saṃsāra' is a form of the general web, in which the soul finding itself, strives to find release (Moksha) from the bonds of its own past deeds (karma). Buddhism, which does not assume the existence of a permanent soul, accepts a semi permanent personality core that goes through the process of Saṃsāra.

The range of Saṃsāra stretches from insects to the generative God Brahma. The rank of one's birth in the hierarchy of life depends on the quality of the previous life. A variety of explanations of the workings of the karmic process within Saṃsāra have been proposed. According to several, the soul after death goes to heaven or hell until it has consumed most of its good or bad karma, then it returns to a new works, the remainder of its karma having determined the circumstances of its next life.

Saṃsāra Realms of Existence

Saṃsāra is also referred as the process of cycling through one rebirth after another within the six realms of existence.

(a) gods (b) demi-gods (c) humans
(d) animals (e) hungry ghosts (e) hell

By following the human realm, we can practice the dharma, and is also able to get liberation from the Saṃsāra.

Mokṣa

Mokṣa, the fourth pumshartha, needs clarification. As stated already, it is said to stand for the spiritual principle and is also said to be a state of bliss. It is supposed to mark the consummation of the process of our moral development and is therefore the ultimate goal of human life.

The common word 'moksha' comes from the Sanskrit root MUC- with the help of the formative -S. It means 'to set free, release, deliver, draw out of. Given this etymology, we may define moksha as the state of being liberated as well as the process of becoming free.

Some of the analogous words used to mean moksha are mukti, Nirvana, Turiya, Kaivalya, Apavarga, Nihsreyasa etc. These are not completely identical terms. However, we stick to the term moksha primarily because in the description of purusharthas it alone occurs in classical as well as modem usage, and secondarily because it is used in a generic sense to denote all that is common to its variety of usages.

The word moksha does not occur in any of the Vedas though the base (root) MUC- is part of the vocabulary of the first Veda where it means 'to release, to let go'. But it occurs in the Brahmanas and is frequent in classical language.

The term is used in Hindu Scriptures to denote both the experience of partial liberation on the earth and the state of total liberation in the divine life.

The Origin of the Concept

(1) **Fear of death.** How did we humans come to have the idea of moksha is an intriguing question, to begin with. Two hypotheses have been formulated. One is that the fear of death might have given rise to the concept of moksha. The other is that the unjust state of affairs might have formed the background for the concept of moksha.

In Ancient India, to take the last of these sources as an example, we find the vedic man tackling the problem of death and looking forward to a blessed life in heaven. What is the nature of this blessed life, if we ask, is clear enough. It was conceived to be the fulfillment of our needs and aspirations.

(2) **Injustice and Pessimism.** According to the second hypothesis, the concept of moksha might have originated depending on how the humans tackled the problem of injustice and pessimism. When we look at time or times what strikes us most is how absent justice seem to be. How the innocent still suffer, how the wicked prosper still and get very little jail sentences if any, and how little seems to have changed since Job (in the Bible) lamented this unjust state of affairs. Most religions seem to tackle this evident pessimism in either of the following two ways: Either they appeal to a dualism between this life and the next. Or, they put most of the divine action in the past. According to the second alternative, the golden age is over, we are now in kaliyuga (the age of moral degeneration).

The Development of the Concept

How the concept of moksha developed in course of time is our next concern.

(1) **Rta.** As we have said, the ideal aimed at, especially, in the Rgveda and the Brahmanas, was length of days on earth and life in the world of heaven in companionship with the gods. Also, it will be of help for us to recall here the idea of Rta we mentioned while dealing with the concept of dharma. The vedic man understood Rta as the cause of integration both personal and social and therefore as the cause of order in the universe.

Man's hope, insight and outlook. His hope of lasting life and his insight into the cosmic order are rendered all the more rich by his positive outlook on life and on all that life could give.

(2) **In the Upanishads.** But when we pass from the Vedas to the Upanishads we find a definite change of view. Why and how did this change occur? Though this question is worth examining, it does not serve our present purpose. Therefore, we only say what that change was. The change of view was from the objective to the subjective, "from brooding on the wonder of the outside world to the meditation on the significance of the self."

How are unity and Brahman and Moksha related? During his inward journey, the Upanishadic man's perception of reality got transformed. All multiplicity gets dissolved in the unity of Brahman. The dissolution of one's ego in the great ocean of being called Brahman became the final goal. And it is this goal that is sought after and experienced as moksha. In other words, it is by becoming part of the ultimate unity of Brahman through knowledge that we attain the state of moksha.

Though the Upanishadic man lived in a world of rich multiplicity he began to ask the penetrating question: "What is that which being known, everything else becomes known?." This search resulted in the perception of unity, a unity that became sacred and holy, divine and normative. This explains why it is identified with Brahman. This concept is not a concept like truth, goodness, etc. It is not even a concept; rather it the limit of a concept. It is this experience of the unity of Brahman that is expressed in the Mahavakyas likc 'tat tvam asi'.

As a result of this shift of interest, intuitive knowledge became the main coocem. 'Aham Brahmasmi', 'I am Brahman' is this special kind of knowledge. This also tells us what the upanishadic conception of moksha is. Moksha consists in the removal of 'all fetters' which is avidyais and in the consequent awakening of the spirit to the true self which is non-different from brahman, the Absolute. So basically the upanishads propose a way of jnana (gnosis) which helps us attain moksha, and consider all other values as relative to it.

(3) According to the Mahabharata also jñāna seems to be the only way to attain emancipation (moksha); knowledge alone is capable of cleansing us of all our sins.

(4) **The Gita concept of Moksha.** Before we begin the discussion of the problems of moksha in the various schools, let us look at the concept presented by one of the texts regarded as sacred – the Bhagavad Gita. While Buddha proposed an eight fold path, the Bhagavad Gita (c. 400 B.C.E.) shows us a three fold path which consists of Jnana (the vision of reality), Bhakti (total surrender to the Lord), and karma (action for the transformation of the world).

We are ruled either by ahamkara (egoism) or by atmabodha (self-awareness). Ahamkara is caused by kama which is the cause of sin and the arch enemy of man. This being the case, Gita understands moksha as freedom from kama. When freed from kama, moksha becomes atmabodha. That is, we begin to see our self in the divine self and to rejoice in it.

How do we explain this world-affirming attitude of the Gita? One explanation is that it is a reaction to the world-negating attitude of the samkhya system. According to samkhya, moksha would mean the emancipation of the spirit from the grips of matter (prakriti).

(5) Without elaborating on the **Gita** stand, let us now look at the various schools meaning styles of thought.

(i) **In Advaita.** One of the best articulations of the Upanishadic concept of moksha is to be found in the Vedanta, one of the orthodox schools. Even here we limit ourselves to the advaita Vedanta of Sankara.

It is important to remember that, according to this school of thought, the identity of the self is not something to be newly anained; rather, it is something that is already there which has only to be realized in our experience. Therefore moksha does not mean any actual change in the nature of the self, but it means a change in standpoint. In other words, moksha is not merely knowing brahman, rather, it is being brahman. This being brahman is moksha in its positive sense.

In its negative sense, moksha means moksha from bondage. As said above, this bondage is destroyed only by destroying avidya because of which we are bound. And this moksha from bondage is to be attained through knowledge; no other path there is. For, knowledge, unlike action, at once removes all avidya and consequently all bondage. Once this knowledge dawns it dawns for ever.

What are the liberated souls supposed to do, it may be asked. They are said to enjoy the four-fold bliss: They are: (a) Salokhya (residence in the same place with God); (b) Samipya (Nearness to God); (c) Sampya (having the external form like that of God); and (d) Sayujya (entering into the body of God and partially sharing his bliss).

(ii) **In Buddhism.** The second example of the concept of moksha is taken from Buddhism, one of the unorthodox systems. This is not the occasion for us to go into questions such as: What is the basis for classifying Buddhism as 'unorthodox' and why is it that buddhism could not strike permanent roots in Hindu India, etc. We only present the Buddhist understanding of moksha. 'sarvam dukha,' discovered Buddha. Suffering is the basic fact of life. Desire (trshna) is what causes this suffering. For, it gives birth to attachment (upadana), greed (kama), anger (krodha), delusion (moha), lust (mada), aggressivity (matsarya) and so on. This is the way desire ties down human life to the cyclic process of birth and death (samsara).

Thus finally we reach nirvana, the word for moksha in Buddhism. The meaning of nirvana is a matter of dispute and is connected with 'anatmavada'. Without getting involved in this dispute, we may take the usual understanding of nirvana as meaning 'extinction of the self.

The Ideal State of Knowledge?

What is the true nature of Moksha? As we have seen, Moksha literally means freedom. This freedom is either freedom from (suffering, birth, etc.) or freedom to. Therefore the concept of moksha is dual in nature, though in the usual descriptions of moksha, the freedom to is not emphasized as much as the freedom from is emphasized.

Also, depending on the variety of schools of thought, there are several theories regarding the nature of moksha. Accordingly, Moksha is described as the positive state of absolute bliss, the state of absolute absence of pain, the state of neither pleasure nor pain, communion with God or the company of God, the realization of the true nature of the self, an experience obtainable even in our embodied state, obtainable only after our physical death, etc. Right now, we may point out one common factor that emerges from these descriptions: Moksha is an ontological state. If so, it is a descriptive concept and not a normative one (evaluative) like justice. The implications of such an understanding of moksha we shall take up later.

One of the impressions that we get from the foregoing account is that moksha represents an ideal state of knowledge. This is also the position that many of the authors like Karl H. Poner have taken. At the same time there are authors like Daya krishna who have argued that moksha does not represent an ideal state of knowledge. Therefore we cannot but examine the question of whether rnoksha really represent an ideal state of knowledge. What follows is a point that Prof. Daya Krishna has made.

In nirvana, according to the Buddhists, the flame is extinguished and what remains can hardly be regarded either as knowledge or its fulfilment in the usual sense of these words. Jainism, of course, has the notion of sawajna, the all-knowing person, in the state of liberation. This is the only view that supports Poner's position that moksha represents an ideal state of cognitive attainment. But one swallow does not a summer make.

The Question of IMMO

1. The Problem

We have not considered all the questions we section. We have only taken a cursive look at the concept of moksha. Some of the problems the concept of moksha gives rise to and remains to be discussed are: (a) What is the nature of the human soul? Is it logically possible for the human soul (consciousness) to continue to exist in the absence of a body? (b) How to explain man's belief in immortality? (c) Can we characterize Indian philosophy as 'spiritual'? (d) What has Indian philosophy to do with moksha? Are they integral to each other?

2. The Distinction between Soul and Body

If we die, shall we cease to live? The widespread belief in the immortality of soul and therefore the belief in moksha are problematic for the philosopher. Can the soul, consciousness, continue to exist in the absence of a body? Is it logically possible?

In the Rig Veda we find the idea of the soul separate from the body. This separate soul can travel around. The problem of immortality presupposes individuality which is denied in Indian Philosophy. All attempts to show that it is logically possible have failed miserably. For, even if we are authorized to distinguish between soul and body, we have no reason to say that one of them (soul) does exist independently.

3. Does moksha Exist?

If the immortality of soul is not beyond doubt, the existence of moksha cannot logically be proved either. Where does the strength of the case for immortality and moksha lie then? Does it lie in ethical considerations? Can we say that immortality and therefore moksha is an ethical postulate without which our moral experience becomes unintelligible?

Moksha, an Ethical Postulate? In so far as there is no logical necessity for an after life, the only way out, in order to explain man's belief in immortality, is to postulate it. Many thinkers have done it, e.g. Kant and Plato, on two grounds. One, we do not see that happiness is always achieved proportionate to moral behavior in this life; two, we can understand the possibility of achieving complete moral perfection only in an infinite series of closer and closer approximations.

4. An Ethical postulate.

(a) There is some truth in this in the sense that we feel it to be inconsistent that our soul which is steadily striving towards the ideal, should be annihilated in the midst of its progress and the elements of value in it lost.

Here we are not saying that mere duration is the essence of immortality. In fact, it cannot be because time is a form for the phenomenal world, and does not apply to the real world at all. Most of the ethical arguments that people advance look like an inference from what ought to be the case to what is the case. But this is as invalid as its counter-argument from what is to what ought to be the case.

The problem of moksha arises because what is ontologically required to be the case is not existentially such - a situation which is radically different from others where what 'ought to be' does not happen to be so as a 'matter of fact'.

(b) **Moksha - a Matter of Faith.** If there is no logical necessity for a person to have a completely disembodied existence, then might he live in another body? Let us take the case of a widow. Wanting to be united with her dead husband, she imagines him as very much as he was before he died. But would he have the body of a man of a certain age, say the age at which he died and remain for ever at this age?

5. The Indian View

But, we the Indians look at it differently. What about our individuality if unity is the ultimate reality? The Upanishadic insight is that the ultimate reality is non-dual. If so, individuality would not be the ultimate truth about ourselves. We have to shed our individuality and all that belongs to it so that the ocean of reality can overwhelm us. It is like a drop of water merging in the sea and losing its dropness and becoming the ocean itself. This way of thinking seems to be one of the meanings of the famous saying of Jesus of Nazareth: "Whoever seeks to gain his life will lose it; but whoever loses his life will preserve it?" Moksha is a concept that can be said to belong to practical philosophy (named by Kant as 'practical Reason? Moksha, therefore, designates an ideal to be actualized. Moksha is an ideal unlike some other ideals pertaining to things outside the self. Moksha is supposed to be the realization of the true nature of the self itself even if it be the case, as in Buddhism, that there is no true nature either of the self or of anything else.

What do we mean by freedom (moksha)? When Indians speak of moksha as freedom what they mean is not the freedom involved in moral action, but the freedom of enjoying a state of being or the freedom of just being. Moksha, therefore, is more talked about in the context of knowledge of what truth is. Here knowledge is the knowledge of the self; and the knowledge of the self here coincides with its own reality.

If so, moksha does not belong to the domain of moral action, dharma. Moksha, in other words, is not dharma even if the latter may prepare the way for it.

Difference between Indian thought and Western Thought

The concept of Mukti also distinguishes Indian thought from Western thought. Western philosophy is quite unaware of a philosophy of the self. All Indian systems, both orthodox and heterodox recognises the idea of the self as the first requisite for any philosophical adventure. This is the spiritual basis of our ethical life.

The three pursuits of human life, namely **Dharma, Artha** and **Kama** are referred as simply subservient to Moksha. It is regarded as the highest pursuit. The genesis of the idea of Moksha is traced in "the endeavour of man to find out ways and means by which we could become happy or at least be free from misery.

No school of Indian philosophy, not even the charvakdency the concept of self. There is absolute unanimity regarding the central conception of moksha which is regarded as the highest goal of life. The different *schools* differ with regard to the nature of Mukti.

Moksha, Nirvana and Kaivalya

The words moksha, nirvana and kaivalya are sometimes used synonymously, because they all refer to the state that liberates a person from all causes of sorrow and suffering. However, in modern era literature, these concepts have different premises in different religions. Nirvana starts with the premise that there is no Self, moksha on the other hand, starts with the premise that everything is the Self; there is no consciousness in the state of nirvana, but everything is one unified consciousness in the state of moksha.

Hinduism

Ancient literature of different schools of Hinduism sometimes use different phrases for moksha. For example, Keval jnana orkaivalya ("state of Absolute"), *Apavarga, Nihsreyasa, Paramapada, Brahmabhava, Brahmajnana and Brahmi sthiti.* Modern literature additionally uses the Buddhist term nirvana interchangeably with moksha of Hinduism.

The six major orthodox schools of Hinduism have had a historic debate, and disagree over whether moksha can be achieved in this life, or only after this life. Many of the 108 Upanishads discuss amongst other things moksha. For example, freedom and deliverance from birth-rebirth, argues Maitrayana Upanishad, comes neither from the Vedanta school's doctrine (the knowledge of one's own Self as the Supreme Soul) nor from the Samkhya school's doctrine (distinction of the Purusha from what one is not), but from Vedic studies, observance of the *Svadharma* (personal duties), sticking to *Asramas* (stages of life).

The six major orthodox schools of Hindu philosophy offer the following views on moksha, each for their own reasons: the Nyaya, Vaisesika and Mimamsa schools of Hinduism consider moksha as possible only after death. Samkhya and Yoga schools consider moksha as possible in this life. Beyond these six orthodox schools, the heterodox schools of Hindu tradition, such as Carvaka, deny there is a soul or after life moksha.

Samkhya, Yoga and Moksa

Both Samkhya and Yoga systems of religious thought are mokshasastras, suggests Knut Jacobsen, they are systems of salvific liberation and release. Samkhya is a system of interpretation, primarily a theory about the world. The eight limbs of yoga can be interpreted as a way to liberation (moksha).

In Samkhya literature, liberation is commonly referred to as kaivalya. In this school, kaivalya means the realization of purusa, the principle of consciousness, as independent from mind and body, as different from prakrti. Like many schools of Hinduism, in Samkhya and Yoga schools, the emphasis is on the attainment of knowledge, vidya or jñana, as necessary for salvific liberation, moksha. It seeks to end ordinary reflexive awareness (cittavrtti nirodhah) with deeper, purer and holistic awareness. Yoga, during the pursuit of moksha, encourages practice (abhyasa) with detachment, which over time leads to deep concentration (samadhi). Detachment means withdrawal from outer world and calming of mind, while practice means the application of effort over time.

Three of four paths of spirituality in Hinduism. Each path suggests a different way to moksha.

Yoga, or marga, in Hinduism is widely classified into four spiritual practices. The first marga is Jñana Yoga, the way of knowledge. The third marga is Karma Yoga, the way of works. The fourth marga is Raja Yoga, the way of contemplation and meditation.

Vedanta and Moksa

The three main sub-schools in Vedanta school of Hinduism - Advaita Vedanta, Vishistadvaita and Dvaita - each have their own views about moksha.

The Vedantic school of Hinduism suggests the first step towards moksa begins with mumuksutva, that is desire of liberation. Shankara cautions that the guru and historic knowledge may be distorted, so traditions and historical assumptions must be questioned by the individual seeking moksha. Those who are on their path to moksha (samnyasin), suggests Klaus Klostermaier, are quintessentially free individuals, without craving for anything in the worldly life, thus are neither dominated by, nor dominating anyone else.

Vivekachudamani, which literally means "Crown Jewel of Discriminatory Reasoning", is a book devoted to moksa in Vedanta philosophy. It explains what behaviors and pursuits lead to moksha, as well what actions and assumptions hinder moksha. The four essential conditions, according to Vivekachudamani, before one can commence on the path of moksha include (1) vivekah (discrimination, critical reasoning) between everlasting principles and fleeting world; (2) viragah (indifference, lack of craving) for material rewards; (3) samah (calmness of mind), and (4) damah (self restraint, temperance).

The Advaita tradition considers moksha achievable by removing avidya (ignorance). Advaita holds there is no being/non-being distinction between Atman, Brahman, and Paramatman. The knowledge of Brahman leads to moksha, where Brahman is described as that which is the origin and end of all things, the universal principle behind and at source of everything that exists, consciousness that pervades everything and everyone.

The Dvaita (dualism) traditions define moksha as the loving, eternal union with God (Vishnu) and considered the highest perfection of existence. Dvaita schools suggest every soul encounters liberation differently. By immersing oneself in the love of God, one's karmas slough off, one's illusions decay, and truth is lived. Both the worshiped and worshiper gradually lose their illusory sense of separation and only one beyond all names remains.

The Vishistadvaita tradition, led by Ramanuja, defines avidya and moksha differently from the Advaita tradition. Such ideas, claims Ramanuja, decay to materialism, hedonism and self worship. Individuals forget Ishvara(God). Mukti, to Vishistadvaita school, is release from such avidya, towards the intuition and eternal union with God (Vishnu).

Moksa in this Life

Among the Samkhya, Yoga and Vedanta schools of Hinduism, liberation and freedom reached within one's life is referred to as jivanmukti, and the individual who has experienced this state is called jivanmukta (self-realized person). Dozens of Upanishads, including those from middle Upanishadic period, mention or describe the state of liberation, jivanmukti. For example, according to Naradaparivrajaka Upanishad, the liberated individual shows attributes such as:

- he is not bothered by disrespect and endures cruel words, treats others with respect regardless of how others treat him;
- when confronted by an angry person he does not return anger, instead replies with soft and kind words;
- even if tortured, he speaks and trusts the truth;
- he does not crave for blessings or expect praise from others;
- he never injures or harms any life or being (ahimsa), he is intent in the welfare of all beings;
- he is as comfortable being alone as in the presence of others;
- he is as comfortable with a bowl, at the foot of a tree in tattered robe without help, as when he is in a mithuna (union of mendicants), grama (village) and nagara (city);
- he doesn't care about or wear sikha (tuft of hair on the back of head for religious reasons), nor the holy thread across his body. To him, knowledge is sikha, knowledge is the holy thread, knowledge alone is supreme.
- for him there is no invocation nor dismissal of deities, no mantra nor non-mantra, no prostrations nor worship of gods, goddess or ancestors, nothing other than knowledge of Self;
- he is humble, high spirited, of clear and steady mind, straightforward, compassionate, patient, indifferent, courageous, speaks firmly and with sweet words.

Moksa in Hinduism

Balinese Hinduism incorporates moksha as one of five tattwas. The other four are: brahman (the one supreme god head, not to be confused with Brahmin), atma (soul or spirit), karma (actions and reciprocity, causality), samsara (principle of rebirth, reincarnation). Moksha, in Balinese Hindu belief, is the possibility of unity with the divine; it is sometimes referred to as nirwana.

Brahmanirvana in the Bhagavad Gita

Brahmanirvana (nirvana in Brahman) is the state of release or liberation; the union with the divine ground of existence (Brahman) and the experience of blissful ego-lessness. The term brahmanirvana is used 5 times in the Bhagavad Gita

(i) verse 2.72: sthitvasyamantakale'pi brahmanirvanamrcchati.

(ii) 5.24 (and following 2 verses): sa yogi brahmanirvanam brahmabhuto'dhigacchati.

(iii) 6.15: santim nirvanvaparamam matsamsthamadhigacchati.

According to Mahatma Gandhi, the Hindu and Buddhist understanding of nirvana are different: The nirvana of the Buddhists is shunyata, emptiness, but the nirvana of the Gita means peace and that is why it is described as brahma-nirvana.

Buddhism

In Buddhism the concept of liberation is Nirvana. It is referred to as "the highest happiness" and is the goal of theTheravada-Buddhist path, while in the Mahayana it is seen as a secondary effect of becoming a fully enlightened Buddha (Samyaksambuddha).

Nirvana literally means "blown out", as in a candle. It is most commonly associated with Buddhism. In Indian religions, the attainment of nirvana is moksha, liberation from the repeating cycle of birth, life and death (reincarnation).

Nirvana is a composed of three phones ni and va and na:

- ni (nir, nis, nih): out, away from, without, a term that is used to negate
- va: blowing as in blowing of the wind and also as smelling
- na: nor, never, do not, did not, should not

Vana is forest in/of the forest/forests; composed of flowers and other items of the forest, but vana has both phonesvan and va. Van has both an auspicious and ominous aspect:

- van: like, love; wish, desire; gain, procure; conquer, win; possess; prepare;
- van:tree; forest; thicket, cluster, group; quantity; wood
- va: blow (of wind); emit (an odor), be wafted or diffused
- va: weave

Abhidharma

The abhidharma-mahavibhasa-sastra, a sarvastivadin commentary, 3rd century BCE and later, describes the possible etymological interpretations of the word nirvana.

Vana	+Nir	Nature of nirvana
The path of rebirth	Leaving off	Being away from the path of rebirth permanently avoiding all paths of transmigration.
Forest	Without	To be in a state which has got rid of, for ever, of the dense forest of the three fires of lust, malice and delusion
Weaving	Being free	Freedom from the knot of the vexations of karmas and in which the texture of both birth and death is not to be woven
Stench or stink	Without	Being without and free from all stench of karmas

Jainism

Moksha (Sanskrit: मोक्ष, leration) or Moksha (Jain Prakrit) means liberation, salvation or soul. It is a blissful state of existence of a soul, completely free from the karmic bondage, free from samsara, the cycle of birth and death. A liberated soul is said to have attained its true and pristine nature of infinite bliss, infinite knowledge and infinite perception. In fact, it is the only objective that a person should have; other objectives are contrary to the true nature of soul. With right view, knowledge and efforts all souls can attain this state. That is why, Jainism is also known as moksamarga or the "path to liberation".

Bhavyata

However, from the point of view of potentiality of moksa, Jain texts bifurcates the souls in two categories-bhavya and abhavya. Bhavya souls are those souls who have faith in moksa and hence will make some efforts to achieve liberation. On the other hand abhavya souls are those souls who cannot attain liberation as they do not have faith in moksa and hence never make any efforts to attain it.

Samyaktva

According to Jainism, Samyak darsana (Rational Perception), Samyak Gyaan(Rational Knowledge) and Samyak Caritra (Rational Conduct) collectively also known as Ratnatraya or the three Jewels of Jainism constitute true Dharma.

Samyak Caritra or rational conduct is the natural conduct of a (soul) living being. It consists in following austerities, engaging in right activities and observance of vows, carefulness and controls. Once a soul secures samyaktva, moksa is assured within a few lifetimes.

Nirvana

Nirvana means final release from the karmic bondage. When an enlightened human, such as, an Arhat or a Tirthankaraextinguishes his remaining aghatiya karmas and thus ends his worldly existence, it is called nirvana. Technically, the death of an Arhat is called nirvana of Arhat, as he has ended his wordly existence and attained liberation.

The terms moksa and nirvana are often used interchangeably in the Jain texts. Uttaradhyana Sutra provides an account of Gautama explaining the meaning of nirvana to Kesi a disciple of Parsva.

Sikhism

The Sikh concept of mukti (moksha) is essentially that of jivan mukti, the one attainable in one's lifetime itself. Sikhism rejects the idea of considering renunciation as the vesture of a jivan mukta. Contrast with it, for example, the Jain view according to which "The liberated persons… have to lead a mendicant's life, for, otherwise, they cannot keep themselves free from karma" (G. N. Joshi: Atman and Moksha. Gujarat University, Ahmedabad, 1965, p. 260).

Jivan mukti itself brings one to the brink of videha mukti (incorporeal emancipation) which is freedom not from the present body, but from any corporeal state hereafter. It spells for the mukta a final cessation of the weals and woes of the cycle of birth-death-birth (janam-maran).

The Sikh mukti is positive concept in two important ways. First it stands for the realization of the ultimate Reality, a real enlightenment (jnana). The mukta is not just free from this or that, he is the master of sense and self, fearless (nirbhai) and devoid of rancor (nirvair), upright yet humble, treating all creatures as if they were he himself, wanting nothing, clinging to nothing.

In Sikhism, one rises from the life of do's and don'ts to that of perfection - a state of "at-one-ment" with the All-self. Secondly, the mukta is not just a friend for all, he even strives for their freedom as well. He no longer lives for himself, he lives for others.

Moksha and the Supreme Being

Hinduism is a theistic religion believing in supreme beings known as gods and demi-gods. Different sects worship different gods or demi-gods; however, **Brahman** is widely believed to be the Supreme Being in the religion. When one achieves moksha, he or she ultimately achieves unity with the Supreme Being.

There are two fundamental schools of thought in Hinduism about the nature of one's unity with the supreme being. The first is known as **Advaita Vedanta**, or non-dualism. This is the belief that one's spiritual self is not separate from the Supreme Being. Giving everything over to the service of the Supreme Being is the path to moksha. One way to visualize this is to think about the human soul as a single blade of grass in a field, with the field being the soul of the Supreme Being. The blade of grass is part of the composition of the field, just as the human soul is part of the soul of the Supreme Being.

The other school of thought is Samkhya. **Samkhya** assumes a dualistic nature between the human soul and the Supreme Being's soul. Each has its own identity and, thus, remains separate, even in moksha. In Samkhya, the unity with the Supreme Being in moksha is not from the joining of souls, but in the existence of two distinct souls on a plane higher than earthly existence. Think of a green frog in a field; it may look like it is part of the field, but it remains very separate.

CĀRVĀKA

There are two main streams in Indian philosophy. First of these streams flows on the basis of vedic authority, while the survival of second one depends on rejecting the authority of Vedas. Nyāya-Vaiśeṣika, Sāṁkhya-Yoga, Mimāṁsa and Vedanta are known as Vedic schools while Cārvāka, Jainism and Buddhism, which are going to be discussed in this chapter, reject the authority of Veda, and are known as Non-Vedic schools of Indian Philosophy.

The School of Materialism in India seems to be very old. References are found to it in the epics and in the early Buddhist Literature. Bṛahaspati, a heretical teacher is regarded as the traditional founder of Chārvāka school. His Sūtra, which we have no reason to doubt, has unfortunately perished. Sometimes this Bṛhaspati is equated with the teacher of the gods who propagated materialism among the Asuras so that they might be ruined. Chārvāka, after whose name this school is so called, is said to be the chief disciple of Bṛhaspati. According to still another view, the word 'Chārvāka' is not a proper name, but a common name given to a materalist, and it signifies a person who believes in 'eat, drink and be merry' (the root 'charv' means to eat), or a person who eats up his own words, or who eats up all moral and ethical considerations, or a person who is 'sweet tongued' (chāruvāk) and therefore whose doctrine is superficially attractive. References to them are also found in mahābharata also. In majjima Nikāya, we find references to a reference to Ajitakeshakambalin, a materialist, probably so called because he must be having a blanket of hair with him, who believed only in perception and in four elements. Shāntarakṣita also refers to him as Kambalāshvatara (the man with a blanket and a mule).

No original work of this school is extant with the single exception of a much later work, Tattvopaplavasimha of Jayarāshi Bhaṭṭa, published by the Oriental Institute of Baroda in 1940. It is therefore very difficult to have a correct idea of it. Out chief sources of information are given in the works of the other schools. The weak points in this school are exaggerated and the strong points are omitted. So we get only a faint caricature and not a true picture. It is indeed very difficult to believe that materialism which is allowed the status of an independent school of Indian Philosophy should really be so crude and degenerate as it is painted. But in the absence of the original works, we have to remain satisfied with these meagre and one-sided accounts.

Sources

In the second Act of the allegorical play called Prabodhachandrodaya, Kṛṣṇapati Mishra sums up the teaching of Materialism thus: 'Lokāyata is the only Shāstra; perception is the only authority; earth, water, fire and ait are the only elements; enjoyment is the only end of human existence; mind is only a product of matter. There is no other world: death means liberation.' Some of the important Sūtras of Bṛhaspati which are quoted in the various philosophical writings may be gleaned as follows:

1. Earth, water fire and air are the elements. (Pṛtuivaptejovāyuriti tattvāni)
2. Bodies, senses and objects are the results of the different combination of elements. (tatsamudāye sharīrendriyaviṣayasamjña.)
3. Consciousness arises from matter like the intoxicating quality of wine arising from fermented yeast (Kiṇvādibhyo madashaktivad vijñanam)
4. The soul is nothing but the conscious body (Chaitanyavishiṣṭaḥ Puruṣaḥ)
5. Enjoyment is the only end of human life. (Kāma evaikaḥ puruṣārthaḥ)
6. Death alone is liberation. (maraṇmevāpavargaḥ)

The Sarva-darshana-saṅgraha gives the following summary of the Chārvāka position:

'There is not heaven, no final liberation, nor any soul in another world; nor do the action of the four castes, orders etc., produce any real effect. If a beast slain in the Jyotiṣṭoma rite will itself go to heaven, why then does not the sacrificer forthwith offer his own father?... If beings in heaven are gratified by out offering the Shrāddha here, then why not give the food down below to those who are standing on the house top? While life remains let a man live happily, let him feed on ghee (clarified butter) even though he runs in debt; when once the body becomes ashes, how can it ever return here?...(All the ceremonies are) a means of livelihood (for) Brāhmaṇas. The three authors of the Vedas were buffoons, knaves and demons'.

Pratyaksa Perception
(The only source of knowledge)

Knowledge of reality or valid cognition is called pramā and the source of such knowledge is called pramāṇa. The Cārvāka holds that perception is the only pramāṇa or dependable source of knowledge. For establishing this position he criticizes the possibility of other sources of knowledge like inference and testimony which are regarded as valid pramāṇas by many philosophers.

Critique of Anumāna

If inference is to be regarded as a pramāṇa, it must yield knowledge about which we can have no doubt and which must be true to reality. But inference cannot fulfil these conditions, because when we infer, for example, the existence of fire in a mountain from the perception of smoke in it, we take a leap in the dark, from the perceived smoke to the unperceived fire. A logician, like the Naiyāyika, will perhaps point out that such a leap is justified by the previous knowledge of the invariable concomitance between smoke and fire and that the inference stated more fully would be : All cases of smoke are cases of fire, this (mountain) is a case of smoke, therefore, this is a case of fire.

The Cārvāka points out that this contention would be acceptable only if the major premise, stating the invariable relation between the middle term (smoke) and the major (fire), were beyond doubt. But this invariable relation (vyāpti) can be established only if we have a knowledge of all cases of smoke and presence of fire. This, however, is not possible, as we cannot perceive even all the cases of smoke and fire existing now in different parts of the world, to speak nothing of those which existed in the past or will exist in the future. No invariable, universal relation (vyāpti) can, therefore, be established by perception. Neither can it be said to be based on another inference, because in will involve a petitio principii, since the validity of that inference again has to be similarly proved. Nor can this vyāpti be based on the testimony (śabda) of reliable persons (who state that all cases of smoke are cases of fire). For, the validity of testimony itself requires to be proved by inference. Besides, if inference always depended on testimony, no one could infer anything by himself.

Therefore it becomes proved that inference can not be regarded as valid source of Knowledge.

Critique of śabda

But can we not regard the testimony of competent persons as a valid and safe source of knowledge? Do we not very often act on knowledge received from authority? The Cārvāka replies that testimony consists of words (śabda). So far as words are heard through our ears, they are perceived. Knowledge of words is, therefore, knowledge through perception and is quite valid. But in so far as these words suggest or mean things not within our perception, and aim at giving us knowledge of those unperceived objects, they are not free from error and doubt. Very often we are misled by so-called authority. The authority of the Vedas, for example, is held in high esteem by many. But in reality the Vedas are the works of some cunning priests who earned their living by duping the ignorant and the credulous. With false hopes and promises the Vedas persuade men to perform Vedic rites, the only tangible benefit of which goes to the priests who officiate and enjoy the emoluments.

But will not our knowledge be extremely limited and practical life sometimes impossible, if we do not accept the words of the experienced and do not depend on expert advice? The Cārvāka reply is that in so far as we depend on any authority, because we think it to be reliable, the knowledge obtained is really based on inference; because our belief is generated by a mental process like this : This authority should be accepted because it is reliable, and all reliable authority should be accepted. Being based on inference, knowledge derived from verbal testimony or authority is as precarious as inference. And as in the case of inference, so here we often act on knowledge derived from authority on the wrong belief that it is reliable. Sometimes this belief accidentally leads to successful results, sometimes it does not. Therefore, authority or testimony cannot be regarded as a safe and valid source of knowledge.

As neither inference nor authority can be proved to be reliable, perception must be regarded as the only valid source of knowledge (pramāṇa).

Rejection of Non-material Elements

If perception is the only reliable source of knowledge, we can rationally assert only the reality of perceptible objects. God, soul, heaven, life before birth of after death , and any unperceived law (like adṛṣṭa) cannot be believed in, because they are all beyond perception. Material objects are the only objects whose existence can be received and whose reality can be asserted. The Cārvākas, thus, come to establish materialism or the theory that matter is the only reality.

Regarding the nature of the material world most other Indian thinkers hold that it is composed of five kinds of elements (pañcabhūta), namely, ether (ākāśa), air (vāyu), fire (agni), water (ap) and earth (kṣiti). But the Cārvākas reject ether, because its existence cannot be perceived; it has to be inferred. The material world is, therefore, held to be composed of the four perceptible elements. Not only non-living material objects but also living organisms, like plants and animal bodies, are composed of these four elements.

Rejection of Soul

The Cārvākas admit that the existence of consciousness is proved by perception. But they deny that consciousness is the quality of any unperceived non-material or spiritual entity. As consciousness is perceived to exist in the perceptible living body composed of the material elements, it must be a quality of his body itself. What people mean by a soul is nothing more than this conscious living body (caitanya viśiṣṭa deha eva ātmā). The non-material soul is never perceived. On the contrary, we have direct evidence of the identity of the self with the body in our daily experiences and judgements like, 'I am fat', 'I am lame', 'I am blind'. If the 'I', the self, were different from the body, these would be meaningless.

But the objection may be raised : We do not perceive consciousness in any of the four material elements. How can it then come to qualify their product, the body? In reply the Cārvāka points out that qualities not present originally in any of the component factors may emerge subsequently when the factors are combined together. For example, betel leaf, lime and nut, none of which is originally red, come to acquire a reddish tinge when chewed together. Or, even the same thing placed under a different condition may develop qualities originally absent. For example, molasses (guḍa), originally non-intoxicant, becomes intoxicant when allowed to ferment. In a similar way it is possible to think that the material elements combined in a particular way give rise to the conscious living body. Consciousness is an epiphenomenon or bye product of matter; there is no evidence of its existence independent of the body.

If the existence of a soul apart from the body is not proved, there is no possibility of proving its immortality. On the contrary, death of the body means the end of the individual. All questions about previous life, after-life, rebirth, enjoyment of the fruits of actions in heaven or hell, therefore, become meaningless.

Rejection of God

God, whose existence cannot be perceived, fares no better than the soul. The material elements produce the world, and the supposition of a creator is unnecessary. The objection may be raised : Can the material elements by themselves give rise to this wonderful world? We find that even the production of an object like an earthen jar requires, in addition to clay which is its material cause, a potter who is the efficient cause, that shapes the material into the desired form. The four elements supply only the material cause of the world. Do we not require an efficient cause, like God as the shaper and designer who turns the material elements into this wonderful world? In reply, the Cārvāka states that the material elements themselves have got each its fixed nature (svabhāva). It is by the natures and laws inherent in them that they combine together to form this world. There is thus no necessity for God. There is no proof that the objects of the world are the products of any design. They can be explained more reasonably as the fortuitous products of the elements. The Cārvākas, therefore, prefer atheism.

In so far as this Cārvāka theory tries to explain the world only by nature, it is sometimes called naturalism (svabhāva-vāda). It is also called mechanism (yadṛcchā-vāda), because it denies the existence of conscious purpose behind the world and explains it as a mere mechanical or fortuitous combination of elements. The Cārvāka theory on the whole may also be called positivism, because it believes only in positive facts or observable phenomena.

Rejection of Dharma and Mokṣa

Some Indian philosophers like the Mimāṁsakas believe that the highest goal of human life is heaven (svarga) which is state of unalloyed bliss that can be attained hereafter by performing here the Vedic rites. The Cārvāka rejects this view, because it is based on the unproved existence of a life after death. 'Heaven' and 'hell' are the inventions of the priests whose professional interest lies in coasing, threatening and making people perform the rituals. Enlightened men will always refuse to be duped by them.

Many other philosophers regard liberation as the highest goal of human life. Liberation, again, is conceived as the total destruction of all sufferings. Some think that it can be attained only after death, when the soul is free from the body; and others believe that it can be attained even in this life. But the Cārvāka holds that none of these views stands to reason. If liberation is freedom of the soul from its bondage to physical existence, it is absurd because there is no soul. But if liberation means the attainment of a state free from all pain, in this very life, it is also an impossible ideal. Existence in this body is bound up with pleasure as well as pain. We can only try to minimise pain and enjoy as much pleasure as we can. Liberation in the sense of complete cessation of sufferings can only mean death. Those who try to attain in life a state free from pleasures and pains by rigorously suppressing the natural appetites, thinking that all pleasures arising out of their gratification are mixed with pain, act like fools. For no wise man would 'reject the kernel because of its husk', nor 'give up eating fish because there are bones', nor 'cease to grow crops because there are animals to destroy them', nor 'stop cooking his food because beggars might ask for a share'. If we remember that our existence is confined to the existence of the body and to this life, we must regard the pleasure arising in the body as the only good thing we can obtain. We should not throw away the opportunities of enjoying this life, in the futile hope of enjoyment hereafter. 'Rather a pigeon today than a peacock tomorrow'. 'A sure shell (courie) is better than a doubtful golden coin'. 'Who is that fool who would entrust the money in hand to the custody of others?' The goal of human life is, therefore, to attain the maximum amount of pleasure in this life, avoiding pain as far as possible. A good life is a life of maximum enjoyment.

A good action is one which leads to a balance of pleasure and a bad action is one which brings about more pain than pleasure. This Cārvāka ethics may be called, therefore, hedonism or the theory that pleasure is the highest goal.

The Existence of Consciousness

The carvakas also says that the existence of consciousness is only proved by perception. According to them, consciousness is not regarded as the quality of any spiritual entity. Consciousness is regarded as the quality of the body only. A soul is regarded as the conscious living body. Soul is made up of four elements which are only perceived. Consciousness is regarded as a by product of matter.

They also say that the death of the body means the end of the individual life. So, all questions about previous life, after life becomes meaningless. They also rejects the existence of God. They say that only material elements produces the world and the thinking of a creator becomes useless. They also say that the material elements have fixed nature. So, there is no necessity of God. The Carvakas believes and supports atheism. Carvaka theory is only known as a naturalist theory. We can give the name of mechanism also to their theory. They are also regarded as positivism.

Liberation

According to many others philosophers, liberation is regarded as the highest goal of human life. Liberation is considered as the total destruction of all sufferings. According to some, it can be attained only after death, when the soul is free from the body and according to others, it can be attained during the life only.

Carvaka don't believe in Dharma and Moksha and he also rejects them. They say that it is an absurd idea that liberation means freedom of the soul from its bondage.

Our work is to minimise pain and enjoy as much pleasure as much possible. Liberation for them, means only death. The goal of human life means to attain the maximum amount of pleasure in this life. A good life is referred as a life of maximum enjoyment. Carvaka theory is also known as a hedonistic theory, which says that pleasure is regarded as the highest goal. There are four human values like Dharma, Artha, Kama and Moksa. But they reject Dharma and Moksa and believes only in Artha and Kama.

JAINISM

Concept of Reality

The Word Jainism is derived from 'Jina' which means 'conqueror' one who has conquered his passions and desires. It is applied to the liberated souls who have conquered passions and desires and karmas and obtained emancipation. The Jainas believe in 24 Tīrthaṅkaras or 'Founders of the Faith' through whom their faith has come down from fabulous antiquity. Of these, the first was Ṛṣabhaveda and the last, Mahāvīra, the great spiritual hero, whose name was Vardhamāna. Mahāvīra, the last of the prophets, cannot be regarded as the founder of Jainism, because even before him, Jaina teachings were existent. But Mahāvīra gave a new orientation to that faith and for all practical purposes, modern Jainism may be rightly regarded as a result of his teachings. He flourished in the sixth century B.C. and was a contemporary of the Buddha. His predecessor, the 3rd Tīrthaṇkara, Pārshvanātha is also a historical personage who lived in the eighth or ninth century B.C.

Knowledge

The Jainas classify knowledge into immediate (aparokṣa) and mediate (parokṣa). Immediate knowledge is further divided into Avadhi, Manaḥparyāa and Kevala; and mediate knowledge into Mati and Śhruta. Perceptual knowledge which is ordinarily called immediate, is admitted to be relatively so by Jainism and therefore included in mediate and not immediate knowledge. It is included under Mati. Pure perception in the sense of mere sensation cannot rank the title of knowledge. It must be given meaning and arranged into order by conception or thought. Perceptual knowledge therefore is regarded as mediate since it presupposes the activity of thought. Mati includes both perceptual and inferential knowledge. Śhruta means knowledge derived from authority. Thus Mati and Śhruta which are the two kinds of mediate knowledge have as their instruments perception, inference an authority, the three Pramāṇas admitted by Jainism. Avadhi-jñāna, Manah-paryāya - jñāna and Kevala - jñāna, are the three kinds of immediate. Knowledge which may be called extra-ordinary and extra-sensory perceptions. Avadhi is clairvoyance; Manaparyaya is telepathy; and Kevala is omniscience. Avadhi is direct knowledge of things even at a distance of space or time. It is called Avadhi or 'limited' because it functions within a particular area and up to a particular time. It cannot go beyond spatial and temporal limits. Manah-paryāya is direct knowledge of the thoughts of others. This too is limited by spatial and temporal conditions.

In both Avadhi and Manaparyāya, the soul has direct knowledge unaided by the senses or the mind. Hence they are called immediate, though limited. Kevala - Jñana is unlimited and absolute knowledge. It can be acquired only by the liberated souls. It is not limited by space, time or object. Besides these five kinds of right knowledge, we have three kinds of wrong knowledge – Samshaya or doubt, Viparyaya or mistake and Anadhyavasāya or wrong knowledge through indifference.

Sat

The Jaina metaphysics is realistic. It gives the doctrine of the monyness of reality. There are innumerable material atoms and innumerable souls which are all separately and independently real. That is why jaina metaphysics is known as pluralistic realism. There are innumerable real substances which are kept under two categories, Jiva and Ajiva. Now we shall discuss these realities one by one.

Druya (Substance)

The Jainas do not hold that being is permanent, without becoming, change and end. Everything is produced, continues and is again destroyed. The definition of substance depends on our standpoint. It is that which always exists, as the universe, which has no beginning or end. It is the subject of qualities and modifications. Anything which has origin, existence and destruction is a substance. The whole universe is brought under the two everlasting, uncreated, eternal and co-existing categories which are called Jiva and Ajiva. Jiva means the conscious spirit and Ajiva means the unconscious non-spirit. Ajiva includes not only matter which is called 'Pudgala', but also space, motion, rest and time. Spirit matter motion, rest and space (respectively called jiva, pudgala, dharma, adharma and ākāsha) are described as asti-kāya dravyas or substances which possess constituent parts extending in space; while time (kāla) is the only anasti-kāya dravya which has no extension in space.

Guṇa (Quality)

Qualities or guṇas inhere in substances as materiality in atoms, and they cannot exist by themselves. The chief qualities are : (1) Existence, (2) Enjoyability, (3) Substantiveness, (4) Knowability, (5) Specific character or identity or essence, (6) the quality of possessing some kind of form. These general qualities are common to dravyas, and each of the latter has also its own specific features. We should not abstract any of these qualities and exalt it to a substantive level. Yet "there is neither quality without substance nor substance without quality". The Nyāya theory of the absolute distinction of substance and quality is refuted. A thing exists in and through the qualities and the qualities constitute the thing. The difference is one of reference and not existence. "If the substance is entirely separate and distinct from its qualities, then it may change into infinite other substances, or again, if the qualities can exist separate from their substance, there will be no necessity for a substance at all". The Nirguṇa Brahman theory as well as the Kṣaṇikavāda are implicitly refuted. Substance and qualities may be externally related as in "Devadatta's cow", or internally as in the "tall cow". "Just as dhana and jñāna (wealth and wisdom) make the owners dhani and jñāni (rich and wise), though expressing two ways of relationship, unity and diversity, even so the relation between substance and qualities implies two aspects of identity and difference." "The relation between substance and quality is one of coeval identity, unity, inseparability and essential simplicity; the unity of substance and qualities is not the result of union or combination."

Paryaya (Mode)

The dravya with the qualities must exist in some form or state. This mode of existence is paryāya and is subject to change. The substance gold with its qualities of malleability and yellowness is not subject to change. The guṇas or qualities continue while the paryāna or forms change. There are two kinds of paryāyas or modifications (1) Modifications of the essential qualities of a thing or substance. The colour of water may change, though colour is a constant property. (2) Modifications of the accidental qualities such as muddiness. Water need not always be muddy.

Jiva (Animate Substance)

Jiva is generally the same as the Ātman or the Puruṣa in other pluralistic schools with this important difference that it is identified with life of which consciousness is said to be the essence. Like the monads of Leibnitz, the Jivas of Jainism are qualitatively alike and only quantitatively different and the whole universe is literally filled with them. The jivas are divided first into those who are liberated (mukta) and those who are bound (baddha). The bound souls are further divided into mobile (trasa) and immobile (sthāvara). The latter live in the atoms of earth, water, fire and air and in the vegetable kingdom and have only one sense—that of touch. The mobile souls are again classified as those who have two senses (e.g. worms), three senses (e.g. ants), four senses (e.g. wasps, bees etc.) and five senses (e.g. higher animals and men).

Consciousness is regarded as the essence of the soul (chetanālakṣaṇo jivaḥ). Every soul from the lowest to the highest possesses consciousness. The degrees of consciousness may vary according to the obstacles of karma. The lowest souls which inhabit material atoms appear to be lifeless and unconscious, but in fact life and consciousness are present in them though in a dormant form. Purest consciousness is found in the emancipated souls where there is no shred to karma. All souls are really alike. The degrees of consciousness are due merely to the karma-obstacles. The soul in its intrinsic nature possesses Infinite Faith, Infinite Knowledge, Infinite Bliss and Infinite Power. In the case of the bound souls these characteristics are obscured by karma. A jiva is a real knower (jñātā), a real agent (kartā) and a real experient (bhoktā). It is included in the astikāya dravyas because its constituents possess extension in space. But it does not extend in space like matter. It is like the light. Just as the light fills the space where it is burning and just as many lights may remain in the same place without coming into conflict with one another, similarly the soul fills the space and many souls may remain together without any conflict. Though itself formless, it takes the form of the body which it illuminates. The soul of an ant is as big as the body of it and the soul of an elephant is as big as the elephant itself. The soul is coextensive with the body. Though we find souls in this world as embodied and as possessing the senses and the manas which help the souls to know, yet really the body, the senses and the manas are obstructions placed by karma and hinder the souls in their direct knowledge. Knowledge is not a property of the soul; it is its very essence. Every soul, therefore, can directly and immediately know everything if it is not obstructed by matter. Freedom from matter means omniscience and emanicipation.

Ajiva (Inanimate Substance)

The category of Ajiva is divided into matter (pudgala), space (ākāsha), motion (dharma), rest (adharma), and time (kāla). They are all without life and consciousness. Time is anastikāya because it does not extend in space. It is infinite. It is not perceived, but inferred from its characteristics which make possible continuity (vartanā), modification (pariṇāma), activity (kriyā), 'now' or 'new' (paratva), and 'then' or 'old' (aparatva). It is one and indivisible. Some Jaina writers have distinguished between real (pāramārthika) and empirical (vyāvahārika) time. The former makes continuity or duration possible and is infinite, one and indivisible. The latter can be divided into moments, hours, days, months and years and makes other changes, except duration, possible.

Like time, space is also infinite, eternal and imperceptible. It is inferred as the condition of extension. All substances except time have extension and extension is afforded only by space. Space itself is not extension; it is the locus of extension. Two kinds of space are distinguished. In one, motion is possible and it is called Lokākāśha or filled space; in the other, motion is not possible and it is called Alokākāśha or empty space. The former contains all the worlds where life and movement are; the latter stretches itself infinitely beyond the former. At the summit of Lokākāśha is Siddhashilā, the Abode of the Liberated Souls.

Dharma and Adharma are used here not in their popular sense of merit and demerit, but in the technical sense of the conditions of movement and rest. Like space and time, these also are eternal and imperceptible. They are inferred as the conditions which help motion and rest respectively. They are formless and passive. Dharma cannot generate motion nor can Adharma arrest it. They only help or favour motion or rest, like water helping the motion of a fish or like earth supporting things which rest on it.

Matter is called Pudgala which means that which is liable to integration and disintegration (pūrayanti galanti cha). This word is used in Buddhism in the sense of a soul, while in Jainism it is used for matter. An atom (aṇu) is supposed to be the smallest part of matter which cannot be further divided. Compound objects (saṅghāta or skandha) of the material world including senses, mind (manas) and breath are the combinations of atoms. Matter possesses the four qualities of colour, taste, smell and touch. Sound is regarded not as a quality, as other systems have done, but only as modification (pariṇāma) of matter. These atoms are supposed to house the souls. Like the ancient Greek atomists Democritus and Leucippus and unlike the Nyāya-Vaiśeṣika thinkers, the Jainas do not maintain any qualitative difference in the atoms. All atoms are qualitatively alike and indistinguishable. They become differentiated by developing the qualities of colour, taste, smell and touch. Hence the distinction of the elements of earth, water, fire and air is secondary and transmutation of elements is quite possible. Matter in its subtle form constitutes karma which infiltrates into the souls and binds them to saṁsāra.

Dharma and Adharma

Dharma is devoid of the sense qualities such as taste, colour, smell, touch and sound. Hence it is different from Pudgala or matter. It pervades the whole world. This description is also applicable to its opposite Adharma. The former is the principle of motion and the latter is the principle of rest. It is Amurtha or non-corporeal. It is not physical and hence sense qualities cannot be associated with it. It is not the aggregate of the simple elements as matter. It is co-existent with the world space. It is permanent and real. It forms indispensable condition of movement of physical objects and living beings. In itself, it is not capable of movement nor is it capable of creating movement in other thing. The analogy of water is used to illustrate its nature. Water is the necessary condition of the movement of fish. But water does not in any way impel the fish to move. Similarly, Dharma is the necessary condition of motion among physical objects of living beings. But it is not the cause of movement of those objects.

Adharma is the principle of rest. Its nature is quite similar to the Dharma. It is also devoid of sense qualities. Hence it is also non-corporeal. It is co-extensive with Loka-Akasa. But it has its own special quality. It is the basic condition of rest. Because of this, the moving objects are brought to rest. The analogy of earth is given in this respect. Earth does not actively arrest the movement of objects - physical and living. But it serves as a place of rest for moving things. The existence of these two principles is postulated as a necessary condition of the world structure. The world is an organised system. It owes its organised systems to these two principles of Dharma and Adharma. Otherwise, material particles will be scattered through the whole space converting the cosmos into chaos. Then there will be no world as such. Though they themselves are Nishkriya Dravyas or non-active things, yet they form the necessary condition of motion or rest of things both living and non-living. In order to explain the systematic structure of the cosmos, Jaina philosophy introduces these two postulates of Dharma and Adharma. If these two principles exist within the limit of world space causing motion and rest, then things in motion must be moved forever and things at rest must be stationary forever. But our experiences are quite different. One and the same thing may be in motion or in rest. Therefore, Dharma and Adharma must not be considered as efficient causes. They are quite neutral in themselves. Without these two entities, the world is impossible and incomplete.

Theory of Knowledge

The Jainas classify knowledge into immediate (aparokṣa) and mediate (parokṣa). Immediate knowledge is further divided into Avadhi, Manahparyāya and Kevala; and mediate knowledge into Mati and Shruta. Perceptual knowledge which is ordinarily called immediate, is admitted to be relatively so by Jainism and therefore included in mediate and not immediate knowledge. It is included under Mati. Pure perception in the sense of mere sensation cannot rank the title of knowledge. It must be given meaning and arranged into order by conception or thought. Perceptual knowledge therefore is regarded as mediate since it presupposes the activity of thought. Mati includes both perceptual and inferential knowledge. Shruta means knowledge derived from authority. Thus Mati and Shruta which are the two kinds of mediate knowledge have as their instruments perception, inference and authority, the three Pramāṇas admitted by Jainism. Avadhi-jñāna, Manahparyāya-jñāna and Kevala-jñāna, are the three kinds of immediate knowledge which may be called extra-ordinary and extra-sensory perceptions. Avadhi is clairvoyance; Manaḥparyāya is telepathy; and Kevala is omniscience. Avadhi is direct knowledge of things even at a distance of space or time. It is called Avadhi or 'limited' because it functions within a particular area and up to a particular time. It cannot go beyond spatial and temporal limits. Manaḥ-paryāya is direct knowledge of the thoughts of others. This too is limited by spatial and temporal conditions. In both Avadhi and Manaḥparyāya, the soul has direct knowledge unaided by the senses or the mind. Hence they are called immediate, though limited. Kevala-jñāna is unlimited and absolute knowledge. It can be acquired only by the liberated souls. It is not limited by space, time or object. Besides these five kinds of right knowledge, we have three kinds of wrong knowledge—Saṁśhaya or doubt, Viparyāya or mistake and Anadhyavasāya or wrong knowledge through indifference.

Knowledge may again be divided into two kinds, namely, Pramāṇa or knowledge of a thing as it is and Naya or knowledge of a thing in its relation. Jaina accepts three pramaṇa-Pratyakṣa, Anumāna and śabda.

Relativity in Jain Philosophy

According to McEvilley, the Jain theory of knowledge is not a phenomenalism but a realistic correspondence view. The Jain doctrine lays a strong emphasis on samyaktva, that is, rationality and logic. Jains suggest that the ultimate principle should always be logical and no principle can be devoid of logic or reason. Thus one finds in the Jain texts, deliberative exhortations on any subject in all its facts. In the process, the Jains came out with three doctrines of relativity used for logic and reasoning:

1. **Nayavada**. The theory of partial standpoints
2. **Syadvada**. The theory of conditioned predication
3. **Anekantavada.** The theory of relative pluralism or manifoldness.

These Jain philosophical concepts made very significant contributions to the ancient Indian philosophy, especially in the areas of skepticism and relativity.

Anekāntavāda

The Jaina metaphysics is a realistic and relativistic pluralism. It is called Anekāntavāda or the doctrine of the manyness of reality. Matter (pudgala) and spirit (jiva) are regarded as separate and independent realities. There are innumerable material atoms and innumerable individual souls which are all separately and independently real. And each atom and each soul possesses innumerable aspects of its own. A thing has got an infinite number of characteristics of its own. Every object possesses innumerable positive and negative characters. It is not possible for us, ordinary people, to know all the qualities of a thing. We can know only some qualities of some thing. To know all the aspects of a thing is to become omniscient. Therefore the Jainas say that he who knows all the qualities of one thing, knows all the qualities of all things, and he who knows all the qualities of all things, knows all the qualities of one thing. Human knowledge is necessarily relative and limited and so are all our judgments. This epistemological and logical theory of the Jainas is called 'Syādvāda'. As a matter of fact, both anekāntavāda and Syādvāda are the two aspects of the same teaching—realistic and relativistic pluralism. They are like the two sides of the same coin. The metaphysical side that reality has innumerable characters is called Anekantavāda while the epistemological and logical side that we can know only some aspects of reality and that therefore all our judgments are necessarily relative, is called Syādvāda.

A thing has many characters and it exists independently. It is called substance (dravya). It persists in and through all attributes and modes. Substance is defined as that which possesses qualities and modes. Out of these innumerable qualities of a substance, some are permanent and essential, while others are changing and accidental. The former are called attributes (guṇa) and the latter modes (paryāya). Substance and attributes are inseparable because the latter are the permanent essence of the substance and cannot remain without it. Modes or modifications are changing and accidental. Reality is a unity-and-difference or difference-and-unity. Viewed from the point of view of substance, a thing is one and permanent and real; viewed from the point of view of modes, it is many and momentary and unreal. Jainism here becomes a 'theological mean, between Brahmanism and Early Buddhism'. Brahmanism emphasizes the one, the permanent, the real; Early Buddhism emphasizes the many, the changing, the unreal; Jainism points out that both are the two sides of the same thing. Substance, therefore, is also defined as that which possesses the three characteristics of production, destruction and permanence. Substance has its unchanging essence and therefore is permanent. But it also has its changing modes and therefore is subject to origination and decay. To mistake any one-sided and partial view as the whole truth is to commit the fallacy of Ekāntavāda. As Jainism takes into account all these partial views, it is calls Anekāntavāda.

Reality of Many Sides

Intellectual Ahimsā and Religious Tolerance

The concept of anekanta and syadvada allows the Jains to accept the truth in other philosophies from their perspective and thus inculcating a tolerance for other viewpoints. Anekantvada is non-absolutist and stands firmly against all dogmatisms, even including any assertion that only Jainism is the right religious path. It is thus an intellectual Ahimsa or Ahimsa of mind.

In Anekantvada, there is no "battle of ideas," because this is considered to be a form of intellectual himsa or damage, leading quite logically to physical violence and war. In today's world, the limitations of the adversarial, "either with us or against us" form of argument are increasingly apparent leading to political, religious and social conflicts.

This ecumenic and irenic attitude, engendered by Anekanta, allowed modern Jain monks like Vijayadharma suri to declare: "...He is neither Jain nor Buddhist, Vaisnava nor Saiva, Hindu nor Muslim, but a traveler on the path of peace shown by the supreme soul, the God who is free from passion."

Even the mounting ecological crisis is linked to adversarialism, because it arises from a false division between humanity and "the rest" of nature. The modern judicial systems, democracy, freedom of speech, secularism, all implicitly reflect an attitude of Anekanta. Many authors like Kamala Jain, have advanced that the Jaina tradition with its emphasis on Ahimsa and Anekanta is capable of providing a solution to a host of problems facing the world: Religious intolerance, terrorism, wars, depletion of natural resources, environmental degradation, and so on.

Influence on Mahatma Gandhi

Since childhood, Gandhi was exposed to the actual practice of non-violence, non-possession and anekantavada. He grew up in an area with a continued Jain population and one of his good friend was a Jain. Mahatma Gandhi, in his writings, attributed his seemingly contradictory positions over a period of time to his learning process, experiments with truth and his belief in anekantavada. He proclaimed that the duty of every individual is to determine what is personally true and act on that relative perception of truth. According to Gandhi, while duty bound to act according to his relative truth, a satyagrahi is equally bound to learn from truth held by his opponent.

Syādvāda

Syādvāda holds all knowledge to be only probable. Every proposition gives us only a perhaps, a may be or a syād. We cannot affirm or deny anything absolutely of any object. There is nothing certain on account of the endless complexity of things. It emphasises the extremely complex nature of reality and its indefiniteness. It does not deny the possibility of predication, though it disallows absolute or categorical predication. The dynamic character of reality can consist only with relative or conditional predication. Every proposition is true, but only under certain condition, i.e. hypothetically.

The Jainas have divided the judgment into seven categories from different standpoints. The judgments, in which an object is related to its own attributes or symptoms, is called Astivachaka Paramarsa. On the other-hand, the judgment in which the absence of relationship is pointed between an object and the attribute and symptoms of other objects, is known as Nastivachaka Paramarsa. The following are the seven categories of Paramarsa.

1. ***Syād asti.*** From the point of view of its own material, place, time and nature, a thing is, *i.e.*, exists as itself. The jar exists as made of clay, in my room at the present moments, of such and such a shape and size.
2. ***Syād nāsti.*** From the point of view of the material, place, time and nature of another thing, a thing is not, *i.e.* it is not nothing. The jar does not exist as made of metal, at a different place or time or of a different shape and size.
3. ***Syād asti nāsti.*** From the point of view of the same quaternary, relating to itself and another thing, it may be said that a thing is and is not. In a certain sense the jar exists and in a certain sense it does not. We say here what a thing is as well as what it is not.
4. ***Syād avaktavya.*** While in three we make statements that a thing is in its own self and is not, as another successively, it becomes impossible to make these statements at once. In this sense a thing is unpredicable. Though the presence of its own nature and the absence of other-nature are both together in the jar, still we cannot express them.
5. ***Syād asti avaktavya.*** From the point of view of its own quaternary and at the same time from the joint quaternary of itself and nothing, a thing is and is unpredicable. We note both the existence of a thing and its indescribability.
6. ***Syād nāsti avaktavya.*** From the point of view of the quaternary of the nothing and at the same time from the joint quaternary of itself and nothing, a thing is not and is also unpredicable. We note here what a thing is not as well as its indescribability.
7. ***Syād asti nāsti avaktavya.*** From the point of view of its own quaternary as well as that of nothing and at the same from the joint quaternary of itself and nothing, a thing is, is not and is indescribable. We bring out the inexpressibly of a thing as well as what it is and what it is not.

Of these possible ways of speaking about a thing or its attributes, the first two are the chief, the simple affirmative that a thing is in its svarupa (own form), svadravya (ownmatter), svakṣsetra (own place), and svakāla (own time), and the simple negative that a thing is not in its pararūpa (other form), paradravya (other matter), parakṣetra (other place), and parakāla (other time). The latter is the negative fact. This doctrine insists on the correlativity of affirmation and negation. All judgments are double-edged in their character. All things are existent as well as nonexistent. This is the theory of syādavāda given by jaina.

Vedantin on Syadvada

The Vedantin levels another charge against Syadvada. He says that no theory can be sustained by mere probability. If everything is probable, then Syadvada, by its own assertion, becomes only probable. The Jainas retort that Syadvada does not mean the theory of probability, that it is not self-condemned scepticism. It means the theory of relativity of knowledge. If all truth is partial, then Syadvada itself is only partially true and therefore, partially false. Relativity itself is related to the Absolute and presupposes its existence.

When we examine the seven steps in the Syadvada, we find that the last three are superfluous and redundant They are merely the combination of the fourth with the first, second and third respectively. If we take to combinations, we may have as many as many steps as we, like. They are borrowed from the famous 'Chatuskotis' or the four categories of thought accepted by Buddhism and Vedanta. It is significant to note in this connection that the doctrine of Syadvada in its fully developed form of seven steps is found perhaps for the first time in Kundakunda's Panchastikaya and Pravachanasara.

Various Books on Syadvada

They are in the Bhagavatisutra and are quoted by Mallavadi in his Naya-chakra. One reference runs thus – 'Relatively, the soul is knowledge relatively, the soul is ignorance' and the other – 'Relatively the soul exists, relatively, the soul does not exist, relatively, the soul is indescribable'. Jainism rightly points out that all our knowledge is necessarily relative conditional and partial. All human knowledge is empirical and therefore relative. The Buddhist Doctrine of Dependent Origination (pratityasamutpada) also tells us that all things have dependent and conditional origination and are therefore relative.

Shunyavada, Vijnanavada and Advaita Vedanta have always maintained the necessarily, relative character of our empirical knowledge. They have made a distinction between the empirical and the absolute, the phenomenal and the noumenal, the conditional and the unconditional, the Samvrti and the Paramartha or the Paratantra and the Parinispanna or the Vyavahara and the Paramartha, Jainism has bluntly refused to make any such distinction. It refuses to rise higher than the relative. It has a bias against absolutism and in favour of common sense realistic pluralism.

Forms of Judgements

Syadvada gives us only seven scattered forms of judgements and makes no attempt to synthesise them. These seven forms of judgement are like scattered pearls or beads or flowers. They cannot be woven into a philosophical garland in the absence of the Absolute which alone can act as the thread. The relatives are bound together in the absolute. It is the absolute which gives life, meaning and significance to the relatives. If you throw away the absolute, you cannot retain even the relatives.

The Jainas do not give us a real identity-in-difference. What they give is merely identity plus difference. But reality is not a mathematical sum total of partial viewpoints. They forget their prejudice against absolutism when they absolutely assert that their teaching alone represents the whole truth, while all other systems give partial truths. Some schools teach being, permanence, identity and universality while others teach non-being, momentariness, plurality and particularly.

The Jainas have combined both, thinking that a mere combination of partial truths will give them the whole truth, But this is not the way of reaching truth. Like the Shunyavadins and the Vedantins the Jainas also have criticised one view by advancing the arguments of its opposite view and the latter by means of the arguments given by the former.

They criticise permanence through the arguments in favour of momentariness and the latter through the arguments supporting the former. They criticise satkaryavada through asatkaryavada and vice versa. All other views are partial and defective, but if they are put down together, they become the Jaina view and Lo! by the magic lamp of Aladin all their defects vanish over night and they represent the whole truth!

Yashovijaya Views on Jainas

Thus, Yashovijaya says that the Jaina view is evidently the best because it has woven together all the nayas in it. But the difficulty is that the nayas have not been woven together, they have been simply put together. The Absolute is the only thread which can weave them together and it has been wantonly thrown away by Jainism.

A proper synthesis is required which will unify all the nayas, preserve their merits and remove their defects. To say that other systems, being relative and partial, are like fire-flies giving only broken light, while Jainism alone, being the complete truth, is like the luminous sun, is to make a half-hearted confession of Absolutism, for by a mere addition of the light of innumerable fire-flies you cannot have the light of the sun.

Thus, by its own assertion Jainism becomes partially false. In practice this relativity is often forgotten. Jainism is often made an exception and absolute validity is claimed for it. While all other teachings are relatively real, the Jaina teaching is held to be absolutely real.

Hemachandra, e.g., commits this fallacy when in his religious zeal he proclaims in a loud and solemn voice before his opponents that Vitaraga is the only God and that Anekanta is the only philosophy. e.g., the Jainas say: If the effect pre exists in its cause, it is already an existent fact and needs no repeated birth; if the effect does not pre-exists in its cause, it is like a sky-flower and cannot be produced.

Metaphysical Thesis

A metaphysical thesis was usually expressed in the canonical literature of Buddhism and Jainism in the form of a question 'Is A B?' 'Is everything F', to which an answer was demanded either yes or no. If yes, the thesis was put forward as an assertion, that is, the proposed position 'A is B' or 'Everything is F' was claimed to be true. Both the Buddha and the Mahavira said that they were followers of a different method or style in answering questions. They were, to be sure, vibhajya-vadin, for they had to analyse the significance or the implications of the questions in order to reach a satisfactory answer. For, it may be that not everything is F, although it may not be true that nothing is F.

The followers of the Mahavira developed their doctrine of anekanta from this clue found in the canonical literature. This is the clue of vibhajya-vada, which originally meant, in both Buddhist and Jam canons, a sort of openness – lack of dogmatic adherence to any viewpoint exclusively. The philosophy of Jainism has been called 'Non-dogmatism' or 'Non-absolutism.' If this is conceded then the main doctrine of Jainism is lost. It is not truly an anekanta, which requires the mixing of the opposite values. This critique, can also be answered. This will lead us to a discussion of saptabhangi.

Proposition

The significant difference between the philosophical motivations of the Jainas and those modem logicians who develop multiple-valued logics or the para-consistent logics. First, the logicians assign truth to the members of a certain set of propositions, falsity to another set and the third value, paradoxicality, to the problem set, i.e., the set of propositions that reveal the various versions of the liar paradox and other paradoxes. The Jainas believe that each proposition, at least each metaphysical proposition, has the value inexpressible. Likewise the same proposition, under another interpretation, could be evaluated true' and under still another interpretation, 'false'.

Second, my reference to the non-bivalence logic or para-consistent logic, in connection with Jainism, should not be over emphasised. Jaina logician did not develop, unlike the modern logicians, truth matrices for Negation, Conjunction etc. Although, the usual law of non-contradiction, which is by itself a very nebulous and vegue concept, is flouted, the Jainas do not land us into the realm of illogic or irrationability.

Limitation on Laws

Lastly the Jainas, in fact, set the limit to our usual under standing of the law of non-contradiction. There are so many determinants and indexicals for the successful application of any predicate that the proper and strict formulation of the ways by which this can be contradicted will always outrun the linguistic devices at our disposal. Rational understanding is possible of the Jaina position in metaphysics. One can say that the Jaina anekanta is a meta-metaphysical position.

They were concerned with the evaluation of propositions, with the general principle of such evaluation. In this way, their view rightly impinged upon the notions of semantics and problems with semantical paradoxes.

Their man argument was intended to show the multi-faceted nature of reality, as well as its ever elusive character such that whatever is revealed to any observer at any given point of time and at any given place, would be only partially and conditionally right, ready to be falsified by a different revelation to a different observer at a different place and time.

Attributes of Metaphysics

The Jaina metaphysics accepts that infinite attributes abide in a single entity, so does its epistemology, as a natural process, that infinite natures can be predicated of a single judgment, whose substantive pertaining to one particular entity. For instance, 'existence' predicated of one single entity is possible only on the presumption of another predicate 'non-existence'.

Thus, any predicate, being accompanied by its counterpart, is made up of a pari of natures of contradictory character, referring to the same entity.

There are number of such correlatives serving as predicate

(i) The first formula describes affirmation only.

(ii) The second formula describes negation only.

(iii) The third formula describes affirmation and negation successively.

(iv) The fourth formula describes affirmation and negation simultaneously. Since, two natures cannot be uttered with equal primacy in the same breath, in regard to a single entity, the term avaktavya (inexpressible) comes into being.

(v) The fifth formula describes affirmation only and then both natures simultaneously.

(vi) The sixth formula describes negation only, and then both natures simultaneously.

(vii) The seventh formula describes both natures successively and then simultaneously.

Criticism of Syadvada

Other philosophical thinkers have bitterly criticized the Jaina Syadvada. The reasons for criticism can be summarized as follows.

The Bauddha and the Vedantius have regarded it as nothing more than a negative theory. They take syad in the sense of probability and they have based their criticism on it. The same things cannot be present and past in the same sense. Philosophers like Dharma Kirti, Santa Raksit and Samkaracharya treat it as the ravings of Mad men for Ramanuja it is as impossible to roll into one thing contradictory qualities of existence and non-existence as it is to bracket light and darkness together. But the clarification given above exposes the ignorance of the Buddhist and Vedantic philosophers about Syadvada. According to Anekantavada everything has more than one quality. Though one sat and eternal from the stand point of Dravya, it is many, asat and ephemeral from the stand point of paryaya. A thing is sat from the view points of its own substance. From, time and space. Thus it admits of no contradiction.

The second objection, raised by Samkaracharya, nevertheless points out the real defect of Syadvada. If everything, argues Samskara, is merely probable, then Syadvada cannot be an exception. In fact, the theory of Anekantika also hinges on Aikantika. The relative is based on the absolute. But for one absolute the seven Nayas of Syadvada are disconnected and cannot be synthesized. Of course, the Jainas believe both in Aikantika and in Anekantika. But they do not seek to effect any synthesis between the two. While propounding Syadvada, they forget it and regard their own theory as the sole gospel of truth. The Jainas criticize satkaryavada by the sole gospel of truth. The Jainas criticize satkaryavada by satkaryavada and vice versa. They differentiate between Sakaladesa and Vikaladesa.

The latter term is applied to scattered groups of particular truths, the former refers to the absolute truths. In the words of Yasovijaya the Jaina out look is the best as all the Nayas are brought together simultaneously in it. But conglomeration does not mean cohesion. In the mere absence of an absolute element, the diverse relative elements can not be united by any means whatever. Yasovijaya further asserts that Anekantavada is characterized by impartiality because it meets out the same treatment to all the different Nayas. Just as a father does not and should not discriminate among his sons, so Anekantavada also does not differentiate among the numerous Nayas. But this quality tends to overlook the diversity. According to Hem Chandra, all the philosophical schools, except the Jaina, are relative, biased and revel in criticizing one another. Only the Jaina Darshan provides a welcome relief as it is free from bias and treats the different Nayas alike.

Of the seven Nayas of Syadvada, the last three appear to be more repetitions of the first four Nayas. According to Kumarila Bhatta, if divided that way, the Nayas can have hundred categories instead of seven.

The Jaina philosophy does not seek to transcend relativism and pluralism and so it does not recognize absolution and monism. It does not distinguish among different relative judgments.

By taking absolute only as a conglomeration of parts, the Jainas have blurred the conception of their Keval Jnana also. They have thus made it ambiguous and indistinct. Kevala Jnana is other worldly, absolute and immediate. But even then the Jainas refuse to differentiate between temporal and other worldly (Paramarthika) knowledge. In fact, Keval Jnana and Syadvada have become contradictory.

Nayavāda

Naya means a standpoint of thought from which we make a statement about a thing. All truth is relative to our standpoints. Partial knowledge of one of the innumerable aspects of a thing is called 'naya'. Judgement based on this partial knowledge is also included in 'naya'.

There are seven 'Nayas' of which the first four are called 'Artha-naya' because they-relate to objects or meanings, and the last three are called 'Śhabda-naya' because they relate to words. When taken as absolute, a 'naya' becomes a fallacy—'nayābhāsa'.

The first is the 'Naigama-naya'. From this standpoint we look at a thing as having both universal and particular qualities and we do not distinguish between them. It becomes fallacious when both universals and particulars are regarded as separately real and absolute, as is done by Nyāya-Vaisheṣika. The second is the 'Saṅgraha-naya'. Here we emphasize the universals qualities and ignore the particulars where they are manifested. It becomes fallacious when universal alone are treated as absolutely real and particulars are rejected as unreal, as is done by Sāṅkhya and Advaita Vedānta. The third is the 'Vyavahāra-naya' which is the conventional point of view based on empirical knowledge. Here things are taken as concrete particulars and their specific features are emphasized. It becomes fallacious when particulars alone are viewed as real and universal are rejected as unreal, as is done by Materialism and Buddhist realistic pluralism. The fourth is called 'Ṛjusūtra-naya '. Here the real is identified with the momentary. The particulars are reduced to a series of moments and any given moment is regarded as real. When this partial truth is mistaken to be the whole truth, it becomes fallacious, as in some schools of Buddhism. Among the nayas which refer to words, the first is called 'Shabda-naya'. It means that a word is necessarily related to the meaning which it signifies. Every word refers either to a thing or quality or relation or action. The seconds is 'Samabhirūḍa-naya' which distinguishes terms according to their roots. For example, the word 'Paṅkaja' literally means 'born of mud' and signifies any creature or plant born of mud, but its meaning has been conventionally restricted to 'lotus' only. Similarly the word 'gauḥ' means 'any thing which moves', but has conventionally become restricted to signify only a 'cow'. The third is called 'Evambhūta-naya' which is a specialized form of the second. According to it, a name should be applied to an object only when its meaning is fulfilled. For example, a cow should be called 'gauḥ' only when it moves and not when it is lying down.

Each naya or point of view represents only one of the innumerable aspects possessed by a thing from which we may attempt to know or describe it. When any such partial viewpoint is mistaken for the whole truth, we have a 'nayābhāsa' or a fallacy. The 'nayas' are also distinguished as 'Dravyārthika' or from the point of view of substance which takes into account the permanent nature and unity of things, and as 'Paryāyāthika' or from the point of view of modes which takes into account the passing modifications and the diversity of things. When a thing is taken to be either as permanent only or as momentary only, either as one only or as many only, fallacies arise.

Bondage and Liberation

Karma is the link which unites the soul to the body. Ignorance of truth and four passions—anger (krodha), greed (lobha), pride (māna) and delusion (māyā) which are called kaṣāya or sticky substances where karmic particles stick, attract the flow of karmic matter towards the soul. The state when karmic particles actually begin to flow towards the soul to bind it is called Āsrava or flow. The state when these particles actually infiltrate into the soul and bind it is called Bandha or bondage. The ideal bondage (bhāva-bandha) of the soul takes place as soon as it has bad disposition and the material bondage (dravya-bandha) takes place when there is actual influx of karma into the soul. In bondage, the karmic matter unites with the soul by intimate interpenetration, just as water unites with milk or fire unites with the red-hot iron ball. It is for this reason that we find life and consciousness in every part of the body. By the possession and practice of right faith, knowledge and conduct, the influx of fresh karma is stopped. This state is called samvara or stoppage. Then, the already existing karma must be exhausted. This state is called nirjarā or wearing out. When the last particle of karma has been exhausted 'the partnership between soul and matter is dissolved', and the soul shines in its intrinsic nature of infinite faith, knowledge, bliss and power. This state is called Mokṣa or liberation. Here kevala jñāna or omniscience is attained. The liberated soul transcends samsāra and goes straight to siddha-shilā at the top of the world and dwells there in eternal knowledge and bliss. Bondage, therefore, means union of the soul with matter and consequently liberation means separation of matter from the soul. We, conscious living souls, find ourselves bound to karmic matter and the end of our life is to remove this karmic dross and regain our intrinsic nature. Hence Jainism is primarily an ethical teaching and its aim is the perfection of the soul. Āsrava or the flow of matter towards the soul is the cause of bondage and Samvara or the stoppage of this flow is the cause of liberation. Everything else in Jainism is said to be the elaboration of this fundamental teaching. These five states together with the Jiva and the Ajiva make the seven principles of Jainism. Sometimes virtue (puṇya) and vice (pāpa) are added to these seven to make up the nine categories of Jainism.

Passions attract the flow of karmic matter into the souls. And passions are due to ignorance. So ignorance is the real cause of bondage. Here Jainism agrees with Sānkhya, Buddhism and Vedānta, Now, ignorance can be removed only by knowledge. So right knowledge is the cause of liberation. This right knowledge is produced by faith in the teachings of the omniscient Tirthaṅkaras. Hence faith is necessary. And it is right conduct which perfects knowledge since theory without practice is empty and practice without theory is blind. Right knowledge dawns when all the karmas are destroyed by right conduct. Hence right faith, right conduct and right knowledge all the three together form the path of liberation which is the joint effect of these three. Right faith (samyak darśana), knowledge (jñāna) and conduct (chāritra) are the three Jewels (tri-ratna) of Jainism. They are inseparably bound up and perfection of one goes with the perfection of the other two.

Union of the Soul

Bondage is referred as the union of the soul with matter. Liberation is referred as the separation of matter from the soul. We are bound to karmic matter. Jainism main aim is to remove this karmic matter. The perfection of the soul is essential for Jainism. Asrava is regarded as the cause of bondage whereas Samvara is regarded as the cause of liberation.

It has been said that passions have a habit of attracting the flow of Karmic matter, which are converted into the souls. Passions arises because of ignorance. Ignorance is regarded as the cause of bondage. Only knowledge is able to remove ignorance. Right knowledge is regarded as the cause of liberation. Faith is essential for the right knowledge. Right conduct perfects right knowledge. Because of right conduct, all the karmas are destroyed.

Three Jewels

- Right faith, right knowledge and right conduct are regarded as the three Jewels of Jainism.
- All these three together form the path of liberation. They are regarded as inseparable.

BUDDHISM

It was in the sixth century B.C. that the world saw the Light of Asia, that perfect embodiment of knowledge, courage, love and sacrifice whose heart overflowed with purest emotion on seeing that human life was essentially fraught with misery and pain, that a shallow optimism was rooted in a deep pessimism, that behind the superficial momentary glow of sensual pleasure there lay the misery of old age, sickness and death; who, moved by that spectacle to sell a remedy for men's ills, at the age of twenty-nine, boldly left not only the material luxuries of the Shākya kingdom but also his believe wife, beloved new-born son, at last found enlightenment as he lay emaciated under a tree near Gaya, dispelling the dark clouds of ignorance and conquering Māra, the Prince of Evil; who then preached the truth he had discovered without distinction of caste, creed or colour. Thus Buddha taught. And Buddhism was embraced by the rich and poor, the high and the low, the intellectual and the dull alike.

Buddhism is divided into many philosophical school and has a vast literature. The teachings of Buddha were oral and were recorded much later by his disciples. Buddha was primarily an ethical teacher and social reformer than a theoretical philosopher. He referred to a number of metaphysical views prevalent in his times and condemned them as futile. Whenever metaphysical questions were put to him, he avoided them saying that they were neither profitable nor conductive to the highest good. 'Philosophy purifies none, peace alone does'.

Buddha's Philosophical teachings and conversations were compiled in the 'Tipiṭaka' or the Three Baskets. The first Basket is the Vinaya -Piṭaka which the discipline of the Order. The second is the Sutta-Piṭaka which is said to be a compilation of the utterance of the Master himself and consists of five collections called Nikāyas - Dīgha, Majjhima, Anguttara, Samyutta and Khuddaka. The third is called Abhidhamma- Piṭaka which deals with philosophical discussions. Besides these, these is a vast non - canonical Pāli literature including Milinda- Pañho, Dīpavamsa, Mahāvamsa, Visuddhi-magga and rich commentary literature of the Tipiṭaka.

Four Noble Truths

The Four Noble Truths (ārya satya) are :

(1) There is suffering (duḥkha). Life is full of misery and Pain. Even the so-called pleasures are really fraught with pain. There is always fear lest we may lose the so-called pleasures and their loss involves pain. Indulgence also results in pain. That there is suffering in this world is a fact of common experience. Poverty, disease, old age, death, selfishness, meanness, greed, anger, hatred, quarrels, bickering, conflicts, exploitation are rampant in this world. That life is full of suffering none can deny.

(2) There is a cause of suffering (duḥkha-samudāya). Everything has a cause. Nothing comes out of nothing—*ex nihilo nihilfit.* The existence of every event depends open its causes and conditions. Everything in this world is conditional, relative, limited. Suffering being a fact, it must have a cause. It must depend on some conditions. This being, that arises, 'the cause being present, the effect arises', is the causal law of Dependent Origination.

(3) There is a cessation of suffering (duḥkha-nirodha). Because everything arises depending on some causes and conditions, therefore if these causes and conditions are removed the effect must also cease. The cause being removed, the effect ceases to exist. Everything being conditional and relative is necessarily momentary and what is momentary must perish. That which is born must die. Production implies destruction.

(4) There is a way leading to this cessation of suffering (duḥkha–nirodha-gāmini pratipat). There is an ethical and spiritual path by following which misery may be removed and liberation attained. This is the Noble Eight-fold Path.

Aṣṭāngamārga (Eight-fold Path)

The Eight fold path contained in the fourth Noble truth of Buddha. The Buddha said, "there are two extremes, o monks from which he who leads a religious life must abstain. One is a life of pleasure, devoted to desire and enjoyment; that is base unworthy, unreal, and unspiritual. The perfect one, O monks, is removed from both these extremes and has discovered the way which lies between them, the middle way enlightens the eye, enlighten the mind, which leads to rest, to knowledge, to enlightenment, to Nirvana". These words of Buddha is the base of eightfold path. The eight fold path consists of the following disciplines .

Right view. As ignorance with its consequences, namely wrong views about the self and the world, is the root cause of our sufferings. It is natural that the first step to moral reformation should be the acquisition of right views or the knowledge truth. So this is the discipline which enable one to see the true nature of the world of experience as being sorrowful, impermanent etc. rights view reveals the four noble truths.

Right mindedness. This refers to the right motivation. Removing all prejudices and evil intentions from ones thoughts, one must cultivate a friendly attitude towards all sentient beings. One should cultivate benevolent thoughts, thoughts of compassion thoughts of sympathy etc.

Rights speech. Right speech is Kind and truthfull, speech, that is less speech. Buddhism preached, "Better than a thousand utterances composed of meaningless words in one sensible word hearing which one becomes peaceful.

Right action. Evil deeds should be avoided. Right deeds do not result in sorrow. One should practice restraint and virtue and one should commit no wrong.

Right Livelihood. The means of living that one adopts should be in agreement with the laws of morality. One should avoid such cruel means of living as that of being a butcher or a huntsman.

Right effort. According to Buddha, self effort is the utmost necessity. Through right efforts, passions should be controlled without right effort one cannot gain enlightenment.

Right Thought. This literally means good memory, not merely the faculty of remembering the past, but also being alert in minds being watchfull and in complete self –possession. It is through right mind fullness that one can control ones acts, feelings and thoughts.

Right Concentration. This is the practice of meditation resulting in the final wisdom. Sense culture should enable one to become discerning and sharp so that one may not be carried away in the storm of sensual pleasure. This should lead one to the development of the power of concentration. Mediation is the way to Nirvana.

Madhyam Pratipada

Buddha's ethical 'middle path' is like the 'golden mean' of Aristotle. Self-indulgence and self-mortification are equally ruled out. In his very first Sermon at Sāranātha he said : 'There are two extremes, O monks from which he who leads a religious life must abstain. One is a life of pleasure, devoted to desire and enjoyment: that is base, ignoble, unspiritual, unworthy, unreal. The Perfect One, O monks, is removed from both these extremes and has discovered the way which lies between them, the middle way which enlightens the eyes, enlightens the mind, which leads to rest, to knowledge, to enlightenment, to Nirvāna'.

Madhyam Pratipada is the theory which avoids both eternalism and nihilism both and find a middle way between them.

Pratityasamutpāda

The doctrine of Pratityasamutpāda or Dependent Origination is the foundation of all the teachings of the Buddha. It is contained in the Second Noble Truth which gives us the cause of suffering, and in the Third Noble Truth which shows the cessation of suffering. Suffering is Samsāra; cessation of suffering is Nirvāṇa. Both are only aspects of the same Reality. Pratityasamutpāda, viewed from the point of view of relativity is Samsāra; while viewed from the point of view of reality, it is Nirvāṇa. It is relativity and dependent causation as well as the Absolute, for it is the Absolute itself which appears as relative and acts as the binding thread giving them unity and meaning. Everything is relative, conditional, dependent, subject to birth and death and therefore impermanent. The causal formula is : 'This being, that arises', i.e., 'Depending on the cause, the effect arises'. Thus every object of thought is necessarily relative. And because it is relative, it is neither absolutely real (for it is subject to death) nor absolutely unreal (for it appears to arise). All phenomenal things hang between reality and nothingness, avoiding both the extremes. They are like the appearances of the Vedāntic Avidyā or Māyā. It is in this sense that Buddha calls the doctrine the Middle Path, Madhyamā Pratipat, which avoids both eternalism and nihilism. Buddha identifies it with the Bodhi, the Enlightenment which dawned upon him under the shade of the bo tree in Gaya and which transformed the mortal Siddhārrtha into the immortal Buddha. He also identifies it with the Dharma, the Law : 'He who sees the Pratityasamutpāda sees the Dharma, and he who sees the Dharma sees the Pratityasamutpāda.' Failure to grasp it is the cause of misery. Its knowledge leads to the cessation of misery Nāgārjuna salutes Buddha as the best among the teachers, who taught the blessed doctrine of Pratityasamutpāda' which leads to the cessation of plurality and to bliss. Shāntarakṣita also does the same.

The twelve chain of dependent origination is given below :

(1) Ignorance (avidyā).
(2) Impressions of Karmic forces (samskāra).
(3) Initial consciousness of the embryo (vijñāna).
(4) Psycho-physical organism (nāma-rūpa).
(5) Six sense-organs including mind (ṣaḍāyatana).
(6) Sense-object-contact (śparsha).
(7) Sense-experience (vedanā).
(8) Thirst for sense-enjoyment (tṛṣṇā).
(9) Clinging to this enjoyment (upādāna).
(10) Will to be born (bhava).
(11) Birth or rebirth (jāti).
(12) Old age and death (jarā-maraṇa)

Out of these twelve links the first two are related to past life, the last two to future life and the rest to present life. This is the cycle of birth-and-death. This is the twelve-spoked wheel of Dependent Origination. This is the vicious circle of causation. It does not end with death. Death is only a beginning of a new life. It is called Bhava-chakra, Samsāra-chakra, Janma-maraṇa-chakra, Dharma-chakra, Pratityasamutpāda chakra etc.

Nirvāṇa

Troubled by the sight of disease, old age and death, Buddha left his home to find a solution of the misery of earthly life. Pratityasamutpāda is the solution which he found. Why do we suffer misery and pain? Why do we suffer old age and death? Because we are born. Why are we born? Because their is a will to be born. Why should there be this will to become? Because we cling to the objects of the world. Why do we have this clinging? Because we crave to enjoy the objects of this world. Why do we have this craving, this thirst for enjoyment? Because of sense experience. Why do we have this sense-experience?

Because of sense-object-contact. Why do we have this contact? Because of the six sense-organs (the sixth sense being the mink). Why do we have the six sense-organs? Because of the psycho-physical organism. Why do we have this organism? Because of the initial consciousness of the embryo. Why do we have this consciousness? Because of our predispositions or impressions of Karma. Why do we have these impressions? Because of Ignorance. Hence Ignorance is the root-cause of all suffering.

In the old books we also find mention of a triple path consisting of Shila or right conduct, Samādhi or right concentration and Prajñā and Charitra of Jainism. Shila and Samādhi lead to Prajñā which is the direct cause of liberation. Hence, perfect wisdom, perfect goodness and perfect equanimity-complete relief from suffering-are- simultaneously attained, therefore, in nirvāna.

Kṣaṇabhangavāda

The doctrine of dependent origination also yields the Buddhist theory of the transitory nature of things. All things, Buddha repeatedly teaches, are subject to change and decay. As everything originates from some condition, it disappears when the condition ceases to be. Whatever has a beginning has also an end. Buddha, therefore, says, "Know that whatever exists arises from causes and conditions and is in every respect impermanent". "That which seems everlasting will perish, that which is high will be laid low; where meeting is, parting will be; where birth is, death will come."

Transitoriness of life and wordily things is spoken of by many other poets and philosophers. Buddha logically perfects this view into the doctrine of *impermanence.* His later followers develop this further into a theory of momentariness (kṣaṇika-vāda), which means not only that everything has conditional and, therefore, non-permanent existence, but also that things last not even for short periods of time, but exist for one partless moment only. This doctrine of momentariness of all things is supported by later writers with elaborate arguments, one of which may be briefly noticed here : The criterion of the existence (sattā) of a thing is its capacity to produce some effect (arthakriys-kāritva-lakṣaṇam sat). A non-existent thing, like a hare's horn, cannot produce any effect. Now, from this criterion of existence, it may be deduced that a thing having existence must be momentary. If, for example, a thing like a seed be not accepted to be momentary, but thought to be lasting for more than one moment, then we have to show that it is capable of producing an effect during each moment it exists. Again, if it really remains the same unchanging thing during these moments, then it should be able to produce the same effect at every one of those moments. But we find that this is not the case. The seed in the house does not produce the seeding which is generated by a seed sown in the field. The seed in the house cannot then be the same as that in the field. But it may be said that though the seed does not actually produce the same effect always, it always has the Potentiality to produce it, and this potentiality becomes kinetic in the presence of suitable auxiliary conditions like earth, water, etc. Therefore, the seed is always the same. But this defence is weak; because then it is virtually confessed that the seed of the first moment is not the cause of the seedling, but that the seed modified by the other conditions really causes the effect. Hence the seed must be admitted to have changed. In this way it may be shown regarding everything that it does not stay unchanged during any two moments, because it does not produce the identical effect during both moments. Hence everything lasts only for a moment.

Anātmavāda

The law of change is universal; neither man, nor any other being, animate or inanimate, is exempt from. It is commonly believed that in man there is an abiding substance called the soul (ātmā), which persists through changes that overcome the body, exists before birth and after death, and migrates from one body to another. Consistently with his theories of conditional existence and universal change, Buddha denies the existence of such soul. But how, it may be asked, does he then explain the continuity of a person through different births, or even through the different states of childhood, youth and old age? Though denying the continuity of an identical substance in man, Buddha does not deny the *continuity of the stream* of successive states that compose his life. Life is an unbroken series of states: each of these states depends on the condition just preceding and given rise to the one just succeeding it. The continuity of the life-series is, therefore, based on a causal connection running through the different states. This continuity is often explained with the example of a lamp burning throughout the night. The flame of each moment is dependent on its own conditions and different from that of another moment which is dependent on other conditions. Yet there is an unbroken succession of the different flames. Again, as from one flame another may be lighted, and though the two are different, they are connected causally, similarly, the end-state of this life may cause the beginning of the next. Rebirth is, therefore, not transmigration, *i.e.*, the migration of the same soul into another body; it is the causation of the next life by the present. The conception of a soul is thus replaced here by that of an unbroken stream of consciousness as in the philosophy of William James. As the present state of consciousness inherits its characters from previous ones, the past in a way continues in the present, through its effect. Memory thus becomes explicable even without a soul. This theory of the non-existence of soul (Anātta-vāda) plays a very important part in understanding the teaching of Buddha. He, therefore, repeatedly exhorts his disciples to give up the false view about the self. Buddha points out that people who suffer from the illusion of the self, do not know its nature clearly; still they strongly protest that they love the soul; they want to make the soul happy by obtaining salvation. This, he wittily remarks, is like falling in love with the most beautiful maiden in the land though she has never been seen nor known. Or, it is like building a stair-case for mounting a palace which has never been seen.

Man is only a conventional name for a collection of different constituents the material body (kāya), the immaterial mind (manas or citta), the formless consciousness (vijñāna), just as a chariot is a collection of wheels, axles, shafts, etc. The existence of man depends on this collection and it dissolves when the collection breaks up. The soul or the ego denotes nothing more than this collection.

From a psychological point of view, man, as perceived from without and within, is analysable also into a collection of five groups (pañca-skandhas) of changing elements, namely, (1) form (rūpa) consisting of the different factors which we perceive in this body having form, (2) feelings (vedanā) of pleasure, pain and indifference, (3) perception including understanding and naming (sañjñā), (4) predispositions or tendencies generated by the impressions of past experience (saṁskāras), and (5) consciousness itself (vijñāna). The last four are together called nāma.

Schools of Buddhism

Buddhism, though primarily an ethical-religious movement thus came to give birth to about thirty schools not counting the minor one. And some of these get into the deep waters of metaphysical speculation, heedless of the founder's warning. Of these many schools we shall first notice the four distinguished in India by Buddhist and non-Buddhist writers. In this account, (1) some Buddha philosophers are nihilists (śūnya-vādī or Mādhyamika), (2) others are subjective idealists (Vijñānavādi or Yogācāra, (3) others again are representationalists or critical realists (Bāhyānumeya-vādī or Sautrāntika), and (4) the rest are direct realists (Bāhyapratyakṣa-vādī or Vaibhāṣika). The first two of the above four schools come under Mahāyāna and the last two under Hīnayāna. It should be noted, however, that under both Mahāyāna and Hinayāna there are many other schools.

Mādhyamika

The founder of this school is said to be Nāgārjuna, who was a Brahmin born in South India about the second century A.D. Aśvaghosa the author of Buddhacarita, is also regarded as a pioneer. In his famous work, Mādhyamikaśātra, Nāgārjuna states, with great dialectical skill and scholarship, the philosophy of the Mādhyamika school. Mādhyamika holds that there is nothing, mental or non-mental, which is real. The universe is śūnya or void of reality. But the Mādhyamika view is not really nihilism, as ordinarily supposed, and that it does not deny all reality, but only the apparent phenomenal world perceived by us. Behind this phenomenal world there is a reality which is not describable by any character, mental or non-mental, that we perceive. Being devoid of Phenomenal characters, it is called śūnya. But this is only the negative aspect of the ultimate reality : it is only a description of what it is not. In the Laṅkāvatāra-sūtra it is stated that the real nature of objects cannot be ascertained by the intellect and cannot, therefore, be described. That which is real must be independent and should not depend on anything else for its existence and origination. But everything we know of is dependent on some condition. Hence it cannot be real. Again, it cannot be said to be unreal. Because an unreal thing, like a castle in the air, can never come into existence. To say that it is both real and unreal or that it is neither real nor unreal, would be unintelligible jargon. Śūnyatā or voidness is the name for this indeterminable, indescribable real nature of things.

Nāgārjuna says, "The fact of dependent origination is called by us śūnyatā'. "There is no dharma (character) of things which is not dependent on some other condition regarding its origin. Therefore, there is no dharma which is not śūnya". It would appear, therefore, that śūnya only means the conditional character of things, and their consequent constant changeability and indeterminability or indescribability.

The view is called the middle (madhyama) path, because it avoids extreme views by denying, for example, both absolute reality and absolute unreality of things and asserting their conditional existence. This was the reason why Buddha, as we saw, called the theory of dependent origination—the middle path. And so Nāgārjuna says that śūnya-vāda is called the middle path because it implies the theory of dependent origination. It can also be interpreted as a theory of relativity. The conditionality of things which makes their own nature (svabhāva) unascertainable, either as real or unreal, etc., may be also regarded as a kind of relativity. Every character of a thing is conditioned by something else and therefore its existence is relative to that condition.

The Mādhyamikas, hold that there is a transcendental reality (noumenon) behind the phenomenal one and it is free from change, conditionality and all other phenomenal characters. As Nāgārjuna says : "There are two truths, on which Buddha's teaching of Dharma depends, one is empirical (saṁvṛti-satya) and meant for the ordinary people, another is the transcendental or the absolutely true one (paramārtha-satya). Those who do not know the distinction between these two kinds of truth, cannot understand the profound mystery of Buddha's teachings."

The truth of the order is only a stepping-stone to the attainment of the higher. The nature of nirvāṇa-experience which takes one beyond ordinary experience cannot be described, it can only be suggested negatively with the help of words which describe our common experience. Nāgārjuna, therefore, describes nirvāṇa with a series of negatives, thus : "That which is not known (ordinarily), not acquired anew, not destroyed, not eternal, not suppressed, not generated is called nirvāṇa". As with nirvāṇa so also with the Tathāgata or one who has realized nirvāṇa. His nature also cannot be described. That is why, when Buddha was asked what becomes of the Tathāgata after nirvāṇa is attained, he declined to discuss the question.

Four Successive Stages

The Indian period of the Madhyamika school is usually divided into four successive stages that can be indicated by listing the philosophers that characterised them :

These are as follows :

1. (Third-fourth century) Nagarjuna and Aryadeva.
2. (Fifth-sixth century) Buddhapalita and Bhavaviveka.
3. (Seventh century-first half of the eighth century) Candrakirti and Shantideva.
4. (Second half of the eighth century-tenth century) Shantarakshita and Kamalashila.

'Nagarjuna summarised the basic themes of his own philosophical doctrine in a series of 445 verses, worded in an extremely concise style, often mnemonic and obscure, which were destined to be learnst by heart and commented upon.

In the literature of the Madhyamika school the term 'Catuskoti' is not expressly used either by Nagarjuna or by Aryadeva, nor by Candrakirti. The four positions of the 'Tetralemma' frequently appear from the very beginning of the literature of this school, where they are either explicitly or implicitly denied each position (koti) the positive one. (i) the negative one, (ii) the one consisting of a combination or union of the positive and negative, (iii) and the one that consists in a double negation of the positive and negative one, (iv) is denied. The negation can be expressed either in a single grammatical word or in the predicate of a sentence.

The positions of the Tetralemma have been used in the 'Stanzas of the Middle Way' to analyse the following :

1. The concept of causation or of non-origin.
2. The totality of the elements on a relative or phenomenal plane.
3. The fact of the condition in the context of the ultimate reality, of the absolute truth.
4. The existence of the talhagata (Thus-gone, it being an epithel for the Buddha).
5. Nirvana.

Illusion in Nirvana

Nirvana itself is an illusion. Bondage and release are relative and therefore unreal. Neither the forces nor the ego can be either bound or liberated. Neither that which is the skandhas nor that which is not the skandhas can be either bound or liberated. Neither that which is bound nor that which is unbound nor that which is both nor that which is neither can be either bound or liberated. He who thinks like this : transcending the five skandhas, I shall obtain liberation', is still entangled in the terrible clutches of the skandhas themselves.

Nirvana cannot be existence because then, like other existing thing, it will be subject to birth and death. It will have a cause also and will be based on the Skandhas like all other Samskrta dharmas. Nirvana cannot be both existence and non-existence together for the very conception is absurd and self-contradictory. Existence and non-existence are absolutely opposed like light and darkness. How can they exist simultaneously in one place? Nirvana cannot be neither existence nor non-existence for then it will not be independent as non-existence necessarily depends upon existence.

Nirvana cannot be both existence and non-existence necessarily depends upon existence. Nirvana cannot be both existence and non existence together for the very conception is absurd and self-contradictory. Existence and non-existence are absolutely opposed like light and darkness. How can they exist simultaneously in one place? Nirvana cannot be neither existence nor non-existence for then it will not be conceived at all. If Nirvana is neither existence nor non-existence nor both nor neither, it is only an appearance, not reality.

Perfections of Perfect Knowledge

There are six perfections of which the last and the highest is the supreme or perfect knowledge. The Astasahasrika Prajna-paramita declares it to be clear and transparent like the sky, to be devoid of plurality, to be beyond finite thought, indescribable, divine mother, one with the Buddha just as Moonlight is one with the Moon, terrible to the fools, but most affectionate to the wise, the seal of the law, the light of existence, the trumpet of religion, the vision of the doctrine, the body of bliss and the only path towards liberation. It is reality itself.

It is indescribable and unthinkable in the sense that intellect fails to describe it adequately. Here, the cries of intellect are satisfied and its contradictions reconciled. It is subtler than the subtle and profounder than the profound. Here all desires and all doubts are set at rest. There are two standpoints-the empirical and the absolute. The former deals with the categories of intellect with name and form, with dependence with relativity with practical compromises, with phenomena or appearances; the latter transcends the former and deals with perfect knowledge which is Non-dual, independent, real and absolute ultimately it is the real, which appears.

Samvrti

Samvrti is covering. It hides the real nature of all things. It also means dependent origination or relativity. It is a practical reality. It is ignorance or delusion which covers reality and gives a false view. The true aspect is reality, the false is appearance. A man of defective vision sees hair floating in the atmosphere. But his experience cannot contradict the true experience of persons of good vision who see no hair. The phenomenal intellect cannot contradict pure knowledge. The empirical truth is only a means the absolute truth is the end Chandrakirti further distinguishes two aspects in the phenomenal reality itself–that which is phenomenally true and that which is phenomenally false. When people with rightly functioning sense-organs, recognise things as real, those things are phenomenally true and those things which are perceived when the sense-organs are not properly functioning, e.g., things in a dream a mirage, hair in the atmosphere, double moon etc. are phenomenally false.

Chandrakirti recognises the Pratibhasa and the Vyavahara of Vedanta by splitting Samvrti into two. Ultimately however, everything phenomental, because realive, is unreal. From the standpoint reality is equated with silence. But because the distinction between the phenomenal and the absolute is itself not absolute, reality from the phenomenal standpoint is heard and preached.

Yogācāra

Asaṅga, vasubandhu, Dinnaga are the famous teachers of this school.

While agreeing with the Mādhyamikas, as to the unreality of external objects, the Yogācāra school differs from them in holding that the mind (citta) cannot be regarded as unreal. For then all reasoning and thinking would be false and the Mādhyamikas could not even establish that their own arguments were correct. To say that everything, mental or non-mental, is unreal is suicidal. The reality of the mind should at least be admitted in order to make correct thinking possible.

The mind, consisting of a stream of different kinds of ideas, is the only reality. Things that appear to be outside the mind, our body as well as other objects, are merely ideas of the mind. Just as in cases of dreams and hallucinations a man fancies to perceive things outside, though they do not really exist there, similarly the objects which appear to be out there, are really ideas in the mind. The existence of any external object cannot be proved, because it cannot be shown that the object is different from the consciousness of the object. An object is never known without the consciousness of it, the object cannot be proved to have an existence independent of consciousness.

The Yogācāra view is called subjective idealism, or vijñānavāda, because according to it the existence of an object perceived is not different from the subject or the perceiving mind. Holding this theory, Yogacāra also accepts that the mind is a stream of momentary conscious states and within the stream there lie, buried the impressions (saṁskāra) of all past experience. At a particular moment that latent impression comes to the surface of consciousness for which the circumstances of the moment are the most favourable. At that moment that impression attains maturity (paripaka), so to say, and develops into immediate consciousness for perception. It is thus that at that particular moment only that object whose latent impression can, under the circumstances, reveal itself becomes perceived; just as in the case of the revival of past impressions in memory, though all the impressions are in the mind, only some are remembered at a particular time. This is why only some object can be perceived at a time and not any at will.

The mind considered in its aspect of being a store-house or home of all impressions is called by the Vijñāna-vādins Ālya-vijñāna. It may be regarded as the potential mind and answers, to the soul or ātman of other systems, with the difference that it is not one unchanging substance like the soul, but is a stream of continuously changing states. Through culture and self-control this Ālaya-vijñāna or the potential mind can gradually stop the arising of undesirable mental states and develop into the ideal state of nirvāṇa. Otherwise, it only gives rise to thoughts, desires, attachment, which bind one more and more to the fictitious external world. The mind, the only reality according to this school, is truly its own place, it can made heaven of hell and hell of heaven.

The Yogācarās are so called either because they used to practise yoga by which they came to realize the sole reality of mind (as Ālayavijñāna) dispelling all belief in the external world, or because they combined in them both critical inquisitiveness (yoga) and good conduct (ācāra). Asaṅga, Vasubandhu, Diṅnāga are the famous leaders of the Yogācāra school. Laṅkāvatāra-sūtra is one of its most important works.

Feature of Asanga

Asanga in the Mahayanasamparigraha-Shastra gives the following ten essential features of the Yogachara School :

1. The Alayavijnana is immanent in all beings.
2. There are three kinds of knowledge-illusory, relative and absolute.
3. The objective world and the subjective ego are only manifestations of the universal consciousness.
4. Six perfections are emphasised.
5. In order to realise Buddhahood, we have to pass through the ten stages of Bodhisattvahood.
6. The goal is to become one, through Bodhi, with the Dharmakaya or Buddha's Body of Pure Existence.
7. The subject-object duality is to be transcended and unity with Pure Consciousness is to be attained.
8. Reality is Dharmakaya or Buddha's body of pure existence which is at once pure consciousness and which manifests itself from the point of view of Samsara, as Nirmanakaya or the body of becoming and from the point of view of Nirvana, as Sambhogakaya or the body of bliss.

Individual Consciousness

Vijnanavada cannot be called subjectivism. It is not the individual consciousness as associated with other momentary functional ideas that creates the external world. The external world is declared to be a manifestation or modification of absolute consciousness. True, the dream state and the waking state are placed on a par. But, it should not be forgotten that the Parikalpita is distinguished from the Paratantra. Both agree in being ultimately, unreal and in existing inside consciousness.

The subject and the object dance within this circle which they cannot overstep. The objectivity of the external world is not denied. The objects appear as objects to the subject which perceives them. Only their objectivity does not fall outside of consciosuness because the distinction of the subject and the object is within consciousness itself which ultimately transcends the subject-object duality.

The Naiyayika and the Mimamsaka were the two major opponents of Buddhism at that time. Uddyotakara in his Nyaya-Vartika refuted the charges of Dinnage and defended the Nyaya position. Dharmakirti in his Pramana-Vartika demolished all the arguments of Uddyotakara in such a merciless manner that the eminent Advaitin, Vachaspati Mishra, at a much later data, had to comment on Uddyotakara in the Nyaya-Vartika-Tatparya-Tika in order to 'rescue the old argument-cows of Uddyotakara which were entangled in the mud of Buddhistic criticism.' Dharmakiriti's attack on Mimamsa also was so damaging that it provoked Kumarila to write his voluminous Sholka.

Vartika

Vartika to refute Buddhism and defend. Mimamsa. The attacks of the Naiyayikas and of the Mimamsakas, in their turn, gave rise to the writings of Shantaraksita and Kamalashila. Shantaraksita in his Tattvasangraha and Kamalashila in his Panjika on it, refute extensively all the charges of the Naiyayikas, especially of Uddyotakara and of the Mimamsakas, especially of Kumarila and criticise all other schools prevalent in their time. Buddhism could not resist the onslaught of Brahmanism and was being rapidly ousted from the land off its birth.

Shantaraksita himself was forced to retire to Tibet, where he called his disciple Kamalashila also. It is that the Svatantra-Vijnanavada school, after producing an enormously rich philosophical literature by way of approval and by way of criticism, came to an end and with it virtually ended Buddhist philosophy in India.

Dharmakirti says that everything is momentary. Whatever is produced must be destroyed. Reality is annihilation. Change exists by itself and always. Reality is such that it is momentary. Annihilation or destruction, therefore, does not required any cause. Annihilation does not mean destruction of a positive entity. Hence, the view that a positive entity is destroyed should be rejected. So, when we say that a thing is destroyed what we really mean is that a thing is momentary.

Shantaraksita also observes that all produced things are necessarily momentary because they do not depend for their destruction on any cause. They are always and everywhere independent of any cause in regard to their destruction. Destruction, therefore, does not depend on any cause except on the fact of being produced.

Destruction Features

Shantaraksita and Kamalashila maintain that destruction is neither an entity nor a non-entity. Destruction is of two kinds. Firstly, it means the 'Momentary character of a thing'. This is transcendental impermanence. Secondly, it means 'Disruption'. This is empirical annihilation. An entity itself, because it exists for a moment only, is called 'Destruction'. When, we admit that transcendental impermanence has a cause what we mean is simply this that an entity it itself the cause of its destruction, because the very fact that a momentary entity is produced implies that it is destroyed.

There can be no other cause of its destruction. 'The character of coming immediately after the thing' does not belong to this destruction because this destruction is born along with the production of the momentary thing itself. Again, disruption too can have no cause.

Only a momentary thing can exist because it alone can be efficient. A permanent entity is inefficient and hence unreal. A permanent entity should produce all its effects simultaneously because the efficient cause being present there is no reason why its effects should be delayed.

If it is urged that a permanent entity can produce successive effects because of its association with successive accessories then the question arises whether the accessories work by producing a peculiar modification in the permanent cause or they work independently.

Apoha

Apoha is the denotation of the word; the positive universal is a false creation of the intellect. Truly speaking, words are neither synonymous nor not-synonymous because they denote neither unity nor plurality. In fact unity and plurality belong to real things only. And these conceptual contents only, not things, differ among themselves. Things-in-themselves are neither unified nor diversified; it is only the conceptual content that appears as diverse. The sified; it is only the conceptual content that appears as diverse.

The object cow and object now-cow both are separate realities. Their reality is well-established. It is only the word which is unreal because it depends on the pure whim of the person using it. Words do not cognise external objects. And on account of the force of ignorance words mistake their own internal reflections to be external objects.

Words can reflect individuals only and so the individuals may be denoted by words. Words cannot reflect universals. So, universals can be neither denoted nor excluded by words. And even if they are excluded they cannot become real. When a thing excludes another, it is called its Apoha. But by this, neither the thing becomes negative nor does the Apoha really become positive.

Sautrāntika

The Sautrāntikas believe in the reality not only of the mind, but also of external objects. They point out that without the supposition of some external objects, it is not possible to explain even the illusory appearance of external objects. It one never perceived anywhere any external object, he could not say, as a Vijñāna-vādin does, that, through illusion, consciousness appears *like* an external object. The phrase 'like an external object' is as meaningless as 'like the son of a barren mother' because an external object is said by the Vijñāna-vādin to the wholly unreal and never perceived. Again, the argument from the simultaneity of consciousness and object to their identity is also defective. Whenever we have the perceptions of an object like a pot, the pot is felt as external and consciousness of it as internal (i.e. to be in the mind. So the object, from the very beginning, is known to be different from and not identical with consciousness. If the pot perceived were identical with the subject, the perceiver would have said, "I am the pot". Besides, if there were no external objects, the distinction between the 'consciousness of a pot' and 'the consciousness of a cloth' could not be explained, because as consciousness both are identical; it is not only regarding the objects that they differ.

The reason why we cannot perceive at will any object at any time and place, lies in the fact that a perception depends on four different conditions and not simply on the mind. There must be the object to impart its form to consciousness, there must be the conscious mind (or the state of the mind at the just previous moment) to cause the consciousness of the form, there must be the sense to determine the kind of the consciousness, that is whether the consciousness of that object would be visual, tactual or of any other kind. Lastly, there must be some favourable auxiliary condition, such as light, convenient position, perceptible magnitude, etc. All these combined together bring about the perception of the object. The from of the object thus generated in the mind, is the effect of the object, among other things. The existence of the objects is not of course perceived, because what mind immediately knows is the copy or representation of the object in its own consciousness. But from this is can infer the object without which the copy would not arise.

The Sautrāntika theory is, therefore, called also the theory of the inferability of external objects (Bāhyānumeya-vāda). The name 'Sautrāntika' is given to this school because it attaches exclusive importance to the authority of the 'Sūtra-piṭaka'. The arguments used by this school for the refutation of subjective idealism anticipated long ago some of the most important arguments which modern Western realists like Moore use to refute the subjective idealism of Berkely. The Sautrāntika position in epistemology resembles 'representationalism' or the 'copy theory of ideas' which was common among Western philosophers like Locke. This exists even now in a modified from among some critical realists.

Vaibhāṣika

While agreeing with the Sautrāntikas regarding the reality of both the mental and the non-mental, the Vaibhāṣikas, like many modern neo realists, point out that unless we admit that external objects are perceived by us, their existence cannot be known in any other way. Inference of fire from the perception of smoke is possible, because in the past we have perceived both smoke and fire together. One who has never perceived fire previously can not infer its existence from the perception of smoke. If external objects were never perceived, as the Sautrāntikas hold, then they could not even be inferred, simply from their mental forms. To one unacquainted with an external object, the mental form would not appear to be the copy or the sign of the existence of an extra-mental object, but as an original thing which does not owe its existence to anything outside the mind. Either, therefore, we have to accept subjective idealism (vijñāna-vāda) or, if that has been found unsatisfactory, we must admit that the external object is directly known. The Vaibhāṣikas thus come to hold a theory of direct realism' (bāhya-pratyakṣa-vāda).

The Abhidhamma treatises formed the general foundation of the philosophy of the realists. The Vaibhāṣikas followed exclusively a particular commentary, Vibhāṣā (or *Abhidhamma-mahāvibhāṣā* on an Abhidhamma treatise (*Abhidharma-jñāna-prasthnāna).* Hence their name.

NYĀYA

Nyāyā school of philosophy is famous for its atomistic pluralism and logical realism. This school, founded by gautama, is allied to the vaiśesika system which is regarded as 'Samāantantra' or similar philosophy. Nyāyā has developed logic and epistemology while, Vaiśesika, metaphysics and ontology. Nyāyā theory of knowledge has great importance in philosophical world. Let us discuss the problems of Nyāya Philosophy schools one by one.

Knowledge, according to Nyāya, reveals both the subject and the object which are quite distinct from itself. This is the reason why Nyāya is called as realist system. Knowledge or cognition is defined as apprehension or consciousness. Knowledge may be valid or invalid. Valid knowledge, is called pramā and, is defined as the right apprehension of an object. Nyāya maintains the theory of correspondence (paratah pramānya). Non-valid knowledge is known as apramā.

Pramāna is valid means of knowledge. Nyāya accepts four valid means of knowledge namely, perception, inference, testimony and comparison.

Prama and Aprama

Pramanya and Apramanya

Nyaya believes in *paratah pramanya* and *paratah apramanya.* Pramanya means a way through which validity of knowledge is known. Apramanya means a way through which invalidity of knowledge is known. Nyaya maintains theory of correspondences which invalidity of knowledge is known. Nyaya says, that validity and invalidity of knowledge arises only after knowledge has arisen. Truth and falsity are regarded as extrinsic characteristics of knowledge. Knowledge is regarded neither as intrinsic nor self-evident. According to Nyaya school, knowledge can be known only through the way of knowing extrinsic qualities of knowledge. Correspondence is regarded as the content and successful activity of the knowledge. Correspondence is regarded as the test of the truth.

Pramana

Pramana is defined a valid means of knowledge. It is also referred as a source of knowing valid knowledge. Nayaya believe in four pramanas. Perception inference comparing and testimony.

Pratyakṣa (Perception)

Gotama defines perception as 'non-erroneous cognition which is produced by the intercourse of the sense-organs with the objects, which is not associated with a name and which is well-defined.' This definition of perception excludes divine and yogic perception which is not generated by the intercourse of the sense-organs with the objects. Hence Vishvanātha has defined perception as 'direct or immediate cognition which is not derived through the instrumentality of any other cognition.' This definition includes ordinary as well as extra-ordinary perception and excludes inference, comparison and testimony. Perception is a kind of knowledge and is the attribute of the self. Ordinary perception presupposes the sense-organs, the objects, the manas and the self and their mutual contacts. The self comes into contact with the manas, the manas with the sense-organs and the sense-organs with the objects. The contact of the sense-organs with the objects is not possible unless the manas first comes into contact with the sense-organs, and the contact of the manas with the sense-organs is not possible unless the self comes into contact with the manas. Hence sense-object contact necessarily presupposes the mans-sense contact and the self-manas contact. The sense-organs are derived from the elements whose specific qualities of smell, taste, colour, touch and sound are manifested by them. The manas is the mediator between the self and the sense-organs. The external object, through the sense and the manas, makes an impression on the self. The theory, therefore, is realistic.

The Two Stages in Pratyakṣa (Savikalpa and Nirvikalpa Pratyakṣa)

The naiyāyika maintains two stages in perception. The first is called indeterminate or nirvikalpa and the second, determinate or savikalpa. They are not two different kinds of perception, but only the earlier and the later stages in the same complex process of perception. These two stages are recognized by Gotama in his definition of perception quoted above.

All perception is determinate, but is necessarily preceded by an earlier stage when it is indeterminate. Bare sensation or simple apprehension is nirvikalpa perception; perceptual judgment or relational apprehension is savikalpa perception. Nyāya avoids the fallacy of the psychical staircase theory that we have first sense experience, then conception and then judgement. Perception is a complex presentative-representative process in which we cannot really separate direct awareness from relational judgement. Indeterminate perception forms the material out of which determinate perception is shaped, but they can be distinguished only in thought and not divided in reality. Nirvikalpa perception is the immediate apprehension, the bare awareness, the direct sense-experience which is undifferentiated and non-relational and is free from assimilation, discrimination, analysis and sysnthesis.

Indeterminate perception presents the bare object without any characterization. In determinate perception we relate the substance with its attributes. The feeling of indeterminate perception is psychological, but its knowledge is logical. As bare awareness, as mere apprehension, we sense indeterminate perception, we feel it, but the moment we try to know it even as 'bare awareness, it has passed into conception and has become determinate'. Hence all our perception being a cognition is determinate and is a perceptual judgement. We can separate indeterminate from determinate perception only in thought and not in reality. Hence, though we feel indeterminate perception as a psychological state of sense-experience, its knowledge even as indeterminate perception is a result of logical deduction. We do feel it directly but only as an awareness, not as a cognition. Mere apprehension, being infra-relational, cannot be cognized. As cognition it is inferred afterwards when conception has transformed mere sensation into a perceptual judgement.

Vātsyāyana says that if an object is perceived with its name we have determinate perception; if it is perceived without its name, we have indeterminate perception. Jayanta Bhaṭṭa says that indeterminate perception apprehends substance, qualities and actions and universals as separate and indistinct something and is devoid of any association with a name, while determinate perception apprehends all these together with a name. Gaṅgesha Upādhyāya defines indeterminate perception as the non-relational apprehension of an object devoid of all association of name, genus, diferentia etc. Annaṁ Bhaṭṭa defines it as the immediate apprehension of an object as well as of its qualities, 'but without the knowledge of the relation between them. The substance and the qualities, the 'that' and the 'what' are felt separately and it is not apprehended that those qualities inhere in that substance or that the 'what' characterizes the 'that'.

The Two Kinds of Pratyakṣa (Laukika and Alaukika)

Again, according to Nyāya, pratyakṣa is of two kinds, namely, laukika (ordinary) and alaukika (extraordinary). When the sense-organs come into contact with the objects present to them in the usual way, we have Laukika perception. And if the contact of the sense-organs with the objects is in an unusual way, i.e., if the objects are not ordinarily present to the senses but are conveyed to them through an extraordinary medium, we have Alaukika perception. Ordinary perception is of two kinds—internal (mānasa) and external (bāhya). In internal perception, the mind (manas), which is the internal organ comes into contact with the psychical states and processes like cognition, affection, conation, desire, pain, pleasure, aversion etc. External perception takes place when the five external organs of sense organs of sight, sound, touch, taste and smell respectively when they come into contact with the external objects. The external sense-organs are composed of material elements of earth, water, fire, air and ether and therefore each senses the particular quality of its element. Thus the sense-organ of smell is composed of the atoms of earth and perceives smell which is the specific quality of earth and so on.

Extra-ordinary perception is of three kinds—sāmānyalakṣaṇa, jñānalakṣaṇa and yogaja. Sāmānyalakṣaṇa perception is the percaption of the universals. According to Nyāya, the universals are a distinct class of reals. They inhere in the particulars which belong to different classes on account of the different universals inhering in them. An individual belongs to a particular class because the universal of that class inheres in it. Thus a cow becomes a cow because it has the universal cowness inhering in it. Ordinarily we perceive only the particulars and not the universals. We perceive particular cows but we do not perceive a 'universal cow'. Hence the Nyāya maintains that the universals are perceived extra ordinarily. The second kind of extraordinary perception is called jñānalakṣaṇa perception. It is the 'complicated' perception through association. Sometimes different sensations become associated and form one integrated perception. Here an object is not directly presented to a sense-organ, but is revived in memory through the past cognition of it and is perceived through representation. Example of it are : 'the piece of sandalwood *looks* fragrant', '*ice looks cold*', 'srone looks hard', 'tea *lookshot*', etc. etc. The theory of illusion accepted by Nyāya called 'Anyathākhyāti' is based on this kind of perception. The third kind of extra-ordinary perception is called yogaja perception. This is the intuitive and immediate perception of all objects, past, present and future, possessed by the Yogins through the power of meditation. It is like the Kevalajñāna of the Jainas, the Bodhi of the Buddhists, the Kaivalya of the Sāṅkhya-Yoga and the Aparokṣānubhūti of the Vedāntins. It is intuitive, supra-sensuous and supra-relational.

Internal and External Perception

Internal and external perception comes under the domain of ordinary perception. In external perception, the five external organs of sense come into contact with the external object. *Samanyalaksana, Jnanalaksana* and *Yogaja* are regarded as three kinds of extraordinary perception. It has been said, that an individual belongs to a particular class because the universal of that class inheres in it.

Jnanalaksana perception is regarded as the complicated perception and this complicated perception is possible only through association. Yogaja perception is regarded as the intuitive and immediate perception of all objects, part, present and future.

Anumāna

The second kind of knowledge is anumāna or inferential or relational and its means is called anumāna or inference. It is defined as that cognition which presupposes some other cognition. It is mediate and indirect and arises through a 'mark', the 'middle term' (linga or hetu) which is invariably connected with the 'major term' (sādhya). It is *knowledge* (māna) which arises *after* (anu) other knowledge. Invariable concomitance (vyāpti or avinābhāvaniyama) is the nerve of inference. The presence of the middle term in the minor term is called pakṣadharmatā. The invariable association of the middle term with the major term is called vyāpti. The knowledge of pakṣadharmatā as qualified by vyāpti is called parāmarsha, *i.e.,* the knowledge of the presence of the major in the minor through the middle which resides in the minor (pakṣadharmatā) and is invariably associated with the major (vyāpti). Like the Aristotelian syllogism, the Indian inference has three terms. The major, the minor and the middle are here called sādhya, pakṣa and liṅga or hetu respectively. We know that smoke is invariably associated with fire (vyāpti) and if we see smoke in a hill we conclude that there must be fire in that hill. Hill is the minor term; fire is the major term; smoke is the middle term.

Indian logic does not separate deduction from induction. Inference is a complex process involving both. Indian logic also rejects the verbalist view of logic. It studies thought as such and not the forms of thought alone. The formal and the material logic are blended here. Verbal form forms no integral part of the inference. This becomes clear from the division of inference into svārtha (for oneself) and parārtha (for others). In the former we do not require the formal statement of the different members of inference. It is a psychological process. The latter, the parārtha which is a syllogism, has to be presented in language and this has to be done only to convince others. There are five members in the Nyāya syllogism. The first is called Pratijñā or proposition. It is the logical statement which is to be proved. The second is Hetu or 'reason' which states the reason for the establishment of the proposition. The third is called Udāharaṇa which gives the universal concomitance together with an example. The fourth is Upanaya or the application of the universal concomitance to the present case. And the fifth is Nigamana or conclusion drawn from the preceding propositions. These five propositions of the Indian syllogism are called 'members' or avayavas. The following is a typical Nyāya syllogism :

(1) This hill has fire (pratijñā).
(2) Because it has smoke (hetu).
(3) Whatever has smoke has fire, *e.g.*, an oven (udāharaṇa).
(4) This hill has smoke which is invariably associated with fire (upanaya).
(5) Therefore this hill has fire (nigamana).

Comparison with Aristotelian's Syllogism

If we compare Nyaya syllogism with the Aristotelian syllogism which has only three propositions, we will also find that this Nyaya syllogism corresponds to the Barbara mood of the first figure, which is the strongest mood of the strongest figure.

The Nyaya syllogism has five and the Aristotelian has three propositions, the terms in both are only three, the sadhya or the major, the paksa or the minor and the hetu or the middle. The first coincides with the fifth and the second with the fourth. If we omit the last two, the first three propositions correspond with the conclusion, the minor premise and the major premise respectively. Hence, if we leave out the first two members of the Nyaya syllogism, which are contained in the last two, we find that it resembles the Aristotelian syllogism in the first figure.

- All things which have smoke have fire (Major premise).
- This hill has smoke (Minor premise).
- Therefore, this hill has fire (Conclusion).

The typical Aristotelian syllogism may be stated in the Nyaya from this

- Socrates is mortal (Pratijna).
- Because he is a man (Hetu).
- Whoever is a man is a mortal, *e.g.* Pythagoras (Udaharana).
- Socrates is a man, who is invariably a mortal (Upanaya).
- Therefore, Socrates is mortal (Nigamana).

Differences between Nyaya and Aristotelian Syllogism

There are certain real differences between the Nyaya and the Aristotelian syllogism apart from the nominal difference between the number of the propositions in each. The Aristotelian syllogism is only deductive and formal, while the Nyaya syllogism is deductive-inductive and formal-material.

Inference, according to Nyaya, is neither from the universal to the particular nor from the particular to the universal, but from the particular to the particular through the universal. The example is a special feature of the Nyaya syllogism and illustrates the truth that the universal major premise is the result of a real induction based on the Law of Causation and that induction and deduction cannot be really separated. While, in the Aristotelian syllogism, the major and the minor terms stand apart in the premises though they are connected by the middle term with each other, in the Nyaya syllogism all the three terms stand synthesised in the Upanaya.

Anayavyatireka

It is referred as one of the classification of inference. It means that the middle term is both positively and negatively related to the major term. The Vyapti should com between the middle and the major term. It is referred as the double agreement between the terms.

Lingaparāmarsha

The Nyāya syllogism has five terms. Among them, middle term works as a bridge between the major and the minor terms. Therefore, the middle term has main responsibility to prove a syllogism valid or invalid. How a middle term is related to major term is lingaparāmarsha. There are five characteristics of a middle term—

(1) It must be present in the minor term (pakṣadharmatā); *e.g.*, smoke must be present in the hill.
(2) It must be present in all positive instances in which the major term is present; *e.g.*, smoke must be present in the kitchen where fire exists (sapakṣasattva).
(3) It must be absent in all negative instances in which the major term is absent; *e.g.*, smoke must be absent in the lake in which fire does not exist (vipakṣāsattva).
(4) It must be non-incompatible with the minor term; *e.g.*, it must not prove the coolness of fire (abādhita).
(5) It must be qualified by the absence of counteracting reasons which lead to a contradictory conclusion; *e.g.*, 'the fact of being caused' should not be used to prove the 'eternality' of sound (aviruddha).

Vyāpti

Vyāpti implies a correlation between two factors of which one is pervaded (vyāpta) and the other pervades (vyāpaka). Vyāpti is of two kinds namely samavyāpti and visamavyāpti. A vyāpti between two terms of equal extension concomitance, so that we may infer either of them from the other, *e.g.*, whatever is nameable is knowable and *vice-versa.* Visamavyāpti is a relation of non-equipollent concomitance between two terms, from one of which we may infer the other, but not vice-versa. We may infer fire from smoke but no smoke from fire. Therefore vyāpti is an invariable the middle and the major term. The Naiyāyikas agree with the vedantins in holding that vyāpti is established by the uncontradicted experience of the relation between two things, and not on any a priory principle like causality or essential identity. They, however go further than the vedantins and supplement uncontradicted experience of the relation between two facts by tarka or indirect proof and by sāmānyalakṣana perception.

The Nyāya method of induction or generalization may be analysed into five steps. These are anavaya, vyatireka, vyabhichārāgraha, upadhinirāsa, tarka and sāmānyalakṣana perception respectively. Anavaya is, when a relation of agreement between two things is in presence, and vyatireka, when this relation is in absence. Vyabhichāragraha is, when we do not observe any contrary instance in which one of them is present without the other. Upādhinirāsa is the elimination of upādhis or conditions on which the relation may possible be dependent. Tarka and sāmānyalakṣana perceptions have their literal meanings about which we have discussed earlier.

Classification of Anumāna

Inference is generally classified into svārtha and parārtha. In svarthanumāna we do not require formal statements of the members of inference. It is a psychological process. And the pararthanumana, which is a syllogism, has to be presented in language and this has to be done only to convince others.

Gotama speaks of three kinds of inference—pūrvavat, sheṣavat and sāmānyatodṛṣṭa. The first two are based on causation and the last one on mere coexistence. A cause is the invariable and unconditional antecedent of an effect and an effect is the invariable and unconditional consequent of a cause. When we infer the unperceived effect from a perceived cause we have pūrvavat inference, *e.g.*, when we infer future rain from dark clouds in the sky. When we infer the unperceived cause from a perceived effect we have sheṣavat inference, *e.g.*, when we infer past rain from the swift muddy flooded water of a river. When inference is based not on causation but on uniformity of co-existences; it is called sāmānyatodṛṣṭa, *e.g.*, when we infer cloven hoofs of an animal by its horns. According to another interpretation, a pūrvavat inference is based on previous experience of universal concomitance between two things, a sheṣavat inference is parisheṣa or inference by elimination, and a sāmānyatodṛṣṭa is inference by analogy.

Another classification of inference gives us the kevalānvayi, kevalavyatireki and anvayavyatireki inferences. It is based on the nature of vyāpti and on the different methods of establishing it. The methods of induction by which universal casual relationship is established may be anvaya, vyatireka or both. The first corresponds to Mill's Method of Agreement, the second to his Method of Difference, and the third to his Joint method of Agreement and Difference or the Method of Double Agreement.

We have kevalānvayi inference when the middle term is always positively related to the major term. The terms agree only in presence, there being no negative instance of their agreement in absence, *e.g.*,

All men are mortal.
Ram is a man.
∴ Ram is mortal.

We have kevalavyatireki inference when the middle term is the differentium of the minor term and is always negatively related to the major term. The terms agree only in absence, there being no positive instance of their agreement in presence, *e.g.*,

All knowable objects are nameable;
The pot is a knowable object;
∴ The pot is nameable

We have anvayavyatireki inference when the middle term is both positively and negatively related to the major term. The vyāpti between the middle and the major is in respect of both presence and absence. There is Double agreement between the terms—they agree in presence in the positive instances and they also agree in absence in the negative instances; *e.g.*,

All things which have smoke have fire;
This hill has smoke;
∴ This hill has fire; and
No non-firey things have smoke;
This hill has smoke;
∴ This hill is not non-fiery;
i.e., This hill has fire.

Classes of Inference

The Kevalanvayi, Kevalavyatireki and Anvayavyatireki are known as another classification of inference. They are all based on the nature of Vyapti, Kevalanvayi says that the middle term is always positively related to the major term. Kevalavyatireki inferences says that the middle term is negatively related to the major term. Anvayavyatireki inference says that the middle term is both positively and negatively related to the major term.

Vyaptigrahopayas

In Vyaptigrahopayas, Vyapti is regarded as an important term. Without Vyapti nothing is possible. It means the division of Vyapti which has been already discussed above.

Hetvābhāsa

In Indian logic a fallacy is called hetvābhāsa. It means that middle term *appears* to be a reason but is not a valid reason. All fallacies are material fallacies. We have mentioned the five characteristics of a valid middle term. When these are violated, we have fallacies. Five kinds of fallacies are recognized :

(1) **Asiddha or Sādhyasama.** This is the fallacy of the unproved middle. The middle term must be present in the minor term (pakṣadharmatā). If it is not, it is unproved. It is of three kinds—

 (a) **āshrayāsiddha.** The minor term is the locus of the middle term. If the minor term is unreal, the middle term cannot be present in it; *e.g.*, 'the sky-lotus is fragrant, because it is a lotus, like the lotus of a lake'.

 (b) **svarūpāsiddha.** Here the minor term is not unreal. But the minor term; *e.g.*, 'sound is a quality, because it is visible'. Here visibility cannot belong to sound which is audible.

 (c) **vyāpyatvāsiddha.** Here vyāpti is conditional (sopādhika). We cannot say, *e.g.*, 'wherever there is fire there is smoke'. Fire smokes only when it is associated with wet fuel. A red-hot iron ball or clear fire does not smoke. Hence 'association with we fuel' is a condition necessary to the aforesaid vyāpti. Being conditioned, the middle term becomes fallacious if we say : 'The hill has smoke because it has fire'.

(2) **Savyabhichara or Anaikāntika.** This is the fallacy of the irregular middle. It is of three kinds.

 (a) **Sādhāraṇa.** Here the middle term is too wide. It is present in both the sapakṣa (positive) and the vipakṣa (negative) instances and violates the rule that the middle should not be present in the negative instances (vipakṣāsattva); *e.g.*, 'the hill has fire because it is knowable'. Here 'knowable' is present in fiery as well as non-fiery objects.

 (b) **Asādhāraṇa.** Here the middle term is too narrow. It is present only in the pakṣa and neither in the sapakṣa nor in the vipakṣa. It violates the rule that the middle term should be present in the sapakṣa (sapakṣasattva); *e.g.*, 'sound is eternal, because it is audible'. Here audibility belongs to sound only and is present nowhere else.

 (c) **Anupasaṁhāri.** Here the middle term is non-exclusive. The minor term is all-inclusive and leaves nothing by way of sapakṣa or vipakṣa; *e.g.*, 'all things are non-eternal, because they are knowable.'

(3) **Satpratipakṣa.** Here the middle term is contradicted by another middle term. The reason is counter-balanced by another reason. And both are of equal force; *e.g.* 'sound is eternal, because it is audible' and 'sound is non-eternal, because it is produced'. Here 'audible' is counter-balanced by 'produced' and both are of equal force.

(4) **Bādhita.** It is the non-inferentially contradicted middle. Here the middle term is contradicted by some other pramāṇa and not by inference. It cannot prove the major term which is disproved by another stronger source of valid knowledge; *e.g.*, 'fire is cold, because it is a substance'. Here the middle term 'substance' is directly contradicted by perception.

(5) **Viruddha.** It is the contradictory middle. The middle term, instead of being pervaded by the presence of the major term, is pervaded by the absence of the major term. Instead of proving the existence of the major term in the minor term, it proves its non-existence therein; *e.g.*, 'sound is eternal, because it is produced'. Here 'produced', instead of proving the eternality of sound, proves its non-eternality.

Upamāna

The third kind of valid cognition is Upamiti and its means is called Upamāna. It is knowledge derived from comparison and roughly corresponds to analogy. It has been defined as the knowledge of the relation between a word and its denotation. It is produced by the knowledge of resemblance or similarity. For example, a man who has never seen a gavaya or a wild cow and does not know what it is, is told by a person that a wild cow is an animal like a cow, subsequently comes across a wild cow in a forest and recognizes it as the wild cow, then his knowledge is due to upamāna. He has heard the word 'gavaya' and has been told that it is like a cow and now he himself sees the object denoted by the word 'gavaya' and recognizes it to be so. Hence upamāna is just the knowledge of the relation between a name and the object denoted by that name. It is produced by the knowledge of similarity because a man recognizes a wild cow as a 'gavaya' when he perceives its similarity to the cow and remembers the description that 'a gavaya is an animal like a cow'.

The Buddhists reduce Upamāna to perception and testimony. The Sāṅkhya and the Vaisheṣika reduce it to inference. The Jainas reduce it to recognition or pratyabhijñā. The Mimāṁsakas recognize it as a separate source of knowledge, but their account of it is different from that of Nyāya, which will be considered in the chapter on Mimāṁsā.

Śabda

Śabda is valid source, of knowledge in all the systems of Indian philosophy. Also in the Nyāya system, the fourth kind of valid knowledge is Śhabda. It is defined, as the statement of a trustworthy person (āptavākya) and consists in understanding its meaning. A sentence is defined as a collection of words and word is defined as that which is potent to convey its meaning. The power is a word to convey its meaning comes, according to ancient Nyāya, from God, and according to later Nyāya, from long established convention. Testimony is always personal. It is based on the words of a trustworthy person, human or divine. Testimony is of two kinds—Vaidika and secular (laukika). The Vaidika testimony is perfect and infallible because the Vedas are spoken by God; secular testimony, being the words of human beings who are liable to error, is not infallible. Only the words of trustworthy persons who always speak the truth are valid; others are not. A word is a potent symbol which signifies an object and a sentence is a collection of words. But a sentence in order to be intelligible must conform to certain conditions. These conditions are four—ākāṅkṣā, yogyatā, sannidhi and tātparya. The first is mutual implication or expectancy. The words of a sentence are interrelated and stand in need of one another in order to express a complete sense. A mere aggregate of unrelated words will not make a logical sentence. It will be sheer nonsense, *e.g.*, 'cow horse man elephant'. The second condition is that the words should possess fitness to convey the sense and should not contradict the meaning. 'Water the plants with fire' is a contradictory sentence. The third condition is the close proximity of the words to one another. The words must be spoken in quick succession without long intervals. If the words 'bring', 'a', 'cow' are uttered at long intervals they would not make a logical sentence. The fourth condition is the intention of the speaker if the words are ambiguous. For example, the word 'saindhava' means 'salt' as well as a 'horse'. Now, if a man who is taking his food asks another to bring 'saindhava', the latter should not bring a horse.

Sakti

It is defined as the causal potency. It also means the power. It has been said that words should have power in themselves, so that they are able to express themselves. It has been said that the power in a word in conveying their meanings.

Laksana

This is very important in shabda. Laksana is referred as a symptom. It has been said that a word is defined as a potent symbol and this potent symbol signifies an object. It has been said that sakti has two meanings. First is Abhidha and second is Laksana. Abhidha sakti means primary or expressive power whereas Laksana sakti means secondary or indicative power. It has been said that through Laksana sakti, indicative feature of a word is delivered.

Akanksa

This is regarded as the first condition of verbal testimony. It means mutual implication or expectancy. It says that the words of a sentence are interrelated. It also expresses a complete sense. It has been said that a mere aggregate of unrelated words are notable to make a logical sentence.

Yogyata

It is referred as the second condition of verbal testimony. It says that the words should possess fitness and this fitness convey the sense also. It should not contradict the meaning.

Sannidhi

It is referred as the third condition of verbal testimony. It is referred as the close proximity of the words. It has been said that one word is connected with another. It says, that the words must be spoken without long intervals.

Tatparya

It is referred as the fourth condition of verbal testimony. It is referred as the intention of the speaker, if the words are found to be ambiguous. The word *Saindhava* is used as an example here. *Saindhava* means both *salt* and *horse*. But, if a person is taking his food, then the salt meaning has to be ascribed to the term Saindhava.

Arthāpatti and Abhāva

Nyāya admits only four pramānas, namely perception, inference, comparison and testimony. Arthāpatti or implication is reduced to inference. For example, when we say : 'Fat Devadatta does not eat during day', the implication is that he must be eating during night otherwise how can he be fat? Mimāṁsā grants the status of an independent pramāṇa to implication. But Nyāya reduces it to inference thus :

All fat persons who do not eat during day, eat during night;
Devadatta is a fat person who does not eat during day;
∴ Devadatta is a fat person who eats during night.

Abhāva or non-existence which also is regarded as a separate pramāṇa by Bhāṭṭa Mīmāṁsā is reduced here either to perceptions or to inference. Abhāva is non-existence of a thing and the same sense-organ which perceives a thing, perceives its non-existence also. If the thing is imperceptible and can only be inferred, then, its non-existence too may be equally inferred.

Concept of God

Nyāyā accepts the metaphysics of the Vaisheṣika School and the accounts of matter, soul and God are almost the same as those in the Vaisheṣika. We have discussed the metaphysics of the Vaisheṣika School and so we need not repeat it here. The categories, the doctrine of asatkāryavāda, the account of creation and destruction, the nature of atoms and souls, the account of bondage and liberation, the authority of the Veda, the nature and function of God, the Unseen Power—all these are accepted by Nyāya. The criticisms which we levelled against the Vaisheṣika also apply against the Nyāya position in so far as both are identical. While Kaṇāda himself has not specifically mentioned God; the later Vaisheṣikas and particularly the later Naiyāyikas have given an elaborate account of God and the latter have made God's Grace an essential thing for obtaining true knowledge of the realities which alone leads to liberation. They refer to God as the creator, maintainer and destroyer of this world and introduce the element of devotion. But in our opinion all this can be done only by courtesy. God, as an eternal external reality, is always limited by the co-eternal atoms and souls and has to be guided by the law of karma. Though the later Naiyāyikas are forced to amend the absurd position that eternal consciousness is not the essence of God by raising consciousness from the position of a separable accident to the position of an inseparable attribute in the case of God, yet they have failed to rise to the correct position by not taking consciousness as the essence of God. An atomistic and spiritualistic pluralism can lead only to an external theism where God, souls and atoms all fall apart and the dualism of matter and spirit can never be overcome. God is said to possess all the six perfections in their fullness—majesty, power, glory, beauty, knowledge and freedom. But then why are the liberated souls not allowed to share these qualities? If liberation consists in getting rid of all qualities, then God will bc regarded as eternally bound. Again, God is called the moral governor of all beings (prayojaka kartā). But then either the souls are not free or the law of karma is thrown overboard. If the law of karma represents the self-determination of God and therefore does not bind God, then Karma and God would become identical and external theism would vanish.

- Gotama (250-450 CE) is the purported author of the Nyaya Sutras, the foundational text for the school.
- Nyaya system is regarded as a system of atomistic ruralism and logical realism.
- The Nyaya school holds that moksha (libration) from samsara (the cycle of birth and rebirth) is brought about through knowledge of the material word and for this reason, they believe that one must first have a complete understanding of what constitutes or knowledge is obtained.
- The Nyaya is also called Tarka-Vidya, science of reasoning or Vada-Vidya, science of discussion.
- Gotama, the founder of Nyaya, is frequently referred in literature as Aksa-Pada, 'eyebooted' and Dirgha Tapas, 'long-penance.'
- Anumana is based upon a well-known or observed connection between two things (cause and effect). *e.g.*, clouds + rain, rain + harvest, smoke + fire, insult + anger, love + attachment.
- There are three types of inference : a priori - from cause to effect, (Purvavat), a posteriori-from effect to cause (Shesavat); or commonly seen (Samanyatodrsta) which is knowledge of one thing derived from the perceptionof another thing with which it is commonly seen.

Proofs for the existence of God

Nyāya-Vaiśeṣika gives the following nine arguments to prove the existence of God :

(1) The world is an effect and hence it must have an efficient cause. This intelligent agent is God. The order, design, co-ordination between different phenomena comes from God (kāryāt).

(2) The atoms being essentially inactive cannot form the different combinations unless God gives motion to them. The Unseen Power, the Adṛṣṭa, requires the intelligence of God. Without God it cannot suply motion to the atoms (āyojanāt).

(3) The world is sustained by God's will. Unintelligent Adṛṣṭa cannot do this. And the world is destroyed by God's will (dhṛtyādeḥ).

(4) A word has a meaning and signifies an object. The power of words to signify their objects comes from God (padāt).

(5) God is the author of the infallible Veda (pratyayataḥ).

(6) The Veda testifies to the existence of God (shruteḥ).

(7) The Vedic sentences deal with moral injunctions and prohibitions. The Vedic commands are the Divine commands. God is the creator and promulgator of the moral laws (vākyāt).

(8) According to Nyāya-Vaisheṣika the magnitude of a dyad is not produced by the infinitesimal magnitude of the two atoms each, but by the number of the two atoms. Number 'one' is directly perceived, but other numbers are conceptual creations. Numerical conception is related to the mind of the perceiver. At the time of creation, the souls are unconscious. And the atoms and the Unseen Power and space, time, minds are all unconscious. Hence the numerical conception depends upon the Divine Consciousness. So God must exist (saṅkhyāvisheṣāt).

(9) We reap the fruits of our own actions. Merit and demerit accrue from our actions and the stock of merit and demerit is called Adṛṣṭa, the Unseen Power. But this Unseen Power, being unintelligent, needs the guidance of a supremely intelligent God (adṛṣṭāt).

Adrsta

It is defined as the unseen power. This unseen power is regarded as not intelligent. It also requires the guidance and this guidance is dependent only on God. God is regarded as intelligent, so only intelligent person can handle unintelligent type of thing.

Nihsryeasa

It is referred as the concept of moksha or liberation. Nyayikas believe in the conception of liberation. Moksha means the concept without anything. It is also referred as the detached attitude.

VAIŚEṢIKA

The word vaiśeṣika is derived from 'Visheṣa' which means particularity or distinguishing feature or distinction. The Vaisheṣika philosophy, therefore, is pluralistic realism which emphasizes that diversity is the soul of the universe. The category of Visheṣa or particularity is dealt with at length in this system, and is regarded as the essence of things. The founder of this system is Kaṇāda who is also known as kaṇabhuk, Uluka and kāshyapa. This system of philosophy was, later on, fused together with the Nyāya which accepted the ontology of the former and developed it in the light of its epistemology.

Concept of Padārtha

As we know that the Vaiśeṣika is ontological aspect of Nyāya system of philosophy, it meditates on metaphysical problems to survive its atomistic pluralism under the shadow of Nyāya's Epistemology. A category is called padārtha and the entire universe is reduced to six or seven padārthas. Padārtha literally means 'the meaning of a word' or 'the object signified by a word'. All object which can be thought (jñeya) and named (abhidheya).

Originally the Vaisheṣika believed in the six categories and the seventh, that of abhāva or negation, was added later on. Though Kanāda himself speaks of abhāva, yet he does not give it the status of a category to which it was raised only by the later Vaisheṣikas. The Vaisheṣika divides all existent reals which are all objects of knowledge into two classes–bhāva or being and abhāva or non-being. Six categories come under bhāva and the seventh is abhāva. All knowledge necessarily points to an object beyond and independent of it. All that is real comes under the object of knowledge and is called a padārtha. The seven padārthas are : (1) substance (dravya), (2) quality (guṇa), (3) action (karma), (4) generality (sāmānya), (5) particularity (visheṣa), (6) inherence (samavāya), and (7) non-being (abhāva).

The Vaisesika system uses the term padartha in a technical sense sanskrit scholars generally seem to be oversee to rendring the term padartha as category. The Doctrine of Padarthas is a characteristically Vaisesika position and the adoption of the term by the other system of Indian its only result in divesting the position of thought strict significance.

Substance (Dravya)

Substance (dravya) signifies the self-subsistence, the absolute and independent nature of things. Therefore, it is defined as the substratum where actions and qualities inhere and which is the coexistent material cause of the composite things produced from it. Without substance, we cannot have qualities and actions for they cannot hang loose in the air, but must be contained somewhere. Substance is the basis of qualities and actions, actual or potential, present or future. Nor can substance be defined apart from qualities and actions. Ultimate substances are eternal, independent and individual and are either infinite or infinitesimal. All compound substances (avayavidravya) which are made of parts and arise out of the simple ultimate substance are necessarily transient and impermanent and subject to production and destruction. But simple ultimate substances which are the material causes of the compound substances are eternal and not subject to production and destruction. The dravyas are nine and include material as well as spiritual substances. The Vaisheṣika philosophy is pluralistic and realistic but not materialistic since it admits spiritual substances. The nine substances are : (1) earth (pṛthivi), (2) water (Ap), (3) fire (tejas), (4) air (vāyu), (5) ether (ākāsha), (6) time (kāla), (7) space (dik), (8) spirit (ātman) and (9) mind or the internal organ (manas).

All of them are objective realisties. Earth, water, fire, air and manas are atomic and eternal. The first four produce composite things; manas does not. Earth, water, fire, air and ether are the five gross elements. These and manas are physical. Soul is spiritual. Time and space are objective and not subjective forms of experience. Ether, space, time and soul are all-pervading and eternal. Atoms, minds and souls are infinite in number. Ether, space and time are one each.

Guṇa (Quality)

Substance is the substratum of qualities and actions. Quality or guṇa is the second category of vaiseṣikas. It inheres in a substance and depends for its existence on the substance and is not a constitutive cause of anything. It is called an independent reality because it can be conceived (prameya), thought (jñeya) and named (abhidheya) independently of a substance where it inheres. The qualities are therefore called objective entities. They are not necessarily eternal. They include both material and mental qualities. They are a static and permanent feature of a substance, while action is a dynamic and transient feature of a substance. A quality, therefore is different from both substance and action. It is defined by Kaṇāda as 'that which inheres in a substance, which does not possess quality or action, which does not produce any composite thing, and which is not the cause of conjunction and disjunction like and action.'

Kaṇāda mentions seventeen qualities to which seven more are added by Prashastapāda. These twenty-four qualities are recognized by the Nyāya-Vaisheṣika School. It is not necessary to mention them all as their importance is not much philosophical. They include material as well as spiritual properties. Smell is the quality of earth; taste of water, colour of fire; touch of air; and sound of ether. Cognition, pleasure, pain, desire, aversion, volition are the mental qualities which inhere in the self.

Karma (Activity)

The third category is Karma or action. Like quality, it belongs to and inheres in a substance and cannot exist separately from it. But while a quality is a static and permanent feature of a substance, an action is a dynamic and transient feature of it. Unlike a quality, an action is the cause of conjunction and disjunction. Action is said to be of five kinds : (1) upward movement (utkṣepaṇa), (2) downward movement (avakṣepana), (3) contraction (ākuñchana), (4) expansion (prasāraṇa), and (5) locomotion (gamana).

Sāmānya (Generality)

The fourth category is Sāmānya or generality. It is class-concept, class-essence or universal. It is the common character of the things which fall under the same class. The sāmānya is more like the 'universal' than like the 'genus'. The genus stands for the class and includes the sub-classes or species. The sāmānya stands, not for the class, but for the common characteristic of certain individuals and does not include the sub-classes. It is the universal by the possession of which different individuals are referred to as belonging to one class. It is called eternal, one and residing in many. It is one, though the individuals in which it resides are many. It is eternal, though the individuals in which it inheres are subject to birth and death, production and destruction. It is common to many individuals. There is the class-essence of the universal of man, called 'man-ness' or 'humanity', which inheres in all individual men. Similarly 'cowness' inheres in all individual cows. Kaṇāda calls generality and particularity as relative to thought (buddhyapekṣa). But this does not mean that the universal and the particular are mere subjective concepts in our mind. Both are objective realities. The system is staunchly realistic. The universal has as much objective reality as the particular. It is not a subjective class-concept in our mind, but an objective eternal timeless entity shared by many particulars and corresponding to a general idea or class-concept in our mind. The universals reside in substances, qualities and actions. They are of two kinds, higher and lower. The higher generality is that of 'being' (sattā). It includes everything and itself is not included in anything. Every other generality is lower because it covers a limited number of things and cannot cover all things. A universal cannot subsist in another universal, otherwise an individual may be a man, a cow, and a horse at the same time. Only one universal subsists in all individuals in either, is not a universal. Conjunction inheres in many substances it conjoins, but it is not a universal since it is not eternal. Non-being is eternal and belongs to many things, but it is not a universal since it does not inhere in them.

The Nyāya-Vaisheṣika School is an advocate of realism. It believes that both the particulars and the universals are separately real.

Viśeṣa (Particularity)

The fifth category is Visheṣa or particularity. It enables us to perceive things as different from one another. Particularity is exclusive. Generality forms the basis of assimilation; particularity forms the basis of discrimination. It is very important to remember that the compositive objects of this world which we generally call 'particular' objects, are not real 'particulars' according to Nyāya-Vaisheṣika. Compound objects can be easily distinguished from one another by the differences of their parts. Thus no compound object, from the dyad to any gross object, is a particular. It is only in the case of the simple ultimate eternal substances which are otherwise alike that a need arises to postulate the category of Visheṣa in order to distinguish them from one another. Thus for example, one atom is similar to another atom of the same element and one soul is similar to another soul. Now, how to account for their separate reality? Nyāya-Vaisheṣika, being a school of staunch realism, maintains not only quantitative but also qualitative pluralism. One atom differs from another not only in numerical existence but also in qualitative existence. The category of Visheṣa or particularity is invented to defend this position and the Vaisheṣika derives its name from this. Each partless ultimate substance has an original peculiarity of its own, an underived uniqueness of its own which is called 'particularity' or Visheṣa. Visheṣa, therefore, is the differentium (vyāvartaka) of ultimate eternal substances (nityadravyavṛtti) which are otherwise alike. There are innumerable eternal Visheṣas. They distinguish the substances where they inhere from other substances and they also distinguish themselves from other particularities. Though they, like qualities and actions, inhere in the substances, yet they are a distinct category. The Vaisheṣika emphasizes realistic pluralism. Atoms, souls, space, time and manas all have their particularities.

Samavāya (Inherence)

Samavāya is different from conjunction or saṁyoga which is a separable and transient relation and is a quality (guṇa). Samavāya is an independent category (padārtha) which means an inseparable eternal relation or inherence. Kaṇāda calls it the relation between cause and effect. Prashastapāda defines it as 'the relationship subsisting among things that are inseparable, standing to one another in the relation of the container and the contained, and being the basis of the idea, "this is in that". The things related by samavāya are inseparably connected (ayutasiddha). It is 'inseparable relationship'. It is eternal because its production would involve infinite regress. It is imperceptible and is inferred from the inseparable relation of two things. The things which are inseparably connected are these : the part and the whole, the quality and the substance, the action and the substance, the particular and the universal, the Visheṣa and the eternal substance. Samavāya is found in these. The whole inheres in the parts; a quality inheres in its substance; an action inheres in its substance; the universal inheres in the individual members of the same class; the particularity (visheṣa) inheres in its eternal substance. Samavāya is one and eternal relationship subsisting between two things inseparably connected.

Abhāva (Non-Being)

The seventh category is Abhāva or non-existence. Kaṇāda does not mention it is a separate category. It is added afterwards. The first six categories are positive. This is negative. The other categories are regarded as absolute, but this category is relative in its conception.

Absence of an object and knowledge of its absence are different. Non-existence is of four kinds: (1) antecedent non-existence (prāgabhāva), (2)subsequent non-existence (pradhvaṁsābhāva), (3) mutual non-existence (anyonyābhāva), and (4) absolute non-existence (atyantābhāva). The first is the non-existence of a thing before its production. The second is the non-existence of a thing after its destruction.

The third is the non-existence of a thing as another thing which is different from it. The fourth is a pseudo-idea, the absence of a relation between two things in the past, the present and the future. Antecedent negation has no beginning, but it has an end. It ends when the thing is produced. Subsequent negation has a beginning, but has no end. It begins when the thing is destroyed and has no end since the same thing cannot be produced again. Mutual negation is exclusion and is opposed to identity. It is both beginningless and endless. Absolute negation is a pseudo-idea. It is both beginningless and endless. Hare's horn, barren woman's child, sky-flower etc. are its classical examples. Mutual negation or anyonyābhāva means non-existence of a thing as another thing—'S' is not P'. The other three negations–antecedent, subsequent and absolute—are called non-existence of correlation or Saṁsargābhāva which implies the non-existence of something in something else—'S is not in P'. If antecedent negation is denied, then all things would become beginningless; if subsequent negation is denied, then all things would become eternal; if mutual negation is denied, then all things would become indistinguishable; and if absolute negation is denied, then all things would exist always and everywhere.

Theory of Causation

Asatkāryavāda

A cause is defined as an unconditional and invariable antecedent of an effect and an effect as an unconditional and invariable consequent of a cause. The same cause produces the same effect and the same effect is produced by the same cause. Plurality of causes is ruled out. The first essential characteristic of a cause is its antecedence; the fact that it should precede the effect (Purvavarti). The second is its invariability; it must invariably precede the effect (Niyatapūrvavrti). The third is its unconditionality or necessity; it must unconditionally precede the effect (Ananyathāsiddha). Unconditional antecedence is immediate and direct antecedence and excludes the fallacy of remote cause.

An effect (kārya) is defined as the 'counter-entity of its own prior non-existence' (prāgabhāvapratiyogi). It is the negation of its own prior-negation. It comes into being and destroys its prior non-existence. It was non-existent before its production. It did not pre-exist in its cause. It is a fresh beginning, a new creation. This Nyāya-Vaisheṣika view of causation is directly opposed to the Sāṅkhya-Yoga and Vedānta view of satkāryavāda. It is called asatkāryavāda or ārambhavāda. The effect (kārya) is non-existent (asat) before its creation and is a new beginning (ārambha), a fresh creation, an epigenesis. It is distinct from its cause and can never be identical with it. It is neither an appearance nor a transformation of the cause. It is newly brought into existence by the operation of the cause.

There are three kinds of causes—samavāyi, asamavāyi and nimitta. The first is the samavāyi or the inherent cause, also called as the upādāna or the material cause. It is the substance out of which the effect is produced. For example, the threads are the inherent cause of the cloth and the clay is the inherent cause of a pot. The effect inheres in its material cause. The cloth inheres in the threads. The effect cannot exist separately from its material cause, through the cause can exist independently of its effect. The material cause is always a substance (dravya). The second kind of cause is asamavāyi or non-inherent. It inheres in the material cause and helps the production of the effect. The conjunction of the threads (tantusaṁyoga) which inheres in the threads is the non-inherent cause of the cloth of which the threads are the material or the inherent cause. The colour of the threads (tanturūpa) is the non-inherent cause of the colour of the cloth. The cloth itself is the inherent cause of its colour. The effect as well as its non-inherent cause both c-oinhere in the material cause. The non-inherent cause is always a quality or an action (guṇa or karma). The third kind of cause is nimitta or efficient. It is the power which helps the material cause to produce the effect. The weaver is the efficient cause of the cloth. The efficient cause includes the accessories (sahakāri), *e.g.*, the loom and shuttle of the weaver or the staff and wheel of the potter. The efficient cause may be a substance, a quality or an action.

Asatkaryavada

Asatkaryavada another name is known as Arambhavada. A cause is regarded as an unconditional and invariable antecedent of an effect whereas an effect is regarded as an unconditional and invariable consequent of a cause.

Asatkaryavada Theory of Causation says that effect is regarded as different from cause. According to Nyaya Vaisesika, effect is regarded as a fresh beginning. They say that cause and effect cannot be regarded as identical. It has been said the Nyaya Vaisesika view of causation is directly opposed to the Samkhya Yoga and Vedanta view of Satkaryavada. According to Nyaya Vaisesika, effect does not pre-exist in the cause.

Samavayi

It is regarded as a kind of causes. It is also known as an inherent cause and the material cause. It is defined as the substance out of which the effect is produced. The example or samavayi causes can be taken as that of the threads, which are regarded as the inherent cause of the cloth. It has been said that the effect always inheres in its material cause. It has been said that the effect cannot exist separately from its material cause.

Asamayayi Nimitta Karana

It is regarded as the third kind of cause. It is also known as an efficient cause. It is regarded the second kind of cause. It is regarded as the power, which helps the material cause to produce its effect. It has been said that the efficient cause also includes the accessories. The efficient cause may be regarded as a substance, quality or an action. God is also regarded as an efficient cause.

Paramāṇuvāda

According to Nyāya-Vaiśeṣika, the effect does not pre-exist in its cause (Asatkāryavāda), but, is a new beginning, a fresh creation (Ārambhvāda). Of course, the effect presupposes a cause. But it is not contained implicitly in the cause nor is it identical with the cause. The doctrine is also known as Paramāṇukāraṇavāda. We find that the material objects of the world are composed of parts and are subject to production and destruction. They are divisible into smaller parts and the latter are further divisble into still smaller parts. By this logic we have to accept the minutest particle of matter which may not be further divisible. This indivisible, partless and eternal particle of matter is called an atom (paramāṇu). All physical things are produced by the combinations of atoms. Creation, therefore, means the combination of atoms in different proportions and destruction means the dissolution of such combinations. The material cause of the universe is neither produced nor destroyed. It is the eternal atoms. It is only the atomic combinations which are produced and which are destroyed. These combinations do not form the essential nature of the atoms nor do they pre-exist in them. Hence the Nyāya-Vaisheṣika advocates Asatkāryavāda.

The atoms are said to be of four kinds—of earth, water, fire and air. These atoms combine in geometrical progression and not in arithmetical one. They increase by multiplication and not by mere addition. When motion is imparted to them by the Unseen Power, they begin to vibrate (parispanda) and immediately change into dyads. A dyad is produced by the combination of two atoms. The atoms are its inherent cause; conjunction is its non-inherent cause; and the Unseen Power is its efficient cause. An atom is indivisible, spherical and imperceptible. A dyad (dvyaṇuka) is minute (aṇu), short (hrasva), and imperceptible. Three dyads form a triad (tryaṇuka) which is great (mahat), long (dīrgha) and perceptible. And so on by geometrical progression till the gross elements of earth, water, fire and air arise.

The Vaisheṣika Atomism is not materialistic because the Vaisheṣika School admits the reality of the spiritual substances—souls and God—and also admits the Law of Karma. The atoms are the material cause of this world of which God, assisted by the Unseen Power, is the efficient cause. The physical world presupposes the moral order. Evolution is due to the Unseen Power consisting of merits and demerits of the individual souls which want to bear fruits as enjoyments or sufferings to be experienced by the souls.

Adrsta

It is referred as an unseen power. This unseen power is regarded as an efficient cause. It has been said that because of unseen power, evolution occurs. The unseen power also consist merits and demerits of the individual souls. Naiyaikas has also discusses about this.

Nihsreyas

It is defined as the attainment or fulfillment. It is referred as moksha. Naiyayikas also speaks about this. Basically, liberation or moksha means the same thing. According to Vaisesika, Nihsreyas is attained only through the knowledge of tattvas.

Vaisesika's Philosophy on God

The Vaisesika also believes in the authority of the Veda and in the moral law of Karma. Kanada himself does not openly refer to God. The expression 'Tadvachana, may mean that the Veda is the word of the seers. All great writers of the Vaisesika and the Nyaya systems, including Prashastapada, Shridhara and Udayana, are openly theistic and some of them, *e.g.*, Udayana give classical arguments to prove the existence of God. Moreover, Kanada believes in spiritualism and makes the physical universe subservient to the moral order.

It is the world of God and this makes it authoritative. God is omniscient, eternal and perfect. He is the lord. The unseen power is unintelligent and needs God as the supervisor and the controller. Atoms and souls are co-present and co-eternal with God. He cannot create them. He simply gives motion to the atoms and sets the ball rolling.

Law of Karma

According to the Law of Karma, one to always reap the fruits of actions one has performed whether they are good or bad, according to the Kamnas, one performed. This Adrsta guided by God, imparts motion to the atoms and leads to creation for the sake of enjoyment or suffering of the individual souls. To get rid of bondage, the soul must stop actions.

Liberation is the cessation of all life, all consciousness, all bliss, together with all pain and all qualities. It is the quality less, indeterminate, pure nature of the individual soul as pure substance devoid of all qualities.

Liberation comes through knowledge. When actions stop, new merits and demerits do not get accumulated and old merits and demerits also are gradually worn out. That is liberation, which is absolute cessation of all pain. The individual soul is treated as a substance and knowledge, bliss etc, are regarded as its accidental qualities, which it may acquire when it is embodied.

Vaisesika Atomism vs. Greek Atomism

The Vaisesika atomism also agrees with the Greek atomism of Leucippus and Democritus in regarding the atoms as the indivisible, partles, imperceptible and ultimate portions of matter which are eternal and are the material cause of this physical universe.

1. The Vaisesika maintains both quantitative and qualitative differences in the atoms. The atoms of Earth, water and air possess different qualities.
2. The Greek atomists regarded atoms as devoid of secondary qualities, while the Vaisesika regards them as possessing secondary qualities.
3. The Greek atomists believed that atoms were essentially active and motion was inherent in them, but the Vaisesika regards the atoms as essentially inactive and motionless.
4. The Greek view held that atoms constituted even the souls, while the Vaisesika distinguishes between the souls and the atoms and regards them as co-eternal distinct entities, each possessing a particularity of its own.
5. The Greek view was materialistic and the evolution was thought of as mechanical, while the Vaisesika view is guided by the spiritual and the moral law and the later Vaisesikas frankly admist God as the efficient cause.

Shankara on Vaisesika Categories

Shankara has pointed out the contradictions in the Vaisesika categories. Firstly, the distinction that Samyoga is a quality and Samavaya is a category cannot be justified because both are relations, may be one is separable and the other inseparable. Again, if Samavaya is not different from the terms it relates, then where does it inhere? If it inheres in the first term, it cannot relate it with the second and if in the second, it cannot relate it with the first and the same Samavaya cannot inhere in both the terms as it cannot be divided.

The categories of the Vaisesika are mere assumptions and if we proceed with assumptions, we may assume any number of categories we like instead of six or seven. The qualitative differences in the atoms cannot be upheld. If the atom of Earth possesses the greatest qualities and the atom of air the least, there should be difference between their weight and magnitude. If the qualities of the atoms are eternal an cannot be separated from them, then why maintain that the qualities of the souls can be separated from them in liberation and why maintain that the substance can remain without qualities.

If the cause transfers its qualities to its effect, then why does the atom not transfer its spherical nature to the adyad and why does the adyad not transfer its minuteness and shortness to the triad etc., which are regarded great and long.

On the Vaisesika hypothesis, there can be no creation and dissolution. Are the atoms essentially active or inactive or both or neither? It this agency seen or unseen? If seen, it could not be present before creation. And if unseen, then it being always present near the atoms, creation would become permanent and if the proximity of the unseen power to the atoms is denied, then creation would be impossible. In all cases, can be no creation from atoms. It is no explanation of this world that it is due to essentially inactive, imperceptible, eternal, abstract material points. It is necessary to synthesise them and reduce them to one common source.

Liberation

The Vaisesika conception of liberation as the real state of the soul, free from all qualities have reduces the soul to a mere nothing. The root fallacy lies in viewing the subject just as an object. The soul is nothing, if it is not a subject and consciousness is not its essence. Discursive intellect also presupposes the foundational consciousness, the transcendental subject and bliss in liberation transcends empirical happiness and pain alike. This truth has been forgotten by the Vaisesika and the resort has been that we are offered a state of petrification as liberation. Starikara calls the vaisesika the semi destroyer of this world as opposed to the Hinayani Buddha who is the full destroyer. Shrinkarsa condemns the vaisesika philosophy as the real Auluka Darshana - owlish philosophy.

SĀṀKHYA

Sāṁkhya, also Sankhya, Sāṁkhya, or Sāṅhya (Sanskrit: सांख्य: IAST : sāṁkhya), is one of the six orthodox (astika) schools of Hindu philosophy and classical Indian philosophy. Sage Kapila is traditionally credited as a founder of the Samkhya school. It is regarded as one of the oldest philosophical systems in India.

Sāṁkhya is an enumerationist philosophy that is strongly dualist. Sāṁkhya philosophy regards the universe as consisting of two realities; Puruṣa (consciousness) and prakriti (phenomenal realm of matter). Jiva is that state in which puruṣa is bonded to prakriti through the glue of desire, and the end of this bondage is moksha.

Sāṁkhya denies the final cause of Ishvara (God). Samkhya does not describe what happens after moksha and does not mention anything about Ishwara or God, because after liberation there is no essential distinction of individual and universal puruṣa.

The word samkhya means empirical or relating to numbers. Although the term had been used in the general sense of metaphysical knowledge before, in technical usage it refers to the Samkhya school of thought that evolved into a cohesive philosophical system in early centuries CE. The Samkhya system is called so because "it 'enumerates' twenty five Tattvas or true principles; and its chief object is to effect the final emancipation of the twenty-fifth Tattva, *i.e.* the Purusa or soul."

Emergence as a Distinct Philosophy

Between 5th and 2nd century BCE, Samkhya thought from various sources started coalescing into a distinct philosophy. Philosophical texts from this era such as the Katha Upanishad, Shvetashvatara Upanishad and Bhagavad Gita have clear references to Samkhyan terminology and concepts. Katha Upanishad conceives the purusha as an individual soul which Atman (Self) inhabits. Other verses of the Upanishad consider purusha to be smaller than the thumb.

Samkhya and Yoga are mentioned together for first time in the Shvetashvatra Upanishad. Bhagavad Gita identifies Samkhya with understanding or knowledge. The three gunas are also mentioned in the Gita, though they are not used in the same sense as in classical Samkhya. The Gita integrates Samkhya thought with the devotion (bhakti) of theistic schools and the impersonal Brahman of Vedanta.

According to Ruzsa, about 2,000 years ago "Senkhya became the representative philosophy of Hindu thought in Hindu circles", influencing all strands of the Hindu tradition and Hindu texts.

Vedic Influences

The ideas that were developed and assimilated into the classical Samkhya text, Samkhyakarika, are visible in earlier Hindu scriptures such as Vedas, Upanishads and Bhagavad Gita. Earliest mention of dualism in the Rig Veda, a Hindu text that was compiled in second millennium BCE, is in the Indra–Vritra myth. In this myth, Indra, leader of the gods, slays Vritra, a serpent demon, to unleash the creative forces held captive by him. Gerald James Larson, a scholar of religions and philosophies of India, believes that this myth contains twofold dualism. He writes On one hand there is dualism of order and chaos. On the other hand, there is dualism of Indra's power over against both the chaos and the order.

The emphasis of duality between existence (sat) and non-existence (asat) in the Nasadiya sukta of the Rig Veda is similar to the vyakta–avyakta (manifest–unmanifest) polarity in Samkhya.

The hymn of Purusha sukta may also have influenced Samkhya. It contains the earliest conception of Purusha, a cosmic being from whom the manifestation arises. Purusha also finds numerous mentions in the hymns of the Atharvaveda. The Samkhya notion of buddhi or mahat is similar to the notion of hiranyagarbha which appears in both the Rig Veda and the Shvetashvatara Upanishad.

Upanishadic Influences

The oldest of the major Upanishads (c. 900–600 BCE) also contain speculations along the lines of classical Samkhya philosophy. The concept of ahamkara in Samkhya can be traced back to the notion of ahamkara in Brihadaranyaka Upanishad and Chhandogya Upanishad. Satkaryavada, the theory of causation in Samkhya, can be traced to the verses in sixth chapter which emphasize the primacy of sat (being) and describe creation from it. The idea that the three gunas or attributes influence creation is found in both Chhandogya and Svetashvatara Upanishads Upanishadic sages Yajnavalkya and Uddalaka Aruni developed the idea that pure consciousness was the innermost essence of a human being. The purusha of Samkhya could have evolved from this idea. The enumeration of tattvas in Samkhya is also found in Taittiriya Upanishad, Aitareya Upanishad and Yajnavalkya–Maitri dialogue in the Brihadaranyaka Upanishad.

Buddhist and Jainist Influences

Buddhism and Jainism had developed in Northeastern India by the 5th century BCE. It is probable that these schools of thought and the earliest schools of Samkhya influenced each other. A prominent similarity between Buddhism and Samkhya is the emphasis on suffering (dukkha). However, suffering is not as central to Samkhya as it is to Buddhism. Therefore, it is likely that Samkhya imbibed this idea from Buddhism. Likewise, the Jain doctrine of plurality of individual souls (jiva) could have influenced the concept of multiple purushas in Samkhya. However Hermann Jacobi, an Indologist, thinks that there is little reason to assume that Samkhya notion of Purushas was solely dependent on the notion of jiva in Jainism. It is more likely, that Samkhya was moulded by many ancient theories of soul in various Vedic and non-Vedic schools.

Satkāryavāda

The sāṁkhya theory of causation on which its doctrine of Prakṛiti is based is known as satkāryvāda. According to this theory the effect is pre-existent in its material cause. Saṁkhya believes that Prakṛti is material cause of the whole universe. All material effects are the modification (pariṇāma) of Prakṛti. Therefore, saṁkhya's satkāryavāda is also known as Prakṛti-pariṇāmavāda. All material effects re-exist in the eternal bosom of Prakṛti and simply come out of it at the time of creation and return to it at the time of dissolution. There is neither new production nor utterdestruction. Production means development or manifestation (āvirbhāva); destruction means envelopment or dissolution (tirobhāva). Production is evolution; destruction is involution. Sāṁkhya five arguments in support of Satkāryavāda:

(1) If the effect does not pre-exist in its cause, it becomes a mere nonentity like the hare's horn or the sky-flower and can never be produced (asadakaraṇāt).

(2) The effect is only a manifestation of its material cause, because it is invariably connected with it (upādānagrahaṇāt).

(3) Everything cannot be produced out of everything. This suggests that the effect, before its manifestation, is implicit in its material cause (sarvasambhavābhāvāt)

(4) Only an efficient cause can produce that for which it is potent. This again means that the effect, before its manifestation, is potentially contained in its material cause. Production is only an actualization of the potential (shaktasya shakyakaraṇāt). Were it not so, then curd should be produced out of water, and cloth out of reeds, and, oil out of sandpaticles.

(5) The effect is the essence of its material cause and as such identical with it. When the obstructions in the way of manifestation are removed, the effect naturally flows out of its cause. The cause and the effect are the implicit and the explicit stages of the same process. The cloth is contained in the threads, the oil in the oil-seeds, the curd in the milk. The effect pre-exists in its material cause (kāraṇabhāvāt).

Prakṛti

The theory that causation means a real transformation of the material cause leads to the concept of Prakṛti as the root-cause of the world of objects. All worldly effects are latent in this uncaused cause, because infinite regress has to be avoided. It is the potentiality of nature, 'the receptacle and nurse of all generation'. As the uncaused root-cause, it is called Prakṛti; as the first principle of this Universe, it is called Pradhāna; as the unmanifested state of all effects it is known as Avyakta; as the extremely subtle and imperceptible thing which is only inferred from its products, it is called Anumāna; as the unintelligent and unconscious principle, it is called Jaḍa; and as the ever-active unlimited power, it is called Shakti. The products are caused, dependent, relative, many and temporary as they are subject to birth and death or to production and destruction; but Prakṛti is uncaused, independent, absolute, one and eternal, being beyond production and destruction. Prakṛti alone is the final source of this world of objects which is implicitly and potentially contained in its bosom. Sāṁkhya gives five proofs for the existence of Prakṛti which are as follows :

(1) All individual things in this world are limited, dependent, conditional and finite. The finite cannot be the cause of the universe. Logically we have to proceed from the finite to the infinite, from the limited to the unlimited, from the peros to the aperos, from the temporary to the permanent, from the many to the one. And it is this infinite, unlimited, eternal and allpervading Prakrti which is the source of this universe (bhedānām parimāṇat).

(2) All worldly things possess certain common characteristics by which they are capable of producing pleasure, pain and indifference. Hence there must be a common source composed of three Guṇas, from which all worldly things arise (samanvayāt).

(3) All effects arise from the activity of the potent cause. Evolution means the manifestation of the hitherto implicit as the explicit. The activity which generates evolution must be inherent in the world-cause. And this cause is Prakṛti (kāryataḥ pravṛttescha).

(4) The effect differs from the cause and hence the limited effect cannot be regarded as its own cause. The effect is the explicit and the cause is the implicit state of the same process. The effects, therefore, point to a world-cause where they are potentially contained (kāraṇakāryavibhāgāt).

(5) The unity of the universe points to a single cause. And this cause is Prakṛti. (avibhāgāt vaishvarūpyasya).

Prakṛti is said to be the unity of the three Guṇas held in equilibrium (guṇānām sāmyāvasthā). The three Guṇas are Sattva, Rajas and Tamas. When these guṇas are held in a state of equilibrium, that state is called Prakṛti. Evolution of worldly objects does not take place at this state. These guṇas are said to be ever-changing. They cannot remain static even for a moment. Change is said to be of two kinds—homogeneous or sarūpa-pariṇāma and heterogeneous or virūpa-pariṇāma. During the state of dissolution (pralaya) of the world, the guṇas change homogeneously, i.e., sattva changes into sattva, rajas into rajas and tamas into tamas. This change does not disturb the equilibrium of the guṇas and unless the equilibrium is disturbed and one predominates over the other two, evolution cannot take place. Evolution starts when there is heterogeneous change in the guṇas and one predominates over the other two and brings about terrific commotion in the bosom of Prakṛti.

The Evolutes

The idea of evolution in Samkhya revolves around the interaction of Prakriti and Purusha. Prakriti remains unmanifested as long as the three gunas are in equilibrium. This equilibrium of the gunas is disturbed when Prakriti comes into proximity with consciousness or Purusha. The disequilibrium of the gunas triggers an evolution that leads to the manifestation of the world from an unmanifested Prakriti. The metaphor of movement of iron in the proximity of a magnet is used to describe this process.

Some evolutes of Prakriti can cause further evolution and are labelled evolvents. For example, intellect while itself created out of Prakriti causes the evolution of ego-sense or ahamkara and is therefore an evolvent. While, other evolutes like the five elements do not cause further evolution. It is important to note that an evolvent is defined as a principle which behaves as the material cause for the evolution of another principle. So, in definition, while the five elements are the material cause of all living beings, they cannot be called evolvents because living beings are not separate from the five elements in essence.

The intellect is the first evolute of prakriti and is called mahat or the great one. It causes the evolution of ego-sense or self-consciousness. Evolution from self-consciousness is affected by the dominance of gunas. So dominance of sattva causes the evolution of the five organs of perception, five organs of action and the mind. Dominance of tamas triggers the evolution of five subtle elements–sound, touch, sight, taste, smell from self-consciousness. These five subtle elements are themselves evolvents and cause the creation of the five gross elements space, air, fire, water and earth. Rajas is cause of action in the evolutes. Purusha is pure consciousness absolute, eternal and subject to no change. It is neither a product of evolution, nor the cause of any evolute.

Evolution in Samkhya is thought to be purposeful. The two primary purposes of evolution of Prakriti are the enjoyment and the liberation of Purusha. The 23 evolutes of prakriti are categorized as follows:

(i) Liberation or Moksa

Like many other major schools of Indian philosophy, Samkhya regards human existence as seat of intense suffering. Ignorance (avidyā) is regarded as the root cause of this suffering and bondage (Samsara). Samkhya offers a way out of this suffering by means of discriminative knowledge (viveka). Such knowledge, that leads to moksa (liberation), involves the discrimination between Prakriti (avyakta-vyakta) and Puruṣa (jña).

Puruṣa, the eternal pure consciousness, due to ignorance, identifies itself with products of Prakriti such as intellect (buddhi) and ego (ahamkara). This results in endless transmigration and suffering. However, once the realization arises that Puruṣa is distinct from Prakriti, the Self is no longer subject to transmigration and absolute freedom (kaivalya) arises. Other forms of Samkhyateach that Mokṣa is attained by one's own development of the higher faculties of discrimination achieved by meditation and other yogic practices as prescribed through the Hindu Vedas.

(ii) Epistemology

Samkhya considered Pratyakṣa or Dṛṣṭam (direct sense perception), Anumāna (inference), and Śabda or Āptavacana (verbal testimony of the sages or shastras) to be the only valid sources of knowledge or pramana.

(iii) Causality

The Samkhya system is based on Sat-kārya-vāda or the theory of causation. According to Satkāryavāda, the effect is pre-existent in the cause. There is only an apparent or illusory change in the makeup of the cause and not a material one, when it becomes effect. Since, effects cannot come from nothing, the original cause or ground of everything is seen as Prakriti.

More specifically, Samkhya system follows the Prakriti-Parināma Vāda. Parināma denotes that the effect is a real transformation of the cause. The cause under consideration here is Prakriti or more precisely Moola-Prakriti (Primordial Matter). The Samkhya system is therefore an exponent of an evolutionary theory of matter beginning with primordial matter. In evolution,Prakriti is transformed and differentiated into multiplicity of objects. Evolution is followed by dissolution. In dissolution the physical existence, all the worldly objects mingle back into Prakriti, which now remains as the undifferentiated, primordial substance. This is how the cycles of evolution and dissolution follow each other. But this theory is very different from the modern theories of science in the sense that Prakriti evolves for each Jeeva separately, giving individual bodies and minds to each and after liberation these elements of Prakriti merges into the Moola Prakriti. Another uniqueness of Samkhya is that not only physical entities but even mind, ego and intelligence are regarded as forms of Unconsciousness, quite distinct from pure consciousness.

Samkhya theorizes that Prakriti is the source of the perceived world of becoming. It is pure potentiality that evolves itself successively into twenty four tattvas or principles. The evolution itself is possible because Prakriti is always in a state of tension among its constituent strands or gunas – Sattva, Rajas and Tamas. In a state of equilibrium of three gunas, when the three together are one, "unmanifest" Prakriti which is unknowable. A guna is an entity that can change, either increase or decrease, therefore, pure consciousness is called nirguna or without any modification.

The evolution obeys causality relationships, with primal Nature itself being the material cause ofall physical creation. The cause and effect theory of Samkhya is called Satkārya-vāda (theory of existent causes), and holds that nothing can really be created from or destroyed into nothingness – all evolution is simply the transformation of primal Nature from one form to another. Samkhya cosmology describes how life emerges in the universe; the relationship between Purusha and Prakriti is crucial to Patanjali's yoga system. The strands of Samkhya thought can be traced back to the Vedic speculation of creation. It is also frequently mentioned in theMahabharata and Yogavasishta.

(iv) Atheism

Samkhya accepts the notion of higher selves or perfected beings but rejects the notion of God. Classical Samkhya argues against the existence of God on metaphysical grounds. Samkhyatheorists argue that an unchanging God cannot be the source of an ever changing world and that God was only a necessary metaphysical assumption demanded by circumstances. The Sutras of Samkhya have no explicit role for a separate God distinct from the Puruṣa. Such a distinct God is inconceivable and self-contradictory and some commentaries speak plainly on this subject.

Arguments for the Existance of Prakriti

(1) Principles of Samkhya

The unity of the three Gunas, which are helpful in equilibrium are defined as Prakriti. Sattva, Rajas and Tamas are regarded as three Gunas. These gunas are regarded as ever-changing. They are not able to remain static even for a moment change includes two kinds, namely homogeneous and heterogeneous. The Guna changes homogeneously, diving the state of dissolution of the world. Evolution occurs during the state of heterogeneous change.

Sattva means goodness, Rajas produces pain whereas. Tamas means darkness. Tamas is opposed to both Sattva and Rajas. The evolutes is very essential for Prakriti. Mahat is regarded as the first product of the evolution. Mahat also means the great. It also includes intellect, ego and mind. It is regarded as cosmic in its nature. Buddhi or intellect means the same thing. Buddhi or intellect has a psychological aspect. Buddhi or intellect is regarded as material. Sattva predominates its. It includes virtue, knowledge and power. Memories and recollections are found only in Buddhi.

(2) Ahankara

Mahat produces Ahankara, according to Samkhya. There are twenty five evolutes which are found. Ahankara is regarded as ego. Ego is regarded as the principle of individualisation. It's also generates self-sense. It also produces the notion of 'I'.

There are three kinds of Ahankara which are as follow :

1. Sattvika, 2. Tamasa, 3. Rajasa

Manas or mind is regarded as same. It arises from the Sattvika Ahankara. It is regarded as the subtle and central sense organ. It come in contact with the several sense organs. The Sattvika Ahankara also produces the five sensory and the five motor organs.

The five sensory organs includes the functions of sight, smell taste, touch and sound. Buddhi has the feature of knowing. Ahankara has the feature of willing and feeling. Manas has the feature of affection. Tanmatras includes the five subtle essences. Tanmatras are arises from the Tamasa Ahankara.

Tanmatras also produces the five Mahabhutas. It includes Earth, water, fire, air and ether. The Purusha comes in the end and is also referred as the 25th evolute. Purusha is regarded as a mere spectator. The Purusha is regarded neither as a cause nor as an effect.

Puruṣa

The other of the two co-present co-eternal realities of Sāṁkhya is the Puruṣa, the principal of pure Consciousness. Puruṣa is the soul, the self, the spirit, the subject, the knower. It is neither body nor senses nor brain nor mind (manas) nor ego (ahaṅkāra) nor intellect (buddhi). It is not a substance which possesses the quality of Consciousness. Consciousness is the essence. It is itself pure and transcendental Consciousness. It is the ultimate knower which is the foundation of all knowledge. It is the pure subject and as such can never become an object of knowledge. It is the silent witness, the emancipated alone, the neutral seer, the peaceful eternal. It is beyond time and space, beyond change and activity. It is self-luminous and self-proved. It is uncaused, eternal and all pervading. It is the indubitable real, the postulate of knowledge, and all doubts and denials pre-suppose its existence. It is called nistraiguṇya, udāsīnā, akartā, kevala, madhyastha, sāksī, draṣṭa sadāprakāshasvarūpa and jñata.

Unlike Advaita Vedānta and like Jainism and Mīmāmsā, Sāṁkhya believes in the plurality of the Puruṣas. Like the Jīvas of the Jainas, the souls of Rāmānuja and the monads of Leibnitz, the Sāṁkhya Puruṣas are subject to qualitative monism and quantitative pluralism. The selves are all essentially alike; only numerically are they different. Their essence is consciousness. Bliss is regarded as different from consciousness and is the product of the sattvaguṇa.

Nature of Purusha

The Puruṣha is regarded as the principle of pure consciousness. Puruṣha regarded as the eternal reality of Sāṁkhya . Purusha is regarded as the soul, the self and the subject. It is also known as the spirit and the knowner. It is regarded neither as body nor-senses. It is also regarded neither as mind nor ego.

Consciousness is regarded as the essence. It is regarded as pure and trancedental consciousness. It is regarded as the foundation of all knowledge. It can never become an object of knowledge. It is regarded as a silent witness and the natural seen. It is regarded as self luminous and self-proved. It is regarded as uncaused, eternal and all pervading. It is regarded as the postulate of knowledge. Sāṁkhya believes in the plurality of the Purushas, according to Sāṁkhya system. It is also regarded as the peaceful eternal.

Proofs for the Existence of Puruṣa

Sāṁkhya gives the following proofs for the existence of the Puruṣa :

(1) All compound objects exist for the sake of the Puruṣa. The body, the senses, the mind and the intellect are all means to realize the end of the Puruṣa. The three guṇas, the Prakṛti, the subtle body—all are said to serve the purpose of the self. Evolution is teleological or purposive. Prakṛti evolves itself in order to serve the Puruṣa's end. This proof is teleological (saṅghātaparārthatvāt).

(2) All objects are composed of the three guṇas and therefore logically presuppose the existence of the Puruṣa who is the witness of these guṇas and is himself beyond them. The three guṇas imply the conception of a nistraiguṇya—that which is beyond them. This proof is logical (triguṇādiviparyayāt).

(3) There must be a transcendental synthetic unity of pure Consciousness to co-ordinate all experiences. All knowledge nessarily presupposes the existence of the self. The self is the foundation (adhiṣṭhāna), the fundamental postulate of all empirical knowledge. All affirmations and all negations equally presuppose it. Without it, experience would not become experience. This proof is ontological (adhiṣṭhānāt).

(4) Non-intelligent Prakṛti cannot experience its products. So there must be an intelligent principle to experience the worldly products of Prakṛti. Prakṛti is the enjoyed (bhogyā) and so there must be an enjoyer (bhoktā), *i.e.*, Puruṣa.

Proofs for the Plurality of Puruṣa

Sāṁkhya gives the following three arguments for proving the plurality of the Puruṣas :

(1) The souls have different sensory and motor organs and undergo separate births and deaths. Had there been only one Puruṣa, the birth or death of one should have meant the birth or death of all and any particular experience of pleasure, pain or indifference by one should have been equally shared by all. Hence the souls must be many.

(2) If the self were one, bondange of one should have meant bondage of all and liberation of one should have meant liberation of all. The activity of one should have made all persons active and the sleep of one should have lulled into sleep all other persons.

(3) Though the emancipated souls are all alike and differ only in number as they are all beyond the three guṇas, yet the bound souls relatively differ in qualities also, since in some sattva predominates, while in other rajas, and in still others tamas. Hence their difference.

Relationship between Puruṣa and Prakṛti

The evolution is teleological. Everything works to serve the purpose of the Puruṣa though unconciously. Just as non-intelligent trees grow fruits, or water flows on account of the declivity of the soil, or ironfilings are attracted towards a magnet, or milk flows through the udders of the cow in order to nourish the calf, similarly everything unconsciously tends to serve the purpose of the Puruṣa, whether it is enjoyment or liberation. Prakṛti is the benefactress of Puruṣa. Though Puruṣa is inactive and indifferent and devoid of qualities, yet the virtuous and the generous Prakṛti which is full of qualities and goodness ceaselessly works through various means in a spirit of detachment for the realization of the Puruṣa, without any benefit to herself. Prakṛti works to liberate the Puruṣa. There is immanent teleology in Prakṛti. Though Puruṣa is neither a cause nor an effect, yet relatively it is he who should be regarded as the efficient cause as well as the final cause of evolution though Sāṁkhya regards Prakṛti as both the material and the efficient cause. He is like Aristotle's God, the unmoved, mover who is beyond evolution. God, the pure intelligence, like the Puruṣa, does not actively participate in evolution. His is the end towards which the creation moves. And the creation moves by his mere presence. The guṇas, which mutually differ and yet always co-operate, work like the oil, wick and flame of a lamp and illuminate the entire purpose of the Puruṣa and present it to the buddhi or the intellect. All the organs work for the realization of the Puruṣa's end and for no other end. The subtle body too works for the sake of the Puruṣa's end. Thus the whole creation unconsciously tends towards the realization of the purpose of the Puruṣa. And creation will continue till all the Puruṣas are liberated. The entire evolution of Prakṛti, therefore, right from the first evolute, the Mahat, up to the last evolutes, the gross elements, is for the purpose of liberating each individuals Puruṣa.

Bondage and Liberation

The earthly life is full of three kinds of pain. The first kind, called ādhyātmika, is due to intraorganic psychophysical causes and includes, all mental and bodily sufferings. The second, ādhibhautika, is due to extra-organic natural causes like men, beasts, birds, thorns, etc. The third, ādhidaivika, is due to supernatural causes, like the planets, elemental agencies, ghosts, demons etc. Wherever there are guṇas there are pains. Even the so-called pleasures lead to pain. Even the life in heaven is subject to the guṇas. The end of man is to get rid of these three kinds of pain and sufferings. Liberation means complete cessation of all sufferings which is the summum bonum, the highest end of life (Apavarga or Puruṣārtha).

Puruṣa is free and pure consciousness. It is inactive, indifferent and possesses no attributes, Really speaking, it is above time and space, merit and demerit, bondage and liberation. It is only when it mistakes its reflection in the buddhi for itself and identifies itself wrongly with the internal organ—the intellect, the ego and the mind, that it is said to be bound. It is the ego, and not the Puruṣa, which is bound. When the Puruṣa realizes its own pure nature, it gets liberated which in fact it always was. Hence bondage is due to ignorance or non-discrimination between the self and the not-self and liberation is due to right knowledge or discrimination between the self and the not-self. Liberation cannot be obtained by means of actions. Karma, good or bad or indifferent, is the function of the guṇas and leads to bondage and not to liberation. Good actions may lead to heaven and bad actions to hell but heaven and hell alike, like this wordly life, are subject to pain. It is only knowledge which leads to liberation because bondage is due to ignorance and ignorance can be removed only by knowledge.

Sāṁkhya admits both Jīvanmukti and Videhamukti. The moment right knowledge dawns, the person becomes liberated here and now, even though he may be embodied due to prārabdha karma.

The final and the absolute emancipation, the complete disembodied isolation automatically results after death. Sāṁkhya liberation is a state of complete isolation, freedom from all pain, a return of the Puruṣa to its pure nature as consciousness. There is no pleasure or happiness or bliss here, for pleasure presupposes pain and is relative to it. Pleasure is the result of sattva guṇa and liberation transcends all guṇas.

Sāṁkhya believes that bondage and liberation alike are only phenomenal. The bondage of the Puruṣa is a fiction. It is only the ego, the product of Prakṛti, which is bound. And consequently it is only the ego which is liberated. Puruṣa, in its complete isolation, is untouched by bondage and liberation. If Puruṣa were really bound, it could not have obtained liberation even after hundred births, for real bondage can never be destroyed. It is Prakṛti which is bound and Prakṛti which is liberated.

Kaivalya

It is referred as a state of liberalisation. This term is found in the Samkhya school. It is also known moksha and redeas release. Consciousness of an individual is regarded as separate from matter Kalvalya means the release from bondage. It also means the total seperateness from Prakriti. Liberation means complete cessation of all suffering. Moksha is regarded as the highest end of life. It has been said that the purusha when realises its own pure nature, become liberated. Bondage occurs due to ignorance. Liberation occurs due to right. Knowledge. It has been said that prakriti is found to be founded whereas Purusha is found to be liberated.

Atheism

The original Sāṁkhya was monistic and theistic. But the classical Sāṁkhya, perhaps under the influence of Materialism, jainism and Early Buddhism, became atheistic. It is orthodox because it believes in the authority of the Veda. It does not establish the non-existence of God. It only shows that Prakṛti and Puruṣas are sufficient to explain this universe and therefore there is no reason for postulating a hypothesis of God. But some commentators have tried to repudiate the existence of God, while the later Sāṁkhya writers like Vijñānabhikṣu have tried to revive the necessity for admitting God. Those who repudiate the existence of God give the following arguments : if God is affected by selfish motives, He is not free; if He is free, He will not create this world of pain and misery. Either God is unjust and cruel or He is not free and all-powerful. If he is determined by the law of Karma, He is not free; if not, He is a tyrant. Again, God being pure knowledge, this material world cannot spring from Him. The effects are implicitly contained in their cause and the material world which is subject to change requires an unintelligent and ever-changing cause and not a spiritual and immutable God. Again, the eternal existence of the Puruṣas is inconsistent with God. If they are the parts of God, they must have some divine power. If they are created by God, they are subject to destruction. Hence there is no God.

Arguments against Ishvara's Existence

According to Sinha, the following arguments were given by the Samkhya philosophers against the idea of an eternal, self-caused, creator God:

- If the existence of karma is assumed, the proposition of God as a moral governor of the universe is unnecessary. For, if God enforces the consequences of actions then he can do so without karma. If however, he is assumed to be within the law of karma, then karma itself would be the giver of consequences and there would be no need of a God.
- Even if karma is denied, God still cannot be the enforcer of consequences. Because the motives of an enforcer God would be either egoistic or altruistic. Now, God's motives cannot be assumed to be altruistic because an altruistic God would not create a world so full of suffering. If his motives are assumed to be egoistic, then God must be thought to have desire, as agency or authority cannot be established in the absence of desire. However, assuming that God has desire would contradict God's eternal freedom which necessitates no compulsion in actions. Moreover, desire, according to Samkhya, is an attribute of prakriti and cannot be thought to grow in God. The testimony of the Vedas, according to Samkhya, also confirms this notion.
- Despite arguments to the contrary, if God is still assumed to contain unfulfilled desires, this would cause him to suffer pain and other similar human experiences. Such a worldly God would be no better than Samkhya's notion of higher self.
- Furthermore, there is no proof of the existence of God. He is not the object of perception, there exists no general proposition that can prove him by inference and the testimony of the Vedas speak of prakriti as the origin of the world, not God.

Therefore, Samkhya maintained that the various cosmological, ontological and teleological arguments could not prove God.

YOGA

Yoga is the physical, mental, and spiritual practices or disciplines which originated in ancient India with a view to attain a state of permanent peace. The term yoga can be derived from either of two roots, yujir yoga (to yoke) or yuj samadhau (to concentrate). The Yoga Sutras of Patañjali defines yoga as "the stilling of the changing states of the mind" (Sanskrit::). Yoga has also been popularly defined as "union with the divine" in other contexts and traditions.

Various traditions of yoga are found in Hinduism, Buddhism and Jainism. In Hinduism, yoga is one of the six āstika schools (accepts authority of Vedas) of Hindu philosophy. Yoga is also an important part of Vajrayana and Tibetan Buddhist philosophy.

Pre–philosophical speculations and diverse ascetic practices of first millennium BCE were systematized into a formal philosophy in early centuries CE by the Yoga Sutras of Patanjali. By the turn of the first millennium, hatha yoga emerged from tantra. It, along with its many modern variations, is the style that many people associate with the word yoga today. Vajrayana Buddhism, founded by the Indian Mahasiddhas, has a parallel series of asanas and pranayamas, such as candāli and true khor. Gurus from India later introduced yoga to the west, following the success of Swami Vivekananda in the late 19th and early 20th century. In the 1980s, yoga became popular as a system of physical exercise across the Western world. This form of yoga is often called Hatha yoga.

Patanjali Citta and Citta-Vṛtti

Yoga is defined as the cessation of the modifications of citta. This cessation is through mediation or concentration which is also called Yoga (yogaḥ samādhiḥ). Chitta means the three internal organs of

(c) **Savanda.** Here the Chitta is concentrated on a still subtler object of meditation.
(d) **Sananda.** Here the Chitta is concentrated on the ego substance.

Role of God

Yoga accepts the existence of God. The interest of Patañjali himself in God seems to be practical, but the later Yogins have taken also a theoretical interest in Him and have tried to prove His existence as a necessary philosophical speculation. Patañjali defines God as a special kind of Puruṣa who is always free from pains, actions, effects and impressions. He is eternally free and was never bound nor has any possibility of being bound. He is above the law of Karma. He is omniscient and omnipotent and omnipresent. He is perfection incarnate. He is purest knowledge. He is the teacher of the ṛsis (sapūrveṣāmpai guruḥ) and the teacher of the Veda, 'Aum' is His symbol. Devotion to God is one of the surest means of obtaining concentration. The proofs advanced one of the surest means of obtaining concentration. The proofs advanced for his existence are : (a) The Veda tell's us that God exists; (b) the law of continuity tells us that there must be the highest limit of knowledge and perfection which is God; (c) God is responsible for the association and dissociation of Puruṣa and Prakṛti; (d) devotion to God is the surest way of obtaining concentration and thereby liberation.

But God of Yoga is not the creator, preserver or destroyer of this world. He is only a special Puruṣa. He does not reward or punish the souls. Innumerable Puruṣas and Prakṛti, all eternals and absolutes, are there to limit him. He cannot grant liberation. He can only remove the obstacles in the upward progress of the devotees. Directly he has nothing to do with the bondage and the liberation of the Puruṣas. Ignorance binds and discrimination between Prakṛti and Puruṣa from Prakṛti. Such a conception of God is certainly unsatisfactory.

PURVA-MIMĀMSĀ

Mimāṁsa and Vedānta are treated as allied systems of thought. Both are based on and both try to interpret the Veda. The earlier portion of the Veda, i.e., the Mantra and the Brāhmaṇa portion, is called Karmakāṇḍa, while the later portion, i.e., the Upaniṣads is called Jñānakāṇḍa, because the former deals with the knowledge of reality. Mimāṁsā deals with the earlier portion of the Veda and is therefore called Pūrva-Mīmāṁsā and also Karma-Mīmāṁsā. Jaimini was the founder of Purva-mīmaṁsā.

ŚRUTI AND ITS IMPORTANCE

The aim of the Mimāṁsā is to ascertain the nature of Dharma. Dharma is not a physical existent, and so it cannot be apprehended through the senses. The other pramānas are of no use, since they all presuppose the work of perception. Perception, inference and such other sources of knowledge have nothing to say on the point that the performer of the Agniṣtoma sacrifice will go to heaven. This knowledge is derived only from the Vedas. Though the pramāṇa of the Veda is the only source of our knowledge of dharma, the others are considered, since it is necessary to show that they cannot give rise to a knowledge of dharma. They are also found useful in repudiating wrong views.

The kernel of the Veda consist of those declarations in injunctive form which prompt men towards certain modes of action by declaring that such action leads to beneficial results. Accepting that ritual is all in all in the Vedas, Jaimini holds that parts apparently unconnected with it are useless, and so they have to be inter-preted as bearing on ritual injunctions. Other texts are authoritative only in so far as they help the individual to action. The Mīmāṁsakas attempt to prove that every part of the sacred text refers to acts of duty.

The Vedas are eternal, since the words of which they are composed are eternal. The relationship between the word and its meaning is natural and not created by convention. The cognitions brought about by Vedic injunctions cannot be set aside at any time or place or under any conditions. It is a self-contradiction to assert that the injunction expresses something which is not true. The Vedas manifest their own validity. Words used by us denote things that can be cognised by other means of knowledge; and, if we cannot know them through other means, then those who utter them must be of unquestionable authority. So non-Vedic utterances do not possess any inherent validity. Prabhākara holds that non-Vedic verbal cognition is of the nature of inference. Only the verbal cognition afforded by the Veda is strictly verbal, but it is not in consistency with the other theory of the self-validity of all cognitions. Since there is no author of Vedic texts, there is no possibility of defects, and so the non-authoritativeness of the Vedas is inconceivable. As the utterances of human beings are valid, if their authors are trustworthy, Kumārila considers them also to be śabdapramāṇa.

Purva-Mimamsa on Existence of God

According to Max Mullers, the Mimamsa is regarded as theistic, the early Mimamsakas are regarded as silent God, but later ones reject the existence of God proofs. According to the Mimamsakas, the deities are regarded as immortal entities. God are not regarded as existing persons.

The Vedic conception of God is regarded as inactive. According to the Mimamsa, God is regarded as an ambiguous position.

Content of Veda

The Mantras and the Brahmanas are regarded as parts of the Vedas.

There are five content of the Veda, which are as follows :

1. Injunctions
2. Hymns
3. Names
4. Prohibitions
5. Explanatory passages.

Injunctions compel one to perform actions in order to achieve certain results. It includes subsidiary injunctions. Subsidiary injunctions describes the details of the sacrifice.

The mantras possesses a mystical effect. It reminds the sacrificer of the different matters. The mantras also contribute directly to the transcendental result. Arthavadas includes the praises of the things that are enjoined. It also includes the description of the doings of others.

Vedas are Eternal

The Vedas are regarded as eternal. The Vedas also includes the words. The relationship between the word and its meaning is regarded as natural. The Vedas are able to manifest their own validity. It has been said that we cannot say that the injunction expresses something that are found as untrue. The verbal cognition afforded by the Veda is regarded as verbal. No author of Vedic tests are found. No defects is found in Vedas.

Classification of Śrutivākyas, Vidhi, Niṣêdha and Arthvāda

Vedas are broadly divided into the Mantras and the Brahmanas. Which we have already discussed about in first chapter.

The contents of the Veda are also classified into 1. injunctions (vidhi), 2. hymns (mantras), 3. names (nāmadheya), 4. prohibitions (niṣedha), and 5. explanatory passages (arthavāda).

Injunctions which impel one to action in expectation of certain results, such as "One who is desirous of heaven is to sacrifice" (svargakāmo yajeta), are the most important. There are subsidiary injunctions which describe the details of the sacrifice, the order in which the several parts of it are to be carried out, as well as the persons who are entitled to perform them. The mantras are largely useful in reminding the sacrificer of the different matters connected with the sacrifice, such as the deities to whom oblations are to be made. Some of the mantras are said to possess a mystical or supersensuous effect and to contribute directly to the transcendental result, apūrva. Names indicate the results to be obtained by the sacrifices. Niṣedhas are only vidhis in disguise, Arthavādas comprise the sentences which contain either praise of the things enjoined (praśaṁsa), or a censure of things prohibited (nindā), as well as description of the doings of others (parakṛti) and instances from history (purākalpa) (Arthasaṁgraha).

Atheism of Purva-mimaēsa

Max müller's view that the Mīmaṁsā is theistic can be accepted if the Mīmaṁsā is to be judged by the vedic ancestry. But judged by what the Mīmāṁsā itself does and says, his contention cannot be fully accepted. When we fined that the early Mīmāṁsakas are silent God and later ones reject the proofs for the existence of God, like the Jainas, without replacing them by any other, we have no positive proof that the early Vedic faith was still alive in them. The different Vedic deities of course still form necessary parts of the sacrifices performed. Depending on this evidence one might say at best that the Mīmāṁsā believes in polytheism. But even such a view is rendered doubtful by the facts that these deities are not regarded as objects of worship, nor even believed to have any existence any where except in the Vedic hymns (mantras) that describe them While the Vedic hymns are inspired by the living presence of the deity in the place of worship, the Mīmāṁsaka wonders how the deity can be simultaneously present in different places where he is invoked. So polytheism of the ordinary kind cannot also be attributed to Mīmāṁsā without some qualification. The deities of the Mīmāṁsaka are immortal entities. They are not existing persons, belonging to the space-time world. But they are not the products of our imagination either; they are eternal and self-manifesting entities described by the eternal, self-revealing Vedas. There may be some grandeur and even purity in such a conception of deities, but one would miss here the living faith of the Vedas. It would not be fair, then, to judge the Mīmāṁsa simply by its Vedic ancestry. Inherited elements of a faith, like inherited limbs, become atrophied by disuse. The Vedic conception of God had no active place in the Mīmāṁsā scheme of life, as it had in the Vedānta one, and it is natural that it should gradually fade away. The Mīmāṁsā is one of the many examples in human history of how an overemphasized means becomes its own end, and how gods are sacrificed for temples, prophets and books. In its great anxiety to maintain the supremacy of the Vedas, the Mīmāṁsā relegates God to an ambiguous position.

Śabdanityavāda

The Mīmāṁsakas propound the theory that words (śabdas) are not really the perceived sounds (dhvanis). The sound produced by the speaker and perceived by the hearer are only the revealers of the words which are not themselves produced. Words are really the letters which are partless and uncaused. A letter, like 'K', is pronounced (and revealed) by different persons at different places and times in different ways. Though these letter-sounds vary, we recognise that the same letter is pronounced by all of them. This identity of the letter shows that it is not produced at any time and place, but transcends them. So the words as letters may be regarded as eternal, that is, as having existence, but being uncaused. This Mimaṁsakas theory is known as śabdanityavāda.

Jaimini sets forth positive considerations in support of this view. The word is ever present, since the utterance of it is only for the purpose of manifesting it to others. There cannot be any effort manifest a non-existing thing. For non-eternal things, cause of destruction are found, but we do not find causes for the destruction of words. The sound produced from air is distinct from the word which it serves to manifest. Besides, we have many Vedic texts insisting on the eternal nature of words.

Jātiśaktivāda

Mimaṁsakas' theory of jatiśaktivāda states that universals (Jāti) are eternal and have potency (śakti) to manifest ākritis and seem as different kinds of individuals. Words denote classes and not individuals. When we say "bring a cow", we do not mean a particular cow, but any animal possessing the features of a cow. The word denotes the class or form, since it has action for its objects. If individuals are denoted by words, a generic idea like 'cow' would be impossible. Again, a word cannot denote all the individuals, since then it would possess as many potencies as there are individuals. It cannot denote a collection of individuals, since then it would be undergoing changes, as some individuals die out and others get in. Again, if the word means a single individual only, there cannot be an eternal connection between word and meaning, and action would be impossible, as it would be difficult to decide which individual is meant. If individuals are objects denoted, then since they are not omnipresent, there cannot be a relation between a word and its meaning. Ākṛti is eternal, and is therefore capable of relationship with the eternal word.

Dharma and Bhāvanā

Dharma is the subject of inquiry in Mīmāṁsā. Jaimini defines dharma as a command or injunction which impels men to action. It is the supreme duty, the 'ought', the 'categorical imperative'. Artha and Kāma which deal with ordinary common morality are learnt by worldly intercourse. But Dharma and Mokṣa which deal with true spirituality are revealed only by the Veda. Dharma is supra-sensible and consists in the commands us to do certain acts and to refrain from doing certain other acts. The authoritativeness of the Veda is supported by social consciousness as well as by individual conscience. Dharma and adharma deal with happiness and pain to be enjoyed or suffered in the life beyond. Actions performed here produce an unseen potency (apūrva) in the soul of the agent which yields fruit when obstructions are removed and time becomes ripe for its fructification. The apūrva is the link between the act and its fruit. It is the causal potency (shakti) in the act which leads to its fructification. Actions are first divided into three kinds—obligatory (which must be performed, for their violation results in sin though their performance leads to no merit); optional (which may or may not be performed; their performance leads to merit, though their non-performance does not lead to sin); and prohibited (which must not be performed, for their performance leads to sin, though their non-performance does not lead to merit).

The earlier Mīmāṁsaka believed only in dharma (and not in mokṣa) and their ideal was the attainment of heaven (svarga). But later Mīmāṁsakas believe in mokṣa and substitute the ideal of heaven by that of liberation (apavarga). Prabhākara and Kumārila both believe that the goal of human life is liberation, though both conceive it in a negative manner like the Nyāya-Vaisheṣika. The soul is chained to Saṁsāra on account of its association with the body, the senses, the mind and the understanding. Through this association, the soul becomes a knower, an enjoyer and an agent. This association is due to karma which is the cause of bondage. When the cause is removed, the effect also ceases to exist. So abstention from karma automatically leads to the dissolution of the 'marriage-tie' of the soul with the body, the senses, the mind etc. and consequently to the return of the soul to its pure nature as a substance rid of all qualities and modes including consciousness and bliss also.

Kumarila and Prabhakara Schools of Mīmaṁsā

Jaimini's Sutra, in twelve elaborate chapters, laid the foundation of the Pūrva Mīmāṁsā. Śabarasvāmī wrote the major commentary or Bhāṣya on this work. He is followed by a long line of commentators and independent writers. The two most important among them are Kumārila Bhaṭṭa and Prahākara (nicknamed 'Guru'), who founded the two schools of Mīmāṁsā named after them, and thus the Mīmāṁsā philosophy gradually developed. The defence of vedic supremacy from Buddhist criticism was also a major cause of coming these schools in light. Shabarasvāmin's commentary on 'Mimaṁsa-sutra' has been explained by Prabhākara and Kumārila Bhatta who differ from each other in certain important respects. Prabhakara's commentary Bṛhati has been commented upon by Shālikanātha who has also written another treatise Prakaraṇa-pañchikā. Kumārila's huge work is divided into three parts-Shlokavārtika, tantravārtika and Tupṭikā, the first the which has been commented upon by Pārthasārathi Mishra who has also written his shāstradipika. Tradition makes Prabhākara a pupil of Kumārila who nicknamed him as 'Guru' on account of his great intellectual powers. But some scholars like Dr. Gangānātha Jha believe that the Prabhākara school is older and seems to be nearer the spirit of the original Mimaṁsā.

Differences in Philosophy = Perception, Inference, Consciousness, Self.

Their Major Points of Difference

Validity of Knowledge

Similarity—Both accept svataḥpramāṇyavāda.

Difference—Prabhākara—defines valid knowledge as apprehension (anubhuti). All apprehension is direct and immediate and valid per se.

Kumārila—defines valid knowledge as apprehension of an object which is produced by causes free from defects and which is not contradicted by subsequent knowledge.

Pramāṇa

Similarity—

1. Both regard knowledge itself as pramāṇa or means of knowledge.
2. Both recognize two kinds of knowledge-immediate and mediate.
3. Perception is regarded as immediate knowledge by both.
4. Both admit two stages in perception-indeterminate and determinate.
5. Both accept that inferential argument has only three members—pratijña, major premise and minor premise.
6. Both accept the eternity of veda and of words.
7. Both argues that significance belongs to the letters themselves and not to any special sphoṭa.

Difference—

1. Prabh.—accepts five pramāṇas-perception, inference, testimony, Comparison and Implication.
   Kuma.—accepts six pramaṇas-perception, inference, testimony, Comparison, Implication and non-apprehension.
   (Jaimini accepts only three-perception, inference and testimony)
2. P.—Defines perception as direct apprehension. (sākṣāt pratitiḥ pratyakṣaṁ)
   K.—Defines perception as direct knowledge produced by the proper contact of the sense organs with the presented objects, which is free from defects.
3. P.—Holds that inference involves a previous knowledge of the general relation and refers to things already known.
   K.—Makes novelty an essential feature of inference. The object of the inferential cognition is something that is not already known.
4. P.—The facts observed by implication remain inconsistent or doubtful until the assumption is made. In inference there is no room for any element of doubt.
   K.—Arthāpatti helps us to reconcile two apparently incosistent facts. There is no such incosistency between well-ascertained facts in inference.
5. P.—Does not accept non-apprehension as an independent source of knowledge.
   K.—Accepts non-apprehension as an independent source of knowledge.

Error

P.—Prabhākara's theory of error is known as Akhyātivāda.

K.—Kumārila's theory of error is Viparitakhyāti.

Self

Similarity—Both admit the plurality of the individual souls and regard the self as an eternal, omnipresent, ubiquitous, infinite substance which is the substratum of consciousness and which is a real knower, enjoyer and agent.

Difference—

1. P.—Consciousness is only an accidental quality of soul.
   K.—Consciousness is modal change in the self.
2. P.—Advocates the theory of simultaneous revelation of knower, known and knowledge (triputipratyakṣavāda).
   K.—advocates the theory of cognizedness of objects (jñatatavāda).
3. P.—accepts self as a subject of every knowledge.
   K.—Accepts self as the object of self-consciousness.

Liberation

Similarity—

1. Both believe that the goal of human life is liberation, though conceive it in a negative sense.
2. Both admit that abstention from karma means abstention from the optional and the prohibited kinds of karma only.

Difference—

1. P.—Believes in 'duty for duty's sake'. Obedience to the veda is an end in itself and is of ultimate value (purusartha).
   K.—Believes in psychological hedonism and makes the performance of these actions a means to realize the ultimate end, *i.e.* liberation.

2. P.—Does not regard liberation as a state of bliss.
   K.—(i) does not regard liberation as a state of bliss. (According to Pārthasārathi)
   (ii) regard liberation as a state of bliss. (According to Nārayana Bhaṭṭa)

Tripuṭi-Saṃvit

Prabhākara is an advocate of tripuṭisaṁvit, according to which the knower, the known and the knowledge are given simultaneously in every act of cognition. Knowledge reveals itself as well as the knower and the known. In the consciousness, "I know this" (aham idaṁ jānāmi), we have the three or the object (viṣayavitti), and the conscious awareness (svasaṁvitti). All consciousness is at the same time whether inferential or verbal, the self is known directly through the agency and the contact of the manas. While there is always a direct and immediate knowledge of self in every act of cognition, there is not always a direct. In recollection and inference the object is not directly presented to consciousness. Though in indirect knowledge the object is not directly presented to consciousness, yet the indirect knowledge itself is directly presented to consciousness. Cognition is also self-cognised by direct apprehension. The cognition which is of the nature of light or illumination does not stand in need of any other thing to manifest it. Therefore, the cognition is said to be self-apprehended. The cognising self and the cognised object are not of the nature of light, and so they require for their manifestation the aid of something different from themselves which is of the nature of light. Cognitions are self-illumined, and not perceived as objects. They are not cognised by other cognitions. They are never objects, and so cannot be cognised, as pleasure and pain are cognised. They are cognised as cognitions, but not as objects. If cognitions are cognised as objects, then each individual cognition may require another cognition to cognise it, and so on *ad infinitum.* Prabhākara feels that his theory is not evidently consistent with Śabara's observation that we perceive objects in apprehension and not cognitions, and so argues that, though cognitions are self cognised, their presence is known through inference. Inference tells us that there is a cognition from the fact that we have the apprehension of the object. The cognition is a prameya, or the object of right knowledge, but it is not saṁvedya, or apprehended in its fullness. According to Prabhākara, we have a case of saṁvedya only when the form of the object is manifested, and this is possible with the objects perceived by the senses. As cognitions have no form, they cannot be perceived. Their presence is only inferred. Inference does not apprehend the form or content of the object, but only its existence. Both Prabhākara and Kumārila admit that cognitions, which are products (pariṇāma) of ātman, are objects of inference.

Jñātāta

Kumarila's theory of knowledge is known as jñātatavāda. Knowledge is a movement brought about by the activity of the self, which results in producing consciousness of objective things. Cognition of a certain object ends not in a further cognition of that cognition, but in the cognisedness (prakaṭatā) of the object. An act of knowledge has four elements in it : 1. the knower (jñātā); 2. the object of knowledge (jñeya); 3. the instrument of the cognisedness of the object (jñātatā). According to Kumārila, a cognition is not directly perceived, but is inferred from the cognisedness (jñātatā, prākaṭya) of the object produced by the cognition. Every act of cognition implies a certain relationship between the perceiver and the perceived, which involves some activity on the part of the perceiver. The presence of the relationship enables us to infer the action of the agent, which is cognition, in the case of knowledge. The cognition is inferred from the relation between the knower and the known, which is apprehended by internal perception (mānasapratyakṣa).

Apprehendedness (jñatatā) is nothing but the character of being the object of cognition. The nature of objectivity is hard to define. If objectivity means that cognition is produced by the object, then even sense-organs and other conditions producing the cognition have to be regarded as objects. Again, it is not possible for a property to be produced in an object at a time when the object does not exist. Apprehendedness is a property of the objects, though it cannot be produced in past and future ones, which are also apprehended.

Abhāva and Anupalabdhi

Kumārila admits non-apprehension (anupalabdhi) as an independent source of knowledge. Dissimilarity is only want of similarity, and it is accounted for by the principle of non-apprehension. When we say "There is no jar in this place", we cognise the absence of the jar. Absence (abhāva) cannot be apprehended by perception, which stands in need of sense-contact with a present object, which is not possible in the case, nor can non-existence be apprehended by the other pramānas. Non-apprehension is a means of knowledge (mānam) with reference to the object negated. We perceive the vacant space and think of the absence of the jar. We may say that the non-existence of the jar is as much perceived as the vacant space, yet, since perception involves contact of an actual object with the senses, we cannot identify the act of non-apprehension with perception. We perceive the vacant space, remember the jar that is absent, and then we have the knowledge of the absence of the jar, which has no reference to the act of perception. Apprehension of non-existence is through anupalabdhi. Abhāva is side to be a positive object of knowledge. What we call emptiness is the locus unoccupied by any object.

Prabhākara does not accept non-apprehension as an independent source of knowledge. The cognition of non-existence is inferred from the non-perception of something that would have been perceived if it were present. When we perceive the mere space and no jar in it, we say that there is no jar. The cognition of the substratum by itself (tanmātradhī) is what answers to non-apprehension. Kumārila disputes that view. We may perceive not merely empty space, but space filled by books and paper, but that will also give us a knowledge of the non-existence of the jar. If we say that we apprehend space as not qualified by the jar, we are admitting negative knowledge. Therefore, abhāva, cannot be reduced to perception, and, is an independent valid source of knowledge.

Anvitābhidhānavāda

According to Prabhākara, who accepts the theory of Anvitābhidhānavāda, the meanings of words can be known only when they occur in a sentence enjoying some duty, and so words denote objects only as related to the other factors of such a sentence. If they are not related to an injunction, but simply remind us of meanings, it is case of remembrance, which is not valid cognition.

Since the potency of the word originates from the separate potencies of the letters, the latter are said to be the direct cause of verbal cognition. The cognition of the meaning of the word is not obtained through sense-perception. The senses present the letters which possess the power to bring about the words have naturally denotative powers by which they refer to objects whether we understand their meanings or not.

Abhihitānvayavāda

According to the abhihitānvayavāda accepted by Kumārila's followers, the knowledge of meanings is due to words; but this knowledge is not due to recollection or apprehension, but to denotation. Words denote meanings which, when combined, give rise to a knowledge of there is such a relationship between the word and its meaning is directly cognisable. If one does not recognise it, when one hears the word for the first time, it only means that the accessories are absent, but that does not makes the relationship non-existent. It the eye cannot see without light, it does not mean that the eye is incapable of seeing altogether. The accessory is the knowledge that such and such a word denotes such and such and object, which is gained from experience. The expressiveness of the word belongs to it by its very nature. This is absolutely true of common names like jar and the like, where the relation of the words to their meanings is independent of any convention.

VEDĀNTA

The Vedānta philosophy of Bādarāyana is also known as the Uttara Mimāṁsā system and is said to have been written down sometime between 500 and 200 B.C.E. The Vedānta Sutras (also called Brahma Sutras) that form the foundation of the philosophy systematize the teachings of the Upanishads. The 555 sutras are often terse and consequently, over the centuries, many scholars and philosophers have written commentaries based on this work. In commenting upon the work, it can be said that the commentaries founded new schools of philosophy. Most notable among these were Shankara (788-820 C.E.) and his school of non-dualism (*advaita*), Rāmānuja (11th century) and qualified non-dualism (*visista advaita*) and Madhva (1197-1267) with his school of dualism (*dvaita*). All three schools come under the heading of Vedānta.

The word *vedānta* can be split into two: *veda* and *anta* and literally means "end of the Vedas." This is taken to mean the distilling of the philosophy of the Vedas and the Upanishads into its essential components. Shankara builds upon Gaudapāda's commentary (*kārikā*) of the Māndūkya Upanishad, the shortest of the Upanishads dealing with the four states of consciousness. In his commentary of the Vedānta Sutras, Shankara begins by asking if there is anything in our experience that we can be certain of. This is the question of the philosopher and we find echoes of the same question in the later writings of René Descrates and Bertrand Russell. "Our senses may deceive us; our memory may be an illusion. The forms of the world may be pure fancy. The objects of knowledge may be open to doubt, but the doubter himself cannot be doubted. ... It cannot be proved, because it is the basis of all proof. The self is self-established and is different from all else, physical and mental. As the subject it is not the object. ... It is undifferentiated consciousness, which remains unaffected even when the body is reduced to ashes and the mind perishes. Reiterating the Upanishadic teaching, Shankara explains the eternal Self is the *ātman* and the universal Self is *Brahman.* "The world is bound up by the categories of space, time and cause. These are not self-contained or self-consistent. They point to something unalterable and absolute ... *Brahman* is different from the space-time-cause world. ... The empirical world cannot exist by itself. It is wholly dependent on *Brahman* ... but *Brahman* depends on nothing. Ignorance affects our whole empirical being. It is another name for finitude. To remove ignorance is to realize the truth. ... While absolute truth is *Brahman*, empirical truth is not false."

ADVAITA VEDĀNTA

Advaita or monism means one and only one reality. Śaṁkarācārya, the founder of Advaita Vedānta, accepts this view of monism and states that Brahman is one and only one reality while all the things seen in this world is only a mere appearance of him. A gold chain is gold in real sense; Difference between a gold chain and a gold ring appears because of their different formation in different shapes and sizes made of a single metal, *i.e.*, gold.

Rejection of Difference

Śaṅkara says that there is no multiplicity here (neha nānā asti kiñcana), that one who sees the many here is doomed to death ('mṛtyoḥ as mṛtyum āpnotiāya miha nāneva paśyati'). In explanation of the unity of all things, which appear to be many, examples like these are cited : Justnas different articles made of gold are all really one, gold is the only real substance in them and the different names and forms (nāma-rūpa) which make them appear as many, are merely matters of verbal distinction, similarly in all objects there is the same Reality, and their differences are merely verbal designation.

The objects of the world are denied separate, individual existence. Brahman (or Ātman) is also described not as Creator, but as a Reality which is indescribable, being not only unspeakable but even unthinkable. Difference or multiplicity seen in this world is only due to Māyā, Māyā is also known as avidyā, ajñāna, adhyāsa etc.

Adhyāsa

It is self-evident, says Shaṅkara, that the subject and the object are absolutely opposed to each other like light and darkness. The subject is Pure Consciousness; the object is Unconsciousness. The one is the ultimate 'I'; the other is the 'non-I'. Neither these two nor their attributes can, therefore, be identified. Yet it is the natural and common practice of people that they wrongly superimpose the object and its attributes upon the subject and error, this coupling of the real and the unreal (satyānṛte mithuṅikṛtya) is called superimposition (adhyāsa) or error (bhrama) or illusion (māyā) or ignorance (avidyā). All definitions of error agree in maintaining that error is the superimposition of one thing on another, *e.g.*, the superimposition of silver on shell or the illusion of the moons on a single moon. This superimposition the learned call 'ignorance', and the realization of the true nature of reality by discarding error, they call 'knowledge'. This transcendental Ignorance is the presupposition of all practices of this phenomenal world. Superimposition, therefore, is the notion of a thing in something else (atasmin tadbuddiḥ). This unreal beginningless cycle of superimposition goes on leading to the false notions of the agent and the enjoyed and to all phenomenal practices. The study of the Vedānta texts is undertaken in order to free oneself from this false notion of superimposition and thereby realize the essential unity of the Self.

Māyā

Brahman is the only Reality; the world is ultimately false; and the individual soul is non-different from Brahman. Brahman and Ātman or the Supreme Self are synonymous terms. The world is a creation of Māyā. The individual selves on account of their inherent Avidyā imagine themselves as different from Brahman and mistake Brahman as this world of plurality, even as we mistake a rope as a snake. Avidyā vanishes at the dawn of knowledge—the super-relational direct and intuitive knowledge of the non-dual self which means liberation.

It is regarded as Shakti under this domain, we mistake shell as silver. The shell is regarded as the ground on which the silver is superimposed. It has been said that, when right knowledge arises, this error Vanishes. The relation between the shell and the silver is regarded as neither of identity nor of difference nor of both. It is regarded as unique. It is also referred as non-difference. Brahman is regarded as the ground on which the world appears through the power of Maya. Maya vanishes, when right knowledge dawns and the essential unity of the jiva with the Paramatman is realised.

The words Māyā, Avidyā, Ajñāna, Adhyāsa, Adhyāropa, Akṣara, Bījashakti, Mūla-prakṛti etc. are recklessly used in Vedānta as very nearly synonymous. Of these Māyā, Avidyā, Adhyāsa and Vivarta are very often used as interchangeable terms. There are two schools among later Advaitins divided on the question whether Māyā and Avidyā are identical or different. The general trend of the Advaitins including Shaṅka himself has been to treat these two terms as synonymous and to distinguish between the two aspects of Māyā or Avidyā which are called āvaraṇa and vikṣepa, the former being the negative aspect of concealment and the latter the positive aspect of projection.

Māyā or Avidyā is not pure illusion. It is not only absence of knowledge. It is also positive wrong knowledge. It is a cross of the real and the unreal (satyānṛte mithunī kṛtya). In fact it is indescribable. For the appearance of the Brahman as the world. It cannot be both existent and non-existent for this conception is self-contradictory. It is called neither real nor unreal (sadasadvilakṣana). It is false or mithyā. But it is not a non-entity like a hare's horn (tuchchha). It is positive (bhāvarūpa). It is potency (shakti). It is also called superimposition (adhyāsa). A shell is mistaken as silver. The shell is the ground on which the silver is superimposed. When right knowledge (pramā) arises, this error (bhrānti or bhrama) vanishes. The relation between the shell and the silver is neither that of identity nor of difference nor of both. It is unique and is known as non-difference (tādātmya). Similarly, Brahman is the ground on which the world appears through Māyā. When right knowledge dawns and the essential unity of the jīva with the Paramātman is realized, Māyā or Avidyā vanishes.

Avidyā as Māyā

Māyā is not only absence of knowledge; it is also positive wrong knowledge. It is not only non-apprehension, but also misapprehension. It makes the infinite appear as finite. It produces the manifold phenomena, which in fact there is only the non-dual Atman. It makes the unlimited Atman appear as limited jivas. Brahman, through Avidyā, appears as the manifold world of names and forms, just as pure water appears as dirty foam. Brahman itself is the locus and object of Avidyā. Avidyā is the darkening power. Its essential nature is to cover or hide the real.

It operates in three ways:

(i) as positive wrong knowledge
(ii) as doubt
(iii) as absence of knowledge. Really it can do no harm to reality, just as migrate-water cannot make the sandy desert muddily.

Condemnation of World

The phenomenal world is often condemned by Shankara as unreal exactly in the spirit of Mahayana Buddism and of Gaudapada. It is said to be like **mirage-water** rope-snake, shell silver dusty surface of the sky, plantain-trunk, dream bubble foam, moving fire-brand magical elephant hair etc., seen floating in the atmosphere on account of defective vision, illusion of **double-moon** pure magic etc.

We have already remarked that such words were the heritage of the common language and not the monopoly of Mahayana. *e.g.*, Shankara observes knowing the true nature of all phenomena, which represent the cycle of birth and death, which are manifest and unmanifest, which are beset with innumerable evils, which are unreal like plantain-trunk, illusion, mirage, sky-castle, dream, bubble, foam, which are being destroyed every moment and which are the result of ignorance, attachment and other defiled actions.

The beginningless samsara, which is of the nature of suffering and which is rotted in ignorance, is like a continually flowing stream of water. Just as a person of defective vision sees double-moon or mosquitoes and flies floating in the **atmosphere** or just as a dreamer sees many things in a dream, similarly this world of plurality of names and forms, is imagined through ignorance.

Criticism of Mayā Opponents

The opponents says, that he fails to understand as how unreal Maya can cause the real Brahman to appear. If the world is unreal, unreal means like the Vedanta texts cannot lead to real liberation; if the world is real, it cannot be Maya.

Shankara replies that the objection is wrong. If a person imagines is very strong, it may result in heart-failure or in some psychological disaster. The water in a dream can quench the thirst in a dream and a person bitten by a snake in dream may feel himself to be dead in the dream. We have seen that even unreal things can cause real things. The opponent hopelessly confuses the two different standpoints the empirical and the absolute, even as he is confusing the imaginary with the empirical. The unreality of the empirical standpoint can be realised only from the absolute standpoint (paramarthika). And even then, though these dream-objects are sublated, the consciousness that the dreamer had experienced these objects in the dream is not sublated even in the waking state. Right knowledge is not useless because, it removes ignorance and secondly, it cannot be sublated. It is only from the absolute stand point, when right knowledge attained that the Vedanta declares the world to be unreal.

Significance of Māyā

Many critics have failed to understand the real significance of Maya or Avidya they have charged Shankara with explaining that world away. This charge is based on a shifting of the standpoint Shankara, as we have shown above, has granted some degree of related even to dreams, illusion and errors.

Unreal means absolutely unreal like the here's horn, which this phenomenal world is not this world is neither real nor unreal. This shows its self-contradictory and therefore, incomprehensible nature. *It is true for all practical purposes.* What does it matter to us, worldly people, if it is not absolutely true in the philosophical sense? When the 'Reality', which is denied to this world means. Who can stand up and say that the world is not 'Unreal' if 'unreal' means 'Non-eternal'? The world will be sublated only, when knowledge dawns and not before.

Three Grades of Sattā

The world possesses three different grades of existence. The first kind of facts possesses only ephemeral existence (prātibhāsika sattā or apparent existence); the second empirical or virtual existence, the sort of existence necessary for ordinary life and practice (vyāvahārika sattā or practical existence) and the third absolute existence (pāramārthika sattā or supreme existence). The world is thus not a homogeneous conception; and if, in spite of this, one insists on being told what such a world (as a whole) is, the fairest reply can only be, what Śaṅkara gives, namely that it is indescribable (anirvacanīya) either as real or as unreal. But if the word, world, is confined only to the second aspect, it would be again fair to say, that the world is real only for practical purpose, more real than the first and less real than the third kind of existence. But if the word is taken in the third sense, Śaṅkara would emphatically assert that the world is eternally real. As he puts it : "As the cause, Brahman, does not lack existence at any time, past, present or future, so does the world not lack existence in any of the three periods of time". Again, "All particular modes of existence with different names and forms are real as existence, but unreal as particulars."

Jīva

Jīva or the individual self is a subject-object complex. Its subject-element is Pure Consciousness and is called the Sākṣin. Its object-element is the internal organ called the antaḥkaraṅa which is bhautika as it is composed of all the five elements, with the predominance of tejas which makes it always active except in deep sleep or states like swoon or trance. The source of the internal organ is Avidyā which causes individuality. In perception, the internal organ, when a sense-organ comes into contact with an object, assumes the 'form' of that object. It is the vṛtti or the mode of the internal organ. This vṛtti inspired by the Sākṣin takes the form of empirical knowledge. In waking state, the internal organ is aided by the senses; in dream state, it functions by itself; and in deep sleep it is lost in its cause Avidyā. In this state too individuality persists because the Sākṣin is associated with Avidyā. In liberation, Avidyā is destroyed by Jñāna and the Sākṣin is realized as the Brahman which it always is.

Jīvanmukti

Shankara repeatedly asserts that the Absolute can be realized through knowledge and knowledge alone; karma and upāsanā are subsidiary. They may help us in urging us to know Reality and they may prepare us for that knowledge by purifying our mind (sattvashuddhi), but ultimately it is knowledge alone which, by destroying ignorance, the root-cause of this world, can enable us to be one with the Absolute. The opposition of knowledge and action stands firm like a mountain. They are contradictory (viparīte) and are poles apart (dūramete). Those who talk of combining knowledge with action, says Shaṅkara, have perhaps not read the Bṛhadāraṇyaka nor are they aware of the glaring contradiction repeatedly pointed out by the Shruṭi and the Smṛti. Knowledge and action are opposed like light and darkness. Actions are prescribed for those who are still in ignorance and not for those who are enlightened. Knowledge only removes ignorance and then Reality shines forth by itself. A liberated sage, however, performs actions without any attachment and works for the uplift of humanity. Shaṅkara's own life bears ample witness to this fact.

Vivartavāda

It is defined as the theory of creation. This theory of creation is given by Sanikara. It is referred as an illusory modification of any subsistence. The rope to the Snake is defined as Vivartā.

Vivartā is defined as change and transformation. It also means appearing altered theory. It is referred as appearance theory. It is defined as the relation, which exists between an actual object and its reflection with in a mineral. It has been said that in Advaitā Vedantā, Vivartā is illustrated through two popular example Sarparajha Maya and Shuktirajata Maya.

Ultimate Reality

Ultimate reality, according to Shankara, is Atman or Brahman, which is pure consciousness or consciousness of the pure self, which is devoid of all attributes and all categories of the intellect. Brahman associated with its potency maya or mulavidya appears as the qualified Brahman or the Lord, who is the creator, preserver and destroyer of this world which is his appearance.

Jiva or individual self is a subject-object complex. It subject-element is pure consciousness and is called the Saksin. It subject element is the internal organ called the antahkarana, which is bhautika as it is composed of all the five elements, with the predominance of tejas, which makes it always active except in deep sleep or states like swoon or trance. The source of the internal organ is Avidya, which causes individuality. In perception the internal organ. When a sense-organ comes into contact with an object, assumes the 'form' of that object.

It is the urtti or the mode of the internal organ. This vrtti inspired by the Saksin takes the form of empirical knowledge. In waking state, the internal organ is aided by the senses; in dream state, it functions by itself; and in deep sleep it is lost in its cause Avidya. In this state too, individuality persists because the Saksin is associated with Avidya. In liberation, Avidya is destroyed by Jnana and the Saksin is realised as the Brahman, which it always is.

Criticism of the Prakrti-Parinama-Vada of Sankhya

Shankara agrees with Sankhya in maintaining that the design, harmony or order in the universe must presuppose a single cause which is eternal and unlimited. According to Shankara, the intelligent Brahman only can be such as cause. How can immanent teleology in nature be explained by unintelligent Prakrti. Only the conscious Brahman associated with its Maya Shakti can be the creator, preserver and destroyer of this world.

Unintelligent Prakrti is too poor and tow powerless to be its cause. We see the stones, bricks and mortar cannot fashion themselves into a well-designed buildings without the help of intelligent workmen. How can, then, the unintelligent symmetry, order and harmony of this great universe – internal and external? Mere clay, without a potter, cannot fashion itself into pot. Chariots cannot move without horses etc.

The argument of Sankhya that just as unintelligent milk flows for the nourishment of the calf, similarly unintelligent Prakrit works for the emancipation of the Purusa is untenable because milk flows as there is a living cow and a living calf and there is also the motherly love in the cow for the calf. Purusa who can neither energise nor restrain it. Prakrti should sometimes evolve and sometimes should not evolve.

Nor can the modification of Prakrti be compared to that of grass, which turns into milk. 'Grass becomes milk only when it is eastern by a milch cow, not when it lies uneaten or is eaten by a bull.

Criticism of Asat-Karyavada

Shankara believes in sat-karyavada. By it he really means satkaranavada. His view is known as *vivartavada*. The effect, must pre-exist in the cause. The cause alone is real; the effect is only its appearance. Shankara agrees with the Shunyavadins and the Svatontra-Vijnana vadins in maintaining, against Sankhya, that if the effect were real and if it really pre-existed in the cause, then it is already an accomplished fact and its production will be a vain repetition.

He also agrees with them, against Nyaya-Vaishesika, that if the effect were a non-entity, it would be like a hare's horn and its production would be impossible. Reality itself, to him, is efficient causation. Shankara, agrees with the Shunyavadin, against **Svatantra-Vijnanavadin**, in maintaining that causation in a real sense in an impossibility.

Criticism of the Paramanu-Karana-Vada of Nyaya Vaishesika

This school maintains that the four substances (Earth, water, fire and air) in their subtle (amurta) from as causes are eternal and atomic. The atoms of Democritus are only quantitatively different, are in motion and make up souls also. God assisted by the unseen power of the jivas generates motion in the atoms. This motion joins two atoms together which make a dyad. Four dyads form a quartered and so on till the gross objects of the world are produced.

An atom is infinitesimal and spherical; a dyad is minute and short and a triad and others are great and long. The things produced are not mere aggregates, but wholes composed of parts, the parts and the whole being related by inherence.

Criticism of the Categories of Nyaya-Vaishesika

This school assumes six categories, which unlike the Aristotelian categories which are mere logical predicates, are metaphysical objects. If so then substance alone should exist. If in order to avoid this difficulty it is maintained that substance and qualities are inseparably connection then this inseparable connection must be either in space or in time or in itself and none of these alternatives can support the Vaishesika theory. If it is inseparable in time, then the two horns of a cow would be inseparably connected.

Criticism or Brahma-Parinama-Vada

Shankara maintains Brahma-karana-vada as he recognises that Brahman is cause of the world. He theory is called Brahma-vivart-vada because it takes the world to be only a phenomenal appearance of Brahman. Shankara is opposed to Brahma-parinama-vada. Brahman associated with its power Maya is the ground, on which the phenomenal world is super-imposed. When true knowledge dawns and the essential unity of the jivatman with the Paramatman is realised, the world is sublated.

Modification or change in a realistic manner, like the change of gold into ornaments or clay into pots or of milk into curd, is called parinama or vikara. They are not, as Sarvajnatma Muni rightly points out, absolutely opposed; parinamavada logically leads to vivartavada, which is only a step ahead of it.

This entire diverse universe of names and forms, of agents and enjoyers, of space, time and causality, says Shankara, proceeds from that omniscient, omnipotent and omnipresent cause, the Brahman which alone is the creator, preserver and destroyer of it. Brahman is the material cause, as well as the efficient cause. Their real aim is to teach that the world is only a phenomenal appearance of Brahman, which is beyond all plurality and phenomena, and which is the same as the Real self.

Criticism of Jainism

Shankara, like Dharmakirti and Shantaraksita, criticises this theory. He points out that contradictory attributes like existence and non-existence, unity and plurality, eternity and momentariness etc., cannot belong to the same thing, just as light and darkness cannot remain at the same place or just as the same thing cannot be hot and cold at the same time. According to this view, the theory of Syadvada itself may not be correct. The theory looks like the words of a lunatic. Again, the judgments cannot be indescribable, for they are clearly set forth.

Criticism of Buddhism

This is the most important School of Hinayana. It is divided, according to Shankara, into two major schools the Vaibhasika and the Sautrantika. The former attaches itself to Vibhasa, a Commentary on an Abhidharma work and may be called presentationism or naive realism as it maintains the independent existence of mind and matter. But both these schools are equally realistic and reduce mind to fleeting ideas and matter to fleeting sensation.

Shankara takes both these schools under the name of **'Sarvastivada'** and says that its followers hold that external reality is either element or elemental and that internal reality is either mind or mental. The internal world consists of the five skandhas-of sensation, idea, feeling, conception and forces.

Criticism of the Theory of Momentariness

The antecedent link in the causal series, says Shankara, cannot even be regarded as the efficient cause of the subsequent link because, according to the theory of momentariness, the preceding link ceases to exist when the subsequent link arises. Again, if it is urged that the mere existence of the preceding moment means its causal efficiency this too is impossible, because no effect can arise without imbibing the nature of the cause and to admit this is to admit that the cause is permanent as it continues to exist in the effect and thus to throw overboard the doctrine of momentariness.

There, are production and destruction in the nature of a thing or another state of it or different thing. All these alternatives are impossible. It is said that production is the thing, is the middle and destruction is the end, then a thing, being connected with three moments, would not be momentary. If production and destruction are regarded as perception and non-perception, being the attributes of the perceiving mind and not of the thing, the thing would become permanent.

Criticism on Vijnanavada and on Gaudapada

In regard to those views, which Vijnanavada shares in common with **Svatantra-Vijnanavada**, Shankara's criticism applies to Vijnanavada also. It is very important to note that here Shankara's criticism loses much of its force. The Alambana-Pariksa of Dinnage is not a very original work. All its ideas are based on Vasubandhu's works. We also know that he declared external objects to be inside consciousness, we also know that he placed dream state and waking state almost on equal footing.

This criticism loses much of its force because, firstly, Vasubandhu and Gaudapada do not deny the objectivity of the external world, as the objects appear as objects to the knowing subject and secondly, because they hold pure consciousness, which is the same as the self-luminous self to be the permanent background of all phenomena.

The difference between Vasubandhu and Gaudapada on the one hand and Shankara on the other, is not the difference of kind, but only of degree. The difference is only of emphasis. We know that Vasubandhu and Gaudapada distinguish between the **illusory** (paraklpita) and the **relative** (paratantra) aspects. Shankara says that the subject and the object are absolutely opposed to each other like light and darkness. The subject is pure consciousness; the object is unconsciousness. This co-mingling of the subject and the object, this mixing up of truth and error, this coupling of the real and the unreal is called superimposition or error or illusion or ignorance.

All definitions of error agree in maintaining that error is the superimposition of one thing on another, *e.g.*, the superimposition of silver on shell or the illusion of the moons on a single Moon. This **superimposition** the learned call 'Ignorance' and the realisation of the true nature of reality by discarding error, they call 'Knowledge'.

VIŚIṢTĀDVAITA

According to Rāmānuja, all knowledge involves distinctions and there is no undifferentiated pure consciousness exist. Pure identity and pure difference are alike unreal. Rāmānuja here agrees with Hegel. Identity is always qualified by difference. Unity is always in and through and because of diversity.

Pure being is pure nothing. Shaṅkara is wrong in saying that Brahman is pure differenceless being. Brahman or Reality cannot be indeterminate, undifferentiated, qualityless substance. It is determinate and qualified (savisheṣa). When the Upaniṣads speak of Brahman as 'devoid of qualities', they only mean that Brahman has no bad qualities and not and is the incarnation of all perfection. The upanishad says that Brahman is regarded as devoid on qualities.

Saguṇa Brahman

In Rāmānuja's account of God, we may notice three points of importance. First, God is identified with the Absolute. He is Brahman and Brahman must be a savisheṣa or a qualified unity. God stands for the whole universe and matter and souls form his body. He being their soul. As the Absolute, the ultimate unity-in-and-through-trinity, the concrete Whole, God may be viewed through two stages—as cause and as effect. During the state of dissolution (pralaya), God remains as the cause with subtle matter and unembodied souls forming His body. The whole universe lies latent in Him. During the state of creation (sṛṣṭi), the subtle matter becomes gross and the unembodied souls (except the nitya and mukta souls) becomes manifest. The former state is called the causal state (kāraṇāvasthā) of Brahman, while the latter state is the effect-state (kāryāvasthā) of Brahman. Secondly, God is considered as the immanent inner controller (antaryāmī), the qualified substance (visheṣya or prakārī) who is in Himself changeless and is the unmoved Mover of this world-process.

Features of Brahman

God, as the perfect personality, is devoid of all demerits and possesses all merits. He has infinite knowledge and bliss. He has a Divine body and is the creator, preserver and destroyer of this universe. He has his consort Lakṣmī, the symbol of power and mercy. He is called Nārāyana or Vāsudeva. He lives in his citadel Vaikuṇṭha which is made of Pure Sattva (shuddha sattva) or Nityavibhūti. His qualities like knowledge, power and mercy etc. are eternal, infinite, numberless unlimited, undefined and matchless. He is knowledge to ignorant, power to the powerless, mercy to the guilty, grace to the afflicted, parental affection to the impure, perennial attachment to those who fear separation, nearness to those who pine to see Him, and kindness to all. Though One in Himself, He manifests Himself in five forms in order to help his devotees. As the immanent soul of the universe, He is Antaryāmī (first form). As the transcendent personal Lord, Nārāyaṇa or Vāsudeva, He is Para or Supreme (second form). As the creator, preserver and destroyer, He reveals himself through four-fold Vyūha (third form). His manifestation as the Lord is called Vāsudeva (this should be distinguished from the Para Vāsudeva of whom this is the first manifestation). He manifestation as the ruler of the cognitive aspect of the souls (buddhitattva or jīvatattva) and as the destroyer of this universe is called Saṅkarṣaṇa. His manifestation as the ruler of the emotional aspect of the souls (manastattva) and as the creator of this universe is called Pradyumna. His manifestation as the ruler of the volitional aspect of the souls (ahaṅkāratattva) and as the preserver of this universe is called Aniruddha. All these four manifestations are called Vyūha and they are the partial and incomplete manifestations of the Supreme Lord (Para). Avatāra (incarnation) (fourth form). He does so in order to protect the good, punish the wicked and restore the dharma, the Law. Vibhava is of two kinds—primary (mukhya) when the Lord Himself descends, like Kṛṣṇa, and secondary (gauṇa) when the souls are inspired by the seekers for liberation. The fifth and the last form of God is when out of his extreme mercy. He takes the forms of the holy idols (archāvatāra).

Refutation of Māyā

Rāmānuja imposes following important charges (anupapatti) on the theory of Māyā.

1. **Āshrayānupapatti**. What is the locus or support of Māyā? Where does Avidyā reside? If there is any such thing as Māyā or Avidyā, we are justified in asking for its seat or abode. Verily, it cannot exist in Brahman, for then the unqualified monism of Brahman would break down. Moreover, Brahman is said to be pure self-luminous Consciousness or Knowledge and Avidyā means ignorance. Then how can Ignorance exist in Knowledge? Again, Avidyā cannot reside in the individual self, for the individuality of the self is said to be the creation of Avidyā. How can the cause depend on its effect? Hence Avidyā cannot exist figment of the Advaitin's imagination. If it resides anywhere, it resides only in the mind of the Advaitin who has imagined this wonderful pseudo-concept, this logical myth.

2. **Tirodhānānupapatti.** How can Avidyā conceal Brahman? If it does, then Brahman is not self-conscious and self-luminous subject. If Brahman is of the nature of self luminosity and self-proved pure knowledge, Ignorance cannot cover or veil its essence. It is as absurd as to say that darkness can hide light or that night can act as a veil on day.
3. **Svarūpānupapatti.** What is the nature of Avidyā? Is it positive or negative or both or neither? If it is positive then how can it be Avidyā? Avidyā means Ignorance and Ignorance means absence of knowledge. To regard ignorance as positive is to accept self-contradiction. Moreover, if Ignorance is positive how can it be ever destroyed? No positive entity can be destroyed. As the Advaitin admits that ignorance is removed by knowledge, Ignorance can never be positive. And if Avidyā is negative, then how can it project this world-illusion on Brahman? To say that Avidyā is both positive and negative is to embrace self-contradiction. And to say that it is neither positive nor negative is to give up all logic.
4. **Anirvachanīyatevānupapatti.** According to Advaitin, Avidyā is defined as indefinable and indescribable. Advaitin also that Avidyā is also regarded as not absolutely in describable. But, according to Ramanuja, this only shows, that Advaitin is giving up all logic.
5. **Pramananupapatti.** Avidyā is recognised by which pramana is not clear. It has been said that Avidyā cannot perceived nor inferred as well as nor can be maintained by the authority.
6. **Nivartakanupapatti.** It has been said that there is no remover of Avidyā. According to Shankara, Brahman knowledge removes Avidyā. But such knowledge is not possible. No knowledge of an undifferentiated attributeless thing exist.
7. **Nivrtyanupapatti.** It has been said that there is no removal of Avidyā. Avidyā is regarded as positive entity, according to Shankara. All these charges of Ramanuja, against Avidyā are based on the misunderstanding of the meaning of this term.

Aprthaksiddhi

This concept is given by Ramanuja. This concept emphasizes on both unity and difference, which exist between Brahman and Jiva. It has been said that the universe of finite and imperfect beings and the Brahman, forms one organic whole. The entities, which are found in relation of Aprthasiddhi are recognised together, through the statement, which says that, 'I am human being.' The unity here is referred as Visishtaaikya. It is not regarded as absolute. It has been said that there is a strong relation between Brahman and Jiva.

Pariṇāmavāda

Rāmānuja believes in the pariṇāmavāda form of satkāryavāda which means that the material cause really changes itself in the form of its effect. The effect is a real transformation of its material cause, just as curd is a real transformation of milk or a gold ornament is of gold or an earthen pot is of earth. Change is not apparent but real. His view is known as Brahmāpariṇāmavāda because according to it the entire universe including the material world and the individual souls is a real modification of Brahman.

Jīva

Though the individual soul is an attribute or mode (prakāra) of God and forms part of His body, yet it is also a spiritual substance in itself and in absolutely real. It is an eternal point of spiritual light. It is beyond creation and destruction. It the state of creation, it is embodied according to its karmas, while in the state of dissolution (pralaya), it is tinged with karmas so that in the next cycle of creation, it has to descend to the mundane life and to become embodied in order to reap the fruits of its karmas.

The soul is different from its body, sense-organs, mind, vital breaths and even cognition. In saṁsāra, it wrongly identifies itself with these due to ignorance and karma. There are innumerable individual souls. They are essentially alike, like the monads of Leibnitz or the jīvas of the Jainas, and they differ only in number. Rāmānuja advocates qualitative monism and quantitative pluralism of souls. The soul is conceived as a real knower (jñātā), a real agent (kartā) and a real enjoyer (bhoktā). Action and enjoyment are regarded as merely different states of knowledge which is said to be the essence of the soul. The soul is a self-luminous substance as well as a self-conscious subject. It is the substance of knowledge which is its essential and inseparable attribute. Knowledge always belongs to the self and persists even in deep sleep and in liberation. Knowledge does not manifest itself in deep sleep for there are then no objects to be revealed.

Though the individual soul is absolutely real, yet it is not independent. It is utterly dependent on God. It is an attribute or a mode of God Who is its substance. It is the body of God Who is its soul. It is supported by God, controlled by God and utilized by God. It is the supported (dhārya) and God is its support (dharta). It is the means (sheṣa) and God is its end (sheṣī). It is a mode (prakara) and God is its substance (prakrtī). It is a part (aṁsha) and God is the Whole (aṁshī). It is the body (sharīra) and God is its soul (sharīrī). And yet it is a real agent and performs and reaps the fruits of its actions. Its defects and imperfections and miseries do not affect God. Rāmānuja tries to reconcile human freedom with Divine sovereignty. God is the master of the Law of Karma. He is the inner controller of the soul. Yet the soul has got freedom of will and God, as a self-determined Whole, does not interfere with it.

Rāmānuja describes three classes of souls. To the first belong the ever free (nitya-mukta) souls which were never bound. They are ever free from Karma and prakṛti and live in Vaikuṇṭha in constant service of the Lord. They are Sheṣa, Garuḍa, Viṣvaksena etc. To the second belong the Released or Liberated (mukta) souls who were once bound but who obtained liberation through their action, knowledge and devotion. To the third belong the Bound (baddha) souls who are wandering in saṁsāra on account of ignorance and bad karmas. These are further divided into four classes : superhuman, human, animal and immobile.

Qualitative Monism

Ramanuja advocated qualitative monism and quantitative pluralistic souls. The soul is referred as a real knower and as well as real agent. Action and enjoyment are regarded as the essence of the soul. The soul is regarded as a self-luminous substance. It is also regarded as a substance of knowledge. Knowledge is belonged to the self only. The individual soul is regarded as real, but is not regarded as independent.

It is dependent on God. It is regarded as a mode of God. It is supported by God only. It is also controlled by God. It is regarded as the means, whereas God is regarded as the end. It is regarded as a part only. He reconcile human freedom with Divine sovereignty. God is regarded as the inner controller of the soul.

Bhakti and Prapatti

The study of the Vedānta produce only book learning and does not bring about liberation. It is true, as the Upaniṣads say, that liberation is brought about by knowledge. But that real knowledge is not a verbal knowledge of scriptures; for then everyone who reads them would be liberated at once. Real knowledge is a steady, constant remembrance of God (dhruvā smṛti). This is variously described as meditation (dhyāna), prayer (upāsanā), devotion (bhakti). Constant meditation on God as the dearest object of love, should be practised continuously along with the performance of the obligatory rituals which remove the obstacles to knowledge. Intense remembrance of God, or devotion thus practised, ultimately matures into an immediate knowledge (darśana or sākṣātkāra) of God. This is, therefore, the final means to liberation. Thus brings about the destruction of all ignorance and karmas by which the body is caused. Therefore, the soul that realizes God is liberated from the body for ever, without any chance of rebirth. We should remember, however, that liberation cannot be attained simply by human efforts. God, pleased by devotion, helps the devotee to attain perfect knowledge by removing obstacles. God lifts from bondage and misery the man who flings himself at the mercy of God and constantly remembers him as the only object of love. Such complete self-surrender is called prapatti.

The Vaisnava Schools

Ramanujacharya attempts to show a harmonious combination of absolutism with personal theism. In the Mahabharata in the section called Narayaniya and in the Puranas, notably in the Visnu and the Bhagavata. The attempt to combine personal theism with absolutism took three main lines Vaisnavism, Shaivism and Shaktism, according as the personal divinity was identified with Visnu or Shiva or Shakti. Chaitanyasampradaya is treated as a branch of Madhvism.

The Vaisnavas, the Shaivas and the Shaktas all have their different sacred literature called the Agamas, which are placed side by side with the Vedas and sometimes treated as the real Vedas. Yoga or concentration, Kriya or acts connected with the founding of temples and installing of idols and Charya or the methods of worship.

The cultural history of South India records a triangular fight among the Vaisnavas, the Shaivas and the Jainas and whoever succeeded in winning over a ruler often indulged in persecuting the members of the other two sects in that territory.

The eyes of Mahapurna, the maternal uncle and teacher of Ramanuja were put out by the Chola king, Rajendrachola or Krmikantha, who was Shaiva and Ramanuja himself was forced to take refuge in the Hoysala province where he converted the Jaina king Bittideva, renamed Visnuvardhanadeva, who constructed a temple at Melukot where Ramanuja lived for twelve years and returned to Shrirangam only after the death of Kulottunga.

The Authority of Pancharatu

All the Vaisnava schools recognise the authority of the Pancharatra, but it is most sacred and important for the Shriaisnavasampradaya of Ramanuja. The Shatapatha Brahmana tells us that Narayana by performing the Pancharatra sacrifice became the great being, the transcendent as well as the immanent. In the Mahabharata we find Nara and Narayana worshipping the changeless Brahman.

Yamunacharya in his Agamapramanya tells us that the Pancharatra-samhita is as valid as the Veda, since both are derived from the same divine source, Narayana or Vasudeva.

The Visnu, Bhagavata, Garuda, Padma and Varaha Puranas favour the Pancharatras, while the Kurma, Vayu Aditya, Agni and Linga Puranas strongly condemn them as absolutely non-vedic low caste sinners. According to Shankara, Badarayana criticises the Vyuha doctrine of the Pancharatra in the Tarkapada of the Brahmasutra. Pancharatra was, so named because it deals with the five philosophical topics or because it incorporates the essence of the four Vedas and the Sankhya yoga or because it was taught by Narayana to his five disciples during five nights.

The Alvars

Ramanuja was also greatly indebted to the Alvars, the Acharyas and to his former teacher Yadavaprakasha. Ramanuja tells us that he is carrying on the Vishistadvaita tradition of the ancient writers like Bodhayana, Tanka, Dramida, Guhadeva, Kapardi and Bharuchi. Sudarshana Suri says, that Yadava has carried on the Vedantic tradition of Ashmarathya. Shankara has mentioned and criticised the bhedabheda view of Bhartrpiapancha. Ramanuja, in his Vedarthasangraha, has criticised both Bhaskara and Yadava.

Ramanuja tells us in his Shribhasya that he has closely followed the interpretations of the Sutras given by Bodhayana. Shankara has referred to Upavarsa and Venkatanatha has identified Upavarsa with Bodhayana. Ramanuja owes much to all these Vedantins, the Alvars, Nathamuni, Yamuna. Bhaskara, Bodhayana, Dramida, Bhartiprapancha, Ashmarathya and others though the greatest influence on him is exercised by Yamuna and Bhaskara and Yadava.

Sources of Knowledge

Ramanuja recognises three sources of knowledge, perception inference and verbal testimony and is indifferent to the rest. Indeterminate perception is not the bare apprehension of an absolutely undifferentiated object. This a psychological myth. All that is known necessarily involves some differentiation.

Discrimination is essential to all knowledge. Whatever is known is known as characterised is some way, as qualified by some specific attribute.

Impressions

Determinate perception occurs, when the sight of an object revives its former impression and it is apprehended as qualified by the class character. In indeterminate perception the object is perceived together with its class character, yet there the class character is not apprehended as such. Recognition or remembrance is regarded as valid knowledge and is granted a separate place.

Recognition refers specially to time and place when and where the same object was previously cognised, while in determinate perception no such specific reference is necessary. Ramanuja's treatment of inference is almost similar to that of the Nyaya-Vaishesika.

He advocates karma-jnana-samuchchaya. The karma-kanda and the Jnana-kanda of the Veda are complementary to each other. He differs from Shankara, who subordinates karma-kanda to jnana-kanda and who maintains that the former is desirable only from a lower standpoint to purify the self.

Self, Knowledge and Error

According to him all knowledge involves discrimination and it is impossible to know an undifferentiated object. Ramanuja agrees with the Naiyayika and the Mimamsaka in maintaining that all knowledge points to a corresponding object existing really and outside of it. Ramanuja defines a substance as a substratum or support of qualities.

The light is an attribute in relation to the lamp, but it is a substance in relation to its rays. Knowledge is both a substance as well as an attribute. It is a substance because it possesses the qualities of contraction and expansion and it is also an attribute because it belongs to a self or to God.

Ramanuja assigns a curious place to knowledge. Substances are generally classified into spiritual and material. It is called ajada or immaterial and is distinguished from both matter and spirit. It is unlike unconscious material substances since it can unaided manifest itself as well as other objects.

The self is also self-luminous, but it can only reveal itself and cannot reveal the object. Knowledge can show itself as well as its object just as a lamp can show itself as well as a pot, but it cannot know either itself or its object.

Distinction between Self Luminous and Consciousness

Ramanuja distinguishes self-luminosity from self-consciousness. Knowledge is self-luminous, but it is not self-conscious. Ramanuja agrees with Prabhakara in maintaining that knowledge is self-luminous and that it reveals its object, that knowledge is a subject-object relation and as such possible only in relation to an object. Ramanuja agrees with Shankara in maintaining that the self is an eternal self-conscious subject and the knowledge is its essence. But, he differs from Shankara in refusing to identify the sell with pure consciousness.

There is nothing like pure consciousness. Consciousness is always qualified and possesses specific attributes. The self is a substance, is incapable of contraction and expansion, cannot reveal the object, can reveal itself and can know itself and the object and is atomic in nature, while knowledge is an attribute, is capable of contraction and expansion, can reveal the object as well as itself, cannot know either itself or the object and is all-pervading in nature.

Knowledge is like the light; the self is like the lamp; the dharma-bhuta-jnana is like the rays. The light constitutes the essence of the lamp and cannot be separated from it. Knowledge is a unique adjunct of the self and is eternally associated with it. The self is eternal and so is knowledge. Ramanuja agrees with Jainism except in that he holds the self to be atomic and to be a part of God and that he regards the presence of the objects as essential for the function of knowledge.

Metaphysical Views

Three things becomes clear and all the three are directly opposed to the Advaitic position of Shankara. First, all knowledge involves distinctions and there is no undifferentiated pure consciousness. Identity is always qualified by difference. Unity is always in and through and because of diversity. Shankara is wrong in saying that Brahman is pure differenceless being. It is determinate and qualified. When the Upanisads speak of Brahman as 'Devoid of qualities', they only mean that Brahman has no bad qualities and not that it has no qualities whatsoever. Shankara's distinction between Brahman and Ishvara, between higher and lower Brahman, is unwarranted and unjustifiable. Brahman is God ànd he is not a formless identity. The self is distinct from knowledge. It is undoubtedly an eternal self-conscious subject, but it is also a self-luminous substance possessing dharmabhuta-jnana as its essential attribute. The self is not pure consciousness, but only the eternal substratum of consciousness.

Brahman as Atomic in Nature

They are atomic in nature and in liberation they do not merge in God, but only become similar to him and serve him realising themselves as the body of God. Thirdly, knowledge not only belongs to a subject, but also points to an object, which exists really and outside of it.

Shankara is wrong in saying that whatever becomes an object is false. God, souls and knowledge are presented as objects, the first two are spiritual and the last is non-material. Shankara's distinction between the higher and the lower standpoints is also unwarranted and wrong.

Creation is Real

Creation, according to Ramanuja, is regarded as absolutely real. The world and souls are as real as God himself. Ramanuja believes in satkaryavada, the theory that the effect necessarily pre-exists in its material cause. Ramanuja believes in the parinamavada form of satkaryavada, which means that the material cause really changes itself in the form of its effect. Change is not apparent but real. His view is known as Brahmaparinamavada because according to it the entire universe including the material world and the individual souls is a real modification of Brahman.

Ramanuja, like Sankhya, believes in Prakrti, yet, unlike it, he makes Prakrti absolutely dependent on God and controlled by God from within just as the body is controlled from within by the soul. Independence, according to Ramanuja, does not constitute the essence of reality. A thing in order to be real need not be independent. Though substances in themselves, in relation to God they are merely. His attributes or modes.

They always qualify God and form his body and he is their soul. They are organically related to him and are not external to him. Matter and souls are different from each other and also different from God, the controller, though they are not external to him.

Creation means that the subtle matter called Prakrti evolves into gross elements and the immaterialised souls become housed in gross bodies according to their karmas. The law of Karma, necessitates creation. And yet Ramanuja says, that creation and dissolution of the world are due to the sweet will of God; they are his lila or sport. The contradiction has to be reconciled by supposing that the Law of Karma represents the will of God.

Vishistadvaita or Identity-in-Difference

Ramanuja's view is Vishistadvaita or non-dualism, which is qualified by difference. It is a concrete whole which consists of the interrelated and inter-dependent subordinate elements which are called 'Vishesanas' and the immanent and controlling spirit which is called 'Vishesya'. He is the immanent inner controller, the supreme real who holds together in unity the dependent matter and individual souls as his body. Ramanuja recognises three things as ultimate and real. These are matter souls and God. Though all are equally real, the first two are absolutely dependent on God. They are the body of God who is their soul. God is the soul of nature. God is also the soul of souls. The relation between the soul and the body is that of inner inseparability. This is also the relation between substance and attribute.

External and Internal Relation

The Nyaya inherence is an external relation, which is rejected by Ramanuja because it involves infinite regress. It is an inner, inseparable, vital and organic relation. God is qualified by matter and souls. They form his body and are inseparable from and utterly dependent on him. Matter and souls are called attributes of God; they are the controlled the supported the parts and the accessory means, while God in their substance controller, support , the whole and the principal end.

The are eternal with God, but are not external to him. God is free from all external differences, homogeneous as well as heterogeneous, since there is nothing either similar or dissimilar which is external to or other than him. His relation with them is natural and eternal. God is both the material and the instrumental cause of the world. He is the immanent as well as the transcendent ground of the world. He is full of all good qualities, existence, knowledge and bliss; truth, goodness and beauty; lustre, love and power.

Ramanuja finds justification for his doctrine of the absolute as a triune unity in such following Upanishadic passages. The eternal powerless soul and the eternal matter and these three constitute the Absolute. The same Upanisad further tells us. This alone need be known and there is nothing else to be known, that there are three entities, the enjoyer the enjoyed and the mover, which constitute the Absolute. There is nothing greater than he, there is nothing external to him, he fills the whole universe. The Taittiriya tells us that all beings arise from, live in and return to this Brahman.

Criticism of Ramanuja

All the charges of Ramanuja against Avidya or Maya are based on the misunderstanding of the meaning of this term. It is called 'Indescribable either as real or as unreal' due to the genuine difficulty of our finite intellect to reach reality. Avidya being not real, the monism of Brahman is not destroyed. Brahman is not really affected by it. The rope is not really affected if it is mistaken as a snake. The shell does not become silver if it is mistaken as that. Mirage cannot make the sandy desert muddy. The power of the magician does not affect his knowledge.

Ramanuja himself, when he fails to explain the cause of bondage of the pure soul, falls back upon the notion that the relation of Karma and ignorance with the soul is beginingless. Avidya does not really conceal Brahman even as a cloud does not really conceal the Sun. Again, Avidya is called positive only to emphasise the fact that it is not merely negative. It is neither positive nor negative. There is no point in saying that indescribability of Avidya is a self-contradictory notion, when the Advaitin himself admits it. These two terms an not contradictories and hence the laws of contradiction and excluded middle are not overthrown. The Law of excluded middle is not overthrown since 'Absolutely real' and 'Absolutely unreal' are not exhaustive. Avidya is not 'Real', but only a superimposition, it vanishes when the ground-reality is known.

Charges Against Advaita

The most important charges levelled against Advaita by Venkatanatha and try to answer them.

It Brahman is a qualityless homogeneous entity, the word 'Brahman' cannot denote it either in a primary' sense of in an implied sense and hence it becomes useless.

Venkatanatha forgets that words according to Shankara himself, can never denote the absolute, which can be realised only by direct spiritual vision. Language and though would become insignificant only when they are transcended.

There can be no inquiry into the nature of Brahman, for all inquiries are possible about qualified objects only. If it is said that this knowledge about Brahman is ultimately false, then no purpose would be served by such false knowledge.

Real Brahman Knowledge

Venkata forgets that real Brahman knowledge is not verbal knowledge, otherwise all those scholars who know Vedanta-texts should have obtained liberation. Venkata also forgets the distinction between the relative and the absolute standpoints, so much emphasised by Shankara. He forgets the detailed classical exposition by Shankara or the view that even 'Unreal' means like the Vedanta-texts lead to real knowledge, just as 'Unreal' dream-experiences lead to real physiological reactions and that the 'Unreality' of the Vedanta-texts can be realised only after Brahman- realisation not before.

Liberation as Unreal

He forgets the fact that bondage and liberation are equally unreal ultimately, that ignorance means bondage and knowledge means liberation. If we do not take advantage of their teaching, it is our fault, not theirs.

The final knowledge of unity be attained, the world-appearance may still continue due to vasana until the body is destroyed.

Venkata forgets that the world-appearance may continue due to the force of vasana, just as a potter's wheel may continue to revolve for some time even though the potter has withdrawn his hand from it.

If liberation cannot be attained in this life, it is futile to talk of it as happening alter death. Shankara believes in Jivanmukti; it is Venkata who rejects it.

If the world is false because it is knowable, then Brahman too, being knowable, would be equally false. Difference cannot be denied. The so-called 'Absence of difference' is itself different from 'difference' and therefore establishes the reality of difference.

Relative Concepts

It is true that difference and difference and identity are relative and one cannot remain without the other. It is further true that bare identity and bare difference are mere abstractions. Identity, in the empirical world, is always qualified by difference. There is a higher 'Unity' which is above this notion of 'Unity-in-difference.

This 'Unity' or 'Identity' is not abstract identity, which alone is relative and opposed to difference. Shankara's system called 'Advaita' is not bare identity, but the highest identity which transcends the intellectual notions of identity, difference and even identity-in-difference.

The falsity of the world is proved by logical proofs which are themselves false. The distinction between the two supposed standpoints is a distinction within though itself and therefore, by its won logic, false. These charges are based on a confusion between the two standpoints.

'Neither real nor unreal'. Brahman is indescribable because it, being the self-proved Real, cannot be fully described by the intellect.

Ramanuja was Influenced by the Alvars

It has been already pointed out that Ramanuja was much influenced by the Alvars and the Acharyas and by the bhedabhedavadins who preceded him. He wanted to find philosophical justification for the Vaisnava theism in the Prasthana-trayạ of the Vedanta and thus tried to harmonise the demands of religious feeling with logical thinking.

Shankara has attempted the former, while Ramanuja has attempted the latter. For Shankara, the only scriptures were the Vedantic texts and he interpreted them, so as to harmonise logical thinking with religious feeling.

There are some doctrines of the Vaisnava theism, which can be harmonised with the Vedantic absolutism, but not all. Ramanuja failed, his failure is due not to his personal incapacity, but due to the very nature of the difficult task he undertook to perform.

He has given us the best type of monotheism pregnant with immanentism. He has emphasised on the religious side, but not at the cost of the philosophical. His intense religious fervour and his bold logic undoubtedly make him one of the immortals in Indian Philosophy.

And yet there is much truth in the remark that Ramanuja's position is essentially similar to the position of Shankara viewed from the practical or phenomenal standpoint.

For all practical purposes Shankara too maintains the reality of all secular and Vedic acts. Though the universe is only a vivarta or an appearance of Brahman, yet as long as it lasts it is as good as real. Sarvajnatma-Muni is right in holding that Parinamavada is an earlier stage of Vivartavada.

Critical Estimation on Relation

Ramanuja has failed to express the relation between the universe and God. He identifies the absolute with God, who is only one of the three realities. God is the underlying substratum of matter and souls which are said to be his attributes. But, if they are his attributes or modes, how can they be as real as God?

Ramanuja abolishes the distinction between attributes and modes and though he explicitly maintains the distinction between attributes and substance. According to him a thing can be a substance as well as an attribute. The distinction is relative. The very definition of Substance' is that it has an independent existence.

Ramanuja undermines this definition, when he says that independence does not constitute the essence of substance, that a thing may be dependent and yet be a substance. Shankara defines the real as that which has independent existence for all times and tells us that Brahman alone is real.

Loyalty to the Upanisads makes him cling to absolutism, while sympathy for Vaisnavism makes him recognise ultimate distinctions. Thus Vishistadvaita is a house divided against itself. He has stated that the universe is organically related to the Absolute, that it is the body of God, that though it has a right to exist separately it is not external to God who is all-inclusive, that identity is always qualified by difference. But, he fails to explain his position further.

Difference belongs to and cannot remain separate from identity. This relation is not that of identity-and-difference for it is self-contradictory. Both identity and difference, like light and darkness, cannot belong to the same thing in the same sense. It is an inner relation and is replace the Nyaya-Vaishiesika relation of samavaya which is rejected as external by Ramanuja.

Matter and Souls

Ramanuja says, that matter and souls form the body of God. The distinction between the body of God and the soul of God is not clearly brought out. He is both the material cause and the efficient cause of the universe. God's body is the material cause, while his soul is the efficient cause of this universe. The soul does not create the body.

But the distinction between the body and the soul of God is not logical. Ramanuja says, that God is not affected by the change of the universe and the imperfections and pains of the souls, even as a soul is not affected the change and the pains of the body. But if a soul is not affected by the change and the pains of the body, it cannot be identified with the empirical ego.

DVAITA (MĀDHVĀCĀRYA)

Mādhva is the champion of unqualified dualism (dvaita) and accuses Shankara of teaching the false doctrines of Shūnyavāda Buddhism under the cloak of Vedānta. His hatred of Advaita is so great that he called Advaitins 'deceitful demons' who play in the darkness of Ignorance Madhya advocates the reality of five-fold differences—between soul and God, between soul and soul, between soul and matter, between God and matter, and between matter and matter. His bias for difference is so great that he advocates difference of degrees in the possession of knowledge and in the enjoyment of bliss even in the case of liberated souls.

Mādhva, like Rāmānuja, accepts the three sources of knowledge—perception, inference and testimony, and like him holds that God who is Hari, Viṣnu, Nārāyaṇa or Vāsudeva can be known only by the scriptures. Like Rāmānuja, Madhva also regards the Pūrva and the Uttara Mīmāṁsā as forming a single science. Like the Mīmāṁsaka, Madhva upholds the authorlessness of the Veda. Madhva, unlike Nyāya which regards God as the author of the Veda, regards God as the great teacher (mahopādhyāya) of the Veda. Like the Mimāṁsaka, Madhva believes that knowledge reveals the knower and the known as independently real and upholds the intrinsic validity of knowledge. The world is real and so are the differences that constitute it. Difference is the very nature of things. To perceive things is to perceive their uniqueness which constitutes difference. Distinctions of things account for the distinctions of ideas.

Madhva, like Rāmānuja, believes in God and souls and matter as the three entities which are eternal and absolutely real, though souls and matter are absolutely dependent on God. God alone is independent. He possesses infinitely good qualities. Existence, knowledge and bliss constitute He essence. He is the creator, preserver and destroyer of this universe. He has a divine body and is transcendent. But he is also immanent as the inner ruler of all souls. He damns some and redeems others. His is a perfect personality. He manifests himself in the various Vyūhas and in incarnations and is present in sacred images. Lakṣmī is his consort. She is all pervading and eternal like him, but her qualities are a little less than those of her Lord. She is ever-liberated (nityamukta) and possesses a divine body. She is the Power of God. The individual souls are numberless and are atomic in size. The soul is by nature conscious and blissful. It becomes subject to pains and imperfections on account of its connection with the material body, sense-organs, mind etc. which connection is due to its past karmas. The souls are eternal and are of three kinds—eternally free (nityamukta), freed (mukta) and bound (baddha). Though God controls the soul from within, yet it is a real agent and a real enjoyer and is responsible for its acts. Bhakti is the only means of liberation. It is defined as the Eternal Love for God with a full sense of His Greatness. Prakṛti is primal Matter. Under the influence of God when he wants to create the world, it evolves itself into the various material products which return to it again at the time of dissolution. Creation means manifestation of subtle matter as gross and the embodiment of the souls in order to reap the fruits of their acts.

Mādhva does not regard the universe of matter and souls as the body of God. Matter and souls are different from each other and from God. They do not qualify God because they have substantive existence themselves. Though God is the immanent ruler of the souls and though the souls as well as matter depend on God, yet they are absolutely different from God and cannot form his body. Madhva advocates both quantitative and qualitative pluralism of souls. No two souls are alike. Each has, besides its individuality, its peculiarity also. He, therefore, believe that even in liberation the souls differ in degrees regarding their possession of knowledge and enjoyment of bliss (ānandatāra-tamya). Rāmānuja rejects this. Madhva does not make any distinction between the body and soul of God. Hence, he regards God as only the efficient cause of the world and not its material cause which is Prakṛti. God creates the world out of the stuff of Prakṛti. Rāmānuja regards God as both the efficient and the material cause of the world. While Rāmānuja makes the liberated soul similar to God in all respects except in some special respects like the possession of the power of creation, preservation and dissolution of this world, and the power of being the inner ruler of the universe, Madhva emphasizes the difference of the liberated soul from God. The soul becomes similar to God in some respects when it is liberated, yet even in these respects it is much inferior to God. It does not enjoy the full bliss of God. The bliss enjoyed by the redeemed souls in fourfold; sālokya or residence in the same place with God: sāmīpya or nearness to God; sārūpya or having the external form like that of God; and sāyujya or entering into the body of God and partially sharing his bliss with him. Thus, though according to Rāmānuja the liberated soul enjoys the full bliss of the realization of Brahman which is homogeneous, ubiquitous and supreme, according to Madhva even the most qualified soul which is entitled to sāyujya form of liberation can share only partial bliss of Brahman and cannot become similar to Brahman (Brahma-prakāra) in the strict sense of the term.

Rejection of Nirguna Brahman

Nirguna Brahman means Brahman without attributes. Brahman is regarded as infinite. But according to Ramanuja and Madhva, Nirguna Brahma concept is totally refuted. This concept is totally refuted. This concept is based on Shankara ideology.

According to Madhva, if Brahman is regarded as only Nirguna, then how we can do bhakti? For Madhva, Brahman is regarded as Saguna only. Saguna Brahman means Brahman with attributes. This God or Ishvara, is possible only through Bhakti.

So, Nirguna concept is refuted. If we will take Nirguna Brahman concept, them no praying is possible. Brahman without attributes is not prayed.

It is regarded as the basis of the impersonal Nirguna Brahman. Nirguna Brahman means Brahman without material forms. Without Saguna Brahman , Nirguna Brahnan is regarded as non-agent.

Bheda and Shakti

By Bheda, Madhva means the notion of difference. He taught the fundamental difference, which exist between the self and the ultimate reality of Brahman. These fundamental differences are referred as Bheda. Madhva is also regarded as Dvaita Vedanta. He advocates five differences.

(i) First difference exist between God and the self.

(ii) Second difference exist between God and the matter.

(iii) Third difference exist between the self and the matter.

(iv) Fourth difference exist between one self and another.

(v) Fifth difference exist between one form of matter and another

Madhva says, that matter, souls and God constitutes the three major realities. The difference between these are very essential. If there will be no difference, then nobody can analyse anything.

Brahman and Maya

Madhva is also against the notion of maya, which is given by Shankara. He says that imaginative notion of Maya is not possible. He says that Maya only exist, in the mind of Shankara. He also applies the same points which is given by Ramanuja.

Features of Saksi

Saksi is referred as witness. By witness, we means a person who witnesses the thing which is going on. Saksi is defined as the ultimate criterion of truth. This criterion of truth is regarded as infallible. It is also regarded intrinsically valid. It is regarded as an instrument of knowledge. It is valid in itself only.

Saksi is also known as the knowing self. This knowing self is capable of both Svaprakasaka and Paraprakasaka. It has been said that both knowledge and its validity is able to be grasped only by Saksi. Saksi is also referred as truth-determining principle. Saksi knows the true from the false. Saksi is regarded as true and valid for all time. It has been said that the validity of knowledge is apprehended only by Saksi directly. It is also defined as the name of spiritual sense organ of the self.

Bhakti

Bhakti for Madhva is very important. According to Madhva, without Bhakti we cannot attain liberation. Bhakti is regarded as a way or means to attain liberation. He also believes in Bhakti, like of Ramanuja. For both of them, Bhakti is regarded as a self surrender or devotion method for attaining liberation.

It is also regarded as the steady flow of deep attachment to God. Bhakti function is to manifest the true relation of jiva to Brahman.

According to Madhva, there are three stages of devotee which are as follows:

(i) Uttama Bhaktas (ii) Madhyama Bhaktas (iii) Adhama Bhaktas

These three bhaktas depend upon the nature of devotee. Taratamya in Bhakti is referred as the doctrine of Bhakti which is propounded by Madhva.

He says that there are three stages of Bhakti which are as follows:

(a) **Mediate knowledge of the Deity**. It precedes paroksajnana.

(b) One that follows it.

(c) **Aparoksajnana.** That comes after direct realisation. It wins the absolute grace of the Lord. It also means God-Realisation.

DVAITADVAITA

Achaarya Nimbarka (14th century CE) is said to be the founder of this school of Vedanta which presents another variation of the bhedaabheda. Nimbarka was a Brahmin from Andhra and his school is identified as the Sanakasampradhaya of Vaishnavism. The works attributed to him are Vedantapaarijaatasaurabha – a short commentary on the Brahma Sutras, Dashashloki, Shrikrishnastavaraaja and Madhvamukavardhana.

Shrinivasa comments on Nimbarka's bhashyam in his Vedantakaustubha, on which Keshava Kashmiri has written his Kaustubhaprabhaa. Purushottama has written commentaries on Dashashloki and Stavaraaja called Vedaantaratnamanjushaa and Shrutyantasuradruma respectively. Maadhava Mukunda's Para-paksha-giri-vajra engages in polemics against Advaita.

IDENTITY AND DIFFERENCE

Nimbarka revives the bhedaabheda of earlier Vedantins like Ashmarathya, Bhartrprapancha, Bhaskara and Yadhava Prakasha. He is also heavily indebted to Ramanuja from whom he seems to have borrowed wholesale, making significant enhancements and modifications here and there.

Nimbarka rejects Ramanuja's conception of souls and matter as qualities of God. The function of quality is either to differentiate a thing from other things or to make the object better known. Matter and souls as the qualities of God serve no such purpose. As there's nothing other than God what can they distinguish him from? Nor can they throw light on his true nature as they do not form his essence. Nimbarka also disputes Ramanuja's view that matter and souls constitute the body of God. It is wrong to distinguish between the body and soul of God. If so, then God being the soul would experience all the miseries and imperfections of the body. One part of God cannot present eternity and perfection, while the other part presents transience and imperfection.

Matter and souls are therefore not the body of God, but his powers. So the truth is not identity qualified by difference, but identity and difference. Both identity and difference are separately and equally real.

God, souls and matter are all real, but the last two are absolutely dependent on God.

The relation between God and universe is one of identity and difference. The universe cannot be absolutely identical with God, for then God himself will be bound and experience all the imperfections and miseries of samsaara. The universe cannot be absolutely different from God either - for then it would constitute a limit to God and he could not be its all pervading inner ruler and controller. Matter and souls do not have an independent existence of God and hence are not different from him. But since there are dependent and limited, they are different from God who is independent and unlimited. Even as the rays of the Sun and the Sun are both distinct and non-distinct, so is the relationship between the soul and God. In "tat tvam asi", 'tat' refers to the all pervading Brahman, 'tvam' refers to the dependant soul and 'asi' refers to the relation of difference cum non-difference between them.

GOD, MATTER AND SOULS

Krishna is the highest Brahman who by his very nature is free from all defects and is filled with all perfections. He manifests himself in the four Vyuhas and in incarnations. He is the ruler of the universe and Radha is his consort. Souls and matter are his powers. He is the material as well as the efficient cause of the universe. He is the efficient cause because as the Lord of karma and the inner ruler of souls, he brings about creation in order to enable the souls reap the fruits of their karma. He is the material cause because creation means the manifestation of his powers of chit and achit. Creation is a real transformation (parinaama) of his powers.

Souls are essentially of the nature of knowledge (jnanasvarupa) and also form the substratum of knowledge. Quite like the Sun which is of the nature of light as well as substratum of light which is its attribute, the relation between soul and knowledge is like the one between the qualified and qualification - identity as well as difference. The soul which is atomic in size is the real knower, agent and enjoyer. It is dependent on God who pervades, supports and controls it from within. Though the soul is eternal, still it suffers the misery of samsara due to its embodiment which itself is due to karma and avidhya. Bhakti to God results in knowledge which brings about liberation.

The inanimate is of three kinds :

1. Apraakrta is the super matter out of which the divine body is made.
2. Praakrta which is derived from praakriti with its three gunas - sattva, rajas and tamas and
3. Kaala or time.

SHUDDHADVAITA

Vallabhacharya is the founder of this school of Vedanta which is also known as the Rudrasampradhaaya of Vaishnavism. Pushtimaarga is another name for this school since it believes that liberation is obtained by the grace of God due to devotion. Vallabha was a Brahmin from Andhra who is said to have developed the views of Vishnusvamin into ShuddhAdvaita or pure non-dualism i.e, undefiled by the Advaitic maya – mayasambhandharahitam shuddham ityuchyate budhaih ShuddhAdvaitamaartanda. Vallabha has written a commentary on the Brahma Sutras called the Anubhaashya and a commentary on the Bhagavatam called Subhodini.

Vallabha's son Vitthalanaatha has written Vidvanmandana. The commentary on the Anubhaashya is the Bhaashyaprakaasha by Purushottama, which itself has been commented on by Gopeshvara in his Rashmi. Gopeshvara has also commented on the Subhodini and Vidvanmandana in his Suvarnasutra. Giridhara's Shuddhadvaitamaartaanda and Balakrishnabhatta's Prameyaratnaarnava are other important works of this school.

AVIKRTAPARINAAMAVAADA

According to the Upanishads Brahman made the world out of itself. Advaita interprets this as there's no real modification (parinaama) of Brahman into the universe and that the manifestation of Brahman as the universe is only an appearance (vivarta). Vallabha on the other hand holds that the manifestation is real. But again it is not parinaama as this manifestation doesn't involve any change or transformation in Brahman. This view of Vallabha which is takes a middle place between vivarta and parinaama is called avikrtaparinaamavaada.

Vallabha rejects the relation of samavaaya between substance and attribute and advocates tadaatmaya or identity. Attributes are identical to the substance and effects are identical to the cause. The substance really appears as the attributes and the cause really appears as the effect. As Brahman is the inherent material cause of this world he is identical with the effect (the universe) but still as far as Brahman is concerned the manifestation doesn't involve any change in him.

Brahman is also the efficient cause. He manifests himself as the universe without undergoing any change. Creation basically means manifestation of Brahman into the universe without involving any change in Brahman and dissolution means withdrawal of this manifestation by Brahman into himself. Like sparks spring forth from fire, the universe springs forth from Brahman. Just like cotton spreads itself as threads, Brahman spreads himself as this universe.

GOD, SOULS AND MATTER

Brahman is Shri Krishna and his essence is sat-chit-ananda - existence, knowledge and bliss. Matter and souls are his parts and real manifestations. He is the abode of all good qualities and includes even seemingly contrary ones - he is smaller than the smallest, greater than the greatest, one as well as many. It is by his power or maya that he manifests himself as this diverse universe revealing his natures of existence, knowledge and bliss in different proportions. From his nature as existence springs forth life(prana), senses and bodies. From his nature of knowledge springs forth infinite atomic souls which are the subjects of bondage. And from his nature as bliss spring forth the antaryaamins (inner controllers) who are the presiding deities of the souls and are as many in number as the souls.

God is the supreme antaryaamin – the inner ruler of the universe. In the material world only the existence aspect of God is manifested while knowledge and bliss are obscured. In the souls existence and knowledge are manifested while bliss is obscured. In the antaryaamins all the three aspects are manifested. All the three forms - jagat, jiva and antaryaamins - are essentially identical with God. While jagat is dissimilar from him (vijaatiya), the jivas are similar to him (sajaatiya) and the antaryaamins are inside him (svagata). He pervades all the forms which are non-different from him. There's no difference either homogeneous or heterogeneous or internal in God.

Jagat is different from samsara. Jagat is the real manifestation of God, while samsara is the cycle of births and deaths imagined by the soul due to ignorance which is fivefold :

1. ignorance of its real nature,
2. false identification with the body,
3. false identification with the senses,
4. false identification with the vital breaths and
5. with the mind.

With the dawn of knowledge ignorance vanishes and with it vanishes samsara. But jagat being a real manifestation of God, endures.

The soul as it is a part of God is identical with him and only appears as different due to the limited manifestations of some divine aspects and obscuration of others.

PUSHTIMAARGA

Bhakti as a firm and all surpassing affection (sneha) for God with a full sense of his greatness is the only means to liberation. It is the loving service of God which means attachment to God and detachment from all other things. It is neither worship nor knowledge, but prema (affection). In Pushtimaarga bhakti, is attained without any individual effort simply by the grace of God who destroys all sins forthwith. Pleased with devotion, God either takes the devotee within himself and keeps him near Himself to enjoy the sweetness of service.

UNIT 2

CLASSICAL WESTERN: ANCIENT, MEDIEVAL, AND MODERN: EPISTEMOLOGY AND METAPHYSICS

PRE-SOCRATIC PHILOSOPHERS

Ancient Greece was the cradle of western civilization. Its earliest known thinkers around the year 500 B.C are called the Pre- Socratic philosophers. The contributions of this period could be well studied through the major schools of this time.

Ionian School

The **Ionian School** refers to a group of Greek philosophers who were active in Miletus, an Ionian colony in Asia Minor, during the sixth century B.C.E., and some of their successors who lived about one hundred years later and modified their doctrines in several respects. They are considered to be the earliest of the Greek philosophers, and therefore of the Western tradition of philosophy. It is notable that the birth of Greek thought took place, not in Greece, but in the colonies on the Eastern shores of the Aegean Sea.

The philosophers of the Ionian school include Anaximander, Anaximenes, Heraclitus, Anaxagoras, Diogenes Apolloniates, Archelaus, Hippon and Thales, and had such diverse viewpoints that they cannot be considered to have followed one specific tradition. While some of these scholars are included in the Milesian school of philosophy, others are more difficult to categorize. Aristotle called them physiologoi meaning 'those who discoursed on nature', but he did not group them together as an "Ionian school." The classification "Ionian" can be traced to the second century historian of philosophy Sotion. The Ionian philosophers are sometimes referred to as cosmologists, since they were largely physicalists who tried to explain the nature of matter.

The Ionian philosophers sought a rational explanation for the origins of the world and physical phenomena, rather than resorting to supernatural explanations and mythology. They all sought to explain the material universe as it could be perceived by the physical senses, in terms of matter, movement, and energy. They differed from the Eleatics and the Pythagoreans, who explained knowledge and existence in metaphysical terminology.

It is customary to divide the Ionian school into the **Earlier Ionians**, including Thales Anaximander, and Anaximenes; and the **Later Ionians** including Heraclitus and those who followed him. The earliest thinkers sought to describe the material substance from which all things are constituted. Heraclitus, and those who came after him, sought to describe the motive force by which everything came into being and continued in existence.

Thales of Miletus

Thales was born in Miletus. The exact date of his birth is unknown. Probably, he must have flourished in the early part of sixth century BCE. He is said of have predicted the eclipse of the sun mentioned by Herodotus. Since, that eclipse occurred on May 28th, 585 BCE, it is one of the reasons to believe that he must have begun his philosophical career in the early part of 6th Century BCE. He is traditionally regarded as the first philosopher. Some other scientific activities are ascribed to Thales such as, the construction of an almanac and the introduction of the Phoenician practice of steering a ship's course by the Little Bear. However, there is little information about his philosophical doctrine since he did not commit his thoughts to writing. According to Aristotle, Thales taught two fundamental philosophical ideas. They are, one, the water is the first absolute principle and, second, the soul is the principal motor. How did Thales arrive at the conclusion that the water is first absolute principle? Besides the mere fact that he lived in a place virtually surrounded by water. Though the explanation might look simple to our intellectual minds, his attempt was to give a rational account of the principle of things. Thus, be broke away from myths and poet-theologians. The second philosophical idea of Thales according to Aristotle is the soul as the principle of movement. According to Aristotle, "Thales, too, to judge from what is recorded about him, seems to have held the soul to be a motive force, since he said that the magnet has a soul in it because it moves the iron.... Certain thinkers say that the soul is intermingled in the whole universe, and it is perhaps for this reason that Thales came to the opinion that all things are full of gods." Perhaps, the best way to understand "all things are full of gods" is to say that everything is fundamentally alive. Not only magnetic stones are endowed with souls but everything else, the whole universe is impregnated with life. How does Thales earn his place as the first Greek philosopher? It is from the fact that he conceives the notion of unity in difference. While holding firm the idea of unity, he philosophically accounted for diversity.

Anaximander

Anaximander was born in Miletus around the year 611 BCE and was a disciple of Thales. He was concerned about the scientific pursuits and he is credited with having constructed a map –most probably for the Milesian sailors on the Black Sea. He wrote a book entitled *On Nature*. Like Thales, he showed keen interest in cosmology. For Anaximander, the *archç* is *ápeiron* –'the infinite' or 'the unlimited.' What does Anaximander refer to by the *ápeiron*? *Ápeiron* means that which is devoid of limit. In other words, it refers to infinite. Probably it would be herculean task to figure out what exactly Anaximander meant by infinite, Aristotle understood it to mean unlimited extension in space and qualitative indetermination. It has no positive identity. It is neither water, nor air, nor any one of the known elements. *Ápeiron* can function in two ways: as a material cause and as a divine principle. *Ápeiron* as a material cause is an important discovery of Anaximander, which Aristotle would fully develop later. Unlike the principle of Thales, the *ápeiron* is not one of the elements (in Aristotelian terms, it is not a substance). It is of an indeterminate nature, and therefore, is different from and prior to all other existing substances. *Ápeiron* as divine causes encompasses and governs all things. Besides this, Anaximander also explains the genesis of all things. For the questions how does the *ápeiron* encompass and govern all things and how it is related to finite things, Anaximander would reply saying that all things proceed necessarily from the *ápeiron* by means of separation of contraries, and return to it in a necessary manner as well. All the same, Anaximander does not explain the process of separation of contraries but one might say that it is caused by the eternal movement of the *ápeiron.* All things are subject to this law of generation and corruption as a punishment. It is the retribution they pay for the commission of an injustice. This punishment restores the equality of the different parts with the passing of time. This is achieved by virtue of the imposition of a limit to each contrary that brings to an end the dominion of one over the other. This is the way Anaximander explains the continuity and stability of material changes, the formation of the world and the governing role of the *ápeiron.*

Anaximenes

For Anaximenes air is the fundamental stuff of which the world is composed.

Anaximenes chose air as the first thing because of its mobility, changeability, and inner vitality. As a matter of fact air was considered to be the breath of the universe. Hence this breathing universe was considered to be a living organism. For this reason Anaximenes is really a hylozoist.

For Anaximenes, this primary air is regulated by the opposed principles of condensation and rarefaction. Condensation simply means compression of the air in a narrow space and rarefaction means expansion of the air in the greater space. By rarefaction air assumes the form of fire, and, by successive condensation it gives rise to water, earth and stone.

Anaximenes accounts for all the important elements and states of material things through his fundamental stuff of air. He tells us, how air accounts for the formation of water, fire and earth. It is the knowing-how, which alone constitutes scientific explanation. Hence the two principles of condensation and rarefaction are important steps in developing the scientific thinking about the universe. There is also another point which must be noted.

The world is not only vapours, liquid and solid, but is also sound, colour, rough-smooth etc. Then, how to explain this world of quality? The principle of condensation and rarefaction admit of quantitative differences. Hence, here is involved the principle that quantity can explain the quality. Later on Pythagoras laid down his famous statement 'what exists, exists in number'. In the modern times no scientific explanation is considered reliable unless it is put into quantitative formulae. Hence, the thinking of Anaximenes is a step forward towards the scientific worldview.

Heraclitus

Heraclitus was born in the middle of 6th Century BCE and died around 480 BCE. He came from Ephesus and belonged to an aristocratic family. He was known as a conceited, proud person who looked down upon the rest of humanity because of its blindness to the truth of his teachings. His philosophy is found in a book entitled *On Nature*, quite a few fragments of which have been preserved. Since it was not easy to determine the exact nature of his thought on account of the cryptic and occult nature of his writings, he was also known as "the obscure one" even during his lifetime. Following are a few important philosophical ideas of Heraclitus. First, Heraclitus affirmed that everything is in constant flux, or, "everything changes." He explains this with an analogy of the river saying, "It is certainly not possible to enter twice into the same river." This is the original contribution of Heraclitus to the history of pre-Socratic thought. For Heraclitus, movement is the central theme and point of departure of his philosophy. All the Miletian philosophers attempted to account for the multiplicity of things and explained that multiplicity by affirming different solutions to the question of the *archç*. This is the widely known thought of Heraclitus. Second, Heraclitus explains the universal process of becoming as a never-ending alternation of contraries. The opposites not only account for the transformation of one substance to another but they constitute the very essence of all things. Third, Heraclitus considered fire as the *archc*: "This world, as well as all other worlds, was not made by the gods or by men. It always was, is, and will be, an ever living fire, which is enkindled according to a certain measure and extinguished according to a certain measure." According to Heraclitus, fire, more than any other *archç*, reflects the constant change and harmony that lies at the root of reality. "The transformations undergone by fire are as follows: first it becomes the sea; then half of the sea becomes land, while the other half becomes burning wind." Most interpreters of Heraclitus understand fire in the metaphorical sense rather as a material cause. Taking fire metaphorically might cause many difficulties as Heraclitus himself uses the term *logos* to refer to the first principle. Understood as such, it means the principle that governs every transformation; it is the law that is inherent in everything. And for Heraclitus, to know the *logos* means to know the truth. Fourth, Heraclitus identifies the nature of the soul with that of the first principle and the soul is infinite part of human being: "No matter how much you journey, though you travel every road, you will never be able to discern the soul's limits, so deep as its *logos*."

It is indeed interesting to note the gradual maturing and refinement of philosophical speculation and concepts from Thales to Heraclitus. Heraclitus probably is the most accomplished thinker of this school. He has a defining influence on Stoics, especially as regards his doctrine of the logos. Hegel saw in him a predecessor.

PYTHAGOREAN'S

Pythagorean's main problem was the harmony, order, unity and proportion in the world. The world is a harmonious order, a cosmos. The Pythagorean account actually begins with Anaximander's teaching that the ultimate substance of things is "the boundless," or what Anaximander called the "*apeiron.*"

The main characteristic of Pythagorean School was its ascetic and religious character. Philosophy was for salvation, it is a way of life not so much knowledge of cause of ultimate things. The school was influenced by Orphicism, which had a common way of life and believed in transmigration of soul. According to the tradition, Pythagoreanism developed at some point was seen as two separate schools of thought, the *mathematikoi* and the *akousmatikoi* ("listeners"). The *mathematikoi* were supposed to have extended and developed the more mathematical and scientific work begun by Pythagoras, while the *akousmatikoi* focused on the more religious and ritualistic aspects of his teachings.

Pythagoras

Pythagoras declared that whatever exists, exists in number. This is not a wild statement. Mathematics means proportion, order and harmony. Pythagoras was a geometrician he is credited to have discovered the theorem that in a right-angled triangle, the sum of the squares on the sides is in equal to the square on the hypotenuse.

For Pythagoras the soul is immortal. He believed in rebirths and even the transmigration of the soul. The whole wheel of rebirths is essentially painful and it is the duty of man that he should put an end to this wheel of rebirths.

The body is the tomb of the soul and the visible world in which man lives is false and illusive. How to get one's release from the round of endless reincarnations in this false world? By means of mystic meditation. This meditation is intellectual and not emotional. No doubt the Pythagoreans had ceremonies and rituals and a recommendation for an ascetic life. But the most important thing was the disinterested pursuit of science and the contemplation of the ultimate things of the universe. This sort of contemplation was considered most conducine towards release from the chain of endless rebirths. Scientific pursuit was also the religious duty of man.

Pythagoras founded an order in which men and women were regarded as equal. They led a common way of life. Even the mathematical discoveries were regarded as collective achievement.

Pythagoras laid emphasis on asceticism and the purity of conduct. In later pythagoreanism vegetarianism was also accepted. Though life was deemed essentially full of miseries and the soul immortal, yet suicide was not deemed desirable. The reason is that suicide instead of putting an end to the wheel of transmigration, really strengthens it.

The most important belief of Pythagoreanism lays streets on the doctrine of transmigration of the soul, and, the main prohibition on taboo was not to eat beans. Along with asceticism, Pythagoras mentioned some taboo-restrictions :

1. To abstain from beans.

2. Not to touch a white cock.
3. Not to stir the fire with iron.
4. Not to eat the heart.
5. And many other such prohibitions.

According to Pythagoras there is a central fire around which the earth, the sun, the moon and five planets move. In this speculation Pythagoras was nearer the truth in not regarding the earth as the centre of the universe.

The Pythagoreans tired to show that things are but number in some arbitrary manner. According to them the world is composed of the opposites. This formula was certainly laid down by Anaximenes too. But the Pythagoreans have ten opposites, namely, (1) Odd and even, (2) Limited and unlimited, (3) One and many, (4) Right and left, (5) Masculine and feminine, (6) Rest and motion, (7) Straight and crooked, (8) Light and darkness, (9) Good and evil, (10) Square and oblong.

Then again in the most arbitrary manner, the Pythagoreans called point 'one', line 'two', plane 'three', solid 'four' material qualities 'five', animal animation 'six' etc. Similarly justice is four or nine, because four is the square of equal numbers 2 × 2, and nine is of three × three.

The Ephesian School

The Ephesian School of philosophy of the 5th Century B.C. essentially refers to the ideas of just one man, Heraclitus who did not have any direct disciples or successors that we are aware of. He is a native of Ephesus in the Greek colony of Ionia. Along with his fellow Ionians of the Milesian School, he looked for a solution to the problem of change, but his view was that the world witnesses constant change, rather than no change at all. Panta Rei which means "everything is in a state of flux", nothing is permanent. "One cannot step into the same river twice." Reality is becoming rather than being. Unity exists in tension of opposites. Reality is at the same time one and many, opposites are composites. This he exemplified by the idea that, although the waters in it are always changing, a river stays the same.

The transformation of material from one state into another does not happen by accident, he held, but rather within certain limits and within certain time and according to law or "logos", according to which all things are one. The difference is essential to unity. He considered that the basis of the entire universe is an ever-living fire (although this is used more as a symbol of change and process, rather than actual fire), so that the world itself consists of a law-like interchange of elements, symbolized by fire.

The Eleatic School

The school took its name from Elea, a Greek city of lower Italy, the home of its chief exponents, Parmenides and Zeno. Its foundation is often attributed to Xenophanes of Colophon, but, although there is much in his speculations which formed part of the later Eleatic doctrine, it is probably more correct to regard Parmenides as the founder of the school. The fundamental reality for him is permanence, not change, being and not becoming, one and not many. Plurality and change are illusion. If A is being and B is being, A is the same as B. A cannot become B for both are Being. He held the view of 'ontological monism.' Being (*ontos*) is one (*Monos*). It is also called 'absolutism' there exists only one absolute independent and unrelated reality and nothing else. Parmenides argued that the first principle of being was One, indivisible, and unchanging. What will bring us to this knowledge is not opinion but reason. The former is the wrong way and relies on sense experience and erroneously takes plurality change as real. But with the way of reason, the right way reveals the truth, namely that reality is one and stable. This is the way that leads the knower behind the false appearances of sense knowledge.

Parmenides

Xenophanes had declared 'All is one'. This was the starting-point of Parmenides. How could he establish this truth? He like the rest of the people found that the world of sensible things is always becoming. Things come into the world and the next moment they perish. They are as much are as also they are not. What can we say about this flux? Heraclitus declared that flux alone is real. To Parmenides it appeared impossible. For him, real is eternal, unchangeable and indestructible. Of course it was left for his pupil Zeno to give reason for regarding the real as one, unchangeable and eternal. For Parmenides it appeared self-contradictory to hold that a thing which is passing away to be real. What is the point involved in saying that the real is permanent and unchangeable?

For Parmenides, One alone is real and manyness and changes are unreal. This distinction is a matter of intuition and at most a postulate of his philosophy. But in real life changes and plurality of things are palpable. What can we say about them? For Parmenides plurality and changes are given by the sense. At most they can be called 'mere appearances'. But what is the reason for regarding them as 'appearances'. Quite obviously they are and yet they cease to be. They appeared to be shot through with self-contradiction, as H. Bradley said and which Zeno, the disciple of Parmenides, tried to prove.

If the world of senses is illusory, then how do we know the one? Of course, through thought. Hence, Parmenides makes a distinction between the appearance and reality, sense and thought. He gives predominance to thought.

If in one way Parmenides teaches the primacy of thought, then in another way he teaches that his 'One' is corporeal, a spherical being with filling space or plenum. If plenum is being, then empty space alone is non-being or unreal. Hence there can be no empty space.

Parmenides Views on Sense and Reason

Parmenides had clearly made the distinction between sense and reason. Truth according to Parmenides lies only in reason therefore, being is known to us only by reason, by thought. The senses for Parmenides is the source of illusion and error. But parmenides is not, as some suggests, the father of idealism. Being which for him is the ultimate reality occupies space, is finite and is spherical shaped. The ultimate reality of things conceived by Parmenides as material is the cardinal thesis of materialism.

It is not in any place or time. This idea is formed by the process of abstraction. Therefore, Parmenides actually placed the absolute reality of things in an idea, though he might have conceived it in a material and sensuous way. Parmenides on this view was an idealist. These two sides are mutually contradicting though Parmenides himself did not see the contradiction. This way he became the father of both materialism and idealism. He makes a distinction between appearance and reality. For him, one above is real and many and changes are unreal.

Zeno of Elea

Very little is known about life of the Zeno of Elea. We certainly know that he was a philosopher and he is said to have been the son of Teleutagoras. Parmenides written by Plato, has been the main source of knowledge about zeno. Pupil and friend of the philosopher Parmenides, Zeno studied with him in Elea. His philosophy of monism claimed that the many things which appear to exist are merely a single eternal reality which he called being. His principle was that all is one and that change or non-being are impossible.

Plato tells us that the young Socrates, met. Zeno and Parmenides on their visit to Athens and discussed philosophy with them. Thus, Plato's claim is certainly possible. Zeno had already written a work on philosophy before his visit to Athens and Plato reports that Zeno's book meant that he had achieved a certain fame in. The book Zeno wrote before his visit to Athens was his famous work which according to Proculus, contained forty paradoxes concerning the continuum. Four of the paradoxes, which we shall discuss in detail below, were to have a profound influence on the development of mathematics.

Details of Zeno Life

Diogenes Laertius gives further details of Zeno's life, which are generally thought to be unreliable. According to Diogenes Laertius, Zeno returned to Elea after the visit to Athens and that he met his death in a heroic attempt to remove a tyrant from the city of Elea. Diogenes Laertius also writes about Zeno's cosmology and again there is no supporting evidence regarding this, but we shall give some indication below of the details.

Zeno's book of Forty Paradoxes was, according to Plato, a youthful effort and it was stolen by someone, so that the author had no opportunity of considering whether to publish it or not.

Proclus also described to work and confirms that Proclus. Zeno elaborated forty different paradoxes following from the assumption of plurality and motion, all of them apparently based on the difficulties deriving from an analysis of the continuum.

In his arguments against the idea that the world contains more than thing. Zeno derived his paradoxes from the assumption that if a magnitude can be divided then it can be divided infinitely often. Writing in the first half of the 6th century he explained Zeno's argument, why something without magnitude could not exist.

This argument makes us realise that we can never get started since we are trying to build up this infinite sum from the 'wrong'.

Zeno uses dichotomy paradox and attacks, on simple pluralism he says that once a thing is divisible, then it is infinitely divisible. Other paradoxes given by Zeno causes problem precisely. He considers that seemingly continuous magnitudes are made up of indivisible elements.

Zeno's paradoxes are important in the development of the notion of infinitesimals. Anaxagoras and the followers of Pythagoras, with their development of incommensurables, are also thought by some to be the targets of Zeno's arguments defend Parmenides' philosophical position, is the whole explanation of why Zeno wrote his famous work on paradoxes.

Russell Views on Zeno Arguments

In this capricious world, nothing is more capricious than posthumous fame. One of the most notable victims of posterity's lack of judgement is Eleatic Zeno. After two thousand years of continuous refutation, the sophists were reinstated and made the foundation of a mathematical renaissance.

Here, Russell is thinking of the work of Cantor, Frege and himself on the infinite and particularly of Weierstrass on the calculus. The relation of the paradoxes to mathematics are also discussed and the author comes to a conclusion.

Although, they have often been dismissed as logical nonsense, many attempts have also been made to dispose of them by means of mathematical theorems, such as the theory of convergent series or the theory of sets.

Mathematicians however, ... realising that Zeno's arguments were fatal to infinitesimals, say that they could only avoid the difficulties connected with them by once and for all banishing the idea of the infinite, even the potentially infinite, altogether from their science; hence forth, therefore, they made no use of magnitudes increasing or decreasing and infinitum, but contented themselves with finite magnitudes that can be made as great or as small as we please.

Pluralist School

Empedocles of Agrigentum (490-430 BCE) was from the ancient Greek city of Akragas, Agrigentum in Latin, modern Agrigento, in Sicily. He appears to have been partly in agreement with the Eleatic School, partly in opposition to it. On the one hand, he maintained the unchangeable nature of substance; on the other, he supposes a plurality of such substances - i.e. four classical elements, earth, water, air, and fire. Of these the world is built up, by the agency of two ideal motive forces - Love as the cause of union, Strife/Hate as the cause of separation. Anaxagoras of Clazomenae (500-428 BCE) in Asia Minor, also maintained the existence of an ordering principle as well as a material substance, and while regarding the latter as an infinite multitude of imperishable primary elements; he conceived divine reason or Mind (*Nous*) as ordering them. He referred all generation and disappearance to mixture and resolution respectively. To him belongs the credit of first establishing philosophy at Athens.

An Attempt at Synthesis: The Atomists

Human being, rather than admit defeat, rather than let him/herself remain confounded and despairing over the apparent contradiction, tries to find a way to reconcile conflicting opinions and harmonize with the all the possible data. Such was the case with Atomists. They noted the clash of view between the first two great schools of Greek philosophy, concerning even so elementary a datum of experience as movement and change. In their response, they seem to have saved the Being so beloved of the Eleatics as well as becoming rigorously championed by Ionians. Reality, according to Atomists, is composed of atoms moving in a void. The individualistic atom, itself unchanging, is the element of permanence whereas its incessant motion provides the element of change. We shall briefly note the important philosophical ideas of a few atomists such as Leucippus, Democritus, Empedocles and Anaxagoras.

Democritus

Democritus, the disciple of Leukippus, accepted the theory of atoms and void and extended this theory to explain epistemology, ethics and metaphysics. The problem of Democritus was to establish the possibility of knowledge, consequently science which the sophists has denied. The second thing was the problem of morality which again was considered to be mere expediency and relative by the sophists. Democritus tried to explain scientific knowledge and absolute morality with the help of his thoroughgoing mechanism and materialism.

For Democritus even the soul is nothing but an aggregate of atoms. However, the soul consists of those atoms which have the essence of fire. These fiery atoms are the finest, smoothest and most mobile. These atoms are distributed throughout the whole universe including animals, plants and other things, but these fiery atoms are found in the largest number in man.

Democritus explains his epistemology on the basis of mechanism and materialism. But he makes a sharp distinction between perception and thought. They do not differ in kind but only in degree. But even then the two are sharply distinguished. For Democritus, perception gives us the information about the world of becoming, but thought gives us the knowledge of being. Indeed knowledge given by sense perception is relative and transitory. The same honey tastes sweet to a healthy man, but in fever it may taste bitter. Besides, thought gives us universal and objectively valid knowledge. In contrast, perception gives us knowledge of what is fleeting and transitory. As the sophists had maintained the knowledge is perception, and as perception is relative and transitory, so they denied the possibility of scientific knowledge which is universally valid for all the scientists. Hence, by upholding the claim of thought over senses, Democritus defended science against the epistemological scepticism of the sophists.

True happiness follows the gentle movement of the fiery atoms, which happiness results from the right insight into fiery atoms. This insight alone secures peace, guards the soul from emotional disturbance and yields mastery over passions through knowledge. This is really Socratic inasmuch as the aphorism of Socrates is 'Virtue is knowledge, and Vice is ignorance'. Democritus does not favour sex-pleasure, for it is disturbing, fleeting and follows from crude images. Democritus teaches the cultivation of true friendship. The ideal of Democritus resting as it does on materialism teaches the steadfastness and tranquillity of the inward soul, which ideal has been taught by the Gita also.

Democritus Atomic Theory

The Greek philosopher Democritus suggested that all matter was formed of different types of tiny discrete particles and the properties of these particles also determined the properties of matter. This theory had some support from other philosophers, but the methods to verify it did not exist in that era, so it was not widely adopted from many centuries.

It re-emerged in the early 19th century in order to explain many laws that had been established in the previous century, when chemists had begun to measure the mass of reactants and products. Today, it is known that some compounds, particularly metal oxides and sulphides, exit in ratios that vary slightly from simple whole number and they are known as non-stoichiometric compounds.

The law of multiple proportions was also given stated that given masses of different elements always combine in small whole number ratios. The English scientist John Dalton also revived that atomic theory in order to explain these observations. In 1808, he also proposed that a chemical element consisted of tiny particles, all with the same chemical properties. The atoms of different elements have different properties and these atoms are not changed during ordinary chemical reactions.

The atomic theory is referred as fundamental to the physical sciences. As the eminent 20th century, scientist Richard Feynman succinctly put it – Everything is made of atoms. Democritus is regarded as a Molecular dynamics simulation programme. It is named after the Greek Philosopher who first introduced the word 'atom' (atomon in Greek means indivisible).

The programme uses molecular dynamics to control the motion of a group of atoms with the ability to change the temperature and the density. It study the effects also. The system is displayed on the screen. It represents the element Argon (Ar). The same things happen in all molecular systems that why can are discover a lot from this.

Empedocles

Empedocles was born in Agrigento, Sicily, in the beginning of the 5th century BCE. He was the first philosopher to harmonize the being of Parmenides with the testimony of the senses. His ideas are found in two of his works: *On Nature* and *The Purifications. On Nature* explains Empedocles' cosmology while the other work contains his ethico-religious teachings. But as a philosopher, he subscribes to the

Eleatic principle of the immutability of the real without denying the existence of sensible reality. We shall briefly study his basic ideas. First, Empedocles says that a certain number of substances, ungenerated, incorruptible and always remaining the same, constitute the origin of all things. As we have already noted, the Ionians explained the origin of all things through the qualitative changes undergone by the first principle. But for Empedocles, the four elements never change; they remain always the same, and it is through their different combinations that other beings are brought into existence. We can say that Empedocles is the origin of the notion of an unchangeable material cause, irreducible to no other thing, and capable of uniting and separating itself from other elements. Second, it is love and hate principle which makes four elements unite with or separate themselves from one another. Love brings things together, and therefore, it is at the origin of the generation of things. Hate is divisive and brings about corruption. Love and hate are two principal forces constantly at odds with each other. There is an alternation of the predominace of one force with the predominance of the other, and this gives rise to the cycles of generation and corruption present in the world. Third, the principle of knowledge lies in a material likeness between the sensible object and our senses. According to Empedocles when there is a continuous effusion of elements from things, and when this comes in contact with the sense, sensible knowledge is produced. The intellectual knowledge too, is brought about in a similar way.

Anaxagoras

Anaxagoras was born in Clazomenae, near Miletus, around the year 500 BCE. Probably, he was the first one to transfer the center of philosophy to Athens. He remained in Athens teaching for about thirty years, until a charge of impiety forced him to transfer to Lampsacus, where he died around the year 428 BCE. He wrote a book titled *On Nature* and his philosophy closely resembles the philosophy of Empedocles. *First*, beings are immutable, indestructible and indivisible. They bring about multiplicity of things according to the way they mix and combine with one another. Hence, the first principle of Anaxagoras, according to Aristotle, is a great mixture: an indeterminate mixture composed of an infinite number of substances, each one of them infinitely small in size. *Second*, to explain the multiplicity of substances, Anaxagoras concludes that the first principle must, in a way, embody all things in itself. He believed that everything must come from something that already exists. They are seeds of all things. Aristotle called them "*homeomeries,*" which means things which remain qualitatively the same even if they are divided into smaller parts. All things are composed of a mixture of *homeomeries*; different mixtures bring about different beings. Since all things come from the first principle, whatever nature things may have, "everything is found in everything:" the qualitative differences of all things are found in everything though some elements may be minimally represented in nature. Third, alongside the *homeomeries*, Anaxagoras adds another principle: the *Nous* or intelligence. The *Nous* is the most subtle and pure of beings. It knows everything completely and has maximum power. "The intelligence ordains everything that is brought into being –those things that existed in the past and exist no longer, those that exist at present and those that will exist in the future." In other words, for Anaxagoras, the *Nous* functions only as the origin of movement. Since the seeds of all things are eternal, the *Nous* merely starts the cosmic movement whereby thing begin to differentiate themselves from one another, and take on their particular characteristics. This observation is criticized by Aristotle, who says that Anaxagoras "uses reason as a *dues ex machina* for making of the world, and when he is at a loss to them from what cause something necessarily is, then he drags reason in, but in all other cases ascribes events to anything rather than to reason." However, Anaxagoras first introduces a spiritual and intellectual principle, though he might have failed to grasp the full import of that difference between that principle and the matter which it forms or sets in motion.

THE SOPHISTS AND SOCRATES

The beginning of 5th century saw a change of focus in Greek philosophy. The Greek philosophical speculation began to shift from the world to the human beings; from the macrocosm to the microcosm, or, in the precise philosophical language, from the object to the subject. Besides, democracy was introduced into Athens, which was also at the time (492-429 BCE) the commercial, cultural and political centre of Greece. With democracy, the 'common man' began to realize that s/he could play an important role in the affairs of the city-state, s/he wanted to equip her/himself with knowledge in practical affairs, especially in rhetoric and the art of persuading. In this, h/she was ably (?) aided by a band of self-appointed itinerant teachers who were willing to offer him/her the fruit of their expertise, of course for a fee! This practice of dispensing knowledge for a rate was something wholly out of keeping with the Greek wisdom and earned the "Sophists," as they were called the epithet, "shopkeepers with spiritual wares" from Socrates. To out-smart other rival teachers, they did not hesitate to clad their speeches with all manner of obscurisms to appear more profound. Moreover, in order to appear more original, they worked out various fine-sounding and specious arguments to attack established norms, which draw enthusiastic support of younger generation and the irk of the elders. Sooner than later, whatever their initial motives and ideals were, sophistry had acquired that connotation of quackery and fraud that it has today. And the terms still has this implication today. However, one must not forget that no less than Socrates himself could be, historically speaking, classed in this "school," but with a difference, of course. For in Socrates we can see the nobility and grandeur of what must have been the pristine sophist ideal. Both Socrates and Sophists gave importance to virtue. For Socrates, it concerned the formation and development of the whole person. Be that it may, properly speaking, sophism was more of a philosophical movement than a school of philosophy. There were difference of opinion among sophists themselves and later, between the first sophists and their disciples. The first sophists were respected personages and were esteemed or the new forms of culture they ushered in, the latter were known to have cared little for content and were more for external form. With them, sophism became barren form of debate and empty rhetoric.

The Sophist Epistemology (Protagoras)

For Sophists Knowledge is perception.

In perception there is the motion from the external object towards the sense-organ. And yet again there is also a corresponding motion of the sense-organ towards the motion of the external object. Hence there is a double motion, one from the external thing and another from the sense-organ of the percipient. But quite obviously perceiving is not the object perceived, and, yet again perceiving is quite different from the perceiving subject. Thus perception is the product of both the object moving towards the subject, and the subject moving towards the object. This perception alone is knowledge. Thus Man is the measure of all things, of what is, that it is; of what is not, that it is not.

Knowledge means that which is true for all and for all the movements of human life. And yet for all practical purpose perception alone is knowledge. This knowledge is relative to different men at different times. Hence the famous saying of Protagoras Homo Mensura, *i.e.*, man is the measure of all things. In other words, what appears to me is true for me and what appears to you is true for you. Hence there is no knowledge. Which is valid and acceptable to all men universally. The conclusion of homo mensura not only shows the relativism of knowledge, but also its universality as impossibility. This is known as scepticism. In others respects, it also means all statements are true and none are false. It is not self-contradictory to say that the same object is x as it appears to me, and, is not x as it appears to you, because I may be talking about one object and you might be speaking about a different object. But from this very statement, it appears that there is not anyone object about which two persons can communicate. And this is what Gorgias holds that no knowledge is possible, and even if knowledge be available it cannot be communicated.

Teachings of Protagoras

This saying puts the whole teaching of Protagoras into a **nutshell**. The earlier Greek philosophers had made a distinction between sense and reason. The teaching of Protagoras rests fundamentally upon denying this distinction. First of all, it is important to understand that reason is a law universally binding upon all men and sensations are the particular element in man. It is particularly this distinction that is denied by Protagoras. By man, he means the individual man and not mankind at large. Each individual man, according to Protagoras, is the standard of what is true to himself. What is true to me is true for me. What is true for you is true for you.

One commonly distinguishes between subjective impressions and objective truth, *e.g.*, one's subjective impression of Earth may be flat, but the objective truth is that the Earth is round. According to this two contradictory, propositions must both be true. Protagoras understood this clearly. In this regard, he says that it makes no difference, whether we say all opinions are true or whether all opinions are false. The word truthhood or falsehood in this context has no meaning. Whatever, I feel I feel, to call it truth for me adds no meaning.

Traits

The traits or rather the words which name and characterise them and enabled them to be socially recognised traits, belong to a vocabulary, which presupposes an established web of social and moral relationships. Where three are not normal standards there is no possibility of failing to come up to them, of doing more or less than is expected of one, or of elaborating and using names and descritions of the traits and dispositions of those who so behave. Thus, the description of the so-called natural man is formed in a vocabulary drawn from social life; what was alleged to be presocial turns out to presuppose the existence of some social order.

One factual and one conceptual point about this particular Greek version of the doctrine of natural man has been made. What he expresses is not nature, but the social attitudes of the Homeric hero. He is a man transposed from a social order where his attitudes and actions are accepted forms of move in the social game and have accepted forms of response, into a quite different social order where he can appear only as an aggressive outsider. But this does not mean that he is a social impossibility. Natural man is merely a man from another and earlier culture. The conceptual point is that this is no accident.

Differences

What the sophists and the long tradition which was later to follow them, failed to distinguish was the difference between the concept of a man who stands outside and is able to question the conventions of some one given social order and the concept of a man who stands outside social life as such. What follows from this error? Natural man portrayed in Thrasymachean guise has two main characteristics. His psychological make up is simple; he is out to get what he wants and what he wants is narrowly circumscribed. His masquerade can only be carried through by putting the conventional moral vocabulary to the service of his private purposes.

Moral Conservatives

Socrates found himself confronted both by moral conservatives using an incoherent moral vocabulary as if they were sure of its meaning and by sophists whose innovations he found equally suspect. It is scarcely surprising that he appears different from different points of view. Plato's mouthpiece. It is clear, then, that the task of delineating the historical Socrates is inherently controversial. But one may perhaps not solve, but avoid the problem by trying to paint a composite portrait from two palettes.

The second is the set of dialogues by Plato which are accepted as chronologically early and in which Plato's own metaphysical doctrines of the soul and of the forms are not yet elaborated.

Aristotle ascribes to Socrates what he calls universal definitions and what he calls inductive arguments and he makes to statements about Socrates' intentions which are of peculiar interest in the light of Plato's portrait. A few lines farther on Aristotle remarks that it was natural that Socrates should be seeking the essence, for he was seeking to syllogise and "what a thing is' the starting point of syllogisms."

Questions given by Socrates

Socrates repeatedly puts such questions as, What is piety? What is courage? What is justice? We see him use what Aristotle calls inductive arguments and we see him syllogising. He does this with the apparent intention of convicting his interlocutors of inability to answer the question rather than with the intention of supplying an answer.

When the Delphic oracle described Socrates as the wisest of the Athenians he concluded that he deserved this title because only he, among them all, knew that he knew nothing. It would not be surprising if Socrates envisaged his duty as a teacher as that of making his pupils wiser by making them discover their own ignorance. But infuriating someone may indeed be the only method of disturbing him sufficiently to force him into philosophical reflection upon moral matters. For the majority of those so assaulted there will be no admirable consequences of this kind. But there is no evidence that Socrates expected the activity of an intellectual gadfly to benefit more than a tiny minority.

Nihilism (Gorgias)

Gorgias was a master of rhetoric and has developed the art of persuasion by means of artistic prose. For this reason he was not interested in the search for truth. For him any weapon is good enough to beat his adversary. Hence his philosophy is eclectic. But for explaining his tenets he took the help of Zeno's arguments, the epistemology of Protagoras with its sceptical conclusion. Gorgias has written a book On Nature or the Non-existent. In this book he laid down three of his tenets, namely.

1. There is Nothing

If there be anything then it can be known only through perception. But perception tells us that things are many and that they are in motion. But Zeno has shown that plurality and motion are shot through with self-contradiction. So they do not exist. Hence, there is nothing.

Perception is the only knowledge. And perception tells us that everything has come into being from its earlier state. But this arising of things can be either from being or non-being. But quite obviously a world of becoming cannot come from an unchanging Being. Again, nothing can arise from non-being. Hence, there is nothing in the world.

2. Even if there be anything it cannot be known

The second tenet of Gorgias is, 'Even if there be anything, we cannot know it'. Protagoras has informed us that perception is a joint product of the object perceived and percipient. But a perceived object is not the external object in itself (as Kant would say), nor is it the perceiving act (as G.E. Moore would say). Hence, we do not know what the real object is.

3. Knowledge cannot be communicated

Things and knowledge are quite separate. Hence, whatever our knowledge be, it cannot be about things (as shown in the first tenet). Hence, what kind of knowledge can be obtained to be communicated at all? Further, we have already seen that according to Protagoras, knowledge is perception, and, perception is true for the perceiver alone and that also at the moment of its occurrence. It cannot be shared with anybody at all, 'My perception is mine, and yours is yours'. There is nothing which two persons can perceive alike. Hence each man is shut up in his cocoon-like existence from which nothing can go out and into which nothing can enter. Hence, no knowledge can ever be communicated.

Rhetorical Innovation

Gorgias rhetorical innovations invokes structure and ornamentation and the introduction of paradoxologia – the idea of paradoxical though and paradoxical expression. Gorgias is also known for contributing to the diffusion of the Attic dialect as the language of literary prose.

There are paraphrases of the treatise **On Nature of the Non-Existent**. These works are each part of the Diels-Kranz collection, and although academics consider this source reliable, many of the works included are fragmentary and corrupt.

Gorgias' writings are both **rhetorical** and **performative**. He goes to great lengths to exhibit his ability of making an absurd, argumentative position appear stronger. Each of his works defend positions that are unpopular, paradoxical and even absurd. Gorgias argues that persuasive words have power that is equivalent to that of the gods and as strong as physical force.

PLATO AND ARISTOTLE

Plato: The Gorgias

It is impossible to produce more than a plausible account of the historical Socrates; and the most obvious reason for this is that it is impossible to say at what point in Plato's dialogues the character called Socrates became merely a mouthpiece for the mature Plato. In the Meno and the Phaedo a metaphysical background is being constructed, which in the republic provides an essential part of a proposed solution to problems which are a restatement of those in the Gorgias. In the dialogues after the republic there is a sustained critique of the metaphysics, but there are also two substantial afterthoughts on the problems of ethics, the Philebus, on pleasure and the Laws.

Three Sections of Gorgias

The Gorgias falls into three sections, in each of which Socrates has a different interlocutor and each of which establishes certain positions once and for all before passing on. The function of the first part is to dispose of the claims of rhetoric. Virtue is taught and also to establish a distinction between two senses of persuasion. For the supreme good is freedom and by freedom is meant the freedom to have one's own way in everything. In order to have one's own way in the city-state, one must be able to sway one's fellow citizens.

Socrates introduces a distinction between the kind of persuasion which produces knowledge in the man who is persuaded and the kind that does not. Gorgias makes it plain that rhetoric is persuasion not of the former, but of the latter king.

One of the praises of the orator is that he can persuaded audiences upon topics on which he himself is unskilled; Gorgias' example is the success of Themistocles and Pericles in persuading the Athenians to build the docks, harbors and defense works necessary for Athenian imperialism, although they themselves were politicians and neither naval nor military engineers. Socrates inquire whether the orator needs a knowledge or right and wrong, any more than he needs a knowledge of engineering. Gorgias is not entirely consistent on this point; he appears to suggest that an orator will on occasion need to be a just man, but is vague as to how he may become just.

Gorgias has been replaced in the argument by his pupil Polus, Polus reiterates that the moral point of the use of rhetoric is the acquisition of power. The successful orator can do whatever he wants. Socrates' retort to this is that a man may do whatever he thinks it good to do and nonetheless not be doing what he desires. The despot who inflicts injury and death upon others may be doing what appears to him to minister to his own good, but he is mistaken. For Socrates, it is worse for a man to inflict wrong than to suffer it.

Counter Example

Polus's counter example is the tyrant Archelaus of Macedon, who had acquired power by successive episodes of treachery and assassination; everybody, says Polus, would like to be Archelaus if he could. Socrates' point is, however, that whether that is what people wish or not is irrelevant. For if that is what they wish, it can only be because of a mistake on their part as to what is for their own good.

Polus is not prepared to admit that it is worse inflict injury without due cause than to suffer it, but he is prepared to concede that it is more disgraceful. In order to understand this we must recall the contrast between the pairs of adjectives, good-bad and honorable-disgraceful.

The reference is to show how a man appears. Polus is prepared to redefine notion because the customary sense has become unclear. But because precisely of his commitment to winning popular favour, he is committed to popular estimations of reputation. He cannot commend his own valuations to his hearers unless at some point at least he appears to accept theirs.

Polus accepts the view that it is more disgraceful to inflict injury undeservedly than it is to suffer it. But Socrates forces upon him the recognition that the predicates are not criterionless. It polus agrees that to suffer injury undeservedly is more honorable it must be because it is pleasanter and more beneficial.

Callicles

Callicles is involved at once in two disagreements with Socrates. The first is over the concept of desire. Socrates argues that the man of boundless desires is like a leaky sieve, never filled, never satisfied; therefore, to have great and violent desires is to make it certain that you will not get what you want.

Secondly, when Callicles at an earlier stage in the dialogue proclaimed the right of the strong man to rule he clearly intended by this to glorify the despot. Socrates, however, points out that the populace are in an obvious sense stronger than the tyrant and therefore on Callicles' view ought to rule. Callicles has to redefine the concept of the 'stronger' as meaning the 'more intelligent'.

The opposite point that Socrates made is that good and bad cannot be synonymous with pleasant and painful. We use good and bad in evaluating pleasures and pains. A coward may feel more relief than a courageous man when danger is avoided and so more pleasure.

And anything that is to count as a 'way of living' will necessarily have some order or form, by which we can distinguish it from other ways of living.

Toward the close of the Gorgias there are two other important moments. One is when Socrates attacks bitterly the line of Athenian statesmen from Miltiades to Pericles whose expansionist policies taught the Athenians to have desires without teaching them the connection between the goods they might desire and the rule-governed order within which alone goods can be realised. Both the political and the religious attitudes exemplified here are recurrent features of Plato's thought which are treated very misleadingly if conceived of as external to his moral analyses.

Justice of Plato

Plato's try to show what justice is, first in the state and then in the soul. He outlines a state in which all basic needs are met. Three classes of citizen are required: artisans and laborers to produce the material needs of society; soldiers to defend the state; and rulers to organise its social life. Plato relies for this transition upon two beliefs, one not certainly true and one certainly false.

The belief which is not certainly true is that one man is better to stick to one job, that this form of the division of labour is under all possible circumstances the best form; the belief which is certainly false is that men are by nature divided up into men best suited for each of these functions. But Plato's beliefs on this point were powerfully reinforced by his doctrine of the tripartite soul.

The Tripartite Soul

The arguments for the tripartite soul are independent of those for the tripartite state but it is necessary for the doctrine of the tripartite state that at least something like the doctrine of the tripartite soul should be true.

The assumption which underlies this argument is that a man cannot simultaneously desire to do something and desire not to do it, in the same sense in which a man cannot simultaneously move in a given direction and not move in that direction. But where desires are concerned a man may desire some end envisaged under a particular description and not desire it under some other description. So a man may want to drink the water, because he is thirsty, but want not to drink, in case he risks an illness. It might perhaps seem that the short way to escape Plato's argument here is to say that the man just does not have incompatible desires. He desires to quench his thirst and he desires not to be ill and it is merely a contingent fact that this water would both quench his thirst and make him ill.

But to this the rejoinder might be that his desires remain incompatible: for what the man desires is to drink this particular water and what he fears is to drink this same water. Yet Plato is only right in a sense about these being incompatible desires and that they are does not have any of the consequences which he supposes to follow. And this is because the incompatibility belongs to the possibility of satisfying both desires, not of having both desires.

Souls

Plato's picture of the parts of the soul is not in fact coherent. Sometimes he speaks as though the rational part of the soul had one set of desires and the appetitive part another; at other times, as if the appetites were the desires and reason essentially a check and restraint upon them. But in fact we do not first have desires and then afterwards reason about them; we learn and we use our reason in learning-to desire certain things and the desire to quench one's thirst is as rational as the desire not to be injured by poison in the water.

It is just not true that only our restraint upon ourselves derives from reflection; it is often upon reflection that we decide that we need to drink. What makes a desire reasonable or unreasonable is its relation to our other purposes and choices, possible as well as actual. A man may behave unreasonably by not allowing his desires play and desire may on occasion correct an agent's would be rational assessments.

Allegiances

Plato's doctrinal allegiances lead him in the Republic not merely to draw false conclusions from the facts of conflict but also, as I have just suggested, to misdescribe them. Nor is Plato consistent here with his other writings. The Greek word for soul, means originally simply that which makes the difference between life and death, between a man and a corpse.

Some early Greek thinkers identify the soul with a material substance; the Pythagoreans with a harmony between the elements of the body, a balance. Plato argues against both in Phaedo that the soul is an immaterial simple substance; that to be destroyed is to be divided up into parts; and that since the soul has no parts it must be immortal.

The Platonic moral is that anger and appetite can conflict. The spirited part of the soul acts, when "it is not corrupted by a bad upbringing," as an agent of reason, being indignant when reason is overborne.

Men fall into three classes depending upon which part of the soul is dominant; this division is that required by the tripartite state. Into which class a man falls may in part be a matter of his early training, but cannot fundamentally be so determined. Plato believes that there are born shoemakers and born rulers. Justice in the state is a matter of everyone knowing his place. Temperance is a virtue not of a class, but of the society as a whole because "the desires of the inferior multitude will be controlled by the desires and wisdom of the superior few."

Justice in the Soul

Justice in the soul is likewise a matter of each part of the soul performing its proper and allotted function. An individual is wise in virtue of reason ruling in him and brave in virtue of the spirited part playing its role; an individual is temperate if his inferior bodily appetites are ruled by his reason. But justice belongs not to this that part or relationship of the soul, but to its total ordering.

When, later on, Plato comes to discuss the corruption of state and soul he treats them as belonging together. Moreover, the just man will rarely exist except in the just state, where at least some men the future rulers- are systematically educated in justice.

An Account of Knowledge

Plato defines a philosopher by setting out an account of knowledge and belief and then contrasting the philosopher, who knows, with the non-philosophical man, who at best has only true belief or opinion. The argument begins from considering the meaning of pairs of predicates and the examples used are beautiful and ugly, just and unjust and good and bad.

Plato says that "Since beautiful and ugly are opposite, they are two; and so each of them is one." But many things exhibit beauty and many things are ugly. So that there is a difference between those who are aware of this or that object as beautiful and those who grasp what 'beautiful itself' is. The identification comes about in this way. Plato makes just this mistake. The identification comes about in this way. Plato contrasts the man who uses the word beautiful in an ordinary, confused way with the man who has really grasped what beautiful means and he interprets this contrast as the contrast between the man who happens to be acquainted with a number of beautiful objects and the man who is acquainted with that which beautiful stands for. The former man is in possession only of 'belief'; his judgements are not reinforced by a well grounded understanding of the meaning of the expression which he uses. The latter is in possession of knowledge; for he really understands what he says.

On the Non-Existent

Gorgias was the author of a lost work On Nature or the Non-Existent. The presented a theory of being. It was at the same time refuted and parodied in the Eleatic thesis. The original text was lost and today there remain just two paraphrases of it. The first is preserved by philosopher Sextus Empiricus in Against the Professors and the other by the anonymous author of On **Melissus, Xenophanes** and **Gorgias**, Each work, excludes material that is discussed in the other, which suggests that each version may represent intermediary sources. It is clear, that the work developed a skeptical argument, which has been extracted form the sources and translated as below:

1. Nothing exists;
2. Even if something exists, nothing can be known about it; and
3. Even if something can be known about it, knowledge about it can't be communicated to others.
4. Even if it can be communicated, it cannot be understood.

The argument has been seen as an ironic refutation of Parmenides' thesis on Being. Gorgias set out to prove that it is as easy to demonstrate that being. Gorgias set out to prove that it is as easy to demonstrate that being is one, unchanging and timeless as it is to prove that being has no existence at all. It seems clear that Gorgias was focused instead on the notion that true objectivity is impossible since the human mind can never be separated form its possessor.

"How can anyone communicate the idea of color by means of words since the ear does not hear colors, but only sounds?" This quote, written by the Sicilian philosopher Gorgias, was used to show his theory that 'there is nothing,' 'it there were anything no one would know it', 'and if anyone did know it, no one could communicate it'. This argument has led some to label Gorgias a nihilist (one who believes nothing exists, or that the world is incomprehensible and that the concept of truth is fictitious).

Arguments Given by Gorgias

For the first main argument where Gorgias says, "there is on-thing" he also to persuade the reader and days that thought and existence are not the same. He claim that if thought and existence truly were the same, then everything that anyone thought world suddenly exist. Plato was regarded as the critics. Plato's dislike for sophistic doctrines is well known and it is in his eponymous dialogue that both Gorgias himself as well as his rhetorical beliefs are regarded as ridiculed. In the Gorgias, Plato distinguishes between philosophy and rhetoric. In the dialogue, Gorgias responds to one of Socrates' statements as follows; Rhetoric is the only area of expertise you need to learn.

Plato answers Gorgias by reaffirming the **Parmenidean idea** which says that being is the basic substance and reality of which all things are composed, insisting that philosophy is a dialectic distinct form and superior to rhetoric.

Every Judgement is Tautology

To sophists were interested in the refutation of the statements of their opponents. Naturally they concentrated on the logic of proof and contradiction. Most probably, following Eleatism, Protagoras had developed the theory of refutation. That is, any judgement can really be a tautology. For example.

This table is black.

Either, the predicate 'black' is the same as 'this table' or not. Quite obviously the predicate is quite different from its subject term. Hence, it tells us something of the subject term (this table) which it is not. So it is false. Similarly, whatever synthetic judgement we frame it becomes false. Hence, we are permitted to say, "This table is this table', which is really a tautology and really says nothing at all. Therefore, we cannot know anything at all.

The Socrates Age

Socratic School. Socrates [469-399 BCE], of Xenophon, the key figure in transforming Greek philosophy into a unified and continuous project is the one still being pursued today by many. The Socratic problem was to meet the challenge of sophistry, which, in undermining knowledge, threatened the foundations of morality and state." Socratic method: includes the elements: (1) skeptical, (2) conventional, (3) conceptual or definitional, (4) empirical or inductive, (5) deductive a "dialectical" process for improving understanding of a subject, he convinced that truth is in every man's heart.

This method of Socratics has two aspects: Ironic- it is a process to help clear notions. He approaches as if seeking knowledge, confesses his utter ignorance and asks questions. Maieutic (mid wifery) – drawing truth out of mind or art of delivering truth. This method helps to clear the mind of the inquirer of all over-hasty, inadequate and mistaken notions and prejudices. Thus philosophy is centred on truth and being. Every human being is pregnant with the truth and the teacher is nothing more than a helpful midwife. Man knows thyself and you will be virtuous. Knowledge is the highest good. Knowledge is virtue and ignorance is a vice. Self knowledge is the foundation of all true and certain knowledge. Self knowledge means the knowledge of powers hidden in the mind, pointing towards the existence of an innate knowledge. Knowledge is formed in the mind by the capacity of intellect which elaborates the findings of the senses.

Plato's Academy. The groundwork of Plato's scheme is the threefold division of philosophy into dialectic, ethics, and physics; its central point is the theory of forms. This theory is a combination of the Eleatic doctrine of the One with Heraclitus's theory of a perpetual flux and with the Socratic method of concepts. These forms are eternal, changeless and incorporeal which can be known only through thought. The things which we see around are only shadows or poor copies of the things that exist in the ideal world. The highest form is that of the Good, which is the ultimate basis of the rest, and the first cause of being and knowledge. Apprehensions derived from the impression of sense can never give us the knowledge of true being — *i.e.* of the forms. It can only be obtained by the soul's activity within itself, apart from the troubles and disturbances of sense; that is to say, by the exercise of reason. Dialectic, as the instrument in this process, leading us to knowledge of the ideas, and finally of the highest idea of the Good, is the first of sciences (*scientia scientiarum*).

The school founded by Plato, called the Academy (from the name of the grove of the Attic hero Academus where he used to deliver his lectures). Plato's Academy is often said to have been a school for would-be politicians in the ancient world, and to have had many illustrious alumni. In at least Plato's time, the school did not have any particular doctrine to teach; rather, Plato posed problems to be studied and solved by the others. There is evidence of lectures given, most notably Plato's lecture "On the Good" but probably the use of dialectic was more common. The academy was divided into three periods of the Old, Middle, and New Academy. The chief personages in the first of these were Speusippus (son of Plato's sister), who succeeded him as the head of the school (till 339 BCE), and Xenocrates of Chalcedon (till 314 BCE). Both of them sought to fuse Pythagorean speculations on number with Plato's theory of ideas. The two other Academies were still further removed from the specific doctrines of Plato, and advocated skepticism.

Aristotle's Peripatetic School

While Plato had sought to elucidate and explain things from the supra-sensual standpoint of the forms, his pupil preferred to start from the facts given us by experience. Philosophy to him meant science, and its aim was the recognition of the purpose in all things. Hence he establishes the ultimate grounds of things inductively — that is to say, by a posteriori conclusions from a number of facts to a universal. Matter is the basis of all that exists; it comprises the potentiality of everything, but of itself is not actually anything. A determinate thing only comes into being when the potentiality in matter is converted into actuality. This is effected by form, inherent in the unified object and the completion of the potentiality latent in the matter. For reason alone can attain to truth either in cognition or action. The end of human activity, or the highest good, is happiness, or perfect and reasonable activity in a perfect life. To this, however, external goods are more of less necessary conditions.

The followers of Aristotle, known as Peripatetics (Theophrastus, Strato of Lampsacus, Lyco of Troas, Aristo of Ceos, Critolaus Diodorus of Tyre,). The school originally derived its name Peripatos from the *peripatoi* ("colonnades") of the Lyceum gymnasium in Athens where the members met. A similar Greek word *peripatetikos* refers to the act of walking, and as an adjective, "peripatetic" is often used to mean itinerant, wandering, meandering, or walking about. The Peripatetic School tended to make philosophy the exclusive property of the learned class, thereby depriving it of its power to benefit a wider circle. This soon produced a negative reaction, and philosophers returned to the practical standpoint of Socratic ethics. The speculations of the learned were only admitted in philosophy where serviceable for ethics. The chief consideration was how to popularize doctrines, and to provide the individual, in a time of general confusion and dissolution, with a fixed moral basis for practical life.

MEDIEVAL PHILOSOPHY

ST. AUGUSTINE

Augustine is a fourth century philosopher who infused his Christian religious doctrine with Plato and Neo-Platonism. He is also famous for his contributions to Western philosophy along with Plato, Aristotle, and Aquinas. Augustine's doctrine stood between the extremes of Pelagianism and Manichaeism. Against Pelagian doctrine, he held that human spiritual disobedience had resulted in a state of sin that human nature was powerless to change. For him, human beings are dependent on divine grace; against Manichaeism he vigorously defended the place of free will in cooperation with grace.

Augustine, also known as Aurelius Augustine was born at Thagaste in North Africa. He was one of the key figures in the transition from classical antiquity to the middle Ages. He lived nearly eighty years of the social transformation, political upheavals, and military disasters that are often referred to as the 'decline of the Roman Empire.' Augustine was a confirmed Manichaean during his early years as a student and teacher of rhetoric at Carthage and Rome. But in Milan, during his early thirties, he began to study Neo-Platonic Philosophy under the guidance of Ambrose. An account of his early life and conversion, together with a reasoned defence of his Neo-platonic principles, may be found in the confessions (confessions). He was named the Bishop of Hippo (Annaba, Algeria) in 396, and devoted the remaining decades of his life to the formation of an ascetic religious community.

Problem of Evil

In order to maintain God's omnipotence, benevolent, omniscient and his goodness to man Augustine is driven to the position that is God is the cause of everything at the same time either he has to exclude the evil or explain it away. Evil is a fact of life, physical and moral. Physical evil can be allowed under the seminal good but what about the moral evil? As a metaphysician how can one explain it. He was not bound and compelled but rather his love inclined him to create. In other words creation is free act of God. Therefore existence if of every kind is good; one should judge its value in relation to the divine will, not from the point of view of human utility. And so even the evil must be good in its way. In other words evil is necessary for the enhancement of the greater good, in the same manner in which the shadow in the moon enhances the beauty of the full moon. The reason is that for Augustine even matter was created by God. Hence if matter be the cause of evil, then God will directly become the cause of evil. Secondly, God is omnipotent and so he could not be imagined to be limited by pre-existing matter. Evil is not good, but it is good that evil is Firstly, what appears as evil is not really evil. Secondly evil is conceived as a defect, as a privation of essence (privatio substantiae), as an omission of the good; for example, there is the evil of blindness; it is simply an absence of the power of vision; in due course this vision (or good) can be restored. Privation of good is evil because it means an absence of something nature ought to have. All kinds of evil including moral evil, are brought under the concept of privation. Moral evil cannot mar the beauty of universal creation, since it springs from the will of man or the fallen angels; it is the result of an evil or defective will, which is nothing positive, but merely represents a privation of good *(privatio boni)*. The worst evil is privation Dei, the turning away from God, or the highest good to the perishable world.

Moral Evil

The first man called Adam was given free will. He misused free will be his disobedience. He ate the forbidden fruit. He became a fallen man. A fallen man can produce only a fallen being. All the descendants of Adam have become fallen disobedient persons. They all are sinners. They all love the world. They have lost free will. Hence for the sin of one man, all have sinned. The is known as the doctrine of Original Sin. All have earned eternal hell-fire. Are they no longer free to rise? No.

A sinner cannot do real good, for real good means free act. Free will means free choice or decision for assent to a definite course of action. St. Augustine who taught the doctrine of indefeasible free will in man in his epistemology, now teaches its absolute denial in his theology. In his theory of knowledge, St. Augustine taught that not even sensation is possible without free will. In theology he restricts this free will only to one man Adam and denies this to all sub sequent human beings.

God by His Grace can redeem some men. Instead of being given to corruptible things, God by His Grace turns some men towards, Himself, preparing them for communion with God. It is God's doing and God's doing alone. Man cannot earn his Godward tendency. God's grace cannot be earned.

St. Augustine maintains the absolute freedom of God and as such cannot be questioned because of His absolute Goodness. No damned person can question this Grace, for he is absolutely corrupt and deserves no salvation but ultimate condemnation. But how do we know that a particular individual has been saved by His Grace? By receiving the baptism, sacrament (holy communion), fasting and prayer.

Epistemology

Augustine time and again attacks the sceptic thesis that a high degree of probability is the most that the human mind can attain. In other words man cannot attain certain knowledge. He refutes this thesis in his book Contra Academicos saying that a man can attain certain knowledge. In his reply to the question of scepticism 'how do you know that this world (even) exists, if the senses are mistaken?" He can refer to the world, so understood, and say, without chance of error, that either it is one or it is not. By which he means, even if it were true that I am mistaken about nearly everything that I suppose to be true, he argued, one inescapable truth will remain : "Si falloor, sum" ("If I am mistaken, Iexist"). His answer certainly suggests the Cartesian 'cogito, ergo sum.'

Conditions of Intellectual Knowledge

After having established knowledge is certain and it is attainable he moves on to the conditions of intellectual knowledge. There are two ways by which man can arrive at knowledge of intelligible objects viz., 1. By rising from the data of sense to an understanding of the hidden causes of things, and ultimately to a knowledge of Him who is the Highest Cause. 2. The truth is indwelling in us and the most excellent means of attaining higher intellectual knowledge is the contemplation and study of our own intellectual life. It is of introspection, for which purity of heart and the practice of virtue are necessary. Here Augustine rejects the Platonic doctrine of anamnesis as an explanation of the presence in the human mind of knowledge that is not derived from sense-experience. Knowledge is recollection, an exercise of the memory but in the sense that when I know I actualize what is learned in my mind, eliciting truths by a process of concentration. This sounds Platonian, but it is combined with a reluctance to believe in the pre-existence of the soul. Nor is the human mind able to realize knowledge unaided.

Theory of Divine Illumination

For Augustine, it is in the light of God, by which the mind is said to be able to discern the objects of intellectual vision. Some thinkers/readers have supposed that it is only a priori truths that Augustine thinks, are made intellectually visible by divine illumination. But it is not correct. When he teaches that we know the essences of things in rationibus aeternis, he is careful to point out that we rise from the data of sense or from a study of our own intellectual life to knowledge of these essences. Whether we are pointing to something to show what 'blue' means, or showing someone a blue colour sample to illustrate what the word signifies, any given effort at ostensive teaching is open to misunderstanding. How can one know whether what is being pointed out is the colour blue, a particular shade of blue, a hue, a coloured object, its shape, or something quite different?

Perhaps Augustine's idea of divine illumination is meant to invoke supernatural aid in dealing with the problem of ambiguity. Again, the inner Teacher, can perhaps, non-naturally, point to walking without pointing to hurrying, or to taking so and so many steps. If that is right, the learner who is intelligent enough will be precisely the one who is able to profit from this ambiguity free inner ostension that only the Divine, the Teacher can perform.

Concept of Man

Man is the calumniation of God's creation. He says man has soul using a mortal and earthly body as one unitary entity. For him, man is 'rational soul which has a body.' His identification of soul to human being reinforces the platonic tendency to identify the person with the mind of soul. He places human being beneath God and above bodies. Among the things it is nobler than sensible things which God created. 'There is something inferior and something equal; something inferior such as the soul of an animal, and something equal such as that of an angel, but there is nothing better." The soul is not what God is, but a creature made by God, made not out of God, but out of nothing. Though the human soul is immortal because it does not cease to live, it is in some sense mortal. For in every changeable nature the change itself is a death, because it causes something which was in it to exist no more. The soul as changeable in time, but not inplace, holds the mid-rank position below the highest and above the lowest.

Origin and Destiny of Soul

From the above paragraph it is very clear that God created the soul, it would mean that the soul of Man is created by God, now the question is that what about the subsequent souls of human being. It posed the problem for Augustine. To answer he listed four hypotheses concerning the origin of souls with a view of defending the justice of God, no matter which one would be correct one. There are as follows :

(a) One soul was created and from it the souls of those who are now born are drawn.

(b) Souls are individually created in each child who is born.

(c) Souls already existing in some secret place are sent by God to animate and rule the bodies of individuals who are born.

(d) Finally, the souls existing elsewhere are not sent by God, but 'come of their own accord to inhabit bodies.

To sum up this view souls come from propagation, created new in each individual; they exist elsewhere and are sent into the bodies of the newborn; or they exist elsewhere and fall of their own accord in these bodies. It is nonetheless, quite possible that he once thought that he knew the answer to the question about the soul, namely the souls existed before their embodiment and fell through sin into bodies or at least into these mortal bodies. He accepts the immortality of the soul and it is created by God. Here only three hypotheses regarding the origin of souls subsequent to Adam are present :

(a) All souls were created in the soul of Adam on the first day.

(b) All subsequent souls come from the soul of Adam by propagation.

(c) The new individual souls are created in the course of time.

The first two theories fit best with Genesis 2 : 2 which teaches that creation was completed on the sixth day, and with Sirach 18 : 1 which affirms that everything was created simultaneously. Hence the first hypothesis seems least problematic as representing Augustine's view at this point.

Concept of God

His understanding of God is influenced by Christian understanding of God, Platonism, and Manichaeism. Christian understanding : God is eternal, transcendent being, all powerful, created the world out of nothing, etc. Platonism: it provided him with important strategic and methodological principles for his thinking about the divine. Manichaeism: God to be a luminous amass extended infinitely through space; God is subject to attack, corruption, violation at the hands of rival power; again he believed that there were two independent divine substances in conflict with one another; his vision own allows him to see that the true God is being itself, the one source of everything exists, and He is true God Who is incorporeal and infinite without extension.

Augustine also believes God is incorruptible, inviolable, and immutable. But the interesting is that his ground of argument i.e. the supremacy of God. The same pattern of reasoning, mutatis mutandis, yields the divine inviolable and immutability. For Augustine, God is immutable, eternal, all-powerful, and all-knowing absolutely devoid of potentiality or composition, a pure spirit, a personal, intelligent being. The mystery of the Trinity of God induces Augustine to consider God as being, knowledge, and love, and since the world has been created by God, it reveals a reflection of these three attributes of God : every creature should consist essentially of being, knowledge and volition.

Proof for God's Existence

Augustine proves God's existence from a priori and a posteriori and point of view basing on the existence of reason. Because the essentially true character of the concepts of reason is the chief of the many witness to the existence of God.

A Priori Argument

Augustine began by proving that human reason exists, something with which no one could argue. He begins to prove that God exists by proving that there is something higher than reason - appears to rely on the assumption that what is higher than reason must be God.

A Posteriori Argument

In order to prove anything, we must first start with a foundation that is accepted as truth. Augustine beings with the platform that we exist. We cannot argue this because if we do, it is proving ourselves wrong. The mere fact that we can argue is a proof of our existence. Now he asks us if we understand these two steps to be true. If we do, then he has proven his next step, we have reason. For without reason, we could not understand these two basic concepts.

ST. ANSELM

Anselm was regarded as a devout Christian. He made sincere efforts to understand his Christian faith. Anselm followed St. Augustine and was regarded as a pronounced platonist. This concept is discussed in Anselm theory. He also accepted the priority and primacy of faith over reason. For him, faith is very important.

Saint Anselm of Canterbury (1033-1109) was regarding as outstanding Christian philosopher and theologian of the 11th century. He is also best known for the celebrated 'ontological argument' for the existence of God in chapter 2 of the Proslogion, but his contributions to philosophical theology go well beyond the ontological argument.

Ontological Argument

One of the most fascinating arguments for the existence of an all perfect God is the ontological argument. While there are several different versions of the argument, all purport to show that it is self-contradictory to deny that there exists a greatest possible being. This article explains and evaluates classic and contemporary versions of the ontological argument.

Most of the arguments for God's existence rely on at least one empirical premise. Likewise, cosmological arguments depend on certain empirical claims about the explanation for the occurrence of empirical events.

In contrast, the ontological arguments are conceptual in roughly the following sense : just as the propositions constituting the concept of a bachelor imply that every bachelor is male, the propositions constituting the concept of God, according to the ontological argument, imply that God exists. Even so, the basic idea is the same : ontological arguments attempt to show that we can deduce God's existence from, so to speak, the very definition of God.

1. The Non-Empirical Nature of the Ontological Arguments

It is worth reflecting for a moment on what a remarkable (and beautiful) undertaking it is to deduce God's existence from the very definition of God. Normally, existential claims don't follow from conceptual claims. I need to go out into the world and conduct some sort of empirical investigation using my senses. Likewise, if I want to prove that bachelors, unicorns, or viruses don't exist, I must do the same.

There is, however, one class of exceptions. We can prove certain negative existential claims merely by reflecting on the content of the concept. We can do so merely by consulting the definition and seeing, that it is self-contradictory. Thus, the very concepts imply that there exist no entities that are both square and circular.

The ontological argument, then, is unique among such arguments in that it purports to establish the real (as opposed to abstract) existence of some entity.

2. The Classic Version of the Ontological Argument

(a) The Argument Described

St. Anselm, Archbishop of Cantebury (1033-1109), is the originator of the ontological argument, which he describes in the Proslogium as follows :

[Even a] fool, when he hears of....a being than which nothing greater can be conceived...understands what he hears, and what he understands is in his understanding...And assuredly that, than which nothing greater can be conceived, cannot exist in the understanding alone. But obviously this is impossible. Hence, there is no doubt that there exists a being than which nothing greater can be conceived, and it exists both in the understanding and in reality.

(b) Gaunilo's Criticism

Gaunilo of Marmoutier, a monk and contemporary of Anselm's, is responsible for one of the most important criticisms of Anselm's argument. As the objection is sometimes put, Anselm simply defines things into existence-and this cannot be done.

Gaunilo shared this worry, believing that one could use Anselm's argument to show the existence of all kinds of non existent things :

Now if some one should tell me that there is .... an island [than which none greater can be conceived], I should easily understand his words, in which there is no difficulty. But suppose that he went on to say, as if by a logical inference: "You can no longer doubt that this island which is more excellent than all lands exists somewhere, since you have no doubt that it is in your understanding.

If it does not exist, any land which really exists will be more excellent than it; and so the island understood by you to be more excellent will not be more excellent."

C. Aquinas's Criticisms

While St. Thomas Aquinas (1224-1274) believed that God's existence is self-evident, he rejected the idea that it can be deduced from claims about the concept of God. Aquinas argued, plausibly enough, that "not everyone who hears this word 'God' understands it to signify something than which nothing greater can be thought, seeing that some have believed God to be a body."

The problem with this criticism is that the ontological argument can be restated without defining God. To see this, simply delete premise 1 and replace each instance of "God" with "A being than which none greater can be conceived."

One natural interpretation of this somewhat ambiguous passage is that Aquinas is rejecting premise 2 of Anselm's argument on the ground that, while we can rehearse the words "a being than which none greater can be imagined" in our minds, we have no idea of what this sequence of words really means. On this view, God is unlike any other reality known to us; while we can easily understand concepts of finite things, the concept of an infinitely great being dwarfs finite human understanding.

Nevertheless, the success of the argument doesn't depend on our having a complete understanding of the concept of a being than which none greater can be conceived. Consider, for example, that, while we don't have a complete understanding (whatever this means) of the concept of a natural number than which none larger can be imagined, we understand it well enough to see that there does not exist such a number.

3. Anselm's Second Version of the Ontological Argument

As it turns out, there are two different versions of the ontological argument in the Prosologium. The second version does not rely on the highly problematic claim that existence is a property and hence avoids many of the objections to the classic version.

God is that, than which nothing greater can be conceived.... And [God] assuredly exists so truly, that it cannot be conceived not to exist. For, it is possible to conceive of a being which cannot be conceived not to exist; and this is greater than one which can be conceived not to exist. But this is an irreconcilable contradiction. There is, then, so truly a being than which nothing greater can be conceived to exist, that it cannot even be conceived not to exist; and this being thou art, O Lord, our God.

This version of the argument relies on two important claims. As before, the argument includes a premise asserting that God is a being than which a greater cannot be conceived. But this version of the argument, unlike the first, does not rely on the claim that existence is a perfection; instead it relies on the claim that necessary existence is a perfection. Otherwise put, then, the second key claim is that a being whose non-existence is logically impossible is greater than a being whose non-existence is logically possible.

More formally, the argument is this:

1. By definition, God is a being than which none greater can be imagined.
2. A being that necessarily exists in reality is greater than a being that does not necessarily exist.
3. Thus, by definition, if God exists as an idea in the mind but does not necessarily exist in reality, then we can imagine something that is greater than God.
4. But we cannot imagine something that is greater than God.
5. Thus, if God exists in the mind as an idea, then God necessarily exists in reality.
6. God exists in the mind as an idea.
7. Therefore, God necessarily exists in reality.

This second version appears to be less vulnerable to Kantian criticisms than the first. Notice, for example, that the claim that x necessarily exists entails a number of claims that attribute particular properties to x. And this seems to entail that x has the reason for its existence in its own nature. But these latter claims clearly attribute particular properties to x.

And only a claim that attributes a particular property can entail claims that attribute particular properties. While the claim that x exists clearly entails that x has at least one property, this does not help. This distinguishes the claim that x exists from the claim that x necessarily exists and hence seems to imply that the latter, and only the latter, expresses a property.

Moreover, one can plausibly argue that necessary existence is a great-making property. To say that a being necessarily exists is to say that it exists eternally in every logically possible world; such a being is not just, so to speak, indestructible in this world, but indestructible in every logically possible world - and this does seem, at first blush, to be a great-making property. As Malcolm puts the point:

If a housewife has a set of extremely fragile dishes, then as dishes, they are inferior to those of another set like them in all respects except that they are not fragile. There is a definite connection between the notions of dependency and inferiority, and independence and superiority. To say that something which was dependent on nothing whatever was superior to anything that was dependent on any way upon anything is quite in keeping with the everyday use of the terms superior and greater.

Nevertheless, the matter is not so clear as Malcolm believes. It might be the case that, other things being equal, a set of dishes that is indestructible in this world is greater than a set of dishes that is not indestructible in this world. From our perspective, there is simply nothing to be gained by adding transworld indestructibility to a set of dishes that is actually indestructible.

And the same seems to be true of God. Suppose that an omniscient, omnipotent, omnibenevolent, eternal (and hence, so to speak, indestructible), personal God exists in this world but not in some other worlds. It is very hard to make sense of the claim that such a God is deficient in some relevant respect. God's indestructibility in this world means that God exists eternally in all logically possible worlds that resemble this one in certain salient respects. From our perspective, necessary existence adds nothing in value to eternal existence. If this is correct, then Anselm's second version of the argument also fails.

ST. THOMAS AQUINAS

Faith and Reason

From the beginning Thomistic philosophy we can notice a steady exploration of the relation between faith and reason, with systematic and complete analysis of this relation. He filled his writings with reason, especially in his Summa Theologica. His vision about the relation between faith and reason can be summarized under three points.

Faith and reason are two different modes of knowing. Reason accepts a truth as known by the light of reason. Faith accepts a truth as known by the light of divine revelation.

The distinction between theology and philosophy does not consist in the fact that theology treats of God, for philosophy also treats of God and divine truths. The distinction consists rather in this, that theology views truth in the light of divine revelation, while philosophy views truth in the light of human reason.

Faith and reason do not contradict. They have their respective juridical boundaries. Truths of faith and truths of reason derive from the same origin, god who is the Truth.

God is the source of all truth. He communicates it to us directly by revelation and indirectly by giving us the power by which we acquire it. Science acquired in the former manner would be divine and it is through experience and reason is human.

Faith and reason are complementary. Faith renders valuable service to reason by elevating the mind on its natural functioning. Reason, in turn renders a valuable service to faith by the role it plays in theology. Reason can come to the aid of faith in various ways. Reason can also use philosophy to refute doctrines contrary to the faith.

For Aquinas, philosophy helps theology in as much as it enables the theologian to deduce scientific conclusions from articles of faith. Theology serves philosophy in as much as it acts as a guide or as a light upon that of the philosopher showing him fields of research and making him convinced of the limitations of his powers. He insisted that reason and faith are not contrary but are two distinct sources of knowledge, both ultimately from god. Some Truth comes through man's reason, some through God's revelation.

Essence and Existence

It has been said that everything has two principles like of essence and existence. Both essence and existence are regarded useful for the existing individual thing. Each is regarded as distinct from the other. This distinction is regarded as real. Aristotle gives matter and form as two realistic thing. According to St. Thomas, all the existences of same essences are regarded as same. They are regarded as different because of their different accidental attributes.

St. Thomas says that essences exist in the divine mind only. Essences exist before the creation of individual things. Essences are regarded as universals, whereas existence is regarded as individual entity. Essence is described as that what of a thing, whereas existence is regarded as the act of being which is exercised only by beings. According to Thomas, form and existence are regarded as same.

Distinction between Essence and Existence

Aquinas makes a distinction between essence and existence in order to solve the problem of universals. Essence is regarded as something which is common to all natures.

Existence means something real being. It has been also said that we can think about and essence without thinking of it as actually excising. It has been also said that everything whose existence in other than its nature get its existence from something other than itself. God's essence is regarded as his existence. God's essence and existence are taken as identical. God is also regarded as simple.

According to Aquinas, existence along with essence means "what intellect first conceives". It has been said that the only other thing that the intellect first conceives is regarded as essence only.

The Existence of God

The proofs for the existence of God are also means of knowing something of God's essence. This knowledge, however, remains always essentially inadequate and incomplete. In other words, by this method we arrive at the knowledge of God through considering what He is not.

A second method is that of analogy. God is the cause of the world. Now every object reflects some perfection of the cause from which it proceeds. Hence it is possible for the human mind to rise to the perfections of God from the consideration of the perfection it finds in creatures. The resultant idea of the nature of God is thus had through analogy with the perfections of the created universe.

But, according to Aquinas, any natural intuitive knowledge of God is precluded to man. For us, only the visible world, which is capable of impressing our senses, the object of natural intuitive knowledge. Such demonstrations are possible and are accommodated to anyone who is simply capable of reflecting.

There are five ways in which the human intellect can prove the existence of God. All have a common point of resemblance. The starting point is a consideration of the sensible world known by immediate experience. Such a consideration of the sensible world would remain incomprehensible unless it was related to God as author of the world. All his proofs for the existence of God bring two distinct elements into play:

1. The existence of a sensible reality whose existence requires a cause;
2. The demonstration of the fact that its existence requires a finite series of causes and consequently a prime cause, which is what we call God.

The Five Ways to Prove the Existence of God

- **Movement.** Movement is any transit, any change from one state of being to another. According to Aristotle 'Movement is a passage from potency to act.' Thus, if there is a movement ultimately there should be a mover; as we know there is a movement. Therefore, there is an ultimate mover whom we call God.
- **Causality.** A cause is anything that contributes to the producing of a thing. That which is produced by cause is effect. God alone can be attributed as creator because He creates everything out of nothing. Therefore, there is a cause, ultimately the First Cause whom we call God.
- **Contingency.** Contingency means dependency. Our existence is not of our own. We have received it from the one who has existence on his own; He is God alone. So we are contingent (dependent) beings. But God is self sufficient; such self sufficient being is necessary. Therefore, there should be a necessary being whom we call God.
- **Grades of perfection.** We see in the life on the world some things are more perfect, better; at the same time some are not like that; thus the grades of perfection (e.g. stone, vegetation, animal kingdom, human kingdom, and god). If there are grades of perfection, there should be a higher perfection; as we know there exists grades of perfection.
- **Teleological (order and purpose).** This is an argument from the design. Paley argues that the natural world is as complex a mechanism, and as manifestly designed as any watch. The rotation of the planets in the solar system and, on earth, the regular procession of the seasons and the complex structure and mutual adaptation of the parts of a living organism, all suggest design. In a human brain, for example, thousands of millions of cells functions together in a coordinated system. The eye is a superb movie camera, with self-adjusting lenses, a high degree of accuracy, colour sensitivity, and the capacity to operate continuously for many hours at a time. Thus according to him nothing is created by chance but well planned and with a purpose.

Philosophy of Human Soul and Goal of Human Life

Besides God, the spiritual substances are the angels and human souls. Angels are not destined to inform any matter; the human soul, on the contrary, is ordered to be the form of the body. Hence the question arises as to the nature of the soul and its relations with the body. Some of man's activities are obviously very like to those of brutes, but the intellectual and volitional functions transcend materiality by virtue of their universal and abstracted character.

The soul is a real part of man and, it is spiritual. The intellect and the will are the faculties of the soul, the means through which it operates. The intellect has for its object the knowledge of the universe, and operates by judging and reasoning.

From an analysis of the intellect and the will, Aquinas proves the spirituality, the simplicity, and the immortality of the soul. The intellect has, in fact, for its proportionate object the universal, the understanding of which is a simple and spiritual act. Since it is simple and spiritual, it is by nature also immortal. The will also is free, i.e., not determined by any cause outside itself. In the physical world everything is determined by causal necessity, and hence there is no liberty. The soul upon which such a faculty depends must be of the same nature as the faculty; that is, the soul must be immaterial.

The human soul since it is immaterial and performs acts which are not absolutely dependent upon the bodily organs, does not perish with the body—although, as Aquinas says, the soul separated from the body is not entirely complete but has an inclination to the body as the necessary instrument for its complete and full activity. The doctrine of Aquinas concerning the soul in general and the human soul in particular, may be summed as follows: When the form in matter is the origin of immanent actions, it gives origin to life and as such is more particularly called the "soul." Superior to the vegetative is the sensitive soul, which is present in animals; besides the processes of nutrition, growth and reproduction the sensitive soul is capable of sensitive knowledge and appetite. Superior still to the sensitive soul is the rational soul.

The rational soul is created directly by God; it is distinct for each man; it is the true form of the body.

Goal of Human Life

In Thomas's thought, the goal of human existence is union and eternal fellowship with God. Specifically, this goal is achieved through the beatific vision, an event in which a person experiences perfect, unending happiness by seeing the very essence of God.

This ultimate goal carries implications for one's present life on earth. Thomas stated that an individual's will must be ordered toward right things, such as charity, peace, and holiness. He sees this as the way to happiness. Thomas orders his treatment of the moral life around the idea of happiness. Those who truly seek to understand and see God will necessarily love what God loves. Such love requires morality and bears fruit in everyday human choices.

Theory of Knowledge

Knowledge, when we reflect upon it as a fact of psychic life, presents itself to us as an extension of the knower. The knower possesses both his own nature and the nature of the thing he knows. Knowledge liberates and extends the self, so that it possesses the other. Knowledge in its very actuality is liberation from the confines of matter. Knowledge is a spiritual act uniting the knower with the thing known.

Thomas Aquinas holds the Aristotelian doctrine that knowing entails some similarities between knower and the known; a human's corporeal nature therefore requires that knowledge starts with sense perception. The same limitation does not apply to beings further up the chain of being, such as angels. God's essence is identified with his existence as pure actuality. God is simple containing no potentiality.

The Thomistic theory of knowledge is realistic. Men obtain their knowledge of reality from the initial data of sense experience, apart from supernatural experiences that some mystics may have. Agreeing with Aristotle, Thomas limited human cognition to "sense perception" and "intellectual understanding" of it, which are intimately related to one another. He distincts the sources of knowledge; the first one is the sense experiences or empiricism, the second one is the intellectual or the rational knowledge. Since both are in potency – the sense, toward the individual form; and the intellect, toward the form of the universal.

- Sense experience is acquired through the sense organs. Sense organs are stimulated by the coloured, audible, odours, gustatory and tactical qualities of extra mental bodies; and sensation is the vital response through man's five external sense powers to such stimulation.
- Aquinas assumed that man's cognitive is aware of red flowers, noisy animals, and cold air and so on. Internal sensation works to perceive, retain, associate, and judge the various impressions (the phantasm) through which things are directly known. Man's higher cognitive functions, those of understanding, judging and reasoning have as their objects the universal meanings that arise out of sense experience.

According to Thomas Aquinas, this is just what happens through the action of a special power of the intellect, *i.e.*, the power by which the phantasm (sense image) is illuminated. Under the influence of this illumination, the form loses its materiality; that is, it becomes the essence or intelligible species.

For Aquinas all the data of sense knowledge and all intelligible things are essentially true. Truth consists in the equality of the intellect with its object, and such concordance is always found, both in sensitive cognition and in the idea. Error may exist in the judgment, since it can happen that a predicate may be attributed to a subject to which it does not really belong.

Besides the faculty of judgment, Aquinas also admits the faculty of discursive reasoning, which consists in the derivation of the knowledge of particulars from the universal. Deductive, syllogistic demonstration must be carried out according to the logical relationships which exist between two judgments. However, he believed that human beings have the natural capacity to know many things without special Divine Revelation, even though such revelation occurs from time to time, "especially in regard to a faith."

MODERN WESTERN PHILOSOPHY

Rationalism is a philosophical movement which gathered momentum during the Age of Reason of the 17th Century. It is usually associated with the introduction of mathematical methods into philosophy during this period by the major rationalist figures, Descartes, Leibniz and Spinoza. The preponderance of French Rationalists in the 18th Century Age of Enlightenment, including Voltaire, Jean-Jacques Rousseau and Charles de Secondat (Baron de Montesquieu) (1689 - 1755), is often known as French Rationalism.

Rationalism is any view appealing to intellectual and deductive reason (as opposed to sensory experience or any religious teachings) as the source of knowledge or justification. It relies on the idea that reality has a rational structure in that all aspects of it can be grasped through mathematical and logical principles, and not simply through sensory experience.

Rationalists believe that, rather than being a *"tabula rasa"* to be imprinted with sense data, the mind is structured by, and responds to, mathematical methods of reasoning. Some of our knowledge or the concepts we employ are part of our innate rational nature: experiences may trigger a process by which we bring this knowledge to consciousness, but the experiences do not provide us with the knowledge itself, which has in some way been with us all along. See the section on the doctrine of Rationalism for more details.

Rationalism is usually contrasted with Empiricism (the view that the origin of all knowledge is sense experience and sensory perception), and it is often referred to as Continental Rationalism because it was predominant in the continental schools of Europe, whereas British Empiricism dominated in Britain.

Although Rationalists asserted that, in principle, all knowledge, including scientific knowledge, could be gained through the use of reason alone, they also observed that this was not possible in practice for human beings, except in specific areas such as mathematics.

It has some similarities in ideology and intent to the earlier Humanist movement in that it aims to provide a framework for philosophical discourse outside of religious or supernatural beliefs. But in other respects there is little to compare.

René Descartes is one of the earliest and best known proponents of Rationalism, which is often known as Cartesianism (and followers of Descartes' formulation of Rationalism as Cartesians). He believed that knowledge of eternal truths (*e.g.* mathematics and the epistemological and metaphysical foundations of the sciences) could be attained by reason alone, without the need for any sensory experience.

Descartes held that some ideas (innate ideas) come from God; others ideas are derived from sensory experience; and still others are fictitious (or created by the imagination). Of these, the only ideas which are certainly valid, according to Descartes, are those which are innate.

Baruch Spinoza expanded upon Descartes' basic principles of Rationalism. His philosophy centred on several principles, most of which relied on his notion that God is the only absolute substance (similar to Descartes' conception of God), and that substance is composed of two attributes, thought and extension.

Gottfried Leibniz attempted to rectify what he saw as some of the problems that were not settled by Descartes by combining Descartes' work with Aristotle's notion of form and his own conception of the universe as composed of monads.

During the middle of the 20th Century there was a strong tradition of organized Rationalism (represented in Britain by the Rationalist Press Association, for example), which was particularly influenced by free thinkers and intellectuals. It accepted the supremacy of reason but insisted that the results be verifiable by experience and independent of all arbitrary assumptions or authority.

RENE DESCARTES

René Descartes was born in 1596 at La Haye, Touraine in central France. He was the son of a minor nobleman and belonged to a family that had produced a number of learned men. Besides the usual classical studies, Descartes received instruction in mathematics and scholasticism, which attempted to use human reason to understand Christian doctrine.

Upon finishing school, he studied law at the University of Poitiers, graduating in 1616. He never practised law, however; in 1618 he entered the service of Prince Maurice of Nassau, leader of the United Provinces of the Netherlands, with the intention of following a military career.

One of the important influences on Descartes during this period was Dutch mathematician Isaac Beeckman, who encouraged him to pursue his studies.

On November 10, 1619 he had three consecutive dreams which convinced that his mission was to seek truth by reason and vowed to make a pilgrimage to the shrine of Our Lady at Loreto In Italy.

But he went there in 1623. He lived for a while in Paris where he enjoyed the friendship of men like Mercenre and Cardinal de Berulle. Finding Paris life too distracting, in 1628 he retired to Holland where he remained till 1649.

In Holland, Descartes worked at his system, and by 1634 he had completed a scientific work called Le Monde (the world). When he heard, however, of the condemnation of Galileo for teaching the Copernican system, as did Le Monde, he immediately had the book suppressed. The Swedish winter proved too harsh for Descartes and the Queen's habit of having his tuition at 5 in the morning was too much for him.

Conception of Method

Descartes was very much concerned with the enquiry into the method of philosophising. He had proposed to lay down thirty six rules of which he mentioned thirty one in the Regulae. The object of Cartesian methodology was to apply mathematical method of philosophy with a view to obtaining certitude in knowledge. As a result of his enquiry, he laid down four broad rules for his self-guidance.

1. Never to accept anything as true unless I clearly know it as such.

   Descartes believes that errors arise from poorly comprehended experiences or from hasty, groundless and preconceived notions. The only remedy, therefore, he thinks, lies in resolute refusal to believe in what is not clearly and distinctly perceived.

2. Divide up each of the difficulties, under examination into as many parts as possible.

   We begin with something vague and indefinite and later on, step by step, attain clearness and distinctness.

3. Commerce with the simplest objects and ascend, step by step to the more complex.

   The explanation must be ordered and systematic. Here Descartes is in favour of deductive use in philosophical thinking, for he implies that later steps should be clearly deducible from earlier ones.

4. In every case make the enumeration so complete that I might be assured that nothing was omitted.

   The complex thing can be understood when we know its (i) several constituent factors separately, clearly and distinctly, and when we (ii) know the order or system in which they are found. Therefore, the first task of philosophy is analytic, the second synthetic.

Need for Method

Descartes was very much worried by the uncertain state of philosophy in his times. He saw that philosophy was cultivated for many centuries by the best minds that had ever lived and there was yet not a single proposition in it which was not under dispute. However, Descartes did not despair of knowledge, and knowledge for him, must attain a certitude equal to that of the demonstrations of Arithmetic and Geometry. This knowledge, he thought, could be attained if we use an appropriate method of enquiry. Seeing that knowledge proper has already been attained in Arithmetic and Geometry, he was surprised to find that philosophers had not reared a lofty edifice on such a firm and solid foundation. However, it was the method and not the subject-matter so much which had enabled mathematics to attain certitude. So Descartes attempted to understand the method of mathematics which could be utilised for advancing knowledge in any subject. He called his own enquiry as 'Universal Mathematics' in Rule IV of his *Regulae.* This will be called 'meta-mathematics' today. "Such a science", according to Descartes, "should contain the primary rudiments of human reason, and its province ought to extend to the eliciting of true results in every subject."

Clarity and Distinctness

Criterion for Truth

Descartes says that clarity and distinctness are regarded as the criterion of truth and as well as the criterion of doubt and methodological scepticism. He says that by a clear perception, he means that which is present and open to the attending mind. That kind of perception is contained in itself only.

He says that an idea must be present to the mind, open to the mind and as well as the mind also must attend to it. This whole procedure is regarded as clarity. He uses clearness and distinctness for the representative functions of ideas.

An idea is regarded as clear, when the mind includes in it that content, which is referred as integral and complete. It is also regarded as distinct when the content of the mind includes nothing other that this. So, clarity and distinctness are regarded as the criterion of truth and as well as the criterion of such doubt and methodological scepticism

Doubt to Reveal Truth

Descartes says that the single certain truth is regarded as a deliberate doubt. It has been also said that doubt when pushed to its farthest limited way, then it is able to reveal something, which is regarded as indubitable. So, he says that sense-testimony can be doubted. Even the truths of science can be doubted But that I doubt cannot be doubted.

'The I Doubt'

It has been said that 'I doubt' cannot be doubted because it is referred as a self-evident truth. It has been also said that I may doubt anything', but I cannot doubt that 'I am doubting'. According to Descartes, I must exist always as a doubting or thinking being.

It is also referred as cogito, ergo sum. The doubt of Descartes and psychological doubt are regarded as different.

Descartes doubt is not regarded as a thing of direct experience, but psychological doubt is regarded as a thing of direct experience. Descartes doubt is not directly determined by the nature of objects, but psychological doubt is caused by the nature of object.

Doubt and Scepticism

It has been said that Descartes doubt should not be confused with scepticism. He is not asserting that whatever can be doubted is regarded as false.

The scepticism denies any certain knowledge whatsoever. It finishes the conclusion about knowledge. So, clarity and distinctness are regarded as the criterion of methodological scepticism. Method with scepticism goes together.

Doubt and Methodological Scepticism

Now how can we find something which is sure and certain? Descartes believes that the single, certain truth can be systematically sought be deliberate doubt. When doubt is pushed to its farthest limited then it will reveal something which is indubitable, which is clearly perceived. Now in order to discover the indubitable intuition, let us doubt all that can be doubted.

(i) **Sense-testimony can be doubted.** Things of our daily life like tables, chairs, etc., we know through the senses. But the senses deceive us as is clear from illusions, hallucinations etc. Now prudence demands that we should not rely on things which deceive us even once.

(ii) **Even the truths of science can be doubted.** At this stage, it might be objected that the truth of sciences like 2 + 2 = 4 cannot be doubted, even in dreams. However, the case does not seem to be quite clear. We cannot know whether any truth of knowledge is at all intended for us finite beings; whether God has not created us rather for mere opinion and error. Besides, who knows there might be no God at all. There might be a demon at once potent and malignant who tricks us to believe in falsehood.

That **I doubt cannot be doubted**. When the doubt has done its worst it finds a fact of completely unassailable certainty. I may doubt anything but I cannot doubt that I am doubting. Whether it be a dream or a real consciousness, I must exist as a doubting or thinking being. Let there be a demon to deceive me, but then I must exist as a thinking being to be deceived. Hence, I doubt or think, therefore, I exist, *i.e.*, cogito crgo sum is the one certain truth which may be taken as the foundation of philosophy.

The doubt of Descartes should not be confused with psychological doubt. For example, in darkness, when a small creature crosses our path, we may doubt whether it was a mouse or a mole. The two may be thus contrasted.

Descartes's Doubt	Psychological Doubt
1. It is not a thing of direct feeling and experience but is a deliberate and dispassionate attitude towards human experience in general.	1. This is directly felt and experienced by us as such, as in the previous example.
2. It is not directly determined by the nature of objects.	2. It is caused by the nature of object about which we want to know.
3. The logical doubt of Descartes is deliberate, depending on the will.	3. It is independent of our will. However, hard we may will, the doubt continues.
4. This is concerned with attitude towards total things or ultimate things.	4. It is concerned with particular things of daily life.

Again, the doubt of Descartes should not be confused with Scepticism. Descartes is not asserting that whatever can be doubted is false, but he is only supposing it to be false. Again, the scepticism is the finished conclusion about knowledge which professes the denial of any certain knowledge whatsoever. However, the Cartesian doubt is only a starting point to find out that which cannot be further doubted.

The Cogito-Intuition or Inference

Descartes did not try to establish Inference. He wanted to establish a simple fact of a self-evident axiom. He says that an inference is depended on premises for its certainty. And this would lead to infinite regress. This infinite regress doesn't reach to the indubitable truth.

The certainty of the Cogito is regarded as clear and distinct. It has been said that nothing else could be intuited with the same certainty. This is also regarded as the indubitable truth of the inseparability of thought and thing.

My being' implied in my being conscious is regarded as the first principle and this principle is referred as both logical and psychological. The term 'therefore' is regarded as unfortunate. It bed to the interpretation of the cogito as an inference.

Descartes Notion. According to Descartes if a notion is complete, *i.e.*, is such that from it a reason can be given for all According to Descartes, the predicates of the subject to which this notion can he attributed, this will be the notion of an individual substance and conversely. A reason can be given from the notion of the individual substance and from it alone, as it is clear from the second axiom. The notion which affords this is the notion of the individual substance.

What Descartes tried to establish is not an inference but a simple fact of primitive knowledge or a self-evident axion. Had it been an inference, then it would be merely dependent on premises for its certainty and then again these premises on other premises for their certainty. This would lead to infinite regress without reaching the indubitable truth. However, the certainty of the cogito is clear and distinct, and, that nothing else could be perceived or intuited with the same certainty. *Cogito ergo sum* means that my consciousness is the means of revealing myself as something existing. Here is the indubitable truth of the inseparability of thought and thing. My being implied in my being conscious is the first principle both logically and psychologically. Of course the use of the term 'therefore' was unfortunate for it led to the interpretation of the *cogito* as an inference. However, 'therefore' primarily means a step in inference but secondarily it means a relation of necessary connection. Descartes uses the term 'therefore' in the secondary sense.

Innate Ideas

It has been said that no sense-experience can give us universal knowledge. The universal principle is supplied by the mind to the sense data. The doctrine of innate ideas says that mind is not regarded as totally receptive. It is also regarded as active. Innate ideas supplies the active formative principles of knowledge. Kant says that general principles and concepts, are regarded as an inherent contribution of the mind to the sense-data.

Descrates was vague in regard of his doctrine of innate ideas. He recognised that the dual mode of innate ideas. It has been said that the essence of the mind is regarded as consciousness, that's why certain ideas belongs only to mind alone. The innate ideas have the feature of clearness and distinctness. Innate ideas is also referred as pure and abstract thoughts. Descartes extend the innateness to sense ideas. They are caused by something external and this something external goes to the mind.

The sense-experience belongs to the physical existence. The sense experience is not found in objects. The ideas of sense must be regarded as natural and this natural ideas belongs to the mind. Innateness become characteristics of every idea, according to Descrates.

The 'Real' Distinction between Mind and Matter

Descartes method of Cogito ergo sum is regarded as a method of abstraction. He also talks about not essential things that are found in thinking. He also discards these things and arrives to consciousness. It has been said that in order to know consciousness, we don't need extension.

By extension, he refers matter. Consciousness and extension is referred as mind and body. Mind and body are regarded as independent of one another. They do not involve each other's existence. It has been said that there are two independent substances and these two independent substances are referred as mind and body.

It has been said that dualism of mind and body is important. Because human beings have both body and soul. Machine moving principle is regarded as the heat, which is found in the heart. It has been said that the death comes because of the destruction of some important parts of the body machine.

God alone by a special creation adds soul in human beings. It has been said that no real relation between body and soul exist. Both are regarded as diametrically opposed.

Rene Descartes. Rene Descartes often called 'The father of modern philosophy' shaped the view that humans are distinctly different from other animals and rest of the natural world. In Descartes, view, language and reason are the features the set humans apart from all other species-using the principle of parsimony, Descartes argues that the observed behaviours of all non-human features can be explained without as ascribing minds and consciousness to them.

Role of God

We should rehabilitate the world, which the doubt has destroyed. Ideas are regarded as true or false because they have the criterion of clearness and distinctness. This being is regarded as omnipotent, source of all goodness and truth and creator of all things.

This innate being also have perfection and this perfection is regarded as infinite. This idea of innate being is caused by an equally perfect cause. This equally perfect cause also refers the infinitely perfect being. God is referred as the infinitely perfect being.

Mind and matter are dependent on God. Mind and matter are regarded as two relative substances.

Clarity and Distinctness as the Criterion of Truth

Descartes says, "A clear perception I call that which is present and open to the attending mind, just as we say that those things are clearly seen by us which, being present to the regarding eye, move it sufficiently strongly and openly. But that perception is distinct which is not only clear but is so precise and so separated from all others that it plainly contains in itself nothing other than which is clear."

Hence to be clear an idea must be *present* to the mind, *open* to the mind and the mind also must *attend* to it. Similarly, distinct is that which is precisely determined so that it may not be confused with anything else. Again, Descartes uses clearness and distinctness in relation to the representative functions of ideas also. Now an idea is clear when the mind includes in it that content, which is 'integral and complete' in relation to the mind's interpretation of it, and it is distinct when the content of the idea includes nothing other than this. For example, the idea of God is clear when it includes all that which goes to constitute the idea of God, and distinct when it includes nothing else.

Regarding truth, Descartes says that if idea of a thing is clear and distinct, it does not mean that the thing really exist (true); but all the ideas of existent things must be clear and distinct to be existent. Our judgments should be based on this assumption, *i.e.*, clarity and distinctness as the criterion of truth.

Role of God

Let us try to rehabilitate the world which the doubt has destroyed. Now with the criterion of clearness and distinctness let us see which ideas are true or false. Now ideas are either innate or those derived from outside or are pure inventions. But of all the ideas there is one innate idea of being who is 'eternal, omniscient, omnipotent, source of all goodness and truth, creator of all things and in sum having in himself all those things in which we can clearly note some perfection which is infinite, or tainted by no imperfection. Now what can be the cause of this idea? At least the cause must be equal to the effect. I cannot be the cause for I know myself to be finite being. Hence this idea must have been caused by an equally perfect cause, namely, the infinitely perfect being called God.

God is the absolute of metaphysics on which everything depends, but which depends on nothing else. He is independent substance on which mind and matter, the two relative substances, depend. He is eternal, omnipotent, omniscient, creator of all things and source of all goodness and truth.

Existence of God

We now have a fundamental principle and a criterion of true knowledge. What else can we know? It is doubtful whether anything can be certain, so long as we are confronted with the possibility of a deceiving God; we do not know as yet whether there is a God, and, if there is, that he is not a deceiver. Certain ideas we regard as effects or copies of an external world. But all this may be illusion. One of the ideas I find in myself is the idea of God. Now, nothing can come from nothing, whatever exists must have a cause for existing; this, too, is a self-evident proposition. The principle of Descartes argument is actually the long established principle of medieval philosophy is that ex nihilo nihil fit: out of nothing can come nothing. Hence, I myself cannot be the cause of the idea of God, for I am a finite, imperfect being, while the idea of God is the idea of a perfect, infinite being. It must have been placed in me by an infinite being, or God, and hence God must exist.

This proof for the existence of God is not the ontological proof of Anselm, but a causal proof, which begins with the idea of a perfect being existing in my mind. The argument differs from the ontological proof in two respects: (1) its starting point is not the concept of God as a formal essence, but the actual existing idea of God in the mind of a man; (2) it proceeds by causal inference from the idea of God to God himself and not, as in the case of the ontological argument, by strict formal implication from the essence of God to his existence. This cannot be so, according to Descartes, for the idea of finitude implies the idea of infinity, or of God; how could I doubt or have desires if I did not have in myself the idea of a being more perfect than myself, by comparison with whom I recognize the defects of my nature? Doubt implies a standard of truth, imperfection a standard of perfection. Again, I could not have been the cause of my own existence; for I have an idea of perfection, and if I had created myself. If my parents had created me, they could also preserve me, which is impossible.

Finally, it also follows from the very notion of God as a perfect being that he exists. It is not in my power to conceive a God without existence, that is, a being supremely perfect and yet devoid of an absolute perfection. This is the ontological argument used by both Anselm and Augustine they would not be perfect; to be perfect there must be one cause only, one God. God must be self caused, for if he is the effect of another being, then that being is the effect of another, and so on ad infinitum: we have an infinite regress and never can reach a causal explanation of the effect with which we began. The idea of God I have received from God; it is innate. God is not only the cause, but the archetype of our existence; he has created man in his own image. If God did not exist, we could not possibly be what we are, nor could we have an idea of God. We know more of God himself and of the human mind than we know of corporeal objects.

Reflecting upon the idea of God, we perceive that he is eternal, omniscient, omnipotent, the source of all goodness and truth; the creator of all things. He is not corporeal and does not perceive by means of the senses, as we do. He has intellect and will, but not like ours; and he does not will evil or sin, for sin is the negation of being. This is the usual theistic position with which we have become acquainted in scholasticism. Descartes agrees with Duns Scotus that we can accept reason only in so far as it does not conflict with revelation. He also holds with him that God could have arranged the world otherwise than it is; and that a thing is good because God makes it so; he does not make it so because it is good.

Innate Ideas

Descartes distinguishes three kinds of ideas namely those that are fabricated, adventitious, or innate. Fabricated ideas are mere inventions of the mind. Adventitious ideas are sensations produced by some material thing existing externally to the mind. But, unlike fabrications, adventitious ideas cannot be examined and set aside at will nor can their internal content be manipulated by the mind. For example, no matter how hard one tries, if someone is standing next to a fire, he cannot help but feel the heat as heat. He also cannot change its internal content so as to feel something other than heat—say, cold. Finally, innate ideas are placed in the mind by God at creation. These ideas can be examined and set aside at will but their internal content cannot be manipulated. Geometrical ideas are paradigm examples of innate ideas. Other examples of innate ideas would be metaphysical principles like "what is done cannot be undone," the idea of the mind, and the idea of God.

The aim of Descartes is to reach clear and certain knowledge, such as arises when we judge that it is impossible for a thing to be otherwise than as we conceive it. Certainty is a property of truths which are clearly and distinctly perceived. Now, certain knowledge cannot spring from the senses, for the senses do not reveal what things are in themselves, but only how they affect us. If we cannot derive true knowledge from sense experience, if genuine knowledge is the result of reasoning from certain basic concepts and principles, these must be inherent in the mind itself- *i.e.*, innate or a priori. The mind has its own standards or norms, which guide it in the pursuit of truth. Principles of knowledge can become explicit only in the course of experience, as the mind exercises itself in thought, but they are somehow present from the beginning.

By innate knowledge he means at times ideas or truths impressed upon the mind, principles which the soul finds in itself, and at other times, the native capacity of the soul to produce such knowledge in the course of human experience.

Mind and Body

Descartes maintains that we do indeed have both minds and bodies- and that the two are not ultimately one and the same thing, but rather are radically and irreducibly different sorts of thing, which exist in an intimate union. Attribute of body is extension. These two substances are absolutely distinct. Mind/ soul is *res cogitans*; as far as I am a thinking and unextended thing I have clear and distinct idea of myself. I can conceive myself as entire without the faculties of imagination and perception, but I cannot conceive these without the faculties of imagination and perception, but I cannot conceive these without an intelligent substance in which they reside. Descartes includes will and also such higher emotions as are not the result of the union of mind and body in thought. According to Descartes, a thinking thing is one that doubts, understands, conceives, affirms, denies, wills, refuses, imagines as well as feels.

Neither extension nor figure, nor notion pertains to the thinking thing. My knowledge about my mind precedes that of any corporal thing. I may not doubt whether there is any body in existence, while I already perceive that I think.

Descartes follows this extreme dualism between mind and body so that the nature is left free for the mechanical explanations of natural science. Mind is separated from nature with its own territory. On the other hand, he does not want to accept the conclusion that the soul is lodged in the body which it uses as an instrument. This is the conclusion that Descartes could not accept. Empirical data went against such a conclusion, leave alone the theological objection. Descartes tries to explain this problem by locating the soul and its activity in a gland in the very centre of the body. He tries to get out of the problem finally by saying that mind and body are incomplete substances viewed in relation to man who is unity which they for together. A clearly unsatisfactory solution to the problem.

According to Descartes, mind and body compose a substantial unity. Motion in animals, and often in ourselves, occurs without the intervention of reason; the senses excited by external objects simply react to the animal spirits and the reactions are mechanical-the animal is nothing but a machine. But in man bodily motion may produce sensations.

Just how this intimate union is to be conceived, is not made clear by Descartes and indeed, it is not possible within the framework of his dualism. Descartes warns against confounding mind and body with one another. Thought and extension are combined in man, in unity of composition but not in unity of nature: the union should not be compared with a mixture of two bodies.

Descartes suggested that the body works like a machine, that it has the material properties of extension and motion, and that it follows the laws of physics. The mind (or soul), on the other hand, was described as a nonmaterial entity that lacks extension and motion, and does not follow the laws of physics. This form of dualism or duality proposes that the mind controls the body, but that the body can also influence the otherwise rational mind, such as when people act out of passion.

Descartes suggested that the pineal gland is "the seat of the soul" for several reasons. First, the soul is unitary, and unlike many areas of the brain the pineal gland appeared to be unitary (though subsequent microscopic inspection has revealed it is formed of two hemispheres). Second, Descartes observed that the pineal gland was located near the ventricles. He believed the animal spirits of the ventricles acted through the nerves to control the body, and that the pineal gland influenced this process. Finally, Descartes incorrectly believed that only humans have pineal glands, just as, in his view, only humans have minds. The question of how a nonmaterial mind could influence a material body, without invoking supernatural explanations, remains controversial to this day.

Mind-Body Interactionism

We intuitively know that there is some relationship between mind and body but we must decide the precise nature of it. Descartes wavers between interactionism which he seems to suggest and parallelism which follows logically from his absolute dualism. A great many bodily activities can be explained in terms of reflexes and his acute observation in this connection makes him the precursor of modern behaviourism. But bodily activities are to some extent influenced by the mind, and the mind is also influenced by the body. He regard sensing, imagining, remembering as mental acts but the objects referred to are not mental. But can the mental ideas tell us anything of the material bodies? No, for the sole function of the ideas is to guide us to what is harmful or beneficial to us and not to represent things external to us. However, Descartes believes that there are real material bodies. This general belief in material bodies is based on divine veracity. If we want to know definitely about the particular material bodies, then we can know only their primary qualities but the so-called secondary non-quantitative qualities are nothing but confused ideas. The confused ideas, however, are caused by external objects as is clear from his explanation of perception. In perception the material bodies effect the mental states through the human body.

(i) Firstly, the exciting body affects the sense-organs of the percipient's own body.

(ii) This bodily affection moves the subtle animal spirits in the nerves. The movement of the animal spirit terminates in the pineal gland which he considers to be the seat of the soul. The soul is indivisible substance and therefore occupies the pineal gland which is the only undivided portion of the brain.

(iii) Lastly, a physical impress or seal is left on the pineal gland which serves as the occasion of the origin of consciousness.

Descartes seems to have explained away the mechanical pressure of the body on the mind by the mediating services of the animal spirits terminating in the pineal gland. Similarly, the mind acts on the body by moving the animal spirits in the pineal gland which coursing through the muscles leads to bodily movement. This direct interactionism he tries to conceal with the help of the analogy of the rider and the horse. Just as the rider spurs on the horse to run fast with his own energy, so the mind only excites the bodily movement without imparting its own energy into the material series.

SPINOZA

Born in 1632, he was the son of Marrano parents. They had immigrated to Amsterdam from Portugal in order to escape the Investigation that had spread across the Iberian Peninsula and live in the tolerant atmosphere of Holland. Just before Spinoza was to turn six, his mother, Hanna, the second of Michael's three wives, died in 1638. As a boy—known to his fellow Portuguese as Bento—he had been one of the shining pupils in the congregation's Talmud Torah school. As Spinoza made progress through his studies, he was being groomed for a career as a rabbi. Spinoza's intellectual orientation, however, came at a cost. On July 27, 1656, Spinoza was issued the harshest writ of cherem, or excommunication, ever pronounced by the Sephardic community of Amsterdam. In 1661, he settled near Leiden, in the town of Rijnsburg. His critical exposition of Descartes's Principles of Philosophy, the only work he published under his own name in his lifetime, was completed in 1663. By this time, he was also working on what would eventually be called the Ethics, his philosophical masterpiece. When Spinoza died in 1677, in The Hague, he was still at work on his Political Treatise; which was soon published by his friends along with his other unpublished writings, including a Compendium to Hebrew Grammar. Spinoza died peacefully in his rented room in The Hague in 1677.

Substance

Spinoza had the vision of the unity of all things. At such he starts with something from which everything can be shown to follow necessarily. This something he calls substance which following Descartes he defines "that which is in itself and is conceived through itself, i.e., the conception of which does not need the conception of another thing in order to its formation." Of course, Descartes had called mind and body also dependent substances on God but Spinoza points out that the phrase 'dependent substances' is contradiction in terms. A substance cannot depend on anything else. As such there can be only one substance. If there were more than one substance then they would limit each other and thus would take away their self-sufficiency. This one substance, he also calls God whom he defines as a "Being absolutely infinite; that is, substance consisting in infinite attributes each of which expresses eternal and infinite essence." Thus the substance is infinite or unlimited. By infinite, firstly he understands that which is uniquely individual for the substance can be conceived only 'in itself.'

Spinoza points out that every determination is negation. Hence his substance becomes most positive without any limitation.

Spinoza has so defined substance that it cannot but be *infinite*, since if it were finite it would mean that it is limited by something else. However, the substance is self-determined and self-contained and nothing can affect or modify it. He also calls it causa sui. A cause, according to him, explains phenomena and does not simply *describe* them. By 'explanation' is meant the showing of necessary connexion between phenomena which means, the establishment of a logical relationship between them. For example, a conclusion is said to be necessarily connected with its premises. Similarly, by saying that the substance is the cause of the universe, Spinoza wants to hold that it follows necessarily from the substance. Hence, the often-repeated statement of Spinoza is that everything follows from substance in the same way in which all the angles of a triangle are together equal to two right angles follows from the definition of a triangle. Hence, by describing substance as *Causa sui,* Spinoza means that the reality is a self-explanatory, all inclusive, inter-related whole.

There is also another characteristic of substance, according to Spinoza, namely, it is *one* or simple. If there were more than one substance, then they would limit one another, and none of them, therefore, would be infinite in the sense of being unaffected by another. Therefore there is one substance which is infinite.

Attributes

There can be no substance without attributes. However, they may be either *essential or accidental.* The essential attributes define a substance, *i.e.,* without which the substance would cease to be substance. The accidental attributes are those variable characters which a substance can lose without ceasing to be what it is.

As the substance is self-contained and is infinite, so it has an infinite number of attributes. Hence, the substance of Spinoza has an infinite number of attributes, each of which expresses the essence of the substance infinitely.

Under two conditions an attribute can limit the substance, namely,

(1) If an attribute excludes the possibility of other attributes, *i.e.,* if one determination negates other determinations, and

(2) If an attribute by itself is finite. Now God has infinite attributes which neither limit one another, nor the substance. They are co-existent properties each of which equally manifests the essence of the substance. Thus the infinite number of attributes, each infinite in itself leaves the substance indeterminate. Further, each attribute taken by itself does not limit the substance, but manifests its nature infinitely and boundlessly.

One wonders whether an infinite number of attributes can co-exist without mutual exclusion. By way of illustration his point on this score, Spinoza holds that out of an infinite number of attributes, human intellect can perceive only two, namely, extension and thought. Here thought and extension, as Descartes had made familiar, are quite independent of each other. As such these two attributes do not limit each other. Further, each of them is infinite in its own kind. Thus, there is possibility of an infinite number of attributes, coexisting together which neither limit one another nor the substance.

Modes

"By mode", says Spinoza, "I understand affections of substance, or that which is in another, through which it is also conceived". The modes are individual things of finite experience. They are to the substance what the waves are to the sea, shapes that perpetually die away that never are. They can never exist without the substance though the substance can exist without them. He seems to hold that they are either in another or in God. Every mode is in God for nothing can exist without God.

Modes are said to be *actual* in so far as they exist at a certain time and place. Viewed in this way they do not follow from God but from the interminable series or connection of finite things. But modes are said to real when we conceive them under the form of eternity. As such they are to be viewed as they are in God. Every mode is rot lost for every idea of an individual thing actually existing necessarily involves the idea of the eternal and infinite essence of God . . . for the force by which individual *thing preserves* in its own existence follows from the eternal necessity of the divine nature. Thus Spinoza sometimes regards the modes to be real affections actually existing in God and sometimes looks upon them as mere illusions created by abstract imagination which views things as separated and unrelated.

Two Types of Modes

Into this relatively simple picture, Spinoza introduces a complication. There are, he says, two types of modes. The first consists in what he calls infinite and eternal modes. Examples include motion and rest under the attribute of extension and infinite intellect under the attribute of thought. The second consists in what may be called finite and temporal modes, which are simply the singular things that populate the universe. Modes of this type follow from the divine nature as well, but do so only as each follows from one or another of God's attributes insofar as it is modified by a modification that is itself finite and temporal.

Unfortunately, Spinoza does little to explain either what these infinite and eternal modes are or what relation they have to finite and temporal modes. For example, if laws of impact are somehow embedded in the infinite and eternal mode motion and rest, then the outcome of any particular collision will be determined by that mode together with the relevant properties (speed, direction, size, etc.) of the bodies involved.

The Concept of 'God or Nature'

"On God" Spinoza begins with some deceptively simple definitions of terms that would be familiar to any seventeenth century philosopher. His definitions begins in following order "By substance I understand what is in itself and is conceived through itself", "By attribute I understand what the intellect perceives of a substance, as constituting its essence"; "By God I understand a being absolutely infinite, i.e., a substance consisting of an infinity of attributes, of which each one expresses an eternal and infinite essence." The definitions of Part One are, in effect, simply clear concepts that ground the rest of his system. From these, the first proposition necessarily follows, and every subsequent proposition can be demonstrated using only what precedes it. There is only one substance in the universe; it is God; and everything else is in God.

Modes of God

This proof that God—an infinite, necessary and uncaused, indivisible being—is the only substance of the universe proceeds in three simple steps. First, establish that no two substances can share an attribute or essence. It follows, in conclusion, that the existence of that infinite substance precludes the existence of any other substance. It follows, in conclusion, that the existence of that infinite substance precludes the existence of any other substance. This second substance would be one of the attributes already possessed by God. But it has already been established that no two substances can have the same attribute. Therefore, there can be, besides God, no such second substance. Those things that are "in" God (or, more precisely, in God's attributes) are what Spinoza calls modes.

God Existing only in A Philosophical Sense

As soon as this preliminary conclusion has been established, Spinoza immediately reveals the objective of his attack. His definition of God—condemned since his excommunication from the Jewish community as a "God existing in only a philosophical sense"—is meant to preclude any anthropomorphizing of the divine being. In the scholium to proposition fifteen, he writes against "those who feign a God, like man, consisting of a body and a mind, and subject to passions. Besides being false, such an anthropomorphic conception of God can have only deleterious effects on human freedom and activity.

World and Its Relation to God

Much of the technical language of Part One is, to all appearances, right out of Descartes. But even the most devoted Cartesian would have had a hard time understanding the full import of propositions one through fifteen. What does it mean to say that God is substance and that everything else is "in" God? Is Spinoza saying that rocks, tables, chairs, birds, mountains, rivers and human beings are all properties of God, and hence can be predicated of God (just as one would say that the table "is red")? It seems very odd to think that objects and individuals—what we ordinarily think of as independent "things"—are, in fact, merely properties of a thing. Spinoza was sensitive to the strangeness of this kind of talk, not to mention the philosophical problems to which it gives rise. Conundrums such as this may explain why, as of Proposition Sixteen, there is a subtle but important shift in Spinoza's language. "From the necessity of the divine nature there must follow infinitely many things in infinitely many modes, (i.e., everything that can fall under an infinite intellect)". According to the traditional Judeo-Christian conception of divinity, God is a transcendent creator, a being who causes a world distinct from himself to come into being by creating it out of nothing. By contrast, Spinoza's God is the cause of all things because all things follow causally and necessarily from the divine nature. Or, as he puts it, from God's infinite power or nature "all things have necessarily flowed, or always followed, by the same necessity and in the same way as from the nature of a triangle it follows, from eternity and to eternity, that its three angles are equal to two right angles". This does not mean that God does not cause the world to come into being freely, since nothing outside of God constrains him to bring it into existence. But Spinoza does deny that God creates the world by some arbitrary and undetermined act of free will. God could not have done otherwise. Everything is absolutely and necessarily determined. In nature there is nothing contingent, but all things have been determined from the necessity of the divine nature to exist and produce an effect in a certain way.

There are, however, differences in the way things depend on God. Some features of the universe follow necessarily from God—or, more precisely, from the absolute nature of one of God's attributes—in a direct and unmediated manner. They include the most general laws of the universe, together governing all things in all ways.

The Mind-Body Problem

Spinoza rejected cartesian dualism and rejected the substantiality of mind and body. He regarded mind and body, extension and thought as two of the many inseparable aspects of a single, all-inclusive reality. Being co-existent attributes of the substance, thought and extension cannot interact.

How are they related? Well, only like can cause the like. The two therefore, cannot interact, but they run parallel to each other. They are infinite but independent of one-another, each capable of expressing God infinitely in its own way. God is extended as well as thinking. These two are but two inseparable aspect of the same thing, like the convex and concave of the same lens. From one viewpoint God appears as infinite extension, as from another angle, he appears as infinite intellect in the same way in which the same person is known as Jacob as well as Israel. No one aspect can exist without the other. Substance thinking and substance extended are one and the same substance, apprehended now through one Attribute, now through the other. To every mode of extension corresponds a mode of thought, in the same order or series. A circle and an idea of a circle are one and the same thing, looked at from the angle of extension and thought respectively. But this parallelism excludes materialism as well as idealism, for matter cannot explain mind, nor mind can explain matter.

This parallelism, with the doctrine of infinite attributes, shows that not only God but everything has an aspect of infinite viewpoints but we human beings can know only two, namely, extension and thought. But we may legitimately ask, why are we condemned to two attributes alone? If thought can know extension, why can it not know the other attributes as well? Both these questions Spinoza could not answer satisfactorily. He pointed out that human beings can know only two for they are embodied spirits. But then everything is endowed with infinite viewpoints and so human beings too have many more aspects than two. Besides, in intellect can know something other than itself, extension, than how can it not know other attributes as well? Once grant that thought can overstep its boundary, there is nothing which can be excluded from its grasp. Again, in strict parallelism, this concession to intellect shows something corresponding to which there is nothing in extension. Hence, in spite of parallelism Spinoza has his idealistic leaning.

The Mind as the Idea of the Body

To understand Spinoza's account of the mind we must begin with that for each finite mode of extension there exists a finite mode of thought that corresponds to it and from which it is not really distinct. More elaborately, it commits him to the thesis that:

(a) for each simple body there exists a simple idea that corresponds to it and from which it is not really distinct and

(b) for each composite body there exists a composite idea that corresponds to it and from which it is not really distinct, composed, as it were, of ideas corresponding to each of the bodies of which the composite body is composed. Spinoza counts all of these ideas, whether simple or composite, as minds. In this respect he does not consider the human mind to be unique. It is simply the idea that corresponds to the human body.

[I]n proportion as a body is more capable than others of doing many things at once, or being acted on in many ways at once, so its mind is more capable than others of perceiving many things at once. And in proportion as the actions of a body depend more on itself alone, and as other bodies concur with it less in acting, so its mind is more capable of understanding distinctly. And from these [truths] we know the excellence of one mind over the others. Here lies the explanation of the excellence of the human mind. The human mind, as an expression of that body in the domain of thought, mirrors the body in being a highly complex composite of many simple ideas and is thus possessed of perceptual capacities exceeding those of other, non-human minds. Only a mind that corresponds to a body of complexity comparable to that of the human body can have perceptual abilities comparable to those of the human mind.

Pantheism

Pantheism is the doctrine according to which the things or modes have no existence of their own. They are mere illusion or abstractions drawn by imagination. In this definition pantheism lays down that God alone is real and all other finite things are suppressed or annulled in the existence of God. This question has to be answered for Spinoza regards modes sometimes as fictitious and at times he regards them as real. As held before the modes are said to be in God and as such they are eternal and real. But he also holds that the modes to be modes are determined not directly by God but by other modes and as such the modes being temporal and finite cannot follow from the infinite substance and therefore are unreal.

Each mode is *real* when it participates in the nature of God and is *unreal* though actual, when it is seen to be determined by the infinite multiplicity of all other finite things. Spinoza is really pantheistic for he negates the actuality of things. The same trend is to be detected in his theory of Infinite modes. The doctrine of infinite modes aims at reconciling the multiplicity of things with the infinite substance. But here as elsewhere what Spinoza gives with one hand he takes away with the other. There are places where Spinoza says that the nature is God and God is nature. He himself points out that God is *natura naturata* looked as the total aggregate of the finite things. This infinite mode in the form of the whole universes he says, is the first in the descent from the substance and the last in ascent of finite things. But then, nature naturata does not mean the sum-total of the modes as actual things for the following reason:

1. Finite things, like squares on the graph, come much later. The substance, as the infinitely extended plane, remains the only eternal reality. As such the sum total of the squares cannot be said to constitute the original plane.
2. Besides, the original infinitely extended plane can be reached, not be adding the squares but by removing them away. The natura naturata to be merged in natura naturans means the negation of all finite things.

This pantheistic tendency in negating the world of finite things is further seen in Ethics and his theory of knowledge. A point as point cannot be understood as long as it is not viewed in a line; a line as line does not exist as long as it is not viewed in relation to a surface and the upward urge for the completion of knowledge continues. However, though a point cannot exist without a line yet it ceases to be a point when merged in a line. Similarly, the finite things as finite cannot exist without the substance but being merged in the substance they cease to be.

Three Orders of Knowing

With the distinction between adequate and inadequate perception in place, Spinoza introduces a set of further distinctions. He begins with inadequate perception, which he now calls knowledge of the first kind, and divides it into two parts.

Experientia Vaga

The first consists of knowledge from random experience (experientia vaga). This is knowledge "from singular things which have been represented to us through the senses in a way which is mutilated, confused, and without order for the intellect".

Ex signis

The second consists of knowledge from signs (ex signis), "for example, from the fact that, having heard or read certain words, we recollect things, and form certain ideas of them, like those through which we imagine the things". What links both of these forms of knowledge is that they lack a rational order. It is obvious that knowledge from random experience follows the order of the affections of the human body, but so does knowledge from signs. A Roman who hears the word 'pomum', for instance, will think of an apple, not because there is any rational connection between the word and the object, but only because they have been associated in his or her experience.

Ratio

When we reach what Spinoza calls the second kind of knowledge, reason (ratio), we have ascended from an inadequate to an adequate perception of things. This type of knowledge is gained "from the fact that we have common notions and adequate ideas of the properties of things". Unlike in the case of knowledge of the first kind, this order of ideas is rational.

Scientia Intuitive

We might think that in attaining this second kind of knowledge we have attained all that is available to us. However, Spinoza adds a third type, which he regards as superior. Unfortunately, Spinoza is once again obscure at a crucial junction, and it is difficult to know what he has in mind here. He seems to be envisioning a type of knowledge that gives insight into the essence of some singular thing together with an understanding of how that essence follows of necessity from the essence of God.

Problems of obscurity aside, we can still see something of the ideal at which Spinoza is aiming. Inadequate ideas are incomplete. What Spinoza is offering with the fourth kind of knowledge is a way of correcting this. It is important to note, however, that he is not proposing that we can have this knowledge with respect to the durational existence of any particular item. Rather, he is proposing that we can have it with respect to the essence of a singular thing as it follows from the essence of God. To have this kind of knowledge is to understand the thing as necessary rather than contingent. It is, to use Spinoza's famous phrase, to regard it *sub quadam specie aeternitatis*, under a certain aspect of eternity.

LEIBNITZ

Leibnitz was born in 1646. He was a great mathematician and scientist. He shared with Newton the honour of having discovered infinitesimal calculus. Some of the popular and important works of Leibniz are :

(a) New Essays on Human Understanding
(b) Monadology
(c) Discourse on Metaphysics.
(d) Theodicy

Like Descartes and Spinoza, Leibniz continued to employ the geometrical method, and based his philosophy on the notion of substance, but he differed radically from them as regards the relation of mind and matter and the number of substances. Spinoza admitted God alone. For Descartes extension is the essence of matter and for Spinoza both extension and thought are attributes of God. According to Leibniz extension involves plurality and belongs to an aggregate of substances. Each single substance must be unextended. He, therefore, believed in an infinite number of substances, which he called "Monads".

Monadology

The Nature of Monads

Monads are real and infinite in number. They are eternal and can not be destroyed. They are indivisible self contained and exclusive of everything else. Being a real unit, each monad contains the whole infinity of existence (*i.e.*, a macrocosm in microcosm). It has no windows through which anything might come in or go out.

The infinite number of monads are qualitatively unlike, so that no two monads are alike. They are found in a hierarchical order of existence. Each monad imperceptibly leads to others. There is no abrupt change anywhere in the *connexion graduelle*. Only with the help of the absolute continuity between the monads we can explain every variety of experience. Besides, with the help of the law of continuous series we bridge the gulf between mind and matter, men and animals, conscious and unconscious states.

Monads being spiritual have two important characteristics of perception and appetition. By virtue of its perception each monad mirrors the whole infinity of existence. The more developed monad in the series has clear perception and the less developed monad has confused perception. The infinite gradations in the monads correspond to their stages of development, there are different degrees of perception. Because each monad is a force, therefore, it has appetition by virtue of which it tends to become the whole. Again, by virtue of its appetition each monad tends to pass from obscure to clear perception. If an action is done from very obscure perception then it is known as impulse and if it is done from clear perception, then it is known as will. Thus the activity of the low monads is prompted by will and desire. However the distinction between impulse and desire is one of degree and, not kind.

The monads are found in a continuous series, one imperceptibly passing into the other. However, in this series we can note the main types of monads. The lowest or bare monads are those in which the perception is most obscure. They go to make the inorganic bodies. They are scarcely more than centres of forces and they express themselves in the form of motion which appears to us purely mechanical. They may be said to be in profound stupor or deep sleep. Then there are conscious monads endowed with memory. This may be called souls. They go to make the plant and animal world. However, the highest monads are called *spirits* having reason and universal, necessary knowledge. They are raised to the knowledge of the self as well as of God.

The Cartesians called spirits alone as souls but called the former two namely, bare monads and animals, automata. However, the difference between the monads is one of degree. In the bare monads the force appears only in the form of mechanical movement as instinct, self-conscious desire and will works for the appetite and spirit (necessity with freedom).

The Truths of Reason and the Truths of Fact

Leibniz was a great logician and believed that logic is the basis of Metaphysics. He even worked on Mathematical Logic but he abstained from publishing it. He felt that even in Metaphysics and morals we should be able to solve problems like in Geometry.

While discussing Leibniz's logical principles the first point to be explained is the distinction between truths of reason and truths of fact. Leibniz based his philosophy on two logical premises – the Law of Contradiction and the Law of Sufficient Reason. The propositions of this form are of two kinds-Truths of reason and Truths of facts. Truths of reason are necessary propositions because they are either self-evident or reducible to self-evidence. By knowing its meaning we know that it's opposite or contradictories cannot be true.

Truths of fact are not necessary propositions, but they are contingent. When we deny them, there will be no logical contradiction... Quoting Leibniz from 'Monodology', "Truths of reason are necessary and their opposite is impossible; truths of fact are contingent and their opposite is possible". Leibniz makes one exception, saying that 'God Exists' is a proposition embracing truths of reason. It is a necessary proposition whose denial would be a logical contradiction. To state that God is possible is to state that God exists. They are known by intuition, their truth being self-evident, like, A is A or what is A cannot be not A. In this manner Leibniz shows that truths of reason are finitely analytic propositions. For Leibniz all true propositions in a sense are analytic. The existence of the world and the whole harmonious system of finite things requires a sufficient reason which Leibniz finds in a free decree of God. No finite mind can perform this analysis. It is in this sense Leibniz calls truths of fact as 'incapable of analyses. Only God can possess that complete and perfect idea of individuality of a being in order to know apriori all that will be predicted of him. It is therefore clear that applying the law of sufficient reason Leibniz affirms that all true propositions are analytic and this rule applies to even empirical statements concerning matters of fact. But this difference arises only because of ignorance and intellectual limitation. For God this difference does not exist.

Proofs for the Existence of God

Leibniz gives following proofs for the existence of God.

1. **Ontological Proof.** Every monad has two aspects, namely, actual and possible, activity and passivity. The less developed monad is more passive and less active, the more developed monad is more active and actual, and, less passive and possible. In the hierarchical series God is the most developed monad the actus purus, *i.e.*, every possibility of which has become actual and fully existent. Now his proof runs thus: 'If God is possible, He exists, for His Existence is a necessary consequence of his possibility. If he did not exist, He would not be possible, nor would any thing outside of him be possible.' In other words, every monad has both actuality and possibility, but in the case of God what is possible is also actual. Hence the existence of God follows from the very possibility of him.
2. **Cosmological Proof.** Every particular thing is contingent for we can always think its non-existence. Not only particular things but the universe as a whole can be easily imagined to be non-existent. As such it is contingent. But every contingent truth is based on sufficient reason. Hence the universe as a whole, being contingent must have a sufficient reason outside the universe. This sufficient reason is God. This proof depends on the validity of the law of sufficient reason which is rather unclear. Besides, it depends on the ontological proof for it assumes the existence of a necessary being who can be the sufficient reason.
3. **Proof based on eternal truths.** There are certain propositions which are always true like 2 + 2 = 4. The basis of eternal truths cannot be contingent but must be found in eternal truths. But a reason for what exists must itself exists. Therefore, the eternal truths must exist and they can exist as thoughts in the mind of God.
4. **Proof based on harmony.** Lastly, from the monadology it is clear that there is a Harmony in the monads. This harmony supposes that there is a being who has regulated and introduced this harmony from outside and this is God.

Leibniz believes in the existence of a good, just and loving God. Man differs from other souls not only in being a clear image of the universe but in being a conscious image of God. By virtue of being a conscious image of God, man can know and imitate him. It is this higher knowledge which tells him that 'he is not only what an inventor is to him machine, but also what a prince is to his subjects, or indeed, what a father is to his children.' Here he emphasizes the conscious devotion and participation of simple mind in the divine one.

Freedom and Necessity

Man, according to Leibniz, is free to pursue his perfection. This perfection consists in the enlightened benevolence of all. But the free action does not mean an action without determinism. Nothing can start *de novo*. Every action has its root in antecedent movements. A purely undetermined action means an abrupt action. But this will break the law of continuity. Hence every action is determined by the past antecedents. The more ignorant we are of past antecedents, the more determined is our action. The more we act from clear ideas or distinct perceptions, the freer we are. This freedom consists in self-determinism. The clear ideas or eternal truths have their special seat in the mind and the more we act according to them, the more self-determined and freer we are. Besides, the clearer we are about the goal, the more rationally we will have to decide between the various possibilities and the choice will be guided more by the law of sufficient reason.

Thus true freedom consists neither in necessity nor in strict spontaneity but in the spontaneous unfolding of the action guided by clear perception. Thus God is most free not because he can do whatever he pleases, nor because his action is dictated by his rational nature; but because his every act is determined by infinite wisdom for the best possible end.

Principles of Non-Contradiction

Fundamental principles of the philosophy of Leibnitz are known as 'principles of non contradiction'. Which are as follows :

Law of continuity. Following his mathematical bent he believed in the law of *continuity.* "It was originally a generalisation of the property of numbers—viz., that they can be continued without end, and divided without limit,—and referred, in this respect, to the infinitely large, in which everything is contained, and to the infinitely small of which everything is made up." This observation coupled with the infinitesimal calculus showed that there is no abrupt change but every change is followed by another, through an infinite number of infinitely imperceptible changes. This law of continuity affirms his thought that lines are generated by the movements of points, surfaces by the movements of lines and solids by the movements of surfaces.

Law of individuality. There is yet another principle which he draws from his mathematical discipline. In mathematics a lengthy chain of reasoning can be compressed in extremely abbreviated formulae. He who knows them can at once draw out much invaluable information and can achieve logical and intellectual satisfaction. This led him to establish the principle of individuality. Everything is real. To the course of imagination the connection between things is one of causal nexus. But everything is real and as such no external influence can change it. Leibnitz, in spite of his opposition to Descartes and Spinoza, looks upon the real in terms of self-containedness. However, this principle of individuality gives his system the appearance of great contrast to Spinoza. Spinoza gives us the whole or the blank universal from which parts have disappeared; but Leibnitz begins with the reality of parts, the extreme multiplicity of finite experience and tries to determine their nature in order to discover the real parts of the real whole. Now parts in order to be real parts must be as real as the whole of which they are parts. Each part somehow must be the whole and contains the whole. The insistence on the reality of individual things made him believe in pluralism.

Principle of harmony. To the above two principles may be added a third principle of hermony which partly arises from his mathematical discipline and partly from the deisre to concede the Spinozistic truth of unity and partly from the necessity of reconciling the first two laws of continuity and extreme individuality. He maintained that everything is real for it contains the whole and in some sense is a whole, i.e., a unity within itself. Now this unity in plurality is called harmony. The law of harmony plays the some role in Leibnitz which the abstract unit played in the philosophy of Spinoza. For this reason his philosophy has been called the philosophy of pre-established harmony.

God the creator of harmony. With the law of harmony the inner circle of the thought of leibnitz is closed but it seems certain that he believed also in God. He further held that individual things no doubt are real but they are knitted together in a grand harmony. This presupposes that some giant intellect has brought about the harmony. This giant intellect is called God. Hence Leibnitz, like Descartes and Spinoza, chooses to make his system *Theocentric, i.e.* God-centred.

Theory of Knowledge

(Truths of Reason and Truths of Facts)

There are two kinds of truth involved in knowledge, namely, necessary and contingent. Necessary truth follow with logical and mathematical certainty their opposite is inconceivable. They are self-evident, self-consistent and based on the law of contradiction. They are so eternal and unchangeable that even the will of God cannot alter them. Such truths no doubt may be complex but they can be analysed into simple identical propositions. Leibnitz did not agree with Locke in disparaging identical propositions. In the last resort the truths of reason can be analysed into ideas so simple as to be indefinable, axions so simple as to be indemonstrable, and postulates which neither need nor admit of proof. Leibnitz himself pointed out that the axioms of Geometry are very near examples of what he aims at expressing by necessary truths.

Descartes laid down that there is only one kind of truth, namely, necessary. However, there is another kind of truth called contingent or truth of fact. We can always think the opposite of any contingent truth. For example, it is fact that the table is before me, but I can always think the possibility of something else instead of the table just now and here. As the necessary truth depends on the law of contradiction, so, the contingent truth depends on the law of sufficient reason. Leibnitz makes very greater use of Sufficient Reason which he expresses thus. It is that "by which we believe that no fact can be true or real, no statement trustworthy, unless there is a sufficient reason. Why it should be so and not otherwise although in a greater number of cases we cannot know these reasons."

The law of sufficient reason teaches the harmony theory of truth. In this connection Leibnitz makes a distinction between possible and compossible. To say that a thing is free from contradiction is to maintain that it is possible, but that alone is actual which is compossible or that which in conformity with the actual system of things. Thus the reason for the existence of a particular thing is the system of the actual things. This system is the sole sufficient reason which explains a particular thing. This doctrine comes very near to the harmony theory of truth according to which a statement is true which harmonises with all other things known.

But can we not say that we, being limited beings, cannot know all the reason for the existence of any particular thing, but cannot God know all the reasons for the existence of a thing? Surely God knows that given a certain arrangement of doors, windows, light etc., the table must be here and nowhere else. Thus for God it is unthinkable that a certain table be somewhere else. In his case then the law of sufficient reason becomes identical with the law of contradiction? Leibnitz is not very clear there. In spite of his strong tendency for compromise he has not been able to harmonise between these two kinds of truth. In one sense, we can say, that the law of sufficient reason is wide enough to include the law of contradiction for there must be some reason why the necessary truth are clear and self-evident. But Leibnitz rather makes a sharp distinction between them. The necessary truths are abstract but the contingent ones are concrete. The knowledge of facts cannot, according to Leibnitz, be reduced necessary truth. God cannot think of a particular thing otherwise than what it is in a system of facts, but the whole system itself can be otherwise. God has chosen this world out of all the infinite possibilities because it is the best possible world for achieving the moral value in his mind. Hence contingent truth is dictated by moral necessity but truths of reason have absolute, compelling and metaphysical necessity.

Identity of Indiscernibles

From the fact of each monad representing the universe from its individualistic standpoint emerges the theory or law of identity of indiscernibles, the basis of the philosophy of Leibnitz. According to him, all the monads of the universe are linked to each other in an ascending order in which one can find all the stages, beginning with the lowest and ending at the highest. Monads differ because they exist at different levels but even at the same level no two monads are identical because they possess their own specific existence in relation to time and space. No two things in the universe can therefore be said to be identical. Had there been no difference between the monads they should have been identical, and therefore they should have been referred to as one rather than as two. It is this which is called the law of identity of indiscernibles. It implies that things between which there is no difference are one, and things that are not identical are not one. But because monads differ from each other in respect of their stages in the order of continuity and in their respective positions in time and space, there can be no identity among them. The law of identity of indiscernibles is intimately connected with the theory of continuity. Thus, no two monads in the universe are alike and neither is their any identity between two monads. When force of the second attribute of monads becomes active the monads evolve. All monads possess their own centres of force. Potential energy or force is everywhere being expressed in ever different forms. No monad can be influenced from outside, and anything that exists in it lies there in nascent form.

Substance

To describe the nature of substance Leibnitz starts with the opposite thesis of pluralism. His problem is, "what must be the nature of parts which can in some way contain or express the whole within itself?" In order to account for the reality in which individual things are real he begins with the notion of substance. However, Descartes had defined it as that which is in itself and conceived through itself, i.e. the existence of which does not involve the existence of anything else. This definition, if followed to the extreme logical consequence, says Leibnitz, leads to the dangerous pantheism of Spinoza. Besides, even in Descartes it leads to dualism and to true unity. Descartes had rightly established the importance of the self and should have established a reality on the pattern of the self. But apart from mind he believes also in the existence of matter which is taken to be mere extension.

Leibnitz rejects matter and the reality of extension and defines substance as indivisible, self active and spiritual units. Therefore, according to Leibnitz the real elements must be spiritual. He calls these indivisible, self-active and spiritual units as monads. They are the true metaphysical points which though indivisible are non-existent. They are, again, different from atoms which though existent are not indivisible. Only a spiritual unit is indivisible like our own self-conscious existence, and yet in real. Hence the monads alone are real.

Sufficient Reason

Principle of Sufficient Reason

Leibniz's view about sufficient reason seems to be not just that it provides a good maxim for the conduct of intellectual enquiry, but that were it not to hold in some domain there could be no truth there at all. Confirmation of this may be found in the 1712 paper *'Metaphysical Consequences of the Principle of Reason,"* which at its outset asserts.

Why should Leibniz have thought any such thing? What support can he offer for it? Reflecting on these questions sixty years after Leibniz's death.

To deny it would be to accept the seeming absurdity that something can come from nothing, ex nihilo aliquod! Yet even though we may suppose that to be a brute impossibility reason requires that we should be able to say something to show why it is, just as we did in the case of the Principle of Contradiction.

Reflecting on Leibniz's division of truths into necessary truths of reasoning and contingent truths of fact one may well suppose that he can not have held his principle to express a very general but merely contingent truth of fact. One may well suppose that he can not have held his principle to express a very general but merely contingent truth of fact.

We might conclude that it must express a necessary truth a truth of reasoning, explicable by the Principle of Contradiction. Its assertion will then either explicitly express an identity or else be reducible to one with the help of definitions, axioms and postulates.

Nor does it seem at all promising to attempt to reduce it or analyse it in other terms than this terms more acceptable to Leibniz, which then reveal its denial to be a contradiction. This is unsatisfactory because Leibniz believes that those primitive principles are loosely speaking identities and this principle does not appear to be one.

Doctrian of Pre-established Harmony

In order that there may be any unity the monads must be related, yet being windowless they cannot be related. "Each spirit being like a world apart, sufficient to itself, independent of every other created thing, involving the infinite, expressing the universe, is as lasting as continuous in its existence, and as absolute as the very universe of created being." But in spite of the monads being independent, working according to their inner urge, the world is a harmony and a cosmos. The monads are not separate stories and events beginning and ending at odd intervals. But we have to explain this harmony between self-contained and exclusive monads. Leibnitz assumed that the harmony between the monads has been pre-established by God., He has so arranged the series of monads in their hierarchical order that the change in one is preceded and followed in other monads harmoniously. To the beholder it appears that the change in A is the cause of the change in B, but really the monads being windowless cannot interact on one another. What appears to us as inter-action is really concomitant relation. For example, we press the button and the fan moves. According to Leibnitz a change in the button-monad takes place as a result of its own preceding movement but a corresponding and correlative change takes place in the fan-monad. We wrongly interpret the independent but concomitant changes between the fan and button due to interaction. God has arranged the order and the working of all the monads in such a way that a grand plan in his mind may be fulfilled. The monads, no doubt, work independently of all other monads according to their own inner urge, but this inner plan coincides with the realisation of the masterplan in the mind of the creator. Because each monads tries to realise in the same final end in the mind of the creator, therefore, a harmony is reached in their working. "This combination of independence and harmony may be compared to different chairs of musicians playing their parts separately, and so situated that they do not see or even hear one another. Nevertheless they keep perfectly together, by each following their own notes, in such a way that one, who hears them all, finds in them a harmony that is wonderful and much more perfect than if there had been any connection between them."

God and Monadology

In his Theodicee Leibnitz tries to reconcile science with theology, monadology with the dogmas of faith. It seems certain that Leibnitz was a confirmed theist, but then his theism is not so intimately connected with his monadology. Sometimes by God he understands not the creator but the very harmony of the monads. In this sense his connection would have been the same as that of Spinoza, i.e., the nature itself would have become God. At times, he thinks God to be the very crown in the series of monads. But in many places he also thinks God to be the creator of the Monads. If the monads be created, then they cease to be eternal and if the monads be uncreated then God becomes unnecessary. Hence monadology and theology go ill together in the system of Leibnitz. Again, if the monads proceed from God, then how are they related to Him? He describes the monads as proceeding from God by constant radiations. But if the metaphor means that monads emanate from God as light emanates from the sun or as thought is the fulguration from the mind, then the monads are reduced just to the status of 'the modes' of Spinoza. Even when Leibnitz consciously tries to recoil from Spinoza, his ghost seems to haunt his monadology.

LOCKE

John Locke was born in 1632; he was the apostle of the Revolution of 1688, which successfully brought in reforms in England. Most of Locke's works appeared within a few years of 1688. His chief work in theoretical philosophy is the Essay concerning Human Understanding. This work was published in 1690.

Locke may be regarded as the founder of Empiricism; according to which sense experience is the only source of philosophic knowledge. The conception of substance was the dominant category during the time of Locke. Locke thought in terms of concrete detail rather than of large abstractions. Locke wanted to break from the bondage of words, from the bondage of wrong methods and from the bondage of the assumption that philosopher's business is to speculate.

Ideas and their Classification

Locke also determines the nature, function and limit of knowledge. According to Locke ideas means the perception of the convection or repugnance of ideas,

The idea has two distinct meanings which are as follow:

(i) It also means a mode of individual consciousness.

(ii) It also means a represent action of something other than itself,

It has been said, that when we say that we have an idea of the table, it only signifies that we are conscious of something that comes before us.

Idea as an event can be studied in two ways which are as follow:

(i) It can be studied in a purely psychological way. We can describe any idea in terms of images.

(ii) It can be also studied in a categorical way. We can also discover the logical content that are involved in the ideas.

He never ignored the representative character of an idea. We can not say, that whether Locke was regarded as a realist or not. He believed only in an extramental world to which our ideas refer. It has been said that there are two kinds of ideas, which are referred as simple and complex ideas.

Simple Ideas

A simple idea is referred as one which is regarded as a 'being in itself uncompounded.' It contains nothing in itself. It is not distinguishable into different ideas. He is not able to explain the way through, which an idea is regarded as unanalysable. His simple ideas are not regarded as the elements of logical empiricism. They are also not regarded as the sensation of the present day psychologies

It has been said, that all ideas originate with and form experience. He says that mind at birth time is always referred as a clean state. It is also known as a tabula rasa. He says, that all the characters of knowledge are acquired through experience only.

Sensation and Reflection

Sensation helps the mind to acquire all knowledge about the determinations of the external world. Reflection is used to receive information about the operations of its own process. A sensation is arised by the affection of the body. Sensation is also related to external material things.

Bodily affection is conveyed to the brain and the knowledge, which is conveyed to the brain gives rise to sensation only. He says, that a sensation always represents something that are found real in the real world. Sensation only tells about the external world.

Locke mentions two other marks of simple ideas which are as follows :

- The mind is regarded as the passive. It has been said that when the mind becomes active, we are able to get complex ideas.
- Simple ideas are directly known as the actual experience content. The simple ideas enters the mind one by one. They also refers to the qualities that are found together.

Reflection. Reflection only tells us about the internal world. In this reflection method, the mind becomes aware of its own action. It always differs from sensation. In reflection, the mind is present directly to the ideas.

A sensation is referred as a representative function of external things.

It has been said that attention is necessary for the reception of all simple ideas. In reflection, greater attention is needed. In sensation, lesser attention is needed. He also likened the mind to a mirror. He also believes in the positivity of the mind. He says, that the passivity of the mind saves the knowledge from fictitious knowledge.

Complex Ideas

According to Locke, a complex whole is regarded as a sum total of simple parts. Knowledge can be explained only by reducing it to simple ideas.

The complex ideas consists of three ideas which are as follows :

1. **Ideas of Modes.** It includes mixed modes and simple modes. Modes are referred as a part of the *complex ideas.* They are also referred as compounded. They are considered as an affections of substances. He talks very little about the mixed modes. They also forms a single complex ideas. Obligation and life are considered as the example of mixed modes. We can also give the example of beauty for it.

   Simple modes are referred as variations of the same simple idea. It has no mixture of any other. The idea of one unit is regarded as simple. Simple modes are also found in spatial forms.
2. **Ideas of Substance.** It is regarded not as a simple idea. It is implied by it. It is regarded as the idea of a support, which underlie a number of simple qualities that are experienced together. It

has been said that the qualities cannot exist by themselves. They always take the help of a substance. He also believes in primary and secondary qualities.

3. **Ideas of Relation.** Ideas of relation includes causality and identity. It has been said that the simple ideas of sensation and reflection suggest the idea of substance only. The experienced data of change is used to imply the necessary ideas of power and causality. Active efficiency is also known by the experienced data of change. This idea of relation also implies the capacity of producing changes and these changes are found in another body. The ideas of power and causality are regarded as subordinate to that active changes.

Causality

Causality is derived only from voluntary action. It has been said, that the idea of active efficiency is derived from our experience of willing. It has been said, that the idea always becomes necessary for understanding all kinds of changes.

It has been said that everything has a beginning and that beginning always have a cause. It has been also said, that the idea of beginning is always convected with the idea of some operation. Everything have a cause.

It has been said that no necessary convection is found in object. According to Locke, the idea of causality is not convected with uniformity. Berkeley also adopts the view of Locke that there is no causality, which are found in things.

By identity, Locke means a continuity of existence. Locke says, that its idea varies with the nature of different objects. It has been said that a material thing is regarded as identical with itself These things also exists at a particular place, at a particular time. The mass of atoms remains same in the same order. A living thing has its atoms constantly changed. The identity of man is regarded as a participation of the same continued life. He says that personal identity depends upon the sameness of consciousness. It has been said that the same self-depends upon the judgement of the same consciousness.

Ideas

Locke tries to determine the nature, function, origin and limit of knowledge. He defines it as the perception of the connection or repugnance of ideas.

The idea has two distinct meanings :

1. It may mean a mode of individual consciousness. As such it becomes a subjective modification without any necessary reference to objective things.
2. Or else, an idea may mean a representation of something other than itself.

Locke does not make any such clear distinction and continues to use the term in both senses. When we say that we have an idea or thought of the table, then ordinarily we mean that we are conscious of something before us. If we further analyse this then we find that the idea of table consists of some images, sensations and feeling standing for something independent of the mind. Thus each idea is a modification of an individual's consciousness pointing out and representing something in the extra-mental world.

Again, idea as an event in individual's consciousness can be studied in two ways.

(a) We may just analyse and describe any idea in one's consciousness in terms of sensation, images and feeling. It turns out to be a purely psychological study.

(b) Again, we may just try to discover the fundamental, timeless and logical content involved in it. This kind of content is known as categories which are formed in all ideas.

Locke uses the term 'idea' in all these senses and as such nothing but confusion arose in his and subsequent philosophy. Nonetheless there is little doubt that Locke was a realist and believed in an extramental world to which our ideas refer. Thus an idea for him 'is at once the apprehension of a content and the content apprehended; it is both a psychical existent and a logical meaning'. He never ignored the representative character of an idea for it refers to something really existent. Eut the confining of knowledge to ideas led to the development of epistemological explanation of knowledge in terms of subjective process in the philosophy of Berkeley.

Classification of Ideas

There are two kinds of Ideas, namely, simple and complex ideas.

1. Simple Ideas

A simple idea is one which 'being in itself uncompounded, contains in it nothing but one uniform appearance or conception in the mind and is not distinguishable into different ideas.' In other words it is an unanalysable simple datum of knowledge. However, Locke does not explain how an idea is to be regarded as unabalysable. He points out that the ideas of extension and duration are simple, yet none of the distinct ideas we have of either is without all manner of composition; it is the very nature of both of them to consist of parts. He once more confuses logical simplicity of conception with the simplicity of sensible presentation. His simple ideas are not the sensation or feeling of the present-day psychologies nor are they elements of logical empiricism. Besides unanalysability Locke mentions two other marks of simple ideas, namely.

(i) The mind is passive in the reception of simple ideas and when the mind becomes active, then we get complex ideas.

(ii) Simple ideas are directly known as the contents of actual experience. For example, we at once know the colour, heat, extensity through sensation. Again the simple ideas enter the mind one by one, though the qualities to which they refer are found together. For instance, we get the ideas of colour, smell, taste, touch of the apple one by one.

All ideas originate with and form experience. Mind at birth is a clean slate or tabula rasa and all the characters of knowledge are acquired through experience. Experience is found in two forms of sensation and reflection. By sensation the mind acquires all knowledge about the determinations of the external world and by reflection it receives information about the operations of its own process.

(a) **Sensation.** A sensation arises by the affection of the body by external material things. This bodily affection is conveyed to the brain which gives rise to sensation. Locke mentions all these distinctions but how bodily motion gives rise to consciousness, he tells us, is unintelligible though the fact is undeniable. Again, as a realist he maintained that a sensation always represents or stands for something in the real world.

(b) **Reflection.** As sensation tells us about the external world, so likewise reflection tells us about the internal world. We can also characterise it as an internal sense by which the mind becomes aware of its own action. It differs from sensation, not only in having a distinct sphere of its own but also in two other respects, namely.

   (i) A sensation performs a representative function by standing as a symbol of external things. However, in reflection the mind is present directly without being represented by an idea as a sign.

   (ii) Secondly, noticing or attention is necessary in the reception of all simple ideas but in reflection there is greater attention needed than in sensation.

We might note with Kant that knowledge begins with experience but it does not originate from it. Experience may simply afford an opportunity for the full exercise of the mental activity. In many places Locke himself seems to point to this theory of active mind but he suffered from the assumption of his own times in regarding knowledge as purely receptive and representative. Any recognition of constructiveness in knowledge, according to this view, will reduce knowledge to invention. Thus the copy-theory of knowledge, is responsible for his rejection of the theory of an active mind. Thus he likened the mind to a mirror. But even this Baconian nature of mind does determine the nature of images reflected by it. Therefore, like all pre-Kantians he held the passivity of the mind to save knowledge from becoming arbitrary and fictitious.

2. Complex Ideas

Locke lived in an age of composition theory according to which a complex whole is only a sum-total of simple parts. This ignored the fact that the whole itself may have a characteristic by virtue of its being a whole and, again, a part is greatly changed by the whole of which it becomes a part. Nonetheless, Locke believed that he could explain knowledge by reducing it to simple ideas.

Following three ideas are the complex ideas.

(a) Ideas of Modes

Mixed Modes. Modes are those 'complex ideas which however compounded contain not in them the supposition of subsisting by themselves but are considered as dependences on or affections of substances's *e.g.*, the ideas of number, duration, triangle and gratitude. Modes have been further sub-divided into simple and mixed. Locke says very little about the mixed modes which consist of simple ideas of different ends, combined by the mind, and considered as forming a single complex idea, which is consolidated and fixed by means of a name. However, we should be careful in being consistent in forming mixed modes. Under this, he gives the instances of obligation, drunkenness and lies. Again, let us take the example of beauty which consists of certain composition of colour and figure, causing delight in the beholder.

Simple modes. Simple modes are 'variations, or different combinations of the same simple idea, without the mixture of any other.'

Here there is the repetition or combination of the same kind of ideas. This is best illustrated in the counting of dozen or score. In the case of number of conception of the combination of identical elements to form the complex ideas of simple modes, seems to work most smoothly. Here the idea of one unit is simple and can be added into any increasing number. Similarly, in spatial forms we can get simple modes. If we settle about some determinate length as our unit, then we can variously repeat the units to arrive at the mixed mode of a mile or any such distance. In all combinations, it is necessary that they should be fixed for the mind, by means of a name. But this adding unit to unit and the fixing of the whole by means of a name, goes beyond the mechanical composition to which Locke drew our attention.

Of simple modes two are worthy of note. First, according to Locke, the idea of infinite is a purely negative simple mode. Starting with numerical unit or with spatial unit of finite space, we can repeat the same kind of ideas to form larger wholes. But we find that there is no reasonable limits to the enlarging of the ideas. Hence we arrive at the infinite, in a purely quantitative, comparative and negative way.

(b) Ideas of Substance

In explaining the complex ideas of Substance and Relations, Locke departs from the purely sensationalistic account of knowledge. They are not given by sensation or reflection, but they appear after the simple ideas are supplied to the mind. Hence they are derivative or secondary rather than complex.

A substance is not any simple ideas but is implied by it. It is the idea of a substratum or support underlying a number of simple qualities experienced together. For example, greenness, a certain size, weight, smell, taste, etc., go to make an apple. But these qualities cannot exist by themselves. There must be something in which they inhere. Nor can we think that an experienced thing like an apple or mango is simply a sum-total of these qualities. Hence all simple ideas, all sensible qualities, carry with them a supposition of a substratum to exist in.' Apart from this common view of substance, he points out that it rests upon the necessity of thought. We apply the idea of substance to simple qualities because we cannot conceive of the simple qualities existing by themselves. Sometimes like Hume he tries to explain the origin of substance in terms of custom or habit. When a certain number of these simple ideas go constantly together, we accustom ourselves to suppose some substratum of the qualities we experience.

Matter. When Locke comes to give an account of the qualities of matter he comes to take the help of the scientific theory of his day. Besides, here he quite definitely takes the copy-theory of ideas.

Locke believes that there are two kinds of qualities, namely primary and secondary. The Cartesian dualism of qualities was maintained by a criticism of matter regarded as pure extension. According to Locke, the real quality of matter is not extension but solidity which really depends on the insensible, minute particles of matter called atoms.

Primary and Secondary qualities. Now the primary qualities are utterly inseparable from the material bodies, in all their different sizes and various changes. There are six such original or primary qualities, namely, solidity, extension, figure, motion, rest and number. They are constantly found in the bodies. The secondary qualities, 'which in truth are nothing in the objects themselves, but powers to produce various sensations *in us by their primary qualities*'. They include colour, sounds, tastes, etc. Again, 'primary qualities of bodies are resemblances of them and their patterns do really exist in the bodies themselves; but the ideas produced in us by the secondary qualities have no resemblance of them at all.' Closely following this distinction, Locke points out that primary qualities of solidity, extension etc., are found in their objective right. They are really existent whether there be any person to perceive them or not. But secondary qualities are totally dependent on human subjects and their various sense-organs. Without eyes, there are no colours, without ears there are no sounds. Besides, secondary qualities are relative for the same bucket of water may be cold or hot, according to different arrangement. Finally, secondary qualities are produced by the primary qualities of bulk, solidity etc.

As pointed out before, Locke pointed out that the material substance is unknown. But his account of the primary and secondary qualities points out that the matter is much more than 'I-know-not-what'.

Mind. We get the knowledge of mind through reflection. We know that it has the qualities of perceiving, thinking, memory and willing with the idea of an unknown Substratum. Hence the real nature of mind is unknown, though its qualities are known. The primary qualities of mind are (i) thinking and (ii) the ability to initiate movement willing. How does the mind move the body by willing? This remains a mystery, but the fact is undeniable.

God. In relation to God, Locke does not apply the conclusions of the unknowability of substance. He seems to tell us that God is knowable and his nature is purely immaterial. The content of the idea of God consists of those qualities and powers which we experience in ourselves by reflection and which it is "better to have than to be without", each enlarged by the idea of infinity.

(C) Ideas of Relation

Causality and Identity. The simple ideas of sensation and reflection suggest the idea of substance; similarly, the experienced data of change imply the necessary ideas of power, causality and active efficiency. The power or causality is an idea of relation for it implies the capacity of producing changes in another body. However, it seems clear that the ideas of power and causality are subordinate to that of active initiation of changes.

Causality derived from voluntary action. How do we derive this idea of active initiative? Do we get it from the examination of impact and motion between external bodies? The idea is not derived from the examination of the movement of external bodies for we never experience the activity in one leading to changes in the other, though we observe the impact and consequent movement in the bodies. The idea of active efficiency is really derived from our experience of willing in producing movements or controlling thought.

Though the idea of active efficiency involved in causality has been derived from voluntary action, the idea becomes necessary in understanding all kinds of changes. Thus we derive the proposition "Everything that has a beginning must have a cause....by contemplating our ideas, and perceiving that the idea of beginning to be, is necessarily connected with the idea of some operation, and the idea of operation with the idea of something operating, which we call a cause."

No necessary connection in object. The idea of causality, for Locke, is not necessarily connected with uniformity. The law in nature is essentially a thing of divine pleasure. Hence we do not see any real or intrinsic connection between the phenomena of nature. The experienced regularity in nature depends on laws implanted by God which we must not be too presumptuous to penetrate.

This view of Locke led Berkeley to hold that there is no causality in things. This led to the further denial of causal connection in the objects by Hume.

Thus Locke concludes that one thing causes change in another is undeniable, but the fact is most unintelligible.

Identity. In general by identity is meant nothing but a continuity of existence. "That, therefore, that had one beginning is the same things; and that which had a different beginning in time and place from that, is not the same but diverse." However, in the treatment of identity, Locke shows that its idea varies with the nature of different objects. A material thing is identical with itself when it exists at a particular place, at a particular time, excluding all other things from occupying that particular place or time. But this consideration of identity seems to be appropriate in the case of individual atoms. A material object is said to be identical with itself when the mass of atoms remains to be in the same order and number.

Identity of atoms, plants and men. A living thing, however, has its atoms constantly changed and still we call it the same Oak or tree. Here identity consists in the sameness of the organisation of the parts in one coherent body, partaking of one common life. The identity of man as a living creature is 'nothing but a participation of the same continued life by constantly fleeting particles of matter, in succession of vitally united to the same organised body.' However when he comes to personal identity then he thinks that it depends upon the sameness of consciousness. This immediacy of the same self does not depend on the immediacy of feeling but of judgement of the same consciousness involving past and present consciousness for it is by the consciousness it has of its present thoughts and actions that it is self to itself now, and so will be the same self, as far as the same consciousness can extend to actions past or to come."

Locke did not co-ordinate all these different ideas of Identity. He, without disbelieving in the existence of substance, causality and identity, declared that they are not intelligible to us.

Refutation of Innate Ideas

According to Locke, the originator of empiricism, the mind is a tabula rasa or blank plate. Locke does not accept the theory of innate ideas, for had ideas been innate they should have been known to children as well as to insane individuals. People who believe that ideas are innate are normally lazy, for they want to avoid the effort of searching for ideas and for that reason like to presume that they are innate. Secondly, once it has been established that ideas are innate, it becomes impossible to analyse them. It should also be kept clearly in mind that Locke's criticism of the theory of innate ideas applies to the theories of the British Platonists and Lord Herbert, but not to Descartes' philosophy.

Proofs against Innate Ideas

In order to disprove the theory of innate ideas Locke tried to establish the fact that man can possess all undeniable knowledge by the application of his normal natural powers that no innate ideas are required to assist this process. Locke presents the following arguments against the theory of innate ideas:

1. Why do children and mad people have no experience of innate ideas – In disproving the existence of innate ideas that are universal in character, Locke has objected that if any truth is impressed upon the soul, then the soul should be aware of it. Putting it differently, it cannot be claimed that the soul can remain unaware of any truths that have been impressed upon it or have been part of it since its creation.
2. Innate ideas should precede all experience and intellectual development – If there are some innate ideas, by implication, they should be prior to any acquired knowledge. On the other hand, it has been seen that ideas that are said to be innate normally follow or come after considerable knowledge which children possess. This, too, cannot be accepted as strictly tenable for in experience knowledge will be equated with ideas that originate in experience and are acquired.
3. Space and time, relative ethical and religious concepts cannot be innate - Some people hold that ethical and moral or religious concepts are innate, and try to use them as examples in order to prove the theory of innate ideas. But Locke has demonstrated that in fact, no religious or ethical idea can be said to be universal.
4. Innate ideas cannot be known in the absence of external influence – One argument put forward in support of the theory of innate ideas is that these ideas are destroyed and even destroyed by nature, education or other external influence. This argument can be objected to. It follows that whenever such external influences are absent these innate ideas should be known, that is, the individual should become aware of them. Children and in same individuals are not influenced by external factors and hence they should be the first to realize the presence of innate ideas but they do not do so. Having argued against the theory of innate ideas successfully Locke comes to the conclusion that this concept is baseless.

Theory of Knowledge

Knowledge, according to Locke, consists in 'perception of the connection and agreement, or disagreement and repugnancy of any of our ideas.' First, knowledge depends on the mental power to perceive or apprehend ideas and not in the mere receptivity of ideas. Secondly, knowledge is rational for it consists in seeing the agreement or disagreement between ideas. Further, he confined knowledge to ideas alone without reference to real things.

So far Locke has finished the account of all kinds of ideas which are the materials and instruments of knowledge. As pointed out before, according to Locke, knowledge as against opinion is certain, instructive, agreeing with the reality of things. Thus there are three important problems in relation to knowledge.

1. Objective certainty as against the probability of opinions,
2. Reality and validity of knowledge, and
3. Instructiveness. Knowledge proper must be instructive as against trifling knowledge in tautological propositions.

Knowledge, according to Locke is universal, certain, instructive and real. Now let us see how far we can know. He divides knowledge into four sorts, namely, (i) Identity or diversity, (ii) Relation, (iii) Co-existence or necessary connection, and (iv) Real existence.

(i) **Knowledge of Identity.** By identity is meant the identity of the content of an idea and its distinction from the content of every other idea. Though the power of perceiving similarity of difference is fundamental yet knowledge of mere identity, can give only a trifling proposition. If each idea is absolutely distinct from each other, then how can we unite the ideas in real knowledge? According to Locke, any "significant predication involves the assertion, not of bare identity or diversity, but of other and more determinate relations between the contents of our ideas." Thus the proposition 'a man is white' means that the thing which has the quality of man has also the quality of whiteness. Thus he advances the relational nature of knowledge.

The consideration to identity gives rise to the knowledge of relations, which is really important in the epistemology of Locke. This kind of knowledge consists of a perception of relations between the content of one idea and that of another after abstracting them from the spatial, temporal and other circumstances of sensible existence.

(ii) **Knowledge of Relations.** This is the fundamental assumption of Locke for explaining the universal and necessary knowledge in science. The perception of these relations between abstracted contents adds to knowledge. Besides, the perception of the relation of agreement or disagreement is necessary for its arises from the very nature of the ideas. For example, 2 + 2 = 4 follows from the very nature of the ideas. Knowledge thus gained is *universal* for it is true of ideas which are timeless and free from concrete details. The knowledge being necessary in the abstract ideas will be true in all cases where they will be embodied in some concrete setting. Such knowledge also may be said to be eternal for it is based on ideas abstracted from all time relations.

The best kind of knowledge in sciences is best seen in mathematics. This is possible because it does not deal with concrete or sensible experience but with ideal construction. The knowledge of mathematics is not due to any innate ideas but because the least difference between different ideas is clearly perceptible. The demonstrative character of mathematics depends on the perfect determination or precision of the ideas with which it is concerned. Besides, the subject-matter of mathematics is formed of discrete ideas. The same thing may be shown in Geometry. Here the subject-matter is continuous, instead of discrete extension, but the value of Geometry depends, like Arithmetic on the ideal construction.

Besides, it has been able to discover the just equality of two angles or ideal elements of extension or figures. Lastly, it has been able to make use of visible and lasting marks in the form of diagrams. The great merit of diagrams lies in checking the tendency towards variation and thereby in securing a common understanding with others.

(iii) **Knowledge of Co-existence.** Locke gradually now makes transition from the abstract ideas to ideas referring to the reality. He turns to the knowledge of co-existence and necessary connection. Now any knowledge worthy of the name must have necessary connection. Let us see whether we can know substance involving co-existence of several qualities. In coming to the knowledge of co-existence "What Locke has in mind is really a distinction between the relations which our thought discovers between the contents of our ideas, when abstraction is made from the conditions of actual existence, and the special relations which are involved in the fact of concrete existence itself." Here he points out that the most part of the material knowledge consists of the knowledge of co-existence, namely, our idea of fire is a body hot, luminous and moving upward; of gold, our idea is a body heavy, yellow, malleable and fusible. But this kind of knowledge is inadequate for the majority of such propositions are lacking intellectual necessity. No doubt we frame such necessary propositions regarding co-existence as 'figure necessarily supposes extension', 'two bodies cannot be in the same place' etc. Unfortunately, such propositions are trifling. The knowledge of actual substance is confined to particular instances and this cannot be raised to the status of the universal and certain knowledge.

(iv) **Knowledge of existence.** All the while Locke believes that there is a real objective world existing in its own right but he confines knowledge to ideas alone. This dualism he could not overcome. He finds that knowledge about existential things is not possible, in general. There are only two things whose existence we know with perfect transparency of knowledge. First, we have the intuitive knowledge of our own self. The unique nature of self-knowledge depends on the fact that the mind and mind alone is present to the understanding.

Intuitive knowledge of self-existence. However, the intuitive knowledge of self differs from the intuitive knowledge about abstract ideas in one important respect. The immediate apprehension of abstract ideas is possible because our abstraction from concrete settings makes it independent of the intervention of many other ideas; whilst the intuitive self-judgement is so perceived because it is self-sufficient, without needing any idea.

The existence of the material world is possible. The existence of God is also known to be real because his existence can be demonstrated. But apart from the existence of self and God, the existence of particular substances cannot be known with certainty. Should we deny, then, the existence of the material world? Locke was not a subjective idealist like Berkeley for he believed that ideas are mere signs, pointing something real beyond themselves. He also granted that the knowledge of the primary qualities is possible. He could not deny the existence of the material world because of the following reasons :

1. There is a peculiar tang of reality found in sense-perception for any one will be able to make a difference between an actual taste and an imagined taste.
2. Besides, there is a certain amount of coerciveness of forcefulness in actual sensation pointing out of something real as their cause. "If I turn my eyes at noon towards the sun I cannot avoid the ideas which the light or sun then produces in me." This independence of the subjective control is not found concerning an imaginal product.
3. Lastly, our sense-organs are not the instruments of creating ideas but only of receiving them. If a person has no eyes, then he can have no ideas of colour or light. Thus the dependence of sensation on our sense-organs points to the existence of something existing outside of us.

Instructiveness of Knowledge

Locke emphasizes on instructiveness of knowledge. According to him, trifling propositions are those which do not add to our knowledge. Under this heading he found identical propositions like A is A or substance is substance. No doubt such propositions are certain but are tautologous. Again, the socalled analytic propositions in which a part of the connotation of the subject is predicated, also come under trifling propositions, e.g. 'Lead is a metal' or 'men are animals'. Hence in an instructive proposition, which adds to our knowledge, there must be something more than the relation the whole and part. In an instructive proposition we may affirm something which is not contained in the subject.

Three Grades of Knowledge

The clarity of man's knowledge depends upon the correlation between the ideas in his mind. In the process of correlation of ideas, at times this relation becomes obvious almost immediately but, at other times it takes a longer period. On the basis of this Locke has given three grades of knowledge.

1. **Intuitive Knowledge.** "Sometimes the mind perceives the agreement or disagreement of two ideas immediately by themselves, without the intervention of any other and this, I think, we may call *intuitive* knowledge." Here we see the agreement or disagreement as directly as we see the light with our eyes. Thus we at once see that white is not black, that a circle is not a triangle.

This knowledge is most clear and certain and is the highest kind of knowledge which human faculty is capable of achieving.

2. **Demonstrative Knowledge.** Next in the degree of knowledge comes the demonstrative knowledge, in which we perceive the agreement or disagreement between two ideas by the *mediation or intervention of other* ideas. For example, we see that A and B are equal to one another because each is equal to C. We express the reasoning like this :

A = C
C = B,
Therefore, A = B.

The separate steps in the reasoning, however, should be immediately clear. Thus demonstrative knowledge consists in a series or chain of intuitions.

The knowledge gained by demonstrative method is certain but it is indirect, requiring proof depending on the quickness and sagacity of the mind. It is not very easy either, for it involves many steps in which a steady application and pursuit is required to this discovery. Again, in intuitive knowledge there is no doubt anywhere but in the demonstrative knowledge, before a demonstration takes place, there is doubt. Besides, demonstrative knowledge is not so clear for it passes through different stages. Lastly, it requires the memory of the previous steps or intuitions. However, memory opens the door to the possibilities of errors and mistakes. Thus, we conclude that the demonstrative knowledge is inferior to intuitive knowledge in degree of certainty.

Locke thought that demonstrative knowledge is not confined to mathematics alone but could be applied to Ethics as well. However, in spite of repeated requests he never carried a demonstration of ethical principles.

3. **Sensitive knowledge.** Anything that comes to acquire the certainty of intuitive or demonstrative knowledge is knowledge and anything which comes short of it is not knowledge but is an opinion. "There is, indeed, another perception of the mind employed about the particular existence of finite beings without us; which, going beyond bare probability, and yet not reaching perfectly to either of the foregoing degrees of certainty, passes under the name of knowledge." This knowledge regarding the particular external objects is called *sensitive knowledge.* Locke does not find the element of certainty in sensitive knowledge but could not deny the name of knowledge to it. Though it may not be knowledge proper, still it guides our happiness or misery, 'beyond which we have no concernment to know or to be'.

Theory of Substance

It has been said that sensation or reflection cannot gives us the knowledge of the theory of substance. Substance appears after the simple ideas and these simple ideas are supplied to the mind.

It is regarded as the idea of a substratum. A substance is regarded not as a simple idea. Qualities needs substance. Qualities inheres in the substance. It has been said that all simple ideas carry with them a supposition of a substratum and this substratum exist in itself only.

It has been said, that we are able to apply the idea of substance to simple qualities. It has been also said that we can not conceive the simple qualities that exist by themselves. When simple ideas are able to go constantly together, then we are able to suppose the qualities substratum.

Distinction between Primary and Secondary Qualities

Primary and secondary qualities comes under the domain of ideas of substance. He says that only two kinds of qualities exist namely primary and secondary. Under the domain of matter so, primary and secondary qualities comes.

The real quality of matter is regarded as a solidity. It does not mean extension. Solidity depends upon the insensible minute particles of matter and these particles of matter is known as atoms.

Primary qualities are regarded as utterly inseparable from the material bodies, According to Locke, *there are six original or primary qualities which are as follows*

1. Solidity
2. Extension
3. Figure
4. Motion
5. Rest
6. Number

These qualities are constantly found in the bodies. The secondary qualities are defined as powers, which produces various sensations in us by their primary qualities. It includes colour, sounds etc. Primary qualities of bodies really exist in the b lies themselves.

The primary qualities are found in their objective aspect. Secondary qualities are dependent only on human subjects. There are no colours without eyes. There are no sounds without ears. Secondary qualities are said to be relative.

It has been said that secondary qualities always needed primary qualities. He says that the material substance is regarded as unknown. The real nature of mind is regarded as unknown, although, its qualities are known.

Thinking and the ability to initiate movement willing are regarded as the primary qualities of mind. It has been said that the content of the idea of God only consists qualities and powers.

Primary and Secondary Qualities

Contained within this section on simple and complex ideas is a very important discussion by Locke on qualities.

1. **Two types of qualities.** Qualities correspond to the ideas derived by Sensation. A quality is whatever it is in the external objects that produces ideas in us when we use Sensation to perceive them. In other words, ideas are the things that are IN US, while qualities are the corresponding things that are IN OBJECTS. Locke is careful to explain that these "qualities" may be divided into two fundamentally different categories: (2.8.9-10)
   a. **Primary qualities.** The first sort of quality is the sort that every object necessarily has, no matter what. These are things like size, shape, and motion or rest.
   b. **Secondary qualities.** The second sort of quality are the sort that can be added to or taken away from objects. These are things like colors, sounds, tastes, warmth, etc.

2. **Defending the distinction.** Locke provides several reasons for thinking that there is such a distinction. (2.8.9-10, 16-17, 19, 21)
   a. **Inseparability.** No matter what you do to an object, you can't take away its primary qualities. For instance, cut a grain of wheat in two, and it will still have size and shape, no matter how many times you divide it. On the other hand, turn off the lights and a jar WILL lose its color (but not its size and shape).
   b. **Non-resemblance.** Things like size and shape DO seem to be in the objects themselves, but it is absurd to think, e.g., pain is IN a fire. Nothing at all in the fire resembles pain.
   c. **Relative to the perceiver.** It seems that secondary qualities are relative to the perceiver. For, if there is a bucket of lukewarm water, one hand may perceive the water as cold, and the other perceive it as warm—for instance if the first hand is already warm, and the second hand is already cold. Primary qualities are not relative in this way.
3. **Some implications.** There are a couple of interesting implications of this distinction. (2.8.11-15, 20)
   a. **Secondary qualities reduce to primary ones.** It seems as if the only thing that reaches our eyes are tiny particles. These stimulate some motion in our nerves and this motion produces ideas in the mind. But, then, COLORS do not reach our eyes, but only particles with particular sizes, shapes, and motions do. This means that all secondary qualities are really just the powers that objects have to produce certain sensory ideas in us via the sizes, shapes, and motions of their particles. This seems supported by the following: Pound an almond and its color and flavor will be altered, but it seems that all you have done to the almond is alter its texture. Therefore, color and flavor seem to be nothing more than something caused by the sizes and shapes of the parts of the almond.
   b. **Secondary qualities do not at all resemble anything in objects.** It seems that the IDEAS produced by secondary qualities do not at all resemble the things in the objects themselves. For instance, the idea of heat is produced in us by the motion of an object's particles, but heat does not at all resemble motion. (Recall Galileo, who said that "tickling" was not in the feather, but only certain shapes, sizes, and motions of its particles) Primary qualities DO really exist in bodies, however. But note: Even our ideas of primary qualities are merely "resemblances" of those qualities.

Skepticism. All we have access to are ideas. Our ideas of secondary qualities do not resemble anything in objects; i.e., the world doesn't have anything like the sensation of colors, odors, pain, or warmth, etc. in it.

Furthermore, even our ideas of primary qualities merely RESEMBLE the actual primary qualities in objects. But, then, how do we know that these ideas really DO resemble those qualities? In order to know for sure, wouldn't we have to compare the REAL qualities with our ideas of them? But, this seems impossible, even in principle. Consider the following argument. What do you think?

1. In order to know if A resembles B, one must be able to compare A and B with one another.
2. Locke claims that we can know that our ideas of primary qualities (A) resemble those qualities (B). Yet, all we have direct access to are our ideas; i.e. (A), we do not have direct access to the actual qualities in objects (B). Therefore, since we only perceive A, and we never perceive B, we cannot compare A with B.
3. Therefore, we cannot know that our ideas of primary qualities resemble the actual qualities in objects.

GEORGE BERKELEY

As a critic of John Locke and precursor of David Hume, George Berkeley presented a profoundly original perspective on some of the crucial questions in epistemology and metaphysics. Denying the existence of matter with remarkable ingenuity Berkeley initiated an outlook to which philosophy has been indebted ever since. George Berkeley, an Irish man, was born in 1685. After his schooling in Kilkenny he entered Trinity College, Dublin in his sixteenth year where he had a brilliant career, first as a graduate student and later as a tutor and fellow, for about thirteen years. In those days Trinity was deeply impacted by Newtonian science and the new philosophies of Descartes, Locke and Malebranche, and Berkeley with his keen intellect soon involved the young minds in scientific and philosophical deliberations.

Visiting London in 1713 he made an indelible impression upon the great literary men of the age like Swift, Steele, Addison and Pope. He devised a scheme for a college in Bermudas and for this purpose he went to America. But having spent three years (1728-31) in Rhode Island he relinquished the project and returned to England being excited about the future possibility of the new world. He wrote the poem containing the frequently quoted line, 'Westward the course of Empire takes its way' on account of which the town of Berkeley in California was called after him.

He married a young girl and said of her, 'I chose her for the qualities of her mind and her unaffected inclination to books. She goes with great cheerfulness to live a plain farmer's life and wears stuff of her own spinning wheel.'

In 1734 he became Bishop of Cloyne in the south of Ireland, where he led a retired life, engrossed with scholarly studies publishing books and articles from time to time but, above all, striving to ameliorate the wretched economic conditions of the peasants. When Berkeley's health began to fail he left Cloyne for Oxford at the age of sixty-seven and a year later in 1753 while sitting quietly at tea with his family he died. He was buried in Christ Church Chapel in Oxford.

Berkeley, with all his scholarship, lived a pious life and was described by Pope to possess every virtue under heaven. Alterbury said of Berkeley that he had, 'so much understanding, so much knowledge, so much innocence, and such humility I did not think had been the portion of any but angels till I saw this gentleman.' Berkeley wrote extensively but his best work was over while he was still quite young. Some of his famous works are: Commonplace Book (1706-08), A New theory of Vision (1709), The Principles of Human Knowledge (1710), The Dialogues of Hylas and Philonous (1713), Alciphron (1732) and Siris (1744). His writings after the age of twenty-eight were of less consequence. Berkeley wrote with great elegance and lucidity.

Refutation of Distinction Between Primary and Secondary Qualities

Primary qualities of extension, solidity etc., never exist apart from the secondary ones. Who can imagine extension without its being coloured etc. What right have we to say, then, that primary qualities can also exist in things apart from the secondary ones? This is nothing but vicious abstraction. Hence we must conclude that both must have the same kind of existence. As the secondary qualities are taken to be mental, so the so-called primary should also be regarded as mental.

Besides, the experiment of Locke showed that the same bucket of water may seem hot or hotter, cold or colder by suitably interchanging one's hands in buckets of cold and hot water. Therefore, he held that the secondary qualities are relative. But this relatively is true of the primary qualities as well. Against Newton, he holds that every motion is relative. The same man on the boat is said to be stationary in relation to the moving steamer and, again, moving in relation to the man standing on the bank. The same relativity is true of number as well. The same yardstick may be called either three feet long or thirty six inches long. Thus if the secondary qualities are said to be subjective because they are relative, then the primary ones should also be regarded as subjective for they are also relative.

Lastly, the primary qualities can no more be perceived without the sense-organs than the secondary ones. Extension, as he shows in The New Theory of Vision, is entirely dependent on our touch and vision.

Thus all qualities are really subjective and mind-dependent and there is no necessity of assuming matter in which the primary qualities are wrongly supposed to be existing.

Immaterialism

Berkeley has rejected matter on many grounds, some of them are given below :

(A) **The Refutation of Matter as an Abstract idea.** Berkeley's whole aim was religious. He refuted the doctrine of abstract ideas not so much because it was inconsistent with empiricism but because it support matter. He believed in sensationism because it at once gave him a weapon of attack against the sciences which supported the reality of matter and motion. Thus Berkeley believed in spiritualism, for which he hardly adduced any real proof, but this necessitated the refutation of materialism. This negative task was the most serious thing he ever undertook to prove. We have already seen the general refutation of matter on the ground that it is abstract idea. But the attempts this refuation most systematically.

(B) **On the Basis of Rejection of Distinction Between Primary and Secondary Qualities.** According to Locke and Descartes, the primary qualities of extension, figure, solidity, motion, rest and number are supposed to be really in things and the secondary qualities of colour, heat, cold etc., are supposed to be in the perceiver and not in the things. But obviously the so-called primary qualities are also ideas. Ideas are mental. Therefore, even the primary qualities are mental. And, hence there is no matter.

(C) **A systematic refutation.** Now Berkeley undertakes to refute the existence of matter on any doctrine whatsoever. If there is matter then it can be shown to have the following alternatives.

1. Matter is directly perceptible.
2. If it be not immediately perceptible then its existence is inferred either on the strength of the
   (i) Likeness of our ideas, or
   (ii) As the cause of the ideas, or
   (iii) As the instrument of our ideas, or
   (iv) As the occasion of the ideas.
3. If matter be shown to be neither perceived nor inferred, then it must be shown to have some use, either religious, moral or practical.

Now Berkeley takes up all these alternatives one by one and shows that matter is neither perceived nor inferred nor has any use. Thus it does not exist at all.

Critique of Abstract Ideas

Berkeley refutes the doctrine of abstract ideas on logical and psychological grounds. His first point may be called the fallacy of vicious abstraction concerning abstract ideas. Any perceived quality is found inseparably mixed with other qualities. Now what is the guarantee that any quality isolated from the rest can also exist in separation from them? The redness of the rose is always found with other qualities of smell, softness, smoothness etc., of the rose. How can we think of the redness existing apart from the other qualities of the rose? This is too arbitrary an assumption to be accepted.

Again Locke points out that the abstract idea of man will be one which is tall and short, fair and dark, dull and intelligent and so on. But how one and the same idea will contain all and yet none of these? To believe in abstract ideas, is clearly to accept a manifest contradiction.

Lastly, Berkeley takes the help of the psychological method of Introspection. We have no faculty for framing abstract ideas. "For myself, I find I have indeed a faculty of imagining, or representing to myself the idea of those particular things I have perceived.....But then whatever hand or eye I imagine, it must have some particular shape and colour. Likewise the idea of man that I frame to myself must be either of a white, or a black, or a tawny, a straight, or crooked, a tall, or a low, or a middle-sized man." Thus we think only of the particular and not of any general man. "And it is equally impossible for me to form the abstract idea of motion distinct from the body moving, and which is neither swift nor slow, curvillinear nor rectilinear; and the like may be said of all abstract ideas whatsoever."

The real aim in the refutation of abstract ideas was to establish *immaterialism.* Matter is an abstract idea for it means something which is moving and stationary, hard and soft etc., all and yet none of these. Besides, it means something existing apart from its being perceived. But this is a vicious abstraction for what right have we to maintain that there can be something independent of our perception when everything in our actual experience is always in our perception? Thus matter is an abstract ideas but an abstract idea does not exist. Hence matter does not exist. This is the general refutation of matter.

Esse Est Percipi

Berkeley's astounding and provocative statement was that 'to be is to be perceived,' or esse est percipi, which entailed that if something were not perceived, it would not exist. This most naturally raises the question whether it exists when it is not being perceived. For Berkeley the entire issue depends on how we understand or interpret the word 'exists'. By this he means to say that there can be no imaginable situation where the term 'exists' is put to use without simultaneously assuming that a mind is constantly perceiving it.

The impossibility of an unperceived body follows from the idea of body as held by Locke. A body according to Locke is a solid, extended, figured substance possessing the power of motion, a certain colour, weight, taste, smell and sound. This latter set of qualities are simply the effects of the body that are produced in the perceiving subject and hence are present in the perceiver and do not reside in the body itself. They are not inherent in the body and are for that matter to be called secondary qualities. On the other hand are the qualities that are inherent in the substance, i.e. the body itself. These are primary qualities. Extension, figure, solidity, motion and rest are such primary qualities. He says that the ideas of solidity and extension which Locke claims to be of primary qualities, are acquired through the sense of touch and become sensations in my mind much like the secondary qualities. It is not possible to disentangle the idea of extension from the idea of colour and other such secondary qualities. Besides, an extended thing which is not at the same time coloured cannot be perceived. If we examine an object of our knowledge, a table, for instance, we do not find that its shape is 'out there' while its color is 'in here.' Thus the distinction that Locke makes between primary and secondary qualities is redundant.

Locke had said that substance, or matter, supports or acts as a substrate to the qualities we sense. Philonous answers that the word substratum has no clear meaning for him and he needed to 'know any sense, literal or not literal, that you understand in it.' Hylas conceded his inability to assign a definite meaning to the term substratum, saying, 'I declare I know not what to say.'

This is however not to say that sensible things do not possess reality but only that sensible things exist only insofar as they are perceived. This in other words means that only ideas exist. To this Berkeley adds that 'I hope that to call a thing 'idea' makes it no less real.' To this the question arises as to why should one say that only ideas, instead of things exist? This, Berkeley says, was to eliminate 'the futile concept of matter:' 'I do not argue against the existence of any one thing that we can apprehend, either by sense or reflection…. The only thing whose existence we deny is that which philosophers call matter or corporeal substance.'

Since it was the science of his day, in particular, physics that leaned so heavily on the notion of matter, Berkeley realized the necessity to challenge its basic assumptions and methods. What agitated Berkeley most was that scientists made use of general and abstract terms as though they had reference to real entities, in particular to an underlying material substance in nature. He said, 'As several of these (qualities) are observed to accompany each other, they come to be marked by one name, and so to be reputed as one thing. Thus for example, a certain colour, taste, smell, figure and consistence having been observed to go together, are accounted as a distinct thing, signified by the name 'apple'; other collections or ideas constitute a stone, a tree, a book and the like sensible things.' He aspired to clarify the approach of scientific language wherein terms such as force, gravity and causality refer to nothing more than an assembly of ideas, which our minds derive from sensation.

The more Berkeley examined the functioning of his mind and grappled with the relation of his ideas with objects outside his mind the more certain he became that no object independent of his ideas could be discovered. He said there is nothing out there of which we do not have some perception.

As a clinching argument Berkeley remarked that 'an idea can be like nothing but an idea,' and so when Locke says that ideas and real things are different; ideas being mental and real things material and mental and material being disparate in nature, there is a contradiction evident in his views. Berkeley says if mind and matter are unlike each other and if knowledge depends upon the likeness of the unlike then it is an absurdity. Since he had refuted Locke's distinction between primary and secondary qualities, which is the very essence of Locke's thought, he has in effect refuted the entire system of representative realism.

The Problem of Solipsism

The term 'subjective' is rather vague. Most probably it means that only 'subjects' are real and 'objects' as independent of the mind are not real. Hence, nature, which is considered to be 'to other' of mind, according to subjective idealism is not real. Therefore, subjective idealism holds that Nature is merely the projection of some minds and has no existence of its own. In this sense, Berkeley's idealism is subjective, since according to it nothing exists apart consciousness, then this interpretation would reduce subjective idealism to solipsism, according to which theory all things and other spirits are so many states of consciousness of a single individual thinker. For simple, we say that this blade of grass is green. Now how can we be certain that A or B is not enough, for we know that to the colour-blind nothing appears red or green. Yet he learns to call a certain patch as 'green' which really appears to him as a shade of grey or brown. Similarly, nobody can ever verify that a certain shade of colour or a certain degree of sweetness or warmth is actually experienced by another individual. If it is so, then what appears to me is real for me and has no validity for others. But who are others? How can we be sure of the existence of other spirits? According to Berkeley, we know the existence of other spirits by the effects they produce on the perceiver and other objects. But certainly those effects are ideas and ideas are the furniture of an individual mind at the time they are entertained. In dreams also we perceive many individuals and many objects, though all of them are the projections of the dreamer's mind alone, who knows we are dreaming all the time? Most probably there can be no way out of solipsism, if we accept the subjectivity of an idea. The sense-data theory is a way out of solipsism. This supposes that our sense data are neither mental nor material. They are the simples, rockbottom, primary elements of knowledge. But the whole sense-data theory is only a procedural presupposition, a mere convention or recommendation is epistemology. Berkeley did not suspect that his 'idealism' would lead to solipsism. He assumed the reality of other finite spirits besides himself and certainly of God. Hence, Berkeley was not a solipsist.

God and the Self

The essence of a thing, as distinguished from that of spirits, consists in being perceived. But the essence of spirits consists in their being perceived or perceiving. If spirits were nothing but ideas, then everything would have been reduced to mere succession of ideas and no permanence could be established. Thus in order to explain the permanence of things, the existence of spirits must be granted. The very essence of a spirit consists in activity,—in its active principle of producing motion and change. Now there are three kinds of spirits, namely, (i) Myself, (ii) Other finite spirits like myself, and (iii) The infinite spirit or God.

I am intuitively aware of my own existence. First, I am aware of the happening of the ideas of colour, heat etc., as mine. Besides, I am immediately aware of myself in my activity of (a) calling up mental images, and (b) of producing changes in my body and other things through volition. Thus perceptually and volitionally I am conceived of my existence.

The existence of other spirits is based on inference by analogy. The finite spirits are passive in the reception of presentations but they are active in the reproduction of images and in existing changes in their own bodies or in the bodies of others and other things to a limited extent. Now we can know the presence of other finite spirits by virtue of their exciting changes in things. We know our own activities in causing changes and when we find that similar changes are taking place, then we can infer the existence of other finite spirits like ourselves. For example, we have made a table and when we find a similar table, then we can infer that there are similar beings like ourselves who have made the table.

The existence of the infinite spirit can be known in the following way : 1. I am aware of a succession of ideas in me. 2. There must be some cause of them which is either, (a) matter, or (b) some other idea or (c) spirit. Now (a) and (b) being passive cannot be active agents or causes. 3. Now the causes must be a spirit, but the finite spirits are incapable of producing ideas of fixed order on such a vast scale. Besides, many of the ideas which compose nature like the rivers, mountains and falls are independent of their will. 4. Therefore, God alone is the cause of all ideas. Besides, the surprising magnificence, beauty and perfection of nature confirm us in this belief. Thus if we know other spirits by their operations in us, through finite and narrow assemblage of ideas they excite in us, then the existence of God is more manifest to us. We know God "withersoever we direct our view, we do at all times and in all places perceive manifested tokens of the Divinity....everything we see, hear, feel, or any wise perception by Sense, being a sign or effect of the power of God". The whole of Nature is the living language of God, and, be-speaking of his Goodness, Wisdom and Presence to all.

DAVID HUME

Born on April 26, 1711, in Edinburgh, Scotland, David Hume attended Edinburgh University from the ages of eleven to fifteen, in which city he remained to study law. Finding this not to his taste, Hume read widely in ancient and modern literature, improved his knowledge of science and languages, and devoted himself above all to philosophy. However, reviewers were mostly hostile and uncomprehending. Having wisely taken the precaution to publish anonymously, Hume soon recovered from his failure and decided to apply his immense literary gifts to the more widely accessible medium of the essay. Hume presented a selection of the doctrines of the Treatise with some previously unpublished material in the form of Philosophical Essays concerning Human Understanding in 1748. A sea change in the reception of Hume's theory of understanding occurred in 1783, when Immanuel Kant declared that Hume's treatment of cause and effect was responsible for awakening him from his dogmatic slumber.

Impressions and Ideas

Hume points out that there are two kinds of contents of the mind, namely, impressions and their ideas. These are the only perceptions which compose the human mind. First, impressions and ideas have been divided into simple and complex. All ideas or impressions are those which admit of no separation or distinction, like the sensation of red or cold or smell. Complex ideas or impressions are those which are composed of simple parts like the idea of an apple, having the parts of colour, taste, smell etc. Again, impressions may be divided into sensation and reflection. Sensations seem to arise from unknown causes but the reflection of passions, desires, emotions and the felt inclination of the mind is 'derived in a great measure from our ideas, Thus reflection is secondary and sensation is primary. But reflection though secondary is not the copy of the sensation because like all other true elements the impressions of reflection are original facts and realities, complete in themselves, and implying no reference to other passions, volitions and actions."

Now let us turn to the important distinction between impressions and ideas. Simple impressions are the originals of which the simple ideas are the copies. Thus impressions are prior and the ideas are posterior. There can be no simple ideas without their corresponding original impressions. The complex ideas however, compounded in fancy need not correspond to their impressions but their elements do correspond to the impression.

For example, we may fancy a new Jerusalem whose pavements are made of gold and whose walls are build of rubies. However, the elements of pavement, gold, wall etc., are all derived from simple impressions. Further, the impressions have superiority in force, liveliness and vivacity; but the ideas, for the most part, are weak and faint. Thirdly, the simple ideas are representative and the simple impressions are represented, but the simple impressions themselves are not representative of anything else. We cannot say that the perceptions are the copies of the extra-mental thing. The cause of the sense-impressions is inexplicable by human reason for we do not know whether they arise immediately from the object, or are produced by the creative power of the mind or are derived from 'the author of our being'. However, the simple ideas are the copies of the original impressions. Lastly, the impressions, strictly speaking, are always simple but the ideas can be both simple and complex.

Ideas, again, may appear either in the form of memory or imagination. The distinction between the memorial and imaginal ideas is not well marked. To a certain extent memorial ideas are strong and lively, and the imaginal ideas are weak and faint. Secondly, in imagination we are freer to produce complex ideas, though not so much the simple ones which are tied to their original impressions; but memory is tied down to their corresponding impressions.

In determining the simple elements of which the mind is composed, Hume takes the help of his famous dogma: *What is distinguishable is separable.* All impressions as such are distinct and separate with no logical connection between them. This is known as Humean atomism. As such the impressions knowledge is a unified whole and a connected system. Hence, Hume supplements his atomism with the Principles of 'union and cohesion' amongst the separate impressions. He points out that there is a gentle force which attract the separate impressions into union. This gentle force is nothing but the law of association working according to the principles of resemblance and continuity. Because of these bonds 'one idea naturally introduces another', and even the product of fancy cannot be arbitrary. This law of association is the all-pervasive principle which binds the separate ideas in every sphere of imagination and science. In the sequel it will be shown that the so-called disciplined reasoning of science does not show any logical or necessary connection. In the last resort the necessary connection will be shown to be one of the association of Ideas. Hence there is connection amongst the impressions which is not rational but is effected through custom and imagination.

Knowledge Concerning Relations of Ideas and Matters of Fact

According to Hume, all knowledge begins with your experiences. Your experiences includes various 'Sense impressions'. He says, that there were just two kinds of reliable human understanding.

According to Hume, all knowledge is divided into 'Matters of fact' and 'Relations of ideas'. This is also referred as Hume's Fork. Without matter of fact and relation of ideas, all knowledge does not exist. He talks about this in his book 'The Treatise on Human Nature'. He says that matters of fact is regarded as a posteriori whereas relations of ideas is regarded as a priori. Hume says, that propositions of mathematics differ from propositions that are based on matters of fact. No amount of experiment will guarantee the truth of future events. The certainty of mathematical reasoning is also not guaranteed.

Why a Cause is Always Necessary

The first question concern the necessity of a cause. This deal with a general maxim in philosophy, which says that whatever begins to exist, must have a cause of existence. This is founded on intuition. But, if we examine this maxim by the idea of knowledge, then we shall discover in it no mark of any such intuitive certainty. All certainty arises from the comparison of ideas and from the discovery of such relations as are unalterable, so long as the ideas continue the same.

That proposition is not intuitively certain. At least any one, who would assert it to be intuitively certain, must deny these to be the only infallible relations and most find some other relation of that kind to be imply in it; which it will then be time enough to examine.

Knowledge : Dependent on Ideas or on Matters of Fact

Hume has given some points which helps him not only in rejection of others' false assumptions but also in building of his own philosophical palace.

1. Propositions of mathematics differ in kind from propositions concerning matters of fact. Naturally factual propositions cannot be confused with mathematical propositions. In other words, mathematical certainty with regard to factual propositions cannot be obtained or demonstrated.
2. No amount of observation or experiment can guarantee the truth of future events. Nay, every rational attempt to base factual proposition on uniformity of nature did the law of causation is bound to fail.

3. Even the certainty of mathematical reasoning cannot be ultimately guaranteed because of the frailty of the judging powers of man.
4. However, Hume holds that man is not guided by reason alone. Nature, custom and habits determine human thinking. This natural propensity in man leads him to believe in causal relation, external world, moral principles and God.

Points (3) and (4) will be included under Hume's scepticism.

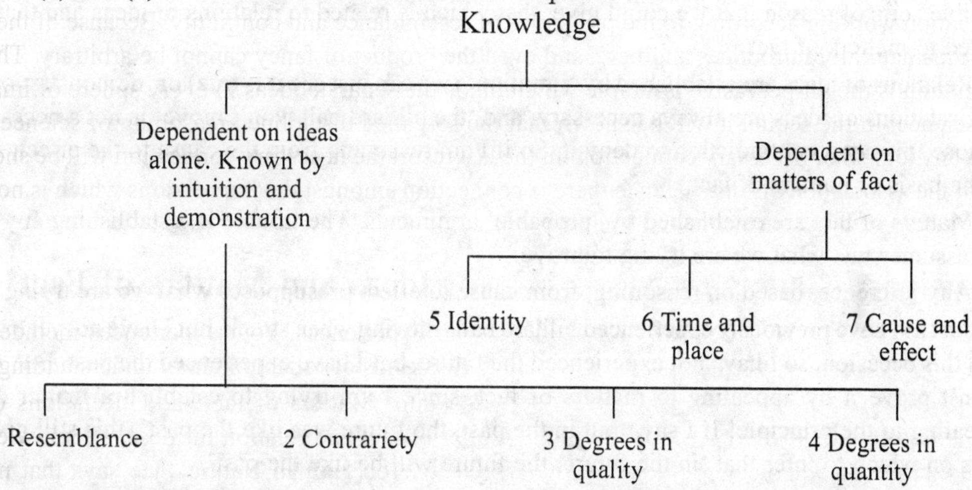

Induction and Causality

Hume's arguments on induction occur in the middle of his exploration of the idea of causation. He is seeking to establish the foundation for our knowledge of matters of fact, and has argued that all our knowledge that goes beyond what is present to our senses or memory rests on causal inference. We have experience that, in the past, whenever a cause of a particular type occurs, *e.g.*, a billiard ball striking another, it was followed by an effect, the second ball moving; but why think that this succession will occur again?

Reasons for Thinking the Future will Resemble the Past

There are two ideas connected with causation which we might think provided us with good grounds for thinking that causes always cause the same effects; and so we can reason from the occurrence of the cause to the effect.

Necessary Connection

If a cause is necessarily connected to its effects, then if we perceive the cause occurring, we can infer the effect. But Hume argues that we are unable to find any impression of this necessity in the objects themselves (this is discussed in the handout 'Hume on causation'). Perhaps because our minds are caused to move from one idea to another like this, we think that the effect must follow the cause. As Hume points out, there is no contradiction in supposing that the second billiard ball won't move when struck. So this can't be the reason we think the future will resemble the past.

Similarity

Philosophers before Hume often thought that an effect must resemble its cause. For example, Descartes argues that only God could have caused the idea of God; Locke argues that only an intelligence could have caused intelligence. We can't figure out what something will cause, or what caused it, just by considering the one object. But if effects had to be similar to their causes, we could. So we can't argue that on this occasion, we can know what effect will follow the cause, because it must be similar to the cause.

The Objection to Reason

Hume argues that our belief that the future will resemble the past is not based on reason at all:

When I infer, from perceiving the cause, that the effect will occur, I'm not reasoning. There are two possible sorts of reason that we could give, that which is related to relations of ideas and that which is related to matters of fact.

Relations of ideas are established by 'intuition' (we can just see it is true) or 'demonstration'. In any case, relations of ideas are always necessary; and 'the billiard ball won't move' is not a necessary truth because it is not a contradiction to deny it. So if I am reasoning from the cause to the effect, it must be on the basis of matters of fact.

Matters of fact are established by 'probable' arguments. The trouble is, establishing any matter of fact assumes just what we are trying to prove.

Any inference, based on reasoning, from cause to effect presupposes what we are trying to show.

Just as I have previously experienced billiard balls moving when struck, but I have not yet experienced it on this occasion, so I have not experienced the future, but I have experienced the past. But, of course, I can't prove it by appealing to matters of fact, since I am trying to establish a matter of fact by appealing to the principle! If I say, 'but in the past, the future was like the past', this still gives me no basis on which to infer that 'in the future, the future will be like the past'.

Hume has argued not just that there isn't a reason on the basis of which we make our causal inferences, he has argued that there is no type of reason which could serve. He finishes his argument by remarking that children are capable of learning from experience, and yet here we are, professional philosophers, struggling to produce the reasoning which we suppose the child easily employs! We can't, because the inference is not based on reasoning at all.

The Positive Account

Hume's account is this: on the basis of past experience of constant conjunction between a cause and its effect, when we perceive the cause again, our minds are caused to infer the effect. That principle Hume calls 'Custom', without pretending that such a label explains it at all. Custom is not a reason or principle of reasoning. It is not that we think 'this object has constantly been conjoined to this second object, so the second will occur again'. Custom is, instead, a natural instinct of the mind, a disposition we simply have in the face of experience of constant conjunction. Without custom, we would be unable to draw causal inferences, and so we would have no knowledge of anything beyond what was present to our senses and memory.

Is Hume's Account 'Sceptical'?

Hume's attack on reason, and his resulting account of induction and causal inference, have traditionally been understood to produce scepticism. We have no rational justification for our causal inferences. But more recently, philosophers have argued that this was not Hume's intention, and pointed out the textual support for this interpretation.

He is not sceptical about the inference or its use:

> My practice, you say, refutes my doubts. But you mistake the purport of my question. As an agent, I am quite satisfied in the point; but as a philosopher…

He clearly claims that we do have knowledge of matters of fact and of how to adjust means to ends.

We may go further and say that Hume believes we have this knowledge through reasoning. Finally, Hume even distinguishes between 'good' and 'bad' causal inferences, which entails that not all beliefs about what will happen next are equal.

What, then, can we make of Hume's declaration that custom is a principle of the imagination, which ties the ideas of cause and effect together? Hume uses the term 'imagination' in two senses: in the narrow sense, he contrasts causal inference producing beliefs about reality with ideas in imagination; in the broad, sense, he includes causal reasoning. This again suggests that the fact that our minds are caused, by experience of constant conjunction, to move from perception of cause to belief in the effect, plays an important role for Hume's account.

The Return of Scepticism

Induction, based on custom, lies at the heart of causal reasoning; and causal reasoning is the foundation of all knowledge of matters of fact. The basis on which we believe that it does are the principles of the imagination, narrowly understood. In fact, he claims that causal reasoning not only doesn't support this belief, it actually opposes it.

Hume Causation

Hume's investigation of causation occurs in the context of thinking about what and how we can know about 'matters of fact'.

Hume argues that we can't deduce what something will cause from examining it alone. 'If that object be entirely new to, he will not be able, by the most accurate examination of its sensible qualities, to discover any of its causes or effects'. But you are being swayed by your experience here. In the absence of any experience of 'what happens next', imagining that the second ball moves is arbitrary; there are so many other things it could do, *e.g.*, stay still and the first ball bounce off it. From this perspective, just considering the qualities of the 'cause', the effect that follows must seem completely arbitrary.

So from examining the first object, we can't infer the thought that it causes 'what happens next'. We can't, from this single experience, infer that the first event caused the second. We have seen that the second follows the first; but to say that it is an effect of the first is to claim much more. The second event follows many events, *e.g.*, your eye blinking as you look at the two balls, someone sneezing outside the room. Perhaps either of these is what caused the second ball to move...

Hume's argument is not just that we cannot gain knowledge of what causes what on the basis of single objects or single instances. It is that we cannot even form the idea of causation from these sources.

Constant Conjunction and Custom

The idea of causation enables us to infer an effect from a cause or vice-versa. You say 'I know what happens next'. You can't make this prediction on the basis of one experience. Instead, you need repeated experiences of the same event following the first. The basis for our idea of causation and our causal inferences, claims Hume, is constant conjunction. Once I've seen enough times one billiard ball strike another, and the second move, when I see a billiard ball moving towards another, I immediately believe that the second one will move when it is struck.

So the idea of causation is derived from our experience of constant conjunction. This experience is, of course, past experience.

Again, it is important to note that we do not infer the effect by saying that because there has been constant conjunction in the past, this new instance will conform to it. Rather, the simple fact that we have experienced constant conjunction sets up the link between cause and effect in our minds. We can give two points in support of this claim:

1. We often don't, and don't need to, call on our memory when making the inference; e.g. when seeing a body of deep water, I immediately think that it could drown me, without calling to mind past experiences of this.
2. Animals are clearly capable of making these causal inferences (p. 118), but animals don't construct arguments with general principles like 'there has been constant conjunction in the past'.

Objection

Is Hume right that we must always have repeated experience in order to associate cause and effect? He gives the example of a child feeling pain when putting its hand in the candle flame, and learning not to put its hand near the candle. But how many times must a child do this before becoming cautious? We can test this claim (a bit unethical, but possible!). I would predict that children burned just once would be cautious. If I am right, Hume's account that the inference of effect from cause depends on repeated experience must be wrong.

Hume can reply that even if we can, in some cases, infer that one event causes another from a single instance, we nevertheless need experience of constant conjunction to form the idea of causation in the first place. The general claim that causal inference is based on custom, and custom is based on constant conjunction would remain, even if in certain instances we can make a particular causal inference from experiencing just one instance of cause-effect.

The Idea of Necessity

To say that one event causes another, we commonly think, is not just to say that the second follows the first (constant conjunction), but that the second must follow the first. Experience shows us what follows what; but, Hume argues, experience does not show us that the effect must follow. Since we have this idea of a necessary connection, so Hume must explain its origins in accordance with his theory of ideas. What is the impression from which the idea is derived?

The Search

Hume begins with our experience of the events themselves. There is no impression of the 'necessary connection' deriving from our sense experience of the objects. If there were, then even in one instance of seeing an event cause its effect, we would immediately have the sense that the second event had to follow. But, he has argued, we don't. There is no impression that the effect had to occur just as it did. How about constant conjunction? Could we gain an impression of necessary connection through repeated experience? This can't be right either. Surely everything we can experience that belongs to the objects is there, present, is just one occasion.

If it is not an impression of sense, could it be an impression of reflection? Hume considers and rejects the suggestion that the idea derives from our experience of willing. The necessary connection would connects one's will as the cause to its effects, *e.g.*, moving part of one's body.

Hume then turns (p. 141) to the philosophical theory that the connection between cause and effect is the will of God. It is God who brings about the effect when the cause occurs. The theory is unpersuasive and certainly no explanation for the origin of the idea of necessary connection.

The idea of necessary causation is part of the idea of causation, and this, Hume has argued, derives from the relation of constant conjunction. This relation, as already argued, doesn't change the objects or our sense impressions of them. But the experience of constant conjunction does change the mind.

So Hume claims that the idea of necessary connection, an essential component of the idea of causation, derives from an impression of reflection. We experience this automatic movement, and it is the feeling of this movement, that is the impression from which we form the idea of necessary connection. The imagination has connected the two events; and the movement of mind from one to the other happens automatically, outside our will. We thereby come to believe that the events themselves are necessarily connected.

The Implication

To say that two objects are necessarily connected, Hume argues, can have no other meaning than that they have acquired this association in our minds. We have a tendency to form the belief that the objects resemble our impressions of reflection. It occurs with secondary qualities, aesthetic properties and moral properties. We think objects are themselves coloured or beautiful, that actions are right or wrong; but in each case, the idea (colour, beauty, right) derives from an impression of reflection, not sense.)

We can have no reason to suppose objects themselves are necessarily connected. If the property of necessary connection was in the two objects, we would be able to infer causes and effects from a single instance.

Is Hume's Account Circular?

Experiencing constant conjunction leads the mind to set up a connection in imagination between the two events. So Is the new habit of the mind an effect of experiencing constant conjunction? In the Treatise I.iii.xiv, Hume explicitly says that it is.

We might well doubt this! It has taken a lot of hard work on Hume's part to demonstrate the connection between experience of constant conjunction and custom – hardly an automatic transition. Hume's theory does not deny this. He claims that the idea of cause originates, in part, in something that does happen automatically; and that in coming to believe that two events are causally related, our minds move from one to the other automatically.

Hume's Definitions of 'Cause'

Hume ends his discussion in §VII by providing two definitions of 'cause', one that refers to the relation between the objects themselves, the other that relates the objects to the mind of the observer. These two definitions of 'cause' are not equivalent. The first definition of cause picks out an objective relation between the objects; the second picks out a relation between the objects and our minds.

Or again, our thought may be conveyed from one to the other – because they have been conjoined in our experience so far – even though the two objects are not constantly conjoined, and in unobserved cases come apart.

Does Hume intend that something is a cause only if it satisfies both conditions? He does not say so. Judging from the context of discussion, we can say instead that Hume is giving us two views of causation.

Objections

However, both definitions are problematic. The first definition is that of 'constant conjunction'. It reduces causation to simple 'regularity', the regularity of one event following another. But this faces two objections. First, Hume refers to causes being 'similar'. But he does not, at any point, give us guidance on what counts as similar. And judgments of similarity are famously dependent on the mind of the observer.

Hume's available only response is to argue that similarity is not always subjective, that some objects just are objectively similar to each other; and that real causal relations are the ones that hold between these objects. But this is not a very Humean idea.

Second, there is a difficulty in distinguishing between constant conjunctions that are accidental from ones which are genuinely causal. For example, it just so happens that you and I both finish work at 5.00 pm.

We can reply that we only need to introduce the idea, present in the Treatise, that the objects related as cause and effect are contiguous to each other as well. But, in fact, Hume does not claim that cause and effect must be spatially contiguous, only temporally. Even if we did introduce spatial contiguity, there are counter examples to this.

The Counterfactual Analysis of Causation

In response, Hume can appeal to the supplementary sentence, that 'if the first object had not been, the second would never had existed'. This does answer the objection – for instance, it is not true that if my alarm hadn't gone off, you wouldn't have stopped work. But this is a completely different idea from mere regular succession, and not one that Hume has addresses in any part of his discussion so far.

The counterfactual analysis itself continues to face problems. When is it true to say that 'if the water hadn't spilled, the table would be dry'; and does this always capture the cause? Suppose, in the actual situation. The counterfactual turns out false, and yet it is obvious that the water spilling is the cause of the water being wet in the actual situation.

The second definition faces a different kind of problem, viz. that it is circular. To rephrase: A cause is an object, followed by another, whose appearance causes the mind to think of that other. In other words, a cause is 'an object, followed by another, whose appearance to the mind is followed by the idea of the second object, where all the objects similar to the first are followed by a similar transition in the mind to objects similar to the second object'.

The External World and the Self

To reach up to the personal identity and to the self we shall have to begin with Hume's idea of substance. According to him any knowledge in order to be real must have elements corresponding to some impressions. Now if there is something permanent, as the supporter of qualities, then it must be traced to some sensation or reflection. If it is a sensation, that it must be either a sensation of colour or heat or cold. But then it is regarded as none of these. Again, if it comes from reflection, then it must be either an emotion or some passions. But a substance is derived neither from sensation nor from reflection. Thus substance as understood by philosopher is an, 'unintelligible chimera'. The idea of a substance, for Hume means, a collection of simple ideas, united by imagination, which have a common name assigned to it.

Hume seems to accept the refutation of material substance by Berkeley, but he goes beyond Berkeley in refuting the spiritual substance also. Hume asked the same question regarding the self which Berkeley had raised with regard to 'matter'. Please show me any impression from which the idea of permanent self is derived, "For my part, when I enter most intimately into what I call *myself,* I always stumble on some particular perception or other, of heat or cold, light or shade, love or hatred, pain or pleasure. I never can catch myself at any time without a perception, and never can observe anything but the perception. When my perceptions are removed for any time, as by sound sleep; so long am I insensible of myself, and may truly he said not to exist.....If any one upon serious and unprejudiced reflection, thinks he has a different notion of himself, I must confess I can reason no longer with him."

If the identity of the self is purely fictitious, then how does it arise at all? According to Hume, the fiction of personal identity is the work of imagination. The succession of pleasure, pain, sensations and images are connected together by resemblance, contiguity and causation. Our notion of personal identity, for Hume, proceeds entirely from the smooth and uninterrupted progress of the thought along a train of connected ideas, according to the principles of resemblance, contiguity and causation. This resemblance is sustained by our memory. Again, causation also produces the notion of personal identity. The human mind, according to Hume, is 'a system of different perceptions or different existences, which are linked together by the relation of cause and effect, and mutually produce, destroy, influence, and modify each other. Our impressions rise to their correspondent ideas; and these ideas in their turn produce other impressions.'

Thus, the subject, self or mind, for Hume, is just a construct of sensations, feeling and images.

The so-called self, according to Hume, "is nothing but a heap or collection of passing sensations." About this refutation of self, Russell writes very approvingly thus : This conclusion is important in metaphysics for it takes away the last vestige of substance; it is important in theology and morality as it abolishes the doctrine of the permanent and immortal soul. In epistemology it is important for it shows that the category of subject and object is not fundamental.

Personal Identity

There are some philosophers, who imagine we are every moment intimately conscious of what we call our self. We feel its existence and its continuance in existence and are certain beyond the evidence of a demonstration, both of its perfect identity and simplicity. To attempt a farther proof of this were to weaken its evidence. No proof can be derived from any fact, of which we are so intimately conscious; nor is there any thing of which we can be certain, if we doubt of this.

All these positive assertions are contrary to that very experience, which is pleaded for them, nor have we any idea of self, after the manner it is here explained. This is a question which must necessarily be answered, if we would have the idea of self pass for clear and intelligible. It must be some one impression, that gives rise to every real idea.

But self or person is not any one impression, but that to which our several impressions and ideas are supposed to have a reference. If any impression gives rise to the idea of self, that impression must continue invariably the same, through the whole course of our lives; since self is supposed to exist after that manner. But there is no impression constant and invariable. It cannot from any of these impressions or from any other, that the idea of self is derived and consequently these is no such idea.

For my when I enter most intimately into what I call myself, I always stumble on some particular perception or other, of heat or cold, light or shade, love or hatred, pain or pleasure. When my perceptions are removed for any time, as by sound sleep; that time am I insensible of myself and may truly be said not to exist.

Rejection of Metaphysics

Hume's scepticism lies complctely under his rejection of metaphysics. According to him reason easily shows that the belief in the continued existence is illusory, for our own reality is of the passing and interrupted impressions only. "This propensity to bestow an identity on our resembling perceptions, produces the fiction of a continued existence; since that fiction, as well as the identity, is really false, as is acknowledge by all philosophers, and has no other effect than to remedy the interruption of our perceptions, which is the only circumstances that is contrary to their identity." But instead of discarding the fiction of the continued existence, human beings inconsistently enough form the hypothesis of double existence. The perceptions are supposed to be interrupted, perishing and different at every different return. But the objects are uninterrupted and preserve a continued existence and identity. Thus both the contradictory verdicts of reason and imagination are inconsistently retained by us.

Sceptical Doubts

All the objects of human reason or enquiry may naturally be divided into two kinds, relations of ideas and matters of fact. Of the first kind are the sciences of Geometry, Algebra and Arithmetic.

That three times five is equal to the half of thirty. It expresses a relation between these numbers. Propositions of this kind are discoverable by the mere operation of thought without dependence on what is anywhere existent in the universe.

Matters of fact, which are the second objects of human reason are not ascertained in the same manner; nor is our evidence of their truth, however great of a like nature with the foregoing. That the Sun will not rise tomorrow is no less intelligible a proposition and implies no more contradiction, than the affirmation, that it will rise. We should in vain, attempt to demonstrate its falsehood.

Subject Worthy of Curiosity

It may, be a subject worthy of curiosity, to enquire what is the nature of that evidence which assures us to any real existence and matter of fact.

They may even prove useful by exciting curiosity and destroying that implicit faith and security, which is the bane of all reasoning and free enquiry. The discovery of defects in the common philosophy, if any such there be will not. All reasonings concerning matter of fact seem to be founded on the relation of Cause and Effect. By means of that relation alone we can go beyond the evidence of our memory and senses. He would give you a reason and this reason would be some other fact, as a letter received from him or the knowledge of his former resolutions and promises. It is constantly supposed that there is a connexion between the present fact and that which is inferred from it. Were there nothing to bind them together, the inference would be entirely precarious. If we anatomise all the other reasonings of this nature, we shall find that they are founded on the relation of cause and effect and that this relation is either near or remote, direct or collateral. Heat and light are collateral effects of fire and the one effect may justly be inferred from the other.

Scepticism

In anylysing the nature of knowledge, Hume never took the notice of objects. According to him, seen objects may be mere 'hide and seek' game played by mind. Hume analysed the furniture of the mind in terms of fleeting impressions. Anything called knowledge not derived from impressions, according to him, could not be based on reason. Taking impression as his touchstone he called in question the validity of the concepts of substance, causality etc., which make up knowledge proper. He after a careful analysis of the main categories of thought came to the conclusion that there is no substance, neither matter nor self. We are left with passing impressions only. Is there any necessary connection between the impressions so that we could pass with certainty from the one to the other? His most careful search into causation showed that there could be no necessary connection between the impressions. Nothing remains,—the vast structure of philosophy crumbles to dust. In Hume, philosophy finds itself in the midst of ruins of its own making. Yes, the result of Humean inquiry appears to us sceptical. Yet lived in an age in which men entertained the highest hope in the possibility of knowledge. Hume's too much attention towards psychology was the main cause of his scepticism.

Reason and the Passions

He says that reason allow can not establish the existence of an object. The sensory perception of an object is regarded necessary for proving the existence of that object. The reason excite passion and emotion. The reason can prevent the expression of a passion or emotion.

It has been said that passions have no representative content. They are regarded as mere original existence. Passion is also regarded as desire. The passions arises directly from the sensations of pleasure of rain. Our actions are determined only by our passions. Actions are not determined by our powers of reason. Our passions are excited by our powers of reason. The moral quality of an action is determined only by the motives. The moral quality is not determined by the consequences of the action. The knowledge is not based on reason. We are left with passing impressions only. No necessary convictions exist between the impressions.

Expression of Passion

Reason promotes the expression of passion. Reason also allows the passions to have a motivating force for its moral conduct. Reason is used for the production of action. Reason is regarded as the slave of the passions. Reason also obey passions.

Reason is not able to oppose passion in the regard of the direction of the will. The reason is regarded as operative. It helps in matters of demonstration. It also helps in the matters of probability.

Importance of Belief

Belief is the true and proper name of feeling. No one is ever at a loss to know the meaning of that term; because every man is every moment conscious of the sentiment represented by it. It may not, be improper to attempt a description of this sentiment; in hopes we may, by that means, arrive at some analogies, which may afford a more perfect explication of it.

This variety of terms, which may seem so unphilosophical, is intended only to express that act of the mind, which renders realities or what is taken for such, more present to us than fictions, causes them to weight more in the thought and gives them a superior influence on the passions and imagination. It is needless to dispute about the terms. It may set them, in a manner, before our eyes, in their true colours, just as they might have existed. It is impossible that this faculty of imagination can ever, of itself, reach belief.

We may make use of words which express something near it. But its true and proper name, as we observed before, is belief; which is a term that every one sufficiently understands in common life. It gives them more weight and influence; makes them appear of greater importance. It enforces them in the mind. It renders them the governing principle of our actions.

Let us then, take in the whole compass of this doctrine and allow, that the sentiment of belief is nothing, but a conception more intense and steady than what attends the mere fictions of the imagination and that this manner of conception arises from a customary conjunction of the object with something present to the memory of senses.

Connections Among Ideas

Nature has established connections among particular ideas. No sooner one idea occurs to our thoughts than it introduces its correlative and carries our attention towards it, by a gentle and insensible movement. These are the only bonds that unite our thoughts together and beget that regular train of reflection or discourse, which in a greater or less degree, takes place among all mankid.

Does it happen, in all these relations, that when one of the objects is presented to the senses or memory, the mind is not only carried to the conception of the correlative, but reaches a steadier and stronger conception of it than what otherwise it would have been able to attain? The appearance of the picture of an absent friend give us our idea of him, which is evidently enlivened by the resemblance and that every passion, which that idea occasions, whether of joy or sorrow acquires new force and vigour. There concur both a relation and a present impression.

Where the picture bears him no resemblance, at least was not intended for him. And where it is absent, as well as the person, though the mind may pass from the thought of the one to that of the other, it feels its idea to be rather weakened than enlivened by that transition.

Custom

Custom is that principle, by which the correspondence has been effected. It is necessary to the subsistence of our species and the regulation of our conduct, in every circumstance and occurrence of human life. It had not effected the presence of an object instantly which excites the idea of those objects, that are conjoined with it. Those, who delight in the discovery and contemplation of final causes, have here ample subject to employ their wonder and admiration.

Custom as Guide

Custom is the great guide of human life. It is that principle alone which renders out experience useful. It makes us to expect for the future, a similar train of events with those which have appeared in the past. Without the influence of custom, we should be entirely ignorant of every matter of fact. It goes beyond what is immediately present to the memory and senses.

Causes and Effects

The causes and effects are discoverable, not by reason, but by experience. Present two smooth pieces of marble to a man who has no tincture of natural philosophy; he will never discover that they will adhere together in such a manner as to require great force to separate them in a direct line, while they make so small a resistance to a lateral pressure.

Such events, as bear little analogy to the common course of nature are also readily confessed to be known only by experience nor does any man imagine that the explosion of gunpowder or the attraction of a loadstone, could ever be discovered by arguments a priori.

External Objects Features

External objects as they appear to the senses, give us no idea of power or necessary connexion, by their operation in particular instances, let us see, whether this idea be derived from reflection on the operations of our own minds and be copied from any internal impression.

This influence of the will we know by consciousness. We acquire the idea of power or energy and they are certain, that we ourselves and all other intelligent beings are possessed of power.

Resemblance

We begin with resemblance and observe that succession of perceptions, which constitutes his mind or thinking principle and suppose that he always preserves the memory of a considerable part of past perceptions. For what is the memory, but a faculty by which we raise up the images of past perceptions? An image necessarily resembles its object must not be the frequent placing of these resembling perceptions in the chain of thought, convey the imagination more easily from one link to another. The memory not only discovers the identity. It also contributes to its production by producing the relation of resemblance among the perceptions.

As to causation, the true idea of the human mind is to be considered as a system of different perception. Our impressions give rise to their correspondent ideas and these ideas in their turn produce other impressions. One thought chases another and draws after it a third, by which it is expelled in its turn.

The soul cannot compare more properly to anything than to a republic or commonwealth in which the several members are united by the reciprocal tries of government and subordination and give rise to other persons, who propagate the same republic in the incessant changes of its parts.

Endurance

Whatever changes he endures, his several parts are still connected by the relation of causation.

Features of Memory

Memory does not so much produce as discover personal identity, by showing us the relation of cause and effect among our different perceptions. It will be incumbent on those, who affirm that memory produces entirely our personal identity to give a reason why we can, thus extend our identity beyond our memory.

As memory alone acquaints us with the continuance and extent of this succession of perceptions. Had we no memory, we never should have any notion of causation, nor consequently of that chain of causes and effects, which constitute our self or person.

But having once acquired this notion of causation from the memory, we can extend the same chain of cause and consequently the identity of our persons beyond our memory and can comprehend times and circumstances and actions which we have entirely forgot, but suppose in general to have existed.

Reasoning

All reasonings may be divided into two kinds; namely, demonstrative reasoning and moral reasoning. That there are no demonstrative arguments. May, I not clearly and distinctly conceive that a body, falling from the clouds and which in all other respects, resembles snow has yet the taste of salt or feeling of fire?

Is there any more intelligible proposition than to affirm, that all the trees will flourish in December and January and decay in May and June? Now whatever is intelligible and can be distinctly conceive implies no contradiction and can never be proved false by any demonstrative argument or abstract reasoning a priori.

It should be regard as matter of fact and real existence, according to the division. But that there is no argument of this kind, must appear, if our explication of that species of reasoning be admitted as solid and satisfactory. To endeavour, the proof of this last supposition by probable arguments or arguments regarding existence, must be evidently going in a circle and taking that for granted, which is the very point in question.

All arguments from experience are founded on the similarity which we discover among natural objects and by which we are induced to expect effect similar to those which we have found to follow from such objects. From causes which appear similar we expect similar effects.

Uniform Experiments

This is the sum of all our experimental conclusions. Now it seems evident that if this conclusion were formed by reason, then it would be as perfect at first and upon one instance as after ever so long a course of experience. It is only after a long course of uniform experiments in any kind, that we attain a firm reliance and security with regard to a particular event.

It is that process of reasoning which from one instance, draws a conclusion so different from that which it infers from a hundred instances that are nowise different from that single one? This question I propose as much for the sake of information as with an intention of raising difficulties cannot find, I cannot imagine any such reasoning.

Identity Attribute

The controversy concerning identity is not merely a dispute of words. For, when we attribute identity, in an improper sense, to variable or interrupted objects our mistake is not confined to the expression.

What will suffice to prove this hypothesis to the satisfaction of every fair enquirer is to show from daily experience and observation, that the objects, which are variable or interrupted.

For, as such a succession answers evidently to our notion of diversity, it can only be by mistake we ascribe to it an identity and as the relation of parts, which leads us into this mistake is really nothing, but a quality, which produces an association of ideas and an easy transition of the imagination from one to another, it can only be from the resemblance, which this act of the mind bears to that, by which we contemplate one continued object, that the error arises.

KANT

Immanuel Kant is a very special philosopher for various reasons. By the time of his birth in 1724, the great epistemological traditions of empiricism and rationalism have already reached their heights and enlightenment Europe was struggling to arrive at a consensus with regard to the central issues related to theory of knowledge. Both the traditions have their influences and given the apparently contradicting presuppositions of their theoretical positions it was hard to find a meeting point or arrive at a consensus. There was a need for a synaptical mind with extraordinary philosophical virtuosity to reconcile them and to derive from their counterproductive opposition something more enlightening. Kant endeavours to do this by adopting the essential features of modern philosophy; its critical attitude, its reluctance to accept authority and tradition and its faith in human understanding to arrive at knowledge.

On the one hand, Kant was inspired by the Wolfian tradition of rationalism and was also influenced by Leiniz, but soon he found some of the assumptions of the rationalist thinkers too simplistic and dogmatic. In his search for a more reasonable account of human knowledge Kant turned to the British Empiricist thinkers, and all the three great empiricists, Locke, Berkeley and Hume have attracted his attention. He was particularly fascinated by the radical criticism of David Hume. Kant has stated that it was Hume who had awakened him from his dogmatic slumbers.

Kant had written three Critiques, apart from some other books dealing with various aspects of philosophy. The three Critiques are : Critique of Pure Reason, Critique of Practical Reason and the Critique of Judgement. The first Critique examines the process of knowledge acquisition that happens in the domain of natural sciences and eventually draws a limit to our understanding with respect to this realm. The second Critique addresses the problem of moral judgement and here too Kant examines the preconditions that enable the human mind to arrive at such judgements. The third Critique deals with the problem of aesthetic judgement and in a sense attempts to unify the domains of pure natural sciences with the domain of ethics.

The Critical Philosophy

Kant is considered as the most important philosopher of the enlightenment and is often called the prophet of enlightenment as the spirit of enlightenment finds its most comprehensive expression in his Critical Philosophy. In the very conceptualization of Critical philosophy, the influence of Hume is visible. Hume's philosophy has expressed a radical doubt about the power of human mind in gaining genuine knowledge with certainty, particularly about the natural world which deals with "matters of fact", about which he affirms only probability is possible. Hume's philosophy is an instance where reason turns its critical gaze on itself. The spirit of modern philosophy consists in its undermining all authority and tradition and in Hume's philosophy it reaches a point where reason turns to itself and attempts to find out the limitations of our understanding.

Hume had contended that necessary knowledge is possible only in relations of ideas and not with regard to matters of fact. He had exhibited that causal relationship, the validity of which is presupposed in natural sciences, is actually based on custom and attributed it to the habit of the mind. Kant has observed that if Hume is right, then there will be only empirical sciences and formal exercises of calculation. In this context Kant's objective can be understood as consisting in endeavouring "to limit Hume's skepticism on the one hand, and the old dogmatism on the other, and to refute and destroy materialism, fatalism, atheism, as well as sentimentalism and superstition."

Unlike Hume, Kant never doubted the possibility of genuine knowledge. Nor did he doubt the powers of human understanding in arriving at knowledge about matters of fact. He endeavours to understand in what way reason has arrived at these principles. In his explanation of this process Kant's synoptical mind attempts reconciling the different and contradictory views held by his predecessors. He thus develops a method which examines the nature and limit of human knowledge by analyzing the knowing mind.

One important feature of the philosophy of the Enlightenment is its separation between the world and knowledge about the world, which is also a separation between the knowing mind and its object of knowledge and between thought and reality. The critical method he proposes addresses this issue by examining what lies at the basis of the distinction between the a priori and the a posteriori sources of knowledge, which would also establish the exact scope and function of such forms of knowledge. In other words, he endeavours understanding the distinction between what the mind discovers to be necessary and universal and what it gains from experience.

Important Features of Critical Method

By understanding the distinction between the necessary knowledge that is a priori and experiential knowledge that is contingent and a posteriori, Kant's critical philosophy attempts to know the nature and limitation of human knowledge. Kant sees that this distinction can be understood also as a distinction between the analytical and synthetical judgments.

The critical method employs a transcendental critique of reason. It seeks to locate the universal and necessary elements in all knowledge in the nature of our thought and is not interested in any specific instance of knowing. In other words, it focuses on the unique kind of knowledge which is common to all experience.

The Critical investigation begins with Kant highlighting the limitations of the two available models of cognition; rationalism and empiricism. He disagreed with Locke's crude empiricism which argued that all our concepts are ultimately derived from experience. There must be something which enables the experience to appear in a meaningful manner. Here Kant agrees with the rationalists who emphasize on the innate structures of the mind. But he nevertheless disagreed with them with regard to the notion of innate ideas which assumes that all human knowledge are native to the mind. They are preconditions which would find their application on the data supplied by empirical experience.

In other words, these a priori concepts are grounded in the mind's own structure. These pure concepts are devoid of all empirical content. They are not derived from experience but is applied to and governs experience. In this sense they do not transcend experience, but are the preconditions of the latter. Instead, but our reason derives it from within itself. Kant carries out his further analysis with an examination of the various kinds of judgements as he thought that the structure of the human mind can be derived by analyzing the structure of judgements.

Classification of Judgements

Analysis of Judgements

The first classification is between the analytic and synthetic judgements. The analytic are judgements whose predicate is already contained in the subject and hence is merely explicative. It simply explicates some obvious and essential characteristic of the subject. Such judgements give us information about some aspect of the subject which we do not get through a mere analysis of the idea of the subject. For example, my car is white.

Kant argues that all analytic statements are a priori, as they are true by definition and certain, though they contain no information about the factual world. Since their predicate is logically contained in the subject their negation would be meaningless. On the other hand synthetic judgements are of two types: synthetic a posteriori and synthetic a *priori.* The other type of synthetic propositions Kant calls synthetic a priori propositions. The first Critique deals with these type of judgements.

By distinguishing synthetic a posteriori from synthetic a priori, Kant dismisses Hume's dichotomy between analytic and synthetic (relations of ideas and matters of fact). He asserted the possibility of our forming any synthetic judgments which have a purely a priori origin. Kant never doubts the possibility of such judgements, as he affirms that they are possible and the very possibility of natural sciences like physics testify their existence. For example, "2+2=4", "a straight line is the shortest distance between two points" and "Every event has a cause" are synthetic a priori statements. He rather raises the question, how such judgements are possible.

According to Kant, all mathematical propositions apply such a priori concepts to space and time, which are also a-priori. Geometry and physics too employ them. Kant maintains that their truth is dependent on intuition, but independent of empirical experience. They rather make empirical experience possible. Physics on the other hand, has both synthetic a posteriori or empirical propositions and synthetic a priory proposition. As mentioned above, synthetic a priori propositions are judgements that are both synthetic and demonstrable a priori. To answer the question, how are synthetic a priori propositions possible. In other words, their truths are necessary like mathematics but they are applied to experience and explain the very possibility of sense impressions.

By explaining the possibility of synthetic a priori propositions Kant intends to overcome the skeptical threat posed by Hume. Their possibility would demonstrate the possibility of natural sciences which presuppose the possibility of experience which is universal and necessary. Hence synthetic a priori judgements also say something about ourselves: about the structure of our mind. What the world is to us is the world as we experience it. But our capacities for experiencing anything would impose a restriction on the kind of world our world could be. With this Kant reconciles rationalism with empiricism and explains the possibility of genuine scientific knowledge.

The transcendental critique of reason thus demonstrates the preconditions of knowledge. Kant admits that all our knowledge begins with experience. The mind plays a crucial role in this process by determining and providing that a priori. Preconditions of the very possibility of knowledge. They is known as Kant's copernican Revolution in Philosophy.

Synthetic *A Priori* Judgements

The Critical Philosophy

Next we turn to the philosophy of Immanuel Kant, a watershed figure who forever altered the course of philosophical thinking in the Western tradition. Long after his thorough indoctrination into the quasi-scholastic German appreciation of the metaphysical systems of Leibniz and Wolff, Kant said, it was a careful reading of David Hume that "interrupted my dogmatic slumbers and gave my investigations in the field of speculative philosophy a quite new direction." This central idea became the basis for his life-long project of developing a critical philosophy that could withstand them.

Kant's aim was to move beyond the traditional dichotomy between rationalism and empiricism. The rationalists had tried to show that we can understand the world by careful use of reason; this guarantees the indubitability of our knowledge but leaves serious questions about its practical content. Both approaches have failed, Kant supposed, because both are premised on the same mistaken assumption.

Progress in philosophy, according to Kant, requires that we frame the epistemological problem in an entirely different way. This is the purpose of Kant's Critique of Pure Reason (1781, 1787): to show how reason determines the conditions under which experience and knowledge are possible.

Varieties of Judgment

In the Prolegomena to any Future Metaphysic (1783) Kant presented the central themes of the first Critique in a somewhat different manner, starting from instances in which we do appear to have achieved knowledge and asking under what conditions each case becomes possible.

The first distinction separates a priori from a posteriori judgments by reference to the origin of our knowledge of them. A priori judgments are based upon reason alone, independently of all sensory experience, and therefore apply with strict universality. A posteriori judgments, on the other hand, must be grounded upon experience and are consequently limited and uncertain in their application to specific cases.

But Kant also made a less familiar distinction between analytic and synthetic judgments, according to the information conveyed as their content. Synthetic judgments, on the other hand, are those whose predicates are wholly distinct from their subjects, to which they must be shown to relate because of some real connection external to the concepts themselves. Hence, synthetic judgments are genuinely informative but require justification by reference to some outside principle.

In fact, Kant held, the two distinctions are not entirely coextensive; we need at least to consider all four of their logically possible combinations:

- Analytic *a posteriori* judgments cannot arise, since there is never any need to appeal to experience in support of a purely explicative assertion.
- Synthetic *a posteriori* judgments are the relatively uncontroversial matters of fact we come to know by means of our sensory experience (though Wolff had tried to derive even these from the principle of contradiction).
- Analytic *a priori* judgments, everyone agrees, include all merely logical truths and straight forward matters of definition; they are necessarily true.
- Synthetic *a priori* judgments are the crucial case, since only they could provide new information that is necessarily true. But neither Leibniz nor Hume considered the possibility of any such case.

Unlike his predecessors, Kant maintained that synthetic a priori judgments not only are possible but actually provide the basis for significant portions of human knowledge. What is more, metaphysics—if it turns out to be possible at all—must rest upon synthetic a priori judgments, since anything else would be either uninformative or unjustifiable.

Mathematics

Consider, for example, our knowledge that two plus three is equal to five and that the interior angles of any triangle add up to a straight line. These (and similar) truths of mathematics are synthetic judgments, Kant held, since they contribute significantly to our knowledge of the world; the sum of the interior angles is not contained in the concept of a triangle.

Kant's answer is that we do it ourselves. Conformity with the truths of mathematics is a precondition that we impose upon every possible object of our experience. Just as Descartes had noted in the Fifth Meditation, the essence of bodies is manifested to us in Euclidean solid geometry, which determines a priori the structure of the spatial world we experience.

Understanding mathematics in this way makes it possible to rise above an old controversy between rationalists and empiricists regarding the very nature of space and time. Leibniz had maintained that space and time are not intrinsic features of the world itself, but merely a product of our minds.

This is our first instance of a transcendental argument, Kant's method of reasoning from the fact that we have knowledge of a particular sort to the conclusion that all of the logical presuppositions of such knowledge must be satisfied. We will see additional examples in later lessons, and can defer our assessment of them until then. Since mathematics derives from our own sensible intuition, we can be absolutely sure that it must apply to everything we perceive, but for the same reason we can have no assurance that it has anything to do with the way things are apart from our perception of them.

Preconditions for Natural Science

In natural science no less than in mathematics, Kant held, synthetic a priori judgments provide the necessary foundations for human knowledge. The most general laws of nature, like the truths of mathematics, cannot be justified by experience, yet must apply to it universally. But of course Kant's more constructive approach is to offer a transcendental argument from the fact that we do have knowledge of the natural world to the truth of synthetic a priori propositions about the structure of our experience of it.

As we saw last time, applying the concepts of space and time as forms of sensible intuition is necessary condition for any perception.

First, it must be possible in principle to arrange and organize the chaos of our many individual sensory images by tracing the connections that hold among them.

Second, it must be possible in principle for a single subject to perform this organization by discovering the connections among perceived images.

Deduction of the Categories

Since (as Hume had noted) individual images are perfectly separable as they occur within the sensory manifold, connections between them can be drawn only by the knowing subject, in which the principles of connection are to be found.

Consider, then, the sorts of judgments distinguished by logicians (in Kant's day): each of them has some quantity (applying to all things, some, or only one); some quality (affirmative, negative, or complementary); some relation (absolute, conditional, or alternative); and some modality (problematic, assertoric, or apodeictic).

The result of this "Transcendental Logic" is the schematized table of categories, Kant's summary of the central concepts we employ in thinking about the world, each of which is discussed in a separate section of the Critique:

Quantity	**Quality**
Unity	Reality
Plurality	Negation
Totality	Limitation
Axioms of Intuition	Anticipations of Perception
Relation	**Modality**
Substance	Possibility
Cause	Existence
Community	Necessity
Analogies of Experience	Postulates of Empirical Thought

Our most fundamental convictions about the natural world derive from these concepts, according to Kant.

The Copernican Revolution

Kant's transcendental critique thus deals with the general conditions of the employment of human faculties. It affirms that, though on the one hand our knowledge should conform to objects, the objects also must conform to our knowledge in the sense that the nature of our faculties determines what the case in the world is.

In this regard, it has been argued that Kant has initiated a Copernican revolution in philosophy; a revolution in philosophy which is akin to the revolution Copernicus initiated in astronomy by proposing a helaeo-centric view. The empiricists, particularly John Locke argues for a representationalist model of knowledge acquisition, where the ideas received by the mind were assumed to have their originals in an external world. The rationalists, he felt are too dogmatic in assuming that the a priori ideas alone world explain the process.

Kant's Copernican revolution thus attempts presenting a more satisfactory, more convincing model, which would also simultaneously reconcile the contradicting views proposed by his predecessors. He keeps the thinking mind at the center and emphasizes its crucial role in knowing the world, which however are accessed only through perception. This regularity is imposed by the mind even at the very stage of having sensations. The mind is thus at the center of the knowing process, though knowledge is not purely innate as the rationalists thought it was. Kant concludes: "Percepts without concepts are blind and concepts without percepts are empty".

The Copernican revolution of Kant has very important consequences. If the objects must conform to our cognition as stated by Kant, then that would imply certain limitations of our knowledge and our understanding. This would definitely reject any possibility of having knowledge about a world or reality that is not given to us through our senses. We would never have a direct access to the world outside us, as all our knowledge is necessarily mediated through our sensations and the a priori structure of our mind.

Forms of Sensibility

Concept of Understanding

The concept of understanding contains pure synthetic unity of the manifold in genera. Time, as the formal condition of the manifold of inner sense and therefore, of the connection of all representations, contains as a priori manifold in pure intuition. Now a transcendental determination of time is so far homogeneous with the category, which constitutes its unity, in that it is universal and rests upon an a priori rule. Thus, an application of the category to appearances becomes possible by means of the transcendental determination of time, which as the schema of the concepts of understanding, mediates the subsumption of the appearances of the appearances under the category.

The Schematism of the Pure Concepts of Understanding

In all subsumptions of an object under a concept the representation of the object must be homogeneous with the concept; in other words the concept must contain something which is represented in the object that is to be subsumed under it. The roundness, which is thought in the latter can be intuited in the former.

Pure concepts of understanding being quite heterogeneous from empirical intuitions and indeed from all sensible intuitions can never be met with in any intuition. For no one will say that a category, such as that of causality, can be intuited through sense and is itself contained in appearance. A Transcendental Doctrine of Judgement is necessary just because of this natural and important question. We must be able to show how pure concepts can be applicable to appearances.

Obviously there must be some third thing, which is homogeneous on the one hand with the category and on the other hand with the appearance and which thus makes the application of the former to the latter possible. This mediating representation must be pure, *i.e.*, void of all empirical content, and yet at the same time, while it must in one respect be intellectual, it must in another be sensible. Such a representation is the transcendental schema.

Schemata

The schema is in itself always a product of imagination. The synthesis of imagination aims at no special intuition, but only at unity in the determination of sensibility, the schema has to be distinguished from the image.

But if, on the other hand, I think only a number in general, whether it be five or a hundred, this thought is rather the representation of a method whereby a multiplicity, for instance a thousand, may be represented in an image in conformity with a certain concept, than the image itself. This representation of a universal procedure of imagination in providing an image for a concept, is know as schema of this concept.

It is schemata, not images of objects, which underlie our pure sensible concepts. No image could ever be adequate to the concept of a triangle. The schema of the triangle can exist nowhere, but in thought. It is a rule of synthesis of the imagination in respect to pure figures in space.

Schemata of Sensibility

The schemata of sensibility first realise the categories, they at the same time restrict them, *i.e.*, limit them to conditions, which lie outside the understanding and are to sensibility. If we omit are stricting condition, we would seem to entend the scope. The concept was preciously limited. They ought, we conclude, to possess a meaning independent of all schemata and of much wider application.

The Faculty of Understanding

Categories of Understanding

Categories is referred as an important part of understanding. By categories, Kant means universal necessary features of experience that are found in all mental experience.

Twelve categories are found in understanding. If there is an absence of categories, then thinking about an object becomes useless. They are present before experience always.

A category is referred as a pure concept of the understanding. A category is regarded as an attribute, property that can be predicated of a thing. Categories do not give us the knowledge of individual. But categories are essential for every object. Every object should have attributes.

For Kant, judgement is also necessary. Ability of judgement is needed for everyone. It also signifies the ability of thinking.

Forms of Judgement

The forms of judgements:

Quantity

- Universal
- Particular
- Singular

Quality

- Affirmative
- Negative
- Infinite

Relation

- Categorical
- Hypothetical
- Disjunctive

Modality

- Problematic
- Assertoric
- Apodictic

Kant uses these table of judgements for the table of categories.

The table of categories are as follows:

Quantity

- Unity
- Plurality
- Totality

Quality

- Reality
- Negation
- Limitation

Relation

- Inherence and Subsistence
- Causality and Dependence
- Communicy Modality
- Possibility
- Existence
- Necessity

Transcendental Deduction of the Categories

Kant says that in the metaphysical deduction, we use to establish the priori origin of the categories. These deductions also helps in the universal logical functions of thought. By logic, Kant means the study of the rules. These rules are derived from experience. He makes a distinction between types of logic. He makes a distinction between general and special logic. Applied logic deals with attention whereas pure general logic deals with a priori understanding only.

Transcendental deduction means that there are a *priori* categories of the understanding which determine the objectivity of empirical statements and that by their means alone such statements can ever be obtained.

From the *Transcendental Aesthetic* one might get the false impression that percepts do not involve any other synthesizing process over and above those provided for by space and time. Now we see that the perception of even a 'line' requires the synthesizing activity of the understanding. In other words, without the synthesizing activity of the understanding there can be no object of any empirical knowledge. This spontaneous activity of the understanding in synthesizing the discrete data is the a priori ground of any empirical knowledge, and is expressed in threefold syntheses, namely,

1. **The synthesis of apprehension in intuition.** Ultimately any perceptions, whether of outer objects or of inner process, is given in time. Now suppose there is aline A B having various parts. Unless the divisions of A B are held together in one single apprehension, we cannot have the idea of A B as a whole. If we could perceive the parts alone, say, AX, AX^1, AX^2 etc. then we would perceive separate parts AX, AX^1, AX^2 etc., but not a complete line composed by these parts as A B. Hence, the multiplicity of parts must first be run through and grasped together in one whole. This is know as 'the synthesis of apprehension in intuition.'
2. **The synthesis of reproduction in imagination.** Again, when we look at the line A B, we successively perceive the parts AX, AX^1, AX^2 etc. This observation would be clearer still if we take for example the perception of a building or a long wall. When we have to perceive the whole line A B or the whole long wall, then at the time we are perceiving the part AX^2, then the image of the previous parts AX and AX^1 must be faithfully reproduced and must fuse into AX^2 and other successive parts. If we drop out AX, AX^1 at the moment of perceiving AX^2 and other successive parts and do not faithfully reproduce them in our further successive perceptions, then no object can ever be correctly perceived as one whole thing. According to Kant, if this condition be not granted then even the most elementary perception of objects in space and time would not be possible.
3. **The synthesis of recognition in a Concept.** The consciousness which apprehends the parts severally which later *reproduces* the various images of its past and which finally *recognizes* them as one and the same parts belonging to one related whole must be the one and the small all through. If we, like Miss Lucky or Beauchamp, what we perceive a moment before forget in the next, then we can have no knowledge at all.

Phenomenon and Noumenon

The consciousness of 'I am' or the synthetic unity of appreciation which accompanies every item of our knowledge of objects is only an a *priori* logical condition. This is never *known.* So the only empirical self which we know is a bundle of successive changes. And this kind of self is not possible without reference to outer things. In this contention of Kant much food for thought is contained, which was fully exploited by Fichte, Schelling and Hegel.

If the forms of sensibility and the concepts of the understanding be constitutive of objects, as objects of knowledge, then this view supports what Kant has termed Transcendental Idealism. According to this view subjects are objects within phenomena and we can never style them as things-in-themselves. Of course, we have full scientific knowledge of the phenomena. Yet we cannot assert that only phenomena are and noumena are not, or that any talk of noumena is self-contradictory.

'Noumenon' for Kant has purely *negative* sense. The term means a thing so far as it is *not an object of our sensible intuition.* The term may acquire a positive sense when it refers to an object of non-sensible intuition. It may mean that a noumenon is an object of knowledge, possibly for an intuitive intellect. However, the notion of an intuitive intellect is only problematic and human intellect can say nothing about it. Human knowledge cannot know non-sensible objects. We cannot legitimately apply to them the concepts of existence, causation or even of 'non-existence'. Hence, for Kant 'noumenon' stands in *negative sense only.*

Thus, the concept of noumena, for Kant, served the purpose of guarding philosophy from the errors of subjective idealism, materialism and even realism. But in due course there were many things in Kant's philosophy which paved the ground for objective Idealism.

The Ideas of Reason (Soul, God and World as a Whole)

Kant holds that thinking, being an active and spontaneous activity, unlike the passive sensibility, can continue to combine and synthesize pure concepts alone, even in the absence of appropriate percepts. This might give us the semblance of knowing, but which really can yield no knowledge proper. In metaphysics we think about God, soul and the world, though we can never know them. Hence thinking is much wider than knowing, and, the limit of knowing is not the limit of thinking.

According to Kant, knowing consists in thinking about percepts. To think means to combine the percepts into judgements with the help of concepts. Ordinarily, we combine the ideas in judgements which have been empirically acquired and associated. For example, this grass is green. We have already acquired the empirical concepts of 'grass' and 'green'. Further, this combination of 'grass' and 'green' appears to us to be objective, that is, the same for all persons. The question is, how can this objectivity of empirical judgements be explained? There are only two ways in which we can explain this : (i) The combination involved in objective empirical judgements is really so in its own right in nature, independent of any human knower; or, (ii) this combination is a *priori,* being introduced by the faculty of thinking called understanding.

If the combination between ideas, as in the greenness of the grass, were objective in its rights; apart from human knowers, then it can be known only by being experienced. But experience can never bestow strict universality and necessity. But natural science, which for Kant meant physics, does contain synthetic judgements a priori. Obviously then the objective combination of ideas in judgements cannot be empirical explained.

Hence, as we have already seen in the case of space and time, the objectivity of empirical judgements can ultimately be explained only if we could show that there are a priori forms of thinking which are also termed as *categories.* Unfortunately, as observed just before, thinking need not be confined to percepts and may be applied to concepts also; and when it does so it leads to transcendental illusions.

Ideas of reason has two parts :

I. **Transcendental Analytic** Dealing with the discovery and proof of the a priori categories of the understanding	A. (i) Discovery of the 12 concepts of the understanding by reflecting upon the 12 kinds of formal judgements give in Logic (ii) Transcendental proof of these 12 concepts showing that by their means alone and object can be thought to be empirical and objectively actual.
II. **Transcendental** (Dialectic) :	B. Use and application of the concepts. This deals with the illegitimate use of the concepts with regard to the supersensible objects yielding the transcendental illusions of paralogisms, antimonies and Ideals of reason.

Reason is the faculty inference and as there are three kinds of inference, so corresponding to them there are three ideas. From the categorical syllogism has been derived the idea of an absolute subject which can be identified with an immortal Soul. The hypothetical syllogism yields the idea of the final synthesis of all phenomena called the World. From the disjunctive syllogism is derived the idea of an absolute unity of all phenomena called God. As said above these ideas only regulate and guide our intellect in the pursuit of knowledge but they do not constitute knowledge, for knowledge proper is confined to perceptible alone. However, these ideas are so captivating that we treat them to be real objects of knowledge and so they give rise to the transcendental illusions.

Freedom and Immortality

'Faith', for Kant has a moral and a pietistic suggestion. It shows that Kant used the term 'reason' in a much broader sense than mere cognition. The importance of Practical Reason and Judgement implied for. Kant the recognition of non-discursive mode of apprehension. Further, Practical Reason gives one the apprehension of the self as 'free', which cannot be scientifically cognised.

First, the freedom of will is the most important and direct postulate of mortality. The categorical imperative or 'ought' implies that we are free to choose between two possible courses of action. If we are not free to choose, then any act becomes absolutely determined. And if I cannot act otherwise than what I do, then there will be no room for blame or praise and consequently there will be no meaning of 'ought'.

Holiness is the supreme end of moral will. But in this life we can never be holy for our action is never out of pure reason only. The struggle of reason continues with the senses and the struggle is only partially won. We must postulate an infinite series of life in which the senses are completely overcome and perfect holiness results. Hence there must be an immortality of soul to give meaning to our moral struggle. Hence we must so act as if there is a life beyond. Of course, 'the immortality of soul' can now be demonstrated but is "an inseparable corollary of an a priori unconditionally valid practical law."

Immortality and God are only indirect postulates of mortality, for moral law is autonomous. They are objects of faith. Thus we find that the metaphysical problems of God, soul and immortality were raised in The Critique of Pure Reason but only the practical reason partially solves by showing them to be the necessary postulates of morality.

Rejection of Speculative Metaphysics

For Kant, rejection of speculative metaphysics is very necessary. The metaphysical problems of God, soul and immortality were found in the critique of pure reason.

In metaphysics, we deal with the super sensible entities like of God, immortal soul etc. We are not able to experienced it. A priori principles are not applicable to them, because they are unnatural entities.

GEORGE WILHELM FRIEDRICH HEGEL

Hegel is a German thinker who devoted his life wholly to academic purists. His science of logic, dialectical reasoning, encyclopaedia of philosophical sciences, philosophy of Right – all provide an intellectual foundation for modern nationalism. Hegel was an idealist who methodically constructed a comprehensive system of thought about the world. He took a much more systematic approach than Kant by making absolute consciousness as the key source of ultimate connections among all other things. Hegel held that Reality must be Rational and that its ultimate structure is revealed in the structure of our thought. He attempts to give an elaborate, comprehensive and systematic ontology from a logical standpoint.

As Kant has noted in antinomies that one general description of the world commonly leads us into a contemplation of the opposite, Hegel made a further supposition that the two concepts so held in opposition can always be united by a shift to some higher level of thought. Thus, the human mind invariably moves from thesis to anti-thesis and then to synthesis, employing each synthesis as the thesis for a new opposition to be transcended by yet a higher level continuing, in a perpetual walk of intellectual achievement.

Compared to other philosophers, it is rather very difficult and harder to understand Hegel. He differs from Parmenides and Spinoza in conceiving the whole, not as a simple substance, but as complex system like an organism. In Hegel's view, world is not an illusion. The apparently separate things of the world have a greater or a lesser degree of reality and their reality exists in the aspect of the whole. Hegel calls, 'The Whole', in all its complexity as 'The Absolute'.

The Conception of Geist (Sprit)

Hegel's absolute idealism tries to arrive at an all-encompassing theory to bridge the finite with the infinite. He proclaims that, only the whole is real and hence all particular facts and concepts are incomplete and only partially true. Hegel advances a very interesting theory, which considers contradictions as natural. Hegel's new way of thinking suggests that we can take the irrational approach of contradicting ourselves. He thus proposes to resolve the problem of antinomies exposed by the Kantian framework. We thus encounter certain irresolvable contradictions. Kant suggests that to avoid this situation we should keep away from such ventures. He declares the impossibility of metaphysics as a science based on this scenario.

Hegel on the other hand approaches reason from a different perspective. He was not prepared to accept the traditional view about the nature of reason, where the latter is conceived as a static faculty. He conceived the Geist as rational and hence essentially dynamic. Hegel's idealism asserts that the absolute encompasses everything. This Spirit is universal and is concrete within itself. As mentioned above the Spirit is a process and hence is dynamic and its intelligent comprehension of itself is at the same time the progression of the total evolving reality.

Hegel divides philosophy into three broad categories: logic, naturphilosophy and the philosophy of the Giest. We can see that all the three sections deal with forms of thought and the fundamental unity of the rational forms. Hegel affirms that everything coincides in the Absolute.

The Absolute is conceived by Hegel as the ultimately real, which is the whole process that encompasses, the subjective and the objective, internal and external and all the three dimensions of time. In this sense, the absolute incorporates both the finite and the infinite and it bridges the finite with the infinite.

Hegel is careful in providing an account of the Geist. It is not the reality that appears before us. He thus categorizes the phenomena that appears before us as inferior or even not completely real, although his all-encompassing theory is not prepared to conceive the appearances as completely unreal. In this process of philosophical contemplation, one may encounter contradictions, as one is focusing solely on understanding. Hegel argues that we have to allow contradictions to take place and reconcile them.

Here the concept of reality advocated by Hegel is unique and different. He argues that it is governed by the principle of teleological causality and not mechanical efficient causality.

The most important feature of this idealism is the conception of the Spirit as activity. In this conception, Hegel is visibly influenced by Aristotle and proposes a principle of teleological causality. In

Aristotle's philosophy we find an identification of the fully substantial being with spirit, which in its essence is activity.

In Aristotle's framework, since reality is rational we can understand it. It is therefore reflected in a unity of logic and metaphysics. According to the teleological process, reality, world, thought and reason are not static, but are dynamic and they move and evolve.

The recognition of such diversity and differences is essential for adopting a teleological approach. The absolute is thus a unity in diversity. Hegel declares that the Real is Rational and rational is Real. According to him, the absolute spirit, or God, is the ultimate reality, which is the Geist or objective mind. Therefore, reality is a complex totality of rational concepts constituting absolute spirit.

Hegel maintains that, contrary to the finite minds of humans, which are nothing, but manifestations of the universal, objective mind, this totality of thought is absolute and infinite.

This rational Absolute or the universal mind, which constitutes the totality of conceptual truths, reveals itself in all areas of human experience and knowledge. Hegel maintains that, though the Absolute is infinite and universal, it is not different from what is existent. He thus affirms that the rational is the existent object more deeply understood. It encompasses the deeper understanding of the vast realms of physical and organic nature and society.

As discussed in the previous chapter, contrary to Kant, who held that the noumena or the real is unknowable, Hegel holds that reality is knowable, since its rational structures are knowable. Every finite stage is both a product and a prophecy. We have examined in the previous chapter how the lower forms are not only negated in the higher forms but also are preserved. The lower forms were carried over and sublated in the higher.

As indicated above, ends or purposes are realized in the process of evolution. Hegel says that, the purposes of universal reason are realized in the process. According to him, the truth lies in the whole, which is the truth of the organism. Thinking, like reality itself, evolves rationally, moves logically, genetically and dialectically. Hegel further maintains that the absolute or Geist is the creative logos or reason and it contains in it the entire logical-dialectical process which unfolds itself in a world.

Hegel's conception of God calls our attention once again in this context. Contrary to the predominant view held by enlightenment reason, Hegel does not conceive God as separate from the world. On the other hand, God is the living and moving reason of the world. God reveals himself in the world, in nature and in history. He rather maintains that, God cannot be without creating a world and without knowing himself in his other in the dialectic.

The absolute is therefore, a unity in opposition, as it includes the world, God and the human mind. Through them it rises to self-consciousness. Hegel describes this process of evolution, a phenomenon where the absolute thinks itself in its object. It comes to know its own essence only in evolution and this happens only in man. It is only in the human mind's thinking process which is dialectical the absolute realizes its essence.

Hegel thus interestingly maintains that in all aspects of human life; in nature itself, in individuals, human institutions, history, law, morality, custom, ethical observances of human beings, we find nothing but the expression of universal reason.

This absolute mind involves everything. The phenomenology of Spirit, which is an attempt to outline the biography of the spirit of humanity will explain this further.

The Phenomenology of Spirit

The phenomenology of spirit outlines the evolution of the human spirit from lesser stages of existence and realization to higher and ultimately to the highest stage. This is very important in Hegelian philosophy, because according to him, it is only in the human mind the absolute Spirit comes to know its own essence in evolution. In a sense it is a description of the history of consciousness.

Phenomenology is a science of consciousness that tries to study the mind in relation to external or internal objects. In this process, the mind evolves to higher and higher stages of consciousness. The first is the stage of consciousness, which is also the stage of sensecertainty.

Here the mind is aware of the presence of other objects around it. It uncritically apprehends particular objects by the senses. He says that, in order to describe such an object of immediate acquaintance we need to employ universal categories. For example, when we say that there are five fingers in a hand, we employ universal categories of quantity, quality, modality, relations etc., which Kant had demonstrated in his first Critique. In science, for instance, we invoke metaphenomenal or unobservable entities to explain sense phenomena. To understand the source of these a priori structures, consciousness has to turn back on itself and become self-conscious.

In the stage of self-consciousness, the self is concerned with the external object. This is a more advanced state where the self subordinates the object to itself. It approaches the object in order to comprehend it, use it to its purposes, tries to appropriate it and consume it. Here the self encounters other selves, an encounter which makes it uncomfortable, as it realizes that it cannot approach other self as an object. It cannot objectify another subject, owing to its subjectivity.

Hegel argues that, this endeavour to cancel others' subjectivity is bound to be counterproductive, as the consciousness of one's own selfhood presupposes the recognition of this selfhood by another self. To further explicate this position, Hegel refers to the master-slave relationship.

In the stage of self-consciousness, one is intimidated by the presence of other subjects, who can cancel one's subjectivity. The other, who is not just an object and is a subject, may enslave one. Here one may try to enslave the other in order to assert one's own selfhood and freedom. Here one enslaves the other and becomes a master and does not recognize the latter as a real person. But by doing this the master deprives himself of that recognition of his own freedom, which he wanted to be preserved. This freedom was precious for him because it was essential for the development of self-consciousness. The slave on the other hand frees himself through labour, which transforms material things.

Hegel summons that, the final solution to this problem consists, not in enslaving the other but in recognizing the latter's subjectivity. But, as pointed out above, this may pose a threat to one's freedom, as the other as a distinct individual subject poses a threat to one's selfhood.

Reason therefore, is the ultimate stage, where the finite subject rises to universal self-consciousness. It consists in the realization that we are all manifestations of the universal Spirit. On the other hand, it involves a full recognition of selfhood in oneself and in others. The highest stage of reason is therefore, a synthesis of the first two stages of consciousness and self-consciousness.

Dialectic Method

In order to comprehend the ideas of Hegel, the starting point is to begin by imagining the universe totally empty. All that exists is Geist, which is mind or spirit; not a particular mind or spirit, but mind or spirit in general (it is also God, but a very strange and peculiar notion of God).

It contains just one idea, the concept of being, although this idea is, so to speak, pregnant with other ideas. From which in turn further concepts flow: one and many, substance and accident, cause and effect, time and space and so on. In this way, all the basic concepts we need to understand the world are deduced, or rather deduce themselves, according to Hegel's own special kind of logic, which he calls the dialectic logic.

In the dialectic logic, things turn into their opposites and then into something that brings together the two opposites in a higher synthesis. So, having deduced the possibility of the world, the next thing that happens is that mind (still entirely unconscious) turns itself into its opposite, which is matter.

But if the question, how mind does this, is deeply mysterious, the question of why it does so is not. It is because mind has a destiny. All that happens—the creation of matter, the emergence of organized life, the appearance of mankind and the whole of human history—all happens so that mind can fulfill that destiny, which is for mind to achieve self-understanding and therefore freedom.

When mind becomes matter, mind is, so to speak, buried in matter, and gradually emerges again over time. Organic life represents progressively higher levels of complexity and rational organization that finally culminate in the emergence of humanity.

Hegel sees human history as a kind of growing up of mind, modeled on the stages of human development—babyhood, infancy, childhood, adolescence and so forth—with a succession of civilizations representing the different stages. From Ancient China, to India, to Ancient Greece, Rome, to medieval Europe and on to modern Europe, each of these civilizations represents a new advance of spirit's self-understanding.

Hegel sometimes speaks of it as the world spirit passing from civilization to civilization as each level of maturity is reached. It is portrayed as a painful process of struggle and self-doubt, involving different forms of alienation, which is the feeling of estrangement from the world.

In each civilization, spirit or mind objectifies itself, expresses itself in the forms of social life, morality, politics, science, art, religion and, above all, philosophy. All the elements of a given civilization are united by a common theme or quality or essence: the Zeitgeist, the spirit of the age.

It is just as when human beings are growing up: they do things, form relationships, test themselves and in doing so find out who they are and what kind of people they are.

The entire historical or cosmological process reached its climax and conclusion, according to Hegel, in the Germany of his own day: the contemporary Prussian state was the highest possible achievement of mind as expressed in social life; Protestantism, the highest expression of religion; Romanticism the highest perfection of art—all of which, in their different ways, expressed the full maturity of spirit. But over and above all was philosophy, the crowning achievement of any age. In this case, it was his philosophy that summed up his age.

Further, he saw his philosophy as summing up the whole process, including the whole of history, the whole development of the universe and the whole evolution of mind since before the universe was formed.

Thus, only in Hegel's philosophy does mind (or spirit or God) become fully developed, fully self-conscious and fully free, which is its final destiny, the point and purpose of the whole process.

In Hegel's philosophy, the ultimate destiny of mind or spirit or God is fulfilled. Mind or God is not some separate being but ourselves, each one of us is part of the whole— the collective mind—and it is only through human thought that mind or spirit or God can express or understand itself.

In achieving self-understanding, God or mankind is no longer alienated; the world is no longer a strange place, but is an objectification of mind, which is the ultimate reality.

The Concepts of Being, Non-being and Becoming

Important Features of Hegelian Philosophy

The central idea of Hegel's philosophy is "only the whole is real." He thus introduces a concept of the Geist or Spirit as a totalizing central concept that unifies everything. He thus attempts to avoid immediacy, the view which holds that something can be itself independently of its relations to anything else. Such an approach, according to Hegel, results in many unwarranted philosophical perplexities and problems, which can be resolved only by emphasizing the importance of highlighting the perspective of the whole. Reality, affirms Hegel, is the whole and the self-subsistence of finite things is an illusion. In this propensity to see everything as a homogeneous whole, Russell sees the influence of mysticism.

Hegel's Concept of Reality

Like Spinoza, who too has emphasized the essential homogeneous nature of the ultimate reality, which is Substance or God, for Hegel too reality, which is the whole, is homogeneous. Therefore, unlike Spinoza he maintains that separate things are not illusory, as each has a greater or lesser degree of reality.

Again, Hegel holds that the reality is governed by the principle of teleological causality and not by mechanical efficient causality. He thus identifies the Spirit with activity. The influence of Aristotle is visible in this teleological conception. We shall explore this aspect in detail in the next chapter.

Contrary to this, the absolute, which is the whole, is like an organism that is rational, purposive and with full of meaning. Hegel realizes that the Kantian approach is not suitable to know such a reality and his conception of rationality is insufficient in knowing the process. Kant maintains that the ego or mind is the condition of the possibility of things appearing to the subject. An account of the ego in Kantian philosophy is nothing but an abstract account of the forms of thought or categories of understanding. Or in other words, the forms of thought are separated from what they are forms of. Kant imagines that there is a gap between mind and world or the noumena and phenomena.

Hegel's Phenomenology of Spirit attempts to give an alternate account of this relationship and show how that gap can be bridged. Here he proposes to go beyond Kant. For Kant thinking is confined to the scientific level and for Hegel it is an activity of spirit or reason and hence is not simply confined to the scientific level.

Hegel views reason as the law according to which being is produced, constituted and unfolded. It is both a subjective faculty and an objective reality. He maintains that the categories of thinking are not just subjective elements of our thinking. In this respect, Hegel opposes Kant's idea of pure concepts. He opposes Kant's approach that limits the number of concepts and also limits these categories to the use in sensory experience. The root problem in Kant's enlightenment conception lies in his limiting the knowledge gained by the categories to the status of mere appearance. Hegel thus opposes the deduction of categories in terms of empirical enumeration of pure concepts.

There are certain fundamental ways in which Hegel's view of the categories of thinking differs from that of Kant's. For Kant the categories are separate from each other, though they are intimately interconnected. Unlike in Kant they are not merely empirical enumeration but are known through real deduction. Nevertheless, like Kant, Hegel too holds that the categories have some supremacy over sense impressions. He thus proposes to further build upon Kant by combining the idea of critical philosophy with the totalizing approach of Romanticism.

Hegel thus proposes the construction of a new theory of reality and a new metaphysics that intends to bring the vast reaches of the human spirit into unification in a single theory. He envisages bringing together the totality of concepts used in the vast stretches of all knowledge, all the arts and sciences, religion, political thought and history.

Geist is the German word, which means spirit, mind or soul. According to Hegel, the Geist is both rational and rationally comprehensible. Its logical structure is manifested in natural sciences and in historical progress. The whole of reality which includes nature, humanity, history etc., is shaped by the Geist, mind or spirit. It manifests through self-consciousness or self-articulation in these human endeavours. In all these diverse fields of human endeavours like psychology, history, religion, drama, art, and philosophy, we find only but the manifestations of the self- consciousness of Geist. In this context Hegel proclaims that the real is rational and the rational is real.

Since this Absolute Spirit encompasses everything, it is God and also the ultimate reality. It thus is a complex totality of rational concepts constituting absolute spirit or God. This totality of thought is absolute and infinite unlike the finite minds of humans. Hegel calls the Geist the objective mind. On the other hand, it is immanent in it. Mind and nature are not mere aspects of the absolute. As Russell says, they are not like a screen, behind which an indifferent and lifeless God lies concealed. Nor is the absolute the principle of nature and of mind, but is itself successively nature and mind. This succession, this process, this perpetual generation of things, is the absolute itself. [History of Philosophy]. The absolute is not immovable, but active.

Hegel's absolute idealism thus presents a very unique account of realify where the latter is conceived as rational and as a conceptual totality and an integrated and total structure of conceptual truths.

But the absolute Spirit is not a mere abstract category of thought. Nor is it a formal or ideal archetype as Plato conceives reality. Hegel maintains that it is not different from what is existent. He asserts that the rational is the existent object more deeply understood.

From these assumptions, Hegel derives his all-inclusive idealism. Opposing Kant he argues that since reality is rational, it is knowable, as its rational structures are knowable. The absolute mind is a unity-in-diversity and it incorporates all differences.

As mentioned above, the absolute being is the common root of the categories or pure concepts. There are certain difficulties in rationally comprehending this concept, as it is the emptiest and at the same time the most comprehensive reality. To repeat, it is everything and hence involves everything. Therefore, it is the most universal being. Logically speaking, this absolute being, which is absolutely infinite and is "everything", cannot be any specific "thing", as any specific thing is essentially a limited and finite entity.

In other words, being is the most universal notion, and hence the poorest and emptiest, the absolute Spirit seems to be " no specific entity" or "no thing". To be something it needs to be determined as a thing and finite. But being without any determination is non-being, or being pure and simple is equal to non-being. The absolute, according to Hegel, is both being and non-being and hence, paradoxically, both itself and its opposite. Since it is infinite and complete in itself, it should be an immovable and barren thing.

There is therefore, a fundamental contradiction in the conception of being, which Hegel says can be overcome if we really understand the implications of such a contradiction, where being is both itself and its opposite. The contradiction present in its conceptualization as a being, results in the dynamism that makes the being an eternal process. Becoming is both being and non-being, as both are contained and reconciled in it. This new contradiction that results from the process of becoming is further resolved by a new synthesis, and so on, until we reach the absolute idea.

Hegel thus explains the concept of reality with an explication of the process of becoming where contradictions are continuously encountered, resolved and synthesized. Each contradiction is reconciled in a unity or a synthesis.

Hegelian system thus conceives contradictions, not as hindrances or as absolutes. Hegel argues that contradictions exist not only in thought, but also in the things themselves. They form the very nature of reality. Hegel says that, in the process of becoming, being determines itself. With an exposition of this process where contradictions are encountered and synthesized, Hegel brings out the dialectical element in thought and reality. He affirms that this process and the immanent dialectical element will also explain the process of historical development. Hegel attempts to expose the dialectic that is manifest in every phenomena; natural, organic, political and historical.

Hegel also tells us how to deal with the contradictions. Opposing the traditional apprehensions about them, Hegel holds that they are not unthinkable. They constitute the root of all life and movement. Therefore, truth is the whole. All individual concepts are partial truths. Reality as a whole consists of oppositions and contradictions and their eventual overcoming. Nature does not stop at contradictions, but overcomes it. All oppositions are resolved in the absolute.

Absolute Idealism

The greatest of all the German idealists was George Wilhelm Friedrich Hegel, who methodically constructed a comprehensive system of thought about the world. Focussed like Kant on the goal of showing how some fundamental unity underlies the confusing multiplicity of experimental contents, Hegel took a much more systematic approach by making absolute consciousness the key source of ultimate connections among all other things. In what follows, we will examine in detail the logical apparatus Hegel employed in pursuit of knowledge.

Even more than Aristotle and the Stoics, Hegel believed that the study of logic is an investigation into the fundamental structure of reality itself. According to Hegel, all logic (and, hence, all of reality) is dialectical in character. But Hegel did not suppose this to be the end of the matter; he made the further supposition that the two concepts so held in opposition can always be united by a shift to some higher level of thought.

Being, for example, is a basic concept that serves as a clear starting-point for any serious thinker, but serious contemplation of its nature reveals it to be so utterly devoid of specific content that the mind is naturally led to the thought of Nothing as its opposite; but these two are not really contradictory, since both may be unified under the more sophisticated and comprehensive notion of Becoming. If, on the other hand, our thesis is the concept of Being as a naive immediate presentation of experience, then its natural antithesis is the idea of Essence as knowledge mediated by classification; and the synthesis that unites these concepts is that of the Notion as a self-mediating interpretation of thought and reality combined.

On the grandest scale of conceivability, all of thought (including the dialectical logic itself) is comprised by the thesis Idea, whose natural antithesis is Nature, the otherness of the known considered independently of its relation to the knower; and the grand synthesis of the two is Spirit, the self-knowing, self-actualizing totality of all that is—namely, the Absolute itself. Even this development, as Hegel described it in the Phenomenology of Spirit, is best understood as the triadic transition from subjective to objective to absolute Spirit.

Subjective Spirit

Considered as subjective, Spirit may be observed, through truths about human nature described by the discipline of psychology, in the structure of thought exhibited by each individual human being.

Recognition of the role we ourselves play in the origination of these Kantian regulative principles, Hegel supposed, leads us directly to the antithesis of sensory experience, the self-conscious awareness of the individual thinker, who acknowledges self as individual ego.

But Hegel held that these levels are transcended by their synthesis in universal consciousness, an abstract awareness of one's own place within the greater scheme of absolute spirit. Here the faculty of reason is crucial, since it most clearly draws upon what is common to us all.

Objective Spirit

Considered objectively, Spirit involves the interaction among many selves that are the proper subject of ethics and social or political theory.

Ethics, on Hegel's view, begins with the concept of freedom understood as the right of each individual human being to act independently in pursuit of its own self-interest. The antithesis to this is the emergence of moral rules, which require the imposition of duty as a constraint upon the natural liberty of human desire.

Political order has its origins in family life, in which the basic needs of all individuals are served by mutual feeling, without any formal principle of organization. The synthesis of the two, then, is the State, which Hegel believed to unite society into a sort of civil family, organized in legal fashion but bound together by a profound emotional sense of devotion.

According to Hegel, then, the modern nation must serve as an actualization of the self-conscious ethical will of a people {Ger. Völk}. Although this sounds something like Rousseau's general will, Hegel's version puts all of the emphasis on the collective expression of what is best for the people rather than on each individual's capacity to discover it for herself or himself.

Absolute Spirit

Finally, when considered most purely, as absolute in itself, Spirit is just the historical process of human thought toward ever-greater awareness of the fundamental unity of all reality.

Since it appreciates and evaluates the Absolute entirely through its presentations among the senses, Art is first to be considered. Effective artistic expression, Hegel supposed, must always transcend the subject/object dichotomy by leading us to awareness of some underlying unity.

The antithesis of Art as a whole is the abstract notion of the Absolute as an objectified other, the divine being contemplated by Religion. Although traditional religion often speaks of god in personal terms, its theological exposition usually emphasizes the radical differentness of the deity and its incomprehensibility to us.

This leaves room for the grand culminating synthesis of human culture, which is (of course!) Philosophy, in which the Absolute learns to cognize itself in perfectly literal terms. As the self-conscious awareness of the Absolute, Hegel's philosophy unifies the sensibility of art and the objectivication of religion by regarding the dialectical logic of reason as the ultimate structure of reality.

UNIT 3

INDIAN ETHICS

CONCEPT OF PURUSĀRTHA, ŚREYAS AND PREYAS

Purusārtha

Purusārtha literally means an "object of human pursuit". It is a key concept in Hinduism, and refers to the four proper goals or aims of a human life. The four purusārthas are Dharma (righteousness, moral values), Artha (prosperity, economic values), Kama (pleasure, love, psychological values) and Moksha (liberation, spiritual values).

All four Purusarthas are important, but in cases of conflict, Dharma is considered more important than Artha or Kama in Hindu philosophy. Moksha is considered the ultimate ideal of human life. At the same time, this is not a consensus among all Hindus, and many have different interpretations of the hierarchy, and even as to whether one should exist.

Historical Indian scholars recognized and debated the inherent tension between active pursuit of wealth (Artha purusartha) and pleasure (Kama), and renunciation of all wealth and pleasure for the sake of spiritual liberation (Moksha). They proposed "action with renunciation" or "craving-free, dharma-driven action", also called Nishkam Karma as a possible solution to the tension.

Etymology

Purusārtha is a composite Sanskrit word from Purusha and Artha. Purusha means "human being", "soul" as well as "universal principle and soul of the universe". Artha in one context means "purpose", "object of desire" and "meaning". Together, Purusartha literally means "purpose of human being" or "object of human pursuit".

Alf Hiltebeitel translates Purusartha as "Goals of Man". Prasad clarifies that "Man" includes both man and woman in ancient and medieval Indian texts. Olivelle translates it as the "aims of human life".

Sreyas and Preyas

The paths of Sreyas and Preyas clearly point to the goals they lead to, namely moksha and worldly aspirations respectively. Vedanta teaches the way to distinguish the real from the unreal by explaining the truth about the Absolute Brahman as that which always exists and hence is not subject to change. But the world, with its infinite variety and charms and attractions, enthrals the jivatmas easily into believing these as real and wishing to possess these. Vidhura blends such Vedanta truths with the tenets of Dharma Sastra to make Dhritarashtra realise his own failings that have deprived him of any peace of mind, pointed out Sri C.L. Ramakrishnan in a discourse.

The Isa Vasya Upanishad states that the entire creation and the universe belong to God. "In the heart of all things, of whatever there is in the universe, dwells the Lord. He alone is the reality. Wherefore, renouncing vain appearances, rejoice in Him. Covet no man's wealth." What better explicit advice for individual happiness than to internalise this mantra as an inner experience and realise that whatever one thinks is his possession is actually sourced from God?

If whatever exists is the wealth of God, it automatically is not any individual's possession — neither yours nor the belonging of others. There is no higher principle than the Lord and the existences in the world are held together by Him even as the gems are by the string. A flower garland is supported by the thread which is hidden. God is behind the entire creation as the material and efficient cause of the world.

He is the abiding force in every aspect of creation. Vidhura states: "Taking the wealth of others, coveting another's wife and forgetting the good deeds of others are the causes for mental unrest in a person."

Varnashrama

Human society is inherently divided into four orders. The first order is the intelligent class, second is the martial class, third is the productive class and the fourth is the labour class. The emergence of these divisions has been touched upon by many scholars and different reasoning have been put up for the same. This project has been taken up to explore such various possible interpretations for the emergence of Varnashrama Dharma.

Varnashrama Dharma is a Sanskrit name given to the divisional structure of the Indian society. When this order of society is intertwined with the four orders of life or the *ashramas*, i.e. *Brahmacharya* or the student life, *Grihastha* or the householder's life, *Vanaprastha* or the retired life and *Sanyasa* or the devotional life, it gives rise to the Varnashrama dharma. It can also be put as the presence of *varna* in different *ashramas* of life. This term paper will delve into the deeper questions of the origin of this dharma in the Indian subcontinent. The description of the emergence of this dharma supported by texts from ancient epics will support the theory of origin. Subsequently different interpretations or theories of emergence would be deliberated upon. Often *Varnashrama dharma* is also thought to be synonymous with the caste system which is very much endemic to India.

In order to bring out the meaning of the word – Varnashrama dharma, delving deeper to bring out the meaning of the fragments in required. According to Manu, Dharma is that which is practised by those who know the Vedas and the Shastras and are people without any bad quality like jealousy and passion. It includes practices recognised by the mind as correct. Varna is the organised division of the human society into four blocks depending upon the occupation which one pursues and *Ashramas* are the four stages in a person's life i.e. celibacy, family life, semi saintly life and life after renunciation. The Varna system mingled with the four Ashramas of one's life on the path of dharma becomes the Varnashrama Dharma.

In Hindu society this dharma was divided into four different groups of people who pursued four different dharmas in their life to attain the ultimate goal of their life, i.e. realisation of god. The first of such kind was the Brahmana Dharma. According to Manu, learning Vedas, teaching of Vedas, conducting yagnas and conducting yagnas for others, giving alms and taking alms for others are the six important duties in a Brahman's life. The greatest Tapas a Brahman can do is to chant Vedas again and again. The next group of people were the Kshatriyas. They were those people who belonged to the clan of the kings and soldiers and used to look after the safety of their territory and the people. Looking after people, collecting weapons to punish those who did wrong, engaging in dharmic wars, winning over enemies' army and ruling the world were the essential duties of a kshatriya. The third varna was the Vaishya Dharma. Manu says that the vaishyas should give charity, perform yajnas, should get knowledge, carry out trade in cereals, gems, gold, silver and other articles, should give money on loan and cultivate the land. The fourth Varna, i.e. the Shudra dharma encompassed service to people of other dharmas. He has also talked about Varna Sadharana Dharma which included those dharmas which would have been common to the people of all the four varnas.

The first reference to the Varnashrama system is made in Purush Sukta verses of the Rig Veda (book 10, hymn 90) where the different sections of the society are regarded as the limbs of the great self. When objectively viewed, these Varnas were sophisticated organisation of the society that intelligently divided the population into different groups that would help the society function smoothly. Another property of the varna system was that what may be desirable for one section of the society could be degrading for another. For example: absolute non violence which includes refraining from animal sacrifice is considered unworthy of a Kshatriya. Underlying all these differences is the one common goal of advancing in spiritual life based on Sanatana dharma.

The complicacies of this fourfold division of the society lead us to think about the main question on which this paper is based, i.e. the origin of this dharma. This organisation of the society has been there in Indian society since time immemorial but there are different theories regarding the emergence of this dharma. *Firstly*, it should be accepted that in any kind of society, different fragments of people perform different services and based on such services a division is formed. Such division among the intelligentsia and the working class existed in all civilisations. It has been deduced that such division was healthy. For instance, the clergy, the nobility, the burghers and the serf and proletariat into which European society was divided was similar to the four varnas. Even Iran was divided into four fold divisions namely Atharva (priest), Rathestha (warrior), Vastrya Fsuvant (head of the family) and Huiti (manual worker) which corresponds to the four fold division in our society.

The origin of the Varnashrama dharma is traced by two theories. One is the Brahmanical view and the other is the western view. The western view mainly focuses on the existence of this organisation in the Aryan society. It is believed that the Aryans brought this sophistication into Indian land which was subsequently adopted by other tribes of that time. At that time, the *dasyus* were the original inhabitants of India who are said to be the ancestors of the Sudras. When the Aryans conquered India, they suppressed and enslaved the *dasyus* who were dark in colour. Varna also means colour. So it was also proposed that the division was also based on the colour of one's skin but then division existed even among the fairer group. History suggests that there was always a rift between the Aryans and the *dasyus* (and between their religious observances) and that might be the reason for the exclusion of the Sudras from the religious rites of a vedic type.

The Rig Vedic society was mostly composed of pastoral lands and cattle were considered to be the wealth. War was a means of livelihood. The chief income of the king used to come from the spoils of war. The priest also used to take a substantial share from it. In the later vedic period, the society got fragmented from a tribal set up to a kind of occupational segregation in which the intellectual class started asserting its power over the serving class subsequently.

The other theory is the Brahmanical view which supports the divine sanction. The Purusha Sukta in Rig veda mentions the purusha who is the world spirit who has produced the Brahmana from his mouth, the Kshatriya from his arms and the Vaishya from his thighs. The Shudra is said to have sprung from his feet. Manu states the reason of such creation of different groups as "for the sake of preserving the universe the being (Brahma, the creator) devoted separate duties to those who sprang respectively from his mouth, his arms, his thighs and his feet". But it has always been meant to be guna karma, i.e. quality work rather than body based restricted scope of work to each of the four groups, i.e. varna karma. Backing the divine origin theory, Geeta says that the order is created on the basis of quality work- *Chaturvarnayam mayasrushtam gunakarma vibhagasaka.* This fourfold division was not meant to be a rigid compartment of fixed occupations and it is quite clear when Geeta says – *tasya kartaramapi mam vidyakartaramavyayam.* According to the divine origin theory, the organisation of this fourfold division was to serve the society but with the coming of Kali yuga, this division which was flexible before became rigid due to the formation of many sub castes and with one sect at loggerheads with the other. Sticking to one's own caste became the norm. The Marxist theory gives another interpretation to this division and bases the varna system on class division.

The Varnashrama dharma is often confused to be the same as the caste system imbibed in the Indian society. The Varnashrama is a natural organised division of the society which would lead to a content society that would be interdependent on each other. The purpose of the *Varnashrama* social system is to provide a structure allowing people to work according to their natural tendencies and to organize society so that everyone, regardless of their position, makes spiritual advancement. This philosophy says that people can only work together with a co-operative spirit if there is a central point of focus. It is different from the caste system in a way that it has not got a hint of racial prejudice.

With the passage of time, Varnashrama got rigidly compartmentalised and rituals and traditions started to be followed very strictly. With the coming of the Muslim empire, the Hindus got aware of their identity and the constant 'identity tussle' made them exhibit their religion as superior to that of the others. Mingling with other factors, this led to the transformation of the Varnashrama dharma to a compulsory form of segregation that accepted the form of caste system in India. The orthodoxy that fell on the defence at the very approach of Islam thought it wise to respond to the new challenges by imposing restrictions on marriage and other ceremonies. Anuloma or Exogamy was no more practised and the group within which one could marry shrinked smaller and smaller. No varna remained a single unit and groups among them based on diet, religious practices etc. were formed. The all embracing idea that people from all caste are children of the god was now practised only on spiritual sphere. There was no equality on the social sphere because of the accretion of *parrabdha* and *sancit* karma. The decline in harmony in the society was reemphasised by the inferior position of women and people from the lower castes. This led to the advent of social evils like sati, child marriage, child widows etc.

Lord Metson quoted in "The Untouchables of India" that caste moderates personal ambition and checks the bitterness of competition. It gives a man, whatever his station in life, a society in which he can be at home even when he is among strangers. For the poor man, it serves as a club, as a trade union and a mutual benevolent society, all rolled into one. It ensures continuing and a certain inherited skill in the arts and crafts. And in the moral sphere it means that every man lives in content with that place which destiny has allotted him, and uncomparingly does his best." But practically none of the plight of those who were the victim of the system was beyond addressable. But with the coming of the European and the spread of English culture in some parts of India, the Indian scholars who took up to rational thinking found the system too suffocating to live in. And from there started the string of reforms. A pioneer of such reform movements was Raja Ram Mohun Roy who raised his voice against social evils.

With the advent of twentieth century and the coming of many modern means of communication, the hiatus between different caste and religious groups got plugged in. Some famous reformers introduced various societies to cover up the social evil of untouchability. The Brahmo Samaj founded by Raja Ram Mohun Roy was one of the societies that aimed at removed social evils like sati, untouchability, etc. He was a great social thinker to suggest inter-caste marriage as the only remedy for breaking down barriers of caste system. The leading social reformer Mahadev Govind Ranade founded the Prarthna Samaj under the inspiration of Keshab Chandra Sen. It also aimed at forming a heterogeneous society where no social impediments would exist nurturing a healthy environment for budding India. The Arya Samaj which was inspired by the Brahmo Samaj was founded by Dayanand Saraswati, made Veda as the centre of purifying all the evils gulping the rational behaviour of human beings at that time. The efforts of Ramakrishna Paramhansa and Swami Vivekanand could not be left behind while counting the number of steps that we have moved ahead of the unfortunate days. The Theosophical society founded by Madame H.P. Blavatsky and Colonel H.S. Olcott has also contributed its part. The contribution of all these enlightened men has brought us to a phase which is vastly different from the landscape of ancient

India. The evil of casteism is not totally obliterated from the social picture but the condition has substantially improved giving rise to a harmonious heterogeneous existence.

Tracing the path of origination of the varna system, this project acquaints us to the Brahmanical and the western theory of interpretation of the emergence of the varna system. Taking in excerpts from the Geeta and emphasising on the words of Manu, it can be concluded that the varna system has reshaped itself over time. Four major varnas were formed due to societal segregation for various reasons but it has eventually taken a rigid form. The contribution from various scholars in transformation of this system has led to a different picture that exists in today's time. The division of society has existed in all times and will keep on existing in some other form if not in this form.

Dharma

There is no Hindu term corresponding to what we call religion, because Dharma and religion are not the same and Hinduism is in fact a Dharma rather than a religion in the restricted sense of the word.

Religion is the response of man to apprehend the forces which are beyond his control and which are supernatural and supersensory.

Hence, religion means those powers and forces which are supernatural, super-social and superhuman. Religion is a belief in some divine power. It may be pointed out that religion has two aspects, namely some sort of belief system and the rituals or the observance of certain actions to establish contact between the individual, and the supernatural power. Real meaning of Dharma is something different from the pure religion.

Dharma means the righteous way of living. It is intended to provide guidelines in all social action and to harmonize relation between Kama and Artha. According to R.V. Kane, "The writers on Dharma Sastras meant by Dharma not a creed or religion but a mode of life or code of conduct which regulated a man's work and activities as a member of society and as an individual and was intended to bring the gradual development of man and to enable him to reach what was deemed to be the goal of human existence. "Therefore, Dharma implies those rules according to which a man must behave as a member of society.

B.G. Gokhale has written, *"And if there is any one concept that has permeated Indian thinking through the ages and created a consistent pattern of thought and behaviour for the large majority of the people it is that of Dharma. The term is of such wide implication that it is applied to determination and evaluation of all forms of human activities."*

Dharma has been equated to the performance of duties. It is said, do the duty even if it be humble, rather than other persons' duty even if it be great. Dharma is the doctrine of the duties and rights of each in the ideal society and as such the law or mirror of all moral actions.

It is clear that Dharma has special significance for Hindus because Dharma is not a creed worship but a mode of life. Dharma represents social values and cultural norms. It is created for the welfare and happiness of man. It is a doctrine of duties and rights.

Dharma has been viewed in a larger sense to mean the duties a person has to perform. The Hindu social organization views the individual not only in terms of the personality of the individual but also as a member of the group. In this manner, Dharma can be understood at several levels of human existence.

The theory of Purushartha explains the management and conduct of life of the individual with regard to the group. Dharma has been given the most important place in the Purushartha system. If man pursues Artha and Kama without Dharma, he cannot attain Moksha. Dharma is the very basis of human life. Devoid of Dharma, man cannot pursue the correct course of life.

The theory of Purushartha finds concrete expression in the Ashrams system. The Ashrams system has been regarded as a place of work and the stages of life through which-a man passes his whole span of life. Accordingly, there are four Ashrams namely Brahmacharya, Grihastha, Vanaprastha and Sanyasa. A man is supposed to pay off three Rinas, namely Deva Rina, Rishi Rina and Pitri Rina. These Rinas can be fulfilled only by passing through the Ashrams system, particularly Grihastha Ashrams. In the Vanaprastha Ashrama, a man goes to the forest and lives the life of a hermit. In the Sanyasa Ashrams, a man has to free himself from all worldly bondage. In this way the Ashrams system prescribed Dharma or duties for every stage of human life.

In ancient Hindu society there were four Varnas or classes. Each Varna was assigned a particular duty to perform and this duty was performed as a matter of Dharma. Whatever might have been the connotation of the Varna, one thing is clear that it was the division of society into various groups. Accordingly, Varna and Dharma meant the prescription of duties for various groups of people. According to Varna system, a man must follow the duties prescribed by his Varna. The Brahmin Varna is to teach, the Kshatnya Varna has to organize and manage the affairs of the society. The Vaishya Varna has to manage the economic affair and the Sudra Varna has to offer his service to the above three Varnas. The Varna Dharma defines the code of conduct and mode of life a person to follow.

Hinduism can also be understood in terms of the religion of humanity. The aim of Manava Dharma or religion of humanity is to know the ultimate truth. According to Manava Dharma Sastra, Dharma is satisfaction, forgiveness, self-control, abstaination from irregular encroachment upon other's life, control of the senses, and ultimately to know the truth and reality. According to Vishnu Dharma Sastra, the religion of humanity includes tolerance, control" non-violence, devotion to teachers, sympathy and freedom from desires, and respect to elders.

The kula Dharma includes the duties of a person and he has to perform his duties in accordance with Dharma prescribed for the householder. The Hindu Sastrakaras are of the opinion that man should not confine himself only to his own selfish interests. A person should not confine himself only to his own selfish interests. A person should offer part of his meals to Gods. Bhutas, guests, animals and saints and only after that he should at his own meal.

The Hindu Sastrakaras have made Hindu Dharma very dynamic and changeable. According to each age and circumstances, a man has to act and it is his duty to move and work according to the needs of times. Prabhu has remarked that Hindu Dharma has so fluctuations that even Adharma becomes Dharma if the situations so demands.

Under this category, the duties have been mentioned according to which the ruler and the ruled must conduct their lives. The duty of Kshatriya is to protect the population. It is the duty of king to protect and safeguard the interests of the public. It is the duty of the public to obey the rules of the land and the dictates of the king.

Duties have been prescribed to face the complexity of life. It is said that in times of emergency a Brahmin is allowed to follow the Dharma of Kshatnya and if it's not possible then he should follow the Dharma of Vaishya. In times of emergency even those things which are generally prohibited become the duty of individual if it can save the atma and Dharma. ,

It is clear that Dharma has been regarded as not only a moral scheme of life but also as the duties prescribed for various sections of the society. Dharma has great significance m Hindu society. It reminds all of their duties and social responsibilities. It is Dharma which acts as an arbitrator between Arha and Karma. Since Dharma is righteousness, therefore, it leads society on right path.

Sadharana Dharma

Sadharana Dharma is the general code of conduct which are said to be binding on every individual of the society irrespective of the caste, creed, sex, place, time etc. It is said that we are all required to cultivate certain general virtues such as truthfulness, compassion, forgiveness, charity, kindness, non-violence etc. just by being a member of the class of human species. It is otherwise known as Samanya Dharma.

Ṛna and Yajña, Concept of Duty

Indian ethics has a special characteristic of Ashram system. Every individual by nature passes through various stages of life.

Indian thinkers correlate the stages of individual to the society. Indian thinkers prescribed duties to every stages of life. The prescribed duties contribute to the social welfare and social stability. Ashram system has four stages. Every individual passes through the stages of a Brahmacharin (a student), a Grihastha (a house holder), a Vanaprastha (retired) and a Sanyasin (a wandering monk.)

The stage of a householder is very important for the stability of the society. The individual enters in to the first unit of society *i.e.,* family, by entering Grihasth ashrama. A householder enjoys the pleasures of life. At the same time, he has many responsibilities. He has to take care of his family, the guests and other society members.

The concept of Ṛna implies obligation and responsibility. Man is a social animal. His development is possible, because many other fellow beings have, in some or other way, contributed to his progress. The individual is under obligation of many members of his society.

The individual is born with 3 Ṛnas namely Rishi Ṛna (debt of sages / teachers), Pitri Ṛna (debt of the ancestors) and Deva Rna (Divine debt)

1. Rishi Ṛna

Rishi Ṛna is also called as Guru Ṛna. The first stage in the life of an individual, *i.e.,* Brahmacharya ashrama (a student) is spent with teacher. In ancient time, the sages, wise people were guide posts of society. The wisdom of the sages was passed from one generation to another generation. The sages played important role in the development of the individual as well as in the social progress. By learning Vedas by giving fees, by showing respect by being grateful, Rishi Rna can be discharged. In Brahmacharya ashrama, an individual becomes free from Rishi Rna.

2. Pitri Ṛna

An individual owes many things including his own existence to his ancestors. It becomes responsibility of the individual to sustain the family by giving birth to next generation. By begetting children the individual becomes free from the debt of his ancestors. Thus in Grihasthashrama, an individual becomes free from Pitri Ṛna.

3. Deva Ṛna

God has created this universe. God is sustainer of this universe. Whatever we receive from nature, is due to the blessings of God. The forces of nature are beyond the control of human beings. To please these forces, men used to perform sacrifices. Performance of sacrifices was a way to show respect to deities. Forces of nature are like supernatural, mighty, powerful agents. A man in such a world is at the mercy of God. By performing sacrifices, man becomes free from the Divine debt. In Grihastha and in Vanaprastha Ashrama, an individual becomes free from Deva Ṛna.

By repaying three Rnas the individual reaches the stage of 'Annrunya' which means freedom from all Rnas. Only after reaching the stage of Annrunya, an individual can prepare himself for the highest purushartha- Moksha

The concept of Rna-traya [3 debts] is a commonly known concept. However, "Shataphath Brahman" refers to fourth debt Viz. Manushya Rna. It is obligation towards humanity. By helping other human beings an individual becomes free from debt towards humanity.

Yajnas

Yajna is a ritual of offerings accompanied by chanting of vedic mantras, derived from the practice in Vedic times. It is called worship or prayer or praise or sacrifice. Yajna is an ancient ritual of offering and sublimating the havana samagri in the fire. The sublime meaning of the word 'yajna' is derived from the sanskrit verb 'yaj', which has a three-fold meaning of worship of deities or devapujana, unity or Saogati karana and charity (dana). An essential element is the ritual fire-the divine Agni-into which oblations are poured, as everything that is offered into the fire is believed to reach God.

Vedic yajnas are typically performed by four Vedic priests :

(i) **The Hota** recites invocations and litanies drawn from the Rigveda. The Verses recited by hota are of three kinds - introductory verses, verses pertaining to yajna and eulogistic verses. The hota is also supposed to contemplate on and identify with the deity of the speech-fire.

(ii) **The Adhvaryu** is an charge of the physical details of the ritual like measuring the ground, building the altar etc. mentioned in the Yajur-veda. The adhvaryu offers three kinds of obligation those that blaze up, those that make great noise and those that sink. Adhvaryu is supposed to contemplate one and identify with the deity of the eye-sun.

(iii) **The Udgata** is the chanter of hymns set to melodies drawn from the Samveda. Those three types of hymns like hota; (chants the introductory, yajna and eulogistic verses) are identified with the three kinds of vital breath prana, Apana and Vyana in the body and the Udgatra himself contemplates on the Vital breath.

(iv) **The Brahman** is the superintendent of the entire performance and is responsible for correcting mistakes by means of supplementary verses invoking the Visvedevas. Brahman has to identify himself with the deity of the mind-moon.

Types of Yajnas

Four hundred yajnas are described in the Vedas, of which 21 are deemed compulsory. These compulsory yajnas are also called 'Nitya Karmas'. The rest of the yajna are optional and are performed for kamyakarma (particular wishes and benefits). The Aupasana Yajna, though not a part of these 21 is still compulsory.

Out of the 21 Nityakarmas, only the Agnihotra and the Aupasana are to be performed twice daily, at dawn and at dusk. The remaining are performed over the course of the year.

1. First seven yajnas are called **Pakayajnas:** They are astaka, sthalipaka, parvana, sravani, agrahayani, caitri and asviyuji. These involve consecrating cooked items.
2. Second sevens are called **Waviryajnas:** They are agniyadhana, agnihotra, Darsapurnamasa, agrayana, caturmasya, nirudha pasu bandha, Sautramani. These involving offering havis or oblations.
3. Remaining sevens are called **Somayajnas**: They are Agnistoma, Atyagnistoma, Uktya, Shodasi, vajpeya, atiratra and aptoryama. These involve the extraction utility and consumption of soma (an extract of a particular chosen tree.)

There are five Panch Maha Yajnas :

(i) Rishi yajna : honouring Rishis by the study of holy scriptures.

(ii) Deva yajna : Worship of the Celestials by pouring oblations into the sacred fire.

(iii) Pitri-yajna : offering libations to ancestors or pitrs.

(iv) Manushya-yajna : Charitable offerings of food to fellow humans.

(v) Bhuta-yajna : feeding animals, especially cows and birds.

Effects of Doing Yajna

Through, bond petitions, we can rouse God to do an action. The words are known as an artificial sounds and these artificial sounds have occult powers. The mystery of, it is not understood by anyone. But the priest are able to understand the mystery of it. The priest referred themselves as the dignity of a God on Earth.

There was only one ambition, which is referred as to become immortal like the Gods. By performing sacrifices, we can become immortal. Without sacrifice, the Sun would not rise. It has been also said that we can depose Indra from his throne in heaven, if we are able to perform a hundred horse-sacrifices. The sacricfies has an essential feature of pleasing the Gods and by doing this men will get the profit.

By performing sacrifices Gods become the friends of men. By performing sacrifices we can gain Earthly profits. The sacrifices has become a rule, which have to be followed. Heavenly bliss is not gained through the sacrifices. The Vedic hymns sacrifices are regarded as a superfluous method of prayers indicate true religion.

Every syllable, which is uttered at the ceremony is regarded as an essential feature of sacrifice. Every act done is also regarded as the essential feature of the sacrifice. The Brahmanas religion includes symbolic subtleties and are also lost in a soulless mechanism of idle rites. Yajna is defined as a ritual of offering, which is accompanied by chanting of Vedic mantras, according to Hinduism.

Karma Yoga

The law of karma is the counter-part in the moral world of the physical law of uniformity. It is the law of the conservation of moral energy. The vision of law and order is revealed in the Ṛta of the Ṛg-Veda. According to the principle of karma there is nothing uncertain or capricious in the moral world. We reap what we sow.

Since the sense of individual responsibility is emphasised, there are critics who think that the karma doctrine is inconsistent with social service. It is said that there is no emphasis on the bearing of one another's burdens. As a matter of fact, the Upaniṣads hold that we can be free from karma only by social service. So long as we perform selfish work we are subject to the law of bondage. When we perform disinterested work we reach freedom. "While thus you live there is no way by which karma clings to you". What binds us to the chain of birth and death is not action as such but selfish action. In an age when the individual was ever ready to shirk responsibility for what he did by throwing the burden on providence or stars or some other being than his own self, the doctine of karma urged that a man "fetters himself by himself, like a bird by its nest". What looms over us is no dark fate but our own past. We are not the victims of a driving doom. Suffering is the wages of sin. There is no question that such an idea is a great incentive to good conduct.

Man is not a mere product of nature. He is mightier than his karma. If the law is all, then there is no real freedom possible. Man's life is not the working of merely mechanical relations. There are different levels—the mechanical the vital the sentient the intellectual and the spiritual—these currents cross and recross and inter-penetrate each other. The law of karma, which rules the lower nature of man, has nothing to do with the spiritual in him. The infinite in man helps him to transcend the limitations of the finite. The essence of spirit is freedom. By its exercise man can check and control his natural impulses. That is why his life is something more than a succession of mechanically determined states.

Karma has a cosmic as well as a psychological aspect. Every deed must produce its natural effect in the world; at the same time it leaves an impression on or forms a tendency in the mind of man. It is this tendency or saṁskāra or vāsanā that inclines us to repeat the deed we have once done. So all deeds have their fruits in the world and effects on the mind. So far as the former are concerned, we cannot escape them, however, much we may try. But in regard to mental tendencies we can control them. Our future conduct hoids all possibilities. By self-discipline we can strengthen the good impulses and weaken the bad ones.

The principle of karma is not inconsistent with the reality of the absolute Brahman. The moral law of karma is the expression of the nature of the absolute. Anthropomorphically we can say a divine power controls the process. Ṛta is the law in the Vedas. Varuṇa is the lord of Ṛta. Karma refers to the unchanging action of the gods. It is an expression of the nature of reality.

There is no doctrine that is so valuable in life and conduct as the karma theory. Whatever happens to us in this life we have to submit in meek resignation, for it is the result of our past doings. Yet the future is in our power, and we can work with hope and confidence. Karma inspires hope for the future and resignation to the past.

Sthitaprajna

Sthitaprajna is not a state of experience. Sthitaprajna begins from the moment you begin to make a differentiation through words when you say, *"This is the Atma and it is separate from everything else."* The state of sthitaprajna begins from the moment you utter the difference till the moment you attain the experience of the Soul (the Self). That is the state of sthitaprajna. The path that Lord Krishna has shown comes all the way to sthitaprajna, however there is a lot more beyond that. When 'we' give you the knowledge of the Self, you experience a state much higher than the state of sthitaprajna. There is tremendous difference between the state of sthitaprajna and attaining the Self. Sthitaprajna means to be stable in pragnya; but that is the relative pragnya (through the medium of intellect). After that one has to attain the experience of the Self. Our pragnya (real) is the one that is established after attaining the awareness of the Self, thereafter all matters are settled without raag-dwesh and a state of equanimity arises. Sthitaprajna means to recognize and know the attributes of the Self through the intellect that has become pure, but not the actual experience of these qualities. With the state of sthitaprajna, one knows and recognizes the universe and its elements; that verily is called the state of 'shuddha samkit'. However, the knowledge of the Self that 'we' give you, gives you the direct experience of the Self and that is called 'parmartha samkit', and with that state one sees, recognizes and experiences the universe and its elements.

One does not become emotional in the state of sthitaprajna, however this state does not lead one to a state of samadhi (uninterrupted bliss). Samadhi can only occur upon attaining the Self. When the illusion of 'I am Chandulal' leaves, a state of samadhi occurs.

Which is the last station Lord Krishna refers to in the Gita? The state of sthitaprajna is the last station in the Gita. He says, "Attain the state of sthitaprajna," but people had to question, "What does sthitaprajna do?" The Lord had to explain what sthitaprajna is. That which becomes stable in pragnya; that which pushes away the non essence (the non-self) and makes you attain the essence (the Self) is sthitaprajna. And your state of the Shuddhatma (the Self) is much higher than the state of sthitaprajna.

Swadharma

In the Indian spiritual tradition, dharma means the way, literally law or duty. Everything and everyone in existence has its own dharma — its essential way of being in the world — that is in harmony with the overriding dharma of nonviolence that applies to all life (ahimsa paramo dharma). Thus a person's swadharma (swa, own, and dharma, duty) is their own unique role in life or way of being in the world, which it is their duty to realize and fulfill. Swadharma is not destiny, which would deny the reality of human choice, but rather a set of capacities that when fully developed allow us to take our place in the world. The Gita warns strongly against attempting to live out the dharma of another, but discovering our own capacities and using them in selfless service is described as the goal of human life.

Lokasaṃgraha

Lokasamgraha is a compound word of two component words, loka and samgraha. The first word 'Loka' denotes, in different contexts, either human beings or the world. The second word, 'samgraha' similarly has more than one meaning, ranging from 'keeping together' to 'protecting' as also to 'regulating'. Samkara defined the world Lokasamgraha as 'weaning people from the tendency to take to the path of wrong.' Vivekananda translated Lokasamgraha as 'working for the good of others', and added that this is "a very powerful idea-which has become the ideal in India".

Tilak has suggested two meanings, one referring to man kind and another referring to various worlds. Since he is the first commentator to highlight, most forcefully and with a detailed explanation, the concept of Lokasamgraha in the Gita, his opinion about both the meanings is noteworthy. First, taking loka to mean mankind, Tilak writes:

> The last and the most important direction of the Blessed Lord to Arjuna in support of the doctrine of karma-yoga is centred on Lokasamgraha.... Taking all the meanings of samgraha as given in dictionaries, Lokasamgraha means 'binding men together, and protecting, maintaining and regulating them in such a way that they might acquire that strength which results from mutual cooperation, thereby putting them on the path of acquiring merit while maintaining their good condition.... (After looking at Samkara's definition) it will be clear that my interpretation of Lokasamgraha as 'making wise, those persons who behave recklessly as a result of ignorance, and keeping them together in a happy state, and putting them on the path of self-amelioration' is neither strange nor without authority.

Apurva

The Sanskrit word apurva in its common usage means 'one of a kind', 'unique', 'like none-other', 'like never before' or 'unprecedented', it is something not foreseen, unpreceded, unprecedented, never seen before; in brief it means that which did not exist before or is newly born. Apurva cannot be denoted through any noun or by any verb; it is comprehended as a result of an act.

Apurva of Hindu philosophy

Bhartrhari explains that pravrtti can be viewed in four ways as apurva, kala-sakti, kriya and kala. Kumarila Bhatta explains that Apurva is the newly known vidhi or that what is not known before hearing a vedic sentence. Salikanatha explains that Apurva is that which is not cognisable by any of the ordinary means of knowledge. And, according to Nagesa, the conclusion that if pravrtti is identified with the universal Dharma it can be properly called Apurva, is the view adopted by Prabhakara who holds that the meaning of verbal endings is karya; and niyoga (obligation) is the very karya that prompts a man to fulfil itself . Karya is apurva or niyama (restriction), apurva is something which has not arisen before the performance of the sacrifice but newly born after it. Niyoga or Apurva is the supersensuous result of an action which later on produces the sensible result or prayojana, the final purpose of the action, Therefore, Apurva is something different from action itself and it is to be understood with regard to its capability of bringing about the heavenly world.

Adrsta

Adrsta is a concept in Indian philosophy which means that which is "unobserved, not seen, invisible". The concept of adrsta is discussed in the Vaiseshika Sutra, the main text of the Vaisheshika Hindu school of philosophy, as part of its philosophical discussion on the nature of the universe. After explaining the atomistic cosmology that this school theorizes as the constituents of universe, it focuses on explaining phenomena such as motion and change. These occurrences are attributed to manifestations of adrsta, or invisible forces and fields as causative reasons behind change. Vaiseshika scholars explain Adrsta as what intermediates between cause and effect but is not seen. The Vaisheshika school also uses Adrsta concept in its formulation of the Karma doctrine.

Sādhya-Sādhana, Itikartavyata

Sadhana, literally "a means of accomplishing something", is a generic term coming from the yogic tradition and it refers to any spiritual exercise that is aimed at progressing the sadhaka towards the very ultimate expression of his or her life in this reality. It includes a variety of disciplines in Hindu, Buddhist, Jain and Sikh traditions that are followed in order to achieve various spiritual or ritual objectives.

Sadhana can also refer to a tantric liturgy or liturgical manual, that is, the instructions to carry out a certain practice. A contemporary spiritual teacher and yogi Sadhguru defines sadhana thusly:

Everything can be Sadhana. The way you eat, the way you sit, the way you stand, the way you breathe, the way you conduct your body, mind and your energies and emotions – this is sadhana. Sadhana does not mean any specific kind of activity, sadhana means you are using everything as a tool for your wellbeing.

According to **N. Bhattacharyya**, *"[R]eligious sadhana, which both prevents an excess of worldliness and molds the mind and disposition (bhava) into a form which develops the knowledge of dispassion and non-attachment. Sadhana is a means whereby bondage becomes liberation."*

According to **B.K.S. Iyengar**, *"Sadhana is a discipline undertaken in the pursuit of a goal. Abhyasa is repeated practice performed with observation and reflection. Kriya, or action, also implies perfect execution with study and investigation. Therefore, sadhana, abhyasa, and kriya all mean one and the same thing. A sadhaka, or practitioner, is one who skillfully applies...mind and intelligence in practice towards a spiritual goal."*

Law of Karma: Ethical Implications

The Law of Karma is infallible and everyone invariably is subjected to it. Sometimes we are oblivious to the fact that most of our lifetime is spent in undergoing destiny which is created by our karmas or deeds in our past births. As per the law of karma, every positive deed which we do, generates a 'merit'; while every negative deed results in a 'demerit or sin' which subsequently we need to repay by enduring happiness or unhappiness. All major events in our life are predestined – for instance the family that we are born into, to whom we will get married etc. During our day-to-day interactions, we are either settling an old account or creating a new one. If an account is not settled in the present birth it is carried over to the next birth. Although, we are not consciously aware of the give-and-take karmic accounts generated in our previous births. In our subsequent births, we may or may not be equipped to settle our destiny and the paradox is that at the same time we are creating new karmic accounts. Thus, this loop of karma and destiny binds us and we remain entangled in it. The only way through which we can nullify our give and take account and destiny is through sustained and regular spiritual practice. In understanding the Law of Karma, we can see how spiritual practice can be useful to even those of us who have absolutely no spiritual interest and who only wish to be immersed in worldly pursuits. Even for those worldly relations to be fruitful they need to be insulated from destiny.

Ṛta and Satya

In the Vedic religion 'Ṛta' is the principle of natural order which regulates and coordinates the operation of the universe and everything within it. 'Ṛta' is properly joined order, rule and truth. In the hymns of the Vedas 'Rta' is the described as that which is ultimately responsible for the proper functioning of the natural, moral and sacrificial orders. The action of the individual in relation to those ordinances, referred to as 'Karma' - two terms which eventually eclipsed. 'Ṛta' in importance as signifying natural, religious and moral order in later Hinduism. 'Rta' is one of the most important religious conceptions of the 'RigVeda'.

'Ṛta' appears most frequently as representing abstract concepts such as "law", "Commandment", "Order", "sacrifice", "truth" and "regularity", but also occasionally or concrete objects such as the waters, the heavens or the sun as manifestations of the operation of 'Rta' in the physical universe, 'Rta' is also frequently used to reference to various Vedic deities.

While the concept of Ṛta as an abstract, universal principle generally remained resistant to the anthropomorphic tendencies of the Vedic period, it became increasingly associated with the actions of individuals deities, in particular with those of the god Varuna as the omniscient, all-encompassing sky. The connection of Varuna and Ṛta extended beyond the physical realm and into the sphere of ritual worship, with the sacrificial for itself being landed as that which "harnesses the steeds and holds the reins of Ṛta, becoming Varuna when he strives for 'Ṛta'.

Consequently, Rta finds a conspicuous place in the Mantras (Hymns). Expressions Like, 'guardians of Ṛta' (Rtasyagopa) and 'Practisers of Ṛta' (Rtayu) occur frequently in the description of the gods. This word originally meant uniformly of nature or the ordered course of things such as in indicated by the regular alter nation of day and night, while in Mantras is not only bears this significance but also the additional one of 'moral order'. The Vedic gods are accordingly to by viewed not only as the maintainers of cosmic order but also as upholders of moral law. This equal responsibility of divinity for the maintenance of cosmic as well as moral order is particularly dear in the conception of Varuna. He represents the sky and is the God of heavenly light. He is described as having fixed the laws of the physical universe which no one can violate.

The great importance given to Ṛta in the Vedas can be appreciated from the description of there laws in Rigveda 1-75-5 where it says, "ritam satyam vijnani" which would literally mean knowing of truth, which is Ṛta, is the only true knowledge. There laws are part of Vedic higher knowledge. According to these laws one is only free to do any action if he obeys and follow these commands of the God and without following them no individual can seek Moksha-the state of eternal bliss. It is also the state when one reaches the abode of God and avoid rebirth in the phenomenal world.

Vedic Metaphysicists have found that having created these laws God himself follows them sternly, lest a cosmic disorder or chaos may result in the destruction of the universe.

Astānga Yoga

Yoga advocates control over the body, the senses and the mind. It does not want to kill the body; on the other hand, it recommends it perfection. A sound mind needs a sound body. Sensual attachment and passions distract the body as well as the mind. They must be conquered. To overcome them, Yoga gives us the Eightfold Path of Discipline (Aṣtāṅga Yoga):

(1) **Yama.** It means abstention and includes the five vows of Jainism. It is abstention from injury through thought, word or deed (ahimsā), from falsehood (satya), from stealing (asteya), from passions and lust brahmacharya), and from avarice (aparigraha).

(2) **Niyama.** It is self-culture and includes external and internal purification (shaucha), contentment (santoṣa), austerity (tapas), study (svādhyāya) and devotion to God (Īshvaraprāṇidhāna).

(3) **Āsana.** It means steady and comfortable posture. There are various kinds of postures which are a physical help to meditation. This is the discipline of the body.

(4) **Prāṇāyāma.** It means control of breath and deals with regulation of inhalation, retention and exhalation of breath. It is beneficial to health and is highly conducive to the concentration of the mind. But it must be performed under expert guidance otherwise it may have bad after-effects.

(5) **Pratyāhāra.** It is control of the senses and consists in which drawing the senses from their objects. Our senses have a natural tendency to go to outward objects. They must be checked and directed towards the internal goal. It is the process of introversion.

These five are called external aids to yoga (bahiraṅga sādhana), while the remaining three which follow are called internal aids (antaraṅga sādhana).

(6) **Dhāraṇā.** It is fixing the mind on object of meditation like the tip of the nose or the mid-point of the eyebrows or the lotus of the heart or the image of the deity. The mind must be steadfast like the unflickering flame of a lamp.

(7) **Dhyāna.** It means meditation and consists in the undisturbed flow of thought round the object of meditation (pratyayaikatānatā). It is the steadfast contemplation without any break.

(8) **Samādhi.** It means concentration. This is the final step in Yoga. Here the mind is completely absorbed in the object of meditation. In dhyāna the act of meditation and the object of meditation remain separate. But here they become one. It is the highest means to realize the cessation of mental modifications which is the end. It is the ecstatic state in which the connection with the external world is broken and through which one has to pass before obtaining liberation.

Jainism: Saṃvara-nirjarā, Tri-ratṇa, Panch-vrata

Samvara (saṃvara) is one of the tattva or the fundamental reality of the world as per the Jain philosophy. It means stoppage—the stoppage of the influx of the material karmas into the soul consciousness. The karmic process in Jainism is based on seven truths or fundamental principles (tattva) of Jainism which explain the human predicament. Out of the seven, the four influxs (asrava), bondage (bandha), stoppage (saṃvara) and release (nirjarā)—pertain to the karmic process.

Saṃvara is the first step in the destruction of accumulated harmful karmas. The world or the samsara is often described as an ocean and the soul as a boat trying to cross it and reach the shores of liberation. The boat is leaking i.e. karmic particles are getting attached to the soul. Hence the first step is to stop the leak and prevent new water from entering the boat. This is saṃvara. Jains assert that emancipation is not possible as long as the soul remains unreleased from the bondage of these karmas. Release is made possible by saṃvara; that is, the stopping of inflow of new karmas, and nirjara; the shedding of existing harmful karma through conscious efforts.

Means of Saṃvara-nirjarā

Samvara or stoppage of karmic influx is achieved through practice of:

(a) Three guptis or three controls of mind, speech and body,

(b) Five samitis or observing carefulness in movement, speaking, eating, placing objects and disposing refuse.

(c) Ten dharmas or observation of good acts like – forgiveness, humility, straightforwardness, contentment, truthfulness, self-control, penance, renunciation, non-attachment and continence.

(d) Anuprekshas or meditation on the truths of this universe.

(d) Parisahajaya, that is, a man on moral path must develop a perfectly patient and unperturbed attitude in the midst of trying and difficult circumstances.

(e) Caritra, that is, endeavour to remain in steady spiritual practices.

Tri-ratṇa

In Jainism the three jewels (also referred to as ratnatraya) are understood as samyagdarshana ("right faith"), samyagjnana ("right knowledge"), and samyakcharitra ("right conduct"). One of the three cannot exist exclusive of the others, and all are required for spiritual liberation. The Triratna is symbolized frequently in art as a trident.

Panch-vrata

Right knowledge, right faith, and right conduct are the three most essentials for attaining liberation in Jainism. In order to acquire these, one must observe the five great vows:

Non-violence (Ahimsa)

Among these five vows, non violence (Ahimsa) is the cardinal principle of Jainism and hence it is known as the cornerstone of Jainism. Non violence is the supreme religion (Ahimsa parmo dharma). It is repeatedly said in Jain literature; "Do not injure, abuse, oppress, enslave, insult, torment, torture, or kill any creature or living being."

According to Jainism all living beings, irrespective of their size, shape, or different spiritual developments are equal. No living being has a right to harm, injure, or kill any other living being, including animals, insects, and plants. Every living being has a right to exist and it is necessary to live with every other living being in perfect harmony and peace.

Nonviolence in Jainism is not a negative virtue. It is based upon the positive quality of universal love and compassion. One who is actuated by this ideal cannot be indifferent to the suffering of others.

Violence of every type should be completely forbidden. Mental tortures by way of harsh words, actions, and any type of bodily injuries should also be avoided. Even thinking evil of some one is considered violence in Jainism.

Practically, it is impossible to survive without killing or injuring some of the smallest living beings. Some lives are killed even when we breathe, drink water, or eat food. Therefore, Jainism says that minimum killing of the lowest form of life should be our ideal for survival.

In the universe, there are different forms of life, such as, human beings, animals, insects, plants, bacteria, and even smaller lives, which cannot be seen even through the most powerful microscopes. Jainism has classified all the living beings according to their senses.

The five senses are touch, taste, smell, sight, and hearing.

One Sense	Touch	plants, water, air, earth, fire, etc.
Two Senses	Touch, Taste	worms, leeches, etc.
Three Senses	Touch, Taste, Smell	ants, lice, etc.
Four Senses	Touch, Taste, Smell, Sight	flies, bees, etc.
Five Senses	Touch, Taste, Smell, Sight, Hearing	humans, animals, birds, heavenly and hellish beings

It is more painful if a life of the higher forms (more than one sense) is killed. Hence Jainism allows lay people to use only vegetables as a food for survival. All non vegetarian food is made by killing living beings with two or more senses. Therefore, Jainism preaches strict vegetarianism, and prohibits non vegetarian foods.

Jainism explains that violence is not defined by actual harm, for this may be unintentional. It is the intention to harm, the absence of compassion, unawareness, and the ignorance that makes an action violent. Without violent thought there can be no violent actions. Non violence is to be observed in action, speech, and thought. One should not be violent, ask others to do so, or approve of such an activity.

Truth (Satya)

Anger, greed, fear, and jokes are the breeding grounds of untruth. To speak the truth requires moral courage. Only those who have conquered greed, fear, anger, jealousy, ego, and frivolity can speak the truth.

Jainism insists that one should not only refrain from falsehood, but should always speak the truth, which should be wholesome and pleasant. One should remain silent if the truth causes pain, hurt, anger, or death of any living being.

Truth is to be observed in speech, mind, and deed. One should not utter an untruth, ask others to do so, or approve of such activities.

Non-stealing (Achaurya or Asteya)

Stealing consists of taking another's property without his consent, or by unjust or immoral methods. Further, one should not take anything which does not belong to him. It does not entitle one to take away a thing, which may be lying, unattended or unclaimed. One should observe this vow very strictly, and should not touch even a worthless thing, which does not belong to him. When accepting alms, help, or aid one should not take more then what is minimum needed. To take more than one's need is also considered theft in Jainism.

The vow of non stealing insists that one should be totally honest in action, thought, and speech. One should not steal, ask others to do so, or approve of such activities.

Celibacy/Chastity (Brahmacharya)

Total abstinence from sensual pleasure and the pleasure of all five senses are called celibacy. Sensual pleasure is an infatuating force, which sets aside all virtues and reason at the time of indulgence. This vow of controlling sensuality is very difficult to observe in its subtle form. One may refrain from physical indulgence but may still think of the pleasures of sensualism, which is prohibited in Jainism.

Monks are required to observe this vow strictly and completely. They should not enjoy sensual pleasures and pleasure of all five senses, ask others to do the same, nor approve of it. There are several rules laid down for observing this vow for householders. They should not have any physical relationship other than own spouse. The relationship with your own spouse should be of limited nature.

Non-attachment/Non-possession (Aparigraha)

Jainism believes that the more worldly wealth a person possesses, the more he is likely to commit sin to acquire and maintain the possession, and in a long run he may be unhappy. The worldly wealth creates attachments, which will continuously result in greed, jealousy, selfishness, ego, hatred, violence, etc. Lord Mahavir has said that wants and desires have no end, and only the sky is the limit for them.

An attachment to worldly objects results in the bondage to the cycle of birth and death. Therefore, one who desires of spiritual liberation should withdraw from all attachments to pleasing objects of all the five senses.

Monks observe this vow by giving up attachments to all things such as:

(i) Material things: wealth, property, grains, house, books, clothes, etc.

(ii) Relationships: father, mother, spouse, children, friends, enemies, other monks, disciples, etc.

(iii) Pleasure of Five Senses: touch, taste, smell, sight, and hearing

(iv) Feelings: pleasure and painful feelings towards any objects

They have the equanimity towards music and noise, good and bad smells, soft and hard objects for touch, beautiful and dirty sights, etc. They do not eat food for taste but for survival with the intention to continue to progress spiritually and ultimately to attain liberation. Non possession and non attachment are to be observed in speech, mind, and deed. One should not possess, ask others to do so, or approve of such activities.

Jainism has lay down and described in much detail these five great vows for the path of liberation. These are to be observed strictly and entirely by the monks and nuns. Partial observance is laid down for the householders with additional seven vows.

Buddhism: *Upāya-Kaushal, Brahma-vihāra: Matri, Karuṇā, muditā, upeksha, bodhi-sattva*

Upāya-Kaushal

Upaya (Sanskrit: upāya, expedient means, pedagogy) is a term used in Buddhism to refer to an aspect of guidance along the Buddhist paths to liberation where a conscious, voluntary action is driven by an incomplete reasoning about its direction. Upaya is often used with kaushalya, upaya-kaushalya meaning "skill in means".

Upaya-kaushalya is a concept emphasizing that practitioners may use their own specific methods or techniques that fit the situation in order to gain enlightenment. The implication is that even if a technique, view, etc., is not ultimately "true" in the highest sense, it may still be an expedient practice to perform or view to hold; i.e., it may bring the practitioner closer to the true realization in a similar way. The exercise of skill to which it refers, the ability to adapt one's message to the audience, is of enormous importance in the Pali Canon.

The Digital Dictionary of Buddhism notes that rendering the Chinese term fāngbiān into English as 'skillful' or as 'expedient' is often difficult, because the connotations shift according to the context as: (1) the teaching being something to marvel at — the fact that the Buddha can present these difficult truths in everyday language (thus, skillful), yet that (2) they are teachings of a lower order as compared to the ultimate truth, and are far removed from reflecting reality, and are a kind of 'stopgap' measure (thus, expedient).

Brahma-vihāra

Brahmavihara, (Sanskrit: "living in the Brahman-heaven"), in Buddhist philosophy, the four noble practices of mental development through which men can attain subsequent rebirth in the Brahman heaven. These four practices are: (1) perfect virtue of sympathy, which gives happiness to living beings (Sanskrit: maitrī; Pāli: metta); (2) perfect virtue of compassion, which removes pain from living beings (karuna); out of karuna the bodhisattva postpones entrance into nirvana to work for the salvation of others; (3) perfect virtue of joy, the enjoyment of the sight of others who have attained happiness (mudita); (4) perfect virtue of equanimity, being free from attachment to everything and being indifferent to living beings (Sanskrit: upekā; Pāli: upekkha). These are also called the four apramānas (infinite feelings), since these four practices give happiness to infinite living beings.

Maitri

Maitri is a Sanskrit word which can be translated as "friendship," "friendliness" or "benevolence." It can also be used to describe the mental union that takes place when two people are on the same wavelength. The Pali version of this word that is often used is metta. Another way of describing maitri is a form of love which excludes the suffering that can arise from attachment (known as upadana).

Karuṇā

Karuṇā (in both Sanskrit and Pali) is generally translated as compassion. It is part of the spiritual path of both Buddhism and Jainism. Karuṇā is important in all schools of Buddhism. For Theravāda Buddhists, dwelling in karuṇā is a means for attaining a happy present life and heavenly rebirth. For Mahāyāna Buddhists, karuṇā is a co-requisite for becoming a Bodhisattva.

In Theravāda Buddhism, karuṇā is one of the four "divine abodes" (brahmavihāra), along with loving kindness (Pāli: *mettā*), sympathetic joy (*mudita*) and equanimity (*upekkha*). In the Pali canon, the Buddha recommends cultivating these four virtuous mental states to both householders and monastics. When one develops these four states, the Buddha counsels radiating them in all directions, as in the following stock canonical phrase regarding karuṇā:

> He keeps pervading the first direction—as well as the second direction, the third, and the fourth—with an awareness imbued with compassion. Thus he keeps pervading above, below, and all around, everywhere and in every respect the all-encompassing cosmos with an awareness imbued with compassion: abundant, expansive, immeasurable, free from hostility, free from ill will.

Such a practice purifies one's mind, avoids evil-induced consequences, leads to happiness in one's present life and, if there is a future karmic rebirth, it will be in a heavenly realm.

The Pali commentaries distinguish between karuṇā and mettā in the following complementary manner: Karuna is the desire to remove harm and suffering (ahita-dukkha-apanaya-kāmāta) from others; while metta is the desire to bring about the well-being and happiness (hita-sukha-upanaya-kamata) of others. The "far enemy" of karuṇā is cruelty, a mind-state in obvious opposition. The "near enemy" (quality which superficially resembles karuṇā but is in fact more subtly in opposition to it), is (sentimental) pity: here too one wants to remove suffering, but for a partly selfish (attached) reason hence not the pure motivation. In the Pali Canon, buddhas are also described as choosing to teach "out of compassion for beings."

Muditā

Muditā is word from Sanskrit and Pali that has no counterpart in English. It means sympathetic or unselfish joy, or joy in the good fortune of others. In Buddhism, mudita is significant as one of the Four Immeasurables (Brahma-vihara).

Defining mudita, we might consider its opposites. One of those is jealousy. Another is schadenfreude, a word frequently borrowed from German that means taking pleasure in the misfortune of others. Obviously, both of these emotions are marked by selfishness and malice. Cultivating mudita is the antidote to both.

Mudita is described as an inner wellspring of joy that is always available, in all circumstances. It is extended to all beings, not just to those close to you. In the Mettam Sutta the Buddha said, "I declare that the heart's release by sympathetic joy has the sphere of infinite consciousness for its excellence."

Sometimes English-speaking teachers broaden the definition of mudita to include "empathy."

The 5th-century scholar Buddhaghosa included advice on growing mudita in his best-known work, the Visuddhimagga, or Path of Purification. The person just beginning to develop mudita, Buddhaghosa said, should not focus on someone dearly loved, or someone despised, or someone one feels neutral about.

Instead, begin with a cheerful person who is a good friend. Contemplate this cheerfulness with appreciation and let it fill you. When this state of sympathetic joy is strong, then direct it toward a dearly loved person, a "neutral" person, and a person who causes difficulty.

The next stage is to develop impartiality among the four--the loved one, the neutral person, the difficult person and oneself. And then sympathetic joy is extended on behalf of all beings.

Obviously, this process is not going to happen in an afternoon. Further, Buddhaghosa said, only a person who has developed powers of absorption will succeed. "Absorption" here refers to the deepest meditative state, in which sense of self and other disappear.

Mudita also is said to be an antidote to indifference and boredom. Psychologists define boredom as an inability to connect with an activity. This may be because we're being forced to do something we don't want to do or because, for some reason, we can't seem to keep our attention focused on what we're supposed to be doing. And plugging away at this onerous task makes us feel sluggish and depressed.

Looked at this way, boredom is the opposite of absorption. Through mudita comes a sense of energized concern that sweeps away the fog of boredom.

In developing mudita, we come to appreciate other people as complete and complex beings, not as characters in our personal play. In this way, mudita is something of a prerequisite for compassion (Karuna) and loving-kindness (Metta). Further, the Buddha taught that these practices are a prerequisite for awakening to enlightenment.

Here we see that the quest for enlightenment does not require detaching from the world. Although it may require retreating into quieter places to study and meditate, the world is where we find practice--in our lives, our relationships, our challenges. The Buddha said,

> "Here, O, Monks, a disciple lets his mind pervade one quarter of the world with thoughts of unselfish joy, and so the second, and so the third, and so the fourth. And thus the whole wide world, above, below, around, everywhere and equally, he continues to pervade with a heart of unselfish joy, abundant, grown great, measureless, without hostility or ill-will."

The teachings tell us that the practice of mudita produces a mental state that is calm, free and fearless, and open to deep insight. In this way, mudita is an important preparation for enlightenment.

Upeksha

Upeksha is a Sanskrit term that describes non-attachment, a balanced mind and tolerance. In Buddhism, it is one of the four elements of true love, together with loving-kindness (maitri), compassion (karuna) and joy (mudita). In yoga, these four elements are seen as different features of universal kindness and are considered the four qualities of a jivanmukta, or one who has achieved liberation (moksha). Abiding in upeksha means inhabiting the mental state of non-self and non-possessive love.

Bodhi-sattva

In Buddhism, Bodhisattva is the Sanskrit term for anyone who has generated Bodhicitta, a spontaneous wish and compassionate mind to attain Buddhahood for the benefit of all sentient beings. Bodhisattvas are a popular subject in Buddhist art.

In early Buddhism, the term bodhisattva was primarily used to refer specifically to Gautama Buddha (a contemporary of Mahavira) in his former life. The Jataka tales, which are the stories of the Buddha's past lives, depict the various attempts of the bodhisattva to embrace qualities like self-sacrifice and morality. The bodhisattva is also called a pusa. This is one who had achieved Buddhahood but chooses to remain in merciful attachment to the world. In Sanskrit this is called a Avalokitesvara.

According to the Jataka tales, the term "bodhisattva" originally referred to the pre-enlightened practitioner of austerities that surpassed Sravakayana and Pratyekabuddhayana by far and completed the "Bodhisattvayana" (Mahayana Buddhism). Mount Potalaka, for example, is one of Bodhisattvayana. The term for practitioners who have not yet reached Bodhisattvayana was not fixed, but the terms Sravaka-Bodhisattva and Pratyekabuddha-Bodhisattva had already appeared in the Agamas of early Indian Buddhism.

Mahayana Buddhism did not place much emphasis in honoring the Sravakayana or Pratyekabuddhayana since they were classified as part of the "Hinayana", but praise of the general Bodhisattvayana was commonplace. Because Hinayana was disliked and the terms Sravaka-Bodhisattva or Pratyekabuddha-Bodhisattva were not widely used, while usage of the general term "bodhisattva" had grown in popularity. Nevertheless, "bodhisattva" retained an implied reference to someone on the path to become an arhat or pratyekabuddha. In contrast, the goal of the bodhisattva path is to achieve samyaksambodhi.

Carvaka's Hedonism

The term "hedonism," from the Greek word (*hedone*) for pleasure, refers to several related theories about what is good for us, how we should behave, and what motivates us to behave in the way that we do. All hedonistic theories identify pleasure and pain as the only important elements of whatever phenomena they are designed to describe. If hedonistic theories identified pleasure and pain as merely two important elements, instead of the only important elements of what they are describing, then they would not be nearly as unpopular as they all are. However, the claim that pleasure and pain are the only things of ultimate importance is what makes hedonism distinctive and philosophically interesting.

Philosophical hedonists tend to focus on hedonistic theories of value, and especially of well-being (the good life for the one living it). As a theory of value, hedonism states that all and only pleasure is intrinsically valuable and all and only pain is intrinsically not valuable. Hedonists usually define pleasure and pain broadly, such that both physical and mental phenomena are included. Thus, a gentle massage and recalling a fond memory are both considered to cause pleasure and stubbing a toe and hearing about the death of a loved one are both considered to cause pain. With pleasure and pain so defined, hedonism as a theory about what is valuable for us is intuitively appealing. Indeed, its appeal is evidenced by the fact that nearly all historical and contemporary treatments of well-being allocate at least some space for discussion of hedonism. Unfortunately for hedonism, the discussions rarely endorse it and some even deplore its focus on pleasure.

Carvaka

Perhaps the earliest written record of hedonism comes from the Carvaka, an Indian philosophical tradition based on the Barhaspatya sutras. The Carvaka persisted for two thousand years (from about 600 B.C.E.). Most notably, the Carvaka advocated scepticism and Hedonistic Egoism – that the right action is the one that brings the actor the most net pleasure. The Carvaka acknowledged that some pain often accompanied, or was later caused by, sensual pleasure, but that pleasure was worth it.

UNIT 4

WESTERN ETHICS

Concepts of Good and Bad

The term "value theory" is used in at least three different ways in philosophy. In its broadest sense, "value theory" is a catch-all label used to encompass all branches of moral philosophy, social and political philosophy, aesthetics, and sometimes feminist philosophy and the philosophy of religion — whatever areas of philosophy are deemed to encompass some "evaluative" aspect. In its narrowest sense, "value theory" is used for a relatively narrow area of normative ethical theory particularly, but not exclusively, of concern to consequentialists. In this narrow sense, "value theory" is roughly synonymous with "axiology". Axiology can be thought of as primarily concerned with classifying what things are good, and how good they are. For instance, a traditional question of axiology concerns whether the objects of value are subjective psychological states, or objective states of the world.

But in a more useful sense, "value theory" designates the area of moral philosophy that is concerned with theoretical questions about value and goodness of all varieties — the theory of value. The theory of value, so construed, encompasses axiology, but also includes many other questions about the nature of value and its relation to other moral categories. The division of moral theory into the theory of value, as contrasting with other areas of investigation, cross-cuts the traditional classification of moral theory into normative and metaethical inquiry, but is a worthy distinction in its own right; theoretical questions about value constitute a core domain of interest in moral theory, often cross the boundaries between the normative and the metaethical, and have a distinguished history of investigation. This article surveys a range of the questions which come up in the theory of value, and attempts to impose some structure on the terrain by including some observations about how they are related to one another.

Claims about good simpliciter are those which have garnered the most attention in moral philosophy. This is partly because as it is usually understood, these are the "good" claims that consequentialists hold to have a bearing on what we ought to do. Consequentialism, so understood, is the view that you ought to do whatever action is such that things would be best if you did it. This leaves, however, a wide variety of possible theories about how such claims are related to other kinds of "good" claim.

Other kinds of views understand good simpliciter in terms of attributive good. What, after all, are the kinds of things to which we attribute goodness simpliciter? According to many philosophers, it is to propositions, or states of affairs. This is supported by a cursory study of the examples we have considered, in which what is being said to be good appears to be picked out by complementizers like "if", "that", and "for": "it would be good if you did that"; "it's good that you came"; "it's better for it to end now". If complementizer phrases denote propositions or possible states of affairs, then it is reasonable to conjecture, along with Foot [1985] that being good simpliciter is being a good state of affairs, and hence that it is a special case of attributive good (if it makes sense at all — Geach and Foot both argue that it does not, on the ground that states of affairs are too thin of a kind to support attributive good claims).

Some philosophers have used the examples of attributive good and good for in order to advance arguments against non-cognitivist metaethical theories (See the entry cognitivism and non-cognitivism). The basic outlines of such an argument go like this: non-cognitivist theories are designed to deal with good simpliciter, but have some kind of difficulties accounting for attributive good or for good for. Hence, there is a general problem with non-cognitivist theories, or at least a significant lacuna they leave. It has similarly been worried that non-cognitivist theories will have problems accounting for so-called "agent-relative" value, again, apparently, because of its relational nature. There is no place to consider this claim here, but note that it would be surprising if relational uses of "good" like these were in fact a deep or special problem for non-cognitivism; Hare's account in The Language of Morals was specifically about attributive uses of "good", and it is not clear why relational non-cognitive attitudes should be harder to make sense of than relational beliefs.

Justice

The idea of justice occupies centre stage both in ethics, and in legal and political philosophy. We apply it to individual actions, to laws, and to public policies, and we think in each case that if they are unjust this is a strong, maybe even conclusive, reason to reject them. Classically, justice was counted as one of the four cardinal virtues (and sometimes as the most important of the four); in modern times John Rawls famously described it as 'the first virtue of social institutions'. We might debate which of these realms of practical philosophy has first claim on justice: is it first and foremost a property of the law, for example, and only derivatively a property of individuals and other institutions? But it is probably more enlightening to accept that the idea has over time sunk deep roots in each of these domains, and to try to make sense of such a wide-ranging concept by identifying elements that are present whenever justice is invoked, but also examining the different forms it takes in various practical contexts. This article aims to provide a general map of the ways in which justice has been understood by philosophers, past and present.

We begin by identifying four core features that distinguish justice from other moral and political ideas. We then examine some major conceptual contrasts: between conservative and ideal justice, between corrective and distributive justice, between procedural and substantive justice, and between comparative and non-comparative justice. Next we turn to questions of scope: to who or what do principles of justice apply? We ask whether non-human animals can be subjects of justice, whether justice applies only between people who already stand in a particular kind of relationship to one another, and whether individual people continue to have duties of justice once justice-based institutions have been created. We then examine three overarching theories that might serve to unify the different forms of justice: utilitarianism, contractarianism, and egalitarianism. But it seems, in conclusion, that no such theory is likely be successful.

Philosophers writing on justice have observed that it has two different faces, one conservative of existing norms and practices, the other demanding reform of these norms and practices. Thus on the one hand it is a matter of justice to respect people's rights under existing law or moral rules, or more generally to fulfil the legitimate expectations they have acquired as a result of past practice, social conventions, and so forth; on the other hand, justice often gives us reason to change laws, practices and conventions quite radically, thereby creating new entitlements and expectations. This exposes an ambiguity in what it means to 'render each his due'. What is 'due' might be what a person can reasonably expect to have given existing law, policy, or social practice, or it might be what the person should get under a regime of ideal justice: this could mean what the person deserves, or needs, or is entitled to on grounds of equality, depending on which ideal principle is being invoked.

Conceptions of justice vary according to the weight they attach to each of these faces. At one extreme, some conceptions interpret justice as wholly concerned with what individuals can claim under existing laws and social conventions: thus for Hume, justice was to be understood as adherence to a set of rules that assign physical objects to individuals (such as being the first possessor of such an object). These rules can be explained by reference to the natural associations that form in people's minds between persons and external objects, and although the system of justice as a whole can be shown to be socially useful, there are no relevant independent standards by which its principles can be assessed (Hume briskly dismissed *equality* and *merit* as principles for allocating property to persons). In similar vein, Hayek argued that justice was a property of individual behaviour, understood as compliance with the 'rules of just conduct' that had evolved to enable a market economy to function effectively. For Hayek, to speak of 'social justice' as an ideal standard of distribution was as meaningless as to speak of a 'moral stone'.

At the other extreme stand conceptions of justice which posit some ideal principle of distribution such as equality, together with a 'currency' specifying the respect in which justice requires people to be made equally well off, and then refuse to acknowledge the justice of any claims that do not arise directly from the application of this principle. Thus claims deriving from existing law or practice are dismissed unless they happen to coincide with what the principle requires. More often, however, ideal justice is seen as proposing principles by which existing institutions and practices can be assessed, with a view to reforming them, or in the extreme case abolishing them entirely, while the claims that people already have under those practices are given some weight. Rawls, for example, whose two principles of justice count as ideal principles for this purpose, is at pains to stress that they are not intended to be applied in a way that disregards people's existing legitimate expectations. About the 'difference principle', which requires social and economic inequalities to be regulated so that they work to the greatest benefit of the least advantaged members of society, he says:

It applies to the announced system of public law and statutes and not to particular transactions or distributions, nor to the decisions of individuals and associations, but rather to the institutional background against which these transactions and decisions take place. There are no unannounced and unpredictable interferences with citizens' expectations and acquisitions. Entitlements are earned and honored as the public system of rules declares.

Here we see Rawls attempting to reconcile the demands of conservative and ideal justice. Yet he does not directly address the question of what should happen when changing circumstances mean that the difference principle requires new laws or policies to be enacted: do those whose prior entitlements or expectations are no longer met have a claim to be compensated for their loss? We could call this the question of transitional justice.

When we raise questions about the scope of justice, we are asking about *when* principles of justice take effect and *among whom*. We have already, when discussing Hume, encountered the idea that there might be circumstances in which justice becomes irrelevant – circumstances in which resources are so abundant that it is pointless to allocate individual shares, or, as Hume also believed, in which resources are so scarce that everyone is permitted to grab what he can in the name of self-preservation. But even in circumstances that are less extreme than these, questions about scope arise. Who can make claims of justice, and who might have the corresponding obligation to meet them? Does this depend on the kind of thing that is being claimed? If comparative principles are being applied, who should be counted as part of the comparison group? Do some principles of justice have universal scope – they apply whenever agent *A* acts towards recipient *B*, regardless of the relationship between them – while others are contextual in character, applying only within social or political relationships of a certain kind? The present section examines some of these questions in greater detail.

What does a creature have to do, or be like, to be included within the scope of (at least some) principles of justice? Most past philosophers have assumed that the line should be drawn so as to exclude all non-human animals, but more recently some have been prepared to defend 'justice for animals'.

Against this, Rawls asserts that although we have 'duties of compassion and humanity' towards animals and should refrain from treating them cruelly, nonetheless they are 'outside the scope of the theory of justice'. How could this claim be justified?

We can focus our attention either on individual features that humans possess and animals lack, and that might be thought relevant to their inclusion within the scope of justice, or on asymmetries in the relationship between humans and other animals. To begin with the latter, Hume claimed that the domination humans exercised over animals – such that an animal could only possess something by virtue of our permission – meant that we were 'bound by the laws of humanity to give gentle usage to these creatures, but should not, properly speaking, lie under any restraint of justice with regard to them'. For Rawls and those influenced by him, principles of distributive justice apply among agents who are related to one another as participants in a 'cooperative venture for mutual advantage', and this might seem to exclude animals from the scope of such principles. Critics of this view have pointed to cases of human-animal co-operation; however these arguments focus mainly or entirely on the special case of *dogs*, and it seems implausible to generalise from them in an attempt to show that human-animal relationships generally have a co-operative character.

But the claim that justice only applies to participants in co-operative practices is anyway vulnerable to the objection that it risks excluding seriously disabled people, people living in isolated communities, and future generations from the scope of justice, so it does not seem compelling as a claim about justice in general. Might there be other reasons why animals cannot make claims of justice on us? Another Rawls-inspired suggestion is that animals lack the necessary moral powers, in particular the capacity to act on principles of justice themselves. They cannot distinguish what is justly owed to them from what is not; and they cannot determine what they owe to others – whether to humans or to other non-human animals – as a matter of justice. This suggestion interprets justice as involving a kind of reciprocity: an agent to whom justice is due must also in principle be an agent who could dispense justice to others, by virtue of having the relevant capacity, even if for physical reasons – such as suffering from severe disability – they cannot do so in practice.

If this suggestion is rejected, and we allow that some animals, at least, should be included within the scope of justice, we can then ask about the form that justice should take in their cases. It appears that justice for animals must be non-comparative. For example, we might attribute rights to the animals over whom we exercise power – rights against cruel treatment, and rights to food and shelter, for instance. This would involve using a sufficiency principle to determine what animals are owed as a matter of justice. It is much less plausible to think that comparative principles might apply, such that giving special treats to one cat but not another could count as an injustice.

Once institutions are established for the purpose (among other things) of delivering justice on a large scale, we can ask what duties of justice individual people have in consequence. Is their duty simply to support the institutions, and comply with whatever rules of conduct apply to them personally? Or do they have further duties to promote justice by acting directly on the relevant principles in their daily lives? No one doubts that *some* duties of justice fall directly on individuals, for example duties not to deceive or defraud when engaging in commercial transactions (and duties of corrective justice where behaviour is faulty), or duties to carry out one's fair share of an informally organized project from which one expects to benefit, such as cleaning up the neighbourhood park. Others fall on them because they are performing a role within a social institution, for example the duty of an employer not to discriminate on grounds of race or gender when hiring workers, or the duty of a local government officer to assign public housing to those in greatest need. But what is much more in dispute is whether individual people have more extensive duties to promote social justice.

Consider two cases: the first concerns parents who confer advantages on their children in ways that undermine fair equality of opportunity. If the latter principle of justice requires, to cite Rawls, that 'those who have the same level of talent and ability and the same willingness to use these gifts should have the same prospects of success regardless of their social class of origin' then there are myriad ways in which some parents can bestow advantages on their children that other parents cannot – financial benefits, educational opportunities, social contacts, and so forth – that are likely to bring greater success in later life. Are parents therefore constrained as a matter of justice to avoid conferring at least some of these advantages, or are they free to benefit their children as they choose, leaving the pursuit of equal opportunities entirely in the hands of the state?

The second example concerns wage differentials. Might individuals whose talents can bring them high rewards in the labour market have a duty not to make use of their bargaining power, but instead be willing to work for a fair wage – which if fairness is understood in egalitarian terms might mean the same wage as everyone else (perhaps with extra compensation for those whose labour is unusually burdensome)? Rawls, as we saw above, argued that economic justice meant arranging social and economic inequalities to the greatest benefit of the least advantaged, and in formulating the principle in this way he assumed that some inequalities might serve as incentives to greater production that would also raise the position of the worst-off group in society. But if individuals were willing to forego incentives, and so economic inequalities served no useful purpose, then the arrangement that worked to the greatest benefit of the least advantaged would be one of strict equality. Cohen (2008) argues that Rawls' position is internally inconsistent. As citizens designing our institutions we are supposed to be guided by the difference principle, but as private actors in the marketplace, we are permitted to ignore that principle and bargain for higher wages, even though doing so will work to the disadvantage of the worst-off group. Justice, according to Cohen, requires us to embrace an ethos of service that disdains material incentives.

Duty

Immanuel Kant (1724–1804) argued that the supreme principle of morality is a standard of rationality that he dubbed the "Categorical Imperative" (CI). Kant characterized the CI as an objective, rationally necessary and unconditional principle that we must always follow despite any natural desires or inclinations we may have to the contrary. All specific moral requirements, according to Kant, are justified by this principle, which means that all immoral actions are irrational because they violate the CI. Other philosophers, such as Hobbes, Locke and Aquinas, had also argued that moral requirements are based on standards of rationality. However, these standards were either instrumental principles of rationality for satisfying one's desires, as in Hobbes, or external rational principles that are discoverable by reason, as in Locke and Aquinas.

Kant agreed with many of his predecessors that an analysis of practical reason reveals the requirement that rational agents must conform to instrumental principles. Yet he also argued that conformity to the CI (a non-instrumental principle), and hence to moral requirements themselves, can nevertheless be shown to be essential to rational agency. This argument was based on his striking doctrine that a rational will must be regarded as autonomous, or free, in the sense of being the author of the law that binds it. The fundamental principle of morality — the CI — is none other than the law of an autonomous will.

Thus, at the heart of Kant's moral philosophy is a conception of reason whose reach in practical affairs goes well beyond that of a Humean 'slave' to the passions. Moreover, it is the presence of this self-governing reason in each person that Kant thought offered decisive grounds for viewing each as possessed of equal worth and deserving of equal respect.

Kant's most influential positions in moral philosophy are found in *The Groundwork of the Metaphysics of Morals* (hereafter, "*Groundwork*") but he developed, enriched, and in some cases modified those views in later works such as *The Critique of Practical Reason, The Metaphysics of Morals, Anthropology from a Pragmatic Point of View, Religion within the Boundaries of Mere Reason* as well as his essays on history and related topics. Kant's *Lectures on Ethics*, which were lecture notes taken by three of his students on the courses he gave in moral philosophy, also include relevant material for understanding his views. We will mainly focus on the foundational doctrines of the *Groundwork*, even though in recent years some scholars have become dissatisfied with this standard approach to Kant's views and have turned their attention to the later works. We find the standard approach most illuminating, though we will highlight important positions from the later works where needed.

The most basic aim of moral philosophy, and so also of the *Groundwork*, is, in Kant's view, to "seek out" the foundational principle of a "metaphysics of morals," which Kant understands as a system of a *priori* moral principles that apply the CI to human persons in all times and cultures. Kant pursues this project through the first two chapters of the *Groundwork*. He proceeds by analyzing and elucidating commonsense ideas about morality, including the ideas of a "good will" and "duty". The point of this first project is to come up with a precise statement of the principle or principles on which all of our ordinary moral judgments are based. The judgments in question are supposed to be those that any normal, sane, adult human being would accept on due rational reflection. Nowadays, however, many would regard Kant as being overly optimistic about the depth and extent of moral agreement. But perhaps he is best thought of as drawing on a moral viewpoint that is very widely shared and which contains some general judgments that are very deeply held. In any case, he does not appear to take himself to be primarily addressing a genuine moral skeptic such as those who often populate the works of moral philosophers, that is, someone who doubts that she has any reason to act morally and whose moral behavior hinges on a rational proof that philosophers might try to give. For instance, when, in the third and final chapter of the *Groundwork*, Kant takes up his second fundamental aim, to "establish" this foundational moral principle as a demand of each person's own rational will, his conclusion apparently falls short of answering those who want a proof that we really are bound by moral requirements. He rests this second project on the position that we — or at least creatures with rational wills — possess autonomy.

The argument of this second project does often appear to try to reach out to a metaphysical fact about our wills. This has led some readers to the conclusion that he is, after all, trying to justify moral requirements by appealing to a fact — our autonomy — that even a moral skeptic would have to recognize.

Kant's analysis of the common moral concepts of "duty" and "good will" led him to believe that we are free and autonomous as long as morality, itself, is not an illusion. Yet in the *Critique of Pure Reason*, Kant also tried to show that every event has a cause. Kant recognized that there seems to be a deep tension between these two claims: If causal determinism is true then, it seems, we cannot have the kind of freedom that morality presupposes, which is "a kind of causality" that "can be active, independently of alien causes *determining* it"

Kant thought that the only way to resolve this apparent conflict is to distinguish between *phenomena*, which is what we know through experience, and *noumena*, which we can consistently think but not know through experience. Our knowledge and understanding of the empirical world, Kant argued, can only arise within the limits of our perceptual and cognitive powers. We should not assume, however, that we know all that may be true about "things in themselves," although we lack the "intellectual intuition" that would be needed to learn about such things.

These distinctions, according to Kant, allow us to resolve the "antinomy" about free will by interpreting the "thesis" that free will is possible as about noumena and the "antithesis" that every event has a cause as about phenomena. Morality thus presupposes that agents, in an incomprehensible "intelligible world," are able to make things happen by their own free choices in a "sensible world" in which causal determinism is true.

Many of Kant's commentators, who are skeptical about these apparently exorbitant metaphysical claims, have attempted to make sense of his discussions of the intelligible and sensible worlds in less metaphysically demanding ways. On one interpretation (Hudson 1994), one and the same act can be described in wholly physical terms (as an appearance) and also in irreducibly mental terms (as a thing in itself). On this compatibilist picture, all acts are causally determined, but a free act is one that can be described as determined by irreducibly mental causes, and in particular by the causality of reason. A second interpretation holds that the intelligible and sensible worlds are used as metaphors for two ways of conceiving of one and the same world.

When we are engaging in scientific or empirical investigations, we often take up a perspective in which we think of things as subject to natural causation, but when we deliberate, act, reason and judge, we often take up a different perspective, in which we think of ourselves and others as agents who are not determined by natural causes. When we take up this latter, practical, standpoint, we need not believe that we or others really are free, in any deep metaphysical sense; we need only operate "under the idea of freedom" (G 4:448). Controversy persists, however, about whether Kant's conception of freedom requires a "two worlds" or "two perspectives" account of the sensible and intelligible worlds.

Although the two most basic aims Kant saw for moral philosophy are to seek out and establish the supreme principle of morality, they are not, in Kant's view, its only aims. Moral philosophy, for Kant, is most fundamentally addressed to the first-person, deliberative question, "What ought I to do?", and an answer to that question requires much more than delivering or justifying the fundamental principle of morality. We also need some account, based on this principle, of the nature and extent of the specific moral duties that apply to us. To this end, Kant employs his findings from the *Groundwork* in *The Metaphysics of Morals*, and offers a categorization of our basic moral duties to ourselves and others. In addition, Kant thought that moral philosophy should characterize and explain the demands that morality makes on human psychology and forms of human social interaction. These topics, among others, are addressed in central chapters of the second *Critique*, the *Religion* and again in the *Metaphysics of Morals*, and are perhaps given a sustained treatment in *Anthropology from a Pragmatic Point of View*. Further, a satisfying answer to the question of what one ought to do would have to take into account any political and religious requirements there are. Each of these requirement turn out to be, indirectly at least, also moral obligations for Kant, and are discussed in the *Metaphysics of Morals* and in *Religion*. Finally, moral philosophy should say something about the ultimate end of human endeavor, the Highest Good, and its relationship to the moral life. In the *Critique of Practical Reason*, Kant argued that this Highest Good for humanity is complete moral virtue together with complete happiness, the former being the condition of our deserving the latter. Unfortunately, Kant noted, virtue does not insure well-being and may even conflict with it.

Further, he thought that there is no real possibility of moral perfection in this life and indeed few of us fully deserve the happiness we are lucky enough to enjoy. Reason cannot prove or disprove the existence of Divine Providence, on Kant's view, nor the immortality of the soul, which seem necessary to rectify these things. Nevertheless, Kant argued, an unlimited amount of time to perfect ourselves (immortality) and a commensurate achievement of well-being (insured by God) are "postulates" required by reason when employed in moral matters.

Throughout his moral works, Kant returns time and again to the question of the method moral philosophy should employ when pursuing these aims. A basic theme of these discussions is that the fundamental philosophical issues of morality must be addressed *a priori*, that is, without drawing on observations of human beings and their behavior. Kant's insistence on an *a priori* method to seek out and establish fundamental moral principles, however, does not always appear to be matched by his own practice. The *Metaphysics of Morals*, for instance, is meant to be based on *a priori* rational principles, but many of the specific duties that Kant describes, along with some of the arguments he gives in support of them, rely on general facts about human beings and our circumstances that are known from experience.

In one sense, it might seem obvious why Kant insists on an *a priori* method. A "metaphysics of morals" would be, more or less, an account of the nature and structure of moral requirements — in effect, a categorization of duties and values. Such a project would address such questions as, What *is* a duty? What *kinds* of duties are there? What *is* the good? What *kinds* of goods are there?, and so on. These appear to be metaphysical questions. Any principle used to provide such categorizations appears to be a principle of metaphysics, in a sense, but Kant did not see them as external moral truths that exist independently of rational agents. Moral requirements, instead, are rational principles that tell us what we have overriding reason to do. Metaphysical principles of this sort are always sought out and established by *a priori* methods.

Perhaps something like this was behind Kant's thinking. However, the considerations he offers for an *a priori* method do not all obviously draw on this sort of rationale. The following are three considerations favoring *a priori* methods that he emphasizes repeatedly.

The first is that, as Kant and others have conceived of it, ethics initially requires an analysis of our moral concepts. We must understand the concepts of a "good will", "obligation", "duty" and so on, as well as their logical relationships to one another, before we can determine whether our use of these concepts is justified. Given that the analysis of concepts is an *a priori* matter, to the degree that ethics consists of such an analysis, ethics is *a priori* as a well.

Of course, even were we to agree with Kant that ethics should begin with analysis, and that analysis is or should be an entirely *a priori* undertaking, this would not explain why *all* of the fundamental questions of moral philosophy must be pursued *a priori*. Indeed, one of the most important projects of moral philosophy, for Kant, is to show that we, as rational agents, are bound by moral requirements and that fully rational agents would necessarily comply with them. Kant admits that his analytical arguments for the CI are inadequate on their own because the most they can show is that the CI is the supreme principle of morality *if there is such a principle*. Kant must therefore address the possibility that morality itself is an illusion by showing that the CI really is an unconditional requirement of reason that applies to us. Even though Kant thought that this project of "establishing" the CI must also be carried out *a priori*, he did not think we could pursue this project simply by analyzing our moral concepts or examining the actual behavior of others. What is needed, instead, is a "synthetic", but still *a priori*, kind of argument that starts from ideas of freedom and rational agency and critically examines the nature and limits of these capacities.

This is the second reason Kant held that fundamental issues in ethics must be addressed with an *a priori* method: The ultimate subject matter of ethics is the nature and content of the principles that necessarily determine a rational will.

Fundamental issues in moral philosophy must also be settled *a priori* because of the nature of moral requirements themselves, or so Kant thought. This is a third reason he gives for an *a priori* method, and it appears to have been of great importance to Kant: Moral requirements present themselves as being *unconditionally necessary*. But an *a posteriori* method seems ill-suited to discovering and establishing what we *must* do whether we feel like doing it or not; surely such a method could only tell us what we *actually* do. So an *a posteriori* method of seeking out and establishing the principle that generates such requirements will not support the presentation of moral "oughts" as unconditional necessities. Kant argued that empirical observations could only deliver conclusions about, for instance, the relative advantages of moral behavior in various circumstances or how pleasing it might be in our own eyes or the eyes of others. Such findings clearly would not support the unconditional necessity of moral requirements. To appeal to *a posteriori* considerations would thus result in a tainted conception of moral requirements. It would view them as demands for which compliance is not unconditionally necessary, but rather necessary only if additional considerations show it to be advantageous, optimific or in some other way felicitous. Thus, Kant argued that if moral philosophy is to guard against undermining the unconditional necessity of obligation in its analysis and defense of moral thought, it must be carried out entirely *a priori*.

Kant's analysis of commonsense ideas begins with the thought that the only thing good without qualification is a "good will". While the phrases "he's good hearted", "she's good natured" and "she means well" are common, "the good will" as Kant thinks of it is not the same as any of these ordinary notions. The idea of a good will is closer to the idea of a "good person", or, more archaically, a "person of good will". This use of the term "will" early on in analyzing ordinary moral thought prefigures later and more technical discussions concerning the nature of rational agency. Nevertheless, this idea of a good will is an important commonsense touchstone to which Kant returns throughout his works. The basic idea, as Kant describes it in the Groundwork, is that what makes a good person good is his possession of a will that is in a certain way "determined" by, or makes its decisions on the basis of, the moral law. The idea of a good will is supposed to be the idea of one who is committed only to make decisions that she holds to be morally worthy and who takes moral considerations in themselves to be conclusive reasons for guiding her behavior. This sort of disposition or character is something we all highly value, Kant thought. He believes we value it without limitation or qualification. By this, we believe, he means primarily two things.

First, unlike anything else, there is no conceivable circumstance in which we regard our own moral goodness as worth forfeiting simply in order to obtain some desirable object. By contrast, the value of all other desirable qualities, such as courage or cleverness, can be diminished, forgone, or sacrificed under certain circumstances: Courage may be laid aside if it requires injustice, and it is better not to be witty if it requires cruelty. There is no implicit restriction or qualification to the effect that a commitment to give moral considerations decisive weight is worth honoring, *but onlyunder such and such circumstances*.

Second, possessing and maintaining a steadfast commitment to moral principles is the very condition under which anything else is worth having or pursuing. Intelligence and even pleasure are worth having only on the condition that they do not require giving up one's fundamental moral convictions. The value of a good will thus cannot be that it secures certain valuable ends, whether of our own or of others, since their value is entirely conditional on our possessing and maintaining a good will. Indeed, since a good will is good under any condition, its goodness must not depend on any particular conditions obtaining. Thus, Kant points out that a good will must then also be good *in itself* and not in virtue of its relationship to other things such as the agent's own happiness, overall welfare or any other effects it may or may not produce A good will would still "shine like a jewel" even if it were "completely powerless to carry out its aims".

In Kant's terms, a good will is a will whose decisions are wholly determined by moral demands or, as he often refers to this, by the Moral Law. Human beings inevitably feel this Law as a constraint on their natural desires, which is why such Laws, as applied to human beings, are imperatives and duties. A human will in which the Moral Law is decisive is motivated by the thought of *duty*. A*holy* or *divine* will, if it exists, though good, would not be good because it is motivated by thoughts of duty because such a will does not have natural inclinations and so necessarily fulfills moral requirements without feeling constrained to do so. It is the presence of desires that *could* operate independently of moral demands that makes goodness in human beings a constraint, an essential element of the idea of "duty." So in analyzing unqualified goodness as it occurs in imperfectly rational creatures such as ourselves, we are investigating the idea of being motivated by the thought that we are constrained to act in certain ways that we *might* not want to simply from the thought that we are morally required to do so.

Kant confirms this by comparing motivation by duty with other sorts of motives, in particular, with motives of self-interest, self-preservation, sympathy and happiness. He argues that a dutiful action from any of these motives, however praiseworthy it may be, does not express a good will. Assuming an action has moral worth only if it expresses a good will, such actions have no genuine "moral worth." The conformity of one's action to duty in such cases is only related by accident to morality. For instance, if one is motivated by happiness alone, then had conditions not conspired to align one's duty with one's own happiness one would not have done one's duty. By contrast, were one to supplant any of these motivations with the motive of duty, the morality of the action would then express one's determination to act dutifully out of respect for the moral law itself. Only then would the action have moral worth.

Kant's views in this regard have understandably been the subject of much controversy. Many object that we do not think better of actions done for the sake of duty than actions performed out of emotional concern or sympathy for others, especially those things we do for friends and family. Worse, moral worth appears to require not only that one's actions be motivated by duty, but also that no other motives, even love or friendship, cooperate. Yet Kant's defenders have argued that his point is not that we do not admire or praise motivating concerns other than duty, only that from the point of view of someone deliberating about what to do, these concerns are not decisive in the way that considerations of moral duty are. What is crucial in actions that express a good will is that in conforming to duty a perfectly virtuous person always would, and so ideally we should, recognize and be moved by the thought that our conformity is morally obligatory.

The motivational structure of the agent should be arranged so that she always treats considerations of duty as sufficient reasons for conforming to those requirements. In other words, we should have a firm commitment not to perform an action if it is morally forbidden and to perform an action if it is morally required. Having a good will, in this sense, is compatible with having feelings and emotions of various kinds, and even with aiming to cultivate some of them in order to counteract desires and inclinations that tempt us to immorality. Controversy persists, however, about whether Kant's claims about the motive of duty go beyond this basic point.

Suppose for the sake of argument we agree with Kant. We now need to know what distinguishes the principle that lays down our duties from these other motivating principles, and so makes motivation by it the source of unqualified value.

According to Kant, what is singular about motivation by duty is that it consists of bare respect for the moral law. What naturally comes to mind is this: Duties are rules or laws of some sort combined with some sort of felt constraint or incentive on our choices, whether from external coercion by others or from our own powers of reason. For instance, the bylaws of a club lay down duties for its officers and enforce them with sanctions. City and state laws establish the duties of citizens and enforce them with coercive legal power. Thus, if we do something because it is our "civic" duty, or our duty "as a boy scout" or "a good American," our motivation is respect for the code that makes it our duty. Thinking we are duty bound is simply respecting, as such, certain laws pertaining to us.

However intuitive, this cannot be all of Kant's meaning. For one thing, as with the Jim Crow laws of the old South and the Nuremberg laws of Nazi Germany, the laws to which these types of "actions from duty" conform may be morally despicable. Respect for such laws could hardly be thought valuable. For another, our motive in conforming our actions to civic and other laws is rarely unconditional respect. We also have an eye toward doing our part in maintaining civil or social order, toward punishments or loss of standing and reputation in violating such laws, and other outcomes of lawful behavior. Indeed, we respect these laws to the degree, but only to the degree, that they do not violate values, laws or principles we hold more dear. Yet Kant thinks that, in acting from duty, we are not at all motivated by a prospective outcome or some other extrinsic feature of our conduct except insofar as these are requirements of duty itself. We are motivated by the mere conformity of our will to law as such.

To act out of respect for the moral law, in Kant's view, is to be moved to act by a recognition that the moral law is a supremely authoritative standard that binds us and to experience a kind of feeling, which is akin to awe and fear, when we acknowledge the moral law as the source of moral requirements. Human persons inevitably have respect for the moral law even though we are not always moved by it and even though we do not always comply with the moral standards that we nonetheless recognize as authoritative.

Kant's account of the content of moral requirements and the nature of moral reasoning is based on his analysis of the unique force moral considerations have as reasons to act. The force of moral requirements as reasons is that we cannot ignore them no matter how circumstances might conspire against any other consideration. Basic moral requirements retain their reason-giving force under any circumstance, they have universal validity. So, whatever else may be said of basic moral requirements, their content is universal. Only a universal law could be the content of a requirement that has the reason-giving force of morality. This brings Kant to a preliminary formulation of the CI: "I ought never to act except in such a way that I could also will that my maxim should become a universal law". This is the principle which motivates a good will, and which Kant holds to be the fundamental principle of all of morality.

Kant's first formulation of the CI states that you are to "act only in accordance with that maxim through which you can at the same time will that it become a universal law". O'Neill and Rawls, among others, take this formulation in effect to summarize a decision procedure for moral reasoning, and we will follow their basic outline:

First, formulate a maxim that enshrines your reason for acting as you propose.

Second, recast that maxim as a universal law of nature governing all rational agents, and so as holding that all must, by natural law, act as you yourself propose to act in these circumstances.

Third, consider whether your maxim is even conceivable in a world governed by this law of nature. If it is, then, fourth, ask yourself whether you would, or could, rationally will to act on your maxim in such a world. If you could, then your action is morally permissible.

If your maxim fails the third step, you have a "perfect" duty admitting "of no exception in favor of inclination" to refrain from acting on that maxim. If your maxim fails the fourth step, you have an "imperfect" duty requiring you to pursue a policy that can admit of such exceptions. If your maxim passes all four steps, only then is acting on it morally permissible. Following Hill, we can understand the difference in duties as formal: Perfect duties come in the form "One must never (or always) Ṅ to the fullest extent possible in C", while imperfect duties, since they require us to adopt an end, at least require that "One must sometimes and to some extent Ṅ in C." So, for instance, Kant held that the maxim of committing suicide to avoid future unhappiness did not pass the third step, the contradiction in conception test. Hence, one is forbidden to act on the maxim of committing suicide to avoid unhappiness. By contrast, the maxim of refusing to assist others in pursuit of their projects passes the contradiction in conception test, but fails the contradiction in the will test at the fourth step. Hence, we have a duty to sometimes and to some extent aid and assist others.

Kant held that ordinary moral thought recognized moral duties toward ourselves as well as toward others. Hence, together with the distinction between perfect and imperfect duties, Kant recognized four categories of duties: perfect duties toward ourselves, perfect duties toward others, imperfect duties toward ourselves and imperfect duties toward others. Kant uses four examples in the *Groundwork*, one of each kind of duty, to demonstrate that every kind of duty can be derived from the CI, and hence to bolster his case that the CI is indeed the fundamental principle of morality. To refrain from suicide is a perfect duty toward oneself; to refrain from making promises you have no intention of keeping is a perfect duty toward others; to develop one's talents is an imperfect duty toward oneself; and to contribute to the happiness of others is an imperfect duty toward others. Again, Kant's interpreters differ over exactly how to reconstruct the derivation of these duties. We will briefly sketch one way of doing so for the perfect duty to others to refrain from lying promises and the imperfect duty to ourselves to develop talents.

Kant's example of a perfect duty to others concerns a promise you might consider making but have no intention of keeping in order to get needed money. Naturally, being rational requires not contradicting oneself, but there is no self-contradiction in the maxim "I will make lying promises when it achieves something I want." An immoral action clearly does not involve a self-contradiction in this sense (as would the maxim of finding a married bachelor). Kant's position is that it is irrational to perform an action if that action's maxim contradicts itself *once made into a universal law of nature*. The maxim of lying whenever it gets you what you want generates a contradiction once you try to combine it with the universalized version that all rational agents must, by a law of nature, lie when doing so gets them what they want.

Cardinal Virtues

The cardinal virtues are the four principal moral virtues. The English word cardinal comes from the Latin word cardo, which means "hinge." All other virtues hinge on these four: prudence, justice, fortitude, and temperance.

Plato first discussed the cardinal virtues in the Republic, and they entered into Christian teaching by way of Plato's disciple Aristotle. Unlike the theological virtues, which are the gifts of God through grace, the four cardinal virtues can be practiced by anyone; thus, they represent the foundation of natural morality.

Prudence. St. Thomas Aquinas ranked prudence as the first cardinal virtue because it is concerned with the intellect. Aristotle defined prudence as recta ratio agibilium, "right reason applied to practice." It is the virtue that allows us to judge correctly what is right and what is wrong in any given situation. When we mistake the evil for the good, we are not exercising prudence—in fact, we are showing our lack of it.

Because it is so easy to fall into error, prudence requires us to seek the counsel of others, particularly those we know to be sound judges of morality. Disregarding the advice or warnings of others whose judgment does not coincide with ours is a sign of imprudence.

Justice. Justice, according to Saint Thomas, is the second cardinal virtue, because it is concerned with the will. As Fr. John A. Hardon notes in his Modern Catholic Dictionary, it is "the constant and permanent determination to give everyone his or her rightful due." We say that "justice is blind," because it should not matter what we think of a particular person. If we owe him a debt, we must repay exactly what we owe.

Justice is connected to the idea of rights. While we often use justice in a negative sense ("He got what he deserved"), justice in its proper sense is positive. Injustice occurs when we as individuals or by law deprive someone of that which he is owed. Legal rights can never outweigh natural ones.

Fortitude. The third cardinal virtue, according to St. Thomas Aquinas, is fortitude. While this virtue is commonly called courage, it is different from what much of what we think of as courage today. Fortitude allows us to overcome fear and to remain steady in our will in the face of obstacles, but it is always reasoned and reasonable; the person exercising fortitude does not seek danger for danger's sake. Prudence and justice are the virtues through which we decide what needs to be done; fortitude gives us the strength to do it.

Fortitude is the only one of the cardinal virtues that is also a gift of the Holy Spirit, allowing us to rise above our natural fears in defense of the Christian faith.

Temperance. Temperance, Saint Thomas declared, is the fourth and final cardinal virtue. While fortitude is concerned with the restraint of fear so that we can act, temperance is the restraint of our desires or passions. Food, drink, and sex are all necessary for our survival, individually and as a species; yet a disordered desire for any of these goods can have disastrous consequences, physical and moral.

Temperance is the virtue that attempts to keep us from excess, and, as such, requires the balancing of legitimate goods against our inordinate desire for them. Our legitimate use of such goods may be different at different times; temperance is the "golden mean" that helps us determine how far we can act on our desires.

Eudaemonism

Eudaimonism is an ethical theory which maintains that happiness (eudaimonia) is reached through virtue (aretṃ). Eudaimonia and aretṃare two central concepts in ancient Greek ethics. Eudaimonia, which literally means "having a good guardian spirit," is often translated into English as "happiness," and while this is adequate in so far as it goes, it does not entirely capture the meaning of the Greek word. One important difference is that happiness seems closely bound up with a subjective assessment of the quality of one's life, whereas eudaimonia refers to an objectively desirable life. Eudaimonia is then a more encompassing notion than happiness since bad events that do not contribute to one's experience of happiness do affect one's eudaimonia.

All ancient ethical theorists understand eudaimonia to be the highest human good, but they differ from one another regarding how to achieve it in its relation to aretm. Specifying the relation between these two central concepts is one of the important preoccupations of ancient ethics, and a subject of much disagreement. As a result, there are a various forms of eudaimonism. Two of the most influential forms are those of Aristotle and the Stoics. Aristotle takes virtue and its exercise to be the most important constituent in eudaimonia but does acknowledge the importance of external goods such as health, wealth, and beauty. By contrast, the Stoics make virtue necessary and sufficient for eudaimonia and thus deny the necessity of external goods.

Eudaimonism has been largely forgotten since the Renaissance, but it has seen a revival after the middle of the twentieth century thanks to the works of ethicists such as Elizabeth Anscombe and Alasdair MacIntyre. Perhaps, one task of contemporary eudaimonism is to remember ancient Greek ethics' understanding of eudaimonia as rooted in the Form of the Good (Plato) or in the contemplative activity of God (Aristotle).

In terms of its etymology, eudaimonia is an abstract noun derived from the adjective, eudaimon. This adjective is, in turn, a compound word comprised of eu, meaning "well," and daimon(daemon), which refers to a sort of guardian spirit. Therefore, to be eudaimon is to live well, protected and looked after by a benevolent spirit. Despite this etymology, however, discussions of eudaimonia in ancient Greek ethics are often conducted independently of any supernatural significance.

The standard English translation of eudaimonia is "happiness." In the Nicomachean Ethics, however, Aristotle (384-322 B.C.E.) says that eudaimonia means "living well and doing well." It is significant that synonyms for eudaimonia are living well and doing well. So, "happiness" seems not to entirely capture the meaning of the Greek word. One important difference is that happiness often connotes being or tending to be in a certain pleasant state of consciousness. For example, when people say of someone that he is a happy man, they usually mean that he seems subjectively contented with the way things are going in his life. In contrast, eudaimonia is a more encompassing notion than happiness, since events that do not contribute to one's experience of happiness may affect one's eudaimonia.

Eudaimonia depends on all the things that would make people happy if they knew about them, but quite independently of whether they do know about them. Ascribing eudaimonia to a person, then, may include ascribing such things as being loved by family and having fine friends. These are all objective judgments about someone's life: They concern a person really being loved by family and really having fine friends. This implies that a person who has evil sons and daughters will not be judged to be eudaimon, even if he or she does not know that they are evil and therefore feels pleased and contented with the way he or she thinks they are. Conversely, being loved by one's children would not count towards your happiness, if you did not know that they loved you; but it would count towards your eudaimonia, even if you did not know that they loved you. So, eudaimonia corresponds to the idea of having an objectively good or desirable life, to some extent independently of whether one knows that these things obtain. It includes not only conscious experiences of well-being and success but a whole lot more. Regarding this, see Aristotle's discussion in the 10th and 11th chapters of Book I of the Nicomachean Ethics.

Because of this discrepancy between the meaning of eudaimonia and happiness, some alternative translations have been proposed. W.D. Ross (1877-1971) suggests "well-being," and John Cooper proposes "flourishing." These translations may avoid some of the misleading associations carried by "happiness," although each tends to raise some problems of its own. Perhaps the safest alternative is to leave the term untranslated (transliterated), allowing its meaning to emerge by considering how it is actually used by the ancient ethical philosophers.

The Greek word aretṃ is usually translated into English as "virtue." One problem with this is that we are inclined to understand virtue in a moral sense, which is not always what the ancients had in mind. For a Greek, aretṃ pertains to all sorts of qualities we would not regard as relevant to ethics, such as physical beauty. So it is important to bear in mind that the sense of "virtue" operative in ancient ethics is not exclusively moral and includes more than states such as wisdom, courage, and compassion. The sense of virtue which aretṃcon notes would include saying something like "speed is virtue in a horse," or "height is a virtue in a basketball player." Doing anything well requires virtue, and each characteristic activity (such as carpentry or flute playing) has its own set of virtues. The alternative translation "excellence" might be helpful in conveying this general meaning of the term. The moral virtues are simply a subset of the general sense in which a human being is capable of functioning well or excellently.

Intuition

The teleological/deontological distinction was introduced in 1930 by C.D. Broad,' and since then it has come to be accepted as the fundamental classificatory distinction for moral philosophy. I shall argue that the presupposition that there is a single fundamental classificatory distinction is false. There are too many features of moral theories that matter for that to be so. I shall argue furthermore that as it is usually drawn the teleological/deontological distinction is not even a fundamental distinction. Another distinction, that between theories that make the right depend solely on considerations of goodness (axiological theories) and those that do not, is significantly more important.

Deteological

Act utilitarianism is a paradigm teleological theory, and The Divine Command Theory and Kant's moral theory are paradigm deontological theories. It is unclear, however, which of the many features of these theories are the defaming characteristics of teleological and deontological theories respectively. In order to assess the importance of the teleological/deontological distinction, we need first to clarify the nature of the distinction. Let us start therefore by examining some of the different characterizations that have been given. Often authors characterize deontological theories simply as theories that are not teleological. So characterized, the nature of deontological theories depends on how teleological theories are characterized. In a later section we shall examine some of the characterizations of teleological theories. In this section we shall examine some of the characterizations of deontological theories that are in dependent of the characterization of teleological theories.

It is often claimed that deontological theories — but not teleological theories — are rule-based, i.e., assess the permissibility of actions in terms of whether they conform to some specified set of rules. The problem with this characterization of deontological theories is that all theories other than those that merely specify prima facie considerations are rule-based. Act utilitarianism, for example, is rule based, since it assess the permissibility of actions in terms of whether they con form to the rule "Maximize the goodness of consequences!".

Both deontological and teleological theories may be (and generally are) rule-based. The difference between the two lies in the kinds of rules that they invoke. In a similar vein it is sometimes claimed that deontological theories, or at least one type thereof, are absolutist in that they claim that there are certain kinds of actions that are absolutely obligatory or forbidden (i.e., such that all actions of that There type are obligatory two problems or forbidden with this respectively.) claim First of all, without some restriction on the admissible action-types all theories are absolutist in this sense, since all theories hold that all actions of the type "is permissible" are permissible. Secondly, even if an appropriate restriction is placed on the admissible action-types to avoid this trivialization (perhaps allowing only non-normative action types). The claim is still false. Act utilitarianism, a paradigm non-deontological theory, is absolutist in this sense. This is because any action that falls under the description "does not have consequences that contain as much happiness as is feasible" is judged forbidden — no matter what its other characteristics are. Furthermore, Ross's intuitionist theory, a paradigm deontological theory, is non-absolutist, because it provides neither necessary nor sufficient conditions for the permissibility of action, but only prima facie considerations that must somehow be weighed together.

The characterization of deontological theories as absolutist is thus inadequate. A closely related characterization of deontological theories is as theories for which there are certain kinds of actions that are always (or never) forbidden, where whether or not a given action is of the specified kinds does not depend on what its outcome is.

The distinction between theories that base the permissibility of actions on their outcomes and those that do not is an important distinction. The outcome of an action is a state of affairs that would be realized if the action were performed. It is objectively determined in that its determination is independent of what the agent, or anyone else, believes (e.g., about what would happen if the action were performed). Theories that do not base the permissibility of actions on their out comes generally base it on their intended, anticipated, or reasonably anticipatable outcomes. Unlike (objective) outcomes, neither intended nor anticipated outcomes are objectively determined, since what they are depends only on the agent's mental state (what he/she intends or believes), and not on what would happen if the action were performed. And the reasonably anticipatable outcome is neither objectively determined, nor determined on the basis of the agent's mental state, but rather on the basis what it would be (intersubjectively) reasonable to anticipate happening.

Teological

Teleological theories are a particular kind of axiological theory. As we shall see, however, authors disagree about the exact defining characteristics. Indeed, we shall uncover four different characterizations of teleological theories. Almost all (if not all) authors require that a theory maximize the good in order to be teleological. As we shall see, most impose further requirements, but some do not, and at least in certain passages, Rawls,' characterizes teleological theories as theories that direct the agent to maximize the good, where the good ness in question may be that of the action's outcome, of its anticipated outcome and the like, or even of the action itself — no matter how this is evaluated (e.g., even if it is in terms of the agent's motives). This, then, is one way of characterizing teleological theories. Let us call theories that direct the agent to maximize the good goodness maximizing.

Most authors are more specific in their characterization of teleological theories. They require not merely that the theory direct the agent to maximize the good, but rather that they direct the agent to maximize the goodness of their outcomes, or of their intended, anticipated, or reasonably anticipatable outcomes.

For brevity, let us use the term 'quasi-outcome' as a generic name for outcomes, intended outcomes, anticipated outcomes, reasonably anticipatable outcomes, and the like. A second way of characterizing teleological theories, then, is as theories for which there is a specified kind of quasi-outcome such that an action is judged permissible just in case its specified quasi-outcome is maximally good. Let us call such theories quasi-outcome-teleological. Many authors' are even more specific in that they require the theory direct the agent to maximize the goodness of (objectively determined) outcomes — as opposed to the intended, anticipated, or reasonably anticipatable outcomes.

Let us call such theories outcome-teleological. This, then, is a third way of characterizing theories. There is yet another condition that is sometimes, but not always, invoked in the characterization of teleological theories: that the viewpoint from which the goodness of the outcomes is assessed be agent-invariant, i.e., the same no matter who the agent is. Classical act utilitarianism (which directs the agent to maximize the goodness of outcomes from the viewpoint of the universe as a whole) satisfies this condition, but ethical egoism (which directs the agent to maximize the good ness of outcomes from his/her viewpoint) and community utilitarianism (which directs the agent the maximize the goodness of outcomes from the viewpoint of his/her community) do not. The distinction between teleological theories for which the viewpoint of evaluation is agent-invariant and those for which it is not is a special case of a more general (and more important) distinction between theories that are agent-sensitive and those that are not. A theory (teleological or not) is agent-sensitive just in case its permissibility conditions make an essential reference to the agent qua agent.

Agent-sensitive theories may make the permissibility of actions depend in a special way on how they affect the agent and/or those bearing special relationships to the agent (e.g., friends, family, neighbors, etc.).'

Teleological theories are agent insensitive just in case their viewpoint for the evaluation of outcomes is agent in variant. As we saw above, some teleological theories are agent-sensitive (e.g., ethical egoism), and some are not (e.g., classical utilitarianism), likewise, some non-teleological theories are agent-sensitive and some are not. For example, a theory that forbids the agent to kill or allow to die any member of his/her family is agent-sensitive, whereas a theory whose sole injunction forbids killing or allowing anyone to die is not.

Egoism

In philosophy, egoism is the theory that one's self is, or should be, the motivation and the goal of one's own action. Egoism has two variants, descriptive or normative. The descriptive (or positive) variant conceives egoism as a factual description of human affairs. That is, people are motivated by their own interests and desires, and they cannot be described otherwise. The normative variant proposes that people should be so motivated, regardless of what presently motivates their behavior. Altruism is the opposite of egoism. The term "egoism" derives from "ego," the Latin term for "I" in English. Egoism should be distinguished from egotism, which means a psychological overvaluation of one's own importance, or of one's own activities.

People act for many reasons; but for whom, or what, do or should they act—for themselves, for God, or for the good of the planet? Can an individual ever act only according to her own interests without regard for others' interests. Conversely, can an individual ever truly act for others in complete disregard for her own interests? The answers will depend on an account of free will. Some philosophers argue that an individual has no choice in these matters, claiming that a person's acts are determined by prior events which make illusory any belief in choice.

Nevertheless, if an element of choice is permitted against the great causal impetus from nature, or God, it follows that a person possesses some control over her next action, and, that, therefore, one may inquire as to whether the individual does, or, should choose a self-or-other-oriented action. Morally speaking, one can ask whether the individual should pursue her own interests, or, whether she should reject self-interest and pursue others' interest instead: to what extent are other-regarding acts morally praiseworthy compared to self-regarding acts?

The descriptive egoist's theory is called "psychological egoism." Psychological egoism describes human nature as being wholly self-centered and self-motivated. Examples of this explanation of human nature predate the formation of the theory, and, are found in writings such as that of British Victorian historian, Macaulay, and, in that of British Reformation political philosopher, Thomas Hobbes. To the question, "What proposition is there respecting human nature which is absolutely and universally true?", Macaulay, replies, "We know of only one . . . that men always act from self-interest." (Quoted in Garvin.) In Leviathan, Hobbes maintains that, "No man gifter but with intention of good to himself; because gift is voluntary; and of all voluntary acts the object to every man is his own pleasure." In its strong form, psychological egoism asserts that people always act in their own interests, and, cannot but act in their own interests, even though they may disguise their motivation with references to helping others or doing their duty.

Opponents claim that psychological egoism renders ethics useless. However, this accusation assumes that ethical behavior is necessarily other-regarding, which opponents would first have to establish. Opponents may also exploit counter factual evidence to criticize psychological egoism— surely, they claim, there is a host of evidence supporting altruistic or duty bound actions that cannot be said to engage the self-interest of the agent. However, what qualifies to be counted as apparent counter factual evidence by opponents becomes an intricate and debatable issue. This is because, in response to their opponents, psychological egoists may attempt to shift the question away from outward appearances to ultimate motives of acting benevolently towards others; for example, they may claim that seemingly altruistic behavior (giving a stranger some money) necessarily does have a self-interested component. For example, if the individual were not to offer aid to a stranger, he or she may feel guilty or may look bad in front of a peer group.

On this point, psychological egoism's validity turns on examining and analyzing moral motivation. But since motivation is inherently private and inaccessible to others (an agent could be lying to herself or to others about the original motive), the theory shifts from a theoretical description of human nature—one that can be put to observational testing—to an assumption about the inner workings of human nature: psychological egoism moves beyond the possibility of empirical verification and the possibility of empirical negation (since motives are private), and therefore it becomes what is termed a "closed theory."

A closed theory is a theory that rejects competing theories on its own terms and is non-verifiable and non-falsifiable. If psychological egoism is reduced to an assumption concerning human nature and its hidden motives, then it follows that it is just as valid to hold a competing theory of human motivation such as psychological altruism.

Psychological altruism holds that all human action is necessarily other-centered, and other-motivated. One's becoming a hermit (an apparently selfish act) can be reinterpreted through psychological altruism as an act of pure noble selflessness: a hermit is not selfishly hiding herself away, rather, what she is doing is not inflicting her potentially ungraceful actions or displeasing looks upon others. A parallel analysis of psychological altruism thus results in opposing conclusions to psychological egoism. However, psychological altruism is arguably just as closed as psychological egoism: with it one assumes that an agent's inherently private and consequently unverifiable motives are altruistic. If both theories can be validly maintained, and if the choice between them becomes the flip of a coin, then their soundness must be questioned.

A weak version of psychological egoism accepts the possibility of altruistic or benevolent behavior, but maintains that, whenever a choice is made by an agent to act, the action is by definition one that the agent wants to do at that point. The action is self-serving, and is therefore sufficiently explained by the theory of psychological egoism. Let one assume that person A wants to help the poor; therefore, A is acting egoistically by actually wanting to help; again, if A ran into a burning building to save a kitten, it must be the case that A wanted or desired to save the kitten. However, defining all motivations as what an agent desires to do remains problematic: logically, the theory becomes tautologous and therefore unable to provide a useful, descriptive meaning of motivation because one is essentially making an arguably philosophically uninteresting claim that an agent is motivated to do what she is motivated to do. Besides which, if helping others is what A desires to do, then to what extent can A be continued to be called an egoist? A acts because that is what A does, and consideration of the ethical "ought" becomes immediately redundant. Consequently, opponents argue that psychological egoism is philosophically inadequate because it sidesteps the great nuances of motive. For example, one can argue that the psychological egoist's notion of motive sidesteps the clashes that her theory has with the notion of duty, and, related social virtues such as honor, respect, and reputation, which fill the tomes of history and literature.

David Hume, in his Enquiry Concerning the Principles of Morals, offers six rebuttals of what he calls the "selfish hypothesis," an arguably archaic relative of psychological egoism. First, Hume argues that self-interest opposes moral sentiments that may engage one in concern for others, and, may motivate one's actions for others. These moral sentiments include love, friendship, compassion, and gratitude. Second, psychological egoism attempts to reduce human motivation to a single cause, which is a 'fruitless' task—the "love of simplicity…has been the source of much false reasoning in philosophy." Third, it is evident that animals act benevolently towards one another, and, if it is admitted that animals can act altruistically, then how can it be denied in humans? Fourth, the concepts we use to describe benevolent behavior cannot be meaningless; sometimes an agent obviously does not have a personal interest in the fortune of another, yet will wish her well. Any attempt to create an imaginary vested interest, as the psychological egoist will attempt, proves futile. Fifth, Hume asserts that we have prior motivations to self-interest; we may have, for example, a predisposition towards vanity, fame, or vengeance that transcends any benefit to the agent. Finally, Hume claims that even if the selfish hypothesis were true, there are a sufficient number of dispositions to generate a wide possibility of moral actions, allowing one person to be called vicious and another humane; and he claims that the latter is to be preferred over the former.

The second variant of egoism is normative in that it stipulates the agent ought to promote the self above other values. Herbert Spencer said, "Ethics has to recognize the truth, recognized in unethical thought, that egoism comes before altruism. The acts required for continued self-preservation, including the enjoyments of benefits achieved by such arts, are the first requisites to universal welfare. Unless each duly cares for himself, his care for all others is ended in death, and if each thus dies there remain no others to be cared for." He was echoing a long history of the importance of self-regarding behavior that can be traced back to Aristotle's theory of friendship in the Nichomachaean Ethics. In his theory, Aristotle argues that a man must befriend himself before he can befriend others. The general theory of normative egoism does not attempt to describe human nature directly, but asserts how people ought to behave. It comes in two general forms: rational egoism and ethical egoism.

Rational egoism claims that the promotion of one's own interests is always in accordance with reason. The greatest and most provocative proponent of rational egoism is Ayn Rand, whose The Virtue of Selfishness outlines the logic and appeal of the theory. Rand argues that: first, properly defined, selfishness rejects the sacrificial ethics of the West's Judaic-Christian heritage on the grounds that it is right for man to live his own life; and, Rand argues that, second, selfishness is a proper virtue to pursue. That being said, she rejects the "selfless selfishness" of irrationally acting individuals: "the actor must always be the beneficiary of his action and that man must act for his own rational self-interest." To be ethically selfish thus entails a commitment to reason rather than to emotionally driven whims and instincts.

In the strong version of rational egoism defended by Rand, not only is it rational to pursue one's own interests, it is irrational not to pursue them. In a weaker version, one may note that while it is rational to pursue one's own interests, there may be occasions when not pursuing them is not necessarily irrational.

Critics of rational egoism may claim that reason may dictate that one's interests should not govern one's actions. The possibility of conflicting reasons in a society need not be evoked in this matter; one need only claim that reason may invoke an impartiality clause, in other words, a clause that demands that in a certain situation one's interests should not be furthered. For example, consider a free-rider situation. In marking students' papers, a teacher may argue that to offer inflated grades is to make her life easier, and, therefore, is in her self-interest: marking otherwise would incur negative feedback from students and having to spend time counseling on writing skills, and so on. It is even arguably foreseeable that inflating grades may never have negative consequences for anyone. The teacher could conceivably free-ride on the tougher marking of the rest of the department or university and not worry about the negative consequences of a diminished reputation to either. However, impartiality considerations demand an alternative course—it is not right to change grades to make life easier. Here self-interest conflicts with reason. Nonetheless, a Randian would reject the teacher's free-riding being rational: since the teacher is employed to mark objectively and impartially in the first place, to do otherwise is to commit a fraud both against the employing institution and the student. (This is indeed an analogous situation explored in Rand's The Fountainhead, in which the hero architect regrets having propped up a friend's inabilities).

A simpler scenario may also be considered. Suppose that two men seek the hand of one woman, and they deduce that they should fight for her love. A critic may reason that the two men rationally claim that if one of them were vanquished, the other may enjoy the beloved. However, the solution ignores the woman's right to choose between her suitors, and thus the men's reasoning is flawed.

Ethical egoism is the normative theory that the promotion of one's own good is in accordance with morality. In the strong version, it is held that it is always moral to promote one's own good, and it is never moral not to promote it. In the weak version, it is said that although it is always moral to promote one's own good, it is not necessarily never moral to not. That is, there may be conditions in which the avoidance of personal interest may be a moral action.

In an imaginary construction of a world inhabited by a single being, it is possible that the pursuit of morality is the same as the pursuit of self-interest in that what is good for the agent is the same as what is in the agent's interests. Arguably, there could never arise an occasion when the agent ought not to pursue self-interest in favor of another morality, unless he produces an alternative ethical system in which he ought to renounce his values in favor of an imaginary self, or, other entity such as the universe, or the agent's God. Opponents of ethical egoism may claim, however, that although it is possible for this Robinson Crusoe type creature to lament previous choices as not conducive to self-interest (enjoying the pleasures of swimming all day, and not spending necessary time producing food), the mistake is not a moral mistake but a mistake of identifying self-interest. Presumably this lonely creature will begin to comprehend the distinctions between short, and long-term interests, and, that short-term pains can be countered by long-term gains.

In addition, opponents argue that even in a world inhabited by a single being, duties would still apply; (Kantian) duties are those actions that reason dictates ought to be pursued regardless of any gain, or loss to self or others. Further, the deontologist asserts the application of yet another moral sphere which ought to be pursued, namely, that of impartial duties. The problem with complicating the creature's world with impartial duties, however, is in defining an impartial task in a purely subjective world. Impartiality, the ethical egoist may retort, could only exist where there are competing selves: otherwise, the attempt to be impartial in judging one's actions is a redundant exercise. (However, the Cartesian rationalist could retort that need not be so, that a sentient being should act rationally, and reason will disclose what are the proper actions he should follow.)

If we move away from the imaginary construct of a single being's world, ethical egoism comes under fire from more pertinent arguments. In complying with ethical egoism, the individual aims at her own greatest good. Ignoring a definition of the good for the present, it may justly be argued that pursuing one's own greatest good can conflict with another's pursuit, thus creating a situation of conflict. In a typical example, a young person may see his greatest good in murdering his rich uncle to inherit his millions. It is the rich uncle's greatest good to continue enjoying his money, as he sees fit. According to detractors, conflict is an inherent problem of ethical egoism, and the model seemingly does not possess a conflict resolution system. With the additional premise of living in society, ethical egoism has much to respond to: obviously there are situations when two people's greatest goods – the subjectively perceived working of their own self-interest – will conflict, and, a solution to such dilemmas is a necessary element of any theory attempting to provide an ethical system.

The ethical egoist contends that her theory, in fact, has resolutions to the conflict. The first resolution proceeds from a state of nature examination. If, in the wilderness, two people simultaneously come across the only source of drinkable water a potential dilemma arises if both make a simultaneous claim to it. With no recourse to arbitration they must either accept an equal share of the water, which would comply with rational egoism. (In other words, it is in the interest of both to share, for both may enjoy the water and each other's company, and, if the water is inexhaustible, neither can gain from monopolizing the source.) But a critic may maintain that this solution is not necessarily in compliance with ethical egoism. Arguably, the critic continues, the two have no possible resolution, and must, therefore, fight for the water. This is often the line taken against egoism generally: that it results in insoluble conflict that implies, or necessitates a resort to force by one or both of the parties concerned. For the critic, the proffered resolution is, therefore, an acceptance of the ethical theory that "might is right;" that is, the critic maintains that the resolution accepts that the stronger will take possession and thereby gain proprietary rights.

However, ethical egoism does not have to logically result in a Darwinian struggle between the strong and the weak in which strength determines moral rectitude to resources or values. Indeed, the "realist" position may strike one as philosophically inadequate as that of psychological egoism, although popularly attractive. For example, instead of succumbing to insoluble conflict, the two people could cooperate (as rational egoism would require). Through cooperation, both agents would, thereby, mutually benefit from securing and sharing the resource. Against the critic's pessimistic presumption that conflict is insoluble without recourse to victory, the ethical egoist can retort that reasoning people can recognize that their greatest interests are served more through cooperation than conflict. War is inherently costly, and, even the fighting beasts of the wild instinctively recognize its potential costs, and, have evolved conflict-avoiding strategies.

On the other hand, the ethical egoist can argue less benevolently, that in case one man reaches the desired resource first, he would then be able to take rightful control and possession of it – the second person cannot possess any right to it, except insofar as he may trade with its present owner. Of course, charitable considerations may motivate the owner to secure a share for the second comer, and economic considerations may prompt both to trade in those products that each can better produce or acquire: the one may guard the water supply from animals while the other hunts. Such would be a classical liberal reading of this situation, which considers the advance of property rights to be the obvious solution to apparently intractable conflicts over resources.

A second conflict-resolution stems from critics' fears that ethical egoists could logically pursue their interests at the cost of others. Specifically, a critic may contend that personal gain logically cannot be in one's best interest if it entails doing harm to another: doing harm to another would be to accept the principle that doing harm to another is ethical (that is, one would be equating "doing harm" with "one's own best interests"), whereas, reflection shows that principle to be illogical on universalistic criteria. However, an ethical egoist may respond that in the case of the rich uncle and greedy nephew, for example, it is not the case that the nephew would be acting ethically by killing his uncle, and that for a critic to contend otherwise is to criticize personal gain from the separate ethical standpoint that condemns murder. In addition, the ethical egoist may respond by saying that these particular fears are based on a confusion resulting from conflating ethics (that is, self-interest) with personal gain; The ethical egoist may contend that if the nephew were to attempt to do harm for personal gain, that he would find that his uncle or others would or may be permitted to do harm in return. The argument that "I have a right to harm those who get in my way" is foiled by the argument that "others have a right to harm me should I get in the way." That is, in the end, the nephew variously could see how harming another for personal gain would not be in his self-interest at all.

The critics' fear is based on a misreading of ethical egoism, and is an attempt to subtly reinsert the "might is right" premise. Consequently, the ethical egoist is unfairly chastised on the basis of a straw-man argument. Ultimately, however, one comes to the conclusion reached in the discussion of the first resolution; that is, one must either accept the principle that might is right (which in most cases would be evidentially contrary to one's best interest), or accept that cooperation with others is a more successful approach to improving one's interests. Though interaction can either be violent or peaceful, an ethical egoist rejects violence as undermining the pursuit of self-interest.

A third conflict-resolution entails the insertion of rights as a standard. This resolution incorporates the conclusions of the first two resolutions by stating that there is an ethical framework that can logically be extrapolated from ethical egoism. However, the logical extrapolation is philosophically difficult (and, hence, intriguing) because ethical egoism is the theory that the promotion of one's own self-interest is in accordance with morality whereas rights incorporate boundaries to behavior that reason or experience has shown to be contrary to the pursuit of self-interest. Although it is facile to argue that the greedy nephew does not have a right to claim his uncle's money because it is not his but his uncle's, and to claim that it is wrong to act aggressively against the person of another because that person has a legitimate right to live in peace (thus providing the substance of conflict-resolution for ethical egoism), the problem of expounding this theory for the ethical egoist lies in the intellectual arguments required to substantiate the claims for the existence of rights and then, once substantiated, connecting them to the pursuit of an individual's greatest good.

A final type of ethical egoism is conditional egoism. This is the theory that egoism is morally acceptable or right if it leads to morally acceptable ends. For example, self-interested behavior can be accepted and applauded if it leads to the betterment of society as a whole; the ultimate test rests not on acting self-interestedly but on whether society is improved as a result. A famous example of this kind of thinking is from Adam Smith's The Wealth of Nations, in which Smith outlines the public benefits resulting from self-interested behavior (borrowing a theory from the earlier writer Bernard Mandeville and his Fable of the Bees). Smith writes: "It is not from the benevolence of the butcher, the brewer, or the baker, that we expect our dinner, but from their regard to their own interest. We address ourselves, not to their humanity but to their self-love, and never talk to them of our own necessities but of their advantages".

As Smith himself admits, if egoistic behavior lends itself to society's detriment, then it ought to be stopped. The theory of conditional egoism is thus dependent on a superior moral goal such as an action being in the common interest, that is, the public good. The grave problem facing conditional egoists is according to what standard ought the limits on egoism be placed? In other words, who or what is to define the nature of the public good? If it is a person who is set up as the great arbitrator of the public, then it is uncertain if there can be a guarantee that he or she is embodying or arguing for an impartial standard of the good and not for his or her own particular interest. If it is an impartial standard that sets the limit, one that can be indicated by any reasonable person. then it behooves the philosopher to explain the nature of that standard.

In most "public good" theories, the assumption is made that there exists a collective entity over and above the individuals that comprise it: race, nation, religion, and state being common examples. Collectivists then attempt to explain what in particular should be held as the interest of the group. Inevitably, however, conflict arises, and resolutions have to be produced. Some seek refuge in claiming the need for perpetual dialogue (rather than exchange), but others return to the need for force to settle apparently insoluble conflicts; nonetheless, the various shades of egoism pose a valid and appealing criticism of collectivism: that individuals act; groups don't. Karl Popper's works on methodological individualism are a useful source in criticizing collectivist thinking (for example, Popper's The Poverty of Historicism).

Psychological egoism is fraught with the logical problem of collapsing into a closed theory, and hence being a mere assumption that could validly be accepted as describing human motivation and morality, or be rejected in favor of a psychological altruism (or even a psychological ecologism in which all actions necessarily benefit the agent's environment).

Normative egoism, however, engages in a philosophically more intriguing dialogue with protractors. Normative egoists argue from various positions that an individual ought to pursue his or her own interest. These may be summarized as follows: the individual is best placed to know what defines that interest, or it is thoroughly the individual's right to pursue that interest. The latter is divided into two sub-arguments: either because it is the reasonable/rational course of action, or because it is the best guarantee of maximizing social welfare.

Egoists also stress that the implication of critics' condemnation of self-serving or self-motivating action is the call to renounce freedom in favor of control by others, who then are empowered to choose on their behalf. This entails an acceptance of Aristotle's political maxim that "some are born to rule and others are born to be ruled," also read as "individuals are generally too stupid to act either in their own best interests or in the interests of those who would wish to command them." Rejecting both descriptions (the first as being arrogant and empirically questionable and the second as unmasking the truly immoral ambition lurking behind attacks on selfishness), egoists ironically can be read as moral and political egalitarians glorifying the dignity of each and every person to pursue life as they see fit. Mistakes in securing the proper means and appropriate ends will be made by individuals, but if they are morally responsible for their actions they not only will bear the consequences but also the opportunity for adapting and learning. When that responsibility is removed and individuals are exhorted to live for an alternative cause, their incentive and joy in improving their own welfare is concomitantly diminished, which will, for many egoists, ultimately foster an uncritical, unthinking mass of obedient bodies vulnerable to political manipulation: when the ego is trammeled, so too is freedom ensnared, and without freedom ethics is removed from individual to collective or government responsibility.

Egoists also reject the insight into personal motivation that others – whether they are psychological or sociological "experts"– declare they possess, and which they may accordingly fine-tune or encourage to "better ends." Why an individual acts remains an intrinsically personal and private act that is the stuff of memoirs and literature, but how they should act releases our investigations into ethics of what shall define the good for the self-regarding agent.

Altruism

Altruism (or Ethical Altruism) is an ethical doctrine that holds that individuals have a moral obligation to help, serve or benefit others, if necessary at the sacrifice of self interest. More precisely, an action is morally right if the consequences of that action are more favorable than unfavorable to everyone except the agent.

The term "altruism" (initially derived from the Latin "alter" meaning "other") was coined by Auguste Comte, the French founder of Positivism, in order to describe his ethical doctrine, which he summed up in the phrase: "Live for others". In more general terms, Altruism is selfless concern for the welfare of others (although its common usage does not necessarily entail any ethical obligation).

Altruism is often seen as a form of Consequentialism, as it indicates that an action is ethically right if it brings good consequences to others. It may be seen as similar to Utilitarianism, although an essential difference is that Utilitarianism prescribes acts that maximize good consequences for all of society, while Altruism prescribes maximizing good consequences for everyone except the actor. It is the opposite of Egoism, which holds that individuals should do what is best for themselves, that it is not only their right but their duty to look after their own interests first.

Friedrich Nietzsche held that the idea that it is virtuous to treat others as more important than oneself is degrading and demeaning to the self, and hinders the individual's pursuit of self-development, excellence and creativity. He maintained that it was an ideology fabricated by the weak for the weak, and masks self-poisoning resentment about individual and collective powerlessness.

The Objectivist Ayn Rand (1905-1982) is on record as stating that most problems in the world come from the doctrine of Altruism, and argues that there is no rational ground for asserting that sacrificing yourself in order to serve others is morally superior to pursuing your own self-interest. Furthermore, if the state were to enforce Altruism as a moral ideal, this could ultimately result in the state forcing everyone into a collectivist political system.

Others have argued that actions formerly seen as altruistic are in reality just a form of enlightened self-interest.

Universalism

Since the late nineteenth century, the debate around issues concerning universalism and universalizability has intensified. Against the claims to universal knowledge made on behalf of Christianity, the West, rationality, and mankind, feminist, critical race, and post colonial scholars and activists have shown that the issues are more complicated. Notwithstanding the validity of their criticism, universalism is not only compatible with the approaches that have condemned it, but is importantly in a sense presupposed by them.

First, we need to distinguish between different kinds of universalism. Universalism, in its most sophisticated form as it appears in the philosophy of science, defends the idea that thinking about any problem in science always leads to reasoning and that this reasoning will always seek the outermost limits through attempts to be universally valid, and to discover non-relative truth. There are two forms of this simple and elegant idea about reason. One argues that this submission to an order of reason is a demand of reason itself. The other disagrees with the idea that we are ultimately submitting ourselves to an order of reason that is there for us to discover. Following Charles Peirce, this view argues that even as we try to think of this order of nature and of rationality, we are always doing so through a community of inquirers, so that this convergence of opinion about universally valid scientific laws always retains its ideal aspect. Here, Peirce sought to update Immanuel Kant's transcendental idealism, and show its relevance to the philosophy of science. For Kant, our scientific laws are valid for rational creatures such as us, and we can show their validity through transcendental deduction. But we cannot ultimately reach beyond the synthetic imagination and the categories of space and time that shape our world to reach into the world of things themselves. Convergence, for Peirce, means that divergent opinions can actually come to agreement on specific scientific laws and that unless there is a significant challenge to that agreement it will remain valid as true. But it is precisely because it is an agreement of a community of inquirers that also makes it open-ended, since such agreements can, at least in principle, always be challenged or re-elaborated by new paradigms of scientific truth. In some sense then, we are creating the order of reasons through the articulation of scientific laws. Simply put, there is always more to know, and as we know more, scientific laws that we previously thought of as unshakeable can either be criticized, extended, or in some cases, downright rejected. Peirce further argues that how well we think is ultimately dependent on the ethics of the scientific community to which we belong. Ethics then, as critiques of a community of knowledge, including scientific knowledge, can be fore grounded without necessarily losing the appeal to scientific laws as justifiable and as universally valid.

Feminists writing in the philosophy of science, such as Evelyn Fox Keller and Sandra Harding, have made important contributions in critiquing claims of universality for scientific law from at least two vantage points. The first and most important is that the community of knowledge is corrupt at the deepest level. It has adopted an ethics of scientific inquiry that, for the most part, has excluded women. Moreover, by so excluding women, it has in fact adopted notions of instrumental rationality that fail to achieve true objectivity because they relate to nature from a masculine or patriarchal viewpoint in which nature is reduced to something only valuable for its use to us. There is a rich and important literature in feminist epistemology and it is obviously impossible for me to be fair to the extent of the varieties of critique offered there. But even when such a feminist critique is allied with the searing analysis of the destructiveness of instrumental rationality as it takes over what we can even think of as reason—an analysis put forth by thinkers of the Frankfurt school such as Theodor Adorno and Max Horkheimer—it does not in itself necessarily lead to the rejection of a universality understood as always taking reason to its limit. This is true even if one allows, following Peirce, that limit might always recede under the changing principles of scientific knowledge. Again, for Peirce, as for many feminists and other critical theorists, convergence remains always and still an ideal.

Indeed, we could argue that Peirce, following Kant, offers us a powerful critique of the pretensions of reason. This critique forces us to see how a thoroughgoing rationalism always is thrown back on the finitude of any actually given community of inquirers, humbled before their own historical position, even as they aspire to the scientific grandeur of ultimately trying to grasp the meaning of the universe. If Kant is right, we will never be able to think God's thoughts. But if Albert Einstein is also right, and the basic argument about reason is compelling, then any given community of inquirers will never stop trying.

Another central question in the debates surrounding universalism has been raised in ethics; precisely, the question is whether we need to rationalize ethical reasons into something more than a circular procedure for moral reasoning. In the famous case of John Rawls's proceduralism, he defends the hypothetical experiment of putting ourselves behind the veil of ignorance to imagine what Kant would have called our noumenal selves unbounded at least as imagined by the contingencies of our own history. Unlike Jürgen Habermas, Rawls does not want to defend his theory of justice or his own political liberalism through an overarching philosophical conception of reason and history that explains ethical and moral principles by an appeal to something outside of them.

Famously, Habermas argued against his predecessors, and indeed Kant himself, by trying to show us that reason can ground itself in universal principles of communicative action when combined with an empirically validated notion of evolutionary learning processes. This attempt to rationalize moral reason has been criticized extensively by theorists of language and of communication who have argued that first of all, no presuppositions can be found. Further, even if they could be found, they would not be strong enough to ground a normative theory, let along an overarching normative conception of modernity and of human moral learning leading to the oneway street of modern Europe. Habermas is adding an empirical dimension to the general and comprehensive worldview of strong universalism advocated by Hegel. For Hegel, the universal ideal of humanity unfolds in all its greatness and, despite its floundering, finally culminates in a grand unity of our particular historical expression and our universal moral selves in what some may have seen as a rather limited embodiment, i.e. the German state. Habermas, in other words, attempts a general and comprehensive theory, to use John Rawls's expression that justifies universalism through a connection of reason and an overarching concept of rationality. But, as mentioned earlier, Rawls himself rejects this as the basis of the universalizable ideals of what he calls political liberalism. Rawls, one of the greatest voices of this vision, argued that at least hypothetically, we should be able to imagine ourselves as noumenal beings that could idealize themselves so as to articulate and defend as reasonable certain universal principles of justice. Rawls certainly defends the universality of the principles of justice. But he refuses universalism understood as the attempt to ground moral reason in an order of reason outside of the procedure, such as in the case of Habermas, who seeks to ground morality and ethics in the presuppositions of language.

In her own work in moral philosophy, Martha Nussbaum has tried to defend universalism in the sense of defending an Aristotelian notion of a moral view of human nature. Her view too should be considered universalism in the sense that she argues that we can know what our nature is and derive from that knowledge a strong commitment to values, universalizable because they are true to the substance of our human nature. By universalizable, I mean to indicate ideals that purport to include all of humanity and therefore can be accepted by all of us. This way of thinking about what is universalizable emphasizes the idea of the scope of who should be included in the ideal of humanity, and the rights that are accorded to those so included. But universalism as defended by either Nussbaum or Habermas ultimately denies the central importance of the insight of the Kantian proceduralism of Rawls. That insight is for a norm to be truly universalizable, it cannot be based on a notion of the human that generalizes out of a particular experience. Again, the feminist critiques of man were not arguing against the aspiration to universalizability of the rights of man, but claiming instead that those rights were indeed only for men, in many instances being granted to men only, and thus fail the test of universalizability that they purported to meet. Feminists, of course, have been joined by postcolonial theorists who have reminded us that the identification of humanity as an ideal, including as a moral ideal, with European modernity, not only risks reducing the universal to the particular, but has also justified the worst forms of colonial cruelty.

A critique then, of European modernity as other than a particular form of history is crucial for the unmooring of the ideal of universality and even the ideal of humanity itself from its implications in a brutal imperialist history. Universalizable norms, in this sense, carry with them a specific kind of self-reflexivity in which universality as an ideal must always lead to critical analysis. The danger is not only of confusing generality with universality, but also of proclaiming a particular form of being human as if this were the last word on who and what we could be. Universality, in other words, as a claim to cover the scope even of rights to be protected is always open to the moral contest it protects.

When Hegel is removed from his presumptuous philosophy of history, the lingering truth of Hegel's insight is that the re-articulation of universality and universalizable norms always takes place through a struggle. Karl Marx saw that struggle, or at least the struggle that could ultimately bring us to our truest humanity, as the battle between classes. History in other words, had not stopped with the bourgeois German state, but would only reach its culmination when humanity realized itself in communism. The lingering importance of German idealism is that it teaches us that at the end of the day we are left with a struggle—the struggle to see that taking reason to its limit also takes us back to the limit of reason itself, as Kant so powerfully taught us. Therefore, Kant's critique itself is integral to what is understood as an ideal in which the procedures by which we seek to universalize a norm or an ideal are always themselves open to question and re-articulation.

This notion of universality, as an ideal whose meaning can be reinterpreted in order for it to be able to live up to its own claims, should not be confused with relativism. Relativism, which argues that norms, values, and ideals are always relative to culture, actually turns on a strong substantive claim about the nature of moral reality. Relativists have to become the strongest kinds of rationalists in order to defend their position. To defend relativism as a substantive truth about moral reality clearly has to appeal to a form of universal knowledge. After all, if the claim is that principles are always inevitably relative to culture, then that claim is one that must defend itself as a universal truth. In our globalized world, the remembrance and the commitment to universality demands nothing less of us than a commitment to the critique and the corresponding imaginative openness to the re-articulations of the ideal.

Subjectivism

Subjectivism teaches that there are no objective moral truths out there.

- There are no objective moral facts. Therefore 'murder is wrong' can't be *objectively* true

  Many forms of subjectivism go a bit further and teach that moral statements describe how the speaker feels about a particular ethical issue.
- Moral statements are just factual statements about the attitude *the speaker* holds on a particular issue
- So if I say "Lying is wrong", all I'm doing is telling you that I disapprove of telling lies

Some forms of subjectivism generalise this idea to come up with:

- Moral statements are just factual statements about the attitude *normal human beings* hold on a particular issue

And this may ultimately lead us to this conclusion about moral truths:

- Moral judgements are dependent on the feelings and attitudes of the persons who think about such things

Good points of subjectivism

Reflects the subjective elements of morality:

- it reflects the close relationship between morality and people's feelings and opinions - indeed it can cope with the contradictory moral views we often find ourselves wrestling with

Reflects the evaluative elements of moral statements

- moral statements in everyday life make judgements ("lying is wrong"), factual statements ("cats have fur") don't

Shows that moral judgements communicate disapproval

- it reflects the communication of approval and disapproval that seems to go along with the everyday making of moral statements

May clarify what people are arguing about

- subjectivism may enable people disagreeing over the rightness or wrongness of some issue to see that the real dispute is not about objective truth but about their own preferences

Reflects the persuasive intentions behind ethical discussions

- subjectivism may also enable people engaging in moral argument to realise that they are not arguing about objective truths but trying to persuade their opponent to adopt their point of view

Bad points of subjectivism

The problem with subjectivism is that it seems to imply that moral statements are less significant than most people think they are - this may of course be true without rendering moral statements *in*significant.

"If I approve of something, it must be good"

- Subjectivism seems to tell us that moral statements give information only about what we feel about moral issues.
- If the simplest form of subjectivism is true then when a person who genuinely approves of telling lies says "telling lies is good" that moral statement is unarguably true. It would only be untrue if the speaker didn't approve of telling lies.
- So under this theory it seems that all the speaker has to do to prove that lying is good is to show lots of evidence that *they do indeed approve of lying* - perhaps that they tell lots of lies and feel good about it, indeed are surprised if anyone criticises them for being a liar, and that they often praise other people for telling lies.
- Most people would find this way of approaching ethics somewhat unhelpful, and wouldn't think it reflected the way in which most people talk about ethical issues.

Moral statements seem more than statements about feelings

- By and large if a person says something is wrong we usually get the message that they disapprove of that something, but most of us probably think that the other person is doing more than just telling us about their feelings.

How can we blame people if moral truths are always subjective?

- If moral statements have no objective truth, then how can we blame people for behaving in a way that 'is wrong', i.e. if "murder is wrong" has no objective truth, then how can we justify punishing people for murder?
- One answer is that we can justify punishment for murder on the basis of the objective truth that most normal people in society disapprove of murder. If we do this, we should not pretend that our justification is based on anything other than the majority view.

Cultural Relativism

Cultural Relativism is the view that moral or ethical systems, which vary from culture to culture, are all equally valid and no one system is really "better" than any other. This is based on the idea that there is no ultimate standard of good or evil, so every judgment about right and wrong is a product of society. Therefore, any opinion on morality or ethics is subject to the cultural perspective of each person. Ultimately, this means that no moral or ethical system can be considered the "best," or "worst," and no particular moral or ethical position can actually be considered "right" or "wrong."

Cultural relativism is a widely held position in the modern world. Words like "pluralism," "tolerance," and "acceptance" have taken on new meanings, as the boundaries of "culture" have expanded. The loose way in which modern society defines these ideas has made it possible for almost anything to be justified on the grounds of "relativism." The umbrella of "relativism" includes a fairly wide range of ideas, all of which introduce instability and uncertainty into areas that were previously considered settled.

Stepping up to the edge of a cliff gives you a good perspective of the terrain below. Taking one step too far, as cultural relativism does, is simply a disaster.

Obviously, perspective is important to our understanding of history, psychology, and politics. Cultural perspective can help us understand why certain actions are considered right or wrong by a particular culture. For example, an ancient society might have considered dyeing one's hair green to be a punishable offense. Most modern societies would find that strange, if not oppressive. Yet, good cultural perspective might tell us more. If we were to find out that green hair was a sign of a prostitute, we would understand that it wasn't the hair color itself, but the prostitution that was truly considered "wrong."

However, the problem with moving from cultural perspective to cultural relativism is the erosion of reason that it causes. Rather than simply saying, "we need to understand the morals of other cultures," it says, "we cannot judge the morals of other cultures," regardless of the reasons for their actions. There is no longer any perspective, and it becomes literally impossible to argue that anything a culture does is right or wrong. Holding to strict cultural relativism, it is not possible to say that human sacrifice is "wrong," or that respect for the elderly is "right." After all, those are products of the culture. This takes any talk of morality right over the cliff, and into meaningless gibberish.

Cultural Relativism: Absolutely Impossible

The contradiction of cultural relativism becomes immediately apparent. A society that embraces the notion that there is no ultimate "right" or "wrong" loses the ability to make any judgments at all. The way in which relativism, including cultural relativism, has permeated modern society is demonstrated in the bizarre ways in which we try to deal with this contradiction. "Tolerance" has mutated to imply unconditional support and agreement for all opinions or lifestyles. However, those who choose to be "intolerant" are not to be supported or agreed with. Tolerance, therefore, becomes an "ultimate good" in and of itself, which is contradictory to the entire idea of relativism. In the same way, heinous crimes such as rape and murder demand a moral judgment — but strict cultural relativism cannot say that such things are always wrong.

Relativism in general breaks down when examined from a purely logical perspective. The basic premise is that "truth is relative." If every truth statement is valid, then the statement "some truths are absolute" must be valid. The statement "there are no absolute truths" is accurate, according to relativism — but it is an absolute truth itself. These contradict the very concept of relativism, meaning that absolute relativism is self-contradictory and impossible.

Cultural Relativism: Crumbling Away

In practice, cultural relativism cannot overcome the boundaries of logic, nor can it override the sense of morality inherent to mankind. We instinctively know that some things are wrong, so cultural relativists attempt to tweak their philosophy to fit that need. Declaring certain actions "mostly" wrong, or "mostly" right is nothing more than making up the rules as one goes. Saying that some morals are "better," even if they aren't "the best," still implies some ultimate standard that's being used to make that judgment. How do you know which cloud is higher unless you know which way "up" is? To firmly state that anything at all is always wrong is to reject relativism itself. In the end, those who insist on clinging to cultural relativism must jettison logic, because there isn't room for both. It is literally impossible for a person to rationally believe that there are no moral absolutes, or at least to live out that belief in any meaningful way.

Since this philosophy is nonsensical, there must be some fundamental absolutes of right and wrong, regardless of the opinions of any given society. Since there are disagreements among different cultures, we cannot assume that these truths are developed by one particular group of people. In fact, the only logical place for these concepts to originate from is something more universal, or at least more fundamental, than culture.

Super Naturalism

Evidence of neither the idea of nature nor the experience of a purely natural realm is found among primitive people, who inhabit a wonderworld charged with the sacred power (or mana), spirits, and deities. Primitive man associates whatever is experienced as uncanny or powerful with the presence of a sacred or numinous power; yet he constantly lives in a profane realm that is made comprehensible by a paradigmatic, mythical sacred realm. In the higher religions a gulf usually is created between the sacred and the profane, or the here and the beyond, and it is only with the appearance of this gulf that a distinction becomes drawn between the natural and the supernatural, a distinction that is not found, for example, in the classical religious traditions of Greece and China. Both the Olympian deities of ancient Greece and the Tao ("Way") of ancient China were apprehended as lying at the centre of what today is commonly known as the natural; yet they were described in language that was imbued with concepts of the sacred.

Paradoxically, the most radical division between the natural and the supernatural is established by those forms of religion that posit a final or ultimate coincidence between the natural and the supernatural, or the sacred and the profane. This is true both in Indian mystical religion and in Near Eastern and Western eschatological religions, which are concerned with the last time that inaugurates a new sacred age. Buddhism, from its very beginning, established a total distinction between the realm of life and individual (samsara), which it identified interiorly as the arena of pain and suffering, and the goal of the Buddhist way, Nirvana, which is understood in wholly negative terms as a final and total release from samsara. As Buddhism developed in India, however, and did so in part by way of making the distinction between Nirvana and samsara ever more comprehensive and pure, it gradually but decisively reached the point of identifying Nirvana and samsara, and this identification, according to some scholars, became the foundation of Mahyna ("Greater Vehicle") Buddhism.

Zoroastrianism, Judaism, Christianity, and Islm, which emphasize eschatology (the doctrine of last times), posit a radical dichotomy between the old aeon and the new aeon, or this world and the Kingdom of God. While normative Judaism cast off eschatology, although it was reborn in a mystical form in the Kabbala (Jewish mysticism), Christianity arose with an eschatological expectation of the immediate coming of the Kingdom of God. Primitive Christianity identified Jesus with the eschatological figure of the Son of man, a divine redeemer whose coming would inaugurate the Last Judgment and the end of the world. This early Christian faith went hand in hand with the belief that all things whatsoever will be transfigured into the Kingdom of God. Such a form of faith refuses to accept the world as simply world or nature but rather understands both nature and history as constantly undergoing a process of transformation that will issue in a wholly new creation or new world.

The secularization of modern Western civilization has created a gulf between the natural and the supernatural because of modern conceptions of the physical universe as being controlled by scientifically knowable and predictable laws and as existing apart from the influence or control of God. Hence, the world becomes a profane reality that is wholly isolated from both the sacred and the supernatural.

Ethical Realism

The moral realist contends that there are moral facts, so moral realism is a thesis in ontology, the study of what is. The ontological category "moral facts" includes both the descriptive moral judgment that is allegedly true of an individual, such as, "Sam is morally good," and the descriptive moral judgment that is allegedly true for all individuals such as, "Lying for personal gain is wrong." A signature of the latter type of moral fact is that it not only describes an enduring condition of the world but also proscribes what *ought to be* the case (or what ought not to be the case) in terms of an individual's behavior.

The traditional areas of disagreement between the realist camp and the antirealist camp are cognitivism, descriptivism, moral truth, moral knowledge, and moral objectivity. The long and recalcitrant history of the realism/antirealism debate records that the focal point of the debate has been shaped and reshaped over centuries, with a third way, namely, Quasi-realism, attracting more recent attention. Quasi-realism debunks the positions of both realism and antirealism.

On the one hand, considering cognitivism, descriptivism, moral truth, moral knowledge, and moral objectivity as specifying the sufficient conditions for moral realism ignores the quasi-realist way. On the other hand, defining moral realism in a way that accommodates quasi-realism ccncedes too much: unlike the moral realist, the quasi-realist denies that moral facts are explanatory. Consequently, one can view quasi-realism as the contemporary heir of antirealism.

If there are moral facts, how can we know them? For a realist, moral facts are as certain as mathematical facts. Moral facts and mathematical facts are abstract entities, and as such, are different in kind from natural facts. One cannot literally display moral facts as one could display, say, a plant. One can display a token of the type, for example one can write "lying for personal gain is wrong" or one can write an equation; however, one cannot observe moral and mathematical facts in quite the same way as one can observe, with the aid of a microscope, clorophyll in a leaf. Such limitations of experience do not stop realists and antirealists from disagreeing on virtually every aspect of the moral practices that seem to presuppose the existence of moral facts. The list of contested areas includes moral language, moral truth, moral knowledge, moral objectivity, moral psychology, and so on. These areas are not discrete but intermingle.

The moral realist may argue for the view that there are moral facts as follows:

(1) Moral sentences are sometimes true.

(2) A sentence is true only if the truth-making relation holds between it and the thing that makes it true.

(3) Thus, true moral sentences are true only because there holds the truth-making relation between them and the things that make them true.

Therefore,

(4) The things that make some moral sentences true must exist.

It is a short inference from the existence of the things that make some moral sentences true to the existence of moral facts.

The moral antirealist can respond to the argument by denying any of the three premises. The antirealist could be a non-descriptivist in rejecting premise (1): no moral sentences are true for they do not describe how the world is; or, she may reject a version of the correspondence theory of truth by denying premise (2): she may argue that a sentence can be true even if there holds no truth-making relation between it and the thing that makes it true. For instance, she may be a proponent of the coherence theory of truth, which holds that a sentence can be true only when there is a truth making relation between it and other sentences relevant to it. Or, she may even reject as illegitimate the inference from "things that make some moral sentences true" to the "existence of moral facts."

In the past, many antirealists were noncognitivists, holding that moral judgments are not cognitive states like ordinary beliefs: that is, antirealists hold that unlike beliefs, the essential function or aim of moral judgments is not to represent the world accurately. (A non-descriptivist claim is that cognitivism

—more specifically descriptivism— is necessary, but not sufficient for moral realism, as will be shown presently.) Moral judgments are, according to the noncognitivist, mental states of some other kind: they are emotions, desires, or intentions of the sort that are expressed by commands or prescriptions.

If moral judgments are expressed by commands or prescriptions, then there cannot be literal moral truths. (Cf. Wright 1993. He argues that the focal discussion in the realist/antirealist debate should be about the acceptable theories of truth.) If there are no literal moral truths, then no moral judgments may be cited as evidence for knowing how the world is. Moral knowledge can no longer be considered as descriptive or propositional; or, no one is justified in believing certain things about the world in making moral judgments. This illustrates how the noncognitivist analysis of moral judgments can be escalated into the antirealist rejection of (those good names that we take for granted when we participate in moral practices such as) "moral truths" and "moral knowledge." The antirealist's noncognitivism threatens moral objectivity as well. Objectivity is to be found within the world. If moral judgments are not about accurately describing the world —for example, if moral judgments are about us —then moral objectivity will not be found within the world. If moral objectivity is to be found within us, then it is not the same objectivity with which we began, or, so had been the old antirealist's way.

If it is noncognitivism that provides the antirealist a way of rejecting moral truth, moral knowledge, and moral objectivity, the denial of noncognitivism (that is, cognitivism) must be necessary for the realist to properly claim them. Cognitivism is the view that moral judgments are cognitive states just like ordinary beliefs. It is part of their function to describe the world accurately. The realist argument that stems from cognitivism — as we saw from the above argument— is often times guided by the apparent difficulties that the noncognitivist analysis of moral judgments faces. For instance, there is the famous Frege-Geach problem, namely, the noncognitivist difficulty of rendering emotive, prescriptive or projective meaning for embedded moral judgments.

Geach (1965) uses the "the Frege point," according to which "a proposition may occur in discourse now asserted, now unasserted, and yet be recognizably the same proposition," to establish that no noncognitivist ("the anti-descriptive theorist") analysis of moral sentences and utterances can be adequate.

Consider a simple moral sentence: "Setting a kitten on fire is wrong." Suppose that the simple sentence means, "Boo to setting a kitten on fire!" The Frege point dictates that the antecedent of "if setting a kitten on fire is wrong, then getting one's friends to help setting a kitten on fire is also wrong" must mean the same as the simple sentence. But this cannot be because the antecedent of the conditional makes no such assertions while the simple moral sentence does. In other words, the noncognitivist analysis of moral sentences cannot be given to the conditional sentences with the embedded simple moral sentence. The problem can be generally applied to cases of other compound sentences such as "It is wrong to set a kitten on fire, or it is not." Even if the noncognitivist analysis of the simple sentence were correct, compound sentences within which a simple moral sentence is embedded should be given an analysis independently of the noncognitivist analysis of it. This seems unacceptable to many. For the following argument is valid: "It is wrong to set a kitten on fire, or it is not; it is not 'not wrong'; hence, it is wrong to set a kitten on fire." If the argument is valid, then the conclusion must mean the same as one of the disjuncts of its first premise. The argument would be otherwise invalid because of an equivocation, and the noncognitivist seems to be forced to say that the argument is invalid.

The cognitivist understanding of moral judgments is at the center of moral realism. For the cognitivist, moral judgments are mental states; moral judgments are of the same kind as ordinary beliefs, that is, cognitive states. But how are we to know this? One manageable way is to focus on what we intend to do when we make moral judgments, and also on how we express them. Moral judgments are intended to be accurate descriptions of the world, and statements express moral judgments (as opposed to command or prescription) just as statements express ordinary beliefs. That is, statements express moral language. The statements that express moral judgments are either true or false just as the statements that express ordinary beliefs are. Moral truths occur when our signs match the world.

Language allows us to communicate with one another, typically using sentences and utterances. A large part of language involves, among many other things, influencing others and us. Normative language, in contrast with descriptive language, includes moral language (that is, moral language is part of evaluative or normative language). It is even more important not to be swayed by moral language because moral reality grips us. It is bad that others try to deceive us, but it is worse that we deceive ourselves into accepting moral facts simply because of the language that we use. That is, moral language — if it is not to describe the world —must not be mistaken as descriptive. Moral language binds us in a certain manner, and the manner in which it binds us is important.

From this, must we then infer that there are entities like "moral goodness" and "obligation" to which moral language refers in the world? Are the three characteristics of structural similarity between moral and descriptive languages, the equal ease with which we employ them, and the logical interplay between them good enough reasons for thinking that there are moral facts? Is it not possible that our ways of influencing others and ourselves are exactly where syntax and semantics of our language betray us and, consequently, that moral language suffers from a lack of referents analogous to terms such as "nothing," the "present king of France," do?

Quasi-realists such as R. M. Hare, Gilbert Harman, and Simon Blackburn promise to set people free from the unduly rigid ontology of moral realism, namely, the existence of moral facts. Quasi-realism would allow people to enjoy the traditional realist comforts such as moral truths, moral knowledge, and moral objectivity, without the realists' baggage of commitments, theoretical burdens, and practical costs, or so they contend. It all sounds too good to be true, but such a possibility seems exciting: why insist on the existence of moral facts if all aspects of our moral practices, especially the realist-sounding ones, could be understood without the fact-multiplying realist ontology? Of course, the real question is this: is there anything significant that will be lost in our understanding of our moral practices if we were to settle for quasi-realism? A definite "yes" to the question has to be given, and we shall see why in this section.

The possibility that the quasi-realist extends to people is that quasi-realism poses no serious threat to the moral realist position. However, this quasi-realist contention— that by siding with quasi-realism nothing significant will be lost in our understanding of our moral practices—is simply mistaken. The quasi-realist loses some of the best explanations of events, states of affairs, and phenomena within the world: the quasi-realist must reject folk moral explanations. This is so, it will be argued, because the quasi-realist cannot accommodate folk moral explanations without reducing them to naturalistic explanations.

Intuitionism

The study of institutions has a long pedigree. It draws insights from previous work in a wide array of disciplines, including economics, political science, sociology, anthropology, and psychology. The reappearance of interest in institutions in the early 1980s followed a familiar pattern: it was a reaction to dominant strands of thought that neglected institutions, historical context, and process in favour of general theorizing. Accordingly, institutionalism is frequently characterized by the attention it gives to history. The institutionalism that emerged in the 1980s is called new institutionalism (NI), but it is less "new" than it is a restatement of previous scholarship. The following discussion traces the development of institutionalism from the 19th century to the emergence of NI in the last decades of the 20th century.

A full overview of the institutionalist tradition would go back to Aristotle's discussion of regime types (politeia). More recent interest in institutions emerged during the 19th century among the German historical economists (GHE), also called the institutional economists. Providing a critical response to the universal theories of the classical economists, these scholars disparaged deductive work, which they considered to be self-referential mathematical modeling. They argued that economic life is better understood through empirical work rather than through logical philosophy.

Their key insight was the need for historically and sociologically informed empirical analysis of reality. The earliest figure from this group was the German economist Wilhelm Roscher. His work insisted on the importance of context—historical, social, and institutional—for understanding the laws of political economy, economic behaviour, and the empirical diversity of social life. Early research focused on the relationship between the social and economic organization of society, stages of development, and evolutionary processes. Bitter conflicts with their Marxist contemporaries (followers of the theories of Karl Marx) notwithstanding, some scholars have come to see a close analytical affinity between the two traditions.

It is customary to divide the GHE into three generations: Early, Younger, and Last. The latter is noteworthy because it encapsulates some of the work of the German sociologist Max Weber, who was influenced by early GHE. Weber is perhaps the most influential modern institutionalist. Contemporary institutional works that posit institutions as an independent and non-epiphenomenal variable are indebted to Weber's theorizing a political realm that is autonomous from economics and ideas. In his discussion of the state and bureaucracy, he proposes a macrosociological theory of institutions.

Institutionalist insights are also present in Weber's theory of authority. For Weber, charismatic authority is inherently transient. As charisma exhausts itself and becomes routinized, traditional or rational-legal forms of authority take its place. With routinization, social relations and interactions become increasingly regular, predictable, and impersonal. Under modern capitalism, these take on a rational-legal form and become more extensive and elaborate. Some usages of the term institutionalization are thus a subset of Weber's process of routinization.

After World War II, institutionalism lost some of its prominence in the social sciences, displaced by theories focusing on social structures or individual behaviour. In the 1980s, however, research on social structures led to a revival of interest in institutions and the emergence of new institutionalism (NI). Theorists of comparative politics suggested that the state was autonomous and called for bringing the state back in as an explanatory variable. The study of institutions was significantly advanced with research in political economy on the state-led development of the Asian NIEs, as well as institutional reforms in the developed countries. Researchers also became increasingly interested in cross-national comparison of institutions, with a view to understanding the process of democratization. Finally, the global expansion of capitalism and European Union (EU) integration led to significant research demonstrating the role of institutions as intermediaries between structures and outcomes.

Some social scientists explicitly referenced earlier institutional works in their call for bringing institutions back in. This new body of work that came to be labelled NI sought to investigate among other things the interaction of society and institutions, the sources of institutional coherence, how historical processes lead to delayed outcomes, and non-utilitarian models of behaviour.

Utilitarianism

Utilitarianism is one of the best known and most influential moral theories. Like other forms of consequentialism, its core idea is that whether actions are morally right or wrong depends on their effects. More specifically, the only effects of actions that are relevant are the good and bad results that they produce. A key point in this article concerns the distinction between individual actions and types of actions. Act utilitarians focus on the effects of individual actions (such as John Wilkes Booth's assassination of Abraham Lincoln) while rule utilitarians focus on the effects of types of actions (such as killing or stealing).

Utilitarians believe that the purpose of morality is to make life better by increasing the amount of good things (such as pleasure and happiness) in the world and decreasing the amount of bad things (such as pain and unhappiness). They reject moral codes or systems that consist of commands or taboos that are based on customs, traditions, or orders given by leaders or supernatural beings. Instead, utilitarians think that what makes a morality be true or justifiable is its positive contribution to human (and perhaps non-human) beings.

The most important classical utilitarians are Jeremy Bentham (1748-1832) and John Stuart Mill (1806-1873). Bentham and Mill were both important theorists and social reformers. Their theory has had a major impact both on philosophical work in moral theory and on approaches to economic, political, and social policy. Although utilitarianism has always had many critics, there are many 21st century thinkers that support it.

The task of determining whether utilitarianism is the correct moral theory is complicated because there are different versions of the theory, and its supporters disagree about which version is correct. This article focuses on perhaps the most important dividing line among utilitarians, the clash between act utilitarianism and rule utilitarianism. After a brief overall explanation of utilitarianism, the article explains both act utilitarianism and rule utilitarianism, the main differences between them, and some of the key arguments for and against each view.

Utilitarianism is a philosophical view or theory about how we should evaluate a wide range of things that involve choices that people face. Among the things that can be evaluated are actions, laws, policies, character traits, and moral codes. Utilitarianism is a form of consequentialism because it rests on the idea that it is the consequences or results of actions, laws, policies, etc. that determine whether they are good or bad, right or wrong. In general, whatever is being evaluated, we ought to choose the one that will produce the best overall results. In the language of utilitarians, we should choose the option that "maximizes utility," i.e. that action or policy that produces the largest amount of good.

Utilitarianism appears to be a simple theory because it consists of only one evaluative principle: Do what produces the best consequences. In fact, however, the theory is complex because we cannot understand that single principle unless we know (at least) three things: (a) what things are good and bad; (b) whose good (i.e. which individuals or groups) we should aim to maximize; and (c) whether actions, policies, etc. are made right or wrong by their actual consequences (the results that our actions actually produce) or by their foreseeable consequences (the results that we predict will occur based on the evidence that we have).

Theories of Punishment

Each society has its own way of social control for which it frames certain laws and also mentions the sanctions with them. These sanctions are nothing but the punishments. 'The first thing to mention in relation to the definition of punishment is the ineffectiveness of definitional barriers aimed to show that one or other of the proposed justifications of punishments either logically include or logically excluded by definition.' Punishment has the following features:

- It involves the deprivation of certain normally recognized rights, or other measures considered unpleasant
- It is consequence of an offence
- It is applied against the author of the offence
- It is applied by an organ of the system that made the act an offence.

The kinds of punishment given are surely influenced by the kind of society one lives in. Though during ancient period of history punishment was more severe as fear was taken as the prime instrument in preventing crime. But with change in time and development of human mind the punishment theories have become more tolerant to these criminals. Debunking the stringent theories of punishment the modern society is seen in loosening its hold on the criminals. The present scenario also witnesses the opposition of capital punishment as inhumane, though it was a major form of punishing the criminals earlier. But it may also be observed till recently the TALIBANS used quite a harsh method for suppression. The law says that it does not really punish the individual but punishes the guilty mind.

As punishment generally is provided in Criminal Law it becomes imperative on our part to know what crime or an offence really is. Here the researcher would like to quote Salmond's definition of crime: Crime is an act deemed by law to be harmful for the society as a whole though its immediate victim may be an individual. He further substantiates his point of view through the following illustration a murderer injures primarily a particular victim, but its blatant disregard of human life puts it beyond a mater of mere compensation between the murderer and the victim's family.

Thus it becomes very important on behalf of the society to punish the offenders. Punishment can be used as a method of educing the incidence of criminal behavior either by deterring the potential offenders or by incapacitating and preventing them from repeating the offence or by reforming them into law-abiding citizens. Theories of punishment, contain generally policies regarding theories of punishment namely: Deterrent, Retributive, Preventive and Reformative.

Punishment, whether legal or divine, needs justification. Because the justification of legal punishment has been given greater consideration by philosophers than has the justification of divine punishment by theologians, the philosophical concepts and 'theories of punishment' (i.e. the justifications) will be used as a basis for considering divine punishment.

Many a time this punishment has been termed as a mode of social protection. The affinity of punishment with many other measures involving deprivation by the state morally recognized rights is generally evident. The justifiability of these measures in particular cases may well be controversial, but it is hardly under fire. The attempt to give punishment the same justification for punishment as for other compulsory measures imposed by the state does not necessarily involve a particular standpoint on the issues of deterrence, reform or physical incapacitation. Obviously the justification in terms of protection commits us to holding that punishment may be effective in preventing social harms through one of these methods.

As punishments generally punish the guilty mind it becomes very important on the part of the researcher to what crime really is. But it is quite difficult on the part of the researcher to say whether or not there must be any place for the traditional forms of punishment. In today's world the major question that is raised by most of the penologist is that how far are present 'humane' methods of punishment like the reformative successful in their objective. It is observed that prisons have become a place for breeding criminals not as a place of reformation as it was meant to be.

It may be clearly said that the enactment of any law brings about two units in the society- the law-abiders and the law-breakers. It is purpose of these theories of punishment to by any means transform or change these law-breakers to the group of abiders. To understand the topic the researcher would like to bring about a valid relation between crime, punishment and the theories.

For that purpose the project is divided into three parts:

• Crime and Punishment • Theories of punishment • Conclusion

The researcher due to certain constraints of limited time and knowledge is unable to cove the area of the evolution of these theories separately but would include them in the second chapter. The researcher would now like to move on to his first chapter in which he would be vividly discussing 'crime and punishment.'

One can surely observe how closely are crime and punishment related. The researcher would in this chapter precisely like to stress on this point itself.

Crime is behaviour or action that is punishable by criminal law. A crime is a public, as opposed to a moral, wrong; it is an offence committed against (and hence punishable by) the state or the community at large. Many crimes are immoral, but not all actions considered immoral are illegal.

In different legal systems the forms of punishment may be different but it may be observed that all arise out of some action or omission. All these constitute all moral as well as legal wrongs such as murder, rape, littering, theft, trespass and many more. As crime is quite different in different geographical area it is quite evident that the forms of punishment would vary as it was mentioned earlier that punishment as well as crime are socially determined. A type of action may be a crime in one society but not in another. For example euthanasia is an offence in India, but in many European countries such as Holland it is legalized. But there are certain offences which are recognized almost universally like murder.

Durkheim explains crime, as crime exists in every society which do and do not have laws, courts and the police. He asserts that all societies have crime, since all societies involve a differentiation between two kinds of actions, those that are allowed and those that are forbidden. He calls the latter type criminal.

Law is the string that binds society, and he who attempts to break the string is a danger to the society as a whole and dealt with sternly by the powerful arms of law. Punishment though most times confused with imprisonment is something much different from it. Punishment though most times confused only with sanctions may also be of moral nature like ostracism. Punishment, whether legal or divine, needs justification. Because the justification of legal punishment has been given greater consideration by philosophers than has the justification of divine punishment by theologians, the philosophical concepts and 'theories of punishment, (i.e. the justifications) will be used as a basis for considering divine punishment.

A complete definition will now be made in such a way as to include both legal and divine punishment. A. Flew first suggests that punishment must be an evil, an unpleasantness to the victim. J. Mabbot objects to the use of the word 'evil' in connection with punishment. He maintains that 'evil' carries too much moral flavour and also that it suggests positive suffering. Mabbot states: The world is a worse place the more evil there is in it and perhaps the more suffering. But it does not seem to me necessarily a worse place whenever men are deprived of something they would like to retain; and this is the essence of modern punishment. While deprivation may be a more appropriate description of modern punishment this does not necessarily exempt it from being an evil. Nor does the suggestion that 'evil' carries a moral flavour, for in fact the word punishment itself carries a moral flavour. (Like 'evil', punishment is not in itself a moral term but it is suggested that it usually occurs in an ethical context.) While we must eventually come to some conclusion as to whether punishment is an evil, it would be preferable at present to use, as does W. Moberly, the slightly more neutral term 'ill'.

Both of these thinkers of punishment believe that the offender must be answerable for any wrong that he has done. K. Baier explains punishment as law-making, penalisation, finding guilty, pronouncing a sentence. In a legal context law-making is a necessary condition, but it is possible to commit a wrongdoing intentionally although no law has been made, in fact it is because certain acts are considered wrong that laws are made in the first place. What is important to note is that punishment is a conditional act and cannot be isolated from its total context.

But Durkhaeim has a different approach to punishment altogether. He treats punishment as the reaction of the society against a crime. According to him a if punishment be a proportionate response to the harm caused to the society then the extent of the punishment inflicted must be clearly sorted out. He also stressed on the point that punishment can never be calculated; it is an intensely emotional- sense of outrage- the desire to exact punishment. He says, It is not the specific nature or result of the offending action as such which matter, but he fact that the action transgresses widely shared ad strongly held sentiments, whatever these might be in any particular case. He explains that if punishment is a reaction of the society against the offenders then it is generally in the form of an outrage or anger thus rather being reparative or reformative becomes punitive. This approach of the society towards the criminals is what makes us treat them as outcasts and treated as an deviant from the social norms. This two-fold approach has been criticized severely by various penologists, as at one time there is the use of both reformative and retributive theories.

Punishment and crime are very strange phenomena to deal with. It is only if the acts done are within the course of the provisions provided under the Code then any benefits take out of it is not questioned. But any action through which maybe the same benefit is gained still the person may be punished as because his action was not within the scope of the provisions. Also there are certain elements in the society who though do many immoral acts but as because any provisions or sanctions are not mentioned so that they can be punished they continue to do that act. One should not earn any benefits or satisfaction out of such acts.

The legitimacy of any form of has always been criticized. Though there are many legal coercive measures but it is quite different from punishment. If the punishment were any retribution to an evil done then regardless of any consequence it would try to end that evil in itself. But if the objective of the punishment given is to prevent the crime from further occurrence then it would rather than using coercive methods it would be using persuasive measures and discourage the offender from committing that act in the future. Treating punishment as a conventional device for the expression of resentment, indignation, disappointment felt either by the sufferer and his family or the punishing authority as such J.Feinberg argues that certain kinds of severe treatment become symbolic of the of the attitudes and judgement of the society or community in the face of the wrongdoing, and constitute a stigma which castes shame and ignominy on the individual on whom the punishment is applied. The distinctiveness of the unpleasant measure could consist of the way of executing them. Thus, summarizing the concept of punishment one can suggest that punishment includes the following areas:

- Punishment inflicted is a feeling of uncomfortable and unpleasant circumstances.
- It is a sequel of a wrongful act.
- There must be some relationship between the punishment inflicted and the crime committed.
- The punishment is a form by which a criminal is made answerable to the society.

Theories of Punishment

With change in the social structure the society has witnessed various punishment theories and the radical changes that they have undergone from the traditional to the modern level and the crucial problems relating to them. Kenny wrote: "it cannot be said that the theories of criminal punishment current amongst our judges and legislators have assumed...."either a coherent or even a stable form. B.Malinowski believes all the legally effective institutions....are....means of cutting short an illegal or intolerable state of affairs, of restoring the equilibrium in the social life and of giving the vent to he feelings of oppression and injustice felt by the individuals.

The general view that the researcher finds is that the researcher gathers is that the theories of punishment being so vague are difficult to discuss as such. In the words of Sir John Salmond, "The ends of criminal justice are four in number, and in respect to the purposes served by the them punishment can be divided as:

1. Deterrent
2. Retributive
3. Preventive
4. Reformative

Of these aspects the first is the essential and the all-important one, the others being merely accessory. Punishment before all things is deterrent, and the chief end of the law of crime is to make the evil-doer an example and a warning to all that are like-minded with him.

The researcher in this chapter would like to discuss the various theories and explain the pros and cons of each theory. The researcher's main aim in this chapter is to show the evolution of the theories as such.

One of the primitive methods of punishments believes in the fact that if severe punishments were inflicted on the offender would deter him form repeating that crime. Those who commit a crime, it is assumed, derive a mental satisfaction or a feeling of enjoyment in the act. To neutralize this inclination of the mind, punishment inflicts equal quantum of suffering on the offender so that it is no longer attractive for him to carry out such committal of crimes. Pleasure and pain are two physical feelings or sensation that nature has provided to mankind, to enable him to do certain things or to desist from certain things, or to undo wrong things previously done by him. It is like providing both a powerful engine and an equally powerful brake in the automobile. Impelled by taste and good appetite, which are feelings of pleasure a man over-eats. Gluttony and surfeit make him obese and he starts suffering disease. This causes pain. He consults a doctor and thereafter starts dieting . Thus the person before eating in the same way would think twice and may not at all take that food. In social life punishment introduces the element of 'pain' to correct the excess action of a person carried out by the impulse (pleasure) of his mind. We all like very much to seize opportunities, but abhor when we face threats. But in reality pain, threat or challenges actually strengthens and purifies a man and so an organization.

J. Bentham, as the founder of this theory, states:

"General prevention ought to be the chief end of punishment as its real justification. If we could consider an offence, which has been, committed as an isolated fact, thė like of which would never recur, punishment would be useless. It would only be only adding one evil to another. But when we consider that an unpunished crime leaves the path of crime open, not only to the same delinquent but also to all those who may have the same motives and opportunities for entering upon it, we perceive that punishment inflicted on the individual becomes a source of security for all. That punishment which considered in itself appeared base and repugnant to all generous sentiments is elevated to the first rank of benefits when it is regarded not as an act of wrath or vengeance against a guilty or unfortunate individual who has given way to mischievous inclinations, but as an indispensable sacrifice to the common safety."

Bentham's theory was based on a hedonistic conception of man and that man as such would be deterred from crime if punishment were applied swiftly, certainly, and severely. But being aware that punishment is an evil, he says, If the evil of punishment exceeds the evil of the offence, the punishment will be unprofitable; he will have purchased exemption from one evil at the expense of another.

The basic idea of deterrence is to deter both offenders and others from committing a similar offence. But also in Bentham's theory was the idea that punishment would also provide an opportunity for reform.

"While a person goes on seeking pleasure, he also takes steps to avoid pain. This is a new system of political philosophy and ethics developed by Jerome Bentham and John Stuart Mill in the 19th century called Utilitarianism. It postulates human efforts towards "maximization of pleasure and maximum minimization of pain" as the goal. "The main ethical imperative of utilitarianism is: the greatest good for the largest number of people; or the greatest number of goods for the greatest number of people" The fear of consequent punishment at the hands of law should act as a check from committing crimes by people. The law violator not merely gets punishment, but he has to undergo an obnoxious process like arrest, production before a magistrate, trial in a criminal court etc. that bring about a social stigma to him as the accused. All these infuse a sense fear and pain and one thinks twice before venturing to commit a crime, unless he is a hard-core criminal, or one who has developed a habit for committing crimes. Deterrent theory believes in giving exemplary punishment through adequate penalty."

In earlier days a criminal act was considered to be due to the influence of some evil spirit on the offender for which he was unwillingly was made to do that wrong. Thus to correct that offender the society reto ed to severe deterrent policies and forms of the government as this wrongful act was take as an challenge to the God and the religion.

But in spite of all these efforts there are some lacunae in this theory. This theory is unable to deter the activity of the hard-core criminals as the pain inflicted or even the penalties are ineffective. The most mockery of this theory can be seen when the criminals return to the prisons soon after their release, that is precisely because as this theory is based on certain restrictions, these criminals are not effected at all by these restrictions rather they tend to enjoy these restrictions more than they enjoy their freedom.

Preventive Theory

Unlike the former theories, this theory aims to prevent the crime rather then avenging it. Looking at punishments from a more humane perspective it rests on the fact that the need of a punishment for a crime arises out of mere social needs i.e. while sending the criminals to the prisons the society is in turn trying to prevent the offender from doing any other crime and thus protecting the society from any antisocial elements.

Fitchte in order to explain this in greater details puts forward the an illustration, An owner of the land puts an notice that 'trespassers' would be prosecuted. He does not want an actual trespasser and to have the trouble and expense of setting the law in motion against him. He hopes that the threat would render any such action unnecessary; his aim is not to punish trespass but to prevent it. But if trespass still takes place he undertakes prosecution. Thus the instrument which he devised originally consist of a general warning and not any particular convictions.

Thus it must be quite clear now by the illustration that the law aims at providing general threats but not convictions at the beginning itself. Even utilitarian such as Bentham have also supported this theory as it has been able to discourage the criminals from doing a wrong and that also without performing any severity on the criminals. The present day prisons are fallout of this theory. The preventive theory can be explained in the context of imprisonment as separating the criminals from the society and thus preventing any further crime by that offender and also by putting certain restrictions on the criminal it would prevent the criminal from committing any offence in the future. Supporters of this theory may also take Capital Punishment to be a part of this theory. A serious and diligent rehabilitation program would succeed in turning a high percentage of criminals away from a life of crime. There are, however, many reasons why rehabilitation programs are not commonly in effect in our prisons. Most politicians and a high proportion of the public do not believe in rehabilitation as a desirable goal. The idea of rehabilitation is considered mollycoddling. What they want is retribution, revenge, punishment and suffering.

Thus one an easily say that preventive theory though aiming at preventing the crime to happen in the future but it still has some aspects which are questioned by the penologists as it contains in its techniques which are quite harsh in nature. The major problem with these type of theories is that they make the criminal more violent rather than changing him to a better individual. The last theory of punishment being the most humane of all looks into this aspect.

Emotivism

Emotivism is no longer a view of ethics that has many supporters. Like subjectivism it teaches that there are no objective moral facts, and that therefore 'murder is wrong' can't be objectively true.

Emotivists teach that:

- Moral statements are meaningless.

This means that the first half of the statement 'it was wrong to murder Fred' adds nothing to the non-moral information that Fred has been murdered.

- Moral statements only express the speaker's feelings about the issue.

Later emotivists added this idea to Emotivism:

- By expressing the speaker's feelings about a moral issue moral statements may influence another person's thoughts and conduct.

In Emotivism a moral statement isn't literally a statement about the speaker's feelings on the topic, but expresses those feelings with emotive force.

When an emotivist says 'murder is wrong' it's like saying 'down with murder' or 'murder, yecch!' or just saying 'murder' while pulling a horrified face, or making a thumbs-down gesture at the same time as saying 'murder is wrong'.

The reasons why some philosophers thought this are technical - they thought that ethical statements could not be converted into statements that could be empirically tested, and thus failed the verifiability criterion of meaning - which meant that they were meaningless.

Emotivism pays close attention to the way in which people use language and acknowledges that a moral judgement expresses the attitude that a person takes on a particular issue. It's like shouting "hurray", or pulling a face and going "ugh".

That's why this theory is called Emotivism, because it's based on the emotive effect of moral language.

Perspectivism

Perspectivism is the philosophical position that one's access to the world through perception, experience, and reason is possible only through one's own perspective and interpretation. It rejects both the idea of a perspective-free or an interpretation-free objective reality.

In visual perception, the appearance of an object changes according to a viewer's relative position to the object. This human experience was developed in philosophy as perspectivism. Although Leibniz integrated this view into his philosophy, it was Nietzschewho fully developed it. His perspectivism challenged the entire history of Western philosophy, including the thoughts of Plato, Descartes, and Kant.

Nietzsche explicated this perspectival or interpretive nature of human existence and attempted to justify the richness of the world that his perspectivism can depict. He shifted traditional questions of epistemology into the realms of axiology, aesthetics, and his unique philosophy of life. After Nietzsche, perspectivism has been taken up in phenomenology, postmodernism, and others. Perspectivism also highlighted the irreplaceable unique value of each individual and the value of differences and diversity.

Perspective, in the context of vision and visual perception, is the way in which objects appear to the eye based on their spatial attributes, or their dimensions and the position of the eye relative to the objects.

As objects become more distant, they appear smaller, because their angular diameter (visual angle) decreases. The visual angle of an object is the angle subtended at the eye by a triangle with the object at its base. The further the height of this triangle, the distance of the object from the eye, the less the visual angle. This follows simply from Euclidean geometry.

The Sun and the Moon appear to be roughly the same size because the Sun, although much, much larger, is also much farther away. The relationship between distance and apparent height of objects is not a linear pattern. If an object were actually touching the eye, thus being no distance away, it would appear infinitely tall.

In our everyday life, a round table does not generally appear as round but as an oval. A rectangular table also appears to us not as a perfect rectangle but, rather, as a diamond-like shape. We seldom see a round table as a perfect circle or a rectangular table as rectangular. Although the appearances of the table are not round or rectangular, we understand the table to be round or rectangular. To see the table as round or rectangular, we need to see it from a particular point of view. When we identify the table as round or rectangular regardless of the variety of its appearances, we tacitly give a particular vantage point to the point of view to which a round or rectangular shape is presented.

Non-perspectivist philosophers such as Plato, Descartes, Kant, and others presupposed the existence of objective reality (Ideas for Plato; objective world for Descartes; thing-in-itself for Kant) and contrasted it with the variety of appearances we experience. The philosophical quest for the one self-identical, unchanging reality is thus accompanied by cognitive powers and conditions of human beings, which allow them to see this reality. Perspectivism rejects these presuppositions held by such philosophers. It rejects the idea of the existence of an unchanging, self-identical objective reality and any privileged cognitive capacity of human beings such as reason.

Descriptivism

The Description Theory of names (a.k.a. descriptivism) says that each name N has the semantic value of some definite description 'the F'. For instance, 'Aristotle' might have the semantic value of 'the teacher of Alexander the Great'. As stated, this view is consistent with Millianism (it would be Millianism if we assumed that the semantic value of a definite description was the individual it referred to), however in practice it is always coupled with a view on which definite descriptions have either a Russellian (see the section on Russell's theory in the entry on descriptions) or an intensional semantics (see the section on Sense Theories above). In the latter case, descriptivism corresponds to the intensional interpretation of Frege's sense theory. It should be noted that Montague's (1973) treatment of names as denoting higher-order functions (i.e., quantifier denotations) does not belong under this heading. It was adopted for reasons of type consilience, rather than descriptivist intuitions. Moreover, his first meaning postulate imposes an intensionally rigid (see the next section) interpretation on names.

Russell is thc carliest proponent of the Description Theory (see Sainsbury 1993 for a dissenting view). He applied it to ordinary, but not what he called "logically proper" names (the latter were in fact demonstratives like 'this' and 'that', and he gave them a Millian semantics). In conjunction with his semantics for definite descriptions, he used the theory to solve the puzzles mentioned in the last section, without resorting to a two-tiered semantic theory (see Sense Theories above). 'The Morning Star' and 'the Evening Star' (as well as 'Atlantis' and 'El Dorado') might correspond in semantic value to different definite descriptions, and so would make different semantic contributions to the sentences in which they occur (semantic contribution must, as on the sense theory, be connected with cognitive significance, if Russellian descriptivism is to answer Frege's puzzle). Moreover, a thinker can often be acquainted (on Russell's view) with the property F in the semantic value of the corresponding description where they cannot be acquainted with the individual the name refers to.

Famous deeds descriptivism is exemplified by the interpretation of 'Aristotle' as 'the teacher of Alexander the Great'. Note that the latter description also contains a proper name, which will in turn be interpreted as a definite description. The hope is that this description will not mention Aristotle, and indeed that ultimately every description will bottom out in irreducible predicates (or "logically proper" names) rather than entering a loop (which would mean that we have not specified, only constrained, the semantic values in question). Like many exercises of this sort, this translation has never been carried out.

Tyler Burge (1973) finds support for the metalinguistic view in non-argumental occurrences of names, which often take on a metalinguistic interpretation, as in:

- There are relatively few Alfreds in Princeton.
- There are relatively few Picassos at the Met.

Burge overcomes the problem of the impropriety of the metalinguistic description by treating names used as arguments as complex demonstratives, so he is properly speaking a "demonstrativist."

Metalinguistic descriptivism is commonly presented in a package with the view that proper rominals (see Syntax above) are metalinguistic predicates (so the nominal 'Alfred' is a predicate true of individuals that are so called). The latter view accounts for on its metalinguistic interpretation, and provides a compositional analysis of proper names consisting of 'the' followed by a proper nominal as metalinguistic definite descriptions. An unvoiced definite article must be posited for proper names that do not carry one overtly, so that all proper names, under analysis, resemble those of Modern Greek (a less remarked-upon fact about Modern Greek is that the definite article also shows up between demonstrative and nominal in complex demonstratives).

Compositional metalinguistic analyses of names have recently been defended by linguists and philosophers. Nevertheless, considerable obstacles remain for such analyses and for the general treatment of proper nominals as metalinguistic predicates. Most straightforwardly, it is not strictly speaking true to say that the Raritan River is called Raritan, or that the Bronx is named Bronx. Nor is a Bronx resident a resident called Bronx, but rather one who resides in the Bronx. Even worse difficulties crop up for views that attempt to analyze the meaning of a nominal like 'George Washington Bridge' as the intersection of the meanings of its component nouns.

UNIT 5

CONTEMPORARY INDIAN PHILOSOPHY

VIVEKANANDA

Swami Vivekananda was a spiritual leader and chief exponent of Vedanta philosophy. He was born of a well-to-do family in Calcutta and his given name was Narendra Nath Datta. As a young man he met Ramakrishna and thereafter devoted himself completely to his teachings. After Ramakrishnan's death in 1886, he traveled throughout India as a wandering monk. In 1893 he went to United States where he represented Hinduism at the World Parliament of Religions in Chicago. After four years of teaching in the west he returned to India where he organized the Ramakrishna Mission and engaged in a strenuous campaign to encourage a national renaissance.

India has produced a number of geniuses in education, science, literature, politics and spiritual regeneration. On of the greatest among them is Swami Vivekananda. He was the embodiment of the spirit of the country and also a symbol of its spiritual aspiration and fulfillment. Swamiji has a unique place in the history of India. He was a spiritual teacher who taught "Work is Worship". He taught humanity, a philosophy which combines external action in a spirit of service for the enrichment of society, with internal action for the spiritual enrichment of the individuals. In the language of Bhagavat Gita, Karma and Jnana, action and inaction became one. This question is the essence of Swami Vivekananda's spiritual message.

Everywhere he taught man to realize his divine heritage. The innate divinity of man was the constant theme of all his teachings. He held that spirituality is the core of every religion. The more spiritual a man the more universal he is. Swamiji concentrated his attention on the essence religion and not on the superficial like habits and customs. Swamiji says "religion is a matter of personal experience and realization. Religion is a realization, no talk, nor doctrines nor theories.

Swami Vivekananda, in accordance with our ancient scriptures and traditions advocated four important methods of God realization which are of universal application irrespective of religion. They are the four Yoga's namely- karma, Jnana, Bhakthi and Raja Yogas.

Swami Vivekananda classifies all the people in the world into four categories, they are

1. The active who wants to work. He follows the path of Karmayoga.
2. The emotional man who follows the path of Bhakthiyoga.
3. The mystic who wants to analyze his own mind and discipline. He follows the path of Raja yoga.
4. The philosopher whose mind wants to weigh everything and use his intellect to know the truth follows the path of Jnanayoga.

Four paths are however mutually exclusive but overlaps each other. But the universal religion of Viveknanada's conception will comprise all the above 4 paths as well as the religious practices. He does not indicate any particular method of faith as superior. Every one can follow his own path without prejudice or hatred towards others.

Freedom

Vivekananda accepts karmayogins to practice nivritti marga and not pravritti marga. The pravritti marga or ordinary life leads us to attachment and bondage whereas the former which is the action of self denial and self sacrifice leads one to self abnegation and detachment from his empirical self, will easily help to attain self realization or God realization.

Vivekananda accepts with samkhya that nature is composed of three forces namely satva, rajas and tamas. In every man there are these forces in varying equilibrium. Karma yoga deals with these forces.

Vivekananda calls Buddha and Christ as the "second rate heroes" because they were the men with move(rajas) and inactivity who takes up the ideas of perfect ones and preach them to the world.

The Spiritual Nature of Man

The uniqueness of his physical nature is also due to the presence of spirituality in him. Vivekananda describes the true nature of man is soul force or Atman. Atman has essentially two characters. Firstly, this aspect of man is similar to divine nature and secondly it is not possible for us to give an exact description of this aspect of man. They are basically identical and that their difference is only apparent. Vivekananda tries to explain the difference between soul's real nature and its nature in various ways.

Vivekananda presents some of the conclusions of the speculation and philosophic inquiry of ideas about Atman. The different philosophies seem to agree that this Atman has neither form nor shape and hence is omnipresent spirit.

Vivekananda's Concept of Man

He says that an ideal society can be established only when man realizes his real nature. The picture of man that emerges in the philosophy of Vivekananda is an organized unity of the physical and the spiritual. Man is a spirit. But Vivekanada never undermines the importance of the physical nature of man. The very fact that man is always asked to awaken his spirituality, presupposes that there is a side of man that is some what different from and yet akin to his spiritual nature. That is his physical nature.

Vivekananda believes that even in his physical capacitics man is superior to other beings because his physical nature is better organized and exhibits a greater unity. The presence of the brain system in the body distinguishes man from every other species and gives him a unique status in the world.

Practical Vedanta

As a philosopher Vivekananda's main contribution lies in his attempt to present Advaita Vedanta in an intelligible, concrete, scientific and practical form. Vivekananda, the stormy messenger of Indian spiritualism was the first effective expound of the Vedanta in the modern age. In a lecture at Harward he described the main of his machinery efforts. The abstract Advaita he said must became living, poetic in our everyday life. Out of the hopeless intricate mythology must comes concrete moral forms and out of bewildering yogism must come the most scientific and practical psychology. He points out the basic strength of Vedanta as

1. Vedanta adheres to the fundamental principles on which a sound philosophy should be based. He explains the particular through the general and moves on to the universal.
2. The Vedanta is routed in the great idea, the ideal of magnificent harmony. The idea of oneness of all of the infinite and impersonal, the wonderful idea of the eternal soul of man of the unborn continuity in the march of things of the infinity of the universe.

The first of these tribute paid to Vedanta is a philosophers tribute while the second is poet's tribute. In the first Vivekananda speaks in terms of rational criteria. In the second he expresses his fascination for an idea rather than a system of thought. This is the characteristic of his approach which is logical and more than logical.

3. Vivekananda mentions a third and strong point of Vedanta, that is its universality and objectivity. Vedanta consists of eternal principle which has their own foundation without depending upon the authority of persons or incarnations. The sanction of Vedanta is the eternal of man. Its ethics are based upon the eternal spiritual solidity of man, already attained. Here Vivekananda is speaking in the context of the Indian tradition in which philosophy and religion have not been sharply demarcated from each other.

Universal Religion

The Swami made a distinct and notable contribution to world religion in his championship of Hinduism as a universal gospel of ethical humanism and spiritual idealism. Hinduism had been the subject of intense misrepresentation at the hands of Christian missionaries who suffered from 'imperialism complex' and were actuated with a sense of burden to 'civilize' the black men and brown men by clearing the road for the economic exploitation of Asia and Africa. But Hinduism was, to Vivekānanda, a comprehensive gospel which could shelter within its bosom the profound philosophic intellect by its Nyaya, Samkhya and Vedanta, could offer to the psychologist its vast store of psychic wisdom of the Rajayoga, could inspire the devotee with the enchanted hymns of the Samaveda and the devotional songs of Tulsidas or of the Alvaras and Naynars (saints of the South), and finally could give to the puissant and hectic worker the doctrine of selfless action as enunciated in the celestial song of Sri Krishna.

He defined religion as the vital and moral force which gives strength to a person or to a nation. In thundering words, he said, "Strength is life, weakness is death". Jawaharlal Nehru in his The Discovery of India had pointed out that the great refrain of Vivekānanda's teaching was abhayam (fearlessness). The Mundakopanished says, "Nāmamātmā balahinena labhyah" Vivekananda wanted to make a harmonious fusion of the Kshatriya manhood and Brahman intellectualism. He shunned all weakening mysteries. Melamed in his book Spinoza and Buddha wants to differentiate between Hebraism and Hinduism and says that the former is individualistic, theistic, optimistic and presents an anthropocentric view of the world. As distinct from it, the latter is universalistic, pessimistic, cosmocentric and world-negating. Mauryan imperialism and Maratha polity were not vague sentimentalists. Vivekāṇanda, although a monist, always stood for a vigorous and valiant action in the secular sphere and heroically inculcated that absolute bravery and firm bold faith could shake history.

Vivekānanda was a representative of entire Hinduism from the Vedas to Vaisanavism. He did not emphasize the Samhitas of the Veda to the same extent as did the late Swami Dayananda. He was impressed greatly by the Jñānakānda of the Upanishads. The universalism of Vivekananda reminded one of the catholic culture of Asoka. He had been brought up under the influence of his teacher Ramkrishna whose whole personality was a demonstration and vindication of the inherent spiritual truth in all the various religions. The Swami partly introduced once more the practice of proselytism in Hinduism which was falling into oblivion. Hindus did not mean to him the cluster of obscure cults and ritualistic superstitions, orthodox dogmas and primitive ceremonialism which, unfortunately, the European critic is very keen in observing, but it signified to him a body of moral and spiritual injunctions and primordial supertemporal laws for the uplift of humanity.

Views of Vivekananda

The Vedas Views on Hindus

The Vedas teach that the soul is divine, only held in the bondage of matter; perfection will be reached, when this bond will burst and the word they use for it is therefore, Mukti-freedom, freedom from the bonds of imperfection, freedom from death and misery.

So, far all the Hindus are agreed. This the common religion of all the sects of India; but, then, perfection is absolute and the absolute cannot be two or three. It cannot have any qualities. It cannot be an individual. We have often and often read this called the losing of individuality and becoming a stock or a stone.

Therefore, to gain this infinite universal individuality, this miserable little individuality must go. Then alone can death cease, when I am one with life, then alone can misery cease, when I am one with happiness itself, then alone can all errors cease, when I am one with knowledge itself and this is the necessary scientific conclusion. Science has proved to me that physical individuality is a delusion, that really my body is one little continuously changing body in an unbroken ocean of matter and Advaita (unity) is the necessary conclusion with my other counter part, soul.

Science is nothing, but the finding of unity. As soon as science would reach perfect unity, it would stop from further progress, because it would reach the goal. Physics would stop, when it would be able to fulfil its services in discovering one energy of which all the others are, but manifestations and the science of religion become perfect, when it would discover him who is the one life in a universe of death, him who is the constant basis of an ever-changing world.

The Hindus have associated the idea of holiness, purity, truth, omnipresence and such other ideas with different images and forms. But with this difference, while some people devote their whole lives to their idol of a church and never rise higher, because with them religion means an intellectual assent to certain doctrines and doing good to their follows, the whole religion of the Hindu is centred in realisation.

Vivekananda's Views on God

He is everywhere, the pure and formless one, the Almighty and the All-merciful. "Thou art our father, thou art our mother, thou art our beloved friend thou art the source of all strength; give us strength. Thou art, he that brethren the burdens of the universe, help me bear the little burden of this life."

Reality View

Reality is one, but is apprehended differently and act to Vivekananda, natures are different, so understand reality differently, but reality is one. Every religion is only evolving a God out of the material man and the same God is the inspirer of all of them.

It is the same talking of different interpretations light coming through glasses of different colours. And these little variations are necessary for purposes of adaptation. But in the heart of everything the same truth regions. One thing more. How, then can the Hindu, whose whole fabric of thought centres in God, believe in Buddhism which is agnostic or in Jainism which is atheistic?

Vivekananda's Views on Hinduism

Swami Vivekananda says that "As the different streams having their sources in different place all mingle their water in the sea, so, O Lord, the different paths which men take through different tendencies, various though they appear, crooked or straight, all lead to Thee." There is only one God.

The Hindus received their religion through revelation, the Vedas. They hold that the Vedas are without beginning and without end. It may sound ludicrous to his audience, how a book can be without beginning or end. But by the Vedas no books are meant.

The Hindu believes that he is a spirit. Him the sword cannot pierce him the fire cannot burn him the water cannot melt him the air cannot dry. The Hindu believes that every soul is a circle, whose circumference is nowhere, but whose centre is located in the body and that death means the change of this centre from body to body. Nor is the soul bound by the conditions of matter. In its very essence it is free, unbounded, holy, pure and perfect. But somehow or other it finds itself tied down to matter and thinks of itself as matter.

I am a Hindu. I am sitting in my own little well and thinking that the whole world is my little well. The Christian sits in his little well and thinks the whole world is his well. I have to thank you of America for the great attempt your are making to break down the barriers of this little world of ours and hope that, in the future, the Lord will help you to accomplish your purpose.

The present convention, which is one of the most August assemblies ever held, is itself a vindication. It is declaration to the world of the wonderful doctrine preached in whichever path, your will take, your will reach to same reality, the Gita.

Vivekananda's Views on Human Soul

The human soul is eternal and immortal, perfect and infinite and death means only a change of centre from one body to another. But here is another questions. Is man a tiny goat in a tempest, raised one moment on the foamy crest of a billow and dashed down into a yawning chasm the next, rolling to and fro at the mercy of good and bad actions—a powerless, helpless wreck in an ever-raging, ever-rushing, uncompromising current of cause and effect; a little moth placed under the wheel of causation which rolls on crushing everything in its way and waits not for the widow's tears or the orphan's cry? The heart sinks at the idea, yet this is the law of nature.

It reached the throne of mercy and words of hope and consolation came down and inspired a Vedic sage and he stood up before the world and in trumpet voice proclaimed the glad tidings: "Children of immortal bliss' '—what a sweet, what a hopeful name! Allow me to call you, brethren, by the sweet name—heirs of immortal bliss—yea, the Hindu refuses to call your sinners. They are the children of God, the shares of immortal bliss, holy and perfect beings. Come up. 0 lions and shake off the delusion that your are sheep; your are souls immortal, spirits free, blest and eternal; the are not matter, the are not bodies; matter is your servant, not your the servant of matter.

Vivekananda's Views on Immortality of Soul

The Swami starts by quoting that in Bhagwad Gita: "None has power to destroy the unchangeable". In Mahabbarata, Yama Raj asks Yudhisthira: "What is the most wonderful thing within this world." Yudhisthira replied "It is the belief of mankind in their own deathlessness despite witnessing death around every moment." The swami says". ...man is thoroughly persuaded that he cannot die".

The Swami notes "The body is dying every minute. The mind is constantly changing. ..But beyond this momentary sheathing of gross matter.., is the Atman, the true self of man permanent,.. ever-free". Not the body, not the mind, the Atman is the real man, the fearless one, the deathless one, the free.

Swami find that although soul is seen in a higher level, the importance of body and mind gets unnecessarily severe relegation as if they are non-entities! According to Vivekananda, it happens in spiritual discourses only. Secondly, he talks about human souls alone, ignoring other living things, make us highly anthropocentric, elevating man to a near-godly pedestal, unfairly ignoring other living creatures altogether.

In Hinduism, soul goes with reincarnation only. In some other religions soul is conceived, but reincarnation is not visualised. The Swamiji begins the chapter by citing from Gita. "Both your and I have passed through many births. You know them not, I know them all. Swamiji says, that man has faced many mysteries from the dawn of history.

Swami states; "Of all the theories that have been held by man about himself, that of a soul entity, separate from the body and immortal, has been the most widespread". The concept of soul depends only on the nature of the religion we are taking about.

The Swamiji says, that Hinduism is the first religion in the world to talk about a permanent and independent soul. The Aryans believed in the impermanence of the body and the permanence of the soul. The body was therefore, not kept indefinitely, but was at once cremated.

The Babylonians, they say that the Assyrians and the Chaldeans believed in a soul almost the way of the Egyptians. The soul was not free to got to other body entities. The ancient Hebrews did not bother with the idea of a soul and for them death was a complete end.

Swami Vivekananda on Maya Concept

He talks about the meaning of Maya. According to him, it is regarded as a contradiction of our intellect. He says that, Maya is not a theory for the explanation of our world'. It is regarded as a statement of facts. It refers only the basis of contradiction. There is neither a how nor why, we only know that it is and that we cannot help it. Even to grasp it, to draw an exact image of it in our minds is beyond our power Thus, it cannot be solved

Speech of Vivekananda on Buddhism : The Fulfilment of Hinduism

I am not a Buddhist, as you have heard and yet I am. If China or Japan or Ceylon follow the teachings of the Great Master, India worships him as God incarnate on Earth. Your have just now heard that I am going to criticise Buddhism, but by that I wish you to understand only this.

The relation between Hinduism (by Hinduism, I mean the religion of the Vedas) and what is called Buddhism at the present day is nearly the same as between Judaism and Christianity. Jesus Christ was a Jew and Shakya Muni was a Hindu. The Jews rejected Jesus Christ, may crucified him and the Hindus have accepted Shakya Muni as God and worship him.

The Religious Ideas

A short sketch of the religious ideas of the Hindus is discussed. The Hindu may have failed to carry out all his plans. Which will be infinite like the God, it will preach and whose Sun will shine upon the followers of Krishna and of Christ, on saints and sinners alike, which will not be Brahminic or Buddhistic, Christian or Mohammedan.

The sum total of all these and still have infinite space for development, which in its catholicity will embrace in its infinite arms and find a place for, every human being, from the lowest grovelling savage not far removed from the brute, to the highest man towering by the virtues of his head and heart almost above humanity, making society stand in awe of him and doubt his human nature.

It will be a religion, which will have no place for persecution or intolerance in its polity. But at the same time, Brahmanism lost something reforming real, wonderful sympathy and charity for everybody, wonderful leaven, which Buddhism had brought to the masses and which had rendered Indian society so great that a Greek historian who wrote about India of that time was led to say that no Hindu woman was known to be unchaste.

Hinduism cannot live without Buddhism, nor Buddhism without Hinduism. This separation between the Buddhists and the Brahmins is the cause of the downfall of India. That is why India is populated by three hundred millions of beggars and that is whv India has been the slave of conquerors for the last thousand years.

AUROBINDO

Sri Aurobindo Ghosh (1872-1950) has been one of the finest thinkers and philosophers of modern India. He was also a popular leader of the freedom movement who went on to become a yogi and a mystic. Aurobindo was born in Konnanagar (West Bengal) on August 15, 1872. After securing a senior classical scholarship, he joined King's College, Cambridge in 1890.

After returning to India, he studied Sanskrit and Indian culture, religion and philosophy. And then till 1910, he devoted himself to the freedom cause by introducing radical Programmes for the Bengal Congress while urging Indians to boycott all foreign made goods and programmes of the British Government. He was arrested for his proswaraj activities in 1910 and jailed for a year.

It was during his imprisonment that he underwent an intense mystical experience that was to have a profound impact on him. From then onwards, he assumed the life of a yogi and went to reside at Pondicherry in Tamil Nadu where he also founded an ashram. The town of Auroville in pondicherry, the 'universal town', was later conceived by one of his chief disciples, known as 'the Mother', to bear out Aurobindo's philosophical principles. Auroville, symbolising the universal spirit, was then opened in 1968.

Aurobindo's political ideas and his philosophy cannot be distinguished as two separate sets of thoughts. This is because all his political ideas are based on those very spiritual and moral concepts that form the essence of his philosophical thoughts. Thus, nationalism for Aurobindo is not simply a political programme or a concept of the intellect. It is an active religion whose main weapons are spiritual. Aurobindo believed that India's national movement had to succeed so that India could complete her destined task and "become herself.

To deal with national oppression, Aurobindo advocated passive as well as active resistance depending upon the type of pressures applied. As political liberty is of the greatest importance to a nation, it has to be guarded or secured by any means. Aurobindo was of the opinion that individuals must be ready to lay down their lives in their nation's interests. But the nation itself was not simply a group of individuals, as Aurobindo saw it. It was an organism just as the individual is one, and a nation has its own personality as well. The function of a society is to help an individual achieve the human ideals and so, a society's ideals have to be based on an accurate understanding of human existence. Man needs to realize that his essential being does not rely on scientific and technological advancement as those made in the West but is a result of living in the spirit.

The revolution conceived by Aurobindo was spiritual in nature. It involved a realization based on the concepts of the Supreme Reality (Sachchidananda), Supermind (the Truth Consciousness) and Evolution. The Brahma (super-consciousness) is related to the Mind (consciousness) through the supermind, the most complete spiritual consciousness. And spiritual evolution was a process that spread over the whole of reality itself.

Sri Aurobindo's theory of evolution is a philosophical theory of evolution based upon philosophical speculation and not an empirical investigation. Aurobindo stated that the ultimate reality is of the nature of a dynamic principle. Reality is all attempting to manifest itself and through its self-manifestation is trying to come back to itself. So, there are two processes going on in the Universe. One is the process of downward movement called involution. The other is the process of upward movement called evolution. Evolution presupposes involution, in fact, evolution is possible only because involution has already taken place.

In simple language it means that at first it involves an extension of scope and the incorporation of co-existence forms, and then it involves a development and growth towards higher form. But, in this process nothing is to be completely rejected, everything finally has to be integrated. The process of widening, therefore, means providing greater scope for the operation of every new element or principle. The second process of heightening means ascent from one step or grade to another higher grade. But the most important character of the evolutionary process is integration.

The first is the process of widening. That means in the process of evolution there is a widening of the field. In this process greater room is provided for each principle it emerges.

Secondly there is the process of heightening. In the process of evolution there is a movement from the lower to the higher. Every new stage that emerges is higher than the earlier one. In the process of evolution there is a movement from higher to still higher one. This is indicated by the term heightening.

The third component factor of evolution is the process of integration. In the process of evolution, Aurobindo pointed out, the lower grades are not discarded. They are taken up, lifted up and transformed. By transformation they are incorporated into the higher grades. That is indicated by the term integration. For integration the descent of the higher principle into the lower principle is required. Without the descent the lower principle cannot be incorporated into the higher principles. So it is clear that for Aurobindo the process of evolution requires prior involution. Understood in this sense evolution is an ascent through descent. On the contrary, it implies that the lower ones are uplifted and transformed. Integration in the philosophy of Sri Aurobindo means ascent through descent. The higher descends into the lower and transforms it completely, in that way the lower ascends to the higher.

Mind and Supermind

The realm of reality has been divided into tow hemispheres, the higher and the lower. The trinue principle of Saccidānanda (The Pure Existent, Consciousness–force and Bliss) represents the higher sphere and Matter, Life, Psyche and Mind belong to the lower hemisphere. We have also seen that evolution has reached the level of mind and is preparing for its Mind is essentially a consciousness which measures, limits and cuts out forms of things from indivisible wholes and treats them as if each were a separate element. It perceives, senses or conceives things by analysing them into their component parts. We have also seen that reality cannot be known by such a process, for that mind somehow has to rise above its normal activities and try to cultivate some capacity for unification.

The difference between mind and Supermind consists in the difference between their manners of apprehending reality. While Supermind essentially gets the unitary picture of reality, mind, by its very nature, breaks and cuts as under a whole into its parts. Mind essentially creates divisions not only between the knower and the known, but also in the objects that it apprehends.

Mind, after all, belongs to the lower hemisphere and it has to ascend to the higher sphere. Therefore, there must be some intermediary steps through which this transition will be brought about. The order of ascent from mind to Supermind is through the following intermediary steps: (Mind), *Higher Mind, Illumined Mind, Intuition, Overmind,* (Supermind). The passage from mind to Supermind is a passage from Nature as we know it to Super-Nature, and as such, mind must pass through some stages which would demonstrate the continuous nature of this transition.

Supermind belongs to the higher hemisphere and yet it is the end and the ideal of mind—that which mind is going to be. As belonging to the higher hemisphere it must have a full consciousness of Saccidananda. It is not Saccidananda itself, and yet it is akin to its nature because it is the consciousness of Saccidananda. Likewise, it is not mind itself, and yet it is its culmination and fulfilment.

Now, it is apparent that any attempt to determine the nature of Supermind must throw light on these two aspects of Supermind: (a) Supermind as Truth-Consciousness—as the spiritual principle having complete knowledge of Saccidananda and (b) Supermind as the ideal and the culmination of mind. In what follows an attempt will be made to explain the nature of Supermind in the light of these two characters of Supermind. Sri Aurobindo describes the Supermind by calling it the *Creator, the Real-idea* and the *Supreme Truth-Consciousness.*

The Supramental Change

Our mind cannot give its complete description, for, as Sri Aurobindo says, "what is magic to our finite reason is the logic of the Infinite." The supramental change, he says, "is a thing decreed and inevitable in the evolution of the Earth-consciousness; for its upward ascent is not ended and mind is not its last summit. But that the change may arrive, take form and endure there is needed the call from below with a will to recognise and not deny the light, when it comes and there is needed the sanction of the supreme from above." The integral Yoga of Sri Aurobindo aims at ascending to the supermind.

Mind cannot describe this state through its categories. It can give a vague and a general description. Sri Aurobindo himself attempts this description thus, 'As if honey could taste itself and all its drops together and all its drops could taste each other and each the whole honey-comb as itself, so should the end be with God and the soul of man and the universe.

Self-Consciousness

The self-consciousness of Brahman called the power of self manifestation is also called by Sri Aurobindo, "the supermind'. The supermind, is a 'Real-Idea', a 'Truth-consciousness'. It is, says Sri Aurobindo, 'conscious reality throwing itself into mutable forms of the own imperishable and immutable substance. It is the divine alone who can know himself in all his aspects. It is with the supermind that the process of self-limitation and self-individualisation starts in Brahman. The unitary Sachchidanada, out of sheder joy, puts himself under self-limitation.

The true self is the unborn and immutable spirit of man, who always lives in the divine plane. He is not involved in the world of ignorance. It sends down a ray, a spark of divinity, as it were, into this world. The psyche, though it does not change its essential spiritual nature yet, is subject to evolution. The psychic element is inherent in matter and evolves towards a fuller existence in life.

The man normally is not aware of his own soul. Mind, life and matter are the instruments, which are available to the soul defective they may ultimately be, the soul has to work in and through them for its knowledge and activity. Hence, in spite of being spiritual and blissful, the soul is actually subject to mentality, vitality and physicality. To have absolute knowledge and absolute power, the soul must attain to supermind, which is the source of mind, life and matter. To merge the consciousness in the divine, write sri Aurobindo and to keep the psychic being controlling and changing all the nature and keeping it turned to the divine till the whole being can live in the divine is the transformation we seek.

Mind Functions

Mind can know the supreme in one or more of its aspects. It can never know it completely and as a whole. Only the supermind can do that. Great sages, according to Sri Aurobindo, have achieved salvation. It has been individual salvation. They have freed themselves from the cycle of birth and death. Some of them have realised Brahman. Mind by its very nature breaks the indivisible reality into bits. It must divide and exclude. It cannot function without the subject-object duality. 'Mind, says Sri Aurobindo, 'cannot possess the infinite, it can only suffer or be possessed by it; it can only lie blissfully helpless under the luminous shadow of the real cast down on it from planes of existence beyond it reach.'

Some of the great sages through their intuitions did have the glimpses of the Supreme. Its action is largely hidden by the interventions of our normal intelligence, for what we call by the name is usually a point of direct knowledge, which is immediately caught and coated over with mental stuff, so that it serves only as an invisible or a very tiny nucleus of a crystallisation, which is in its mass intellectual or otherwise mental in character.

'The Lite Divine' is inspired by the creative vision of the seers of the Vedas and the sages of the Upanisads. As a free commentator on Vedanta, Sri Aurobindo comes after the great Acharyas of Vedanta, like Shankara, Ramanuja, Madhva, Vallabha and Nimbarka.

The supreme reality, according to Sri Aurobindo, is Brahman, the divine. It is eternal, absolute and infinite. It is absolutely indeterminate, indefinable and free. It cannot be completely described as either positively or negatively. Though, it is indescribable in itself. It is not absolutely unknowable to us. The Spiritual Being in us is regarded as essence. It means the divine itself.

The existence of Brahman appears to us as Atma, Ishwara and Purusa. The Consciousness of Brahman, which is always a force manifests itself as Maya, Shakti and Prakriti.

The Bliss of **Brahman** underlies all these manifestations. It is out of sheer bliss. The divine manifests himself as this world. These three aspects and these powers embrace all reality. When taken as a whole, reconcile all apparent contradictions. The supreme in itself is regarded as the timeless and spaceless pure existence, one and stable, to which measure and measurelessness are inapplicable. It manifests itself as the 'measureless movement in time and space'.

Evolution of Mind

The evolution of mind introduces a very great change in life and matter. The evolution has been up to the mental plane and has been through ignorance. Consciousness in mind itself is feeling an I urge to evolve into supermind. The supramental descent is a logical necessity.

The supramental being is called Gnostic being. With the descent of the supermind, mind, life and matter will be radically transformed. Their defects and mutability will vanish.

Integral Yoga

This yoga accepts the value of cosmic existence and holds it to be a reality; its object is to enter into a higher Truth-Consciousness or Divine Supramental Consciousness in which action and creation are the expression not of ignorance and imperfection, but of the Truth, the Light, the Divine Ananda (Bliss). Only those who can accept the call to such a change should enter into this yoga.

The Sādhanā or practice of the Integral Yoga does not proceed through any set mental teaching or prescribed forms of meditation, mantras or others, but by aspiration, by a self-concentration inwards or upwards, by a self-opening to an Influence, to the Divine Power above us and its workings, to the Divine Presence in the heart and by the rejection of all that is foreign to these things. It is only by faith, aspiration and surrender that this self-opening can come.

The method we have to pursue is to put our whole conscious being into relation and contact with the Divine and to call Him in to transform our entire being into His, so that in a sense God Himself, the real Person in us, becomes the saṭdhaka of the saṭdhana as well as the Master of the Yoga by whom the lower personality is used as the centre of a divine transfiguration and the instrument of its own perfection. In effect, the pressure of the Tapas, the force of consciousness in us dwelling in the Idea of the divine Nature upon that which we are in our entirely, produces its own realisation.

It is not merely to rise out of the ordinary ignorant world-consciousness into the divine consciousness, but to bring the supramental power of that divine consciousness down into the ignorance of mind, life and body, to transform them, to manifest the Divine here and create a divine life in Matter. This yoga can only be done to the end by those who are in total earnest about it and ready to abolish their little human ego and its demands in order to find themselves in the Divine.

To concentrate, preferably in the heart and call the presence and power of the Mother to take up the being and by the workings of her force transform the consciousness.

When the mind falls quiet and the concentration becomes strong and the aspiration intense, then there is the beginning of experience. The more the faith, the more rapid the result is likely to be. For the rest one must not depend on one's own efforts only, but succeed in establishing a contact with the Divine and a receptivity to the Mother's Power and Presence.

The object of the Integral Yoga is to enter into and be possessed by the Divine Presence and Consciousness, to love the Divine for the Divine's sake alone, to be tuned in our nature into the nature of the Divine, and in our will and works and life to be the instrument of the Divine.

The whole principle of Integral Yoga is to give oneself entirely to the Divine alone and to nobody else, and to bring down into ourselves by union with the Divine Mother all the transcendent light, power, wideness, peace, purity, truth-consciousness and Ananda of the Supramental Divine.

The psychic change so that a complete devotion can be the main motive of the heart and the ruler of thought life and action in constant union with the Mother and in her Presence. The perception of the One and Divine infinitely everywhere, the Mother everywhere and living in that infinite consciousness.

Thus, integral yoga is integral, or total, in ways more than one. It accepts all methods, uses all life, and helps all humanity. It seems an easy yoga because it does not prescribe a single rigid path for all.

IQBAL

Allama Muhammad Iqbal was born at Sialkot in the year 1877, and died on April 21, 1938 at Lahore. His family had inherited strong Sufi tendencies. The environment in which he was brought up, made a significant mark on Iqbal's growing mind. Iqbal's ancestors hailed from Kashmir and were Brahmin and had embraced Islam. Iqbal's grandfather Sheikh Muhammad Rafiq, had migrated from Kashmir Valley and was peddler of Shawls.

Though the family never returned to Kashmir, the memory of the land and its people was never erased from the mind of Iqbal. As Iqbal has said about himself that his body comes from the earthly paradise of Kashmir; and his heart belongs to the Holy Land of Hijaz and song of Shiraz.

Inspite of his vocational engagements, Iqbal's father Sheikh Noor Muhammad, used to spare time for the company of good scholars and Sufi Saints, from whom he acquired a great deal of mystic knowledge and developed insight in the affairs of religion. Before the birth of Iqbal; Sheikh Noor Muhammad had seen a dream. He used to tell his friends, in the latter part of his life, that the birth of his son, Iqbal was made known to him in a dream. A lovely coloured bird was flying over our heads, and every one tried to catch it, but no one succeeded. At last, it came down and flew right into my hands. The personality qualities of Noor Muhammad like humility, sobriety etc., impressed Iqbal much. Iqbal reminds this impact in Remuz-e-Be-Khudi. It caused great distress to his father. "What shall I reply to the Prophet (PBUH) on the 'Day of Judgement', said Sheikh Noor Muhammad to his son Iqbal, with tears in his eyes, when he asks me why I fail to teach you the essence of humanity.

In the early choice of Iqbal's education, his parents enrolled him in the Maktaba of Molvi Mir Hassan, who had recognized in his first glance Iqbal's poetic talent, was an acknowledged scholar of Arabic and Persian literatures and Islamic studies. Iqbal passed his matriculation examination in 1893, from Scottish Mission School, Sialkot. Iqbal passed his B.A. from the Government Collage Lahore. In 1899, he completed his M.A. in philosophy. In Arnold, Iqbal found a loving teacher, who combined in himself, a profound knowledge of the western philosophy and deep understanding of Islamic culture and Arabic literature. At the Government College, Lahore Iqbal came under the influence of Prof. Arnold, an influence which in its capacity and potency can be well compared with that of Molvi Mir Hassan. He paid there his gratitude and indicated his future aspirations and quest of knowledge.

In spite of having post graduate qualification, Iqbal was enrolled in B.A. in Cambridge, and he took Ph.D from Munich (Germany) in 1907. His thesis, "The Development of Metaphysics in Persia was published in 1908 in London and was dedicated to his teacher Thomas Arnold. Their relationship as teacher and student was ideal one. Iqbal was called to the bar at the Lincoln Inn in 1908. On return from Europe, Iqbal joined the Government College Lahore, as assistant professor but left it for law practice.

Self

Iqbal states the organic view of man, and then refers to some of the interpretations of this view by the different seats and schools of Islam. In particular he makes a mention of the views of Devotional Sufism, specially to the famous expression of Hallaj–'Anal Haq' or 'I am the creative truth'. He tries to organise the salient features of all these ideas and then arrives at his own conception of the self. 'Anal Haq' particularly seems to have provided to Iqbal the rudiments of his own notion of the self.

Iqbal says that the Quran emphasises the individuality and uniqueness of man. According to him the Quranic conception of man lays emphasis on at least three aspects of man, (a) that man is the chosen of God, (b) that man, with all his faults, is meant to be the representative of God on earth, (c) that man is the trustee of a free personality which he accepted at his own peril. The description of the nature of the relation between the body and the soul throws light on character of the self. The self is a series of activities, and as such must need an environment on which it will act or to which it will react. In his actions and reactions he will utilise even the body. Thus, the egos cannot remain in complete isolation, they must have a world. The ego is confronted with the world of the non-ego, and it is through his experiences of this world of the non-ego, that the life of the ego grows and develops.

From this Iqbal deduces two other characters of the ego (a) Firstly, the life of the ego is not a mechanical life, it is steadily trying to realise some purpose. (b) The life of the ego is constituted by the experiences, feelings and volitions of the ego. One of the most prominent characters of the self is freedom.

Iqbal feels that the ego potentially is capable of infinite freedom. In his finite activities it appears to be limited, but if its powers are cultivated fully its freedom would know no bounds.

An important character of the self has to be emphasised in order to clarify its nature fully. That character is *Immortality*. Iqbal believes in the doctrine of Personal immortality and substantiates his view by referring to the Quran. According to him immortality appears to be both the nature of the self and his ultimate destiny. The self is immortal in spite of the apparent fact of death. There is no inconsistency in believing that immortality represents both the nature and the destiny of the individual. One can never become anything which he is not already.

God

Iqbal believes in Monotheism. He conceives God as one, omnipotent, all-knowing, and supremely good creator of the world. It believes that God is a personal God. The distinction between God and the Absolute appears to be irrelevant to Islam. Iqbal tries to develop such a notion of God and shows that it satisfied not only the religious urge of man, but also his metaphysical curiosity. The nature and at tributes of God have been interpreted from that point of view.

Iqbal does not attach much value to the traditional proofs for God's existence. He feels that the Cosmological, Ontological and the Teleological proofs for God's existence are attempts on the part of our limited intellect to comprehend the nature of God. He feels that as proofs they are utterly inadequate because they are somehow based on a superficial interpretation of experience and not on an intuitive experience of reality. According to Iqbal 'proofs' do not give the knowledge of God. For this Iqbal leans on the authority of Intuition. Just as an intuition reveals the nature of the self or of the world so an intuition reveals the nature of God also. Iqbal is convinced that this is the only way in which God's existence can be apprehended.

Man and Superman

According to Iqbal the universe is of the nature of a free creative force. He also says that the world-process is not blind but purposive. The teleological character of the world shows that the world process is being rationally directed. He says further that rational egos have the capacity to regulate and direct their own creative life. Therefore we are constrained to think that there is a Being directing the creative life of the universe. That Being cannot be Outside the universe, because in that case the end and the goal of the world would become external. Thus, the supreme Ego is conceived as guiding the creative progress of the world.

Iqbal believes that individuality is a matter of degrees. There is a rising note of egohood through out the universe, it has not reached perfection even in human beings. Therefore, Iqbal comes to conceive God as the Supreme Ego–as the ideal of egohood. It is from this point of view that Iqbal interprets the Quranic description of God as Light. Iqbal says that the teaching of modern Physics is that the velocity of light cannot be exceeded and that it is independent of perspectives and remains the same for all observers. Thus, the analogy of light gives an impression of immense dynamism–of continuous and ceaseless movement. Iqbal thinks that light is the nearest metaphor for understanding the nature of the Absolute Ego, which is the most perfect embodiment of dynamic and creative life.

If God is an ego, can we conceive him as infinite? Iqbal says that this problem appears to be a problem because we place the infinite in space-time-dimension. We have seen that space and time are not absolute dimensions that can limit the Supreme ego. The Supreme Ego is infinite in the sense that it has infinite creative possibilities within it, of which creation is only an expression. God's infinity involves an infinite series of expression, even space and time are expressions of the possibilities of God.

RABINDRANATH TAGORE

Rabindranath Tagore was a great philosopher, poet, novelist, dramatist and a prophet. He was born on May 07, 1961 in Calcutta in an educated, rich and respected family. The responsibility of his education remained mainly on the shoulders of his father Mahrishi Devandranath Tagore. He provided Rabindranath with education of Sanskrit language, Indian philosophy and astronomy. Soon he was fed up with the rigid and lifeless education imparted there. Thus, he developed aversion for the prevalent dull education and he left the Bengal academy. In 1877, Rabindranath was sent to England for receiving education in law. There too he got fed up and returned to India without obtaining any degree. As such, Tagore got his education mostly at home through tutors and private readings. He had started writing articles for Bengali magazines very early in life.

Rabindranath Tagore developed into a renowned poet, writer, dramatist, philosopher and painter soon that people began to address him reverently as Gurudev. Tagore translated Gitanjali into English which brought him noble prize and worldwide recognition. In the same year, Calcutta University adored him with the degree of Doctor of Literature. In 1915, the Indian government endowed him with knighthood which he returned after the notorious Jallianwala Bagh massacre to express his emotions of anger at the episode. He went to Japan, Europe and U.S.A. In 1921, his school previously known as Shantiniketan ashram became a world famous university known as Vishwa Bharti University.

Religion of Man

Tagore conceives humanistic conception of religion for a man and gives the theory of spiritual humanism. Tagore was a prophet of love, harmony and fellowship. Rejecting the narrow dividing walls and concentrating his attention on concrete humanity as an organic whole, Tagore gave to the organised man the gospel of unity and harmony. His vision of peace, love and humanism was nurtured on spiritual foundations demanding that man be treated in the perspective of the eternal. He stood for spiritual equality and moral equanimity. Believing that man is only a unique model of God, Tagore desired the exaltation of the spirit of man. Stressing on the liberty of the human spirit, he stood for the idealisation and perfection of the neglected human spirit. Tagore regarded man as the culmination of the creative process of a superior great power. The inner being of man is organic with the heart of eternity. He said, 'Truth, which is one with the Universal Being, must essentially be human, otherwise whatever we individuals realise as true can never be called truth... In any case, if there be any truth absolutely related to humanity then for us it is absolutely non-existing....My religion in the reconciliation of the super-personal man, the universal human spirit, in my own individual being..."

Accepting the sanctity of human conscience, he stood for synthesis between philosophic contemplation, devotional adoration and affirmative action. Realising that God belongs to the broken home as well as to magnificent temples and churches, his, humanism pleads for social mutualistic co-operation, love and service.

Ideas on Education

Tagore had a philosophy of life, and his theory of education was accordingly shaped. Generally, education is dominated by the ideal of attaining technical efficiency in order to get on in life. Such an education is incomplete according to Tagore. Tagore regarded education as the basis of the true, the complete life. Perfect knowledge is the basis of all true freedom; it is avidya which forges fetters that bind. That is why the wise man comes and says, "Set yourselves free from avidya; know your true soul and be saved from the grasp of the self which imprisons you."

Tagore felt that the education of a child is the most important work in building up the life of the nation. He wanted to train human beings for freedom, for peace, for justice. Accordingly, in his school he brought about an atmosphere of freedom, of sympathy and of service and these are Tagore's cardinal ideals of education. According to Tagore, no nation can be alive and strong, unless its children receive proper education, nor mere book knowledge. The stress on book knowledge was given in our country by the foreign rulers on political considerations. Every imperial government avoids spreading true enlightenment; the strength of foreign government lies in the people's ignorance." Tagore believed that the provision for the training of the children must begin from the earliest stage. He turned to this vital task unaided and he began his experiments at Santiniketan. True education is the basis of all constructive work, according to him. Further Tagore enunciated that the aim of the school should be the highest degree of individual development in each of its pupils. He could not accept the view that true education would in any way stifle the very essence of freedom. Free minds, nurtured on free criticism, must seek for profound changes in the foundations of society resulting in the triumph of reason over human conduct.

Tagore was an advocate of the medium of instruction through the mother tongue. In a speech read before the Rajshahi Association in 1892 which was published under the title of Siksher Her-Pher (Topsyturvydom in Education), Tagore pointed out the folly of imparting education through the vehicle of a foreign language. English is a completely alien tongue, its association of themes and ideas are foreign and the education we receive through the medium of English is 'inadequate to our life.'

Tagore favoured open-air classes. The deadness of the walls made everything dull and gloomy. Discipline was not imposed upon children : they had the freedom of movement as he believed that a moving mind had more power to assimilate facts and to gather knowledge from the outside world. In Tagore's opinion, the school must be an 'ashram where men have gathered to attain the highest end of life, in the peace of nature, where life is not merely meditative, but fully awake in its activities, where boys's minds are not being perpetually drilled into believing that the ideal of the self-idolatry of the nation is the trust ideal for them to accept, where they are bidden to realise man's world as God's kingdom to whose citizenship they have to aspire." He lamented that the system of folk education, which was indigenous to India, was dying out. An educational institution, in Tagore's vision, should not exist in isolation; it should have a close contact with the socio-economic conditions prevalent in the locality.

Fear of Teaching

He says that teaching should not be artificial and theoretical. It should be practical and real. He says that the practicality of education will increase the creative skill within a learner. He says that by using this creativity the student will become master in his own field.

He says, that fine arts should be used as a subject in his education curriculum. He says that educational process important parts are game, music, drama, dance etc. to him, education is regarded as the basis of the true notion of the complete life. He says, that the training of the children must begin from the earliest stage. According to him, true education is the basis of all constructive work.

He says, that English is a completely Alien language. He says, that we should focus on our mother tongue which is Hindi. He favoured open air classes for students. He says, that the school should not impose their useless rules on the students.

Religion

Religion consists in the, endeavour of men to cultivate and express those qualities which are inherent in the nature of man the, eternal and to have faith in him. We begin our history with all the original promptings of our brute nature, which helps us to fulfil those vital needs of ours that are immediate. But deeper within us there is a current of tendencies, which runs in many ways in a contrary direction, the life current of universal humanity.

Religion has its, function in reconciling the contradiction,' by subordinating the brute nature to what we consider as the truth of man. This is helped when our faith in the eternal man, whom we call by different names and imagine in different images, is made strong.

It proves that man has a feeling that he is truly represented in something which exceeds himself. He is aware that he is not imperfect, but incomplete. He knows that in himself some meaning has yet to be realised. We do not feel the wonder, of it, because it seems so natural to us that barbarism in man is not absolute, that its limits are like the limits of the horizon.

Unity Idea

The divine principle of unity has ever been that of an inner interrelationship. This is revealed in some of its earliest stages in the evolution of multicellular life on this planet. He misses himself when isolated; he finds his own larger and truer self in his wide human relationship.

The idea of the humanity, of our God or the divinity of man the eternal, is the main subject of this book. This thought of God has, not grown in my mind through any process of philosophical reasoning. On the contrary, it has followed he current of my temperament from early days until it suddenly flashed into my consciousness with a direct vision.

It very often-contradicts. The trivialities of our daily life and upsets the, arrangements made for securing our personal exclusiveness behind the walls of individual habits and superficial conventions.

Creation in Religion of Man

Creation has been made possible through the continual self-surrender of the unit to the universe. And the spiritual universe of man is also ever claiming self-renunciation from the individual units.

It is said in a verse of the Upanishad that this world, which is all movement is pervaded by one supreme unity and therefore, true enjoyment can never be had through the satisfaction of greed, but only through the surrender of our individual self to the universal self.

We must know that the evolution process of the world has made its progress towards the revelation of its truth that is to say some inner value which is not in the extension in space and duration in time. When life came out it did not bring with it any new materials into existence. Its elements are the same which are the materials for the rocks and minerals. The same thing is true with regard to mind and the consciousness of self; they are revelations of a great meaning; the self-expression of a truth.

The Law of Nature

The laws of nature through the help of the invention of new instruments plays an important role. This field of life's onward March is a field of ruthless competition. Because the material world is the world of quantity, where resources are limited and victory waits for those who have superior facility in their weapons, therefore, success in the path or progress for one group most often runs parallel to defeat in another.

Any new chance of a too obviously physical variation is certain to meet with a determined disapproval from man, the most powerful veto being expected from his aesthetic nature, which peremptorily refuses to calculate advantage, when its majesty is offended by any sudden license of form. We all know that the back of our body has a wide surface practically unguarded. From the strategic point of view this oversight is unfortunate, causing us annoyances and indignities, if nothing worse, through unwelcome intrusions.

The Spirit of Life

The spirit of life boldly declared for a further freedom and decided to eat of the fruit of the tree of knowledge. This time her struggle was not against the inert, but against the limitation of her own overburdened agents. She fought against the tutelage of her prudent old Prime Minister, the faithful instinct. She took a bold step in throwing open her gates to a dangerously explosive factor which she had cautiously introduced into her council – the element of mind.

Imagination

We must realise not only the reasoning mind, but also the creative imagination, the love and wisdom that belong to the supreme person, whose spirit is over us all, love for whom comprehends love for all creatures and exceeds in depth and strength all other loves, leading to difficult endeavours and martyrdoms that have no other gain than the fulfilment of this lover itself.

Man Development Process in Religion of Man

Man desired in his completeness to be the one great representative of multiform life, not through wearisome subjection of opportunities with the help of his reasoning mind. It enables the schoolboy who is given a pen-knife on his birthday to have the advantage over the tiger in the fact that it does not take him a million years to obtain its possession, nor another million years for its removal, when the instrument proves unnecessary or dangerous.

The new organs that today are being added as a supplement to man's original vital stock are too quick and too numerous for his inner nature to develop its own simultaneous concordance with them.

Detachment of Man

The detachment achieved by man is physical. It represents his freedom from the necessity of developing the power of his senses and limbs in the limited area of his own physiology, having for itself an unbounded background with an immense result in consequence. Nature's original intention was that man should have the allowance of his sight-power ample enough for his surroundings and a little over. But to have to develop an astronomical telescope on our skull would cause a worse crisis of bankruptcy than it did to the Mammoth whose densely foolish body indulged in an extravagance of tusks.

Man, in his mission to create himself, tries to develop in his mind an image of his truth according to an idea which he believes to be universal and is sure that any expression given to it will persist through all time. This is a mentality absolutely superfluous for biological existence. It represents his struggle for a life which is not limited to his body. For our physical life has its thread of unity in the memory of the past, whereas this ideal life dwells in the prospective memory of the future. In the records of past civilisations, unearthed from the closed records of dust, we find pathetic efforts to make their memories uninterrupted through the ages, like the effort of a child who sets adrift on a paper boat his dream of reaching the distant unknown.

K.C. BHATTACHARYA

Concept of Philosophy

Usually it is believed that philosophy is an attempt to construct a world-view. In India philosophy is made to serve a practical–more accurately a religious–purpose. It aims at freeing man from suffering. The path leading to this state of complete freedom from suffering consists in a kind of knowledge. This knowledge is conceived as the knowledge of the distinction between the 'real' and the 'unreal'. That means that philosophy has to give a world-view, it has to analyse the nature of the world in order to discover the real and unreal aspects of the world.

But, Krishnachandra does not agree with this fully. In this respect his position is similar to that of Kant, or even to that of the Logical Positivists. Like them, K.C. Bhattacharya also believes that it is not an essential function of philosophy to construct a synthetic view of the world. He feels that judgements of philosophy are not factual; they are not related to facts in so far as they do not claim facticity like the empirical judgements.

Features of Philosophy

The concept of philosophy is the most comprehensive and perhaps the best paper of Professor K.C. Bhattacharya. His concept of philosophy represents the central tenets of his philosophical understanding. For him, the study of philosophy is the understanding of the speakable. These are not speakable and also not believed. Therefore, propositions and judgements, which are not speakable do not come under the province of philosophical study. But, the judgements and propositions which refer to the self-subsistence of objects, the subject and the absolute are speakable, though they are not literally thinkable, but they come under the scope of philosophical study.

K.C. BHATTACHARYA
Maya or Avidy
1. The subject as freedom.
2. Swaraj in ideas.
3. The concept of the absolute and its alternative forms
4. Knowledge and truth
5. Fact and thought of fact
6. Concept of value
7. Reality of the future.

In philosophy, the content is spoken and as well as is particularly symbolised. He propounds his philosophy of theoretic consciousness. By theoretic consciousness; he means the minimum understanding of a speakable. Bhattacharya's idea of thinking is different from that of Kant. Bhattacharya makes a distinction between Thinking and Speaking. He says that thinking is related to science and speaking is related to philosophy.

Subject as Freedom

K.C. Bhattacharya talks about subject as freedom. He says that the subject can, at times be spoken as the object, although not meant as the object, but the object, can never be spoken as the subject. The first stage of subjectivity is an awareness of the distinction of the subject and the object.

The subject frees itself from the object and the object is that from, which the subject frees itself subject and object are inter-related. Subjectivity is the cult of the subjects is non-objective.

Three Stages of Subjectivity

There are three stages of subjectivity *i.e.,*

(a) Bodily subjectivity
(b) Psychic subjectivity and
(c) Spiritual Subjectivity
(a) In the bodily stage, the self identifies itself with the body. The stage of psychic subjectivity includes image and thought.
(b) In this stage, the subject identifies itself with the psychic life. A vegetation of this stage of subjectivity leads to the third stage of subjectivity, the spiritual subjectivity.
(c) The spiritual subjectivity means 'the positive, freedom from objective meaning.'

Spiritual subjectivity has also been subdivided into three sub-grades (a) Feeling, (b) Introspection and (c) Beyond Introspection. In the first stage of feeling, there is a feeling of freedom from actual thought and in its second stage there is a feeling of freedom from possible thought. He says that subject first identifies itself with the perceived body and then with the felt body. The body perceived externally is called the perceived body and the felt body is the body felt from within. The subject disassociate itself from the external body and also from the body which is felt.

The distinction between subject as free and subject as freedom subject as free is the introspective stage of subjectivity. Subject as freedom is the realm of the indefinite, the absolute.

The Doctrine of Maya

The doctrine of Maya, for him is an illusory world. Maya means Avidya, Mithya, or Adhysa. Maya is indeterminable indescribable. It means the world, which we see. When illusory world is negated, then the original world of Brahman is known. He takes Maya doctrine from Sankara. Sankara says that maya is the inherent power of Brahman. Maya is superimposition. Maya is error. The correct knowledge indicates the knowledge of absolute, Brahman. Brahman indicates Nirguna Brahman. It is without attributes.

RADHAKRISHNAN

Sarvapalli Radhakrishnan was born on September 5, 1888 at a small place Triputi, Chitoor district, Madras Presidency. He was the second child of the Hindu parents who were conventional in their religious outlook. Radhakrishnan received his education at Madras Christian College. He joined as Assistant Professor of Philosophy at Presidency College, Madras in 1911. He remained engaged in the serious study of Indian philosophy and religion.

He was appointed King George V. Professor of Philosophy at the Calcutta University in 1921. He was appointed as Vice-Chancellor of Andhra University in Waltair from 1931 to 1936 and vice chancellor of Banaras University from 1939 to 1948. In the independent India, he was appointed the ambassador to U.S.S.R. He was made the chairman of the University Commission appointed in 1948 to examine the working of the various universities in the countries and suggest remedies for reforms. He was elected as vice-president of Indian Republic in 1950 and again in 1957, he also held the position of chancellor of Delhi University. He went on goodwill tours of European countries namely East and Central Africa in June-July 1956. He went on a three week tour of Indo-China states in September-1957. He attended East West philosophers' Conference in Honolulu and visited U.S.A. also. He also attended the UNESCO Conference at Paris in November-1960.

In 1967, he retired from his office and engaged himself in his academic pursuits. At the ripe age of 86 years, he left this world on April 17, 1975 for his heavenly abode.

Dr. Radhakrishnan was a versatile genius who rendered services not only as a philosopher but also an intellectual reformer and a clear farsighted statesman. His service to philosophy has been recognized equally by the West and the East. He succeeded happily in evolving a mean between the oriental and accidental thinking.

In Dr. Radhakrishnan, wisdom and power went together. The world knows him as a philosopher, statesman, world teacher and cultural ambassador. Indian nation was enriched in having him as a President. He served India in a most dignified way and was very popularly known as Philosopher-Statesman.

Why Intuition?

Radhakrishnan feels that sense-experience or Intellectual Cognition cannot give the knowledge of reality, although in practical life they are useful as sources of knowledge. He thinks that both of them are inherently limited, and in a sense, even defective. As such they are incapable of comprehending the reality.

Through the senses only external features of the objects are known. These sensory impressions do not touch the core of the object, they are too superficial to be able to give an idea of the reality. And, hence, senses are not always reliable. They very often deceive us. Illusions and hallucinations occur quite naturally without even letting us suspect that we are being deluded. Therefore it is not safe to pin absolute faith on the senses. Again, sense-impressions themselves, at times, conflict with each other. The same thing appears differently to different viewers and also to the same viewer at different times.

Thus, Radhakrishnan feels that although sense-impressions are otherwise useful they cannot give the knowledge of reality.

Intellectual Cognition also is unable to give us the knowledge of reality on account of the following reasons :

(a) Intellectual deliberation rests on the presupposition of the duality of the subject and the object. That which is non-dual–the Absolute–cannot be known through a process that knows only after creating a separation between the knower and the known.
(b) Intellect moves in the realm of relations only. Relations presuppose multiplicity. Thus, Intellectual knowledge is knowing by relating different entities with each other. Reality is One, and therefore above diversity and relations. Consequently, it cannot be known by intellectual or relational ways.
(c) Intellectual Cognition is symbolic in nature and, as such, moves in the world of symbols. For knowing reality, on the other hand, it is essential to go beyond the symbols to the symbolised.
(d) Intellect, in its deliberations, separates the what from 'the that', and then by a kind of an intellectual synthesis tries to restore the unity of the two. But no amount of conceptual synthesis can restore the original unity of the reality, just as no treatment of a deep cut-wound can restore the original smoothness of the skin.
(e) Intellect is not primary or original. It works on materials and data supplied by other sources. Hence, if any view of reality has to be based on intellect, it will have to pre-suppose not only intellect but those other sources also.
(f) Intellect, in fact, is merely an aspect of our mental life; feeling, conation etc. are other aspects which also are equally important. A complete comprehension of reality will be possible only when all these aspects are taken into account and satisfied.

Intuition has certain clear advantages over sense-impression and intellectual deliberation. Sense-experience can explore only external or superficial aspects of the object, whereas Intuition can apprehend its essence. Senses are liable to error. Intuition is infallible, it does not even need verification for judging the veracity of truths intuited. The need for verification is felt only when ideas are related to objects–only when there remains a difference between 'knowing a thing' and 'being a thing'.

In spite of this there is one point common to them both, which brings them closer to each other. Both of them apprehend their objects directly and immediately. Like sense-experience Intuition is knowing without the medium of anything and without the intervention of anything. That is why it is said that Intuition possesses the directness of the senses, and that Intuition is, in a sense, an extension of the process of perceiving to regions beyond the reach of the senses.

Intuition and Intellect

Intuition is the faculty by which the mystics come into contact with Reality or God or the ground of the universe. Intuition gives us integral knowledge, which is different and superior to the discursive knowledge given by the intellect and sensuous knowledge. The intellect is not creative and productive. It is logical in nature, and is necessary for communication, proof or demonstration. It creates the duality of the subject and the object. Intuition is creative. It gives us certain knowledge, which is free from the subject object distinction. In it knowing and being are one. This faculty, though present in almost every one, is highly developed only in a few individuals. It is through intuition that, we are aware of certain basic self-evident truths regarding the world and ourselves which are not derived through experience nor through reason and so can neither be verified nor be disproved by them.

It is the conviction of Dr. S. Radhakrishnan that mystics everywhere and at all times are in contact with the same living reality and that their experience of it is the same. Though the experience is the same the expressions of it in language are more or less adequate. It is also the strong conviction of Dr. S. Radhakrishnan that all Philosophy must be a systematization of the expressions of mystic experience.

Since Dr. S. Radhakrishnan admits that intuition is present in every one in some degree or other, that there might be different degrees of intensity even in religious experience, that after all, it may not be permanent in any individual, and that religious experience has to be identified with moksha, it follows that everybody is liberated sometime or other in his life, at least to some extent, and that moksha admits of degrees. All the religions in the world are the manifold expressions of the identical experience of the mystics who are the founders of those religions. Believing in the principle of emergent evolution, Dr. S. Radhakrishna asserts that mind emerges out of life, but that with mind the process of evolution does not come to a stop, and that it will proceed further, the last emergent being Spirit or Ananda which comprises of all the rest. Human beings, being free, can create evil in the world, though evil still forms part of the Divine purpose.

Dr. S. Radhakrishnan's epistemological study is nothing but the explanation on to the possible source of knowledge. He is aware that the East generally emphasizes the ultimacy of creative intuition and that the West lays emphasis on the critical intelligence.

According to him there are three possible sources of knowledge. Dr. S. Radhakrishnan's sense experience is noting different from what psychology describes as sense perceiving. His function is together impressions of the philosophical objects. Intellectual cognition on the other hand is almost the same as conceptual knowledge.

He feels that some experience or intellectual cognition can not give the knowledge or reality but in practical life they are useful as sources of knowledge. This definition is not to be presented too closely. It is relative and not absolute.

For Dr. S. Radhakrishnan sense experience and intelligence are incapable of giving the knowledge of reality hence he developed a third source of knowledge that of intuitive apprehension.

It is knowledge by being and not by sense for by symbols. Intuition is the direct realization of its object. In this apprehension the distinction between the knower and the known completely vanishes and their duality is completely destroyed. In it the knower establishes an identity with the known. Intellect studies both the outer and inner aspects of objects and it is indirect and symbolic. Its main tool is analysis so it fails to grasp the whole nature of objects. The function of intellect is analysis but there must be a whole, the whole as whole can be grasped by intuition alone.

Intuition is related to intellect as a whole is to a part. It comprehends sense and intellectual knowledge. Intuition is knowledge by identity. It is the final and supreme knowledge, whereas the intellect grows and develops from error to truth. Both intuition and intellect belong to the self. Intuition carries with it its own guarantee; it has the character of revelation. In intuition, we become one with the truth, one with the object of knowledge. "The object known is seen not as an object outside the self, but as a part of the self."

In fact, Intuition needs intellect for the expression, elaboration and justification or its result. Intuition in itself is dumb. Its results, in order to be communicated to others have to be put in under poses Intuition, without which its deliberations cannot start. The function of Intellect is 'analysis', but there must be something to be analysed, and that something must be a 'whole'. The whole as a whole can be grasped by Intuition alone. That gives to Intuition its primary.

Intuition and Life

Intuition is direct and immediate because it deals with the objects themselves and not with their signs or symbols. It deals with them without taking help from or without the intervention of anything else. Intuition is self evident. It is self-evident because it does not need the support of anything else for its expression. It is its own guarantee, its validity and truth become evident as soon as it takes place. Intuition gives a very intimate knowledge of its object because it is knowing by becoming. It is not unpractical or impossible, on the other hand, it is natural to man. Every one of us is capable of some intuition; ordinary examples taken from life can prove this.

Intuition thus conceived performs the functions of sense, instinct and intellect and does something more. It is on account of this special peculiarity of Intuition that it is capable of knowing reality.

A strong evidence of the exclusiveness of Intuition lies in the fact that certain aspects of life are open only to Intuition. The emotion of love, for example, baffles intellect. In order to know it one has to become a lover.

Judgments of value are possible only through Intuition. The worth of life, the belief in the highest good, and the belief in the moral nature of the universe are all realised through Intuition. We appreciate the beauty of Nature, we perceive moral qualities in human conduct–in these examples of aesthetic and moral sensibility we do not pause and think and then come to know; we come to know almost in a flash. Intuition, thus, makes us aware of the object in an act of sudden insight. This is evident even in the examples of ordinary Intuitions.

The general principle of life and logic and the basic assumptions of sciences are all known through Intuition. Unity, for instance, is one such assumption and we are aware of unity only intuitively. The deepest convictions by which we live and think', and 'the root principles of our thought and life' are not derived from perceptual experience or logical knowledge, but from intuition. Great Truths are not proved, but seen.

The knowledge of the self also is possible only through Intuition. How do I know that I am? Self-awareness, according to Radhakrishnan, is an intuitive awareness. In every act of feeling, wiling and knowing the self is intuitively aware of itself as feeling, willing and knowing.

The Idealist View of Life

He wrote a book on An Idealist View of Life. It includes many topics like intellect and intuition, the spirit in man, (Matter, Life and Mind), ultimate reality etc. He was a spiritual idealist. Beliefs can be known only through intuition. Atoms and material objects in general are not fixed 'Things', 'substance', but rather are on-going events. Physical objects are moving points in a continuous change. Matter are abstractions from the concrete fact, which is a set of events. Matter is not a thing, but a system of interrelated events. Life and matter are two different kinds of activity. Matter is regressive, while life is regarded as progressive activity. There is no impassable gulf between matter and life. Matter is as truly creative as mind.

Behaviour of Living Organisations

There is something specific in the behaviour of living organisms, which is not traceable in the non-living. A living organisms maintains its specific structure and activities throughout all changes. Life is a dynamic equilibrium, which tends to maintain itself. In living organisms, form, structure and composition are interdependent. The living organism is regarded as a whole, do things that no atomic system could ever do.

A living organism adapts itself to its environment. An atom can neither mend itself nor reproduce itself. A living organism replies to the changes of the environment. A sense of environment enters into its very life of organism. Both, environment and life are inextricably interuined. They are regarded as expressions of a larger whole. Matter does not help us to understand the coordinated maintenance of life. Life is a different order of fact.

Mental phenomena are different from vital activities. The living organism manifest only the organic wholeness and persistence. Though, the organism seem to have a 'Mind' of their own, it is only seeming. We discern the activity of the mind in relation to physical change in complex parts of the body, though we have no direct knowledge of the nature of this relation.

Features of Spirituality

The spirit in man. Besides consciousness in the animal world and self-consciousness in the human, we have spiritual consciousness or super-consciousness. While in, the first case we have a psychological unity between the animal and the environment, in the second we have a logical unity and in the third a spiritual unity. At the spiritual level, the individual becomes aware of the substance of spirit, not as an object of intellectual cognition, but as an awareness in which the subject becomes its own object.

The spirit which is inclusive of both self and object is self-subsistent and self-consistent. It above satisfies the total desire and whole intelligence. It is all that there is, all being and all value. Spirit is regarded as both real and individual without qualification. Universal spirit is higher than the self-conscious individual. The reality of universal spirit is an obvious implication of our daily life. For the spiritual being religion is a vital contact with reality, which is the source of all values. Spirit is something essentially and purely inward to be known only from within and yet, when it is known it leaves nothing outside. In the language of religion, spirit is God, the ultimate reality, which is one and all comprehensive. The spiritualised man is a new genus of man exhibiting a new quality of life.

JIDDU KRISHNAMURTI

Jiddu Krishnamurti was born on May 11, 1895 in a middle class family, in a small town of Madanapallein Chittoor district in Andhra Pradesh. His father, Jiddu Narainiah, was employed as an official of the then colonial British Administration. Krishnamurti was very fond of his mother, Sanjeevamma, who died when he was ten. He and his brother were adopted in their youth by Dr. Annie Besant, the then president of Theosophical society. Dr. Besant and others proclaimed that Krishnamurti would be a world teacher.

However, from childhood, Krishnamurti had a unique temperament of thoughtful nature with a habit of quiet observation.

In 1911, the leadership of the Theosophical Society at Adyar established a new organization, called the 'Order of the Star in the East' (OSE) to prepare the world for the expected appearance of the world teacher. Krishnamurti was named as its head, while senior Theosophists were installed in the various other positions.

In 1929, Krishnamurti renounced the role that he was expected to play, dissolved the Order with its huge following and returned all the money and property that had been donated for this work. Krishnamurti Foundation of India (KFI), originally, charitable institution under the name of the Rishi Valley Trust, was set up by Krishnamurti in 1928. Later, this trust became the foundation for new education in 1953 and eventually the Krishnamurti Foundation India in 1970. The work of the Foundation includes education, research and environmental programs conducted in an overall perspective deriving from Krishnamurti's thought.

Krishnamurti until death on Feb 17, 1986, travelled throughout the world talking to large audience and to individuals about the need for the radical change in mankind. Krishnamurti is regarded globally as one of the greatest thinkers and religious teachers of all time. He did not expound any philosophy or religion, rather talked to the concerns of our everyday lives, of the problems of living in modern society with its violence and corruption, of the individual's search for security and happiness and the need for mankind to free itself from inner burdens of fear, anger, hurt and sorrow. For his uniqueness, he appears to be standing alone away from traditional thinking. His uniqueness is also his greatness.

Jiddu Krishnamurti was born on 1895/1896. He was an Indian speaker and writer on philosophical and spiritual objects. The date of birth of Krishnamurti is a matter of dispute. Lutyens determines it to be 12th May, 1895, but Williams says that no one is sure on his birth registrations, that's why we think that his birth dates ranges from 4th May, 1985 to 25th May, 1896. His subject matter included psychological revolution, the nature of mind, meditation. He was born into a Telugu Brahmin family in India (British India).

Freedom from the Known

A book known as *The First and Last Freedom* was written by him. He says that "Truth is a pathless land". The uniqueness of man does not lie in the superficial, but in the complete freedom from the content of his consciousness, which is common to all humanity. So, he is not individual. Freedom is not a reaction, freedom is not choice. It is man's pretence because he has choice he is free. Freedom is pure observation without direction, without fear of punishment and reward. Freedom is without motive; freedom lies in the first step of his existence. Freedom is found in the choiceless awareness of our daily existence.

Freedom

Freedom from the known indicates the true worth of the environment. It refers intelligence faculty. He says that a mind always remain in conflict, the function of memory is to escape from the present. But, when mind ceased to escape through memory, then we are able to know the supreme intelligence, which is truth, which is without effort which is timeless. After then only, we are able to have no fear of not living in the present.

Fear as the Greatest Problems

Fear is one of the greatest problems in life A mind that is caught in fear lives in confusion, in conflict and therefore must be violent, distorted and aggressive. The freedom from fear is very essential. If you observe very closely what is taking place and examine it, you will see that it is based on an intellectual conception and the intellect is a fragment. Our main focus is to be the totality of life and, when we look at what is taking place in the world we begin to understand that there is no outer and inner process; there is only one unitary process, it is a whole. To be able to look at this seems to Krishnamurti all that is needed. Fear, pleasure, sorrow, thought and violence all are interrelated. The freedom from all these possessions are essential.

Krishnamurti says that when mind is completely free, then we are able to know truth. By freedom, he means complete freedom or of freedom from undesirable thing. Freedom comes only when you see and act, never through revolt. Freedom is a state of mind not freedom from something, but a sense of freedom. Freedom implies being completely alone. The man who is completely alone is innocent and it is this innocency that frees the mind from sorrow.

Analysis on Self

The self is a problem that thought cannot resolve. There must be an awareness, which is not of thought. To be aware, without condemnation or justification of the activities of the self-just to be aware is sufficient. The self must cease through awareness of its own limitation,, the falseness of its own existence. However, deep, wide and extensive it may become, the self is always limited and until it is abandoned, the mind can never be free. The self is still the self at any level you may place it.

Self-sacrifice is an extension of the self. The sacrifice of the self is a refinement of the self and however, subtle the self may make itself, it is still enclosed, petty, limited. The self, in its very structure, is contradictory, it is made up of many entities with different masks each in opposition to the other. The whole fabric of the self is the result of contradictory interests and values.

Freedom from Gendage

The creativeness comes into being when there is freedom from the bondage of craving with its conflict and sorrow. With the abandonment of the self with its assertiveness and ruthlessness and its endless struggle to become, there comes creative reality. When, the self is temporary absent, then we are open to reality. Freedom from self demands no enjoyment. Freedom from self gives us self-knowledge. Without self-knowledge you merely live in a state of contradiction and uncertainty without self-knowledge what you think-feel has no basis; without self-knowledge enlightenment is not possible. Thus, through constant awareness there comes deep and wide self-knowledge.

What we are going to do is to learn about ourselves not according to the speaker or to Freud or to Jung, to some analyst or philosopher, but to learn actually what we are to learn about one self means an end of all authority.

Educational Aims as propounded by J. Krishnamurthy's philosophy are specifically stated as below:

1. Education should aim at establishing a good society which is without violence and contradictions of various beliefs.
2. Education should aim at peace and harmony in society.
3. Education should lead to complete development of body, mind and heart of pupils.

4. Education should aim at aesthetic development of the pupils.
5. Education should aim at developing a child in a manner that he can do his work independently.
6. Education should lead to self knowledge which means understanding by his own efforts.
7. Education should aim at development of critical thinking in teachers and pupils.
8. Education should awaken the intelligence of pupils so that they can think objectively.
9. Education should aim at inculcating love for knowledge which is without conflicts and confusions.
10. Education should aim at bringing proper balance between inner and outer world of knowledge. Inner world includes opinions, fears, miseries and confusions and outer world includes knowledge, technology and computers etc.

M.K. GANDHI

Non-Violence

In an issue of Young India, Gandhi gave a comprehensive definition of non-violence to be practised by a Congress satyagrahi in his relationship with a person who had behaved with him in a fashion which had violent ingredients. Gandhi did not relish the idea of retaliation of any kind on a wrong-door. He preached, instead, the gospel of non-violence for his true followers and workers. When a person claims to be non-violent, he is expected not to be angry with one who has injured him. He will not wish him harm; he will wish him well. He will not swear at him, and he will not cause him any physical hurt. He will put up with all the injury to which he is subjected by the wrong-doer. Thus non-violence is complete innocence. Complete non-violence is complete absence of ill-will against all that lives. It, therefore, embraces even sub-human life not excluding noxious insects or beasts. Non-violence is, therefore, in its active form goodwill towards all life. It is pure love.

According to Gandhi non-violence is a perfect state. It is a goal towards which all mankind moves naturally though unconsciously. If, says Gandhi, we can manage to apply non-violence successfully at home, it will in its pure form become an irresistible power in the service of the State. Non-violence is the law of our species as violence is the law of the brute. Non-violence in its dynamic condition means conscious suffering. It does not mean meek submission to the will of the evil-doer, but it means putting one's whole soul against the will of the tyrant.

The Gandhian concept of non-violence is dharma in action, and truth translated. It is not a static code of morality ready for adoption. It evolves and is in essence 'creative morality', in the language of Bergson. Non-violence is a dynamic and creative concept centred on truth. Truth, the supreme Gandhian value, is the consummation of all that is spiritual in man. Gandhi's interpretation of the concept of ahimsa is a glorious chapter in the history of Indian ethical thought. He regards violence as an evil in. He does not consider it to be neutral.

To him, while truth was the end non-violence was the means. They were so intertwined that it was critically impossible to disentangle and separate them. They were like the two sides of a coin.

He is of the opinion that killing or injury to life can be an act of violence only under certain conditions. These conditions are anger, pride, hatred, selfish consideration, bad intention and similar her considerations. Any injury to life done under these motives is himsa. Thus, the negative meaning Ahimsa is 'non-killing or non-injury', but this presupposes that a non-violent act is free from hatred, anger, malice and the like.

He preached, the gospel of non-violence for his true followers and workers. Non-violence is the practice of being harmless to self and others under every condition, it means abstention from violence based on moral religious or spiritual principles. The Gandhian ahimsa is a philosophy and strategy for social change that rejects the use of violence. Mahatma Gandhi long non-violence struggle against British rule in India, eventually helped India to win its independence in 1947. Non-violence is linked with peace, passivity and pacifism. Love of the enemy or the realisation of the humanity of all people, is a fundamental concept of non-violence. Struggle associated with non-violence is the non-cooperation campaign for Indian independence led by Gandhi. The notion of Satya or Truth, is central to the Gandhian conception of non-violence. Gandhi advocated vegetarianism as part of his non-violent philosophy.

Features of Non-Violence

Non-violent action generally comprises three categories : Act of Protest and Persuasion which includes speeches, art public communication, non-cooperation includes labour strikes, economic boycotts, tax refusal and non-violent intervention includes fasting, blockades, truck cavalcades. He was no the originator of the principle of non-violence, but he was the first to apply it in the political field on a large scale. Gandhi explains his philosophy and way of life in his autobiography. The Story of My Experiments with Truth. In Young India, he gave a comprehensive definition of non-violence. Non-violence means conscious suffering, it converts, the brute force into soul force. It says that 'Hate the sin and not the sinver.'

The ahimsa main task is to soften and not to stiffen our opponents attitude towards us. Non-violence refers strength, whereas violence refers weakness only. Non-violence refers soul force whereas violence refers brute force. Non-violence is linked with Satyagraha. Non-violence needs sacrifice, love, sympathy, whereas violence includes greed, anger, desire. Non-violence is the law of the human race and is infinitely greater than and superior to brute force. It affords the fullest protection to one's self-respect and sense of honour. It means uttermost selflessness. Selflessness means complete freedom from a regard for one's body.

It does not simply mean non-killing. Himsa means causing pain to or killing any life out of anger. Refraining from so-doing is ahimsa. Violence will be violence for all time and all violence is sinful. Anger is the enemy of ahimsa and pride is a monster that swallous it up. It means absence of hatred.

Hateis the subtlest form of violence. We can only win over the opponent by love, never by hate. Love and patience is regarded as the positive aspects of ahimsam. In its positive form, it means the largest love, greatest charity. It includes fearlessness. It calls forth the greatest courage. He rejects passive resistance, because of its insufficiency.

Satyagraha

According to Gandhi it is based on the assumption that 'the world rests on the bedrock of satya or truth.' Gandhi explained the term 'satyagraha' from various viewpoints. Satyagraha is not a weapon of the weak, the coward, the unarmed and the helpless. It is a weapon of the morally vigilant and the active. As Simone Panter-Brick significantly puts it, Gandhi's satyagraha rejects violence but not fighting; it is a war without violence. Satyagraha is not the traditional resistance of evil by evil. It is the resistance of evil by its opposite, *i.e.*, by good. Satyagraha requires a very strict moral and religious discipline, Gandhi has in course of his numerous references to this subject, mentioned a number of qualities and characters which a Satyagrahi must possess. Some of the basic ones are given below :

1. A Satyagrahi must be basically honest and sincere.
2. A Satyagrahi must not have any mental reservations, he must be open-minded.
3. A Satyagrahi must be a disciplined soldier. Truth alone should be his master and conscience his guide. He should be loving, but firm.
4. This means that a Satyagrahi must be completely fearless. He must not fear anything worldly—even death.
5. Fearlessness leads to another virtue, sacrifice. A Satyagrahi must be prepared for the greatest possible sacrifice.
6. Suffering and Sacrifice have to be undergone in an attitude of simplicity and humility.
7. Gandhi asserts that a Satyagrahi is required to practise truthfulness and non-violence not only in his actions, but also in thought and speech.
8. A Satagrahi must be firm in his dealings and behaviour.
9. There must be a conformity between the thought and action of a Satyagrahi.
10. Gandhi also recommends that the Satyagrahi must learn to put on restraints upon his own self.

A Satyagrahi has various methods at his disposal. Non-cooperation is the refusal to cooperate with an oppressor or evil force. Civil disobedience is a form of non-cooperation in which the satyagrahi refuses to comply with lays or orders incompatible with morality or general good. Gandhi was particular that civil disobedience never degenerated into criminal disobedience; only laws that go against people's welfare were to be disobeyed. Defiance and disrespect have no place in Gandhi's form of civil disobedience. The principles that a satyagrahi must learn to follow are the ideas of truth and non-violence, non-possession and non-stealing and brahmacharya. It is only on sublimating one's desires that one can achieve the physical, moral and spiritual strength necessary to fight a just war non-violently and fearlessly.

Swaraj

The Gandhian concept of Swaraj has a far broader and deeper significance that English terms like freedom or independence. Swaraj for Gandhi had both a negative and a positive implication. Negatively speaking Swaraj meant freedom from alien rule and its influence on civilisation. Positively Swaraj meant freedom for the whole people, the peasants, the workers, the women, everyone included.

The people's Swaraj of Gandhi is four dimensional: the four dimensions being provided by the political, social, economic and the moral facets. Gandhi considered them as constituting the 'square of Swaraj'. Unless these four dimensions are in perfect trim and properly adjusted and co-ordinated, the square of Swaraj will present a distorted picture or as Gandhi said, "it will be out of shape if any of its angles is untrue". He insisted on dimocratisation in the matter of possession and on the exercise of governmental authority 'for the people'. To him Swaraj meant that people shall constitute the sovereign power. Swaraj is 'perfect democracy, in which inequalities based on possession, colour, race, creed or sex vanishes. In it land and state belong to the people, justice is prompt, perfect and cheap and there is freedom of worship, speech and the press."

Gandhi's Swaraj is a state of existence where all social distinctions wither away. He said, "Every community would be on a par with every other, under the Swaraj constitution'. Gandhi treated Swaraj as a synonym of Rama Rajya. Profoundly non-doctrinaire in his approach to religion and as much a

Christian, a Muslim and a Jew as a Hindu in respect of his religious belief, he did not consider Rama Rajya in any Hindu doctrinaire sense of the term. He said, "By Rama Rajya, I do not mean Hindu Rajya. I mean by Rama Rajya Divine Rajya, the Kingdom of God."

Emphasis on self-restraint and self-rule remained a significant cornerstone of Gandhi's moral dimension of Swaraj. He also laid stress on performance of duty. To him, "performance of duty and observance of morality are conceivable terms.' As Wilfred Wellock has observed the basis of Gandhian Swaraj is 'the small community such as the village and the small marker town. Only in such society where politics are local and vital since they have to do with the organisation of the local economic life can there be real political and economic freedom and full personal responsibility."

Features of Satyagrahi

A satyagrahi must be sincere and honest. He must be open-minded, must be a disciplined teacher, he must learn to put on restraints upon his own self. Simplicity and humility are regarded as the key factors of a satyagrahi. A satyagrahi practice truth in his actions, in thought and also in speech. Truth and non-violence with love is essential for satyagrahi. Satyagraha is not a weapon of the coward and the helpless. Gandhi's Satyagraha rejects violence. It is a war without violence. It refers the active force and not the inactive force. Gandhi's Satyagraha never rejects fighting.

Principles of Satyagraha

Satyagraha should follow the following principles :

- Non-violence
- Truth
- Non-stealing
- Chastity
- Non-possession
- Body labour
- Fearlessness
- Equal respect for all religions.
- Freedom from untouchability. Every Satyagrahi in India should follow seven rules.
- Must have a living faith in God.
- Must believe in truth and non-violence.
- Must be leading a chaste life.
- Must be a habitual Khadi wearer and spinner.
- Must abstain from alcohol.
- Must willingly carry out all the rules of discipline that are issued.
- Must obey the jail rules.

Impacts of Swaraj

Swaraj has to be experienced by each one for himself. Swaraj for Gandhi means freedom for the meanest of our countrymen. Constructive work was considered as a continuous programme of socio-economic upliftment of the poor and weaker sections. It is considered as an important part of Swaraj. Swaraj can only be attained, through truth and non-violence.

Swaraj has both a negative and a positive implication. Negatively, Swaraj means freedom from alien rule. Positively, Swaraj means freedom for the whole people, everyone is included. In Swaraj, inequalities based on colour, race, sex vanishes. Gandhi Swaraj is treated as Rama Rajya. By Rama Rajya, he means the Kingdom of God.

Critique on Modern Civilization

Gandhi's critique of modern civilisation is far more complex than is generally imagined and quite different from that of such other thinkers as Rousseau, Carlyle, Ruskin, Tolstoy and Thoreau, by the last three of whom he was deeply influenced. In Gandhi's view, modern civilisation is grounded in a fatally flawed theory of man. Unlike ancient civilisation which was soul or spirit centred, the modern one was body-centred and in that sense 'materialistic'. Gandhi argues that modern civilisation suffered from several basic and interrelated limitations. First, it lacked moral and spiritual depth. Secondly since it had no guiding principles to decide what desires deserved to be satisfied and within what limits, it led to a way of life devoid of meaning and purpose. Thirdly, it dehumanised man and had a profound anti-human bias. Fourthly, it perverted the human psyche and was suffused with the spirit of violence. Finally, it reduced wisdom to knowledge and the latter to a form of power only useful as an instrument of control over nature and other men. It thereby not only perverted the pursuit of truth but also lacked a system of knowledge capable of critically evaluating its basic assumptions and objectives.

Following are given some points on which Gandhi has criticized on modern civilization–

1. For Gandhi modern civilisation was propelled by the two interrelated principles of greed and want.
2. For Gandhi machines relieved drudgery, created leisure, increased efficiency and were indispensable when there was a shortage of labour. Their use must therefore be guided by a well-considered moral theory indicating how men should live, spend their free time and relate to one another. Since the modern economy lacked such a theory and was only propelled by the search for profit, it mechanised production without any regard for its wider moral, cultural and other consequences.
3. For Gandhi the mechanisation or fetishism of technology was closely tied up with the larger phenomenon of industrialism, another apparently self-propelling and endless process or creating larger and larger industries with no other purpose than to produce cheap consumer goods and maximise profit. He argued that since modern economic life following an inexorable momentum of its own, it reduced men to being its helpless and passive victims and represented a new form of slavery, more comfortable and invidious and hence more dangerous than the earlier ones.
4. Modern man, Gandhi went on, spent most of his energy trying to steady himself in a hostile and unsteady environment. He had neither the inclination nor the ability to slow down the tempo of his life, relax, compose himself, reflect on his pattern of life and nurture the inner springs or energy.
5. Gandhi believed that modern civilisation rested on and was sustained by massive violence.

Although convinced that the foundation of modern civilisation was 'rotten', Gandhi did not dismiss it altogether but praised what he took to be its three great achievements. Firstly, he admired its scientific spirit of inquiry. The second great achievement of modern civilisation consisted in understanding and bringing the natural world under greater human control. Thirdly, in Gandhi's view, modern civilisation had greatly contributed to the organisational side of life.

Features of Modern Man

Modern man lives outside himself and exhausts himself physically and spiritually. Gandhi thought that modern civilisation had a depressed air of futility and madness about it, He accepts the utility of machines, but not at the cost of human beings. These professions have become limited because of the craze behind functional specialisation of the modern age. For him, modern society is referred as the most depended society. He says that modern medical science is representing a severe form of violence.

European doctors are the worst of all. For the sake of a mistaken care of the human body, they kill thousands of animals. They practice dissection. No religion sanction this. He says that every profession like lawyers, politicians are suffering from the same tendency. They all are seeing life in parts. He had a problem with domineering rational tendency of modernity.

Gandhi's Concept of Women

Sita Damyanti and Draupazdi were the three ideals of Indian womanhood that Gandhi repeatedly invoked as inspirations for the downtrodden women of India. They were symbols versatile enough to incorporate the qualities that the chose to endow them with. He tended to overburden the symbols with meanings they were ill equipped to carry.

Sita only wore cloth made in India or home-spun and thus, kept her heart and body pure. Furthermore, 'Sita was no slave of Rama.' Gandhi's Sita was no helpless creature. Even the great physical might of Ravan dwindled, when pitched against her superior moral courage. This is the ideal, he presented for Indian women to emulate. From Sita, who was gentleness incarnate.....a delicate flower', to Draupadi, giant oak' in her strength and resoluteness. To Olive Doke a (young girl who had worked among the unclad primitive negro tribes of Africa) a symbol of absolute fearlessness, courage and will to serve a cause Gandhi saw no contradiction in the transition.

Features of Indian Women

Even if all women could not become. Ranis of Jhansi they could emulate the still better example of Sita who even the mighty Ravava dared not touch. He would far rather see India's women trained to wield arms....than that they should feel helpless. But arms, for Gandhi, were a symbol of one's weakness. The real strength of a woman was her consciousness of her purity and 'Chastity'. This equation of rape with loss of virtue reflects the age-old patriarchal bias.

This was Gandhi's standard advice to women for defence against male aggression. Even though he admitted that he was himself incapable of this kind of courage, he felt sure that a truly chaste and brave woman would not find it difficult to kill herself at the altar of her chastity. Women should be as 'self-reliant' as Draupadi was. Krishna here represents no physical man, but as in the Bhagvad Gita the voice of one's conscience and resolute will to follow one's chosen path.

Gandhi's Imagination of Womenhood

Gandhi's ideal of womanhood was Sita, but his message to Indian women was to rise above wifehood and become sisters. He felt a wife could never become a sister in the full sense of the word. He lamented that our women 'know how to be wives not sisters'. It was possible to become the world's sister only by making Brahmacharya' a natural condition and being fired by the spirit of service.

Gandhi's ideal of a wife is Sita was willing to concede that every husband was not likely to be an ideal man. In this regard, he felt the famous 16th century saint poet Mirabai had shown the way. He saw her as one who had the courage to reject the confining role of wife and mother and to remain undaunted by the persecution, which she had to suffer at the hands of her husband and his powerful family. By sheer dint of her moral courage and determination to continue on her chosen path in defiance of all norms of social behaviour, she was even able to convert her husband into a devotee.

Women's Issues

Women were not to confine their concerns only to what are normally seen as women's issues, but have a say in the rebuilding of the whole society. This question of liberation of women, liberation of India, removal of untouchability, amelioration of the economic condition of the masses and the like resolve themselves into penetration into the villages, reconstruction or rather reformation of the village life.

He did not see marriage and motherhood as the only mission in life for every young woman. He repeatedly lamented that 'a vast majority of girls disappear from public life as soon as they are discharge from schools and colleges.' He would rather they were inspired by better examples. "Every Indian girl, is not born to many."

Thought of Gandhi

Gandhi encouraged those who wanted to life a socially useful life to stay unmarried. He did not altogether reject the institution of marriage. Because he realised that sexuality could not be eliminated, no matter how much he propagandised in favour of conquering, it altogether, he saw marriage as the only existing, though inadequate, restraint on sexuality. 'Marriage is a fence that protects religion. If the fence were to be destroyed, religion would go to pieces. The foundation of religion is restraint and marriage is nothing, but restraint.

Passive Resistance

Passive resistance is a method of securing rights by personal suffering. It is the reverse of resistance by arms. When, I refuse to do a thing that is repugnant to my conscience, I use should force. For instance, the government of the day has passed a law, which is applicable to me. I do not like it. It by using violence.

But to insist on absolute uniformity in a system like that of untouchability which after all is a matter of social behaviour and which must therefore vary with the circumstances of each province and also of each individual is simply to trifle with the problem. Passive resistance cannot proceed a step without fearlessness. Those alone can follow the path of passive resistance, who are free from fear, whether as to their possessions, false honour their relatives, the government, bodily injuries, death.

Machinery Impact on Human

It is machinery that has impoverished India. It is difficult to measure the harm that Manchester has done to us. But, I make a mistake. How can Manchester be blamed? We wore Manchester cloth and that is why Manchester wove it. I was delighted when, I read about the bravery of Bengal. There are no cloth-mills in that Presidency. It is true, Bengal encourage the mill industry of Bombay. If Bengal had proclaimed a boycott of all machine-made goods, it would have been much better.

Condition of Labour

The workers in the mills of Bombay have become slaves. The condition of the women working in the mills is shocking. When. there were no mills, these women were not starving. And those who have amassed wealth out of factories are not likely to be better than other rich men.

It would be folly to assume that an Indian Rockefeller would be better than the American Rockefeller. Impoverished India can become free, but it will be hard for an India made rich through immorality to regain its freedom. I fear we will have to admit that moneyed men support British rule, their interest is bound up with its stability. Money renders a man helpless.

Features of Complete Independence

Complete Independence through truth and non-violence means the independence of every unit, it means the humblest of the nation, without distinction of race, colour or creed. This independence is never exclusive. It is wholly compatible with interdependence within or without. Practice will always fall short of the theory, even as the drawn line falls short of the theoretical line of Euclid.

It has three definite functions which are as follows :

- It can be effectively offered for the redress of a local wrong.
- It can be offered without regard to effect, though aimed at a particular wrong or evil, by way of self-immolation in order to rouse local consciousness or conscience. Such was the case in Champaran, when I offered Civil Disobedience without any regard to the effect and well knowing that even the people might remain apathetic.
- In the place of full response to constructive effort, it can be offered as it was in 1941. The issue must be definite and capable of being clearly understood and within the power of the opponent to yield. This method properly applied must, lead to the final goal.

Features of Gandhi's Theory

Gandhi was not only a politician par excellence, but also an individual, integrated within his social milieu and aware of his internal contradictions and the need to transcend them. Chastity is one of the greatest disciplines without which the mind cannot attain requisite firmness.

A man who is unchaste loses stamina, become emasculated and cowardly. He whose mind is given over to animal passions is not capable of any great effort. This can be proved by innumerable instances. Such an indulgence, except for perpetuating the race, is strictly prohibited. A passive resister has to avoid even that very limited indulgence, because he can have no desire for progeny. How is one to carry one's wife with one? What are her rights and other such questions? Yet those who wish to take part in a great work are bound to solve these puzzles.

Gandhi's Efforts in Nationalist Movement

Gandhi advocates the use of the spinning wheel in a series of writings mainly meant for women, wherein he has given his new message for the women of India, spin for the upliftment of the country.

It was not only an effective strategy for increasing the involvement of women in the national struggle, but it also made possible their involvement, without shifting the terrain of the movement and struggle from the household.

Gandhi is not only bringing the nationalist programme within the four walls of the household, but he is also redefining political participation. Participation for the women in the nationalist awakening means spinning at home. Gandhi, it seems, has a very clear idea of the characteristics that define public and private space. The private is the domestic sphere, the household, a sphere where he seems to he affirming the complete legitimacy of the woman by creating a new role for her in it.

Gandhi on the Concepts of States

Men and women are of equal rank, but they are not identical. They are a peerless pair being supplementary to one another each helps the other, so that without the one, the existence of me other cannot be conceived.

On the other hand, home life is entirely in the sphere of women and therefore, in domestic affairs, in the upbringing and education of children, women ought to have more knowledge and these very biological characteristics of having productive capacities and of being mother are give are women only.

The power, denied to men of creating new ideals and transiting them into action. By comparison man is thoughtless, impatient and given to the pursuit of novelty. When, therefore, she has a new idea, it seems to have its birth in the tender depths of her heart.

Framework of Gandhi

Gandhi's writings till 1916, on women, have been couched in a frame work, which were common to the reformists. Gandhi specially seems to have close affinity with Ishwar Chandra Vidyasagar and his ideas on women's education with which he agreed and whose cause he advocates. Only once, in 1906-07, does he strike a different note whilst commenting on the struggle being waged by the upper class suffragettes for their political rights in England.

Gandhi does not make any disparaging remarks on their confrontation with the police or their, fight for political equality, but he also does not draw out any implications for this movement for the women of India. As yet, in Gandhi there does seem to be any consciousness of the distinct place of women in the national awakening. Women cannot think of themselves as weak creatures. Sita, Draupadi and other women (have) filled the wicked with awe', he states. They cannot be weak if they have been 'mothers of sons. Men being physically stronger should not become a monster and oppress woman, but on the contrary, 'he must do her service by protecting her and providing her with the means through, which she may cultivate strength of soul.'

Weakness Turns into Strength

For in Gandhi, women's weakness is now turned into strength. Satyagraha is indeed the weapon of the weak against the strong. The fight by the Indians against the British, of weak against the strong, is only possible, when the weak perceive their weakness as strength and as a strategy to overpower their enemy. Gandhi links his understanding of women's weakness and its transformation into strength as part of the same strategy and as embodied in the conceptions of Satyagraha and Ahimsa. "The non-violent movement,' he asserts, 'is to enable the weakest human beings to Vindicate their dignity.' Woman is the weakness personified. Yet, 'she may be weak in body, but she can be as strong in soul.' The spinning wheel with all its implications is the weapon in India at least for the strong in soul.

Gandhi on Untouchability

From 1925, onwards, Gandhi starts a campaign against untouchability and writes a series of articles against the evils of Hinduism. As part of this campaign, he also introduces the problem of child widows and actively advocates the remarriage of these widows.

In a stringent critique, he exposes in detail the contemporary discriminatory practices that legitimise male widower's remarriage, while not allowing women to remarry. He criticises the argument that early marriage makes possible the retention of purity in women and their adjustment into the new family. Gandhi instead argues that the shastras, which have affirmed the early marriage of girls are not depicting the true essence of Hinduism but are in fact interpolations. It is sinful and illegal to marry off girls at a young age.

Gandhi now creates a god-like woman leader fighting violence and justice. As the embodiment of the universal mother, she is the repository and the symbol of all that is morally good of mankind. It is not necessary for her to involve herself, in politics to fight injustice because she is now the personification of renunciation and thus can now 'adorn both her sex and nation'. She is no longer weak and at the mercy of men. She is Sabala.

Non-Violence as a Good Weapon

Gandhi's insistence on non-violence as a revolutionary weapon contributed to creating favourable conditions for mass participation of people, especially women. More and more people felt encouraged to come out of their homes, instead of hiding in fear, as they tend to do, when movements encourage the use of violence. Thus women's traditional qualities, such as their lesser capacity for organised violence, were not downgraded, but were held up as models of superior courage. When, used consciously and collectively, their form of non-violence could put the mightiest weapons to shame.

Different Aspects

The three aspects social political, and personal are inextricably linked because it is only with Gandhi's emergence as a political leader, when he confronted the problem of mass mobilisation, that he became aware of women not only in terms of their problems, but also as a powerful potential force in society, hitherto over looked and kept suppressed.

If most Indian women had lost 'the spirit of strength and courage, the power of independent thinking and initiative, which actuated the women of ancient India. They should begin by imparting education to their own wives, mothers and daughters. To those who argued that the political struggle ought to have primacy over everything else, he answered. To postpone social reform, till after the attainment of Swaraj, is not to know the meaning of Swaraj.

Major Contribution of Gandhi

The main contribution of Gandhi to the cause of women lay in his absolute and unequivocal insistence on their personal dignity and autonomy in the family and in society. Personal and social experience had convinced him that hitherto 'Man has regarded woman as his tool.'

She has learnt to be his tool and in the end found it easy and pleasurable to be such, because when one drags another in his fall the descent is easy. While, he agreed with those who felt that 'these is no power of resistance left' in the women of India 'to fight against any evil whatever', yet he emphasised that women needed to take the task of their upliftment into their own hands.

The Custom of Child Marriage

In Gandhi's view, one of the glaring abuse of Indian womanhood was the custom of child marriage. This evil as intimately related to that of child widowhood. 'It is religion, not religion, to give religious sanction to a brutal custom' and by countenancing them 'we recede from God as well as Swaraj. Thus, the question of women's oppression was linked to social and national health.

Parents who committed the sin of 'marrying' their daughters of tender age should expiate for the sin by remarrying these daughters, should they become widowed while they are yet in their teens.' Gandhi felt that the presence of thousands of such widows in any society was a serious menace. It was like 'setting on a mine, which may explode at any moment.'

But his advocacy of remarriage was not based on seeing ascetic widowhood as an inherent part of the patriarchal Ideology for women's repression. Remarriage was advocate in the interest of social health. Every sexual relationship outside of marriage was seen as sinful. That is why, while in the case of child widows, Gandhi was emphatically in favour of remarriage.

Gandhi on Prostitution

The fight against prostitution and the rehabilitation of 'our fallen sisters' was an integral part of the programme for national reconstruction and purification, which Gandhi urged women to take up. There are quite a few instances of prostitutes, young and old, having given up their calling and taken to Charkha as a means of livelihood, in response to (Gandhi's call. This happened at Madaripur and Noakhali in Bengal. But beyond khadi and Charkha, Gandhi's panacea for all evils, he had no clear programme for these women and their rehabilitation nor did he put forth any ideas about how to combat the institution.

On the other hand, Gandhi displayed an insufferable kind of self-righteousness, quite out of character, when he heard the form and shape the movement for the reclamation of fallen sisters was taking at Barisal.

He admitted, that they were 'intelligent, modest and dignified' and that their 'determination was as firm as that of any satyagrahi, he declined to accept them as Congress members or even to accept their donations unless they gave up being prostitutes. He was alarmed that the 'corporate activity' of these women was tending to make them unhealthily forward.

He declared : 'We will not incorporate an association of known thieves for the purpose for which these women have formed their association! Yet he considered them even worse than thieves because, while thieves stole material possessions, these women steal virtue. Gandhi never displayed this kind of self-righteousness *vis-a-vis* better known exploiters of society. The doors of the Congress were not closed to even the most tyrannical of landlords or the most corrupt of businessmen.

Women's Role in the Struggle for Swaraj

Gandhi's first encounter with woman-power took place in Africa. This was during the agitation against the Black Act in 1913, when instead of eliminating the disabilities already imposed on Indians, a new Supreme Court ruling, in a test case, declared all Hindu, Muslim and Parsee marriages invalid, Gandhi 'suddenly found himself heading or rather swept along by, a cohort of furious and exalted maenads.' The long-delayed entry of women in the satyagraha gave the movement a new force. Their impassioned appeals instantly brought out thousands of miners in a protest strike.

The success of this satyagraha was in no small measure due to the new moral force that women's entry brought into the movement. Gandhi was quick to learn this lesson. 'Many of our movements stop halfway because of the condition of our women.

D.D. Upadhyaya

Deen Dayal Upadhyaya (1916-68) was one of the founders of the Jana Sangh, which later became the Bhartiya Janta Party. He has been the source of ideological guidance and moral inspiration for the Bhartiya Janata Party since its inception. He advocated the doctrine of Integral humanism, which was adopted by the Jaṇa Ṣangh in 1965 and later by Bharatiya Janata Party as its official doctrine. It aims to appeal to broad sections of Indian society by presenting an indigenous economic model that puts human being at center of development.

Before independence all the movements and policies in the country had one principal 'aim to drive out the foreign rulers and to achieve independence'. There was less thought or debate over the face of the new Bharat after independence. Although leaders like Gandhiji discussed the idea of independent India in his book 'Hind Swaraj' and Lokmanya tilak in 'Gita Rahasya' yet there was no coherent ideology. All ideological differences were kept aside in order to achieve the collective goal of independence and self-rule. In the aftermath of the independence struggle, differences soon surfaced between political ideologies and groups. This phase soon followed by political opportunism with the sole purpose to gain power without any principles. Many in the political were of the viewpoint that one could adopt anything from extreme Marxism to capitalism just to remain in power. In this environment, Deen Dayal felt that the rise in opportunism in the political parties was detrimental to national interest. Lack of national identity has led to "confusion about our goal and the direction". Further he felt that the present political establishment was getting suffocated by Western theories and ideologies and consequently there was a big roadblock on the growth and expansion of original Bharathiya thought. In this background gave the so called doctrine of integral humanism based on the values of Sanatana dharma, in the form of four lectures.

He was of the view that an independent nation cannot progress if it relies upon the Western concepts like individualism, democracy, socialism, communism, capitalism etc. It does not mean that he was critical of these concepts. According to him modern technology and western science should be welcomed but wanted it to be adapted to suit Indian requirements. He explains that western science and the western way of life are two different things. Whereas western science is universal and must be absorbed by us if we wish to go forward, the same is not true about the western way of life and values. In fact he advocated that thoughtless imitation of the West must be discarded. He even exhorts Indian leaders to shun away the superficial Western foundations which became the basis of Indian polity after independence and take inspiration from timeless traditions of our ancient culture. He also envisaged the concept of Dharma Rajya for Indian state which is duty oriented unlike other concepts which are right-oriented. Dharma Rajya does not recognize any individual or body as sovereign. Every individual is subject to certain obligations and regulations. Rights of the executive, of the legislature, as well as of the people, are determined and regulated by Dharma. Naturally, therefore, there is no scope here for rights being trampled upon or for any hankering after unlimited rights. Also, there is no danger of dereliction of duty, of power-madness, or of any conflict of rights. Therefore the purpose of Upadhyaya was to identify desirable goals for Indian society and the intellectual and spiritual basis for their attainment. But, his political philosophy has remained largely undebated and now in era of neo liberalism researchers should consider its broad agenda seriously so that we remain adhere to our national identity.

Narayana Guru

"Swamiji and Narayana Guru were the spiritual emancipators of India. They took inspiration from the Indian philosophical traditions, especially Vedanta. On the basis of which they presented a new design for life: a model contentment, compassion, balance, and harmony. Both of them accepted religion as one of the most important aspects of human life."

"Both of them tried to base a religion on the rational ground by accepting reason as the final guide even in the field of religion and the aim of religion as realisation. One of the most important things in these two rishis is that they conducted and participated in religious conferences. The religious ideas of these two rishis suggest some new ideas and could throw new light on religious concepts."

"Sri Narayana Guru was a wisdom teacher of India whose life followed the ancient and immemorial pattern of oriental saints and prophets. His basic stand was that of a non-dualist Vedantic visionary. This made it possible for him to appreciate the value elements of all traditions and to view all religions with the attitude of a devoted lover of beauty, goodness, and truth. Hence his philosophy is at once traditional and modern, as well as scientific and religious; which makes it all comprehensive, universal, and unitive."

"Swamiji and Guru have the same opinion that religion was not theoretical but can be applied in daily life. They gave a practical demonstration of Advaita in real life. The unique trend of their philosophies is that religion was brought down from the whimsical heights to the midst of the masses. In their views, we have seen a lot of similarities and slight differences. But their formation of a new ideal of universal religion and one religion can be called universal love or universal brotherhood. It has given an equal value for all the religions of the world, as they truly exist. Their identification of truth was absolute and scientific, and they showed that religion can be practised by each and everybody. They made all understand that it is not necessary to have a vast literary knowledge, but the practice—it is verv much needed. Therefore, it can be applied to all nations, all societies, and individuals. It is the harmony of all religions and one of the best solutions for the prevalent religious conflicts in the world, and to make the people aware that essentially all religions are one and the same."

The Guru's slogan of 'one caste, one religion, one god' is an elevated expression of humanism which recognises the value of a human being as being supreme. A value that simultaneously recognises all human beings as being equal, irrespective of all social divisions. This universality of oneness of humanity, in a sense, crystallises the finest elements of rational thought and philosophy that emerged in the course of the advance of human civilization in these lands. As "different rivers flow through different courses to merge in the ocean", so do different human beings through the practice of individual beliefs and faith eventually merge with humanity as a whole. This is humanism of the highest variety.

In the context of the concrete conditions in India today, the Guru's philosophy has a very strong relevance. The recent incidents of attacks on the dalits and other marginalised sections of the Indian people highlight the need to adhere to the values propagated by the Guru – 'the oneness of humanity'. Likewise, the growing communal polarisation in India which targets and attacks religious minorities requires to be combated with the Guru's values and philosophy. In that sense, this 160th birth anniversary of Sree Narayana Guru has an important relevance to meet the current challenges that threaten the unity and integrity of India whose religious, linguistic, ethnic, cultural, regional diversity is unmatched by any country in the world today. India's unity and integrity can only be protected and strengthened by strengthening the bonds of commonality that run through this diversity. India's social stability and equanimity will only implode if any effort is made to impose any form of uniformity – religious, linguistic, cultural etc – upon this diversity. Unfortunately, it is precisely this that is being sought by the current campaigns of the communal forces in India.

These campaigns to sharpen communal polarisation are conducted also through unleashing violence and terror which targets some political parties like the CPI(M) apart from religious minorities and dalits. The recent developments in Kannur district, Kerala, confirm this pattern. Since the LDF victory in the recent assembly elections was declared, six CPI(M) workers have been killed and around 300 of its members injured in brutal attacks launched by the RSS. 35 offices of our Party have been attacked and destroyed and 80 houses of Party workers vandalised and damaged.

Ironically, the RSS/BJP organised a demonstration outside the CPI(M) headquarters in New Delhi alleging CPI(M) terror. At that very moment, a CPI(M) local committee member, K Mohanan, was hacked to death in the chief minister's constituency.

The CPI(M) state secretary and the chief minister have both appealed for peace and invited the RSS for talks to end such violence. We continue to await their response.

The Guru's philosophy is, thus, a weapon to safeguard and cherish India as we know of it today. This growth of rabid communal polarisation that we see around us today, in India, runs completely in contradiction with the body of thought and action that the Guru has bequeathed to us. This rich legacy and the philosophical activities that the Guru undertook had heralded a movement for social renaissance in Kerala. Remember, Swami Vivekananda had once described the Kerala society as a 'mad house' of casteism. The Guru, through his philosophy of oneness of humanity, spread the indomitable values of equality and humanism. Kerala was a society where caste prejudices went beyond even the obnoxious practice of untouchability. In Kerala, there was the practice of unseability. Comrade EMS Namboodiripad used to tell us that in his childhood, it was not unusual to see some 'unfortunate' human beings carrying a bell around their neck whose sound would warn the upper castes, to take a different path!

It was the social renaissance heralded by the Guru, amongst others, that has transformed this society into one with the most progressive values in the country today. In the process, Kerala society has achieved such advances in its human development indices that it matches and, in some cases, outstrips the standards existing in the developed capitalist countries today. In the field of literacy, education, gender equality, religious harmony and other social parameters, Kerala proudly stands at the top on the rest of India.

The Guru used spirituality as a propelling force for upward social mobility of the people. The Guru, thus, gave a new weapon in the struggle against caste based social oppression. In this process, he developed a unique combination of materialism and spiritualism, propagating the Buddha's preachings of the control over the body, word, mind, food and deed. The consecration of the Shiva Lingam in 1888 – the Aruvippuram Prathishta - remains a landmark that has gone way beyond being a symbolic gesture, in this struggle against caste based social oppression.

The Guru's humanism has a strong resonance with the Communist philosophy and worldview. The overriding concern of Marxism is humanism. In fact, Karl Marx had once said, "Nothing human is alien to me". It is the pursuit of the simple question of what constitutes the real freedom of a human being and his consequent liberation from all forms of bondage, Marx proceeded to reject the Hegelian idea of the revolution of the mind as articulated by Feuerbach, during his time, to come to a conclusion of seminal importance. This was: consciousness of a human being is determined by the social conditions and not vice a versa.

Marxism's focus, thus, is on changing the concrete conditions of material existence, as the basic pre-requisite for human liberation. This emerges from the understanding that without changing the material conditions of existence to eliminate human exploitation of all forms, liberation of human beings is not possible. Thus, followed Marx's own scientific study of the real living conditions of the people and his consequent dissection of capitalism.

A great deal of controversy is always generated regarding the Marxist understanding of religion. The popular perception is the normally out of context quotation that "religion is the opium of the people". In fact, deliberately, the passage in which this statement finds place is never quoted in the full.

Marx had stated :"Religious distress is at the same time the expression of real distress and the protest against real distress. Religion is the sigh of the oppressed creature, the heart of the heartless world, just as it is the spirit of the spiritless situation. It is the opium of the people".

For a human being who is oppressed, religion provides the escape for relief, it provides a "heart in a heartless world, a spirit in a spiritless situation." This is the strength and power of religion.

Marxism does not attack religion *per se.* Marxism's quest is to change the real world; to transform the comforts that religion provides – "heart of a heartless world, a spirit in a spiritless situation" – into concrete reality. Therefore, as a Communist, we can assure you that the CPI(M) will be the foremost upholder of every individual's right to his/her choice of their faith and their right to maintain their beliefs and propagate them. We will defend, till the last breath, this right of the individual choice and protect the faith of every individual. It, therefore, necessarily follows that we shall also protect everybody against any attempt to interfere into the rights of individual liberty of faith by any body of thought or action. However, this is precisely what the communal forces are doing in India today by sharpening communal polarisation. The CPI(M)'s opposition to communalism is, hence, integral to both its philosophy and practice.

Yet another resonance with Marxist philosophy is the Guru's emphasis on "*freedom through education, strength through organisation, economic independence through industry*". Guru, thus, emphasises the strengthening of the material basis of human existence as a prerequisite for the realisation of his vision of the `oneness of humanity'. The radical change in the material conditions of existence of human beings is precisely what we, Marxists, are seeking to achieve in India.

The Guru's philosophy spread far and wide beyond the confines of Kerala. I am told that Mahatma Gandhi came to the Guru's ashram thrice during our freedom movement. Gurudev Rabindranath Tagore came to meet the Guru in 1922. This, surely, was a meeting of great minds. Tagore had by then penned the Nobel Prize winning immortal lines to awaken India: *"Where the mind is without fear and the head is held high; Where knowledge is free; Where the world has not been broken up into fragments by narrow domestic walls;…."*

The Guru's teachings and personal example are, thus, not merely relevant but more necessary to meet the challenges before us in India today.

On the one hand, the material basis of existence for the vast mass of our people and the country, as a consequence of embracing the neo-liberal policy trajectory by the Indian ruling classes, is deteriorating. We have a situation in India today where, despite bombastic sloganeering like 'Make in India', 'Stand up India', 'Digital India' etc., industrial growth is stagnating, if not declining, unemployment is growing, the rise in prices of all essential commodities is relentless imposing greater economic burdens on the people. Hunger and malnutrition, especially among women and children, continue to place vast sections of the Indian people in poverty and misery. The Global Hunger Index, released last week, ranks India at 97 out of 118 countries. With 215 million Indians going hungry, India is behind countries like Bangladesh and Rwanda. India's agrarian distress is intensifying leading to thousands of Indian farmers committing distress suicides.

This situation has to change. India has no dearth of resources. What India requires is pro-people economic policies whereby our resources can be used to create a better India for all Indian people. Instead, what we see today is that there are two Indias in the making – a 'shining India' for a few and a 'suffering India' for the most. This gap between the two Indias continues to widen. Unless this process is reversed by alternative policies, Indian people cannot realise their inherent potential.

Unless material needs are satisfied, the growth of spiritualism leading to social renaissance and, therefore, to cultural renaissance would be simply impossible. The economic policies followed by the current central government in India only buttresses such material regression of our people's lives. These policies need to be resisted and reversed. This is one focus of CPI(M)'s activities today.

On the other hand, the CPI(M)'s other focus is against the growing communal polarisation and the vicious pursuit of consolidating the Hindutva communal vote bank politics which is leading to severe ruptures in our society that can well destroy the unity and integrity of India. Under the present central government, both these aspects of anti-people economic reforms and communal polarisation constitute its singular agenda. In the process, the communal forces even make an attempt to forcibly appropriate the Guru's philosophy and legacy.

This, simply, cannot be allowed. Such efforts, in particular, have to be defeated in order to carry ourselves to higher levels of social and material existence as envisaged and propagated by the Guru. The efforts to replace the rich Indian history with Hindu mythology and the evolution of the syncretic Indian philosophy with a monolithic Hindu theology will have to be resisted and defeated.

Tiruvallur

Tirukkural is a 2000 year old Tamil book that compresses 133 different topics in beautiful poetry. The topics range from war [like Sun Tzu] to economics [like Kautilya] to religion, politics, family life to even beautiful ways to woo your girl. It is among the most complete philosophica works in terms of breadth.

Unlike religious works, it is practical and simple that we make our 5 year olds read it among their first things. Even after 2000 years, those ideas look as fresh as when it was written. These are allover Tamil Nadu, but the translations are quite common across the world.

Background

Tirukkural is the core of Tamil philosophy. It is a 2000 year old text that feels as good as new. The language is fresh, readable, super concise and packs an extraordinary level of education for politicians, lovers, devotees, leaders and businessmen. The intense handling of diverse philosophy is unmatched. You will be surprised how much insights you can draw today from this ancient work. In this post, I will attempt to translate the key poems of this magnificent text.

We don't know either the original name of the book nor the author. The book name merely translates to "Verses of God" and the author's name Thrivalluvar is also made up. It is considered to be an equivalent of the Vedas by the Tamils and finds a lot of similarities with the Hindu texts.

Some classic couplets of 2000 year old work:

1. The people who are praising flute and lute as the sweetest in the world have not paid attention to their toddler's baby talk.
2. Great is the joy of the mother when a child is born to her; but greater is her joy when she hears his unblemished character and scholarliness from others.
3. Better to lose fighting an elephant than to feel elated winning a rabbit.
4. Retaliation will bring joy only for a day. Patience and forgiveness will bring joy for life.
5. Even the most powerful person in the world will get into serious trouble with a loose tongue.

6. Even fire burns will heal easily. But burns from loose words will never be.
7. Even if God doesn't help you, your efforts will eventually bear fruits.

Structure

It is comprised of 1330 couplets each with exactly 7 words.

There are 133 chapters and 3 parts. The 3 main parts are:

1. Aram (Dharma / Justice)
2. Porul (Artha / Wealth & power)
3. Inbam (Kama / Love & Sex).

Jyotiba Phule

JOTIRAO GOVINDRAO PHULE occupies a unique position among the social reformers of Maharashtra in the nineteenth century. While other reformers concentrated more on reforming the social institutions of family and marriage with special emphasis on the status and right of women, Jyotiba Phule revolted against the unjust caste system under which millions of people had suffered for centuries and developed a critique of Indian social order and Hinduism. During this period, number of social and political thinkers started movement against such systems and methods. These thinkers aimed at upliftment of the status of women socially, economically, educationally and politically. Of these socio-political thinkers Mahatma Phule, Mahatma Gandhi, Dr. B.R. Ambedkar, Raja Ram Mohan Roy, Ishwar Chandra Vidyasagar, and such other have organized movement for striving equality for dalits, backward classes and women. As such, Mahatma Phule was an earliest leader, who strongly opposed gender inequality. He was in the real sense a great thinker finder of truth... He was severely criticized by Brahmin samaj for his noble work and attacked by them. But he continued with his movement. He sacrificed his life for the upliftment of untouchables, peasants and women. Mahatma Jyoti Rao Phule is regarded as the most important figure of social reform movement in India. He is regarded as the father of Indian social revolution.

Some important Facts about Mahatma Jotiba Phule:

There are some important facts to consider about this great personality. He is a real inspiration and ideal reformer of India:

- Phule had read biographies of George Washington and Chhatrapti Shivaji. They were source of inspiration for him. Phule was influenced by Thomas Paine's ideas and his book "The Rights of Man". Phule himself has recorded that he was influenced by the ideas of Paine. In place of exploitative Indian social order, Phule wanted to establish a society founded on principles of Individual liberty and equality and in place of Hinduism he would have like to put universal religion.
- Mahatma Phule was the first defender of human equality and rights. We should understand and appreciate the profound significance of his unflinching espousal of the rights of man which remained till the end of his life a major theme of his writings and a goal of his actions.
- He was First revolutionary and leader of downtrodens, peasants and supporter of women's education. He paved the way for the new era of social activism. He established many institutions and tried to remove manmade inequality. He was the first active leader of downtroddens and introduced us to humanity. He was propagator of Human unity and national progress.

- Dr. B.R. Ambedkar said "Mahatma Phule the greatest Shudra of modern India who made the lower classes of Hindus conscious of their slavery to the higher classes who preached the gospel that for India social democracy was more vital than independence from foreign rule."
- Phule's views and philosophy was based on facts, reality, experiences and observation. In that sense his philosophy was not utopiean but realistic. He was a source of inspiration for Maharshi Shinde, Dr. Babasaheb Ambedkar, Gadgebaba and Sahu Maharaj.
- He was a Founder of many movements –
  (1) Movement against discrimination (2) Movement of Dalit (3) Movement of women's education. (4) peasant's movement (5) movement against blind faith.

We can define "Philosopher" a person who establishes the central ideas of some movement, cult, etc., or a person who regulates his or her life, actions, judgments, utterances, etc., by the light of reason." There are several other titles which can be used for Mahatma Jyotiba Phule like educationist, social revolutionary, humanist, feminist and so on. But if we can use only single word for him it cannot explain his enlightening personality. Since we can find several ideas related to metaphysics, epistemology, ethics, socio-political philosophy in his writing, so here we used the title "Philosopher" for him. A philosopher is that person who contributed in more than one knowledge discipline. In modern Indian philosophy we can consider him and also include in the core philosophical courses which can be teach at graduation and postgraduate level. This is the tragedy of our Indian education system that those thinkers who really contributed in the educational, socio-political and other aspects of Indian peoples are remained far from core academic environment. This is the real need of our education system that ideas of revolutionaries like Mahatma Jyotiba Phule, Dr. B.R. Ambedkar and Shaheed Bhagat Singh should be reached to every Indian. Here we will discuss Mahatma Jyotiba Phule's ideas with the titles which have been already established:

A. Feminism and Women Empowerment

B. Philosophy of Education

C. Ideas on Social Justice and Equality

D. Philosophy of Politics and Economics

E. Philosophy of Religion

Mahatrna Jyotiba Phule do not want be a religious thinker, religious guru or a philosopher of religion. Also he was not interested to prove the existence of God, relation of God and the world etc. His intention was to show the dilemma created by religious authorities who bound man in religious rituals and made peoples enemy of each other. His thinking was that Hindu religion not only give spiritual knowledge to man but also bound his social and personal life in religious bigotries. He wants that religion which gives man a true freedom to grow socially and spiritually. Phule influenced by radical religious ideas of Thomas Paine could succeed in doing this kind of a theoretical exercise. Phule believed in one God (Nirmik). He regarded God as a creator of this world and all men and women his children. There are thirty-three articles in the Sarvajanik Satyadharma, which define the rules for the creation of a world-family based on basic human rights as well as the social and intellectual attitudes essential for it...

In the end, it is also added that various great personalities were inspired by the personality of Mahatma Jyoti Rao Phule who brought great changes in social and economic fields of India. Dr. Babasaheb Bhim Rao Ambedkar, first law minister of the Republic of India and the architect of Indian Constitution was inspired by his noble work towards humanity and he followed the philosophy of Mahatma Jyotiba Phule based upon justice, equality, liberty and fraternity. He followed all the suggestions given by Jyotiba as right to education to all, special provisions for women, minorities, downtrodden etc. It is also important to note that Mahatma Phule has left, grappling with issues that we have still not resolved more than 125 years after his death in 1890, he could have deserved better recognition in the society. Government should have to make proper provisions of Mahatma Jyotiba Phule books in schools and colleges. Mahatma Jyotiba Phule 's philosophy of education, human rights, women empowerment, socio-political and religious ideas needs to be initiated actively in the society for its betterment.

M.N. Roy

M.N. Roy was a twentieth century Indian philosopher. He began his career as a militant political activist and left India in 1915 in search of arms for organizing an insurrection against British rule in India. However, Roy's attempts to secure arms ended in a failure, and finally in June 1916, he landed in San Francisco, California. It was there that Roy, who was then known as Narendra Nath Bhattacharya, changed his name to Manbendra Nath Roy. Roy developed friendships with several American radicals, and frequented the New York Public Library. He began a systematic study of socialism, originally with the intention of combating it, but he soon discovered that he had himself become a socialist! Roy met Lenin in Moscow in 1920, and went on to become an international ranking communist leader. Nevertheless, in September 1929 he was expelled from the Communist International for various reasons. He returned to India in December 1930 and was sentenced to six years imprisonment for his role in the Kanpur Communist Conspiracy Case.

Roy's real philosophical quest began during his prison years which he decided to use for writing a systematic study of 'the philosophical consequences of modern science', which would be a re-examination and re-formulation of Marxism to which he subscribed since 1919. The reflections, which Roy wrote in jail over a period of five years, grew into nine rigorous volumes. The 'Prison Manuscripts' have not yet been published in their totality, and are currently preserved in the Nehru Memorial Museum and Library Archives in New Delhi. However, selected portions from the manuscript were published as separate books in the 1930s and the 1940s.

In his philosophical works, Roy has made a clear distinction between philosophy and religion. According to Roy, no philosophical advancement is possible unless we get rid of orthodox religious ideas and theological dogmas. On the other hand, Roy has envisaged a very close relationship between philosophy and science. Moreover, Roy has given a central place to intellectual and philosophical revolution in his philosophy. Roy maintained that a philosophical revolution must precede a social revolution. Besides, Roy has, in the tradition of eighteenth century French materialist Holbach, revised and restated materialism in the light of twentieth century scientific developments. In the context of Indian philosophy, Roy could be placed in the tradition of ancient Indian materialism—both Lokayata and Carvaka.

Philosophy, according to Roy, is contemplation, study and knowledge of nature. Its function is "to know things as they are, and to find the common origin of the diverse phenomena of nature, in nature itself".

Philosophy, says Roy, begins when "spiritual needs" of human beings are no longer satisfied by primitive natural religion, which imagines and worships a variety of gods as personification of the diverse phenomena of nature. The grown-up human is no longer satisfied with the nursery-tales, with which "he was impressed in his spiritual childhood".. Intellectual growth emboldens him to seek the causes of all natural phenomena in nature itself and to "find in nature a unity behind its diversity." (Roy 1951)

In his book *Science and Philosophy*, Roy defines philosophy as "the theory of life". The function of philosophy, in words of Roy, "is to solve the riddle of the Universe". According to Roy, philosophy is born out of the efforts of man to explain nature and to understand his own relationship with it.

A. Philosophy and Metaphysics

Roy has made a distinction between philosophy and metaphysics. According to him, metaphysics also begins with the desire to discover the unity behind the diversity. However, it leaves the ground of philosophy in its quest for a "noumenon" beyond nature, something that is distinct from "phenomena". Thus, it abandons the inquiry into what really exists, and "plunges into the wilderness of speculation". It takes up the absurd task of knowing the intangible, as the condition for the knowing the tangible.

It is obvious that Roy was opposed to speculative philosophy, which set for itself the impossible task of prying into the transcendental being "above and behind" the physical universe - of acquiring the knowledge of the reality behind the appearance. According to Roy, an inquiry, which denies the very existence of the object to be enquired, is bound to end in idle dreams and hopeless confusion.

B. Philosophy and Religion

Roy was opposed not only to speculative philosophy but also to the identification of philosophy with poetic fancy or theology and religion. According to him, for the average educated human, the term philosophy has a very vague meaning. It stands not only for speculative thought, but also for poetic fancy. Not only that, in India, philosophy is often not distinguished from religion and theology. "Indeed," according to Roy, "what is generally believed to be the distinctive feature of Indian philosophy is that it has not broken away from the medieval tradition, as modern Western philosophy did in the seventeenth century."

According to Roy, faith in the supernatural does not allow the search for the causes of natural phenomena in nature itself. Therefore, rejection of orthodox religious ideas and theological dogmas is the precondition for philosophy. Roy was of the view that, religion will certainly be liquidated by the rise of science, because scientific knowledge enables humankind to answer questions, confronted by which in its childhood, it was forced to assume super-natural forces or agencies. Therefore, according to Roy, in order to perform its function, "philosophy must break away from religion" and start from the reality of the physical universe.

C. Philosophy and Science

On the one hand, Roy regards rejection of orthodox religious ideas and theological dogmas as the essential precondition of philosophy, and on the other, he envisages a very intimate relationship between philosophy and science. In fact, according to Roy, the philosophical significance of modern scientific theory is to render untenable the old division of labor between science and philosophy. Science is, says Roy, stepping over the old boundary line, "Digging deeper and deeper into the secrets of nature, science has come up against problems, the solution of which was previously left to philosophy. Scientific inquiry has pushed into what is traditionally regarded as the 'metaphysical' realm."

The problems of philosophy - cosmology, ontology and epistemology - can all be progressively solved, according to Roy, in the light of scientific knowledge. The function of philosophy is, points out Roy, to explain existence as a whole. An explanation of existence requires knowledge of existence. Knowledge about the different phases of existence is being gathered by the various branches of science. Therefore, says Roy, the function of philosophy is to coordinate an entire body of scientific knowledge into a comprehensive theory of nature and life. Philosophy can now exist only as the science of sciences - a systematic coordination, a synthesis of all positive knowledge, continuously readjusting itself to progressive enlargement of the store of human knowledge. A mystic metaphysical conception of the world is no longer to be accorded the distinction of philosophy. Thus, according to Roy, philosophy is a logical coordination of all the branches of positive knowledge in a system of thought to explain the world rationally and to serve as a reliable guide for life.

Roy's New Humanism: Twenty-Two Theses on Radical Democracy

"New Humanism" is the name given by Roy to the "new philosophy of revolution" which he developed in the later part of his life. This philosophy has been summarized by Roy in the "Twenty-Two Theses" and elaborated in his *New Humanism - A Manifesto.*

New Humanism, as presented in the Twenty-Two Theses, has both a critical and a constructive aspect. The critical aspect consists of describing the inadequacies of communism (including the economic interpretation of history), and of formal parliamentary democracy. The constructive aspect, on the other hand, consists of giving highest value to the freedom of individual, presenting a humanist interpretation of history, and outlining a picture of radical or organized democracy along with the way for achieving the ideal of radical democracy.

a. Basic Tenets of New Humanism

Apart from Roy's effort to trace the quest for freedom and search for truth to the biological struggle for existence. The basic idea of the first three theses of Roy is individualism. According to Roy, the central idea of the Twenty-Two Theses is that political philosophy must start from the basic idea *that the individual is prior to society, and freedom can be enjoyed only by individuals.*

Quest for freedom and search for truth, according to Roy, constitute the basic urge of human progress. The purpose of all-rational human endeavor, individual as well as collective, is attainment of freedom in ever-increasing measure. The amount of freedom available to the individuals is the measure of social progress. Roy refers back the quest for freedom to human being's struggle for existence, and he regards search for truth as a corollary to this quest. Reason, according to Roy, is a biological property, and it is not opposed to human will. Morality, which originates from the rational desire for harmonious and mutually beneficial social relations, is rooted in the innate rationality of man.

b. Humanist Interpretation of History

In his humanist interpretation of history, presented in theses four, five and six, Roy gives an important place to human will as a determining factor in history, and emphasizes the role of ideas in the process of social evolution. Formation of ideas is, according to Roy, a physiological process but once formed, ideas exist by themselves and are governed by their own laws. The dynamics of ideas runs parallel to the process of social evolution and both of them influence each other. Cultural patterns and ethical values are not mere super structures of established economic relations. They have a history and logic of their own.

c. Inadequacies of Communism

Roy's criticism of communism, contained in theses seven to eleven is based mainly on the experience of the former Soviet Union, particularly the "discrepancy between the ideal and the reality of the socialist order." According to Roy, freedom does not necessarily follow from the capture of political power in the name of the oppressed and the exploited classes and abolition of private property in the means of production. For creating a new world of freedom, revolution must go beyond an economic reorganization of society. A political system and an economic experiment which subordinate the man of flesh and blood to an imaginary collective ego, be it the nation or class, cannot possibly be, in Roy's view, the suitable means for the attainment of the goal of freedom.

The Marxian doctrine of state, according to which the state is an instrument of exploitation of one class by another, is clearly rejected by Roy. According to Roy, the state is "the political organization of society" and "its withering away under communism is a utopia which has been exploded by experience".

Similarly, Roy rejects the communist doctrine of the dictatorship of the proletariat. "Dictatorship of any form, however plausible may be the pretext for it, is," asserts Roy, "excluded by the Radical-Humanist perspective of social revolution".

d. Shortcomings of Formal Parliamentary Democracy

Roy has discussed the shortcomings of formal parliamentary democracy in his twelfth and thirteenth theses. These flaws, according to Roy, are outcome of the delegation of power. Atomized individual citizens are, in Roy's view, powerless for all practical purposes, and for most of the time. They have no means to exercise their sovereignty and to wield a standing control of the state machinery.

"To make democracy effective," says Roy, "power must always remain vested in the people and there must be ways and means for the people to wield sovereign power effectively, not periodically, but from day to day."

e. Radical Democracy

Thus, Roy's ideal of radical democracy, as outlined in theses fourteen to twenty-two consists of a highly decentralized democracy based on a network of people's committee's through which citizens wield a standing democratic control over the state.

Roy has not ignored the economic aspect of his ideal of radical democracy. He argued that progressive satisfaction of the material necessities is the pre-condition for the individual members of society unfolding their intellectual and other finer human potentialities. According to him, an economic reorganization, which will guarantee a progressively rising standard of living, is the foundation of the Radical Democratic State. "Economic liberation of the masses", says Roy, "is an essential condition for their advancing towards the goal of freedom."

The ideal of radical democracy will be attained, according to Roy, through the collective efforts of mentally free men united and determined for creating a world of freedom. They will function as the guides, friends and philosophers of the people rather than as their would-be rulers. Consistent with the goal of freedom, their political practice will be rational and, therefore, ethical.

Roy categorically asserts that a social renaissance can come only through determined and widespread endeavor to educate the people as regards the principles of freedom and rational co-operative living. Social revolution, according to Roy, requires a rapidly increasing number of men of the new renaissance, and a rapidly expanding system of people's committees and an organic combination of both. The program of revolution will similarly be based on the principles of freedom, reason and social harmony.

As pointed out by Roy himself in his preface to the second edition of the *New Humanism: A Manifesto*, though new humanism has been presented in the twenty-two theses and the Manifesto as a political philosophy, it is meant to be a complete system. Because of being based on the ever-expanding totality of scientific knowledge, new humanism cannot be a closed system. "It will not be", says Roy, "a dogmatic system claiming finality and infallibility."

f. Philosophical Revolution or Renaissance

It is obvious from the foregoing that Roy was a great supporter of philosophical revolution or renaissance, and he has given a central place to it in his radical humanism. Roy was an admirer of European renaissance and drew inspiration from it. For him, "the renaissance was the revolt of man against God and his agents on this earth". According to Roy, the renaissance "heralded the modern civilization and the philosophy of freedom". He strongly believed that India, too, needed a renaissance on rationalist and humanist lines. According to him, this was a necessary condition for democracy to function in a proper manner. He believed that "a new Renaissance based on rationalism and cosmopolitan humanism" was essential for democracy to be realized. (Roy has used the word "rationalist" not in the Cartesian sense but in the *popular* sense. In this sense, a "rationalist" regards *reason* including both perception and inference as a source of knowledge.)

According to Roy, a philosophical revolution must precede a social revolution. He was opposed to blind faith and superstitions of all kinds and supported rationalism. As a physical realist, he rejected all allegedly supernatural entities like god and soul. Similarly, he was opposed to fatalism and the doctrine of *karma.* He unequivocally rejected the religious mode of thinking and advocated a scientific outlook and a secular morality. As noted earlier, he was in favor of delinking philosophy with religion and associating it closely with science. He believed that science would ultimately liquidate religion.

According to Roy, a revolutionary is one who has got the idea that the world can be remade, made better than it is today, that it was not created by a supernatural power, and therefore, could be remade by human efforts.

Further, according to Roy, "the idea of improving upon the creation of God can never occur to God-fearing. We can conceive of the idea only when we know that all gods are our own creation, and we can depose whomsoever we have enthroned."

Roy's critical approach towards religion comes out very clearly in the preface of his book, *India's Message*, where he asserts that a criticism of religious thought and a searching analysis of traditional beliefs and the time-honored dogmas of religion is essential for the belated Renaissance of India. "The spirit of inquiry should overwhelm the respect for tradition."

According to Roy, "a critical examination of what is cherished as India's cultural heritage will enable the Indian people to cast off the chilly grip of a dead past. It will embolden them to face the ugly realities of a living present and look forward to a better, brighter and pleasanter future." Thus, Roy was opposed to an uncritical and vain glorification of India's so-called "spiritual" heritage. However, he did not stand for a wholesale rejection of ancient Indian thought either. He favored a rational and critical approach towards ancient traditions and thoughts. Roy believed that the object of European renaissance was to rescue the positive contributions of ancient European civilization, which were lying buried in the

Maulana Azad

Universalising education was the master key. India needed an education that was 'rooted to its culture and committed to progress'. Great stalwarts around Mahatma Gandhi realised the criticality of ensuring the best features of Indian tradition: Equal respect for all religions, beliefs and diverse practices gets its traditional due. Muslims, who refused to migrate to the promised paradise called Pakistan, loved India and its tradition of unity in diversity. Maulana Abul Kalam Azad, one of the stalwarts of the freedom struggle and a great scholar of international repute in matters of religions and spirituality, elaborates it: "The acceptance of unity in diversity has been (India's) motto throughout the ages. The essence of this principle is a large and wide-hearted

toleration in which differences are recognised and given their due. The Indian genius has always recognised that truth as many faces and conflict and hatred have arisen because people claim a monopoly of truth and virtue." One wonders why India has not paid due attention to the perception of the Maulana who had, in his own way, strived hard to prepare people who understood the Indian diversity in its full glory and glare. Maulana's concern to see India as a nation of people proud of their heritage and, simultaneously, also of their readiness to accept and acknowledge all that contributes to the growth and well-being of India and its people.

There are occasions when, one single sentence or a small statement could project the total personality of a visionary leader. Here is an example from his presidential address delivered in the 1940 annual session of the Indian National Congress: "I am a part of this indivisible unity that is Indian nationality. I am indispensible to the noble edifice and without me, this splendid structure of India is incomplete. I am an essential element which has gone to build India. I can never surrender this claim." Sadly enough, India was partitioned but Maulana remained steadfast in his views. He became the first Education Minister of India. Apart from the formal celebrations of the National Education Day every year on November 11, it would be prudent that the contemporary relevance of Maulana's views is thoroughly discussed and incisively debated amongst the policy makers and implementers. Education, in its present shape, is certainly not 'bringing out the best from the body, mind and spirit'!

During the last over-six decades, India has much to project as its achievements are under progress and development. This includes the international chorus about India being a young nation that could provide skilled manpower to the nations facing 'ageing societies'! We have a far-more literate, modern and forward-looking India today than in Maulana's times. There is the other side as well: We have far more violence, bigotry, distrust and unrest in the country today than fifty years ago. The dream — post-independence — was that things would just be the other way round: More peace, intense social cohesion, ever-increasing religious harmony, peace, mutual trust and equal distribution of the fruits of progress and development. Obviously, something has gone wrong during the intervening period. It deserves to be analysed and pragmatic remedial steps should be initiated to redress the situation.

Did Maulana anticipate the negative developments of tomorrow in his times? A couple of instances would indicate that he was a visionary scholar who understood and contributed effectively in the freedom struggle and in the much-needed transformation towards a fully literate India comprising of a just and value-based society. Addressing a meeting of the vice-chancellors of Indian universities in Delhi on November 3, 1951, Maulana said: "The basis of our life is still agriculture and a vast majority of our people depend on agriculture for their livelihood....Our agriculture graduates are fit for almost everything except becoming agriculturists themselves." Even in times of globalisation, vast number of Indians remain dependent on agriculture, which has continuously remained ignored. The growth rate in this sector is abysmally low.

The result: Young persons are migrating to cities and towns and often leading a far miserable life which they could have improved upon if agricultural operations were given the much needed support. He had suggested a way out to overcome the deficiency by giving an extra bias to agriculture in school education and introducing agricultural education in the universities: "In addition, schools and colleges in the rural and semi-rural areas must encourage all students — whatever may be their subjects of study — to devote a part of their normal scholastic routine to work on land. For schools and colleges in cities and towns, I would suggest their adoption of villages where students may participate in a programme of complete reconstruction of village life."

The Maulana gave a great and scholarly speech while inaugurating the symposium on the Concept of Man and Philosophy of Education in East and West, New Delhi, December 13, 1951: "The Greek approached the concept of man from an external point of view. Hence we find that, from the early times, Greek philosophy devotes far greater attention to what man does than what man is."

UNIT 6

RECENT WESTERN PHILOSOPHY

NIETZSCHE

Critique of Western Culture

Freiderich Nietzsche is arguably the most important philosopher of 20th century in terms of his influence on many contemporary thinkers, like Heidegger, Foucault, Rorty and many others who belong to the different schools of thought.

Nietzsche was born in 1844 in Rocken in Prussia and his early education was on literature, particularly, Greek and German literature. In 1889 he had a sudden mental breakdown and became psychotic and he died in 1890.

Nietzsche was the advocate of a culture and society that would create stronger and more fully-developed individuals. He thought that, the major hurdle in realizing this is the moral and ideological spirit of the modern age. While many of his contemporaries saw modernity as a boon, offering humanity a more meaningful world, Nietzsche conceived it as the major obstacle towards human development. [Nietzsche: Preface to *The Antichrist*] It will be interesting to read these lines along with what another great thinker of 20th century, Sigmund Freud said about modern culture.

Nietzsche's critique of Western Civilization begins with his comparison of the nineteenth-century European and German culture with the culture of ancient Greece. He argues that, compared to the high culture of the latter, the former is sick and inferior and it worships weakness and mediocrity. The creative conflicts between these two contrasting traits were responsible for the superiority of Greek civilization and were responsible for all the fabulous achievements it made in various fields of human enquiries.

Apollo and Dionysus are the two Greek Gods, who exhibit contrasting characters. Apollo is the god of medicine, music and poetry. On the other hand, Dionysians are wild, frenzied and sensuous, as Dionysus is the god of ecstasy, terror, guilt and atonement, death and resurrection, vegetation, trees, wine, madness, and drama. According to Nietzsche, all forms of enthusiasm and ecstasy are Dionysian. The ancient Greek civilization had witnessed a fruitful merger of these two contradictory traits, where the principle of individuation, self-control, order, and equilibrium was merged with the inclination to break any border and norm, and to lose self-control.

The Greek culture soon encountered more rational and systematic philosophical systems sphere headed by Socrates, Plato and Aristotle. He introduces the notion of will to power in this context, which are the fundamental driving forces of all living creatures and the basic impulse of all our acts.

According to Nietzsche, life is an instinct of growth, for survival, for the accumulation of forces and for power. Life itself is Will to Power, he affirms. It is essentially an instinct for growth and for continuance. He affirms that, where the will to power is lacking there is decline. Criticizing the so-called supreme values of mankind, he argues that they all are characterized by a lack of will to Power.

This will to power is not just a will to survive or preserve one's existence. Instead, it is a proactive force: to act in life and not just to react. But at the same time, it is not a power over others, but the feelings of creative energy and control over oneself that are necessary to achieve self-creation, self-direction and to express individual creativity.

The most important obstacle in the path of realizing this will is moral and religious beliefs and the social establishments created to promote them. According to Nietzsche, all of them are anti-nature and anti-body and they attempt to discipline the body and to kill the will to power.

Ancient culture was free from the grip of these moral and religious traditions. With the emergence of the rational philosophical tradition of Plato and Aristotle, the decline begins. According to Nietzsche, they discounted the body as the seat of emotions and idealized the rational mind over the passionate will.

The Church demanded complete submission and it developed a morality that idealized obedience and loyalty. The creation of mediocrity has become the central motif of Western civilization. As a result of all these, the Western civilization has been dominated by a morality of the good and evil.

To clarify this further, Nietzsche introduces a distinction between master morality and herd morality. It rejects the fundamental distinction every moral traditions make; between good and evil. In this sense, it is beyond good and evil and even, beyond morality.

On the other hand, slave morality is the morality of submission and slavery. It is created by domesticating the body. Nietzsche says that the ascetic priests have created the slave morality as negating the body was essential in their programme. He says that slave morality "channels resentment inward against the body and outward against enemies of the herd".

This morality, which insists on disciplining the body by suppressing all bodily drives and passions, is the morality of the herd. It negates and sacrifices the body. As mentioned above, it insists that the individual should submit him/herself and be obedient to the social forces and institutions for the sake of salvation in a future heaven. They universalized slavery and insisted that everyone should observe the authority of the Church and its doctrines, which was intolerant to all forms of individual brilliance.

The herd morality works on the basis of the dichotomy of good and evil. Nietzsche thus calls it a morality of good and evil. Since all are God is creations, Christianity propagates a form of equality, a form of soul atomism, which asserts that all souls are at the equal level.

Nietzsche says that, for these reasons the slaves viewed the behavior of the powerful warrior types as evil. The latter are uninhibited by conscience and hence are considered as ruthless. Such men are capable of realizing their desires directly by freely exercising their passions and will to power. On the other hand, the weak represents cowardice and helplessness and find themselves overshadowed by the strong. Despite being a minority the strong exercises their will to power and dominates. They have eventually invented the notion of evil to characterize what is at the corc of the behaviour of the strong.

The herd morality, with its conception of good and evil thus rescued them from their enslavement. The weak liberated themselves by making everyone weak. They were intolerant towards all who exhibit independent brilliance and therefore, are capable of defining their own place in the world.

He thus wages a war against the very underlying conception of the morality that maintains a distinction between good and evil. Opposing the ways in which morality was conceived in human societies, Nietzsche argues that since morality is not a science, there cannot be any moral facts. He then argues that moral and religious judgments belong to a level of ignorance, as all value judgments concerning life are stupidities.

Nietzsche makes a detail analysis of what is understood as modern morality, which according to him is characterized by its complete neglect of the will to power and other important passions of life. They have contributed to creating and strengthening the herd morality, which in its essence consists in a denial of life. On the other hand Nietzsche maintains that life is essentially appropriation, injury, conquest of the strange and weak, suppression, severity, obtrusion of peculiar forms, incorporation, and at the least, putting it mildest, exploitation.

Nietzsche then examines what constitutes the basis of morality and affirms that it is the conception of universal and unchanging Truth. Since Plato onwards this tendency was strong in Western thought. Christianity divinized this notion and postulated its conception of good on the basis of the idea human nature, which by virtue of being a creation of God, is divine in nature. In the enlightenment era, philosophers like Kant further developed the idea of the essential rational faculty in man and tried to base their ethical theories upon it.

During the modern age this idea of unchanging universal truth has undergone some changes, particularly with the historical approach initiated by Darwin and Hegel. In other words, this position makes the idea of a perspectival truth sensible. This changed perspective on truth has also challenged conceptions of universal truth and universal human nature.

Following these insights Nietzsche argues that the notion of other worldliness, which is central to Christian morality, is invented in order to ensure smooth succession of the status quo.

Nietzsche develops his moral nihilism, from this general nihilistic position, which denies truth any universal value. This nihilism makes everything permitted, a position which will open up a boundless area of freedom of strong men and races to freely exercise their will to power and dominate and realize their development.

Nietzsche argues that modern age has made this nihilism inevitable and this had ultimately resulted in the death of God, where the latter stood for all that is universally and eternally divine and right.

With this death of God the moral foundations of Christianity was shattered and the "thou shalt" which contains the gist of the Christian moral commandment lost its meaning. He insists on creating new meaning out of the chaotic aftermath of God's death. The concept of overman or superman is introduced in this context. This overcoming of man has to be achieved undergoing three stages of moral development: the stages of the Camel, the Lion and the Child.

The Camel represents the average man, who unquestionably accepts the authority of the "thou shalt". The camels attitude of kneeling down in accepting its load is comparable to the average human beings attitude of kneeling down to carry the weight of what he/she believe are his/her duties. Their major purpose is to normalize the individual, to control his/her individual brilliance and merge him/her with the common moral framework of the society. As the camel who does not will what it does and only simply obeys what it "ought to do", the average man gives his will to what he believes are his duties.

In the next stage in the path of moral transformation, the camel converts itself into a lion. Nietzsche says that, like the camel that moves in the desert the spirit moves in its own desert and in the loneliest desert the spirit becomes a lion.

Nietzsche observes that, even after killing the "thou shalt", the lion is not completely free from the morality of good and evil. He once loved the "thou shalt" and has treated it as most sacred and now he seeks freedom from this love. Moreover, it has still not completely liberated itself from its past. It has succeeded in negating the existing moral frameworks by killing the "thou shalt", but it fails to fill the vacuum with a new morality, which is completely free from the parameters of the earlier one.

The child thus represents the real character one aspires to attain. It is absolutely unremorseful of what it does, as it is unaffected by the morality of the good and evil. The child applies its will in developing and achieving unique values and developing autonomy. It creates itself, as no models whatsoever influences it.

Nietzsche's overman is a strong and free individual who has overcome the man in himself. This overman has overcome his trivial, weak, petty tendencies that make him a lover of the status co. and worshipper of the "thou shalt" through a process of self-overcoming. In other words, he exercises his will to power. He creates his own values, and lives fully and passionately.

Nietzsche adds that, the overman creates a unique new master morality, which is free from the old values and customs. In this sense he is his own judge. He self-creates by overcoming, mastering and transforming his inner chaos into a new order. This however is not an easy task and Nietzsche reminds that only a few individuals succeed in this.

Though they exercise the will to power, among them they practice a different and unique morality. They recognize that they have equal strength and consequently they form a social body existing without necessarily injuring or exploiting others.

In the history of European philosophy, particularly the modern western thought, Nietzsche is a seminal thinker who entertained unique ideas and his theories still exert phenomenal influence on many of the contemporary thinkers. Nevertheless, his teleology is characteristically different from that of many other thinkers. For instance, Aristorle propagates a teleological outlook where he posits eudemonia as the ultimate human goal.

The Will to Power

The will to power is perhaps the key concept in Nietzsche's philosophy. It is strongly connected to his concept of 'life'. And he claims that 'all animals… strive instinctively for an optimum combination of favourable conditions which allow them to expend all their energy and achieve their maximum feeling of power'. Each form of life has a particular constitution, with its instincts having different strengths, such that certain conditions will favour its form of life.

And 'life' does not refer just to biological life; the same is true of societies, of classes within society, wherever we find different 'types' of people. The 'original fact of all history' is that society originates in and is based upon 'exploitation'. The will to power, claims Nietzsche, even underpins philosophical theories.

So what exactly is the will to power? There are three possible interpretations:

1. The Metaphysical Interpretation

Two passages in Beyond Good and Evil seem to support the metaphysical interpretation, 22 and 36. In 22, Nietzsche argues that the scientific idea of 'laws of nature' is an interpretation driven by the value of equality. But Nietzsche does not say that such a reading would be more correct or that we should read nature in this way.

Nietzsche has argued repeatedly that how we understand what appears depends on our perspective, which embodies our values, which originate in our instincts. We cannot go beyond the reality we experience, grounded in our instincts, to some 'deeper' reality. So The hypothesis to be tested is whether 'all mechanical events, is so far as an energy is active in them, are really the energy of the will'.

But is Nietzsche asserting that this is how we should understand the world? Boscovich, an 18th century physicist, argued that matter is comprised of force fields. Is Nietzsche suggesting that each force field is essentially a drive to expand its field and so increase its power relative to other force fields? Some philosophers have interpreted Nietzsche this way, but there are three good reasons to resist. First, Nietzsche says that the question comes down to 'whether we believe in the causality of the will', then arguing that it is the only form of causality. But he explicitly rejects both causality (as real) and the causality of the will. If we think the world 'itself' contains causation, which the metaphysical interpretation claims, we project our concepts mistakenly onto it.

Third, as discussed below, he claims that some forms of life can 'lack' the will to power.

2. The Organic and Psychological Interpretations

The organic interpretation has a stronger basis in the text – Nietzsche explicitly asserts that life is the will to power. Will to power would then be the force that distinguishes what is living from what is inanimate. Furthermore, Nietzsche talks of societies being 'alive' and exhibiting the will to power (259), which again indicates that 'life' is not meant biologically. So what does he mean 'life' in this context?

One passage in particular helps: 'Life itself is...the instinct for growth,... for power: where the will to power is lacking there is decline. It is my contention that all the supreme values of mankind lack this will'. The psychological interpretation of 'will to power' is therefore best, bearing in mind that for Nietzsche psychology is very firmly rooted in physiology, in biology. It also fits with Nietzsche's use of the idea of will to power in providing accounts for a wide variety of human behaviour and thought.

The will to power is the basic character of our drives or instincts. The essence of a drive is to assert itself. To do so successfully, to achieve expression, is for it to have power.

Power is not a separate aim of the drives. In asserting itself, each drive comes into competition with others, and with the drives of other individuals. And so drives are always in relations of power to each other. The will to power is not, therefore, a will to political power, although this may be one form it can take. Instead, Nietzsche understands its greatest expression to be a genuine creativity – of art, of insight, and of course, of new values.

3. The will to Power, Physiology and Psychology

Nietzsche emphasises that we cannot be 'great' simply through aspiration or education: 'There is no way to efface from a person's soul what his ancestors best and most regularly like to do... It is simply impossible that a person would not have his parents' and forefathers' qualities and preferences in his body'. He subscribes to a form of Lamarckism, the theory that the characteristics an organism acquires in its lifetime, *e.g.,* certain preferences, can be passed on to its offspring. So you do not carry your ancestors' preferences in your 'body'.

But Nietzsche doesn't distinguish biological inheritance (via the genes) from social inheritance and there is a strong tendency for people to have the same values and preferences as their parents. He is concerned with the idea of inheritance in general, not biological inheritance specifically.

However, this forms an objection. If there is a gap between genetics (physiology) and psychology, then the 'will to power' is not as connected to 'bloodlines' as Nietzsche claims. We therefore need to reconsider his claim that we are each a 'psycho-physiological type'. If psychological types, e.g. having a strong or weak will, having the instinct for commanding or obeying, are not based in physiology, then we need to reinterpret many of his analyses and criticisms of people with weak will.

Furthermore, if a strong will to power is not based in a healthy physiology, a weak will in a sickly physiology, then Nietzsche's claims about life itself being the will to power must be reconsidered.

This is too quick. Suppose the 'vitality' Nietzsche values is a psychological vitality, not a physiological one. As human beings, we are not concerned with, nor do we value, mere physiological life. For example, in 200, he speaks of the degeneration that occurs when the 'races' are mixed. But his concern is that such a person embodies contradictory values, and so feels in conflict with himself. As a result, his idea of happiness will be tranquillity. A stronger person, he continues, will exercise his will to power to make something productive of the tension within him. So while Nietzsche bases his remarks in 'race', his concern is psychological throughout. We can read the story of mixed 'races' in terms of mixed value systems instead.

GEORGE EDWARD MOORE

G.E. Moore (1873-1958) was an important British philosopher of the first half of the twentieth century. He was one of the trinity of philosophers at Trinity College Cambridge who made Cambridge one of centres of what we now call 'analytical philosophy'. But his work embraced themes and concerns that reach well beyond any single philosophical programme.

The Refutation of Idealism

Moore was first drawn to philosophy through contact with McTaggart and under McTaggart's influence he fell briefly under the spell of British idealism, especially the work of F. H. Bradley. One element of this theory is what he calls 'the fallacy involved in all empirical definitions of the good', which is immediately recognisable as a precursor of his famous claim in Principal Ethical that there is a fallacy, the 'naturalistic fallacy', in all naturalistic definitions of goodness.

A substantial part of this early dissertation is devoted to a critical discussion of Kant's moral philosophy, and it is striking that although in his general approach and conclusions Moore endorses the kind of idealism advanced by Bradley, he is already critical of Kant's conception of practical reason. He argues that Kant's use of this conception blurs the distinction between 'the psychological faculty of making judgments and inferences' and that which is 'true and objective'. It is easy to see how this line of thought could be extended to a general criticism of Kant's conception of the a priori; and it is precisely this generalisation that Moore undertakes in his successful 1898 dissertation. At the same time he comes to see that his previous enthusiasm for Bradley's idealism was not well founded (though it still takes him a little time to accept that the arguments of Bradley and McTaggart against the reality of time are flawed).

There are several aspects to this. As I have indicated, he rejects Kant's conception of the a priori as a muddled form of subjectivism or psychologism. The following passage from Principal Ethical (1903) is indicative of his polemic which can be found in many of his writings of this period:

The distinction Moore is drawing on here between thought on the one hand and what is objective or real on the other is one that runs through his critique of idealism. An important early context in which he elaborates it is his discussion of meaning in his famous paper 'The Nature of Judgement' (1899), which comes largely from his 1898 Dissertation. This is a mistake, but what is important is what follows: as against this view Moore holds that meanings, which he calls 'concepts', are entirely non-psychological. He put this point very clearly in a short entry written a year later on 'Truth':

> it seems plain that a truth differs in no respect from the reality to which it was supposed merely to correspond: e.g. the truth that I exist differs in no respect from the corresponding reality — my existence. So far, indeed, from truth being defined by reference to reality, reality can only be defined by reference to truth.

As Moore came to see ten years later, this radical metaphysics of true propositions is too simple. But in the present context what is striking about it is the way in which by itself it hovers between idealism and realism.

Moore's most famous criticisms of idealism are contained in his paper 'The Refutation of Idealism'. The basic theme of this paper is the extension to sense-experience of the strong distinction between the mind and its objects which we have encountered in connection with meaning. His argument here is in part phenomenological: 'when we try to introspect the sensation of blue, all we can see is the blue'; but he also argues that to suppose otherwise, that the 'blue' is merely a content of the experience is to suppose that it is a quality of the experience, so that the experience is blue in much the way in which a blue bead is blue, which he takes to be absurd. Not surprisingly Moore's critics were not happy with this comparison, but it was not until the formulation of the 'adverbial' theory of experience by Ducasse in the 1940's, according to which someone who has a sensation of blue is someone who 'senses bluely', that there was a reasonably robust response to Moore's criticism. What is, nonetheless, odd about Moore's paper is that he makes no attempt to address the famous 'argument from illusion'.

The final aspect of Moore's critical response to idealism concerns his rejection of the monism which was characteristic of British idealism. This is the holistic thesis that ordinary things are essentially interrelated in such an intimate way that they constitute together an 'organic unity' which is, in a sense, the only thing that 'really' exists, since it is the only thing whose existence is not dependent on the existence of anything else. Rather later, however, in his paper 'External and Internal Relations' (written in 1919) Moore focused on the idealist conception of internal relations which lies at the heart of the monist thesis. Moore then argues that the best reason one could have for the thesis involves a logical fallacy; he shows how the thesis that all relations are internal might be plausibly, but fallaciously, inferred from Leibniz' Law, the uncontentious principle that things which differ in their relations must differ in their identity. Simplifying a bit, and using Moore's concept of entailment (see below), his argument runs as follows:

1. Leibniz' Law states that
   xRy entails ($z = x \rightarrow zRy$),
   where '$\rightarrow$' is the truth-functional conditional
2. Since entailment is a necessary connection, one might infer
   $xRy \rightarrow$ Necessarily ($z = x \rightarrow zRy$)
3. From (2) one can immediately infer
   $xRy \rightarrow$ Necessarily ($x = x \rightarrow xRy$)
4. Since $x = x$ is itself a necessary truth, one can now infer
   $xRy \rightarrow$ Necessarily (xRy)
   which expresses the thesis that all relations are internal.

So, on the face of it, this thesis has here been inferred from Leibniz' Law. Moore observes, however, that the step from (1) to (2) is invalid; it confuses the necessity of a connection with the necessity of the consequent. In ordinary language this distinction is not clearly marked, although it is easy to draw it with a suitable formal language.

Moore's argument here is a sophisticated piece of informal modal logic; but whether it really gets to the heart of the motivation for Bradley's Absolute idealism can be doubted.

Defence of Common Sense

A Defence of Common Sense is an influential 1925 essay by philosopher G. E. Moore. In it, he attempts to refute absolute skepticism (or nihilism) by arguing that at least some of our established beliefs - facts - about the world are absolutely certain. Moore argues that these beliefs are common sense.

In section one, he argues that he has certain knowledge of a number of truisms, such as "My body has existed continuously on or near the earth, at various distances from or in contact with other existing things, including other living human beings".

In section two, he argues that there is a distinction between mental facts and physical facts. He says there is no good reason to hold, as many philosophers of his time did, that every physical fact is logically dependent on mental facts, or that every physical fact is causally dependent on mental facts. An example of a physical fact is "The mantelpiece is at present nearer to this body than that bookcase is." Mental facts include "I am conscious now" and "I am seeing something now."

In section three, he affirms that not only does he not think there are good reasons for believing that all material objects were created by God, but neither does common sense give reasons to think that God exists at all or that there is an afterlife.

The fourth section considers how common sense propositions like "Here is my hand" are to be analysed. Moore considers three possibilities that occur to him for how what we know in these cases is related to what we know about our sensedata, i.e. what he sees when looking at his hand.

The fifth section is an examination of the problem of other minds. Moore argues that "there are other 'selves'", but explains why this question has baffled philosophers. In other words, the sense data that he perceives through his senses are facts about the interaction of the external world and himself, but he (and other philosophers) do not know how to analyze these interactions.

Philosophical Analysis

By the time Moore returned to Cambridge in 1911 to a lectureship there, Russell and Whitehead were finishing off their massive project of exhibiting the logical foundations of mathematics — Principal Mathematical. One example of this concerns the status of propositions, the 'objects' of thought. As we saw above, in his early work Moore had been emphatic that propositions are altogether independent of thought and had even proposed that facts are just true propositions. But as he came to think more about falsehood in his lectures Some Main Problems of Philosophy of 1910–11, it became clear to him that this position was a mistake, since the truth of a proposition should not affect its ontological status and yet it would be absurd to give false propositions the status of facts. According to Moore, philosophers talk legitimately of propositions in order to identify the aspects of thought and language which are crucial to questions of truth and inference, and in doing so it may appear that they regard propositions as genuine entities. Moore does not allude here explicitly to Russell's theory of incomplete symbols and logical fictions, but it is clear that this is the kind of position he has in mind. The new logic enables one to preserve realist appearances without accepting realist metaphysics.

Yet Moore was not an uncritical follower of Russell. He was critical of Russell's account of implication in which Russell proposes that the truth-functional conditional expresses all there is to the logical relationship of implication between propositions, and introduced instead the term 'entailment' for this latter relationship. While recognising that entailment is closely connected to logical necessity he came to think that entailment is not just a matter of the necessity of the truth-functional conditional, thereby setting off a debate about this relationship which continues to this day. While agreeing with Russell that existence is not a straightforward first-order predicate (so that the logical form of 'Tame tigers exist' is not the same as that of 'Tame tigers growl'), Moore argued that statements such as 'This might not exist' make perfectly good sense and that they could not do so unless the simpler statement 'This exists' also makes sense.

Moore's uses of Russell's logic take place in the broader context of his use of analysis as a method of philosophy. Although Moore always denied that philosophy is just analysis, there is no denying that it plays a central role in his philosophy and it is therefore important to determine what motivates this role. In addition Moore held that it is just not true that all necessity is logical necessity, as Wittgenstein maintained; in his early writings, despite his hostility to Kant, he had explicitly defended the conception of necessary synthetic truths and he did not change his mind on this point. This point also provides a reason for his rejection of logical empiricism, since this position famously includes the thesis that all necessary truths are 'analytic'. But Moore also recognised that his early criticisms of William James' pragmatism can be applied to the logical empiricist position. But, he argued, it does not follow that we cannot now affirm that either the proposition or its negation is true, thanks to the Law of Excluded Middle; in which case it cannot be that truth is verifiability—contrary both to James' pragmatism and to logical empiricism.

BERTRAND RUSSELL

Russell's Refutation of Idealism

Idealism is the view, which proclaims that reality is fundamentally mental. Russell's refutation of idealism is unique, as he applies the method of language analysis in order to expose the flaws of idealism as a philosophical position.

Since idealism asserts a form of monism—all reality is a single spiritual entity—it rejects the plurality of things, which we normally experience as mere appearance. According to the idealist, everything is related to everything else in the universe and the universe is ultimately a single thing. Russell, on the other hand held a realist view, which affirmed that objects of experience were independent of the experience of them.

They affirm that the relation of experience to its objects are internal and hence in reality there are no such relations and therefore, all relations are unreal.

Russell initiates a linguistic analysis of this idealistic view in order to refute it. He holds that both idealism and monism are the results of a linguistic confusion. The idealist holds a fundamentally mistaken view about relations. Consequently, the relationship between them is not something between two things. In other words, they are not different from each other and hence the so-called relationship is unreal.

From this simple fact the idealist argues that every proposition constitutes a predication on reality as a whole. Since all relations are internal and therefore are unreal, the relationship articulated by all propositions is unreal. There exists only one entity, which is homogenous and spiritual. Russell argues that, the mistake of the idealist is to consider all propositions, including relational propositions as possessing a subject-predicate form.

Again, for A to be the left of B there should be two separate entities of A and B. This refutes the fundamental position of idealism and advocates pluralism. Hence Russell's approach is characterized by the method of language analysis. He approaches the philosophical position of idealism from the point of view of language analysis and examines how legitimate is their monism and idealism, so that they can logically argue for pluralism. Russell seeks to expose the logical contradictions inherent in this view and argues that by analysing the structure of the propositions held to be true by the idealists we can expose these logical contradictions.

Russell's Logic as the Essence of Philosophy

Logic as Essence of Philosophy is a lecture/essay by Bertrand Russell that breaks all of the principles down to their bare minimums. Russell does a lot for epistemology when he brings everything down to philosophy only mattering to logic and sense data. In this lecture he makes logic the bare essence of philosophy.

Logic is our rules for making judgments and thoughts and without it, we would not be able to get anything out of what we philosophize. We have observations, and we have a desire to make something out of them. Logicians like Frege establish formally these rules for philosophizing and the boundaries to maintain.

Metaphysics is a branch of philosophy that aims to help us understand the being around us, and what all this actually is.

Russell calls logic the essence of philosophy, because whether it is metaphysics or not, any philosophical relation can be reduced to pure logical sentences. Metaphysics is just discredited among them because before it is reduced, it means even less than the other philosophies.

I bring Russell's essay up for discussion just to lay some foundation in what metaphysics and epistemology do in fact have in common. My aim in my progressing writings is to shoot down empiricism and positivism in their elimination of metaphysics, and defend metaphysics to its stronghold. Metaphysics and epistemology have this quality in common. I feel little further need to explain this relation, in that I feel that my readers have a strong understanding and feel for logic without my need to explain it.

If theres pink shoes, then theres fogoters. There are pink shoes, so there must be fogoters. This is a perfectly logical statement, yet we cannot know for sure if this true because we cannot know what fogoters are. I push this concept so hard because I want to clarify that empiricists and positivists do not discredit metaphysics because of its logic, but because of its definitions. I used Russell's lecture to base my discussion off of, and to lay some foundation for some writings that will be here in the future.

This thought brings me to address the actual defining of A, B, C, D, fogoters, rooters, and beezers. It is not until here where metaphysics begins to be discredited and eliminated by the positivists and empiricists. We can assign a letter like A to the first spot to mean anything, but when we define it, metaphysicians use relations with these undefineds and make properties out of them. It all works out agreeably until the variables are assigned definitions, and at that point, disputes are had and philosophy divides itself.

One of the bigger problems of metaphysics is that a newly defined term is often needed to be set forth to say what a metaphysician means. Empiricists and positivists dislike this action. After stating what i have said before this point, I want to portray metaphysics as a plethora of definitions that are scattered about, and then I want to further organize that beyond this writing to arrange all of the conflicting metaphysics together like Carnap began to organize the analytic and synthetic definitions.

The taking upon the action of defining a term is something that puts you in an infinite regress of referrals. Lets define the word 'braggadocio' to help understand how defining something puts us in an infinite regression. Language: a body of words and the systems for their use common to a people who are of the same community or nation, the same geographical area, or the same cultural tradition. Okay, so what if we don't know what words or common means. Then we would define those, and so on, and so forth.

I state that defining things puts us in an infinite regression because this sets the stage for a metaphysical buildup to have a stronghold instead of speculative things based on faith. I want to create a metaphysical buildup just like Carnap did so in an epistemological way.

This was only a preconcerning discussion about my intentions and thoughts. I did however want to root some things in this essay by Russell (even if most of this writing goes beyond what the his lecture actually adresses).

Logical Atomism

Russell initially adopted a form of phenomenalism, which held that perceptual knowledge could be analyzed in terms of our acquaintance with the fundamental data of sensory experience. His book Our Knowledge of the External World and his paper "The Relation of Sense-Data to Physics" advocate this position. In his 1927 book, The Analysis of Matter Russell analyses the chief concepts of physics, such as force and matter, in terms of events and here he had adopted a realist position.

Logical atomism is a philosophical view about language, which aims at explaining the relationship between language and the world. It was primarily developed in order to resolve questions about the nature of perception and its relation to physics. It aims at establishing the empirical basis for physical science. Hence it comes up with a theory of the world. Russell thus initiates a metaphysical theory about the physical world and tries to give an account of the nature of reality by exposing its logical structure.

Russell argues that all propositions are not of the subject-predicate form. According to him, the surface grammar of statements may often mislead us. Russell proposes a logical analysis of language in order to resolve such confusions. Such an analysis can bring this out by revealing the structure of propositions. In the above-mentioned paper "On Denotation" Russell takes up an expression "The present King of France is bald" for analysis. His analysis shows that this statement asserts three things:

1. There exists at present at least one person who reigns in France.
2. There exists at present at most one person who reigns in France.
3. Whoever reigns in France is bald.

Now Russell proceeds further and tells that the statement "There exists at present at least one person who reigns in France" is false, as France is not a monarchy. Therefore, concludes Russell, the conjunction of the three statements is also false.

Russell thus affirms that the logical structure of the world and of language is revealed in the proper logical analysis of language. He conceives the world as consisting of facts, which are things with many qualities related in different ways. Russell contends that, a fact can be analyzed into its constituents like things, qualities, and relations.

From these basic contentions Russell examines the basic features of language that are revealed in its logical analysis. The analysis of propositions brings out their logical structure. We can analyze propositions into more and more elementary forms of propositions, which express basic facts and Russell calls them atomic propositions. Russell affirms that, if all the atomic facts are known, and that they are all the atomic facts, we could infer all other truths from them, as they are the most elementary forms of expressions that represent facts in the world.

Therefore, the logical analysis of language exposes the ultimate simple units of linguistic expressions that have immediate acquaintance with the world of facts. We can thus proceed to more and more precise, clear and definite knowledge from the obvious and vague ordinary beliefs about the world. We thus arrive at the simple symbols, which immediately refer to facts from the complex symbols or propositions, which we analyze.

Our ordinary languages have misleading structures. The logical structure of linguistic expressions is not apparent from the surface grammar of ordinary languages. Hence they should be logically analyzed. The ambiguous, misleading expressions of ordinary languages can be logically analyzed through descriptions. This according to Russell will reveal the logical structure. It thus brings out the logical structure or the depth grammar of linguistic expressions and leaves no room for doubts or confusions. In such a language, each word will have an object to represent and an object will have one and only one symbol. This notion of an ideal language is not Russell's creation, as it has been existent in philosophical circles since long. But Russell's idea of logical analysis had given it a new life. Many philosophers, particularly the thinkers of the logical positivism movement were inspired by such Russelian ideas.

L. WITTGENSTEIN

According to Wittgenstein philosophy is nothing but analysis and discussion of language. The language is nothing but a symbolic expression of the facts of experience. The language is comprised of two types of expressions or statements : the simple and compound. The entire fabric of language is analyzable is compound statements, which in turn, are analyzable in simple statements. Thus language is nothing but "the totality of propositions." A simple of atomic proposition is a mirror or reflection of the reality. According to Wittgenstein, "proposition is a picture of reality." Since language represents the facts of experience, the relationship between facts and the linguistic expressions there of must indeed by very close. It is the fact which makes a proposition true or false. If the proposition is correspondent to the facts it is true : otherwise false. Wittgenstein is here reviving the correspondence theory of truth, according to which a proposition is true if and only if it asserts what the facts indeed are. For example, if we say that a ripe Dusseri mango is sweet, what we are asserting in according to the nature of Dusseri, that is, our statement of Dusseri mango corresponds to the fact. On the contrary if we say, "King of Nepal is a Moslem" our statement is untrue because King of Nepal happens to be a Hindu.

Thus we learn that a compound proposition can be to translated or analyzed as to give us simple proposition and that each simple proposition is a symbolic expression for a single fact. Since a simple proposition stands for some simple fact, the truth of the proposition can be determined by comparing the two. A momentous and crucial fact which follows from this analysis is that each linguistic expression is, directly or indirectly, overtly or covertly, connected with some or the other fact of experience. Therefore, if there is any linguistic expression which masquerades as a proposition but on analysis fails to show any connection with any fact of experience, then that linguistic expression is not a proposition but a pseudo-proposition. A pseudo proposition is not merely not connected with any fact but it is impossible to think that it can be so connected. This is the basic difference between pseudo-propositions and false propositions. Thus difference can be best explained by examples. Let us have two following propositions : (1) "Aspirin causes headache" and (2) "God exists". Now (1) is false because aspirin is a pain remover but aspirin and headache are facts whereas (2) is neither true nor false or meaningless because there is and cannot be a fact which will answer to or correspond with our idea of god. Thus a pseudo proposition is neither true nor false because the criterion of truth has no relevance to it.

The precise and scientific explanation of Wittgenstein conception of the meaning is in the following words: "The sense of a proposition is the method of its verification." That is, a proposition is a proposition if and only if some empirical facts are to be found which may confirm or disconfirm the proposition in question. Those propositions which can neither be confirmed nor disconfirmed by the empirical evidence are meaningless. It is a mistake to call these propositions.

Language and Reality

To *imagine* a language, according to Wittgenstein is to imagine a form of life. Thus language is a style of life and the activity of man is a game. The terms used in a language have some special meaning. If a word has no special meaning it is senseless. For example, the words, 'sky' and 'flower' each has meaning and refer to something particular, but the word 'sky flower' is devoid of meaning because no special meaning is inherent in it. It refers to nothing.

Applying the analogy of 'sky flower' to the philosophical problem, Wittgenstein asserts that though sky and flower each has meaning, yet the syntax of two 'sky flower' fails to convey and meaning. In the same manner, the words used in asserting metaphysical problem may each have meaning but the assertion taken as a whole may be syntactically defective and therefore has no meaning. A simple example would explain the point. The metaphysical assertion "All reality is ideal" has no meaning though each word in it is meaningful. We can only talk of this or that real object or fact but to say, "All reality" makes no sense because there is nothing corresponding to all reality as we have objects corresponding to a red rose, a philosophy book etc. In order to resolve metaphysical puzzle the philosophical usages should be, according to Wittgenstein, reinterpreted as commonsense usages of daily life. "What we do is to bring words back from their metaphysical to their every day use." In an ideal language, according to Wittgenstein, only the words which are symbols for some real state of affairs are used. The philosophic problems crop up when we deviate from this principle and use words having no referents. The philosophic language usually is immaturish and imperfect. This is the reason for the lack of clarity in the philosophic assertions. Wittgenstein disregards grammar.

The grammar sometimes meisleads and systematically misleading expressions produce in us illusion of a problem and we feel restless. Once we let reality juncture and dispel the illusion, our problem vanishes into thin air. The one-sidedness of philosophy is responsible for the puzzles of philosophy. In *Philosophical Investigations,* Writtgenstein says that "philosophy is a battle against the betwitchment of intelligence by language." The role of philosophy is to protect us against falling into illusions due to grammatical similarities. For example, a noun is a name of something and it follows that to every name there must correspond an objective fact. This may lead us to believe that since God is a noun, there must be some person, place or thing which is called God. By avoiding these errors we find almost all metaphysical problems disappear. They are dissolved like a dream dissolving on waking.

Fact and Objects

The facts and objects are very essential. He says that the world is regarded as the totality of facts and not of things. He says that the world description depends upon all the facts and not on all the objects.

The atomic facts are regarded as state of affairs. He says that object is linked together to the formation of the fact. He says that there is no need for the logical objects. He says that objects are regarded as simple. He says that the configuration of objects produces state of affairs.

The state of affairs may or may not exist, but objects have no alternative. He never offers an example of an object. It has been said that only objects have names. In a state of affairs, objects fit into one another. A relation is not regarded as an object.

Name and Propositions

The 'names' are not regarded as mere signs. 'Names' are regarded as signs with their meanings names are identified in the context of sentences only. Names and propositions are interrelated. A thought in a proposition finds an expression that can only be perceived by the senses. A proposition includes all that which the projection also includes.

A proposition contains only the possibility of expressing its meaning. A propositions also contains the form. For understanding a proposition, the facts are very important. A proposition only shows its sense. A propositions are able to 'picture' the world.

The Picture Theory

The picture theory is talked in the Tractatus. It represents the proposed description of the relation of representation. It is also called as the picture theory of language. Pictures defines that pictorial form. Through picturing relationship, we are able to understand the relationship of a proposition.

The pictorial form of a proposition is best known through the pictorial form of a thought. He says that this pictorial form is defined as a logical structure. This logical structure of thought should correspond to words. He says that a picture cannot express it own pictorial form.

Philosophy and Language

Philosophy has no propositions. Philosophy is defined as the activity of clarifying language. We should remain silent. He says that we should speak only when people misuse language.

All the propositions are regarded as meaningless. He says that philosophy also fight against the bewitchment of our intelligence by means of our language. Philosophy cannot find any truth because it's task is to only clarify our thoughts by the use of language.

It has been said that the tractatus precludes philosophical theories whereas the investigations points out the non-dogmatic nature of philosophy. The language is defined as a symbolic expression of the facts of experience. Language is very important for both early and later **Wittgenstein.**

Meaning and Use

Meaning and use theory comes in the philosophical investigation of Wittgenstein. Meaning of a word lies only in its usage which is presented in the language. Without use, nothing can be known. He says that only in language, we can use the meaning. Usage theory signifies only meaning.

Forms of Life

Forms of life is very essential. He talked about this concept in this book name 'Philosophical Investigation'. He says forms of life represents our living conditions. It represents our surroundings. It means changes which has inculcated in out life's. Our use of language represents our form of life. Form of life is common to human kind. It also represents the common behaviour of mankind.

HUSSERL

The Husserlian Method

The true founder of modern phenomenology, of which Brentano and Meinong were the forerunners, was Edmund Husserl (1859-1938). Husserl set himself the task of describing in general terms the method and subject matter of a new science of pure phenomenology; he also executed numerous detailed and penetrating phenomenological investigations. Phenomenology is an investigation of phenomena—*i.e.*, items displayed or found in experience.

Phenomenology as the descriptive analysis of subjective phenomena, independently of any philosophical or epistemological presuppositions or commitments, is advocated by Husserl as an indispensable preliminary to all other sciences. Husserl conceived pure phenomenology as a necessary preparatory science much as Aristotle considered logic as a propaedeutic science.

Phenomenology is subjectivistic in that its investigation are initially directed, in Cartesian fashion, towards the ego and its presentations. Indeed, Husserl discerns in Descartes' *Mediatations* the first halting steps in the direction of pure phenomenological inquiry. Phenomenology, however, is not subjectivistic in a psychological or mentalistic sense.

Husserl insists on the autonomy of rational inquiry into the ideal relational factors in experience. Phenomenology is philosophical science prior to and independent of psychology, yet it does not preclude legitimate psychological investigation. Husserl's polemic against psychologism is directed only against the presumptuous claims of psychology to supersede logical and phenomenological inquires–not against psychology as a special, factual science.

An essential feature of the phenomenological method is its technique of 'bracketing' or 'elimination' of the factual dimension of our experience, in order to focus attention on its essential, ideal aspect—the proper subject matter of philosophical inquiry. The phenomenologist is not concerned with particular facts as such, but with the ideal essences which shine through the particulars. Husserl frequently uses the expression *Epoche* (suspension of judgement) to refer to the purification of experience of its factuality; the characteristic phenomenological attitude involves in initial suspension of judgement regarding the existence—whether physical or psychical—of the presentations of consciousness. The phenomenological bracketing or elimination of existence is a methodological attitude which must be preserved throughout to insure investigation of the essential constitution of experience. Phenomenology, like mathematics, says Husserl, is "the science of pure possibilities [which] must everywhere precede the since of real facts."

Intentionality

Phenomenological analysis and description is conversant with the ideal entities with which we are confronted after we have bracketed or eliminated factuality. The question suggests itself whether these ideal objects of phenomenological inquiry are Platonic universals. Husserl's reply is in the negative: he refuses to commit himself to Platonic realism by entifying or hypostatizing these idealities. Instead, like Meinong, he invokes the theory of intentional reference in his interpretation of the objects of phenomenological study. Intentionality (*Intentionalität*) is an intrinsic trait of the subjective processes of consciousness whereby they refer to objects; the objects of phenomenological inquiry are intentional objects. The phenomenologist is not committed to assigning to these objects any ontological status beyond the mere fact that they are envisaged. From the point of view of phenomenology, the important thing is not the status of ideal objects but the fact that such objects may be investigated in their interrelations; and that the results of such descriptive analysis and coercive and communicable. They then possess the only kind of objectivity which is necessary or desirable for the purposes of genuine knowledge.

M. HEIDEGGER

Being and Nothingness

In metaphysical investigation, Heidegger is interested in three things; Dasein (Being-there), Time and Being. Like all other existentialists, Heidegger believes that science investigates the Being-there, the objective reality, whereas philosophy studies the Being per se, The Being per se is beyond our commonsense experience, it is beyond both the knower and the known. Thus expistemological studies always miss the Being. Being can be studied only by inwardisation, by self-knowledge.

The mystery of Being cannot be resolved unless we understand the mystery of non-being, that is "what is" can be known by the exclusion of "what is not". The being manifested itself by negating the negation. In the words of Heidegger. "Nothing nothings itself." This negative approach to being is remniscient of Upanishad's approach of *neti* to the ultimate reality." As a matter of fact the conception of nothingness is included in the conception of being. This fact was also emphasized by Hegel when he asserted that pure being is pure Nothing. According to Heidegger, the negative judgement is based upon nothingness. Thus *Nothingness* is the source of negation and not vice versa. If an objection is raised that nothingness signifies not just lack but the lack or absence of something, and, therefore, pure nothingness is a merely theoretical concept and in reality it is not and is incapable of experience. Heidegger's reply is that experience of dread proves that nothingness is experienced. As Heidegger puts it. "Dread reveals Nothing." Dread is psychologically very different from fear, in as much as fear is of something this or that whereas dread is a fear which threatens the very being. For example, fear of death is a dread in as much as dread of death threatens annihilation. In withdrawal from the world man has a positive experience of nothingness. In withdrawal we not only experience *nothingness* but being also, because it is being to which we return and which is our source and 'enduring home'. Heidegger says, "An experience of Being as sometimes 'other' than every thing that has come to us in dread to dread, i.e., in sheer timidity, shut our ears to the soundless voice which attunes us to the horrors of the abyss." All great philosophers, saints and thinkers have emphasized that the quest for truth and reality requires great courage and tremendous effort but the reward of this courage and effort is realisation of the truth. In the words of Heidegger, "The clear courage for essential dread guarantees the most mysterious of all possibilities, the experience of Being." The ability and capacity to confront non-thinness with courage opens the pathway to the experience of being. The confrontation with nothingness nothings or annihilates our being as well the being of the world. If we are able to bear this terrible and dreadful situation without willing, without caving in, we pass through it and experience an amazing peace, tranquility of mind, nay, we realize the being. The realization of being equips our minds with the ability to fore sake, to renounce the Dasein, being there. Thus only by diving deep into Nothingness can we have the courage to realize the reality. By this process all the veils covering the being start receding. It is not the destiny of man to remain confined to the world around him. The realization of the totality of the being requires the sacrifice of Dasein. The pinnacle of human life, according to Heidegger, "comes from the inwardness out of which historical man dedicates the Being-there he has won for himself to the preservation of the dignity of being." But the sacrifice of the Dasein, in fact, represents the gratitude of man to the being, from which he derives his Dasein. As Heidegger puts it, "In sacrifice there is experienced and expressed the hidden thinking which alone does homage to grace where with the being has endowed the nature of man."

It is the duty of each man to transcend the Dasein, the being there are to experience a harmony of being and truth and listen to the prompting of being truth unity, only thus will he be able to understand the language of the Reality. Having realised this being, the philosopher tries to make it manifest, The success in this is automatic and for this purpose he has to make use of symbols. This is the condition of homecoming that is, man returns to the source of his being. But the man is unable to fathom the depths of being even though he has attained it. Being in its totality is unfathomable; therefore, in the ultimate analysis, its knowledge is impossible; its mystery is irresoluble. Man's duty is to guard this mystery. Therefore, though being is never understood, its realisation nonetheless changes the reality around us;

outlook is transformed. Man experiences great beatitude. He looks upon the world not merely as world but the manifestation of the Invisible and Unknown. Our attitude to everything becomes reverential.

Man as Being-in-the World

According to Heidegger man finds himself in a world, which is *dasein,* and which he cannot but be related to or concerned about. There may be no validity or reason of the world which surrounds him, but once there he can not but be concerned about. In the world certain things happen over which he has no control; on the other hand, there are things which he uses as tools. He operates on the world with their help. The inner principle which organizesis relations to the world is Care or Concern. "Care" is, therefore, the basis of being-there. In his relation to the world, man experiences various moods like curiosity, anxiety, boredom, fear and angst (dread). The mood of boredom signifies that the whole world affects us and that nothing of permanent interest or value is there in the world for us.

Death is an inescapable fact of human existence: it can not be evaded. Ordinarily we remain oblivious of this or suppress it. But the moment it emerges in our consciousness, it produces dread, a violent fear. It pulls man out of his self-forgetfulness and confronts him with the reality, his authentic existence. In face of death man's eye shifts from the external world and concentrates on his personal being. He begins to think seriously about his past, present and future. He recognizes that future depends upon his present acts and he realizes the opportunities lost by him to lead an authentic life. This produces in him a sense of guilt. He resolves to wake up and be an authentic person who freely chooses to be.

Critique of Technological Civilization

The central problem of the modern highly complex world is not ideological but practical. It is neither relevant nor important today to win followers for a particular ideology or theory but to inspire in men a sense of responsibility and freedom. If there is this sense the process of communication is facilitated. The world peace cannot be accomplished by raising slogans. We require for this purpose individuals who are free, who communicate freely and above all, who respect theirs as well as others personalities. A fortiori the peace is possible if and only if there is peace in each heart; if each man is free from inner conflicts, if each can be from the desire to subject others to his will. That is why existentialists attach from the desire to subject others to his will. That is why existentialists attach so great importance to the problem of inner conflict. The traditional philosophies do not consider these problems philosophically worthwhile; but for existentialists these are extremely crucial and fundamental. The source of modern philosophical issues is the feeling of alienation from world, society as well as self. If we regard the existence cannot be rationally solved. These can be resolved in practice only.

A true harmony is not a harmony of ideas or thoughts but a harmony of desires. A true philosophy is not a philosophy of substance but rather a philosophy of existents, a philosophy of immediate experiences. The true nature of this philosophy is not thinking about the being but participating in its movement, that is, commitment. The existentialist philosophy does not have any definite aim because life being movement and flow which is not mere mechanical change but a creative advance, it is not possible to tie down life to any particular aim. Life cannot be aimless or having an aim but only inauthentic and authentic. An authentic existence is the only aim that life has but this is not some future state but a present quality of life. An authentic existence is the only aim that life has but this is not some future state but a present quality of life. An authentic life can be personal only. The existentialism condemns both historicism and the scientific philosophy.

LOGICAL POSITIVISM

This chapter discusses one of the very significant developments the 20th century European philosophy has witnessed; logical positivism, which is also known as neo empiricism. It is rather a movement that reflects the dominant scientific outlook of 20th century European civilization and its extension to all spheres of life. The logical positivists thus advocated a unique conception of knowledge which considered the scientific model as paradigm. They were tremendously influenced by many philosophical approaches, notably, the positivism of Augustine Comte, the logical atomism of Bertrand Russell, and most significantly, by the peculiar conception of language and meaning developed by Ludwig Wittgenstein in his early work, the Tractatus Logico Philosophicus.

The fact that almost all major advancements in knowledge have been in the field of natural sciences have prompted the logical positivists to consider scientific conception of knowledge as paradigmatic. They found that the theories of speculative philosophy advocated by different thinkers were merely personal interpretations about reality. On the other hand, science provides a totally different picture. It approaches reality and life from a different perspective. The story of humanity has never been the same after enlightenment, which had witnessed the emergence of modern science.

Following Wittgenstein who declared that philosophy is not a science, and there are no philosophical theories, the logical positivists too have affirmed that philosophy does not contribute to the increase of human knowledge. 20th century philosophy was characteristically different from the philosophical thinking of early centuries. Earlier, philosophy was the handmaid of theology and with the civilization turning more and more towards science, the 20th century philosophy has become a handmaid of science.

The Emergence of Logical Positivism

After the World War I, a group of intellectuals comprising of mathematicians, scientists, and philosophers, began meeting in Vienna under the leadership of the German philosopher and physicist, Moritz Schlick. They began contemplating about the possibility of a systematic reduction of human knowledge to logical and scientific foundations, as they believed, science alone is capable of providing universal and certain knowledge. The most notable members of the Vienna Circle were Moritz Schlick, Hans Reichenbach, Rudolf Carnap, Herbert Feigl, Philipp Frank, Kurt Grelling, Hans Hahn, Carl Gustav Hempel, Victor Kraft, Otto Neurath and Friedrich Waismann.

Logical Positivism formally began in 1929 with the publication of a manifesto entitled The Vienna Circle; Its Scientific Outlook, jointly written by Carnap, Neurath and Hahn. One of the most important features of logical positivism was the advocacy of the principle of verification, which states that, in order to be meaningful a statement needs to be empirically verifiable, though ironically, this statement itself is not verifiable.

As mentioned above, the logical positivists were influenced by many factors that contributed in determining the social and cultural life of 20th century Europe. Einstein's theory of relativity and quantum mechanics were other factors that influenced their thinking. But the single most important influence was Wittgenstein's Tractatus, to which they developed their own unique reading and interpretation.

The logical positivists adopted uncompromising positivism and proposed a blanket rejection of metaphysics. Being faithful to the empiricist tradition, it was natural for the logical positivists to be influenced by the radical empiricist philosophy of David Hume. Subsequently, they have rearticulated Hume's division of Relations of Ideas and Matters of Facts as tautologies and factual propositions. The theory of verifiability is proposed in this context, which came to be identified as the hallmark feature of the logical positivists.

Logical Positivism and the Question of Meaning

Like many others who consider language analysis constituting the core of philosophy, the logical positivists too have treated language analysis as vital. According to them, there are different types of meaningful statements. Therefore, they contend that the meaning of a proposition is known if we know the method by means of which we verify it. In other words, we know the meaning if we know the conditions under which the statement is true or false.

Subsequently, they argue that many metaphysical utterances are due to the commission of logical errors. They begin their analysis with an examination of statements that express the so-called metaphysical truths. As A. J. Ayer says, the traditional disputes of philosophers are, for the most part, as unwarranted as they are unfruitful. He then asserts that the surest way to end them is to establish beyond question 'what should be the purpose and method of a philosophical inquiry?'

Rejection of Metaphysics and Language Analysis

The logical positivists reject metaphysics in a characteristically different manner than many others who ventured doing so. For instance, Immanuel Kant had demonstrated that metaphysics as a science is impossible. He treated the impossibility of metaphysics as a matter of fact and he attempted to draw a limit to our thinking. They intend to show how metaphysics is impossible by a criticism of the nature of the actual statements which comprise metaphysics. Applying the verification principle as a criterion for meaningfulness they assert that statements that transcend the limits of all possible sense experience have no literal significance. As the so-called metaphysical propositions transcend such limits, they are bound to be meaningless.

The logical positivists thus maintain that all propositions about God or absolute, transcendent entities, substance, destiny of man, meaning of human life, goodness etc. are metaphysical. These propositions look like other meaningful propositions that are about matters of fact.

Employing the method of the logical analysis of language in order to demonstrate the meaninglessness of metaphysical propositions, the logical positivists were influenced by Wittgenstein's Tractatus. Wittgenstein talks about those elementary propositions which a logical analysis of language may expose.

We may need to examine a little more the important features of the principle of verification in this context. As indicated above, this principle asserts that the meaning of a proposition is its method of verification. They argue that all meaningful statements can be ultimately analyzed to the elementary statements which stand for observable events.

According to A.J. Ayer, the principle of verification affirms that a sentence is factually significant to any given person, if, and only if, he knows how to verify the proposition which it purports to express - that is, if he knows what observations would lead him, under certain conditions, to accept the proposition as being true, or reject it as being false. Ayer discusses different types of verification such as practical verifiability, verifiable in principle, strong verifiability and weak verifiability.

The criterion of strong verification insists that a statement is meaningful if and only if, its truth could be conclusively established in experience. They are therefore, not conclusively verified. On the other hand, the criterion of weak verification states that a statement is meaningful if it is possible for experience to render it probable. It only says that if some experiential propositions can be deduced from it in conjunction with certain other premises without being deducible from those other premises alone, then it is meaningful.

The very idea of conceiving verifiability as a criterion for meaningfulness encounters several difficulties. The idea of verifiability is based on the notion of elementary statements which are direct observation statements. But these elementary statements themselves are not infallible, as they may not refer to anything other than the private sensations of the speaker. They may not be anything more than mere records of the subject's immediate experiences.

Logical Positivism and the Idea of Unified Science

The logical positivists have advocated an idea of unified science, which affirms that all genuine knowledge can be equated with scientific knowledge. They thought that they could materialize the unity of all sciences by developing a common language in which all scientific propositions can be expressed.

The logical positivists maintain that scientific theory represents an axiomatic system, which is not directly verifiable. It is an abstract formal system. Theoretical statements are formed out of theoretical terms and logical terms. The logical positivists thus hold that all sciences share a common language and all scientific terms could be restated as, or reduced to, a set of basic statements, or protocol sentences, describing immediate experience or perception. In other words, the logical positivists envisage a reduction of all scientific terms into terms of physics. They argue that the procedures for testing statements in the various sciences are basically the same.

Inspired by Wittgenstein, the logical positivists argue that the primary function of philosophy is not to propose basic principles of knowledge. Philosophy does not aim at constructing a deductive system of meaningful propositions by offering the consequences of basic principles of knowledge as a complete picture of reality.

Like most other philosophical movements, historical and cultural factors have played a crucial role in the emergence of logical positivism. The beginning of 20th century was an era of reason and scientific rationality. Though the logical positivists have generated a lot of interest from different quarters, they failed to sustain and consolidate as a movement. Their theories derived a lot from the thoughts of Russell and Wittgenstein. Putnam has demonstrated that the distinction the logical positivists made between "observational" and "theoretical" statements is meaningless. W. V. Quine has criticized the distinction between analytic and synthetic statements, and the reduction of meaningful statements to immediate experience.

PRAGMATISM C.S. PEIRCE

Peirce's pragmatic doctrine of belief involves both his account of meaning and his special ideas on belief; and those familiar with Dewey's step in a complete act of reflective thinking will recognize his indebtedness to Peirce's account of belief. For example, Peirce's irritation or indecision of doubt becomes Dewey's problematic situation the former's struggle to rid ourselves of doubt and establish a belief (which he equates with inquiry) parallels the latter's reflective process, and Pierce's beliefs which will truly guide our action correspond to Dewey's hypotheses which will solve our problems.

For Pierce the meaning of a concept is to be found in "all the conceivable experimental phenomena which the affirmation or denial of the concept could imply. "Or as he sometimes puts it, the meaning of any idea is the habit which it establishes. The difference in ideas or beliefs is to be seen in the habits established: and if there are no differences in practice, the ideas mean the same thing.

A belief affects our action. It prepares us to act. It initiates a habits or rule of action. Doubt interferes with habits, is unpleasant. When we get rid of a doubt, we have a belief and consequently a habit. Thus doubt indicates a kind of temporary breakdown in our habitual responses, and until the doubt or perplexity has been removed normal action is held up.

It is worth noticing that the "practical consequences" or "conceivably experimental phenomena" with which Peirce is concerned are not private but instead are phenomena open to all investigators. The problem of fixing beliefs is not simply an individual problem but rather a social one-one for the community of investigators or practicing scientists. Truth for him is public : it is "that which is fated to be ultimately agreed to by all who investigate" : and the real is the object represented in this true opinion. It seems clear that he wished to dissociate himself from the individualistic, relativistic, and utilitarian interpretations of his doctrine. He was intellectualistic rather than voluntaristic. To dissociate his views from the broader pragmatism of James he suggested calling his view "pragmaticism".

PRAGMATISM WILLIAM JAMES

James early developed the idea that concepts are not copies of abstract reality but primarily relations between parts of perceptual experience, affording a kind of map of relations among the elements of things. Though he distinguished three ends or parts served by concepts, their most important function is to steer us practically. They are ways of handling the perceptual or experiential flux and of making connections with distant parts of it. They start from and come back to this perceptual flux. As James puts it, "We *harness* perceptual reality in concepts in order to drive it better to our ends." The consequence to which a concept leads constitutes the more important part of its significance." To understand what it means and to weight its importance, by the pragmatic rule, we ask what sensible difference to anybody its being true will make. If two concepts lead us to identical consequences, they mean the same thing. Thus to know the world in its useful functions we must know it in its relations and the instruments of knowledge are concepts.

One of James's most important doctrines was that of the streams of thought, or consciousness, or the subjective life. On his view mind is not made up of atomic sensations. We have rather a stream of sensations from it; but there is far more to the stream than the sensations. Actually they are found in relations, and when we abstract them, we too frequently neglect the relations, which are as real as the sensions.

In his *philosophy* he used the figure of the bird's life, with a combination of perching and flights, to describe it. The perchings or resting places correspond to the sensations or substantive parts, and the flights between perches to the feeling of relations. IF we limit our attention to the substantive parts, we omit what gives continuity to the steam of consciousness directs attention, of course, to the continuity of "James's saddle-back present which looks towards both the past and the future exemplifies this. No matter how small a section of the perceptual flux we take, "It always a much a once, and contains innumerable aspects of the characters which conceptions pick out, isolate, and thereafter always intend. It shows duration, intensity, complexity or simplicity, interestingness, exactingness, pleasantness, or their opposites. Data for all our sense enter into it, merged in a general extensiveness of which each occupies a big or little share. Yet all these parts leave its unity unbroken.

One must remember here James's view of concepts, his theory of meaning. Facts, events, experiences, percepts are neither true nor false. They simply are. Truth is applicable to concepts, theoretical relations between facts, to a short-hand rendering of facts or experience. Truth is instrumental. A belief is true in so far as it leads to something useful (works) and fits in with other beliefs. According to James, the test is "what works best in the way of leading us, what fits every part of life best and combines with the collectivity of experience's demands, nothing being omitted." "The ideas are those that we can assimilate, validate, corroborate, and verify. False ideas are those we cannot. That is the practical difference it makes to us to have true ideas; that therefore is the meaning of truth, for it is all that truth is known as."

On this view truth is primarily a matter of consequences, of the way ideas work out in practice. It is something that happens to an idea in becoming verified or validated. It is an affair of leading us to objects useful for our purposes, and "true ideas lead us into useful verbal and conceptual quarters as well as directly up to useful sensible termini. "Though James spoke of the true as the satisfactory in the sense of that which leads satisfactorily or by satisfactory conjunctions, this, of course, is not to be interpreted as meaning that the true is to be equated with whatever is pleasant; and at times he complained of a certain paucity of philosophical imagination which could lead his critics to think that this was what he meant. Pent in as the pragmatist sees himself to be "between the whole body of funded truths squeezed from the past and the coercions of the world of sense about him," there is little danger that he will jack objective control and think of satisfactory leadings in terms of merely subjective satisfactions or pleasures.

GILBERT RYLE

Gilbert Ryle was a philosopher and a founding representative of the Oxford-based British ordinary language philosophers who were influenced by Wittgenstein's insights into language. He is principally known for his critique of Cartesian dualism, for which he coined the phrase "the ghost in the machine." He referred to some of his ideas as "behaviourism" (not to be confused with the psychological Behaviorism of B. F. Skinner and John B. Watson), and he claimed that much of his philosophical work amounted to "Occamizing" (the reference is to William of Occam and his so-called "Occam's razor," which states that the best explanation is the simplest, the overly-complicated concepts and work of other philosophers. Gilbert Ryle was born in 1900, at Brighton, Sussex, England.

Among other things, Ryle became interested in the work of Bertrand Russell on logic. Ryle did fail to appreciate Plato's Republic, an attitude that would remain with him throughout his life. For seven terms he worked on ancient and modern philosophy and Greek and Roman history. H. J. Paton was his tutor. He also spent some time learning languages, especially Italian, and learning some Italian philosophy, especially that of Benedetto Croce and Giovanni Gentile. In October 1924 he became a lecturer in philosophy at the prestigious Christ Church College at Oxford, and began teaching.

Concept of Mind

Ryle says that by a person's mind he does not mean the existence of any incident of special status, but of different ways in which the different incidents of his life are ordered. Thus he says that it is not proper to ask the question about the relation between a person and his mind or the relation between a person's body and his mind. He further says that the activities of knowing or choosing is not done by some one's mind but by the person himself though these actions can be classified as mental acts. Similarly, he says that instead of saying that my eyes see this or my nose smells that, we say I see this or I smell that. But in these activities my eyes and my nose have contributions because these are organs of senses. But he denies treating 'mind' as an organ of sense like the eyes or the nose. He says that it is logically improper to make conjunctions, disjunctions and cause-effect relation about mind and body.

Thus after rejecting Descartes mind body dualism Ryle says that when we talk about a person's mind we actually talk about person's abilities, liabilities and inclinations to do. Mind is composed of sensations, feelings and images which are the stuff of mind. Thus Ryle's analysis of mind is very much close to Hume's and Russell's analysis of mind.

Ryle says that to talk about mind or consciousness as some counterpart of human behaviour or some world behind or beyond the activities is a mistake. The meaningful referent of the concept of mind is a description of how people behave. The words like 'intelligence' or 'stupidity' that express mental concepts do not name occult, private entities that are spiritual.

Category Mistake

This is how Ryle analyses the official theory which he calls 'Descartes' Myth'. This analysis is often called by Ryle as "the dogma of the ghost in the Machine." Ryle's main aim is to prove the above theory as totally false. He says that the entire theory is false in principle. It is not the fact that this theory suffers from different kinds of particular mistakes combined together but from one big mistake which is named by Ryle as a 'Category Mistake.' This is a special kind of mistake according to him. He says, "Category mistakes are those made by people who are perfectly competent to apply concepts, at least in the situations with which they are familiar, but are still liable in their abstract thinking to allocate those concepts to logical types to which they do not belong."

This mistake arises in the theory of mind when the mental life is assumed to belong to one category when it really belongs to another category. The philosopher's myth is therefore called by Ryle as 'dogma.' Ryle's aim is to prove the falsity of the myth. But he anticipates that his effort of doing so may be taken by the critics as denying the mental life of human beings. He says that his aim is just to rectify the mental-conduct concept which is falsely described by the official theory.

The concept of 'category mistake' is enumerated by Ryle in a very funny way by giving a series of examples. One of them is that- a foreigner when for the first time visits Oxford or Cambridge to see the university and he is shown all the colleges, libraries, playgrounds, museum, scientific departments and administrative offices. But after seeing all these he assumes that he has not seen the university. He admits that he has seen all these shown but asks whereabouts of the university. He forgets that the university is nothing but the organized whole of all the things shown to him. Understanding the co-ordination of all the things shown is the seeing university. If the foreigner assumes that like other institutions such as, the Christ Church or the Bodleian Library or the Ashmolean Museum, university stood for an extra member of the class then it is an innocent but mistaken assumption. He mistakenly believes that the university is like other institutions and thus he allocates it to the category to which other institutions belong.

The destructive purpose of Ryle is to show that the source of double life theory is a family of category mistakes. The official theory tries to prove that the ghost of a person is somehow embodied in a machine. He says that a person's thinking, feeling and purposive doing is impossible to describe in an idioms of physics, chemistry and physiology alone and so they must be described in a different way. Like the human body, the human mind is complex organized unit though these two differ in stuff and structure. He says, "as the human body, like any other parcel of matter, is a field of causes and effects, so the mind must be another field of causes and effects, though not (Heaven be praised) mechanical causes and effects."

A. J. AYER: THE PROBLEM OF KNOWLEDGE

Brief Summary of Book

Knowing as having the right to be sure

The answers which we have found for the questions we have so far been discussing have not yet put us in a position to give a complete account of what it is to know that something is the case. The first requirement is that what is known should be true, but this is not sufficient; not even if we add to it the further condition that one must be completely sure of what one knows. For it is possible to be completely sure of something which is in fact true, but yet not to know it.

The circumstances may be such that one is not entitled to be sure. For instance, a superstitious person who had inadvertently walked under a ladder might be convinced as a result that he was about to suffer some misfortune; and he might in fact be right. But it would not be correct to say that he knew that this was going to be so. He arrived at his belief by a process of reasoning which would not be generally reliable; so, although his prediction came true, it was not a case of knowledge. Again, if someone were fully persuaded of a mathematical proposition by a proof which could be shown to be invalid, he would not, without further evidence, be said to know the proposition, even though it was true.

But while it is not hard to find examples of true and fully confident beliefs which in some ways fail to meet the standards required for knowledge, it is not at all easy to determine exactly what these "standards are. One way of trying to discover them would be to consider what would count as satisfactory answers to the question How do you know? Thus people may be credited with knowing truths of mathematics or logic if they are able to give a valid proof of them, or even if, without themselves being able to set out such a proof, they have obtained this information from someone who can. Claims to know empirical statements may be upheld by a reference to perception, or to memory, or to testimony, or to historical records, or to scientific laws. But such backing is not always strong enough for knowledge. Whether it is so or not depends upon the circumstances of the particular case. If I were asked how I knew that a physical object of a certain sort was in such and such a place, it would, in general, be a sufficient answer for me to say that I could see it; but if my eyesight were bad and the light were dim, this answer might not be sufficient. Even though I was right, it might still be said that I did not really know that the object was there. If I have a poor memory and the event which I claim to remember is remote, my memory of it may still not amount to knowledge, even though in this instance it does not fail me. If a witness is unreliable, his unsupported evidence may not enable us to know that what he says is true, even in a case where we completely trust him and he is not in fact deceiving us. In a given instance it is possible to decide whether the backing is strong enough to justify a claim to knowledge. But to say in general how strong it has to be would require our drawing up a list of the conditions under which perception, or memory, or testimony, or other forms of evidence are reliable. And this would be a very complicated matter, if indeed it could be done at all.

Moreover, we cannot assume that, even in particular instances, an answer to the question How do you know? will always be forthcoming. There may very well be cases in which one knows that something is so without its being possible to say how one knows it. I am not so much thinking now of claims to know facts of immediate experience, statements like 'I know that I feel pain', which raise problems of their own into which we shall enter later on. In cases of this sort it may be argued that the question how one knows does not arise. But even when it clearly does arise, it may not find an answer. Suppose that someone were consistently successful in predicting events of a certain kind, events, let us say, which are not ordinarily thought to be predictable, like the results of a lottery. If his run of successes were sufficiently impressive, we might very well come to say that he knew which number would win, even though he did not reach this conclusion by any rational method, or indeed by any method at all. We might say that he knew it by "intuition, but this would be to assert no more than that he did know it but that we could not say how. In the same way, if someone were consistently successful in reading the minds of others without having any of the usual sort of evidence, we might say that he knew these things telepathically. But in default of any further explanation this would come down to saying merely that he did know them, but not by any ordinary means. Words like 'intuition' and 'telepathy' are brought in just to disguise the fact that no explanation has been found.

But if we allow this sort of knowledge to be even theoretically possible, what becomes of the distinction between knowledge and true belief? How does our man who knows what the results of the lottery will be differ from one who only makes a series of lucky guesses? The answer is that, so far as the man himself is concerned, there need not be any difference. His procedure and his state of mind, when he is said to know what will happen, may be exactly the same as when it is said that he is only guessing. The difference is that to say that he knows is to concede to him the right to be sure, while to say that he is only guessing is to withhold it. Whether we make this concession will depend upon the view which we take of his performance. Normally we do not say that people know things unless they have followed one of the accredited routes to knowledge. If someone reaches a true conclusion without appearing to have any adequate basis for it, we are likely to say that he does not really know it. But if he were repeatedly successful in a given domain, we might very well come to say that he knew the facts in question, even though we could not explain how he knew them. We should grant him the right to be sure, simply on the basis of his success. This is, indeed, a point on which people's views might be expected to differ. Not everyone would regard a successful run of predictions, however long sustained, as being by itself a sufficient backing for a claim to knowledge. And here there can be no question of proving that this attitude is mistaken. Where there are recognized criteria for deciding when one has the right to be sure, anyone who insists that their being satisfied is still not enough for knowledge may be accused, for what the charge is worth, of misusing the verb 'to know'. But it is possible to find, or at any rate to devise, examples which are not covered in this respect by any established rule of usage. Whether they are to count as instances of knowledge is then a question which we are left free to decide.

It does not, however, matter very greatly which decision we take. The main problem is to state and assess the grounds on which these claims to knowledge are made, to settle, as it were, the candidate's marks. It is a relatively unimportant question what titles we then bestow upon them. So long as we agree about the marking, it is of no great consequence where we draw the line between pass and failure, or between the different levels of distinction.

If we choose to set a very high standard, we may find ourselves committed to saying "that some of what ordinarily passes for knowledge ought rather to be described as probable opinion. And some critics will then take us to task for flouting ordinary usage. But the question is purely one of terminology. It is to be decided, if at all, on grounds of practical convenience.

One must not confuse this case, where the markings are agreed upon, and what is in dispute is only the bestowal of honours, with the case where it is the markings themselves that are put in question. For this second case is philosophically important, in a way in which the other is not. The sceptic who asserts that we do not know all that we think we know, or even perhaps that we do not strictly know anything at all, is not suggesting that we are mistaken when we conclude that the recognized criteria for knowing have been satisfied. Nor is he primarily concerned with getting us to revise our usage of the verb 'to know', any more than one who challenges our standards of value is trying to make us revise our usage of the word 'good'.

The disagreement is about the application of the word, rather than its meaning. What the sceptic contends is that our markings are too high; that the grounds on which we are normally ready to concede the right to be sure are worth less than we think; he may even go so far as to say that they are not worth anything at all. The attack is directed, not against the way in which we apply our standards of proof, but against these standards themselves. It has, as we shall see, to be taken seriously because of the arguments by which it is supported.

I conclude then that the necessary and sufficient conditions for knowing that something is the case are first that what one is said to know be true, secondly that one be sure of it, and thirdly that one should have the right to be sure. This right may be earned in various ways; but even if one could give a complete description of them it would be a mistake to try to build it into the definition of knowledge, just as it would be a mistake to try to incorporate our actual standards of goodness into a definition of good. And this being so, it turns out that the questions which philosophers raise about the possibility of knowledge are not all to be settled by discovering what knowledge is. For many of them reappear as questions about the legitimacy of the title to be sure. They need to be severally examined; and this is the main concern of what is called the theory of knowledge.

W.V.O. QUINE: TWO DOGMAS OF EMPIRICISM

"Two Dogmas of Empiricism" is a paper by analytic philosopher Willard Van Orman Quine published in 1951. According to City University of New York professor of philosophy Peter Godfrey-Smith, this "paper [is] sometimes regarded as the most important in all of twentieth-century philosophy". The paper is an attack on two central aspects of the logical positivists' philosophy. One is the analytic–synthetic distinction between analytic truths and synthetic truths, explained by Quine as truths grounded only in meanings and independent of facts, and truths grounded in facts. The other is reductionism, the theory that each meaningful statement gets its meaning from some logical construction of terms that refers exclusively to immediate experience.

"Two Dogmas" has six sections. The first four focus on analyticity, the last two on reductionism. There, Quine turns the focus to the logical positivists' theory of meaning. He also presents his own holistic theory of meaning.

Analyticity and Circularity

Most of Quine's argument against analyticity in the first four sections is focused on showing that different explanations of analyticity are circular. The main purpose is to show that no satisfactory explanation of analyticity has been given.

Quine begins by making a distinction between two different classes of analytic statements. The first one is called logically true and has the form:

(1) **No unmarried man is married.** A sentence with that form is true independent of the interpretation of "man" and "married", so long as the logical particles "no", "un-" and "is" have their ordinary English meaning.

The statements in the second class have the form.

(2) **No bachelor is married.** A statement with this form can be turned into a statement with form (1) by exchanging synonyms with synonyms, in this case "bachelor" with "unmarried man". It is the second class of statements that lack characterization according to Quine. The notion of the second form of analyticity leans on the notion of synonymy, which Quine believes is in as much need of clarification as analyticity. Most of Quine's following arguments are focused on showing how explanations of synonymy end up being dependent on the notions of analyticity, necessity, or even synonymy itself.

How do we reduce sentences from the second class to a sentence of the first class? Some might propose definitions. "No bachelor is married" can be turned into "No unmarried man is married" because "bachelor" is defined as "unmarried man". But, Quine asks: how do we find out that "bachelor" is defined as "unmarried man"? Clearly, a dictionary would not solve the problem, as a dictionary is a report of already known synonyms, and thus is dependent on the notion of synonymy, which Quine holds as unexplained.

A second suggestion Quine considers is an explanation of synonymy in terms of interchangeability. Two linguistic forms are (according to this view) synonymous if they are interchangeable in all contexts without changing the truth-value. But consider the following example:

(3) **"Bachelor" has fewer than ten letters.** Obviously "bachelor" and "unmarried man" are not interchangeable in that sentence. To exclude that example and some other obvious counterexamples, such as poetic quality, Quine introduces the notion of cognitive synonymy. But does interchangeability hold as an explanation of cognitive synonymy? Suppose we have a language without modal adverbs like "necessarily". Such a language would be extensional, in the way that two predicates which are true about the same objects are interchangeable again without altering the truth-value. Thus, there is no assurance that two terms that are interchangeable without the truth-value changing are interchangeable because of meaning, and not because of chance. For example, "creature with a heart" and "creature with kidneys" share extension.

In a language with the modal adverb "necessarily" the problem is solved, as salva veritate holds in the following case.

(4) Necessarily all and only bachelors are unmarried men while it does not hold for

(5) Necessarily all and only creatures with a heart are creatures with kidneys.

Presuming that 'creature with a heart' and 'creature with kidneys' have the same extension, they will be interchangeable salva veritate. But this interchangeability rests upon both empirical features of the language itself and the degree to which extension is empirically found to be identical for the two concepts, and not upon the sought for principle of cognitive synonymy.

It seems that the only way to assert the synonymy is by supposing that the terms 'bachelor' and 'unmarried man' are synonymous and that the sentence "All and only all bachelors are unmarried men" is analytic. But for salva veritate to hold as a definition of something more than extensional agreement, i.e., cognitive synonymy, we need a notion of necessity and thus of analyticity.

So, from the above example, it can be seen that in order for us to distinguish between analytic and synthetic we must appeal to synonymy; at the same time, we should also understand synonymy with interchangeability salva veritate. However, such a condition to understand synonymy is not enough so we not only argue that the terms should be interchangeable, but necessarily so. And to explain this logical necessity we must appeal to analyticity once again.

Reductionism

Analyticity would be acceptable if we allowed for the verification theory of meaning: an analytic statement would be one synonymous with a logical truth, which would be an extreme case of meaning where empirical verification is not needed, because it is "confirmed no matter what". "So, if the verification theory can be accepted as an adequate account of statement synonymy, the notion of analyticity is saved after all."

The problem that naturally follows is how statements are to be verified. An empiricist would say that it can only be done using empirical evidence. So some form of reductionism - "the belief that each meaningful statement is equivalent to some logical construct upon terms which refer to immediate experience" - must be assumed in order for an empiricist to 'save' the notion of analyticity. Such reductionism, says Quine, presents just as intractable a problem as did analyticity.

In order to prove that all meaningful statements can be translated into a sense-datum language, a reductionist would surely have to confront "the task of specifying a sense-datum language and showing how to translate the rest of significant discourse, statement by statement, into it." To illustrate the difficulty of doing so, Quine describes Rudolf Carnap's attempt in his book Der logische Aufbau der Welt.

Quine first observes that Carnap's starting point was not the strictest possible, as his "sense-datum language" included not only sense-events but also "the notations of logic, up through higher set theory... Empiricists there are who would boggle at such prodigality." Nonetheless, says Quine, Carnap showed great ingenuity in defining sensory concepts "which, but for his constructions, one would not have dreamed were definable on so slender a basis." However, even such admirable efforts left Carnap, by his own admission, far short of completing the whole project.

Finally, Quine objects in principle to Carnap's proposed translation of statements like "quality q is at point-instant x;y;z;t" into his sense-datum language, because he does not define the connective "is at". Without statements of this kind, it is difficult to see, even in principle, how Carnap's project could have been completed.

The difficulty that Carnap encountered shows that reductionism is, at best, unproven and very difficult to prove. Until a reductionist can produce an acceptable proof, Quine maintains that reductionism is another "metaphysical article of faith".

Quine's Holism

Instead of reductionism, Quine proposes that it is the whole field of science and not single statements that are verified. All scientific statements are interconnected. Logical laws give the relation between different statements, while they also are statements of the system. This makes talk about the empirical content of a single statement misleading. It also becomes impossible to draw a line between synthetic statements, which depend on experience, and analytic statements, that hold come what may. Any statement can be held as necessarily true according to Quine, if the right changes are made somewhere else in the system. In the same way, no statements are immune to revision.

Even logical laws can be revised according to Quine. Quantum logic, introduced by Garrett Birkhoff and John von Neumann, abandons the law of distributivity from classical logic in order to reconcile some of the apparent inconsistencies of classical Boolean logic with the facts related to measurement and observation in quantum mechanics. Quine makes the case that the empirical study of physics has furnished apparently credible grounds for replacing classical logic by quantum logic, rather as Newtonian physics gave way to Einsteinian physics. The idea that logical laws are not immune to revision in the light of empirical evidence has provoked an intense debate (see "Is Logic Empirical?").

According to Quine, there are two different results of his reasoning. The first is a blurring of the line between metaphysics and natural science. The common-sense theory about physical objects is epistemologically comparable to the gods of Homer. Quine is a physicalist, in the sense that he considers it a scientific error not to adopt a theory which makes reference to physical objects. However, like Gods of Homer, physical objects are posits, and there is no great epistemic difference in kind; the difference is rather that the theory of physical objects has turned out to be a more efficient theory. As Quine states in "Two Dogmas", "The myth of physical objects is epistemologically superior to most in that it has proved more efficacious than other myths as a device for working a manageable structure into the flux of experience".

The second result is a move towards pragmatism. Since, Quine says, the function of science is to predict future experiences in the light of past ones, the only ground for choosing which explanations to believe is "the degree to which they expedite our dealings with sense experiences." While pragmatic concerns are important for Carnap and other logical positivists when choosing a linguistic framework, their pragmatism "leaves off at the imagined boundary between the analytic and the synthetic". For Quine, every change in the system of science is, when rational, pragmatic.

Critique and Influence

Rudolf Carnap prepared a reply entitled "Quine on Analyticity", but this was not published until 1990. Addressing Quine's concern over the status of the sentence "Everything green is extended", Carnap wrote "the difficulty here lies in the unclarity of the word 'green', namely in an indecision over whether one should use the word for something unextended, i.e., for a single space-time point. In daily life it is never so used, and one scarcely ever speaks of space-time points." Carnap then puts forward that an exact artificial language ought to clarify the problem by defining 'green' (or its synonym) as something that is either necessarily or contingently not applied to space-time points. He wrote that once that decision is made, the difficulty is resolved. Carnap also answers Quine's argument on the use of sets of formal sentences to explain analyticity by arguing that this method is an explication of a poorly understood notion.

Paul Grice and P. F. Strawson criticized "Two Dogmas" in their (1956) article "In Defense of a Dogma". Among other things, they argue that Quine's skepticism about synonyms leads to a skepticism about meaning. If statements can have meanings, then it would make sense to ask "What does it mean?". If it makes sense to ask "What does it mean?", then synonymy can be defined as follows: Two sentences are synonymous if and only if the true answer of the question "What does it mean?" asked of one of them is the true answer to the same question asked of the other. They also draw the conclusion that discussion about correct or incorrect translations would be impossible given Quine's argument. Four years after Grice and Strawson published their paper, Quine's book Word and Object was released. In the book Quine presented his theory of indeterminacy of translation.

In "'Two Dogmas' revisited", Hilary Putnam argues that Quine is attacking two different notions. Analytic truth defined as a true statement derivable from a tautology by putting synonyms for synonyms is near Kant's account of analytic truth as a truth whose negation is a contradiction. Analytic truth defined as a truth confirmed no matter what however, is closer to one of the traditional accounts of a priori. While the first four sections of Quine's paper concern analyticity, the last two concern apriority. Putnam considers the argument in the two last sections as independent of the first four, and at the same time as Putnam criticizes Quine, he also emphasizes his historical importance as the first top rank philosopher to both reject the notion of apriority and sketch a methodology without it.

Jerrold Katz, a onetime associate of Noam Chomsky's, countered the arguments of "Two Dogmas" directly by trying to define analyticity non-circularly on the syntactical features of sentences.

In his book Philosophical Analysis in the Twentieth Century, Volume 1 : The Dawn of Analysis Scott Soames has pointed out that Quine's circularity argument needs two of the logical positivists' central theses to be effective:

All necessary truths (and all a priori truths) are analytic

Analyticity is needed to explain and legitimate necessity.

It is only when these two theses are accepted that Quine's argument holds. It is not a problem that the notion of necessity is presupposed by the notion of analyticity if necessity can be explained without analyticity. According to Soames, both theses were accepted by most philosophers when Quine published "Two Dogmas". Today however, Soames holds both statements to be antiquated.

H.P. GRICE AND P.F. STRAWSON: IN DEFENSE OF A DOGMA

The analytic/synthetic distinction brought to prominence by Immanuel Kant in his Critique of Pure Reason, in his distinction between analytic and synthetic judgments, occupies an essential place in the empiricist view of knowledge as lucidly reflected in the views of the logical positivists. Before Kant, Leibniz and Hume had made similar distinction between "truth of reason/truth of fact" and "relations of ideas/matters of fact" respectively1 W. V. O. Quine in his paper; "Two Dogmas of Empiricism" has subjected this distinction to criticisms by identifying two dogmas in it which, he says, are not justifiable.

The first of these dogmas insists on a "fundamental cleavage between truth which are analytic or grounded in meaning independently of matters of fact, and truth which are synthetic, or grounded in fact. The other dogma is reductionism; the belief that each meaningful statement is equivalent to some logical experience? One major reasons for supposing this distinction right is that: "A statement is analytic if it can be shown to be ultimately reducible to a form governed by the logical law of identity. 'A is A' (and) a statement is synthetic if it cannot be shown to be reducible to a statement that is basically of the form of an identity statement." Quine, on examining this distinction, says it cannot be justified since it is not a clear one and therefore seems unwarranted and useless. He therefore outrightly rejects it.

In their paper "In Defence of a Dogma" H. P. Grice and P. F. Strawson attack Quine's position by arguing that the criticisms raised by Quine do not, at all "justify the rejection, as illusory, of the analytic synthetic distinction and the notions which belong to the same family." Put differently, Grice and Strawson opines that the criticisms given by Quine against the distinction, or simply because the distinction falls short of Quine's expectations does not justify the rejection of the distinction neither does it imply that the distinction does not exist. They also contend that even the criticisms and points raised by Quine for the rejection of the distinction tend to allow for or accommodate the distinction itself.

It is important at this point that we examine more vividly the reason(s) for Quine's rejection of the distinction, and also to see if Grice and Strawson are right to say that they are not enough for the rejection of the analytic/synthetic distinction.

Quine's Reasons for Rejection of the Analytic/Synthetic Distinction

The major reason why Quine rejects the distinction is due to the nature of analyticity. He distinguishes: between two types of analytic statements, that of logical truths and those believed to be convertible to logical truths. The former are statements that are true under all reinterpretation of their components with the exception of the logical particles, which should be left unuttered. e.g. "no married man is unmarried" or "A triangle has three angles." The later are those that depend on synonymity; e.g., "no married man is a bachelor" which could be turned into a logically true statement by substituting "unmarried man" for it synonym "bachelor."

Quine contends that the major difficulty with analyticity lies with this second clarification of analytic statements and not with the first because it depends on synonymity which itself cannot be clarified.

He says thus that, We still lack a proper characterization of the second class of analytic statements and therewith of analyticity generally inasmuch as we have ... to learn on a notion of "synonymy" which is no less in need of clarification than analyticity itself.

In other words, it is not clear what is meant when two expressions are said to be synonymous. This is because whenever an attempt is made to explain synonymy, it is done with the concept of analyticity which is in turn in need of clarification, and whatever clarification that is sought for analyticity is again based on synonymy. This therefore tends to lead to a circular form of reasoning. Hence, there is no adequate clarification of synonymy and analyticity. The problem Quine is trying to bring out here, says Grice and Strawson, is this; "There is a certain circle or family of expressions of which "analyticity" is one of such that if any one member of the circle could be taken to be satisfactorily understood or explained, then other members of the circle could be verbally, and hence satisfactorily explain in terms of it.

Other members of the family include "self-contradictory," (in a broad sense), "necessary," "synonymous," "semantical rule" and perhaps definition (but again in a broad sense). Unfortunately, each member of the family is in as great need of explanation as any other... To make "satisfactory sense" of one of these expressions would seem to involve two things: (1) it would seem to involve providing an explanation which does not incorporate any expression belonging to the family circle (2) it would seem that the explanation provided must be of the same general character as those rejected explanations which do incorporate members of the family–circle (i.e., it must specify some features common and peculiar to all cases to which, for example, the word "analytic" is to be applied; it must have the same general form as an explanation beginning "a statement is analytic if and only if ..." ... if we take these two conditions together and generalize the results, it would seem that Quine requires of a satisfactory explanation of an expression that it should take the form of a pretty strict definition but should not make use of any member of a group of interdefinable terms to which the expression belongs."

Quine says, for instance, that though "definition" seems to solve the problem of synonymy faced by the second class of analytic statements, it, on a very careful examination, doesn't but rather reaffirms it. He remarks that definition does not, as some have supposed, hold the key to synonymy and analyticity since definition—except in the extreme case of the explicitly conventional introduction of new notations––hinges on prior relations of synonymy. He also attempts to see how cognitive synonymy not presupposing analyticity can help reduce the problem. He however, sees this as difficult to achieve since there can be no adequate explanation of cognitive synonymy that would not incorporate directly or indirectly the notion of analyticity. This is because interchangeability without change in the truth value of the resultant statements is meaningless until it is relativised to a language whose extent is specified in relevant respects.

The reason being that it is easy to construct truths which become false under substitution, say of "unmarried man" for "bachelor" for example with the aid of phrases like "bachelor of arts" etc., and with the aid of single quotes to mention either of both of such pairs of words or expressions, e.g., "bachelor has four letters." By specifying an extensional language with one and many place predicates, truth functions, and quantifications as its primitives, we could, according to Quine, obtain such interchangeability. But then, the best that such interchangeability (salva veritate) in such an extensional language can guarantee for us is the truth of the resultant statements, not their analyticity. In other words it would not guarantee the necessity of their truth because all that such interchangeability entails in such a language is extensional isomorphism. And, as Quine is quick to point out, mere extensional agreement falls short of cognitive synonymy. On the other hand, language that contains intentional adverbs like "necessarily" guarantee cognitive synonymy. However, the interchangeability in such a language presupposes the understanding of the concept of analyticity. So we are back to where we started.

Quine also makes an attempt to explain analyticity by drawing on the resources of the verification theory of meaning. On this theory, two statements would supposedly be held synonymous if they are susceptible to identical mode of empirical confirmation or disconfirmation. If that supposition is true, it seems that the notion of analyticity is saved after all. For then we could explain the notion of analyticity in terms of synonymy of statements together with logical truths.

But Quine holds that the verification principle is fundamentally wrong; its supposed validity rests on a defective conception of meaning which regards individual statements as independent or primary units of meaning. Quine maintains that it is this defective conception of meaning which in turn produces the two problematic results, the two dogmas of empiricism.

For the above reasons, Quine insists that the distinction made between analyticity and synthetic statements and the reason given for such, are not clear and are totally misunderstood by those who use the expressions; that the stories they tell themselves about the distinction are full of illusions. Hence he says it is a distinction which he rejects as insensible, useless and illusory. But, how plausible are these criticism against the distinction and, even if plausible, do they amount to such a rejection of it?

Replies from Grice and Strawson

The reason why Quine sees the analytic/synthetic distinction as inadequately clarified, hence useless and although illusory, the reason why he says the belief in the existence of such a distinction is a philosophical mistake, an unempirical dogma of empiricism, a metaphysical article of faith, as we have seen above, is the circular nature of explaining analyticity, synonymy and other members of the circle of interdefinable concepts. To make satisfactory sense of analyticity or any other member of the family, Quine has insisted above, involves two conditions which are: providing an explanation which does not incorporate any expression belonging to the family circle, and that the explanation provided must specify some features common and peculiar to all cases to which thee expression is to be applied. According to Grice and Strawson, we may begin to feel that such a satisfactory explanation is hard to come by. But how does it follow that not having a satisfactory explanation of X is enough reason to say X doesn't make sense? It would seem fairly clearly unreasonable to insist in general that the availability of a satisfactory explanation in the sense sketched above is a necessary condition of an expression making sense. It is perhaps dubious whether any such explanation can ever be given (the hope that there can be is, or was, the hope of reductive analysis in general). Even if such explanation can be given in some cases, it would be pretty generally agreed that there are other cases in which they cannot.

One might think, for example, of the group of expressions which include "morally wrong," "blameworthy," "breach of moral rules," etc., or of a group which include the propositional connections and the words "true," and "false," "statement," "fact," "denial," "assertion." Few people would want to say that the expression belonging to either of these groups were senseless on the ground that they have not been formally defined (or even on the ground that it was impossible formally to define them) except in terms of members of the same group.

Besides, according to Grice and Strawson, simply because the expression cannot be explained in Quine's terms does not mean that they cannot be explained at all. They can be, and are explained, though in other and less formal ways than that required by Quine, which implies that, though there is no one way of explaining them, there is a generally agreed philosophical (and ordinary usage for them. To illustrate this point, they (Grice and Strawson) use a member of the analyticity family namely logical impossibility which Quine regards as not clearer than the others, by bringing out the contrast between logical and natural impossibility. They use the instance of the logical impossibility of a child of three's being an adult, and the natural impossibility of a child of three's understanding Russell's theory of types. Ultimately, the distinction between such statements, they claim, will amount to the distinction between not believing something and not understanding something.

In other words, the distinction is between lack of belief and lack of understanding, or between incredulity yielding to conviction and incomprehension yielding to comprehension. It would be rash to maintain that this distinction does not need clarification, but it would be absurd to maintain that it does not exist. In the face of the availability of this informal type of explanation for the notions of the analyticity group, the fact that they have not received another type of explanation seem a wholly inadequate grounds for conclusion that the notions are pseudo-notions, that the expressions which purport to express them have no sense. Hence, Quine's argument that the notions of the analyticity group have not been satisfactorily explained does not justify his extreme position for their rejection. This is because even though the distinction demands for better clarification, there is a strong presumption in favour of the existence of the distinction which he challenges, a presumption resting both on philosophical and ordinary usage.

Another point of criticism raised by Grice and Strawson against Quine is on his notion of definition and synonyms. As noted earlier, in criticizing definition as depending on synonymy, he, however, excluded what he calls extreme cases of explicitly conventional introduction of new notations. In the extreme case, the definiendom becomes synonymous with the definiens simply because it has been expressly created for the purpose of being synonymous with the definiens. This is, however, incoherent according to Grice and Strawson. As they say, it is like the position of a man to who you are trying to explain, say, an idea of one thing fitting into another thing, or two things fitting together, and who says, "I can understand what it means to say that one thing fits into another, or that two things fit together, in the case where one was specifically made to fit to the other but I cannot understand what it means to say this in any other case. This is because Quine's extreme case are in reality indifferent from those he condemns and hence, it will be improper for him to accept one and reject the others. For these and other reasons, they conclude that Quine's case against the analytic/synthetic distinction is not well made out, it is incoherent and unjustified. This is seen once more in their attack on Quine's positive theory or scientific holism as affirming, rather than refuting the distinction, though Quine insist that it is incompatible with the distinction.

Quine's Positive Theory and the Affirmation of the Analytic/Synthetic Distinction

Having rejected the analytic/synthetic distinction, Quine boldly sketches his own positive theory that will aid in determining the relation between the statements we accept as true or reject as false on the one hand, and the experiences in the light of which we do so, on the other. His positive theory can be summarized in these five propositions.

(1) Taken collectively, science has its double dependence upon language and experience; (though) … this duality is not significantly traceable into the statement of science.

(2) (our) statements about the eternal world face the tribunal of sense experience not individually but only as a corporate body

(3) thus, the unit of empirical significance is the whole of science.

(4) consequently, any statement can be held true, come what may, if we make drastic enough adjustment elsewhere in the system.

(5) And conversely, by the same token, no statement is immune to revision.

These five propositions are what constitute Quine's positive theory or scientific holism which advocates a new theory of meaning not predicated on individual words or statements, but on science as a whole. It can be summarized as follows. Whatever our experiences maybe, it is in principle possible to hold on to, or reject any statement we like, so long as we are prepared to make extensive enough revisions elsewhere in our system of beliefs. In practice, our choices are governed largely by consideration of convenience. We wish our system to be as simple as possible, but we also wish disturbances to it as it exists to be as small as possible.

Quine maintains that his positive theory is in no way compatible with the analytic/synthetic distinction. Grice and Strawson, however, contends that Quine's position is compatible with, and gives room for the kind of explanation that he rejects of analytic/synthetic distinction. Grice and Strawson say, for instance, concerning Quine's supposition that "no statement is immune to revision" that;

Since it is an illusion to suppose that the characteristics of immunity in principle from revision, come what may, belongs or could belong to any statement, it is an illusion to suppose that there is a distinction to be drawn between statements which posses this characteristics and statement which lacks it. Yet Quine suggest, this is precisely the distinction which those who use the terms "analytic" and synthetic" suppose themselves to be drawing. Quine's view would perhaps be… that those who believe in the distinction are inclined, at least sometimes to mistake the characteristics of strongly resisting revision (which belongs to beliefs very centrally situated in the system) for the mythical characteristics of total immunity from revision.

Therefore, Quine, while positing his own dogma of revisability, endorses the distinction in contention in the sense that even though this implies that there is no absolute necessity about the adoption or use of any conceptual scheme whatever or more narrowly in terms that he would reject, that there is analytic proposition such that we must gave linguistic forms bearing just the sense required to express that proposition, it is not possible to deny the existence of necessities within any conceptual scheme we adopt or use or, more narrowly again, that there are no linguistic forms which do express analytic propositions.

It is therefore the conclusion of Grice and Strawson that Quine's rejection of the analytic/synthetic distinction is not justified by his criticism of the distinction. Hence, the distinction still remains, even in the light of not being able to satisfy Quine's ideals.

PHENOMENOLOGY AND EXISTENTIALISM

The relationship between phenomenology and existentialism is a close one. Phenomenology shares several of the same ideas as its sibling, and the line between the two is often unclear.

Founded by Edmund Husserl, phenomenology is a philosophical model that was made to be free of presupposition. The idea is to study and describe objects and events from the position of observers, rather than to make claims about some objective reality. Anything that is not immediately concious is to be excluded. Rather than deductive or empirical methods, Husserl's method was to rely on the information gathered by the senses and to throw away all scientific or metaphysical knowledge or beliefs in order to study phenomenon more accurately.

Phenomenology is sometimes compared to idealism, the metaphysical claim that all that truly exist are minds. Phenomenology does not make this claim. Instead, phenomenology merely focuses on the epistemological claim that all we know is our subjective reality, coupled with the normative claim that we ought to avoid the meaningless attempt to seek out some objective reality. The importance is placed on the subjective.

This importance on human cognition rather than belief or assumption is mirrored in existentialism. Albert Camus takes a phenomenological view to the world with his descriptions of knowledge:

This heart within me I can feel, and I judge that it exists. This world around me I can feel, and I likewise judge that it exists. There ends all my knowledge, and the rest is construction.

While the rest of philosophy is often focuses on how things are and how we are able or unable to perceive the truth in the world, phenomenology counts that our perceptions and internal experience are what matters. Existentialism mirrors this idea in its description of human nature. Psychologists, sociologists and philosophers alike have searched for so-called "truths" of human nature. Existentialism holds that there are no (or at least few) universal truths about human nature — the individual is what is important, and the individual is free to make his or her life in any way imaginable.

Together, existentialism and phenomenology move the focus away from facts about the world towards facts about the individual self. For phenomenology, that means changing the way we view metaphysics and epistemological claims. For existentialism, it generates a normative ethic on how to live a worthwhile life.

KIERKEGAARD: SUBJECTIVITY AS TRUTH, LEAP OF FAITH

The philosophy of Soren Kierkegaard has been a major influence in the development of 20th-century philosophy, especially existentialism and postmodernism. Kierkegaard was a 19th-century Danish philosopher who has been labeled by many as the "Father of Existentialism", although there are some in the field who express doubt in labeling him an existentialist to begin with. His philosophy also influenced the development of existential psychology.

Kierkegaard criticized aspects of the philosophical systems that were brought on by philosophers such as George Wilhelm Friedrich Hegel before him and the Danish Hegelians. He was also indirectly influenced by the philosophy of Immanuel Kant. He measured himself against the model of philosophy which he found in Socrates, which aims to draw one's attention not to explanatory systems, but rather to the issue of how one exists.

One of Kierkegaard's recurrent themes is the importance of subjectivity, which has to do with the way people relate themselves to (objective) truths. In Concluding Unscientific Postscript to Philosophical

Fragments, he argues that "subjectivity is truth" and "truth is subjectivity." What he means by this is that most essentially, truth is not just a matter of discovering objective facts. While objective facts are important, there is a second and more crucial element of truth, which involves how one relates oneself to those matters of fact. Since how one acts is, from the ethical perspective, more important than any matter of fact, truth is to be found in subjectivity rather than objectivity.

Subjectivity

Johannes Climacus, in Concluding Unscientific Postscript to Philosophical Fragments, writes the following cryptic line: "Subjectivity is Truth". To understand Climacus's concept of the individual, it is important to look at what he says regarding subjectivity. What is subjectivity? In very rough terms, subjectivity refers to what is personal to the individual—what makes the individual who he is in distinction from others. Another way to interpret subjectivity is the unique relationship between the subject and object.

Johann Fichte wrote similarly about subjectivity in his 1799 book The Vocation of Man.

I must, however, remind my reader that the "I" who speaks in the book is not the author himself, but it is his earnest wish that the reader should himself assume this character, and that he should not rest contented with a mere historical apprehension of what is here said, but really and truly, during reading, hold converse with himself, deliberate, draw conclusions, and form resolutions, like his representative in the book, and, by his own labour and reflection, developed out of his own soul, and build up within himself, that mode of thought the mere picture of which is laid before him in the work. Preface

Scientists and historians, for example, study the objective world, hoping to elicit the truth of nature—or perhaps the truth of history. In this way, they hope to predict how the future will unfold in accordance with these laws. In terms of history, by studying the past, the individual can perhaps elicit the laws that determine how events will unfold—in this way the individual can predict the future with more exactness and perhaps take control of events that in the past appeared to fall outside the control of humans.

In most respects, Climacus did not have problems with science or the scientific endeavor. He would not disregard thc importance of objective knowledge. Where the scientist or historian finds certainty, however, Climacus noted very accurately that results in science change as the tools of observation change. But Climacus's special interest was in history. His most vehement attacks came against those who believed that they had understood history and its laws—and by doing so could ascertain what a human's true self is. That is, the assumption is that by studying history someone can come to know who he really is as a person. Kierkegaard especially accused Hegel's philosophy of falling prey to this assumption. He explained this in, Concluding Unscientific Postscript:

> It is the existing spirit who asks about truth, presumably because he wants to exist in it, but in any case the questioner is conscious of being an existing individual human being. In this way I believe I am able to make myself understandable to every Greek and to every rational human being. If a German philosopher follows his inclination to put on an act and first transforms himself into a superrational something, just as alchemists and sorcerers bedizen themselves fantastically, in order to answer the question about truth in an extremely satisfying way, this is of no more concern to me than his satisfying answer, which no doubt is extremely satisfying-if one is fantastically dressed up. But whether a German philosopher is or is not doing this can easily be ascertained by anyone who with enthusiasm concentrates his soul on willing to allow himself to be guided by a sage of that kind, and uncritically just uses his guidance compliantly by willing to form his existence according to it. When a person as a learner enthusiastically relates in this way to such a German professor, he

> accomplishes the most superb epigram upon him, because a speculator of that sort is anything but served by a learner's honest and enthusiastic zeal for expressing and accomplishing, for existentially appropriating his wisdom, since this wisdom is something that the her Professor himself has imagined and has written books about but has never attempted himself. It has not even occurred to him that it should be done. Like the customers clerk who, in the belief that his business was merely to write, wrote what he himself could not read, so there are speculative thinkers who merely write, and write that which, if it is to be read with the aid of action, if I may put it that way, proves to be nonsense, unless it is perhaps intended only for fantastical beings.

Hegel wanted to philosophize about Christianity but had no intention to ever become a Christian. For Climacus, the individual comes to know who he is by an intensely personal and passionate pursuit of what will give meaning to his life. As an existing individual, who must come to terms with everyday life, overcome its obstacles and setbacks, who must live and die, the single individual has a life that no one else will ever live. In dealing with what life brings his way, the individual must encounter them with all his psycho-physical resources.

Subjectivity is that which the individual—and no one else—has. But what does it mean to have something like this? It cannot be understood in the same way as having a car or a bank account. It means to be someone who is becoming someone—it means being a person with a past, a present, and a future. No one can have an individual's past, present or future. Different people experience these in various ways—these experiences are unique, not anyone else's. Having a past, present, and future means that a person is an existing individual—that a person can find meaning in time and by existing. Individuals do not think themselves into existence, they are born. But once born and past a certain age, the individual begins to make choices in life; now those choices can be his, his parents', society's, etc. The important point is that to exist, the individual must make choices—the individual must decide what to do the next moment and on into the future. What the individual chooses and how he chooses will define who and what he is—to himself and to others. Kierkegaard put it this way in Works of Love, 1847:

> We are truly reluctant to make a young person arrogant prematurely and teach him to get busy judging the world. God forbid that anything we say should be able to contribute to developing this malady in a person. Indeed, we think we ought to make his life so strenuously inwardly that from the very beginning he has something else to think about, because it no doubt is a morbid hatred of the world that, perhaps without having considered the enormous responsibility, wants to be persecuted. But on the other hand we are also truly reluctant to deceive a young person by suppressing the difficulty and by suppressing it at the very moment we endeavor to recommend Christianity, inasmuch as that is the very moment we speak. We put our confidence in boldly daring to praise Christianity, also with the addition that in the world its reward, to put it mildly, is ingratitude. We regard it as our duty continually to speak about it in advance, so that we do not sometimes praise Christianity with an omission of what is essentially difficult, and at other times, perhaps on the occasion of a particular text, hit upon a few grounds of comfort for the person tried and tested in life. No, just when Christianity is being praised most strongly, the difficulty must simultaneously be emphasized. (….) Christianly the world's opposition stands in an essential relationship to the inwardness of Christianity. Moreover, the person who chooses Christianity should at that very moment have an impression of its difficulty so that he can know what it is that he is choosing.

The goal of life, according to Socrates, is to know thyself. Knowing oneself means being aware of who one is, what one can be and what one cannot be. Kierkegaard uses the same idea that Socrates used in his own writings. He asks the one who wants to be a single individual the following questions in his 1847 book, Upbuilding Discourses in Various Spirits

Everyone must make an accounting to God as an individual; the king must make an accounting to God as an individual, and the most wretched beggar must make an accounting to God as an individual – lest anyone be arrogant by being more than an individual, lest anyone despondently think that he is not an individual, perhaps because in the busyness of the world he does not even have a name but is designated only by a number. What else, indeed, is the accounting of eternity than that the voice of conscience is installed eternally in its eternal right to be the only voice!...

Are you now living in such a way that you are aware of being a single individual and thereby aware of your eternal responsibility before God; are you living in such a way that this awareness can acquire the time and stillness and liberty to withdraw from life, from an honorable occupation, from a happy domestic life – on the contrary, that awareness will support and transfigure and illuminate your conduct in the relationships of life. You are not to withdraw and sit brooding over your eternal accounting, whereby you only take on a new responsibility.

You will find more and more time for your duties and tasks, while concern for your eternal responsibility will keep you from being busy and from busily taking part in everything possible – an activity that can best be called a waste of time...

Have you made up your mind about how you want to perform your work, or are you continually of two minds because you want to be in agreement with the crowd? Do you stick to your bid, not defiantly, not despondently, but eternally concerned; do you, unchanged, continue to bid on the same thing and want to buy only the same thing while the terms are variously being changed?...

Are you hiding nothing suspicious in your soul, so that you would still wish things were different, so that you would dare robber-like to seize the reward for yourself, would dare to parade it, would dare to point to it; so that you would wish the adversity did not exist because it constrains in you the selfishness that, although suppressed, yet foolishly deludes you into thinking that if you were lucky you would do something for the good that would be worth talking about, deludes you into forgetting that the devout wise person wishes no adversity away when it befalls him because he obviously cannot know whether it might not indeed be a good for him, into forgetting that the devout wise person wins his most beautiful victory when the powerful one who persecuted him wants, as they say, to spare him, and the wise one replies: I cannot unconditionally wish it, because I cannot definitely know whether the persecution might not indeed be a good for me. Are you doing good only out of the fear of punishment, so that you scowl even when you will the good, so that in your dreams at night you wish the punishment away and to that extent also the good, and in your daydreams delude yourself into thinking that one can serve the good with a slavish mind?

Subjectivity comes with consciousness of myself as a self. It encompasses the emotional and intellectual resources that the individual is born with. Subjectivity is what the individual is as a human being. Now the problem of subjectivity is to decide how to choose—what rules or models is the individual going to use to make the right choices? What are the right choices? Who defines right? To be truly an individual, to be true to himself, his actions should in some way be expressed so that they describe who and what he is to himself and to others. The problem, according to Kierkegaard, is that we must choose who and what we will be based on subjective interests—the individual must make choices that will mean something to him as a reasoning, feeling being.

Kierkegaard decided to step up to the Tree of the knowledge of good and evil for himself, replacing Adam, and make his choice in the presence of God, where no one was there to accuse or judge him but his Creator. This is what he had Abraham do in Fear and Trembling. This is how Kierkegaard thought learning about oneself takes place. Here is where the single individual learns about guilt and innocence. His book, The Concept of Anxiety, makes clear that Adam did have knowledge when he made his choice and that was the knowledge of freedom. The prohibition was there but so was freedom and Eve and Adam decided to use it.

In Kierkegaard's meaning, purely theological assertions are subjective truths and they cannot be either verified or invalidated by science, i.e. through objective knowledge. For him, choosing if one is for or against a certain subjective truth is a purely arbitrary choice. He calls the jump from objective knowledge to religious faith a leap of faith, since it means subjectively accepting statements which cannot be rationally justified. For him the Christian faith is the result of the trajectory initiated by such choices, which don't have and cannot have a rational ground (meaning that reason is neither for or against making such choices). Objectively regarded, purely theological assertions are neither true nor false.

Leap of Faith

A leap of faith, in its most commonly used meaning, is the act of believing in or accepting something outside the boundaries of reason.

The phrase is commonly attributed to Soren Kierkegaard; however, he never used the term, as he referred to a qualitative leap. A leap of faith according to Kierkegaard involves circularity insofar as the leap is made by faith. In his book Concluding Unscientific Postscript, he describes the core part of the leap of faith: the leap. "Thinking can turn toward itself in order to think about itself and skepticism can emerge. But this thinking about itself never accomplishes anything." Kierkegaard says thinking should serve by thinking something. Kierkegaard wants to stop "thinking's self-reflection" and that is the movement that constitutes a leap. He is against people thinking about religion all day without ever doing anything; but he is also against external shows and opinions about religion. Instead, Kierkegaard is in favor of the internal movement of faith. He says, "where Christianity wants to have inwardness, worldly Christendom wants outwardness, and where Christianity wants outwardness, worldly Christendom wants inwardness." But, on the other hand, he also says: "The less externality, the more inwardness if it is truly there; but it is also the case that the less externality, the greater the possibility that the inwardness will entirely fail to come. The externality is the watchman who awakens the sleeper; the externality is the solicitous mother who calls one; the externality is the roll call that brings the soldier to his feet; the externality is the reveille that helps one to make the great effort; but the absence of the externality can mean that the inwardness itself calls inwardly to a person - alas - but it can also mean that the inwardness will fail to come." The "most dreadful thing of all is a personal existence that cannot coalesce in a conclusion," according to Kierkegaard. He asked his contemporaries if any of them had reached a conclusion about anything or did every new premise change their convictions.

H_2 plus O becomes water, and water becomes ice, by a leap. The change from motion to rest, or vice versa, is a transition which cannot be logically construed; this is the basic principle of Zeno's dialectic, and is also expressed in Newton's laws of motion, since the external force by which such change is effected is not a consequence of the law, but is premised as external to the system with which we start. It is therefore transcendent and non-rational, and its coming into existence can only be apprehended as a leap. In the same manner, every causal system presupposes an external environment as the condition of change. Every transition from the detail of an empirical induction to the ideality and universality of law, is a leap. In the actual process of thinking, we have the leap by which we arrive at the understanding of an idea or an author.

Kierkegaard agreed with Lessing, a German dynamist, that truth lies in the search for an object, not in the object sought. It is another case of "act accomplishing itself." If God held truth in one hand and the eternal pursuit of it in the other, He would choose the second hand according to Lessing. Religious truth concerns the individual and the individual alone, and it is the personal mode of appropriation, the process of realization, the subjective dynamism that counts. Of Lessing, Kierkegaard writes approvingly. But if we are constantly occupied in the immanent striving of our own subjectivity, how are we to ascend to knowledge of a transcendent God whom traditional thought declares to be known even by reason. Lessing and Kierkegaard declare in typical fashion that there is no bridge between historical, finite knowledge and God's existence and nature. This gap can only be crossed by a "leap." Faith is a completely irrational experience, and yet it is, paradoxically, the highest duty of a Christian. Though as Thomte observes, it is not a spontaneous belief, faith is nevertheless something blind, immediate, and decisive. It has the character of an "act of resignation." It is unmediated and a-intellectual, much like Kant's proof for the existence of God. Nature makes no leaps, according to the maxim of Leibniz. But faith, according to Kierkegaard must do so in a radical way.

Like Dostoevsky, Kierkegaard, who plays an important role in the spiritual struggle for meaning on the part of the modern writer, cast off the bondage of logic and the tyranny of science. By means of the dialectic of "the leap," he attempted to transcend both the aesthetic and the ethical stages. Completely alone, cut off from his fellow-men, the individual realizes his own nothingness as the preliminary condition for embracing the truth of God. Only when man becomes aware of his own non-entity — an experience that is purely subjective and incommunicable — does he recover his real self and stand in the presence of God. This is the mystique which has been rediscovered by twentieth-century man, the leap from outwardness to inwardness, from rationalism to subjectivity, the revelation, that is ineffable, of the reality of the Absolute.

SARTRE: CONCEPT OF FREEDOM, BAD-FAITH, HUMANISM

Sartre's primary idea is that people, as humans, are "condemned to be free". This theory relies upon his position that there is no creator, and is illustrated using the example of the paper cutter. Sartre says that if one considered a paper cutter, one would assume that the creator would have had a plan for it: an essence. Sartre said that human beings have no essence before their existence because there is no Creator. Thus: "existence precedes essence". This forms the basis for his assertion that because one cannot explain one's own actions and behavior by referring to any specific human nature, they are necessarily fully responsible for those actions. "We are left alone, without excuse." "We can act without being determined by our past which is always separated from us."

Sartre maintained that the concepts of authenticity and individuality have to be earned but not learned. We need to experience "death consciousness" so as to wake up ourselves as to what is really important; the authentic in our lives which is life experience, not knowledge. Death draws the final point when we as beings cease to live for ourselves and permanently become objects that exist only for the outside world. In this way death emphasizes the burden of our free, individual existence.

As a junior lecturer at the Lycée du Havre in 1938, Sartre wrote the novel La Nausée (Nausea), which serves in some ways as a manifesto of existentialism and remains one of his most famous books.

Taking a page from the German phenomenological movement, he believed that our ideas are the product of experiences of real-life situations, and that novels and plays can well describe such fundamental experiences, having equal value to discursive essays for the elaboration of philosophical theories such as existentialism. With such purpose, this novel concerns a dejected researcher (Roquentin) in a town similar to Le Havre who becomes starkly conscious of the fact that inanimate objects and situations remain absolutely indifferent to his existence. As such, they show themselves to be resistant to whatever significance human consciousness might perceive in them.

He also took inspiration from phenomenologist epistemology, explained by Franz Adler in this way: "Man chooses and makes himself by acting. Any action implies the judgment that he is right under the circumstances not only for the actor, but also for everybody else in similar circumstances."

This indifference of "things in themselves" (closely linked with the later notion of "being-in-itself" in his Being and Nothingness) has the effect of highlighting all the more the freedom Roquentin has to perceive and act in the world; everywhere he looks, he finds situations imbued with meanings which bear the stamp of his existence. Hence the "nausea" referred to in the title of the book; all that he encounters in his everyday life is suffused with a pervasive, even horrible, taste—specifically, his freedom. The book takes the term from Friedrich Nietzsche's Thus Spoke Zarathustra, where it is used in the context of the often nauseating quality of existence. No matter how much Roquentin longs for something else or something different, he cannot get away from this harrowing evidence of his engagement with the world.

The novel also acts as a terrifying realization of some of Immanuel Kant's fundamental ideas about freedom; Sartre uses the idea of the autonomy of the will (that morality is derived from our ability to choose in reality; the ability to choose being derived from human freedom; embodied in the famous saying "Condemned to be free") as a way to show the world's indifference to the individual. The freedom that Kant exposed is here a strong burden, for the freedom to act towards objects is ultimately useless, and the practical application of Kant's ideas proves to be bitterly rejected.

Also important is Sartre's analysis of psychological concepts, including his suggestion that consciousness exists as something other than itself, and that the conscious awareness of things is not limited to their knowledge: for Sartre intentionality applies to the emotions as well as to cognitions, to desires as well as to perceptions. "When an external object is perceived, consciousness is also conscious of itself, even if consciousness is not its own object: it is a non-positional consciousness of itself."

MORLEAU-PONTY: PERCEPTION, EMBODIED CONSCIOUSNESS

Consciousness

In his Phenomenology of Perception (first published in French in 1945), Merleau-Ponty developed the concept of the body-subject (le corps propre) as an alternative to the Cartesian "ego cogito." This distinction is especially important in that Merleau-Ponty perceives the essences of the world existentially. Consciousness, the world, and the human body as a perceiving thing are intricately intertwined and mutually "engaged." The phenomenal thing is not the unchanging object of the natural sciences, but a correlate of our body and its sensory-motor functions. Taking up and "communing with" (Merleau-Ponty's phrase) the sensible qualities it encounters, the body as incarnated subjectivity intentionally elaborates things within an ever-present world frame, through use of its pre-conscious, pre-predicative understanding of the world's makeup. The elaboration, however, is "inexhaustible" (the hallmark of any perception according to Merleau-Ponty). Things are that upon which our body has a "grip" (prise), while the grip itself is a function of our connaturality with the world's things. The world and the sense of self are emergent phenomena in an ongoing "becoming."

The essential partiality of our view of things, their being given only in a certain perspective and at a certain moment in time does not diminish their reality, but on the contrary establishes it, as there is no other way for things to be co-present with us and with other things than through such "Abschattungen" (sketches, faint outlines, adumbrations). The thing transcends our view, but is manifest precisely by presenting itself to a range of possible views. The object of perception is immanently tied to its background—to the nexus of meaningful relations among objects within the world. Because the object is inextricably within the world of meaningful relations, each object reflects the other (much in the style of Leibniz's monads). Through involvement in the world – being-in-the-world – the perceiver tacitly experiences all the perspectives upon that object coming from all the surrounding things of its environment, as well as the potential perspectives that object has upon the beings around it.

Each object is a "mirror of all others." Our perception of the object through all perspectives is not that of a propositional, or clearly delineated, perception; rather, it is an ambiguous perception founded upon the body's primordial involvement and understanding of the world and of the meanings that constitute the landscape's perceptual gestalt. Only after we have been integrated within the environment so as to perceive objects as such can we turn our attention toward particular objects within the landscape so as to define them more clearly. This attention, however, does not operate by clarifying what is already seen, but by constructing a new Gestalt oriented toward a particular object. Because our bodily involvement with things is always provisional and indeterminate, we encounter meaningful things in a unified though ever open-ended world.

Perception

From the time of writing Structure of Behavior and Phenomenology of Perception, Merleau-Ponty wanted to show, in opposition to the idea that drove the tradition beginning with John Locke, that perception was not the causal product of atomic sensations. This atomist-causal conception was being perpetuated in certain psychological currents of the time, particularly in behaviourism. According to Merleau-Ponty, perception has an active dimension, in that it is a primordial openness to the lifeworld (the "Lebenswelt").

This primordial openness is at the heart of his thesis of the primacy of perception. The slogan of Husserl's phenomenology is "all consciousness is consciousness of something", which implies a distinction between "acts of thought" (the noesis) and "intentional objects of thought" (the noema). Thus, the correlation between noesis and noema becomes the first step in the constitution of analyses of consciousness. However, in studying the posthumous manuscripts of Husserl, who remained one of his major influences, Merleau-Ponty remarked that, in their evolution, Husserl's work brings to light phenomena which are not assimilable to noesis–noema correlation. This is particularly the case when one attends to the phenomena of the body (which is at once body-subject and body-object), subjective time (the consciousness of time is neither an act of consciousness nor an object of thought) and the other (the first considerations of the other in Husserl led to solipsism).

The distinction between "acts of thought" (noesis) and "intentional objects of thought" (noema) does not seem, therefore, to constitute an irreducible ground. It appears rather at a higher level of analysis. Thus, Merleau-Ponty does not postulate that "all consciousness is consciousness of something", which supposes at the outset a noetic-noematic ground. Instead, he develops the thesis according to which "all consciousness is perceptual consciousness". In doing so, he establishes a significant turn in the development of phenomenology, indicating that its conceptualisations should be re-examined in the light of the primacy of perception, in weighing up the philosophical consequences of this thesis.

JOHN DEWEY: CONCEPT OF TRUTH, COMMON-FAITH, EDUCATION

Concept of Truth

In "The Problem of Truth" Dewey presents a critique of the two traditional theories of truth– Correspondence (realism) and Coherence (idealism) theories of truth, and he argues that a pragmatic theory truth will overcome some of the insurmountable difficulties the two traditional theories face. His goal is not to present a final and complete theory but simply one that improves upon the traditional ones. He writes, "We are concerned with the definition of truth; we have seen how the orthodox consistency and correspondence theories break down at just the critical points where the theory ought to be in use. If the account of the nature of a proposition, just given, leads to an account of truth all that recommends the two opposed orthodox theories and escapes the factors that bring them to a deadlock, we shall at least have reason for accepting this account [the pragmatic account] of truth as compared with either of the others, no matter how much may remain undone in its development on its own account". Dewey considers three logical steps to understand the pragmatic theory of truth: (1) reconsidering the meaning of a proposition or judgment, (2) refocusing of the meaning of truth from a past to a future outlook and reference, and (3) considering a proposition's future performance. Let us see how these three steps help develop a pragmatic theory of truth.

First, however, let us consider the problems related to the coherence and correspondence theories of truth. The coherence theory claims that a proposition is true if and only if it is consistent with existing beliefs. We may add that a beliefs truth is sustained through the continued consistency with new experiences and new beliefs. However, Dewey notes that while such as theory may be a sine qua non of truth it cannot be the essence of truth. In other words, we might argue that truth requires consistency, and thus a necessary condition for a new belief to be true is that it be consistent with our existing beliefs. However, dreams or delusions may be consistent and not true. Therefore, consistency alone does not guarantee truth. Dewey argues, "Enlarge the mental factor as you will; give it the utmost self-consistency of which it is capable; you have increased, doubtless, the chances of its being true, but to say that truth itself lies that way is to make fancy the measure of reality".

The correspondence theory of truth claims that a proposition is true if and only if the proposition agrees with reality. While this theory appears to be appeal to our common sense, it also has its challenges. First, notice that a statement is true if it describes the world as it really is. But how do we know how the world really is? This shifts the attention to reality. The only way we can determine whether a proposition agrees or disagrees with reality is by introducing a third element that can provide the necessary comparison. Dewey continues, "Now this [third thing] is either itself a proposition or it is not. If it is a proposition, it claims to be true or to agree with its object; this object is beyond itself, and hence another proposition is required for its comparison, and so on ad infinitum". If it is not a proposition, Dewey claims it is difficult to imagine what this could be.

A second difficulty with the correspondence theory of truth is that the theory seems to beg the question, insofar as it assumes what it intends to demonstrates. It reports what is discovered in our past experiences of reality as truth. The proposition is posited as a guaranteed conclusion and as the end of the inquiry process. However, for this very reason, Dewey claims, it assumes the essence of what is at stake, namely, the truth of the proposition. Dewey claims, "the primary common assumption of both realistic and idealistic conceptions is that a statement by its nature implies an assertion of its own truth". This ushers us into the first step of the pragmatic theory of truth: a reexamination of the nature of a proposition.

What is a proposition? According to Dewey, a proposition is an intellectual judgment that begins (and not ends) an inquiry. It is not something that is assumed to be true but rather something that needs to be investigated and verified. If the proposition is certain (or if it is uttered with an attitude of certainty), then it is not a genuine intellectual judgment but rather a truism or a prejudiced claim or dogmatic claim. This first step is essential in understanding pragmatism because it highlights the fallibilistic attitude that permeates the pragmatic theory of truth. All genuine intellectual propositions should be understood as propositions whose truth requires justification and our attitudes toward these propositions should be one of openness to its truth or falsity, depending on the future evidence relevant to the proposition. Dewey explains, "The first step in the pragmatic criticism of both realistic and idealistic notions is, then, questioning the idea that every statement by its own nature implies as assertion of it own truth. For that conviction it substitutes the hypothesis that every proposition (so far as genuinely intellectual in quality, not mere dogmatic prejudice or memorandum for further guidance) is a hypothesis concerning some state of affairs; and that it is of its nature to be doubtful, not assured, of truth; and that its assertion of its own truth is only conditional; that it is a means of setting on foot activities of inquiry which will test the worth of its claim".

The second step of the pragmatic theory of truth is related and dependent on the first step. Given our interpretation of an intellectual proposition as a hypothesis, we now must focus all of our efforts on the future success or failure of the proposition. Unlike the correspondence and coherent theories of truth, in which the truth or falsity of a proposition relies on antecedent conditions and the past, a proposition, considered as a hypothesis, must look into the future for its confirmation or rejection. Dewey notes, "No one who has genuinely taken the first step-that of apprehending that an intellectual statement, in proportion to the degree of its being genuinely intellectual is hypothetical and tentative- will have any difficulty with the second".

The importance of the future for a theory of truth can be shown in another way. Consider how the realistic and idealistic theories of truth rely on the past for their truth status determination. If propositions are simply reports of the past then positions must all be true. If, however, we consider this only a subjective form of truth, that is, not really truth at all, then we have to forgo an objectivist form of truth since truth from an absolutists or neutral perspective is simply impossible. Therefore, any theory of truth that only looks into the past can never provide a satisfactory conception of a working and meaningful theory of truth. On the other hand, by looking into the future, pragmatism can avoid situations in which propositions are either all true or all false. Instead, pragmatism can test the propositions with future experiences and see whether they work. Pragmatism can consider the past, too, since all propositions have a connection with its past; however, pragmatism also considers how the proposition forged from the past will work in the future, which brings us to the third step of a pragmatic theory of truth.

The third step of the pragmatic theory of truth follows logically from the second step. Given our attention to the future of the position, we have to understand the proposition within its proper context. In this case, Dewey believes that the proposition does not exist in a vacuum but rather within a situation that has a projected outcome. In other words, the proposition is in use and it is part of a larger project with a specific end in mind. How the position functions within this situation and the position's consequences with respect to the intended goal will determine the instrumental value of the position and the position's truth-value. This is the proposition's test. Dewey explain: "The point and reference of the statement is in the use to which the thing is to be put; the matter of the statement is in the use to which the thing is to be put; the matter of the statement is some existing fact or antecedent. The report, the proposition, is stating this antecedent existence, as having a bearing and certain kind of bearing upon the attaining of an end. It is inevitable an estimate, am interpretation, just because it is concerned with existence and the bearing it has upon an end as yet an uncertain and unattained".

Consider Dewey's analogy with the compass and its ability to direct the ship to port. The compass, like a proposition, has a past and this past is responsible for the compass's present state. But whether the compass is a good compass relies more (or at least as much) on its future success than on its past successful journey's. Dewey says, "It is the sign of the progress of events toward their termination, their fulfillment, their consequences". He continues, "When a question of further use, of reference to future consequences enters in, we are inevitably concerned with fitness, the adaptability, of the things for the use intended". It is within this scientific context that we should interpret the pragmatic idea that what is true is what works and what works is what is true.

Common-faith

A Common Faith is a compilation of John Dewey's writings based on the Terry Lectures at Yale University. It consists of three chapters: "Religion Versus the Religious," "Faith and Its Object," and "The Human Abode of the Religious Function."

Dewey's overarching theme in A Common Faith is the role of distinct religious experience in realizing human potential through action and imagination. Dewey lays out the direct purpose of this work in his closing statement at the end of the third chapter: "Here are all the elements for a religious faith that shall not be confined to sect, class, or race. Such a faith has always been implicitly the common faith of mankind. It remains to make it explicit and militant". Much like in many of Dewey's other works, democracy is a common theme throughout his statements in A Common Faith.

There are three major themes present in A Common Faith. The first establishes distinct differences between "the religious" and religions themselves as experience. The second affirms God as "creative intersection of the ideal or possible and the real or actual," while the third establishes "the infusion of the religious as a pervasive mode of experience into democratic life".

In his review of A Common Faith, A. E. Elder states that "There is potential in man a religious attitude towards life - a natural capacity for faith - which can so enrich life and advance human well-being, that if through misunderstanding or other causes it is suppressed, then human life as a whole is adversely affected and remains a poor and stunted thing". However, this religious attitude is not necessarily expressed through devotion to one particular religion; Dewey argues that this faith is present in experience itself. R.S. states in his review of A Common Faith that "...the central argument, as those who are acquainted with Professor Dewey's philosophy might expect, is designed to show that religion should be detached from its supernatural associations within organized historical institutions, and widened, on the basis of its function in experience, so as to cover all devotion to ideal ends inclusive enough to integrate a whole self and arouse emotional support".

In reference to the idea of the religious in A Common Faith, Baurain states that for Dewey, "...the religious is characterized by a rejection of creeds, doctrines, rituals, and other elements of organized religion. Instead, an authentically religious attitude or orientation is existential and humanist. Moral faith rests not upon a divine Supreme Being or divinely revealed truths, but upon the dynamic potential of inquiry to discover knowledge and pursue ideals, that is, to act on experiential knowledge in order to improve life". Central to this work is the idea that religious experience itself is not explicitly tied to singular religions, and that experience can and should be creatively harnessed to enrich life.

However, Dewey carefully defines the difference between 'religion' and 'the religious' in the first chapter of A Common Faith. M. C. Otto traces this difference, stating of A Common Faith that "Perhaps the most arresting thing is the distinction insisted upon between religion, any religion past or present, and the religious attitude or function. This is so sharply drawn that it almost seems as if Mr. Dewey were saying that every activity in the world may take on a religious character, excepting religion".

Alexander posits that "...one of the central points Dewey seeks to make in A Common Faith is that both "faith" and the religious attitude have nothing to do with "doctrines" of any sort… Dewey states explicitly that his lectures were addressed to the antireligious naturalists and humanists who, he feared, had set up a new dualism, that between "Man vs. Nature," in place of the old". In this way, this common faith is a push against the strict, binding doctrines of religious creed or scientific law that suppressed creativity and lived experience, disenfranchising many. In fact, in direct reference to A Common Faith, Dewey himself states that "…my book was written for the people who feel inarticulately that they have the essence of the religious with them and yet are repelled by the religions".

Dewey utilizes the word 'common' in the title of this body of work, referring to the potential for religious expression and spirituality in everyone and echoing his views on democracy. Alexander states, "To see something as "common," for Dewey, is to grasp it imaginatively in terms of its possibilities for growth. Dewey's use of the word "common" should not be taken to indicate a complacent optimism based on satisfaction with things as they are now. To grasp the possibilities in the present requires creative exploration and struggle". Much in line with Dewey's other philosophies, Alexander goes on to say that "…a "common faith" means a faith in the potentialities of human life to become genuinely fulfilled in meaning and value, but only if those potentialities are actualized through action".

Ultimately, in order to achieve this 'common faith,' Alexander states, "Dewey urges that we put the question of revealed truth aside and look at the effect such experiences have on the lives of the individuals who undergo them".

Education

John Dewey was a strong proponent for progressive educational reform. He believed that education should be based on the principle of learning through doing.

In 1894 Dewey and his wife Harriet started their own experimental primary school, the University Elementary School, at the University of Chicago. His goal was to test his educational theories, but Dewey resigned when the university president fired Harriet.

In 1919, John Dewey, along with his colleagues Charles Beard, Thorstein Veblen, James Harvey Robinson and Wesley Clair Mitchell, founded The New School for Social Research. The New School is a progressive, experimental school that emphasizes the free exchange of intellectual ideas in the arts and social sciences.

During the 1920s, Dewey lectured on educational reform at schools all over the world. He was particularly impressed by experiments in the Russian educational system and shared what he learned with his colleagues when he returned to the States: that education should focus mainly on students' interactions with the present. Dewey did not, however, dismiss the value of also learning about the past.

In the 1930s, after he retired from teaching, Dewey became an active member of numerous educational organizations, including the New York Teachers Guild and the International League for Academic Freedom.

RICHARD RORTY: CRITIQUE OF REPRESENTATIONALISM, AGAINST EPISTEMOLOGICAL METHOD, EDIFYING PHILOSOPHY

The Philosophy of Richard Rorty is the thirty-second volume in the *Library of Living Philosophers series*, which commenced with a volume on the philosopher with whom Rorty is most often compared, John Dewey. With this volume, the series title serves as a sad reminder of Rorty's death at the age of 75 in 2007, while the collection was still in preparation. For many who, like the reviewer, were in the early stages of a university career in philosophy at the time, the publication of Rorty's Philosophy and the Mirror of Nature in 1979 was a very significant event indeed. I imagine that the attitude towards Rorty expressed by James Edwards in his contribution to the volume is far from unusual: "I am one of those who admire the work (and the man) almost without reservation; one of those who would not want to imagine what recent ... philosophy would have been if Rorty had not been around to shake things up and to forge some unexpected linkages" (658). Of course not everyone, even from that particular generation, reacted to this work, and the stream of writings following it, with admiration. While many saw in Rorty a Socratic gadfly, to another wing of the profession he was closer to an ancient sophist. And even among those who do admire, admiration rarely means whole-hearted agreement -- many admirers still find troubling elements within Rorty's philosophy, as Edwards himself seems to.

With Philosophy and the Mirror of Nature and the series of collections of essays that started with Consequence of Pragmatism in 1982, Rorty's thought-provoking ideas began to find a wide readership beyond the bounds of professional philosophy and started to attract the combination of applause and condemnation that has continued to this day. In fact, collections of critical essays on Rorty, similar in conception and format to the Library of Living Philosophers series, have been appearing on a reasonably regular basis since Alan Malachowski's Reading Rorty in 1990. Even omitting non-English language volumes and ones with very specific themes, such as one on "Rorty and Confucianism", there have been, on my count, seven prior to this volume. Of these, a number, like the Malachowski volume, have followed the LLP practice of having paired replies by Rorty to the interpretative and critical pieces. Both Malachowski's collection and the impressive 2000 volume edited by Robert Brandom, Rorty and His Critics, while large at around 400 pages each, are dwarfed by the LLP volume. With the standard introductory "Intellectual Autobiography", twenty-nine substantial essays, most with replies by Rorty, and an extensive bibliography of Rorty's writings, it is roughly the size of the other two combined.

So much has already been written about the philosophy of Richard Rorty that one might wonder whether there will be much new left to say. But while it is true that many of the general themes invoked in the essays in this book have a familiar ring, the majority of contributors manage to find new and illuminating ways of articulating their senses of agreement and disagreement to make it a very worthwhile addition to the literature. And as always, Rorty's replies are masterly in their ability to articulate economically the conceptual structure of the issues under dispute and, typically, to defuse criticisms by questioning distinctions presupposed by them. That there are still avenues of Rorty's thought to explore and take issue with might alone be taken as testifying to the breadth as well as the richly inventive nature of his philosophizing.

Clearly then, Rorty has been an eminently discussible as well as criticizable philosopher, and one of the reasons for this seems to lie in the fact that since the eighties he has been regarded as a philosopher who, emerging from the heartland of the fast-professionalizing world of American analytic philosophy – the philosophy department at Princeton – started to write about and engage with what he calls the "line of thought that leads from Hegel through Kierkegaard and Nietzsche to Heidegger and Derrida" – a line of thought clearly outside the bounds of philosophy to many within the analytic tradition. In the late sixties and early seventies, Rorty might have appeared to the casual observer as a philosopher working centrally within the type of analytic philosophy represented by the Princeton department – a mode of philosophy that was to shape the image of what professionalized Anglophone philosophy would become during the next decades. For example, he was anthologized as the advocate of a radical "eliminative materialist" position within the early philosophy of mind and had edited a volume on analytic method, The Linguistic Turn. But from the autobiographical essay with which the volume commences one gets an interesting overview of his early years. Thus he describes his first years at Princeton, where he started as a junior academic in 1960, as ones in which he felt the need "to speak to some of the issues with which [his colleagues] were concerned and to write in somewhat the same vein as they did". The reception of some of this work "made [him] feel that perhaps [he] had a future in the analytic philosophy business", but in the course of putting together The Linguistic Turn, in particular, and in "figuring out what Carnap and Wittgenstein agreed about, the better to highlight their obvious differences", he bolstered his "own preference for Wittgensteinian dissolutions of philosophical problems over constructive solutions", preferences that had also been acquired by his earlier immersion in the pragmatists. And in the course of the seventies, as he tells it, he was struck

> by the fact that Wittgenstein's debunking approach to philosophical problems could as easily be applied to what my Princeton colleagues thought of as the 'principal problems of analytic philosophy' as to the problems of the metaphysicians at whom Ayer had jeered.

"Both sets of problems", he had begun to think, "were equally artificial". This then led him "to construct a historical narrative about the development of modern philosophy designed to support Wittgenstein's suggestion that philosophical problems were just cul-de-sacs down which philosophers had wandered". The result was Philosophy and the Mirror of Nature.

On its appearance, many analytic philosophers responded to this work as a betrayal by one of their own, some seeing it as a cynical courting of the emerging "post-modernism" that seemed to be taking over the humanities. But as Rorty tells it, he had already acquired "a taste for ambitious, swooshy, Geistesgeschichte" in his undergraduate years at the Richard McKeon-dominated department at the University of Chicago, and on going to Yale, where he did his PhD, he had been at home in another analytic-lite department, where versions of absolute idealism were still defended along with attempts to synthesize Whitehead and Hegel. A quick survey of the 1960s section of Rorty's bibliography reveals how his more standardly "analytic" publications were interspersed with articles and reviews devoted to traditional pragmatism as well as thinkers like Blanshard, Hartshorne and Weiss, his erstwhile teachers. Against this background it is easy to see how the more "professional" analytic concerns that were then developing at Princeton could become fodder for an historicizing approach to philosophy that had predated any serious engagement with developments in analysis. But Rorty's pre-analytic stance now became importantly modified by his assimilation of "what Carnap and [the latter] Wittgenstein agreed about", giving his thought its familiar "debunking" stamp.

It was this early attraction to Hegel and "swooshy" grand tellings of the history of philosophy that allowed Rorty in the seventies to massage into his ongoing narrative, in a seemingly effortless way, philosophical voices new to the Anglophone scene such as those of the late Heidegger, Hans-Georg Gadamer and Jacques Derrida, creating the sorts of "unexpected linkages" to which Edwards refers. And yet this is not enough to capture just those features of Rorty's philosophizing that makes him such a fascinating, discussible and objection-attracting figure. Others were reacting against what they took to be the narrowness of the type of emerging professionalized philosophy, with its focus on technical semantic problems, that Rorty complained about at Princeton. Thus "continental philosophy" was splitting away to accommodate types of philosophy that had always been at best marginal to the analytic movement, while some analytic philosophers such as Hilary Putnam and Stanley Cavell were going in purportedly "post-analytic" directions. But neither of these movements shared Rorty's resolutely debunking attitude to the tradition of philosophy itself. Crudely, it might be said that these movements tended to advocate that there was more to philosophy than what was perceived as the narrow technical issues that were coming to define the discipline, but for Rorty there was little worth saving from the "Plato-Kant tradition" that analytic philosophy had displaced. That is, it must be remembered that Rorty's objections to professionalized philosophy Princeton-style were themselves an extension of the objections of the early analytic positivists to the "Plato-Kant tradition" itself.

This meant that while Rorty in Philosophy and the Mirror of Nature could compare his "conversational" historicism with the type of Hegel- and Heidegger-inspired "dialogical" historicism of Hans-Georg Gadamer, Rorty's debunking attitude to philosophy was not that of Heidegger nor philosophers inspired by him. For Heidegger, as Peter Dews makes clear in his essay, freedom from the sorts of linguistic enchantments expressed in the metaphysics from which Wittgenstein (and following him, Rorty) sought to liberate thought was

> not so much the driving force, as itself an expression of a fateful failure to respect the 'ontological difference' between 'Being' and 'beings'. For Rorty, by contrast, however innovative and insightful a metaphysician may have been in his own day, his ideas no longer carry any live charge; metaphysical theories have ceased to address the problems with which we are concerned, even obliquely.

In short, Rorty's attitude to traditional philosophy had more in common with the views of Carnap than his bmte noir, Heidegger.

In her contribution Susan James rightly attributes Rorty's vast influence to the "scope and grandeur" of his philosophy, "so rich in thought-provoking asides and quickly sketched connections". But I suggest that the set of features alluded to above has also contributed to Rorty's peculiar status within intellectual life and has prompted the particular combinations of agreement and disagreement that can be seen to play out within the essays in this and other similar volumes. Thus, many of the authors here start from a reasonably-to-strongly sympathetic position but quickly come to what has been bothering them in Rorty's particular approach to this or that topic. What one tends to find here are critics intent on getting more truth out of philosophy than Rorty is willing to allow, even if they are in agreement with his critique of a model of philosophical knowledge that aims at some divinely eternal overview.

The essays here are divided up into four sections: "Pragmatism Old and New", with essays by Cheryl Misak, James W. Allard, Harvey Cormier, Jacquelyn Ann K. Kegley, Robert Cummings Neville, Jean-Pierre Cometti, Aldo Giorgio Gargani, and María Pía Lara; "The World Well Lost: Language Representation, and Truth" with Jaroslav Peregrin, János Boros, Huw Price, Yasuhiko Tomida, Albrecht Wellmer, Michael P. Lynch, David Detmer and Andrzej Szahaj; "Conversation Stoppers: Politics, Progress, and Hope" with Susan James, Richard A. Posner, Yong Huang, J. B. Schneewind, William L. McBride and Jeffrey Stout; and "A Kind of Writing: Edifying Conversations" with Raymond D. Boisvert, Gianni Vattimo, Jolán Orbán, Pascal Engel, Miguel Tamen, Peter Dews and James C. Edwards. The borders between these groupings are understandably very porous with common themes crossing the boundaries. It is impossible, of course, in even a long review to do justice to individual essays and to Rorty's replies, or even survey all of them. In the remainder of this review I will focus on two or three representatives from each of the sections, although not necessarily in their particular order, in an attempt to give an impression of the sorts of issues raised and pursued throughout this volume.

Rorty is often cited as the most influential figure in the recent revival of interest in American pragmatist philosophy and, as one might expect, the essays in Section I tend to compare the sort of pragmatism revitalized by him in the wake of figures such as Sellars, Quine and Davidson with classical pragmatism and the idealist philosophy from which it emerged. Of the classical pragmatists it is to the work of James and, especially, Dewey that Rorty mostly appeals. In the course of his essay from Section III, and drawing on the work of Robert Brandom, Stout gives a nice thumb-nail sketch of the particularly Deweyan dimension to Rorty's pragmatism. At the heart of this position is "the social-practical conception of norms that the classical pragmatists took over from Hegel". Rorty's way of understanding this is to see the source of such norms as "social agreement among human beings" and it is this that ties his pragmatism into his political advocacy of Deweyan democracy and Millian liberalism. To understand that we are the ultimate sources of the norms according to which we think and act is to see claims by particular sections of the community to unilaterally determine those norms as dangerous attempts to dominate the rest, hidden behind a quasi-clerical pretense of access to some ultimate truth existing independently of humans. And for Rorty, as for Mill, the good community is one which maximizes the chances of individuals creating unique lives, which for Rorty implies fashioning the "vocabularies" with which they shape their outlooks and behaviors. To the extent that traditional philosophy seeks a source for norms in something other than human agreement, it is to be regarded as just an extension of religion. In short, to see our ideas or language as trying to represent something essentially independent from us – seeing philosophical knowledge as ideally a "mirror of nature" – is just another instance of thinking of ourselves as responsible to something other than other human beings.

A number of papers attempt to bring out features and shortcomings of Rorty's brand of pragmatism by usefully comparing him to earlier figures. In "Idealism, Pragmatism and the World Well Lost", Allard insightfully compares Rorty to the nineteenth-century Scottish idealist Edward Caird, seeing both as responding to the "broken harmony of spiritual life" in their own times. Caird had been concerned to reconcile science with religion, while for Rorty the analogous task is to somehow reconcile science with literary culture regarded as a provider of new vocabularies within which individuals may articulate their values, aspirations and hopes. But while Caird had appealed to idealist metaphysics to do this, Rorty, of course, rejects any metaphysical solution. Allard, however, like a number of others in the volume, is skeptical of Rorty's strategy for defending humanistic culture in the face of the sciences' perceived monopolization of truth by simply abandoning the idea that it is the function of language in any context to truly represent the world. And while Dewey had similarly protested against such a representationalist conception of language, Dewey's earlier version of pragmatism, thinks Allard, did not face potential incoherencies that Rorty's Wittgenstein/Davidson-based version of pragmatism does. In his response to Allard, Rorty clarifies how he sees the relation between his pragmatism – which is more a form of "romanticism" – and nineteenth-century idealism. "Like idealism, romanticism resists the claim that natural science tells us how reality really is. But romanticism does not go on to offer an alternative account". And we just don't need the sorts of answers that Allard says Rorty's pragmatism cannot provide: "After we cease asking which entities are available to serve as truth makers, we can forget about metaphysics".

Kegley, in "False Dichotomies and Mixed Metaphors: Genuine Individuals Need Genuine Communities", also has reservations about the capacity for Rorty to do justice to the aspirations he can be seen as sharing with earlier idealists once the metaphysical project is abandoned in its entirely, and to this end she contrasts Rorty with the American idealist Josiah Royce. Like Rorty, Royce rejected any Cartesian conception of the human subject linked to the "mirroring" conception of knowledge and stressed the idea of the self as coming to be through a type of self-interpretation. Thus she quotes Royce's claim that "my idea of myself is an interpretation of my past – linked also with an interpretation of my hopes and intentions as to my future". This is an idea that looks similar to Rorty's idea that freedom is a product of constructing narratives of the self in which one frees oneself from the way others try to pin one down in their accounts. But Royce, she thinks, has a more concrete sense of the type of community in which this type of self-creation via redescription can find a place. In comparison to the set of criteria Royce comes up with for the sort of genuine community in which self-creation is possible, Rorty's invocation of the ironist who merely recognizes the ultimate contingency of her values looks too thin. But Rorty replies that one's ability to identify those "anticommunities" unworthy of one's loyalty will depend on one's belonging to some other. "But what criterion should somebody raised in the bosom of the Mafia use when deciding whether to rat out her friends and relatives?"

In her essay from Section III, "Politics and the Progress of Sentiments", James pursues different but linked concerns in the context of Rorty's political thought. One of Rorty's important contributions to contemporary political theory has been to revive Hume's suggestion that sees "social and political advance as a progress of sentiments" and to focus on the role of "imagination, redescription, and narrative" in this process. Integral to "the capacity of more and less powerful individuals to imagine the sufferings and humiliations of others, and to conceive of better ways of life in which these deprivations are overcome" is "redescription – the capacity to reconfigure and re-evaluate existing practices by challenging the terms in which they are normally discussed and by inventing new normative vocabularies". But James questions the "excessively sharp opposition between reason and passion" which leads Rorty to minimize the role of reason here. "Rorty's emphasis on narratives", she states, "sometimes blurs the important difference between narratives about mainly imaginary states of affairs and narratives that are already realized in more or less powerful practices". In his response, Rorty reemphasizes that in the light of the failure to rationally ground hope in progress, all that is available for us is a type of ungrounded "romantic, utopian hope" sustained by the types of narratives to which he appeals.

The essays of section II "The World Well Lost: Language, Representation, and Truth" tend to focus on these issues in ways they have come to be discussed in contemporary analytic philosophy. Peregrin, in "Language, the World, and the Nature of Philosophy", develops a sympathetic sketch of Rorty's pragmatism while pointing to its dangers. With the claim that pragmatism is a "good servant" but "bad master", he is concerned lest pragmatism comes to be taken as an "ultimate philosophical doctrine" that does more harm than good. "The point is that pragmatism is powerful only if it is entertained within the context of philosophy carried out as a cooperative enterprise". Outside this context "pragmatism merely furnishes the combatants with an extra lethal weapon: that of simply dismissing the opponent's views on the score of not being helpful or interesting". In response Rorty enlarges on the role of theorizing within the pragmatist's practice. "Though sometimes it works best to say 'that's a bad question, one that we pragmatists don't ask', with some interlocutors it is more effective to reply, 'here's an answer to that question, since you insist on asking it'". It is in such contexts that new philosophical theories, like those of Davidson and Brandom, are useful, despite the fact that they don't claim to say something about the way the world really is.

In her contribution in Section I, "Richard Rorty's Place in the Pragmatist Pantheon", Misak appeals to Peirce as an early pragmatist whose "pragmatic elucidation" of truth offers a way around problems found in William James and, by implication, Rorty, given the Jamesian quality of some of his early statements about truth. Rorty had become aware of the problems of James's definitions of truth and modified his own position by introducing a "cautionary" dimension to truth to accompany the "endorsing" view according to which we apply the term true "to all the assertions we feel justified in making, or feel others are justified in making". By itself, the endorsing view seems to reduce truth to justification, but the "cautionary" use breaks this by reminding us that what we take to be justifications are likely to change in the future, the distinction between present and future justifications now preventing the collapse of truth into justification. But this, she thinks, leads to a thought that Rorty is "loathe to accept. There is something at which we aim that goes beyond what seems right to us here and now". Peirce's elucidation of this idea is of truth as a belief that would remain forever justified. In his response, Rorty appeals to the Jamesian requirement that conceptual differences make a difference. He cannot see how the Peircean idea amounts to anything more than the "banal thought that we might be wrong… . The Peircean thought seems to me merely to cloak a commonplace in a metaphor (aiming at a far-off target) [that] provides no practical guidance".

Misak's concerns intersect with those expressed in Lynch's contribution to Section II, "Truth and the Pathos of Distance". Lynch also rejects the type of deflationary approach to truth that Misak calls the "endorsement" view and, in ways similar to Allard, wants to defend humanistic culture by ways other than Rorty's general deflation of the notion of truth. The humanities construct narratives and offer coherent explanations that we evaluate in terms of the notion of truth, and so we need a way of capturing their capacity for truth. Rather than deflate truth, Lynch recommends that we be pluralists about truth and acknowledge that the features that make humanistic narratives truth-apt are different from those that make the natural sciences so. Rorty in reply writes that while Lynch thinks it appropriate to ask the question "what makes it true?", he doubts that "talk of truth-makers has any useful function except to instill the comforting feeling that we have, somewhere out there in the distance, an invisible friend called Reality".

In his "One Cheer for Representationalism?", Price is happy to accept the deflationary approach to truth and neatly traces a path to the evisceration of the notion of representation from within analytic philosophy itself. One can extend the early positivists' "expressivist" treatments of moral claims globally with the aid of deflationary or "minimalist" treatments of truth to a type of antirepresentationalist stance akin to Rorty's. Price shares Rorty's generally Wittgenstein-Carnap approach to language, as well as his strong resistance to "metaphysics", but, parallel to Brandom, he finds more coherence among the functions of the truth predicate than Rorty or Wittgenstein allow, given the fundamental role of assertion within our language games. Brandom's position, however, threatens to lapse into a metaphysical account of representation, and so Price contrasts his own one cheer for representationalism with Rorty's none and Brandom's two. Rorty in his response doesn't see much difference between the stances of all three, but among other things Price's approach draws into question Rorty's consistent identification throughout the volume of his own position with that of Brandom, an issue to which I will return.

Boisvert, in "Richard Rorty: Philosopher of the Common Man, Almost", finds Rorty's contributions to philosophy to reside in the historicist, pluralist and anti-foundationalist ideas he so successfully spread, as well as his powerful reinterpretation of the notion of democracy. But like Peregrin and others, Boisvert is concerned about the potential for Rorty's position to transform into a non-therapeutic dualistic theorizing, noting, as had Kegley and James, the "pairs of 'either-ors'" pervading some of Rorty's texts. Rather than Rorty's "blanket rejection of 'essences'", he recommends an attitude to the idea of essence that recontextualizes "what was best about that term".

Boisvert's criticism allows Rorty to expand on the significance for him of Hegel, whose historicizing approach he constantly invokes throughout the volume. What Rorty exactly recommends of Hegel's approach to philosophy is hard to pin down, as it is clearly Hegel stripped of the metaphysics with which he is usually identified. Hegel himself portrayed his philosophy as the culmination of the Plato-Kant tradition that Rorty abjures, but for Rorty he is the first name in the series that passes through Kierkegaard and Nietzsche to Heidegger and Derrida. And many of course will find Hegel an odd precedent for any approach to philosophy that can be found as common to Wittgenstein and Carnap. In his response to Price, Rorty opposes his Hegelian stance to Price's Humean one, but one might have difficulty with what this distinction could count for in Rorty. Price appeals to a type of "anthropology" as the self-image for philosophy and one might wonder if this term might not often capture Rorty's position as well, as he commonly portrays the virtues of "history" as residing primarily in the fact that it allows us to grasp the contingency of the ideas we come up with. Might not anthropology do this too?

To the differences Price finds between Rorty and Brandom, one might add their respective attitudes to Kant. For Brandom, Hegel correctly grasps the spirit of Kant, but for Rorty Hegel is Kant's antithesis. Rorty's antipathy to Kant is the focus of Boros's essay "Representationalism and Antirepresentationalism: Kant, Davidson, and Rorty", where he points to the oddness of not taking Kant as a type of proto-antirepresentationalist. In his reply, Rorty can only find value in the Critique of Pure Reason in that "by exasperating Hegel, it led him to give up on epistemology and to take the historicist turn". Hegel is often taken to be a critic of "dichotomous" forms of thinking, but, in his reply to Boisvert, Rorty justifies his either-orism once again by invoking Hegel:

> I think of Hegel as having shown us that promoting such divisions – insisting on sharp either-ors – is necessary to keep the conversation going. Without the great nay-sayers, and what Bosvert calls 'dreams of radical fresh starts,' we will not have what Hegel called the 'struggle and labor of the negative'.

Dews, in his "'The Infinite is Losing its Charm': Richard Rorty's Philosophy of Religion and the Conflict Between Therapeutic and Pragmatic Critique", places Rorty accurately, I believe, in relation to Hegel by putting him in the company of the nineteenth-century "Left Hegelians", in particular Feuerbach and Stirner:

> It is hard to overlook the parallels between Feuerbach's effort to define a radically new mode of philosophizing, and Rorty's advocacy of a post-philosophical thinking, which has abandoned the quest for timeless truths and immutable structures, in favor of cultural-political intervention.

But Feuerbach's anthropology was in turn open to Stirner's critique of his appeal to "essences", in this case, anthropological ones. Stirner's construal of "the very notion of objective truth as an outdated trammel, a redundant constraint on the agency of the self" sounds very Rortyan, and if Rorty's appeal to the communal basis of knowledge and morals seems to separate him from Stirner's "rampaging egoism", there are core elements of his thinking that makes it difficult for him to "hold the line against the Stirnerian anarchist".

Dews wonders if it had been this concern that had led Rorty in the last decade of his life to "a conception of human emancipation able to house aspirations formerly nurtured by religion". If Rorty's resistance to religion had come to soften, then one might wonder at the persistence of his antipathy to the Plato-Kant tradition, given his essentially left-Hegelian conception of it as no more than a continuation of religion. Stout, in "Rorty on Religion and Politics", sees only the "smallest possible adjustment in his original secularism" in Rorty's later attitudes to religion, however. Stout questions the compatibility of Rorty's "de-divinizing" form of pragmatism – which he shares with Dewey, but with neither Peirce nor James – with other features of his pragmatism. Thus he sees "Rorty's generalized anticlericalism" as "in tension with his antiessentialism" and his exclusion of religiously articulated claims from the public sphere as in tension with his advocacy of democracy.

As with a small number of other essays in the volume, Dews's is not accompanied by Rorty's response because it had been finished too late. With this essay in particular, I had been looking forward to Rorty's reply, wondering if and how he was going to slip through the nets Dews had fashioned for him. Unfortunately, we no longer have the benefit of his table-turning rejoinders. From the evidence provided from this volume, however, this is unlikely to stop the man and his ideas from remaining, for many, foci of admiration and provocation and a continuing source of both inspiration and frustration.

IMMANUEL LEVINAS: ETHICS AS A FIRST PHILOSOPHY, PHILOSOPHY OF 'OTHER'

Ethics as First Philosophy

What Levinas tries to point out here refers to the necessity of the direct interrogation of consciousness. Further, in reference to Aristotle, he identifies metaphysics, which he considers as "the first philosophy" with ethics rather than reducing it to ontology, and claims that ethics proceeds ontology. Ontology leads the Other to the identical and does not permit the identical to be alienated by the Other. Therefore, this elevates freedom standing as the identification of the identical. At this point, theory denies metaphysical desire and externality which reinforces it. However, the source of metaphysical desire refers to an ontological way and if it only remained as a theory, it would not make any progress. Thus, the source of metaphysical desire should be brought beyond theory and ontology by critical intentionality since, as opposed to ontology, critique does not reduce the Other into the identical. On the contrary, it questions the function of the identical (Direk 2000). Levinas explains that:

> The other metaphysically desired is not "other" like the bread I eat, the land in which I dwell, the landscape I contemplate, like, sometimes, myself for myself, this "I," that "other". I can "feed" on these realities and to a very great extent satisfy myself, as though I had simply been lacking them. Their alterity is thereby reabsorbed into my own identity as a thinker or a possessor. The metaphysical desire tends toward something else entirely, toward the absolutely other.

Apart from the singular pretension of desire cannot be clarified the customary analysis of desire, for desire comes out a being indigent and incomplete of fallen from its past grandeur. According to Levinas, the metaphysical desire doesn't long to return because it is desire for a land not of our birth so that we should never mention about ourselves. And also, the metaphysical desire has different intention. It is like goodness, but the desire cannot fulfill it; however, it has confidence in it. Therefore, Levinas especially says that desire is a desire for the definitely other and metaphysics desires the other on the further side of satisfactions.

Levinas extends his criticisms regarding the dominance of the Other over the identical and the analysis of ontology through metaphysics against Husserl and Heidegger. He also makes reference to the tradition of Western philosophy in his criticism since he refuses the dominance of the identical which resides in the foundations of the Western metaphysics. He puts difference of the different against dominance of the identical. By this, he aims at initiating a philosophical tradition which bases itself on responsibility without using violence against difference of the different. According to Levinas, in a society composed of differences, the most significant problem refers to ruling out the issue of responsibility.

In Heidegger's early work, ontology – the science of Being in the Aristotelian sense – is fundamental, and Dasein is the fundament or condition of possibility for any ontology, a being whose 'a priori' structure must first be clarified in an existential analysis. For Levinas, the exceptional character of Heideggerian ontology is that it presupposes the factual situation, or existential facticity, of the human being.

According to Levinas, the fundamental character of Heideggerian ontology is that it firstly presumes the factual situation of the human being because the comprehension of being does not approve a solely intellectual attitude. Ontology is not only or just a science but it also forms the anthropological preparation for the particular of the problem of Being. Levinas calls: "The profound need to leave the climate of that philosophy". Because of the comprehension of being, Heidegger reunites the Platonic tradition of Western Philosophy. A relation with an entity cannot be for Levinas, "unless it is the other (autrui)".

The identification of the understanding of being with the fullness of concrete existence initially risks drowning ontology in existence. This philosophy of existence, which Heidegger rejects as a designation of his own work, is merely the counterpart – but an inevitable one – of his conception of ontology. Historical existence which interests the philosopher in that it is ontology is of interest to human beings and literature because it is dramatic. When philosophy and life are confused, we can no longer know whether we are interested in philosophy because it is life, or whether we care about life because it is philosophy. The essential contribution of the new ontology may appear in its contrast to classical intellectualism. To understand a tool is not to see it, but to know how to use it; to understand our situation in reality is not to define it, but to be in an affective state. To understand being is to exist.

The fact that we are responsible beyond our intentions means that the domination via our consciousness and our mastery of reality through consciousness is not the only way to have relation with the reality. We are already present in the reality with our being. According to Heidegger's philosophy, our consciousness of reality does not match with our existence in the world. However, the philosophy of existence suddenly is wiped out in the face of ontology. Levinas expresses the existence as understanding. Thus, the transcendence of the verb of knowing is connected to the verb of existing. Therefore, "All men by nature desire to know" which is the first sentence of Aristotle's Metaphysics stays true for a philosophy. And in consequence, Levinas indicates that:

> Its responsibility for the other, the proximity of the neighbor, does not signify a submission to the non-ego; it means an openness in which being's essence is surpassed in inspiration. It is an openness of which respiration is a modality or a foretaste, or, more exactly, of which it retains the aftertaste. Outside of any mysticism, in this respiration, the possibility of every sacrifice for the other, activity and passivity coincide.

Philosophy of Other

Levinas' concept *'the Other in the identical'* both summarizes his major idea and indicates the relationship between his and Husserl's phenomenology. According to Levinas, Husserl especially focuses on and stresses the concept of the self-identical which coincides with itself and it isn't possible that we may comprehend Plato's realism and also what he tries to emphasize. The self-identical is tried to be clarified through the feeling of reality resulting from the influences of phenomenological consciousness. According to Husserl, the reality of world is not a natural, if, and only if, it is a positive reality because it is provided by consciousness. He claims that the existence which is admitted through the statement "Cogito ergo sum" by Descartes is not an objective existence because reaching the objective reality from "sum" is impossible. Besides, Descartes thought that every experience, however passive it may be, is made over a "constitution of being" immediately, supposing that the given were drawn from oneself or by me, so we might say that being resists in itself the possibility of idealism. Levinas also explains the idea of infinity as well:

> But the relation with infinity-the idea of the Infinite, as Descartes calls it-overflows thought in a wholly different sense than does opinion. Opinion vanishes like the wind when thought touches it-or is revealed to be already within that thought. What remains ever exterior to thought is thought in the idea of infinity. It is the condition for every opinion as also for every objective truth. The idea of infinity is the mind before it lends itself to the distinction between what it discovers by itself and what it receives from opinion.

The relation with infinity will have to be specified by terms aside from those of objective experience. On the other hand, if experience definitely has a relation with the Other, the relation with infinity is experienced successfully in the sense of the word. The production of the infinite entity is not separable from the idea of infinity, this is because the idea of infinity is the form of being, the infinition. Yet, infinity is not initial existing, after then reveals itself, whose infinition is indicated as revelation.

According to Husserl, who intends to tailor philosophy as an objective science, efforts to provide an objective science with a natural belief in the existence of the world are futile. The first thing to be done is to question the objectivity of natural sciences which are accepted as certain, since that objectivity of natural sciences is founded on a general assertion constituted by them. Thus, since it is based on some prejudices, they are not open to discussion.

Husserl indicates that the objectivity of the natural sciences alone is derived not only from themselves but also from the necessity of separating the real world from the world of scientific reality in order to reach to a certain science.

Even though, the world looks as if it loses its existence, we cannot claim that it completely disappears precisely disappearing of the world because, according to Husserl, the world continues in its existence as a phenomenon after this situation. The world as a phenomenon reflects a directly obvious and a substantial life since it is possible to have an access to the consciousness which enables us to reach the source of every knowledge and the knowing subject. That effect of consciousness on the world is a thing termed by Husserl "the first presence". Therefore, according to Husserl, the thing formed the content of the first presence, can only be grasped in a present which does not belong to itself anymore after it happens, only by the eclipse of reason. For this reason, he especially emphasizes that the reality of the present can only be realized by the eclipse in reason. It shows that we can never apprehend the present solely in its absolute.

Levinas states that the first impression presented as open or closed form in Husserlian phenomenology is not a notion but life itself. Since the first impression is a thing which cannot be comprehended, it is not thinking content but it is life itself. Levinas, thus defines life as:

> The permanent effort of the transcendental reduction comes down to leading "mute consciousness" to speech and to not taking the exercise of constituent intentionality led to speech for a being placed in the positivity of the world. The life of consciousness is excluded from it and, precisely as excluded from the positivity of the world, as a "mute subject," it allows beings of the world.

Essentially, Levinas passes to life notion from notion. Although Husserl agrees with the opinion at this point, Levinas's qualification about life reveal the differentiation between Husserl and Levinas. Along with this differentiation, Levinas underlies the basics of deconstruction.

His perspective which sees both identicalness and deconstruction in between the identical and the Other unfolds the meaning of the concept of "the Other in the identical". How could the Other in the identical be comprehended? In order to explain the Other, he mentions the conspiration between the Other and the identical. This conspiration reveals the fact that the Other in the identical already exists for the subject which enables the unfolding of its existence. In his opinion, the conspiration emerges at this point. With the conspiration between the identical and the Other, the Other ensures its superiority over the identical since during this conspiration, there happens a powerful conflict and opposition between the Other and the identical which will lead to domination of either of them over the Other.

One of the main problems here is how the conflict between the identical and the Other ends up in the victory of the identical. The relation with the Other has a different quality compared to the structure of intentionality. The Other is not only involved in the tendency of inclining.

Initially, the Other as absolute resists the unconventionality of intentionality. In the face of this resistance, the Other cannot be even be transformed into the content of consciousness, and the resistance against the unconventionality of the Other's intentionality destroys the dominance of the identical. A substitution of me for the others, is then not an alienation because I exist through the other. Furthermore, this is my inspiration which is the psyche that can be a sign for this alterity in the same without alienatio.

UNIT 7

SOCIAL AND POLITICAL PHILOSOPHY: INDIAN

MAHABHARATA

In the Shanti Parvan ("Book of Consolation," 12th book) of the Mahabharata, there is also a notable account of the origin of kingship and of rajadharma, or the dharma (law) of the king as king. Bhishma, who is discoursing, refers with approval to two different theories of the origin of kingship, both of which speak of a prior period in which there were no kings. According to one account, this age was a time characterized by insecurity for the weak and unlimited power for the strong; the other regards it as an age of peace and tranquillity. The latter account contains a theory of the fall of humankind from this ideal state, which led to a need for institutionalized power, or kingship; the former account leads directly from the insecurity of the prekingship era to the installation of king by the divine ruler for the protection and the security of humankind. Kingship is thus recognized as having a historical origin. The primary function of the king is that of protection, and dandaniti, or the art of punishment, is subordinated to rajadharma, or dharma of the king. Though it recognizes a quasi-divinity of the king, the Mahabharata makes the dharma, the moral law, superior to the king.

The Bhagavadgita ("Song of the Lord") forms a part of the Mahabharata and deserves separate consideration by virtue of its great importance in the religious life and thought of the Hindus. Not itself a shruti, it has, however, been accorded the status of an authoritative text and is regarded as one of the sources of the Vedanta philosophy. At a theoretical level, it brings together Samkhya metaphysics, Upanishadic monism, and a devotional theism of the Krishna-Vasudeva cult. In its practical teaching, it steers a middle course between the "path of action" of the Vedic ritualism and the "path of renunciation" of the Upanishadic mysticism, and it accommodates all the three major "paths" to moksha: the paths of action (karma), devotion (bhakti), and knowledge (jnana). This synthetic character of the work accounts for its great hold on the Hindu mind. The Hindu tradition treats it as one homogenous work, with the status of an Upanishad.

Neither performance of the duties prescribed in the scriptures nor renunciation of all action is conducive to the attainment of moksha. If the goal is freedom, then the best path to the goal is to perform one's duties with a spirit of non-attachment without caring for the fruits of one's actions and without the thought of pleasure or pain, profit or loss, or victory or failure, with a sense of equanimity and equality. The Kantian ethic of "duty for duty's sake" seems to be the nearest Western parallel to Krishna's teaching at this stage. But Krishna soon went beyond it by pointing out that performance of action with complete non-attachment requires knowledge (jnana) of the true nature of the self, its distinction from prakriti, or Matter (the primeval stuff, not the world of matter perceived by the senses), with its three component elements (sattva—i.e., tension or harmony; rajas—i.e., activity; and tamas—i.e., inertia), and of the highest self (purushottama), whose higher and lower aspects are Matter and finite individuals, respectively. This knowledge of the highest self or the supreme lord, however, would only require a devotional attitude of complete self-surrender and performance of one's duties in the spirit of offering to him. Thus, karma-yoga ("discipline of action") is made to depend on jnana-yoga ("discipline of knowledge"), and the latter is shown to lead to bhakti-yoga ("discipline of devotion"). Instead of looking upon Krishna's teaching as laying down alternative ways for different persons in accordance with their aptitudes, it would seem more logical to suppose that he taught the essential unity and interdependence of these ways. How one should begin is left to one's aptitude and spiritual makeup.

Rajdharma

Rajdharma as a concept constitutes the judicious duties of the King towards his subjects. The basic concern of the rajdharma is welfare of the people. The King and Kingship is associated with the concept and concern of the prajapalanah. In ancient Indian classics the spirit of rajdharma was to ensure peace, justice and prosperity to the people. Rajdharma is described as an essential element of state even in saptanga theory but it was expected from the King to perform his duties in such a righteous manner so that the state should be called as dharmarajya and King as the dharmrajah. Practice of Dharma and maintaining impartiality are the only means through which rajdharma may be practiced and dharmarajya or Ramrajya is achieved. The concept of rajdharma as enunciated in the past still holds value as orderly, peaceful and prosperous life for society and good ethical conduct in polity. Society has changed much even then the tenor or norms of political life require the basic principle of rajdharma for better governance of the society. Unethical, unprincipled politics is reality of the political life to regulate the affairs of the governance and justice. It is essential to observe the rajdharma.

Study of political traditions and civilisational values reveal an unbroken continuity of Indian culture and civilisational practices. C. Rajgopalachari rightly philosophised in very lucid words: "There is no country which can be governed more easily than India. You have only to appeal to traditions. All the great old kings of the past, Janaka and Shri Rama are still alive and governing our hearts. I am not the Governor General, Shri Rama is". Political tradition of India has been referred to as one of the most ancient and most extensive and varied one. The keynote of Indian political culture is its eternal values and Sanatana Dharma.

However, the beginning of India's civilisation is traced so long back in time that often it appears to be lost in the twilight of history, yet retaining much of its basic identity. Dr. Arnold Toynbee, after surveying the history of the entire mankind in his book; A Study of History observed, "it is already becoming clear that a chapter which has a western beginning will have to have an Indian ending if it is not the end in the self-destruction of the human race..... At this supremely dangerous moment in human history, the only way of salvation for mankind is the Indian way, emperor Ashoka's and Mahatma Gandhi's principle of non-violence and Sri Ramakrishna's testimony to the harmony of religions. Here we have an attitude and spirit that can make it possible for the human race to grow together into a single family and, in the Atomic Age, this is the only alternative, to destroy ourselves." Here Toynbee was actually echoing the idea placed before the mankind by India's ancient Rishis – Vasudhaiva Kutumbakam – "The World is one Family." This Indian way has come to us in unbroken continuity through Vedas, Upanishadas, Puranas, Smrities, Dharma-Sutras, Dharma-Sastras, Niti-Sastras, Epics, Arthasastras, Rishies, Maharishies and Brahmarishies from the ages. Moreover, India's culture is primarily concerned with spiritual development and is of special significance in our age which is marked by the materialistic civilisation. In the words of Sri Aurobindo: "India of the ages is not dead, nor has she spoken her last creative word, She lives and has still something to do for herself and the human race".

There are a number of authoritative treatises on ancient Indian culture, civilisation and heritage. The literature is quite voluminous and is extensively used. However, the time has come to outline the foundations of classical Indian philosophical and political essence. The aim of this article is to explore the underlying essence of rajdharma in popular traditional treatise or often referred to as Adi-Kavya: Ramayana and Mahabharata with a view to set an inextricable linkage between the past and present.

The Ramayana and the Mahabharata, the two great epics are replete with sound political and economic theories. Today's most resonating term 'good governance' and its veracities had sufficient traces in these two texts in varied forms. Both the epics deal with the deeds of kings and heroes, descriptions of wars and practical philosophy. "The epics alone are a good answer to those tall-talkers, pseudo-intellectuals and pseudo-secularists who make some sweeping and negational statements that the Indian political theory has not so far been constructed even in rudimentary form". In fact, both the great epics are of perennial interest for understanding, ancient Indian social and political life and thought".

The Ramayana, which is the earlier of the two epics, contains references to principles of good governance, diplomacy, war and peace. It contains prescriptions regarding the manner in which the king should consult his ministers, learned men, and the chief officer of the army in formulating the policies of the state on various issues and matters. The Ramayana of Maharishi Valmiki gives multi-sided picture of a perfect life. Valmiki's main theme is inner perfection, virtuous actions, overcoming evils and transforming the evildoers. In this epic, stress is laid everywhere on the importance of moral values.

Notwithstanding the Ramayana, a sacred text teaching righteousness, is also regarded as Dharma-Shastra. Besides, it expounds the principles of eternal law and presents the ideals of good conduct, which is one of the bases of Dharma.

The Ramayana of Valmiki is a text of ethics which deals with polity, administration, diplomacy, war and other statecraft related issues, which fall within the domain of politics, justice and governance. The Ramayana has perennial influence on the minds and attitudes of men and women in India down the centuries. Even today the teachings of Ramayana as moral values obedience, simple living, high thinking, sacrifices, devotion, dedication, commitment, charity and humanity, etc. are highly significant in changing modern societies. Being a society having religious bent, these texts bear great importance for its social as well as political life. Ramrajya/ Dharmrajya, contrary to its meaning often misconstrued, is equivalent to present day's well-ordered political society, good governance, su-rajya and swarajya as its driving principles. However, this appears to be still a distinct dream. It is pertinent to argue that Ramrajya is not associated with any kind of worship method, but it advocates ethical governance with principles of morality, justice to all, peace, prosperity and Lok-kalyana (welfare).

The benefits of good government and democracy are exemplified in the Rama Rajya. According to Mahatma Gandhi, Ram-Rajya means a return of the ultimate Indian values of Dharma, upheld since time immemorial. The pictures drawn in the Ramayana, of happiness, harmony and understanding in domestic and social spheres are ideal. It provides detailed guidelines for rulers, for statesmen, for policy-makers and for the persons belonging to the four stages (Ashramas) of life.

During the Gupta period (320 A.D.-413 A.D.), Rama was considered as a great king of the past also as God. Harivansa, a Sanskrit classic of 2nd and 3rd A.D., held the reign of Rama as the most righteous time on earth. Vayupurana, 5th century A.D., says that there was all-round prosperity, peace and dharma at the time of Rama and Ramayana. In Ramayanamanjari, Kashmiri Poet Kshemendra described that during Rama's time the whole earth became like heaven and all the people performed well their proper duties, following strictly the path of Dharma. Ramacharitamansa written in 16th Century by Tulsidasa has been extremely popular and it comprises some of the most poetic verses, deeply embedded in the cultural realm of the Indian society.

There is no language in India in which the Ramayana is not translated. Kamban Ramayana in Tamil 9th and 10l Century A.D., Ranganath Ramayana, 12th Century A.D., Telugu, Madhya Kandali's Ramayana in Assamia 14th Century A.D., Jagmohan Ramayana, Bala Ramadasa Ramayana in Oriya in 15th Century A.D. are the forms of Ramayana in different languages. All these texts have profound impact on the minds of men and women in India. Not only in India, the Ramayana has left undying influence in the countries abroad. In Java the entire story of Ramayana was carved on stone. Such deep influence is also found in Cambodia, South Annam and Malaya. The Rama tradition is very much alive in these countries.

The Ramayana believes in the divine origin of the King, but does not concede that a king can do whatever he likes; he has to follow the dictates of dharma. His powers are limited. He can be deposed, disobeyed or killed if he does not follow the dharma. In Ramayana, "Rajnam manusam prahardevatav samato bhan "it is clearly narrated that blemishes kill a king who does not protect his people. In Balkanda of Valmiki Ramayana we learn from the epic that a king who went astray from the path of Dharma could be openly accused, scolded, imprisoned, banished or even killed. In Uttarakanda "Ramasya Dushkartam" the Brahmana! whose son died young, accused Rama openly of having done some unrighteous deed.

The sages of Dandakarnya spoke to Rama of not being provided protection even after extracting 1/6 part of earning of the subjects in the form of Bali (Tax). In Ayodhyakanda the younger brother of King Rama, Shatrughana proclaimed that a King who took the unrighteous path should be imprisoned after considering his case on merit. The king in the epic has been addressed as Nardeva, Dharmapala, Lokpala.11 The Ramayana allots a very high place to personal righteousness and conduct of the king and his men. The State is regarded in the epic Ramayana as an essentially beneficial institution for the efficient protection of human life and for the better realisation of the higher ideals.

The duties of the people described in Ramayana are to obey the king who rightly performs his dharma. According to Ramayana the king first took upon himself the duty to provide complete protection to all the people from all sorts of fear (bhaya) and that the people agreed to pay him one sixth of their earnings and share with him the merit of their good deeds allowing one fourth of it for the King. Though the king was the fountain-head of all the activities of the state, the Ramayana does not conceive of him as an autocrat.

Like the Ramayana, the Mahabharata also has been the source of spiritual strength to the people of India. The authorship of the Mahabharata is attributed to Vedvyasa. According to Vedvyasa (200 B.C. - 200 A.D.) the epic is intended to be a treatise on life itself, including Dharma and ethics, polity and government, philosophy and the pursuit of salvations. In the Mahabharata among all the parva, Shantiparva is more relevant to our present study because this parva deals with the duties of the king and the obligations of the subject, which is known as Raj dharma. It provides a theory of state which is remarkable for the age as it deals with such fundamental questions as the importance of the state and science of politics, the origin of state, the functions of the government, welfare state, obligation, etc. This section of the Mahabharata contains the most profound body of political ideas in our ancient literature. For example, we can refer these texts (slokas) from Shantiparva

The king is vested with the authority and power of governance, the true sovereignty belongs to dharma, not to King. The Mahabharata states it again and again that in all the acts of the governance, the goal of the king, or the state is the protection of the people. Protection supports the world, protected people prosper, prospering they endow the king in turn.

The text (sloka) says: Dharmo Yat raja rakshati prajah Bhutanam hiyatha dharmo rakshanamparma daya1.

In other words, protecting of all living beings with kindness towards them is the highest Dharma. In Shantiparva, Bhishma said to Yudhishtira, "He is the best of kings in whose dominations men live fearlessly like sons in the house of their sire". If the king did not exercise the duty of protection, the strong would forcibly appropriate the possessions of the weak, and if the latter refused to surrender them with ease, their very lives would be taken. Wives, sons, food and other kinds of property would not then exist.

The text (sloka) says: Putra eevpitugrahe vishyeyasya manvah Nirbhaya vicharishyanti sa raja rajasattam.

In Shantiparva like other Indian classics danda is also described as a means rajdharma because the fear of punishment is the basis of governance; and the purpose of governance is to secure the people's freedom from fear.

The text (sloka) says: Dandah shasti prajah, sarva danda evami rakshati \ Dandah sapteshu jagarti dandam dharm vidurvdha.

According to Yudhisthir, rajadharmas are the refuse of all creatures; and not only the threefold end of life, but salvation itself depends upon them. The Mahabharata contrary to the Arthasastra postulations, categorically declares the fulfillment of righteousness to be bounden duty of the king. Dharma is the fundamental principle of human conduct. The King upholding dharma is the very epitome of ethical conduct. The creatures are grounded in the King. The King who rightly upholds dharma is indeed a King.

The text (sloka) says: Ḋharme tishthanti bhutani dharmo raajani tishthanti \ Tarn raja sadhuyah shasti sa raja prithvipatiah.

It is clearly stated in Shantiparva "Dharme vardhanti vardhanti sarvbhutani sarvada".

In reference to it we can say that the royal power should obtain power through dharma because it nourishes and enhances. The prosperity that comes through dharma neither decreases nor dies; all living beings have dharma as the foundation of their existence, and dharma exists over and above the King. Only he remains the King, who lives and governs in accordance with dharma. When dharma prospers, all living beings prosper. Scores of references can be cited from the Ramayana and the Mahabharata to establish the practices of rajdharma at the time of Rama and Krishna.

Rajdharma as explained above suggests that it contains some universal principles of governance. It means a body of principles such as providing security and safety to the its subjects displacing the law of jungle (matsyanyaya) by equitable law and justice in society. Rajdharma is not limited to the safety and security alone rather it is extended to secure material prosperity and peace to the people as text (sloka) says that praja kite hetang rajyah, praja sukhe sukhah rajyah. In other words, happiness of the king lies in the happiness his people and their welfare lies in his welfare. This reflects the ideals of rajdharma.

Both the texts, the Ramayana and the Mahabharata, provide a theory of the state which is remarkable for this age. It deals with every fundamental question as the importance of dharma, importance of governance and art of politics. Both the texts are focused on welfare of the people and clearly define the obligations of the king towards his subjects. It is important to recognise a new conception of rajdharma which is required for present day politics where moral crisis is writ on every facet of our social and political life. In this context an honest evaluation of Indian classics such as the Ramayana and the Mahabharata can be more meaningful.

Law and Governance

The king, according to Valmki, cannot be a despot. We find in Ramayan the king consulting ministers, learned men and the principal officers of the army in shaping the policy of the State. Not only this, but a wider consultation with the people from different parts of land was held.

Ramayana indicates that free expression of opinion was invited in such assemblies. As an example, for finalizing Rama's installation as heir apparent, Dasaratha invited an exceptionally large gathering.

. Announcing his intention of retiring from administration, he said, 'If what I have proposed is proper' and is to your liking, do you accord approval to it, and advise me as to what else I am to do and in what manner'. He then invited free discussion for obtaining dispassionate decisions. Even when the leaders, and the citizens took counsel together and gave their unanimous support, the king wanted to make them think a second time and so he spoke again as if he had not known their minds.

'You have wished for Rama', said he, 'as soon as you have heard my speech. This raises doubts in my mind. Do you, therefore, speak out your minds truly? Why, while I am righteously ruling the land, do you wish to see my son installed?'

It would be interesting to note that the epic describes that even Ravana as an obstinate and wilful ruler allowed free discussion in his assembly; where not only Bibhisana but also Kumbhakarna vehemently criticized his conduct towards Sita. Says Kumbhakarna in a blunt and fearless manner. 'all this that thou has done', says he to Ravana, 'is not worthy of thee.'

The main feature of the governance of the descendents of Iksvaku was their commitment to righteousness and devotion to the welfare of their subjects. Under Dasaratha's efficient administration a state where no one was slenderly read or illiterate or untruthful existed in Ayodhya and its provinces with a high level of culture and affluence.

King's concern for the welfare of the people is reflected during a conversation when Bharat was pursuing Rama to return to the palace, the latter asks about the welfare of people in Kosala: '

Dharma is not yet another 'religious' faith among many mutually contesting 'religious faiths'. But neither is dharma antagonistic to any religious faith. Rather, dharma is the foundation of 'religion' itself. Thus religion in its institutional form divides, while dharma unites.

The goal of the king, or of the state, is the protection of all living beings with kindness towards them and that is the highest dharma The Rajdharma of the king (state).

'Do you look favourably to the welfare of agriculturists and cowherds? And do they, remaining in their respective vocations, receive from you what they want and get over what they find harmful? See the people not suffer from lack of water supply and so on?'

Rama further asks Bharat to take good care of the soldiers and servants by timely payment of their salary and supply of provisions. He warns that if these people get angry with the king great disaster comes to the state.

Though Ramayana is a Kavya, it also deals with polity, administration, diplomacy and war and other topics. War according to Valmiki, is not to occupy the land or properties of the vanquished but its purpose is to remove an obstruction.

Rama did not kill Ravana for occupying Lanka but to remove an impediment in the rule of dharma and that is the righteous war. We shall see later that Mahabharata also deals with the concept of dharma and Rajdharma in its manifold aspects.

We have seen that the king or state in Ramayana is to observe certain norms of Maryada, during governance, based on dharma. The Mahabharata enquires about the political theory of which law and governance are essential components.

The greatest part of the political thought in the Mahabharata unfolds in Shantiparva in the form of a long conversation between Yudhishthira and the dying Bhishma. Asks Yudhishthera: What is governance? What is its origin and its purpose? What is it like? What are its forms and structure? To this Bhishma replies:

> There was a time when kingdom or king (state) did not exist and there was; neither governance nor governor. The people protected each other by means of dharma which sustained them. But this state did not last long and after sometime people lost their sense of duty and obligations. Driven only by their greed, people started doing violence to each other which created anarchy. Thus arose the need for a governing force, to bring order in the people and the king or state was invested with the authority of governance or power of danda (punishment).

It is through governance order is created and the material conditions of life are protected. Protection is the first foundation of all social order and the justification of the existence of the state. The Mahabharata declares that the power of danda or the authority to govern is drawn from the tenets of dharma. It is, therefore, essential to enquire into the attributes of dharma.

Narada's Questions to King Yudisthir

Before taking charge of the sabha made for him by the danava Maya, king Yudhisthira pays homage to ten thousand brahmans with garments, garlands and eatables. We again see how every grand event among the kshatriyas — even one involving an exchange between kshatriyas and a danava — becomes a rent-seeking opportunity for the brahmans. The epic, certainly written by the priest class, does not miss many opportunities to show the kshatriyas as making deep obeisance to the brahmans.

At any rate, the upkeep of the varna system is an attitude central to the Mahabharata, and in as much as evidences of this attitude today rightly attract criticism, the Mahabharata also cannot save itself from the same. The impulse to rewrite the epic, to alter the shlokas where the epic reinforces the caste system, stems from identifying the text as a text of its times, from seeing it as a political tool more than itihaas.

Saying that the original text needs to be criticised in places does not mean that the epic, in and of itself, has no value for our times. There is a lot of wisdom that can be drawn from it. For one, the text alludes to, and promotes, strict principles of governance and proper conduct for kings. Perhaps the best example of this is seen in Narada rishi's visit to king Yudhisthira's sabha, in which the sage interrupts the revelries in the court and then poses a flurry of questions to the king. Note, here, that it is Narada's second visit to the Pandavas. In the first visit, he had advised them to establish a protocol of exclusivity with Draupadi and set up rules for punishment in case that protocol was breached.

Narada asks Yudhisthira many questions, one after the other, never waiting to get an answer to any one question. This method implies that the questions are rhetorical, their purpose not to see if Yudhisthira knows the answer but only to remind him of their relevance and complexity. Narada is giving a lecture.

Narada asks Yudhisthira if he uses "the six royal qualities to judge the seven means?", or does he "follow the eight duties before concluding an alliance?", or are his "six chief officers" devoted to him? The usage of numbers in Narada's speech tells the reader that the details about royal qualities and means and duties, et cetera, have been enumerated in other texts which are available for the king to study.

Particularly interesting are the instances when Narada asks Yudhisthira about his mental health and personal habits. E.g. "Do you find happiness without making your mind suffer?" Or, "In the dead of night, do you think about what should be done and what should not?" Such questions suggest that while the ruler is expected to stay awake with the concerns of good governance, his (it's always a 'he' here) mental health is clearly seen as a crucial element in the overall structure.

Narada's questions thus provide valuable insights into the persistent issues of governance and jurisprudence.

KAUTILYA

The sole leader of the entire territory or the kingdom was the monarch or the sovereign who has an absolute control over the entire state. Kautilya favored hereditary monarchy as it ensured continuity. He had great faith in the law of primo-geniture, that is, the eldest son taking over the reigns from the father or the king Kautilya emphasized on the need for proper upbringing of the prince in order to avoid future problems.

Kautilya also explained the plausible dangers that a king can encounter with reference to his sovereign power. Kautilya made it very clear that dangers to the sovereignty come from three quarters, viz., from the enemy, within the territory and sometimes the wrong policy of the king himself.

In some cases, even the ministers might be a part of the trouble when they feel neglected. It is for this reason that the king must always respect the ministers all the time. Further, weak fortification of the territory can be a serious threat to the sovereignty of the king.

Similarly, lack of enough funds can also be a danger and efforts have to be made for the constant flow of funds to the treasury. It is also stated that a well-equipped and prepared army would ward off any dangers to the sovereign power of the king. Finally, if the king lacks enough number of allies or friends, then again his power would be in danger.

As regards the internal troubles, these are considered much more dangerous than the external troubles. In order to make sure that there is less likelihood of trouble within the kingdom, a king must be able to control the army as well the finances of the kingdom. It is for his own good that he must follow the policy of divide and rule.

It is also important for the king to strictly audit the national income and sources of expenditure. Kautilya suggested that the construction of more forts on the borders and friendlier relations with the neighbours saves the sovereign power of the king or the monarch.

The historical process of tradition of Indian Politics is primeval and traced back to the period of Vedas. The deliberations regarding politics are found in 'smritis' and 'puranas' by the name 'dandaniti'. References to various political texts are available which studied and discovered the concept of 'dandaniti'. It is possibly Kautilya's Arthashastra which stands out to be systematically scientific and most authoritative explanations of these prehistoric studies. Arthashastra was Transcribed in around 4th century BC by the Prime Minister of The Great Mauryan Empire Kautilya, also called Chanakya or Vishnugupta. Arthashastra is one of the most persuasive and comprehensive treatises in Political Science in the Indian Vedic Civilization. Regarded as essence of ancient Vedic wisdom in politics and economics, Arthashastra has noteworthy significance in modern times with some inquisitive resonance with the thoughts and theories of various philosophers, economists and political scientists around the globe.

Arthashastra

The Arthashastra is a primeval Indian discourse on statecraft, economic policy and military strategy, written in Sanskrit. It had wide influence on Sanskrit literature. The Mahaubhaurata mentions a number of schools of Arthashastra principle, and the names of previous writers from the fifth century B.C. agreed with those found in the Arthasastra of Kautilya. Kautilya, also recognized as Vishnugupta and Chanakya, is traditionally credited as the author of the text.

Arthashastra entails the science (sastra) of wealth/earth/polity (artha). 'Artha' however is bit wider and an all-embracing term with different meanings. In 'Arthashastra' itself, it is being used in various contexts, indicated by L.N. Rangarajan in his translation of Kautilya -Arthashastra. It is used in the sense of material well-being, in livelihood, economically productive activity trade etc. This is alike with 'wealth' which is defined in 'Wealth of Nations'. In simple way, 'arthashastra' can be explained as 'science and art of politics and diplomacy'. This treatise is divided into sixteen books dealing with virtually every topic concerned with the running of a state, taxation, law, diplomacy, military strategy, economics, bureaucracy etc. The book is a masterwork which includes an array of topics like statecraft, politics, strategy, selection and training of employees, leadership skills, legal systems, accounting systems, taxation, fiscal policies, civil rules, internal and foreign trade etc. Arthashastra backs rational ethic to the conduct of the affairs of the state. The emphasis is on systematisation of law and uniformity of law throughout the empire.

Kautilya's Arthasashtra is magnificent work on ancient political thought which was undoubtedly composed between 3rd-2nd Century B.C. Kautilya was the great Prime Minister of Chandragupta Maurya. Kautilya's Arthashastra is mainly a work on the art of government. In his political and administrative ideas, the focus of attention was the king. According to his beliefs, for the smooth functioning of administration and for the welfare of the people, the king had to be acquainted in the four Vedas and four sciences of government (Anvikashaki Trai, Varta and Dandniti). Kautilya's administrative and judicial structure was hierarchical in nature. As for impartiality, he emphasised on the principal of equity and immediacy. As for law and order, he believed that law was an imperial command enforced by sanctions. Dissimilar many other authors in the community, Kautilya is exceptional Indian political philosopher who was both thinker and statesman. He contributed in various social and political revolutions of his Age and abstracted from his study of conflicts some general principles capable of universal application and effective in all times and ages. With more and more studies in the field of politics and economics and with a modern outlook and understanding of world affairs, the significance and indebtedness of Kautilya's 'arthashastra' is incontrovertible.

Kautilya's arthshastra had wide influence of Sanskrit literature (Sharma, 2001). In the previous stages of its history, the science of politics was termed raujadharma, but when the study was extended to include both politics and economics, it was called arthasastra, (In treatises which emphasize that fear of retribution is the real basis of order, the term dandaniti is sometimes employed.) Most political thought presumed the existence of a monarchical form of government, and politics was consequently demarcated as the science of monarchy. The intent of arthshastra texts was to guide the king and his ministers, and they included such subjects as public administration, economic regulation, foreign policy, techniques of warfare, and civil law. The most significant of these works is the treatise generally attributed to Kautilya, the minister of the first Mauryan ruler.

Arthasastra, written in Sanskrit debates theories and principles of governing a state. It is not an account of Maurya administration. The title Arthashastra, which means "the science of material Gain" or "science of Polity", does not leave any doubts about its ends. Kautilya asserted that the ruler should use any means to attain his goal and his actions required to moral sanction. The only problems debated are the most practical kind. Though the kings were allowed a free restraint, the peoples were subject to set of rules. This double standard has been cited as an excuse for undesirability of the Arthashastra, though the real cause of its ultimate neglect was the creation of a totally different society to which these methods were no longer applied.

Arthashastra remains exclusive in all of Indian literature because of its total absence of specious reasoning, or its unabashed support of scholars continued to study it for its clear cut opinions and formal prose till the twelfth century. Espionage and the liberal use of challenging agents is recommended on a large scale. Murder and false accusations were to be used by a king's secret agents without any thoughts to morals or ethics. There are chapters for kings to help them keep in check the premature desires of their sons and similarly chapters intended to help princes to prevent their fathers' authoritarian authority. However, Kautilya regretfully admits that it is just as difficult to detect on official's fraudulence.

Economic ideas of Kautilya in Arthshastra: Kautilya's economic treatise Arthshastra is an idea work, a perfect balance between State management and people's welfare which was created 2,500 years before. He was a great statesman as well as great intellectual. He described Economics as the most important aspect as it provides the basis for human existence and survival. He performed a dominant role in the formation of Maurya Dynasty. With his guidance, empire conquered growth with stability with the help of strong administration and efficient fiscal management. He believed in public welfare because when his work gave a strong focus on the wealth, effectiveness and wellbeing of the king, his actual objective was not to benefit the king but to benefit the people.

Welfare State

Arthsashtra sets the conceptual groundwork for making India the first welfare state. He backed welfare in all spheres. He did not talk only about human welfare but paid attention to animal welfare also. He states that "In the happiness of his subjects lies the king's happiness, in their welfare lays his welfare. He shall not consider as good as only that which pleases him but treat as beneficial to him whatever pleases his subjects" He supported the protection of livelihood, of weaker section, consumer protection and even the welfare of prisoners also. The King's dharma is to be just, fair and liberal in protecting his people. His boldness to his people should be like attitude of a father towards his children. Kautilya demarcated the model ruler as one "who is ever active in promoting the welfare of the people and who endears himself by enriching the public and doing well to them."

Kautilya is not principally concerned with broad political speculation on the origin and nature of the state (India provides no philosophical text that can be compared with the major theoretical works of Europe), and his originality is not to be found in the monarchy of abstraction. The treatise is a collection and summary of earlier Arthasastra writings. Of the three ends of human life, virtue, wealth, and enjoyment, Kautilya allocates first importance to wealth, but he is always aware of the instrumental value of religion and principled norms in preserving the structure of society. He permitted the king to determine for himself what shall have the sanction of law, although the Vedas are accepted as sources of dharma, and statute law must be well-matched with the sacred texts. Despite the importance he ascribed to the role of the king, Kautilya is practical in his approach and would give importance to that component of dominance which happens to be of most consequence at any particular time.

In Indian theory, independence was usually thought to cover seven elements:

- The king
- The ministers
- The populace
- The fort
- The treasury
- The army
- The ally

The theory, in which diplomacy is made an integral part of politics, is intended to show the necessary conditions for the effective functioning of the state.

Good Governance

Governance generally incorporates all aspects of the way a country is governed, including its economic policies and regulatory framework. Arthashastra stated that good governance comes with peace and order which can be accomplished through the partnership of different factors in a community. The first of these factors is the leader. The leader is the one held responsible for everything that is happening in a community. In Indian society, the leader or the king plays a vital role as he is the one leading the nation and thus, must display a lot of virtues.

Kautilya had enormous knowledge about different aspects of governance such as taxation, diplomacy, trade, business, administration etc. It is supposed that he also had a good knowledge of medicine and astrology as well. It is a discourse on political economy alike to Machiavelli's, The Prince and hence he has been compared to Machiavelli by some and Aristotle and Plato by others. Kautilya explained the way a state's economy is organized, how ministers should be selected, war conducted, and how taxation should be organized and distributed. He put more emphasis on the importance of a network of detectives and informers which function as an investigation corps for the king, focusing on external threats and internal dissidence.

The Arthashastra provides various qualities that defines a good leader and most of stresses on honesty and responsibility. Kautilya gave much emphasis on this issue as corruption ravaged the Indian society during his time. Even through the passage of time, dishonesty still remains up to the present society.

He followed a general approach to governance and enlightened several areas critical to the operation of a country in depth. The main sections deal with National security and Foreign Policy, Administration of Justice, Strategies related to economic development, Taxation, Labour Management, and Financial Management. According to him, attainment of good governance requires that the objectives of the state are fulfilled and realized. This is possible through accurately organized and guided administration. He proposed that good governance should avoid extreme decisions and actions. Decisions should be taken according to the situation. When assessing Kautilya's four-pronged approach to public finance and state planning, which was actually economics, monetarism and much more, based on "dharma, artha, kama and moksha," many thinkers agreed that understanding human welfare was the basis of Arthshastra. It is said to be the ancient and most extensive treatise on governance and administration of state in the world, which describe theories of state craft and monetarism and also a code of civil and criminal law still applicable currently.

The Arthashastra also dealt with the magistrates of their jobs. In the 4th chapter, it elaborates that, "The magistrate should be impartial, and decide on a case, remaining neutral between the King and the subjects." This indicates that they should be impartial in every trial or case they are handling no matter who the people are involved. This echoes true justice: punishing the guilty and releasing the innocent, an ideal justice system where everyone is judged similarly.

Key element in effective governance is the existence and accomplishments of projects that will enhance the nation. In the Arthashastra, Kautilya offered concrete proposals that must be implemented appropriately. The most important of these is the prioritization of education. This is because in any society, having a good number of human capital is necessary good financial development. In the Arthashastra, Kautilya cited the requirement of extensive training of the people in various fields which resulted to a good outcome in those times. Currently, there is an immense importance of education in all sectors and growth of nation.

Although the Arthashastra's main goal and responsibility is the welfare of the people, Kautilya still includes rules in his treatise the maintenance of the environment and other living things. This is due to the fact that the Indian society values all living things because of their belief.

The Arthshastra linked political governance with economic governance. The end is economic governance while political governance is the means. But as economic objectives are not understood in the absence of political ones, then political governance becomes an end and economic governance the means. 'The end justifies the means', this is supposed to be the basis of Kautilyan beliefs. Political power and material wealth are the means and ends of governance. And good governance – political or economic – depends upon justifying the ends and means as the socio, economic and political circumstances.

Arthashastra explicated that there is a sturdy connection between good governance and the economy of a nation. Kautilya's Arthashastra elaborated that it is contemporary Relevance, "the end is economic governance while political governance is the means". It means that appropriate management and good governance has an effect on the economic aspect of a nation. The Arthashastra offered the basic guidelines for the proper management of the economy of the country. Ruler must know how to manage resources, such as monetary funds. It can contribute to the development of the economy. Major factor emphasized by the Arthashastra is agriculture. "The importance of irrigation and providing amenities could be taken up on a priority basis. Systematic cropping patterns and irrigation systems followed by Kautilya is what today's experts need to recognize". Kautilya also identifies organic farming because of its non-usage of chemicals. Beside from this, it is also required to learn different agricultural processes because it will aid in the production and storage of sources that will be used by the society.

Kautilya asserted that to guarantee good governance, there must be a suitably guided public administration, where the ruler should surrender his likes and dislikes in the interest of his subjects, and the personnel running the Government should be responsive. Additionally, Kautilya highlighted that for citizen friendly good governance, there should be consistency in the administrative practices as well as competent ministers and officials owning qualities of leadership, accountability, intellect, energy, good moral conduct, and physical fitness, capable of taking quick decision. Kaufmann and Kraay stated that the concept of Governance is not new. Kautilya presented key pillars of the art of governance emphasizing justice, ethics and anti-autocratic tendencies. He further detailed the duty of the king to protect the wealth of the state and its subjects, to enhance, maintain, and it does also safeguard such wealth as well as the interests of the subjects." A ruler must administers justice on the basis of four principles: righteousness, evidence, history of the case, and the prevalent law, shall conquer the earth. Kautilya articulated in the Arthashastra that a nation would benefit from trade if certain "safeguards and policy measures" are present. The trade policies of the country are implemented and are not offensive for the other parties would ensure the benefits of the nation when it comes to trading. This promotes trust and well-being for both parties.

Kautilya on Law and Justice: Kautilya upheld that it is indispensable duty of government to maintain order. He describes 'order' broadly to include both social as well as order in the sense of thwarting and punishing criminal activity. Arthashastra incorporate both the civil law and criminal law. Kautilya attributed a lot of importance to 'dharma'. According to him, 'the ultimate source of all law is dharma'. He enticed in the name of 'dharma' to the sense of honour and duty and to human dignity, to moral responsibility and to enlightened loyalty. It is quite understandable that the judge in the arthashastra was called 'dharmashta' or upholder of dharma. He said that so long every 'Arya' follows his 'svadharma' having due regard to his 'varna' and 'ashrama' and the king follows his 'rajdharma', to sustain social order.

Kautilya mainly focused on duties of King to maintain law and order in the society. He writes in Arthashastra, "Because the King is the guardian of right conduct of this world with four 'varnas' and four 'ashramas' he can enact and promulgate laws when all traditional codes of conduct perish." The King was looked upon an embodiment of virtue, a protector of dharma. He too was overseen by his dharma as any other citizen was. Thus, if any actions of the King went against the predominant notion of dharma, associations and/or the individual citizens were free to question him. He recalls every time that 'dharma' alone is guiding star for every king, or rather every individual and that following 'dharma' one shall have a life of dignity while social order prevailing in society.

He comments, "A King who administers justice in accordance with 'dharma', evidence, customs, and written law will be able to conquer whole world". Kautilya acknowledged the importance of rational law or King's law and its importance to 'dharma', 'vyayhara' and 'charitra'. He upheld that King's law was to be in harmony with the injunctions of the three Vedas wherein the four 'varnas' and 'ashramas' are defined. King was not the only interpreter of dharma. In fact, there was no specific institution devolved with the authority of interpreting dharma. Every individual was believed competent to interpret it. This was an important factor in guaranteeing the non-religious character of the Vedic state.

Kautilya did not interpret law to be a manifestation of the free will of the people. Thus sovereignty, the authority to make laws, did not vest with inhabitants. Laws were derived from four sources, dharma (scared law), vyavhara (evidence), charita (history and custom), and rajasasana (edicts of the King). Kautilya recommended that any matter of dispute shall be judged according to four bases of justice. These in order of increasing importance are:

- 'Dharma', which is based on truth
- 'Evidence', which is based on witnesses
- 'Custom', i.e. tradition accepted by the people
- 'Royal Edicts', i.e. law as promulgated.

If there is conflict among the various laws, dharma was supreme. The ordering of the other laws was case specific. Rajasasana ordered the relationship between the three major social groupings, the citizen, the association, and the state. The constitutional rules at the state level were specified in the rajasasana but the constitutional rules at the level of the association were to be decided by the members of the association. The mutual choice and the operational level rules of the association were also decided by the members of the association though the state did promulgate laws to safeguard the individual member from the oppression of the majority in the association. Arthashastra sketches a system of civil, criminal, and mercantile law (now it is called business laws).

Foreign Trade

Foreign trade is vital element of any economic system. Kautilya accepted that foreign trade in goods and services is a major source for snowballing the state wealth. He ascribed that foreign trade should be stimulated by providing some incentives such as exemption from taxes so that foreign traders to make a profit. He gave huge importance to imports. He further spoke that foreign trade is supportive to increase the supply of those goods which may not be available domestically. Through imports, a state can obtain goods more cheaply from foreign sources. In this way, he framed a comparative advantage view of foreign trade. He said that it is beneficial for the different kingdoms when the product being imported are cheaper than those can be obtained domestically. He accepted that trade based on the principal of comparative advantage would be beneficial for both exporting and importing nations. Trade is an important source of revenue for the Treasury.

The Arthashastra favours foreign trade and urges the king to take part in it through his overseer of trade. He should encourage the import of goods produced in foreign countries by permitting concessions. And those to bring such products in ships. He should grant exemption from taxes that would enable them to make a profit. And no lawsuit in money matters should be allowed against foreign trades except such as members of local guilds and their associates (Tom Trautmann, 2016). Thus the import of goods is treated as desirable practice. But at the same time exporting should be permitted for those goods that are abundant in quantity (Tom Trautmann, 2016).

Kautilya supports the use of tariffs, both export and import duties. Kautilya backed attracting foreigners who possess good technical knowledge. He Supports the use of tariffs, both import and export duties. He suggested heavy taxation on those foreign goods which are items of luxuries and on the other hand on the articles of common consumption light duties were imposed. Any item which is highly beneficial for the country should be free from any import duties. He was the first person to discuss the passport is necessary to cross the boundaries.

Taxation

Jha and Jha (1997) indicated that "Chankya paid supreme importance to the maintenance of a rich treasury, which positively affected entire activities of the administration." He focused on good fiscal management and the ways to development of all the sectors of the economy. According to him, public revenue does not exist for the desire of the king but as a fund to be utilised to augment the wealth of nations. He confessed the taxation is the main source of revenue. The power of taxing of the state is boundless but taxation should not be excessive. He supported that tax base should be increased not the tax rate. He commented the excessive burden of tax on people. Kautilya stated that King must collect taxes like honey bee, enough to sustain but not too much to destroy."

Kautilya indirectly suggests a linear income tax. He highlights fairness, stability of tax structure, fiscal federalism, avoidance of heavy taxation, ensuring of tax compliance and subsidies to encourage capital formation. He advocated limiting the taxation power of the State, having low rates of taxation, maintaining a gradual increase in taxation and most importantly devising a tax structure that ensured compliance many postulates of Kautilya's philosophy of political economy are applicable to modern times. Preferably, the government should collect taxes and do welfare of people. Kautilya's system of taxation involved the elements of sacrifice by the taxpayer, direct benefit to the taxpayers, redistribution of income, and tax incentives for desired investments. He suggested tax holiday as an incentive which means if any one brings new land under cultivation, he should be relieved from agricultural tax for at least two years. He advocates a mixed economy and argued for a very active role of government. His conversation on taxation gave an idea of three principles that include, taxation power is limited, taxation should not be heavy and excessive and tax increase should be reasonable. He recommended a system of tax collection and public expenditure of revenue in such a way as to build up the permanent revenue yielding capacity of the economy. He stated that tax base should be increased not the tax rate. The functional relationship which conversed kautilya in Arthsashtra between the rate of income tax and the magnitude of tax revenue is now said in terms of Laffer curve.

He encouraged indirect taxes such as excise and custom duties and direct taxes as income tax on individuals, wealth tax, and profession tax. He also promoted land revenue, water tax and toll, fine and penalties. According to him, tax receipts can be divided into three parts; income earned through taxes on goods produced within a country, Income earned through taxes on goods produced in the capital and income earned through taxes on imports and exports. He supported that wealthy people should pay higher tax according to their paying capacity. In this way, he considers the ability to pay approach. Tax should be levied one in a year.

Growth Oriented Public Expenditure

Kautilya supported that most of the revenue generated from taxation should be spent on creative activities and public welfare. He argued different items where state should incur expenditure such as on national defence, public administration and salaries of the ministers, government departments, maintenance of national store house and granaries, maintenance of armies and on the acquisition of valuable gems, stones and ornaments and whatever was left should be deposited to the treasury.

In Arthashastra, it is elucidated that law was not viewed just as code of prohibition, nor was it limited to corrective justice of law courts. Its range was wider than ethics itself and institutions were creation of law while traditions and customs rested on its sanctions. All philosophies of society were formed by it and law was blended with religion, with morality and with public opinion and by its subtle operations subjected the society to its will. The role of law in the society was to bring a just order in society and the remarkable task was to be carried by the King along with his assistants.

Kautilya indicated in his famous verse:

"In the happiness of his subjects lies the King's happiness;

In their welfare his welfare.

He shall not consider as good only that which pleases him but,

Treat as beneficial to him whatever pleases his subjects".

The Arthashastra treatise elaborated that writer is slightly concerned with ethical considerations. Political expedience had been a characteristic of the Arthasastra tradition, and in such works as the Santi Parvan right is likened with might in a world in which the stronger live upon the weaker. Kautilya generally recommends unprincipled tactics only against those who would undermine the social order, and he is aware of that power, if not restrained in its use, can be unhelpful of itself. The writer of the Arthasastra was sensitive to the economic bases of power and opposed any distributing tendency that would wane the control of the state over the economic life of society. Yet the state should not seek to eradicate the independent group life of the community. The caste structure was recognized as long as the general well-being was not prejudiced by narrow class rights. The Arthasastra signifies an important step in the direction of authority based on the interests of all. The king was recommended to see no interest other than the interest of his subjects. However, Kautilya clarified that affluence rests on the good will of the people and that the power of the state depends on wealth. This idea of authority must necessarily include many functions formerly reserved to institutions that were not considered political.

The Nutisaura of Kamandaka, usually retained in the Gupta period (fourth or fifth century A.D.), is basically an synopsis of the Arthasaustra, although the later writer disregards a number of subjects that Kautilya clearly believed of great importance. Two-thirds of the Kamandaklya Nitisara relates to foreign policy and the conduct of conflicts. All the literature that has been considered far was shaped in northern India, and, except for Buddhist writings, in Sanskrit. Several Jaina texts can be categorized among the Arthasastra literatures.

A Western Perspective on Kautilya's Arthashastra

However, the influence of Kautilya to economy has been ignored by western researchers despite the fact that his coverage of this subject was perhaps the most sophisticated and broadly based on internationally until Adam Smith published his Wealth of Nations in 1776.

The influential treatise, Arthashastra discovers issues of social welfare, the collective ethics that hold a society together, counselling the king that in times and in areas distressed by famine, epidemic and such acts of nature, or by war, he should initiate public projects such as building irrigation projects, building forts around major strategic holdings and towns, and exempt taxes on those affected. The text was powerful on other Hindu texts that followed, such as the sections on king, governance and legal procedures included in Manusmriti. The Arthashastra was written at the end of the fourth century BC, it seems to have been revived only in 1905, after centuries of oblivion. The dissertation in its present shape is most likely not the text written by Kautilya, though it is perhaps based on a text that was authored by Kautilya; and is no case can the text in its completely be credited to Kautilya on account of numerous stylistic linguistic distinctions.

Relevance of Arthsashtra in Modern Time

Kautilya is one of the most renowned Indian political philosophers. Though, he lived a long time ago, certain philosophies from his theory are still applicable in modern political framework. The book, written in Sanskrit elucidates theories and principles of governing a state. Kautilya established an extremely vital imperative: governance, polity, politics, and progress have to be linked to the welfare of the people. When assessing the some economic ideas of kautilya, it can be understood that even the terminology employed in Arthsashtra may have changed but the nature and role of state in the economic system seem persistent in all settings. Covering various topics on administration, politics and economy, it is a book of law and a treatise on running a country, which is pertinent even today. His philosophies remain prevalent today in India.

He offered cherished basis for economic science. It comprises of very useful economic ideas on foreign trade, taxation, public expenditure, agriculture and industry. Good governance and stability are inseparably linked. If rulers are responsive, accountable, removable, recallable, there is stability. If not, there is uncertainty. This is even more applicable in the present democratic system. He recommended that heavy taxation should be avoided. If tax rates are high, public will not be willing to pay the tax and discover the ways of tax evasion. Low rate of taxation will produce more revenue to the state.

He was well mindful that terms of trade were not just depending on economics but also on various factors. There is no autonomous mechanism that will ensure that a nation would benefit from trade in the absence of certain precautions and policy measures. Social welfare is the main focal point of Kautilya's economic notions. The State was required to help the poor and helpless and to be proactive in contributing to the welfare of its citizens. Kautilya gave more emphasis to human capital formation that is relevant in current times because development is not possible without human capital growth. Besides these ideas, there are a number of things in Arthsashtra which is very significant such as conservation of natural resources. Arthsashtra provides much basic knowledge about economics, and several of his ideas are still important in today's economic system.

To summarize, Arthashastra is an exceptional test in all of Indian literature because of its total absence of erroneous reasoning, or its blatant support of real politic, and scholars continued to study it for its clear cut arguments and formal style till the twelfth century. The Arthashastra provides broad coverage on the overall economy, which includes: infrastructure (roadwork, irrigation, forestry, and fortification), weights and measurements, labour and employment, commerce and trade, commodities and agriculture, land use and property laws, money and coinage, interest rates and loan markets, tariffs and taxes, and government expenditures and the treasury. It is noteworthy that a book such as 'Arthashastra' should have been written more than 2000 years ago in northern India. It is a book of substantial size. It includes economics, political science, public administration, low and statecraft. It is projected to provide practical advice for the management of the state and thereby enhance the wealth of the nation.

Especially, Arthashastra is a discourse on political economy interpreted in its broadest sense. It was written somewhere between 321 and 286 BC. A Modern of Aristotle, Kautilya, a Brahmin, played a governing role in the formation and functioning of Maurya Empire. Afterward under his leadership, growth with stability was conquered in the empire with the help of strong administration and efficient monetary management. His accomplishment in the domain of scholarship is certainly creditable. The 'Arthashastra' consists of detailed analysis of different aspects of ancient Indian economy." Intelligence and the liberal use of stimulating agents is suggested on a large scale, Kautilya remorsefully acknowledges that it is not easy to identify an official's deceit. Kautilya has delivered a comprehensive and explanatory description of the duties, responsibilities and role of the king, prince(s), ministers, and other state officials. As for the state's political administration, Kautilya provided a complete commentary as to how this should be effectively undertaken. He gave instructions about the defence of the state's limits, protection of the forts, and the manner in which the attack by the rival must be controlled. The Arthashastra categorizes legal matters into civil and criminal and it stipulates extravagant strategies for administering justice in terms of evidence, procedures and witnesses. It can be said that Kautilya's Arthshastra offers valuable foundation for economy. It consists of valuable insights about finances. It can be used to glen of significance to modern time and can be useful to exemplify several contemporary economic thoughts. He offered a set of different economic policy measures to encourage economic development.

CONSTITUTIONAL MORALITY

The phrase 'constitutional morality' has, of late, begun to be widely used. Yet the phrase rarely crops up in discussions around the Constituent Assembly. Of the three or four scattered uses of the phrase, only one reference has any intellectual significance. This is, of course, Ambedkar's famous invocation of the phrase in his speech 'The Draft Constitution', delivered on 4 November 1948. In the context of defending the decision to include the structure of the administration in the Constitution, he quotes at great length the classicist, George Grote. The quotation is worth reproducing in full:

The diffusion of 'constitutional morality', not merely among the majority of any community, but throughout the whole is the indispensable condition of a government at once free and peaceable; since even any powerful and obstinate minority may render the working of a free institution impracticable, without being strong enough to conquer ascendance for themselves.

What did Grote mean by 'constitutional morality'? Ambedkar quotes Grote again:

By constitutional morality, Grote meant... a paramount reverence for the forms of the constitution, enforcing obedience to authority and acting under and within these forms, yet combined with the habit of open speech, of action subject only to definite legal control, and unrestrained censure of those very authorities as to all their public acts combined, too with a perfect confidence in the bosom of every citizen amidst the bitterness of party contest that the forms of constitution will not be less sacred in the eyes of his opponents than his own.

In Grote's rendition, 'constitutional morality' had a meaning different from two meanings commonly attributed to the phrase. In contemporary usage, constitutional morality has come to refer to the substantive content of a constitution. To be governed by a constitutional morality is, on this view, to be governed by the substantive moral entailment any constitution carries. For instance, the principle of non-discrimination is often taken to be an element of our modern constitutional morality. In this sense, constitutional morality is the morality of a constitution.

There was a second usage that Ambedkar was more familiar with from its 19th century provenance. In this view, constitutional morality refers to the conventions and protocols that govern decision-making where the constitution vests discretionary power or is silent.

But Grote's use of the term was different from these two uses, and more important for Ambedkar's purposes. Ambedkar was making a series of historical claims about constitutionalism. Like Grote, he had little doubt that constitutional morality was rare. It was not a 'natural sentiment'. The purpose of Grote's History of Greece had been, in part, to rescue Athenian democracy from the condescension of its elitist critics like Plato and Thucydides, and argue that Athenian democracy had, even if briefly, achieved elements of a genuine constitutional morality.

For Grote, there were only two other plausible instances of a constitutional morality having been remotely realized: the aristocratic combination of liberty and self-restraint experienced in 1688 in England, and American constitutionalism. All other attempts at enshrining a constitutional morality had grievously foundered. For Ambedkar, this note of historical caution simply added to his worries about India. Democracy in India was only, as he put it, 'top dressing on Indian soil, which is essentially undemocratic.' Our people have 'yet to learn' constitutional morality.

What are the elements of constitutional morality that Ambedkar is so concerned about? His invocation of Grote is meant not as a reference merely to historical rarity, but also as a pointer to the distinctiveness of constitutionalism as a mode of association. In both the 4 November 1948 speech and the final 'Reply to the Debate' on 25 November 1949, Ambedkar – amidst discussions of a whole range of substantive issues such as federalism, rights, decentralization, and parliamentary government – returns to elements of constitutional morality prefigured in his use of Grote. For him, the real anxiety was not 'Constitution' the noun, as much as the adverbial practice it entailed.

For Grote, the central elements of constitutional morality were freedom and self-restraint. Self-restraint was a precondition for maintaining freedom under properly constitutional government. The most political expression of a lack of self-restraint was revolution. Indeed constitutional morality was successful only in so far as it warded off revolution. Ambedkar also takes on the explicitly anti-revolutionary tones of constitutionalism. In a strikingly odd passage, he says that the maintenance of democracy requires that we must 'hold fast to constitutional methods of achieving our social and economic objectives. It must mean that we abandon the bloody methods of revolution. It means we must abandon the method of civil disobedience, non-cooperation and satyagraha.'

In one stroke, both violent revolution and passive resistance are equated as exemplifying a kind of excess and lack of self-restraint incompatible with constitutional morality. The tacit equivalence he posits between satyagraha and violence has roots in Ambedkar's experience of satyagraha as a form of coercion. It is a feature of constitutional morality that while government is subject to the full force of criticism, this criticism must, in some sense, be 'pacific' criticism.

Ambedkar dismisses an entire repertoire of political action used during the nationalist movement as being incompatible with the demands of constitutional morality, as he understood it. These forms of political action continue to be seen by many as essential to democracy, though it is doubtful that Ambedkar would have admitted them within the ambit of constitutional morality. But there is perhaps a deeper element at play in his ruling out satyagraha as incompatible with the basics of constitutional morality. And this in part springs from his understanding of the distinctiveness of constitutional morality.

For the second element of constitutional morality is the recognition of plurality in its deepest form. What is surprising is that Ambedkar turns out to be as, if not more, committed to a form of non-violence as Gandhi. For him, respecting constitutional forms is the only way in which a genuinely non-violent mode of political action can come into being. For the central challenge in a political society is the management and adjudication of differences – though what Ambedkar had in mind were more differences of opinion than of identity.

The only way of non-violent resolution amidst this fact of difference is securing some degree of unanimity on a constitutional process, a form of adjudication that can mediate difference. Unilaterally declaring oneself to be in possession of the truth, setting oneself up as a judge in one's own cause, or acting on the dictates of one's conscience might be heroic acts of personal integrity. But they do not address the central problem that a constitutional form is trying to address, namely the existence of a plurality of agents, each with his/her own convictions, opinions and claims.

Constitutional morality requires submitting these to the adjudicative contrivances that are central to any constitution – parliament, courts and so on. In the face of difference, the only point of unanimity that one can seek is over an appropriately designed adjudicative process. This is one reason, for example, why Ambedkar does not think socialism should be part of the constitution, even though equality is of paramount concern to him. What the parties have to agree to, as Ambedkar recognizes over and over, is an allegiance to a constitutional form, not an allegiance to a particular substance.

Therefore, constitutional morality requires that allegiance to the constitution is non-transactional. The essence of constitutional morality is that allegiance to the constitution cannot be premised upon it leading to outcomes that are a mirror image of any agent's beliefs. A constitutional morality requires putting up with the possibility that what eventually emerges from a process is very different from what citizens had envisaged.

The third element of constitutional morality is its suspicion of any claims to singularly and uniquely represent the will of the people. This is most deeply manifest in Ambedkar's hostility to any personification of political authority. In part what rendered satyagraha ominous, from a constitutional point of view, was not just its uncompromising character; it was also the fact that its agents saw themselves as personifying the good of the whole. Ambedkar is hugely suspicious of any form of hero worship – now a rather ironic fear in an age in which Ambedkar himself has been deified. But this suspicion of personification was part of a larger sensibility that formed a crucial element of his constitutional morality: he was suspicious of any claims to embody popular sovereignty. This may be a somewhat surprising claim to attribute to Ambedkar, and with him other architects of the Constitution. But the evidence of this is unmistakable.

Thus Ambedkar is very reluctant to see any branch of government, whether it be the legislature or the courts, or even the Constituent Assembly itself, as being able to claim authoritatively that it embodies popular sovereignty and can speak in its name. He is often suspicious of the legislature's claim to do so (for instance, in his argument for why the form of administration should not be entrusted to the legislature). His defence of a relatively easy process of amending the constitution rests on a halfway compromise between, on the one hand, a radical Jeffersonianism that would subject the constitution to renegotiation at every generation and, on the other, a rigid constitution that would deeply entrench the present generation's preferences.

In short, any appeal to popular sovereignty has to be tempered by a sense that the future may have at least as valid claims as the present. Indeed, it has to be said of the Constituent Assembly as a whole, that there is very little demagoguery in the name of popular sovereignty. Almost never is a claim advanced or defended on the ground that it somehow represents the will of the people. Often the discourse is more centred on the responsibility to the people. This is not simply because the Constituent Assembly was not elected by universal suffrage; nor was it simply a product of elitism trying to keep popular sovereignty at bay. It was rather because there was a deeper grasp of a political truth: any claims to speak on behalf of popular sovereignty are attempts to usurp its authority. No claim to represent popular sovereignty therefore, should ever be considered fully convincing; the chief purpose of constitutional government is to challenge governmental, or any other claims to represent the people.

One piece of evidence for this is Ambedkar's defence of the parliamentary form of government because it embodies what he calls the principle of 'responsibility'. By this he means that the executive will be subject to 'daily assessment'. While elections will give an opportunity for the people to engage in what he calls 'periodic assessment', the arsenal of parliamentary democracy will facilitate daily assessment in the form of resolutions to no confidence motions, debates to adjournment motions, etc. Whether or not he was right about a parliamentary system of government is debatable, but it is deeply interesting that he sees parliament's function as questioning any claims the government might make to embody popular opinion or sovereignty simply on account of its majority.

The function of parliament is not so much to represent popular sovereignty as it is to debate and constantly question government. But, paradoxically, this is to prevent government from claiming monopoly over popular will. There is not a single place in the debates where the protagonists raise the following questions: What form of democracy will best represent the will of the people? The predominant focus is on multiplying rather than on questioning claims to represent the people. Although someone like Nehru was occasionally impatient with institutions like the court, the subsequent contest between the judiciary and legislature can be seen as yet another exemplification of the Constitution's impulse that there should be no singularly authoritative arbiter of either popular will, or constitutional interpretation.

It is a concern for criticism rather than representation of popular will that ties Ambedkar most closely to Grote's invocation of constitutional morality. After all, the burden of Grote's great history of Athenian democracy was to defuse the criticism of Athens that popular sovereignty was a threat to freedom and individuality. Once popular sovereignty or the authority of the people had been invoked, who else would have any authority to speak? Grote defused this anxiety in a novel way. Allegiance to forms of constitution was not to be confused with deference to popular sovereignty. The claim by a government that it represented popular sovereignty did not, by itself, have any authority. Its claims and decisions could still be interrogated, censured and subject to unrestrained criticism. Indeed, what Athenian constitutional practice had achieved was precisely this: the space for unrestrained criticism that was nevertheless 'pacific and bloodless' and not silenced by claiming the authority of the people.

This account of constitutional morality may seem to emphasize the formal elements: self-restraint, respect for plurality, deference to processes, scepticism about authoritative claims to popular sovereignty, and the concern for an open culture of criticism that remains at the core of constitutional forms. These may seem rather commonplace, but Ambedkar had little doubt that the subjectivity that embodied these elements was rare and difficult to achieve. Ambedkar grasped singularly the core of the constitutional revolution: it was an association sustained not by a commonality of ends, or unanimity over substantive objectives (except at perhaps a very high level of generality). It was rather a form of political organization sustained by certain ways of doing things. It was sustained not so much by objectives as by the conditions through which they were realized. This was the core of constitutional morality.

A constitution thus was not a relationship between concrete persons, but rather a relationship between abstract personae bound together by abstract rules. It is precisely this abstraction, this distance from specific persons and wished for substantive outcomes that allowed a constitutional culture to emerge. Ambedkar was a powerful and trenchant critic of caste. In this context, caste was an impediment to constitutional morality in a very specific way. It is the form of social existence that prevented the emergence of those abstract personae so central to constitutional morality. It is the one particularity that constantly undermines the formation of the self, central to constitutional morality. For constitutional morality requires various forms of dissociation: the ability to dissociate a person from their views; the ability to trust someone despite deep disagreement based on the knowledge that there is a shared agreement on processes to adjudicate that disagreement. Caste identity, by its very character, made such dissociation impossible.

For Ambedkar, without fraternity, 'equality and liberty would be no deeper than coats of paint.' Nowhere does Ambedkar make the argument that the Constitution is about distribution of power among different castes. Caste embodies a principle of social separation, and is, to use his phrase, 'anti-national'. Its very existence precludes an ability to abstract from one's identity. It ensures that the relationship between groups is perpetually competitive. A constitutional morality, by contrast, requires both these features – abstraction and agreement or cooperation. It requires the presumption that we are equal. However, that equality is possible only when for constitutional purposes our caste identities do not matter. A constitutional morality requires the sense that despite all differences we are part of a common deliberative enterprise.

But there are still several good reasons to unpack the references to constitutional morality. First, we simply need to complicate our understanding of how our framers understood the Constitution. Formalism of a certain kind was central to their imagination of the Constitution as a mode of association. Second, it is a striking fact that while Ambedkar recognized the contradictions between the actual injustice and constitutional aspirations, he did not collapse the Constitution into a doctrine of distributive justice. Implicit in his invocation of the contradiction is a dual-track conception of justice. There is constitutional justice, defined by certain rights and procedures. There is also substantive justice, embodied in debates over private property and the rival claims of socialism versus capitalism.

In a way the constitutional discourse is caught between two impulses. On the one hand it wants to say that we can rise above these particular disagreements and provide a framework where both parties can contend; the rights of those who build billion dollar homes can contend with the claims of those who demand more radical forms of redistribution. Our Constitution has space for both socialists and capitalists or, to take another example, those who radically disagree over reservation. Constitutional morality is simply the conditions one subscribes to in determining the outcome, whatever that might be.

On the other hand, we might feel that there is something unstable about the political psychology associated with this dissociation of constitutional from distributive justice. Can citizens really be committed to a framework that allows both goals at once: the rights of the billion-dollar home owner and a commitment to redistribution? In almost all his speeches, Ambedkar himself wrestles with this tension: Can a constitution survive without a singular conception of distributive justice underlying it?

In the final analysis, he pitches for constitutional morality, an allegiance to constitutional forms, rather than collapsing the domains of constitutional and distributive justice. He doesn't cheat by giving us the (false) assurance that the forms of constitutional morality will produce deep substantive equality; nor does he cheat by saying that substantive equality simply is the same thing as constitutional morality. No society has yet adequately negotiated the tension between the domain of constitutional morality and the domain of substantive justice. He wanted a revolution, but never became a revolutionary.

The final reason for focusing on constitutional morality is historical. What was the nature of the Constituent Assembly's achievement? It is fair to say that it became a supreme exemplar of what Ambedkar defined as constitutional morality. This is a sensibility that few analysts of the Constitution can recover. They are often fixated on transactional views of the Constitution, measuring it by a yardstick of justice external to its purposes. Perhaps the frame of constitutional morality can direct our attention to a crucial question: What kind of a political sensibility was required to make a constitution possible?

Constitutions not only allocate authority, define the limits of power or enunciate values. They also constitute our sense of history and shape a sense of self. They often mark a new beginning and define future horizons. Despite the centrality of the Constitution to our social and political life, it has been ill-served by our historical imagination. In a very mundane sense, with a handful of exceptions, there is no serious or deep historiography associated with our Constitution, one that can put it in proper historical and philosophical perspective.

The promulgation of India's Constitution was made possible by a sensibility that few contemporary historians can recover. While the Constitution was an extraordinary work of synthesis, our historical imagination is given to divisiveness. There is no more striking example of this than the way in which members of the Constituent Assembly have been divided up and appropriated, rather than seen in relation to each other. Ambedkar, Patel, Nehru, Prasad and a host of others are now icons in partisan ideological battles, as if to describe Ambedkar as a Dalit, or Patel as proto-BJP, or Nehru as a Congressman exhausts all that needs to be said about them.

The greatness of each one of them consists not just in the distinctive points of view they brought together, but their extraordinary ability to work together despite so many differences. Congress itself facilitated the entry of so many people with an anti-Congress past into key roles in the Assembly. It takes a willful historical amnesia to forget the fact that the men and women of the Assembly worked with an extraordinary consciousness that they needed and completed each other. The historiography of the Constituent Assembly has not regarded it as an exemplar of constitutional morality. It has rather assessed it on a much more ideological yardstick.

The ability to work with difference was augmented by another quality that is rarer still: the ability to acknowledge true value. This may be attributed to the sheer intellectualism of so many of the members. Their collective philosophical depth, historical knowledge, legal and forensic acumen and sheer command over language is enviable. It ensured that the grounds of discussion remained intellectual. Also remarkable was their ability to acknowledge greatness in others. It was this quality that allowed Nehru and Patel, despite deep differences in outlook and temperament, to acknowledge each other. Their statesmanship was to not let their differences produce a debilitating polarization, one that could have wrecked India. They combined loyalty and frankness. Even as partial a biographer of Nehru as S. Gopal conceded that what prevented the rupture was their 'mutual regard and Patel's stoic decency.'

The third sensibility so many leaders of the Constituent Assembly carried was a creative form of self-doubt. They were all far more self-conscious that they were taking decisions under conditions of great uncertainty. Was it that easy to know what the consequences of a particular position were going to be? They also understood their mutual vulnerabilities. Nehru's answer to Patel's worry that Nehru was losing confidence in him was that he was losing confidence in himself. And anyone who has read the tortured last pages of The Discovery of India will understand how much Nehru meant it. Much of the cheap condescension of posterity heaped upon these figures would vanish if we could show as much self-awareness and a sense of vulnerability as our founding generation did. Many of them made mistakes of judgment. But one has the confidence that they were more likely to acknowledge their mistakes than most of those who comment upon them. They embodied the central element of a constitutional morality: to treat each other as citizens deserving equal regard, despite serious differences.

The fourth sensibility which we have lost sight of is the importance of form. We are all instinctive Marxists in the sense that we think of institutions, forms and laws as so many contrivances to consolidate power. But this was a generation with a deep sense that forms and institutions are not merely instrumental for an immediate goal; they are the enabling framework that allows a society the possibilities of self-renewal. Forms also allow trust to be built; they give a signal that power, even when it seeks to do good, is not being exercised in a way that is arbitrary. This is exactly why the members took the Assembly and its deliberations seriously.

The fifth feature of their sensibility is a sense of judgment. This is a very intangible political quality. Part of it is the ability to deliberate in a way that takes on board all the relevant considerations, and does not make politics hostage to a single mission. Another is the ability to judge one's own power and place in relation to others and the public at large. This gives a better sense of when to compromise and when to press a point, when to curb one's ego and when to project power.

The Constitution was made possible by a constitutional morality that was liberal at its core. Not liberal in the eviscerated ideological sense, but in the deeper virtues from which it sprang: an ability to combine individuality with mutual regard, intellectualism with a democratic sensibility, conviction with a sense of fallibility, deliberation with decision, ambition with a commitment to institutions, and hope for a future with due regard for the past and present.

Secularism and Fundamental Rights

The constitution of India is the most significant document which is fundamental to the governance of the state. Fundamental Rights constitute a salient feature of Indian constitution. These are the basic rights of the individual which are contained in Part III of the constitution and these rights ensure an effective guarantee against any antidemocratic action of the state.

The inclusion of Fundamental rights from Article 12 to 35 in chapter III of Indian constitution is an important landmark in the process of making available to every Indian citizen social, economic and political justice. Pt. Nehru described it as the conscience of the constitution. Constitution of India provides for both the Fundamental Rights to safeguard the individuals liberty and dignity, — and the Directive Principles to ensure social, economic and political justice to every member of the community. Therefore Indian Constitution provides all the people of India; social, economic and political justice.

The Courts (Supreme Court and High Court) have the power to declare the laws as void which contravenes the fundamental rights. So, fundamental rights are protected from any state or any law which infringes on them or takes away any of them.

Originally the Indian constitution described seven fundamental rights. But after the 44th Constitutional Amendment of 1979, their number has come down to six. Right to property under Article 31 has been deleted from the list of fundamental rights and it has been made a legal right under Article 300 A.

I. The Right to Equality (Article 14-18)
II. The Right to Freedom (Article 19-22)
III. The Right against Exploitation (Article 23, 24)
IV. The Right to Freedom of Religion (Article 25-28)
V. The Cultural and Educational Rights (Article 29-30)
VI. Right to Constitution Remedies (Article 32)

Recognising fully the importance of right to equality in a democratic country, the constitution assigns first place to the right to equality in the list of fundamental rights. Infact right to equality is the very basis of a democratic state. Before political independence of Indian people were discriminated against on the basis of caste, religion, colour and race etc. But after the attainment of political independence of the country it became essential to abolish all these discriminatory measures. With this objective the flight to equality was incorporated in the Indian constitution from Article 14-18.

Its description is as under:

I. Right to Equality

1. Equality before Law – Article 14

The Right to Equality before law is the very basis of the 'rule of law' in the country. This right is also enjoyable by the foreigners living in India.

Article 14 of the Indian Constitution prøvides that "The state shall not deny to any person equality before law or the equal protection of law within the territory of India."

Equality before law, however, does not mean absolute equality or equality among the un-equals. It means equality among the people similarly situated. It does not prohibit the classification of persons into different groups. It also admits the right of the state to establish special courts for trying cases involving specific offences by certain persons.

Exceptions

The exceptions to this Right are as under. The President of India and Governors of various states while performing their executive functions connected with their respective offices, cannot be held responsible for any such act nor can they be tried before any court, in a criminal case. In order to file a civil suit against the President of India or the governors of states, a notice for a period of two months must be served.

The executive heads of foreign countries and their ambassadors would be out of the purview of the Indian law.

2. Prohibition of Discrimination—Article 15

Article 15, prohibits discrimination on the grounds of religion, race, caste, sex or place of birth. No person on any of these grounds can be denied access to shops, hotels, public restaurants and places of public entertainment or the use of wells, tanks, bathing ghats, roads and places of public resort maintained wholly or partly by the state funds or dedicated to the use of general public.

Exceptions

The State will be empowered to undertake special measures in order to protect the interests of children and the women. The State will be empowered to undertake special measures in order to protect the interests of the citizens of the socially or educationally backward classes or those of the members of Scheduled Castes or Scheduled Tribes. The constitution nowhere, defines the socially and educationally backward classes of citizens. By implication it gives this Right to define them to the State.

3. Equality of Opportunity—Article 16

The constitution provides for equality of opportunity for all citizens in matters relating to employment or appointment to any office under the state. Article 16 further states that no citizen shall on grounds of religion, race, caste, sex, place of birth, residence or any of them ineligible for or discriminated against in respect of any employment under the state.

Exceptions

(i) Article 16 will not be applicable in case of appointments in religious or communal institutions.

(ii) It is also laid down that this right shall not prevent the state from making provision for reservation of appointments or posts in favour of any backward class of citizens which in the opinion of the state, is not adequately represented in the services under the state. The expression 'Backward Classes of Citizens' in this Article includes scheduled castes, scheduled tribes and other weaker sections of society.

(iii) The Indian Parliament is empowered to determine or fix residential qualifications for appointment to any particular post.

4. Abolition of Untouchability—Article 17

The centuries-old malady of untouchability has been abolished. Article 17 of the Indian Constitution states that "Untouchability is abolished and its practice in any form is forbidden. The enforcement of inability arising out of untouchability shall be an offence punishable in accordance with law. "

In fact, it is a solid measure undertaken to abolish untouchability. Article 17 of the Indian Constitution is an Article of Deliverance for crores of Indian people. M.V. Pylee has rightly said that "It is a charter of deliverance to one sixth of the total population of India from perpetual subjugation and despair, from perpetual humiliation and disgrace."

For the realisation of this Right, the Government passed 'The Untouchability Offence Act-1995' and 'The Protection of Civil Rights Act 1976.' By these Acts discrimination against Scheduled Castes has been held unlawful. The provision has been made that whatever facilities will be available to the Hindus of high caste will also be available to the members of scheduled castes.

Under the Act of 1976, to practice untouchability or to propagate it directly or indirectly, or to justify it on historical, philosophical, religious and traditional basis has been declared a crime. Anybody found guilty of practicing it can be imprisoned from six months to 2 years and fined Rs 100/- to Rs 1000/-. Any person who has been punished under the above-cited acts for the abolition of untouchability will be disqualified for the purpose of seeking elections to the Indian Parliament or State Legislature.

5. Abolition of Titles—Article 18

The conferment of titles creates unnatural classes in the society which is against the principle of social equality. By abolishing titles, our constitutional fathers have tried to establish democratic equality in the true sense of the term. It has been done so before in other countries. Titles of nobility were abolished in U.S.A. in 1787.

Under this Article following provisions have been made:

1. The state shall not confer any other title except the military and academic ones.
2. No Indian citizen will accept any title from a foreign State.
3. No person who is not an Indian citizen but holds an office of profit under the state will accept any title from a foreign state without the permission of the President.
4. No person who is occupying an office of profit under the state shall accept any gift, salary or title of any kind from any foreign state.

The Govt. of India began to confer in 1954 titles of Bharat Ratna, Padam Vibhushan, Padam Bhushan and Padam Shri. The critics were of the opinion that this act of the Government do not conform with Article 18 of the Constitution. In July 1977, by an ordinance issued by the President, conferment of these titles was stopped but with the Congress (I) coming into power in January 1980, the Government has once again started conferring these titles.

II. Right to Freedom—Article 19 to 22

Right to Freedom is the most important of all fundamental rights. The freedoms granted to citizens from Article 19—22 have been called 'soul and spirit of the constitution. 'Herein, the constitutional fathers have tried to strike a compromise between personal liberty and public authority.

1. Freedom under Article 19

Article 19 of the constitution confers the following six freedoms to the citizens of India:

(i) Freedom of speech and expression.
(ii) Freedom to assemble peacefully without arms.
(iii) Freedom to form associations or unions.
(iv) Freedom to move throughout the territory of India.
(v) Freedom to reside and settle in any part of India.
(vi) Freedom to practice any profession, occupation, trade or business.

(i) **Freedom of Speech and Expression.** Indian Constitution grants freedom of speech and expression to every citizen of India. Every citizen can express himself by writing or speaking. The freedom of the press has not been separately mentioned but this freedom comes under the freedom of expression. Dr. Ambedkar was of the view that newspapers are a means for man to express his opinion and the freedom of press need not to be separately mentioned.

Freedom of speech and expression is not absolute. Keeping in view the sovereignty and integrity of India, security of the state, friendly relations with foreign countries, public order, morality, contempt of the court, activities which incite crimes—the state has the power to impose reasonable restrictions on this right.

During internal emergency, restriction was imposed on the publication of the proceedings of Parliament and State Legislatures by the Press but by the 44th Constitutional Amendment 1979, a provision was made that the Press has full freedom to publish the proceeding of Parliament and State Legislatures. No restriction in this matter shall be imposed on the press.

(ii) **Freedom to Assemble Peacefully without Arms.** By this freedom, the citizens can assemble to express themselves and hear the views of others, but the assembly should be peaceful and the people should attend such meetings or rallies without arms. Indian Constitution like the U.S.A. Constitution does not give the right to bear arms. The people cannot keep unlicenced arms. The Sikhs have been made special exception because to bear 'Kirpan' (sword) comes under their religious principles.

(iii) **Freedom to form Associations or Unions.** Indian constitution grants to its citizens the right to form associations or unions so that they may achieve their economic, political, social, religious and cultural objectives. A citizen may or may not become the members of any association or union. No one can force him against his will to become member of a particular union or association.

All the citizens do not have the equal right to form associations or unions. Government servants cannot enjoy this right like other citizens of the country because they are governed by government rules and regulations. Indian Government is empowered to limit the right to freedom to form associations or unions in the name of the country's public order and ethics etc.

(iv) **Freedom to Move Freely throughout the Territory of India.** All the citizens of India have been given the right to move freely in any part or region of the country. They do not require any permit to go to any part of the country.

The state can impose restrictions on the Right of the citizens to move freely in any part of the country in view of the common public interests and the interests of scheduled tribes.

(v) **Freedom to Reside and Settle in any Part of the Country.** The India citizens have been given the right to freedom to reside and settle in any part of the country.

The state can impose reasonable restrictions on the right of the citizens to reside or settle in any part of the country in the name of common public interest and the interests of the members of Scheduled Tribes.

(vi) **Freedom to Practice any Profession or to Carry on any Occupation, Trade or Business.** In India, for quite a long time people have been adopting professions on the basis of caste and religion. Therefore a progressive and prosperous society could not be evolved. The makers of Indian Constitution deemed professional dynamism necessary for the establishment of progressive democracy and gave it a place in the form of fundamental rights in the constitution. According to the constitution of India every citizen has been given the freedom to practice any profession of his or her choice. No individual can be compelled against his will to adopt any particular profession. The state can impose restrictions on this right for public interest.

The state can fix professional or technical qualifications for profession, job, trade or business.

The state can make provision to give business, trade or industrial services by itself or by corporation made under its ownership or control.

2. Protection in Respect of Conviction of an Offence – Article 20

Under Article 20, the constitution provides protection against arbitrary conviction in respect of offences committed by the people.

It lays down that:

(i) Do person can be convicted of an offence except for the violation of a law in force at the time of the commission of the act charged as an offence. This provision prevents ex-post- facto legislation which makes an innocent act an offence, which when committed was not an offence.

(ii) No person can be subjected to a penalty greater than the one which might have been indicated under the law in force at the time of commission of an offence.

(iii) No person can be arrested and punished for the same offence more than once.

(iv) No person accused of an offence can be forced to be a witness against himself.

This Article provides protection against arbitrary and excessive punishment, prevents double prosecution and punishment and it warrants against the forcible securing to statements/confessions from an accused.

44th Amendment to the constitution has laid down that the executive will have no power under Article 359 to suspend Article 20 during the emergency. The provision highlights the importance attached to this right.

3. Protection of Life and Personal Liberty—Article 21

Article 21 provides protection to the life and liberty of citizens as well as non-citizens. It states "No person shall be deprived of his life and liberty except according to procedure established by law." It provides the right not to be subjected to imprisonment, arrest or physical coercion in any manner without legal jurisdiction. The term 'procedure established by law' means the awarding of punishment in accordance with law and according to the set procedure.

The 44th Amendment of the constitution has made the right of life and personal liberty inviolable even during an emergency. It means that Article 21 of the Indian Constitution cannot be suspended even during emergency. However, 59th Amendment of the constitution has laid down that this right can be suspended by the President.

4. Protection against Arrest and Detention—Article 22

This Article of the constitution provides for protection against arbitrary arrest and detention.

It lays down that a person who is arrested and detained shall be:

(i) Informed of the ground of his arrest and shall have the right to consult and be defended by a legal practitioner of his choice.

(ii) Produced before the nearest magistrate within a period of 24 hours of his arrest. He cannot be detained in custody beyond 24 hours without the authority of the state.

These safeguards do not apply.

(i) To any person who for the time being is an enemy alien.

(ii) To any person who is arrested or detained under any law providing for preventive detention.

In other words, the constitution authorises preventive detention which involves arrest, detention and imprisonment without trial and before any crime has actually been committed. The provision of preventive detention is required in the interest of national unity and integration.

III. Right against Exploitation (Article 23, 24)

Articles 23 and 24 of the Constitution provide against human exploitation.

1. Prohibition of Traffic in Human Beings and Forced Labour – Article 23

Under Article 23, the constitution prohibits traffic in human beings, beggar and similar forms of forced labour. This Article makes the selling and buying of men and women and exploitation of people by forcing them to work as bonded labourers or work without remuneration, an offence. For protecting women against selling and buying for immoral purposes, the Suppression of Immoral Traffic in Women and Girls Act (SITA) has been in operation since 1956.

2. Prohibition of Employment of Children (Article 24)

Article 24 provides that no child below the age of fourteen years shall be employed to work in any factory or mine or engaged in any other hazardous employment. This Article provides protection to children from exploitation which can adversely affect their health.

IV. Right to Freedom of Religion—Article 25-28:

Right to freedom of religion ensures the positive aspect of secularism as it gives to the people the right to freely adopt and propagate any religion.

The freedoms granted under these Articles are as under:

1. Freedom of Conscience—Article 25

This Article guarantees to all persons, the freedom of conscience and the right of profess, practice and propagate any religion. Forcible conversions stand prohibited in India. There is no state religion in India. All religions are equal.

2. Freedom to Manage Religious Affairs—Article 26

Under Article 26 of the Constitution, the Indian citizens have been given the following rights in managing their religious affairs subject to the public health and morality.

They are:

(a) To establish and maintain institutions for religious and charitable purposes.

(b) To manage its own affairs in matters of religion.

(c) To own and acquire movable and immovable property in name of religion.

(d) To administer such religious property in accordance with law.

3. Freedom for Paying Taxes for the Promotion of any Religion —Article 27

Under Article 27, the constitution lays down that no person shall be compelled to pay any taxes, the proceeds of which are specifically appropriated in payment of expenses for the promotion or maintenance of any particular religious denomination.

4. No Religious Instructions in Government Educational Institutions— Article 28

Article 28 prohibits the imparting of religious instructions in any educational institution which is wholly maintained out of state funds or receiving aid from the state.

According to Article 28 (3) in private educational institutions which are recognised by the government or which receive financial aid of any kind from the state, no person shall be compelled to get religious education or attend religious worship against his will.

The right to religious freedom, like other fundamental rights, has certain limitations. This right can be exercised subject to public order, morality and health. It also provides that the state shall have the right to regulate or restrict any economic, financial, political or other secular activity that may be associated with a religious practice or to provide for social welfare and reform or the throwing open Hindu religious institutions of public character to all classes and sections of the Hindus. The term Hindus, include person professing the Sikh, Jain and Buddhist religions. The Constitution recognises the right of the Sikhs to wear and carry Kirpan as a part of professing the Sikh religion.

V. Cultural and Educational Rights – Articles 29, 30

The Constitution provides special protection to the minorities. Articles 29 and 30 of the Part III of the constitution guarantee to the minorities cultural and educational rights.

1. Right to Protect Language, Script and Culture – Article 29

The Constitution lays down that any section of the citizens residing in the territory of India or any part thereof having a distinct language, script or culture of its own shall have the right to conserve the same. This right is absolute as the constitution does not lay down that state can impose reasonable restrictions on it. The objective of this right is to protect the minorities in maintaining their language and culture and to prevent the majority from imposing its language and culture on the minorities.

2. Right to Establish and Administer Educational Institutions – Article 30

Under Article 30, the Constitution admits that all minorities whether based on religion or language, shall have the right to establish and administer educational institutions of their choice. They have the right to admit students to their institutions and to have their own governing bodies. The State Universities cannot impose a particular medium of instructions on the minority institutions. Further, the state while providing grant-in-aid to educational institutions cannot discriminate against such minority institutions. The minority character of such institutions cannot be destroyed by the state.

VI. Right to Constitutional Remedies – Article 32

The Rights given in the constitution become absolutely fruitless if adequate provisions are not provided for their protection. With this objective, the following four provisions have been made for the protection of Fundamental Rights under Article 32.

They are:

1. Article 32 (1) of the Constitution provides that a citizen can approach the Supreme Court of India by the process of law for the implementation of Fundamental Rights included in chapter III of the Indian Constitution.
2. According to Article 32 (2) of the Constitution, the Supreme Court of India has the right to issue writs in the nature of the Habeas Corpus, Mandamus, Prohibition, Quo-warranto and Certiorari.
3. According to Article 32 (3) of the Constitution, the Indian Parliament can power any court to issue notice within its jurisdiction without infringing or influencing the powers of the Supreme Court of India.
4. According to Article 32 (4) of the constitution, the state cannot suspend the right to constitutional remedies except in cases provided in the Constitution.

The Fundamental Rights given in Part III of the Constitution mark the beginning of a new era in the constitutional history of India. They are the foundation stone of democratic system in India. They defend individual's freedom from the autocracy of executive and legislature. They give to the people the trust that state is an instrument of social welfare but individual is not a means for the state.

They create for man an atmosphere in which he may get economic, social and political justice and fully develop his life. They determine relations between man and state. Fundamental Rights protect the interests of minorities and provide them constitutional guarantees to preserve their language, script and culture. They establish the rule of law in India. Fundamental Rights have psychological importance which no government can undermine.

The importance of Fundamental Rights is as under:

1. **Foundation of Democracy.** India earns the privilege of being the most populous democracy in the world. Fundamental Rights create an atmosphere of freedom and democracy. In Chapter III of the Constitution such rights and liberties are given to the Indian citizens which are the sheet anchor of democracy in the country.
2. **Establish Relations between the Individual and the State.** The inclusion of the long list of Fundamental Rights in the Indian Constitution is a sure indication that the main aim of the state is to protect the interests of the people. With the help of Fundamental Rights an attempt is made to establish balance between the rights of the citizens and the state because a citizen can enjoy freedom only in a state.
3. **Check on the Arbitrariness of the Government.** The Fundamental Rights impose checks on the government and thus limits the arbitrary attitude of the government. Article 15 of the constitution prohibits the government to discriminate against people in respect of color, caste, religion, race etc. All such provision tries to limit the dictatorial attitude of the government.

4. **Create Proper Conditions for the Development of Man.** Fundamental Rights create congenial and appropriate conditions for the development of the personality of the individual. These rights provide to the citizens the right to life and liberty etc. A person can choose any profession, trade or service according to his bent of mind. He can live, reside, settle and move about in any part of the country. The state services are open to all people of the country. All these conditions create favourable environment for the development of personality of the individual.
5. **Foundation of Social Democracy.** The Fundamental Rights embodied in the Indian Constitution abolish all types of discriminations based on color, caste, creed, race, religion and sex etc. The citizens have been given the right to go to public places like hotels, shops, entertainment houses, wells, tanks, and public baths etc. without any sort of discrimination. According to Article 17 untouchability has been regarded as a punishable crime. Similarly Article 18 of the Indian Constitution puts limitation on the bestowal or receipt of titles and prizes etc.
6. **Protection of the Interests of Minorities.** The Fundamental Rights make adequate provisions for the protection of the interests of various minorities. These minorities enjoy all the rights which the majority community enjoys and in addition to these they also enjoy certain other rights and privileges. The Indian Constitution provides these minorities the right to establish and administer their own educational institutions. The government cannot discriminate against such institutions while giving grants to them. In addition to this, the minorities also enjoy the right to preserve their own language, script and culture.
7. **Foundation of Rule of Law.** Article 14 of the constitution provides equality before law to all people living in the Indian territory. It implies that no discrimination will be made on the basis of the status or title of an individual. In case of violation of the laws of the land every individual is subject to the same punishment. None can be deprived of his life, liberty or property except by the rule of law established in the country. The administration of the country is being run not according to will of some individual but according to the law of the land.
8. **Establishment of Secular State.** The Fundamental Rights embodied in the Indian Constitution also provide for the establishment of a secular state. According to Article 25 to 28 of the Constitution, the individual is given the right to adopt, profess and profess any religion which he likes. These Articles also make provision for the establishment and administration of educational rights by the various minorities. The Indian citizens cannot be forced to pay any box in the name of any religion. Besides this, there is a ban on religious education being imported in government educational institutions. The State has no religion of its own but the individual possesses religious freedom.

Constitutionalism

Constitutionalism, doctrine that a government's authority is determined by a body of laws or constitution. Although constitutionalism is sometimes regarded as a synonym for limited government, that is only one interpretation and by no means the most prominent one historically. More generally constitutionalism refers to efforts to prevent arbitrary government.

At its most generic level, arbitrariness consists in the capacity of rulers to govern willfully – that is, with complete discretion – and to serve their own interests rather than those of the ruled. Constitutionalism attempts to avoid these dangers by designing mechanisms that determine who carr rule, how, and for what purposes. However, constitutional traditions differ as to what precisely counts as an arbitrary act and which mechanisms offer the best defense against arbitrary acts occurring. The classical republican tradition, as related by its neorepublican interpreters to political constitutionalism, identifies arbitrariness with domination of the ruled by their rulers and seeks to avoid it by establishing a condition of political equality characterized by a balance of power between all the relevant groups and parties within a polity, so that no one can rule without consulting the interests of the ruled. The more modern, liberal tradition identifies arbitrariness with interference with individual rights and seeks to establish protections for them via the separation of powers and a judicially protected constitution.

Both traditions are present within most democracies and can be found side by side in many constitutions. The first tradition focuses on the design and functioning of the democratic process, including the selection of electoral systems and the choice between presidential or parliamentary forms of government, of unitary or federal arrangements, and of unicameralism or bicameralism. Although the detailing of these procedural mechanisms and the relations between them usually forms the bulk of most constitutional documents, their constitutional importance has come to be eclipsed – in legal circles particularly – by the second tradition. This view emphasizes the specification and judicial protection of the different competencies of the political system and of constitutionally entrenched rights by a constitutional court. Political theorists and scientists disagree, however, on whether these two traditions are complementary, mutually entailed, or incompatible. The second is often seen as necessary to ensure the fairness of the procedures and/or the outcomes of the first. Yet it lays itself open in turn to doubts about whether courts are, or could ever be, truly bound by constitutions so that law rather than judges rule and, if so, whether judicial processes are not more arbitrary and prone to error for deciding constitutional outcomes than the democratic procedures and outcomes they are often thought to legitimately limit. In the following sections, this entry traces these two traditions and then turns to exploring their respective advantages and disadvantages and any tensions and complementarities that exist between them.

Total Revolution

Jaya Prakash once stated that Total Revolution is a combination of seven revolutions, viz., political, social, economic, cultural, ideological or intellectual, educational and spiritual; and the main motive being to bring in a change in the existing society that is in tune with the ideals of the Sarvodaya. JP had a very idealistic notion of society and it is in this endeavor, he shifted from Marxism to Socialism and later towards Sarvodaya.

By the early 1970s, JP completely withdrew from party and power politics, and con-centrated more on social regeneration through peaceful means. This did not mean that JP kept quiet while there was social and political degeneration taking root in political freedom. In order to better the situation, despite his old age, he embarked on the task of working towards bringing in a complete change in the political and economic life of India.

Initially, he tried to organize people and make them conscious or aware of the situations and then appealed to the leaders. But with no response, he began to organize youth to save the democracy from degeneration and called this revolution as Total Revolution. The momentum to the movement came when there were agitations in Gujarat and followed in Bihar as well.

In 1974, the Bihar agitations spiralled into massive protests by the people to bring about a change in the political, social and educational system. At this juncture, JP announced a fourfold plan of action that aimed to paralyze the administration, introduction of Gram Swarajya and establishing people's government.

Explaining the term 'peoples government', JP stated that it would be a small unit of democracy at the village, panchayat, or the block level, at all the three levels, if possible.

These units were regarded as the sources of the power of the people in times of peace, as well injustice or tyranny, and mainly for the reconstruction of the society on the basis of equality and the elimination of poverty, oppression and exploitation. JP further called upon the people of Bihar as well as the entire India to unite by cutting across their individual and party interests.

His motive behind charging up the Bihar students was to bring about a complete change in the entire governmental structure and the system of Indian polity. It is for this reason he called it a Total Revolution. JP presented the concept of total revolution in a very comprehensive manner. His commitment to socialist and humanistic ideas was very evident in the idea of total revolution.

He was aiming at uprooting of corruption from political and social life in India. Besides this, JP wanted to create conditions wherein the people living below the poverty line could get the minimum necessities of life. Thus, total revolution was a device for bringing about a Gandhian humanist version of an ideal society.

In his prison dairy, JP once stated that Total Revolution is a combination of seven revolutions, viz., political, social, economic, cultural, ideological or intellectual, educational and spiritual; and the main motive being to bring in a change in the existing society that is in tune with the ideals of the Sarvodaya. JP had a very idealistic notion of society and it is in this endeavor, he shifted from Marxism to Socialism and later towards Sarvodaya.

Like Gandhi, he also experimented with his own beliefs, tested his notions and modified his ideas. The inherent contradictions within the Parliamentary democracy made JP lose any faith he had in it. He opined that democracy gives no assurance for a better life to the people in the future when they are socially and economically neglected. He opined that only a peaceful revolution could bring about some change in the society.

One of the main reasons for lack of development in India, according to JP, was the widespread corruption in all walks of life. He believed that the multiparty system and general elections every five years had reared corruption. Further, the failure of economic planning and public investments is also due to this corruption.

Through this revolution, JP aimed at changing the society and also the individuals' outlook towards the society. He also asked the workers in Bihar to prepare for the long struggle for achieving the objectives of total revolution.

He laid out a plan for the movement; on how the revolution should move on the propaganda for public education, and constructive programmes consisting of creating consciousness about various social evils such as dowry system, caste conflicts, communalism and untouchability. Thus, JP had a very clear perspective of the social ideals and objectives when he took upon the task of guiding the Indian masses for a concrete action.

JP strongly believed that for democracy to be a lively and effective instrument there is an urgent need for a strong opposition, powerful public opinion, free and fear-less press, ideological and moral pressure from the academicians, and trade unions. He, in fact, advised the people to revise their thinking and attitude towards democratic functioning in India.

When Janata Party came to power, JP was hopeful that there would be a change in socio-political and economic situation in India. But unfortunately, the party leaders pursued their political ambitions and were attracted towards the corrupting influence of power, despite their pledge that they would aim at bringing about a just society. Naturally, the country slipped into old order of political rivalry and infighting.

Towards the end of his life, JP revealed his thoughts about India and the ideals for which he struggled all these years. He explained saying, India of my dreams is a community in which every individual, every resource is dedicated to the service of the weak community, dedicated to 'Antyodaya' to the well-being of the poorest and the weakest.

India of my dreams is a community in which every citizen participates in the affairs of the community. It is a community in which the weak are organized and awakened to implement reforms and to keep an eye on the rulers … it is a community in which the people have a right to and opportunity to bring them to book if they go astray in which office is not looked upon as a privilege, but as a trust given by the people … in short, my vision is of a free progressive and Gandhian India. However, his dream remained unfulfilled despite his long struggle throughout his life.

Swadeshi

The word swadeshi derives from Sanskrit and is a conjunction of two Sanskrit words. Swa means self or own and desh means country. So Swadesh means own country. Swadeshi, the adjectival form, means of one's own country, but can be loosely translated in most contexts as self-sufficiency.

Like many of Gandhi's terms, swadeshi can be used to describe the state of an individual or a community. In the case of an individual, swadeshi means acting from a position of strength to solve problems, by drawing on one's own capacities, and addressing one's own weaknesses. One person cannot solve another person's problems and proposed solutions must be made based on personal experience.

In the other, more common usage, swadeshi is the focus on acting within and from ones own community, both politically and economically. In other words, it is the interdependence of community and self-sufficiency. Gandhi believed this would lead to independence (Swaraj), as British control of India was rooted in control of her indigenous industries. Swadeshi was the key to the independence of India, and was represented by the charkha or the spinning wheel, the "center of the solar system" of Gandhi's constructive program.

Gandhi said of swadeshi:

> "The cleanest and the most popular form of Swadeshi is to stimulate hand-spinning and hand-weaving and to arrange for a judicious distribution of yarn and cloth so manufactured."
>
> "Swadeshi is an eternal principle whose neglect has brought untold grief to mankind. It means production and distribution of articles manufactured in one's own country… Swadeshi is a constructive program."
>
> "Swadeshi is that spirit in us which restricts us to the use and service of our immediate surroundings to the exclusion of the more remote… In the domain of politics, I should make use of the indigenous institutions and serve them by curing them of their proved defects. In that of economics, I should use only things that are produced by my immediate neighbours and serve those industries by making them efficient and complete where they might be found wanting. It is suggested that such Swadeshi, if reduced to practice, will lead to the millennium, because we do not expect quite to reach it within our times, so may we not abandon Swadeshi even though it may not be fully attained for generations to come."

It seems that Gandhi's prediction is becoming a reality. Swadeshi is what the progressive movement of today is calling, think globally act locally. Swadeshi is a call to the consumer to be aware of the violence caused by supporting industries that result in poverty and harm to workers and environmental degradation. In a world moving towards decentralized, localized organization, we might adapt Gandhi's strategy, replacing mass production and consumerism with community, and then form the community of communities: the Earth Community.

Satyagraha

Satyagraha, (Sanskrit and Hindi: "holding onto truth") concept introduced in the early 20th century by Mahatma Gandhi to designate a determined but nonviolent resistance to evil. Gandhi's satyagraha became a major tool in the Indian struggle against British imperialism and has since been adopted by protest groups in other countries.

According to this philosophy, satyagrahis—practitioners of satyagraha—achieve correct insight into the real nature of an evil situation by observing a nonviolence of the mind, by seeking truth in a spirit of peace and love, and by undergoing a rigorous process of self-scrutiny. In so doing, the satyagrahi encounters truth in the absolute. By refusing to submit to the wrong or to cooperate with it in any way, the satyagrahi asserts that truth. Throughout the confrontation with evil, the satyagrahi must adhere to nonviolence, for to employ violence would be to lose correct insight. Satyagrahis always warn their opponents of their intentions; satyagraha forbids any tactic suggesting the use of secrecy to one's advantage. Satyagraha includes more than civil disobedience. Its full range of application extends from the details of correct daily living to the construction of alternative political and economic institutions. Satyagraha seeks to conquer through conversion: in the end, there is neither defeat nor victory but rather a new harmony.

Satyagraha draws from the ancient Indian ideal of ahimsa ("noninjury"), which is pursued with particular rigour by Jains, many of whom live in Gujarat, where Gandhi grew up. In developing ahimsa into a modern concept with broad political consequences, as satyagraha, Gandhi also drew from the writings of Leo Tolstoy and Henry David Thoreau, from the Bible, and from the Bhagavadgita, on which he wrote a commentary. Gandhi first conceived satyagraha in 1906 in response to a law discriminating against Asians that was passed by the British colonial government of the Transvaal in South Africa. In 1917 the first satyagraha campaign in India was mounted in the indigo-growing district of Champaran. During the following years, fasting and economic boycotts were employed as methods of satyagraha in India, until the British left the country in 1947.

Critics of satyagraha, both in Gandhi's time and subsequently, have argued that it is unrealistic and incapable of universal success, since it relies upon a high standard of ethical conduct in the opponent, the representative of evil, and demands an unrealistically strong level of commitment from those struggling for social amelioration. Nonetheless, satyagraha played a significant role in the civil rights movement led by Martin Luther King, Jr., in the United States and has spawned a continuing legacy in South Asia itself.

Sarvodaya

21st century is the era of globalization. New economic policy of globalization moves on to make the world a global village. New challenges and problems have emerged before youth. The belief that all emergent problems - ecological, social, economical, political and moral-could be resolved by discoveries and technological innovations persists, filatures in the past notwithstanding. What is happening today is in line with what Gandhi almost predicted in Hind Swaraj as he prepared its manuscript in 1908. Gandhi put forward four main goals before youth for humanity, so as to move towards its destiny. These are Swaraj, Non-violence, Swadeshi and Sarvodaya. These are the main pillars of the thesis he has propounded in the Hind Swaraj. In this paper an attempt is made to focus on Sarvodaya as one of the pillars to bring Hind Swaraj. Objectives of this research paper are to know Gandhian philosophy of Sarvodaya for changing attitude of youth & aware youth for their rights & duties. Primary & secondary resources are used for this paper.

Sarvodaya is a term meaning *'Universal Uplift'* or *'Progress of All'*. The term was first coined by Mohandas Gandhi as the title of his 1908 translation of John Ruskin's tract on political economy, *"Unto This Last"*, and Gandhi came to use the term for the ideal of his own political philosophy. Later Gandhian, like the Indian nonviolence activist Vinoba Bhave, embraced the term as a name for the social movement in post-independence India which strove to ensure that self-determination and equality reached all strata of India society.

Gandhi received a copy of Ruskin's "Unto This Last" from a British friend, Mr. Henry Polak, while working as a lawyer in South Africa in 1904. In his *Autobiography*, Gandhi remembers the twenty-four hour train ride to Durban (from when he first read the book, being so in the grip of Ruskin's ideas that he could not sleep at all: "I determined to change my life in accordance with the ideals of the book." Gandhi advances the concept of Sarvodaya, which were the based on three basic principles:

- That the good of the individual is contained in the good of all.
- That a lawyer's work has the same value as the barber's in as much as all have the same right of earning their livelihood from their work.
- That is a life of labour, i.e., the life of the tiller of the soil and the handicraftsman is the life worth living.

The first of these I knew. The second I had dimly realized. The third have never occurred to me. *'Unto This Last'* made it clear as daylight for me that the second and third were contained in the first. I arose with the dawn, ready to reduce these principal to practice."

The Sarvodaya Movement has as its target the establishment of a whole network of such self-supporting village communities. The family relationships which are confined at present to the blood group will be extended to cover the whole village where distinctions based on race, creed, caste, language and so forth will completely be eliminated. Agriculture will be so planned that all the people will have enough to consume. Industry will be conducted on a cottage basis till all the people in the village are gainfully employed. The needs of the village will be determined by the people of the village themselves, through Village Council, representative of the whole village.

Principles of the Sarvodaya

- There is no centralized authority, and there is political and economic atmosphere in the villages.
- Politics will not be the instrument of power but an agency of service and *Rajnity* will yield place to *Loknity.*
- All people will be imbued with the spirit of love, fraternity, truth, non-violence and self-sacrifices. Society will function on the basis on the non-violence.
- There will be no party system and majority rule and society will be free from the evil of the tyranny of the majority.

- The sarvodaya society is socialist in the true sense of the term. All calling will be the same moral, social and economical values. The individual personality has the fullest scope for development.
- The sarvodaya society is based on equality and liberty. There is no room in it for unwholesome some competition, exploitation and class-hatred.
- Sarvodaya stands for the progress of the all. All individual should do individual labour and follow the ideal of non possession. Then it will be possible to realize the goal of: from each according to his work and to each according to his needs.
- There will be no private property, the instrument of exploitation and the source of social distinctions and hatred. Similarly, the profit motive will disappear, rent and interest to will go.
- The Sarvodaya Movement is based on Truth, Non-violence and Self-denial.
- The Sarvodaya Movement makes a sincere and bold attempt to create the necessary atmosphere to bring together such individuals with an unwavering faith in the Welfare of all.
- The gain to the individual would be small. The development of each quality depends upon every other. If all the qualities are improved a little, then the individual would gain more.

Social Democracy

Social democracy, political ideology that originally advocated a peaceful evolutionary transition of society from capitalism to socialism using established political processes. In the second half of the 20th century, there emerged a more moderate version of the doctrine, which generally espoused state regulation, rather than state ownership, of the means of production and extensive social welfare programs. Based on 19th-century socialism and the tenets of Karl Marx and Friedrich Engels, social democracy shares common ideological roots with communism but eschews its militancy and totalitarianism. Social democracy was originally known as revisionism because it represented a change in basic Marxist doctrine, primarily in the former's repudiation of the use of revolution to establish a socialist society.

The social democratic movement grew out of the efforts of August Bebel, who with Wilhelm Liebknecht cofounded the Social Democratic Workers' Party in 1869 and then effected the merger of their party with the General German Workers' Union in 1875 to form what came to be called the Social Democratic Party of Germany (Sozialdemokratische Partei Deutschlands). Bebel imbued social democracy with the belief that socialism must be installed through lawful means rather than by force. After the election of two Social Democrats to the Reichstag in 1871, the party grew in political strength until in 1912 it became the largest single party in voting strength, with 110 out of 397 seats in the Reichstag. The success of the Social Democratic Party in Germany encouraged the spread of social democracy to other countries in Europe.

The growth of German social democracy owed much to the influence of the German political theorist Eduard Bernstein. In his Die Voraussetzungen des Sozialismus und die Aufgaben der Sozialdemokratie; "The Preconditions of Socialism and the Tasks of Social Democracy"; Eng. trans. Evolutionary Socialism), Bernstein challenged the Marxist orthodoxy that capitalism was doomed, pointing out that capitalism was overcoming many of its weaknesses, such as unemployment, overproduction, and the inequitable distribution of wealth. Ownership of industry was becoming more widely diffused, rather than more concentrated in the hands of a few. Whereas Marx had declared that the subjugation of the working class would inevitably culminate in socialist revolution, Bernstein argued that success for socialism depended not on the continued and intensifying misery of the working class but rather on eliminating that misery. He further noted that social conditions were improving and that with universal suffrage the working class could establish socialism by electing socialist representatives.

The violence of the Russian Revolution of 1917 and its aftermath precipitated the final schism between the social democratic parties and the communist parties.

After World War II, social democratic parties came to power in several nations of western Europe – e.g., West Germany, Sweden, and Great Britain (in the Labour Party) – and laid the foundations for modern European social welfare programs. With its ascendancy, social democracy changed gradually, most notably in West Germany. These changes generally reflected a moderation of the 19th-century socialist doctrine of wholesale nationalization of business and industry. Although the principles of the various social democratic parties began to diverge somewhat, certain common fundamental principles emerged. In addition to abandoning violence and revolution as tools of social change, social democracy took a stand in opposition to totalitarianism. The Marxist view of democracy as a "bourgeois" facade for class rule was abandoned, and democracy was proclaimed essential for socialist ideals. Increasingly, social democracy adopted the goal of state regulation of business and industry as sufficient to further economic growth and equitable income.

State Socialism

The year 1848 is very significant in the history of Socialist thought. It was the period when one phase of socialism had ended and the latter was to be started. By this time, all Utopian socialists, viz., Robert Owen, Fourier, Blanc, St. Simonians and Proudhon proved to be utter failures.

In the trial of their schemes. When the Revolution of 1848 was over, a class of Socialism appeared, known as State Socialists who recognised STATE as an instrument for the execution of their socialists schemes. In this way, socialism developed mainly in France and England till 1848, was to a great extent utopian and idealistic and moreover, it was dominated by the middle-class spirit.

State Socialism developed in Germany during the second half of the 19th century which was based on scientific realism. State Socialism was not merely an economic doctrine; but it was also a moral and social movement. It was based upon "a certain ideal of justice and particular conception of function of society and of the State."

Since reforms, both social and economic were to be executed through a nation state, State socialism had a nationalistic character. The socialists, namely Rodbertus and Lassalle presented this idealistic doctrine; they wanted to bring a radical change in the social order with the help of the government.

State socialism has also been known as socialism of the chain in Germany because a large number of intellectuals – Professors and writers of contemporary Germany were associated with it; and as Internationalism in France.

The main tenet of State Socialism was that the State should improve and consolidate its position by bringing about legislation for the uplift of the downtrodden. Strictly speaking, it is wrong to call this socialist movement, for it did not advocate abolition of private property and unearned income. It was content with some reforms which were not very socialistic in nature.

The movement developed in two stages. In the first stage, the Laissez-faire was criticised. In the second stage Socialism proper emerged and a manifesto containing objectives of State Socialism was issued. Wagner was the leader of this new movement.

Phases of State Socialism

First Phase of State Socialism

In the formative stage, the state socialism began in Germany in the early 19th Century as an economic movement. It was not an organised one, and in fact it was a loose mingling of economic thoughts which generally criticised the free competition. There were several classical economists who criticised the ideal of free competition or Laissez-faire. They were also against individualism.

Besides, Sismondi and Cournot in France, Herman and List in Germany, and John Stuart Mill in England felt that the ideal of liberty (which classicists upheld) was likely to create a conflict between individual and social interests.

The struggle could only be resolved by seeking state intervention in these matters. Thus, these thinkers and writers were not the forerunners of State Socialism; but their criticism of Laissez-faire and their advocacy of state intervention were unconscious contributions to the tendencies which led to the growth of State Socialism.

Second Phase of State Socialism

A clear-cut formulation of the doctrine of State Socialism took place in 1872 when a historical conference of economists, jurists, administrators, politicians and professors was held at Eisenach. The leaders of this conference were Schmoller Schaffle, Buvhart and Wagner.

The Eisenach conference formulated the doctrine of State Socialism, as follows:

> "The State was a great moral institution for the education of humanity, which could enable an increasing number of people to participate in highest benefits of civilisation." The citizens of the nation were not merely in economic association with each other but were bound together by the ties of common languages, culture and political constitution. The State was the organ of the moral solidarity of the nation and hence was responsible towards the poorer sections of the society.

The following arguments were put forward by the state socialists in support of their case for state and against individualism and laissez-faire:

(i) Based on the theory of conjectures propounded by Lassalle, they argued that the weakness of individual judgement often led to economic crisis.

(ii) As Sismondi, St. Simon and Louis Blanc had stressed, the State Socialists argued that the troubles and uncertainties caused by competition among individual producers should be checked and curbed in the social interest.

(iii) The functions of the State were historically evolving. In the early stages of development, individual actions and private charity were adequate. In modern life greater 'Social character' in economic matters is expected out of necessity.

It can be seen that State Socialism was a sharp reaction against the extreme Laissez-faire of classical economists. Schmoller gave the name "MANCHESTERISM" for the extremely optimistic and liberal aspects of classicism which was fully elaborated by Cobden and Bright in England, and Bastiat in France. Thus, State Socialism was opposed to 'Manchesterism', but it qualified its stand. Individual initiative as such, was to be fostered.

State interference was to be prevailed upon in such spheres, where individual interest came to clash with the general social interest. In pursuance of this stand, the Socialists did not condemn private property and its fruits, viz., rent and interest. What they wanted was a more equitable social system to give tine worker due profit of his labour. In the sphere of distribution, they advocated a step of progressive taxation system which would bring about a leveling of social classes.

In the sphere of production, they stood for state control of such industries which are in the nature of public utilities and are likely to become monopolies, if left in the hands of individuals. Thus, they advocated the State administration of transport system, nationalisation of railways, canals, roads, municipalisation of water, gas and electricity and State operation of the banking system.

It would be wrong to presume that this programme of socialists was scarcely socialist in character, because, it upheld private property, rent and interest. It was, in reality a well-meaning programme of reform for national prosperity through state agency. The programme had a moral and ethical, rather than an economic basis. It was a far cry from the militant Marxists Socialist Programme. In fact, it was the nature of compromise.

Assessment of State Socialism

Though State Socialism remained an intellectual rather than a working class movement, its programme was tried and experimented extensively in almost all democratic countries of the world. The German Chancellor, BIS-mark applied this programme when he provided sickness and old-age insurance measures for the working class.

All the state socialist programmes were adopted and implemented in England and France with the beginning of the 20th century. It was not implemented as an application of the theory, but to meet the demand put forth by the progressive democratic opinion.

Public control and operation of utility services and progressive taxation and control of employer-employee relations were steps in recognition of more "social" character of modern life in which state interference was essential to preserve the individual's interest. The modern Welfare State when it resorts to a "Controlled" economy, only implements the programme of State Socialism.

Affirmative Action

"Affirmative action" means positive steps taken to increase the representation of women and minorities in areas of employment, education, and culture from which they have been historically excluded. When those steps involve preferential selection—selection on the basis of race, gender, or ethnicity—affirmative action generates intense controversy.

The development, defense, and contestation of preferential affirmative action has proceeded along two paths. One has been legal and administrative as courts, legislatures, and executive departments of government have made and applied rules requiring affirmative action. The other has been the path of public debate, where the practice of preferential treatment has spawned a vast literature, pro and con. Often enough, the two paths have failed to make adequate contact, with the public quarrels not always very securely anchored in any existing legal basis or practice.

The ebb and flow of public controversy over affirmative action can be pictured as two spikes on a line, the first spike representing a period of passionate debate that began around 1972 and tapered off after 1980, and the second indicating a resurgence of debate in the 1990s leading up to Supreme Court's decisions in 2003 and 2016 upholding certain kinds of affirmative action. The first spike encompassed controversy about gender and racial preferences alike. This is because in the beginning affirmative action was as much about the factory, the fire-house, and the corporate suite as about the college campus. The second spike represents a quarrel about race and ethnicity. This is because the burning issue at the turn of the twentieth-first century is about college admissions. At selective colleges, women need no boost; African-Americans and Hispanics do.

In 1972, affirmative action became an inflammatory public issue. True enough, the Civil Rights Act of 1964 already had made something called "affirmative action" a remedy federal courts could impose on violators of the Act. Likewise, after 1965 federal contractors had been subject to President Lyndon Johnson's Executive Order 11246, requiring them to take "affirmative action" to make sure they were not discriminating. But what did this 1965 mandate amount to? The Executive Order assigned to the Secretary of Labor the job of specifying rules of implementation. In the meantime, as the federal courts were enforcing the Civil Rights Act against discriminating companies, unions, and other institutions, the Department of Labor mounted an ad hoc attack on the construction industry by cajoling, threatening, negotiating, and generally strong-arming reluctant construction firms into a series of region-wide "plans" in which they committed themselves to numerical hiring goals. Through these contractor commitments, the Department could indirectly pressure recalcitrant labor unions, who supplied the employees at job sites.

While the occasional court case and government initiative made the news and stirred some controversy, affirmative action was pretty far down the list of public excitements until the autumn of 1972, when the Secretary of Labor's Revised Order No. 4, fully implementing the Executive Order, landed on campus by way of directives from the Department of Health, Education, and Welfare. Its predecessor, Order No. 4, first promulgated in 1970, cast a wide net over American institutions, both public and private. By extending to all contractors the basic apparatus of the construction industry "plans," the Order imposed a one-size-fits-all system of "underutilization analyses," "goals," and "timetables" on hospitals, banks, trucking companies, steel mills, printers, airlines—indeed, on all the scores of thousands of institutions, large and small, that did business with the government, including a special set of institutions with a particularly voluble and articulate constituency, namely, American universities.

At first, university administrators and faculty found the rules of Order No. 4 murky but hardly a threat to the established order. The number of racial and ethnic minorities receiving PhDs each year and thus eligible for faculty jobs was tiny. Any mandate to increase their representation on campus would require more diligent searches by universities, to be sure, but searches fated nevertheless largely to mirror past results. The 1972 Revised Order, on the other hand, effected a change that punctured any campus complacency: it included women among the "protected classes" whose "underutilization" demanded the setting of "goals" and "timetables" for "full utilization". Unlike African-Americans and Hispanics, women were getting PhDs in substantial and growing numbers. If the affirmative action required of federal contractors was a recipe for "proportional representation," then Revised Order No. 4 was bound to leave a large footprint on campus. Some among the professoriate exploded in a fury of opposition to the new rules, while others responded with an equally vehement defense of them.

As it happened, these events coincided with another development, namely the "public turn" in philosophy. For several decades Anglo-American philosophy had treated moral and political questions obliquely. On the prevailing view, philosophers were suited only to do "conceptual analysis"—they could lay bare, for example, the conceptual architecture of the idea of justice, but they were not competent to suggest political principles, constitutional arrangements, or social policies that actually did justice. Philosophers might do "meta-ethics" but not "normative ethics." This viewed collapsed in the 1970s under the weight of two counter-blows. First, John Rawls published in 1971 A Theory of Justice, an elaborate, elegant, and inspiring defense of a normative theory of justice (Rawls 1971). Second, in the same year Philosophy & Public Affairs, with Princeton University's impeccable pedigree, began life, a few months after Florida State's Social Theory and Practice. These journals, along with a re-tooled older periodical, Ethics, became self-conscious platforms for socially and politically engaged philosophical writing, born out of the feeling that in time of war (the Vietnam War) and social tumult (the Civil Rights Movement, Women's Liberation), philosophers ought to do, not simply talk about, ethics. In 1973, Philosophy & Public Affairs published Thomas Nagel's "Equal Treatment and Compensatory Justice" and Judith Jarvis Thomson's "Preferential Hiring", and the philosophical literature on affirmative action burgeoned forth.

In contention was the nature of those "goals" and "timetables" imposed on every contractor by Revised Order No. 4. Weren't the "goals" tantamount to "quotas," requiring institutions to use racial or gender preferences in their selection processes? Some answered "no". Properly understood, affirmative action did not require (or even permit) the use of gender or racial preferences. Others said "yes". Affirmative action, if it did not impose preferences outright, at least countenanced them. Among the yea-sayers, opinion divided between those who said preferences were morally permissible and those who said they were not. Within the "morally permissible" set, different writers put forward different justifications.

The essays by Thomson and Nagel defended the use of preferences but on different grounds. Thomson endorsed job preferences for women and African-Americans as a form of redress for their past exclusion from the academy and the workplace. Preferential policies, in her view, worked a kind of justice. Nagel, by contrast, argued that preferences might work a kind of social good, and without doing violence to justice. Institutions could for one or another good reason properly depart from standard meritocratic selection criteria because the whole system of tying economic reward to earned credentials was itself indefensible.

Justice and desert lay at the heart of subsequent arguments. Several writers took to task Thomson's argument that preferential hiring justifiably makes up for past wrongs. Preferential hiring seen as redress looks perverse, they contended, since it benefits individuals (African-Americans and women possessing good educational credentials) least likely harmed by past wrongs while it burdens individuals (younger white male applicants) least likely to be responsible for past wrongs. Instead of doing justice, contended the critics, preferential treatment violated rights. What rights were at issue? The right of an applicant "to equal consideration", the right of the maximally competent to an open position, or the right of everyone to equal opportunity. Moreover, according to the critics, preferential treatment confounded desert by severing reward from a "person's character, talents, choices and abilities", by "subordinating merit, conduct, and character to race", and by disconnecting outcomes from actual liability and damage.

Defenders of preferences were no less quick to enlist justice and desert in their cause. Mary Anne Warren, for example, argued that in a context of entrenched gender discrimination, gender preferences might improve the "overall fairness" of job selections. Justice and individual desert need not be violated.

If individual men's careers are temporarily set back because of...[job preferences given to women], the odds are good that these same men will have benefited in the past and/or will benefit in the future—

not necessarily in the job competition, but in some ways—from sexist discrimination against women. Conversely, if individual women receive apparently unearned bonuses [through preferential selection], it is highly likely that these same women will have suffered in the past and/or will suffer in the future from…sexist attitudes.

Likewise, James Rachels defended racial preferences as devices to neutralize unearned advantages by whites. Given the pervasiveness of racial discrimination, it is likely, he argued, that the superior credentials offered by white applicants do not reflect their greater effort, desert, or even ability. Rather, the credentials reflect their mere luck at being born white. "Some white…[applicants] have better qualifications…only because they have not had to contend with the obstacles faced by their African-American competitors". Rachels was less confident than Warren that preferences worked uniformly accurate offsets. Reverse discrimination might do injustice to some whites; yet its absence would result in injustices to African-Americans who have been unfairly handicapped by their lesser advantages.

Rachels' diffidence was warranted in light of the counter-responses. If racial and gender preferences for jobs (or college admissions) were supposed to neutralize unfair competitive advantages, they needed to be calibrated to fit the variety of backgrounds aspirants brought to any competition for these goods. Simply giving blanket preferences to African-Americans or women seemed much too ham-handed an approach if the point was to micro-distribute opportunities fairly.

SOCIAL INSTITUTIONS

The term, "social institution" is somewhat unclear both in ordinary language and in the philosophical literature. However, contemporary sociology is somewhat more consistent in its use of the term. Typically, contemporary sociologists use the term to refer to complex social forms that reproduce themselves such as governments, the family, human languages, universities, hospitals, business corporations, and legal systems. A typical definition is that proffered by Jonathan Turner: "a complex of positions, roles, norms and values lodged in particular types of social structures and organising relatively stable patterns of human activity with respect to fundamental problems in producing life-sustaining resources, in reproducing individuals, and in sustaining viable societal structures within a given environment." Again, Anthony Giddens says: "Institutions by definition are the more enduring features of social life." He goes on to list as institutional orders, modes of discourse, political institutions, economic institutions and legal institutions. The contemporary philosopher of social science, Rom Harre follows the theoretical sociologists in offering this kind of definition: "An institution was defined as an interlocking double-structure of persons-as-role-holders or office-bearers and the like, and of social practices involving both expressive and practical aims and outcomes." He gives as examples schools, shops, post offices, police forces, asylums and the British monarchy.

In this entry the above-noted contemporary sociological usage will be followed. Doing so has the virtue of grounding philosophical theory in the most salient empirical discipline, namely, sociology.

At this point it might be asked why a theory of social institutions has, or ought to have, any philosophical interest; why not simply leave such theorising to the sociologists? One important reason stems from the normative concerns of philosophers. Philosophers, such as John Rawls, have developed elaborate normative theories concerning the principles of justice that ought to govern social institutions. Yet they have done so in the absence of a developed theory of the nature and point of the very entities (social institutions) to which the principles of justice in question are supposed to apply. Surely the adequacy of one's normative account of the justice or otherwise of any given social institution, or system of social institutions, will depend at least in part on the nature and point of that social institution or system.

The entry has five sections. In the first section various salient accounts of social institutions are discussed. Accounts emanating from sociological theory as well as philosophy are mentioned. Here, as elsewhere, the boundaries between philosophy and non-philosophical theorising in relation to an empirical science are vague. Hence, it is important to note the theories of the likes of Durkheim and Talcott Parsons as well as those of John Searle and David Lewis.

Any account of social institutions must begin by informally marking off social institutions from other social forms. Unfortunately, as noted above, in ordinary language the terms "institutions" and "social institutions" are used to refer to a miscellany of social forms, including conventions, rules, rituals, organisations, and systems of organisations. Moreover, there are a variety of theoretical accounts of institutions, including sociological as well as philosophical ones. Indeed, many of these accounts of what are referred to as institutions are not accounts of the same phenomena; they are at best accounts of overlapping fields of social phenomena. Nevertheless, it is possible, firstly, to mark off a range of related social forms that would be regarded by most theorists as being properly describable as social institutions; and, secondly, to compare and contrast some of the competing theoretical accounts of the "social institutions" in question.

Social institutions need to be distinguished from less complex social forms such as conventions, rules, social norms, roles and rituals. The latter are among the constitutive elements of institutions.

Social institutions also need to be distinguished from more complex and more complete social entities, such as societies or cultures, of which any given institution is typically a constitutive element. A society, for example, is more complete than an institution since a society—at least as traditionally understood—is more or less self-sufficient in terms of human resources, whereas an institution is not. Thus, arguably, for an entity to be a society it must sexually reproduce its membership, have its own language and educational system, provide for itself economically and—at least in principle—be politically independent.

Social institutions are often organisations. Moreover, many institutions are *systems* of organisations. For example, capitalism is a particular kind of economic institution, and in modern times capitalism consists in large part in specific organisational forms—including multi-national corporations—organised into a system. Further, some institutions are *meta-institutions*; they are institutions (organisations) that organise other institutions (including systems of organisations). For example, governments are meta-institutions. The institutional end or function of a government consists in large part in organising other institutions (both individually and collectively); thus governments regulate and coordinate economic systems, educational institutions, police and military organisations and so on largely by way of (enforceable) legislation.

Nevertheless, some institutions are not organisations, or systems of organisations, and do not require organisations. For example, the English language is an institution, but not an organisation. Moreover, it would be possible for a language to exist independently of any organisations specifically concerned with language. Again, consider an economic system that does not involve organisations, e.g. a barter system involving only individuals. An institution that is not an organisation or system of organisations comprises a relatively specific type of agent-to-agent interactive activity, e.g. communication or economic exchange, that involves: (i) differentiated actions, e.g. communication involves speaking and hearing/understanding, economic exchange involves buying and selling, that are; (ii) performed repeatedly and by multiple agents; (iii) in compliance with a structured unitary system of conventions, e.g. linguistic conventions, monetary conventions, and social norms, e.g. truth-telling, property rights.

In this entry the concern is principally with social institutions (including meta-institutions) that are also organisations or systems of organisations. However, it should be noted that institutions of language, such as the English language, are often regarded not simply as institutions but as more fundamental than many other kinds of institution by virtue of being presupposed by, or in part constitutive of, other institutions. Searle, for example, holds to the latter view. A case might also be made that the family is a more fundamental institution than others for related reasons, e.g. it is the site of sexual reproduction and initial socialisation.

Note also that uses of the term "institution" in such expressions as "the institution of government", are often ambiguous. Sometimes what is meant is a particular token, e.g. the current government in Australia, sometimes a type, i.e. the set of properties instantiated in any actual government, and sometimes a set of tokens, i.e. all governments. Restricting the notion of an institution to organisations is helpful in this regard; the term "organisation" almost always refers to a particular token. On the other hand, the term "institution" connotes a certain gravity not connoted by the term "organisation"; so arguably those institutions that are organisations are organisations that have a central and important role to play in or for a society. Being central and important to a society, such roles are usually long lasting ones; hence institutions are typically trans-generational.

Having informally marked off social institutions from other social forms, let us turn to a consideration of some general properties of social institutions. Here there are four salient properties, namely, structure, function, culture and sanctions.

Roughly speaking, an institution that is an organisation or system of organisations consists of an embodied (occupied by human persons) structure of differentiated roles. These roles are defined in terms of tasks, and rules regulating the performance of those tasks. Moreover, there is a degree of interdependence among these roles, such that the performance of the constitutive tasks of one role cannot be undertaken, or cannot be undertaken except with great difficulty, unless the tasks constitutive of some other role or roles in the structure have been undertaken or are being undertaken. Further, these roles are often related to one another hierarchically, and hence involve different levels of status and degrees of authority. Finally, on teleological and functional accounts, these roles are related to one another in part in virtue of their contribution to (respectively) the *end(s)* or *function(s)* of the institution; and the realisation of these ends or function normally involves interaction among the institutional actors in question and external non-institutional actors. (The assumption here is that the concept of an end and of a function are distinct concepts.) The constitutive roles of an institution and their relations to one another can be referred to as the *structure* of the institution.

Note that on this conception of institutions as *embodied* structures of roles and associated rules, the nature of any institution at a given time will to some extent reflect the personal character of different role occupants, especially influential role occupants, e.g. the British Government during the Second World War reflected to some extent Winston Churchill's character. Moreover, institutions in this sense are dynamic, evolving entities; as such, they have a history, the diachronic structure of a narrative and (usually) a partially open-ended future.

Aside from the formal and usually explicitly stated, or defined, tasks and rules, there is an important implicit and informal dimension of an institution roughly describable as institutional *culture*. This notion comprises the informal attitudes, values, norms, and the ethos or "spirit" which pervades an institution. Culture in this sense determines much of the activity of the members of that institution, or at least the manner in which that activity is undertaken. So while the explicitly determined rules and tasks might say nothing about being secretive or "sticking by one's mates come what may" or having a hostile or negative attitude to particular social groups, these attitudes and practices might in fact be pervasive; they might be part of the culture. Naturally, there can be competing cultures within a single organisation; the culture comprised of attitudes and norms that is aligned to the formal and official complex of tasks and rules might compete with an informal and "unofficial" culture that is adhered to by a substantial sub-element of the organisation's membership.

It is sometimes claimed that in addition to structure, function and culture, social institutions necessarily involve sanctions. It is uncontroversial that social institutions involve informal sanctions, such as moral disapproval following on non-conformity to institutional norms. However, some theorists, e.g. Jon Elster, argue that formal sanctions, such as punishment, are a necessary feature of institutions. Formal sanctions are certainly a feature of many institutions, notably legal systems; however, they do not seem to be a feature of all institutions. Consider, for example, an elaborate and longstanding system of informal economic exchange among members of different societies that have no common system of laws or enforced rules. Again, a spoken language such as pidgin English, is presumably an institutions; yet breaches of its constitutive norms and conventions might not attract any formal sanctions.

Thus far we have informally marked off social institutions from other social forms, and we have identified a number of general properties of social institutions. It is now time to outline some of the main theoretical accounts of social institutions.

Notwithstanding our understanding of social institutions as complex social forms, some theoretical accounts of institutions identify institutions with relatively simple social forms—especially conventions, social norms or rules. At one level this is merely a verbal dispute; contra our procedure here, such simpler forms could simply be termed "institutions". However, at another level the dispute is not merely verbal, since what we are calling "institutions" would on such a view consist simply of sets of conventions, social norms or rules. Let us refer to such accounts as *atomistic* theories of institutions . Schotter is a case in point as is North. The best known contemporary form of atomism is rational choice theory and it has been widely accepted in, indeed it is in part constitutive of, modern economics. The most influential philosophical theory within a broadly rational choice framework is David Lewis' theory of conventions. According to Lewis, conventions are regularities in action that solve coordination problems confronted by individual agents. Agents conform to the regularity because they prefer to do so, given others conform, and they believe that others will conform.

The "atoms" within atomistic accounts themselves typically consist of the actions of individual human persons, e.g. conventions as regularities in action. The individual agents are not themselves defined in terms of institutional forms, such as institutional roles. Hence atomistic theories of institutions tend to go hand in glove with atomistic theories of all collective entities, e.g. a society consists of an aggregate of individual human persons. Moreover, atomistic theories tend to identify the individual agent as the locus of moral value. On this kind of view, social forms, including social institutions, have moral value only derivatively, i.e. only in so far as they contribute to the prior needs, desires or other requirements of individual agents.

The regularities in action (or rules or norms) made use of in such atomistic accounts of institutions cannot simply be a single person's regularities in action (or a single person's rules or norms prescribing his or her individual action alone); rather there must be interdependence of action such that, for example, agent *A* only performs action *x*, if other agents, *B* and *C* do likewise. Moreover, some account of the interdependence of action in question is called for, e.g. that it is not the sort of interdependence of action involved in conflict situations (although it might arise as a solution to a prior conflict situation).

Assume that the conventions, norms or rules in question are social in the sense that they involve the required interdependence of action, e.g. the parties to any given convention, or the adherent to any such norm or rule, conform to (respectively) the convention, norm or rule on the condition that others do. Nevertheless, such interdependence of action is not sufficient for a convention, norm or rule, or even a set of conventions, norms or rules, to be an institution. Governments, universities, corporations etc. are structured, unitary entities. Accordingly, a mere *set* of conventions (or norms or rules) does not constitute an institution. For example, the set of conventions comprising the convention to drive on the left, the convention to utter, "Australia", to refer to Australia, and the convention to use chopsticks does not constitute an institution. Accordingly, a problem for atomistic accounts of social institutions is the need to provide an account of the structure and unity of social institutions, and an account that is faithful to atomism, e.g. that the structure is essentially aggregative in nature.

By contrast with atomistic accounts of social institutions, *holistic*—including *structuralist-functionalist*—accounts stress the inter-relationships of institutions (structure) and their contribution to larger and more complete social complexes, especially societies (function). Thus according to Barry Barnes: "Functionalist theories in the social sciences seek to describe, to understand and in most cases to explain the orderliness and stability of entire social systems. In so far as they treat individuals, the treatment comes after and emerges from analysis of the system as a whole. Functionalist theories move from an understanding of the whole to an understanding of the parts of that whole, whereas individualism proceeds in the opposite direction". Moreover, "such accounts list the "functions" of the various institutions. They describe the function of the economy as the production of goods and services essential to the operation of the other institutions and hence the system as a whole." Such theorists include Durkheim, Radcliffe-Brown and Parsons. Of particular concern to these theorists was the moral decay consequent (in their view) upon the demise of strong, mutually supportive social institutions. Durkheim, for example, advocated powerful professional associations. He said:

> A system of moral morals is always the affair of a group and can operate only if the group protects them by its authority. It is made up of rules which govern individuals, which compel them to act in such and such a way, and which impose limits to their inclinations and forbid them to go beyond. Now there is only one moral power—moral, and hence common to all—which stands above the individual and which can legitimately make laws for him, and that is collective power. To the extent the individual is left to his own devices and freed from all social constraint, he is unfettered by all moral constraint. It is not possible for professional ethics to escape this fundamental condition of any system of morals. Since, then, the society as a whole feels no concern in professional ethics, it is imperative that there be special groups in the society, within which these morals may be evolved, and whose business it is to see that they are observed.

Moreover, here the meta-institution of government obviously has a pivotal directive and integrative role in relation to other institutions and their inter-relationships, even though government is itself simply one institution within the larger society. Further, holistic accounts of institutions lay great stress on institutional roles defined in large part by social norms; institutional roles are supposedly largely, or even wholly, constitutive of the identity of the individual human agents who occupy these roles. (Individuals participate in a number of institutions and hence occupy a number of institutional roles; hence the alleged possibility of their identity being constituted by a number of different institutional roles.)

Many such holistic accounts deploy and depend on the model, or at least analogy, of an organism. A salient historical figure here is Herbert Spencer. On this holistic, organicist model, social institutions are analogous to the organs or limbs of a human body. Each organ or limb has a function the realisation of which contributes to the well-being of the body as a whole, and none can exist independently of the others. Thus the human body relies on the stomach to digest food in order to continue living, but the stomach cannot exist independently of the body or of other organs, such as the heart. Likewise, it is suggested, any given institution, e.g. law courts, contributes to the well-being of the society as a whole, and yet is dependent on other institutions, e.g. government. Here the "well-being" of the society as a whole is sometimes identified with the stability and continuation of the society as it is; hence the familiar charge that holistic, organicist accounts are inherently politically conservative. This political conservatism transmutes into political authoritarianism when society is identified with the system of institutions that constitute the nation-state and the meta-institution of the nation-state—the government—is assigned absolute authority in relation to all other institutions. Hence the contrasting emphasis in political liberalism on the separation of powers among, for example, the executive, the legislature and the judiciary.

Holistic accounts of social institutions often invoke the terminology of internal and external relations. An internal relation is one that is definitive of, or in some way essential to, the entity it is a relation of; by contrast, external relations are not in this way essential. Thus being married to someone is an internal relation of spouses; if a man is a husband then necessarily he stands in the relation of being married to someone else. Likewise, if someone is a judge in a court of law then necessarily he stands in an adjudicative relationship to defendants. Evidently, many institutional roles are possessed of, and therefore in part defined by, their internal relations to other institutional roles.

However, the existence of institutional roles with internal relations to other institutional roles does not entail a holistic account of social institutions. For the internal relations in question might not be relations among institutional roles in different institutions; rather they might simply be internal relations among different institutional roles in the same institution. On the other hand, the existence of institutional roles with internal relations does undermine the attempts of certain forms of atomistic individualism to reduce institutions to the individual human agents who happen to constitute them.

Here it is important to distinguish the plausible view that institutions are not reducible to the individual human persons who constitute them from the controversial view that institutions are themselves agents possessed of minds and a capacity to reason. Peter French is an advocate of the latter view (French 1984). (See also Margaret Gilbert's notion of a "plural subject"). If we ascribe intentions to organisations, e.g. ascribe to Gulf Oil the intention to maximise profits, then we are apparently committed to ascribing to Gulf Oil a whole network of sophisticated propositional attitudes concerning economic production, the workings of markets, and so on. Moreover, a being with such a network of propositional attitudes would be capable of high level thought, and therefore be possessed of a language in which to do this thinking. Further, this agent's thought processes would include planning for its future and doing so on the basis of its past mistakes, and the likely responses of other corporations. Such a corporate agent is self-reflective; it not only distinguishes its present from both its past and its future, and itself from other corporations, it reflects on itself for the purpose of transforming itself. Such a being has higher order propositional attitudes, including beliefs about its own beliefs and intentions, and conceives of itself as a unitary whole existing over time. In short, it looks as though we now have a fully conscious, indeed self-conscious, being on our hands. Nor do matters rest here. For if we are prepared to grant Gulf Oil a mind, then why not all its subsidiaries, as well as all other companies and subsidiaries worldwide. Indeed how can we stop at corporations? Surely governments, universities, schools, supermarkets, armies, banks, political parties, trade unions, English soccer teams' supporters' clubs (at least) now all have minds, albeit in some cases smaller minds (so to speak). Not only do we have a self-conscious mind, but apparently we have an ever expanding community of self-conscious minds; or so it could be argued.

Thus far we have discussed atomistic and holistic accounts of social institutions. However, there is a third possibility, namely, (what might be termed) *molecular* accounts. Roughly speaking, a molecular account of an institution would not seek to reduce the institution to simpler atomic forms, such as conventions; nor would it seek to define an institution in terms of its relationships with other institutions and its contribution to the larger societal whole. Rather, each institution would be analogous to a molecule; it would have constitutive elements ("atoms") but also have its own structure and unity. Moreover, on this conception each social institution would have a degree of independence vis-a-vis other institutions and the society at large; on the other hand, the set of institutions might itself under certain conditions form a unitary system of sorts, e.g. a contemporary liberal democratic nation-state comprised of a number of semi-autonomous public and private institutions functioning in the context of the meta-institution of government.

A general problem for holistic organicist accounts of social institutions—as opposed to molecular accounts—is that social institutions can be responses to *trans-societal* requirements or needs. Accordingly, an institution is not necessarily a constitutive element of some given society in the sense that it is both in part constitutive of that society and wholly contained within that society. Examples of such trans-societal institutions are the international financial system, the international legal system, the United Nations and some multi-national corporations. Indeed, arguably any given element of such a trans-societal institution stands in some *internal* relations to elements of other societies.

This raises the question as to whether or not the category of social institution might be *conceptually* independent of the category of society in the sense that it might be conceptually possible for there to be an institution without there being a society. This is consistent with the impossibility of there being a society without institutions. That is, perhaps societies presuppose social institutions, but not vice-versa.

Here we need to distinguish conceptual (or logical) impossibility from *practical* impossibility. For example, it might well be that no society and no system of institutions can exist, practically speaking, without the meta-institution of government; absent government, societies and social institutions tend to disintegrate. However, it would not follow from this that the institution of government is logically necessary for the existence of societies and (non-government) institutions.

The claim that institutions are conceptually independent of societies goes hand in glove with the proposition that human social life is dependent on institutions, but not necessarily on societies as such. The picture here is of human beings who are members of many different social groups, e.g. academic philosophers, EU citizens, speakers of the Spanish language, each of which group is sustained by one or more social institutions; however, there are no societies as such. For those who lived, or are living, in traditional tribes or clans this picture might be incomprehensible. However, it does have some resonance for those living in contemporary cosmopolitan settings.

In response to this claim of the independence, and perhaps priority, of institutions vis-ā-vis societies it can be pointed out that trans-*societal* institutions presuppose societies. This is true enough. However, this would not rescue the holistic organicist conception; for such trans-societal institutions are not generally—and certainly not necessarily—constitutive "organs" of some larger society. Moreover, international institutions presuppose only nation-states, and the latter might be conceived of in narrowly political terms. Contemporary nation-states are not, it might be insisted, complete and self-sufficient societies, such as traditional tribes or clans might have been.

In this section atomistic and holistic accounts of institutions have been discussed in general terms. It is now time to focus on two recent molecular theories, namely, the collective acceptance theory and the teleological theory.

UNIT 8

SOCIAL AND POLITICAL PHILOSOPHY: WESTERN

PLATO: IDEAL STATE AND JUSTICE

Ideal State

In his most celebrated book the Republic, Plato gives the theory of an ideal state. As far as a state is concerned, Plato gives ideas about how to build an Ideal commonwealth, who should be the rulers of the Ideal state and how to achieve justice in the Ideal state. Plato finds the state as the more suitable place to discuss about the morality than an individual, because everything is easier to see in the large than in the small. A state, says Plato, is a man 'writ' large against the sky. The elements that make up a city correspond to the elements that constitute the individual human soul.

The justice of the city is the same as it is for the individual. For Plato, there is not one morality for the individuals and another for the state. Like the tripartite individual human soul every state has three parts which are its three classes.

The elements that constitute the human soul are as follows:

1. Bodily appetite, 2. Spirited elements 3. Reason

Like the tripartite individual human soul, every state has three parts such as:

1. Producer class, 2. Military class, 3. Ruling class

Plato finds the origin of the state in the various needs of people. Nobody is self-sufficient. So, to meet the various needs men created the political institution. To Plato, in the beginning there was only one class namely the producing class. Then emerged the guardian class. From the guardian class emerged the ruling class.

In a state the producer class will consist of those people to whom the bodily appetites are dominant and who live for money. The producer class is made up of farmer, blacksmiths, fishermen, carpenters, shoe-makers, weavers, labourers, merchants, retailers and bankers. The life of the producer class is much easier than the life of the rulers or the guardians. The life of the produce class follows the old familiar patterns of home and property, family and children, work, rest, and recreation. By nature the producers have money.

Each member of the producer class will be educated by being taught a trade or a profession – farming, banking, carpentry-according to his or her capabilities and to the needs of the society, both of which will be determined by the guardians.

The military class will be drawn from that type of men to whom the spirited element is dominant and who live for success in aggressive and courageous acts. The members of the ruling class will be drawn from that type of man to whom reason is dominant and who lives only for truth. A state should be ruled only by the elite group of the most rational. In the ideal state each of these three classes will perform a vital function on behalf of the organic totality of the state.

Selection of the Ruling Class

Plato gives most emphasis on the selection of the ruling class. The selection of the ruling class is from all classes by natural intellectual capacity. Women as well as men possess the natural capacity of intelligence to become members of the ruling class.

Plato proposes that an ideal state will be governed by a person who is highly educated, has passion for truth and has achieved the greatest wisdom of knowledge of the good. The ruler of this ideal state is called the Philosopher king.

The Philosopher king has several important functions to perform. The rulers, said Plato, should be the one who has been fully educated, one who has come to understand the difference between the visible world and the invisible world, between the realm of opinion and the realm of knowledge, between appearance and reality. The Philosopher king is one whose education, in short, has led him up step by step through the ascending degrees of knowledge of the Divided line until at last he has a knowledge of the good.

To reach this point, the Philosopher King will have progressed through many stages of education. By the time he is eighteen years old, he will have had training in literature, music and elementary mathematics. His literature would be censored. Music also would be prescribed so that seduction music would be replaced by a more wholesome, martial meter. For the next few years there would be extensive physical and military training. At the age twenty a few would be selected to pursue an advanced course in mathematics. At age thirty, a five year course in dialectic and moral philosophy would begin. The next fifteen years would be spent gathering practical experience through public service. Finally, at age fifty, the ablest men would reach the highest level of knowledge, the vision of the good and would then be ready for the task of governing the state.

Both the ruling class and the military class are forbidden to possess any private property or any money. They must live, men and women like soldiers in barracks, with common meals and sleeping quarters. Their food, clothing and equipment will be provided by the producers. This food must be simple and restricted to moderate quantities. They are too have no family life, in order to avoid any conflict between family loyalties and their loyalty to the state.

When they are at the physical prime of life, their sexual gratification is restricted to officially designated and infrequent occasions on which they are required to breed children to maintain the number of the guardian class. These occasions Plato calls sacred Marriage which are temporary unions for the sake of producing children.

Justice in the State

Like the human soul, the justice will be achieved in a state when each class fulfils their respective functions. Justice is a general virtue. It means that all parts are fulfilling their special functions. As the craftsmen embody the element of appetite, they will also reflect the virtue of temperance. Temperance is not limited to the craftsmen but applies to all the classes, for it indicates, when it is achieved, the willingness of the lower to be ruled by the higher. Still temperance applies in a special way to the craftsmen subordinate to the two higher levels.

The guardians, who defend the state, manifest the virtue of courage. To assure the state that these guardians will always fulfill their functions. Special training and provision are made for them. Unlike the craftsmen, who marry and own property, the guardians will have both property and wives in common. Plato considered these arrangements essential if the guardians were to attain true courage, for courage means knowing what to fear and what not to fear. The only real object of fear for the guardian should be fear of moral evil. He must never fear poverty and privation, and for this reason mode of life should be isolated from possessions.

Thus, in his Republic Plato gives the theory of an ideal state. But later the theory of the ideal state was severely criticized by Aristotle.

Justice

Plato in his philosophy gives very important place to the idea of justice. He used the Greek word "Dikaisyne" for justice which comes very near to the work 'morality' or 'righteousness', it properly includes within it the whole duty of man. It also covers the whole field of the individual's conduct in so far as it affects others. Plato contended that justice is the quality of soul, in virtue of which men set aside the irrational desire to taste every pleasure and to get a selfish satisfaction out of every object and accommodated themselves to the discharge of a single function for the general benefit.

Plato was highly dissatisfied with the prevailing degenerating conditions in Athens. The Athenian democracy was on the verge of ruin and was ultimately responsible for Socrate's death. Plato saw in justice the only remedy of saving Athens from decay and ruin, for nothing agitated him in contemporary affairs more than amateurishness, needle someness and political selfishness which was rampant in Athens of his day in particular and in the entire Greek world in general. In additional, Sophistic teaching of the ethics of self-satisfaction resulted in the excessive individualism also induced the citizens to capture the office of the State for their own selfish purpose and eventually divided "Athens in to two hostile camps of rich and poor, oppressor and oppressed. "Evidently, these two factors amateur needle someness and excessive individualism became main targets of Plato's attack. The attack came in the form of the construction of an ideal society in which "Justice" reigned supreme, since Plato found in justice the remedy for curing these evils. Thus, we are to inquire in this study the nature of justice as propounded by Plato as a fundamental principle of well-order society.

It is to be noted that before Plato many theories of justice were prevalent. The inquiry about justice goes from the crudest to the most refined interpretation of it. It remains therefore to inquire what were the reasons for which he rejected those views. Thus before discussing Plato's own concept of justice, it is necessary to analyze those traditional theories of justice were rejected by him.

Cephalus who was a representative of traditional morality of the ancient trading class established the traditional theory of justice . According to him 'justice consists in speaking the truth and paying one's debt. Thus Cephalus identifies justice with right conduct. Polemarchus also holds the same view of justice but with a little alteration. According to him "justice seems to consist in giving what is proper to him". The simple implication of this conception of justice may be that "justice is doing good to friends and harm to enemies." This is also a traditional maxim of Greek morality.

The views propounded by Cephalus and Polemarchus were criticized by Plato. The view point of Cephalus was criticised on the ground that there may be cases in which this formula may involve the violation of the spirit of right and his formula does not admit of being taken as a sound universal principle of life. It is not right to restore deadly weapons to a man after he has gone mad. And the contention of Polemarchus was condemned by Plato on the ground that it was only easy to speak of giving good to friend and evil to enemies. But if the friends only a friend in seeming, and an enemy in reality, then what will happen? Then under such circumstances whether we should rigidly follow the definition and do him good or we may use discretion and do him evil? But to do evil to anybody, including one's enemy was inconsistent with the most elementary conception of morality. Thus, this conception of justice regulated the relations between individuals on individualistic principles and ignores the society as a whole.

Thrasymachus who represented the new and critical view, propounded the radical theory of justice. He defines justice as "the interest of the stronger". In the other words, might is right. For while, every man acts for himself and tries to get what he can, the strongest is sure to get what he wants and as in a state the Government is the strongest, it will try to get and it will get, whatever it wants for itself. Thus, for Thrasymachus justice means personal interest of the ruling group in any state or we can further define it as "another's good". Laws are made by the ruling party in its own interest. Those who violate such laws are punished because violation of such laws is treated as violation of justice. Socrates criticises the definition of justice given by Thrasymachus and he says just as a physician studies and exercises his power not in his interest but in the interest of a patient, the Government of any kind shall do what is good for the people for whom it exercises its art. But Thrasymachus advances some more arguments in support of his concept of justice and injustice.

An unjust is superior to a just in character and intelligence.

Injustice is a source of strength.

Injustice brings happiness.

Socrates attacks these points of Thrasymachus and throws light on the nature of justice.

Justice implies superior character and intelligence while injustice means deficiency in both respects. Therefore, just men are superior in character and intelligence and are more effective in action. As injustice implies ignorance, stupidity and badness, It cannot be superior in character and intelligence. A just man is wiser because he acknowledges the principle of limit.

Unlimited self-assertion is not a source of strength for any group organized for common purpose, Unlimited desire and claims lead to conflicts.

Life of just man is better and happier. There is always some specific virtue in everything, which enables it to work well. If it is deprived of that virtue, it works badly. The soul has specific functions to perform. When it performs its specific functions, it has specific excellence or virtue. If, it is deprived of its peculiar virtue, it cannot possibly do its work well. It is agreed that the virtue of the soul is justice. The soul which is more virtuous or in other words more just is also the happier soul. Therefore, a just man lives happy. A just soul, in other words a just man, lives well; an unjust cannot.

At this juncture the new point of view is stated by Glaucon and he put Forward a form of what was later to be known as a social contract theory, arguing we are only moral because, it pays us or we have to be. Glaucon describes the historical evolution of the society where justice as a necessity had become the shield of the weaker. In the primitive stage of society without law and government, man was free to do whatever he likes. So the stronger few enjoyed the life at the sufferance of the weaker many. The weaker, however, realised that they suffered more injustice. Faced with this situation they came to an agreement and instituted law and government through a sort of social contract and preached the philosophy of just. Therefore, justice in this way something artificial and unnatural. It is the "product of convention". It is through this artificial rule of justice and law that the natural selfishness of man is chained. A dictate of the weaker many, for the interest of the weaker many, as against the natural and superior power of the stronger few.

Plato realises that all theories propounded by Cephalus, Thrasymachus and Glaucon, contained one common element. That one common element was that all the them treated justice as something external "an accomplishment, an importation, or a convention, they have, none of them carried it into the soul or considered it in the place of its habitation." Plato prove that justice does not depend upon a chance, convention or upon external force. It is the right condition of the human soul by the very nature of man when seen in the fullness of his environment. It is in this way that Plato condemned the position taken by Glaucon that justice is something which is external. According to Plato, it is internal as it resides in the human soul. "It is now regarded as an inward grace and its understanding is shown to involve a study of the inner man." It is, therefore, natural and no artificial. It is therefore, not born of fear of the weak but of the longing of the human soul to do a duty according to its nature.

Thus, after criticising the conventional ideas of justice presented differently by Cephalus, Polymarchus, Thrasymachus and Glaucon, Plato now gives us his own theory of justice. Plato strikes an analogy between the human organism on the one hand and social organism on the other. Human organism according to Plato contains three elements-Reason, Spirit and Appetite. An individual is just when each part of his or her soul performs its functions without interfering with those of other elements. For example, the reason should rule on behalf of the entire soul with wisdom and forethought. The element of spirit will sub-ordinate itself to the rule of reason. Those two elements are brought into harmony by combination of mental and bodily training. They are set in command over the appetites which form the greater part of man's soul. Therefore, the reason and spirit have to control these appetites which are likely to grow on the bodily pleasures. These appetites should not be allowed, to enslave the other elements and usurp the dominion to which they have no right. When all the three agree that among them the reason alone should rule, there is justice within the individual.

Corresponding to these three elements in human nature there are three classes in the social organism-Philosopher class or the ruling class which is the representative of reason; auxiliaries, a class of warriors and defenders of the country is the representative of spirit; and the appetite instinct of the community which consists of farmers, artisans and are the lowest rung of the ladder. Thus, weaving a web between the human organism and the social organism, Plato asserts that functional specialization demands from every social class to specialize itself in the station of life allotted to it. Justice, therefore to Plato is like a manuscript which exists in two copies, and one of these is larger than the other. It exists both in the individual and the society. But it exists on a larger scale and in more visible form in the society. Individually "justice is a 'human virtue' that makes a man self consistent and good: Socially, justice is a social consciousness that makes a society internally harmonious and good."

Justice is thus a sort of specialization. It is simply the will to fulfill the duties of one's station and not to meddle with the duties of another station, and its habitation is, therefore, in the mind of every citizen who does his duties in his appointed place. It is the original principle, laid down at the foundation of the State, "that one man should practice one thing only and that the thing to which his nature was best adopted". True justice to Plato, therefore, consists in the principle of non-interference. The State has been considered by Plato as a perfect whole in which each individual which is its element, functions not for itself but for the health of the whole. Every element fulfils its appropriate function. Justice in the platonic state would, therefore, be like that harmony of relationship where the Planets are held together in the orderly movement. Plato was convinced that a society which is so organized is fit for survival. Where man are out of their natural places, there the co-ordination of parts is destroyed, the society disintegrates and dissolves. Justice, therefore, is the citizen sense of duties.

Justice is, for Plato, at once a part of human virtue and the bond, which joins man together in society. It is the identical quality that makes good and social . Justice is an order and duty of the parts of the soul, it is to the soul as health is to the body. Plato says that justice is not mere strength, but it is a harmonious strength. Justice is not the right of the stronger but the effective harmony of the whole. All moral conceptions revolve about the good of the whole-individual as well as social.

LOCKE, HOBBES, ROUSSEAU: SOCIAL CONTRACT THEORY

Thomas Hobbes

Thomas Hobbes, 1588-1679, lived during the most crucial period of early modern England's history: the English Civil War, waged from 1642-1648. To describe this conflict in the most general of terms, it was a clash between the King and his supporters, the Monarchists, who preferred the traditional authority of a monarch, and the Parliamentarians, most notably led by Oliver Cromwell, who demanded more power for the quasi-democratic institution of Parliament. Hobbes represents a compromise between these two factions. On the one hand he rejects the theory of the Divine Right of Kings, which is most eloquently expressed by Robert Filmer in his Patriarcha or the Natural Power of Kings, (although it would be left to John Locke to refute Filmer directly). Filmer's view held that a king's authority was invested in him (or, presumably, her) by God, that such authority was absolute, and therefore that the basis of political obligation lay in our obligation to obey God absolutely. According to this view, then, political obligation is subsumed under religious obligation.

On the other hand, Hobbes also rejects the early democratic view, taken up by the Parliamentarians, that power ought to be shared between Parliament and the King. In rejecting both these views, Hobbes occupies the ground of one who is both radical and conservative.

He argues, radically for his times, that political authority and obligation are based on the individual self-interests of members of society who are understood to be equal to one another, with no single individual invested with any essential authority to rule over the rest, while at the same time maintaining the conservative position that the monarch, which he called the Sovereign, must be ceded absolute authority if society is to survive.

Hobbes' political theory is best understood if taken in two parts: his theory of human motivation, Psychological Egoism, and his theory of the social contract, founded on the hypothetical State of Nature. Hobbes has, first and foremost, a particular theory of human nature, which gives rise to a particular view of morality and politics, as developed in his philosophical masterpiece, Leviathan, published in 1651. The Scientific Revolution, with its important new discoveries that the universe could be both described and predicted in accordance with universal laws of nature, greatly influenced Hobbes. He sought to provide a theory of human nature that would parallel the discoveries being made in the sciences of the inanimate universe.

His psychological theory is therefore informed by mechanism, the general view that everything in the universe is produced by nothing other than matter in motion. According to Hobbes, this extends to human behavior. Human macro-behavior can be aptly described as the effect of certain kinds of micro-behavior, even though some of this latter behavior is invisible to us. So, such behaviors as walking, talking, and the like are themselves produced by other actions inside of us. And these other actions are themselves caused by the interaction of our bodies with other bodies, human or otherwise, which create in us certain chains of causes and effects, and which eventually give rise to the human behavior that we can plainly observe.

We, including all of our actions and choices, are then, according to this view, as explainable in terms of universal laws of nature as are the motions of heavenly bodies. The gradual disintegration of memory, for example, can be explained by inertia. As we are presented with ever more sensory information, the residue of earlier impressions 'slows down' over time. From Hobbes' point of view, we are essentially very complicated organic machines, responding to the stimuli of the world mechanistically and in accordance with universal laws of human nature.

In Hobbes' view, this mechanistic quality of human psychology implies the subjective nature of normative claims. 'Love' and 'hate', for instance, are just words we use to describe the things we are drawn to and repelled by, respectively. So, too, the terms 'good' and 'bad' have no meaning other than to describe our appetites and aversions. Moral terms do not, therefore, describe some objective state of affairs, but are rather reflections of individual tastes and preferences.

In addition to Subjectivism, Hobbes also infers from his mechanistic theory of human nature that humans are necessarily and exclusively self-interested. All men pursue only what they perceive to be in their own individually considered best interests - they respond mechanistically by being drawn to that which they desire and repelled by that to which they are averse. This is a universal claim: it is meant to cover all human actions under all circumstances – in society or out of it, with regard to strangers and friends alike, with regard to small ends and the most generalized of human desires, such as the desire for power and status.

Everything we do is motivated solely by the desire to better our own situations, and satisfy as many of our own, individually considered desires as possible. We are infinitely appetitive and only genuinely concerned with our own selves. According to Hobbes, even the reason that adults care for small children can be explicated in terms of the adults' own self-interest (he claims that in saving an infant by caring for it, we become the recipient of a strong sense of obligation in one who has been helped to survive rather than allowed to die).

In addition to being exclusively self-interested, Hobbes also argues that human beings are reasonable. They have in them the rational capacity to pursue their desires as efficiently and maximally as possible. Their reason does not, given the subjective nature of value, evaluate their given ends, rather it merely acts as "Scouts, and Spies, to range abroad, and find the way to the things Desired". Rationality is purely instrumental. It can add and subtract, and compare sums one to another, and thereby endows us with the capacity to formulate the best means to whatever ends we might happen to have.

From these premises of human nature, Hobbes goes on to construct a provocative and compelling argument for why we ought to be willing to submit ourselves to political authority. He does this by imagining persons in a situation prior to the establishment of society, the State of Nature.

According to Hobbes, the justification for political obligation is this: given that men are naturally self-interested, yet they are rational, they will choose to submit to the authority of a Sovereign in order to be able to live in a civil society, which is conducive to their own interests. Hobbes argues for this by imagining men in their natural state, or in other words, the State of Nature. In the State of Nature, which is purely hypothetical according to Hobbes, men are naturally and exclusively self-interested, they are more or less equal to one another, (even the strongest man can be killed in his sleep), there are limited resources, and yet there is no power able to force men to cooperate. Given these conditions in the State of Nature, Hobbes concludes that the State of Nature would be unbearably brutal. In the State of Nature, every person is always in fear of losing his life to another. They have no capacity to ensure the long-term satisfaction of their needs or desires. No long-term or complex cooperation is possible because the State of Nature can be aptly described as a state of utter distrust. Given Hobbes' reasonable assumption that most people want first and foremost to avoid their own deaths, he concludes that the State of Nature is the worst possible situation in which men can find themselves. It is the state of perpetual and unavoidable war.

The situation is not, however, hopeless. Because men are reasonable, they can see their way out of such a state by recognizing the laws of nature, which show them the means by which to escape the State of Nature and create a civil society. The first and most important law of nature commands that each man be willing to pursue peace when others are willing to do the same, all the while retaining the right to continue to pursue war when others do not pursue peace. Being reasonable, and recognizing the rationality of this basic precept of reason, men can be expected to construct a Social Contract that will afford them a life other than that available to them in the State of Nature.

This contract is constituted by two distinguishable contracts. First, they must agree to establish society by collectively and reciprocally renouncing the rights they had against one another in the State of Nature. Second, they must imbue some one person or assembly of persons with the authority and power to enforce the initial contract. In other words, to ensure their escape from the State of Nature, they must both agree to live together under common laws, and create an enforcement mechanism for the social contract and the laws that constitute it. Since the sovereign is invested with the authority and power to mete out punishments for breaches of the contract which are worse than not being able to act as one pleases, men have good, albeit self-interested, reason to adjust themselves to the artifice of morality in general, and justice in particular.

Society becomes possible because, whereas in the State of Nature there was no power able to "overawe them all", now there is an artificially and conventionally superior and more powerful person who can force men to cooperate. While living under the authority of a Sovereign can be harsh (Hobbes argues that because men's passions can be expected to overwhelm their reason, the Sovereign must have absolute authority in order for the contract to be successful) it is at least better than living in the State of Nature. And, no matter how much we may object to how poorly a Sovereign manages the affairs of the state and regulates our own lives, we are never justified in resisting his power because it is the only thing which stands between us and what we most want to avoid, the State of Nature.

According to this argument, morality, politics, society, and everything that comes along with it, all of which Hobbes calls 'commodious living' are purely conventional. Prior to the establishment of the basic social contract, according to which men agree to live together and the contract to embody a Sovereign with absolute authority, nothing is immoral or unjust - anything goes. After these contracts are established, however, then society becomes possible, and people can be expected to keep their promises, cooperate with one another, and so on. The Social Contract is the most fundamental source of all that is good and that which we depend upon to live well. Our choice is either to abide by the terms of the contract, or return to the State of Nature, which Hobbes argues no reasonable person could possibly prefer.

Given his rather severe view of human nature, Hobbes nonetheless manages to create an argument that makes civil society, along with all its advantages, possible. Within the context of the political events of his England, he also managed to argue for a continuation of the traditional form of authority that his society had long since enjoyed, while nonetheless placing it on what he saw as a far more acceptable foundation.

John Locke

For Hobbes, the necessity of an absolute authority, in the form of a Sovereign, followed from the utter brutality of the State of Nature. The State of Nature was completely intolerable, and so rational men would be willing to submit themselves even to absolute authority in order to escape it. For John Locke,

1632-1704, the State of Nature is a very different type of place, and so his argument concerning the social contract and the nature of men's relationship to authority are consequently quite different. While Locke uses Hobbes' methodological device of the State of Nature, as do virtually all social contract theorists, he uses it to a quite different end. Locke's arguments for the social contract, and for the right of citizens to revolt against their king were enormously influential on the democratic revolutions that followed, especially on Thomas Jefferson, and the founders of the United States.

Locke's most important and influential political writings are contained in his Two Treatises on Government. The first treatise is concerned almost exclusively with refuting the argument of Robert Filmer's Patriarcha, that political authority was derived from religious authority, also known by the description of the Divine Right of Kings, which was a very dominant theory in seventeenth-century England. The second treatise contains Locke's own constructive view of the aims and justification for civil government, and is titled "An Essay Concerning the True Original Extent and End of Civil Government".

According to Locke, the State of Nature, the natural condition of mankind, is a state of perfect and complete liberty to conduct one's life as one best sees fit, free from the interference of others. This does not mean, however, that it is a state of license: one is not free to do anything at all one pleases, or even anything that one judges to be in one's interest. The State of Nature, although a state wherein there is no civil authority or government to punish people for transgressions against laws, is not a state without morality. The State of Nature is pre-political, but it is not pre-moral. Persons are assumed to be equal to one another in such a state, and therefore equally capable of discovering and being bound by the Law of Nature. The Law of Nature, which is on Locke's view the basis of all morality, and given to us by God, commands that we not harm others with regards to their "life, health, liberty, or possessions". Because we all belong equally to God, and because we cannot take away that which is rightfully His, we are prohibited from harming one another. So, the State of Nature is a state of liberty where persons are free to pursue their own interests and plans, free from interference, and, because of the Law of Nature and the restrictions that it imposes upon persons, it is relatively peaceful.

The State of Nature therefore, is not the same as the state of war, as it is according to Hobbes. It can, however devolve into a state of war, in particular, a state of war over property disputes. Whereas the State of Nature is the state of liberty where persons recognize the Law of Nature and therefore do not harm one another, the state of war begins between two or more men once one man declares war on another, by stealing from him, or by trying to make him his slave. Since in the State of Nature there is no civil power to whom men can appeal, and since the Law of Nature allows them to defend their own lives, they may then kill those who would bring force against them. Since the State of Nature lacks civil authority, once war begins it is likely to continue. And this is one of the strongest reasons that men have to abandon the State of Nature by contracting together to form civil government.

Property plays an essential role in Locke's argument for civil government and the contract that establishes it. According to Locke, private property is created when a person mixes his labor with the raw materials of nature. So, for example, when one tills a piece of land in nature, and makes it into a piece of farmland, which produces food, then one has a claim to own that piece of land and the food produced upon it. (This led Locke to conclude that America didn't really belong to the natives who lived there, because they were, on his view, failing to utilize the basic material of nature. In other words, they didn't farm it, so they had no legitimate claim to it, and others could therefore justifiably appropriate it.) Given the implications of the Law of Nature, there are limits as to how much property one can own:

one is not allowed to take more from nature than one can use, thereby leaving others without enough for themselves. Because nature is given to all of mankind by God for its common subsistence, one cannot take more than his own fair share. Property is the linchpin of Locke's argument for the social contract and civil government because it is the protection of their property, including their property in their own bodies, that men seek when they decide to abandon the State of Nature.

According to Locke, the State of Nature is not a condition of individuals, as it is for Hobbes. Rather, it is populated by mothers and fathers with their children, or families - what he calls "conjugal society". These societies are based on the voluntary agreements to care for children together, and they are moral but not political. Political society comes into being when individual men, representing their families, come together in the State of Nature and agree to each give up the executive power to punish those who transgress the Law of Nature, and hand over that power to the public power of a government. Having done this, they then become subject to the will of the majority. In other words, by making a compact to leave the State of Nature and form society, they make "one body politic under one government" and submit themselves to the will of that body. One joins such a body, either from its beginnings, or after it has already been established by others, only by explicit consent. Having created a political society and government through their consent, men then gain three things which they lacked in the State of Nature: laws, judges to adjudicate laws, and the executive power necessary to enforce these laws. Each man therefore gives over the power to protect himself and punish transgressors of the Law of Nature to the government that he has created through the compact.

Given that the end of "men's uniting into common-wealths" is the preservation of their wealth, and preserving their lives, liberty, and well-being in general, Locke can easily imagine the conditions under which the compact with government is destroyed, and men are justified in resisting the authority of a civil government, such as a King. When the executive power of a government devolves into tyranny, such as by dissolving the legislature and therefore denying the people the ability to make laws for their own preservation, then the resulting tyrant puts himself into a State of Nature, and specifically into a state of war with the people, and they then have the same right to self-defense as they had before making a compact to establish society in the first place. In other words, the justification of the authority of the executive component of government is the protection of the people's property and well-being, so when such protection is no longer present, or when the king becomes a tyrant and acts against the interests of the people, they have a right, if not an outright obligation, to resist his authority. The social compact can be dissolved and the process to create political society begun anew.

Because Locke did not envision the State of Nature as grimly as did Hobbes, he can imagine conditions under which one would be better off rejecting a particular civil government and returning to the State of Nature, with the aim of constructing a better civil government in its place. It is therefore both the view of human nature, and the nature of morality itself, which account for the differences between Hobbes' and Locke's views of the social contract.

Jean-Jacques Rousseau

Jean-Jacques Rousseau, 1712-1778, lived and wrote during what was arguably the headiest period in the intellectual history of modern France – the Enlightenment. He was one of the bright lights of that intellectual movement, contributing articles to the Encyclopdie of Diderot, and participating in the salons in Paris, where the great intellectual questions of his day were pursued.

Rousseau has two distinct social contract theories. The first is found in his essay, Discourse on the Origin and Foundations of Inequality Among Men, commonly referred to as the Second Discourse, and is an account of the moral and political evolution of human beings over time, from a State of Nature to modern society. As such it contains his naturalized account of the social contract, which he sees as very problematic. The second is his normative, or idealized theory of the social contract, and is meant to provide the means by which to alleviate the problems that modern society has created for us, as laid out in the Social Contract.

Rousseau wrote his Second Discourse in response to an essay contest sponsored by the Academy of Dijon. (Rousseau had previously won the same essay contest with an earlier essay, commonly referred to as the First Discourse.) In it he describes the historical process by which man began in a State of Nature and over time 'progressed' into civil society. According to Rousseau, the State of Nature was a peaceful and quixotic time. People lived solitary, uncomplicated lives. Their few needs were easily satisfied by nature. Because of the abundance of nature and the small size of the population, competition was non-existent, and persons rarely even saw one another, much less had reason for conflict or fear. Moreover, these simple, morally pure persons were naturally endowed with the capacity for pity, and therefore were not inclined to bring harm to one another.

As time passed, however, humanity faced certain changes. As the overall population increased, the means by which people could satisfy their needs had to change. People slowly began to live together in small families, and then in small communities. Divisions of labor were introduced, both within and between families, and discoveries and inventions made life easier, giving rise to leisure time. Such leisure time inevitably led people to make comparisons between themselves and others, resulting in public values, leading to shame and envy, pride and contempt. Most importantly however, according to Rousseau, was the invention of private property, which constituted the pivotal moment in humanity's evolution out of a simple, pure state into one characterized by greed, competition, vanity, inequality, and vice. For Rousseau the invention of property constitutes humanity's 'fall from grace' out of the State of Nature.

Having introduced private property, initial conditions of inequality became more pronounced. Some have property and others are forced to work for them, and the development of social classes begins. Eventually, those who have property notice that it would be in their interests to create a government that would protect private property from those who do not have it but can see that they might be able to acquire it by force. So, government gets established, through a contract, which purports to guarantee equality and protection for all, even though its true purpose is to fossilize the very inequalities that private property has produced. In other words, the contract, which claims to be in the interests of everyone equally, is really in the interests of the few who have become stronger and richer as a result of the developments of private property. This is the naturalized social contract, which Rousseau views as responsible for the conflict and competition from which modern society suffers.

The normative social contract, argued for by Rousseau in The Social Contract (1762), is meant to respond to this sorry state of affairs and to remedy the social and moral ills that have been produced by the development of society. The distinction between history and justification, between the factual situation of mankind and how it ought to live together, is of the utmost importance to Rousseau. While we ought not to ignore history, nor ignore the causes of the problems we face, we must resolve those problems through our capacity to choose how we ought to live. Might never makes right, despite how often it pretends that it can.

The Social Contract begins with the most oft-quoted line from Rousseau: "Man was born free, and he is everywhere in chains". This claim is the conceptual bridge between the descriptive work of the Second Discourse, and the prescriptive work that is to come. Humans are essentially free, and were free in the State of Nature, but the 'progress' of civilization has substituted subservience to others for that freedom, through dependence, economic and social inequalities, and the extent to which we judge ourselves through comparisons with others. Since a return to the State of Nature is neither feasible nor desirable, the purpose of politics is to restore freedom to us, thereby reconciling who we truly and essentially are with how we live together. So, this is the fundamental philosophical problem that The Social Contract seeks to address: how can we be free and live together? Or, put another way, how can we live together without succumbing to the force and coercion of others? We can do so, Rousseau maintains, by submitting our individual, particular wills to the collective or general will, created through agreement with other free and equal persons. Like Hobbes and Locke before him, and in contrast to the ancient philosophers, all men are made by nature to be equals, therefore no one has a natural right to govern others, and therefore the only justified authority is the authority that is generated out of agreements or covenants.

The most basic covenant, the social pact, is the agreement to come together and form a people, a collectivity, which by definition is more than and different from a mere aggregation of individual interests and wills. This act, where individual persons become a people is "the real foundation of society". Through the collective renunciation of the individual rights and freedom that one has in the State of Nature, and the transfer of these rights to the collective body, a new 'person', as it were, is formed. The sovereign is thus formed when free and equal persons come together and agree to create themselves anew as a single body, directed to the good of all considered together.

So, just as individual wills are directed towards individual interests, the general will, once formed, is directed towards the common good, understood and agreed to collectively. Included in this version of the social contract is the idea of reciprocated duties: the sovereign is committed to the good of the individuals who constitute it, and each individual is likewise committed to the good of the whole. Given this, individuals cannot be given liberty to decide whether it is in their own interests to fulfill their duties to the Sovereign, while at the same time being allowed to reap the benefits of citizenship. They must be made to conform themselves to the general will, they must be "forced to be free".

For Rousseau, this implies an extremely strong and direct form of democracy. One cannot transfer one's will to another, to do with as he or she sees fit, as one does in representative democracies. Rather, the general will depends on the coming together periodically of the entire democratic body, each and every citizen, to decide collectively, and with at least near unanimity, how to live together, i.e., what laws to enact. As it is constituted only by individual wills, these private, individual wills must assemble themselves regularly if the general will is to continue.

One implication of this is that the strong form of democracy which is consistent with the general will is also only possible in relatively small states. The people must be able to identify with one another, and at least know who each other are. They cannot live in a large area, too spread out to come together regularly, and they cannot live in such different geographic circumstances as to be unable to be united under common laws.

Although the conditions for true democracy are stringent, they are also the only means by which we can, according to Rousseau, save ourselves, and regain the freedom to which we are naturally entitled.

Rousseau's social contract theories together form a single, consistent view of our moral and political situation. We are endowed with freedom and equality by nature, but our nature has been corrupted by our contingent social history. We can overcome this corruption, however, by invoking our free will to reconstitute ourselves politically, along strongly democratic principles, which is good for us, both individually and collectively.

ISAIAH BERLIN

Late nineteenth-century German neo-Kantians had regarded philosophy as the 'scientia scientiarum', the science of the sciences. That is, science was concerned with enquiring into, and establishing, how it is possible to know or understand anything else: its goal was to understand understanding, to know what knowledge is and how it can be achieved.

Berlin remained vague about where these concepts and categories came from, and perhaps only once made at all explicit what the distinction was between these two types of element in the structure of our thought. Given his overall outlook, and hints scattered through his writings, it seems likely that he believed they come mainly from culture, education, ordinary experience and common social practices, as well as philosophical theories. Some might be 'inbuilt' to the extent that they are influenced by certain basic needs or tendencies intrinsic to human beings, or (like Kant's examples of space and time) are required to make sense of the world and human existence in ways comprehensible to our brains, given the manner in which these are able to function. But Berlin believed that only a few of the concepts and categories that we use are like this; many are cultural or theoretical artefacts, subject to deliberate alteration or change in response to experience. Examples of basic concepts that have been transient include a teleological conception of nature—that is, the view that everything that exists in the world exists for a purpose, and is defined by the purpose that it pursues—and a conception of human beings as wholly different from animals, as opposed to a view that sees them as (particularly well-developed) animals.

As for the difference between concepts and categories, a passage in Historical Inevitability appears to show that categories (Berlin's examples here are 'the three dimensions and infinite extent of ordinary perceptual space, the irreversibility of temporal processes, the multiplicity and countability of material objects') are more capacious, unspecific and abstract than concepts. However, the boundary between the two is left open, and it is unclear at what point it is crossed in the sequence of increasingly specific and variable examples Berlin gives: colours, shapes, (gustatory) tastes, 'the uniformities on which the sciences are based', 'the categories of value', 'moral standards', 'rules of etiquette', subjective preferences of taste. Concepts are thus perhaps related to categories somewhat as species to genus, though Berlin does not put it in exactly these terms, and the evidence for his view does not point to any precise, or consistent, position.

Berlin did not offer a definitive statement or theory about concepts and categories, not only because to do so involved doing the sort of philosophical work from which he shrank, but also because he thought that different concepts and categories differed in their origins, function, necessity, malleability etc. For him, such concepts and categories were simply facts about the way we think, which were philosophically significant, but best approached in historical or psychological terms, rather than as Kantian transcendental ideas (that is, ideas which are wholly prior to experience, and are necessary conditions for any kind of knowledge).

Berlin believed that philosophers make two kinds of contribution to the consideration of philosophical questions. The first is to reformulate these questions by suggesting a new outlook on the world that liberates the intellect from the state of intellectual quasi-cramp that has caused the problem. The second, critical rather than creative, contribution is to provide a violent shock to dogmatic assumptions about the solutions to philosophical questions, thus creating new problems and inspiring further thought. For a philosopher to do this required considerable force of character, and a certain amount of exaggeration and simplification, as well as self-confidence and persistence. Later in life Berlin described himself as a historian of ideas rather than as a philosopher, despite the fact that his account of the nature of philosophy emphasised philosophy's historical dimension. This reflected his (high) standards—which he did not believe himself to meet—for considering someone a genuine or significant philosopher.

The topics that dominated Berlin's early work on philosophy were the doctrines of verification and phenomenalism, derived from the Vienna Circle by way of A. J. Ayer. In the 1930s Berlin and his philosophical peers at Oxford were occupied primarily with the philosophy of knowledge: How do, or can, we know things, and what does it mean when we say we know something? They argued that these questions were tied up with the use of language, and the evaluation of the meaning of statements with questions such as 'How do we know what a statement means, or if it has any meaning at all?' Verificationism held that the meaning of a statement was to be found in the way in which it could be verified; if it couldn't be verified—that is, shown to be true, or proven false—it had no meaning as a statement of fact, but was merely an expression of personal taste, or meaningless. Phenomenalism held that all our knowledge comes from our sense impressions: we can know only sense data, i.e. the deliverances of perceptual experience. Anything not founded on sensory experience is nonsense.

Berlin regarded these doctrines as beneficial in clearing away confusions and exposing errors. But, while he believed that the world of human experience is all that we can know, he rejected verifiability as the only, or the most plausible, criterion for judging beliefs or hypotheses, and maintained throughout his life that many statements that could not be directly verified by empirical observation were nevertheless clearly meaningful. He therefore warned his colleagues that the principle of verification would lead to untenable consequences, and would, if not abandoned or considerably revised, breed new fallacies in the place of those it had dispelled. Berlin argued that there are conceptual truths, such as relationships of degree, similarity or contrast, which are universal, and which inform our experience, but are not subject to empirical test. These fundamental properties of qualities and relations are brute facts which we cannot deny or think without, but which we can also not verify by inspection.

Berlin's approach in these early years was shaped by the emphasis on the analysis of the meaning of words then being championed by his friend J.L. Austin. As Berlin explained at the time, 'Words are examined by philosophers for the purpose of discovering whether, as they are used in successful communication, they tend to exhibit or obscure some characteristic by which one type of fact differs from another, or alternatively suggest falsely the existence of distinctions which direct inspection of experience fails to reveal. This is done because inattention to either tends to lead to systematic confusion and error, not necessarily in the use of words, which, being conventional and intended for common practice and not the convenience of philosophers, is rightly not altered by their criticisms, but in the accurate discrimination and description of irreducible types of experience'.

The term derives from the Ionian philosophers, the founders of Western philosophy, such as Thales, who offered different theories about the composition of the universe; a hallmark of these theories was the attempt to discover a single substance out of which everything else is composed.

The distinction between the human or cultural sciences—history, philosophy, law and the various social sciences, such as sociology, economics, anthropology etc.—had become a major issue in nineteenth-century German philosophy. It continued to play an important part in Germany in the earlier twentieth century, and also became a significant issue in the English-speaking world, due both to the influence of the Vienna Circle and to the emergence of the social sciences as an increasingly self-confident and respected field of study. Berlin's work, even though it invoked earlier figures such as G. B. Vico and J.G. Herder, closely resembled, and was influenced by, attempts by such thinkers as Heinrich Rickert, Wilhelm Dilthey and Max Weber to explain the nature of the human sciences.

Berlin acknowledged that there were certain human sciences that sought to emulate the aims of the natural sciences, by trying to discover regularities in human behaviour, and refining them into explanatory laws. Berlin was dubious regarding such disciplines—economics, sociology, psychology among them—but acknowledged that such scientific studies of human behaviour had some value. He maintained, though, that history remained fundamentally different from the natural sciences in its aims and techniques. Other human sciences may seek to abstract from a large number of stable similarities and recurrences in human behaviour across many different cases, in order to construct useful, applicable ideal models to help better understand such behaviour.

But history is different: it is concerned with exploring and understanding individual cases as individual, that is, unique, non-recurrent, changing and unstable. It is richer in description and less rigorous in explanation.

Other human sciences necessarily abstract: their descriptive power is extensive rather than intensive, their descriptions thinner. The subject-matter of history, on the other hand, involves a thick texture of criss-crossing, constantly changing and melting conscious and unconscious beliefs and assumptions. History is an 'amalgam, a rich brew composed of apparently disparate ingredients'. In looking for satisfactory and satisfying historical accounts, we look for 'something full enough and concrete enough to meet our conception of public life [...] seen from as many points of view and at as many levels as possible, including as many components, factors, aspects as the widest and deepest knowledge, the greatest analytical power, insight, imagination can present'.

Historical explanation is arrangement of the discovered facts in patterns which satisfy us because they accord with life—the variety of human experience and activity—as we know it and can imagine it. The historian seeks to capture the unique pattern and peculiar characteristics of a particular subject: to paint a portrait, rather than take an X-ray image.

Berlin took up the problem of free will and determinism, and the related topic of the role of individual choice and agency in history, both indirectly, through an examination of Leo Tolstoy's philosophy of history. These questions had, however, likely preoccupied him since his work on Marx in the mid-1930s, when he would have encountered them in the form of Plekhanov's defence of historical determinism. Plekhanov's work served as a challenge to Berlin's belief in the historical importance of individuals, and his conception of morality, based as it was on the human capacity for choice.

The influence on Berlin of Soviet Communism is obvious here; but while this was the main inspiration and target for his attack, his critique could also be, and was, applied to Nazism, and even to the more complacent and inhumane policies of capitalist Western democracies.

Apart from one essay on ancient Greek individualism, he devoted scant attention to the history of the ideas in the ancient world. As for the Middle Ages, while Berlin could admit that the period might have been superior to what followed in some respects—greater public order, intellectual security, social cohesion etc.—he regarded it as by and large an intellectually blank period, because of the very stability and conservatism of its intellectual life. Berlin's interest in Renaissance thought was greater, though it yielded only one essay — an original examination of 'The Originality of Machiavelli'.

Berlin's writings on the history of ideas can be classified in several different ways. One is geographical, yielding as a first category works on Russian intellectual and cultural history, particularly of the nineteenth century; here belong his several essays on Herzen, his two studies of Tolstoy, his pieces on Turgenev, Belinsky and Plekhanov, as well as those on Russian populism and the theme of artistic commitment in Russian thought. The other geographical category covers the history of ideas in Western Europe, primarily focusing on Germany, but also encompassing France and Italy (with glances at England and Switzerland). (A third category may be made of Berlin's several essays on modern, secular Jewish thinkers.) It is also natural to divide his historical essays into portraits of individuals (in addition to those already named, Vico, Herder, Hamann, Rousseau, Kant, Maistre, Saint-Simon, Fichte, Hegel, Hess, Marx, Mill, Sorel, Verdi, Meinecke and others) and examinations of larger epochs, movements and themes—most notably the Enlightenment and the Counter-Enlightenment, the romantic movement and nineteenth-century socialism.

Berlin derived this interpretation of the Enlightenment's assumptions and inconsistencies from Plekhanov's works on the history of materialism.

Berlin focused, in his accounts of the Enlightenment, on the radical, materialist, naturalist, proto-Utilitarian element among the philosophes — Holbach, Helvétius, La Mettrie—and the more mild-mannered Condorcet, though he acknowledged, and sought to encompass, other figures—Montesquieu, Voltaire, Hume, Kant (the last two seen, however, as forerunners of the Enlightenment's critics, however unintentionally), and sometimes Rousseau.

These included the ultramontane Catholic reactionary Joseph de Maistre (whom he portrayed as a precursor of Fascism and the author of a disturbingly compelling, dark and savage vision of human life as essentially characterised by conflict); the Italian antiquarian and critic of scientism Giambattista Vico; and pre-romantic German enemies of Enlightenment rationalism and universalism such as Hamann and Herder.

Berlin used the terms 'values', 'ideals' and 'goals' more or less—but not quite—interchangeably. Values, for Berlin, are ideas about what it is good to be and do—about what sort of life, what sort of character, what sort of actions, what state of being it is desirable to aspire to.

Most prominent among these other pluralist thinkers have been Stuart Hampshire, Bernard Williams, Michael Walzer, Thomas Nagel, John Gray, Steven Lukes, John Kekes, Joseph Raz, William Galston and George Crowder; Robert Nozick, John Rawls, Richard Rorty and Charles Taylor have at times advanced positions which in some ways resemble pluralism, but are difficult to categorise in relation to it.

Berlin did not respond to Leo Strauss's direct and powerful attack; he did respond to Arnaldo Momigliano's criticism, which made the pluralism = relativism accusation through an examination of Berlin's interpretations of Vico and Herder; and he was anxious to draw a sharp distinction between relativism and pluralism in his later work. Nevertheless, the charge continues to be made by critics, and rejected by supporters, of Berlin's pluralism.

One of the best-known forms of relativism is cultural relativism—the view that all values emerge from particular cultures, and are valid within and for those cultures, but not necessarily for others. Berlin sometimes appears to say this; he also seems sometimes to endorse, and sometimes to disavow, a major assumption underlying most versions of cultural relativism, namely, a holistic conception of culture. This regards cultures as unified and wholly separate entities, webs in which each belief is bound together with every other belief, and within which members cannot disentangle their beliefs one from another, rejecting some, retaining others, judging each critically and separately. It remains controversial whether Berlin's view of culture was holistic, and, if so, to what extent and in what way; but it has been maintained—most notably and persistently by Steven Lukes—that pluralism can be rescued from the shoals of relativism if the pluralist rejects a holistic conception of culture, which, Lukes maintains, is fundamentally mistaken. Lukes's critique of holism, and his de-coupling of pluralism from holism, are plausible; it does not however necessarily follow that not accepting holism allows the pluralist to believe consistently in universal standards or values (conflicting though these may be) transcending all cultures.

The rejection of a holistic view of culture does remove a major obstacle to a belief that certain values transcend cultural differences, in suggesting that cultures aren't wholly self-contained, closed-off and non-connecting. However, the occurrence of variety, conflict and dissent within cultures, and the recurrence of certain beliefs in different cultures, need not, in themselves, suggest the existence of a universal human nature or universal values underlying cultural variety.

Gray has sometimes presented his critique of liberalism as a critique only of a certain sort of liberalism, or strain within the liberal tradition, and has opposed to this another, better, more pluralistic liberalism; at other times, he has presented his critique as a more wholesale indictment of liberalism as such.

Gray's arguments can be summarised in vastly simplified form as three main propositions about liberalism. The first of these is that liberalism is absolutist and monistic: it is based on assigning an absolute moral/political priority to liberty as the paramount political value. If values really are incommensurable, then this is unallowable. The second is that liberalism is one value-system or way of life among many. If pluralism is conceived of in terms of ways of life, value-systems, cultures etc., rather than individual values, then the conclusion would be that liberalism is just one of these many valid but conflicting ways of life, with no claim to privilege. Therefore, liberals living in liberal societies are free to be liberal and pursue liberal values; but they have no right to impose their views on others, or regard themselves as superior or their way of doing things as preferable. Finally, Gray charges that liberalism by its nature has historically been a universalist doctrine—that is, that it has denied this last proposition, and indeed claimed to be superior to other forms of life, for all people, everywhere, at all times. Therefore, if pluralism is accepted, and liberals accept liberalism as just one form of life among many, then one of the central goals of traditional liberalism must be abandoned.

Galston has argued that pluralism and liberalism are compatible if neither is seen as a fully comprehensive or encompassing doctrine, and has sought to suggest what a politics that is both truly pluralist and truly liberal would look like. Crowder, in probably the most systematic and careful discussion of the topic to date, has sought to show that Gray's account of value pluralism incorporates a number of assumptions and conclusions that make his position closer to relativism than to a truly objective value pluralism; that genuine value pluralism is wholly consistent with a belief in a core or minimum of universal human values, as well as non-monistic and non-quantitative comparison of and choice between values based on practical reason; and that value-pluralism's recognition of both genuine moral variety and a basic, minimal standard of human decency support liberalism. Steven Lukes has also contributed much to this debate, as have commentary by Hans Blokland, Jeffrey Friedman, Amy Gutmann, Ira Katznelson, Charles Larmore, Pratap B. Mehta, Jonathan Riley, Michael Walzer and Daniel Weinstock;

there is also a significant review of the topic by Albert Dzur, and a collection of essays exploring the political implications of pluralism. Whether these works—in particular, Galston and Crowder's volumes—have exhausted the pluralism/liberalism debate remains to be seen.

The insensitive and authoritarian rule of managerial bureaucrats—those whom Stalin, in one of Berlin's favourite quotations, called 'engineers of human souls'—particularly worried Berlin throughout the 1950s, when most of his work on political judgement was written.

While Herzen's combination of ironic wit, moral passion and vivacity naturally appealed to Berlin, it may seem strange that the biddable British academic should have identified himself with the wayward Russian aristocrat turned wandering revolutionary, or that the very embodiment of cautious, sceptical and moderate liberalism should have regarded a radical malcontent, the father of Russian agrarian socialism, as a political guide.

In fact, Herzen was an ambivalent revolutionary, and Berlin, while certainly every inch the liberal, was a less stolid and more radical thinker than is sometimes recognised. The two men shared a passion for liberty, a suspicion of authority, an opposition to both injustice and intellectual complacency. However, what Berlin seized on in Herzen was the latter's opposition to — and occasional passionate denunciation of— the doctrine of historical inevitability, and the political ethics to which this attack was joined.

The distinction goes back at least to Kant, and it (or something like it) had appeared in the works of T. H. Green, Bernard Bosanquet, and Boris Chicherin, and had more recently been used by Guido de Ruggiero, R. G. Collingwood, John Petrov Plamenatz, and Dorothy Fosdyke, among others; Berlin himself acknowledged Benjamin Constant as the main influence on his thinking. Berlin's conception of positive and negative liberty may also owe something to Rousseau's distinction between the liberty of the man and that of the citizen, and to the more general distinction among earlier theorists, of whom Rousseau was the most prominent, between natural and moral liberty.

Berlin cites Stoicism's preaching of self-discipline and renunciation as a way of resisting, and remaining uncorrupted by, overwhelmingly powerful earthly authorities; Rousseau's insistence that the only just society is one in which people retain their liberty by transmuting it from the individual self-governance of solitary selves in a state of nature to the collective self-rule of the people by the people, so that obedience to the civil authority is really obedience to oneself, and thus freedom rather than subjection; and finally Kant's philosophy of moral autonomy, whereby the individual's inalienable freedom and dignity lie in the fact that the individual acts in accordance with a self-given moral law, and is therefore recognised as a freely choice-making being, dependent on no one and nothing else.

Berlin has considerable sympathy for this last, Kantian, outlook, though he believed that it had inspired profound errors. He acknowledged that the Stoic ideal was admirable, but charged that it rested on a misuse of words: to attain independence through a renunciation of those desires that make one prey to the domination of others might be sublime, and it might be the best that one can do in certain circumstances; but the fact remains that one is then less free than one would be otherwise, in that there are constraints, both internal and, ultimately, external, preventing one from acting with true freedom.

It must be noted that the former part of Berlin's argument here is somewhat stronger than the latter: the conflict of values may mean that the making of choices is an inescapable and even significant part of life, but this is not, in itself, a reason for embracing the making of choices as something valuable and central to both dignity and fulfillment. Indeed, if making choices involves the tragic losses that Berlin claims it sometimes does, one may be inclined to try to escape the painful and difficult position of having to choose, rather than proudly embracing it.

Berlin's Zionism has been the subject of minor controversy. Some critics have complained that it led him to turn a blind eye to injustice and tacitly approve of Israeli chauvinism. This was not so. Berlin was a liberal and humane Zionist; he believed in the justice and necessity of a Jewish homeland, but also opposed violence, nationalist aggression and chauvinism wherever they appeared. Indeed, his aversion to political radicalism led him to support the moderate, pro-British Chaim Weizmann against more assertive Zionist leaders such as David Ben-Gurion in the 1940s, even when it became apparent that Ben-Gurion's strategy was likely to be more effective than Weizmann's in establishing a Jewish state. Later in life Berlin was a quiet but firm, and at times privately vehement, critic of the Likud bloc and of Israeli policy in the West Bank and Gaza, and a supporter of the Peace Now movement and a 'two-state solution' to the Israeli-Palestinian conflict.

BERNARD WILLIAMS

Bernard Williams wrote an introduction and postscript to a 1960 series of BBC Third Programme shows on the topic "Freedom and the Will." The show's hosts included a number of ordinary language philosophers including Peter F. Strawson, Stuart Hampshire, David F. Pears, and Mary and Geoffrey J. Warnock.

Williams' introduction showed an understanding of why Aristotle did not see the "problem of free will".

> "Now Aristotle did believe, I think, that if it could be shown that it was a matter of necessity that men acted in one way rather than another, then our ordinary thought about action and responsibility would be undermined. If human actions were necessitated, there would indeed be something radically wrong with our notions of human action; but, he thought, it was quite certainly false that human actions were necessitated. If this is a correct account of Aristotle, we can see one reason why he does not confront the freewill problem. It is because he thinks that it cannot seriously be doubted that human actions are free from necessitation."

Williams was mistaken about the origin of the free will problem, which he traced to Christian theology and an omniscient, omnipotent God with divine foreknowledge of the future.

> "the problem of freewill makes its first large-scale appearance in a religious context, when men had come to believe that here was one God, omnipotent, omniscient, and concerned with human action. The problem of freewill was first definitely stated as a problem of Christian theology. The problem arose, in fact, from a number of different roots in Christian belief: Christianity asserts on the one hand that man does freely choose his actions, but also asserts on the other hand statements not evidently compatible with this, for instance that God being omniscient knows from all eternity what actions a man will in fact perform."

Williams objected strongly to the idea that the natural laws of science could explain everything, that physical determinism required philosophers to accept Humean compatibilism.

Moral Luck

In his 1981 essay, Moral Luck, williams wrote,

> I entirely agree with [Thomas Nagel] that the involvement of morality with luck is not something that can simply be accepted without calling our moral conceptions into question.

That was part of my original point; I have tried to state it more directly in the present version of this paper. A difference between Nagel and myself is that I am more sceptical about our moral conceptions than he is. "Scepticism about the freedom of morality from luck cannot leave the concept of morality where it was, any more than it can remain undisturbed by scepticism about the very closely related image we have of there being a moral order, within which our actions have a significance which may not be accorded to them by mere social recognition. These forms of scepticism will leave us with a concept of morality."

Freedom and the Will

We can trace back to near the beginning of Western Civilization the notion of individual responsibility: the notion that certain states of affairs in the world can be traced to the actions of human beings, for which those human beings can in various ways be called to account. The actions for which we are in the fullest sense responsible are those for which we can be praised or blamed.

This notion of responsibility is to be found already in the moral and legal thought of the Ancient Greeks. The Greeks already worked with the notion which we have today, that the question whether a man is responsible for something that happens is not just the question whether what happens is a consequence of movements of the man's body. For instance, suppose a man's arm moves in such a way as to knock over and break a valuable vase, someone else's property. In a limited sense, we know already in these circumstances what the cause of the damage was — the movement of this man's arm; but we do not yet know whether the man himself is in the full sense responsible for this damage, whether he is to blame. For that, we want to know more about the movement of his arm. In particular, we want to know whether he intended this movement of his arm, or whether perhaps it was just some nervous twitch, out of his control.

Again, even if the movement was not out of his control, we still want to know, for instance, whether he realized the vase was there: if not, his breaking of the vase will be unintentional, and to that extent free from blame. There are other sorts of situation, too, that relieve people of responsibility for things that they have done, or at least mitigate it ; being in certain peculiar states, for instance, such as sleep-walking or under the influence of drugs ; or, rather differently, being forced to do things by other persons.

Aristotle, in his Ethics, reviews and classifies these sorts of situation that relieve people of responsibility. His account is complex and subtle, but substantially he reduces the types of situation to two classes: those in which the agent is ignorant of relevant matters, and those in which, as he puts it, the originating principle of the action lies outside the agent himself — by which, I think, he principally means cases in which someone is physically forced to do something by someone else.

Aristotle's account is of interest for two reasons in particular. The first is a positive reason: that it is interesting to find a Greek philosopher giving an analysis of responsibility and the conditions that relieve people of it that so remarkably corresponds, in its essentials, to some of the considerations that we still employ today, both in the law and in everyday life. The second reason is a more negative one. Aristotle's account is concerned, as I have said, with the conditions that relieve people of responsibility for what they have done. I mean by this that he considers and classifies certain special circumstances that relieve people of responsibility, while taking it for granted that in the usual circumstances people are responsible. He analyses the framework of praise and blame and responsibility as a going concern, as it were. He never, or scarcely ever, considers the notion that we might never really be responsible, that the going concern of praise and blame, our ordinary notions on these matters, might as a whole he founded on an illusion.

Aristotle, that is to say, is precisely not concerned with that large-scale philosophical problem or set of philosophical problems which in later times has come to be known as the problem of freedom of the will. For the heart of that problem lies in the fundamental and revolutionary suggestion that our ordinary notions of responsibility may be altogether confused, because based on some false or ultimately unintelligible theory about human beings and their actions. I think we may be able to see, in historical terms, how this fundamental and revolutionary suggestion came to be made, if we ask first why Aristotle does not consider it.

One reason is that Aristotle regards it as certain, and indeed makes it a central point of his philosophy, that there is no necessity about human actions – that it is never necessary in any sense that a man should, on a particular occasion, have done this rather than that. For him, necessity is something that applies only to such things as the movements of the heavenly bodies; human actions, on the contrary, are a sort of thing which could always have happened otherwise.

Now Aristotle did believe, I think, that if it could be shown that it was a matter of necessity that men acted in one way rather than another, then our ordinary thought about action and responsibility would be undermined. If human actions were necessitated, there would indeed be something radically wrong with our notions of human action; but, he thought, it was quite certainly false that human actions were necessitated.

If this is a correct account of Aristotle, we can see one reason why he does not confront the freewill problem. It is because he thinks that it cannot seriously be doubted that human actions are free from necessitation.

This is a very important point, because, as we shall see, one reason that the freewill problem did eventually arise was that men did begin to have serious doubts about just this. I shall come back to this point. First, however, it is worth while, for our historical picture, to look briefly at another reason for Aristotle's silence on this subject.

This was his lack of belief in any personal god concerned with human affairs. Some earlier Greek writers, in particular the tragedian Aeschylus, do seem to be concerned with problems not far removed from the problem of freewill. Aeschylus's portrayal of Prometheus, or again of Orestes, seems to be in part a dramatic representation of human freedom as against forces set in motion by the gods, or perhaps we should better say, personified in the gods.

Plato, nearly a century later, could still, in a poetic passage, write in these terms, and assert human freedom: 'the responsibility is with the soul that chooses its destiny: God is not responsible'. For Aristotle, a little later, there are no such gods, there are no such forces, and the question does not arise.

I mentioned earlier that men came eventually to doubt Aristotle's principle that human actions were not necessitated. This they did – or at least, the doubt occurred to them – with the rise of a mechanistic view of the universe, according to which the universe was a closed system, every state of which was determined as a consequence of its earlier states in accordance with natural laws – laws which, in the eighteenth and nineteenth centuries, were believed to have been in essence discovered by Newton. The possibility of such a scientific account of the universe had occurred, indeed, to certain of the Greeks, who realized further that such an account would have consequences for human action. The atomist Epicurus, for instance, was apparently aware of these problems.

The speculations of the atomists, however, remained speculations; and it was only with the rise of a successful experimental and predictive mechanical science in the seventeenth century that the problems became acute. How, it was asked, could a human agent intervene in the world, be, in Aristotle's terms, an 'originating principle of action', if every event in the universe was as it was merely in virtue of the earlier states of the universe, however remote? Would not every human action be a case of `the originating principle lying outside the agent himself', so that there would be no action left for which he would be responsible? Descartes, in the first half of the seventeenth century, both held the mechanistic view of the material universe, and saw this problem; he wished further to safeguard responsible action from the realm of natural necessity.

This he tried to do by distinguishing two quite separate realms, that of mind and that of matter, to the second of which alone, matter, the natural laws applied. But this was a quite inadequate kind of solution, even in Descartes's terms. Descartes himself realized that a bodily human action is itself, from one point of view, an event in the material world.

If all events in the material world are subject to natural law, how does the mind come into it? Descartes' distinction between two realms, designed to insulate responsible human action from mechanical causation, insulated the world of mechanical causation, that is to say, the whole of the external world, from responsible human action.

Man would be free only if there was nothing he could do. Once this way of looking at the problem is accepted, there seem to be only two possibilities. Either all physical changes are subject to natural law, in which case those particular physical changes which constitute human actions are subject to it; or human actions are not subject to natural law, so not all physical changes are subject to it. The belief that all physical changes are subject to natural law has attracted, needless to say, a label: the label 'determinism'. So here we have in outline an apparently simple opposition: either determinism is true, in which case there is no genuine human intervention in the world, that is, no freewill; or there is freewill, in which case determinism is false.

With the rise of Humean compatibilism, most philosophers become compatibilist

The issue has, of course, been endlessly posed in these terms, and in these terms endlessly discussed. But not all thinkers have accepted these terms, either explicitly by rallying to one side or the other, or implicitly by professing ignorance as to which alternative was true. Right from the seventeenth century there have been philosophers who have criticized this opposition itself, and the terms in which the question was posed. Some have claimed, radically, that when the notions involved are properly understood, the alleged opposition dissolves, and the supposed dilemma can be shown to be a set of muddles and misunderstandings. Hobbes, Hume, and in our own time A.J. Ayer and others have taken this view. Others, less ambitious, have held that although there may be one, or probably more than one, genuine opposition here, nevertheless the terms of the discussion are so imprecise and ill understood that, without much further analysis, it is impossible to understand what the oppositions are, if they exist. Such a view is, I think, held by many linguistic philosophers today.

It certainly does seem that a tremendous number of questions have been begged and important distinctions blurred in the simple sort of formulation of the problem that I sketched just now. First of all, the formulation introduced a good deal of metaphor: one spoke of physical changes being 'subject to' natural laws, as though the natural laws exercised some mechanistic tyranny over events. Though an enticing metaphor, it is a very misleading one, and should be eliminated. What then, without benefit of metaphor, will be the formulation of determinism?

It would seem to be something like this: that given any total state-description of the universe, it is in principle possible to predict or retrodict correctly any other, however remote, in virtue of a finite set of scientific laws. But there are still difficulties about this formulation. It is still not free from unclarities and ambiguities — great difficulties, for instance, surround that slippery phrase 'in principle'. Under what conditions could we say that we could in principle predict every state of the universe ? Just when we thought that there were laws in virtue of which we could do it, if only we knew them?

This would surely not be enough — this would only be a situation of faith in determinism, not a situation in which determinism had been shown to be true. So perhaps we should say that determinism had been shown to be true if we knew all the relevant laws, and could predict all the states of the universe if only we took enough trouble.

But then what certainty would we have that we did know all the relevant laws, unless we could actually succeed in making these vast predictions — that is, could not only in principle, but in practice predict? And this even the most fervent determinist would surely agree we could not do.

The difficulties for determinism in the twentieth century are the probabilistic consequences of quantum mechanics

There are other difficulties in the formulation of determinism. What, for instance, are we to make of the phrase 'a total state-description of the universe'? Even if we made more precise – as we should have to – what terms such a description would have to be in, are there not overwhelming reasons for thinking that no such description could ever be completed? The eighteenth century the astronomer Laplace could perhaps talk glibly in these terms; in the twentieth we certainly cannot.

Here someone may say: Good. We now understand that the conditions specified by the determinist could never be satisfied – that is to say, determinism is a false or incoherent doctrine. So the enemy of freewill is out of business, and freewill is all right. Rut such a confident answer would be premature, and this just illustrates the obscurities of the simple opposition we originally set up. For while this extremely grandiose enemy, Laplacean determinism, is perhaps out of business, rather humbler but more effective enemies are certainly still in existence.

Here it is worth while to recall the point we started with right at the beginning: the fact that in ordinary life and the law we admit certain conditions as relieving an agent from responsibility for what he has done : conditions such as somnambulism, force majeure, etc. Now it is a most conspicuous feature of our present moral thought that this list of conditions is gradually being extended in the light of advancing psychological and other scientific knowledge.

For instance, we now recognize in ordinary life, and perhaps even in the law, the existence of certain compulsive conditions – kleptomania is one sort of example. The proof that an agent was in such a state relieves him of responsibility, or at least mitigates it, for actions of the appropriate type.

Now it is not an accident that the discussion of such cases gives rise to constant difficulty and doubt. We feel compelled to admit more and more such conditions into the class of conditions that exonerate, without really being clear on what principle we are doing it. Moreover, there is the lurking feeling that the principle on which we are doing it might be one that eventually might extend to swallow up wide ranges of action now regarded as normal and responsible. For instance, are we to say that a man is not responsible if there is a psychological explanation of what he did ? This by itself is too weak, since the phrase ' psychological explanation' can cover practically anything, including for instance 'he freely chose'. But perhaps some sorts of psychological explanation . . . ? Here we do not know, not just where to draw the line, but how to, and in this ignorance we can feel no a priori confidence how much of our ordinary sphere of action will be left intact by the line when properly drawn. Here we feel the presence perhaps of another type of determinism less grandiose but more pressing than the total physical determinism of Laplace.

In this situation, looking for a criterion, we may turn to the other side of the field. We may ask, not what are the general conditions of non-responsibility, but what are the general conditions of responsibility: perhaps there is some sign that an action is, in the appropriate sense, really ours. Here we meet for the first time a concept that has been absent from the discussion so far – the concept of the will itself. It is in virtue of the operation of the will that some philosophers have tried to distinguish this class of responsible actions. But what is the operation of the will, and what are its signs?

We indeed speak in ordinary life of 'efforts of will', and it is in the occurrence of these that in reflective moments we perhaps feel most conscious in some sense of our freedom. But here there are many difficulties. First, it is certain that only a very few of the actions for which people are normally held responsible are accompanied by efforts of will, in this psychological sense; and the same goes for any other conscious process that might be suggested here instead, such as explicit decision, formulated intention and so on.

Often we just act, without such processes, nor would we regard such actions as any the less responsible of free for that reason. Again, there is a deep difficulty about what an effort of will really is. There is indeed some kind of psychological process in connection with which the term is used – but might it not be just a psychological process which accompanied some actions (perhaps peculiarly difficult ones) and not others? Contrary to what some philosophers have supposed, efforts of will do not wear their metaphysical significance on their face. It may even be that they have nonc.

I have mentioned in the last few pages a good number of problems and difficulties. It is these difficulties that contributors to this book will be considering: in particular, the definition of determinism; the search for general conditions of responsibility; the nature of the will and its connection with what we call efforts of will; the scope and implications of different kinds of psychological explanation. My aim has been to try to link with a few threads these different topics to the history of that set of issues which is over-simply called 'the problem of the freedom of the will'.

I have tried to suggest that there is not one simple issue here, but a great network of difficulties. The difficulties are, however, not unrelated to one another – the network has a centre. This centre lies on a line, which is deeply engraved in human thought, the line between man as a conscious, reflective being and man as part of physical nature, conditioned by and acted upon by his environment. The basic nature of this dividing line appears in the constant preoccupation of philosophy with these difficulties! and it is its very depth that makes it necessary for any serious search for understanding in this region now to distrust grandiose theories, and to take the difficulties, so far as possible, one at a time. They are, after all, no less complex than the human situation.

LIBERALISM

Liberalism includes a broad spectrum of political philosophies that consider individual liberty to be the most important political goal, and emphasize individual rights and equality of opportunity. Although most Liberals would claim that a government is necessary to protect rights, different forms of Liberalism may propose very different policies. They are, however, generally united by their support for a number of principles, including extensive freedom of thought and freedom of speech, limitations on the power of governments, the application of the rule of law, a market economy (or a mixed economy with both private-owned and state-owned enterprises) and a transparent and democratic system of government.

Like the similar concept of Libertarianism, Liberalism believes that society should be organized in accordance with certain unchangeable and inviolable human rights, especially the rights to life, liberty and property. It also holds that traditions do not carry any inherent value, that social practices ought to be continuously adjusted for the greater benefit of humanity, and that there should be no foundational assumptions (such as the Divine Right of Kings, hereditary status or established religion) that take precedence over other aspects of government.

Anarchism is a much more radical form of Liberalism, although, like Anarchism, Liberalism historically stands in opposition to any form of authoritarianism, whether in the form of Communism, Socialism, Fascism or other types of Totalitarianism. Its emphasis on individual rights (Individualism) also puts it in opposition to any kind of collectivism, which emphasize the collective or the community to a degree where the rights of the individual are either diminished or abolished (e.g. Communitarianism).

The word "liberal" derives from the Latin "liber" (meaning "free" or "not a slave"). In everyday use, it means generous and open-minded, as well as free from restraint and from prejudice. Its use as a political term, however, only dates from the early 19th Century.

History of Liberalism

The modern ideology of Liberalism can be traced back to the Humanism which challenged the authority of the established church in Renaissance Europe, and more particularly to the 17th and 18th Century British and French Enlightenmentthinkers, and the movement towards self-government in colonial America.

John Locke's "Two Treatises on Government" of 1689 established two fundamental liberal ideas: economic liberty (meaning the right to have and use property) and intellectual liberty (including freedom of conscience). His natural rights theory ("natural rights" for Locke being essentially life, liberty and property) was the distant forerunner of the modern conception of human rights, although he saw the right to property as more important than the right to participate in government and public decision-making, and he did not endorse democracy, fearing that giving power to the people would erode the sanctity of private property. Nevertheless, the idea of natural rights played a key role in providing the ideological justification for the American and the French revolutions, and in the further development of Liberalism.

In France, the Baron de Montesquieu (1689-1755) advocated laws restraining even monarchs (then a novel concept), rather than accepting as natural the mere rule of force and tradition, and French physiocrats (believers that the wealth of nations was derived solely from the value of land agriculture or land development) established the idea of "laissez-faire" economics as an injunction against government interference with trade.

In the late French Enlightenment, Voltaire argued on intellectual grounds for the establishment of a constitutional monarchy in France, and Jean-Jacques Rousseauargued for a natural freedom for mankind, and for changes in political and social arrangements based around the idea that society can restrain a natural human liberty, but not obliterate its nature.

Rousseau was also instrumental (along with Locke) in the development of a key liberal concept, that of the social contract (the idea that the people give up some rights to a government in order to receive social order). He asserted that each person knows their own interest best, and that man is born free, but that education was sufficient to restrain him within society, an idea that rocked the monarchical society of his age. He also asserted, again in contravention of established political practice, that a nation could have an organic "national will" and a capacity for self-determination which would allow states to exist without being chained to pre-existing social orders, such as aristocracy.

Another major contributing group to the ideas of Liberalism are those associated with the Scottish Enlightenment, especially David Hume and Adam Smith. Possibly Hume's most important contribution to Liberalism was his assertion that the fundamental rules of human behavior would eventually overwhelm any attempts to restrict or regulate them (which also influenced Immanuel Kant's formulation of his categorical imperative theory). Adam Smith expounded on the theory that individuals could structure both moral and economic life without direction from the state, and that nations would be strongest when their citizens were free to follow their own initiative ("The study of his own advantage naturally, or rather necessarily, leads him to prefer that employment which is most advantageous to the society"). In his influential "The Wealth of Nations" of 1776, he argued that the market, under certain conditions, would naturally regulate itself and would produce more than the heavily restricted markets that were the norm at the time, and he agreed with Hume that capital, not gold, is the wealth of a nation.

Much of the intellectual basis for the American Revolution (1775-1783) was framed by Thomas Paine (1737-1809), Thomas Jefferson (1743-1826) and John Adams (1735-1826) who encouraged revolt in the name of "life, liberty and the pursuit of happiness" (echoing Locke), and in favor of democratic government and individual liberty. In particular, Paine's widely-read pamphlet "Common Sense" (1776) and his "The Rights of Man" (1791) were highly influential in this process. The goal was to ensure liberty by preventing the concentration of power in the hands of any one man.

The French Revolution (1789-1799) was even more drastic and less compromising, although in its first few years the revolution was very much guided by liberal ideas. However, the transition from revolt to stability was to prove more difficult than the similar American transition, and later, under the leadership of Maximilien Robespierre (1758-1794) and the Jacobins, power was greatly centralized and most aspects of due process were dispensed with, resulting in the Reign of Terror. Nevertheless, the French Revolution would go further than the American Revolution in establishing liberal ideals with such policies as universal male suffrage, national citizenship and a far reaching "Declaration of the Rights of Man and Citizen".

John Stuart Mill popularized and expanded liberal ideas in the mid-19th Century, grounding them in the instrumental and the pragmatic, particularly in his "On Liberty" of 1859 and other works. He also propounded a utilitarian justification of Liberalism, in which the moral worth of the economic system is determined solely by its contribution to overall utility in maximizing happiness or pleasure among all people.

Gradually, the idea of liberal democracy (in its typical form of multiparty political pluralism) gathered strength and influence over much of the western world, although it should be noted that, for liberals, democracy is not an end in itself, but an essential means to securing liberty, individuality and diversity). Towards the end of the 19th Century, though, splits were developing within Liberalism between those who accepted some government intervention in the economy, and those who became increasingly anti-government, in some cases adopting varieties of Anarchism.

In the 20th Century, in the face of the growing relative inequality of wealth, a theory of Modern Liberalism (or New Liberalism or Social Liberalism) was developed to describe how a government could intervene in the economy to protect liberty while still avoiding Socialism. Among others, John Dewey, John Maynard Keynes (1883-1946), Franklin D. Roosevelt (1882-1945) and John Kenneth Galbraith (1908 - 2006) can be singled out as instrumental in this respect. Other liberals, including Friedrich Hayek (1899-1992), Milton Friedman (1912-2006), and Ludwig von Mises (1881-1973), argued that phenomena such as the Great Depression of the 1930's and the rise of Totalitarian dictatorships were not a result of "laissez-faire" Capitalism at all, but a result of too much government intervention and regulation on the market

Types of Liberalism

There are two major currents of thought within Liberalism, Classical Liberalism and Social Liberalism:

1. Classical Liberalism holds that the only real freedom is freedom from coercion, and that state intervention in the economy is a coercive power that restricts the economic freedom of individuals, and so should be avoided as far as possible. It favors laissez-faire economic policy (minimal economic intervention and taxation by the state beyond what is necessary to maintain individual liberty, peace, security and property rights), and opposes the welfare state (the provision of welfare services by the state, and the assumption by the state of primary responsibility for the welfare of its citizens).
2. Social Liberalism argues that governments must take an active role in promoting the freedom of citizens, and that real freedom can only exist when citizens are healthy, educated and free from dire poverty. Social Liberals believe that this freedom can be ensured when governments guarantee the right to an education, health care and a living wage, in addition to other responsibilities such as laws against discrimination in housing and employment, laws against pollution of the environment, and the provision of welfare, all of which would be supported by a progressive taxation system.

As with many political philosophies, there are several forms and variations of Liberalism, including the following:

- Conservative Liberalism is a variant of Liberalism representing the right-wing of the Liberal movement, and combines liberal values and policies with conservative stances. Unlike Liberal Conservatives, however, who tend to be more committed to authority, tradition and established religion, Conservative Liberals are supporters of the separation between church and state. It also differs from Libertarianism in that it is far less radical in its economic program, and in its support for an active defense policy and military interventions.
- Economic Liberalism is the theory of economics in Classical Liberalism, developed during the Enlightenment, particularly by Adam Smith, which advocates minimal interference by government in the economy. Libertarianism, Neoliberalism and some schools of Conservatism, particularly Liberal Conservatism are often referred to as Economic Liberalism.
- Neoliberalism refers to a program of reducing trade barriers and internal market restrictions, while using government power to enforce opening of foreign markets. In some ways it is a modern attempt, championed by Conservatives like Ronald Reagan (1911-2004) and Margaret Thatcher (1925-2013) since the 1970's, to revert to a purer Classical Liberalism.

- American Liberalism is largely a combination of social liberalism, social progressivism, and mixed economy philosophy. It is distinguished from Classic Liberalism and Libertarianism, which also claim freedom as their primary goal, in its insistence upon the inclusion of positive rights (such as education, health care and other services and goods believed to be required for human development and self-actualization) and in a broader definition of equality.
- National Liberalism is a variant of Liberalism commonly found in several European countries in the 19th and 20th Century, which combines nationalism with policies mainly derived from Economic Liberalism.
- Ordoliberalism is a mid-20th Century school of Liberalism, developed mainly in Germany, emphasizing the need for the state to ensure that the free market produces results close to its theoretical potential.
- Paleoliberalism is a term that has at least a few distinct, though largely ambiguous, meanings, including extreme Liberalism, and very socialist or socially libertarian Liberalism, and opposed to Neoliberalism.
- Cultural Liberalism is a liberal view of society that stresses the freedom of individuals from cultural norms.

MARXISM

Marxism, a body of doctrine developed by Karl Marx and, to a lesser extent, by Friedrich Engels in the mid-19th century. It originally consisted of three related ideas: a philosophical anthropology, a theory of history, and an economic and political program. There is also Marxism as it has been understood and practiced by the various socialist movements, particularly before 1914. Then there is Soviet Marxism as worked out by Vladimir Ilich Lenin and modified by Joseph Stalin, which under the name of Marxism-Leninism became the doctrine of the communist parties set up after the Russian Revolution. Offshoots of this included Marxism as interpreted by the anti-Stalinist Leon Trotsky and his followers, Mao Zedong's Chinese variant of Marxism-Leninism, and various Marxisms in the developing world. There were also the post-World War II non-dogmatic Marxisms that have modified Marx's thought with borrowings from modern philosophies, principally from those of Edmund Husserl and Martin Heidegger but also from Sigmund Freud and others.

The written work of Marx cannot be reduced to a philosophy, much less to a philosophical system. The whole of his work is a radical critique of philosophy, especially of G.W.F. Hegel's idealist system and of the philosophies of the left and right post-Hegelians. It is not, however, a mere denial of those philosophies. Marx declared that philosophy must become reality. One could no longer be content with interpreting the world; one must be concerned with transforming it, which meant transforming both the world itself and human consciousness of it.

This, in turn, required a critique of experience together with a critique of ideas. In fact, Marx believed that all knowledge involves a critique of ideas. He was not an empiricist. Rather, his work teems with concepts (appropriation, alienation, praxis, creative labour, value, and so on) that he had inherited from earlier philosophers and economists, including Hegel, Johann Fichte, Immanuel Kant, Adam Smith, David Ricardo, and John Stuart Mill. What uniquely characterizes the thought of Marx is that, instead of making abstract affirmations about a whole group of problems such as human nature, knowledge, and matter, he examines each problem in its dynamic relation to the others and, above all, tries to relate them to historical, social, political, and economic realities.

Historical Materialism

In 1859, in the preface to his Zur Kritik der politischen Ökonomie (Contribution to the Critique of Political Economy), Marx wrote that the hypothesis that had served him as the basis for his analysis of society could be briefly formulated as follows:

In the social production that men carry on, they enter into definite relations that are indispensable and independent of their will, relations of production which correspond to a definite stage of development of their material forces of production. The sum total of these relations of production constitutes the economic structure of society, the real foundation, on which rises a legal and political superstructure, and to which correspond definite forms of social consciousness. The mode of production in material life determines the general character of the social, political, and intellectual processes of life. It is not the consciousness of men which determines their existence; it is on the contrary their social existence which determines their consciousness.

Raised to the level of historical law, this hypothesis was subsequently called historical materialism. Marx applied it to capitalist society, both in Manifest der kommunistischen Partei (1848; The Communist Manifesto) and Das Kapital (vol. 1, 1867; "Capital") and in other writings. Although Marx reflected upon his working hypothesis for many years, he did not formulate it in a very exact manner: different expressions served him for identical realities. If one takes the text literally, social reality is structured in the following way:

1. Underlying everything as the real basis of society is the economic structure. This structure includes (a) the "material forces of production," that is, the labour and means of production, and (b) the overall "relations of production," or the social and political arrangements that regulate production and distribution. Although Marx stated that there is a correspondence between the "material forces" of production and the indispensable "relations" of production, he never made himself clear on the nature of the correspondence, a fact that was to be the source of differing interpretations among his later followers.
2. Above the economic structure rises the superstructure, consisting of legal and political "forms of social consciousness" that correspond to the economic structure. Marx says nothing about the nature of this correspondence between ideological forms and economic structure, except that through the ideological forms individuals become conscious of the conflict within the economic structure between the material forces of production and the existing relations of production expressed in the legal property relations. In other words, "The sum total of the forces of production accessible to men determines the condition of society" and is at the base of society. "The social structure and the state issue continually from the life processes of definite individuals . . . as they are in reality, that is acting and materially producing."

Analysis of Society

To go directly to the heart of the work of Marx, one must focus on his concrete program for humanity. This is just as important for an understanding of Marx as are The Communist Manifesto and Das Kapital. Marx's interpretation of human nature begins with human need. "Man," he wrote in the Economic and Philosophic Manuscripts of 1844,

is first of all a natural being. As a natural being and a living natural being, he is endowed on the one hand with natural powers, vital powers…; these powers exist in him as aptitudes, instincts. On the other hand, as an objective, natural, physical, sensitive being, he is a suffering, dependent and limited being…, that is, the objects of his instincts exist outside him, independent of him, but are the objects of his need, indispensable and essential for the realization and confirmation of his substantial powers.

The point of departure of human history is therefore living human beings, who seek to satisfy certain primary needs. "The first historical fact is the production of the means to satisfy these needs." This satisfaction, in turn, opens the way for new needs. Human activity is thus essentially a struggle with nature that must furnish the means of satisfying human needs: drink, food, clothing, the development of human powers and then of human intellectual and artistic abilities. In this undertaking, people discover themselves as productive beings who humanize themselves through their labour. Furthermore, they humanize nature while they naturalize themselves. By their creative activity, by their labour, they realize their identity with the nature that they master, while at the same time, they achieve free consciousness. Born of nature, they become fully human by opposing it.

Becoming aware in their struggle against nature of what separates them from it, they find the conditions of their fulfillment, of the realization of their true stature. The dawning of consciousness is inseparable from struggle. By appropriating all the creative energies, they discover that "all that is called history is nothing else than the process of creating man through human labour, the becoming of nature for man. Man has thus evident and irrefutable proof of his own creation by himself." Understood in its universal dimension, human activity reveals that "for man, man is the supreme being." It is thus vain to speak of God, creation, and metaphysical problems. Fully naturalized, humans are sufficient unto themselves: they have recaptured the fullness of humanity in its full liberty.

Living in a capitalist society, however, the individual is not truly free. He is an alienated being; he is not at home in his world. The idea of alienation, which Marx takes from Hegel and Ludwig Feuerbach, plays a fundamental role in the whole of his written work, starting with the writings of his youth and continuing through Das Kapital. In the Economic and Philosophic Manuscripts the alienation of labour is seen to spring from the fact that the more the worker produces the less he has to consume, and the more values he creates the more he devalues himself, because his product and his labour are estranged from him. The life of the worker depends on things that he has created but that are not his, so that, instead of finding his rightful existence through his labour, he loses it in this world of things that are external to him: no work, no pay. Under these conditions, labour denies the fullness of concrete humanity. "The generic being (Gattungwesen) of man, nature as well as his intellectual faculties, is transformed into a being which is alien to him, into a means of his individual existence."

Nature, his body, his spiritual essence become alien to him. "Man is made alien to man." When carried to its highest stage of development, private property becomes "the product of alienated labour…the means by which labour alienates itself (and) the realization of this alienation." It is also at the same time "the tangible material expression of alienated human life."

Although there is no evidence that Marx ever disclaimed this anthropological analysis of alienated labour, starting with The German Ideology, the historical, social, and economic causes of the alienation of labour are given increasing emphasis, especially in Das Kapital. Alienated labour is seen as the consequence of market product, the division of labour, and the division of society into antagonistic classes. As producers in society, workers create goods only by their labour.

These goods are exchangeable. Their value is the average amount of social labour spent to produce them. The alienation of the worker takes on its full dimension in that system of market production in which part of the value of the goods produced by the worker is taken away from him and transformed into surplus value, which the capitalist privately appropriates. Market production also intensifies the alienation of labour by encouraging specialization, piecework, and the setting up of large enterprises. Thus the labour power of the worker is used along with that of others in a combination whose significance he is ignorant of, both individually and socially. In thus losing their quality as human products, the products of labour become fetishes, that is, alien and oppressive realities to which both the individual who possesses them privately and the individual who is deprived of them submit themselves. In the market economy, this submission to things is obscured by the fact that the exchange of goods is expressed in money.

This fundamental economic alienation is accompanied by secondary political and ideological alienations, which offer a distorted representation of and an illusory justification of a world in which the relations of individuals with one another are also distorted. The ideas that people form are closely bound up with their material activity and their material relations:

> "The act of making representations, of thinking, the spiritual intercourse of men, seem to be the direct emanation of their material relations." This is true of all human activity: political, intellectual, or spiritual. "Men produce their representations and their ideas, but it is as living men, men acting as they are determined by a definite development of their powers of production." Law, morality, metaphysics, and religion do not have a history of their own. "Men developing their material production modify together with their real existence their ways of thinking and the products of their ways of thinking." In other words, "It is not consciousness which determines existence, it is existence which determines consciousness."

In bourgeois, capitalist society the individual is divided into political citizen and economic actor. This duality represents his political alienation, which is further intensified by the functioning of the bourgeois state. From this study of society at the beginning of the 19th century, Marx came to see the state as the instrument through which the propertied class dominated other classes.

Ideological alienation, for Marx, takes different forms, appearing in economic, philosophical, and legal theories. Marx undertook a lengthy critique of the first in Das Kapital and of the second in The German Ideology. But ideological alienation expresses itself supremely in religion. Taking up the ideas about religion that were current in left post-Hegelian circles, together with the thought of Feuerbach, Marx considered religion to be a product of human consciousness. It is a reflection of the situation of a person who "either has not conquered himself or has already lost himself again" (the individual in the world of private property). It is "an opium for the people." Unlike Feuerbach, Marx believed that religion would disappear only with changes in society.

Marx analyzed the market economy system in Das Kapital. In this work he borrows most of the categories of the classical English economists Smith and Ricardo but adapts them and introduces new concepts such as that of surplus value. One of the distinguishing marks of Das Kapital is that in it Marx studies the economy as a whole and not in one or another of its aspects. His analysis is based on the idea that humans are productive beings and that all economic value comes from human labour. The system he analyzes is principally that of mid-19th-century England.

It is a system of private enterprise and competition that arose in the 16th century from the development of sea routes, international trade, and colonialism. Its rise had been facilitated by changes in the forces of production (the division of labour and the concentration of workshops), the adoption of mechanization, and technical progress. The wealth of the societies that brought this economy into play had been acquired through an "enormous accumulation of commodities." Marx therefore begins with the study of this accumulation, analyzing the unequal exchanges that take place in the market.

According to Marx, if the capitalist advances funds to buy cotton yarn with which to produce fabrics and sells the product for a larger sum than he paid, he is able to invest the difference in additional production. "Not only is the value advance kept in circulation, but it changes in its magnitude, adds a plus to itself, makes itself worth more, and it is this movement that transforms it into capital."

The transformation, to Marx, is possible only because the capitalist has appropriated the means of production, including the labour power of the worker. Now labour power produces more than it is worth. The value of labour power is determined by the amount of labour necessary for its reproduction or, in other words, by the amount needed for the worker to subsist and beget children. But in the hands of the capitalist the labour power employed in the course of a day produces more than the value of the sustenance required by the worker and his family. The difference between the two values is appropriated by the capitalist, and it corresponds exactly to the surplus value realized by capitalists in the market. Marx is not concerned with whether in capitalist society there are sources of surplus value other than the exploitation of human labour—a fact pointed out by Joseph Schumpeter in Capitalism, Socialism, and Democracy. He remains content with emphasizing this primary source:

Surplus value is produced by the employment of labour power. Capital buys the labour power and pays the wages for it. By means of his work the labourer creates new value which does not belong to him, but to the capitalist. He must work a certain time merely in order to reproduce the equivalent value of his wages. But when this equivalent value has been returned, he does not cease work, but continues to do so for some further hours. The new value which he produces during this extra time, and which exceeds in consequence the amount of his wage, constitutes surplus value.

Throughout his analysis, Marx argues that the development of capitalism is accompanied by increasing contradictions. For example, the introduction of machinery is profitable to the individual capitalist because it enables him to produce more goods at a lower cost, but new techniques are soon taken up by his competitors. The outlay for machinery grows faster than the outlay for wages. Since only labour can produce the surplus value from which profit is derived, this means that the capitalist's rate of profit on his total outlay tends to decline. Along with the declining rate of profit goes an increase in unemployment. Thus, the equilibrium of the system is precarious, subject as it is to the internal pressures resulting from its own development.

Crises shake it at regular intervals, preludes to the general crisis that will sweep it away. This instability is increased by the formation of a reserve army of workers, both factory workers and peasants, whose pauperization keeps increasing. "Capitalist production develops the technique and the combination of the process of social production only by exhausting at the same time the two sources from which all wealth springs: the earth and the worker." According to the Marxist dialectic, these fundamental contradictions can only be resolved by a change from capitalism to a new system.

Class Struggle

Marx inherited the ideas of class and class struggle from utopian socialism and the theories of Henri de Saint-Simon. These had been given substance by the writings of French historians such as Adolphe Thiers and Frannois Guizot on the French Revolution of 1789. But unlike the French historians, Marx made class struggle the central fact of social evolution. "The history of all hitherto existing human society is the history of class struggles."

In Marx's view, the dialectical nature of history is expressed in class struggle. With the development of capitalism, the class struggle takes an acute form. Two basic classes, around which other less important classes are grouped, oppose each other in the capitalist system: the owners of the means of production, or bourgeoisie, and the workers, or proletariat. *"The bourgeoisie produces its own grave-diggers. The fall of the bourgeoisie and the victory of the proletariat are equally inevitable"* because the bourgeois relations of production are the last contradictory form of the process of social production, contradictory not in the sense of an individual contradiction, but of a contradiction that is born of the conditions of social existence of individuals; however, the forces of production which develop in the midst of bourgeois society create at the same time the material conditions for resolving this contradiction. With this social development the prehistory of human society ends.

When people have become aware of their loss, of their alienation, as a universal nonhuman situation, it will be possible for them to proceed to a radical transformation of their situation by a revolution. This revolution will be the prelude to the establishment of communism and the reign of liberty reconquered. "In the place of the old bourgeois society with its classes and its class antagonisms, there will be an association in which the free development of each is the condition for the free development of all."

But for Marx there are two views of revolution. One is that of a final conflagration, "a violent suppression of the old conditions of production," which occurs when the opposition between bourgeoisie and proletariat has been carried to its extreme point. This conception is set forth in a manner inspired by the Hegelian dialectic of the master and the slave, in Die heilige Familie. The other conception is that of a permanent revolution involving a provisional coalition between the proletariat and the petty bourgeoisie rebelling against a capitalism that is only superficially united. Once a majority has been won to the coalition, an unofficial proletarian authority constitutes itself alongside the revolutionary bourgeois authority. Its mission is the political and revolutionary education of the proletariat, gradually assuring the transfer of legal power from the revolutionary bourgeoisie to the revolutionary proletariat.

If one reads The Communist Manifesto carefully one discovers inconsistencies that indicate that Marx had not reconciled the concepts of catastrophic and of permanent revolution. Moreover, Marx never analyzed classes as specific groups of people opposing other groups of people. Depending on the writings and the periods, the number of classes varies; and unfortunately the pen fell from Marx's hand at the moment when, in Das Kapital, he was about to take up the question. Reading Das Kapital, one is furthermore left with an ambiguous impression with regard to the destruction of capitalism: will it be the result of the "general crisis" that Marx expects, or of the action of the conscious proletariat, or of both at once?

COMMUNITARIANISM

Communitarianism, social and political philosophy that emphasizes the importance of community in the functioning of political life, in the analysis and evaluation of political institutions, and in understanding human identity and well-being. It arose in the 1980s as a critique of two prominent philosophical schools: contemporary liberalism, which seeks to protect and enhance personal autonomy and individual rights in part through the activity of government, and libertarianism, a form of liberalism (sometimes called "classical liberalism") that aims to protect individual rights—especially the rights to liberty and property—through strict limits on governmental power.

There are strong communitarian elements in many modern and historical political and religious belief systems—e.g., in the Hebrew Bible (Old Testament) and the Christian New Testament (Acts

4:32: "Now the whole group of those who believed were of one heart and soul, and no one claimed private ownership of any possessions, but everything they owned was held in common"); in the early Islamic concept of shkr ("consultation"); in Confucianism; in Roman Catholic social thought (the papal encyclical Rerum Novarum); in moderate conservatism ("To be attached to the subdivision, to love the little platoon we belong to in society, is the first principle…of public affections"—Edmund Burke); and in social democracy, especially Fabianism. Communitarian ideas have also played a significant role in public life through their incorporation into the electoral platforms and policies of Western political leaders of the late 20th and early 21st centuries, including British Prime Minister Tony Blair, Dutch Prime Minister Jan Peter Balkenende, and U.S. Presidents Bill Clinton and Barack Obama.

The term communitarian was coined in 1841 by John Goodwyn Barmby, a leader of the British Chartist movement, who used it to refer to utopian socialists and others who experimented with unusual communal life-styles. It was rarely used in the generations that followed.

It was not until the 1980s that the term gained currency through its association with the work of a small group of mostly American political philosophers who argued for the importance of the common good in opposition to contemporary liberals and libertarians, who emphasized the good for individuals, particularly including personal autonomy and individual rights. The Canadian philosopher Charles Taylor and the American political theorist Michael Sandel were among the most prominent scholars of this brand of communitarianism. Other political theorists and philosophers who were often cited as communitarians in this sense, or whose work exhibited elements of such communitarian thinking, included Shlomo Avineri, Seyla Benhabib, Avner de-Shalit, Jean Bethke Elshtain, Amitai Etzioni, William A. Galston, Alasdair MacIntyre, Philip Selznick, and Michael Walzer.

During the same period, students of East Asian politics and society used communitarianism to describe the social thinking within authoritarian societies such as China, Singapore, and Malaysia, which extolled social obligations and the importance of the common good and accorded much less weight to autonomy and rights. Indeed, these societies viewed individuals as more or less interchangeable cells who find meaning in their contribution to the social whole rather than as free agents. Scholars of this kind of communitarianism included the American political theorist Russell A. Fox and the Singaporean diplomat Bilahari Kausikan.

In 1990 Etzioni and Galston founded a third school, known as "responsive" communitarianism. Its members formulated a platform based on their shared political principles, and the ideas in it were eventually elaborated in academic and popular books and periodicals, gaining thereby a measure of political currency, mainly in the West. The main thesis of responsive communitarianism is that people face two major sources of normativity, that of the common good and that of autonomy and rights, neither of which in principle should take precedence over the other.

The Common Good Versus Individual Rights

Whereas the classical liberalism of the Enlightenment can be viewed as a reaction to centuries of authoritarianism, oppressive government, overbearing communities, and rigid dogma, modern communitarianism can be considered a reaction to excessive individualism, understood by communitarians as an undue emphasis on individual rights, leading people to become selfish or egocentric. Excessive individualism was discussed in an oft-cited communitarian work, Habits of the Heart: Individualism and Commitment in American Life (1985), by the American sociologist Robert Neelly Bellah, who observed that by the early 1980s most Americans had become self-centred. Increasing prosperity from the 1950s, among other factors, had contributed to a decline in respect for traditional authority and institutions, such as marriage, and fostered a kind of materialistic hedonism, according to many communitarians. Earlier sociologists such as Ferdinand Tónnies and Émile Durkheim had discussed such antisocial tendencies in the context of modernization, which they viewed as a historical transition from oppressive but nurturing communities (Gemeinschaft) to liberating but impersonal societies (Gesellschaft). They warned of the dangers of anomie (normlessness) and alienation in modern societies composed of atomized individuals who had gained their liberty but lost their social moorings. Essentially the theses of Tonnies and Durkheim were supported with contemporary social-scientific data in Bowling Alone: The Collapse and Revival of American Community (2000), by the American political scientist Robert Putnam.

The close relation between the individual and the community was discussed on a theoretical level by Sandel and Taylor, among other academic communitarians, in their criticisms of philosophical liberalism, including especially the work of the American liberal theorist John Rawls and that of the German Enlightenment philosopher Immanuel Kant. They argued that contemporary liberalism and libertarianism presuppose an incoherent notion of the individual as existing outside and apart from society rather than embedded within it. To the contrary, they argued, there are no generic individuals but rather only Germans or Russians, Berliners or Muscovites, or members of some other particularistic community. Because individual identity is partly constituted (or "constructed") by culture and social relations, there is no coherent way of formulating individual rights or interests in abstraction from social contexts. In particular, according to these communitarians, there is no point in attempting to found a theory of justice on principles that individuals would choose in a hypothetical state of ignorance of their social, economic, and historical circumstances (from behind a Rawlsian "veil of ignorance"), because such individuals cannot exist, even in principle.

Liberal scholars argued that this line of criticism is overstated or misconceived. Despite its emphasis on autonomy and rights, they contended, contemporary liberalism is not incompatible with the notion of a socially embedded self. Indeed, Rawls himself, in his foundational work A Theory of Justice, recognized the importance of what he called "social unions" and asserted that "only in a social union is the individual complete." Thus, according to liberals, the communitarian critique does not rebut the core of liberal theory but merely serves as a corrective to "stronger" liberal doctrines such as libertarianism, which does embrace an atomized notion of individual identity (see below A synthesis: Rights and responsibilities).

Academic communitarians also drew upon Aristotle and the German idealist philosopher George Friedrich Wilhelm Hegel to argue that some conception of the good must be formulated on the social level and that the community cannot be a normative-neutral realm. Unless there is a social formulation of the good, there can be no normative foundation upon which to draw to settle conflicts of value between different individuals and groups. Such an overriding good (e.g., the national well-being) enables persons with different moral outlooks or ideological backgrounds to find principled (rather than merely prudential) common ground.

Liberals and libertarians responded by characterizing the communitarian position as akin to East Asian authoritarian communitarianism. They also argued that social formulations of the good—and the obligations they generate, which individuals must then discharge—can sometimes be oppressive. Some libertarians cited taxes and mandatory vaccinations as examples of such obligations.

A Synthesis: Rights and Responsibilities

Responsive communitarianism may be considered a synthesis of both liberal and academic-communitarian concerns. Sandel and Taylor in effect held that many forms of philosophical liberalism, especially libertarianism, overemphasize autonomy and rights at the expense of the common good. However, in doing so, they were less than clear about the standing of individual rights, including human rights. Indeed, Alasdair MacIntyre asserted that rights were merely figments of the imagination, like unicorns. Responsive communitarians attempted to bridge this divide. In their platform and in their academic works, they posited that all societies must heed the moral claims of two core values, the common good and autonomy and rights.

They also held that, because actual societies tend to tilt toward one core value or the other, they need to be pulled back toward the centre. Thus Japan, in their view, was strongly dedicated to the common good but insufficiently committed to the rights of women, ethnic minorities, and the disabled, while the United States during the presidential administration of Ronald Reagan (1981-89) and the United Kingdom during the prime ministership of Margaret Thatcher (1979-90) attached undue importance to individual rights. The early prime ministership of Tony Blair demonstrated a concern for the common good through its policies of devolution and the "stakeholder society" (the idea that businesses should be responsive to workers, consumers, and other groups whose interests they affect), as did the early administration of George W. Bush through its dedication to "compassionate conservatism." After the 2001 September 11 attacks, however, the common good in the United States was increasingly identified with national security, and some individual rights (e.g., the right to habeas corpus) were curtailed.

In the same vein, responsive communitarians also warned against excessively expansive definitions of rights and championed modern communities in which people find both a rich web of social relations and considerable degrees of freedom. In the early 21st century, responsive communitarians believed that the Scandinavian countries had achieved the best balance, though even there some individual rights were being curtailed for security reasons and in response to anti-immigrant sentiment.

Policy Implications

Responsive communitarianism developed criteria for the formulation of policies that would enable societies to cope with the potential conflicts between the common good and individual rights, including in areas such as public health versus individual privacy and national security versus individual liberty. These criteria, which must be applied jointly, included the following:

1. No change is justified in governing public policies and norms unless society encounters serious challenges, because these kinds of changes exact considerable societal costs.
2. Limitations on rights can be considered only if there are significant gains to the common good—what the U.S. courts refer to as a "compelling interest"—and if the intrusion is as limited as possible.
3. Adverse side effects that result from policy changes must be treated, above all, by introducing stronger mechanisms of accountability and oversight.

An example of the application of these criteria can be seen in the debate in the United States concerning whether to improve public health by testing newborn babies for HIV. According to communitarians, such tests would be justified if: (1) they saved lives (an infant infected with HIV has a strong chance of not developing AIDS if it is not breastfed and is treated with the drug AZT), (2) the intrusion were limited to testing blood that would be collected anyway, and (3) the adverse side effects could be limited by regulations that ban the disclosure of test results to nonmedical personnel.

Socially Constructed Preferences

The communitarian approach challenges the liberal view—reflected in many social sciences, especially neoclassical economics and the study of law—that the political and economic preferences of individuals should be respected and that their aggregation should guide the governance of the polity (through voting) and the economy (through the influence of consumer spending on the production and distribution of consumer goods). It is fully legitimate, for example, for public authorities to urge people to resist the appeals of political extremists or to encourage them to save more of their money. Communitarianism also challenges the libertarian position that it is paternalistic to interfere with individual choices based on personal preferences. In keeping with their view concerning the social constitution of individual identity, communitarians argue that personal preferences are to a significant extent not autonomous but rather a reflection of the larger culture, aspects of which can be heavily influenced by non-rational forces such as commercial advertising. Hence, public efforts to influence such preferences in beneficial ways, say in campaigns against smoking and obesity, do not undermine personal autonomy and are not a violation of human dignity.

The Third Sector

Communitarianism adds a major element to a centuries-old debate in the West over the proper roles of government on the one hand and the market on the other. Communitarians argue that attention also must be paid to the role of civil society, including families, local and nonresidential communities, voluntary associations, schools, places of worship, foundations, and nonprofit corporations. It stresses that much of the behaviour that must be regulated in any society, as well as the factors that encourage people to discharge their social responsibilities (e.g., caring for children), are influenced by this third sector. Communitarians point to the importance of social norms and informal social controls in fostering pro-social conduct and in providing the moral foundations (e.g., trust) required for the successful operation of both governments and markets. The American political journalist Jonathan Rauch introduced the term "soft communitarianism" to refer to communitarianism that focuses on the role of civil society, in contrast to "hard," East Asian communitarianism, which views the state as the primary social agent.

Cultural Relativism and the Global Community

Because communitarians favour communal formulations of the good, which are necessarily particular to each community, they are vulnerable to the charge of ethical relativism, or to the claim that there is no absolute good but only different goods for different communities, cultures, or societies. Walzer adopted a clearly relativistic position in his book Spheres of Justice (1983), in which he asserted that the caste system is "good" by the standards of traditional Indian society. Critics argued, however, that his position was untenable. One simply needs to consider a community that champions honour killings, lynchings, or book burnings to realize that communities should not be the ultimate arbiters of that which is good. While acknowledging that different communities may have different ultimate values, Taylor argued—as did Rawls—that an "overlapping consensus" on specific norms and policies is still possible, though different communities may have different reasons for believing that a given norm or policy is right. In the United States, for example, abortion-rights and antiabortion activists have worked together to make adoption easier and to improve the quality of day-care centres. According to a much more-contested argument, advanced by the American scholar of religion Don Browning, there are some substantive universal values, such as human rights and the integrity of the global climate, that can provide a foundation for particularistic, communal ones.

Closely related to the question of the scope of morality is the question of the scope of community itself. Historically, communities have been local. However, as the reach of economic and technological forces extended, more-expansive communities became necessary in order to provide effective normative and political guidance to and control of these forces—hence the rise of national communities in Europe in the 17th century. Since the late 20th century there has been a growing recognition that the scope of even these communities is too limited, as many challenges that people now face, such as the threat of nuclear war and the reality of global environmental degradation, cannot be handled on a national basis. This has led to the quest for more-encompassing communities. The most advanced experiment in building a supranational community is the European Union (EU). However, so far the EU has not developed the kind of social integration and shared values that a strong community requires.

A similar issue arises with regard to the global community, currently more an ideal than a reality. Could such a community be constructed top-down, say, through some kind of enhanced United Nations (UN)? Or will it arise from the bottom up, through societal processes and institutions such as international nongovernmental organizations (NGOs), the transnational sharing of norms (e.g., for protecting the environment), a global second language (about one quarter of the world's population has at least a functional command of English), and other informal social networks? The question remains whether, ultimately, world governance can thrive without a worldwide community.

MULTICULTURALISM

Cultural diversity has been present in societies for a very long time. In Ancient Greece, there were various small regions with different costumes, traditions, dialects and identities, for example, those from Aetolia, Locris, Doris and Epirus. In the Ottoman Empire, Muslims were the majority, but there were also Christians, Jews, pagan Arabs, and other religious groups. In the 21st century, societies remain culturally diverse, with most countries having a mixture of individuals from different races, linguistic backgrounds, religious affiliations, and so forth. Contemporary political theorists have labeled this phenomenon of the coexistence of different cultures in the same geographical space multiculturalism. That is, one of the meanings of multiculturalism is the coexistence of different cultures.

The term 'multiculturalism', however, has not been used only to describe a culturally diverse society, but also to refer to a kind of policy that aims at protecting cultural diversity. Although multiculturalism is a phenomenon with a long history and there have been countries historically that did adopt multicultural policies, like the Ottoman Empire, the systematic study of multiculturalism in philosophy has only flourished in the late twentieth century, when it began to receive special attention, especially from liberal philosophers. The philosophers who initially dedicated more time to the topic were mainly Canadian, but in the 21st century it is a widespread topic in contemporary political philosophy. Before multiculturalism became a topic in political philosophy, most literature in this area focused on topics related to the fair redistribution of resources; conversely, the topic of multiculturalism in the realm of political philosophy highlights the idea that cultural identities are also normatively relevant and that policies ought to take these identities into consideration.

To understand the discussion of multiculturalism in contemporary political philosophy, there are four key topics that should be taken into consideration; these are the meaning of the concept of 'culture', the meaning of the concept of 'multiculturalism', the debate about justice between cultural groups and the discussion regarding the practical implications of multicultural practices.

Multiculturalism is before anything else a theory about culture and its value. Hence, to understand what multiculturalism is it is indispensable that the meaning of culture is clarified. In this section, five concepts of culture that are predominant in contemporary political philosophy are outlined: semiotic, normative, societal, economic/rational choice and the anti-essentialist cosmopolitanism conceptions of culture. As Festenstein points out, these are not competing conceptions of culture, where each selects a distinct set of necessary and sufficient conditions for the right application of the predicate. Contrastingly, all these conceptions of culture defend, even though in slightly different ways, the idea that culture is constitutive of personal identity. Therefore, it is possible to simultaneously defend, say, a semiotic conception of culture and admit that a culture may have normative, societal, economic and cosmopolitan features.

The semiotic conception of culture was very popular in the 1960s, and has its roots in classic social anthropology. Social anthropologists like Margaret Mead, Levi-Straus and Malinowski considered culture as a set of social systems, symbols, representations and practices of signification held by a certain group. Thus, from this perspective, a culture is defined as a system of ideals or structures of symbolic meaning. Put differently, according to this view, culture should be understood as a symbolic system which in turn is a way of communication which represents the world. This form of communication is based on symbols, underlying structures and beliefs or ideological principles. One of the philosophers endorsing this perspective of culture is Parekh. According to Parekh, human life is organized by a historically created system of meaning and significance and in turn this is what we call culture.

Taylor who contends that human beings are self-interpreting animals, that is, human beings' identities depend on the way each individual sees them self, also endorses this viewpoint. These self-understandings necessarily have to have meaning. Hence, the thesis that human beings are self-interpreting animals presupposes that human existence is constituted by meaning. In turn, this implies that human beings are also language animals. By language, what is meant are all modes of expression (music, spoken language, art and so forth). To be language animals means that individuals are capable of creating value and meaning, and in Taylor's view, these meanings have their origins in each individual's cultural community. That is to say, language is, at least primarily, a result of the interaction of individuals with their own cultural community. More precisely, linguistic meanings and self-interpretations have their origins in individuals' linguistic communities. Thus, culture is a system of symbolic meaning.

Bearing this in mind, it can be argued that the study of culture from the semiotic perspective is the analysis or elucidation of meaning. As in hermeneutics, where the reader has to interpret the meaning of a text, in culture one has to interpret its internal logic. An example of interpreting the internal logic of a culture could be given by the story told by Quine regarding the native who says 'Gavagai!' whenever he sees a rabbit. Quine suggests that there may be multiple meanings associated with this actions; it may mean 'rabbit', 'food', 'an undetached rabbit-part', 'there will be a storm tonight' (if the native is superstitious) and so forth. The symbolism, sign process or system of meaning underlying this action is what, according to the point of view of semeiotics, culture is, and this is what should be studied. In short, it is the study of culture's autonomous logic.

The normative conception of culture is usually adopted by communitarians. From this point of view, culture is important because it is what provides beliefs, norms and moral reasons, prompting individuals to act. Hence, part of what a person is includes their moral commitments; their practical identity is made up of these moral commitments, while their reasons to act are motivated by their moral commitments. In other words, according to the normative conception of culture, the term 'culture' refers to a group of norms and beliefs that are distinctive and which constitute the practical identify of a group of individuals; thereby, people's values and commitments result, in part, from culture.

By way of illustration, part of what a Christian, a Muslim and a Jew are is constituted by the fact they abide or follow the moral teachings of the Bible, the Quran and the Torah, respectively. Therefore, understanding who one is about understanding one's moral commitments and therefore culture is norm-providing. Shachar is one of the philosophers who endorses this conception of culture.

According to her, culture is a world view, both comprehensive and distinguishable, whereby community law is able to be created. To minority groups that have a culture, Shachar attaches the label 'nomoi communities'. According to her, this term can apply to religious, ethnic, racial, tribal and national groups, for all these groups exhibit the normative dimension required to be classified as a 'nomoi community'.

The normative conception of culture is usually associated with the semiotic, in the sense that one does not contradict the other; in fact, they may be complementary. For instance, Taylor endorses both perspectives of culture. However, this is not necessary because the system of meaning and significance does not need to provide moral reasons in order to motivate action. From the semiotic perspective, what someone is not necessarily his or her moral commitments; it can be anything within the system. That is, the system of meaning may be based on anything while, according to the normative conception of culture, culture is strong source of one's moral commitments.

To explain how the semiotic and normative conceptions of culture can be compatible, consider Taylor's conception of culture. Taylor considers that individuals are self-interpreting animals. The fact that individuals are thus entails that human existence is constituted by meanings. From the normative point of view, these meanings are moral evaluations/strong evaluations. This refers to the distinctions of worth that individuals make regarding objects of desire. In other words, it is a background of distinctions between things that individuals consider important or worthy and those things which are considered less valuable. From the normative perspective of culture, individuals direct their lives and purposes towards what they consider morally worthwhile.

In short, these strong evaluations or moral frameworks are what indicate to individuals what is meaningful and rewarding. That is, they are motivated by these evaluations. Therefore, the self has a moral dimension, in the sense that rationality and identity refer to moral evaluations. Identity is connected with morality because what individuals are is constituted by their self-interpretations, which are ultimately provided by strong evaluation. These moral beliefs or strong evaluations are in turn provided by an individual's culture–that is why this can be considered a normative conception of culture.

The societal conception of culture is a concept mainly used by the Canadian philosopher Kymlicka. In order to understand this, it is helpful to consider Kymlicka's dual typology of the sources of diversity that exist in contemporary societies; for Kymlicka there are two kinds of diversity: polyethnic minorities and national minorities.

Kymlicka uses the term polyethnicity to refer to the kind of diversity resulting from immigration. Polyethnic minorities refer to what is commonly defined as ethnic groups. According to him, polyethnic groups are usually not territorially concentrated; rather they are dispersed around the country to which they migrated. Furthermore, Kymlicka affirms that they do not usually want to be segregated from the culture of the majority; rather they want to integrate with it, demanding policies that give them equal citizenship. For instance, these groups demand language rights, voting rights, places in parliament and so forth. However, even though this demand for equal citizenship is usually what polyethnic groups aspire to, this is not always the case. Kymlicka contends that polyethnic groups can be sub-divided into liberal and illiberal groups. Liberal polyethnic groups have aspirations that do not go against liberal values, usually aspiring to be integrated into society, demanding policies for equal citizenship. As an example, Kymlicka usually refers to Latin-American immigrants living in the United States, who, in broad terms, make demands for language rights, such as an education curriculum in Spanish.

On the other hand, for Kymlicka, illiberal polyethnic groups are those where the culture and the demands to the state are not in accordance with liberal values. For example, some religious minority ethnic groups advocate the death penalty for gays within their groups; others have gendered and discriminatory norms in relation to divorce and marriage. Some of these groups have demands that are more similar to the ones of national minorities but Kymlicka contends that these cases are the exception, not the rule.

Polyethnic groups are not, in Kymlicka's view, considered a culture; according to him, only nations are a culture. Kymlicka uses the term nation interchangeably with the terms culture, people and societal culture, for example, "I am using 'a culture' as synonymous with 'a nation' or 'a people'—that is, as an intergenerational community, more or less institutionally complete, occupying a given territory or homeland, sharing a distinct language and history". In Kymlicka's view, national minorities are a group in a society with a societal culture and a smaller number of members than the majority. Hence, a national minority is a societal culture where the amount of members is smaller in number than the amount of members of the majority. For Kymlicka a societal culture is a kind of social setting that provides individuals with meaningful ways of life, both in the public and private sphere. These societal cultures are important mainly because they give individuals the groundwork from which they can make choices. More precisely for Kymlicka due to the fact that societal cultures provide meaningful ways of life, they provide the social context that individuals need in order to make their own choices (that is, to be autonomous). Kymlicka's rationale is that autonomy is only possible in certain social contexts and that social context is set up by societal cultures.

From Kymlicka's point of view, national minorities or minority societal cultures usually share a number of characteristics. First, national minorities have settled in the country long ago. For example, most of the Amish communities in Pennsylvania settled there in the eighteenth century, as a result of religious persecution in Europe. Aborigines in Australia and many Native American groups in the USA have lived in that territory for a long period. Second, from Kymlicka's point of view, these groups are often territorially concentrated; for example, Quebec and Catalonia are situated in specific geographic areas of Canada and Spain, respectively. In India, Sikhs are geographically concentrated mostly in the Punjab region. Third, according to Kymlicka, the institutions and practices of these groups provide a full range of human activities; this means that nations are embodied in common economic, political and educational institutions.

These institutions are not based only on shared meanings, memories and values but include common practices and procedures. Put differently, nations are institutionally complete in the sense that they encompass a wide institutional elaboration that encompasses a variety of areas of life; they have their own governments, laws, schools and so forth. In Kymlicka's view, the fourth characteristic that national minorities have in common is that they usually aspire to either total or partial segregation from the larger society. That is, these groups wish to be a totally or partially separate society, with a different state, governed by their own laws and institutions.

Hence, national minorities, in Kymlicka's view, do not want to integrate in the larger society; rather they wish to be able to have a certain degree of autonomy. For example, many Quebecois want to be able to have their own government institutions, run in the way they wish, like schools run in French. Often, the Amish want to be left alone, without intervention from the state in their internal affairs. More precisely, one of the demands of some Amish communities is that they are exempt from the basic educational requirements that other citizens of the USA have to abide by, namely, the minimum literacy requirements.

This, as will be explained later on, relates to other set of normative questions about what groups can and cannot impose to their members. In order to address this problem, Kymlicka draws a distinction between practices that can be imposed (external protections) and practices that cannot be imposed (internal restrictions).

From Kymlicka's point of view, national minorities can further be sub-divided into liberal and illiberal minorities. The former are those whose demands are compatible with liberal values, that is, their demands do not violate individuals' rights and liberties. Under the concept of liberal national minorities are examples like Quebecois and Catalonians; these national minorities usually demand the right to use a different language in schools and their other institutions, and this does not necessarily violate any liberal value. The concept of illiberal national minorities refers to groups that wish to endorse illiberal values, like the death penalty for gays and lesbians.

Rational choice is a theory that aims to explain and predict social behavior. From the viewpoint of rational choice, individuals act self-interestedly when they take into consideration their preferences and the information available. Self-interest means that individuals tend to maximize what is valuable for them. In other words, human behavior is goal-oriented. It is goal oriented by its preferences, that is, individuals act according to their preferences. For instance, if an individual prefers a hot chocolate to a vanilla milkshake or a strawberry milkshake and all the options are available, he will choose hot chocolate (other things being equal).

According to the rational choice view, the information available strongly affects behavior. By way of illustration, if an individual does not know that hot chocolate is available he will not choose it. Thus individuals act according to their self-interest, information and preferences.

If a certain person's preference is to buy the tastiest hot chocolate and this person has the information that the tastiest hot chocolate is sold in a particular store, then this person will act in order to achieve her/his own interest, that is, by going to that store and purchasing it there. Obviously, these actions are limited by the options available and by the actions of others. Therefore, if there is no hot chocolate on the market, this person will not be able to buy it–the option is not available because the suppliers decided not to offer hot chocolate. In this sense, an individual's are dependent on their circumstances and on the actions of others.

With these premises in mind, a possible definition of culture from a rational choice perspective is provided by Laitin, whereby culture is:

an equilibrium in a well-defined set of circumstances in which members of a group sharing in common descent, symbolic practices and/or high levels of interaction—and thereby becoming a cultural group—are able to condition their behavior on common knowledge beliefs about the behavior of all members of the group.

Therefore, there are four key features of this conception of culture. First, a cultural group is a group in which individuals share a certain number of characteristics that differentiate them from other individuals–for example, language or religion. Second, all these individuals share a high degree of common knowledge. What common knowledge means in this context is that the members of a certain culture have shared information and mutual expectations about the actions and beliefs of others in the group. Third, there is a cultural equilibrium when the incentive to act or the self-interest to act is according to the beliefs of his or her own culture. More precisely, a cultural equilibrium occurs when individuals' have an interest in acting in accordance with the norms and practices of their culture. These norms and practices can be any, but Laitin provides an insightful example with respect to the old Chinese tradition of foot binding.

Laitin explains that it was very difficult for Chinese women to marry a man if they did not engage in the foot binding tradition. In this case, most Chinese parents forced their daughters to engage in this practice owing to the fact that their interest in finding a husband to their daughters was in accordance with the cultural practice of foot binding. Finally, a well-defined set of circumstances can be described as a kind of situation where the type of interactions that members have with each other are ones of coordination and not conflict. That is, individuals' actions are ones that are arranged in a way that match or complement each other, rather than being in conflict.

The concepts of culture mentioned above have been strongly criticized by some political theorists. Some of these, who direct their criticisms mostly to the semiotic, normative and societal conceptions of culture, argue that these conceptions are essentialist views of culture that inaccurately describe social reality. However, as Festenstein has pointed out, these criticisms are sometimes misplaced, that is, these conceptions of culture do not necessarily need to be essentialist.

In general terms, from an essentialist point of view, there is a distinction between the essential and accidental properties that the different kinds of objects and subjects may have. Accidental properties are properties that are not necessarily present in all members of a certain group of objects or subjects. Essential properties are those that define the objects or subjects, that is, objects or subjects necessarily need to have these properties in order to be members of a certain group.

Furthermore, members of other groups do not have this property or set of properties; otherwise they too would belong to this group. By way of illustration, a bookshelf in order to be a bookshelf has to necessarily be constructed in a way that makes it possible to hold books–this is its essential property. The fact that a specific bookshelf is brown, black or blue is an accidental property–it does not change what the object is and it is indifferent to its definition.

These properties are necessary and sufficient not only to include a certain object or subject in the group but also to exclude any object or subject which does not share these properties. Bearing this in mind, it can be concluded that essences are given by differences and similarities; for what defines a subject is what it has in common with the subjects of the same group, which in turn is a characteristic that other groups do not have.

In terms of what this means to culture, it means identifying the social characteristics or attributes that make the group what it is, and that all members of that group necessarily share. Moreover, these characteristics are what differentiate members of that group from others and clearly exclude others. For example, for an essentialist, to classify Muslims as Muslims means to identify a certain characteristic, like shared practices and beliefs, common to all of the individuals who identify as Muslims. Thus, essentialism applied to culture would be that a certain culture means having a certain characteristic or set of characteristics that all members share, and which no one outside the group does. Hence, from this point of view, the identity of the group is constituted by the set of properties or attributes which are essential to this particular group.

According to the critics of essentialism, this theory necessarily makes two wrong assumptions about culture. First, the critics state that essentialists wrongly affirm that cultures are clearly demarcated wholes and their practices and beliefs do not overlap with other cultures. Thus, according to this argument, essentialists wrongly affirm that beliefs and practices are exclusive to each culture.

This premise is necessary for defending essentialism because from an essentialist point of view; different groups cannot share the same essential properties; otherwise they would belong to the same group. Second, essentialists, according to these critics, wrongly picture cultures as internally uniform or homogeneous. Put differently, essentialists consider that individuals with the same culture all agree and interpret practices in the same way.

Furthermore, they all place the same value on the practices of the group. This second premise is necessary for essentialist thinking owing to the fact that a group has to have a property or a set of properties that is predicated of all individuals in order for them to be members of this group.

This essentialist perspective of culture has however been widely contested. The general argument is that essentialism stereotypes and makes abusive generalizations of what groups are. That is to say, according to the critics, essentialism is descriptively inaccurate. Criticism of this perspective contends that the first premise lacks empirical evidence. There is no evidence that there is any exclusivity in terms of practices and beliefs, in fact, evidence suggests the opposite; cultures borrow practices and beliefs in order to increase their fitness.

Cultures are not bounded, owing to the fact that culture is constantly changing, influenced by local, national and global resources. Hence, according to this view, it is not possible to clearly demarcate the boundaries of cultures because they share a number of practices and beliefs. There is significant overlapping of cultures, especially in neighboring cultures. The distinction between cultures is, therefore, overemphasized–the boundaries between cultures not being clearly demarcated.

With regards to the second premise, the criticism contends that it is false to say that there is internal homogeneity inside a group in terms of needs, interests and beliefs. Rather, the social actors of cultural groups have different needs, interests and interpretations about the beliefs and practices of groups. Furthermore, in many cases, they consider these practices and beliefs quite contestable, discussable and open to different interpretations. Therefore, there is wide disagreement about cultural meaning. Anti-essentialists contend that there are too many exceptions to make essentialist claims. Therefore, there are a considerable number of counter-examples to this generalization. As a consequence, some anti-essentialists usually argue that these categories should be substituted by thinner categories. Thus, rather than speaking about women, one should speak about black women, or lesbian Muslim women.

Taking this into consideration, different, more flexible conceptions of culture have been suggested; perhaps the most well-known being the cosmopolitan conception of culture, defended by Waldron. In Waldron's view, cultures are dynamic and in continuous creation and interchange. Consequently, cultures overlap with each other, making it impossible to attribute exclusive properties to one single culture and to differentiate between them. In other words, according to this view, there is a melange of cultures because people move between cultures by enjoying the opportunities that each provides. Hence, individuals live in a The term 'multiculturalism' is sometimes used to describe a condition of society; more precisely, it is used to describe a society where a variety of different cultures coexist. Many countries in the world are culturally diverse. Canada is just one example, including a variety of cultures such as English Canadians, Quebecois, Native Americans, Amish, Hutterites and Chinese immigrants. China is another country that can also be considered culturally diverse. In contemporary China, there are 56 officially recognized ethnic groups, and 55 of these groups are ethnic minorities who make up approximately 8.41 percent of China's overall population. The other ethnic group is that of Han Chinese, which holds majority status.

There are a variety of ways whereby societies can be diverse, for example, culture can come in many forms. Perhaps the chief ways in which a country can be culturally diverse is by having different religious groups, different linguistic groups, groups that define themselves by their territorial identity and variant racial groups.

Religious diversity is a widespread phenomenon in many countries. India can be given as an example of a country which is religiously diverse, including citizens who are Sikhs, Hindus, Buddhists, among other religious groups. The US is also religiously diverse, including Mormons, Amish, Hutterites, Catholics, Jews and so forth. These groups differentiate from each other via a variety of factors. Some of these are the Gods worshiped, the public holidays, the religious festivals and the dress codes.

Linguistic diversity is also widespread. In the 21st century, there are more than 200 countries in the world and around 6000 spoken languages. Linguistic diversity usually results from two kinds of groups. First, it results from immigrants who move to a country where the language spoken is not their native language. This is the case for those Cubans and Puerto Ricans who immigrated to the United States; it is also the case for Ukrainian immigrants who moved to Portugal.

The second kind of groups that are a cause of linguistic diversity are national minorities. National minorities are groups that have either settled in the country for a long time, but do not share the same language with the majority. Some examples include Quebecois in Canada, Catalans and Basques in Spain, and the Uyghur in China. Usually, these linguistic groups are territorially concentrated; furthermore, minority groups that fall into this category usually demand a high degree of autonomy. In particular, minority groups usually demand that they have the regional power to self-govern, that is, to run their territory as if it was an independent country or to succeed and become a different country.

A third kind of group diversity can results from distinct territory location. This territory location does not necessary mean that members of distinct cultures are, in fact, different. That is, it is not necessary that habits, traditions, customs, and so forth are significantly different. However, these distinct groups identify themselves as different from others because of the specific geographical area in which they are located. Possibly, in the UK, this is what distinguishes Scots from English. Even though there are historical differences between Scots and English, if one assumes that these two groups have little to distinguish themselves from each other, other than their geographical location, they would fit this third kind of group diversity. As mentioned above, these differences are conceptual and, in practice, cultural groups are characterized by a variety of features and not just one.

The fourth kind of group diversity is race. Races are groups whose physical characteristics are imbued with social significance. In other words, race is a socially constructed concept in the sense that it is the result of individuals giving social significance to a set of characteristics they consider that stand out in a person's physical appearance, such as skin color, eye color, hair color, bone/jaw structure and so forth. However, the mere existence of different physical characteristics does not mean that there is a multicultural environment/society. For instance, it cannot be affirmed that Sweden is multicultural because there are Swedes with blue eyes and others with green.

Physical characteristics create a multicultural environment only when these physical characteristics mean that groups strongly identify with their physical characteristics and where these physical characteristics are socially perceived as something that strongly differentiates them from other groups. That is, racial cultural diversity is not simply the existence of different physical characteristics. Rather, these different physical characteristics must entail a sense of common identity which, in turn, are socially perceived as something that differentiates the members of that group to others. However, many times this idea of common identity is exaggerated, as Waldron's argument suggests.

For instance, even though there is the idea that a black culture exists in the United States, Appiah denies that such black culture exists, since there is no common identity among blacks in the United States. An example of a physical difference that is considered socially significant and, therefore, creates a multicultural society/environment can be seen in the Tutsis and Hutus of Rwanda. In general terms, Tutsis and Hutus are very similar, due to the fact that they speak the same language, share the same territory and follow the same traditions. Nevertheless, Tutsis are usually taller and thinner than Hutus. The social significance given to these physical differences are sufficient for members of both groups, broadly speaking, to identify as members of one group or the other, and subsequently oppose to each other.

Obviously, groups are not, most of the time, identified only by being linguistically different, territorially concentrated or religiously distinct. In fact, most groups have more than one of these characteristics. For instance, Sikhs in India, besides being religiously different, are also characterized, in general terms, by their geographical location. Namely, they are localized in the Punjab region of India. The Uyghur, from China, have a different language, are usually Muslims and are usually located in Xinjiang. Thus, the classification is helpful for understanding the characteristics of each group, but does not mean that these groups are simply defined by that characteristic.

A question that arises is whether this criticism entails that any attempt to define culture is mistaken. Some anti-essentialists like Narayan contend that this is not the case. Rather, she contends that cultures can be defined if two points are taken into consideration. First, cultures are fluid and constantly changing; hence, any definition of culture should consider that cultures are always in flux. Second, broader categories should be substituted by thinner categories. This means that rather than using terms like 'African Culture', one should use terms like 'Tutsi culture in Rwanda'.

The term 'multiculturalism' can also be used to refer to a kind of policy. This kind of policy has two main characteristics. First, it aims at addressing the different demands of cultural groups. That is, it is a kind of policy that refers to the different normative challenges (ethnic conflict, internal illiberalism, federal autonomy, and so forth) that arise as a result of cultural diversity. For example, these are policies that aim at addressing the different normative challenges that arise from minority groups, like Quebecois, wishing to have their own institutions in a different language from the rest of Canada. To contrast with redistributive policies, multicultural policies are not primarily about distributive justice, that is, who gets what share of resources, although multicultural policies may refer to redistribution accidentally (Fraser, 2001). Multicultural policies aim at correcting the kind of disadvantages that some individuals are victims of, and that result from these individuals' cultural identity. For instance, these are policies that aim at correcting a disadvantage that may result from someone being a member of a certain religion. In the case of some Muslims, this can mean addressing the problem of Muslims living in a Christian country and demanding different public holidays than the majority to celebrate their own festivals such as Eid-ul-Fitr.

Second, multicultural policies are policies that aim at providing groups the means by which individuals can pursue their cultural differences. Put differently, multicultural policies have as their objectives, the preservation, allowance or celebration of differences between different groups. Consequently, multicultural policies contrast with assimilation. That is, according to the assimilationist view, it is acceptable that people are different, but the final goal of policies should be to make the minority group become part of the majority group, that is, to be accepted by those in the majority group, and to somehow find a consensus position between different cultures.

Contrastingly, multiculturalism acknowledges that people have different ways of life and, in general terms, the state ought not to assimilate these groups but to give them the tools for pursuing their own ways of life or culture. That is, from a multiculturalist point of view, the final objective of policies is neither the standardization of cultural forms nor any form of uniformity or homogeneity; rather, its objective is to allow and give the means for groups to pursue their differences.

According to Kymlicka, in the context of contemporary liberal political philosophy, there have been two waves of writings on multiculturalism. This discussion of what policies ought to be undertaken in order to protect minority cultures is included in what Kymlicka called the first wave of the wave of writings on multiculturalism. In his view, the first wave of writing focused on assessing to what extent it is just, from a liberal point of view, to give rights to groups so that they can pursue their cultural differences.

In this first wave of writings, contemporary liberal political philosophers have discussed what kind of inequalities exist between majorities and minorities, and how these should be addressed. In other words, the discussion has been about what kind of intergroup inequalities exist, and what the state should do about them. In general terms, contemporary liberal political philosophers who have written about this topic have taken two different stands.

On the one hand, some liberal political philosophers defend that state institutions should be blind to difference and that individuals should be given a uniform set of rights and liberties. In these authors' views, cultural diversity, religious freedom and so forth are sufficiently protected by these sets of rights and liberties, especially by freedom of association and conscience. Therefore, those who stand for a uniform set of rights and liberties contend that ascribing rights on the basis of membership in a group is a discriminatory and immoral policy that creates citizenship hierarchies that are undesirable and unjust. Thus, in the view of these contemporary liberal philosophers, involvement in the cultural character of society is something that the state is under the duty to not do.

On the other hand, some philosophers have taken the opposite view on this matter. For example, there are some contemporary liberal political philosophers who are more sympathetic to the idea of ascribing rights to groups and have defended difference-sensitive policies. As Kymlicka points out, these contemporary liberal political philosophers have tried to show that difference-sensitive rules are not inherently unjust. In general terms, these contemporary political philosophers argue that a regime of difference-sensitive policies does not necessarily entail a hierarchization of citizenship and unfair privileges for some groups. Rather, they argue that difference-sensitive policies aim at correcting intergroup inequalities and disadvantages in the cultural market. Moreover, some of these philosophers contend that difference-blind policies favor the needs, interests and identities of the majority. These philosophers who consider that groups are entitled to special rights can be classified as a form of multicultural citizenship.

Those who defend special rights for groups have suggested a variety of policies. In his book The Multiculturalism of Fear, Levy systematically exposed the kinds of difference-sensitive policies that are usually discussed in the literature. According to him, difference-sensitive policies can be divided into eight categories: exemptions, assistance, symbolic claims, recognition/enforcement, special representation, self-government, external rules and internal rules.

Exemptions to laws are usually rights based on a negative liberty of non-interference from the state in a specific affair, which would cause a significant burden to a certain group. Or, to put it another way, exemptions to the law happen when the state abstains from interfering with or obliging a certain group who desire to practice something in order to diminish their burden.

Exemptions can also be a limitation of someone else's liberty to impose some costs on a certain group. Imagine that there is a general law that decrees corporations have the right to impose a dress code upon their employees. However, having this general law would burden those groups for whom dressing in a certain manner (that is, different from the one required by the company) is a very important value. For example, for many Sikh men and Muslim women it is very important to wear turbans and headscarves, respectively. Hence, it can be claimed that giving these individuals the option of either finding another job or rejecting their dress code can be a significant burden to them; given that the choice of dressing in a certain way is sometimes much harder for Sikh men and Muslim women than for a Westerner, and that it would undermine their identity, an exemption may be justified. Hence, these groups would be able to engage in practices that are not allowable for the majority of citizens.

Assistance rights aim to aid individuals in overcoming the obstacles they face because they belong to a certain group. In other words, assistance rights aim to rectify disadvantages experienced by certain individuals, as a result of their membership of a certain group, when compared to the majority. This can mean funding individuals to pursue their goals or using positive discrimination to help them in a variety of ways. Language rights are an example of this approach. Suppose that some individuals from Catalonia cannot speak Spanish.

An assistance measure would be having people speak both Spanish and Catalan at public institutions, so that they can serve people from the minority as well the minority language group. Another example would be awarding subsidies to help groups preserve their cohesion by maintaining their practices and beliefs, and by allowing individuals from a minority to participate in public institutions as full citizens. Most of these practices are temporary, but they do not need to be (language rights, for example, are often not temporary).

Symbolic claims refer to problems which do not affect individuals' lives directly or seriously, but which may make the relations between individuals from different groups better. In a multicultural country, where there are multiple religions, ethnicities and ways of life, it may not make sense to have certain symbols that represent only a specific culture. Symbolic claims are ones that require, on the grounds of equality, the inclusion of all the cultures in a specific country in that country's symbols. An example would be including Catholic, Sikh, Muslim, Protestant, Welsh, Northern Irish, Scottish, and English symbols on both the British flag and in the national anthem. Not integrating minority symbols may be considered as dispensing a lack of respect and unequal treatment to minorities.

Recognition is a demand for integrating a specific law or cultural practice into the larger society. If individuals want to integrate a specific law, they can ask for the law to become part of the major legal system. Hence, Sharia law could form part of divorce law for Muslims, while Aboriginal law could run in conjunction with Australian property rights law. It could also be a requirement to include certain groups in the history books used in schools–for example, to include the history of Indian and Pakistani immigrants in British history textbooks. Failing to integrate this law may bring a substantive burden to bear on individuals' identity. In the Muslim case, because family law is of crucial importance to their identity, they may be considerably burdened by having to abide by a Western perspective of divorce. With regards to Aboriginal law, because hunting is essential for their way of life, if other individuals own the(ir) land this may undermine the Aboriginal culture.

Special representation rights are designed to protect groups which have been systematically unrepresented and disadvantaged in the larger society. Minority groups may be under-represented in the institutions of a society, and in order to place them in a position of equal bargaining power, it is necessary to provide special rights to the members of these groups. Hence, these rights aim to defend individuals' interests in a more equal manner by guaranteeing some privileges or preventing discrimination. One way to achieve this is by setting aside extra seats for minorities in parliament.

Self-government rights are usually what are claimed by national minorities (for example, Pueblo Indians and Quebecois) and they usually demand some degree of autonomy and self-determination. This sometimes implies demands for exclusive occupation of land and territorial jurisdiction. The reason groups sometimes may need these rights is that the kind of autonomy they give is a necessary condition by which individuals can develop their cultures, which is in the best interest of a culture's members. More precisely, a specific educational curriculum, language right or jurisdiction over a territory may be a necessary requirement for the survival and prosperity of a particular culture and its members. This is compatible with both freedom and equality; it is compatible with freedom because it allows individuals access to their culture and to make their own choices; it is consistent with equality because it places individuals on an equal footing in terms of cultural access.

What Levy classifies as external rules can be considered as kinds of rights for self-government. They involve restricting other people's freedom in order to preserve a certain culture. Hence, Aborigines in Australia employ external safeguards to protect their land. For example, freedom of movement is limited to outsiders who circulate in Aboriginal territory; furthermore, outsiders do not have the right to buy Aboriginal land. Demands that groups make for internal rules are those demands that aim at restricting individuals' behavior within the group.

Stigmatizing, ostracizing or excommunicating individuals from groups because they have not abided by the rules is what is usually meant by internal rules. Thus, this is the power given to groups to treat their members in a way that is not acceptable for the rest of society.

An example can be if a certain individual marries someone from another group, which may then mean he is expelled from his own group. Another case is that of the Amish who want their children to withdraw from school earlier than the rest of society. In contrast to external rules, the restrictions on freedom apply to members of the group and not to outsiders. It is controversial whether internal rules are compatible with liberal values or not. On the one hand, authors like Kymlicka affirm they are not, because they undermine individuals' autonomy, which is, in his view, a central liberal value. On the other hand, philosophers like Kukathas contend that liberals are committed to tolerance and, thereby, should accept some internal restrictions.

FEMINISM

Feminism, the belief in the social, economic, and political equality of the sexes. Although largely originating in the West, feminism is manifested worldwide and is represented by various institutions committed to activity on behalf of women's rights and interests.

Throughout most of Western history, women were confined to the domestic sphere, while public life was reserved for men. In medieval Europe, women were denied the right to own property, to study, or to participate in public life. At the end of the 19th century in France, they were still compelled to cover their heads in public, and, in parts of Germany, a husband still had the right to sell his wife. Even as late as the early 20th century, women could neither vote nor hold elective office in Europe and in most of the United States (where several territories and states granted woman suffrage long before the federal government did so). Women were prevented from conducting business without a male representative, be it father, brother, husband, legal agent, or even son. Married women could not exercise control over their own children without the permission of their husbands. Moreover, women had little or no access to education and were barred from most professions. In some parts of the world, such restrictions on women continue today.

There is scant evidence of early organized protest against such circumscribed status. In the 3rd century BCE, Roman women filled the Capitoline Hill and blocked every entrance to the Forum when consul Marcus Porcius Cato resisted attempts to repeal laws limiting women's use of expensive goods. "If they are victorious now, what will they not attempt?" Cato cried. "As soon as they begin to be your equals, they will have become your superiors."

That rebellion proved exceptional, however. For most of recorded history, only isolated voices spoke out against the inferior status of women, presaging the arguments to come. In late 14th- and early 15th-century France, the first feminist philosopher, Christine de Pisan, challenged prevailing attitudes toward women with a bold call for female education. Her mantle was taken up later in the century by Laura Cereta, a 15th-century Venetian woman who published Epistolae familiares, a volume of letters dealing with a panoply of women's complaints, from denial of education and marital oppression to the frivolity of women's attire.

The defense of women had become a literary subgenre by the end of the 16th century, when Il merito delle donne, a feminist broadside by another Venetian author, Moderata Fonte, was published posthumously. Defenders of the status quo painted women as superficial and inherently immoral, while the emerging feminists produced long lists of women of courage and accomplishment and proclaimed that women would be the intellectual equals of men if they were given equal access to education.

The so-called "debate about women" did not reach England until the late 16th century, when pamphleteers and polemicists joined battle over the true nature of womanhood. After a series of satiric pieces mocking women was published, the first feminist pamphleteer in England, writing as Jane Anger, responded with Jane Anger, Her Protection for Women. This volley of opinion continued for more than a century, until another English author, Mary Astell, issued a more reasoned rejoinder in A Serious Proposal to the Ladies. The two-volume work suggested that women inclined neither toward marriage nor a religious vocation should set up secular convents where they might live, study, and teach.

Influence of the Enlightenment

The feminist voices of the Renaissance never coalesced into a coherent philosophy or movement. This happened only with the Enlightenment, when women began to demand that the new reformist rhetoric about liberty, equality, and natural rights be applied to both sexes.

Initially, Enlightenment philosophers focused on the inequities of social class and caste to the exclusion of gender. Swiss-born French philosopher Jean-Jacques Rousseau, for example, portrayed women as silly and frivolous creatures, born to be subordinate to men. In addition, the Declaration of the Rights of Man and of the Citizen, which defined French citizenship after the revolution of 1789, pointedly failed to address the legal status of women.

Female intellectuals of the Enlightenment were quick to point out this lack of inclusivity and the limited scope of reformist rhetoric. Olympe de Gouges, a noted playwright, published Déclaration des droits de la femme et de la citoyenne (1791; "Declaration of the Rights of Woman and of the [Female] Citizen"), declaring women to be not only man's equal but his partner. The following year Mary Wollstonecraft's A Vindication of the Rights of Woman, the seminal English-language feminist work, was published in England. Challenging the notion that women exist only to please men, she proposed that women and men be given equal opportunities in education, work, and politics. Women, she wrote, are as naturally rational as men. If they are silly, it is only because society trains them to be irrelevant.

The Age of Enlightenment turned into an era of political ferment marked by revolutions in France, Germany, and Italy and the rise of abolitionism. In the United States, feminist activism took root when female abolitionists sought to apply the concepts of freedom and equality to their own social and political situations. Their work brought them in contact with female abolitionists in England who were reaching the same conclusions. By the mid-19th century, issues surrounding feminism had added to the tumult of social change, with ideas being exchanged across Europe and North America.

In the first feminist article she dared sign with her own name, Louise Otto, a German, built on the work of Charles Fourier, a French social theorist, quoting his dictum that "by the position which women hold in a land, you can see whether the air of a state is thick with dirty fog or free and clear." And after Parisian feminists began publishing a daily newspaper entitled La Voix des femmes ("The Voice of Women") in 1848, Luise Dittmar, a German writer, followed suit one year later with her journal, Soziale Reform.

The Suffrage Movement

These debates and discussions culminated in the first women's rights convention, held in July 1848 in the small town of Seneca Falls, New York. It was a spur-of-the-moment idea that sprang up during a social gathering of Lucretia Mott, a Quaker preacher and veteran social activist, Martha Wright (Mott's sister), Mary Ann McClintock, Jane Hunt, and Elizabeth Cady Stanton, the wife of an abolitionist and the only non-Quaker in the group. The convention was planned with five days' notice, publicized only by a small unsigned advertisement in a local newspaper.

Stanton drew up the "Declaration of Sentiments" that guided the Seneca Falls Convention. Using the Declaration of Independence as her guide to proclaim that "all men and women [had been] created equal," she drafted 11 resolutions, including the most radical demand—the right to the vote. With Frederick Douglass, a former slave, arguing eloquently on their behalf, all 11 resolutions passed, and Mott even won approval of a final declaration "for the overthrowing of the monopoly of the pulpit, and for the securing to woman equal participation with men in the various trades, professions and commerce."

Yet by emphasizing education and political rights that were the privileges of the upper classes, the embryonic feminist movement had little connection with ordinary women cleaning houses in Liverpool or picking cotton in Georgia. The single nonwhite woman's voice heard at this time—that of Sojourner Truth, a former slave—symbolized the distance between the ordinary and the elite. Her famous "Ain't I a Woman" speech was delivered in 1851 before the Women's Rights Convention in Akron, Ohio, but Truth did not dedicate her life to women's rights. Instead, she promoted abolitionism and a land-distribution program for other former slaves. In the speech, Truth remarked, "That man over there says that women need to be helped into carriages, and lifted over ditches, and to have the best place everywhere. Nobody ever helps me into carriages, or over mud-puddles, or gives me any best place! And ain't I a woman?"

Although Seneca Falls was followed by women's rights conventions in other states, the interest spurred by those first moments of organizing quickly faded. Concern in the United States turned to the pending Civil War, while in Europe the reformism of the 1840s gave way to the repression of the late 1850s. When the feminist movement rebounded, it became focused on a single issue, woman suffrage, a goal that would dominate international feminism for almost 70 years.

After the U.S. Civil War, American feminists assumed that woman suffrage would be included in the Fifteenth Amendment to the U.S. Constitution, which prohibited disfranchisement on the basis of race. Yet leading abolitionists refused to support such inclusion, which prompted Stanton and Susan B. Anthony, a temperance activist, to form the National Woman Suffrage Association in 1869. At first they based their demand for the vote on the Enlightenment principle of natural law, regularly invoking the concept of inalienable rights granted to all Americans by the Declaration of Independence. By 1900, however, the American passion for such principles as equality had been dampened by a flood of Eastern European immigrants and the growth of urban slums. Suffragist leaders, reflecting that shift in attitude, began appealing for the vote not on the principle of justice or on the common humanity of men and women but on racist and nativist grounds. As early as 1894, Carrie Chapman Catt declared that the votes of literate, American-born, middle-class women would balance the votes of foreigners: "Cutoff the vote of the slums and give to woman…the ballot."

This elitist inclination widened the divide between feminist organizers and the masses of American women who lived in those slums or spoke with foreign accents. As a result, working-class women—already more concerned with wages, hours, and protective legislation than with either the vote or issues such as women's property rights—threw themselves into the trade union movement rather than the feminists' ranks. Anthony, however, ceded no ground. In the 1890s she asked for labour's support for woman suffrage but insisted that she and her movement would do nothing about the demands made by working women until her own battle had been won. Similarly, when asked to support the fight against Jim Crow segregation on the nation's railroads, she refused.

Radical feminists challenged the single-minded focus on suffrage as the sine qua non of women's liberation. Emma Goldman, the nation's leading anarchist, mocked the notion that the ballot could secure equality for women, since it hardly accomplished that for the majority of American men. Women would gain their freedom, she said, only "by refusing the right to anyone over her body…by refusing to be a servant to God, the state, society, the husband, the family, etc., by making her life simpler but deeper and richer." Likewise, Charlotte Perkins Gilman, in Women and Economics, insisted that women would not be liberated until they were freed from the "domestic mythology" of home and family that kept them dependent on men.

Mainstream feminist leaders such as Stanton succeeded in marginalizing more extreme demands such as Goldman's and Gilman's, but they failed to secure the vote for women. It was not until a different kind of radical, Alice Paul, reignited the woman suffrage movement in the United States by copying English activists. Like the Americans, British suffragists, led by the National Union of Woman Suffrage Societies, had initially approached their struggle politely, with ladylike lobbying. But in 1903 a dissident faction led by Emmeline Pankhurst began a series of boycotts, bombings, and pickets. Their tactics ignited the nation, and in 1918 the British Parliament extended the vote to women householders, householders' wives, and female university graduates over the age of 30.

Following the British lead, Paul's forces, the "shock troops" of the American suffrage crusade, organized mass demonstrations, parades, and confrontations with the police. In 1920 American feminism claimed its first major triumph with the passage of the Nineteenth Amendment to the Constitution.

The Postsuffrage Era

Once the crucial goal of suffrage had been achieved, the feminist movement virtually collapsed in both Europe and the United States. Lacking an ideology beyond the achievement of the vote, feminism fractured into a dozen splinter groups: the Women's Joint Congressional Committee, a lobbying group, fought for legislation to promote education and maternal and infant health care; the League of Women Voters organized voter registration and education drives; and the Women's Trade Union Leaguelaunched a campaign for protective labour legislation for women.

Each of these groups offered some civic contribution, but none was specifically feminist in nature. Filling the vacuum, the National Woman's Party, led by Paul, proposed a new initiativemeant to remove discrimination from American laws and move women closer to equality through an Equal Rights Amendment (ERA) that would ban any government-sanctioned discrimination based on sex. Infighting began because many feminists were not looking for strict equality; they were fighting for laws that would directly benefit women. Paul, however, argued that protective legislation—such as laws mandating maximum eight-hour shifts for female factory workers—actually closed the door of opportunity on women by imposing costly rules on employers, who would then be inclined to hire fewer women.

Questions abounded. Could women be freed from discrimination without damaging the welfare and protective apparatus so many needed? What was the goal of the feminist movement—to create full equality, or to respond to the needs of women? And if the price of equality was the absence of protection, how many women really wanted equality? The debate was not limited to the United States. Some proponents of women's rights, such as Aletta Jacobs of the Netherlands or Beatrice Webb of England, agreed with Paul's demand for equality and opposed protective legislation for women. Women members of trade unions, however, defended the need for laws that would help them.

This philosophical dispute was confined to relatively rarefied circles. Throughout the United States, as across Europe, Americans believed that women had achieved their liberation. Women were voting, although in small numbers and almost exactly like their male counterparts. Even Suzanne LaFollette, a radical feminist, concluded in 1926 that women's struggle "is very largely won." Before any flaws in that pronouncement could be probed, the nation—and the world—plunged into the Great Depression. Next, World War II largely obliterated feminist activism on any continent. The war did open employment opportunities for women—from working in factories ("Rosie the Riveter" became an American icon) to playing professional baseball—but these doors of opportunity were largely closed after the war, when women routinely lost their jobs to men discharged from military service. This turn of events angered many women, but few were willing to mount any organized protest.

In the United States the difficulties of the preceding 15 years were followed by a new culture of domesticity. Women began marrying younger and having more children than they had in the 1920s. Such television programs as Father Knows Best and Ozzie and Harriet reflected what many observers called an idyllicsuburban life. By 1960 the percentage of employed female professionals was down compared with figures for 1930.

The women's movement of the 1960s and '70s, the so-called "second wave" of feminism, represented a seemingly abrupt break with the tranquil suburban life pictured in American popular culture. Yet the roots of the new rebellion were buried in the frustrations of college-educated mothers whose discontent impelled their daughters in a new direction. If first-wave feminists were inspired by the abolition movement, their great-granddaughters were swept into feminism by the civil rights movement, the attendant discussion of principles such as equality and justice, and the revolutionary ferment caused by protests against the Vietnam War.

Women's concerns were on Pres. John F. Kennedy's agenda even before this public discussion began. In 1961 he created the President's Commission on the Status of Women and appointed Eleanor Roosevelt to lead it. Its report, issued in 1963, firmly supported the nuclear family and preparing women for motherhood. But it also documented a national pattern of employment discrimination, unequal pay, legal inequality, and meagre support services for working women that needed to be corrected through legislative guarantees of equal pay for equal work, equal job opportunities, and expanded child-care services. The Equal Pay Act of 1963 offered the first guarantee, and the Civil Rights Act of 1964 was amended to bar employers from discriminating on the basis of sex.

Some deemed these measures insufficient in a country where classified advertisements still segregated job openings by sex, where state laws restricted women's access to contraception, and where incidences of rape and domestic violence remained undisclosed. In the late 1960s, then, the notion of a women's rights movement took root at the same time as the civil rights movement, and women of all ages and circumstances were swept up in debates about gender, discrimination, and the nature of equality.

Dissension and Debate

Mainstream groups such as the National Organization for Women (NOW) launched a campaign for legal equity, while ad hoc groups staged sit-ins and marches for any number of reasons—from assailing college curricula that lacked female authors to promoting the use of the word Ms. as a neutral form of address—that is, one that did not refer to marital status. Health collectives and rape crisis centres were established. Children's books were rewritten to obviate sexual stereotypes. Women's studies departments were founded at colleges and universities. Protective labour laws were overturned. Employers found to have discriminated against female workers were required to compensate with back pay. Excluded from male-dominated occupations for decades, women began finding jobs as pilots, construction workers, soldiers, bankers, and bus drivers.

Unlike the first wave, second-wave feminism provoked extensive theoretical discussion about the origins of women's oppression, the nature of gender, and the role of the family. Kate Millett's Sexual Politics made the best-seller list in 1970, and in it she broadened the term politics to include all "power-structured relationships" and posited that the personal was actually political. Shulamith Firestone, a founder of the New York Radical Feminists, published The Dialectic of Sex in the same year, insisting that love disadvantaged women by creating intimateshackles between them and the men they loved—men who were also their oppressors. One year later, Germaine Greer, an Australian living in London, published The Female Eunuch, in which she argued that the sexual repression of women cuts them off from the creative energy they need to be independent and self-fulfilled.

Any attempt to create a coherent, all-encompassing feminist ideology was doomed. While most could agree on the questions that needed to be asked about the origins of gender distinctions, the nature of power, or the roots of sexual violence, the answers to those questions were bogged down by ideological hairsplitting, name-calling, and mutual recrimination. Even the term liberation could mean different things to different people.

Feminism became a river of competing eddies and currents. "Anarcho-feminists," who found a larger audience in Europe than in the United States, resurrected Emma Goldman and said that women could not be liberated without dismantling such institutions as the family, private property, and state power. Individualist feminists, calling on libertarian principles of minimal government, broke with most other feminists over the issue of turning to government for solutions to women's problems. "Amazon feminists" celebrated the mythical female heroine and advocated liberation through physical strength. And separatist feminists, including many lesbian feminists, preached that women could not possibly liberate themselves without at least a period of separation from men.

Ultimately, three major streams of thought surfaced. The first was liberal, or mainstream, feminism, which focused its energy on concrete and pragmatic change at an institutional and governmental level. Its goal was to integrate women more thoroughly into the power structure and to give women equal access to positions men had traditionally dominated. While aiming for strict equality (to be evidenced by such measures as an equal number of women and men in positions of power, or an equal amount of money spent on male and female student athletes), these liberal feminist groups nonetheless supported the modern equivalent of protective legislation such as special workplace benefits for mothers.

In contrast to the pragmatic approach taken by liberal feminism, radical feminism aimed to reshape society and restructure its institutions, which they saw as inherently patriarchal. Providing the core theory for modern feminism, radicals argued that women's subservient role in society was too closely woven into the social fabric to be unraveled without a revolutionary revamping of society itself. They strove to supplant hierarchical and traditional power relationships they saw as reflecting a male bias, and they sought to develop non-hierarchical and antiauthoritarian approaches to politics and organization.

Finally, cultural or "difference" feminism, the last of the three currents, rejected the notion that men and women are intrinsically the same and advocated celebrating the qualities they associated with women, such as their greater concern for affective relationships and their nurturing preoccupation with others. Inherent in its message was a critique of mainstream feminism's attempt to enter traditionally male spheres. This was seen as denigrating women's natural inclinations by attempting to make women more like men.

The Race Factor

Like first-wave feminism, the second wave was largely defined and led by educated middle-class white women who built the movement primarily around their own concerns. This created an ambivalent, if not contentious, relationship with women of other classes and races. The campaign against employment and wage discrimination helped bridge the gap between the movement and white labour union women.

But the relationship of feminism to African American women always posed greater challenges. White feminists defined gender as the principal source of their exclusion from full participation in American life; black women were forced to confront the interplay between racism and sexism and to figure out how to make black men think about gender issues while making white women think about racial issues. Such issues were addressed by black feminists including Michele Wallace, Mary Ann Weathers, bell hooks, Alice Walker, and Bettina Aptheker.

The call by white feminists for unity and solidarity was based on their assumption that women constituted a gender-based class or caste that was unified by common oppression. Many black women had difficulty seeing white women as their feminist sisters; in the eyes of many African Americans, after all, white women were as much the oppressor as white men. "How relevant are the truths, the experiences, the findings of White women to Black women?" asked Toni Cade Bambara in The Black Woman: An Anthology. "I don't know that our priorities are the same, that our concerns and methods are the same." As far back as Sojourner Truth, black feminists had seen white feminists as incapable of understanding their concerns.

Yet some black women, especially middle-class black women, also insisted that it was fundamentally different to be black and female than to be black and male. During the first conference of the National Black Feminist Organization, held in New York City in 1973, black women activists acknowledged that many of the goals central to the mainstream feminist movement—day care, abortion, maternity leave, violence—were critical to African American women as well. On specific issues, then, African American feminists and white feminists built an effective working relationship.

The Globalization of Feminism

By the end of the 20th century, European and American feminists had begun to interact with the nascent feminist movements of Asia, Africa, and Latin America. As this happened, women in developed countries, especially intellectuals, were horrified to discover that women in some countries were required to wear veils in public or to endure forced marriage, female infanticide, widow burning, or female genital cutting (FGC). Many Western feminists soon perceived themselves as saviours of Third World women, little realizing that their perceptions of and solutions to social problems were often at odds with the real lives and concerns of women in these regions. In many parts of Africa, for example, the status of women had begun to erode significantly only with the arrival of European colonialism. In those regions, then, the notion that patriarchy was the chief problem—rather than European imperialism—seemed absurd.

The conflicts between women in developed and developing nations played out most vividly at international conferences. After the 1980 World Conference of the United Nations Decade for Women: Equality, Development and Peace, in Copenhagen, women from less-developed nations complained that the veil and FGC had been chosen as conference priorities without consulting the women most concerned. It seemed that their counterparts in the West were not listening to them.

During the 1994 International Conference on Population and Development, in Cairo, women from the Third World protested outside because they believed the agenda had been hijacked by Europeans and Americans. The protesters had expected to talk about ways that underdevelopment was holding women back. Instead, conference organizers chose to focus on contraception and abortion. "[Third World women] noted that they could not very well worry about other matters when their children were dying from thirst, hunger or war," wrote Azizah al-Hibri, a law professor and scholar of Muslim women's rights. "The conference instead centred around reducing the number of Third World babies in order to preserve the earth's resources, despite (or is it 'because of') the fact that the First World consumes much of these resources." In Beijing, at the Fourth World Conference on Women in 1995, Third World women again criticized the priority American and European women put on reproductive rights language and issues of discrimination on the basis of sexual orientation and their disinterest in the platform proposal that was most important to less-developed nations – that of restructuring international debt.

Still, the close of the 20th century saw women around the world advancing their interests, although often in fits and starts. Feminism was derailed in countries such as Afghanistan, where the staunchly reactionary and antifeminist Taliban banned even the education of girls. Elsewhere, however, feminism achieved significant gains for women, as seen in the eradication of FGC in many African countries or government efforts to end widow burning in India. More generally, and especially in the West, feminism had influenced every aspect of contemporary life, communication, and debate, from the heightened concern over sexist language to the rise of academic fields such as women's studies and ecofeminism. Sports, divorce laws, sexual mores, organized religion – all had been affected, in many parts of the world, by feminism.

UNIT 9

LOGIC

TRUTH AND VALIDITY

The term logic is derived from the Greek word 'logos' which means thought or reason and language or expression. Logic is the study of the methods and principles used to distinguish good (correct) from bad (incorrect) reasoning. The logician is concerned primarily with the correctness of the completed process of reasoning. The central problem of logic is the distinction between correct and incorrect reasoning.

The most important question in connection with reasoning is the question of truth or falsity. Logic being concerned with reasoning must, therefore, deal with the nature and conditions of truth. Truth and falsehood may be predicated of propositions, but never of arguments. And the attributes of validity and invalidity can belong only to deductive arguments, never to propositions. There is a connection between the validity or invalidity of an argument and the truth or falsehood of its premisses and conclusions, but the connection is by no means a simple one.

It is important to realize that an argument may be valid while one or more of its premisses is untrue. Arguments may exhibit differing combinations of true and false premisses and conclusions.

Some valid arguments contain only true propositions, as, for example:

All men are mortal,
All students are men,
Therefore, all students are mortal.

Some valid argument contain entirely false proposition, as, for example:

All ten-legged creatures have wings,
All spiders have ten legs,
Therefore, all spiders have wings.

This argument is valid because, if its premisses were true, its conclusion would have to be true also, even though in fact, they are all false.

Moreover, an argument may have premisses that are all true and may have a true conclusion and may nevertheless be invalid, as in the following example:

If the mining industry were in a sound condition the miners and the mine owners would be contented. The mining industry is not in a sound condition. Therefore the miners and the mine owners are not contented.

Arguments with false premisses and true conclusions may be valid or invalid. Here is an example of a valid argument with false premisses and a true conclusion:

All fishes are mammals.
All whales are fishes.
Therefore all whales are mammals.

And here is an example of an invalid argument with false premisses and a true conclusion:

All mammals have wings. All whales have wings. Therefore all whales are mammals.

Finally, there are invalid arguments whose premisses and conclusions are all false, as, for example:

All mammals have wings.
All whales have wings.
Therefore all mammals are whales.

It is clear from the above examples that there are valid arguments with false conclusions as well as invalid arguments with true conclusions. Hence, it is clear that the truth or falsity of an argument's conclusion does not by itself determine the validity of invalidity of that argument. And the fact that an argument is valid does not guarantee the truth of its conclusion.

If an argument is valid, and its conclusion is false, not all its premisses can be true. And also, if an argument is valid and its premisses are true, we may be certain that its conclusion must be true also. Some perfectly valid arguments do have false conclusions. Such an argument must have at least one false premiss.

When an argument is valid, and all of its premisses are true, we call it 'sound'. The conclusion of a sound argument obviously must be true. If a deductive argument is not sound, either it is not valid or not all of its premisses are true, it fails to establish the truth of its conclusion, even if the conclusion is true.

To test the truth or falsehood of premisses is the task of science in general, since premisses may deal with any subject matter at all. The logician is not so much interested in the truth or falsehood of propositions as in the logical relations between them.

By the 'logical' relations between propositions, we mean those relations that determine the correctness or incorrectness of the arguments in which they occur. The logician is interested in the correctness even of arguments whose premisses may be false.

There might be a suggestion that we ought to confine ourselves to arguments that have true premisses, ignoring all others. But as a matter of fact, we are interested in, and must often depend on, the correctness of arguments whose premisses are not known to be true. Examples of such situations suggest themselves readily.

A scientist who is interested in verifying scientific theories by deducing testable consequences from them does not know beforehand which theories are true. Were that known, there would be no need for further verification. In our everyday affairs, we must often choose between alternative courses of action.

Where these courses are genuine alternatives that cannot all be adopted, we may try to reason about which should be chosen. Such reasoning generally involves figuring out the consequences of each of the different actions among which we must choose.

One might argue, "Suppose I choose the first alternative, then such and such will be the case. On the other hand, assuming that I choose the second alternative, then something else will follow". In general, we are inclined to choose among alternative courses of action on the basis of which set of consequences we prefer.

In each case, we are interested in reasoning correctly, rest we decide ourselves. Were we interested only in arguments that have true premisses, we should not know which line of argument to consider until we knew which of the alternative premisses was true.

And if we knew which premiss was true, we should not be interested in the arguments at all, because our purpose in considering the arguments was to help us decide which alternative premises to make true. To confine our attention to arguments with true premisses alone would be self-defeating and stultifying.

So far, we have discussed only about propositions and arguments that contain them as 'premisses' and 'conclusion'. However, these are not linguistic entities such as sentences, but what sentences may be used to assert.

Whether the actual process of thinking or reasoning requires language or not is an open question. It may be that, thinking requires the use of symbols of some sort: words or images or what not. It is obvious that the communication of any proposition or any argument requires symbols and involves language.

The use of language, however, complicates our problem. Certain accidental or misleading features of their formulations in language may make more difficult the task of investigating the logical relations among propositions. It is part of the task of the logician, therefore, to examine language itself, primarily from the point of view of discovering and describing those aspects of it that tend to obscure the difference between correct and incorrect argument.

DENOTATION AND CONNOTATION

The terms, denotation and connotation, are used to convey and distinguish between two different kinds of meanings or extensions of a word. A denotation is the strict, literal, definition of a word, devoid of any emotion, attitude, or color. The connotation of a word or term adds elements of emotion, attitude, or color. The meaning or use of denotation and connotation depends partly on the field of study.

- In media-studies terminology, denotation is the first level of analysis: What the audience can visually see on a page. Denotation often refers to something literal, and avoids being a metaphor. Here it is usually coupled with connotation, which is the second level of analysis, being what the denotation represents.
- In logic, linguistics, and semiotics, a denotation of a word or phrase is a part of its meaning; however, several parts of meaning may take this name, depending on the contrast being drawn:
- Denotation and connotation are either
  - in basic semantics and literary theory, the literal and figurative meanings of a word, or,
  - in philosophy, logic and parts of linguistics, the extension and intension of a word
- Denotation can be synonymous with reference, and connotation with sense, in the sense and reference distinction in philosophy of language.
- In Computer science, denotational semantics is contrasted with operational semantics.
- In Semiotics, denotation also has its own meaning.

In logic and semantics, denotational always attracts the extension, meaning "in the pair," but the other element genuinely varies.

The distinction between connotation and denotation corresponds roughly to Gottlob Frege's groundbreaking and much-studied distinction between Sinn (sense) and Bedeutung (reference).

Bertrand Russell, in 1905, published a seminal article on the topic of denotation, entitled "On Denoting."

Denotation often links with symbolism, as the denotation of a particular media text often represents something further; a hidden meaning (or an enigma code) is often hidden in a media text.

Within contemporary society, connotation branches into a culmination of different meanings. These could include the contrast of a word or phrase with its primary, literal meaning (known as a denotation), with what that word or phrase specifically denotes. The connotation essentially relates to how anything may be associated with a word or phrase, for example, an implied value judgment or feelings.

- A stubborn person may be described as being either "strong-willed" or "pig-headed." Although these have the same literal meaning (that is, stubborn), strong-willed connotes admiration for someone's convictions, while pig-headed connotes frustration in dealing with someone. Likewise, "used car" and "previously owned car" have the same literal meaning, but many dealerships prefer the latter, since it is thought to have fewer negative connotations.

- It is often useful to avoid words with strong connotations (especially disparaging ones) when striving to achieve a neutral point of view. A desire for more positive connotations, or fewer negative ones, is one of the main reasons for using euphemisms. (Although, not all theories of linguistic meaning honor the distinction between literal meaning and connotation).

In logic and in some branches of semantics, connotation is more or less synonymous with intension. Connotation is often contrasted with denotation, which is more or less synonymous with extension. A word's extension is the collection of things it refers to; its intension is what it implies about the things it is used to refer to. So, the denotation or extension of "dog" is just the collection of all the dogs that exist. The connotation or intension of "dog" is (something like) "four-legged canine carnivore." Alternatively, the connotation of the word may be thought of as the set of all its possible referents (as opposed to merely the actual ones). So saying, "You are a dog," would imply that the subject was ugly or aggressive rather than a literal canine.

NATURE OF PROPOSITIONS

Propositions are the material of our reasoning. A proposition links nouns, pronouns and phrases to other words in a sentence. The word or phrase that the proposition introduces is called the object of the proposition. A proposition is a judgment expressed in a language and a judgment is a mental act in which two or more than two ideas are combined together.

Judgments have two types:

1. Affirmative- Indians are laborious.
2. Negative- Indians are not dull.

A proposition usually indicates the temporal, spatial or logical relationship of its object to the rest of the sentence as in the following examples:

The book is **on** the table.

The book is **beneath** the table.

The book is leaning **against** the table.

The book is **beside** the table.

She held the book **over** the table.

She read the book **during** class.

Components of Proposition

Every proposition has three components called as term. Any word or word phrase, which is used in a proposition as a subject or predicate, is called as term:

1. Subject- About whom something asserts or denies.
2. Predicate-What assert or deny.
3. Copula– Conjunct both subject and predicate terms. Copula will be negative or affirmative.

Difference with Sentences

1. Propositions are different from sentences. Sentences have many kinds like questions, exclamations etc. But none of these can be asserted and denied. Truth and Falsity apply always to proposition, but not apply to questions or commands or exclamations.

2. Propositions must be differentiated from sentences by means of what they are asserted. Two different sentences consisting the same proposition.
3. Sentences are parts of some language, but propositions are not tied to any given language i.e. "It is raining", "Barsat ho rahi hai", both consist the same content.
4. A sentence called as proposition when it's both term (subject and predicate) are nouns i.e. Ram is a man. "Flower is beautiful" is not a proposition because its predicate is adjective.
5. Proposition is always in present tense. But sentences are expressed in all tenses.
6. Proposition explains quantity and quality but sentence does not explain it.
7. All propositions are sentences but not all sentences are propositions.

Types of Proposition

According to the relation of terms proposition has three types:

1. **Categorical Proposition** It is a type of proposition which has no condition for their assertion.– Roshan is a student.
2. **Conditional or Hypothetical Proposition**: A type of compound proposition, it is false only when the antecedent is true and the consequent is false.- If Ram will pass, then he will get a bicycle.
3. **Disjunctive Proposition**: A type of compound proposition; if true, at least one of the component of propositions must be true.-Ram is honest or clever.

Categorical Proposition

A categorical proposition is simply a statement about the relationship between categories. It states whether one category or categorical term is fully contained with another, is partially contained within another or is completely separate.

A dog is an animal.

Some dogs are friendly.

No dog is a cat.

Propositions may have *quality*: either affirmative or negative.

They may also have *quantity*: such as 'a', 'some', 'most' or 'all'. The 'all' quantity is also described as being *universal* and other quantities *particular.*

Aristotelian Four-fold Classification of Categorical Propositions:

Aristotle classified categorical proposition in four, based on Quality and Quantity distribution:

Universal Affirmative – All S is P. – A Type Proposition – All men are mortal.

Universal Negative – No S is P. – E Type Proposition – No men are immortal.

Particular Affirmative – Some S is P. – I Type Proposition – Some men are wise.

Particular Negative – Some S in not P. – O Type Proposition – Some men are not wise.

CATEGORICAL SYLLOGISM

Syllogism is a widely used term in logic. In the previous chapter we mentioned the meaning of syllogism. It has, however, been defined in this chapter as a deductive argument in which a conclusion is inferred from two premises. For brevity, in this section we shall refer to categorical syllogisms simply as "syllogisms" even though there are other kinds of syllogisms that will be discussed in later units. In this section we will try to make you understand the meaning, terms, mode, figures etc. of categorical syllogism. A categorical syllogism is a deductive argument consisting of three categorical propositions that together contain exactly three terms, each of which occurs in exactly two of the constituent propositions.

A syllogism is a deductive argument in which a conclusion is inferred from two premises. A categorical syllogism is a deductive argument consisting of three categorical propositions that together contain exactly three terms, each of which occurs in exactly two of the constituent propositions.

A categorical syllogism is said to be in standard form when its premises and conclusion are all standard-form categorical propositions and are arranged in a specified standard order. To specify that order, it will be useful to explain the logician's special names for the terms and premises of categorical syllogisms.

The conclusion of a standard-form syllogism is a standard-form categorical proposition that contains two of the syllogism's three terms. The conclusion is always used to identify the terms of the syllogism.

- **Major Term.** The term that occurs as the predicate of the conclusion is called the "major term" of the syllogism.
- **Minor Term.** The term that occurs as the subject term of the conclusion is called the "minor term" of the syllogism.
- **Middle Term.** The third term of the syllogism, which does not occur in the conclusion, appearing instead in both premises, is called "middle term".

Let's make the terms clear with an example.

No heroes are cowards.

Some soldiers are cowards.

Therefore some soldiers are heroes.

Here,

Soldiers = Minor term

Heroes = Major term

Cowards = Middle term (which does not appear in the conclusion)

The premises of a standard-form syllogism are named after the terms that appear in them. The major and minor terms must each occur in a different one of the premises. The premise containing the major term is called the "major premise" and the premise containing the minor term is called the "minor premise". In the syllogism given above,

Major premise = No heroes are cowards.

Minor premise = Some soldiers are cowards.

Dear learners, earlier we said that a syllogism is in standard form when its premises are arranged in a specified order. Let's see the order,

1. Major premise
2. Minor premise
3. Conclusion

The mood of a standard-form syllogism is determined by the types (identified by letter: A, E, I or O) of the standard-form categorical propositions it contains. The mood of every syllogism is represented by three letters, in a specific order:

First letter = Type of the syllogism's major premise

Second letter = Type of its minor premise

Third letter = Type of its conclusion

For example, in the illustrative syllogism given above, the major premise is an E proposition, the minor premise is an I proposition, and the conclusion is an O proposition. So the mood of that syllogism is EIO.

Laws of Thought

Laws of thought, traditionally, the three fundamental laws of logic: (1) the law of contradiction, (2) the law of excluded middle (or third), and (3) the principle of identity. That is, (1) for all propositions p, it is impossible for both p and not p to be true, or symbolically ~(p · ~p), in which ~means "not" and · means "and"; (2) either p or ~p must be true, there being no third or middle true proposition between them, or symbolically p ("~p, in which ("means "or"; and (3) if a propositional function F is true of an individual variable x, then F is indeed true of x, or symbolically $F(x) \supset F(x)$, in which $\supset$ means "formally implies." Another formulation of the principle of identity asserts that a thing is identical with itself, or $(\forall x)\ (x = x)$, in which "means "for every"; or simply that x is x.

Aristotle cited the laws of contradiction and of excluded middle as examples of axioms. He partly exempted future contingents, or statements about unsure future events, from the law of excluded middle, holding that it is not (now) either true or false that there will be a naval battle tomorrow but that the complex proposition that either there will be a naval battle tomorrow or that there will not is (now) true. In the epochal Principia Mathematica of A.N. Whitehead and Bertrand Russell, this law occurs as a theorem rather than as an axiom.

That the laws of thought are a sufficient foundation for the whole of logic, or that all other principles of logic are mere elaborations of them, was a doctrine common among traditional logicians. The law of excluded middle and certain related laws were rejected by L.E.J. Brouwer, a Dutch mathematical intuitionist, and his school, who did not admit their use in mathematical proofs in which all members of an infinite class are involved. Brouwer would not accept, for example, the disjunction that either there occur 10 successive 7's somewhere in the decimal expansion of π or else not, since no proof is known of either alternative, but he would accept it if applied, for instance, to the first 10100 digits of the decimal, since these could in principle actually be computed.

In 1920 Jan Aukasiewicz, a leading member of the Polish school of logic, formulated a propositional calculus that had a third truth-value, neither truth nor falsity, for Aristotle's future contingents, a calculus in which the laws of contradiction and of excluded middle both failed. Other systems have gone beyond three-valued to many-valued logics—e.g., certain probability logics having various degrees of truth-value between truth and falsity.

CLASSIFICATION OF PROPOSITIONING

Propositions may be classified into various classes according to different principles, such as the principles of composition, relation, quality, quantity, modality, significance etc. But for our purpose it suffices to consider the classification of propositions according to relation, significance, quality, quantity and both quality and quantity.

(a) Classification of propositions according to relation

According to relation, propositions are of two types namely (i) categorical and (ii) conditional.

This distinction depends on the nature of the relation between subject and predicate of the proposition. A proposition is called categorical if the relation between subject and predicate of the proposition is either affirmed or denied without any condition or restriction.

In other words, a categorical proposition is one in which the predicate in either affirmed or denied of the subject unconditionally. For example, "All men are mortal", "Some men are rich", "Gopal is the author of many books" are propositions in which the predicate is affirmed of the subject without any condition. So, they are all categorical propositions.

Similarly, "No man is perfect", some men are not rich", "Gopal is -not the son of Ram" are propositions in which the predicate is denied of the subject without any condition. Hence, they too are categorical propositions.

On the other hand, in case of conditional propositions, the relation between subject and predicate holds conditionally. It is of three types, namely (i) Hypothetical, (ii) Alternative and (iii) Disjunctive. A hypothetical proposition is a conditional proposition, having the form "if P then Q", where "P" and "Q" stand for any propositions.

In this case, the "if-clause" and "then-clause" of the proposition are respectively called antecedent and consequent. The antecedent (or if clause) always states the condition for asserting the consequent (or the then-clause), For example, I shall go if he comes", here "he comes" is the antecedent and 'I shall go' is the consequent of he above proposition.

Moreover, since "my going" depends on "his coming", "I shall go if he comes" is a hypothetical proposition. The same is the case with the propositions "I shall not go to the college if it is raining". Here "my not going to the college" depends on "raining". So "it is raining" is the antecedent and "I shall not go to the college" is the consequent.

An alternative proposition is a kind of conditional proposition having the form "either P or Q", where P and Q are called alternatives representing propositions. In this case, we cannot assert or deny both the alternatives. The assertion of one of them depends on the denial of the other and vice-versa. For example, "Either Gopal is a student of N. C. College or he is a student of City College", expresses an alternative proposition. Here both the alternative cannot be asserted or denied simultaneously, i.e. given that this proposition in true, if we say that Gopal is both a student of N. C. College as well as City College then we would be making a false statement. The same is the case if we deny both the alternatives. Thus in case of an alternative proposition if we assert one alternative then the other alternative must be denied art vice versa.

A disjunctive proposition is a kind of conditional proposition having the form "either P or Q", where P and Q are called disjuncts, representing propositions. In this case, we cannot deny both the disjuncts, though both of them can be asserted. A disjunctive proposition holds good even if one of its disjuncts is asserted. For example, consider the proposition; either Ashok does yoga or pranayam. The proposition is false if Ashok does not do either of the two. But there is no harm if he does both. In other words, a disjunctive proposition holds good if one of its disjuncts is asserted and false if both are denied.

Though propositions according to relation are divided into categorical and conditional yet the ancient logicians, including Aristotle, were interested only with categorical propositions. This is because, any conditional proposition is built out of categorical propositions by use of propositional operations like "If....... then", either..... Or....." etc.

Hence, categorical proposition is the most basic type of proposition and we shall now develop a system of deductive logic based on the notion of categorical proposition.

(b) Classification of Propositions according to significance

According to significance, a proposition is either analytic (or verbal) or synthetic (or real). We know that a proposition (or more precisely a categorical proposition) expresses a relation between subject and predicate terms.

A proposition is called analytic (or verbal) if and only if either the subject or predicate terms are equivalent in meaning or the predicate states part of the meaning (or connotation) of the subject.

In other words, an analytic proposition is one in which the predicate either partially or wholly contained in the subject. The truth or falsity of such propositions depends entirely on the meaning of the subject as well as the predicate term occurring in the proposition. For example, "Triangle is a plane figure bounded by three straight lines," "All bachelors are unmarried", "All circular figures are figures", "All red things are colored", Black cats are black" are examples of analytic proposition. The truth of such a proposition depends on the meaning of the subject, predicate and copula present in the proposition.

Thus, to accept or reject such a proposition we don't have to see how the things really are on the world but only to know the meaning of the words and terms present in it. Thus to know the truth of "All bachelors are unmarried", we don't have to look at the world to see whether bachelor is unmarried or not. If we know the meaning of terms ('all', 'bachelor', and unmarried") and the copula (is) then we would be in a position to ascertain its truth.

On the contrary, a proposition is called synthetic (or real) if and only if its truth or falsehood depends on facts. In case of synthetic proposition the subject and predicate terms are non-equivalent in meaning. In such a case, the predicate states something new about the subject in the sense that the predicate is not contained either implicitly or explicitly in the subject.

To know the truth of synthetic proposition say "It is raining", "The grass is green", All men are mortal", we have to look at the world to see how the things really are. Without coking at the world, we cannot either reject or accept the truth of a synthetic proposition.

(c) Classification of propositions according to quality

According to quality, a proposition is either affirmative or negative. A proposition is called affirmative if and only if the predicate is affirmed of the subject. For example, in the proposition "Ram is a boy", the predicate 'a boy' is affirmed of the subject "Ram".

A proposition is called negative if and only if the predicate is denied of the subject. For example, in the proposition 'Ram is not rich" the predicate 'rich' are denied of the subject. In case of affirmative proposition, the copula is affirmative whereas in negative propositions the copula carries the sign of negation. But in case of universal negative propositions, the sign of negation is no: attached to the copula but to the subject. For example in "No man is perfect' or 'No S is P' the sign of negation is attached to the subject of the proposition.

However, this is mere a convention of English language. Note that the quality of the hypothetical proposition depends on the quality of the consequent. For example, the negation of "If he comes, I shall go' would be 'If he comes, I shall not go'. Similarly the negation of 'if A is B then C is D' would be 'if A is B then C is not D. Briefly, we may say that if the consequent of a hypothetical proposition is negative (or affirmative), the hypothetical proposition in question is negative (or affirmative). To repeat, the quality of a hypothetical proposition depends on the quality of the consequent.

(d) Classification of proposition according to quantity

According to quantity a proposition is either universal or particular. A proposition is called universal if the predicate of the proposition is either affirmed or denied of the entire denotation of the subject. On the other hand, a proposition is called particular if the predicate of the proposition is affirmed or denied of a part of the denotation of the subject. For example, in the proposition "All men are mortal", the predicate 'mortal' is affirmed of the entire denotation of the subject. Here the word 'all' refers to the entire denotation of the subject term 'man'.

Similarly, in the proposition "Some men are rich", the predicate 'rich' is affirmed of a part of the denotation of the subject term 'men'. Further, in the proposition "Some men are not rich" the predicate term 'rich' is denied of a part of the denotation of the subject term. In "No men is perfect" the predicate term is denied of the entire denotation of the subject.

Thus the words like 'All', 'No', 'Some' etc. are quantity-words specifying the quantity of the term to which it is attached. 'All' and 'No' are marks of universality and the word 'some' indicates particularity. In a logical proposition the quantity - words (or the quantifiers) are attached only to the subject term. According, "All men are mortal", "No men is perfect" are the samples of universal proposition where as "Some men are rich", "Some men are not rich" are examples of particular propositions.

Note that the classification of propositions that we have introduced so far is mutually exclusive and taken it is jointly are exhaustive. For example, the division of proposition according to quality is either affirmative or negative. This division is mutually exclusive because it is impossible of find a proposition, which is both affirmative as well as negative.

In other words, if a proposition is affirmative then it cannot be negative and vice versa. Similarly, this division is also exhaustive, which means that there is no proposition which is neither affirmative nor negative. These two conditions jointly say that any proposition must have exactly one quality i.e. either it is affirmative or negative. The same is the case with other divisions of propositions like division according to relation and division according to quantity.

(e) Classification of propositions according to both quality and quantity

We have already discussed the classifications of propositions according to quality as well as quantity that may be repeated for convenience. According to quality, the propositions are of two types i.e. affirmative and negative and according to quantity, propositions are universal and particular. From these two classifications, we obtain a third type of classification of propositions according to the mixed principle of quality and quantity.

Popularly these four types of propositions are respectively known as A, E, I and O propositions. For example, "All men are mortal" is an A-proposition or universal affirmative proposition. It is a universal proposition because the predicate term 'mortal' is affirmed of the entire denotation of the subject term. It is also affirmative as the predicate is affirmed of the subject.

Thus, for an A-proposition we have to verify two conditions i.e. firstly the predicate must be affirmed of the subject and secondly, it must be affirmed of the entire denotation of the subject. The structure of A-proposition is 'All S is P' where 'S' and 'P' stand for subject term and predicate term respectively.

Universal negative propositions are called E-propositions. 'No man is perfect' is an example of an E-proposition. In this case the predicate term 'perfect' is denied of the entire denotation of the subject term 'man'. Since it is a case of denial of the predicate, it is negative and since the denial is about the entire denotation of the subject, it is universal.

Hence, the proposition "No man is perfect" is an example of universal negative proposition or E-proposition. It has the form "No S is P", where 'S' and 'P' stand for the subject and predicate terms respectively.

"Some men are rich" and "Some men are not rich" are examples of I and O-propositions respectively. In the case of former the predicate term 'rich' is affirmed of a part of the denotation of the subject, where as in case of the predicate term is denied of the part of the denotation of subject.

Further, a categorical proposition in which logicians are interested exhibits its logical constituents explicitly. It states its quantity, quality, subject and predicate in an explicit manner. These four constituents in a categorical proposition should be written in the following order, quantifier, subject term, copula (exhibiting the quality of the proposition) and predicate term.

SQUARE OF OPPOSITION

The square of opposition is a chart that was introduced within classical (categorical) logic to represent the logical relationships holding between certain propositions in virtue of their form. The square, traditionally conceived, looks like this:

Given the assumption made within classical (Aristotelian) categorical logic, that every category contains at least one member, the following relationships, depicted on the square, hold:

Firstly, A and O propositions are ***contradictory***, as are E and I propositions. Propositions are contradictory when the truth of one implies the falsity of the other, and conversely. Here we see that the truth of a proposition of the form *All S are P* implies the falsity of the corresponding proposition of the form *Some S are not P.* For example, if the proposition "all industrialists are capitalists" (A) is *true,* then the proposition "some industrialists are not capitalists" (O) must be *false.* Similarly, if "no mammals are aquatic" (E) is *false,* then the proposition "some mammals are aquatic" must be *true.*

Secondly, A and E propositions are ***contrary***. Propositions are contrary when they cannot *both* be true. An A proposition, e.g., "all giraffes have long necks" cannot be true at the same time as the corresponding E proposition: "no giraffes have long necks." Note, however, that corresponding A and E propositions, while contrary, are not contradictory. While they cannot both be true, they *can* both be false, as with the examples of "all planets are gas giants" and "no planets are gas giants."

Next, I and O propositions are ***subcontrary***. Propositions are subcontrary when it is impossible for both to be *false.* Because "some lunches are free" is false, "some lunches are not free" must be true. Note, however, that it is possible for corresponding I and O propositions both to be *true*, as with "some nations are democracies," and "some nations are not democracies." Again, I and O propositions are subcontrary, but not contrary or contradictory.

Lastly, two propositions are said to stand in the relation of ***subalternation*** when the truth of the first ("the superaltern") implies the truth of the second ("the subaltern"), but *not* conversely. A propositions stand in the subalternation relation with the corresponding I propositions. The truth of the A proposition "all plastics are synthetic," implies the truth of the proposition "some plastics are synthetic." However, the truth of the O proposition "some cars are not American-made products" does not imply the truth of the E proposition "no cars are American-made products." In traditional logic, the truth of an A or E proposition implies the truth of the corresponding I or O proposition, respectively. Consequently, the falsity of an I or O proposition implies the falsity of the corresponding A or E proposition, respectively. However, the *truth* of a particular proposition does not imply the truth of the corresponding universal proposition, nor does the falsity of an universal proposition carry downwards to the respective particular propositions.

The presupposition, mentioned above, that all categories contain at least one thing, has been abandoned by most later logicians. Modern logic deals with uninstantiated terms such as "unicorn" and "ether flow" the same as it does other terms such as "apple" and "orangutan". When dealing with "empty categories", the relations of being contrary, being subcontrary and of subalternation no longer hold. Consider, e.g., "all unicorns have horns" and "no unicorns have horns." Within contemporary logic, these are both regarded as true, so strictly speaking, they cannot be contrary, despite the former's status as an A proposition and the latter's status as an E proposition. Similarly, "some unicorns have horns" (I) and "some unicorns do not have horns" (O) are both regarded as false, and so they are not subcontrary. Obviously then, the truth of "all unicorns have horns" does not imply the truth of "some unicorns have horns," and the subalternation relation fails to hold as well. Without the traditional presuppositions of "existential import", i.e., the supposition that all categories have at least one member, then only the contradictory relation holds. On what is sometimes called the "modern square of opposition" (as opposed to the traditional square of opposition sketched above) the lines for contraries, subcontraries and subalternation are erased, leaving only the diagonal lines for the contradictory relation.

Truth Function and Provisional Logic

Logicians in the Stoic school of philosophy, during the 3rd century B.C., meeting on the painted porch in downtown Athens, were the first to discover and systematize the logical standards for this type of argument, and for a long time it was called "Stoic logic." The system was updated and expanded in the late 19th century by the German logician Gottlob Frege. It is now called "truth-functional logic" for reasons that will be explained shortly.

The logical details are a little harder to explain, compared to the details of categorical logic, even when simplified greatly. For one reason, they are more mathematical in nature. But let's give it a try.

A declarative sentence is **compound** if it contains within itself one or more sentences and one or more sentence operators. (By *sentence* I will always mean "declarative sentence.") A sentence is **simple** if it is not compound. A **sentence operator** is a word or phrase that joins one or more sentences into a compound sentence. A compound sentence is thus composed of one or more sentence operators joining one or more sentences into the compound. In the following compound sentence, *and* is the operator joining the two simpler sentences into the compound:

Plato founded the Academy, and Aristotle founded the Lyceum.

This type of compound sentence is called a "conjunction." The simple sentence to the left of the operator, "Plato founded the Academy," is called the "left conjunct," and the simple sentence to the right of the operator, "Aristotle founded the Lyceum," is called the "right conjunct." The operator (*and*) is called the "conjunction operator" because it is used to form a conjunction.

A sentence will be said to have the "truth-value" of "true" if it expresses a true proposition, and it will be said to have the "truth-value" of false if it expresses a false proposition. These definitions will allow us to express some complicated points more economically.

Now, a compound sentence is truth-functional if the truth-value of the compound as a whole is a strictly defined function of the truth-value or truth-values of the sentence or sentences inside it. A sentence operator is truth-functional if the compound it forms is a truth-functional compound. Finally, an argument is truth-functional if (a) it is composed of truth-functional sentences and (b) its validity is a strict function of nothing but the abstract arrangement of the truth-functional operators in its sentences.

Now we can say: a truth-functional conjunction is "any conjunction formed with an operator asserting that both conjuncts are true and nothing more." The compound sentence, "Plato founded the Academy, and Aristotle founded the Lyceum," is a truth-functional conjunction because it asserts that both of its conjuncts are true and its truth-value as a whole is a function of the truth-values of its parts according to the following exact rule covering all possible cases:

- If the left conjunct is true and the right conjunct is true, then the conjunction as a whole is true.
- If the left conjunct is true and the right conjunct is false, then the conjunction as a whole is false.
- If the left conjunct is false and the right conjunct is true, then the conjunction as a whole is false.
- If the left conjunct is false and the right conjunct is false, then the conjunction as a whole is false.

This rule, or function, applies, of course, to *any* conjunction formed with *and* when the *and* asserts that both conjuncts are true and nothing more. Logicians express this general rule more compactly on a device called a "truth-table."

QUANTIFICATION

Quantification, in logic, the attachment of signs of quantity to the predicate or subject of a proposition. The universal quantifier, symbolized by (∀-) or (-), where the blank is filled by a variable, is used to express that the formula following holds for all values of the particular variable quantified. The existential quantifier, symbolized (∃-), expresses that the formula following holds for some (at least one) value of that quantified variable.

Quantifiers of different types may be combined. For example, restricting epsilon (ε) and delta (δ) to positive values, b is called the limit of a function f(x) as x approaches a if for every ε there exists a δ such that whenever the distance from x to a is less than δ, then the distance from f(x) to b will be less than ε; or symbolically:

$$(\forall \varepsilon)(\exists \delta)(|x - a| < \delta \supset |f(x) - b| < \varepsilon)$$

in which vertical lines mark the enclosed quantities as absolute values, $<$ means "is less than," and ⊃" means "if . . . then," or "implies."

SYMBOLIC LOGIC

1. We are going to set up an artificial "language" to avoid difficulties of vagueness, equivocation, amphiboly, and confusion from emotive significance.
   (i) The first thing is to learn the elements of this "new language."
   (ii) The second is to learn to translate ordinary language grammar into symbolic notation.
   (iii) The third thing is to evaluate arguments in this "new language."

2. Symbolic logic is by far the simplest kind of logic—it is a great time-saver in argumentation. Additionally, it helps prevent logical confusion.
   (i) The modern development begin with George Boole in the 19th century.
   (ii) Symbolic logic can be thought of as a simple and flexible shorthand:
      1. Consider the symbols:
         $[(p \supset q) \cdot (q \supset r)] \supset (p \supset r)$.
      2. This rule was well known to the Stoics, but they expressed it this way:
         "If, if the first then the second and if the second then the third, then, if the first then the third."
      3. We will find that all of the essential manipulations in symbolic logic are about as complex and working with numbers made up of ones and zeros.
3. We begin with the simplest part of propositional logic: combining simple propositions into compound propositions and determining the truth value of the resulting compounds.
   (i) Propositions or statements can be thought of as the "atoms" of propositional logic. ("Proposition" and "statement" are often taken to be equivalent terms.)
      1. Simple propositions are statements which cannot be broken down without a loss in meaning.
         a. *E.g.*, "John and Charles are brothers" cannot be broken down without a change in the meaning of the statement. Note the change in meaning with "John is a brother" and "Charles is a brother."
         b. Whereas, "John and Charles work diligently" can be broken down without a change in meaning:
            "John works diligently." "Charles works diligently." (It is assumed contextually that the meaning of the original statement is not that John and Charles work diligently together but perhaps not so apart.)
      2. Conventionally, capital letters (usually towards the beginning of the alphabet) may be used as abbreviations for specific propositions.
         E.g., "John and Charles are brothers" can be symbolized as **B**.
         and "John and Charles work diligently" can be symbolized as **J** and **C**.
         The logical operator "and," as we will see, will be symbolized as "·".
2. In addition to propositions, propositional logic contains another element: operators on propositions.
   (i) Propositions can be thought of like the sticks of a tinker-toy set.
   (ii) Operators are like the connecting blocks.
   (iii) By adding more and more operators, we get more complex structures.
3. For evaluation of statements, there is only one condition to be learned:
   "In order to know the truth value of the proposition which results from applying an operator to propositions, all that need be known is the definition of the operator and the truth value of the propositions used."

DEDUCTIVE AND INDUCTIVE LOGIC

The process of thinking about something, in a rational manner, so as to draw valid conclusions, is known as Reasoning. It is a daily activity that we use to make decisions, which involves the construction of thoughts and converting them into a proposition to give reasons on why we have opted for a particular alternative over the other. Reasoning (logic) can take two forms – inductive reasoning or deductive reasoning. The **inductive reasoning** follows a particular flow or behaviour so as to make inferences

Conversely, **deductive reasoning** uses available information, facts or premises to arrive at a conclusion. These two logics are exactly opposite to each other. Still, they are often juxtaposed due to lack of adequate information. In this article, we are going to tell you the basic differences between inductive and deductive reasoning, which will help you to understand them better.

Basis For Comparison	Inductive Reasoning	Deductive Reasoning
Meaning	Inductive Reasoning connotes the argument in which the premises give reasons in support of the probable truth of the conjecture.	Deductive reasoning is the fundamental form of valid reasoning, wherein the premises give guarantee of the truth of conjecture.
Approach	Bottom-up approach	Top-down approach
Starting point	Conclusion	Premises
Based on	Patterns or trend	Facts, truths and rules
Process	Observation > Pattern > Tentative Hypothesis > Theory	Theory > Hypothesis > Observation > Confirmation
Argument	May or may not be strong.	May or may not be valid.
Structure	Goes from specific to general	Goes from general to specific
Draws inferences with	Certainty	Probability

In research, inductive reasoning alludes to the logical process, in which specific instances or situations are observed or analysed to establish general principles. In this process, the multiple propositions are believed to provide strong evidence, for the truth of the conclusion. It is used to develop an understanding, on the basis of observing regularities, to ascertain how something works.

These are uncertain arguments; that describes the extent to which the conclusions drawn on the basis of premises, are credible.

In inductive reasoning, there are certain possibilities that the conclusion drawn can be false, even if the all the assumptions are true. The reasoning vests on experience and observations that support the apparent truth of the conclusion. Further, the argument can be strong or weak, as it only describes the likelihood of the inference, to be true.

Deductive Reasoning means a form of logic in which specific inferences are drawn from multiple premises (general statements). It establishes the relationship between the proposition and conclusion. When all the proposed statements are true, then the rules of deduction are applied and the result obtained is inevitably true.

Deductive logic is based on the fundamental law of reasoning, i.e. if X then Y. It implies the direct application of available information or facts, to come up with new information or facts. In this, the researcher takes into account a theory and generates a hypothesis, which can be tested, after that the observation are recorded, which leads to particular data, which is nothing but the confirmation of validity.

UNIT 10

APPLIED PHILOSOPHY

WHAT IS APPLIED PHILOSOPHY?

Applied philosophy is a form of philosophy, albeit one that differs from non applied or, as some put it, "pure philosophy." Presumably, the distinction between applied and pure philosophy is exhaustive and mutually exclusive, though there might be borderline cases. What distinguishes the two? Here is one way to approach the question: When we apply philosophy, we apply it to something. If I say that I am working on a piece of applied philosophy and if, in response to the question what I apply philosophy to, I say "Oh, nothing. I am just writing a piece in applied philosophy," I show myself to be conceptually and/or grammatically confused. "To apply" is a verb that takes an object. On the assumption that applied and non applied philosophy are mutually exclusive, this suggests that pure philosophy has no object. But, non grammatically speaking, this is not so. Work in a field of philosophy outside applied philosophy, such as general metaphysics, has an object – for example, the nature of properties. Hence, applied philosophy does not distinguish itself from pure philosophy in that the former is philosophy applied to an object, whereas pure philosophy is not. Pure philosophy being applied philosophy in this sense is not marked by the use of the term "applied." This is because the problems it addresses are ones that are normally considered philosophical problems in a narrow sense. Metaphorically, pure philosophy is philosophy applied to itself – that is, to philosophical problems such as the fundamental nature of reality, knowledge, morality, and so on – whereas applied philosophy is philosophy applied to non philosophical problems broadly construed.

PHILOSOPHY OF TECHNOLOGY

If philosophy is the attempt "to understand how things in the broadest possible sense of the term hang together in the broadest possible sense of the term", as Sellars put it, philosophy should not ignore technology. It is largely by technology that contemporary society hangs together. It is hugely important not only as an economic force but also as a cultural force. Indeed during the last two centuries, when it gradually emerged as a discipline, philosophy of technology has mostly been concerned with the meaning of technology for, and its impact on, society and culture, rather than with technology itself. Mitcham calls this type of philosophy of technology "humanities philosophy of technology" because it accepts "the primacy of the humanities over technologies" and is continuous with the overall perspective of the humanities (and some of the social sciences). Only recently a branch of the philosophy of technology has developed that is concerned with technology itself and that aims to understand both the practice of designing and creating artifacts (in a wide sense, including artificial processes and systems) and the nature of the things so created. This latter branch of the philosophy of technology seeks continuity with the philosophy of science and with several other fields in the analytic tradition in modern philosophy, such as the philosophy of action and decision-making, rather than with the humanities and social science.

The entry starts with a brief historical overview, then continues with a presentation of the themes on which modern analytic philosophy of technology focuses. This is followed by a discussion of the societal and ethical aspects of technology, in which some of the concerns of humanities philosophy of technology are addressed. This twofold presentation takes into consideration the development of technology as the outcome of a process originating within and guided by the practice of engineering, by standards on which only limited societal control is exercised, as well as the consequences for society of the implementation of the technology so created, which result from processes upon which only limited control can be exercised.

It may come as a surprise to those new to the topic that the fields of philosophy of science and philosophy of technology show such great differences, given that few practices in our society are as closely related as science and technology. Experimental science is nowadays crucially dependent on technology for the realization of its research set-ups and for gathering and analyzing data. The phenomena that modern science seeks to study could never be discovered without producing them through technology.

Theoretical research within technology has come to be often indistinguishable from theoretical research in science, making engineering science largely continuous with 'ordinary' or 'pure' science. This is a relatively recent development, which started around the middle of the nineteenth century, and is responsible for great differences between modern technology and traditional, craft-like techniques. The educational training that aspiring scientists and engineers receive starts off being largely identical and only gradually diverges into a science or an engineering curriculum. Ever since the scientific revolution of the seventeenth century, characterized by its two major innovations, the experimental method and the mathematical articulation of scientific theories, philosophical reflection on science has focused on the method by which scientific knowledge is generated, on the reasons for thinking scientific theories to be true, or approximately true, and on the nature of evidence and the reasons for accepting one theory and rejecting another. Hardly ever have philosophers of science posed questions that did not have the community of scientists, their concerns, their aims, their intuitions, their arguments and choices, as a major target. In contrast it is only recently that the philosophy of technology has discovered the community of engineers.

It might be claimed that it is up to the philosophy of technology, and not the philosophy of science, to target first of all the impact of technology—and with it science—on society and culture, because science affects society only through technology. This, however, will not do. Right from the start of the scientific revolution, science affected human culture and thought fundamentally and directly, not with a detour through technology, and the same is true for later developments such as relativity, atomic physics and quantum mechanics, the theory of evolution, genetics, biochemistry, and the increasingly dominating scientific world view overall. Philosophers of science overwhelmingly give the impression that they leave questions addressing the normative, social and cultural aspects of science gladly to other philosophical disciplines, or to historical studies. There are exceptions, however, and things may be changing; Philip Kitcher, to name but one prominent philosopher of science, has since 2000 written books on the relation of science to politics, ethics and religion.

There is a major difference between the historical development of modern technology as compared to modern science which may at least partly explain this situation, which is that science emerged in the seventeenth century from philosophy itself. The answers that Galileo, Huygens, Newton, and others gave, by which they initiated the alliance of empiricism and mathematical description that is so characteristic of modern science, were answers to questions that had belonged to the core business of philosophy since antiquity. Science, therefore, kept the attention of philosophers. Philosophy of science is a transformation of epistemology in the light of the emergence of science. The foundational issues—the reality of atoms, the status of causality and probability, questions of space and time, the nature of the quantum world—that were so lively discussed during the end of the nineteenth and the beginning of the twentieth century are an illustration of this close relationship between scientists and philosophers. No such intimacy has ever existed between those same philosophers and technologists; their worlds still barely touch. To be sure, a case can be made that, compared to the continuity existing between natural philosophy and science, a similar continuity exists between central questions in philosophy having to do with human action and practical rationality and the way technology approaches and systematizes the solution of practical problems. This continuity appears only by hindsight, however, and dimly, as the historical development is at most a slow convening of various strands of philosophical thinking on action and rationality, not a development into variety from a single origin. Significantly it is only the academic outsider Ellul who has, in his idiosyncratic way, recognized in technology the emergent single dominant way of answering all questions concerning human action, comparable to science as the single dominant way of answering all questions concerning human knowledge. But Ellul was not so much interested in investigating this relationship as in emphasizing and denouncing the social and cultural consequences as he saw them. It is all the more important to point out that humanities philosophy of technology cannot be differentiated from analytic philosophy of technology by claiming that only the former is interested in the social environment of technology.

The close relationship between the practices of science and technology may easily keep the important differences between the two from view. The predominant position of science in the philosophical field of vision made it difficult for philosophers to recognize that technology merits special attention for involving issues that do not emerge in science. This view resulting from this lack of recognition is often presented, perhaps somewhat dramatically, as coming down to a claim that technology is 'merely' applied science.

A questioning of the relation between science and technology was the central issue in one of the earliest discussions among analytic philosophers of technology. In 1966, in a special issue of the journal Technology and Culture, Henryk Skolimowski argued that technology is something quite different from science. As he phrased it, science concerns itself with what is, whereas technology concerns itself with what is to be. A few years later, in his well-known book The Sciences of the Artificial, Herbert Simon emphasized this important distinction in almost the same words, stating that the scientist is concerned with how things are but the engineer with how things ought to be. Although it is difficult to imagine that earlier philosophers were blind to this difference in orientation, their inclination, in particular in the tradition of logical empiricism, to view knowledge as a system of statements may have led to a conviction that in technology no knowledge claims play a role that cannot also be found in science. The study of technology, therefore, was not expected to pose new challenges nor hold surprises regarding the interests of analytic philosophy.

In contrast, Mario Bunge defended the view that technology is applied science, but in a subtle way that does justice to the differences between science and technology. Bunge acknowledges that technology is about action, but an action heavily underpinned by theory—that is what distinguishes technology from the arts and crafts and puts it on a par with science. According to Bunge, theories in technology come in two types: substantive theories, which provide knowledge about the object of action, and operative theories, which are concerned with action itself. The substantive theories of technology are indeed largely applications of scientific theories. The operative theories, in contrast, are not preceded by scientific theories but are born in applied research itself. Still, as Bunge claims, operative theories show a dependence on science in that in such theories the method of science is employed. This includes such features as modeling and idealization, the use of theoretical concepts and abstractions, and the modification of theories by the absorption of empirical data through prediction and retrodiction.

In response to this discussion, Ian Jarvie proposed as important questions for a philosophy of technology what the epistemological status of technological statements is and how technological statements are to be demarcated from scientific statements. This suggests a thorough investigation of the various forms of knowledge occurring in either practice, in particular, since scientific knowledge has already been so extensively studied, of the forms of knowledge that are characteristic of technology and are lacking, or of much less prominence, in science. A distinction between 'knowing that'—traditional propositional knowledge—and 'knowing how'—non-articulated and even impossible-to-articulate knowledge—had been introduced by Gilbert Ryle in a different context. The notion of 'knowing how' was taken up by Michael Polanyi under the name of tacit knowledge and made a central characteristic of technology; the current state of the philosophical discussion is presented in this encyclopedia's entry on knowledge how. However, emphasizing too much the role of unarticulated knowledge, of 'rules of thumb' as they are often called, easily underplays the importance of rational methods in technology. An emphasis on tacit knowledge may also be ill-fit for distinguishing the practices of science and technology because the role of tacit knowledge in science may well be more important than current philosophy of science acknowledges, for example in concluding causal relationships on the basis of empirical evidence. This was also an important theme in the writings of Thomas Kuhn on theory change in science.

To claim, with Skolimowski and Simon, that technology is about what is to be or what ought to be rather than what is may serve to distinguish it from science but will hardly make it understandable why so much philosophical reflection on technology has taken the form of socio-cultural critique. Technology is an ongoing attempt to bring the world closer to the way one wishes it to be. Whereas science aims to understand the world as it is, technology aims to change the world. These are abstractions, of course. For one, whose wishes concerning what the world should be like are realized in technology? Unlike scientists, who are often personally motivated in their attempts at describing and understanding the world, engineers are seen, not in the least by engineers themselves, as undertaking their attempts to change the world as a service to the public. The ideas on what is to be or what ought to be are seen as originating outside of technology itself; engineers then take it upon themselves to realize these ideas. This view is a major source for the widely spread picture of technology as being instrumental, as delivering instruments ordered from 'elsewhere', as means to ends specified outside of engineering, a picture that has served further to support the claim that technology is neutral with respect to values. This view involves a considerable distortion of reality, however. Many engineers are intrinsically motivated to change the world; in delivering ideas for improvement they are, so to speak, their own best customers. The same is true for most industrial companies, particularly in a market economy, where the prospect of great profits is another powerful motivator. As a result, much technological development is 'technology-driven'.

To understand where technology 'comes from', what drives the innovation process, is of importance not only to those who are curious to understand the phenomenon of technology itself but also to those who are concerned about its role in society. Technology or engineering as a practice is concerned with the creation of artifacts and, of increasing importance, artifact-based services. The design process, the structured process leading toward that goal, forms the core of the practice of technology. In the engineering literature, the design process is commonly represented as consisting of a series of translational steps. At the start are the customer's needs or wishes.

In the first step these are translated into a list of functional requirements, which then define the design task an engineer, or a team of engineers, has to accomplish. The functional requirements specify as precisely as possible what the device to be designed must be able to do. This step is required because customers usually focus on just one or two features and are unable to articulate the requirements that are necessary to support the functionality they desire. In the second step, the functional requirements are translated into design specifications, which the exact physical parameters of crucial components by which the functional requirements are going to be met. The design parameters chosen to satisfy these requirements are combined and made more precise such that a blueprint of the device results. The blueprint contains all the details that must be known such that the final step to the process of manufacturing the device can take place. It is tempting to consider the blueprint as the end result of a design process, instead of a finished copy being this result.

However, actual copies of a device are crucial for the purpose of prototyping and testing. Prototyping and testing presuppose that the sequence of steps making up the design process can and will often contain iterations, leading to revisions of the design parameters and/or the functional requirements. Even though, certainly for mass-produced items, the manufacture of a product for delivery to its customers or to the market comes after the closure of the design phase, the manufacturing process is often reflected in the functional requirements of a device, for example in putting restrictions on the number of different components of which the device consists.

The complexity of a device will affect how difficult it will be to maintain or repair it, and ease of maintenance or low repair costs are often functional requirements. An important modern development is that the complete life cycle of an artifact is now considered to be the designing engineer's concern, up till the final stages of the recycling and disposal of its components and materials, and the functional requirements of any device should reflect this. From this point of view, neither a blueprint nor a prototype can be considered the end product of engineering design.

The biggest idealization that this scheme of the design process contains is arguably located at the start. Only in a minority of cases does a design task originate in a customer need or wish for a particular artifact. First of all, as already suggested, many design tasks are defined by engineers themselves, for instance, by noticing something to be improved in existing products.

But more often than not design starts with a problem pointed out by some societal agent, which engineers are then invited to solve. Many such problems, however, are ill-defined or wicked problems, meaning that it is not at all clear what the problem is exactly and what a solution to the problem would consist in. The 'problem' is a situation that people—not necessarily the people 'in' the situation—find unsatisfactory, but typically without being able to specify a situation that they find more satisfactory in other terms than as one in which the problem has been solved.

In particular it is not obvious that a solution to the problem would consist in some artifact, or some artifactual system or process, being made available or installed. Engineering departments all over the world advertise that engineering is problem solving, and engineers easily seem confident that they are best qualified to solve a problem when they are asked to, whatever the nature of the problem. This has led to the phenomenon of a technological fix, the solution of a problem by a technical solution, that is, the delivery of an artifact or artifactual process, where it is questionable, to say the least, whether this solves the problem or whether it was the best way of handling the problem.

A candidate example of a technological fix for the problem of global warming would be the currently much debated option of injecting sulfate aerosols into the stratosphere to offset the warming effect of greenhouse gases such as carbon dioxide and methane. Such schemes of geoengineering would allow us to avoid facing the—in all likelihood painful—choices that will lead to a reduction of the emission of greenhouse gases into the atmosphere, but will at the same time allow the depletion of the Earth's reservoir of fossil fuels to continue. Given this situation, and its hazards, the notion of a problem and a taxonomy of problems deserve to receive more philosophical attention than they have hitherto received.

These wicked problems are often broadly social problems, which would best be met by some form of 'social action', which would result in people changing their behavior or acting differently in such a way that the problem would be mitigated or even disappear completely. In defense of the engineering view, it could perhaps be said that the repertoire of 'proven' forms of social action is meager. The temptation of technical fixes could be overcome—at least that is how an engineer might see it—by the inclusion of the social sciences in the systematic development and application of knowledge to the solution of human problems. This however, is a controversial view. Social engineering is to many a specter to be kept at as large a distance as possible instead of an ideal to be pursued. Karl Popper referred to acceptable forms of implementing social change as 'piecemeal social engineering' and contrasted it to the revolutionary but completely unfounded schemes advocated by, e.g., Marxism. In the entry on Karl Popper, however, his choice of words is called 'rather unfortunate'. The notion of social engineering, and its cogency, deserves more attention that it is currently receiving.

An important input for the design process is scientific knowledge: knowledge about the behavior of components and the materials they are composed of in specific circumstances. This is the point where science is applied. However, much of this knowledge is not directly available from the sciences, since it often concerns extremely detailed behavior in very specific circumstances. This scientific knowledge is therefore often generated within technology, by the engineering sciences. But apart from this very specific scientific knowledge, engineering design involves various other sorts of knowledge. In his book What Engineers Know and How They Know It, the aeronautical engineer Walter Vincenti gave a six-fold categorization of engineering design knowledge (leaving aside production and operation as the other two basic constituents of engineering practice). Vincenti distinguishes

1. Fundamental design concepts, including primarily the operational principle and the normal configuration of a particular device;
2. Criteria and specifications;
3. Theoretical tools;
4. Quantitative data;
5. Practical considerations;
6. Design instrumentalities.

The fourth category concerns the quantitative knowledge just referred to, and the third the theoretical tools used to acquire it. These two categories can be assumed to match Bunge's notion of substantive technological theories. The status of the remaining four categories is much less clear, however, partly because they are less familiar, or not at all, from the well-explored context of science. Of these categories, Vincenti claims that they represent prescriptive forms of knowledge rather than descriptive ones. Here, the activity of design introduces an element of normativity, which is absent from scientific knowledge. Take such a basic notion as 'operational principle', which refers to the way in which the function of a device is realized, or, in short, how it works. This is still a purely descriptive notion. Subsequently, however, it plays a role in arguments that seek to prescribe a course of action to someone who has a goal that could be realized by the operation of such a device. At this stage, the issue changes from a descriptive to a prescriptive or normative one. An extensive discussion of the various kinds of knowledge relevant to technology is offered by Houkes.

Although the notion of an operational principle—a term that seems to originate with Polanyi – is central to engineering design, no single clear-cut definition of it seems to exist. The issue of disentangling descriptive from prescriptive aspects in an analysis of the technical action and its constituents is therefore a task that has hardly begun. This task requires a clear view on the extent and scope of technology. If one follows Joseph Pitt in his book Thinking About Technology and defines technology broadly as 'humanity at work', then to distinguish between technological action and action in general becomes difficult, and the study of technological action must absorb all descriptive and normative theories of action, including the theory of practical rationality, and much of theoretical economics in its wake. There have indeed been attempts at such an encompassing account of human action, for example Tadeusz Kotarbinski's Praxiology, but a perspective of such generality makes it difficult to arrive at results of sufficient depth. It would be a challenge for philosophy to specify the differences among action forms and the reasoning grounding them in, to single out three prominent fields of study, technology, organization and management, and economics.

A more restricted attempt at such an approach is Ilkka Niiniluoto's. According to Niiniluoto, the theoretical framework of technology as the practice that is concerned with what the world should be like rather than is, the framework that forms the counterpoint to the descriptive framework of science, is design science. The content of design science, the counterpoint to the theories and explanations that form the content of descriptive science, would then be formed by technical norms, statements of the form 'If one wants to achieve X, one should do Y'. The notion of a technical norm derives from George Henrik von Wright's Norm and Action. Technical norms need to be distinguished from anankastic statements expressing natural necessity, of the form 'If X is to be achieved, Y needs to be done'; the latter have a truth value but the former have not. Von Wright himself, however, wrote that he did not understand the mutual relations between these statements. Ideas on what design science is and can and should be are evidently related to the broad problem area of practical rationality – see this encyclopedia's entries on practical reason and instrumental rationality – and also to means-ends reasoning, discussed in the next section.

Design is an activity that is subject to rational scrutiny but in which creativity is considered to play an important role as well. Since design is a form of action, a structured series of decisions to proceed in one way rather than another, the form of rationality that is relevant to it is practical rationality, the rationality incorporating the criteria on how to act, given particular circumstances. This suggests a clear division of labor between the part to be played by rational scrutiny and the part to be played by creativity. Theories of rational action generally conceive their problem situation as one involving a choice among various course of action open to the agent.

Rationality then concerns the question how to decide among given options, whereas creativity concerns the generation of these options. This distinction is similar to the distinction between the context of justification and the context of discovery in science. The suggestion that is associated with this distinction, however, that rational scrutiny only applies in the context of justification, is difficult to uphold for technological design. If the initial creative phase of option generation is conducted sloppily, the result of the design task can hardly be satisfactory. Unlike the case of science, where the practical consequences of entertaining a particular theory are not taken into consideration, the context of discovery in technology is governed by severe constraints of time and money, and an analysis of the problem how best to proceed certainly seems in order. There has been little philosophical work done in this direction; an overview of the issues is given in Kroes, Franssen, and Bucciarelli.

The ideas of Herbert Simon on bounded rationality are relevant here, since decisions on when to stop generating options and when to stop gathering information about these options and the consequences when they are adopted are crucial in decision making if informational overload and calculative intractability are to be avoided. However, it has proved difficult to further develop Simon's ideas on bounded rationality since their conception in the 1950s. Another notion that is relevant here is means-ends reasoning. In order to be of any help here, theories of means-ends reasoning should then concern not just the evaluation of given means with respect to their ability to achieve given ends, but also the generation or construction of means for given ends.

A comprehensive theory of means-ends reasoning, however, is not yet available; for a proposal on how to develop means-ends reasoning in the context of technical artifacts. In the practice of technology, alternative proposals for the realization of particular functions are usually taken from 'catalogs' of existing and proven realizations. These catalogs are extended by ongoing research in technology rather than under the urge of particular design tasks.

When engineering design is conceived as a process of decision making, governed by considerations of practical rationality, the next step is to specify these considerations. Almost all theories of practical rationality conceive of it as a reasoning process where a match between beliefs and desires or goals is sought. The desires or goals are represented by their value or utility for the decision maker, and the decision maker's problem is to choose an action that realizes a situation that, ideally, has maximal value or utility among all the situations that could be realized. If there is uncertainty concerning he situations that will be realized by a particular action, then the problem is conceived as aiming for maximal expected value or utility. Now the instrumental perspective on technology implies that the value that is at issue in the design process viewed as a process of rational decision making is not the value of the artifacts that are created.

Those values are the domain of the users of the technology so created. They are supposed to be represented in the functional requirements defining the design task. Instead the value to be maximized is the extent to which a particular design meets the functional requirements defining the design task. It is in this sense that engineers share an overall perspective on engineering design as an exercise in optimization. But although optimization is a value-orientated notion, it is not itself perceived as a value driving engineering design.

The functional requirements that define most design problems do not prescribe explicitly what should be optimized; usually they set levels to be attained minimally. It is then up to the engineer to choose how far to go beyond meeting the requirements in this minimal sense. Efficiency, in energy consumption and use of materials first of all, is then often a prime value. Under the pressure of society, other values have come to be incorporated, in particular safety and, more recently, sustainability. Sometimes it is claimed that what engineers aim to maximize is just one factor, namely market success. Market success, however, can only be assessed after the fact. The engineer's maximization effort will instead be directed at what are considered the predictors of market success. Meeting the functional requirements and being relatively efficient and safe are plausible candidates as such predictors, but additional methods, informed by market research, may introduce additional factors or may lead to a hierarchy among the factors.

Choosing the design option that maximally meets all the functional requirements (which may but need not originate with the prospective user) and all other considerations and criteria that are taken to be relevant, then becomes the practical decision-making problem to be solved in a particular engineering-design task. This creates several methodological problems. Most important of these is that the engineer is facing a multi-criteria decision problem. The various requirements come with their own operationalizations in terms of design parameters and measurement procedures for assessing their performance. This results in a number of rank orders or quantitative scales which represent the various options out of which a choice is to be made. The task is to come up with a final score in which all these results are 'adequately' represented, such that the option that scores best can be considered the optimal solution to the design problem.

Engineers describe this situation as one where trade-offs have to be made: in judging the merit of one option relative to other options, a relative bad performance on one criterion can be balanced by a relatively good performance on another criterion. An important problem is whether a rational method for doing this can be formulated. It has been argued by Franssen that this problem is structurally similar to the well-known problem of social choice, for which Kenneth Arrow proved his notorious impossibility theorem in 1950, implying that no general rational solution method exists for this problem. This poses serious problems for the claim of engineers that their designs are optimal solutions, since Arrow's theorem implies that in most multi-criteria problems the notion of 'optimal' cannot be rigorously defined.

This result seems to except a crucial aspect of engineering activity from philosophical scrutiny, and it could be used to defend the opinion that engineering is at least partly an art, not a science. Instead of surrendering to the result, however, which has a significance that extends much beyond engineering and even beyond decision making in general, we should perhaps conclude instead that there is still a lot of work to be done on what might be termed, provisionally, 'approximative' forms of reasoning. One form of reasoning to be included here is Herbert Simon's bounded rationality, plus the related notion of 'satisficing'. Since their introduction in the 1950s these two terms have found wide usage, but we are still lacking a general theory of bounded rationality. It may be in the nature of forms of approximative reasoning such as bounded rationality that a general theory cannot be had, but even a systematic treatment from which such an insight could emerge seems to be lacking.

Another problem for the decision-making view of engineering design is that in modern technology almost all design is done by teams. Such teams are composed of experts from many different disciplines. Each discipline has its own theories, its own models of interdependencies, its own assessment criteria, and so forth, and the professionals belonging to these disciplines must be considered as inhabitants of different object worlds, as Louis Bucciarelli phrases it. The different team members are, therefore, likely to disagree on the relative rankings and evaluations of the various design options under discussion. Agreement on one option as the overall best one can here be even less arrived at by an algorithmic method exemplifying engineering rationality. Instead, models of social interaction, such as bargaining and strategic thinking, are relevant here. An example of such an approach to an (abstract) design problem is presented by Franssen and Bucciarelli.

To look in this way at technological design as a decision-making process is to view it normatively from the point of view of practical or instrumental rationality. At the same time it is descriptive in that it is a description of how engineering methodology generally presents the issue how to solve design problems. From that somewhat higher perspective there is room for all kinds of normative questions that are not addressed here, such as whether the functional requirements defining a design problem can be seen as an adequate representation of the values of the prospective users of an artifact or a technology, or by which methods values such as safety and sustainability can best be elicited and represented in the design process.

Understanding the process of designing artifacts is the theme in philosophy of technology that most directly touches on the interests of engineering practice. This is hardly true for another issue of central concern to analytic philosophy of technology, which is the status and the character of artifacts. This is perhaps not unlike the situation in the philosophy of science, where working scientists seem also to be much less interested in investigating the status and character of models and theories than philosophers are.

The artifacts that are of relevance to technology are, in particular, made to serve a purpose. This excludes, within the set of all man-made objects, on the one hand byproducts and waste products and on the other hand works of art. Byproducts and waste products result from an intentional act to make something but just not precisely, although the author at work may be well aware of their creation. Works of art result from an intention directed at their creation (although in exceptional cases of conceptual art, this directedness may involve many intermediate steps) but it is contested whether artists include in their intentions concerning their work an intention that the work serves some purpose. A further discussion of this aspect belongs to the philosophy of art. An interesting general account has been presented by Dipert.

Technical artifacts, then, are made to serve some purpose, generally to be used for something or to act as a component in a larger artifact, which in its turn is either something to be used or again a component. Whether end product or component, an artifact is 'for something', and what it is for is called the artifact's function. Several researchers have emphasized that an adequate description of artifacts must refer both to their status as tangible physical objects and to the intentions of the people engaged with them. Kroes and Meijers have dubbed this view "the dual nature of technical artifacts"; its most mature formulation is Kroes. They suggest that the two aspects are 'tied up', so to speak, in the notion of artifact function. This gives rise to several problems. One, which will be passed over quickly because little philosophical work seems to have been done concerning it, is that structure and function mutually constrain each other, but the constraining is only partial. It is unclear whether a general account of this relation is possible and what problems need to be solved to arrive there. There may be interesting connections with the issue of multiple realizability in the philosophy of mind and with accounts of reduction in science; an example where this is explored is Mahner and Bunge.

It is equally problematic whether a unified account of the notion of function as such is possible, but this issue has received considerably more philosophical attention. The notion of function is of paramount importance for characterizing artifacts, but the notion is used much more widely. The notion of an artifact's function seems to refer necessarily to human intentions. Function is also a key concept in biology, however, where no intentionality plays a role, and it is a key concept in cognitive science and the philosophy of mind, where it is crucial in grounding intentionality in non-intentional, structural and physical properties. Up till now there is no accepted general account of function that covers both the intentionality-based notion of artifact function and the non-intentional notion of biological function—not to speak of other areas where the concept plays a role, such as the social sciences. The most comprehensive theory, that has the ambition to account for the biological notion, cognitive notion and the intentional notion, is Ruth Millikan's; Vermaas & Houkes; and Houkes & Vermaas. The collection of essays edited by Ariew, Cummins and Perlman presents a recent introduction to the general topic of defining the notion of function in general, although the emphasis is, as is generally the case in the literature on function, on biological functions.

Against the view that, at least in the case of artifacts, the notion of function refers necessarily to intentionality, it could be argued that in discussing the functions of the components of a larger device, and the interrelations between these functions, the intentional 'side' of these functions is of secondary importance only. This, however, would be to ignore the possibility of the malfunctioningof such components. This notion seems to be definable only in terms of a mismatch between actual behavior and intended behavior. The notion of malfunction also sharpens an ambiguity in the general reference to intentions when characterizing technical artifacts. These artifacts usually engage many people, and the intentions of these people may not all pull in the same direction.

A major distinction can be drawn between the intentions of the actual user of an artifact for a particular purpose and the intentions of the artifact's designer. Since an artifact may be used for a purpose different from the one for which its designer intended it to be used, and since people may also use natural objects for some purpose or other, one is invited to allow that artifacts can have multiple functions, or to enforce a hierarchy among all relevant intentions in determining the function of an artifact, or to introduce a classification of functions in terms of the sorts of determining intentions. In the latter case, which is a sort of middle way between the two other options, one commonly distinguishes between the proper function of an artifact as the one intended by its designer and the accidental function of the artifact as the one given to it by some user on private considerations. Accidental use can become so common, however, that the original function drops out of memory.

Closely related to this issue to what extent use and design determine the function of an artifact is the problem of characterizing artifact kinds. It may seem that we use functions to classify artifacts: an object is a knife because it has the function of cutting, or more precisely, of enabling us to cut. On closer inspection, however, the link between function and kind-membership seems much less straightforward. The basic kinds in technology are, for example, 'knife', 'aircraft' and 'piston'.

The members of these kinds have been designed in order to be used to cut something with, to transport something through the air and to generate mechanical movement through thermodynamic expansion. However, one cannot create a particular kind of artifact just by designing something with the intention that it be used for some particular purpose: a member of the kind so created must actually be useful for that purpose. Despite innumerable design attempts and claims, the perpetual motion machine is not a kind of artifact.

A kind like 'knife' is defined, therefore, not only by the intentions of the designers of its members that they each be useful for cutting but also by a shared operational principle known to these designers, and on which they based their design. This is, in a different setting, also defended by Thomasson, who in her characterization of what she in general calls an artifactual kind says that such a kind is defined by the designer's intention to make something of that kind, by a substantive idea that the designer has of how this can be achieved, and by his or her largely successful achievement of it.

Qua sorts of kinds in which artifacts can be grouped, a distinction must therefore be made between a kind like 'knife' and a corresponding but different kind 'cutter'. A 'knife' indicates a particular way a 'cutter' can be made. One can also cut, however, with a thread or line, a welding torch, a water jet, and undoubtedly by other sorts of means that have not yet been thought of. A 'cutter' would then refer to a truly functional kind. As such, it is subject to the conflict between use and design: one could mean by 'cutter' anything than can be used for cutting or anything that has been designed to be used for cutting, by the application of whatever operational principle, presently known or unknown.

This distinction between artifact kinds and functional kinds is relevant for the status of such kinds in comparison to other notions of kinds. Philosophy of science has emphasized that the concept of natural kind, such as exemplified by 'water' or 'atom', lies at the basis of science. On the other hand it is generally taken for granted that there are no regularities that all knives or airplanes or pistons answer to. This, however, is loosely based on considerations of multiple realizability that fully apply only to functional kinds, not to artifact kinds. Artifact kinds share an operational principle that gives them some commonality in physical features, and this commonality becomes stronger once a particular artifact kind is subdivided into narrower kinds. Since these kinds are specified in terms of physical and geometrical parameters, they are much closer to the natural kinds of science, in that they support law-like regularities; see for a defense of this position.

DEMOCRATISATION OF TECHNOLOGY

In the past, patents dominated the technology industry and it was hard for anyone to replicate someone else's work without being sued. Developers would create an innovative piece of technology and then put a patent on it so that nobody could make exactly the same thing. In these cases, things had to be slightly altered and it made overall progress slow.

Times are changing, though, and now ideas are being shared more frequently in an effort to help push technology forward at a faster rate. In a major shift, technology isn't just available to big corporations and developers nowadays. In fact, consumers are able to gain more access to high-tech equipment and buy sophisticated technological products. In addition to this, these people can participate in the development of products and help push technology further. This means many more people today are working on helping technology progress than there were before, and this is obviously speeding up the overall process.

When thinking about the democratisation of technology, scholars often compare it to when the printing press led to information being brought to the masses in a much broader way. After the invention of the printing press by Johannes Gutenberg in the early 1400s, it was possible to get information to more people and the machine had a major social impact. The internet is the modern-day equivalent of this, and has had the same effect but on a much larger scale. Now people from all over the world can instantly communicate with each other and share ideas in a matter of minutes.

The internet hasn't always been this open to the public, however. It was actually invented in 1969 and was initially used as a method of communication between scientists and within the government. It wasn't until the 1990s that the innovation became available to everyone on the planet. In 1993, the US government made the internet available for commerce, and the conception of HTML at this time meant that accessibility was universal and anyone could create online content. Ever since that time, the internet has got faster and better at an impressive rate. Now, the platform has made it possible for ideas to be shared easily. It is the main reason why we are currently seeing the democratisation of technology.

While the world is doubtlessly moving towards a state where there is complete democratisation of technology, this hasn't quite been achieved yet. There is still a way to go for people all over the world to have access to the same technology. So how can full democratisation be achieved?

One of the ways is to try to reduce the number of developers disparaging new platforms and claiming that they can never replace the traditional methods of old. These people want to steer amateurs away from creating their own things with affordable technology, and instead have them pay the companies huge amounts of money to do it for them. The key for developers with this mindset is teaching them that they need to adapt to this shift in the way technology is used. They could also use new technological advancements to make their own jobs easier, rather than stand in the way of innovations.

The popularity of smartphones, entertainment apps, and casual games could serve as a catalyst for the democratisation of technology as more and more people realise how easy it is to create content in this genre. These games, which are often based on things in other areas of popular culture can also serve to attract more players and get a greater number of people interested in the world of gaming. For instance, at Wink Slots there are online slot games based on popular characters like Dr Jekyll and the Invisible Man, and fans of these fictional icons may seek games in order to experience them on another level. This is why mobile games are also frequently based on things that are popular in other media. There are games based on hugely popular films like Tomb Raider and Jurassic World, and people who enjoyed these films are going to be interested in playing games about them.

Mobile games are fairly easy for amateur developers to make, which is why there are so many more companies coming about in the industry. The start of the hugely successful Roveo Entertainment is a prime example of this. The software company which came up with the record-breaking Angry Birdsapp was started by some Finnish students from the Helsinki University of Technology. Niklas Hed, Jarno Vakevainen, and Kim Dikert started out by winning a mobile game development competition at the Assembly demoparty and this led to the three youngsters setting up their own company. Angry Birds games have now had over 2 billion downloads across all platforms, and the titles have made the Finnish developers exceedingly rich. Stories like this are helping to inspire others to do the same, and highlighting how the democratisation of technology has made previously difficult things possible.

The exciting thing about the democratisation of technology is the fact that it can lead to much faster development in the industry. Advancements which had previously taken years can occur in a much shorter space of time. As the story of the team behind Roveo shows, there will definitely be a rise in programmers as more people have access to the tools necessary to create simple games. These budding developers may then take the knowledge and skills learnt from that and go on to make more advanced titles.

The democratisation of technology has the power to change people's lives, as it opens up a whole host of new opportunities and possibilities. It gives people new ways to make money through development, advertise and promote businesses, and invent new things. The people of today are so lucky to have access to all these things, and dreams that were previously impossible are now achievable.

It is certainly an exciting time to be alive, as we are now witnessing technological progress at its fastest ever rate. There is no limit to what can be achieved through the democratisation of technology, and there is no doubt that the industry is going to continue to develop at a lightning pace from now on.

Public evaluation of science of technology:

> Recently several articles have appeared arguing for a several changes in the kinds of S&T evaluations that are being made. Among other suggestions, the following seem to be of special merit: (1) a more macro and systemic focus; (2) concentrating on the processes of innovation; (3) using theory to guide the S&T evaluation; and (4) identifying blockages and obstacles or what Arnold labels failures. One of the great advantages of concentrating on innovation processes is that it helps identify the causal chain connecting policy intervention and outcome including eventual societal impact, a problem that Molas-Gallart and Davies identify in the medium and long-term evaluations that are more typical. To this list of desiderata, we would add the perspective of the policy maker who wants to know what policy reformulations should be made to correct the blockages and obstacles.

Given these observations, the Center for Innovation has developed the following kinds of theories and frameworks for evaluation of innovation and knowledge production:

- A three level framework, micro, meso, and macro, for evaluation of technological sectors with three sets of indicators at each level for identifying blockages and obstacles.
- Measures of radical innovation in science and technology.
- A focus on evaluating health care in real time.

As an example of the first objective, we presented a new policy model at an International Conference. Several papers were published on this framework. At the meetings of the American Evaluation Association we made a concrete proposal for a new kind of innovation applied to the U.S. that would examine the three levels, micro, meso, and macro, and identify a number of blockages.

This presentation was turned into an entire book, Restoring the Innovative Edge: Driving the evolution of science and technology, was published in May 2011 by Stanford Press. It suggests the following steps needs to be taken:

- Seize strategic opportunities for radical product/process innovations and scientific breakthroughs by knowing the processes of evolution.
- Select the appropriate kinds of complex research teams.
- Stimulate cross-fertilization learning within and between research teams.
- Construct transformational organizations.
- Connect the idea innovation network to overcome gaps.
- Continuously evaluate the innovation process.
- Public and private sector cooperation.
- New kinds of data collection by funding agencies.

Each of these solutions involves various costs because this is a complex social system that has other barriers attached to it. Furthermore, what is the most appropriate solution for one kind of research organization, say a public research laboratory, is not necessarily the best for a private firm or a university. The book provides some consideration of these various kinds of dilemmas.

As an example of successful approaches to radical innovation in science and technology, Hage with a team of historians (Hollingsworth and Hollingsworth), selected some 276 radical innovations across a century of time defined by 8 major prizes or nominations. Only six research organizations accounted for one-fourth of these advances, one of which is the Institut Pasteur. So Hage working with Mott identified the characteristics of why this organization was so successful and published several papers [Summarized in this presentation]. This Institut created the area of biomedical research and transformed the French health care system providing a way of defining institutional innovations.

A special focus of the Center for Innovation has been measuring radical innovation in the health care system and developing new metrics to evaluate the returns from investment R&D funding. The Canadian government asked Hage to develop a comprehensive framework for evaluating health care benefits. In a white paper, he proposed 15 measures of technical advance in a specific health category by examining the stages of health care intervention. In addition three measures of increased knowledge were suggested. Special sections on various topics were created including one on measuring the quality of care and another on detecting gaps in medical research.

As an example of how this framework can be used, we received a grant from the National Science Foundation to measure the various outcomes of investments in medical research. Rather than focus on specific tools and techniques, the intent is to evaluate the clinical research program in its capacity to reduce health care costs and mortality. This project examined four morbidities: melanoma cancer, breast cancer, colorectal cancer, and frailty and falls. The melanoma report provides an example what was accomplished.

We have expanded our evaluation concerns about health to developing countries. Having previously completed a project on the relative merits of network of vs. single founded agencies in Nicaragua, the Liverpool School of Tropical Medicine asked the Center for Innovation to answer the question why leadership in the India health care system was not responsive to recommendations to improve health care delivery. In developing countries, the current technology has been to use LQAS sampling techniques combined with concrete indicators to measure the effectiveness of various interventions to reduce disease and mortality. While the centralization/decentralization of the Indian health care system meant little progress because of LQAS, while Uganda profited for a number of reasons from its evaluations.

A major goal of the Center for Innovation consists of developing the concept of the Gross Domestic Innovation Benefit measure. Much of neo-classical economics has been constructed on the idea of the GDP, which is based on various measures of productivity. The consequence of this has been the emergence of theories that in various ways improve productivity but also at the same time had unfortunate consequences not only for innovation, which is poorly captured in productivity measures, but for other aspects of the health of individuals and the quality of the environment. Our concept of a measure of Gross Domestic Innovation Benefit would include the consequences of innovation not only for economic growth, employment, and positive trade balances but for increased knowledge, external power and health and rehabilitation benefits.

ETHICAL IMPLICATION OF TECHNOLOGY

In the past four decades technology has fundamentally altered our lives: from the way we work to how we communicate to how we fight wars. These technologies have not been without controversy, and many have sparked intense debates that are often polarized or embroiled in scientific ambiguities or dishonest demagoguery.

The debate on stem cells and embryo research, for example, has become a hot-button political issue involving scientists, policy makers, politicians and religious groups. Similarly, the discussions on genetically modified organisms (GMOs) have mobilized civil society, scientists and policy makers in a wide debate on ethics and safety. The developments in genome-editing technologies are just one example that bioresearch and its impact on market goods are strongly dependent on social acceptance and cannot escape public debates of regulation and ethics. Moreover, requests for transparency are increasingly central to these debates, as shown by movements like Right to Know, which has repeatedly demanded the labeling of GMOs on food products.

Ethical and Regulatory Challenges

On March 4 the World Economic Forum released its list of the top 10 emerging technologies for 2015. It includes advances that aim to resolve some of the ethical debates posed by an earlier generation of technologies as well as others that will bring about new ethical and regulatory challenges. The notion of "emerging" technology does not necessarily mean that all such advances are new or revolutionary by themselves. Some have already been around for years or, in various forms, for decades (for example, fuel-cell vehicles, artificial intelligence, the digital genome, additive manufacturing methods). They are now transitioning to a new phase, however, becoming more widely used or incorporated in consumer goods. In one way or another all these technologies are bound to gain more ground in coming years.

Precise genetic-engineering techniques will likely solve some of the main controversial elements in the GMO debate—for example, the fact that genetic engineering was neither precise nor predictable. The range of procedures associated with GM crops is precise in the initial process of cutting and splitting genes in the test tubes. But the subsequent steps are uncontrolled and some mutations can occur and alter the functioning of the natural genes in potentially harmful ways. A technique that would achieve greater accuracy and greater predictability over genetic mutations is, of course, a net improvement on conventional GMOs. It is, however, critical that this technique is properly studied and implemented in a sustainable way and that it doesn't just give renewed legitimacy to genetic engineering in agriculture.

More accuracy is also expected in the operation of drones with the adaptation of the sense-and-avoid equipment. This will have unequivocal security benefits, helping unmanned aerial vehicles avoid collisions with other drones or piloted aircraft. The critical offshoot of this innovation is that it will encourage and enable the operation of a larger number of drones, a development which can be both welcomed (for instance, China flies drones to help fight pollution) and anticipated, as the growth indangerous drone flights around populated areas appears to be developing ahead of regulations.

Autonomous systems, artificial intelligence (AI) and robotics, while already decades-old technologies, will continue to expand their functionalities and enter new eras of continual specialization. More intuitive, emergent AI could change speech and conversational software with unprecedented precision, helping millions of people and also redefining the way we command and interact with computers.

Robots as Intelligent as Humans

New-generation robotics will increasingly have more autonomy and capacity to react without preprogramming, which complicates current debates on robotics: The trust and reliance invested in a robot will have to be greater, bringing robots closer to the point of being on par with us. Neuromorphic chip technology further illustrates this. It is among the most revolutionary developments in AI and a radical step in computing power. Mimicking the intricacies of the human brain, a neuro-inspired computer would work in a fashion similar to the way neurons and synapses communicate. It could potentially learn or develop memory. This would imply that, for instance, a drone equipped with a neuromorphic chip would be better at surveillance, remembering or recognizing new elements in its environment.

Immediate ethical red flags emerge, however: Building neuromorphic chips would create machines as smart as humans, the most intelligent species on the planet. These technologies are demonstrations of human excellence yet computers that think could be devastating for our species and, as Marvin Minsky has put it, they could even keep humanity as pets.

The interest in smart machines is now also pursued in additive manufacturing methods, which are increasingly integrating smart materials into manufacturing. These materials could adapt, change properties, interact or respond to their environments. With 4-D Printing, which takes into account the transformation that occurs over time, some materials will adapt and repair by themselves without maintenance or they could be preprogrammed to disintegrate on their own. This will raise new questions of standardization, traceability and copyright.

More radical disruptions will occur once the technology transitions to the organic world, making it possible to assemble biomaterials that evolve and develop on their own, design cancer-fighting robots that would release antibodies only in contact with cancerous cells, and so on. The moment of the print button for biology is nearing. Effectively, this could also mean that in a not too-distant future smart pharmacology will permit us to receive a continuous supply of antidepressants or neuroenhancers every time our dopamine level drops. The ethical consequences of such developments should be thought through. Having our emotions controlled in detail by smart machines will pave the way for dangerous forms of dependences and new understandings of our humanity and the emotions that define us.

Genome-based treatment, based on wider and cheaper availability of genome data, will provide new ways to customize the therapeutic protocol and enhance our control over diseases and medical treatment. The speed, accuracy and costs of genome-reading have changed dramatically in just a matter of years: A decade ago this process was a billion-dollar effort where as today the price has dropped sharply to around $8,000. In cancer treatment, for instance, this will allow transitioning from broad-spectrum chemotherapies to more individualized diagnoses and targeting of specific malfunctioning genes. As we are truly starting to gain more precise tools to fight life-threatening diseases, a range of other issues arise. Pervasive global inequalities will still prevent millions of people from enjoying the benefits of such treatments, even in a context of decreasing costs of genome sequencing. Furthermore, a range of security and privacy risks associated with data storage of genome data will invariably arise and require protective mechanisms, especially as such databases are often shared for security reasons (for example, between international police forces), increasing the possibility of hacking or abuse by authorities.

Inevitably, the emerging technologies of the future will redefine our understanding of biology, the material world and manufacturing. The implications will further extend into geopolitics and global balances of power. Fuel-cell vehicles are finally expected to make their way to the market and reduce dependency on oil or emissions that contribute to climate change. In the long term, this will accentuate the vulnerability of oil-dependent economies and recalibrate geopolitical relations. Recyclable thermostat polymers, reportedly discovered by accident, will dramatically change fabrication and manufacturing, leading to new standards in industries. Globally, the advent of distributed manufacturing is bound to lead to a reassessment of the meaning of value chains and infrastructure. Rather than ship parts of a given product, some companies will simply trade information, leaving it to the customer to finalize the product's manufacture. A suite of other technologies such as 3-D printing, informatics and robotics are enabling a paradigm shift to a dematerialized future with endless possibilities for customization.

Changes Ahead

As always, we must welcome innovation and the benefits it brings us. But we must also remain committed to sustainable development, taking into account issues of inequality, human dignity and inclusiveness. Finally, this year's top emerging technologies also remind us of the importance of political commitment. Take the example of the transition toward fuel-cell vehicles: it will require huge infrastructural adaptations and conversions. In fact, it's estimated that if the U.S. spent the same amount of money it took to put a person on the moon ($100 billion in today's dollars), the shift to hydrogen-powered cars and refueling stations that pump hydrogen would be significantly eased. Often the technology itself is available but only a massive exercise of political will can bring about change.

Some technologies might progress independently of political support. But good governance, examinations of dual-use risks and ethical considerations must still remain guiding posts at all times. Ultimately, how we approach the regulation of emerging technologies will inevitably have wide implications—not only for security and ethics but for our definition of human dignity and the equality of individuals.

ENVIRONMENTAL ETHICS: NATURE AS MEANS OR END, ALDO-LEOPOLD; LAND-ETHICS, ARNE NAESS: DEEP ECOLOGY, PETER SINGER; ANIMAL RIGHTS

Environmental ethics is the discipline in philosophy that studies the moral relationship of human beings to, and also the value and moral status of, the environment and its non-human contents. This entry covers: (1) the challenge of environmental ethics to the anthropocentrism (i.e., human-centeredness) embedded in traditional western ethical thinking; (2) the early development of the discipline in the 1960s and 1970s; (3) the connection of deep ecology, feminist environmental ethics, animism and social ecology to politics; (4) the attempt to apply traditional ethical theories, including consequentialism, deontology, and virtue ethics, to support contemporary environmental concerns; (5) the preservation of biodiversity as an ethical goal; (6) the broader concerns of some thinkers with wilderness, the built environment and the politics of poverty; (7) the ethics of sustainability and climate change, and (8) some directions for possible future developments of the discipline.

The Challenge of Environmental Ethics

Suppose putting out natural fires, culling feral animals or destroying some individual members of overpopulated indigenous species is necessary for the protection of the integrity of a certain ecosystem. Will these actions be morally permissible or even required? Is it morally acceptable for farmers in non-industrial countries to practise slash and burn techniques to clear areas for agriculture? Consider a mining company which has performed open pit mining in some previously unspoiled area. Does the company have a moral obligation to restore the landform and surface ecology? And what is the value of a humanly restored environment compared with the originally natural environment? It is often said to be morally wrong for human beings to pollute and destroy parts of the natural environment and to consume a huge proportion of the planet's natural resources. If that is wrong, is it simply because a sustainable environment is essential to (present and future) human well-being? Or is such behaviour also wrong because the natural environment and/or its various contents have certain values in their own right so that these values ought to be respected and protected in any case? These are among the questions investigated by environmental ethics. Some of them are specific questions faced by individuals in particular circumstances, while others are more global questions faced by groups and communities. Yet others are more abstract questions concerning the value and moral standing of the natural environment and its non-human components.

In the literature on environmental ethics the distinction between instrumental value and intrinsic value (in the sense of "non-instrumental value") has been of considerable importance. The former is the value of things as means to further some other ends, whereas the latter is the value of things as ends in themselves regardless of whether they are also useful as means to other ends. For instance, certain fruits have instrumental value for bats who feed on them, since feeding on the fruits is a means to survival for the bats. However, it is not widely agreed that fruits have value as ends in themselves. We can likewise think of a person who teaches others as having instrumental value for those who want to acquire knowledge. Yet, in addition to any such value, it is normally said that a person, as a person, has intrinsic value, i.e., value in his or her own right independently of his or her prospects for serving the ends of others. For another example, a certain wild plant may have instrumental value because it provides the ingredients for some medicine or as an aesthetic object for human observers. But if the plant also has some value in itself independently of its prospects for furthering some other ends such as human health, or the pleasure from aesthetic experience, then the plant also has intrinsic value. Because the intrinsically valuable is that which is good as an end in itself, it is commonly agreed that something's possession of intrinsic value generates a prima facie direct moral duty on the part of moral agents to protect it or at least refrain from damaging it.

Many traditional western ethical perspectives, however, are anthropocentric or human-centered in that either they assign intrinsic value to human beings alone (i.e., what we might call anthropocentric in a strong sense) or they assign a significantly greater amount of intrinsic value to human beings than to any non-human things such that the protection or promotion of human interests or well-being at the expense of non-human things turns out to be nearly always justified. For example, Aristotle maintains that "nature has made all things specifically for the sake of man" and that the value of non-human things in nature is merely instrumental. Generally, anthropocentric positions find it problematic to articulate what is wrong with the cruel treatment of non-human animals, except to the extent that such treatment may lead to bad consequences for human beings. Immanuel Kant ("Duties to Animals and Spirits", in Lectures on Ethics), for instance, suggests that cruelty towards a dog might encourage a person to develop a character which would be desensitized to cruelty towards humans. From this standpoint, cruelty towards non-human animals would be instrumentally, rather than intrinsically, wrong. Likewise, anthropocentrism often recognizes some non-intrinsic wrongness of anthropogenic (i.e. human-caused) environmental devastation. Such destruction might damage the well-being of human beings now and in the future, since our well-being is essentially dependent on a sustainable environment.

When environmental ethics emerged as a new sub-discipline of philosophy in the early 1970s, it did so by posing a challenge to traditional anthropocentrism. In the first place, it questioned the assumed moral superiority of human beings to members of other species on earth. In the second place, it investigated the possibility of rational arguments for assigning intrinsic value to the natural environment and its non-human contents. It should be noted, however, that some theorists working in the field see no need to develop new, non-anthropocentric theories. Instead, they advocate what may be called enlightened anthropocentrism (or, perhaps more appropriately called, prudential anthropocentrism). Briefly, this is the view that all the moral duties we have towards the environment are derived from our direct duties to its human inhabitants.

The practical purpose of environmental ethics, they maintain, is to provide moral grounds for social policies aimed at protecting the earth's environment and remedying environmental degradation. Enlightened anthropocentrism, they argue, is sufficient for that practical purpose, and perhaps even more effective in delivering pragmatic outcomes, in terms of policy-making, than non-anthropocentric theories given the theoretical burden on the latter to provide sound arguments for its more radical view that the non-human environment has intrinsic value.

Furthermore, some prudential anthropocentrists may hold what might be called cynical anthropocentrism, which says that we have a higher-level anthropocentric reason to be non-anthropocentric in our day-to-day thinking. Suppose that a day-to-day non-anthropocentrist tends to act more benignly towards the non-human environment on which human well-being depends. This would provide reason for encouraging non-anthropocentric thinking, even to those who find the idea of non-anthropocentric intrinsic value hard to swallow. In order for such a strategy to be effective one may need to hide one's cynical anthropocentrism from others and even from oneself. The position can be structurally compared to some indirect form of consequentialism and may attract parallel critiques.

The Early Development of Environmental Ethics

Although nature was the focus of much nineteenth and twentieth century philosophy, contemporary environmental ethics only emerged as an academic discipline in the 1970s. The questioning and rethinking of the relationship of human beings with the natural environment over the last thirty years reflected an already widespread perception in the 1960s that the late twentieth century faced a human population explosion as well as a serious environmental crisis. Among the accessible work that drew attention to a sense of crisis was Rachel Carson's Silent Spring, which consisted of a number of essays earlier published in the New Yorker magazine detailing how pesticides such as DDT, aldrin and deildrin concentrated through the food web. Commercial farming practices aimed at maximizing crop yields and profits, Carson speculates, are capable of impacting simultaneously on environmental and public health.

In a much cited essay on the historical roots of the environmental crisis, historian Lynn White argued that the main strands of Judeo-Christian thinking had encouraged the overexploitation of nature by maintaining the superiority of humans over all other forms of life on earth, and by depicting all of nature as created for the use of humans. White's thesis was widely discussed in theology, history, and has been subject to some sociological testing as well as being regularly discussed by philosophers. Central to the rationale for his thesis were the works of the Church Fathers and The Bible itself, supporting the anthropocentric perspective that humans are the only things that matter on Earth. Consequently, they may utilize and consume everything else to their advantage without any injustice. For example, Genesis 1: 27–8 states: "God created man in his own image, in the image of God created he him; male and female created he them. And God blessed them, and God said unto them, Be fruitful, and multiply, and replenish the earth, and subdue it: and have dominion over fish of the sea, and over fowl of the air, and over every living thing that moveth upon the earth." Likewise, Thomas Aquinas argued that non-human animals are "ordered to man's use". According to White, the Judeo-Christian idea that humans are created in the image of the transcendent supernatural God, who is radically separate from nature, also by extension radically separates humans themselves from nature. This ideology further opened the way for untrammeled exploitation of nature. Modern Western science itself, White argued, was "cast in the matrix of Christian theology" so that it too inherited the "orthodox Christian arrogance toward nature". Clearly, without technology and science, the environmental extremes to which we are now exposed would probably not be realized. The point of White's thesis, however, is that given the modern form of science and technology, Judeo-Christianity itself provides the original deep-seated drive to unlimited exploitation of nature. Nevertheless, White argued that some minority traditions within Christianity might provide an antidote to the "arrogance" of a mainstream tradition steeped in anthropocentrism.

Around the same time, the Stanford ecologists Paul and Anne Ehrlich warned in The Population Bomb that the growth of human population threatened the viability of planetary life-support systems. The sense of environmental crisis stimulated by those and other popular works was intensified by NASA's production and wide dissemination of a particularly potent image of earth from space taken at Christmas 1968 and featured in the Scientific American in September 1970. Here, plain to see, was a living, shining planet voyaging through space and shared by all of humanity, a precious vessel vulnerable to pollution and to the overuse of its limited capacities. In 1972 a team of researchers at MIT led by Dennis Meadows published the Limits to Growth study, a work that summed up in many ways the emerging concerns of the previous decade and the sense of vulnerability triggered by the view of the earth from space. In the commentary to the study, the researchers wrote:

We affirm finally that any deliberate attempt to reach a rational and enduring state of equilibrium by planned measures, rather than by chance or catastrophe, must ultimately be founded on a basic change of values and goals at individual, national and world levels.

The call for a "basic change of values" in connection to the environment (a call that could be interpreted in terms of either instrumental or intrinsic values) reflected a need for the development of environmental ethics as a new sub-discipline of philosophy.

The new field emerged almost simultaneously in three countries—the United States, Australia, and Norway. In the first two of these countries, direction and inspiration largely came from the earlier twentieth century American literature of the environment. For instance, the Scottish emigrant John Muir (founder of the Sierra Club and "father of American conservation") and subsequently the forester Aldo Leopold had advocated an appreciation and conservation of things "natural, wild and free". Their concerns were motivated by a combination of ethical and aesthetic responses to nature as well as a rejection of crudely economic approaches to the value of natural objects (a historical survey of the confrontation between Muir's reverentialism and the human-centred conservationism of Gifford Pinchot (one of the major influences on the development of the US Forest Service) is provided in Norton; also see Cohen and Nash (ed). Leopold's A Sand County Almanac (, in particular, advocated the adoption of a "land ethic":

> That land is a community is the basic concept of ecology, but that land is to be loved and respected is an extension of ethics. (Leopold 1949)
>
> A thing is right when it tends to preserve the integrity, stability, and beauty of the biotic community. It is wrong when it tends otherwise. (Leopold 1949)

However, Leopold himself provided no systematic ethical theory or framework to support these ethical ideas concerning the environment. His views therefore presented a challenge and opportunity for moral theorists: could some ethical theory be devised to justify the injunction to preserve the integrity, stability and beauty of the biosphere?

The land ethic sketched by Leopold, attempting to extend our moral concern to cover the natural environment and its non-human contents, was drawn on explicitly by the Australian philosopher Richard Routley (later Sylvan). According to Routley, the anthropocentrism imbedded in what he called the "dominant western view", or "the western superethic", is in effect "human chauvinism". This view, he argued, is just another form of class chauvinism, which is simply based on blind class "loyalty" or prejudice, and unjustifiably discriminates against those outside the privileged class. Echoing the plot of a popular movie some three years earlier, Routley speculates in his "last man" (and "last people") arguments about a hypothetical situation in which the last person, surviving a world catastrophe, acts to ensure the elimination of all other living things and the last people set about destroying forests and ecosystems after their demise. From the human-chauvinistic (or absolutely anthropocentric) perspective, the last person would do nothing morally wrong, since his or her destructive act in question would not cause any damage to the interest and well-being of humans, who would by then have disappeared. Nevertheless, Routley points out that there is a moral intuition that the imagined last acts would be morally wrong. An explanation for this judgment, he argued, is that those non-human objects in the environment, whose destruction is ensured by the last person or last people, have intrinsic value, a kind of value independent of their usefulness for humans. From his critique, Routley concluded that the main approaches in traditional western moral thinking were unable to allow the recognition that natural things have intrinsic value, and that the tradition required overhaul of a significant kind.

Leopold's idea that the "land" as a whole is an object of our moral concern also stimulated writers to argue for certain moral obligations toward ecological wholes, such as species, communities, and ecosystems, not just their individual constituents. The U.S.-based theologian and environmental philosopher Holmes Rolston III, for instance, argued that species protection was a moral duty. It would be wrong, he maintained, to eliminate a rare butterfly species simply to increase the monetary value of specimens already held by collectors. Like Routley's "last man" arguments, Rolston's example is meant to draw attention to a kind of action that seems morally dubious and yet is not clearly ruled out or condemned by traditional anthropocentric ethical views.

Species, Rolston went on to argue, are intrinsically valuable and are usually more valuable than individual specimens, since the loss of a species is a loss of genetic possibilities and the deliberate destruction of a species would show disrespect for the very biological processes which make possible the emergence of individual living things. Natural processes deserve respect, according to Rolston's quasi-religious perspective, because they constitute a nature (or God) which is itself intrinsically valuable (or sacred).

Meanwhile, the work of Christopher Stone (a professor of law at the University of Southern California) had become widely discussed. Stone proposed that trees and other natural objects should have at least the same standing in law as corporations. This suggestion was inspired by a particular case in which the Sierra Club had mounted a challenge against the permit granted by the U.S. Forest Service to Walt Disney Enterprises for surveys preparatory to the development of the Mineral King Valley, which was at the time a relatively remote game refuge, but not designated as a national park or protected wilderness area. The Disney proposal was to develop a major resort complex serving 14000 visitors daily to be accessed by a purpose-built highway through Sequoia National Park. The Sierra Club, as a body with a general concern for wilderness conservation, challenged the development on the grounds that the valley should be kept in its original state for its own sake.

Stone reasoned that if trees, forests and mountains could be given standing in law then they could be represented in their own right in the courts by groups such as the Sierra Club. Moreover, like any other legal person, these natural things could become beneficiaries of compensation if it could be shown that they had suffered compensatable injury through human activity. When the case went to the U.S. Supreme Court, it was determined by a narrow majority that the Sierra Club did not meet the condition for bringing a case to court, for the Club was unable and unwilling to prove the likelihood of injury to the interest of the Club or its members. In a dissenting minority judgment, however, justices Douglas, Blackmun and Brennan mentioned Stone's argument: his proposal to give legal standing to natural things, they said, would allow conservation interests, community needs and business interests to be represented, debated and settled in court.

Reacting to Stone's proposal, Joel Feinberg raised a serious problem. Only items that have interests, Feinberg argued, can be regarded as having legal standing and, likewise, moral standing. For it is interests which are capable of being represented in legal proceedings and moral debates. This same point would also seem to apply to political debates. For instance, the movement for "animal liberation", which also emerged strongly in the 1970s, can be thought of as a political movement aimed at representing the previously neglected interests of some animals 1976, Clark 1977, and also the entry on the moral status of animals). Granted that some animals have interests that can be represented in this way, would it also make sense to speak of trees, forests, rivers, barnacles, or termites as having interests of a morally relevant kind? This issue was hotly contested in the years that followed. Meanwhile, John Passmore argued, like White, that the Judeo-Christian tradition of thought about nature, despite being predominantly "despotic", contained resources for regarding humans as "stewards" or "perfectors" of God's creation. Skeptical of the prospects for any radically new ethic, Passmore cautioned that traditions of thought could not be abruptly overhauled. Any change in attitudes to our natural surroundings which stood the chance of widespread acceptance, he argued, would have to resonate and have some continuities with the very tradition which had legitimized our destructive practices. In sum, then, Leopold's land ethic, the historical analyses of White and Passmore, the pioneering work of Routley, Stone and Rolston, and the warnings of scientists, had by the late 1970s focused the attention of philosophers and political theorists firmly on the environment.7

The confluence of ethical, political and legal debates about the environment, the emergence of philosophies to underpin animal rights activism and the puzzles over whether an environmental ethic would be something new rather than a modification or extension of existing ethical theories were reflected in wider social and political movements. The rise of environmental or "green" parties in Europe in the 1980s was accompanied by almost immediate schisms between groups known as "realists" versus "fundamentalists". The "realists" stood for reform environmentalism, working with business and government to soften the impact of pollution and resource depletion especially on fragile ecosystems or endangered species. The "fundies" argued for radical change, the setting of stringent new priorities, and even the overthrow of capitalism and liberal individualism, which were taken as the major ideological causes of anthropogenic environmental devastation. It is not clear, however, that collectivist or communist countries do any better in terms of their environmental record.

Underlying these political disagreements was the distinction between "shallow" and "deep" environmental movements, a distinction introduced in the early 1970s by another major influence on contemporary environmental ethics, the Norwegian philosopher and climber Arne Nnss. Since the work of Nnss has been significant in environmental politics, the discussion of his position is given in a separate section below.

Deep Ecology

"Deep ecology" was born in Scandinavia, the result of discussions between Nnss and his colleagues Sigmund Kvaloy and Nils Faarlund. All three shared a passion for the great mountains. On a visit to the Himalayas, they became impressed with aspects of "Sherpa culture" particularly when they found that their Sherpa guides regarded certain mountains as sacred and accordingly would not venture onto them. Subsequently, Nnss formulated a position which extended the reverence the three Norwegians and the Sherpas felt for mountains to other natural things in general.

The "shallow ecology movement", as Nnss calls it, is the "fight against pollution and resource depletion", the central objective of which is "the health and affluence of people in the developed countries." The "deep ecology movement", in contrast, endorses "biospheric egalitarianism", the view that all living things are alike in having value in their own right, independent of their usefulness to others. The deep ecologist respects this intrinsic value, taking care, for example, when walking on the mountainside not to cause unnecessary damage to the plants.

Inspired by Spinoza's metaphysics, another key feature of Nnss's deep ecology is the rejection of atomistic individualism. The idea that a human being is such an individual possessing a separate essence, Nnss argues, radically separates the human self from the rest of the world. To make such a separation not only leads to selfishness towards other people, but also induces human selfishness towards nature. As a counter to egoism at both the individual and species level, Nnss proposes the adoption of an alternative relational "total-field image" of the world. According to this relationalism, organisms (human or otherwise) are best understood as "knots" in the biospherical net. The identity of a living thing is essentially constituted by its relations to other things in the world, especially its ecological relations to other living things. If people conceptualise themselves and the world in relational terms, the deep ecologists argue, then people will take better care of nature and the world in general.

As developed by Nnss and others, the position also came to focus on the possibility of the identification of the human ego with nature. The idea is, briefly, that by identifying with nature I can enlarge the boundaries of the self beyond my skin. My larger—ecological—Self (the capital "S" emphasizes that I am something larger than my body and consciousness), deserves respect as well. To respect and to care for my Self is also to respect and to care for the natural environment, which is actually part of me and with which I should identify.

"Self-realization", in other words, is the reconnection of the shriveled human individual with the wider natural environment. Nnss maintains that the deep satisfaction that we receive from identification with nature and close partnership with other forms of life in nature contributes significantly to our life quality. (One clear historical antecedent to this kind of nature spiritualism is the romanticism of Jean-Jacques Rousseau as expressed in his last work, the Reveries of the Solitary Walker)

When Nnss's view crossed the Atlantic, it was sometimes merged with ideas emerging from Leopold's land ethic. But Nnss—wary of the apparent totalitarian political implications of Leopold's position that individual interests and well-being should be subordinated to the holistic good of the earth's biotic community—has always taken care to distance himself from advocating any sort of "land ethic". Some critics have argued that Nnss's deep ecology is no more than an extended social-democratic version of utilitarianism, which counts human interests in the same calculation alongside the interests of all natural things (e.g., trees, wolves, bears, rivers, forests and mountains) in the natural environment. However, Nnss failed to explain in any detail how to make sense of the idea that oysters or barnacles, termites or bacteria could have interests of any morally relevant sort at all. Without an account of this, Nnss's early "biospheric egalitarianism"—that all living things whatsoever had a similar right to live and flourish—was an indeterminate principle in practical terms. It also remains unclear in what sense rivers, mountains and forests can be regarded as possessors of any kind of interests. This is an issue on which Nnss always remained elusive.

Biospheric egalitarianism was modified in the 1980s to the weaker claim that the flourishing of both human and non-human life have value in themselves. At the same time, Nnss declared that his own favoured ecological philosophy—"Ecosophy T", as he called it after his Tvergastein mountain cabin—was only one of several possible foundations for an environmental ethic. Deep ecology ceased to be a specific doctrine, but instead became a "platform", of eight simple points, on which Nnss hoped all deep green thinkers could agree. The platform was conceived as establishing a middle ground, between underlying philosophical orientations, whether Christian, Buddhist, Daoist, process philosophy, or whatever, and the practical principles for action in specific situations, principles generated from the underlying philosophies. Thus the deep ecological movement became explicitly pluralist.

While Nnss's Ecosophy T sees human Self-realization as a solution to the environmental crises resulting from human selfishness and exploitation of nature, some of the followers of the deep ecology platform in the United States and Australia further argue that the expansion of the human self to include non-human nature is supported by the Copenhagen interpretation of quantum theory, which is said to have dissolved the boundaries between the observer and the observed. These "relationalist" developments of deep ecology are, however, criticized by some feminist theorists.

The idea of nature as part of oneself, one might argue, could justify the continued exploitation of nature instead. For one is presumably more entitled to treat oneself in whatever ways one likes than to treat another independent agent in whatever ways one likes. According to some feminist critics, the deep ecological theory of the "expanded self" is in effect a disguised form of human colonialism, unable to give nature its due as a genuine "other" independent of human interest and purposes.

Meanwhile, some third-world critics accused deep ecology of being elitist in its attempts to preserve wilderness experiences for only a select group of economically and socio-politically well-off people. The Indian writer Ramachandra Guha for instance, depicts the activities of many western-based conservation groups as a new form of cultural imperialism, aimed at securing converts to conservationism. "Green missionaries", as Guha calls them, represent a movement aimed at further dispossessing the world's poor and indigenous people. "Putting deep ecology in its place," he writes, "is to recognize that the trends it derides as "shallow" ecology might in fact be varieties of environmentalism that are more apposite, more representative and more popular in the countries of the South."

Although Nnss himself repudiates suggestions that deep ecology is committed to any imperialism, Guha's criticism raises important questions about the application of deep ecological principles in different social, economic and cultural contexts. Finally, in other critiques, deep ecology is portrayed as having an inconsistent utopian vision.

Feminism and the Environment

Broadly speaking, a feminist issue is any that contributes in some way to understanding the oppression of women. Feminist theories attempt to analyze women's oppression, its causes and consequences, and suggest strategies and directions for women's liberation. By the mid 1970s, feminist writers had raised the issue of whether patriarchal modes of thinking encouraged not only widespread inferiorizing and colonizing of women, but also of people of colour, animals and nature. Sheila Collins, for instance, argued that male-dominated culture or patriarchy is supported by four interlocking pillars: sexism, racism, class exploitation, and ecological destruction.

Emphasizing the importance of feminism to the environmental movement and various other liberation movements, some writers, such as Ynestra King, argue that the domination of women by men is historically the original form of domination in human society, from which all other hierarchies—of rank, class, and political power—flow. For instance, human exploitation of nature may be seen as a manifestation and extension of the oppression of women, in that it is the result of associating nature with the female, which had been already inferiorized and oppressed by the male-dominating culture.

But within the plurality of feminist positions, other writers, such as Val Plumwood, understand the oppression of women as only one of the many parallel forms of oppression sharing and supported by a common ideological structure, in which one party (the colonizer, whether male, white or human) uses a number of conceptual and rhetorical devices to privilege its interests over that of the other party (the colonized: whether female, people of colour, or animals). Facilitated by a common structure, seemingly diverse forms of oppression can mutually reinforce each other.

Not all feminist theorists would call that common underlying oppressive structure "androcentric" or "patriarchal". But it is generally agreed that core features of the structure include "dualism", hierarchical thinking, and the "logic of domination", which are typical of, if not essential to, male-chauvinism. These patterns of thinking and conceptualizing the world, many feminist theorists argue, also nourish and sustain other forms of chauvinism, including, human-chauvinism (i.e., anthropocentrism), which is responsible for much human exploitation of, and destructiveness towards, nature.

The dualistic way of thinking, for instance, sees the world in polar opposite terms, such as male/female, masculinity/femininity, reason/emotion, freedom/necessity, active/passive, mind/body, pure/soiled, white/coloured, civilized/primitive, transcendent/immanent, human/animal, culture/nature.

Furthermore, under dualism all the first items in these contrasting pairs are assimilated with each other, and all the second items are likewise linked with each other. For example, the male is seen to be associated with the rational, active, creative, Cartesian human mind, and civilized, orderly, transcendent culture; whereas the female is regarded as tied to the emotional, passive, determined animal body, and primitive, disorderly, immanent nature.

These interlocking dualisms are not just descriptive dichotomies, according to the feminists, but involve a prescriptive privileging of one side of the opposed items over the other. Dualism confers superiority to everything on the male side, but inferiority to everything on the female side. The "logic of domination" then dictates that those on the superior side (e.g., men, rational beings, humans) are morally entitled to dominate and utilize those on the inferior side (e.g., women, beings lacking in rationality, non-humans) as mere means.

The problem with dualistic and hierarchical modes of thinking, however, is not just that they are epistemically unreliable. It is not just that the dominating party often falsely sees the dominated party as lacking (or possessing) the allegedly superior (or inferior) qualities, or that the dominated party often internalizes false stereotypes of itself given by its oppressors, or that stereotypical thinking often overlooks salient and important differences among individuals.

More important, according to feminist analyses, the very premise of prescriptive dualism—the valuing of attributes of one polarized side and the devaluing of those of the other, the idea that domination and oppression can be justified by appealing to attributes like masculinity, rationality, being civilized or developed, etc.—is itself problematic.

Feminism represents a radical challenge for environmental thinking, politics, and traditional social ethical perspectives. It promises to link environmental questions with wider social problems concerning various kinds of discrimination and exploitation, and fundamental investigations of human psychology. However, whether there are conceptual, causal or merely contingent connections among the different forms of oppression and liberation remains a contested issue.

The term "ecofeminism" or "ecological feminism" was for a time generally applied to any view that combines environmental advocacy with feminist analysis. However, because of the varieties of, and disagreements among, feminist theories, the label may be too wide to be informative and has generally fallen from use.

Disenchantment and the New Animism

An often overlooked source of ecological ideas is the work of the neo-Marxist Frankfurt School of critical theory founded by Max Horkheimer and Theodore Adorno. While classical Marxists regard nature as a resource to be transformed by human labour and utilized for human purposes, Horkheimer and Adorno saw Marx himself as representative of the problem of "human alienation". At the root of this alienation, they argue, is a narrow positivist conception of rationality—which sees rationality as an instrument for pursuing progress, power and technological control, and takes observation, measurement and the application of purely quantitative methods to be capable of solving all problems. Such a positivistic view of science combines determinism with optimism. Natural processes as well as human activities are seen to be predictable and manipulable. Nature (and, likewise, human nature) is no longer mysterious, uncontrollable, or fearsome. Instead, it is reduced to an object strictly governed by natural laws, which therefore can be studied, known, and employed to our benefit. By promising limitless knowledge and power, the positivism of science and technology not only removes our fear of nature, the critical theorists argue, but also destroys our sense of awe and wonder towards it. That is to say, positivism "disenchants" nature—along with everything that can be studied by the sciences, whether natural, social or human.

The progress in knowledge and material well-being may not be a bad thing in itself, where the consumption and control of nature is a necessary part of human life. However, the critical theorists argue that the positivistic disenchantment of natural things (and, likewise, of human beings—because they too can be studied and manipulated by science) disrupts our relationship with them, encouraging the undesirable attitude that they are nothing more than things to be probed, consumed and dominated. According to the critical theorists, the oppression of "outer nature" (i.e., the natural environment) through science and technology is bought at a very high price: the project of domination requires the suppression of our own "inner nature" (i.e., human nature)—e.g., human creativity, autonomy, and the manifold needs, vulnerabilities and longings at the centre of human life. To remedy such an alienation, the project of Horkheimer and Adorno is to replace the narrow positivistic and instrumentalist model of rationality with a more humanistic one, in which the values of the aesthetic, moral, sensuous and expressive aspects of human life play a central part. Thus, their aim is not to give up our rational faculties or powers of analysis and logic. Rather, the ambition is to arrive at a dialectical synthesis between Romanticism and Enlightenment, to return to anti-deterministic values of freedom, spontaneity and creativity.

In his later work, Adorno advocates a re-enchanting aesthetic attitude of "sensuous immediacy" towards nature. Not only do we stop seeing nature as primarily, or simply, an object of consumption, we are also able to be directly and spontaneously acquainted with nature without interventions from our rational faculties. According to Adorno, works of art, like natural things, always involve an "excess", something more than their mere materiality and exchange value. The re-enchantment of the world through aesthetic experience, he argues, is also at the same time a re-enchantment of human lives and purposes. Adorno's work remains largely unexplored in mainstream environmental philosophy, although the idea of applying critical theory (embracing techniques of deconstruction, psychoanalysis and radical social criticism) to both environmental issues and the writings of various ethical and political theorists has spawned an emerging field of "ecocritique" or "eco-criticism".

Some students of Adorno's work have argued that his account of the role of "sensuous immediacy" can be understood as an attempt to defend a "legitimate anthropomorphism" that comes close to a weak form of animism. Others, more radical, have claimed to take inspiration from his notion of "non-identity", which, they argue, can be used as the basis for a deconstruction of the notion of nature and perhaps even its elimination from eco-critical writing. For example, Timothy Morton argues that "putting something called Nature on a pedestal and admiring it from afar does for the environment what patriarchy does for the figure of Woman. It is a paradoxical act of sadistic admiration", and that "in the name of all that we value in the idea of 'nature', [ecocritique] thoroughly examines how nature is set up as a transcendental, unified, independent category. Ecocritique does not think that it is paradoxical to say, in the name of ecology itself: 'down with nature!'?"

It remains to be seen, however, whether the radical attempt to purge the concept of nature from eco-critical work meets with success. Likewise, it is unclear whether the dialectic project on which Horkheimer and Adorno embarked is coherent, and whether Adorno, in particular, has a consistent understanding of "nature" and "rationality"

On the other hand, the new animists have been much inspired by the serious way in which some indigenous peoples placate and interact with animals, plants and inanimate things through ritual, ceremony and other practices.

According to the new animists, the replacement of traditional animism (the view that personalized souls are found in animals, plants, and other material objects) by a form of disenchanting positivism directly leads to an anthropocentric perspective, which is accountable for much human destructiveness towards nature. In a disenchanted world, there is no meaningful order of things or events outside the human domain, and there is no source of sacredness or dread of the sort felt by those who regard the natural world as peopled by divinities or demons.

When a forest is no longer sacred, there are no spirits to be placated and no mysterious risks associated with clear-felling it. A disenchanted nature is no longer alive. It commands no respect, reverence or love. It is nothing but a giant machine, to be mastered to serve human purposes.

The new animists argue for reconceptualizing the boundary between persons and non-persons. For them, "living nature" comprises not only humans, animals and plants, but also mountains, forests, rivers, deserts, and even planets.

Whether the notion that a mountain or a tree is to be regarded as a person is taken literally or not, the attempt to engage with the surrounding world as if it consists of other persons might possibly provide the basis for a respectful attitude to nature.

If disenchantment is a source of environmental problems and destruction, then the new animism can be regarded as attempting to re-enchant, and help to save, nature. More poetically, David Abram has argued that a phenomenological approach of the kind taken by Merleau-Ponty can reveal to us that we are part of the "common flesh" of the world, that we are in a sense the world thinking itself .

In her work, Freya Mathews has tried to articulate a version of animism or panpsychism that captures ways in which the world (not just nature) contains many kinds of consciousness and sentience. For her, there is an underlying unity of mind and matter in that the world is a "self-realizing" system containing a multiplicity of other such systems. According to Mathews, we are meshed in communication, and potential communication, with the "One" (the greater cosmic self) and its many lesser selves. Materialism (the monistic theory that the world consists purely of matter), she argues, is self-defeating by encouraging a form of "collective solipsism" that treats the world either as unknowable or as a social-construction.

Mathews also takes inspiration from her interpretation of the core Daoist idea of wuwei as "letting be" and bringing about change through "effortless action". The focus in environmental management, development and commerce should be on "synergy" with what is already in place rather than on demolition, replacement and disruption. Instead of bulldozing away old suburbs and derelict factories, the synergistic panpsychist sees these artefacts as themselves part of the living cosmos, hence part of what is to be respected. Likewise, instead of trying to eliminate feral or exotic plants and animals, and restore environments to some imagined pristine state, ways should be found—wherever possible—to promote synergies between the newcomers and the older native populations in ways that maintain ecological flows and promote the further unfolding and developing of ecological processes. Panpsychism, Mathews argues, frees us from the "ideological grid of capitalism", can reduce our desire for consumer novelties, and can allow us and the world to grow old together with grace and dignity.

In summary, if disenchantment is a source of environmentally destructive or uncaring attitudes, then both the aesthetic and the animist/panpsychist re-enchantment of the world are intended to offer an antidote to such attitudes, and perhaps also inspirations for new forms of managing and designing for sustainability.

MEDICAL ETHICS

Medical ethics involves examining a specific problem, usually a clinical case, and using values, facts, and logic to decide what the best course of action should be.

Some ethical problems are fairly straightforward, such as determining right from wrong. But others can also be more perplexing, such as deciding between two "rights"—two values that are in conflict with each other—or deciding between two different value systems, such as the patient's versus the doctor's.

Doctors may deal with a great variety of perplexing ethical problems even in a small medical practice. Here are some common problems identified in a 2016 Medscape survey, where at least some physicians held different opinions [1]:

- Withholding treatment to meet an organization's budget, or because of insurance policies;
- Accepting money from pharmaceutical or device manufacturers;
- Upcoding to get treatment covered;
- Getting romantically involved with a patient or family member;
- Covering up a mistake;
- Reporting an impaired colleague;
- Cherry-picking patients;
- Prescribing a placebo;
- Practicing defensive medicine to avoid malpractice lawsuits;
- Dropping insurers; and
- Breaching patient confidentiality owing to a health risk.

Professional standards are a way to provide some guidance on ethical problems, but they cannot address every issue, and they may not address troubling nuances, such as reconciling two conflicting values.

Many professional ethicists recommend using four basic values, or principles, to decide ethical issues:

1. **Autonomy.** Patients basically have the right to determine their own health care.
2. **Justice.** Distributing the benefits and burdens of care across society.

3. **Beneficence.** Doing good for the patient.
4. **Nonmalfeasance.** Making sure you are not harming the patient.

However, ethical values are not limited to just these four principles. There are other important values to consider, such as truth-telling, transparency, showing respect for patients and families, and showing respect for patients' own values.

In addition, medical ethics is not just a thought process. It also involves people skills, such as gathering the facts needed to make a decision and presenting your decision in a way that wins over the confidence of all parties.

Listening skills are an essential part of medical ethics. Quite often, ethical disputes result from not knowing all the facts, or not providing all the facts to patients. Tactfulness and respect are also important. A well-constructed ethical decision could be ignored if you have not won the patient's confidence.

Ethics is often seen as a proscriptive activity—telling you what you cannot do. But in many cases it can be very freeing. It can affirm that you are doing the right thing. If you go through the proper ethical thought process, you'll have greater certainty that what you're doing is the right thing. Relieved of nagging doubts, you will be able to proceed more directly and more vigorously with your care plan.

As the health system evolves, ethical decisions could become more challenging. For example, mounting difficulties in finding affordable insurance prompt patients to forgo the care they need, and this affects the clinician's care plan.

MEDIA ETHICS

A media revolution is transforming, fundamentally and irrevocably, the nature of journalism and its ethics. The means to publish is now in the hands of citizens, while the internet encourages new forms of journalism that are interactive and immediate.

Our media ecology is a chaotic landscape evolving at a furious pace. Professional journalists share the journalistic sphere with tweeters, bloggers, citizen journalists, and social media users.

Amid every revolution, new possibilities emerge while old practices are threatened. Today is no exception. The economics of professional journalism struggles as audiences migrate online. Shrinkage of newsrooms creates concern for the future of journalism. Yet these fears also prompt experiments in journalism, such as non-profit centers of investigative journalism.

A central question is to what extent existing media ethics is suitable for today's and tomorrow's news media that is immediate, interactive and "always on" – a journalism of amateurs and professionals. Most of the principles were developed over the past century, originating in the construction of professional, objective ethics for mass commercial newspapers in the late 19th century.

We are moving towards a mixed news media – a news media citizen and professional journalism across many media platforms. This new mixed news media requires a new mixed media ethics – guidelines that apply to amateur and professional whether they blog, Tweet, broadcast or write for newspapers. Media ethics needs to be rethought and reinvented for the media of today, not of yesteryear.

The changes challenge the foundations of media ethics. The challenge runs deeper than debates about one or another principle, such as objectivity. The challenge is greater than specific problems, such as how newsrooms can verify content from citizens. The revolution requires us to rethink assumptions. What can ethics mean for a profession that must provide instant news and analysis; where everyone with a modem is a publisher?

The media revolution has created ethical tensions on two levels.

- On the first level, there is a tension between traditional journalism and online journalism. The culture of traditional journalism, with its values of accuracy, pre-publication verification, balance, impartiality, and gate-keeping, rubs up against the culture of online journalism which emphasizes immediacy, transparency, partiality, non-professional journalists and post-publication correction.
- On the second level, there is a tension between parochial and global journalism. If journalism has global impact, what are its global responsibilities? Should media ethics reformulate its aims and norms so as to guide a journalism that is now global in reach and impact? What would that look like?

The challenge for today's media ethics can be summarized by the question: Whither ethics in a world of multimedia, global journalism? Media ethics must do more than point out these tensions. Theoretically, it must untangle the conflicts between values. It must decide which principles should be preserved or invented. Practically, it should provide new standards to guide online or offline journalism.

A lack of clarity over who is a journalist leads to definitional disputes over who is doing journalism. That leads to the question: What is journalism? Many people believe, "What is journalism?" or "Is he or she doing journalism?" is a more important question than whether who can call themselves a journalist.

At least three approaches to this question are possible – skeptical, empirical, and normative. Skeptically, one dismisses the question itself as unimportant. For example, one might say that anyone can be a journalist, and it is not worth arguing over who gets to call themselves a journalist. One is skeptical about attempts to define journalism.

Empirically, there is a more systematic and careful approach to the question. We can look at clear examples of journalism over history and note the types of activities in which journalists engaged, e.g. gathering information, editing stories, publishing news and opinion. Then we use these features to provide a definition of journalism that separates it from novel writing, storytelling, or editing information for a government database.

The normative approach insists that writers should not be called journalists unless they have highly developed skills, acquired usually through training or formal education, and unless they honor certain ethical norms.

The skills include investigative capabilities, research skills, facility with media technology of media, knowledge of how institutions work, and highly developed communication skills. The ethical norms include a commitment to accuracy, verification, truth, and so on.

The normative approach is based on an ideal view of journalism as accurately and responsibly informing the public. One defines journalism by considering the best examples of journalism and the practices of the best journalists.

A writer who has these skills and these ethical commitments is capable of publishing good (well-crafted, well-researched) and ethically responsible journalism. Persons who do not meet these normative requirements may call themselves journalists but they are not considered journalists from this normative perspective. They are at irresponsible, second-rate, or incompetent writers seeking to be journalists, or pretending to be journalists.

Anonymity is accepted more readily online than in mainstream news media. Newspapers usually require the writers of letters to the editor to identify themselves. Codes of mainstream media ethics caution journalists to use anonymous sources sparingly and only if certain rules are followed. The codes warn journalists that people may use anonymity to take unfair or untrue "potshots" at other people, for self-interested reasons.

Online, many commentary and "chat" areas do not require anonymity. Online users resist demands from web site and blogs to register and identify themselves. Anonymity is praised as allowing freedom of speech and sometimes helping to expose wrong doing. Critics say it encourages irresponsible and harmful comments. Mainstream media contradict themselves when they allow anonymity online but refuse anonymity in their newspapers and broadcast programs.

The ethical question is: When is anonymity ethically permissible and is it inconsistent for media to enforce different rules on anonymity for different media platforms? What should be the ethical guidelines for anonymity offline and online?

LEGAL ETHICS

Lawyers are often thought to be hardly better than hired guns, who, in the words of Plato, are paid to "make the weaker argument the stronger" — like the sophists of old. In fact, lawyers are legally and morally bound by stringent codes of ethics. Noted philosopher of law David Luban, of Georgetown University, is the guest as Philosophy Talk explores the ethical obligations of lawyers to their clients, to the court, and to society at large.

John and Ken begin by discussing the common conception of lawyers as ethically challenged and morally reprehensible. John discusses his family's relationship to the law and the respect he has for both lawyers and the legal system, although he acknowledges there are bad apples in the profession. Ken gives the example of a defense witness zealously cross-examining a rape victim. Is this kind of activity ethical? What does the code of ethics for lawyers say? What does human morality require? Are these in conflict? How far can a lawyer go in contemporary times?

In order to answer some of these questions, Ken introduces David J. Luban, Frederick J. Haas Professor of Law and Philosophy from Georgetown University. John begins by asking David what the ethical rules that lawyers impose upon themselves, and whether they differ for different kinds of lawyers. David responds that despite the negative stereotype of lawyers, they impose a strict rule upon their profession never to lie, deceive, or misrepresent themselves. In the court room, the lawyer is supposed to be a zealous representative for their client, and should do whatever is within the bound of the law to help them win, ignoring all other interests. There are also rules about confidentiality and future crimes, but John pushes the conversation towards deception inside and outside of the courtroom. Luban points out that lying anywhere is discouraged, and notes that Bill Clinton lost his law license for this very reason.

Ken points out that there is a big difference between lying and not vigorously seeking the truth, and wonders: since the legal system is about ascertaining the truth, why isn't everyone in the courtroom concerned with finding the truth, instead of just not lying? David discusses our "adversarial" tradition and John asks about some alternative systems that are used in similar societies in South America and continental Europe. Ken steers the discussion away from these inquisitorial systems to the American adversarial tradition, and asks Luban whether or not there is a deep philosophical justification for this structure, and if not, why don't we change it? David Luban defends the adversarial tradition by using similar arguments to those put forward by Karl Popper: in order to arrive at the truth it is necessary to propose bold conjectures and then attempt to refute them. In this way opposing lawyers in America refute each other and end up with a more accurate view of what really happened. Luban thinks that this is a great idea in some scenarios, like theoretical points of law, but in trial situations the system leads to negative results.

John, Ken, and David further discuss a lawyer's role in helping the accused "escape punishment" and also take calls from the listening audience ranging from bad lawyer stories, moral martyrhood, the respect for dignity and self-incrimination in contemporary law.

- **Roving Philosophical Report.** Zoe Corneli discusses the brutal reality of the courtroom and the moral code of public defenders with a Law Professor who spent many years defending rape and other brutal crime defendants.
- **Conundrum on Justice, Jury Duty, and Abusive Relationships.** John and Ken help an Oregon schoolteacher deal with an interesting case he deliberated upon while sitting on a jury.

MULTIPLE CHOICE QUESTIONS

1. Samhitā consists of
   (1) Mantras (2) Brahmanas
   (3) Upanisads (4) All of these
2. Brahmacharya is the means to meet
   (1) Ṛsiṛna (2) Pitṛṛṇa
   (3) Devaṛṇa (4) None of these
3. The havya of Yajña results in benefiting
   (1) Ṛtvik
   (2) Consumer of the havya
   (3) Devatā
   (4) None of the above
4. Which one of the following is an example of Arthaveda?
   (1) Āmnāyasya kriyarthatvāt
   (2) Swargakamo yajet
   (3) Saptadvipa vasumati
   (4) Agnina sinchet
5. In the turīya state, Atman is
   (1) Conscious (2) Unconscious
   (3) Subconscious (4) Non-dual
6. Bhāgvadgitā has been considered as the most important work due to
   (1) Harmonious philosophy of life
   (2) Synthesis of action, devotion and knowledge
   (3) Moral teachings
   (4) All the above
7. What is true about Ṛta?
   (1) a cosmic order
   (2) the settled will of a supreme God
   (3) the law of morality and righteousness
   (4) all of the above
8. The self is
   (1) Universal (2) Immanent
   (3) Transcendent (4) All of these
9. The whole universe is founded on
   (1) Vedas and moves by it
   (2) Śesanaga and stayed on it
   (3) Ṛta and moves in it
   (4) Brahma and moves in him
10. The enjoyment of fruits of the Karma that not yet has been started is called
    (1) Sañcitā Karma
    (2) Sañcīyamāna Karma
    (3) Prārabdha Karma
    (4) Anārabdha Karma
11. Devarna can be repaid by
    (1) Performing yajña
    (2) Giving birth to a son
    (3) Both (1) and (2)
    (4) Neither (1) nor (2)
12. Who are the keepers of Ṛta and forgivers of sin?
    (1) Indra and Varuṇa (2) Mitra and Surya
    (3) Indra and Surya (4) Varuṇa and Mitra
13. Who are called the Adityas (the sons of Adity?)
    (1) Varuṇa and Mitra
    (2) Mitra and Bhaga
    (3) Aryaman and Bhaga
    (4) Varuṇa, Mitra, Aryaman and Bhaga
14. Varuṇa is associated with
    (1) the morning light
    (2) the sunlight

(3) the night-sky
(4) the stars light

15. In Upaniṣadic period Varṇa-system was changeable. This can be inferred by the discussion between
(1) Yajñyavalkya and his wife
(2) Satyakāma and his teacher
(3) Uddālaka and Svetaketu
(4) Naciketa and Yama

16. Bhutayajña is performed for the well-being of
(1) Souls of dead persons
(2) Souls of the ancestors
(3) The Performer
(4) None of the above

17. Which one of the following is the basis of law of Karma, according to Vedic tradition?
(1) God (2) Nature
(3) Human Being (4) Rit

18. Ṛta literally means
(1) the course of things
(2) Seasons
(3) Ceremony
(4) temporal changes

19. Ṛta can be said as
(1) the immanence of justice
(2) chief justice of this world
(3) the supreme administrator
(4) all of the above

20. The regularity of the movements of the sun, moon and stars, the alterations of day and of night, and of the reasons are because of
(1) Ṛta works (2) Ṛta applied
(3) Ṛta fixed (4) Ṛta moves

21. Ṛta denotes
(1) permanency of the world
(2) the order of the world
(3) mortality of living beings
(4) eternity of the absolute

22. Ṛta is the principle for everything
(1) that occurs in the universe
(2) that happens in the universe
(3) that is ordered in the universe
(4) that is related to god

23. Which of the following upanisads expresses the dialogue between Prajapati and Indra to make clear the different states of self as Jagrat, swapna, gahana nidra and turiya
(1) Chāndogya (2) Katha
(3) Mundaka (4) Mandukya

24. The religion of the Brahmanas are
(1) purely formal (2) purely informal
(3) atheistic (4) without text

25. What is true about Brahmanical religion
(1) Prayer comes to mean the muttering of mantras.
(2) Loud petitions were thought necessary to rouse god to action.
(3) Priest claimed for himself the dignity of god on earth.
(4) All of the above.

26. Anyone could become immortal like the gods by
(1) Performing sacrifices
(2) Praying the god
(3) Uttering the mantras
(4) learning the magic

27. We can depose Indra from his throne in heaven if we perform
(1) A thousand horse sacrifice
(2) Our duties well
(3) A hundred horse sacrifice
(4) Kindness in all actions

28. The sacrifices were made as a rule for gaining
(1) earthly profits (2) heavenly bliss
(3) purified soul (4) mearness of god

29. The Yājmana, or the man for whom the rite is performed

(1) is a passive agent (2) is a active agent
(3) prays (4) utters the mantras

30. As a Brahmacarin or student, a Brahmin
(1) must control his passions
(2) wait on his preceptor
(3) beg for his food
(4) all of the above

31. Who says, "A twice-born man, a Brahmin, Kṣatriya, or Vaiśya unlearned in the Vedas, soon falls, even while living, to a condition of Sudra"
(1) Manu (2) Brahaspati
(3) Prajāpati (4) Yajñyavalkya

32. "The order of vānaprasthas, of sages who dwell in forests and live on fruits, roots and air, is prescribed for the three twice-born classes, the order of householders is prescribed for all" is said in
(1) Ramayana (2) Mahabharata
(3) Manusmṛiti (4) Naradsmṛiti

33. Vedas give importance to the
(1) Spiritual profits (2) Physical profits
(3) Economical profits
(4) All of the above

34. Man is said to owe some debts or duties to
(1) the gods (2) seers
(3) the gods and seers
(4) god, seers, manes, men and lower creations

35. In the Satapath Brahmana, what is taught as a means to the attainment of spiritual freedom
(1) Sarvapratibha (2) Sarvamedha
(3) Satsaṁbhaśana (4) Karlavyaniṣtha

36. Godliness, the first duty, consist in
(1) the mechanical performance of fixed ritual
(2) Praise and good works
(3) trying to be divine as much as possible
(4) (2) and (3) both

37. Which one is the correct sequence?
(1) Jāgrat, Susupti, Svapna
(2) Jāgrat, Svapna, Susupti
(3) Svapna, Susupti, Jāgrat
(4) Susupti, Jāgrat, Svapna

38. Who says that 'Upanishad' means 'secret instructions' ?
(1) Paul Deussen (2) Keith
(3) Radhakrishnan (4) Shankar

39. Adultery is condemned as a sin against the god
(1) specially Varuṇa (2) Agni
(3) Vāk (4) none of these

40. In all cases of evil-doing
(1) confession is supposed to make the guilt less
(2) offerings to the gods is supposed to make the guilt less
(3) There is no way to lessen the guilt
(4) Asceticism is the way to lessen the guilt

41. A worthy idea, for the gods are supposed to have obtained divine rank by austerity, is
(1) Asceticism (2) priest-hood
(3) duty-devoted (4) none of these

42. The first reference to the division of Hindu Society into the four classes is found in
(1) Atharvaveda
(2) Mundākopaniśada
(3) Purusha Sukta (4) Ramayana

43. The movements of stars and planets according to Vedic literature is guided by
(1) The Will of God
(2) The Will of the Devatas
(3) Ṛta (4) Yajña

44. By performing what God become the friends of men?
(1) Sacrifices (2) R
(3) Necessary actions
(4) Sensdess actions

45. Theories of creation given in Vedic hymns are
(1) Materialistic (2) Vitalistic
(3) (1) and (2) both (4) None of them

46. The world is created
A. without any pre-existent matter,
B. out of pre-existent matter,
C. out of god's own nature,
D. through god's power acting on pre-existent matter.
Choose the right statements from the codes given below
(1) A & C (2) B & C
(3) C & D (4) A & B

47. First of all there was non-existent from which the whole existence arrives. Here, non existent means
(1) negation of existence
(2) a positive being
(3) nothing
(4) everything

48. Ātma is ________ dehaparima a ' this view is upheld by
(1) Baudha (2) Cārvāka
(3) Both Bauddha & Cārvāka
(4) Jaina

49. Who is the author of the primeval water?
(1) Indra (2) Varuṇa
(3) god (4) Mitra

50. Choose the true statement
(1) Nāsadiya hymn is translated by Maximüller
(2) Brahma is Hiraṇyagarbha
(3) God created chaos by his will
(4) All of the above

51. 'First of all there was non-existent' means
(1) Existent in its manifested form was not then
(2) There was nothing
(3) There was a matter named non-existent
(4) There was a hollow space

52. The first cause of this universe is
(1) absolute consciousness
(2) beyond time and space
(3) beyond age death and immortality
(4) all of the above

53. Tapas is
(1) the rushing forth
(2) the spontaneous outgrowth
(3) the projection of being into existence
(4) all the above

54. Desire or Kāma denotes
(1) Intellectual stir
(2) the sense of defficiency
(3) active effort
(4) all of the above

55. According to the hymns of Ṛig Veda
(1) the world is real
(2) the world is unreal
(3) the world is apparent
(4) the world is indescribable

56. Who among the following divided Veda into four ?
(1) Kṛṣṇa (2) Vyāsa
(3) Manu (4) None of these

57. The right order is
(1) Virat – puruṣa – virat
(2) Puruṣa – virat – puruṣa
(3) Matter – puruṣa – virat
(4) Virat – matter – puruṣa

58. According to Taittirīya Brahmana
(A) formerly nothing existed, neither heaven nor atmosphere nor earth,
(B) In the begining Prajapāti alone existed,
(C) Desire is the seed of existence,
(D) Prajapāti created living beings
(1) A & B (2) B & D
(3) A & C (4) A, B, C & D

59. Upaniṣadic theory of creation says
(1) ānanda is the begining and the end of the world
(2) the efficient and the final causes are one.
(3) matter has more potential in it than life.
(4) all the above

60. In the logical accounts, according to upanisads, a god overlooking matter, stirring it up into motion. This god is
(1) Brahma (2) Indra
(3) Prajñāna (4) Prajapāti

61. Whose ideals resembles with upaniṣadic theory of creations
(1) Aristotle (2) Plato
(3) Socertese (4) None

62. According to Upaniṣads form and matter are
(1) two different realities
(2) aspects of one reality
(3) matter is produced from form
(4) only matter is real

63. What is true above ātman
(1) Ātman is absolute
(2) Ātman is the highest reality
(3) Ātman is the sum of Indriyas
(4) Ātman is the sum of thoughts

64. What type of Satta is ascribable to Brahman?
(1) Vyavaharika
(2) Paramarthika
(3) Both Vyavaharika & Paramarthika
(4) Pratibhasika

65. In which Ashrama Vyavastha, a person leaves for the jungle in order to pray to God and practice Yoga ?
(1) Brahmacharya (2) Garhastha
(3) Vanaprastha (4) Sanyasa

66. Which one of the following is not the correct sequence?
(1) Sainhita, Brahmana, Aranyaka
(2) Brahmana, Aranyaka, Upanishada
(3) Veda, Upanishada, Aranyaka
(4) Sanihita, Aranyaka, Upanishada

67. Rajasuya Yajña is performed
(1) to make the king more powerful
(2) to swear one as king
(3) to bring good to the king
(4) to win a war

68. In the vanaprastha stage the............spends his time in fasting.
(1) devotee (2) rshis
(3) supernatural man (4) restless person

69. Correct number of Samhitās is
(1) One (2) Two
(3) Three (4) Four

70. Which Upanisad calls God as Tajjalān ?
(1) Chāndogya (2) Katha
(3) Māndukya (4) Mundaka

71. The Priest belonging to Sāmaveda is known as
(1) Udgāthā (2) Hotā
(3) Brahmā (4) None of these

72. The Vedic word Rta stands for
(1) moral order
(2) cosmic order
(3) both moral and cosmic order
(4) neither moral nor cosmic order

73. The arguments presented in favour of Vedas include
(1) Power of the authors
(2) Characters of the authors
(3) Purpose of the authors
(4) None of the above

74. The individual self is
(1) a knot of the existent and the non-existent
(2) product of ignorance

(3) the nearest approach to the absolute
(4) all of the above

75. Brahmacharya is the means to meet
(1) Ṛsiṛṇa (2) Pitṛṛṇa
(3) Devaṛṇa (4) Manusyaṛna

76. Which one of the following systems of Indian Philosophy designated Moksha as Nirvana ?
(1) Jainism (2) Buddhism
(3) Yoga (4) Samkhya

77. All the following orders of the Purusharthas are wrong except :
(1) Dharma, Artha, Kāma, Mokṣa
(2) Artha, Kāma, Mokṣa, Dharma
(3) Dharma, Kāma, Artha, Mokṣa
(4) Dharma, Mokṣa, Artha, Kāma

78. What is the Upanishadic view of Mukti?
(1) Knowledge of Atman
(2) Knowledge of Brahman
(3) Unity of Brahman and Atman
(4) None of the above

79. The self is called Prajñana in
(1) jagrat state (2) swapana state
(3) susupti state (4) turiya state

80. The correct sequence of four parts of Vedas is
(1) Samhitā, Āranyaka, Brāhmana, Upanisad.
(2) Samhitā, Brāhmana, Āranyaka, Upanisad.
(3) Upanisad, Āranyaka, Brāhmana, Samhitā.
(4) Samhitā, Brāhmana, Upanisad, Āranyaka.

81. Which statements are true
(1) avyakta is higher than the ātman,
(2) avyakta is higher than manas,
(3) avyakta is higher than the mahat,
(4) avyakta is higher than the intellect

Codes :
(1) A, B, C & D (2) A, B & D
(3) A, B & C (4) B, C & D

82. Arranged ascending order is
(1) objects, senses, mind, intellect
(2) senses, objects, intellect, mind
(3) senses, intellect, mind, object
(4) intellect, senses, object, mind

83. Arranged ascending order is
(1) intellect, mahat, ātman, avyakta
(2) mahat, intellect, avyakta, ātman
(3) intellect, mahat, avyakta, ātman
(4) intellect, avyakta, mahat, ātman

84. Brahman is
(1) objective side of ultimate reality.
(2) subjective side of ultimate reality.
(3) neither objective nor subjective.
(4) none of the above

85. According to Upaniṣads Brahman is
(1) saprapancā, saguna, saviśesa
(2) nisprapanca, nirguna, mirviśesa
(3) (1) and (2) both are accepted
(4) only saguna and anirvacaniya

86. According to saṃkarācārya Iśvara is
(1) saguṇa (2) nirguṇa
(3) indescribable (4) none of the above

87. "The absolute is the personal and the immanent god, and matter and selves alike form his real body".
The above given statement expresses the theory of
(1) Ramānuja (2) Saṃkara
(3) Madhva (4) Nimbarka

88. Select the correct matching from the codes given below
(A) Brahmapariṇamavāda-saṃkarācārya
(B) Brahmapariṇamavāda-Ramanujācārya
(C) Brahmavivartavāda-Ramanujāchārya
(D) Brahmavivartavādā-Saṃkarācārya

Codes :

(1) A & B (2) B & C

(3) C & D (4) B & D

89. That, which inclines us to repeat the deed we have once done, is

(1) impression of Karma on the mind

(2) law of Ṛta

(3) cosmological order

(4) our sinful activities

90. The moral law of Karma is

(1) the expression of nature of absolute.

(2) the expression of the nature of god

(3) regulated by Iśvara

(4) man's nature itself

91. Karma refers to the unchanging actions of

(1) the gods (2) the absolute

(3) the man (4) the nature

92. The law of Karma is related to

(1) morality (2) metaphysics

(3) epistemology (4) axiology

93. The order of human life in traditional Hindu society are arranged in

(1) Brahmacarya, sanyasa, gṛhastha, vanaprastha

(2) Gṛhastha, brahmacarya, vanaprashta, sanyasa

(3) Sanyasa, gṛhastha, vanaprastha, brahmacarya

(4) Brahmacarya, gṛhastha, vanaprastha, sanyasa

94. Saṁsara is real

(1) within the absolute

(2) without the absolute

(3) out of absolute

(4) in itself

95. Reality manifest itself in and through and by means of the

(1) permanency (2) temporal changes

(3) static character (4) unreality

96. Temporal changes occurs

(1) randomly

(2) according to the law of karma

(3) according to the law of Ṛta

(4) according to the law of Ṛna

97. Plurality seen in this world is

(1) real (2) apparent

(3) indescribable (4) nature of absolute

98. Mokṣa is a state of

(1) pain (2) ānanda

(3) confussion

(4) ānanda and non-ānanda

99. During the state of Mokṣa

(1) heaven and earth are felt to flow together

(2) the creature as creature is abolished

(3) creature realises his oneness with creator

(4) all of the above

100. Neti-neti negates

(1) all descriptions about the Brahman

(2) the Brahman

(3) the reality of this world

(4) the reality of ātman

101. Trivarga indicates

(1) Mokṣa, dharma & artha

(2) Dharma, kama and mokṣa

(3) Kama, artha and dharma

(4) Kama, artha and mokṣa

102. The temporal happenings become eternal when viewed in relation to the

(1) absolute (2) ātman

(3) law of karma (4) law of Ṛta

103. Taittirīya upaniṣad postulates the theory of 'five kosas' which hide the identity of soul. These 'five kosas' are

(1) Prithvi, aap, tejas, vayu, ākāsa

(2) Roopa, Vedana, vijñāna, samjñā, saṃskāra

(3) Rupa, rasa, gandha, sparsha and śabda

(4) Anna, prana, manas, vijñāna and ānanda

104. Which one of the following represents the correct meaning of the concept of Aṣrama-dharma.
(1) This a living of Sramaṇa's life
(2) This is to live in a aṣrama made in forests
(3) This is to fulfil ethical duties according to our situation
(4) This is the donation of service for the society.

105. Which one of the following is not included in puruṣārtha-catustaya
(1) Dharma (2) Nyaya
(3) Mokṣa (4) Artha

106. Which one of the following is accepted by Vedic ethics as highest good
(1) dana (2) yajña
(3) Ahiṃsa (4) kṣamasheelata

107. Which one of the following western thinker's social system can be compared with varṇadharma
(1) 'Middle path' of Aristotle
(2) Russoue's 'social contract'
(3) Marx concept of new-society
(4) 'major highest goods' of Plato

108. Upaniṣads can be said as monists because they believe in
(1) one god (2) many gods
(3) one creater (Brahma)
(4) one reality (Brahman)

109. The reason behind the rejection of vedic yajña by upaniṣads is
(1) Yajña is only for sawarnas
(2) This is complicated
(3) This includes the killings of animals
(4) it is not helpful in gaining Mokṣa

110. Which of the following is not harmonical with the law of karma
(1) Punarjanma is controlled by kriyaman karma
(2) Punarjanma is regulated by God's own will
(3) The pleasures and pain of this life are the products of the works of previous life.
(4) Punarjanma is regulated by saṃcit karma.

111. Match the following
Statement :
(a) The several elements are found in the nature of individual.
(b) Fire, water and earth constitute the jivatman, together with the principle of infinite.
(c) Ātman is the ultimate reality.
(d) All birds go towards the tree intended for their abode, so all this goes to the supreme self.
Upaniṣads :
(i) Chāndogya (ii) Taittirīya
(iii) Katha (iv) Praśna
Codes :

	(a)	(b)	(c)	(d)
(1)	(i)	(ii)	(iii)	(iv)
(2)	(iv)	(ii)	(i)	(iii)
(3)	(ii)	(i)	(iii)	(iv)
(4)	(ii)	(iii)	(iv)	(i)

112. Match the following and choose your answer from the codes given below :

Vedas	**Priests**
(a) Sāma	(i) Hota
(b) Yajur	(ii) Udgata
(c) Atharva	(iii) Adhvaryu
(d) Ṛig	(iv) Brahma

Codes :

	(a)	(b)	(c)	(d)
(1)	(iv)	(i)	(iii)	(ii)
(2)	(ii)	(iii)	(i)	(iv)
(3)	(iii)	(ii)	(iv)	(i)
(4)	(ii)	(iii)	(iv)	(i)

113. Match the following

Group X	Group Y
(a) Prāṇa	(i) ākasa
(b) Manas	(ii) vāyu
(c) Mind	(iii) other
(d) Gross body	(iv) physical elements

Codes :

	(a)	(b)	(c)	(d)
(1)	(i)	(ii)	(iii)	(iv)
(2)	(ii)	(iii)	(iv)	(i)
(3)	(ii)	(i)	(iii)	(iv)
(4)	(iv)	(ii)	(i)	(iii)

114. Match the following

(a) Self identifies itself with the objects.

(b) Objects have to be framed by the mind independently of the body.

(c) The self becomes a mere abstraction as there are no contents at all.

(d) The self enjoys positive bliss without subject-object duality.

(i) Jagrat (ii) Swapna

(iii) Susupti (iv) Turiya

Codes :

	(a)	(b)	(c)	(d)
(1)	(i)	(ii)	(iii)	(iv)
(2)	(ii)	(iii)	(iv)	(i)
(3)	(iii)	(iv)	(i)	(ii)
(4)	(iv)	(i)	(ii)	(iii)

115. Match the following

(a) Aumkara	(i) Svapna
(b) A	(ii) Turiya
(c) U	(iii) Jāgrata
(d) M	(iv) Susupti

Codes :

	(a)	(b)	(c)	(d)
(1)	(i)	(ii)	(iii)	(iv)
(2)	(ii)	(i)	(iv)	(iii)
(3)	(iii)	(iv)	(i)	(ii)
(4)	(ii)	(iii)	(i)	(iv)

116. Match the following comparisons

(a) bow	(i) Atman
(b) arrow	(ii) Brahman
(c) mark	(iii) man
(d) hunter	(iv) praṇava

Codes :

	(a)	(b)	(c)	(d)
(1)	(i)	(ii)	(iii)	(iv)
(2)	(ii)	(iii)	(iv)	(i)
(3)	(iv)	(i)	(ii)	(iii)
(4)	(iii)	(iv)	(i)	(ii)

117. Match the following

(a) Punishment for sinful activities	(i) Karma
(b) We reap what we sow	(ii) Ṛna
(c) Offerings to the gods.	(iii) Ṛta

Codes :

	(a)	(b)	(c)
(1)	(i)	(ii)	(iii)
(2)	(ii)	(iii)	(i)
(3)	(iii)	(i)	(ii)
(4)	(iii)	(ii)	(i)

118. Match the following

List-I	List-II
(a) Brahman	(i) Cosmic aspect
(b) Karma	(ii) Liberation
(c) Moksha	(iii) Ultimate witness
(d) Atman	(iv) Subject

Codes :

	(a)	(b)	(c)	(d)
(1)	(i)	(ii)	(iii)	(iv)
(2)	(iv)	(iii)	(ii)	(i)
(3)	(iv)	(ii)	(iii)	(i)
(4)	(iv)	(i)	(ii)	(iii)

119. Match the following

List-I	List-II
(a) Rta	(i) Course of things
(b) Dev-Rna	(ii) Yajna
(c) Rna	(iii) Obligations
(d) Brahmacarin	(iv) Student

Codes :

	(a)	(b)	(c)	(d)
(1)	(i)	(ii)	(iii)	(iv)
(2)	(iv)	(iii)	(ii)	(i)
(3)	(iii)	(ii)	(iv)	(i)
(4)	(iv)	(ii)	(iii)	(i)

120. Match the following

List-I	List-II
(a) Rta	(i) Cosmic order
(b) Rna	(ii) Duty
(c) Brahman	(iii) Non-dual bliss
(d) Atman	(iv) Individual self

Codes :

	(a)	(b)	(c)	(d)
(1)	(ii)	(iii)	(iv)	(i)
(2)	(i)	(ii)	(iii)	(iv)
(3)	(ii)	(iv)	(iii)	(i)
(4)	(i)	(iv)	(iii)	(ii)

121. Match the following

List-I	List-II
(a) Brahmacharin	(i) Vedas
(b) Grhastha	(ii) Householder
(c) Vanaprastha	(iii) Hermit
(d) Sanyasin	(iv) Ascetic

Codes :

	(a)	(b)	(c)	(d)
(1)	(i)	(ii)	(iii)	(iv)
(2)	(iv)	(iii)	(ii)	(i)
(3)	(iii)	(iv)	(ii)	(i)
(4)	(i)	(iv)	(iii)	(ii)

122. Match the following

List-I	List-II
(a) Rta	(i) Divine realms
(b) Hymns	(ii) Mantras
(c) Upanishad	(iii) Chandogya
(d) Karma	(iv) Psychological ashect

Codes :

	(a)	(b)	(c)	(d)
(1)	(i)	(ii)	(iii)	(iv)
(2)	(iv)	(iii)	(ii)	(i)
(3)	(iii)	(iv)	(ii)	(i)
(4)	(ii)	(iv)	(iii)	(i)

123. Match the following

List-I	List-II
(a) Theories of creation	(i) Nasaduja Hymn
(b) Moksha	(ii) Freedom
(c) Preyas	(iii) Material world
(d) Sreyas	(iv) Spiritual world

Codes :

	(a)	(b)	(c)	(d)
(1)	(i)	(ii)	(iii)	(iv)
(2)	(ii)	(iii)	(iv)	(i)
(3)	(iv)	(iii)	(ii)	(i)
(4)	(i)	(iv)	(iii)	(ii)

124. Match the following

List-I	List-II
(a) Jagrat	(i) Waking
(b) Swapna	(ii) Dreaming
(c) Susupti	(iii) Sleep
(d) Turuja	(iv) Deep sleep

Codes :

	(a)	(b)	(c)	(d)
(1)	(i)	(ii)	(iii)	(iv)
(2)	(iv)	(iii)	(ii)	(i)
(3)	(iii)	(ii)	(iv)	(i)
(4)	(iv)	(ii)	(iii)	(i)

125. Match the following

List-I	List-II
(a) Karma	(i) Action
(b) Atman	(ii) Subject
(c) Yajna	(iii) Sacrifice
(d) Rna	(iv) Varuna

Codes :

	(a)	(b)	(c)	(d)
(1)	(ii)	(iii)	(iv)	(i)
(2)	(iv)	(iii)	(ii)	(i)
(3)	(i)	(ii)	(iii)	(iv)
(4)	(iii)	(ii)	(iv)	(i)

Directions. The following items consist of two statements, one labelled the 'Assertion A' and the other labelled the 'Reason R'. You are to examine these two statements carefully and decide if the Assertion A and the reason R individually true and if so, whether the reason is a correct explanation of the assertion. Select your answers to these items using the codes given below.

Codes:

(1) Both A and R are true and R is the correct explanation of A

(2) Both A and R are true but R is not a correct explanation of A

(3) A is true but R is false

(4) A is false but R is true.

126. **Assertion (A).** In the conception of Ṛta there is a development from physical to divine.

Reason (R). Ṛta, after being the cosmic order, becomes the settled will of god, the law of morality and righteousness as well.

127. **Assertion (A).** The world is the working of a harmonious purpose.

Reason (R). Ṛta, is the reason behind the arranged order of the things.

128. **Assertion (A).** The faith in Ṛta gives us solace and security whenever unbelief tempts us the confidence in ourselves is shattered.

Reason (R). Everything that is ordered in the universe has Ṛta for its principle.

129. **Assertion (A).** Indian society was divided in three classes during Brahmanical period.

Reason (R). Sacrifices took the central place.

130. **Assertion (A).** Sacrifices took the central place.

Reason (R). The sacrifices pleased the god and profited men.

131. **Assertion (A).** A rigid soul-deadening, commercialist creed based on a contractual motive took the place of the simple devout religion of the Vedas.

Reason (R). Sacrifices for earthly profits took the central place.

132. **Assertion (A).** Life is a round of duties and responsibilities.

Reason (R). The concept of Ṛṇa is the way to live in harmony with the world around.

133. **Assertion (A).** Hiraṇyagarbha evolved the beautiful world from shapeless chaos.

Reason (R). Hiraṇyagarbha arose in the beginning from the great water which pervaded the universe.

134. **Assertion (A).** The one breathed breathless by its own power.

Reason (R). Other than that there was not anything beyond.

135. **Assertion (A).** The fact of affirmation or positing of the primal 'I' in absolute consciousness evolves the world.

Reason (R). If there is no other there is no ego.

136. **Assertion (A).** The world is always restless.

Reason (R). The timeless whole is ever breaking out in a series of becomings.

137. **Assertion (A).** The first forms of fire, water, air, earth are looked upon as divine.

Reason (R). According to Upaniṣads, matter itself is a god.

138. **Assertion (A).** According to Upaniṣads, the external world is not something separate, existing side by side with the ātman.

Reason (R). The world of plurality can be reduced without residnum into the everlasting one, Brahman.

139. **Assertion (A).** Nature is a system of spontaneity of self-evolving autonomy.

Reason (R). It is the energising of the absolute.

140. **Assertion (A).** The temporal process is an actual process.

Reason (R). Reality manifest itself in and through by means of the temporal changes.

141. Choose the true statements from the codes given below
A. Ṛta corresponds to the universals of Plato,
B. The world of experience is the reflection of Ṛita;
C. Ṛta exists before the manifestation of all phenomena,
D. Ṛta remains unchanged in all the velters of mutation codes
(1) A, B & C (2) B & D
(3) B, C, D (4) A, B, C & D

142. A. Ṛta is called father of all,
B. Marut come from the after from the seat of the Ṛta,
C. Vishnu is the embryo of the Ṛta,
D. What heaven and earth are by the reason of Ṛta Codes
(1) A & C (2) B & D
(3) A, B, D (4) A, B, C, D

143. There are given following three duties which are to be obeyed
(A) Offerings to the seers
(B) offerings to the anscesters
(C) offerings to the gods
Which is the correct order by which these duties are to be obeyed
(1) B, C, A (2) A, B, C
(3) C, A, B (4) C, B, A

144. Doctrine of sheaths mean
A. matter B. form
C. life D. death
Select the correct answer using codes given below
(1) A, B & C (2) A & B
(3) B, C & D (4) A, B & C, D

145. Theories of creation says that
A. water develop the world.
B. water comes first.
C. nothing comes first.
D. nothing develops the world.
Select the correct answer using codes given below
(1) C & D (2) C, B & D
(3) A & B (4) A, B & C

146. Yajna means
A. eventual hell.
B. don't helps anyone.
C. a sacrifice which save the worldly creatures.
D. helps in attaining heaven
Select the correct answer using codes given below
(1) C & D (2) A, B & C
(3) A, B & D (4) C & D

147. Rta is described as
A. course of things
B. course of action
C. human realms
D. course of laws
Select the correct answer using codes given below
(1) A & B (2) B & C
(3) A & C (4) A, B, C & D

148. Rna means
A. duties
B. obligations
C. essentiality
D. sacrifices
Select the correct answer using codes given below
(1) A & B (2) B & C
(3) A & C (4) B & D

149. Atman is described as
A. subject B. object
C. individual self
D. body
Select the correct answer using codes given below
(1) A & B (2) B & C
(3) A & C (4) A, B, C & D

150. Truths given by Nāgārjuna are

A. Pārabhāsikā B. saṁvṛti

C. Parmarth D. Laukika

Choose the answer form the codes given below

(1) A and B (2) A, B and C

(3) B and C (4) A, B, C and D

151. Which of the following doctrines tries to explain mind and consciousness as the products of matter

(1) Nyāya (2) Jaina

(3) Cārvāka (4) Buddhism

152. Which among the following schools holds that matter is the only reality

(1) Jainism (2) Cārvāka

(3) Buddhism (4) Saṁkhya

153. Which among the following doctrines represents the tendency that seeks to reduce the higher to the lower ones

(1) Materialism (2) Idealism

(3) Conceptualism (4) Realism

154. Which of the following doctrines explains the higher phenomenon in the light of the lower ones.

(1) Idealism (2) Realism

(3) Conceptualism (4) Materialism

155. Which of the following schools opposes the spiritual interpretations of the universe

(1) Purva Mimaṁsa (2) Jainism

(3) Cārvāka (4) Nyāya

156. Which of the following schools accepts perception as the only source of knowledge

(1) Nyāya (2) Chārvāka

(3) Jainism (4) Buddhism

157. Which of the following schools criticizes inference and testimony as the valid sources of knowledge

(1) Nyāya (2) Sāṁkhya

(3) Cārvāka (4) Buddhism

158. The no. of pramāṇas accepted by cārvāka

(1) Six (2) three

(3) two (4) one

159. According to Cārvāka the valid source of knowledge is

(1) pratyakṣa (2) Anumāna

(3) Śabda

(4) Pratyakṣa and Anumāna

160. Who among the following Philosophers said, 'Inference is a mere leap in the dark'

(1) Mahāvira (2) Buddha

(3) Cārvāka (4) Gautama

161. 'Deductive inference is initiated by the fallacy of petitio principii'. This argument is accepted by

(1) Cārvāka (2) Mahāvira

(3) Buddha (4) Nyāya

162. Cārvāka rejects the validity of deductive inference because

(1) the conclusion has no relation with major premise

(2) the conclusion is already present in major premise

(3) the conclusion contradicts the major premise

(4) Vyāpti is not established between major premise and conclusion

163. Which among the following schools rejects anumāna as a valid source of knowledge

(1) Nyāya (2) Buddhism

(3) Cārvāka (4) Jainism

164. Cārvāka rejects 'vyāpti' on the basis of

(1) invariable relation or vyapti is not possible between two terms

(2) all the premises represent different aspects of truths

(3) perception does not prove vyāpti

(4) vyāpti can not be taken as invariable association

165. Who says that the vedas are the works of some cunning priests
(1) Jainism (2) Buddhism
(3) Cārvāka (4) sāṁkhya

166. Which among the following knowledges are not valid according to cārvāka
(1) Words which are heard
(2) Smelt fragrance
(3) Seen items
(4) Knowledge obtained from texts

167. Who says that the world comes into existence by the spontaneous combination of material elements
(1) Cārvāka (2) Jainism
(3) Buddhism (4) Nyāya

168. 'The material elements themselves have got each its fix nature. It is by the natures and laws inherent in them that they combine together to form this world'
Above lines expresses the theory of
(1) Vaiśesika (2) Cārvāka
(3) Saṁkhya-yoga (4) Jaina

169. The correct sequence of three jewels of Jainism is
(1) Samyaka Darshan, Samyaka Jnana, Samyaka Charitra
(2) Samyaka, Jnana, Samyaka Darshan, Samyaka Charitra
(3) Samyaka Charitra, Samyaka Jnana, Samyaka Darshan
(4) Samayaka Darshan, Samyaka Charitra, Samyaka Jnana

170. According to Cārvākā, the soul is
(1) a self-conscious eternal being
(2) an unconsious eternal being
(3) a mere form of ultimate reality
(4) the living body, with the quality of consciousness.

171. According to Cārvāka, the purusārthas are
(1) dharma and artha
(2) artha and kāma
(3) kāma and mokṣa
(4) dharma, artha, kāma and mokṣa

172. Cārvāka gives importance to
(1) liberation and virtue
(2) virtue only
(3) wealth and enjoyment
(4) wealth only

173. Who among the following philosophers thinks that all questions about previous life, after-life, rebirth, enjoyment of the fruits of actions in heaven or hell are meaningless
(1) Cārvāka (2) mahāvira
(3) Buddha (4) Gautama

174. Cārvāka accepts mokṣa as
(1) the end of this life
(2) a state of ānanda
(3) cessation of suffering
(4) none of the above

175. Cārvāka believes in
(1) rebirth
(2) achieving mokṣa
(3) living with lust and lull
(4) living with kindness and benevolence

176. How many Tirthānkaras are there in Jainism
(1) 22 (2) 21
(3) 23 (4) 24

177. According to Jainism, reality (sat) consists of
(1) permanence (2) origination
(3) decay (4) all of the above

178. Which among the following can be kept under reality following jaina's theory
(1) Substance (2) permanence
(3) Change (4) Decay
Choose your answer from the codes given below
(1) 2 and 3 (2) 1 and 3
(3) 1, 2, 3 and 4 (4) 1, 2 and 3

179. A substance is
(1) dharma (2) dharmi
(3) guna (4) paryāya

180. A substance, according to Jaina, is possessed of
(1) Changing essential characters and unchanging modes
(2) Unchanging essential characters and changing modes
(3) Only unchanging essential characters
(4) Only unchanging modes

181. Which among the following, according to Jaina, is anastikāya dravya
(1) Jiva (2) Ajiva
(3) Ākasā (4) Kāla

182. The correct sequence of the following in Buddhist Bhavachakra is
(1) Spars', Vedana, Trusna
(2) Trusna, Vedana, Spars's
(3) Trusna, Spars's, Vedana
(4) Vedana, Spars's, Trusna

183. Which among the following is not traśa
(1) Elephant (2) Man
(3) Tirthānkara (4) Ant

184. In Jaina's theory inanimate substances (ajiva) are
(1) dharma, ākāśa and pudgala
(2) dharma and adharma
(3) dharma, adharma, ākāsā and pudgala
(4) ākāśa and pudgala

185. Pudgala is of two kinds namely
(1) aṇu and paramāṇu
(2) parmaṇu and dravya
(3) guna and paryāya
(4) aṇu and saṅghata

186. Syadvada is
(1) sceptical (2) rationalistic
(3) empiricist (4) relativistic

187. 'Tirthankara' is a term associated with
(1) Carvaka (2) Jainism
(3) Buddhism (4) Yoga

188. According to Jaina, the essential character of soul is
(1) consciousness (2) thinking
(3) meditation (4) Intuition

189. Guṇas are the
(1) essential characters
(2) accidental characters
(3) essential and accidental both
(4) neither essential nor accidental

190. Paryāyas are the
(1) essential as well as accidental characters
(2) essential characters
(3) accidental characters
(4) neither essential nor accidental

191. Which of the following character can be kept under guṇa
(1) Desire (2) volitions
(3) pleasure (4) consciousness

192. Which of the following characters is not paryāya
(1) Desire (2) Volitions
(3) pleasure (4) consciousness

193. According to Jaina, a substance is that which
(1) possesses guṇas as well as paryāyas
(2) is free from all modifications
(3) can never be changed
(4) none of the above

194. Which among the following according to Jaina theory, is not a conscious substance
(1) horse (2) ants
(3) aṇu (4) stone

195. In vegetable or in lifeless things, according to Jaina, which kind of consciousness is present

(1) growing kind (2) tactual kind
(3) extensive kind (4) all of the above

196. Which of the following is true according to Jaina theory
(1) the soul manifests itself and others
(2) The soul pervades the entire body in which it lives
(3) The soul is eternal
(4) all of the above

197. Which among the following are the qualities of pudgalas (material substances) given in jaina's metaphysics
(1) only touch
(2) touch and taste
(3) touch, test, smell and colour
(4) touch, taste, smell, colour and sound

198. Which among the following is correct according to jainism
(1) Body, mind, speech and breath are all the products of matter
(2) Sound is not an original quality like other four
(3) Material substances have only four qualities
(4) All of the above

199. Which of the following are the functions of time according to Jainism
(1) Continuity and movements
(2) modification or change of states
(3) Newness and oldness of substances
(4) All of the above

200. Jaina theory distinguishes time between
(1) Bhuta, vartamana and bhaviṣya
(2) Kṣaṣa and prahara
(3) Parmārthika and vyavahārika
(4) Divasa, māsa and varṣa

201. What is the mark of parmārthika kāla?
(1) Parivartana (2) Vartana
(3) Gati (4) Navinata

202. The function of ākāśa, according to Jaina metaphysics is
(1) to save the world like a roof
(2) to secure substances from natural hazards
(3) to afford room for the existence of all extended substances
(4) None of the above

203. The Jaina distinguishes ākāśa between
(1) lokākāśa and alokākāśa
(2) parākāśa and aparākāśa
(3) vyavahārika and parmārthika
(4) none of the above

204. According to Jaina, the knowledge of kāla and ākāsa can be obtained only by
(1) perception (2) testimony
(3) inference (4) comparison

205. According to Jaina, the conditions of movement and rest are
(1) kāla and ākāśa
(2) dharma and adharma
(3) dharma and dharmi
(4) pudgala

206. Dharma and adharma are
(1) formless passive substances
(2) opposed to each other
(3) eternal, non-moving and both pervade the lokākāśa
(4) all of the above

207. Space, time, dharma and adharma are
(1) remote and passive instrumental conditions
(2) remote and active instrumental conditions
(3) the prime matters of this universe
(4) none of the above

208. Anckāntavāda is the theory of
(1) Śaṁkara (2) Ramanuja
(3) Jaina (4) Madhva

209. Jaina metaphysics can be kept under
(1) Realistic pluralism
(2) Idealistic pluralism
(3) Qualified monism
(4) Monism

210. Anekantavāda means
(1) manyness of god
(2) manyness of reality
(3) manyness of individuality
(4) manyness of thing

211. Syādvāda is the theory of
(1) truth and validity (2) error
(3) judgement (4) none of these

212. Nayavāda is the theory related to
(1) error (2) judgement
(3) matter
(4) knowledge of a thing

213. Nayavāda is the principle that
(1) truth is relative to our stand points
(2) truth is same at all the points
(3) truth is nowhere else
(4) none of the above

214. Naigamnaya relates to the purpose or end of a course of activity which is present throughout. This view is adopted by
(1) Siddhasena (2) Pujyapāda
(3) Nagasena (4) Nagarjuna

215. We have naigamanya when we comprehend a thing as having both generic and specific qualities and we do not distinguish between them
This view is adopted by
(1) Pujyapāda (2) Nagasena
(3) Siddhasena (4) Nagarjuna

216. Which one of the following pairs is a correctly matched?
(1) Whatever is sat is momentary : Jaina
(2) The self of an elephant is bigger than that of an ant : Carvaka
(3) Isvara can perceive with out sense-organs : Nyaya
(4) Inference is not a dependable source of knowledge : Vaisesika

217. Which of the following is true about Jaina theory of universals
(1) universals and individuals are both real
(2) only universals are real
(3) individuals are dependent to universals
(4) universals are not real apart from individuals

218. Pratitya samutpada-vada is a
(1) epistemological theory of Nyaya
(2) theory of causation in Buddhism
(3) epistemological theory of Vedanta
(4) metaphysical theory of the Jainas

219. Saṁgrahanaya emphasizes
(1) Particular qualities
(2) Common features
(3) Unreality of sāmāṅya
(4) none of the above

220. Which of the following Nayas is based on empirical knowledge?
(1) Naigamanaya (2) Saṁgrahanaya
(3) Vyavahāranaya (4) Rjusutranaya

221. To which Nayas the real is the momentary
(1) Naigamanaya (2) Saṅgrahanaya
(3) Vyavahāranaya (4) Rjusutranaya

222. Saptabhanginaya or syādvāda is a doctrine related to
(1) Jainism (2) Buddhism
(3) Nayaya-vaiśesike (4) Sāṁkhya

223. Who does hold that even perception is not a valid source of knowledge?
(1) Kanada (2) Jayrasi Bhatta
(3) Dinnaga (4) Mahavira

224. Choose the correct combination
(1) Akasa, Eka, Nitya, Vibhu

(2) Atma, Eka, Nitya, Murta
(3) Kala, Eka, Nitya, Mahat
(4) Samanya, Aneka, Nitya, Vibhu

225. Which of the following knowledges, according to Jaina, cannot be wrong
(1) Mati and śruti
(2) Manaḥparyāya and kevala
(3) Śruti and avadhi
(4) Mati and avadhi

226. Erroneous knowledge 'saṁsaya' affects
(1) Mati and śruti (2) Śruti and avadhi
(3) Avadhi (4) Kevāla

227. Erroneous knowledge viparyāya may be found in
(1) mati and śruti (2) śruti and avadhi
(3) avadhi (4) kevāla

228. Which of the following groups denotes the erroneous knowledges
(1) Mati and śruti
(2) Saṁsaya, viparyāya and anadhya-vasāya
(3) Śruti, avadhi and kevala
(4) mati and avadhi

229. What is true according to Jainism?
(1) Only one kind of knowledge is active at a time
(2) All kinds of knowledge are active simultaneously
(3) Kevāla can be active with mati
(4) Avadhi can be active with śruti

230. In Jaina philosophy, what is true about caitanya?
(1) Caitanya is the essence of jiva
(2) Darśana and jñana are the two manifestations of caitanya
(3) Caitanya is ever active
(4) All of the above

231. Carvaka ethics is called
(1) Hedonistic (2) Idealistic
(3) Marxism (4) Realism

232. According to Jaina, what is not true about perfect knowledge
(1) It is free form saṁśaya
(2) It is free form vimoha
(3) It is free form daśana
(4) It is free from vibhrama

233. Pramānas, accepted by Jainism, are
(1) Pratyakṣa, anumāna and śabda
(2) Pratyakṣa and anumāna
(3) Pratyakṣa and Anumāna
(4) Pratyakṣ

234. According to Jaina, the body is made of pudgalas. The organizers of this body are
(1) Tirthankaras (2) Gods
(3) Karmas or passions
(4) The soul

235. According to Jaina, because of bondage, the soul becomes
(1) Without potentiality
(2) Unknown to its potentiality
(3) Full of potentiality
(4) None of the above

236. The internal and primary cause of bondage is
(1) āsrava (2) saṁvara
(3) nirjara (4) bhāva

237. Āsrva is
(1) influx of matter into the soul
(2) internal and primary cause of bondage
(3) lose of matter from the soul
(4) all of the above

238. Liberation is
(1) influx of matter into the soul
(2) internal and primary cause of bondage
(3) expulsion of matter from the soul
(4) none of the above

239. Saṁvara is
(1) influx of matter into the soul
(2) stopping the influx of new matter into the soul

(3) internal and primary cause of bondage
(4) expulsion of matter from the soul

240. Nirjara is
(1) influx of matter
(2) stopping the influx
(3) expulsion of matter
(4) complete elimination of matter

241. Liberation is the joint effect of triratnas. These triratnas are
(1) right exercise, right speech and right faith
(2) right knowledge, right speech and right exercise
(3) right faith, right speech and right morals
(4) right knowledge, right faith and right conduct

242. Syadvada is the
(1) epistemological theory of Buddhists
(2) epistemological theory of Vedantins
(3) metaphysical theory of Jainas
(4) epistemological theory of Jainas

243. Who among the following holds the view ethical idealism
(1) Mahāvira (2) Buddhā
(3) Gautama (4) Kapila

244. The first Ārya satya 'life is full of suffering' proves
(1) Buddha's pessimistic view
(2) Worthlessness of life
(3) to revolt against evil
(4) Purposelessness of life

245. The number of 'indeterminate questions' mentioned by Buddha is
(1) 10 (2) 5
(3) 20 (4) 3

246. In Pali language the indeterminate questions mentioned by Buddha are known as
(1) avyākatāni (2) avyavahārika
(3) Niṅgula (4) vyākata

247. All the teachings of Gautama centre round
(1) metaphysical topics
(2) four-noble truths
(3) nirvāna
(4) ārhata

248. Pratityasamutpāda (the chain of twelve links) is related to
(1) first noble truth
(2) forth noble truth
(3) second noble truth
(4) third noble truth

249. Which gives us the cause of suffering according to Budha?
(1) Second Noble Truth
(2) First Noble Truth
(3) Third Noble Truth
(4) None of these

250. Who is produced before Jati according to Budha?
(1) jarā-marana (2) avidya
(3) vijñana (4) sadāyatana

251. Who is produced after Bhāva according to Budha?
(1) avidya (2) jāti
(3) vijnana (4) vedanā

252. Who is produced after upadana according to Budha?
(1) avidya (2) jāti
(3) vijnana (4) vedanā

253. Who is produced after tṛsna according to Budha?
(1) sparśa (2) vedanā
(3) bhava (4) tṛsna

254. Who is produced before tṛsna according to Budha?
(1) vedanā (2) upādāna
(3) nāmarupa (4) upādāna

255. Pratityasamutpāda is also known as
(1) Bhava-cakra (2) Saṁsāra-cakra
(3) Dharma-cakra (4) All of the above

256. Who is produced before vedana according to Budha?
(1) upādāna (2) sparśa
(3) jati (4) jarāmarana

257. Who is produced before sparsa according to Budha?
(1) vedanā (2) jāti
(3) ṣaḍāyatana (4) bhava

258. Which shows in the third noble truth?
(1) cause of suffering
(2) samāra
(3) reality
(4) cessation of suffering

259. Who is produced before sadayatana according to Budha?
(1) sparśa (2) nāma-rupa
(3) vedanā (4) tṛṣna

260. Who is produced before name-rupa according to Budha?
(1) sparśa (2) vedanā
(3) vijñāna (4) trsna

261. Pratityasamutpāda expresses
(1) Conditionality of events
(2) Buddha's special conception of neural causation
(3) the cause of suffering
(4) all of the above

262. Who is produced before vijñāna according to Budha?
(1) saṁsakāra (2) nāmarupa
(3) nāmarupa (4) jati

263. Who is produced before saṁsakāra according to Budha?
(1) vijñāna (2) avidyā
(3) nāmarupa (4) jati

264. Buddha says that avidyā is associated with
(1) present life (2) future life
(3) past life (4) none of these

265. Gautama Buddha was the propounder of
(1) Śaśvatavāda (2) Ucchedavāda
(3) Madhyamamārga (4) None of these

266. Gautama Buddha told us a causal chain of suffering, which is known as dvādaśanidāna. Which among the following expresses the causation theory of Buddhism
(1) Satkāryavāda
(2) Asatkāryavāda
(3) vivartavāda
(4) Pratityasamutpadavāda

267. In Buddhism, cessation of suffering is known as
(1) Nirvāna (2) Death
(3) heaven (4) pleasure

268. In Buddhism, the mean to attain nirvāṇa is known as
(1) Triratna
(2) Āṣtangikamarga
(3) Aṣtangayoga
(4) Sādhanacatuṣtaya

269. Which among the following is not included in āstāngikamārga
(1) samyag drsti (2) samyag karmānta
(3) samyag bhoga
(4) samyag samkalpa

270. Buddhas theory, regarding the self, was
(1) Advaitavāda (2) Viśiṣtadvaita
(3) Anātmavāda (4) Śuddhadvaita

271. Buddha's theory related to God was
(1) Polytheism (2) Henotheism
(3) Monism (4) Atheism

272. Sabda is pramana, but not an independent pramana according to
(1) Carvaka (2) Vaisesika
(3) Bauddha (4) None of these

273. According to the Jainas truth is
(1) absolute
(2) relative
(3) Both (1) and (2)
(4) none of these

274. Trikāya theory has brought individual theism in Mahāyāna-buddha-science (Buddhology). Which among the following is the correct sequence of Trikāyas?
(1) Dharmakāya, saṁbhogakaya, Nirmānakāya
(2) Dharmakāya, nirmānakāya, saṁbhogakāya
(3) Saṁbhogakaya, nirmānakāya, dharmakāya
(4) Nirmānakāya, dharmakāya, saṁbhogakāya

275. Which among the following expresses the Triratna in Buddhism?
(1) Dharma, artha, kāma
(2) Duḥkha, samudāya, nirodha
(3) Buddha, dhamma, saṁgha
(4) Bodhisatva, amitābha, nirvāṇa

276. Buddhism accepts
(1) karma theory and eternal soul
(2) karma theory but not eternal soul
(3) eternal soul but not karma theory
(4) Neither eternal soul nor karma theory

277. Three among following are similar in some way. Which one is not among those three
(1) Pratityasamutpāda
(2) Śunyata
(3) Madhyamāpratipada
(4) Aparigraha

278. Which among the following is not the Buddhist theory?
(1) kṣanikavāda
(2) Śunyavāda
(3) Vijñānavada
(4) Tataśtheśvaravāda

279. "There is no reality which is similar to the universal terms like a 'tree' or a 'dog'. These universal terms are only a kind of talking about individuals like a 'Neem' or a 'Pomelian'".
This view is accepted by
(1) Cārvāka (2) Buddhism
(3) Nyāya (4) Mimāṁsa

280. Who holds that the parimana (dimension) of the body is the parimana of atma?
(1) Carvaka (2) Jaina
(3) Vaisesika (4) None of these

281. Sat is a current of the series of such conscious states which are causally related. This theory is accepted by
(1) Jainism (2) Nyāya
(3) Yogācāra (4) Yoga

282. Which of the following schools of Indian philosophy has faith in rebirth but not in transmigration
(1) Buddhism (2) Casvaka
(3) Vaisesika (4) Samkhya

283. Which among the following states that 'soul is not the essence'
(1) Cārvāka (2) Jainism
(3) Buddhism (4) Purva-mimaṁsa

284. The Buddhist doctrine of Pratityasamutpada can be defined as
(1) There is no permanent self
(2) Whatever is, is momentary
(3) There is no origination of some elements
(4) Whatever originates, originate on some conditions

285. Liberation according to Jainism is
(1) freedom from life and death
(2) freedom from Karma
(3) freedom from matter
(4) All of the above

286. Should Buddhism be said as pessimistic school of Indian philosophy?

(1) Yes, because it supposes that the life is full of suffering
(2) Yes, because it gives importance to the sacrificial life
(3) No, because it shows the way leading to cessation of suffering
(4) No, because it supposes that only a general life is full of suffering

287. Astāṅgamarga is given by
(1) Vedas (2) Jainas
(3) Buddhas (4) Upaniṣads

288. Which among the following statements about reality is true according to Buddhism?
(1) Svalakṣana is eternally changeable
(2) Svalakṣana is able to be namified
(3) Salakṣana is real in space and time
(4) Svalakṣana is ever active

289. Which among the following implies the Buddhist conception of universals?
(1) Universals are eternal class ideas which have their own existence
(2) Universals are simple objective ideas which are found in individuals
(3) universals are simple quality less names of the things
(4) Universals are class essence inher in individuals

290. 'Pramā is a knowledge unbounded by the inference' if this statement is true, which among the following statement will be accepted by Dingnāga?
(1) Pramā is a work of mind
(2) Prama produces opposites
(3) Prama is based on similarities
(4) Prama is source of knowledge

291. According to Buddhism Anupalabdhi is not an independent source of knowledge because
(1) Anupalabdhi is a form of anumāna
(2) Anupalabdhi can be included in pratyakṣa
(3) Anupalabdhi is not used as a source of knowledge in Buddhist literature
(4) Anupalabdhi is absence of knowledge

292. According to Buddhism, Vyāpti is adopted in the form of
(1) Tādātmya
(2) Tādātmya and Tadutpatti
(3) Tadutpatti
(4) Neither Tādātmya Nor Tadutpatti

293. Which one of the following is true according to Buddhism?
(1) Nirvāna can be attained in this life
(2) Nirvāna can be attained only after death
(3) Nirvana can be attained in this life as well as after death
(4) Nirvāna can be attained by the Grace of Tathāgata

294. On the question of nature of self the Carvaka philosophy can be classified as
(1) Dehatimavadins
(2) Pranavadins
(3) Indriyatimavadins
(4) All of the above

295. Pratiyasamutpāta is related to
(1) Duḥkha
(2) Duḥkha-samudāya
(3) Duḥkha-nirodha
(4) Duḥkha-nirotha-mārga

296. The meaning of 'samyagsmṛti' is
(1) to keep in memory the words of Buddhist saints
(2) to keep in memory the true meanings of Buddhist literature
(3) to keep in memory the right form of mind and body
(4) to keep in memory the right form of the soul

297. According to Buddhism, the theory related to pudgala-nairatmya means

(1) to neglect any of the eternal substances either spiritual or physical
(2) to accept only an eternal spiritual substance but not the material one
(3) to accept the material substance but to neglect the spiritual
(4) to accept a supreme reality beyond the both material and spiritual

298. In Buddhism, the rejection of substances is mainly based on
(1) the theory of suffering
(2) the theory of anātmavāda
(3) the theory of non-eternity
(4) the theory of pratityasamutpāda

299. By the Buddhist theory of Apohavāda
(1) Idealism is developed
(2) Realism is developed
(3) Pragmatism is developed
(4) Nominalism is developed

300. Which one of the following is accepted in Buddhism
(1) Svataḥ-prāmāṅya, parataḥapramaṅya
(2) Suatah pramaṅya, suataḥapramaṅya
(3) Paratah pramaṅya, svataḥ aprāmāṅya
(4) Paratah Prāmāṅya, parataḥ aprāmāṅya

301. Which one of the following pairs is correctly matches?
(1) Nyāya – Ātmakhyāti
(2) Buddhism – Asatkhyāti
(3) Mimaṁsā – Anyathākhyāti
(4) Advaita – vedant – Vivekakhyāti

302. Which of the following theory is related to sautantrika?
(1) Vijñānavāda
(2) Vāhyapratyakṣavāda
(3) Vahyānumeyavāda
(4) Śunyavāda

303. The view that all types of Pratyaksa are Nirvikalpaka is upheld by
(1) Nyaya (2) Vaisesika
(3) Bauddha (4) Visistadvaita

304. Liberation according to Jainism is termed as
(1) Bhava-Moksa (2) Dravya Moksa
(3) Both (1) and (2) (4) None of these

305. According to Nāgārjuna, the world is
(1) either real or unreal
(2) unreal
(3) neither real nor unreal
(4) indescribable

306. Vijnanavada stands for
(1) subjective idealism
(2) objective idealism
(3) absolute idealism
(4) realism

307. "The blue colour and the consciousness of blue colour are identical, because they are never perceived to exist separately". This statement expresses the theory of
(1) Mādhyamika (2) Yogācāra
(3) Vaibhāsika (4) Sautrāntika

308. Bahyānumeyavāda is the theory accepted by
(1) Mādhyamika (2) Yogācāra
(3) Sautrāntika (4) Vaibhāsika

309. According to Vaibhāsikas
(1) Only mind is real
(2) Mind and external objects are real
(3) Only external objects are real
(4) Nothing is real

310. Copy theory of ideas is accepted by
(1) Mādhyamika (2) Yogacāra
(3) sautrāntika (4) Vaibhāsika

311. In Jainism, the following lacks Kayatva (ṃagnitude)
(1) Dharma (2) Adharma
(3) Kala (4) Pudgala

312. For Carvaka
(1) happiness is liberation

(2) death is liberation
(3) karma is liberation
(4) knowledge is liberation

313. The following Noble Truth of the Buddha includes the doctrine of dependent origination
(1) there is suffering
(2) there is cessation of suffering
(3) theories cause of suffering
(4) path of liberation

314. Match the following and choose your answer from the codes given below

Particulars	Name given by Jaina
(a) Aṇu	(i) Anastikāya
(b) Man	(ii) Pudgala
(c) Kāla	(iii) Guṇa
(d) Cetanā	(iv) Traśa

Codes :	(a)	(b)	(c)	(d)
(1)	(i)	(ii)	(iii)	(iv)
(2)	(ii)	(iv)	(i)	(iii)
(3)	(iii)	(i)	(iv)	(ii)
(4)	(iv)	(iii)	(ii)	(i)

315. Match the following and choose your answer from the codes given below

(a) Dharma (i) Astikāya
(b) Dharmi (ii) Anastikāya
(c) Jiva, ajiva (iii) Dravya
(d) Kāla (iv) Guṇa

Codes :	(a)	(b)	(c)	(d)
(1)	(i)	(ii)	(iii)	(iv)
(2)	(iv)	(iii)	(i)	(ii)
(3)	(i)	(iii)	(iv)	(ii)
(4)	(iv)	(ii)	(iii)	(i)

316. Match the following and choose your answer from the codes given below

(a) men (i) 5-sensed
(b) bees (ii) 4-sensed
(c) ants (iii) 3-sensed
(d) worms (iv) 2-sensed

Codes :	(a)	(b)	(c)	(d)
(1)	(i)	(ii)	(iii)	(iv)
(2)	(ii)	(iii)	(iv)	(i)
(3)	(iii)	(iv)	(i)	(ii)
(4)	(iv)	(i)	(ii)	(iii)

317. Match the following and choose your answer according to the codes given below

Views	Schools
(a) deny sāmāṅya	(i) Nyaya-Vaiśesika
(b) deny viśeṣa	(ii) Jainism
(c) accepts both	(iii) Buddhism
(d) distinction is relative	(iv) Saṁkhya and Advaita Vedanta

Codes :	(a)	(b)	(c)	(d)
(1)	(iii)	(iv)	(i)	(ii)
(2)	(iv)	(iii)	(ii)	(i)
(3)	(ii)	(i)	(iii)	(iv)
(4)	(i)	(ii)	(iii)	(iv)

318. Match the following and choose the answer from the codes given below

(a) Ordinary cognition (i) Mati
(b) Knowledge through words (ii) Śruti
(c) Direct knowledge (iii) Avadhi
(d) Telepathic Knowledge (iv) Manaḥparyāya
(e) Perfect knowledge (v) Kevala

Codes :	(a)	(b)	(c)	(d)	(e)
(1)	(v)	(iv)	(iii)	(ii)	(i)
(2)	(iv)	(iii)	(ii)	(i)	(v)
(3)	(i)	(ii)	(iii)	(iv)	(v)
(4)	(i)	(ii)	(v)	(iv)	(iii)

319. Match the following and choose the answer from the codes given below.

I	II
(a) Desires to know the details	(i) Vyañjanā vagraha
(b) Recognition as this and not that	(ii) Arthāvagraha
(c) Relates subject to the object	(iii) Ihā

(d) An impression results — (iv) Avāya
(e) Consciousness is excited and a sensation felt — (v) Dhāraṇa

Codes :

	(a)	(b)	(c)	(d)	(e)
(1)	(i)	(ii)	(iii)	(iv)	(v)
(2)	(iii)	(iv)	(i)	(v)	(ii)
(3)	(ii)	(iii)	(v)	(i)	(iv)
(4)	(iii)	(iv)	(v)	(i)	(ii)

320. Match the following and choose the answer from the codes given below

Schools	Theories
(a) Jainism	(i) Hedonism
(b) Theravāda	(ii) Anuvrata
(c) Lokāyata	(iii) Sarvāstivāda
(d) Mahāyāna	(iv) Triratna
	(v) Apohavāda

Codes :

	(a)	(b)	(c)	(d)
(1)	(ii)	(iv)	(v)	(iii)
(2)	(ii)	(iii)	(i)	(v)
(3)	(v)	(iv)	(i)	(ii)
(4)	(i)	(iii)	(iv)	(v)

321. Match the following and choose the answer from the codes given below

(a) Vedanā	(i) Be indulged in pleasure
(b) Upādāna	(ii) All the six senses including mind
(c) Ṣaḍāyatana	(iii) Primary consciousness of the embryo
(d) Vijñāna	(iv) Sense perception

Codes :

	(a)	(b)	(c)	(d)
(1)	(i)	(iv)	(ii)	(iii)
(2)	(iv)	(i)	(iii)	(ii)
(3)	(iv)	(i)	(ii)	(iii)
(4)	(i)	(iv)	(iii)	(ii)

322. Match the following pairs and choose the answer from the codes given below

Schools of Buddhism	Theories
(a) Mādhyamika	(i) Śunyavāda
(b) Yogācāra	(ii) Vijñānavāda
(c) Vaibhāṣika	(iii) Vāhyapratyakṣavada
(d) Sautrantika	(iv) Vāhyānumeyavada

Codes :

	(a)	(b)	(c)	(d)
(1)	(i)	(ii)	(iii)	(iv)
(2)	(ii)	(iii)	(iv)	(i)
(3)	(iii)	(iv)	(i)	(ii)
(4)	(iv)	(i)	(ii)	(iii)

323. Match the following and find out the correct answer from the codes given below

(a) Mādhyamika	
(b) Yogācāra	(i) Hinayāna
(c) sautrāntika	(ii) Mahāyāna
(d) Vaibhāṣika	

Codes :	(a)	(b)	(c)	(d)
(1)	(i)	(ii)	(i)	(ii)
(2)	(ii)	(ii)	(i)	(i)
(3)	(i)	(i)	(ii)	(ii)
(4)	(ii)	(i)	(ii)	(i)

324. Match the following

(a) Mādhyamika	(i) External objects are perceived by us
(b) Yogācāra	(ii) External objects are inferred
(c) Vaibhāsika	(iii) External objects are mere ideas of mind
(d) Sautrāntika	(iv) External objects are indescribable

Codes :	(a)	(b)	(c)	(d)
(1)	(i)	(ii)	(iii)	(iv)
(2)	(ii)	(i)	(iv)	(iii)
(3)	(iv)	(iii)	(i)	(ii)
(4)	(iii)	(iv)	(ii)	(i)

325. Match the following

List-I	List-II
(a) Syad asti	(i) Relatively real
(b) Syad-nasti	(ii) Relatively unreal
(c) Syad-asti nasti	(iii) Relatively real and unreal

(d) Syad-avaktavya (iv) Relatively indescribable

Codes :	(a)	(b)	(c)	(d)
(1)	(i)	(ii)	(iii)	(iv)
(2)	(iv)	(iii)	(ii)	(i)
(3)	(i)	(iv)	(iii)	(ii)
(4)	(ii)	(iv)	(iii)	(i)

326. Match the following

List-I	List-II
(a) Nayavada	(i) Jainism
(b) Materialism	(ii) Carvaka
(c) Syad-asti avaktavya	(iii) Relatively real and indescribable
(d) Syad nasti avaktavya	(iv) Relatively unreal and indescribable

Codes :	(a)	(b)	(c)	(d)
(1)	(i)	(ii)	(iii)	(iv)
(2)	(iv)	(ii)	(iii)	(i)
(3)	(iii)	(ii)	(iv)	(i)
(4)	(ii)	(iv)	(iii)	(i)

327. Match the following

List-I	List-II
(1) Four Noble Truth	(i) There is suffering
(2) Theory of Momentariness	(ii) Buddhism
(3) Anekantavada	(iii) Jainism
(4) Hedonistic	(iv) Carvaka

Codes :	(a)	(b)	(c)	(d)
(1)	(i)	(ii)	(iii)	(iv)
(2)	(iv)	(iii)	(ii)	(i)
(3)	(i)	(iv)	(iii)	(ii)
(4)	(ii)	(iv)	(iii)	(i)

328. Match the following

List-I	List-II
(a) Syadvada	(i) Epistemology
(b) Anekantavada	(ii) Metaphysics
(c) No soul theory	(iii) Buddhism
(d) Pleasure	(iv) Carvaka

Codes :	(a)	(b)	(c)	(d)
(1)	(i)	(ii)	(iii)	(iv)
(2)	(iv)	(iii)	(ii)	(i)
(3)	(iv)	(ii)	(iii)	(i)
(4)	(ii)	(iv)	(iii)	(i)

329. Match the following

List-I	List-II
(a) Madhyamika	(i) Nagarjuna
(b) Yogacara	(ii) Dinnaga
(c) Sautrantika	(iii) Critical realist
(d) Vaibhasika	(iv) Direct realist

Codes :	(a)	(b)	(c)	(d)
(1)	(i)	(ii)	(iii)	(iv)
(2)	(iv)	(iii)	(ii)	(i)
(3)	(ii)	(iii)	(i)	(iv)
(4)	(iv)	(ii)	(iii)	(i)

330. Match the following

List-I	List-II
(a) Sunyata	(i) Buddhism
(b) Yogacara	(ii) Subjective idealist
(c) Truth	(iii) Relative
(d) Dinnaga	(iv) Apohavada

Codes :	(a)	(b)	(c)	(d)
(1)	(i)	(ii)	(iii)	(iv)
(2)	(ii)	(iii)	(iv)	(i)
(3)	(iv)	(iii)	(ii)	(i)
(4)	(iv)	(ii)	(iii)	(i)

331. Match the following

List-I	List-II
(a) Syadvada	(i) Seven propositions
(b) Pramana	(ii) Means of valid knowledge
(c) Vaibhasika	(iii) Direct realist
(d) Sautrantika	(iv) Critical realist

Codes :	(a)	(b)	(c)	(d)
(1)	(i)	(ii)	(iii)	(iv)
(2)	(iv)	(iii)	(ii)	(i)
(3)	(iv)	(ii)	(iii)	(i)
(4)	(ii)	(iv)	(iii)	(i)

332. Match the following

List-I	List-II
(a) Nirvana	(i) Buddhism
(b) Critique of inference	(ii) Carvaka
(c) Paryaya	(iii) Jainism
(d) Syad asti, nasti avaktavya	(iv) Relatively real, unreal and indescribable

Codes :	(a)	(b)	(c)	(d)
(1)	(i)	(ii)	(iii)	(iv)
(2)	(iv)	(iii)	(ii)	(i)
(3)	(iv)	(ii)	(iii)	(i)
(4)	(ii)	(iv)	(iii)	(i)

333. Match the following

List-I	List-II
(a) Akasa	(i) Rupa
(b) Ksiti	(ii) Sabda
(c) Tejah	(iii) Gandha
(d) Marut	(iv) Sparsa

Codes :	(a)	(b)	(c)	(d)
(1)	(i)	(ii)	(iii)	(iv)
(2)	(ii)	(iii)	(i)	(iv)
(3)	(i)	(iii)	(ii)	(iv)
(4)	(iii)	(ii)	(iv)	(i)

Directions. In the questions given below are two statements labelled as Assertion (A) and Reason (R). In the context of the two statements which one of the following is correct?

Codes :

(1) Both A and R are true and R is the correct explanation of A

(2) Both A and R are true, but R is not the correct explanation of A

(3) A is true, but R is false

(4) A is false, but R is true

334. **Assertion (A).** Inference as a valid source of knowledge is rejected by cārvāka.

Reason (R). We proceed here from known to the unknown and there is no certainty in this, though some inferences may turn out to be accidently true.

335. **Assertion (A).** According to cārvāka, deductive inference is merely an argument in a circle (the fallacy of petitio principii).

Reason (R). The conclusion is already contained in the major premise.

336. **Assertion (A).** According to Cārvāka, inductive inference is uncertain.

Reason (R). Inductive inference proceeds unwarrentedly from the known to the unknown.

337. **Assertion (A).** Cārvāka criticizes inference.

Reason (R). Perception does not prove vyāpti.

338. **Assertion (A).** Cārvāka says that the Vedas are not reliable.

Reason (R). According to cārvāka, Vedas, the work of cunning priests, are written for the benefits of a particular class.

339. **Assertion (A).** Cārvāka emphasizes that the supposition of God as creator is unnecessary.

Reason (R). The world comes into existence by the spontaneous combination of material elements.

340. **Assertion (A).** Cārvāka accepts soul.

Reason (R). The existence of a soul.

341. **Assertion (A).** According to cārvāka, no wise man would willingly work for liberation.

Reason (R). Liberation in the sense of destruction of the sufferings can be obtained only by death.

342. **Assertion (A).** Wealth is not an end in itself.

Reason (R). Wealth is good only as a means to enjoyment.

343. **Assertion (A).** A substance, according to Jaina, is real.

Reason (R). All the three elements that characterize reality are there in a substance.

344. **Assertion (A).** Jaina theory says that change and permanenence are both real.

Reason (R). Reality consists of three factors : permanence, origination and decay.

345. **Assertion (A).** The essential characters of a substance remain in the substance as long as the substance remains.

Reason (R). Without essential character, the substance will cease to be what it is.

346. **Assertion (A).** Without ākāsā substances could not be extended.

Reason (R). Jainas suppose that the function of akāsā is to provide room for the existence of all extended substances.

347. **Assertion (A).** The self reveals its own nature as well as that of the object, according to Jainism.

Reason (R). The consciousness of the jiva is ever active.

348. **Assertion (A).** The Jaina says that the bondage occurs because of the association of matter with body.

Reason (R). The association of matter with body limitize the soul.

349. **Assertion (A).** Cārvāka did not favour the use of inference to establish metaphysical categories.

Reason (R). He believed that through inference we can acquire indubitable knowledge.

350. **Assertion (A).** According to Jainism liberation is possible only after annihilation of the body.

Reason (R). Only elimination of the matter with which the soul is already mingled will lead to liberation.

351. **Assertion (A).** Perfect peace in Buddhism is not in the pleasures gained through the fulfillment of desires.

Reason (R). Perfect peace in Buddhism is a state of calmness, evenness and passionless self possession.

352. **Assertion (A).** Buddhists deny the reality of pudgals.

Reason (R). All the pudgals are creations.

353. **Assertion (A).** Buddhists deny the universals as independent substance.

Reason (R). Universals are nothing but only mental creations.

354. **Assertion (A).** Astāngamārga of Buddhism teaches us the practice of yoga.

Reason (R). Astāngamārga of Buddhism is an ethical way of living.

355. **Assertion (A).** According to yogācāra mind can not be regarded as unreal.

Reason (R). For them all reasoning and thinking would be false.

356. **Assertion (A).** Materialism is followed by Carvaka.

Reason (R). Carvaka believes in hedomistic world.

357. **Assertion (A).** Carvaka believes in perception only.

Reason (R). Carvaka rejects inference and verbal testimony.

358. **Assertion (A).** Carvaka says that inference is regarded a mere leap in the dark.

Reason (R). Vyapti is not proved by perception.

359. **Assertion (A).** Shunyavada Buddhism rejects inference.

Reason (R). Advaita vedanta also rejects inference.

360. **Assertion (A).** Carvaka criticises shabda.

Reason (R). Vedas are regarded as the works of cunning priests.

361. **Assertion (A).** According to Jainism, everything is regarded as relative.

Reason (R). Everything is regarded as conditional.

362. **Assertion (A).** Jaina metaphysics is referred as Avekantavada.

Reason (R). It means the doctrine of manyness of reality.

363. **Assertion (A).** Jaina metaphysics is regarded as realistic and relativistic pluralist.

Reason (R). Jaina says that truth is regarded as relative.

364. **Assertion (A).** The three basics of Buddhism as a religion are : the Buddha, the Dhamma and the Sangha.

Reason (R). The three basic features of Buddhist Philosophy are : Anicca, Asatta and Dukkha.

365. Cārvāka's theory can be kept under

A. atheism B. naturalism
C. mechanism D. positivism

Choose your answer from the codes given below

(1) only A (2) A and C
(3) A, B, C and D (4) B and D

366. Sautrantika believes in

(1) reality of mind.
(2) reality of external objects.
(3) Non-reality of mind.
(4) Non-reality of external objects.

Select the correct answer using the codes given below :

(1) 1 and 2 (b) 2 and 3
(3) 3 and 4 (d) 1 and 4

367. Find out the conclusion given by syādvāda and choose your answer from the codes given below

A. All judgments are double-edged in their character
B. All things are existent as well as non-existent
C. A thing is what it is and is not what it is not
D. All negation has a positive basis

(1) A and C (b) A, B and D
(3) B, C and D (d) A, B, C and D

368. Four Noble Truth says that

A. there is a suffering.
B. there is a cause of suffering.
C. there is a cessation of suffering.
D. there is a way leading to a cessation of suffering.

Choose your answer from the codes given below

(1) A and B (b) B and C
(3) A and D (d) All of these

369. Yogacara believes in

A. subjective idealism
B. rejection of external objects.
C. non-subjective idealism.
D. non-rejection of external objects.

Choose your answer from the codes given below

(1) A and B (b) B and C
(3) B and D (d) C and D

370. Madhyamika believe in

A. Nagarjuna teachings.
B. dialectical skill.
C. non-dialectical skill.
D. jainism teachings.

Choose your answer from the codes given below

(1) A and B (b) B and C
(3) C and D (d) B and D

371. Liberated souls attain the fourfold perfection (ananta catustaya). These are

A. infinite knowledge B. infinite faith
C. infinite power D. infinite bliss

Choose the answer from the codes given below

(1) A, B and C (2) B, C and D
(3) A, B, C and D (4) A, B and D

372. In the chain of twelve links given by Buddha, which among the following is related to past life?

A. Avidya B. Saṁskāra
C. Bhava D. Jāti
E. Jarāmarana

Choose the answer from the following codes

(1) C & D (2) A & B
(3) C & E (4) A & D

373. Dinnaga believes in

A. Apohavada B. Perception
C. Carvaka D. Jainism

Choose your answer from the codes given below

(1) A and B (2) B and C
(3) B and D (4) A and D

374. Which among the following are accepted by śunyavādin Buddhists?
A. External object are originated
B. External objects are qualityless
C. External objects are a mere form of ideas
D. External objects are nothing but are only matters
Choose your answer from the codes given below
(1) A and B (b) A and D
(3) B and C (d) C and D

375. Hinayana school contains
A. Vaibhasika B. Sautrantika
C. Non-vaibhasika D. Sunyata
Choose your answer from the codes given below
(1) A and B (2) B and C
(3) C and D (4) B and D

376. Mahayana school contains
A. Yogacara B. Madhyamika
C. Sautrantika D. Vaibhasika
Choose your answer from the codes given below
(1) A and B (2) B and C
(3) B and D (4) C and D

377. Buddhism believes in
A. pratityasamutpada
B. non-pratityasamutpada
C. theory of no soul
D. soul theory
Choose your answer from the codes given below
(1) A and B (2) B and C
(3) C and D (4) A and C

378. Which statements are correct about Dinnaga? Choose your answer from the codes given below the statements
A. He accepts only two pramanas-pratyakṣa and anumāna
B. His theory is known as Apohavāda
C. He accepts comparison as a source of knowledge
D. He was the pupil of Dharmakirti
Codes :
(1) A and B (b) A and D
(3) B and C (d) C and D

379. Consider the following statements According to the Nyāya-Vaiśeṣika school
A. light is the absence of darkness
B. darkness is the absence of light
C. darkness is a distinct substance
D. our perception of colour and movement in darkness is illusory.
Which of the above statements are correct?
(1) A and C (2) B and D
(3) A and D (4) C and D

380. Which of the following are acceptable to Nyāya?
A. God is the nimittakāraṇa of the world
B. God is a form of ātman
C. God is the samavāyikāraṇa of the world
D. Is characterised by its power to motivate one to action
Codes:
(1) A alone is true (2) A and C are true
(3) B alone is true (4) B and A are true

381. Which among the following statements is true according to Nyāya system
(1) Knowledge manifests itself
(2) Knowledge manifests nothing
(3) Knowledge manifests only padārthas
(4) Knowledge manifests all its objects

382. According to Nyāya, pramā is
(1) yathārtha smṛti (2) ayathartha smṛti
(3) yathārthānubhavā
(4) ayathārthānubhavā

383. Which among the following knowledges is pramā?
(1) Saṁsaya (2) Pratyakṣa
(3) Bhrama (4) Tarka

384. In how many kinds are the pramās divided in the Nyāya philosophy?
(1) 4 (2) 3
(3) 2 (4) 6

385. Pramā means
(1) Valid representative cognition
(2) Non-valid representative cognition
(3) Valid presentative cognition
(4) Non-valid presentative cognition

386. Apramā means
(1) Valid presentative cognition
(2) Non-valid presentative cognition
(3) Valid representative cognition
(4) Non-valid representative cognition

387. According to Nyāya, the source, by which pramā obtained, is known as
(1) Pramāṇa (2) Pratyakṣa
(3) Anumāna (4) Kaivalya

388. Parimana of manas according to Vaisesika school is
(1) Bibhu Parimana (2) Mahat Parimana
(3) Anuparimana (4) Misra Parimana

389. According to Nyāya Philosophy saṁśaya is an indefinite knowledge. Saṁśaya is obtained when
(1) Mind compares between two objects
(2) Mind replaces one object by other
(3) Mind is presented between two objects
(4) None of the above

390. How many characteristics of pramā is given in Nyāya Philosophy?
(1) 1 (2) 3
(3) 5 (4) 7

391. How many pramānas are accepted by Nyāya?
(1) 1 (2) 2
(3) 3 (4) 4

392. Which among the following is not an independent source of knowledge according to Nyāya?
(1) Authority (2) Comparison
(3) Implication (4) Inference

393. Which among the following are not the kinds of pratyakṣa according to Nyāya Vaiśeṣika
(1) Sāmānyalakṣana and Jñānalakṣana
(2) Laukika and Alaukika
(3) Suvikalpa and Nirvikalpa
(4) Vāhya and Āntara

394. Nyāya theory of knowledge can be kept under
(1) Idealism (2) Realism
(3) Subjective Idealism
(4) None of the above

395. According to Nyāya, Perception is
(1) Presentative process
(2) Representative process
(3) Complex presentative-representative process
(4) None of the above

396. According to Nyāya, In determinate perception we relate
(1) God to human beings
(2) Substance to its attributes
(3) Mind to matter
(4) Attributes to its modes

397. Nirvikalpa pratyakṣa, according to Nyāya, presents
(1) Bare object without any characterization
(2) Object with its characteristics
(3) Only characteristics not objects
(4) None of the above

398. Which system among the following holds that liberated souls lack even consciousness
(1) Nyaya (2) Jaina
(3) Samkhya (4) Yoga

399. Nyāya divides ordinary perception in
(1) mānasa and bāhya
(2) sāmānyalakṣana, Jñānalakṣana and yogaja

(3) savikalpa and nirvekalpa
(4) none of the above

400. Which perception, according to Nyāya, gives the knowledge of pain?
(1) Indeterminate (2) Determinate
(3) Internal ordinary (4) External ordinary

401. The external sense-organs are composed of
(1) earth, water, fire and ether
(2) earth, water, fire, air and space
(3) earth and fire
(4) earth and water

402. The theory of illusion accepted by Nyāya is known as
(1) Khyātivāda (2) Akhyātivada
(3) Anyathākhyātivāda
(4) Anirvacaniyakhyātivāda

403. 'Anyathākyāti' is based on which among the following kinds of perception?
(1) Sāmāanyalkṣana (2) Jñānalakṣana
(3) Yogaja (4) Laukika

404. How many propositions does the Nyāya syllogism have?
(1) 2 (2) 3
(3) 5 (4) 4

405. Which among the following is involved in Nyāya inference?
(1) Deduction (2) Induction
(3) Neither deduction nor induction
(4) Deduction and induction both

406. Which among the following is true meaning of samavyāpti?
(1) Vyāpti between two terms of equal extension
(2) Vyāpti between two terms of unequal extension
(3) Vyāpti between hetu and pratijñā
(4) None of the above

407. In how many steps may the Nyāya method of induction be analysed?
(1) 1 (2) 3
(3) 4 (4) 6

408. According to Vaisesika, 'humanity' in human beings is due to
(1) particularity (2) inherence
(3) coherence (4) generality

409. Liṅgaparāmarśa is
(1) a way of talking
(2) a manner in which middle term is related to major term
(3) a kind of induction
(4) a kind of deduction

410. How many characteristics of middle term are given by Nyāya-Vaiśeṣikas
(1) 1 (2) 3
(3) 7 (4) 5

411. According to Nyāya, which kind of inference is based on mere coexistence?
(1) Parārthānumāna
(2) Purvavat anumāna
(3) Śeṣavat anumāna
(4) Sāmānyatodrṣta anumāna

412. Which among the following anumanās are based on causation?
(1) Svārtha and parārtha
(2) Purvavat and sāmānyatodrṣṭa
(3) Purvavat and śeṣavat
(4) Kevalānvayi and kevalvyatireki.

413. Who reduced Upamana to inference?
(1) Samkhya (2) Vaisesika
(3) Both (1) and (2)
(4) Advaita Vedanta

414. In Pūrvavat anumāna, we infer
(1) the unperceived effect from a perceived cause
(2) the unperceived cause from a perceived effect
(3) not on the basis of causation but on uniformity of co-existence

(4) imperceptible cause from perceptible effects

415. According to Vaisesika, "The donkey is not a horse." is an example of
(1) Pragabhava (2) Dhvamsabhava
(3) Atyantabhava (4) Anyonyabhava

416. Pramāna in Indian philosophy implies
(1) means of knowledge
(2) means of valid knowledge
(3) means of invalid knowledge
(4) the thing to be known

417. The Vaisesikas hold that the parimana of the trasarenu is due to
(1) the parimana of the paramanus
(2) the parimana of the dryanukas
(3) the number of its constituent dryanukas
(4) the number of the paramanus

418. The Naiyāyikas accepts cognition of non-existence as generated by
(1) Perception (2) Inference
(3) Comparison (4) Verbal testimony

419. Which of the following doctrines regarding the validity of knowledge is advocated by the Nyāya-Vaiśeṣika system?
(1) Extrinsic validity of knowledge
(2) Intrinsic validity of knowledge
(3) The idealistic theory of knowledge
(4) The illusory theory of knowledge

420. The Samavayikarana of the world according to the Vaisesikas is
(1) Paramanu (2) Dvyanuka
(3) Trasarenu (4) None of these

421. Which one of the following is correct according to nyāya?
(1) Sāmānya is unreal
(2) Sāmānya is non-eternal
(3) Sāmānya is an objective entity
(4) Sāmānya is a subjective concept

422. Classical Vaisesika system is known as
(1) science of soul
(2) science of thinking
(3) science of meditation
(4) science of categories

423. Which among the following means of knowledge is produced by the knowledge of resemblance or similarity?
(1) Pratyakṣa (2) Anumāna
(3) Upamāna (4) Śabda

424. Which among the following conditions is violated by the statement, 'water the plant with fire'
(1) Ākāṅkṣa (2) Yogyata
(3) Sannidhi (4) Tātparya

425. In which pramāna arthāpatti is reduced by Naiyayikas?
(1) Pratyakṣa (2) Anumāna
(3) Upamāna (4) Śabda

426. Abhāva is reduced to
(1) Pratyakṣa (2) Anumāna
(3) Either to pratyakṣa or to anumāna
(4) Neither to pratyakṣa nor to anumāna

427. According to Nyāya, God is
(1) Creator (2) Maintainer
(3) Destroyer (4) All of these

428. Which of the following is related to the unseen power Adṛṣṭa?
(1) Not able to see (2) Able to see
(3) Stock of merit and demerit
(4) Lord of all the karmas

429. God is known as padāt when he is introduced as
(1) the producer of the significant meaning of the words related to objects
(2) a creater
(3) a maintainer (4) a destroyer

430. Which of the following meanings of padārtha is accepted by Nyāya-Vaiśeṣika?

(1) An object which is base of substance and qualities
(2) An object which can be thought and named
(3) An object which is similar to God
(4) None of the above

431. The theory of atomistic pluralism is accepted by
(1) Saṁkhya-yoga (2) Vedānta
(3) Nyāya-Vaiśeṣika (4) Mimaṁsa

432. According to Nyāya-Vaiśeṣikas which among the following is correct?
(1) Consciousness is the essence of soul
(2) Consciousness resides out of self
(3) Consciousness is not the essence of self
(4) Consciousness is essence of mind

433. How many padārthas are accepted by Vaiśeṣika?
(1) 2 (2) 4
(3) 6 (4) 7

434. Which among the following does not come under Vaiśeṣika's padārtha?
(1) Karma (2) Saṁavaya
(3) Sāmāñya (4) Abhāva

435. God according to Nyaya is
(1) material cause of the world
(2) efficient cause of the world
(3) Both (1) and (2)
(4) Neither (1) nor (2)

436. Which among the following is true about vaiśeṣika's substance
(1) It signifies the self subsistence, the absolute and independent nature of things
(2) It is the substratum where actions and qualities inhere
(3) It is the coexistent material cause of the composite things produced from it
(4) All of the above

437. How many substances are considered by Vaiśeṣikas?
(1) 7 (2) 5
(3) 9 (4) 16

438. Which among the following is the cause of our cognitions of east and west, here and there, near and far
(1) Ākāsha (2) Kāla
(3) Dik (4) Vāyu

439. Which among the following are objective forms of experience
(1) Time and space
(2) Earth, water, fire, and air
(3) Mind and spirit
(4) None of the above

440. How many qualities are mentioned by Kaṇāda?
(1) 7 (2) 17
(3) 16 (4) 24

441. For its existence qualities depend on
(1) Padarthas (2) God
(3) Karma (4) Dravya

442. Who among the following added seven more into the number of qualities mentioned by Kaṇada?
(1) Praśastapāda (2) Vasudeva
(3) Nagarjuna (4) Siṁhamitra

443. Who propounds that there is internal difference in God?
(1) Shankara (2) Ramanuja
(3) Kapil (4) Patanjali

444. The sense-object contact needed for perceiving the abhava of pot on the ground, according to Nyaya is
(1) Visesanata
(2) Samyukta Visesanata
(3) Yogyanupalabdhi
(4) Samavaya

445. According to Nyāya-Vaiśeṣika atoms are different with each other
(1) Only in quality

(2) In quality and quantity both
(3) Only in quantity
(4) None of the above

446. 'The validity and invalidity of knowledge are due to extraneous conditions'. This view is maintained by
(1) Nyāya (2) Sāṁkhya
(3) Mimāṁsa (4) Vedānta

447. The Asamavayi karana of the creation of the world according to the Vaisesikas is
(1) Paramanu (2) Dvyanuka
(3) Paramanusamyoga
(4) Trasarenu

448. According to the Vaisesikas, liberation (nihsreyasa) is attained by
(1) Tattvajnana alone
(2) Practicing the Dharmas prescribed by God
(3) Tattvajnana along with practicing the Dharmas prescribed by God
(4) None of the above

449. According to the Vaisesika school, the universal 'cowness' is
(1) non-eternal and many
(2) eternal and many
(3) eternal, one and residing in many
(4) non-eternal and one

450. Vyapti can be properly defined as
(1) invariable concomitance
(2) causal relation
(3) sequence (4) None of these

451. Which out of the following does not refute perception as a valid means of knowledge?
(1) Jayarashi Bhatta (2) Sri Harsha
(3) Goutama (4) Nagarjuna

452. Sakti has how many meanings?
(1) One (2) Two
(3) Three (4) Four

453. Nyaya-Vaishesika gives how many arguments in favour of the existence of God?
(1) Eight (2) Nine
(3) Ten (4) Five

454. What was the founder name of Nyaya School?
(1) Gotama (2) Purva-Mimamsa
(3) Sankhya (4) Kapila

455. Substance, quality is referred as what?
(1) Padarthas (2) Category
(3) Both (1) and (2) (4) Criteria

456. Guna is regarded as what?
(1) Independent reality
(2) Dependent reality
(3) Actual reality (4) Relevant reality

457. Asatkaryavada is regarded as what?
(1) Arambhaivada (2) Satkaryavada
(3) Rational (4) Adventure

458. According to Nyaya-Vaisesika, effect does not pre-exist in what?
(1) Cause (2) Invariable consequent
(3) Variable (4) Antecelat

459. Samavayi is regarded as what?
(1) Kind of cause (2) Kind of action
(3) No cause (4) Kind of rationality

460. According to Nyāya, Upamāna gives us knowledge about
(1) two similar Vastu in the world
(2) the relation between Vācaka and the Vācya meant by it
(3) similarity in the uses of words
(4) perceived similarity between Vastu

461. Vaiśeṣikas do not accept testimony as an independent source of knowledge because
(1) Testimony can be included under inference
(2) Vedas are not reliable
(3) No one is authorised
(4) Words are non-eternal

462. 'Smṛtirūpaḥ Paratrapūrva Dṛṣtāvabhāsaḥ Adhyasaḥ' is the definition of error given by
(1) Nyāya-Vaiśeṣika (2) Prabhākara
(3) Śankara (4) Kumārila

463. Which one of the following pairs is correctly matched?
(1) Dvaita : Anyathākhyāti
(2) Nyāya-Vaiśeṣika : Satkhyāti
(3) Advaita Vedānta : Anyathākhyāti
(4) Viśiṣtādvaita : Anirvacaniva-khyāti

464. Which one of the following views is not correct according to Vaiśeṣika?
(1) Atoms are eternal
(2) Compounds made of atoms are not eternal
(3) All atoms are of the same kind
(4) Atoms are known by inference

465. According to Nyāya-Vaiśesika sāmānya abides in
(1) quality, relation and particular
(2) substance, quality and action
(3) substance, action and absence
(4) substance, only

466. 'A dog is called a dog'. because it is different from all objects which are not dog. 'A dog therefore, means not a non-dog'. This argument is advanced by
(1) Janism (2) Nyāya-vaiśesika
(3) Buddhism (4) Advaita vedānta

467. Which one of the following is not a component of parārthānumāna?
(1) Jainism (2) Upanaya
(3) Udāharana (4) Parāmarśa

468. Which one of the following is not a case of an ordinary perception?
(1) Dhanaraj is absent in the class
(2) Listen to the melodious tunes of a singer
(3) The piece of a sandalwood on the top of the building is fragrant
(4) I know that potness inheres in the pot

469. According to Nyāya-Vaiśeṣika Abhāva is known by
(1) perception (2) non-apprehension
(3) inference (4) recognition

470. According to Nyāya school, Vyāpti is a
(1) relation and a resemblance
(2) resemblance and recognition
(3) relation and a rule
(4) recognition and a rule

471. Which one of the following is a case of invalid knowledge according to Nyāya school
(1) Horns of hare (2) Tarka
(3) Blue pot
(4) Healthy Devadatta does not eat during the day

472. .... himself has not specifically mentioned God, it was developed by the later Nyāya and Vaiśeṣika school
(1) Gautama (2) Kaṇāda
(3) Sankara (4) Rāmānuja

473. .... aphorism, 'the authority of the Veda is due to its being His word' has been interpreted as 'the Veda is the Word of God' by the commentators.
(1) Gautama's (2) Saṅkara's
(3) Kapila's (4) Kaṇāda's

474. Which one of the following pairs of Schools accept Upamāna as an independent source of knowledge?
(1) Sāṁkhya and Vedānta
(2) Buddhism and Nyāya
(3) Vadānta and Pūrva-mimāmsā
(4) Pūrva-mimāmsā and Yoga

475. Arthāpatti and Anupalabdhi are accepted as valid sources of knowledge by
(1) Sāṁkhya (2) Yoga
(3) Advaita (4) Nyāya

476. 'Error consists in not cognizing the difference between the real and illusory object.' this view is advocated by

(1) Kumārila (2) Prabhākara
(3) Saṅkara (4) Nyāya-vaiśesika

477. According to which school of Indian metaphysics, the atoms of space, time, ether, mind, earth, water, fire and air are perfect, eternal and inorganic?
(1) Sānkhya (2) Nyāya-Vaiśeṣika
(3) Vedānta (4) Buddhism

478. Which one of the following has not been treated as a category in Vaiśeṣika philosophy?
(1) Substance (2) Attributes
(3) Karma (4) Artha

479. Which one of the following theses according to Vaiśeṣika entails that mind (Manas) can perceive things only one at a time?
(1) The order of things being present in succession
(2) Things being different in nature
(3) The mind being atomic in nature
(4) The fact that object cannot come in contact with the senses all at once

480. According to Nyāya-vaiśeṣika consciousness is
(1) the nature of the individual self
(2) a permanent quality of the individual self
(3) an impermanent quality of the individual self
(4) a function of the individual self

481. Sāmānya, in the Vaiśeṣika system stands for
(1) the genus (2) the species
(3) class concept or universal
(4) an idea in the mind

482. According to Nyāya-Vaiśeṣika the number 'one' is directly perceived, but other numbers are
(1) inferred
(2) indirectly perceived
(3) conceived
(4) known by comparison

483. According to the Naiyāyikas the knowledge resulting from upamāna-pramāṇa is that of
(1) similarity
(2) the relation between the name and its object
(3) the relation between a universal type and its particular
(4) a new object

484. According to Nyāya, 'Ice looks cold' is an example of
(1) sāmānyalakṣana (2) jnānalakṣaṇa
(3) yogajalakṣaṇa
(4) laukika ṣannikarṣa

485. According to Nyāya-Vaiśeṣika, the non existence of a jar on the floor is perceived by an eye because
(1) the eye is in contact with the floor, which is qualified by the floorness
(2) the eye is in contact with the floor, which is qualified by the non-existence of the jar
(3) there is no jar qualified by floorness
(4) there is only floor not qualified by jarness

486. Consider the following inference :
'Sky-flower' is fragrant as it has got flowerness in it'.
This inference commits the fallacy of
(1) anaikāntika (2) satpratipakṣa
(3) bādhita (4) āśrayāsiddhi

487. According to the Naiyāyikas prama is
(1) manifestation of objects
(2) apprehension which agrees with the real character of the object apprehended
(3) revelatory of reality
(4) knowledge of an object with qualities which exist in the object

488. 'Nirvāṇa' in Hinayāna Buddhism means
(1) the burning out of a lamp
(2) self-realisation
(3) attaining eternal existence
(4) cessation of all sufferings

489. Which one of the following, according to the Vaiśeṣikas, Justifies the distinction between qualities and actions?
(1) Qualities are characterised by universals, while actins are not characterised by universals
(2) Qualities inhere in substances while actions inhere in qualities
(3) Many qualities may inhere simultaneously in the same substance, but many actions cannot
(4) All qualities are non-eternal, while some actions are eternal

490. Which one of the following arguments according to Nyāya supports the moral law of Karma?
(1) Causal argument
(2) The authority of scriptures
(3) The anti-theistic arguments
(4) The argument from adṛsta (unseen)

491. According to Nyāya logic Implication is included under
(1) Kevalānvayi inference
(2) Kevalavyātireki inference
(3) Anvayvyātireki inference
(4) Sāmānyatodṛsta inference

492. In Advaita Vedānta, the two aspects of Avidyā are called
(1) Māyā and āvaraṇa
(2) Āvaraṇa and avyakta
(3) Avyakta and māyā
(4) Viksepa and āvraṇa

493. According to the Vaiśeṣika School, the Universal 'cowhood' is
(1) eternal, one and residing in many
(2) non-eternal, one and residing in many
(3) non-eternal and many
(4) eternal and many

494. In the statement 'Rose is red' the relation between rose and red, according to vaiśeṣika, is a case of
(1) Saṁyoga (2) Svarūpa
(3) Tādātmya (4) Samavāya

495. According to Nyāya-vaiśeṣika which one of the following represents the correct sequence of the five members of syllogism?
(1) Hetu, Udāharaṇa, Pratijñā, Upanaya, Nigamana
(2) Pratijñā, Udāharaṇa, Hetu, Nigamana, Upanaya
(3) Pratijñā, Hetu, Upanaya, Udāharana, Nigamana
(4) Pratijñā, Hetu, Udāharana, Upanaya, Nigamana

496. According to Nyāya school, vyatireki vyāpti between hetu and sādhya obtains when
(1) all cases of hetu are cases of absence of sādhya
(2) some cases of hetu are cases of sādhya
(3) some cases of sādhya are cases of hetu
(4) all cases of absence of sādhya are cases of absence of hetu

497. Which one of the following alternatives is accepted by the Nyāya system?
(1) Svataḥ-prāmānya, Parataḥ-aprāmānya
(2) Svataḥ-prāmānya, Svataḥ-aprāmānya
(3) Parataḥ-prāmānya, Svataḥ-aprāmānya
(4) Parataḥ-prāmānya, Parataḥ-aprāmānya

498. Which one pair of the following systems accepts correspondence theory of truth?
(1) Vedānta and saṃkhya
(2) Nyāya and vedānta
(3) Mimāmsā and vedānta
(4) Nyāya and cārvāk

499. The substance out of which the effect is produced is known as what?
(1) Material cause (2) Inherent cause
(3) Efficient cause (4) Final cause

500. According to Nyāya, mind is an internal sense organ because it
(1) is assigned the function of thinking and contemplation

(2) cannot establish a direct contact with an object in the external world
(3) can serve as a mediator between soul and the external sense-organs
(4) discriminates between good and bad objects which do not belong to the external world

501. Nyāya maintains two stages in perception, the first is nirvikalpa and the second is
(1) Vikalpa (2) Savikalpa
(3) Avyapadeshya (4) None of these

502. Nyāya-Vaiśeṣika philosophy is both
(1) realistic and dualistic
(2) realistic and monistic
(3) realistic and pluralistic
(4) idealistic and monistic

503. In Vaiśeṣika system, the six positive categories are
(1) Samavāya, Sāmānya, Saṁyoga, Dravya, Guṇa, karma
(2) Samavāya, Sāmānya, Viśeṣa, Dravya, Guṇa, Karma
(3) Atman, Manas Visesa, Dravya, Guṇa, Karma
(4) Samavaya, Samanya Viśeṣa, Dravya, Guna, Paramanu

504. According to vaiśeṣikas, creation of the world begins with
(1) The combination of atoms
(2) The interference of God
(3) The ceremonial performance
(4) combination of five elements

505. 'We accept inference if it is collaborated by perception. But we deny inference if it cannot be so corroborated.'. This view is held by
(1) Vaiśeṣikas
(2) a school of Buddhist logicians
(3) a school of Cārvākas
(4) Tāntrikas

506. According to the Nyāya school, when one visually perceives the fragrance of a distant sandalwood, it is a case of
(1) perception due to sāmānyalakṣaṇa sannikarsa
(2) perception due to vogaja sannikarsa
(3) mrvikalpaka perception
(4) perception due to jñānalaksana sannukarsa

507. In Seṣavat anumana, we infer
(1) the unperceived cause from a perceived effect
(2) by analogy with examples
(3) not on the basis of causation but on uniformity co-existence
(4) the unperceived effect from a perceived cause

508. "Śabda and Upamana are not independent pramana as they are reducible to anumana" This is the view of
(1) Naiyāsyikas (2) Vaiśeṣikas
(3) Vedānta
(4) Prabhākara Mimāṁsakas

509. Which one of the following pairs is not admitted the Vaiśeṣika school?
(1) Savikalpaka pratyakṣa and nirvikalpaka pratyakṣa
(2) Svārthānumana and parārthāmumāna
(3) Ambhava and smṛti
(4) Dṛṣtārthāpātti and śrutārthāpatti

510. Nyāya-Vaiśeṣika believes in
(1) Only nirvikalpa pratyakṣa
(2) Only savikalpa pratyakṣa
(3) Both savikalps and nirvikalpa pratyakṣa
(4) Neither nirvikalpa nor savikalpa pratyakṣa

511. According to the Nyāya school. Anumiti is possible without
(1) Paksa-Jñāna (2) Parāmarsa-jñāna
(3) Sādhva-jñāna (4) Udāharana-jñāna

512. According to Nyāya-Vaiśeṣika Dravya-Guṇa relationship is
(1) Saṁyoga (2) Tādātmya
(3) Samavāya (4) Saṅnikarṣa

513. Which one of the following statements according to the Nvāya-Vaiśeṣikas, does not refer to quality (Guṇa)
(1) Your knowledge about Nyāya-Vaiśeṣika philosophy
(2) Your desire to pass the examination
(3) The white colour of your answer paper
(4) The movement of your hand while writing

514. According to Nyāya, substance and quality are contingently related because
(1) it believes is Asatkāryavād
(2) something can come out of nothing
(3) a change in an object can be noticed only through its qualities
(4) the two belong to two different categories

515. ....literally means a knowable or an object of true knowledge.
(1) Pramāṇa (2) Prameya
(3) Nirṇaya (4) Vitaṇḍā

516. Nyāya-Vaiśeṣika god is
(1) creator (2) destroyer
(3) Administrator (4) Passive agent

517. According to Nyāya which one of the following is not gaṇa?
(1) Nīla (2) Kāla
(3) Utkṣipana (4) sound

518. Which of the following systems is founded by Gautama?
(1) Nyāya (2) Jainism
(3) Sānkhya (4) Buddhism

519. According to Nyāya valid knowledge consists in the manifestation of an object as it really is. It is the application of
(1) Correspondence theory of truth
(2) Coherence theory of truth
(3) Pragmatic theory of truth
(4) Self-evident theory of truth

520. 'Vaiśesikasūtra' is written by
(1) Praśastapāda (2) Kaṇāda
(3) Udayana (4) Sridhara

521. .....literally means 'the meaning of a word' or 'the object signified by a word'.
(1) Padārtha (2) Object
(3) Jñeya (4) Abhidheya

522. Vaiśeṣika divided categories into two classes, bhāva and ....
(1) Dravya (2) Real
(3) Abhāva (4) Abhidheya

523. The vaiśeṣika philosophy is pluralistic and realistic but not.......since it admits spiritual substance.
(1) materialistic (2) Subjective
(3) Idealistic (4) None of these

524. The five gross elements, admitted by the Vaiśeṣikas are earth, water, fire, air and......
(1) Space (2) Ether
(3) Time (4) Mind

525. ....defines indeterminate perception as the non-relational apprehension of an object devoid of all association of name, genus, differentia etc.
(1) Gaṅgeśa (2) Jayanta
(3) Vātsyāyana (4) Gautama

526. The Nyāya philosophy was founded by
(1) Patanjali (2) Gautama
(3) Kaṇāda (4) Udayana

527. Is inference, the second source of knowledge according to Nyāya school?
(1) Yes (2) No
(3) Not certain (4) Question is vague

528. According to Nyāya there are three kinds of alaukika perception viz., sāmānyalakṣana, jñānalakṣaṇa and

(1) Yogaja (2) Mānasa
(3) Ghrāṇja (4) None of these

529. What is an indirect way of justifying a certain conclusion by exposing the absurdity of its contradictory nature?
(1) Nirṇaya (2) Vāda
(3) Tarka (4) Siddhānta

530. The Vaiśeṣika idea of God is wholly transcendent to and separate from
(1) Man and the world
(2) The world
(3) The phenomenal world
(4) None of the above

531. Perception can be classified into..... and alaukika perception.
(1) Laukika (2) Nirvikalpa
(3) Yogaja (4) None of these

532. There are two kinds of testimony, the scriptural and the
(1) Adṛṣṭāntha (2) Secular
(3) Verbal (4) None of these

533. ....is the way of knowing anything truly.
(1) Pramāṇa (2) Prameya
(3) Siddhānta (4) Tarka

534. ....perception is the immediate apprehension, the direct sense experience which is undifferentiated and non-relational and is free from assimilation, discrimination, analysis and synthesis.
(1) Nirvikalpa (2) Savikalpa
(3) Laukika (4) Alaukika

535. The founder of Vaiśeṣika system is
(1) Gautama (2) Patañjali
(3) Udayana (4) Kaṇāda

536. In.............testimony we have the words of God and so it is perfect and infallible by nature.
(1) Vaidika (2) Laukika
(3) Verbal (4) None of these

537. Vaiśeṣika suggests............, guided by God, imparts motion to the atoms and leads to creation for the sake of enjoyment or suffering of the individual souls.
(1) The adṛṣṭa (2) Liberated soul
(3) Absolute knowledge
(4) None of the above

538. ....is the cessation of all life, all consciousness, all bliss, together with all pain and all qualities.
(1) Liberation (2) Creation
(3) Destruction (4) None of these

539. ....is any of the five propositions in which syllogistic inference requires to be stated if it is to prove or demonstrate a doctrine.
(1) Avayava (2) Tarka
(3) Nirṇaya (4) Vitaṇda

540. According to which school, "the atoms of space, time, ether, mind, earth, water, fire and air are perfect and eternal; there can be no question of their creator, they are inorganic"?
(1) Sānkhya (2) Nyāya
(3) Both (1) and (2)
(4) Neither (1) nor (2)

541. ....is certain knowledge about anything, attained by means of any of the legitimate methods of knowledge.
(1) Siddhānta (2) Tarka
(3) Nirṇaya (4) Pramāṇa

542. ....and..............are imperceptible substances, each of which is one eternal and all pervading.
(1) Space, soul (2) Space, time
(3) Manas (4) None of these

543. ....is the internal sense for the perception of the Individual soul and its qualities.
(1) self (2) atman
(3) Manas (4) None of these

544. ....philosophy is mainly interested in the problems of logic and epistemology.
(1) Buddhist (2) Cārvāka
(3) Nyāya (4) Sānkhya

545. The first work of Nyāya philosophy is ....of Gautama.
(1) Nyāyabhāsya
(2) Nyāya-sūtra
(3) Nyāyakusumanjali
(4) Nyāya-darśana

546. Nyāyamañjari is written by
(1) Jayanta (2) Udayana
(3) Uddyotakara (4) Vātsyāyana

547. Nyāya...............suggests, there are four separate sources of true knowledge, these are perception, inference, comparison and testimony.
(1) Theory of knowledge
(2) Theory of physical world
(3) Realism
(4) None of the above

548. 'Tadvachana' means that
(1) The Veda is the Word of the seers
(2) God's word is the basis of all logical statements
(3) God's word is the ultimate judgement
(4) None of the above

549. The Vaiśeṣikas' atomism agrees with the ....atomism.
(1) Nyāya (2) Vedānta
(3) Greek (4) Jaina

550. The atoms are the material cause of this world of which God, assisted by the............, is the efficient cause.
(1) Energy (2) Unseen power
(3) Moral law (4) Soul

551. The Unseen Power, adrṣṭa is..............and needs God as the supervisor and the controller of the world.
(1) Intelligent (2) Unintelligent
(3) Final cause (4) None of these

552. Atoms and.................are co-present and co-eternal with God.
(1) Souls (2) Adrṣṭa
(3) Liberated soul (4) None of these

553. 'These must be an intelligent cause (kartā) for all composite objects of the world's is the...........argument for God's existence.
(1) Causal (2) Ontological
(3) Teleological (4) Metaphysical

554. Our good actions produce a certain efficiency called............and bad actions produce some deficiency called.
(1) Merit, demerit (2) Happiness, sorrow
(3) Joy, sorrow (4) None of these

555. The stock of merit and demerit accruing from good and bad action is called
(1) Adrṣṭa (2) Puṇya-Pāpa
(3) Liberation (4) Bondage

556. Naiyāyikas suggest the authority of the Vedas has its source in the supreme authority of their
(1) Creator (2) Learner
(3) Ruler
(4) Author or āptaprāmanya

557. According to Vaiśeṣika, dharma is that which
(1) Is prescribed by the Veda
(2) Is prescribed by the Veda and has for its purpose and valuable action
(3) Leads to material or spiritual welfare
(4) Is characterized by its power to motivate one to action

558. Nyāya Philosophy is also known as
(1) Akṣapāda system (2) Tarkaśāstra
(3) Both (1) and (2) (4) None of these

559. Ānayanta means
(1) Philosophy (2) Buddhism
(3) Cārvāka (4) Nyāya philosophy

560. The Vaiśeṣika theory of the world is known as
(1) The atomic theory of the world
(2) The ultimate theory of the world
(3) Creation and destruction theory
(4) None of the above

561. I look at a blooming rose from a distance and say 'I see a fragrant rose', it is an example of................perception.
(1) Sāmānyalakṣaṇa (2) Jñānalakṣaṇa
(3) Yogaja (4) None of these

562. According to Vaiśeṣika the first combination of two atoms is called a...............and a combination of three dyads is called a...........
(1) Dvyaṇuka, Tryaṇuka
(2) Trasareṇu, Tryaṇuka
(3) Trasareṇu, Dvyaṇuka
(4) None of the above

563. What is the minimum perceptible object according to Vaiśeṣika philosophy?
(1) Dvyaṇuka (2) Atom
(3) Tryaṇuka (4) None of these

564. Sarva-darśana-saṅgraha is written by
(1) Udayana (2) Gautama
(3) Mādhavācārya (4) Gaṅgeśa

565. ....is the highest universal, since all other universals come under it.
(1) Being-hood (2) Substance
(3) Earth (4) Matter

566. Substantiality is..............universal.
(1) Para (2) Apara
(3) Parāpara (4) None of these

567. The Nyāya-Vaiśeṣikas enunciate the............ theory of the universal.
(1) Materialistic (2) Realistic
(3) Logical (4) Metaphysical

568. Universal is eternal, one and
(1) Uncaused (2) Pure
(3) Residing in many
(4) None of the above

569. The universals reside in substances qualities and
(1) Actions (2) Samavāya
(3) Viśeṣa (4) None of these

570. Conjunction inheres in many substances it conjoins, but it is not a universal, since it is not
(1) Eternal (2) Real
(3) Physical (4) None of these

571. The fourth category recognised by Nyāya-Vaiśeṣikas is
(1) Sāmānya (2) Samavāya
(3) Abhāva (4) Viśeṣa

572. It is the.................by the possession of which different individuals are referred to as belonging to one class.
(1) Universal (2) Guṇa
(3) Samavāya (4) None of these

573. Match List I with List II and select the correct answer by using the codes given below the lists :

List-I	List-II
(a) Perception	(i) Sañjñāsañjñisaṁbandha
(b) Inference	(ii) Dṛstāntha
(c) Comparison	(iii) Vyāpti
(d) Testimony	(iv) Jñānalakṣana

Codes :

	(a)	(b)	(c)	(d)
(1)	(ii)	(i)	(iii)	(iv)
(2)	(iv)	(iii)	(ii)	(i)
(3)	(iv)	(iii)	(i)	(ii)
(4)	(ii)	(iii)	(i)	(iv)

574. Match the following

List-I	List-II
(a) Perception	(i) Ordinary
(b) Inference	(ii) Vyapti
(c) Comparison	(iii) Analogy
(d) Verbal testimony	(iv) Shalda

Codes :	(a)	(b)	(c)	(d)
(1)	(i)	(ii)	(iii)	(iv)
(2)	(iv)	(iii)	(ii)	(i)
(3)	(i)	(iv)	(iii)	(ii)
(4)	(iii)	(iv)	(ii)	(i)

575. Math the following

List-I (Substances)	List-II (Qualities)
(a) Atman	(i) Rasa
(b) Prithvi	(ii) Sabda
(c) Jala	(iii) Gandha
(d) Akasha	(iv) Jnana

Codes :	(a)	(b)	(c)	(d)
(1)	(iv)	(ii)	(i)	(iii)
(2)	(iv)	(i)	(ii)	(iii)
(3)	(ii)	(i)	(iii)	(iv)
(4)	(iv)	(iii)	(i)	(ii)

576. Match the following and choose the answer from the codes given below. Kinds of vyāpti–Meaning

(a) Aṅvaya	(i) A relation of agreement between two things is in presence
(b) Vyatireka	(iii) A relation of agreement is in absence
(c) Vyabhicārāgraha	(iii) Absence of contrary instance
(d) Upādhinirāsa	(iv) Elimination of conditions on which the relation may possible be dependent

Codes :	(a)	(b)	(c)	(d)
(1)	(iii)	(iv)	(i)	(ii)
(2)	(iv)	(i)	(ii)	(iii)
(3)	(i)	(ii)	(iii)	(iv)
(4)	(ii)	(iii)	(iv)	(i)

577. Match the following and choose your answer from the codes given below

Inference	Condition
(a) Kevalānvayi	(i) Middle term is both positively and negatively related to major term.
(b) Kevalavyatireki	(ii) Middle term is positively related to the major term.
(c) Anvayavyatireki	(iii) Middle term is negatively related to major term.

Codes :	(a)	(b)	(c)
(1)	(ii)	(iii)	(i)
(2)	(iii)	(ii)	(i)
(3)	(ii)	(i)	(iii)
(4)	(iii)	(i)	(ii)

578. Match List I with List II and select the correct answer by using the codes given below the lists :

List-I	List-II
(a) Apohavāda	(i) Realism
(b) Jainism	(ii) Nominalism
(c) Nyāya-Vaiśeṣika	(iii) Conceptualism

Codes :	(a)	(b)	(c)
(1)	(i)	(ii)	(iii)
(2)	(ii)	(iii)	(i)
(3)	(i)	(iii)	(ii)
(4)	(ii)	(i)	(iii)

579. Match List-I (Types of Abhāva) with List-II (Statements) and select the correct answer using the codes given below the Lists :

List-I (Types of Abhāva)	List-II (Statements)
(a) Prāgabhāva	(i) Mahatma Gandhi is dead
(b) Pradhvamsābhāva	(ii) Rāma is not Lakṣmana
(c) Anyonyābhāva	(iii) Ratnāvati is not yet born
	(iv) Sachin is not on the cricket-ground

Codes:	(a)	(b)	(c)
(1)	(iii)	(i)	(iv)
(2)	(iii)	(i)	(ii)
(3)	(ii)	(iv)	(i)
(4)	(iv)	(iii)	(ii)

580. Match the following and choose your answer from the codes given below

Hetvābhāsa Meaning (fallacy of)

(a) Asiddha (i) Unproved middle
(b) Anaikantika (ii) Irregular middle
(c) Satpratipakṣa (iii) Middle term is contradicted by another M
(d) Bādhita (iv) Non-inferentially contradicted middle
(e) Viruddha (v) Contradictory middle

Codes :	(a)	(b)	(c)	(d)	(e)
(1)	(v)	(iv)	(iii)	(ii)	(i)
(2)	(iii)	(ii)	(i)	(iv)	(v)
(3)	(i)	(ii)	(iii)	(iv)	(v)
(4)	(ii)	(iii)	(iv)	(v)	(i)

581. Match the following and choose your answer from the codes given below :

Karma	Meaning
(a) Utkṣepana	(i) Expansion
(b) Avakṣepana	(ii) Contraction
(c) Ākuñcana	(iii) Upward motion
(d) Prasārana	(iv) Locomotion
(e) Gamana	(v) Downward motion

Codes :	(a)	(b)	(c)	(d)	(e)
(1)	(i)	(ii)	(iii)	(iv)	(v)
(2)	(ii)	(iv)	(iii)	(v)	(iv)
(3)	(iv)	(v)	(iii)	(ii)	(i)
(4)	(iii)	(v)	(ii)	(i)	(iv)

582. Match the following and choose your answer from the codes given below

(a) Generality (i) Cause of conjuction
(b) Particularity (ii) Inherence
(c) Karma (iii) Cause of assimilation
(d) Samavāya (iv) Cause of discrimination

Codes :	(a)	(b)	(c)	(d)
(1)	(i)	(ii)	(iii)	(iv)
(2)	(ii)	(i)	(iv)	(iii)
(3)	(iii)	(iv)	(i)	(ii)
(4)	(iv)	(iii)	(ii)	(i)

583. Match List-I (Concepts) with List-II (Systems) and select the correct answer using the codes given below the List :

List-I	List-II
(1) Jnānalakṣana Pratyakṣa	(i) Buddhism
(2) Vivarta	(ii) Nyāya
(3) Svarūpabhūtajñāna	(iii) Advaita Vedānta
(4) Pratityasamutpāda	(iv) Viśiṣtnadvaita Vedānta

Codes :	(a)	(b)	(c)	(d)
(1)	(iv)	(iii)	(ii)	(i)
(2)	(ii)	(iii)	(iv)	(i)
(3)	(iii)	(i)	(iv)	(ii)
(4)	(ii)	(iv)	(i)	(iii)

584. Match List-I (Doctrines) with List-II (Philosophers) select the correct answer using the codes given below the Lists :

List-I	List-II
(a) Substance is the compound of from and matter	(i) Desecrates
(b) Substance is that which is conceived in itself	(ii) Locke
(c) Substance is the unknown support of qualities	(iii) Aristotle
(d) Substance is the inherent cause or qualities	(iv) Nyāya-Vaiśeṣika

Codes :	(a)	(b)	(c)	(d)
(1)	(iii)	(iv)	(i)	(ii)
(2)	(iv)	(iii)	(ii)	(i)
(3)	(ii)	(i)	(iii)	(iv)
(4)	(iii)	(i)	(ii)	(iv)

585. Match List-I with List-II and select the correct answer using the codes given below the Lists:

(a) Nyāya (i) Correspondence theory
(b) Sāṁkhya (ii) Coherence theory
(c) Buddhism
(d) Mimāṁsa

Codes : (a) (b) (c) (d)
(1) (ii) (i) (ii) (i)
(2) (i) (ii) (i) (ii)
(3) (ii) (i) (ii) (i)
(4) (i) (i) (ii) (ii)

586. Match, according to the Nyāya-Vaiśeṣika view List-I (Substances) with List-II (Qualities) and select the correct answer using the codes given below the lists :

List-I	List-II
(a) Ātman	(i) Sneha
(b) Pṛthivi	(ii) Śabda
(c) Jala	(iii) Gandha
(d) Ākāśa	(iv) Jnaña

Codes : (a) (b) (c) (d)
(1) (iii) (iv) (i) (ii)
(2) (iii) (iv) (ii) (i)
(3) (iv) (iii) (i) (ii)
(4) (iv) (iii) (ii) (i)

587. Match List I with List II and select the correct answer by using the codes given below the lists :

List-I	List-II
(a) Saṁśaya	(i) The object for which or to avoid which one acts
(b) Prayojana	(ii) An undisputed fact which illustrates a general rule
(c) Dṛṣṭānta	(iii) What is taught and accepted as true
(d) Siddhānta	(iv) A state of uncertainty

Codes :
(a) (b) (c) (d)
(1) (iv) (i) (ii) (iii)
(2) (iv) (i) (iii) (ii)
(3) (i) (iii) (iv) (ii)
(4) (i) (ii) (iii) (iv)

588. Match List I with List II and select the correct answer by using the codes given below the lists.

List I	List II
(a) The starting point of the process of creation or destruction is his will	(i) Anādi
(b) The first combination of two atoms	(ii) Maheśvara
(c) The process of creation and destruction of the world is beginningless	(iii) Brahmā
(d) World-soul who is endowed with supreme wisdom, detachment and excellence	(iv) Dvyaṇuka

Codes : (a) (b) (c) (d)
(1) (iii) (iv) (i) (ii)
(2) (ii) (iv) (i) (iii)
(3) (ii) (iii) (iv) (i)
(4) (iii) (ii) (i) (iv)

Direction. The following items consists of two statements, one labelled the 'Assertion A' and the other labelled the 'Reason R'—you are to examine these two statements carefully and decide it the Assertion and the Reason R are individuality true and it so, whether the Reason is a correct explanation of the Assertion select your answer to these items using the codes given below and mark your answer sheet accordingly.

Codes:

(1) Both A and R are true and R is the correct explanation of A.
(2) Both A and R are true but R is not a correct explanation of A.
(3) A is true but R is false.
(4) A is false but R is true.

589. **Assertion (A).** According to Nyāya Vaiśeṣika, the higher generality is that of being.

Reason (R). It covers all things.

590. **Assertion (A).** The causation theory of Nyāyā-Vaiśeṣika is known as ārambhvāda.

Reason (R). They believe that the effect is not pre-existent in its cause.

591. **Assertion (A).** According to Nyāya-Vaiśeṣika, if antecedent negation is denied, then all things would become beginningless and endless.

Reason (R). They believe that the production is a new creation.

592. **Assertion (A).** Ordinarily we perceive a particular cow and not a universal cow.

Reason (R). Nyāya maintains that the universals are perceived extraordinarily.

593. **Assertion (A).** According to Nyāya quality can not separated from substance.

Reason (R). Samavāya is an inseparable relationship, and also it is a relationship between a quality and a substance.

594. **Assertion (A).** According to Nyāya-Vaiśeṣika, atoms can form different combinations.

Reason (R). God gives motion to them.

595. **Assertion (A).** According to Nyāya-Vaiśeṣika God's existence is proved.

Reason (R). God is the author of the infallible Veda.

596. **Assertion (A).** The World must have an efficient cause.

Reason (R). According to Nyāya Vaiśeṣika, the world is an effect.

597. **Assertion (A).** Nyāya maintains that testimony is always personal.

Reason (R). It is based on the worlds of a trust worthy person.

598. **Assertion (A).** Śamkara criticised the Nyāya theory of khjativāda.

Reason (R). According to Śamkara, effect must exist in the cause before its manifestation.

599. **Assertion (A).** According to Naiyāyikas, the Cārvaka claim that all inferences are invalid, is self-defeating.

Reason (R). The Cārvākas employ inferences for establishing the claim that all inference are invalid.

600. **Assertion (A).** According to Nyāya philosophy pain and pleasure are known by inference.

Reason (R). According to them, pain and pleasure are not the objects of the external sense-organs.

601. **Assertion (A).** Abhāva is an independent category in Nyāya Vaisesika Philosophy.

Reason (R). Abhāva is perceived by sense organs.

602. **Assertion (A).** Adṛṣṭa is passive but works.

Reason (R). God is governor who regulates Adṛṣṭa.

603. **Assertion (A).** God must be omniscient as he has the direct knowledge of absolutely simple and small entity like atoms.

Reason (R). The intelligent cause, *i.e.*, God must have a direct knowledge of the material causes, viz., the atmos as means, a desire to attain some end, the power of will to accomplish or realize the end.

604. **Assertion (A).** The Vaiśeṣika theory of the world is known as the atomic theory of the world.

Reason (R). Vaiśeṣikas reduce all composite objects of the world into four kinds of atoms of earth, water, fire and air.

605. **Assertion (A).** Realism suggests that the relation between an object and its knowledge is internal.

Reason (R). The object of a knowledge exists independently of knowledge or the knower.

606. **Assertion (A).** Realists claim that the object of a knowledge exists independently of knowledge or the knower.

Reason (R). The existence of an object of knowledge never depends on knowing mind.

607. Assertion (A). Realism holds that every knowledge must have an object.

Reason (R). The object is not an integral part of knowledge.

608. Assertion (A). Particularity (viśeṣa) is the extreme opposite of the universal (sāmānya).

Reason (R). There are innumerable particularities, since the individuals in which they subsist are innumerable.

609. Assertion (A). Atoms and souls are copresent and co-eternal with God.

Reason (R). God is the efficient cause of the world of which the eternal atoms are the material cause.

610. Assertion (A). The Nyāya and Vaiśeṣika are allied systems of philosophy.

Reason (R). Both the systems have same end of view, *i.e.,* liberation is absolute cessation of suffering of individual.

611. Assertion (A). Quality is different from both substance and action.

Reason (R). Quality is an unmoving or motionless property of things and it inheres in the thing as something passive and inactive.

612. Assertion (A). Sāmānyalakṣana perception is the perception of the universals.

Reason (R). The universals are a distinct class of reals.

613. Assertion (A). Abhava is an independent category in Nyaya-Vaisesika.

Reason (R). Abhava is perceived by sense organs.

614. Assertion (A). Quality is an independent reality.

Reason (R). Quality can be prameya, jñeya and abhidheya.

615. Laukika perception means

A. ordinary perception
B. usual way perception
C. extra-ordinary perception
D. unusual way perception

Select the correct answer using the codes given below :

(1) A and B (2) B and C
(3) C and D (4) B and D

616. Anumana means

A. inference
B. second kind of knowledge
C. perception
D. third kind of knowledge

Select the correct answer using the codes given below

(1) A and B (2) B and C
(3) C and D (4) B and D

617. Vishesa means

A. particularity B. fifth category
C. particularity D. generality

Select the correct answer using the codes given below

(1) A and B (2) B and C
(3) C and D (4) B and D

618. Which one is the correct sequence of the following choose from the code below

A. Udaharana B. Pratijna
C. Hetu D. Upanaya

Codes:

a. a,b,c,d b. b,c,a,d,
c. b,d,c,a d. c,d,a,b

619. Which among the following are pramā? Choose your answer from the codes given below

a. Pratyaksa b. Anumiti
c. Śabda d. Upamiti
e. Anupalabdhi

Codes:

1. a and b
2. a, b, c and e
3. a, b, d and e
4. a, b, c and d

620. Which among the following is true about indeterminate pratyakṣa?

A. Its feeling is psychological
B. Its knowledge is logical
C. Its knowledge is philosophical
D. It is the knowledge of universals

Choose the correct answer from the codes given below

(1) A and B (2) B and D
(3) C and D (4) 1, B and D

621. Which of the following statements are admitted by the Nyāya school?

A. Non-eternal substances are always characterized by qualities
B. Non-eternal substances are often characterised by qualities
C. Eternal substances are always characterised by qualities
D. Eternal substances are often characterised by qualities

Select the correct answer using the codes given below :

(1) A and C (2) B and C
(3) A and D (4) B and D

622. Consider the following statements concerning Nyāya-Vaiśesika

A. Universals and particulars are mere subjective concepts in mind.
B. Universals reside in substances, qualities and actions.
C. A universal can subsist in another universal.
D. Both particular and universals are separately real.

Which of these statements are correct?

(1) A and B (2) B and D
(3) A and C (4) B and C

623. Which among the following come under Vaiśesika's padarth?

A. Dravya C. Guṇa
B. Samavāya D. Viśesa

Choose your answer from the codes given below

(1) A and B (2) A, B and D
(3) A, B and C (4) A, B, C and D

624. Vaisesika is regarded as

A. pluralist B. atomist
C. monist D. dualist

Select the correct answer using the codes given below

(1) A and B (2) B and C
(3) C and D (4) B and D

625. God is devoid of

A. dwesa B. avidya
C. particularity D. generality

Select the correct answer using the codes given below

(1) A and B (2) B and C
(3) C and D (4) B and D

626. Karma means

A. action
B. it inheres in a substance
C. it inheres in an action
D. it does not inheres in a substance

Select the correct answer using the codes given below

(1) A and B (2) B and C
(3) C and D (4) B and D

627. Nyaya is regarded as

A. realist B. pistemologist
C. rationalist D. metaphysicist

Select the correct answer using the codes given below :

(1) A and B (2) B and C
(3) C and D (4) B and D

628. Padartha means

A. category B. vaisesika notion

C. Samkhya notion D. Mimamsa notion

Select the correct answer using the codes given below

(1) A and B (2) B and C

(3) C and D (4) B and D

629. Vyapti means

A. neric of an inference

B. invariable concomitance

C. existential fallacy

D. referrent fallacy

Select the correct answer using the codes given below

(1) A and B (2) B and C

(3) C and D (4) B and D

630. Consider the following statements about the Nyāya-Vaiśeṣika view.

A. God creates the world by transforming himself into the world

B. God creates the world out of Abhāva

C. God creates the world out pre-existent atoms

D. God creates the world in accordance with the karma of jivas

Which of these statements are correct?

(1) A and D (2) B and D

(3) B and C (4) C and D

631. Which among the following theories of causation is accepted by Sāṁkhya

(1) Asatkāryavāda (2) Āraṁbhavāda

(3) Satkāryavāda (4) Vivartavāda

632. The theory that the effect is pre-existent in its material cause, is known as

(1) Asatkāryavāda (2) Satkāryavāda

(3) Ārambhavāda (4) None of these

633. Saṁkhya's satkāryavāda is also known as

(1) Prakṛti-priṇāmavāda

(2) Brahma-priṇāmavāda

(3) vivartavāda (4) Ārambhavāda

634. 'There is neither new production nor utter destruction. Production means 'avirbhāva' and destruction means 'Tirobhāva'. This theory is accepted by

(1) Nyāya (2) Vaiśeṣika

(3) Sāmkhya (4) Cārvāka

635. The Purusa is referred as what?

(1) 25th evolute (2) 26th evolute

(3) 27th evolute (4) 28th evolute

636. Purusa is regarded as what?

(1) Consciousness

(2) Pure consciousness

(3) Real Consciousness

(4) Normal consciousness

637. According to Samkhya,...........is known as spirit.

(1) Purusha (2) Prakriti

(3) Perception (4) Inference

638. According to ...., Purusha is regarded as pure.

(1) Samkhya (2) Hegel

(3) Mimamsa (4) Shankara

639. Prakriti serves .... end.

(1) perception (2) inference

(3) purusha (4) verbal testimony

640. Purusa is regarded as an .... principle of the universe.

(1) intelligent (2) unintelligent

(3) purposive (4) extension

641. Purusha and..........contains an important relationship.

(1) Prakriti (2) Asatkaryavada

(3) Error theory (4) illusionary theory

642. Purusa is regarded as...........and devoid of qualities.

(1) inactive (2) active

(3) error theory (4) asatkaryavada

643. The original Samkhya was regarded as..........and theistic.

(1) monistic (2) pluralist
(3) relativist (4) none of these

644. The eternal............of the Purusas are inconsistent with God.
(1) interference (2) false
(3) existence (4) inference

645. Samkhya and...........goes together.
(1) Yoga (2) Jaina
(3) Buddhism (4) Vedanta

646. Which of the following guṇas is responsible for the manifestation of objects in consciousness
(1) Rajas (2) Sattva
(3) Tamas (4) None of these

647. Feverish effort and wild stimilation are the results of
(1) rajas (2) tamas
(3) sattva (4) none

648. Passivity and negativity are the results of
(1) Sattva (2) Rajasa
(3) Tamas (4) None

649. Which type of change in guṇas causes the starting of evolution?
(1) Heterogeneous (2) Homogeneous
(3) Sarupa-pariṇāma (4) None

650. Paralaya of the world happen when guṇas change
(1) Homogeneously (2) Heterogeneously
(3) Harmoneously (4) None of these

651. Which of the following statement is correct about the change of guṇas?
(1) Change does not disturb the equilibrium
(2) Change disturbs the equilibrium
(3) Change disturbs in some manner while in some manner does not
(4) None of the above

652. Which of the following is true about Puruṣa?
(1) Pure and transcendental consciousness.
(2) Ultimate knower
(3) Pure subject
(4) All of the above

653. 'It is the silent witness, the emancipated alone, the neutral seer, the peaceful eternal'.
In above statement Śaṁkhya is talking about
(1) Prakṛti (2) Puruṣa
(3) Iṣvara (4) Brāḥman

654. According to saṁkhya, which of the following is the correct discription of Puruṣa?
(1) It is one (2) It is many
(3) It is qualitatively one and qualitatively many
(4) None of the above

655. How many kinds of pain are there in earthly life?
(1) 1 (2) 2
(3) 3 (4) 4

656. Which among the following is a kind of pain of earthly life?
(1) Ādhyātmika (2) Adhibhautika
(3) Adhidaivika (4) All of these

657. Sāṁkhya accepts liberation as
(1) Only jivanmukti
(2) Only videhamukti
(3) Both jivanmukti and videhamukti
(4) None of the above

658. According to Sāṁkhya liberation is a state of
(1) Complete isolation
(2) no pleasure, no pain and no bliss
(3) pure consciousness
(4) all of the above

659. Sāṁkhya believes in
(1) theism (2) atheism
(3) polytheism (4) none of these

660. Patanjali yoga is also known as
(1) Raj yoga (2) Bhaktiyoga
(3) Karmyoga (4) Haṭhayoga

661. According to Yoga citta means
(1) Buddhi, ahaṅkāra and manas
(2) Prakṛti
(3) Mind
(4) None of the above

662. When citta is related to any object it assumes the form of that object. This form is called
(1) Citta-vṛtti (2) Citta-bhumi
(3) Jñāna (4) Klesha

663. Which among the following is not included under the kinds of cittavṛtti?
(1) Pramāna (2) Nidrā
(3) Avidyā (4) Smṛti

664. According to.............philosophy, devotion of God is the best means for the attainment of concentration and restraint of mind
(1) Nyāya (2) Sānkhya
(3) Yoga (4) Vaiśeṣika

665. ....is the person who possesses perfect knowledge and perfect power.
(1) God (2) Lord
(3) Avatāra (4) None of these

666. The Yoga mostly accepts the........... epistemology and admits the three pramāṇas viz., perception, inference and scriptural testimony
(1) Sānkhya (2) Nyāya
(3) Jaina (4) Vedānta

667. There are two main kinds of yoga or samādhi, *viz*..................and..................
(1) Saṁprajñāta, asaṁprajñāta
(2) Primary, secondary
(3) Primary, saṁprajñāta
(4) None of the above

668. Which one of the following shows the correct sequence of the steps involved in the eightfold path of Yoga?
(1) Asana, Prāṇāyāma, Dhyāna, Dhāraṇā, Pratyāhāra, Yama, Niyama, Samādhi
(2) Dhyāna, Āsana, Yama, Niyama, Pratyāhāra, Prāṇāyāma, Dhāraṇā, Samādhi
(3) Niyama, Āsana, Dhyāna, Dhāraṇā, Prāṇāyāma, Yama, Pratyāhāra, Samādhi
(4) Yama, Niyama, Āsana, Prāṇāyāma, Pratyāhāra, Dhāraṇā, Dhyāna, Samādhi

669. Yoga-vārtikā is written by
(1) Vijñānabhiksu (2) Vācaspati
(3) Patañjali (4) Śridhara

670. Which one of the following statements is correct?
(1) Sānkhya school believes Īśvara is Saguṇa Brahama
(2) He is the original cause
(3) Both (1) and (2)
(4) None of the above

671. The Sānkhya school regards error as
(1) Misapprehension
(2) Non-apprehension
(3) Cognition
(4) None of the above

672. The.......are of five kinds, *viz.*, right cognition, wrong cognition, verbal cognition, absence of cognition and memory
(1) Modification of the chitta
(2) Levels of mental life
(3) original knowledge
(4) None of the above

673. The best means of spiritual advancement are found in
(1) Yoga school (2) Nyāya school
(3) Sānkhya school (4) None of these

674. When one of the following is related to 'Āstika' school?
(1) Yoga (2) Cārvākas
(3) Buddha (4) None of these

675. Meditation on God helps the concentration of
(1) Mind (2) Heart
(3) Soul (4) None of these

676. Which among the following school does not believe in God
(1) Advait vedānta (2) Sāṁkhya
(3) Yoga (4) Nyāya

677. Sāṁkhya believe in
(1) Plurality of Purusa
(2) Monism
(3) Theism
(4) None of the above

678. Yoga mostly accepts the metaphysics and the epistemology of
(1) Nyāya (2) Mimaṁsa
(3) Sānkhya (4) Vaiśeṣka

679. Yoga sutra is devided into
(1) two parts (2) three parts
(3) four parts (4) five parts

680. The first part of Yoga-sutra is known as
(1) Kaivalyapāda (2) Sādhanāpāda
(3) Vibhutipāda (4) Samādhipāda

681. Viparyāya is a kind of
(1) Cittabhumi (2) Chittavṛti
(3) Klesha (4) Āṣṭangayoga

682. Cittabhumis mentioned by Yoga are
(1) Pramāna, Viparyāya Vikalpa, Niḍra, smṛti
(2) Avidyā, asmita, rāga, dveṣa, abhiniveśa
(3) Kṛipta, Muḍha, Vikṣipta Ekāgra, Niruddha
(4) Pramāna, Asmita, Muḍha, Niḍra, Smṛti

683. In Yoga, when the citta is concentrated on the ego substance with which the self is generally identified, this state is
(1) Sāsmita samādhi
(2) Sānaṅda samādhi
(3) Savitarka samādhi
(4) Savichāra samadhi

684. Samādhi, in which mediator and the object of meditation are completely fused together, is known as
(1) Savitarka samādhi
(2) Saṁprajñāta samādhi
(3) Asaṁprajñāta samādhi
(4) Sāsmita samādhi

685. The light of consciousness, which comes from the Puruṣa and illuminates Vṛiti, is called
(1) Jñāna (2) Pratyakṣa
(3) Anumāna (4) Viparyāya

686. Which of the following arguments is not given against God in saṁkhya system?
(1) If God is affected by selfive motives he is not free
(2) If he is free, he cannot create this world
(3) The eternal existence of the Puruṣa is inconsistent with God
(4) God cannot be perceived

687. 'God or Brahman cannot be the cause of the world' is suggested by
(1) Sāṅkhya school
(2) Naiyāyikas
(3) Yoga school (4) Saṅkara

688. 'The ultimate cause of the world is the eternal but ever-changing prakṛti' is claimed by
(1) Sāṅkhya and Yoga school
(2) Sāṅkhya philosophers
(3) Naiyāyikas
(4) None of the above

689. ....creates the world unconsciously for the good of the individual selves in the same way in which the milk of the cow flows unconsciously through her udder for the nourishment of the calf
(1) Puruṣa (2) Prakṛti
(3) God (4) Adṛṣta

690. According to Patanjali God is never
(1) Free
(2) In bondage
(3) Without purpose
(4) Cruel

691. God is devoid of

(1) Rāga (2) Dweṣa

(3) Avidyā (4) All of these

692. According to Patanjali God is different even from

(1) Liberated man (2) Man

(3) Woman (4) None of these

693. Patanjali believes that 'Īśvarāpraṇidhāna' is an instrument

(1) To attain Samādhi

(2) To practise yoga

(3) To practise singing of Vedic hymns

(4) None of the above

694. During the state of..........the primal unconscious nature of prakṛti remains in a latent, subtle and undifferentiated form

(1) Creation (2) Dissolution

(3) Maturity (4) None of these

695. Do Sānkhyas believe in God?

(1) Yes (2) No

(3) Not certain (4) None of these

696. ....believes that the Sānkhya system is not atheistic.

(1) Vijñānabhikṣu (2) Udayana

(3) Sridhara (4) S.N. Dasgupta

697. Vijñānabhikṣu claims that the Sānkhya system is

(1) Theist (2) Atheist

(3) Materialistic (4) None of these

698. ....is both the material and efficient cause of the world, according to Sānkhya.

(1) puruṣa (2) Prakṛti

(3) God (4) Adṛsta

699. Sānkhya admits the first cause which is specifically described as the supreme root cause of the world is

(1) Puruṣa (2) Prakṛti

(3) Prakāśaka (4) None of these

700. Prakṛti is constituted by the three guṇas, namely

(1) Primary, secondary, infinite

(2) Bright, laghu, consciousness

(3) Sattva, rajas, tamas

(4) None of the above

701. Sānkhya believes the evolution of the world has its starting point in the contact between

(1) Puruṣa and Prakṛti

(2) Finite material, infinite material

(3) Self, infinite material

(4) None of the above

702. Sānkhya accepts three independent sources of knowledge, these are

(1) Perception, inference and comparison

(2) Perception, scriptural testimony and non-cognition

(3) Perception, inference and scriptural testimony

(4) None of the above

703. Who is the founder of Yoga system?

(1) Sankarāchārya (2) Patañjali

(3) Buddha (4) Mahavira

704. Astika is

(1) Who believes in rebirth

(2) Who believes in God

(3) Who believes in God but not in rebirth

(4) None of the above

705. The............admits the existence of earth, water, fire and air and rejects the ether.

(1) Cārvāka (2) Yoga

(3) Mīmaṁsa (4) Sankhya

706. Five types of Yama according to Patañjali are

(1) Ahimsā, asteya, satya, brahmacarya and asana.

(2) Ahimsā, satya, asteya, brahmacarya, and aparigraha.

(3) Satya, asteya, brahmacarya, aparigraha and dhyāna.
(4) Asteya, brahmacarya, satya, dhyāna and asana.

707. Samkhya theory of causation is based upon
(1) Effect is not related with the cause.
(2) Effect does not pre-exist in the cause.
(3) Effect is produced out of nothing.
(4) Effect pre-exists in the cause.

708. To Patañjali Sāsmita is a kind of
(1) Yoga (2) Samādhi
(3) Āsana (4) Prāṇāyāma

709. According to Samkhya, the first evolute is
(1) Mahābhuta (2) Tanmatras
(3) Mahat (4) Ahaṁkāra

710. According to whom "Yoga is the cessation of the modification of Citta" ?
(1) Patanjali (2) Vijñānabhiksu
(3) Iśvarakṛṣna (4) Vasubandhu

711. Which one of the following schools hold that sufferings are mainly of three types ?
(1) The Buddhist (2) The Jaina
(3) Sāṁkhya (4) Mīmāṁsā

712. The correct sequence of external aids to yoga of Patanjali is
(1) Pratyahara, Pranayama, Asana, Niyama and Yama
(2) Pranayama, Pratyahara, Asana, Niyama and Yama
(3) Asana, Pratyahara, Pranayama, Niyama and Yama
(4) Yama, Niyama, Asana, Pranayama and Pratyahara.

713. Match the following forms of prakṛti with their characteristics and choose your answer from the codes given below :

From	Characteristic
(a) Prakṛti	(i) Uncaused root-cause
(b) Pradhāna	(ii) Unmanifested state of all effects
(c) Jaḍa	(iii) Everactive unlimited power
(d) Avyakta	(iv) First principle of this universe
(e) Śakti	(v) Unintelligent and unconscious principle

Codes :

	(a)	(b)	(c)	(d)	(e)
(1)	(i)	(iv)	(v)	(ii)	(iii)
(2)	(ii)	(i)	(v)	(iv)	(iii)
(3)	(i)	(iv)	(v)	(ii)	(iii)
(4)	(ii)	(i)	(v)	(iv)	(iii)

714. Match the following guṇas with their colours and choose your answer from the codes given below

Guṇa	Colour
(a) Sattva	(i) White
(b) Rajas	(ii) Black
(c) Tamas	(iii) Red

Codes :

	(a)	(b)	(c)
(1)	(i)	(ii)	(iii)
(2)	(i)	(iii)	(ii)
(3)	(ii)	(i)	(iii)
(4)	(ii)	(iii)	(i)

715. Match List I with List II and select the correct answer by using the codes given below the lists :

List-I	List-II
(a) Samādhipāda	(i) Describes the inward aspect of yoga and the supernormal powers acquired by it.
(b) Sādhanāpāda	(ii) Describes the nature and forms of liberation, the reality of the transcendental self, the other world etc.
(c) Vibhūtipāda	(iii) Deals with the Kriyāyoga as a means of attaining samādhi

(d) Kaivalyapāda	(iv)	Deals with the modifications of citta and the different methods of attaining yoga.

Codes :

	(a)	(b)	(c)	(d)
(1)	(iv)	(i)	(ii)	(iii)
(2)	(iii)	(iv)	(i)	(ii)
(3)	(iv)	(iii)	(i)	(ii)
(4)	(iii)	(i)	(iv)	(ii)

716. Match List I with List II and select the correct answer by using the codes given below the lists :

List-I	List-II
(a) Ahimsā	(i) Non-stealing
(b) Satya	(ii) Abstention from all kinds of injury to any life.
(c) Asteya	(iii) Non-acceptance of unnecessary gifts from other people
(d) Brahmacarya	(iv) Truthfulness in thought and speech
(e) Aparigraha	(v) Control of the carnal desires and passions

Codes :

	(a)	(b)	(c)	(d)	(e)
(1)	(ii)	(i)	(iv)	(iii)	(v)
(2)	(ii)	(iv)	(i)	(v)	(iii)
(3)	(v)	(iv)	(i)	(ii)	(iii)
(4)	(v)	(iii)	(ii)	(i)	(iv)

717. Match List I with List II and select the correct answer by using the codes given below the lists :

List-I	List-II
(a) Nyāya	(i) Prayers are offered to liberated souls instead of God.
(b) Jaina	(ii) Prakṛti, not God, is the sufficient cause for the objects of the world
(c) Sānkhya	(iii) God is the supreme self distinct from other selves
(d) Yoga	(iv) God is creator, sustainer, destroyer of universe.

Codes :

	(a)	(b)	(c)	(d)
(1)	(iii)	(iv)	(ii)	(i)
(2)	(iv)	(i)	(ii)	(iii)
(3)	(ii)	(i)	(iii)	(iv)
(4)	(iv)	(iii)	(ii)	(i)

718. Match List I with List II and select the correct answer by using the codes given below the lists :

List-I	List-II
(a) Prakṛti and Kāla	(i) Immaterial or ajada
(b) Chit and Īśvara	(ii) Sattva, rajas and tamas
(c) Dharmabhūtajñāna and Nityavibhui	(iii) Conscious or chetanā
(d) Prakrti	(iv) Unconscious or jada

Codes :

	(a)	(b)	(c)	(d)
(1)	(iii)	(iv)	(i)	(ii)
(2)	(iv)	(iii)	(i)	(ii)
(3)	(ii)	(iii)	(i)	(iv)
(4)	(i)	(iv)	(iii)	(ii)

719. Match List I with List II and select the correct answer by using the codes given below the lists :

List-I (Theories of Causation)	List-II (Systems)
(a) Satkāryavāda	(i) Sānkhya
(b) Asatkāryavāda	(ii) Viśiṣṭādvaita
(c) Vivartavāda	(iii) Nyāya
(d) Brahmapariṇāmavāda	(iv) Advaita Vedānta

Codes :

	(a)	(b)	(c)	(d)
(1)	(i)	(iii)	(iv)	(ii)
(2)	(iii)	(i)	(iv)	(ii)
(3)	(i)	(iii)	(ii)	(iv)
(4)	(iii)	(i)	(ii)	(iv)

720. Match the following

List-I	List-II
(a) Cittavṛtti	(i) Vikṣipta
(b) Cittabhumi	(ii) Nidra
(c) Kleśa	(iii) Rāga
(d) Aṣṭaṅgayoga	(iv) Dhāraṇā

Codes :

	(a)	(b)	(c)	(d)
(1)	(i)	(ii)	(iii)	(iv)
(2)	(ii)	(i)	(iv)	(iii)
(3)	(i)	(iii)	(iv)	(ii)
(4)	(ii)	(i)	(iii)	(iv)

721. Match List I witn List II and select the correct answer by using the codes given below the lists :

List-I	List-II
(a) Nyāyakusumāñjali	(i) Udayana
(b) Ṭattvacintāmani	(ii) Jaimini
(c) Yoga-Sūtra	(iii) Gaṅgeśa
(d) Mimāṁsa-Sūtra	(iv) Patañjali

Codes :

	(a)	(b)	(c)	(d)
(1)	(ii)	(iv)	(iii)	(i)
(2)	(i)	(iii)	(iv)	(ii)
(3)	(i)	(iii)	(ii)	(iv)
(4)	(iii)	(i)	(iv)	(ii)

722. Match the following

List-I	List-II
(a) Savitarka	(i) Citta is concentrated on the tip of the nose.
(b) Savichāra	(ii) Citta is concentrated on tanmātrās
(c) Sānanda	(iii) Citta is concentrated on the senses.
(d) Sāsmita	(iv) Citta is concentrated on the ego substance

Codes :

	(a)	(b)	(c)	(d)
(1)	(i)	(ii)	(iii)	(iv)
(2)	(ii)	(iii)	(iv)	(i)
(3)	(iii)	(iv)	(ii)	(i)
(4)	(iv)	(iii)	(ii)	(i)

723. Match the following

List-I	List-II
(a) Yama	(i) Steady and comfortable posture
(b) Niyama	(ii) Self-culture
(c) Āsana	(iii) Control of breath
(d) Prāṇāyāma	(iv) Abstention

Codes :

	(a)	(b)	(c)	(d)
(1)	(i)	(ii)	(iii)	(iv)
(2)	(ii)	(iii)	(iv)	(i)
(3)	(iv)	(ii)	(i)	(iii)
(4)	(iii)	(ii)	(i)	(iv)

724. Match the following

List-I	List-II
(a) Pratijña	(i) Concentration
(b) Dhāraṇā	(ii) meditation
(c) Dhyāna	(iii) Control of the senses
(d) Samādhi	(iv) Fixing the mind on the tip of the nose

Codes :

	(a)	(b)	(c)	(d)
(1)	(i)	(ii)	(iii)	(iv)
(2)	(iv)	(ii)	(i)	(iii)
(3)	(iii)	(iv)	(ii)	(i)
(4)	(iv)	(iii)	(ii)	(i)

725. Match the following

List-I	List-II
(a) Bhutādi	(i) Sattva predominates
(b) Taijasa	(ii) Rajasa predominates
(c) Vaikarika	(iii) Tamasa predominates

Codes :

	(a)	(b)	(c)
(1)	(i)	(ii)	(iii)
(2)	(ii)	(iii)	(i)
(3)	(iii)	(ii)	(i)
(4)	(i)	(iii)	(ii)

726. Match List-I with List-II and select the correct answer by using the codes given below the List :

List-I	List-II
(a) Kapila	(i) Sāṁkhya-tattvakaumudi
(b) Īśvarakṛṣṇa	(ii) Sāṁkhya-sūtra
(c) Vijñānabhikṣu	(iii) Sāṁkhya-sūtra
(d) Vācaspati Miśra	(iv) Sānkhya-Kārikā

Codes :

	(a)	(b)	(c)	(d)
(1)	(ii)	(iv)	(iii)	(i)
(2)	(ii)	(iii)	(i)	(iv)
(3)	(iii)	(ii)	(i)	(iv)
(4)	(iv)	(iii)	(ii)	(i)

727. Match the following

List-I	List-II
(a) Samkhya	(i) Prakriti
(b) Yoga	(ii) Patanjali
(c) Nyaya	(iii) Logic
(d) Vaisesika	(iv) Ontology

Codes :

	(a)	(b)	(c)	(d)
(1)	(i)	(iv)	(iii)	(ii)
(2)	(i)	(ii)	(iii)	(iv)
(3)	(iv)	(iii)	(ii)	(i)
(4)	(iii)	(iv)	(ii)	(i)

728. Match the following

List-I	List-II
(a) Samkhya	(i) Atheism
(b) Mimamsa	(ii) Jainism
(c) Vaisesika	(iii) Category
(d) Yoga	(iv) Samadhi

Codes :

	(a)	(b)	(c)	(d)
(1)	(i)	(ii)	(iii)	(iv)
(2)	(iv)	(iii)	(ii)	(i)
(3)	(i)	(iv)	(iii)	(ii)
(4)	(iii)	(iv)	(ii)	(i)

729. Match the following

List-I	List-II
(a) Purva Mimamsa	(i) Vedas
(b) Hetabhava	(ii) Fallacy
(c) Perception	(iii) Setraordinary
(d) Inference	(iv) Purvavat

Codes :

	(a)	(b)	(c)	(d)
(1)	(i)	(ii)	(iii)	(iv)
(2)	(iv)	(iii)	(ii)	(i)
(3)	(i)	(iv)	(iii)	(ii)
(4)	(iii)	(iv)	(ii)	(i)

730. Match the following

List-I	List-II
(a) Prabhakara	(i) Triputi samirt
(b) Kumarilla	(ii) Jnatata
(c) Perception	(iii) determinate
(d) Inference	(iv) Shesavat

Codes :

	(a)	(b)	(c)	(d)
(1)	(i)	(ii)	(iii)	(iv)
(2)	(iv)	(iii)	(ii)	(i)
(3)	(i)	(iv)	(iii)	(ii)
(4)	(iii)	(iv)	(ii)	(i)

731. Match the following

List-I	List-II
(a) Prabhakara	(i) Anvitabhidhanavada
(b) Kumarila	(ii) Abhihitanvayadvada
(c) Nyaya	(iii) Logic
(d) Vaisesika	(iv) Atomistic

Codes :

	(a)	(b)	(c)	(d)
(1)	(i)	(ii)	(iii)	(iv)
(2)	(iv)	(iii)	(ii)	(i)
(3)	(iii)	(iv)	(ii)	(i)
(4)	(ii)	(iv)	(iii)	(i)

732. Match the following

List-I	List-II
(a) Carvaka	(i) Materialist
(b) Mimamsa	(ii) Phiralist
(c) Nyaya	(iii) Realist
(d) Samkhya	(iv) Purusa

Codes :

	(a)	(b)	(c)	(d)
(1)	(i)	(ii)	(iii)	(iv)
(2)	(iv)	(iii)	(ii)	(i)
(3)	(iii)	(iv)	(ii)	(i)
(4)	(i)	(iv)	(iii)	(ii)

Directions. The following items consist of two statements, one labelled the 'Assertion A' and the other labelled the 'Reason R'. You are to examine these two statements carefully and decide if the Assertion A and the reason R individually true and if so, whether the reason is a correct explanation of the assertion. Select your answers to these items using the codes given below

Codes:

(1) Both A and R are true and R is the correct explanation of A

(2) Both A and R are true but R is not a correct explanation of A

(3) A is true but R is false

(4) A is false but R is true.

733. **Assertion (A).** All wrodly effects, according to Sānkhya, are latent in prakṛti.

Reason (R). Infinite regress has to be avoided.

734. **Assertion (A).** The individual selves are limited in knowledge and, therefore, cannot control the subtle material cause of the world.

Reason (R). Prakṛti being non-intelligent must be controlled and directed by some intelligent agent to produce the world.

735. **Assertion (A).** The classical Sānkhya philosophers argue against the existence of God, thus the system is regarded as an atheistic system.

Reason (R). Sānkhya traces the whole course of the world to the interplay of two ultimate principles, *viz.,* spirit and primal matter.

736. **Assertion (A).** Sānkhya believes in plurality of puruṣa.

Reason (R). Different souls does not share their experiences of pleasure, pain, death etc.

737. **Assertion (A).** Sāṁkhya believes in plurality of Puruṣa.

Reason (R). Liberation of one does not mean liberation of all.

738. **Assertion (A).** According to Sānkhya the emancipated souls are all alike and differ only in number.

Reason (R). They are all beyond the three guṇas.

739. **Assertion (A).** There is Puruṣa.

Reason (R). Prakṛti evolves itself in order to serve the Puruṣa's end.

740. **Assertion (A).** Puruṣa is the witness of three guṇas and is himself beyond them.

Reason (R). All objects are composed of the three guṇas.

741. **Assertion (A).** According to Sānkhya there must be an intelligent principle to experience the worldly products of prakṛti.

Reason (R). Non intelligent Prakṛti cannot experience its products.

742. **Assertion (A).** According to sankhya there is Puruṣa.

Reason (R). The desire for liberation and emancipation implies the existence of a person who can try for and obtain liberation.

743. **Assertion (A).** Samkhya says that emancipated souls differs.

Reason (R). Emancipated souls are regarded as beyond the three gunas.

744. **Assertion (A).** Purusa is regarded as the witness of three gunas.

Reason (R). All objects are composed of only the three gunas.

745. **Assertion (A).** All morldly effects, are regarded as latent in prakriti.

Reason (R). Infinite regress is avoided.

746. **Assertion (A).** The individual selves are regarded as limited in knowledge.

Reason (R). Prakriti must be controlled.

747. **Assertion (A).** In Sāṁkhya, Puruṣa is pure consciousness.

Reason (R). Puruṣa is both body and mind.

In the context of the above two statements, which one of the following is correct ?

748. **Assertion (A).** Iśhwara is the *nimittākaraṇa* (efficient cause) of the world.

Reason (R). Iśhwara is ominipresent.

749. Which among the following arguments in support of satkāryavāda is given by sāṁkhya?

A. asadakāraṇāt

B. upādānagrahaṇāt

C. sarvasaṁbhāvābhāvāt

D. visamakāranāt

Codes:

(1) A and B (2) A, B and C

(3) B and C (4) A, B, C and D

750. Which among the following are correct according to Sāṁkhya?

A. Puruṣa is neither a cause nor an effect

B. Prakṛti is only a cause and not the effect

C. Mahat, Ahaṅkāra and the five subtle essences are both causes and effect

D. Five sensory, five motor organs, five gross elements and manas are effects only.

Codes:

(1) A and B (2) B and C

(3) A, B and C (4) A, B, C and D

751. Which of the following are the main characteristics of God according to Yoga philosophers?

A. He is the supreme ruler of the world

B. He has infinite knowledge and unlimited power

C. He has created the world according to his will

Codes:

(1) Both A and B are true

(2) B alone is true

(3) A alone is true

(4) B and C are true

752. Which among the followings is/are the kinds of ahainkāra? Select your answer from the codes given below.

A. Tanmātra B. Taijasa

C. Bhutādi D. Vaikārika

Codes:

(1) A, B and C (2) B, C and D

(3) A, B, C and D (4) A, B and D

753. Chitta-Vrth includes

A. right cognition B. wrong cognition

C. restless D. Mudha

Codes:

(1) A and B (2) B and C

(3) C and D (4) B and D

754. Chitta means

A. first evolute of Prakriti.

B. three internal organs of Samkhya

C. second evolute of Prakriti.

D. four internal organs of Samkhya.

Select the correct answer using the codes given below

(1) A and C (2) A and B

(3) C and D (4) A and B

755. Purusha means

A. soul B. eternal

C. Brahman D. self

Select the correct answer using the codes given below

(1) A and B (2) B and C

(3) C and D (4) B and D

756. Which of the following entities would be considered to be a universal (Sāmānya) by the Nyāya-Vaiśeṣika school?

A. The property of being a cow (Gotva)

B. The property of being a universal (Sāmānyatva)

C. The property of being a substance (Dravyatva)

D. The property of being a Viśeṣa (Viśeṣatva)

Select the correct answer from the codes given below

(1) A and B (2) B and C

(3) A and C (4) A and D

757. Mimāṁsa believes in

A. Svatahprāmanyavāda

B. Paratahprāmāṇyavāda

C. Svatahaprāmāṇyavāda

D. Paratah aprāmāṇyavāda

Codes:

(1) A and C (2) A and D

(3) B and D (4) B and C

758. Which of the following pramāṇas are admitted by Jaimini? Select your answer from the codes given below

A. Pratyakṣa B. Anumāna

C. Sabda D. Upamāna

Codes:

(1) A, B, C and D (2) A and B

(3) A, B and C (4) A and C

759. Which among the following statements are true? Select your correct answer from the codes given below—

A. Mimāṁsa is an atheist system of Indian philosophy.

B. According to Mimāṁa Vedas are written by God

C. Mimāṁsa believes in the eternity of the words.

D. Kumārila and Prabhākara are the two major schools of Mimāṁsa

Codes:

(1) A, B and C (2) B, C and D

(3) A, C and D (4) A, B, C and D

760. Which of the following are admitted by both Prabhākara and Kumārila. Select correct answer from the codes given below.

A. Svatahprāmāṇyavāda and paratahapramāṇyavāda

B. Plurality of the individual souls

C. Soul is the substratum of consciousness

D. Abstention from karma means abstention from the optional and the prohibited kinds of karma only.

Codes:

(1) A, B, C and D

(2) B, C and D

(3) C and D

(4) A, B and C

761. Which among the following is Prabhākara's definition of valid knowledge?

(1) Apprehension (anubhuti)

(2) uncontradicted apprehension

(3) produced by causes free from defects

(4) (2) and (3) together

762. Which of the following is the correct definition of valid knowledge given by Kumārila

(1) Apprehension (anubhuti)

(2) Uncontradicted apprehension

(3) Produced by causes free from defects

(4) (2) and (3)

763. Who among the following does not accept memory as valid cognition?

(1) Prabhākara (2) Kumārila
(3) (1) and (2) both
(4) Neither (1) or (2)

764. The Mimāṁsaka upholds the
(1) theory of parataḥ prāmāṇyavāda
(2) theory of svatahprāmāṇyavāda
(3) (1) and (2) both
(4) None of the above

765. Mimāṁsaka advocates the self validity of knowledge in respect of
(1) utpatti (2) Jñāpatti
(3) samudpatti (4) (1) and (2) both

766. Who accepts non-apprehension as a independent source of knowledge?
(1) Prabhakara (2) Kumarila
(3) Gautama (4) Kapila

767. Find out of Mimāṁsaka's meaning of comparison from the following options
(1) It is the knowledge of similarity of a unknown with a known object
(2) It is known through the recollection of what was learnt from the verbal authority of a person
(3) It is a relation of a word with the object denoted by
(4) None of the above

768. Which is the most important pramāna for Mimaṁsakas?
(1) Pratyakṣa (2) Anumāna
(3) Śabda (4) Upamāna

769. Which of the following is not Mimāṁsakas view?
(1) Words and their meanings are eternal.
(2) Words cannot be created or destroyed
(3) Words can be created and destroyed
(4) Words are manifested through human efforts

770. 'Anvitābhidhānavāda' theory is related to
(1) Prabhākara (2) Kumārila
(3) Jaimini (4) Gautama

771. Upaniṣads means
(1) The end of the Vedas
(2) What destroys ignorance and gets man near to God
(3) Revealed texts
(4) None of the above

772. Prabhakara's view of error is known as
(1) Satkhyātivāda
(2) Akhyātivāda
(3) Anyathākhyātivāda
(4) Anirvacaniyakhyātivāda

773. Ṛk, Yajus, Sāma and Atharva are
(1) Different Saṁhitas
(2) Different Upaniṣads
(3) Different Brāhmaṇas
(4) None of the above

774. Which of the following has/have developed Jñāna Kānda?
(1) Shatpat Brahman scriptures
(2) Aranyakas and Upaniṣads
(3) Shrutis
(4) None of the above

775. Philosophy aims at
(1) Criticism (2) Reflection
(3) Both (1) and (2)
(4) Neither (1) nor (2)

776. The Vedanta school lays emphasis on
(1) Karma Kānda
(2) Knowledge, *i.e.*, Jñāna
(3) Both the above
(4) Neither of the above

777. What is regarded as the fountain-head of philosophy?
(1) Vedas (2) Gita
(3) Upanisads (4) None of these

778. Prabhakara's theory is criticised by.......... and..........
(1) Nyāya-Vaiśeṣika, Kumārila

(2) Nyāya, Cārvāka
(3) Mīmāṁsā, Vedānta
(4) None of the above

779. According to Prabhakara's............is only partial truth and it is imperfect knowledge.
(1) Inference (2) Smṛti
(3) Recognition (4) Postulation

780. Prabhakara's is true to his..............position in maintaining that knowledge can never misrepresent its object.
(1) Materialistic (2) Realistic
(3) Conceptualistic (4) None of these

781. Sadasatkhyāti of later Sāṁkhya and Jainism agrees mainly with the view of
(1) Rāmānuja (2) Kumārila
(3) Pravākara (4) None of these

782. 'Error is not akhyāti or non-apprehension but viparīta-khyāti or misapprehension' is maintained by
(1) Rāmānuja (2) Kumārila
(3) Pravākara (4) None

783. ....maintains the logical distinction between truth and error and regards error as a misapprehension.
(1) Kumārila (2) Śaṇkara
(3) Rāmānuja (4) None of these

784. Kumārila holds that error is a..............., a..............knowledge and not a composite of two imperfect cognitions.
(1) Valid knowledge, perfect
(2) Single psychosis, unitary
(3) Temporary knowledge, unitary
(4) None of the above

785. Kumārila claims error is not akhyāti or non-apprehension but..........or..............
(1) Satkhyāti, apprehension
(2) Viparita-khyāti, misapprehension
(3) Viparita-khyāti, apprehension
(4) None of the above

786. The earlier portion of the Veda is called
(1) Uttara-Mimāmsā
(2) Dharma-Mīmāṁsā
(3) purva-Mīmāṁsā
(4) None of the above

787. The................upholds the theory of Svataḥprāmāṇyavāda which may be translated as the theory of self-validity or intrinsic validity of knowledge.
(1) Nyāya-Vaiśeṣika
(2) Mīmamsāka
(3) Advaita Vedānta
(4) None of the above

788. According to the Mīmāṁsākas the performance of sacrifice gives rise to Karmaphala through
(1) Interference of God
(2) Creation of apūrva
(3) Some natural power
(4) Power of mantra

789. Which one of the following theses is acceptable to the Mīmāṁsākas?
(1) Knowledge is self-revealing
(2) Knowledge is revealed by factors other than itself
(3) Knowledge is neither self-revealed nor revealed by factors other than itself
(4) Knowledge is revealed by God

790. ....believes in non-apprehension as the sixth independent Pramāṇa.
(1) Rāmārila (2) Kumārila
(3) Pravākara (4) Kapila

791. ....divides testimony into personal (pauruṣeya) and impersonal (apauruṣeya).
(1) Kumārila (2) Rāmānuja
(3) Pravākara (4) None of these

792. Mīmāṁsā-sūtra is written by
(1) Patañjali (2) Jaimini
(3) Pārthasārathi (4) None of these

793. There are five valid sources of knowledge viz., inference, comparison, testimony, postulation and.......according to the Mīmāṁsākas.
(1) Non-perception (2) Savikalpaka
(3) Arthāpatti (4) None of these

794. According to pūrvamimāṁsā School of prabhākara, illusion can be explained as
(1) a kind of memory cognition
(2) a cognition of some recollected property as the property of the present object
(3) the non-cognition of the difference between the object of perception and the object of memory cognition
(4) the cognition of an entity neither truly real nor truly unreal

795. 'Anumāna can at best provide probable knowledge of an object'. This view is maintained by
(1) Mīmāṁsā (2) Cārvāka
(3) Jainism (4) Buddhism

796. Non-perception is admitted as a valid source of knowledge by..........not by..............
(1) Naiyāyikas, Yoga
(2) Kumārila Bhatta, Prabhākara
(3) Sāṁkhya, Yoga
(4) None of the above

797. ....adopts Pravākara's theory with some modification and his theory is called Satkhyāti.
(1) Naiyāyika (2) Rāmānuja
(3) Kumārila (4) None of these

798. Mimāṁsā accepts
(1) Svatahapramānya
(2) Paratahapramānya
(3) Paratahsvapramanya
(4) None of the above

799. 'The explanatory propositions in the Veda are authoritative only when they help persons to perform their duties'. This view is related to
(1) Anvitābhidhānavāda
(2) Abhihitanvayavāda
(3) Śabdanityavada (4) Jatiśaktivāda

800. The theory of Abhihitanvayavāda is given by
(1) Prabhakara (2) Kumarila
(3) Jaimini (4) Gautama

801. 'The Knowledge of meanings is due to words; but this knowledge is not due to recollection or apprehension, but to denotation'. The theory which accepts the view given above is known as
(1) Sabdanityavāda
(2) Anvitābhidhānavāda
(3) Abhihitanvayavāda
(4) Jātiśaktivāda

802. Jaimini defines dharma as
(1) Performance of vedic ceremonies
(2) Religion
(3) A command or injunction which impels men to action
(4) A network of relationship

803. According to Mimaṁsa, the authoritativeness of the Veda is supported by
(1) Social consciousness
(2) Individual conscience
(3) God (4) (1) and (2) both

804. Mimāṁsa believes liberation in a
(1) Positive manner
(2) Negative manner
(3) (1) and (2) both
(4) None of the above

805. Apurva, according to Mimāṁsa is
(1) An unseen potency produced by actions performed
(2) Actions performed in previous life
(3) Liberation
(4) unique

806. According to Prabhakara, non-apprehension of jar on the ground means

(1) perception of ground
(2) Perception of jar at same other place
(3) Jar is present in smṛti
(4) It is compared that there is not the same thing as a jar seen before

807. The character of being the object of cognition is known as
(1) Jñēya (2) Jñāna
(3) Jñānakaraṇa (4) Jñātātā

808. Both Prabhākra and Kumārila admit that cognitions, which are products of..........are objects of....................
(1) Indrias, knowledge
(2) Impressions, Pratyakṣa
(3) Ātman, Inference
(4) Sensations, perception

809. According to Kumārila, a cognition is not directly perceived, but is inferred from the................of the object.
(1) Jñāna (2) Jñāta
(3) Jñēya (4) Jñātata

810. The theory, according to which the knower, the known and the knowledge are given simultaneously in every act of cognition, is known as
(1) Jñātātāvāda
(2) Triputisaṁvit
(3) Anvitābhidhānavāda
(4) Abhihitanvayavāda

811. Which of the following pramāṇas is rejected by prabhākara as an independent source of knowledge?
(1) Anumāna (2) Abhāva
(3) Arthāpatti (4) Upamāna

812. The relationship between the word and its meaning is...........and not created by..........
(1) Artificial, convention
(2) Natural, authority
(3) Natural, convention
(4) Artificial, authority

813. Which portion of the Veda is called Karmakānda?
(1) Mantras (2) Brahmanas
(3) Upaniṣads (4) (1) and (2) both

814. Which among the following is called Jñānakānda?
(1) Upaniṣads (2) Mantras
(3) Brahmanas (4) (2) and (3) both

815. The Vedas, according to Mimāṁsakas, manifest their own
(1) Words (2) Validity
(3) Invalidity (4) letters

816. Prabhākara holds that non-vedic verbal cognition is of the nature of
(1) Pratyakṣa (2) Anumāna
(3) Śabda (4) Upamāna

817. The utterances of human beings are valid, if their authors are
(1) seers (2) Religious
(3) Politicians (4) Trustworthy

818. Who considers the utterances of trustworthy persons as a śabdapramāna?
(1) Kumārila
(2) Prabhākara
(3) (1) and (2) both
(4) Neither (1) and (2)

819. Kaivalaya means the...........from bondage.
(1) release (2) perception
(3) prakriti (4) inference

820. An unique innovation of Mimamsa Philosophy about the source of knowledge is
(1) Anupalabdhi (2) Inference
(3) Comparison (4) Testimony

821. Which one of following alternatives is accepted by Mimamsa?
(1) Svatah-pramanya, Svatah-apramanya
(2) Paratah-pramanya, Paratah-apramanya
(3) Svatah-pramanya, Paratah-apramanya
(4) Paratah-pramanya, Svatah-apramanya

822. An unique innovation of Mimaṁsā Philosophy about the source of knowledge is

(1) Anupalabdhi (2) Inference

(3) Comparison (4) Testimony

823. The view that Vedas are pauruseya is held by

(1) Jaimini (2) Sankara

(3) Gautama (4) Kapila

824. The main objective of the Mimamsa System is

(1) to establish the authority of the Upanishads

(2) to establish the authority of the Vedas

(3) to establish the authority of the Smrtis

(4) None of the above

825. Match list I with list II and select your answer from the codes given below.

List-I	List-II
(a) Sāṁkhya	(i) Paratahprāmāṇya, Paratah aprāmāṇya
(b) Buddhism	(ii) Svatahprāmāṇya, svatahaprāmāṇya
(c) Nyāya-vaiśeṣika	(iii) Paratahprāmāṇya, svatahaprāmāṇya
(d) Mimāṁsa	(iv) Svatahpramaṇya, paratahaprāmāṇya

Codes :

	(a)	(b)	(c)	(d)
(1)	(i)	(ii)	(iii)	(iv)
(2)	(ii)	(iii)	(i)	(iv)
(3)	(iv)	(iii)	(ii)	(i)
(4)	(iii)	(ii)	(i)	(iv)

826. Match list I with list II and select your answer according to the codes given below :

List-I (Philosophers)	List-II (No. of Pramanas accepted)
(a) Jaimini	(i) 3
(b) Prabhākara	(ii) 4
(c) Kumārila	(iii) 5
(d) Gautama	(iv) 6

Codes :

	(a)	(b)	(c)	(d)
(1)	(i)	(iii)	(iv)	(ii)
(2)	(ii)	(iv)	(i)	(iii)
(3)	(i)	(iv)	(ii)	(iii)
(4)	(ii)	(iii)	(i)	(iv)

827. Match List I with List II and select the correct answer by using the codes given below the lists :

List-I	List-II
(a) Pravākara	(i) Anyathākhyāti
(b) Kumārila	(ii) Yathārthakhyāti
(c) Earlier Sāṁkhya	(iii) Akhyāti
(d) Rāmānuja	(iv) Sadasatkhyāti
(e) Nyāya	(v) Satkhyāti
(f) Later Sāṁkhya and jainism	(vi) Vipparitakhyāti

Codes :

	(a)	(b)	(c)	(d)	(e)	(f)
(1)	(v)	(iii)	(vi)	(ii)	(i)	(iv)
(2)	(vi)	(v)	(iv)	(ii)	(i)	(iii)
(3)	(iii)	(vi)	(v)	(ii)	(i)	(iv)
(4)	(iii)	(ii)	(iv)	(i)	(v)	(vi)

828. Match List I with List II and select the correct answer by using the codes given below the lists

List-I (Philosophical System)	List-II (Book Associated)
(a) Nyāya	(i) Īsha-Bhāṣya
(b) Buddhism	(ii) Shabara-bhāṣya
(c) Pūrva Mimāṁsā	(iii) Ratnāvali
(d) Advaita Vedānta	(iv) Tarkasaṅgraha

Codes :

	(a)	(b)	(c)	(d)
(1)	(iv)	(ii)	(i)	(iii)
(2)	(iv)	(iii)	(ii)	(i)
(3)	(iv)	(i)	(ii)	(iii)
(4)	(iii)	(iv)	(i)	(ii)

829. Match List I with List II and choose the correct matching from the codes given below.

List-I	List-II
(a) Vidhi	(i) Praśaṁsa, ninda, parakṛti purākalpa
(b) Niṣedha	(ii) Only vidhis in disguise
(c) Arthavāda	(iii) Which impel one to action in expectation of certain results.

Codes :

	(a)	(b)	(c)
(1)	(i)	(ii)	(iii)
(2)	(iii)	(ii)	(i)
(3)	(ii)	(iii)	(i)
(4)	(iii)	(i)	(ii)

830. Match List I with List II and choose your answer from the codes given below :

List-I	List-II
(a) Kumārila	(i) Apohvāda
(b) Prabhākara	(ii) Iñātatavāda
(c) Diṁāga	(iii) Triputisamvit

Codes :

	(a)	(b)	(c)
(1)	(i)	(ii)	(iii)
(2)	(ii)	(iii)	(i)
(3)	(iii)	(i)	(ii)
(4)	(ii)	(i)	(iii)

831. Match List I with List II and select the correct answer from the codes given below—

List-I	List-II
(a) Prabhākara	(i) Negation can be reduced to perception
(b) Kumarila	(ii) Negation can be reduced either to perception or to inference
(c) Nyāya	(iii) Negation is an independent pramāna

Codes :

	(a)	(b)	(c)
(1)	(i)	(ii)	(iii)
(2)	(ii)	(iii)	(i)
(3)	(i)	(iii)	(ii)
(4)	(ii)	(i)	(iii)

832. Match List I with List II

List-I	List-II
(a) Prabhākara	(i) Consciousness is only an accidental quality of soul
(b) Kumārila	(ii) Consciousness is modal change in the self
	(iii) Akhyātivāda
	(iv) Viparitakhyātivāda

Codes :

	(a)	(b)	(c)	(d)
(1)	(i)	(ii)	(iii)	(iv)
(2)	(ii)	(i)	(iv)	(iii)
(3)	(iii)	(ii)	(iv)	(i)
(4)	(iv)	(iii)	(i)	(ii)

833. Match List I with List II and select the correct answer from the codes given below :

List-I	List-II
(a) Cārvāka	(i) Pluralism
(b) Śaṅkara	(ii) Materialism
(c) Rāmānuja	(iii) Monism
(d) Mimāṁsa	(iv) Qualified Monism

Codes :

	(a)	(b)	(c)	(d)
(1)	(ii)	(iii)	(iv)	(i)
(2)	(iii)	(ii)	(i)	(iv)
(3)	(iv)	(iii)	(ii)	(i)
(4)	(i)	(ii)	(iii)	(iv)

834. Match the following

List-I	List-II
(a) Mimamsa	(i) Jaimini
(b) Samkhya	(ii) Purusha
(c) Nyaya	(iii) Epistemology
(d) Vaisesika	(iv) Metaphysics

Codes :

	(a)	(b)	(c)	(d)
(1)	(i)	(ii)	(iii)	(iv)
(2)	(ii)	(iv)	(iii)	(i)
(3)	(iv)	(iii)	(ii)	(i)
(4)	(iii)	(iv)	(ii)	(i)

835. Match the following

List-I	List-II
(a) Nyaya	(i) Anyathakhyati
(b) Prabhakara	(ii) Akhyati
(c) Kumarila	(iii) Viparitakhyati
(d) Ramanuja	(iv) Satkhyati

Codes :

	(a)	(b)	(c)	(d)
(1)	(i)	(ii)	(iii)	(iv)
(2)	(iv)	(iii)	(ii)	(i)
(3)	(iii)	(iv)	(ii)	(i)
(4)	(ii)	(iv)	(iii)	(i)

836. Match the following

List-I	List-II
(a) Prabhakara	(i) Triputi-Samirt
(b) Kumarila	(ii) Anupalabdhi
(c) Upanishads	(iii) Jhanakanda
(d) Vaisesika	(iv) Dravya

Codes :	(a)	(b)	(c)	(d)
(1)	(i)	(ii)	(iii)	(iv)
(2)	(iv)	(iii)	(ii)	(i)
(3)	(i)	(iv)	(iii)	(ii)
(4)	(ii)	(iv)	(iii)	(i)

Directions. The following items consist of two statements, one labelled the 'Assertion A' and the other labelled the 'Reason R'. You are to examine these two statements carefully and decide if the Assertion A and the reason R individually true and if so, whether the reason is a correct explanation of the assertion. Select your answers to these items using the codes given below.

Codes :

(1) Both A and R are true and R is the correct explanation of A

(2) Both A and R are true but R is not a correct explanation of A

(3) A is true but R is false

(4) A is false but R is true.

837. **Assertion (A).** Error becomes a single psychosis according to Kumārila.

Reason (R). Error is due to a positive wrong synthesis of the two imperfect cognitions.

838. **Assertion (A).** Akhyātivāda holds that error is due to non-discrimination between the two cognitions of separate objects.

Reason (R). Error is due to a wrong synthesis of the presented and the represented objects.

839. **Assertion (A)** Atmān cannot be the agent of action.

Reason (R). The five causes adhistāna, kartā, karma, ceṣtā and daiva operating together lead to successful completion of action.

840. **Assertion (A)** According to Mimāṁsa Vedas are eternal.

Reason (R). The words are eternal.

841. **Assertion (A)** According to Mimaṁsa, letters are not produced at any time and place, but transcends them.

Reason (R). The same letter is pronounced by different persons at different places and times in different ways.

842. **Assertion (A)** Polytheism of the ordinary kind cannot be attributed to the Mimāṁsa without some qualification.

Reason (R). The Mimāṁsaka wonders how the deity can be simultaneously present in different places where he is invoked.

843. **Assertion (A)** According to Mimāṁsa Vedas are eternal.

Reason (R). The order in which the words occur in the Veda is self-determined and therefore intrinsically valid.

844. **Assertion (A)** According to kumarila Negation cannot be perceived.

Reason (R). There is no sense-object contact in negation.

845. **Assertion (A)** The non-authoritativeness of the vedas is inconceivable.

Reason (R). Since there is no author of Vedic texts, there is no possibility of defects.

846. **Assertion (A)** Prabhakara does not accept non apprehension as an independent source of knowledge.

Reason (R). When we perceive the mere space and no jar in it, we say that there is no jar.

847. **Assertion (A).** Abhava is referred as a regative category.

Reason (R). Abhava is non-perceived by sense organs.

848. **Assertion (A).** Vedas are eternal, according to Mimamsa.

Reason (R). The words are regarded as non-eternal.

849. **Assertion (A).** Negation cannot be perceived, according to Kumarila.

Reason (R). In negation, no sense-object contact is observed.

850. **Assertion (A).** According to Kumarila, error is regarded as a single psychosis.

Reason (R). Error means a positive wrong synthesis.

851. Who among the following does hold that even the liberated souls differ in degrees

(1) Sankara (2) Ramanuja
(3) Madhva (4) Gaudpada

852. Ramanuja's theory of causation is known as

(1) Vivartavāda
(2) Prakriti parināmavāda
(3) Brahma parināmavāda
(4) Asatkāryavāda

853. The word 'māyā' to Sañkara means :

(1) Sat only (2) Asat only
(3) Both sat and asat
(4) Neither sat nor asat but indescribable

854. Prapathi is the relation between

(1) Jiva and Jagat
(2) Brahma and Jagat
(3) Jiva and Iśvara
(4) Jiva and Brahman

855. For Ramanuja, liberation is to attain

(1) Sāmīpya (2) Sānnidhya
(3) Sāyujya (4) Sālokya

856. According to Madhva jīva and Brahman are

(1) Different (2) Non-different
(3) Both different and non-different
(4) None of the above

857. The imposition of some quality on a thing where it is not, is termed as :

(1) Avidyā (2) Adhyāsa
(3) Akhyāti
(4) None of the above

858. Nirguna Brahman is the ultimate truth according to

(1) Rāmānuja (2) Madhva
(3) Śaṁkara (4) Nimbārka

859. Which is not the aim of the study of Vedānta scripture ?

(1) Liberation from avidya
(2) Self realization
(3) Brahma realization
(4) Worldly prosperity

860. Sribhāṣya is the authoritative text of

(1) Viśiṣṭādvaita (2) Advaita
(3) Dvaita (4) Dvaitādvaita

861. Rāmānuja has divided bound souls into four classes : superhuman, human, animal and

(1) Mobile (2) Immobile
(3) Bird (4) Plant

862. Brahman is called as indeterminate or

(1) Nirguṇa (2) Saguna
(3) Infinite (4) None of these

863. Rāmānuja believes the entire universe including the material world and the individual souls is a real modification of Brahman, thus his theory is known as

(1) Pariṇāmvāda
(2) Brahmapariṇāmavāda

(3) Brahmavāda
(4) None of the above

864. What is trivṛtkaraṇa?
(1) The three elements, viz., fire, water and earth become mixed up together and give rise to all gross objects which we perceive in the material world
(2) The three elements are controlled by God
(3) The three elements are the root cause of all changes in the material world
(4) None of the above

865. When the self is in bondage, its knowledge is obscured by its
(1) Ignorance (2) Karmas
(3) Consciousness (4) None of these

866. In............soul enjoys infinite knowledge and everlasting bliss.
(1) Liberation (2) Ultimate state
(3) Divine sovereignty
(4) None of these

867. Soul is the controlled (niyāmya) and .... is its controller (niyantā).
(1) Knowledge
(2) God
(3) True knowledge
(4) None of the above

868. The worship of Shiva goes back to
(1) Atharvaveda (2) Yajurveda
(3) Upaniṣads (4) Puraṇas

869. The commentary on the Bhāgvata called Subodhini is written by
(1) Rāmānuja (2) Śaṅkara
(3) Vallabhacharya (4) Nimbārka

870. Who is known as Ānandatirtha or Pūrṇaprajña?
(1) Rāmānuja
(2) Madhvāchārya
(3) Vallabhacharya
(4) Śaṅkara

871. Māyā or avidyā means
(1) Pure illusion
(2) Positive wrong knowledge
(3) Absolutely wrong knowledge
(4) Non-existence

872. ....is indescribable, thus it is mithyā.
(1) Illusion (2) Consciousness
(3) Māyā (4) None of these

873. ....is the ground on which the world appears through Māyā according to Śaṅkara.
(1) Brahman (2) God
(3) Soul (4) Consciousness

874. Madhvācharya is the champion of
(1) Unqualified dualism
(2) Nominalism
(3) Realism
(4) None of the above

875. According to.............., God is Lord of Karma who is pleased only by bhakti.
(1) Śaṅkara (2) Madhvāchārya
(3) Udayana (4) Śridhara

876. Śaṅkara believes that ultimate reality, Brahman associated with its māyā appears as
(1) Soul (2) Supreme Soul
(3) Īśvara (4) None of these

877. ....is pure consciousness which is pure existence and pure bliss also.
(1) Self (2) God
(3) Supreme Lord (4) None of these

878. Śaṅkara believes...........or.............cannot be negated, for it is the ultimate ground on which all effects or phenomena are superposed.
(1) God, soul (2) Brahman, soul
(3) Brahman (4) None of these

879. According to Śaṅkara, ultimate reality is
(1) God (2) Soul
(3) Brahman (4) None of these

880. Śaṅkara suggests that from the phenomenal point of view the world is
(1) Real (2) Unreal
(3) Illusion (4) None of these

881. World is creation of.................., according to Śaṅkara.
(1) Brahman (2) Īśvara
(3) Supreme soul (4) None of these

882. Śaṅkara's theory of world is known as
(1) Brahmavāda
(2) Brahmavivarta-vāda
(3) Parināmvāda
(4) None of the above

883. .... is the creator, preserver and destroyer of this world which is his appearance.
(1) Brahman (2) Īśvara
(3) Supreme soul (4) None of these

884. ....Brahman or Īśvara in Śaṅkara's philosophy is the object of worship.
(1) Saguna (2) Nirguṇa
(3) Supreme (4) Ultimate

885. Śankara śuggests that from............point of view the world is rcal.
(1) Phenomenal (2) Spiritual
(3) Logic (4) Epistemological

886. Creatorship of the world is God's.......... according to Śaṅkara.
(1) Svarūpa-lakṣaṇa
(2) Taṭastha-lakṣana
(3) Vyāvaharikadṛṣṭi
(4) None of the above

887. ....is like the magician who is a juggler only to those who are deceived by his trick according to Śaṅkara.
(1) God (2) Brahman
(3) Soul (4) None of these

888. The .... is both the locus and the object of Māyā.
(1) Soul (2) God
(3) Highest Brahman
(4) None of the above

889. Creation is nothing but the phenomenal appearance of................due to avidyā, according to Śaṅkara.
(1) Brahman (2) God
(3) Soul (4) None of these

890. Śaṅkara says, Brahman, being super-sensuous, can be realized only through
(1) Knowledge (2) Shruti
(3) Brahamajñāna (4) None of these

891. Śaṅkara assets that the Absolute can be realized only through
(1) Knowledge (2) Brahmajñāna
(3) Pramā (4) None of these

892. Rāmānuja recognises three sources of knowledge, namely
(1) Perception, inference, comparison
(2) Perception, inference, verbal testimony
(3) Inference, verbal testimony, non-perception
(4) Comparison, verbal testimony, non-perception

893. Rāmānuja believes Karmakāṇḍa and the jñānakāṇḍa of the Veda are
(1) Complementary to each other
(2) Similar to each other
(3) Opposite to each other
(4) None of the above

894. According to Rāmānuja, the individual soul is
(1) only Jnātā
(2) Jnātā and Kartā
(3) Kartā and Bhoktā
(4) Jnātā Kartā and Bhoktā

895. Saguṇa Brahman is admitted by Rāmānuja because

(1) Pure identity can only be between two names
(2) Pure difference can only be between any two concepts
(3) any knowledge involves identification and differentiation
(4) the law of identity of logic is essential for any knowledge

896. Rāmānuja believes in................., the theory that the effect necessarily pre-exists in its material cause.
(1) Asatkāryavāda (2) Satkāryavāda
(3) Syādavāda (4) None of these

897. Which one of the following statements is not correct about Rāmānuja's conception of the world
(1) God creates the manifold world by a gracious act of will
(2) The unconscious part of God is the source of the material objects of the world.
(3) The world is as real as God Himself
(4) There is no dissolution of the world

898. Rāmānuja claims that all knowledge is.......... and there is no illusory object anywhere.
(1) True (2) False
(3) Perfect (4) None of these

899. The relation of the individual soul with God according to Rāmānuja, is
(1) Samavāya (2) Saṁyoga
(3) Aprthaksiddhi (4) Bhedābheda

900. According to Rāmānuja, Brahman is devoid of
(1) Sajātiya and vijātiya bheda
(2) Sajātiya vijātiya and Svagatabheda
(3) Sajātiya and Svagatabheda
(4) vijātiya and Svagatabheda

901. Which one of the following distinctions exists in Brahman according to Rāmānuja
(1) Vijatiya (2) Sajatiya
(3) Svagata (4) Bahya

902. Which one of the following is not acceptable to Rāmānuja?
(1) Brahman is qualified
(2) Brahman is Ishvara
(3) Jivas merge in Ishvara and have no separate identity
(4) Jiva is not identical with Brahman

903. Rāmānuja admitted that
(1) the world and souls are as real as God Himself
(2) souls are as real as God, but the world is unreal
(3) God alone is real, the world and souls are unreal
(4) though real, souls are created and destroyed by God.

904. Which one of the following statements is correct according to Rāmānuja?
(1) God can never be proved by inference. His existence is to be admitted on the testimony of scriptural texts and of those.
(2) God can be proved by inference alone. Scriptural sources can only give some secondary support to this proof.
(3) Inference and scriptural texts prove the existence of God independently of each other.
(4) Existence of God is a matter of faith and devotion neither scriptures nor reason can prove it.

905. Rāmānuja agrees with the .... and the .... in maintaining that all knowledge points to a corresponding object existing really and outside of it.
(1) Naiyāyika, sāṅkhya
(2) Naiyāyika, Mīmāṁsaka
(3) Sāṅkhya, Yoga
(4) Mīmāṁsaka, Yoga

906. According to................, knowledge ajada or immaterial and is distinguished from both matter and spirit.

(1) Rāmānuja (2) Śaṅkara
(3) Madhva (4) Nimbārka

907. Who was the chief exponent of Māyavāda?
(1) Śaṅkarāchārya
(2) Rāmānuja
(3) Both (1) and (2)
(4) None of the above

908. In the process of creation, ... is the creative power which at first remains unmanifested, then becomes differentiated into subtle objects, and then into the gross ones.
(1) Atom
(2) Māyā
(3) Three basic elements (fire, water and air)
(4) None of the above

909. Vedārtha-saṅgraha is written by
(1) Vallabha (2) Madhva
(3) Rāmānuja (4) Nimbārka

910. Two centuries after Rāmānuja, his followers became rigidly divided into two school ....and................. .
(1) Vaḍagalai, Teṅgalai
(2) Ubhaya-Vedāntins, Vedāntins
(3) Veṅkaṭanāth, Lokāchārya
(4) None of the above

911. The view of the................is very much similar to vedānta.
(1) Buddhism
(2) Mimaṁsa
(3) Svatantra Vijñānavada
(4) None of the above

912. ....claims that the reality of a permanent self-luminous Self which is a pure consciousness must be admitted.
(1) Śaṅkara (2) Śāntarakṣita
(3) Kamalashila (4) None of these

913. Illusory modification of any substance, as of the rope into the snake is called...............
(1) Vivarta, pariṇāma
(2) Avidyā, result
(3) Illusion, pariṇāma
(4) None of the above

914. Rāmānuja admits that the unconscious element in God really changes into the world, thus his theory known as
(1) Brahmavāda (2) Pariṇāmavāda
(3) Advaita vedānta (4) None of these

915. 'The Life Divine' is written by
(1) M. Hiriyanna
(2) S.N. Dasgupta
(3) Śri Aurobindo
(4) S.S. Sastri

916. Rāmānuja holds that the created world is as real as
(1) God (2) Brahman
(3) Spiritual world (4) None of these

917. The Upaniṣads, the Brahma-Sūtra and the...........are called 'Prasthāna-traya' or the three basic works of Vedānta.
(1) Purāṇas (2) Bhagavad Gītā
(3) Īshā-Bhāsya (4) None of these

918. ....is known as the first available systematic treatise on Advaita Vedānta.
(1) Gauḍapāda-Kārika
(2) Brahma-Sūtra
(3) Shāiriraka-Bhāsya
(4) None of the above

919. The first systematic expounder of Advaita Vedānta is
(1) Gauḍapāda (2) Śaṅkara
(3) Nāgārjuna (4) Rāmānuja

920. The fundamental doctrine of Gauḍapāda, the world, being only an appearance, is in fact never created, is known as
(1) No origination or Ajātivāda
(2) Advaita Vedānta
(3) Dependent origination
(4) None of the above

921. Saṅkara's criticism towards..............is that of hatred and animosity and thus it is not fully justified everywhere.

(1) nyāya (2) Buddhism
(3) jainism (4) Sāṅkhya

922. Jainism and...............maintain that the universal is not a mere name and is identical with the particulars in point of existence.

(1) Vedānta (2) Buddhism
(3) Mīmāṁsāka (4) Cārvāka

923. ....suggests sāmānya as a reality independent of individual objects.

(1) Praśastapāda (2) Naiyāyika
(3) Kaṇāda (4) None of these

924. The phenomenal world is condemned by..........as unreal exactly in the spirit of Mahāyāna Buddhism and of Gaudapāda.

(1) Śaṅkara (2) Rāmānuja
(3) Madhva (4) Vallabha

925. Who is Sat-Chit-Ānanda according to Śaṅkara?

(1) Para Brahma (2) Īśvara
(3) Soul (4) None of these

926. According to..............Īśvara is the reflection of Brahman in Māyā, while jiva is the reflection of Brahman in Avidyā.

(1) Pratibimbavāda
(2) Syādvāda
(3) Appearance theory
(4) None of the above

927. ....theory is not atheism but it is the logical perfection of the theistic faith.

(1) Śaṅkara's (2) Rāmānuja's
(3) Madhva's (4) Vallabha's

928. ....advocates qualitative monism and quantitative pluralism of souls.

(1) Saṅkara (2) Mādhva
(3) Śridhara (4) Rāmānuja

929. Śaṅkara's conception of God as Parābrahman means

(1) Saguṇa Brahman
(2) Nirguna Brahman
(3) Absolute
(4) Non of the above

930. ....like the Upaniṣads believes in the gradual revelation of truth in stages through which spiritual progress takes place.

(1) Advaita Vedānta (2) Nyāya
(3) Vaiśeṣika (4) Yoga

931. In Rāmānuja's philosophy God is identified with the

(1) Universe
(2) Absolute
(3) Ultimate principle
(4) None of the above

932. God may be viewed through causal state of Brahman and the

(1) Last stage of Iśvara
(2) Effect state of Brahman
(3) Effect state of Avidyā
(4) None of the above

933. ....belongs to the self and persists even in deep sleep and in liberation.

(1) Avidyā
(2) Knowledge
(3) Consciousness
(4) None of the above

934. The....................is conceived as a real knower, a real agent and a real enjoyer.

(1) God (2) Soul
(3) Supreme Lord (4) None of these

935. Eternal consciousness is only an inseparable attribute of God, not His very essence, as maintained in the

(1) Vaiśeṣika view
(2) Nyāya philosophy

(3) Advaita Vedānta
(4) Yoga Philosophy

936. What is the cause of bondage according to Rāmānuja?
(1) Embodiment
(2) Karma
(3) Avidyā
(4) Wrong viewpoint about the world

937. Rāmānuja accepts the .... interpretation of creation.
(1) Naiyāyika's (2) Sāṁkhya's
(3) Upaniṣadic (4) None of these

938. Rāmānuja believes that God manifests Himself in.................forms in order to help his devotees.
(1) Three (2) Four
(3) Five (4) Six

939. Rāmānuja suggests that God as............. descends down on this earth in the human or the animal form in order to punish the wicked and restore the dharma.
(1) Antaryāmi
(2) Avatāra
(3) Vyūha
(4) Supreme Lord

940. God's manifestation as the ruler of the cognitive aspect of the souls and as the destroyer of this universe is called
(1) Jivatattva (2) Saṅkarṣana
(3) Avatāra (4) None of these

941. Vibhava or Avatara is two kinds
(1) Primary and secondary
(2) Primary and ultimate
(3) Jiva and Ajiva
(4) None of the above

942. ....believes in the utility of worshipping God and many deities as a state on the way to the highest truth.
(1) Śaṅkara (2) Rāmānuja
(3) Mahāvira (4) Udayana

943. Rāmānuja recognises................, souls and God as ultimate and real.
(1) Matter (2) World
(3) Atoms (4) None of these

944. The..................deny all the predicates of God, even worshipability.
(1) Upaniṣads
(2) Puranas
(3) Vedanta philosophy
(4) Non of the above

945. What is an individual soul according to Rāmānuja?
(1) It is a spiritual substance which is unreal
(2) It is not beyond creation and destruction
(3) It is an attribute or mode of God and forms part of His body
(4) None of the above

946. In the state of creation,................is embodied according to its Karmas, while in the state of dissolution or liberation, it remains in itself
(1) The individual soul
(2) Achit
(3) Consciousness
(4) None of the above

947. As the perfect personality God is devoid of all..............and possesses all
(1) Pleasure, pain
(2) Demerit, merit
(3) Avidyā, pleasure
(4) None of the above

948. Rāmānuja attempts a harmonious combination of absolutism with personal
(1) Realism (2) Nominalism
(3) Theism (4) None of these

949. Gitābhāsya is written by
(1) Śaṅkara (2) Rāmānuja
(3) Vallabhachārya (4) Chaitanyadev

950. Rāmānuja's view is known as
(1) Visiṣṭādvaita (2) Dvaita
(3) Advaita (4) None of these

951. ....is devoid of all distinctions, external as well as internal.
(1) God (2) Soul
(3) Brahman (4) None of these

952. Who among the following philosophers held the view that oneness of ātman and Brahman can be realised in this life itself?
(1) Madhav (2) Kapila
(3) Jayarāsi (4) Śaṅkara

953. ....and...............advocate the view known as anirvachaniyakyāti
(1) Vijñānavāda, Advaita Vedānta
(2) Vijñānavāda, Sāṁkhya
(3) Advaita Vedānta, Yoga
(4) None of the above

954. The subjective error is regarded as pratibhāsa by
(1) Naiyāyika (2) Vedānta
(3) Jain (4) None of these

955. Which one of the following pairs is correctly matched?
(1) Jainism : The soul is the stream of consciousness or mental states.
(2) Nyāya-Vaiśeṣika : The soul is a substance which is partless, eternal and which makes knowledge possible.
(3) Buddhism : The soul is a pure, conscious, blissful reality which appears as divided into many selves.
(4) Śankara : The individual soul is a portion of God, but it is limited and not all pervading.

956. Which one of the following features according to Rāmānuja makes reality qualified?
(1) Heterogeneous distinctions
(2) Homogeneous distinctions
(3) Internal distinctions
(4) Unity in diversity

957. Vedānta literally means
(1) Vedic rituals
(2) Problems discussed in Vedas
(3) The end of the Vedas
(4) None of the above

958. According to Advaita Vedānta, the status of the world is
(1) real
(2) unreal
(3) both real and unreal
(4) neither real nor unreal

959. According to Ramanuja, God is regarded as the .... controller of the soul.
(1) inner (2) ordinary
(3) external (4) extraordinary

960. Which one of the following is not a school of vedānta thought?
(1) Bhaktivāda
(2) Visistadvaita
(3) Dvaita
(4) Shuddhadvaita

961. The most important pramāna which gives the knowledge of Brahman, according to Vedānta, is
(1) Pratyaksa (2) Anumāna
(3) Arthapātti (4) Sabda

962. The relation among Brahman, Maya and Jiva in Advaita Vedanta is such that
(1) Jiva cannot exist without Maya and Maya can not exist without Brahman.
(2) Jiva and Brahman can exist without Maya since Jiva is Brahman only.
(3) Maya can exist alone since it is beginningless.
(4) Brahman is not related to either Jiva or Maya in any sense.

963. Ramanuja advocates
(1) Monism
(2) Dualism
(3) Qualified monism
(4) Dual-dualism

964. According to Śankara the aphrorism 'tattvamast' establishes the identity of the individual soul with reality through
(1) its primary meaning
(2) its secondary meaning
(3) both its primary and its secondary meaning
(4) neither its primary not its secondary meaning

965. According to Saṅkara Vedanta the relation between Maya and Brahman is
(1) Vastavika
(2) Svatah-Siddha
(3) Anupādhika
(4) Kāryakāranabhava

966. Which one of the following holds anirvacaniyakhyati as a theory of error?
(1) Ramanuja-vedanta
(2) Saṁkhaya
(3) Prabhakara-Mimāṁsa
(4) Śankara-vedanta

967. According to Śaṅkara, Brahman is
(1) the totality of mind and matter
(2) pure consciousness
(3) a series of momentary cognitions
(4) identical with Prakṛti

968. Which one of the following pramāṇas according to Advaita Vedānta is recommended for the knowledge of Abhāva?
(1) Shruti (2) Anumāna
(3) Upamāna (4) Anuplabdhi

969. Which one of the following statements according to Advaita Vedānta is true of knowledge of Brahman?
(1) Both Pratykṣa and Anumāna give us knowledge of Brahman
(2) Arthāpatti alone give us knowledge of Brahman
(3) Sruti is the only source of knowledge of Brahman
(4) Both Arthāpatti and Anupālabdhi give us knowledge of Brahman.

970. Who among the following is a staunch protagonist of the doctrine that mokṣa can be attained only by knowledge and not by Karma?
(1) Madhyācārya (2) Vallabhācārya
(3) Śankāracārya (4) Rāmānujacārya

971. Who was the chief exponent of Māyāvāda?
(1) Śaṅkara (2) Rāmānuja
(3) Madhva (4) None of these

972. In the 'rope-snake' illusion according to Advaita Vedānta
(1) The snake is unreal
(2) The snake is real
(3) The snake is neither real nor unreal
(4) The snake is dreamt

973. Where can the roots of most of the philosophy of India be traced?
(1) In Vedas
(2) In Bhagvad Gita
(3) In Ramayan
(4) In Upaniṣads

974. Who calls Advaitins a 'deceitful demons'?
(1) Rāmānujacārya (2) Mādhavacārya
(3) Vallabhācārya (4) Nimbārka

975. How many pramāṇas are accepted by Madhvācārya?
(1) 3 (2) 4
(3) 5 (4) 6

976. Madhvā advocates the reality of differences
(1) five-fold (2) four-fold
(3) three-fold (4) two-fold

977. Which of the following theories of Madhvā is not common to Rāmānuja's?
(1) Three sources of knowledge
(2) God can be known only by the scriptures
(3) Purva and the uttara-Mimāṁsa are forming a single science
(4) Authorlessness of Veda

978. According to Madhva
(1) God is author of the Veda
(2) God is the great binder and collector of the Veda
(3) God is the great teacher of the Veda
(4) None of the above

979. According to Rāmānuja God, pleased by................helps the devotee to attain perfect knowledge by removing............ .
(1) Upāsana, doṣa (2) Dhyana, obstacles
(3) Bhakti, obstacles
(4) Dhruvāsmṛti, doṣa

980. According to Rāmānuja prapatti is necessary for liberation Prapatti is
(1) Constant remembrance of god
(2) Constant uneditation
(3) Complete self-surrender
(4) Prayer

981. According to Advaita Vedānta.............hides the nature of the shell and makes it look like silver
(1) Mithyā (2) Darkness
(3) Avidya (4) None of these

982. Negatively avidyā covers(āvraṇa) and positively it......(vikṣepa) silver on it.
(1) Silver, modifies
(2) Shellness, projects
(3) Brightness, projects
(4) None of the above

983. Vedantins think error is...............superimposition which does not really affect the ground and is removed by right knowledge
(1) Indefinite (2) Indescribable
(3) Infallible (4) None of these

984. Rāmānuja's Satkhyāti is also known as
(1) Anirvacanīyakhyāti
(2) Akhyāti
(3) Sadasatkhyāti (4) Yatharthakhyāti

985. ....goes to the extent of saying that the shell appears as silver because there are some particles of silver in it and explains this by his interpretation of triplication
(1) Saṁkhya (2) Rāmānuja
(3) Kumarila (4) None of these

986. Who says that God is identified with the absolute?
(1) Rāmānuja (2) Hegel
(3) Shankara (4) Jiva

987. Which one of the following is correctly matched?
(1) Anupalabdhi as a Pramāṇa — Advaita Vedānta
(2) Sabda as a Pramāṇa — Buddhism
(3) Arthāpatti as a Pramāṇa — Nyaya Vaiśeṣika
(4) Anumāna as a Pramāṇa — Cārvāka

988. Which one of the following according to Rāmānuja correctly represent the status of soul?
(1) There is unqualified identity between soul and God
(2) God and soul are two separate entities
(3) Soul is same as the body
(4) The relation between soul and God is that of part and whole.

989. Which one of the following represents the correct sequence in the Advaitic tradition ?
(1) Vyas, Śaṅkara, Govindapāda, Goudapāda.
(2) Goudapāda, Vyas, Śaṅkara,

Govindapāda.
(3) Śaṅkara, Vyas, Govindapāda, Goudapāda.
(4) Vyas, Goudapāda, Govindapāda, Śaṅkara.

990. Which charges imposes by Rāmānuja in the theory of Māyā.
(1) Āshrayānupapatti
(2) Tirodhānānupapatti
(3) Svarūpānupapatti
(4) All of the above

991. Match List I with List II and select the correct answer from the codes given below

List-I	List-II
(a) Sālokya	(i) nearness to god
(b) Sāmipya	(ii) having the external form
(c) Sārupya	(iii) residence in the same place with god
(d) Sāyujya	(iv) entering into the body of god

Codes :

	(a)	(b)	(c)	(d)
(1)	(i)	(ii)	(iii)	(iv)
(2)	(ii)	(iii)	(iv)	(i)
(3)	(iii)	(i)	(ii)	(iv)
(4)	(iv)	(iii)	(ii)	(i)

992. Match List I with List II and select the correct answer by using the codes given below the lists :

List-I	List-II
(a) Matter, souls and God and real	(i) Madhva
(b) Soul though a dependent part of God is essentially different from him	(ii) Vallabha
(c) Shiva is the supreme reality who possesses the eight attributes	(iii) Rāmānuja
(d) Distinguishes between jagat or praṇpañch and saṁsāra	(iv) Shaiva Siddhānta

Codes :	(a)	(b)	(c)	(d)
(1)	(iii)	(iv)	(i)	(ii)
(2)	(iii)	(i)	(iv)	(ii)
(3)	(iv)	(iii)	(ii)	(i)
(4)	(ii)	(iv)	(i)	(iii)

993. Match List I with List II and select the correct answer by using the codes given below the lists :

List-I	List-II
(a) Nyāya	(i) Shloka-Vārtika
(b) Buddhism	(ii) Chhāndogya-Bhāṣya
(c) Pūrva-Mīmāṁsa	(iii) Tattvacintāmani
(d) Advaita vedānta	(iv) Pramṇavārtika

Codes :	(a)	(b)	(c)	(d)
(1)	(iii)	(iv)	(ii)	(i)
(2)	(iii)	(iv)	(i)	(ii)
(3)	(iv)	(iii)	(i)	(ii)
(4)	(ii)	(iv)	(i)	(iii)

994. Match List-I with List-II and select the correct answer by using the codes given below the lists

List-I	List-II
(a) Ever-free souls which were not bound	(i) Baddha souls
(b) Liberated souls which were once bound but obtained liberation through their action knowledge etc.	(ii) Nityamukta souls
(c) Bound souls which were wandering in Saṁsāra on account of ignorance and bad Karmas.	(iii) Mukta souls
	(iv) Niyāmya souls

Codes :	(a)	(b)	(c)
(1)	(ii)	(iii)	(i)
(2)	(iv)	(iii)	(i)
(3)	(iv)	(ii)	(iii)
(4)	(iv)	(iii)	(ii)

995. Match List I with List II and select the correct answer by using the codes given below the lists :

List-I	List-II
(a) Viśiṣṭādvaita	(i) Nimbārka
(b) Dvaita	(ii) Mādhva
(c) Śuddhādvaita	(iii) Rāmānuja
(d) Dvaitādvaita	(iv) Viṣṇusvāmi and Vallabha

Codes :

	(a)	(b)	(c)	(d)
(1)	(iii)	(i)	(iv)	(ii)
(2)	(iv)	(iii)	(ii)	(i)
(3)	(iii)	(ii)	(iv)	(i)
(4)	(iv)	(ii)	(iii)	(i)

996. Match List I with List II and select the correct answer by using the codes given below the lists :

List-I	List-II
(a) Vaiṣṇavism	(i) Tipiṭaka
(b) Shaivism	(ii) Tantra
(c) Shāktism	(iii) Shiva Āgama
(d) Buddhism	(iv) Pañcharātra Samhitā

Codes :

	(a)	(b)	(c)	(d)
(1)	(iii)	(ii)	(iv)	(i)
(2)	(iv)	(ii)	(iii)	(i)
(3)	(iv)	(iii)	(ii)	(i)
(4)	(ii)	(iv)	(iii)	(i)

997. Match List I with List II and select the correct answer by using the codes given below the lists :

List-I	List-II
(a) Advaita	(i) Āsteya
(b) Viśiṣṭādvaita	(ii) Spanda
(c) Dvaita	(iii) Bhakti
(d) Kashmir Śaivism	(iv) Prapatti
	(v) Jñāna

Codes :

	(a)	(b)	(c)	(d)
(1)	(v)	(iv)	(iii)	(ii)
(2)	(ii)	(i)	(iii)	(v)
(3)	(v)	(ii)	(iv)	(i)
(4)	(iii)	(iv)	(v)	(ii)

998. Match List I with List II and select the correct answer by using the codes given below the lists :

List-I	List-II
(a) The source of the material objects	(i) Trivṛtkāraṇa
(b) The subtle elements fire, water and earth manifest qualities	(ii) Unconscious matter (acit)
(c) In every object there is a mixture of three elements	(iii) māyā
(d) God is the wieldier of a magical power	(iv) Sattva, rajas tamas

Codes :

	(a)	(b)	(c)	(d)
(1)	(ii)	(iv)	(i)	(iii)
(2)	(ii)	(i)	(iii)	(iv)
(3)	(iii)	(ii)	(i)	(iv)
(4)	(iv)	(iii)	(ii)	(i)

999. Match the following

List-I	List-II
(a) Shankara	(i) Jnana
(b) Mimamsa	(ii) Karma
(c) Madhva	(iii) Bhakti
(d) Acit	(iv) Unconscious matter

Codes :

	(a)	(b)	(c)	(d)
(1)	(i)	(ii)	(iii)	(iv)
(2)	(iv)	(iii)	(ii)	(i)
(3)	(iii)	(iv)	(ii)	(i)
(4)	(i)	(iv)	(iii)	(ii)

1000. Match the following

List-I	List-II
(a) Dravita	(i) Bhakti
(b) Ramanuja	(ii) Prapatti
(c) Vallabha	(iii) Dvaitadvaita
(d) Mukta souls	(iv) Liberated souls

Codes :

	(a)	(b)	(c)	(d)
(1)	(i)	(ii)	(iii)	(iv)
(2)	(iv)	(iii)	(ii)	(i)
(3)	(ii)	(iii)	(iv)	(i)
(4)	(i)	(iv)	(iii)	(ii)

1001. Match the following

List-I	List-II
(a) Shankara	(i) Non-dualist
(b) Ramanuja	(ii) Parinamavada
(c) Madhva	(iii) Dvaita
(d) Jiva	(iv) Individual soul

Codes :

	(a)	(b)	(c)	(d)
(1)	(ii)	(iv)	(iii)	(i)
(2)	(iv)	(iii)	(ii)	(i)
(3)	(iii)	(iv)	(ii)	(i)
(4)	(i)	(ii)	(iii)	(iv)

1002. Match the following

List-I	List-II
(a) Chit	(i) Souls
(b) Acit	(ii) Matter
(c) Ramanuja	(iii) Rejection of Maya
(d) Shankara	(iv) Monist

Codes :	(a)	(b)	(c)	(d)
(1)	(i)	(ii)	(iii)	(iv)
(2)	(i)	(iv)	(iii)	(ii)
(3)	(iii)	(iv)	(ii)	(i)
(4)	(iv)	(iii)	(ii)	(i)

1003. Match the following

List-I	List-II
(a) Advita	(i) Shankara
(b) Maya	(ii) Locus of Brahman
(c) Ramanuja	(iii) Qualified monism
(d) Madhva	(iv) Bhakti

Codes :

	(a)	(b)	(c)	(d)
(1)	(i)	(ii)	(iii)	(iv)
(2)	(ii)	(iv)	(iii)	(i)
(3)	(iv)	(iii)	(ii)	(i)
(4)	(ii)	(iii)	(iv)	(i)

1004. Match the following

List-I	List-II
(a) Baddha souls	(i) Bounds souls
(b) Nityamukti souls	(ii) Ever-free souls
(c) Mukata souls	(iii) Obtains liberation through action
(d) Vallabha	(iv) Suddhavaita

Codes :

	(a)	(b)	(c)	(d)
(1)	(i)	(ii)	(iii)	(iv)
(2)	(iv)	(ii)	(iii)	(i)
(3)	(iv)	(iii)	(ii)	(i)
(4)	(ii)	(iii)	(iv)	(i)

1005. Match the following

List-I	List-II
(a) Shankara	(i) Vivartavada
(b) Ramanuja	(ii) Visistadvaita
(c) Madhva	(iii) Dvaita
(d) Nimbarka	(iv) Dvaita dvaita

Codes :

	(a)	(b)	(c)	(d)
(1)	(i)	(ii)	(iii)	(iv)
(2)	(ii)	(iii)	(iv)	(i)
(3)	(iv)	(iii)	(ii)	(i)
(4)	(iv)	(ii)	(iii)	(i)

Directions. The following items consist of two statements, one labelled the 'Assertion A' and the other labelled the 'Reason R'. You are to examine these two statements carefully and decide if the Assertion A and the reason R individually true and if so, whether the reason is a correct explanation of the assertion. Select your answers to these items using the codes given below

Codes:

(1) Both A and R are true and R is the correct explanation of A

(2) Both A and R are true but R is not a correct explanation of A

(3) A is true but R is false

(4) A is false but R is true.

1006. **Assertion (A).** Madhva advocates both quantitative and qualitative pluralism of souls.

Reason (R). Madhva believes that in liberation, the souls differ in degrees regarding their possession of knowledge and enjoyment of bliss.

1007. **Assertion (A).** According to Rāmānuja Bhakti helps the devotee to attain perfect knowledge by removing obstacles.

Reason (R). God becomes pleased by Bhakti.

1008. **Assertion (A).** According to Rāmānuja, Jiva is a Prakara of God.

Reason (R). Jiva is a transformation of god.

1009. **Assertion (A).** Jagat is a vivarta of Brahman.

Reason (R). Jagat belongs to the Vyavahariki Satta.

1010. **Assertion (A).** According to Śaṅkara the so-called Pramanas remove ignorance but do not give real knowledge.

Reason (R). The Pramānas are based on the distinction between subject and object.

1011. **Assertion (A).** According to Śaṅkara, the individual selves are identical with Brahman.

Reason (R). The Laksyartha of the statement Tattvamasi should be admitted instead of its Śakyārtha.

1012. **Assertion (A).** Śaṅkara repeatedly asserts that the Absolute can be realised through knowledge and knowledge alone.

Reason (R). Knowledge only removes ignorance and then reality shines forth by itself.

1013. **Assertion (A).** An advaitin, 'tat tvam asi' gives an identity statement.

Reason (R). This statement has to be interpreted with the help of lakaṣanāvṛtti.

1014. **Assertion (A).** Rāmānuja believes that the relation of the soul and Karma is said to be beginningless.

Reason (R). In liberation, the soul shines in its pristine purity untouched by Karma and therefore can never descend to the mundane existence any more.

1015. **Assertion (A).** Absolute Existence-Consciousness is nothing other than God described by the Upaniṣads.

Reason (R). Only pure existence is beyond actual and possible contradiction.

1016. **Assertion (A).** There must be an intelligent cause (karta) of the world for all its effects and it is God.

Reason (R). All the composite objects of the world, *e.g.* mountains, seas, the sun, the moon must be the effect of some cause.

1017. **Assertion (A).** The Upaniṣads conceive Brahman not only as the pure ground of all reality and consciousness but also the ultimate source of all joy.

Reason (R). The proof of the Self's being the source of all joy is that it is not dearest thing to man.

1018. **Assertion (A).** God is the object of worship.

Reason (R). Creatorship of the world is God's essence.

1019. **Assertion (A).** Rāmānuja suggests three things, *viz.*, matter, souls and God as ultimate and real.

Reason (R). All these three are equally real, but the first two are absolutely dependent on God.

1020. **Assertion (A).** Māyā is bhāvarūpa according to Śaṅkara.

Reason (R). Māyā is indescribable and indefinable for it is neither real nor unreal nor both.

1021. **Assertion (A).** Māyā, according to Advaita Vedānta, is indescribable.

Reason (R). Māyā cannot be known by any valid means.

1022. **Assertion (A).** Rāmānuja has adopted a kind of realistic epistemology.

Reason (R). He says that the object of knowledge as well as that of illusion is real.

1023. **Assertion (A).** According to Advaita Vedānta to know Brahman is to be Brahman.

Reason (R). There is a relation of non-difference between Ātman and Brahman.

1024. **Assertion (A).** Madhva calls Advaitins 'deceitful demons'.

Reason (R). "They play in the darkness of ignorance and provide false interpretation of Veda", Madhava says.

1025. **Assertion (A).** Māyā is regarded as bhavarupa, according to Shankara.

Reason (R). Māyā is regarded as indefinable, according to Shankara.

1026. **Assertion (A).** God is regarded as the object of worship.

Reason (R). Greatorship of the world is regarded as God's essence.

1027. **Assertion (A).** Madhva believe in quantitative and qualitative pluralism of souls.

Reason (R). He says that in liberation the souls differ in degrees.

1028. **Assertion (A).** Māyā is regarded as indescribable.

Reason (R). Māyā is not known through any valid means.

1029. **Assertion (A).** Jiva is regarded as a Prakara of God, according to Ramanya.

Reason (R). Jiva is regarded as a transformation of God.

1030. **Assertion (A).** Brahman is attained through knowledge, according to Advaitin.

Reason (R). Brahman is regarded as indefinable.

1031. **Assertion (A).** According to Madhva, Advaitins is regarded as 'deceitful demons'.

Reason (R). He says that Advaitins provides false interpretation of Veda.

1032. **Assertion (A).** Ramanuja talks about matter, souls and God.

Reason (R). These are regarded as real and dependent on God.

1033. **Assertion (A).** Advaita accepts the standard of abādhitatva.

Reason (R). Advaita accepts the ontological reality of the world.

1034. **Assertion (A).** Vedanta of Sankara accepts Sadhana Catustaya.

Reason (R). Vedanta of Sankara accepts Sadhana Saptaka.

1035. Consider the following statements

According to Rāmānuja

A. the self can know itself as well as its object

B. the self can reveal the object but can not reveal itself

C. the self is distinct from pure consciousness

D. the relation of the soul and Karma has a beginning.

Which of the above statements are correct?

(1) A and C (2) A and D

(3) B and C (4) B and D

1036. Consider the following statements According to Rāmānuja

A. The souls are ever free, liberated and in bondage

B. consciousness is an accidental property of the soul

C. the relation of the soul and karma is beginning. Of these statements

(1) A, B and C are correct

(2) A and B are correct

(3) B and C are correct

(4) A and C are correct

1037. Complete the following statements Bhakti is considered as

A. highest real knowledge

B. lowest real knowledge

C. devotion D. non-devotion

Select the correct answer from the codes given below :

(1) C and D (2) B and C

(3) A and D (4) A and C

1038. Complete the following statements Ramanuja believes in

A. three classes of souls.

B. four classes of souls.

C. qualitative monism.

D. non-qualitative monism.

Select the correct answer from the codes given below :

(1) A and B (2) A and C

(3) B and C (4) C and D

1039. Consider the following statements regarding Śaṅkara

A. He is responsible for the bhedābheda view in Vedānta.

B. He wrote bhāṣyas on Prasthānatrayi.

C. He maintains Brahma-Parināma-vāda.

D. He accepts the principle of non-contradiction as the test of truth.

Of these statements

(1) A and B are correct

(2) B and D are correct

(3) A and D are correct

(4) B and C are correct

1040. Complete the following statements Prapatti means

A. complete self surrender to God.

B. non-complete self surrender to God.

C. it is open to all.

D. it is not open to all.

Select the correct answer from the codes given below :

(1) A and B (2) A and C

(3) B and C (4) C and D

1041. Complete the following statements Madhva believes in

A. refutation of Māyā.

B. non-refutation of Māyā.

C. Dvaita

D. Dvaitadvaita

Select the correct answer from the codes given below :

(1) A and B (2) A and C

(3) B and C (4) C and D

1042. Advaita Vedānta holds that

A. The knowledge of Ātman is Vidyā

B. The knowledge of Jagat is Vidya

C. The knowledge of Prapañca is avidya

D. The knowledge through sense perception is Avidyā.

Select the correct answer from the codes given below :

(1) C and D (2) B and C
(3) A, C and D (4) B, C and D

1043. Complete the following statements
The released souls means

A. souls which were once found.
B. souls which were not found.
C. These souls are later liberated.
D. These souls are not liberated.

Select the correct answer from the codes given below :

(1) C and D (2) A and C
(3) B and C (4) A and B

1044. Consider the following statements :

A. Souls are bound on account of their ignorance.
B. The soul as to remove its karmic obstacles.
C. Knowledge is the immediate cause of liberation.

Which of these statements are correct according to Ramanuja ?

(1) A, B and C (2) A and B
(3) B and C (4) A and C

1045. Complete the following statements
Shankara believes in

A. Advaita Vedanta
B. Dvaita
C. Non-dualism D. Duality

Select the correct answer from the codes given below :

(1) B and C (2) A and C
(3) A and B (4) C and D

1046. Which of the following is/are held by Śaṅkarācārya?

A. Ātman and Brahman are identical.
B. Ātman is created by Brahman.
C. Ātman and Brahman are nonidentical.
D. Jīva is a product of māyā.

Select the correct answer from the codes givens below

Codes:

(1) A alone (2) B alone
(3) B and C (4) A and D

1047. Complete the following statements
Free souls means

A. souls without any bondage.
B. souls with bondage.
C. souls are free from karma.
D. souls are not free from karma.

Select the correct answer from the codes given below :

(1) C and D (2) A and C
(3) A and B (4) B and C

1048. Consider the following statements
According to Rāmājuna

A. Jivas are nitya, mukta and baddha
B. Jīva is one with Brahman
C. Jīva is a part of Brahman of these statements

(1) A, B and C are correct
(2) A and B are correct
(3) B and C are correct
(4) A and C are correct

1049. Complete the following statements
Bound souls means

A. souls, which wanders in sainsara.
B. souls which don't wanders in sainsara.
C. souls which exist because of ignorance.
D. souls which does not exist because of ignorance.

Select the correct answer from the codes given below :

(1) C and D (2) A and C
(3) A and B (4) B and C

1050. **Assertion (A).** Prabhakara does not accept non-apprehension.
Reason (R). We perceive no jar in the space.

1051. Which of the following two currents flowing almost side by side in the philosophy of Vivekananda?

(1) Nyāya and saṁkhya

(2) Advait Vedānta and Bhakti-cult

(3) Mimāṁsa and Advait Vedānta

(4) Jainism and Buddhism

1052. What is the view of Vivekānanda about the two currents (Advaita and Bhakti-cult) flowing side by side in his philosophy?

(1) these are two different systems of philosophy

(2) these are the same ways targeting towards different goals

(3) these are two ways of looking at the reality

(4) None of the above

1053. Vivekānanda is a........, and yet God, according to him, is personal.

(1) Monist (2) Polytheist

(3) Pantheist (4) Henotheist

1054. According to Vivekānanda, the absolute can be described as

(1) sat-it-ānanda

(2) Nirguṇa

(3) Anirvacaniya

(4) None of the above

1055. Vivekānanda asserts that ānanda is in

(1) sacrifice (2) surrender

(3) Love (4) service

1056. The one watch-word for universal religion, according to Vivekānanda, is

(1) self-service (2) Compromise

(3) Acceptance (4) Perfect-liberation

1057. The believer in the universal religion has to be broad minded and open hearted, he would be prepared to learn from

(1) the scriptures of all religions

(2) Vedas

(3) Bhāgvadgita

(4) Manusmṛti

1058. Which among the following expresses the Vivekānanda's conception about religion?

(1) It is a growth from within

(2) It is inherent in the very constitution of man

(3) Its nature can be known by analysing the religious sense

(4) All of the above

1059. What, according to Vivekānanda, is the nature of supernatural element?

(1) A God, or an impersonal principle

(2) the absolute reality, or the destiny

(3) the law, or anything of this sort

(4) All of the above

1060. Universal religion has to be acceptable to

(1) All minds (2) Only its members

(3) Hindus only (4) Indians only

1061. Creation, according to Sri Aurobindo, is nothing but an

(1) Expression of sorrow

(2) Expression of nothingness

(3) Expression of Joy

(4) None of the above

1062. What is the root of birth, the cause of remaining in existence and that into which creation ceases?

(1) Brahma (2) Delight or ānanda

(3) Ignorance (4) Māyā

1063. The delight of world-process in relation to the saccidananda is called

(1) Māyā (2) Adhyāsa

(3) Lilā (4) Prakṛti

1064. According to Sir Aurobindo, evolution is possible only because....has already taken place

(1) destruction (2) God

(3) involution (4) None

1065. According to Aurobindo, the realm of reality has been divided into two hemispheres, and
(1) Higher, lower (2) North, south
(3) Upper, lower (4) None of these

1066. Evolutionary growth, according to Sri Aurobindo, is a
(1) four-fold process
(2) triple process
(3) two fold process
(4) five-fold process

1067. The most important character of evolutionary process is
(1) Widening (2) Heightening
(3) Integration (4) Combination

1068. Integration in the philosophy of Sri Aurobindo means
(1) Enlargement
(2) Ascent through descent
(3) Expansion
(4) None

1069. The order of ascent from Mind to supermind is through the following intermediary steps
(1) Illumined Mind, Intuition, Higher Mind, Overmind
(2) Intuition, Illumined Mind, Higher Mind, Overmind
(3) Higher Mind, Illumined Mind, Intuition, Overmind
(4) Higher Mind, Intuition, Illumined Mind, Overmind

1070. The difference between Mind and supermind consists in the difference between their
(1) manners of apprehending reality
(2) appearances
(3) structures
(4) None of the above

1071. The supermind is described by Sri Aurobindo by calling it
(1) Omnipotent, omniscient, omnipresent
(2) super-conscious entity
(3) The creator, the real idea and the supreme truth consciousness
(4) A divine being

1072. Which one of the following statements does not truly reflect Gandhiji's philosophy of life?
(1) Hate the sin and not the sinner
(2) Non-violence is an active moral fight against wickedness
(3) Violence is not always wrong
(4) Punishment should always be retributive

1073. Does Aurobindo favour evolutionary theory
(1) Yes (2) No
(3) Not certain (4) Irrelevant

1074. 'Satyartha Prakash' is attributed to
(1) Śaṅkarāchārya
(2) Swami Dayanand
(3) Gautama Buddha
(4) None of these

1075. Yoga, according to Sri Aurobindo, is
(1) Realisation of divinity
(2) Attainment of supernatural existence
(3) Realisation of truth
(4) Attainment of power like God

1076. According to Sri Aurobindo, Yoga means union with the divine. Thus union is
(1) Transcendental (2) Cosmic
(3) Individual
(4) All three together

1077. Which among the following does not come under the three steps of Integral yoga
(1) psychicisation
(2) socialisation

(3) spiritualisation
(4) supermentalisation

1078. According to Iqbal self is
(1) Pure consciousness
(2) Transformed form of God
(3) A series of activities
(4) All of the above

1079. Iqbal describes the self as its life is
(1) mechanical
(2) Teleological
(3) Partially both (1) and (2)
(4) Neither (1) nor (2)

1080. The life of the ego, Iqbal says, is constituted by the
(1) Experiences (2) feelings
(3) Volitions (4) All of these

1081. One of the most prominent characters of the self is
(1) bondage (2) freedom
(3) devotion (4) motion

1082. Which among the following is not the character of the self according to Iqbal?
(1) freedom
(2) Immortality
(3) A series of activities
(4) Attraction and distraction

1083. Iqbal believes in the doctrine of personal immortality and substantiates his view by referring to the
(1) Quran (2) Veda
(3) Geeta (4) Upaniṣads

1084. Iqbal believes in
(1) Monotheism (2) Polytheism
(3) Atheism (4) Pantheism

1085. Which of the following is the proof given by Iqbal to prove the God's existence?
(1) Cosmological
(2) Teleological
(3) Ontological
(4) None of these

1086. Iqbal accepts the only way in which God's existence can be apprehended. That way is
(1) Intuition
(2) The authority of Quran
(3) Teleological
(4) Cosmological

1087. According to Iqbal the universe is of the nature of a
(1) free creative force
(2) mechanical force
(3) Devine force
(4) None of the above

1088. Which of the following statements does not express Iqbal's view?
(1) Individuality is a matter of degrees
(2) Rational egos have the capacity to regulate and direct their own creative life
(3) World process is being rationally directed
(4) Iqbal interprets the quaranie description of God as darkness

1089. According to Iqbal, God is
(1) finite (2) infinite
(3) limited in space-time-dimension
(4) (2) and (3) both

1090. Ordinary religions, according to Tagore, are
(1) Working for the welfare of human beings
(2) Are just aimless wanderings
(3) God's work
(4) None of the above

1091. Tagore recommends the rule of....in religion.
(1) God (2) Man
(3) Love (4) All of these

1092. Which of the following constitute a religious life according to Tagore?
(1) Love (2) Sacrifice
(3) Sincerity (4) Innocence

1093. What is the innermost truth of man according to Tagore?
(1) Animity (2) Manhood
(3) Priesthood (4) All of these

1094. According to Tagore manhood means
(1) Social service
(2) Kind nature
(3) An extra awareness that is greater than his material sense
(4) Animity with adoptation of culture

1095. Which of the following, according to Tagore, is the basis of all true freedom?
(1) devotion (2) social service
(3) perfect knowledge
(4) All of the above

1096. It, Tagore says, is...........which forges fetters that bind.
(1) Avidyā (2) Māyā
(3) Illusion (4) Love

1097. Tagore wanted to train human being for
(1) freedom (2) peace
(3) justice (4) All of these

1098. According to Tagore, the strength of foreign government lies in the
(1) Army power
(2) people's ignorance
(3) political power
(4) All of the above

1099. Tagore was an advocate of the medium of instruction through the
(1) language of majority
(2) language used in administration
(3) (1) and (2) both
(4) Mother tongue

1100. Which among the following is more unique, according to Bhattācārya, than remaining three
(1) 'I' (2) 'He'
(3) 'she' (4) 'you'

1101. K.C. Bhattācārya says that true subjectivity would consist in a
(1) 'I'
(2) 'I' subjected to some object
(3) denial of 'I'
(4) None of the above

1102. Taking subjectivity in a very wide sense Krishnachandra enumerates three stages of subjectivity. Which of the following is not included among them?
(1) Bodily subjectivity
(2) Objective subjectivity
(3) Psychic subjectivity
(4) Spiritual subjectivity

1103. Bhattacharya says that the subject may identify itself with the body
(1) externally (2) internally
(3) as absent (4) All of the above

1104. A person is looking for a book in his study-room, but he does not find it. The former is the—and the latter is perception of the
(1) perception of room, absence
(2) perception of absence, room
(3) perception of absence, absence of absence
(4) None of the above

1105. To construct a synthetic view of the world, according to Krishnanchandra, is
(1) an essential function of philosophy
(2) not an essential function of philosophy
(3) not definite with respect to philosophy
(4) None of these

1106. According to K.C. Bhattācārya, judgements of philosophy are
(1) factual

(2) Either factual or valuable
(3) not factual
(4) None of the above

1107. According to Radhakrisnan there are.......... possible source of knowledge.
(1) 3 (2) 4
(3) 5 (4) 6

1108. Which among the following is not a possible source of knowledge according to Radhakrisnan?
(1) Sense-experience
(2) Implication
(3) Intellectual cognition
(4) Intuitive apprehension

1109. The main tool of Intellectual cognition is
(1) Synthesis (2) Senses
(3) Analysis (4) None of these

1110. The function of intellect, according to Radhakrisnan is
(1) Synthesis (2) Argumentation
(3) Differentiation (4) Analysis

1111. The whole as a whole must be grasped by ....alone.
(1) Intellect (2) Intuition
(3) Sense-experience
(4) Implication

1112. According to Radhakrisnan the general principle of life and logic and the basic assumptions of sciences are all known through
(1) Intuition (2) Intellect
(3) Perception (4) Inference

1113. Gandhi, an idealist, advocates.........as the ultimate destiny of mankind......
(1) Positivism (2) Anarchism
(3) Liberalism (4) None of these

1114. Gandhi is in favour of.............of political power and economic power
(1) Dictatorship
(2) Decentralization
(3) Supremacy
(4) None of the above

1115. Gandhi advocates.........., which implies the greatest good of all' and it includes the good of the greatest number.
(1) Utilitarianism (2) Sarvodaya
(3) Anarchism (4) None of these

1116. Gandhi's altruistic ethics of ahimsa is the .... of Nietzche's individualistic ethics of will to power.
(1) Same (2) Antithesis
(3) Opposite (4) None of these

1117. According to.........., the State is a passing in the life of people. All government is coercion. All coercion is immoral. Coercion of government should be abolished. The State should be superseded by a cooperative society
(1) Socialism (2) Communism
(3) Anarchism (4) Democracy

1118. Ahimsa is not merely a..........virtue of non-killing and non-injury but a.........virtue of doing good to others.
(1) Positive, negative
(2) Simple, complex
(3) Negative, positive
(4) None of these

1119. ....is supreme kindness and supreme self-sacrifice.
(1) Ahimsa (2) Non-violence
(3) Non-injury (4) None of these

1120. Ahimsa is abstinence from causing pain through word or thought and
(1) Jealousy (2) Resentment
(3) Inhumanity (4) None of these

1121. Gandhi believes in the........., therefore, he says, the wealthy should act as trustees of their superfluous wealth and use it for the good of society.

(1) God
(2) Trusteeship of the wealthy
(3) Equal distribution
(4) None of the above

1122. "I often describe my religion as religion of truth.........instead of saying God is truth. I have been saying truth is God"—Who is the speaker?

(1) Tolstoy (2) Gandhi
(3) Rashdall (4) None of these

1123. ....is impossible without a complete merging of oneself in an identification with this limitless ocean of life

(1) Realization of ultimate end
(2) Realization of truth
(3) Understanding of religion
(4) None of the above

1124. .....is the supreme good, according to Gandhi.

(1) Morality (2) Ahimsa
(3) God (4) None of these

1125. Love and.........are the only means of God-realization, according to Gandhi.

(1) Aim (2) Attraction
(3) Ahimsa (4) None of these

1126. ....can never be realized by one who is not pure in heart.

(1) God (2) Truth
(3) Ultimate knowledge
(4) None of the above

1127. ....is necessary for complete self-control including sex-restraint according to Gandhi.

(1) True knowledge
(2) Absolute self-surrender to God
(3) Self-purification
(4) None of the above

1128. "Whosoever will save his life shall lose it and whosoever will lose his life for my sake shall find it"—Who is the speaker?

(1) Gandhi (2) Tolstoy
(3) Jesus Christ
(4) None of the above

1129. A perfect vision of.........can only follow a realization of ahimsa.

(1) God (2) Truth
(3) Love (4) None of these

1130. The doctrine of fearless pursuit of truth is called

(1) Ahimsa (2) Soul force
(3) Satyagraha (4) None of these

1131. Gandhi claims that..........is the end, Ahimsa is our supreme duty.

(1) Truth
(2) Non-violence
(3) Self-purification
(4) None of these

1132. ......in thought, word and deed constitutes the negative aspect of ahimsa.

(1) Non-violence
(2) Non-cooperation
(3) Abstinence
(4) None of the above

1133. Ahimsa is not only complete absence of ill-will towards mankind and sentient creation but involves........and..........for them.

(1) Attachment, affection
(2) Overflowing love, affection
(3) Oveflowing love, attraction
(4) None of the above

1134. Ahimsa in its positive form means......... greatest charity.

(1) Selflessness (2) Fearlessness
(3) Largest love (4) None of these

1135. ....ahimsa necessarily includes truth and fearlessness.

(1) Active (2) Positive
(3) Moderate (4) None of these

1136. The most popular contemporary Indian ethics has been presented by
(1) Mahesh Yogi
(2) Sri Aurobindo
(3) Rabindra Nath Tagore
(4) M.K. Gandhi

1137. The most integral theory of ethics in contemporary Indian thought has been presented by
(1) Rajneesh
(2) Sri Aurobindo
(3) Rabindra Nath Tagore
(4) Mahesh Yogi

1138. According to Gandhi, satyagraha is a
(1) Weapon of the weak
(2) Weapon of the peace wanted people
(3) Weapon of the morally vigilant and the active
(4) Weapon of the kinds

1139. Gandhi's resistance of evil is
(1) Evil (2) Good
(3) Violence (4) None-violence

1140. Which among the following is not a quality of satyagrahi mentioned by Gandhi
(1) A satyagrahi must be honest and sincere
(2) A satyagrahi must be open-minded
(3) A satyagrahi must be a disciplined soldier
(4) A satyagrahi must follow the fine vows—satya, Ahimsa, asteya, brahmacarya, aparigraha

1141. Which among the following is not correct
(1) Gandhi's swaraj is a state of existence where all social distinctions wither away
(2) By Ramarajya Gandhi wanted to regulate Hindu Government in country
(3) Emphasis on self-restraint and self-rule remained a significant cornerstone of Gandhi's moral dimension of swaraj
(4) The people's swaraj of Gandhi is four dimensional

1142. According to Radhakrishnan the ultimate human destiny is
(1) Jeevanmukti
(2) Videhamukti
(3) Sarvamukti
(4) eat, drink and enjoy

1143. Sarvamukti means
(1) To sacrifice all the luxurious things
(2) To die
(3) Universal redemption
(4) To leave all the possessions

1144. How many kinds of Ignorance are mentioned by Sir Aurobindo?
(1) 3 (2) 5
(3) 7 (4) 9

1145. Which of the following is not included under the seven-fold ignorance of Sri Aurobindo?
(1) The Original ignorance
(2) The cosmic ignorance
(3) The egoistic ignorance
(4) The Traditional ignorance

1146. Truth for.........is God, and.........and God are not different things.
(1) Tolstoy, spirit
(2) Gandhi, God's law
(3) Gandhi, spirit
(4) None of the above

1147. The word 'Satya' is derived from the word "—" which means being
(1) Sat (2) Sat-chit-anand
(3) True knowledge
(4) None of the above

1148. What is the essence of violence according to Gandhi?
(1) Hatred (2) Aversion
(3) Exploitation (4) None of these

1149. The principle of non-violence necessitates .....from exploitation in any form.
(1) Complete abstention
(2) Removal
(3) Absence
(4) None of the above

1150. "All wealth belongs to God, and those who hold it are trustees, not possessors"—Who is the speaker?
(1) Gandhi (2) Tolstoy
(3) Aurobindo (4) None of these

1151. What is the meaning of selflessness in Gandhi's view?
(1) It means complete freedom
(2) It means abstinence from violence
(3) It means complete freedom from a regard for one's body
(4) None of the above

1152. Gandhi believes that ahimsa does not simply mean non-killing, it implies
(1) Conquest of anger and pride
(2) Non-cooperation
(3) Absolute truthfulness
(4) None of the above

1153. A.........will always try to overcome evil by good, anger by love, untruth by truth, himsa by ahimsa.
(1) Gandhian thinker
(2) Satyagrahi
(3) Wise person
(4) None of the above

1154. ....is the subtlest form of violence and we can win over the opponent only by love never by it.
(1) Aversion
(2) Hate
(3) Selfishness
(4) None of these

1155. I have intense longing to lose myself in the Eternal and become merely a lump of clay in the........., suggests Mahatma Gandhi.
(1) God's wish-fulfilment
(2) Potter's divine hands
(3) Potter's hand
(4) None of the above

1156. ......and.......are so interwound that it is practically impossible to disentangle and separate them.
(1) Non-violence, truth
(2) Ahimsa, truth
(3) Soul force, Ātman
(4) None of the above

1157. Non-violence implies as complete......as is humanly possible.
(1) Self-purification
(2) Self-estimation
(3) Truth
(4) None of the above

1158. Non-violence implies a living faith in the existence of the soul as apart from
(1) The body
(2) Emotions
(3) Truth
(4) None of the above

1159. The immediate service of all human beings becomes a necessary part of the endeavour, simply because the only way to find.......and be one with it.
(1) Ultimate truth
(2) God is to see him in his creation
(3) The meaning of ultimate truth
(4) None of the above

1160. Gandhi claims there is.........in all mankind.
(1) Unity of Spirit (2) Ahimsa
(3) Truth (4) None of these

1161. Man's ultimate aim is the.......and all his activities, social, political, religious have to be guided by the ultimate aim of the vision of God.

(1) Perfect knowledge
(2) Truth
(3) Realization of God
(4) None of the above

1162. Gandhi's idea of human freedom is borrowed from
(1) Tolstoy's view
(2) The Vedas
(3) The Bhagavad Gitā
(4) None of the above

1163. "I believe in absolute oneness of God and therefore humanity"—Who is the speaker?
(1) Gandhi
(2) Tolstoy
(3) Rabindranath Tagore
(4) None of the above

1164. Gandhi believes in......and in the essential unity of a man and for that matter of all lives.
(1) God (2) Truth
(3) Advaita (4) None of these

1165. According to Gandhi which one of the following is not consistent with non-violence?
(1) Sacrificing one's life
(2) Passive submission
(3) Love for others
(4) Non-cooperation

1166. According to Gandhi
(1) God is in the first place and Ahimsa is in the second place
(2) Truth is in the first place and Ahimsa is in the second place
(3) Truth is in the first place and human dignity is in the second place
(4) Truth is in the first place and God is in the second place

1167. Which one of the following views does Gandhi hold?
(1) Truth is the means and God is the end
(2) Ahimsa is the means and Freedom is the end
(3) Virtue is the means and Ahimsa is the end
(4) Ahimsa is the means and Truth is the end.

1168. Which of the following would Gandhiji not accept?
(1) A good end justifies the means to it
(2) End and means are convertible terms
(3) Satya is the end, ahimsa is the means
(4) End and means are interdependent

1169. Which one of the following is not true of Gandhi's concept of ahimsa?
(1) Ahimsa is the means, Truth is the end
(2) Ahimsa and Truth are inseparable
(3) Ahimsa is the same as non-killing
(4) Ahimsa is the absence of hatred

1170. According to Gandhi, we see Truth in fragment and from different angles of vision, view
(1) God in itself
(2) Nation in its solidarity
(3) Society in its collective wisdom
(4) The individual himself

1171. Which one of the following is not presupposed by Gandhi in his idea of Satyagraha?
(1) Contingency of evil in man
(2) Contingency of goodness in man
(3) Identity of Truth and God
(4) Eventual triumph of non-violence

1172. Swaraj means the government of
(1) A particular religion
(2) A particular country
(3) Public without discrimination of race, caste, religion, class etc.
(4) Gandhi

1173. Which of the following is in correct sequence?

(1) Concept of value, Indian philosophy, Life ahead, India of my dream
(2) India of my dream, Concept of value, Life ahead, Indian philosophy
(3) Indian philosophy, Life ahead, Concept of value, India of my dream
(4) India of my dream, Life ahead, Concept of value, Indian philosophy.

1174. Which of the following pairs is correctly matched?

(1) Gandhi : Non-violence
(2) Ambedkar : Satyagraha
(3) Bhattacharya : The idealist view of life
(4) Radhakrishnan : Critique of modern civilisation

1175. What of the following would Ambedkar not accept?

(1) Neo-Buddhism
(2) Who were Shudras
(3) The Untouchables
(4) Six Varnas

1176. Which of the following would Bhattacharya not accept?

(1) Doctrine of Maya
(2) Concept of philosophy
(3) Religion of man
(4) Swaraj in ideas

1177. Which of the following would Krishnamurti not accept?

(1) Freedom from the known
(2) The first and last freedom
(3) Freedom from the self
(4) Satyagraha

1178. What first position is attached with Ambedkar?

(1) President
(2) Law minister
(3) Prime minister
(4) Finance minister

1179. What do you mean by 'subject as freedom, according to Bhattacharya?

(1) Denial of I (2) I
(3) Negation
(4) Acceptance

1180. What do you mean by philosophy, according to Bhattacharya?

(1) Speaking (2) Awareness
(3) Spirituality (4) Negation

1181. What intelligence, don't have, according to Krishnamurti?

(1) Abnormality (2) Spirituality
(3) Asset (4) Liability

1182. What do you mean by self, according to Krishnamurti?

(1) Idea (2) Memory
(3) Experience (4) All of these

1183. What is important for Krishnamurti?

(1) Creativeness (2) Bondage
(3) Awareness (4) Liberation

1184. Firstly, there were how many Varna's according to Ambedkar?

(1) 1 (2) 2
(3) 3 (4) 4

1185. Whether Bhattacharya, Radhakrishnan, Krishnamurti is in correct sequence?

(1) Yes (2) No
(3) Can't say (4) Don't know

1186. Whether Krishnamurti believes in religion of man

(1) Yes (2) No
(3) Can't say (4) Don't know

1187. Whether Ambedkar believes in superman?

(1) Yes (2) No
(3) Can't say (4) Don't know

1188. Ambedkar don't accept what?
(1) Neo-Buddhism
(2) Who were Shudras
(3) Six Varnas
(4) All of these

1189. From the following............is not accepted by Krishnamurti.
(1) freedom from the known
(2) the first and last freedom
(3) freedom from the self
(4) satyagraha

1190. Ambedkar wrote.......book?
(1) Who Were Shudras
(2) India of My Dream
(3) Young India
(4) Hind Swaraj

1191. What do you mean by felt body according to Bhattacharya?
(1) Body felt from within
(2) Body perceived externally
(3) Body perceiving awareness
(4) Body perceiving nothing

1192. According to Bhattacharya, the subject disassociate itself from what?
(1) External body (2) Fat body
(3) Internal body (4) Thin body

1193. Which awareness has to be negated according to KC Bhattacharya?
(1) Awareness of the subject's freedom
(2) Awareness of no freedom
(3) Awareness of the object
(4) Awareness of the negation

1194. According to KC Bhattacharya, 'subject as free' means what?
(1) An attempt to realise freedom
(2) An attempt to realise ignorance
(3) Implication
(4) Acceptance

1195. According to Ambedkar, Chaturvarnya refers to what?
(1) Inequality (2) Equality
(3) Awareness (4) Negation

1196. According to Ambedkar, the present day Shudras are racially different from what?
(1) Original Shudras
(2) Copied Shudras
(3) Imbied Shudras
(4) Award Shudras

1197. Shudras are subject to what according to Ambedkar?
(1) Pain (2) Penalties
(3) Claims (4) Doctrines

1198. According to Ambedkar, Rigveda supports whom?
(1) Shudras (2) Violence
(3) Irrationality (4) Rationality

1199. According to Ambedkar, for Buddhism what is important?
(1) Noble birth (2) High ideals
(3) High concepts (4) High doctrines

1200. Whose data of birth is in dispute?
(1) Krishnamurti (2) Ambedkar
(3) Gandhi (4) All of these

1201. Krishnamurti was born in which family?
(1) Telugu (2) Marathi
(3) Mahar (4) Hindu

1202. What do you mean by freedom according to Krishnamurti?
(1) Pure non-observation
(2) First step of existence
(3) Second step of existence
(4) Third step of existence

1203. Freedom from what, is important according to Krishnamurti?
(1) Past Completely
(2) Present

(3) Medium Situations
(4) Large Situations

1204. What do you mean by self, according to Krishnamurti?
(1) Accumulated memory of the unconscious
(2) No memory
(3) No mind
(4) No awareness

1205. Self means what?
(1) Power (2) Authority
(3) Negation (4) Positivity

1206. Self is........according to Krishnamurti?
(1) limited (2) unlimited
(3) medium (4) lower

1207. According to Ambedkar, on............., social organisation of the Indo-Aryans was based?
(1) Chatuvarnya
(2) Violence
(3) Externality
(4) Internality

1208. According to KC Bhattacharya philosophy is
(1) the knowledge of the absolute
(2) self-evident elaboration of the self
(3) self-evident elaboration of the self-evident
(4) the study of the self-evident

1209. True knowledge according to J Krishnamurti is as follows
(1) Accepted by religious text
(2) Prescribed by masters
(3) Unconditional awareness
(4) Conditional reactions

1210. Mahatma Gandhi criticised industrialisation in one of the following writings.
(1) Autobiography
(2) Hind Swaraj
(3) Key to health (4) Harijan

1211. Point out from the following reason why Dr. B.R. Ambedkar Opposes the Caste System prevalent in India?
(1) As it creates discrimination social injustice and inequality with in the Indian Nation
(2) As it is Vedic heritage
(3) As it is foreign innovation
(4) As it is suggested by smarties

1212. An Idealist View of Life is writer by
(1) Radhakrishnan
(2) J Krishnamurti
(3) Tagore
(4) KC Bhattacharya

1213. According to whom "Man is the architect of his own destiny."?
(1) B.R. Ambedkar (2) J. Krishnamurti
(3) Tagore (4) Gandhi

1214. According to whom intuition is the way of knowing reality?
(1) Krishnamurti (2) K. C. Bhattacarya
(3) Radhakrishnan (4) Iqbal

1215. Which of the following are the three mantras for Ambedkar?
(1) Caste, Varna and Karma
(2) Karma, Destiny and Rebirth
(3) Educate, Organise and Agitate
(4) None of the above

1216. Ambedkar was very much influenced by
(1) Buddhism (2) Christianity
(3) Hinduism (4) Jainism

1217. J. Krishnamurti said which of the following ?
(1) Truth is God
(2) Truth is what works
(3) Truth is painful
(4) Truth is a pathless land

1218. The Doctrine of Trusteeship is propounded by
(1) J Krishnamurti
(2) Swami Vivekananda
(3) Radhakrishnan
(4) Gandhi

1219. The architect of Indian Constitution is
(1) Gandhi (2) Sri Aurobindo
(3) Tagore (4) Ambedkar

1220. Radhakrishnan is the author of
(1) Sarvodaya (2) Life Divine
(3) Religion and Society
(4) Who are the Sudras

1221. The Journal Harijan was run by
(1) Ambedkar
(2) Sri Aurobindo
(3) Gandhi
(4) Swami Vivekananda

1222. Gandhi means by Sarvodaya
(1) uplift of some
(2) uplift of majority
(3) uplift of all
(4) None of these

1223. According to Gandhi, the goal of constructive program is
(1) Providing economic relief to the unemployed.
(2) Distributing some wages to spinners and weavers.
(3) Creating a non-violent order of society.
(4) None of the above

1224. 'Buddhism is nothing, if not rationalism' according to
(1) Gandhi (2) Ambedkar
(3) Bhagavandas (4) Tilak

1225. Which of the following is not acceptable to Ambedkar ?
(1) Liberty, equality and fraternity
(2) Education, Organisation and agitation
(3) Buddha, Dhamma and Sangha
(4) Caste, Varna and Karma

1226. Who focussed the Upanisadic dictum "Arise, Awake and Stop not till the goal is reached" in modern times ?
(1) Swami Dayanand
(2) Raja Rammohan Roy
(3) Swami Vivekananda
(4) Mahatma Gandhi

1227. Which of the following are admitted by Tagore to be the essential aspects of human self ?
(1) Physical and mental
(2) Vital and mental
(3) Physical and spiritual
(4) Mental and spiritual

1228. The theory of evolution accepted by Sri Aurobindo is known as
(1) Emergent Evolution
(2) Mechanical Evolution
(3) Integral Evolution
(4) None of the above

1229. To whom of the following statement can be rightfully attributed to 'He reads Shankara from a Hegelian point of view' ?
(1) Swami Vivekananda
(2) Sri Aurobindo
(3) Dr. S. Radhakrishnan
(4) J. Krishnamurthy

1230. The champion of 'integral yoga' is
(1) J. Krishnamurti
(2) Vivekananda
(3) M.N. Roy
(4) Sri Aurobindo

1231. Iqbal believes that self is immortal, because
(1) It takes birth and rebirth.

(2) It exists before taking birth in human body.
(3) It survives death and is immortal.
(4) It takes birth at a definite place and time.

1232. 'Man-making Education' is advocated by
(1) Gandhi and Vivekananda
(2) Vivekananda and Sri Aurobindo
(3) Gandhi and Ambedkar
(4) Vivekananda only

1233. The concept of Mānav devatā is advanced by
(1) Swāmī Vivekānanda
(2) Rabindranath Tagore
(3) Sri Aurobindo
(4) B.R. Ambedkar

1234. Sri Aurobindo is a
(1) Purnadvaitin (2) Visistadvaitin
(3) Advaitin (4) Dvaitin

1235. The author of Gitanjali is
(1) Gandhi (2) Tagore
(3) K.C. Bhattacarya (4) Ambedkar

1236. To Vivekananda Māyā is
(1) A power of Brahman
(2) A form of evil
(3) A statement of fact
(4) A state of consciousness

1237. 'Education is the manifestation of the perfection already in man' is the view of
(1) Radhakrishnan (2) Vivekananda
(3) Aurobindo
(4) Rabindranath Tagore

1238. Who has given the concept of 'Integral Yoga' ?
(1) Vivekananda (2) Aurobindo
(3) Gandhiji (4) Radhakrishnan

1239. 'The Human Cycle' is written by
(1) Tagore (2) Gandhi
(3) Radhakrishnan (4) Sri Aurobind

1240. What is the intermediate principle in Sri Aurobindo's Philosophy ?
(1) Psychic Being
(2) Consciousness force
(3) Super mind
(4) Higher mind

1241. The correct sequence of triple transformation in evolutionary theory of Sri Aurobindo is
(1) Supramental, Psychic and Spiritual
(2) Spiritual, Psychic and Supramental
(3) Psychic, Spiritual and Supramental
(4) Psychic, Supramental and Spiritual

1242. Select the correct sequence of triple process in evolutionary theory of Sri Aurobindo
(1) Widening, Heightening and integration
(2) Heightening, Widening and Integration
(3) Integration, Widening and Heightening
(4) Heightening, Integration and Widening

1243. Who propounds that ascent without descent is unthinkable?
(1) Tagore (2) Iqbal
(3) Radhakrishnan (4) Sri Aurobindo

1244. Select the correct sequence of evolutionary journey from higher mind to supermind of Sri Aurobindo.
(1) Higher mind, Over mind, Super mind, illumined mind, Intuitive mind
(2) Intuitive mind, Over mind, Higher mind, Super mind, illumined mind
(3) Illumined mind, Intuitive mind, Over mind, Higher mind, Super mind
(4) Higher mind, Illumined mind, Intuitive mind, Over mind, Super mind.

1245. Match list I with list II and select the correct answer from the codes given below.

List I	List II
(a) Vivekānanda	(i) Religion of man
(b) Sri Aurobindo	(ii) Universal Religion

(c) Tagore (iii) Subject's freedom
(d) K.C. Bhattācārya (iv) Integral yoga

Codes :

	(a)	(b)	(c)	(d)
(1)	(i)	(ii)	(iii)	(iv)
(2)	(i)	(ii)	(iv)	(iii)
(3)	(ii)	(iv)	(iii)	(i)
(4)	(ii)	(iv)	(i)	(iii)

1246. Match the following

List-I	List-II
(a) Radhakrishnan	(i) Subject as freedom
(b) Gandhi	(ii) Neo-Buddhism
(c) Ambedkar	(iii) Non-violence
(d) K.C. Bhatta-charya	(iv) An idealist new of life

Codes :

	(a)	(b)	(c)	(d)
(1)	(i)	(ii)	(iii)	(iv)
(2)	(iv)	(iii)	(ii)	(i)
(3)	(ii)	(iv)	(iii)	(i)
(4)	(i)	(iv)	(ii)	(iii)

1247. Match the following

List-I	List-II
(a) Gandhi	(i) Swaraj
(b) Ambedkar	(ii) Caste system
(c) Krishnamurti	(iii) Freedom from the known
(d) K.C. Bhatta-charya	(iv) Swaraj in ideas

Codes :

	(a)	(b)	(c)	(d)
(1)	(i)	(ii)	(iii)	(iv)
(2)	(iv)	(ii)	(iii)	(i)
(3)	(i)	(iv)	(iii)	(ii)
(4)	(ii)	(iv)	(iii)	(i)

1248. Match the following

List-I (Books)	List-II (Philosophers)
(a) Hind Swaraj	(i) Krishnamurti
(b) Who were Shudras	(ii) Gandhi
(c) The First and Last Freedom	(iii) Ambedkar
(d) Principal Upanishad	(iv) Rahakrishnan

Codes :

	(a)	(b)	(c)	(d)
(1)	(i)	(ii)	(iii)	(iv)
(2)	(ii)	(iii)	(i)	(iv)
(3)	(iv)	(iii)	(ii)	(i)
(4)	(i)	(iv)	(iii)	(ii)

1249. Match the following

List-I	List-II
(a) Young India	(i) Gandhi
(b) Knowledge and truth	(ii) Bhattacharya
(c) Truth and actua-lity	(iii) Krishnamurti
(d) The untouchables	(iv) Ambedkar

Codes :

	(a)	(b)	(c)	(d)
(1)	(i)	(ii)	(iii)	(iv)
(2)	(iv)	(iii)	(ii)	(i)
(3)	(i)	(iv)	(iii)	(ii)
(4)	(ii)	(iv)	(iii)	(i)

1250. Match the following

List-I	List-II
(a) Satyagraha	(i) Gandhi
(b) Varna and caste system	(ii) Ambedkar
(c) Doctrine of Maya	(iii) K.C. Bhatta-charya
(d) Freedom from self	(iv) Krishnamurti

Codes :

	(a)	(b)	(c)	(d)
(1)	(i)	(ii)	(iii)	(iv)
(2)	(iv)	(iii)	(ii)	(i)
(3)	(i)	(iii)	(ii)	(iv)
(4)	(iv)	(ii)	(iii)	(i)

1251. Match the following

List-I	List-II
(a) Ambedkar	(i) Chaturvarnaya
(b) Gandhi	(ii) Swadeshi
(c) Krishnamurti	(iii) Intelligence
(d) Radhakrishnan	(iv) Intuition and intellect

Codes :

	(a)	(b)	(c)	(d)
(1)	(i)	(ii)	(iii)	(iv)
(2)	(i)	(iv)	(iii)	(ii)
(3)	(i)	(iv)	(iii)	(ii)
(4)	(iii)	(iv)	(ii)	(i)

1252. Match the following

List-I	List-II
(a) Gandhi	(i) Trusteeship
(b) Bhattacharya	(ii) Perceived body
(c) Ambedkar	(iii) Dalit
(d) Radhakrishnan	(iv) Intuition and life

Codes :

	(a)	(b)	(c)	(d)
(1)	(i)	(ii)	(iii)	(iv)
(2)	(iv)	(iii)	(ii)	(i)
(3)	(ii)	(i)	(iv)	(iii)
(4)	(iii)	(ii)	(iv)	(i)

1253. Match the following

List-I	List-II
(a) Vivekananda	(i) Universal religion
(b) Iqbal	(ii) Immortality of soul
(c) Tagore	(iii) Religion of man
(d) Aurobindo	(iv) Dualism

Codes :

	(a)	(b)	(c)	(d)
(1)	(i)	(ii)	(iii)	(iv)
(2)	(i)	(iv)	(iii)	(i)
(3)	(iv)	(ii)	(iii)	(i)
(4)	(i)	(iii)	(ii)	(iv)

1254. Match the following

List-I	List-II
(a) Tagore	(i) Spirituality
(b) Vivekananda	(ii) Monist
(c) Aurobindo	(iii) Dualist
(d) Iqbal	(iv) Monotheism

Codes :

	(a)	(b)	(c)	(d)
(1)	(i)	(ii)	(iii)	(iv)
(2)	(ii)	(i)	(iv)	(iii)
(3)	(iii)	(iv)	(ii)	(i)
(4)	(iv)	(iii)	(i)	(ii)

1255. Match the following

List-I	List-II
(a) Aurobindo	(i) Gnostic being
(b) Vivekananda	(ii) Practical Vedanta
(c) Tagore	(iii) Jivan Devata
(d) Iqbal	(iv) Monotheism

Codes :

	(a)	(b)	(c)	(d)
(1)	(i)	(ii)	(iii)	(iv)
(2)	(i)	(iii)	(ii)	(iv)
(3)	(iv)	(i)	(iii)	(ii)
(4)	(iv)	(ii)	(i)	(iii)

1256. Match the following

List-I	List-II
(a) Integral Yoga	(i) Aurobindo
(b) Universal religion	(ii) Vivekananda
(c) Subject's freedom	(iii) KC Bhattacharya
(d) Swaraj	(iv) Gandhi

Codes :

	(a)	(b)	(c)	(d)
(1)	(i)	(ii)	(iii)	(iv)
(2)	(i)	(iii)	(ii)	(iv)
(3)	(ii)	(iv)	(iii)	(i)
(4)	(ii)	(i)	(iii)	(iv)

1257. Match the following

List-I	List-II
(a) Iqbal	(i) Teleological

(b) Tagore (ii) Open-air classes
(c) Aurobindo (iii) Supermind
(d) Vivekananda (iv) Advaita Vedanta

Codes :

	(a)	(b)	(c)	(d)
(1)	(i)	(ii)	(iii)	(iv)
(2)	(ii)	(i)	(iii)	(iv)
(3)	(iv)	(iii)	(ii)	(i)
(4)	(i)	(iv)	(iii)	(ii)

1258. Match the following

List-I	List-II
(a) Tagore	(i) Educational institutionalist
(b) Iqbal	(ii) Monotheist
(c) Aurobindo	(iii) Supreme truth consciousness
(d) Vivekananda	(iv) Spiritual equality

Codes :

	(a)	(b)	(c)	(d)
(1)	(i)	(ii)	(iii)	(iv)
(2)	(ii)	(i)	(iv)	(iii)
(3)	(iii)	(ii)	(i)	(iv)
(4)	(iv)	(iii)	(ii)	(i)

1259. Match the following

List-I	List-II
(a) Vivekananda	(i) Ananda as love
(b) Aurobindo	(ii) Ananda as delight
(c) Tagore	(iii) Ananda as spiritual
(d) Iqbal	(iv) Ananda as God

Codes :

	(a)	(b)	(c)	(d)
(1)	(i)	(ii)	(iii)	(iv)
(2)	(iv)	(ii)	(iii)	(i)
(3)	(i)	(iv)	(iii)	(ii)
(4)	(ii)	(i)	(iv)	(iii)

1260. Match the following

List-I	List-II
(a) Supermind	(i) Highest
(b) Mind	(ii) Lowest
(c) Delight	(iii) Creation
(d) Internal yoga	(iv) Union with divine

Codes :

	(a)	(b)	(c)	(d)
(1)	(i)	(ii)	(iii)	(iv)
(2)	(iv)	(ii)	(iii)	(i)
(3)	(i)	(iv)	(iii)	(ii)
(4)	(ii)	(i)	(iv)	(iii)

1261. Match the following

List-I	List-II
(a) Subject as freedom	(i) Sri Aurobindo
(b) Gnostic being	(ii) Rabindranath Tagore
(c) Universal religion	(iii) Vivekananda
(d) Jivan Devata	(iv) KC Bhattacharya

Codes :

	(a)	(b)	(c)	(d)
(1)	(i)	(ii)	(iii)	(iv)
(2)	(i)	(iii)	(ii)	(iv)
(3)	(iv)	(i)	(iii)	(ii)
(4)	(iv)	(ii)	(i)	(iii)

1262. Match the following

List-I	List-II
(a) Sri Aurobindo	(i) Secrets of the self
(b) Tagore	(ii) Absolute and the alternative forms
(c) KC Bhattacharya	(iii) Sadhana
(d) Iqbal	(iv) Life divine

Codes :

	(a)	(b)	(c)	(d)
(1)	(iv)	(iii)	(ii)	(i)
(2)	(iv)	(iii)	(i)	(ii)
(3)	(iii)	(iv)	(i)	(ii)
(4)	(i)	(ii)	(iii)	(iv)

Directions : The following items consist of two statements, one labelled as the 'Assertion A' and the other labelled as 'Reason R'. You are to examine these two statements carefully and decide if the Assertion 'A' and the Reason 'R' are individually true and if so, whether the Reason is a correct explanation of the Assertion. Select your answer to these items using the codes given below and mark your answer sheet accordingly :

Codes :

(1) Both A and R are true and R is the correct explanation of A.

(2) Both A and R are true but R is not the correct explanation of A.

(3) A is true but R is false.

(4) A is false but R is true

1263. **Assertion (A).** Intellectual cognition is not quite infallible.

Reason (R). Logical arguments are changeable and can be rejected on the strength of equally strong arguments.

1264. **Assertion (A).** 'Ahimsa is our supreme duty' (Gandhi).

Reason (R). 'Ahimsa is the means, truth is the end' (Gandhi).

1265. **Assertion (A).** According to Gandhi the means must be pure as the ends.

Reason (R). According to Gandhi truth is the purest means to all ends.

1266. **Assertion (A).** In Gandhian ethics the golden rule of conduct is mutual toleration.

Reason (R). Conscience is not the same thing for all.

1267. **Assertion (A).** Gandhiji identifies God with Truth.

Reason (R). Truth is universal and all pervasive.

1268. **Assertion (A).** Iqbal rejects the doctrine of parallelism of the body and the soul.

Reason (R). Parallelism makes them (the body and the soul) passive spectators of each-other.

1269. **Assertion (A).** Iqbal rejects the doctrine of Interactionism of the body and the soul.

Reason (R). Interactionism raises the difficulty regarding the exact place or locus where interaction takes place.

1270. **Assertion (A).** According to Iqbal there is no inconsistency in believing that immortality represents both the nature and the destiny of the individual.

Reason (R). One can never become anything which he is not already.

1271. **Assertion (A).** Iqbal says that cosmological, ontological and teleological proofs, as proofs, are utterly inadequate.

Reason (R). They (proofs) are somehow based on a superficial interpretation of experience and not on an intuitive experience of reality.

1272. **Assertion (A).** The supreme ego, according to Iqbal, is infinite.

Reason (R). The supreme ego has infinite creative possibilities within it, of which creation is only an expression.

1273. **Assertion (A).** Tagore favoured open-air classes.

Reason (R). The deadness of the walls made everything dull and gloomy.

1274. **Assertion (A).** According to Tagore, Discipline was not imposed upon children.

Reason (R). He believed that a moving mind had more power to assimilate facts and to gather knowledge from the outside world.

1275. **Assertion (A).** K.C. Bhattacarya prefers the word 'I' to both 'you' or 'he' as subject.

Reason (R). The word 'I' is more unique than either of the two.

1276. **Assertion (A).** The stage of complete freedom of the subject is transcendental.

Reason (R). Transcendence is possible only when some content is negated and superseded.

1277. **Assertion (A).** God is truth, love and bliss according to Gandhi.

Reason (R). God can neither be perceived nor grasped by the intellect, but he can be felt.

1278. **Assertion (A).** Gandhi suggests, when an individual has more than his proportionate portion, he becomes a trustee for that portion for God's people.

Reason (R). The wealthy should not be dispossessed of their possessions, because that would imply resort to violence.

1279. **Assertion (A).** Gandhi says that God is the end.

Reason (R). God can be known through truth, love or non-violence.

1280. **Assertion (A).** K.C. Bhattacharya wrote Swaraj in Ideas.

Reason (R). He believes in subject as freedom.

1281. **Assertion (A).** Krishnamurti believes in freedom from the known.

Reason (R). Mind creates conflicts.

1282. **Assertion (A).** Krishnamurti wrote 'The First and Last Freedom' book.

Reason (R). This book talk about intelligence.

1283. **Assertion (A).** Ambedkar advocated Neo-Buddhism.

Reason (R). He believes in Buddhism.

1284. **Assertion (A).** Ambedkar wrote 'who were Shudras' book.

Reason (R). He says that Shudra can destroy Varna system.

1285. **Assertion (A).** Bhattacharya believes in the Denial of 'I'.

Reason (R). He believes in subject as freedom.

1286. **Assertion (A).** Krishnamurti says that intelligence is an essential power.

Reason (R). Intelligence does not refer to any conflict.

1287. **Assertion (A).** Ambedkar says that caste system is a curse for a society.

Reason (R). He believes in Neo-Buddhism.

1288. **Assertion (A).** Bhattacharya says that freedom as the subject means transcendental world.

Reason (R). Transcendental world means the negation of the content.

1289. **Assertion (A).** Radhakrishnan says that intellectual is not infallible.

Reason (R). He says that both intellect and intuition are needed.

1290. **Assertion (A).** Ambedkar says that first there were three Varnas.

Reason (R). He says that everyone are equal.

1291. **Assertion (A).** Ambedkar believes in Buddhism only.

Reason (R). He departed from Hinduism.

1292. **Assertion (A).** Bhattacharya believes in subject as free.

Reason (R). He believes in the Denial of 'I'.

1293. **Assertion (A).** Krishnamurti says that freedom from self is essential.

Reason (R). He wrote book named 'The First and Last Freedom.'

1294. **Assertion (A).** Bhattacharya believes in the denial of 'I'

Reason (R). He believes in subject as freedom.

1295. **Assertion (A).** Krishnamurti says that intelligence is an essential power.

Reason (R). Intelligence does not refer to any conflict.

1296. **Assertion (A).** Ambedkar says that caste system is a curse for a society.

Reason (R). He believes in Buddhism.

1297. **Assertion (A).** According to Krishnamurti, self creates false existence.

Reason (R). Self is related to the experience.

1298. **Assertion (A).** Gandhiji identifies God with truth.

Reason (R). Truth is universal and all pervasive.

1299. **Assertion (A)** : In Gandhian ethics the golden rule of conduct is mutual toleration.

Reason (R) : Conscience is not the same thing for all.

1300. **Assertion (A).** Iqbal believes in Self.

Reason (R). He was monotheistic.

1301. **Assertion (A).** Aurobindo says that mind and supermind are the two hemispheres of reality.

Reason (R). He was monistic.

1302. **Assertion (A).** For Tagore, mother tongue is essential for education.

Reason (R). He was spiritual.

1303. **Assertion (A).** Vivekananda follows Ramkrishna philosophy.

Reason (R). Ramkrishna was his teacher.

1304. **Assertion (A).** Vivekananda believes in practical Vedanta.

Reason (R). He was dualist.

1305. **Assertion (A).** Tagore wrote a book on Gitanjali.

Reason (R). He also wrote 'A Religion of Man'.

1306. **Assertion (A).** Aurobindo was dualist.

Reason (R). He believe in evolution.

1307. **Assertion (A).** Vivekananda believes in Hinduism.

Reason (R). He don't believes in Quaran.

1308. The triple process of evolutionary growth, according to Aurobindo, involves processes of......., ...and......

A. Widening B. Heightening
C. Integration D. Differentiation
E. Combination F. Distraction

Codes:

(1) A, B and E (2) B, C and D
(3) D, E and F (4) A, B and C

1309. Which of the following belong to lower hemisphere? Select correct answer from the codes given below.

A. Matter B. Life
C. Mind D. Super Mind
E. Psyche

Codes:

(1) A, B and E (2) A, B, C and E
(3) B, C and D
(4) A, B, C, D and E

1310. Which of the following statements are associated with Gandhiji's concept of truth?

A. Truth is an ontological category
B. Truth is an ethical category
C. Truth is only a property of statements

Select the correct answer from the codes given below :

(1) A, B and C (2) A and B
(3) B and C (4) A and C

1311. Integral yoga is also known as

A. Purāṇa yoga B. Purva yoga
C. Inner yoga D. Pṛstha yoga

Codes:

(1) B and C (2) A and C
(3) A and D (4) C and D

1312. In respect of philosophical judgements, Krishnachandra's position is similar to......... Select the correct answer from the codes given below.

A. Kant B. Hegel
C. Hume
D. Logical positivists

Codes:
(1) A and B (2) B and C
(3) C and D (4) A and D

1313. On what ground Gandhi criticizes the modern civilization? Choose the options and select the correct answer from the codes given below.

A. Materialistic view
B. Suffering from several basic and inter-related limitations
C. Lack of moral and spiritual depth
D. Having no guiding principle
E. Dehumanized man and anti-human bias.

Codes:
(1) A and C (2) C and E
(3) B and D (4) All the five

1314. Consider the following statements:
According of Gandhi, the Law of non-violence

A. is good enough for individuals
B. is not meant for the masses
C. implies self-purification
D. is to be used against a government

What of these statements are correct?
(1) A and B (2) B and D
(3) A and C (4) C and D

1315. Consider the following statements :
According to Gandhiji, Non-violence means

A. the moral alternative to war
B. the virtue of the strong
C. the soul-force
D. non-killing

Of these statements
(1) A, B and C are correct
(2) A, B and D are correct
(3) A and D are correct
(4) B, C and D are correct

1316. Which of the following statements are true of Gandhian thought?

A. Truth is a property of statements
B. Truth is God
C. Truth is an ontological category
D. Truth is an ethical category

Select the correct answer using the codes given below :

Codes:
(1) A, B and C (2) B, C and D
(3) A, C and D (4) A, B and D

1317. **Statement.** Krishnamurti wrote the first and last freedom book.

Conclusion.

I. This book Talk about Intelligence.
II. Self is an experience.

Codes:
(1) Conclusion I is correct
(2) Conclusion II is correct
(3) Both are strong.
(4) Neither are strong.

1318. **Statement.** Ambedkar advocated Neo-Buddhism.

Conclusion.

I. He departs from Hinduism.
II. He don't departs from Hinduism.

Codes
(1) Conclusion I is correct
(2) Conclusion II is correct
(3) Both are strong.
(4) Neither are strong.

1319. Which of the following statements are made by J. Krishnamurti?

A. Duty is complete order
B. Freedom and love go together.
C. The mind has to be empty to see clearly.
D. Journey is better than arrival.

Codes:
(1) A, B and C (2) B, C and D
(3) A, C and D (4) All of these

1320. Swami Vivekananda believes in
A. universal religion
B. practical vedanta
C. monism of the Upanishads Hinduism

Codes:
(1) A and B (2) B and C
(3) A and D (4) All of these

1321. Aurobindo believes in
A. integral evolution
B. mind and supermind
C. universal religion
D. religion of man

Codes:
(1) A and B (2) A and C
(3) A and D (4) All of these

1322. Tagore believes in
A. religion of man
B. ideas on education
C. a philosophy of life
D. spirituality

Codes:
(1) A and B (2) B and C
(3) C and D (4) All of these

1323. Iqbal believes in
A. immortality of self
B. man and superman
C. monotheism
D. Quran

Codes:
(1) A and B (2) B and C
(3) C and D (4) All of these

1324. Iqbal conceive God as
A. one B. omnipotent
C. all knowing
D. supremely good creater of the world

Codes:
(1) A and B (2) B and C
(3) A and D (4) All of these

1325. Tagore was
A. a prophet of love
B. a prophet of non-love
C. a prophet of harmony
D. a prophet of non-harmony

Codes:
(1) A and B (2) A and C
(3) B and C (4) C and D

1326. Aurobindo works include
A. the human cycle
B. savitri
C. the Veda D. essays on the sita

Codes:
(1) A and B (2) B and C
(3) C and D (4) All of these

1327. Vivekananda was
A. influenced by Advinta Vedanta
B. influenced by Bhakti cut
C. not influenced by Samkara Upanishad
D. non-monist

Codes:
(1) A and B (2) A and C
(3) C and D (4) None of these

1328. **Assertion (A).** According to Mimamsa, letters are not produced at any time.

Reason (R). The same letter is pronounced by different persons at different places.

1329. Pythagoras says that
A. whatever exists, exists in number.
B. the soul is immortal.
C. all is one.
D. fire is essential.

Select the correct answer from the codes given below :

(1) A and B (2) A, B and D

(3) B and C (4) C and D

1330. Goiges wrote a book on

A. nature

B. non-existent

C. existent

D. Homo Mensura

Select the correct answer from the codes given below :

(1) A and B (2) B and C

(3) A and D (4) C and D

1331. Who established the theory of Becoming?

(1) Plato (2) Parmanides

(3) Heraclitus (4) St. Anselm

1332. For Russell, the father of the line of philosophers was

(1) Thales (2) Socrates

(3) Plato (4) Anaximander

1333. The first man who made a map of the earth is

(1) Thales (2) Anaximander

(3) Heracliturs (4) Anaximenes

1334. "Man is the measure of all things" is said by

(1) Plato (2) Aristotle

(3) Socrates (4) Protagoras

1335. Who affirmed, "what is contradictory to thought cannot be real"?

(1) Plato (2) Aristotle

(3) Parmenides (4) Anaximander

1336. "Knowledge is virtue" is said by

(1) Democritus (2) Socrates

(3) Aristotle (4) Leibnitz

1337. According to Socrates, knowledge is through

(1) concepts (2) percepts

(3) Intuition (4) None

1338. The Idea of the..............is one single reality which underlies all that is called virtue or good.

(1) God (2) Evil

(3) Good (4) Particular

1339. Who was the philosopher interviewed by young Socrates ?

(1) Anaximenes (2) Anaximander

(3) Heraclitus (4) Parmenides

1340. Whose birthday is celebrated as "World Philosophers' Day"?

(1) Thales (2) Pythagoras

(3) Socrates (4) Plato

1341. Who said that all things are full of Gods?

(1) Zeno (2) Thales

(3) Democritus (4) None

1342. Who holds that the philosophy of Milesians to be hylozoistic?

(1) Zeno (2) Windelband

(3) Frank Thilly (4) Russell

1343. According to Anaximander, the fundamental stuff is

(1) water (2) boundless mass

(3) air (4) fire

1344. Anaximander's fundamental stuff is

(1) formless (2) Partless

(3) infinite (4) eternal

Codes :

(1) 1 and 2 (2) 1, 2 and 3

(3) 2, 3 and 4 (4) 1, 2, 3 and 4

1345. What is true for Anaximander?

(1) A formless general principle can account for the particulars

(2) Vice-versa of (a)

(3) A formless general principle can not account for the particulars

(4) Generality has no relation with particularity

1346. According to Anaximander, the world is governed by
(1) God (2) boundless matter
(3) the opposite (4) itself

1347. The world, according to Anaximander, goes on because
(1) of God's grace
(2) matters are active
(3) the opposites work
(4) none of the above

1348. According to the Anaximander
(1) At one time there was water everywhere on this earth.
(2) There were only watery creatures
(3) By drying up of water land appeared
(4) All of the above

1349. According to Anaximander the earth is.
(1) spherical
(2) cylindrical
(3) A disc
(4) solid state of water

1350. According to Anaximander the earth
(1) is hanging in space
(2) moves freely in space
(3) rests on a fixed point
(4) none of the above

1351. Who among the following is known as the first thinker?
(1) Thales (2) Pythagoras
(3) Anaximander (4) Descartes

1352. The fundamental stuff, out of which this universe is made, according to Thales is
(1) Water (2) Air
(3) Soil (4) Fire

1353. The earth, according to Thales, is a
(1) bowl floating on the water
(2) disc floating on the water
(3) plate of any metal
(4) None of the above

1354. Aristotle the biologist conjectured that Thales choose water to be the ultimate stuff, for
(1) body is full of water
(2) food is always wet and this liquid food nourishes the body
(3) water is necessary for life
(4) None of the above

1355. Who among the following gave birth to scientific way of thinking?
(1) Pythagoras (2) Democritus
(3) Thales (4) Plato

1356. Who among the following said that Thales had predicted the eclipse which took place in 585 B.C.?
(1) Pythagoras (2) Aristotle
(3) Russell (4) Moore

1357. Who discovered how to calculate the distance of a ship at sea with the help of observations taken at two points?
(1) Pythagoras (2) Anaximander
(3) Anaximenes (4) Thales

1358. Who discovered how to calculate the height of a tree or pyramid from the length of its shadow?
(1) Pythagoras (2) Anaximander
(3) Anaximenes (4) Thales

1359. Thales' speculation, regarding worldview, was
(1) naturalistic (2) anthropomorphic
(3) theocentric (4) scientific

1360. Who regarded Magnet as something living for it attracts things towards itself?
(1) Thales (2) Pythagoras
(3) Zeno (4) Heraclitus

1361. Which of the following statements expresses Anaximenes's view?
(1) Quality can explain the quantity
(2) Quantity can explain the quality

(3) Quantities and qualities are unknown
(4) Quantity counts, quality controls

1362. 'What exists, exists in numbers' is stated by
(1) Thales (2) Anaximenese
(3) Pythagoras (4) Anaximander

1363. For Pythagoras the soul is
(1) mortal
(2) immortal
(3) a kind of fire
(4) nothing but only consciousness

1364. Which among the following statements is true about Pythagoras?
(1) He believes in rebirths
(2) He does not believe in rebirths
(3) He is a nihilist
(4) He is an atheist

1365. What is body according to Pythagoras?
(1) A mere idea
(2) Combination of atoms
(3) Tomb of the soul
(4) None of the above

1366. The visible world in which man lives is
(1) real
(2) false and illusive
(3) indescribable
(4) ideal world

1367. Pythagoras mentions a way to release from the round of endless reincarnations in this false world. That is
(1) devotion
(2) physical exercise
(3) Mystic meditation
(4) reading the Pythagorean texts

1368. Pythagoras recommended for
(1) an ascetic life
(2) material life
(3) (1) and (2) both
(4) none of the above

1369. Which of the following cannot be related to Pythagoras?
(1) the communistic state of affairs
(2) the essence sect holding all things in common
(3) vegetarianism
(4) None of the above

1370. Pythagoras laid emphasis on
(1) asceticism
(2) Purity of conduct
(3) (1) and (2) both
(4) neither (1) nor (2)

1371. Pythagoras believed in
(1) life is full of miseries
(2) immortal soul
(3) suicide is undesirable
(4) Transmigration of the soul
(5) All of the above

1372. Which one of the following does not come under the taboo-restrictions mentioned by Pythagoras?
(1) To abstain from beans
(2) Not to touch a white cock
(3) Not to stir the fire with iron
(4) Not to wear a white hat

1373. Who has discovered the theorem that in a right-angled triangle, the sum of the squares on the sides is in equal to the square on the hypotenuse?
(1) Thales (2) Anaximander
(3) Pythagoras (4) Zeno

1374. The existence of void was a necessary element in Atomistic theory, given by
(1) Aristotle (2) Democritus
(3) Heraclitus (4) Zeno

1375. The earliest-expressions of empiricism in ancient Greek philosophy were those of the
(1) Stoics (2) Neoplatonists
(3) Sophists (4) None of these

1376. Who were considered as atheist Greek philosophers?
(1) Plato, Aristotle
(2) Aquinas, Plato
(3) Thales, Anaximenes, Heraclitus
(4) None of the above

1377. Which one of the following beliefs was NOT held by Pythagoras?
(1) The universe is an eternal rational unity
(2) The universe functions according to mathematical principles
(3) The universe is composed of monads
(4) Reality cannot be known by means of our senses alone

1378. Which one of the following philosophers is associated with stoicism?
(1) Zeno (2) Thales
(3) Anaximander (4) Heraclitus

1379. Which one of the following statements adequately sums up Heraclitus' philosophy?
(1) All things originate from water
(2) The universe is composed of five great elements
(3) All things are in a state of flux
(4) The originating cause of the universe is air

1380. According to Pythagoras the world is composed of the opposites. How many opposites are there mentioned by Pythagoreans?
(1) 50 (2) 10
(3) 40 (4) 20

1381. Which among the following opposites is not mentioned by Pythagoreans?
(1) Odd and even
(2) Limited and unlimited
(3) One and many
(4) Up and down

1382. Which among the following opposites is not mentioned by Pythagoreans?
(1) Up and down
(2) Right and left
(3) Masculine and feminine
(4) Rest and motion

1383. Anaximander's theory of evolution is
(1) organic (2) natural
(3) based on theology
(4) none of the above

1384. According to Anaximander, God is
(1) water
(2) boundless matter
(3) an stimulating force
(4) mere idea

1385. Anaximander is
(1) Polytheist (2) Henotheist
(3) Monotheist
(4) None of the above

1386. Who said that there is a central fire around which the earth, the sun, the moon and five planets move?
(1) Thales (2) Heraclitus
(3) Pythagoras (4) Anaximander

1387. Who, among the following Greek philosophers, had declared 'one alone is real'?
(1) Anaximander
(2) Pythagoras
(3) Parmenides
(4) None of the above

1388. According to Parmenides, how can we know the one?
(1) through thought
(2) by senses
(3) (1) and (2) both
(4) None of the above

1389. Distinction between the appearance and reality, sense and thought is given by
(1) Thales (2) Anaximenese
(3) Pythagoras (4) Parmenides

1390. For Heraclitus, reality is
(1) Change (2) Flux
(3) Becoming (4) All of the above

1391. Democritus accepts
(1) Hedonism (2) Utilitarianism
(3) Scepticism (4) None

1392. According to Heraclitus all things come from..........and return to............
(1) Water, fire (2) Fire, fire
(3) Air, water (4) Water, water

1393. According to Heraclitus process alone is reality and is best symbolized by
(1) Earth (2) Water
(3) Fire (4) Air

1394. According to Anaximenes, the primary stuff of this universe is
(1) Water (2) Boundless matter
(3) Air (4) Fire

1395. Anaximenes chose air as the first thing because of its
(1) Mobility
(2) Changeability
(3) inner vitality
(4) All of the above

1396. For Anaximenes, the primary air is regulated by
(1) its quality of mobility
(2) the opposed principles of condensation and rarefaction
(3) the grace of God
(4) none of the above

1397. By rarefaction, Anaximenes says, air assumes the form of
(1) water (2) fire
(3) earth (4) stone

1398. By condensation air assumes the form of
(1) water (2) earth
(3) stone (4) All of the above

1399. Who among the following thinks that all the material elements are produced out of air?
(1) Thales (2) Anaximander
(3) Anaximenes (4) Zeno

1400. According to Anaximenes the world is
(1) Vapours, liquid and solid
(2) Sound and colour
(3) rough and smooth
(4) All of the above

1401. Socrates laid down three propositions. Which of the following is not included among them?
(1) Virtue is knowledge
(2) Virtue can be taught
(3) Virtue is one
(4) Virtue continuously varies with the variation of facts

1402. Democritus teaches
(1) Not to tell a lie
(2) Work for society
(3) Cultivation of true friendship
(4) None of the above

1403. Democritus says that............pleasure is lower than...........pleasure.
(1) Mental, sex (2) Physical, sex
(3) Spiritual, sex (4) sex, mental

1404. The theory of atoms is related to
(1) Democritus
(2) Heraclitus
(3) Anaximander
(4) Parmenides

1405. For Democritus, the soul is
(1) A stream of consciousness
(2) A bundle of ideas
(3) Nothing but a conscious body
(4) An aggregate of atoms

1406. For Democritus, the soul consists of those atoms which have the essence of

(1) Fire (2) Water
(3) Change (4) Air

1407. The fiery atoms, according to Democritus, are found in largest number in
(1) Plant (2) Animal
(3) Man (4) God

1408. The sophists had maintained that
(1) Everything is in constant flux
(2) Perception gives the knowledge of becoming
(3) Knowledge is perception
(4) None of the above

1409. For Democritus perception gives us the information about the world of
(1) being (2) becoming
(3) reality (4) None of these

1410. For Democritus, thought gives us the knowledge of
(1) being (2) becoming
(3) Reality (4) None

1411. The man who declared himself first "I am a Philosopher" is
(1) Socrates (2) Pythogoras
(3) Bacon (4) Heraditus

1412. The expounder of dialectical method in early Greek Philosophy was
(1) Socrates (2) Aristotle
(3) Zeno (4) Plato

1413. Who ultimately reduced the number of causes from four to two only ?
(1) Parmanides (2) Pythagoras
(3) Plato (4) Aristotle

1414. For Democritus, atoms do not differ in........but only in............. .
(1) Degree, Kind
(2) Kind, Degree
(3) Substances, Attributes
(4) None of these

1415. According to sophists, for all practical purposes, what alone is knowledge?
(1) Intuition (2) Intellect
(3) Perception (4) Reason

1416. For Socrates, by conception is meant
(1) Particular idea
(2) Universal idea of a class
(3) Universal and particular both
(4) None of the above

1417. 'Homo mensura (man is the measure of all things)' is famous saying of
(1) Protagoras (2) Gorgius
(3) Socrates (4) Plato

1418. Which of the following is not accepted by Gorgius?
(1) There is nothing
(2) Even if there be anything it cannot be known
(3) Knowledge cannot be communicate
(4) None of the above

1419. 'Non-existent' is written by
(1) Protagoras (2) Gorgius
(3) Democritus (4) Parmenides

1420. The conversational method of Socrates took the form of
(1) Sceptic (2) Doubt
(3) Dialectic (4) None of these

1421. Protagoras famous .... is Homo Mensura.
(1) saying (2) notion
(3) doctrine (4) term

1422. The thing which is valid and acceptable to all men is considered as what?
(1) Universal (2) Particular
(3) Relevant (4) Rational

1423. The universal deal with what, according to Socrates?
(1) Being (2) Man
(3) Human (4) God

1424. Who believed that "good and ill are one"?
(1) Thales (2) Heraclitus
(3) Aristotle (4) Anaximenes

1425. Socrates wrote _____ number of books/articles.
(1) Three (2) Four
(3) One (4) None

1426. Greek Philosophy begins with
(1) An inquiry into the essence of the objective world.
(2) By studying body and mind problem.
(3) Accepting received opinions.
(4) Accepting customary set forth doctrines.

1427. 'Socratic Irony' means
(1) Lecturing on the street corners.
(2) Ready to face death for the sake of truth.
(3) Evolving truth through dialogue.
(4) Acting as that one knew less.

1428. Who among the following is an Ionic Philosopher ?
(1) Heraclitus (2) Zeno
(3) Thales (4) Anaxagoras

1429. Socrates did not advocate that
(1) Right thinking leads to right action.
(2) No man is voluntarily bad or voluntarily good.
(3) Doubt implies a doubter.
(4) An un-examined life is not worth-living.

1430. The prominent sophists were
(1) Leucippus and Democritus
(2) Socrates and Plato
(3) Protagoras and Gorgias
(4) Anaxagoras and Tuucydides

1431. The Sophists did not propose
(1) 'Proper study of mankind is man.'
(2) 'Morality is mere convention.'
(3) 'Man is the measure of all things.'
(4) 'Knowledge is virtue.'

1432. Who declared, 'whenever the shadow of a man is equal to his height, the height of a pyramid is equal to its shadow' ?
(1) Thales (2) Pythagoras
(3) Socrates (4) Plato

1433. Match list I with list II in the manner that the matching should be correct according to Pythagorean assumptions and select the appropriate answer from the codes given below;

List-I	List-II
(a) Animal animation	(i) 3
(b) Material qualities	(ii) 4
(c) Solid	(iii) 5
(d) Plane	(iv) 6

Codes :

	(a)	(b)	(c)	(d)
(1)	(i)	(ii)	(iii)	(iv)
(2)	(iv)	(ii)	(iii)	(i)
(3)	(iv)	(iii)	(ii)	(i)
(4)	(i)	(iii)	(ii)	(iv)

1434. Match list I with list II in same manner as given in question no. 103.

List-I	List-II
(a) Point	(i) 3
(b) Line	(ii) 9
(c) Plane	(iii) 2
(d) Justice	(iv) 1

Codes :

	(a)	(b)	(c)	(d)
(1)	(iv)	(iii)	(i)	(ii)
(2)	(iii)	(iv)	(ii)	(i)
(3)	(iv)	(i)	(iii)	(ii)
(4)	(iii)	(ii)	(iv)	(i)

1435. Match the following

List-I	List-II
(a) On nature	(i) Gorgias
(b) No book	(ii) Socrates

(c) Homo Mensura (iii) Protagoras
(d) Atomism (iv) Democritus

Codes :

	(a)	(b)	(c)	(d)
(1)	(i)	(ii)	(iii)	(iv)
(2)	(ii)	(iii)	(iv)	(i)
(3)	(iv)	(iii)	(ii)	(i)
(4)	(ii)	(iii)	(i)	(iv)

1436. Match the following

List-I	List-II
(a) Gorgias	(i) Nihilism
(b) Protagoras	(ii) Homo Mensura
(c) Sophist	(iii) Refutation of the statements
(d) Judgement	(iv) Tantology

Codes :

	(a)	(b)	(c)	(d)
(1)	(i)	(ii)	(iii)	(iv)
(2)	(iv)	(iii)	(ii)	(i)
(3)	(iv)	(ii)	(iii)	(i)
(4)	(ii)	(iv)	(iii)	(i)

1437. Match the following

List-I	List-II
(a) Knowledge	(i) Perception
(b) Sophist Epistemology	(ii) Protagoras
(c) Rhetoric	(iii) Gorgias
(d) Judgement	(iv) Tantology

Codes :

	(a)	(b)	(c)	(d)
(1)	(i)	(ii)	(iii)	(iv)
(2)	(ii)	(iv)	(iii)	(i)
(3)	(ii)	(iv)	(iii)	(i)
(4)	(i)	(iv)	(iii)	(ii)

1438. Match list I with list II and select the correct answer from the codes given below:

List-I	List-II
(a) Thales	(i) Number
(b) Anaximander	(ii) Water
(c) Anaximenese	(iii) Air
(d) Pythagoras	(iv) Boundless mass

Codes :

	(a)	(b)	(c)	(d)
(1)	(ii)	(iv)	(iii)	(iii)
(2)	(iii)	(i)	(iv)	(ii)
(3)	(iv)	(ii)	(i)	(iii)
(4)	(i)	(iii)	(ii)	(iv)

1439. Match the following

List-I	List-II
(a) Gorgias	(i) Art of persuasion
(b) Protagoras	(ii) Man is the measure of all things
(c) Earlier Greek philosophers	(iii) Distinction between sense and reason
(d) Sophist	(iv) Humanistic

Codes :

	(a)	(b)	(c)	(d)
(1)	(i)	(ii)	(iii)	(iv)
(2)	(iv)	(iii)	(ii)	(i)
(3)	(iii)	(ii)	(iv)	(i)
(4)	(ii)	(i)	(iii)	(iv)

1440. Match the following

List-I	List-II
(a) Sophist	(i) Protagoras
(b) Socrates	(ii) Dialectic
(c) Virtue	(iii) Taught
(d) Knowledge	(iv) Supreme source of good

Codes :

	(a)	(b)	(c)	(d)
(1)	(i)	(ii)	(iii)	(iv)
(2)	(iv)	(iii)	(ii)	(i)
(3)	(iii)	(ii)	(iv)	(i)
(4)	(i)	(iv)	(iii)	(ii)

1441. Match the following

List-I	List-II
(a) Conversational	(i) Method
(b) Virtue	(ii) Ethics

(c) Nothing (iii) Gorgias
(d) Knowledge (iv) Sophist

Codes :

	(a)	(b)	(c)	(d)
(1)	(i)	(ii)	(iii)	(iv)
(2)	(iv)	(iii)	(ii)	(i)
(3)	(iv)	(ii)	(iii)	(i)
(4)	(ii)	(iii)	(iv)	(i)

1442. Match the following

List-I	List-II
(a) Thales	(i) one
(b) Parmenides	(ii) atoms
(c) Heraclitus	(iii) flux
(d) Democritus	(iv) water

Codes :

	(a)	(b)	(c)	(d)
(1)	(i)	(ii)	(iii)	(iv)
(2)	(i)	(iii)	(ii)	(iv)
(3)	(iv)	(i)	(iii)	(ii)
(4)	(i)	(iii)	(iv)	(ii)

1443. Match the following

List-I	List-II
(a) Gorgias	(i) Ecletic philosophy
(b) Protagoras	(ii) Perception
(c) Zeno	(iii) Dialectic
(d) Socrates	(iv) Three propositions

Codes :

	(a)	(b)	(c)	(d)
(1)	(i)	(ii)	(iii)	(iv)
(2)	(iv)	(iii)	(ii)	(i)
(3)	(ii)	(iv)	(iii)	(i)
(4)	(i)	(ii)	(iii)	(iv)

1444. Match the following

List-I	List-II
(a) Heraclitus	(i) flux
(b) Democritus	(ii) atoms
(c) Pythagoras	(iii) Numbers
(d) Anaximenese	(iv) air

Codes :

	(a)	(b)	(c)	(d)
(1)	(iv)	(i)	(ii)	(iii)
(2)	(iii)	(iv)	(i)	(ii)
(3)	(ii)	(iii)	(iv)	(i)
(4)	(i)	(ii)	(iii)	(iv)

1445. Match the following

List-I	List-II
(a) Conception	(i) Universal idea of a class
(b) Socrates	(ii) Virtue
(c) Knowledge	(iii) Concept
(d) Perceptions	(iv) Recollection

Codes :

	(a)	(b)	(c)	(d)
(1)	(i)	(ii)	(iii)	(iv)
(2)	(iv)	(iii)	(ii)	(i)
(3)	(iii)	(ii)	(iv)	(i)
(4)	(i)	(iv)	(iii)	(ii)

1446. Match the following

List-I	List-II
(a) Protagoras	(i) Homo mensura
(b) Gorgius	(ii) Nihilism
(c) Socrates	(iii) Virtue is knowledge

Codes :

	(a)	(b)	(c)
(1)	(i)	(iii)	(ii)
(2)	(i)	(ii)	(iii)
(3)	(ii)	(i)	(iii)
(4)	(ii)	(iii)	(i)

1447. Match the following

List-I	List-II
(a) Democritus	(i) Happiness as a state of soul
(b) Parmenides	(ii) One alone is real
(c) Heraclitus	(iii) Being is identical with not being

(d) Pythagoras (iv) Transmigration soul

Codes :

	(a)	(b)	(c)	(d)
(1)	(i)	(ii)	(iii)	(iv)
(2)	(i)	(iv)	(iii)	(ii)
(3)	(ii)	(iv)	(iii)	(i)
(4)	(ii)	(iii)	(iv)	(i)

1448. Match the following

List-I	List-II
(a) Pythagoras	(i) Numbers
(b) Parmenides	(ii) Appearance and reality
(c) Democritus	(iii) Perception and thought
(d) Thales	(iv) Water

Codes :

	(a)	(b)	(c)	(d)
(1)	(i)	(ii)	(iii)	(iv)
(2)	(iv)	(iii)	(ii)	(i)
(3)	(iv)	(ii)	(iii)	(i)
(4)	(i)	(iv)	(iii)	(ii)

1449. Match the following

List-I	List-II
(a) Democritus	(i) Fiery atoms are man
(b) Heraclitus	(ii) Reality is becoming
(c) Pythagoras	(iii) Tomb of the soul
(d) Anaximenes	(iv) The world is rough and smooth

Codes :

	(a)	(b)	(c)	(d)
(1)	(i)	(ii)	(iii)	(iv)
(2)	(ii)	(iii)	(iv)	(i)
(3)	(iv)	(iii)	(ii)	(i)
(4)	(i)	(ii)	(iii)	(iv)

1450. Match the following

List-I	List-II
(a) Pre-Socratic	(i) Heraclitus
(b) Sophist to Aristotle	(ii) Plato
(c) Post-Aristotelian	(iii) Stocis
(d) Classical Western philosophy	(iv) Ancient Greece

Codes :

	(a)	(b)	(c)	(d)
(1)	(i)	(ii)	(iii)	(iv)
(2)	(iv)	(iii)	(ii)	(i)
(3)	(ii)	(iii)	(iv)	(i)
(4)	(i)	(iv)	(iii)	(ii)

Directions. The following items consist of two statements, one labelled the 'Assertion A' and the other labelled the 'Reason R'. You are to examine these two statements carefully and decide if the Assertion A and the reason R individually true and if so, whether the reason is a correct explanation of the assertion. Select your answers to these items using the codes given below

Codes :

(a) Both A and R are true and R is the correct explanation of A

(b) Both A and R are true but R is not the correct explanation of A

(c) A is true but R is false

(d) A is false but R is true.

1451. **Assertion (A).** Thales claims that water is the fundamental stuff of which the universe is made.

Reason (R). Water succeeds in explaining all the possible states of being solid, liquid and vaporous.

1452. **Assertion (A).** Windelband holds that the philosophy of Thales and of other Milesians to be hylozoistic.

Reason (R). Thales is said to have said that all things are full of gods.

1453. **Assertion (A).** Anaximander claims that the earth, air, water and fire cannot be the ultimate stuff of the universe.

Reason (R). They have opposite characters.

1454. **Assertion (A).** Anaximander is accepted as the first theist.

Reason (R). Anaximander has given the first philosophical concept of God.

1455. **Assertion (A).** Anaximander is a monotheist.

Reason (R). Anaximander calls his infinite, boundless matter 'God'.

1456. **Assertion (A).** Anaximenese chose air as the first things.

Reason (R). Air has the qualities of mobility, changeability and inner vitality.

1457. **Assertion (A).** The two principles of condensation and rarefaction are important steps in developing the scientific thinking about the universe.

Reason (R). Anaximenese tells us how air accounts for the formation of water, fire and earth on the basis of condensation and rarefaction.

1458. **Assertion (A).** According to Pythagoras suicide is not deemed desirable.

Reason (R). Suicide can not help in putting an end to the wheel of transmigration.

1459. **Assertion (A).** For Parmenides, real is eternal, unchangeable and indestructible.

Reason (R). For Parmenides it appeared self contradictory to hold that a thing which is passing away to be real.

1460. **Assertion (A).** For Parmenides, movement or motion is unreal.

Reason (R). Parmenides says that the empty space is illusory.

1461. **Assertion (A).** The sophists denied the possibility of scientific knowledge.

Reason (R). The sophists had maintained that knowledge is perception and perception is relative and transitory.

1462. **Assertion (A).** The famous saying of Protagoras is 'Homomensura'.

Reason (R). Protagoras thinks that for all practical purposes perception alone is knowledge.

1463. **Assertion (A).** Sophists were concentrated on the logic of proof and contradiction.

Reason (R). The sophists were interested in the refutation of the statement of their opponents.

1464. **Assertion (A).** The sophists held that morality consists in pleasure.

Reason (R). For sophists, feeling was taken to be the seat of morality.

1465. **Assertion (A).** For Socrates knowledge is through concept.

Reason (R). The universals deal with Being.

1466. **Assertion (A).** All the men have knowledge of absolute equality, justice, virtue, goodness etc., but these become dim and dormant in them.

Reason (R). See the men have deception of senses.

1467. **Assertion (A).** Gorgias took the help of Zeno's argument.

Reason (R). He also took the help of Protagoras epistemology with its sceptical conclusion.

1468. **Assertion (A).** Knowledge of absolute justice become dimin all men.

Reason (R). Because of the deception of senses which is present every time in men.

1469. **Assertion (A).** The logic of proof and contradiction was important for Sophist.

Reason (R). The refutation of the statement of their opponents were given by the Sophists.

1470. **Assertion (A).** Thales says that the Earth is regarded as a disc which floats on the water.

Reason (R). Because for him, water is regarded as the ultimate stuff of the universe.

1471. **Assertion (A).** Parmenides starting point was Xenophares 'All in one'.

Reason (R). Because reality alone is one and changes are regarded as unreal.

1472. **Assertion (A).** Heraclitus talks about the downward and upward way.

Reason (R). Condensation and rarefaction comes under the domain of the downward and upward way.

1473. **Assertion (A).** Scientific knowledge is not possible according to Sophists.

Reason (R). Knowledge is perception.

1474. **Assertion (A).** Morality means pleasure, according to Sophist.

Reason (R). Feeling is regarded as the seat of morality according to Sophist.

1475. **Assertion (A).** For Heraclitus, fire keeps on changing every moment.

Reason (R). Because everything is in fuse and is also momentary.

1476. **Assertion (A).** According to Parmenides, the empty space is regarded as illusory.

Reason (R). Because movement is regarded as unreal.

1477. **Assertion (A).** Perception is relative, according to the Sophists.

Reason (R). Perception is transitory, according to the Sophists.

1478. **Assertion (A).** Pythagoras says that, the soul is immortal.

Reason (R). Because he believes in rebirths and also in the transmigration of the soul.

1479. **Assertion (A).** Knowledge is known only through concepts, according to Socrates.

Reason (R). Being is dealt by the universals.

1480. **Assertion (A).** The whole of being cannot be plurality according to Zeno.

Reason (R). For Zeno to say that one and the same whole is both infinitely small and infinitely great is absurd.

1481. **Assertion (A).** Anaximender distinction between formless matter and particular is found in the theory of Aristotle.

Reason (R). Aristotle doctrine is known as matter and form.

1482. **Assertion (A).** Pythagoras believes in fire.

Reason (R). Because, according to him the Earth, the Sun, the Moon and the five plants move around this fire which is also regarded as central.

1483. **Assertion (A).** Homo Mensura was given by protagoras.

Reason (R). Protagoras says that perception alone is knowledge.

1484. Which among the following opposites are mentioned by Pythagoreans? Select the correct answers from the codes given below :

A. Straight and crooked
B. Light and darkness
C. Good and evil
D. Square and oblong

Codes :

(1) A and B (2) B and C
(3) B, C and D (4) A, B, C and D

1485. Heraclitus believes in

A. Harmony of opposites
B. Only one reality
C. All is flow and becoming
D. The doctrine of flux

Codes:

(1) A and B (2) B and C
(3) A, C and D (4) A and D

1486. The method of enquiry of Socrates was regarded as

A. conversational
B. dialectic
C. non-dialectic
D. non-conversational

Select the correct answer from the codes given below :

(1) A and B (2) B and C
(3) C and D (4) A, B, C and D

1487. Gorgias says that

A. there is nothing.
B. knowledge can not be communicated.
C. Homo Mensura.
D. virtue is one.

Select the correct answer from the codes given below :

(1) A and B (2) A and C
(3) B and C (4) C and D

1488. Democritus says that

A. sex-pleasure is not needed.
B. the cultivation of true friendship is needed.
C. the world is governed by the opposites.
D. scientific way of thinking is needed.

Select the correct answer from the codes given below :

(1) A and B (2) A and C
(3) A and C (4) A and D

1489. Heraclitus says that

A. reality is becoming.
B. reality is non-becoming.
C. fire is the ever-changing reality.
D. the theory of atoms are essential.

Select the correct answer from the codes given below :

(1) A, B and C (2) A and D
(3) B, C and D (4) A, B and D

1490. Parmenides says that

A. reality is one.
B. reality is many.
C. reality is non-eternal.
D. changes are unreal.

Select the correct answer from the codes given below :

(1) A and B (2) A and C
(3) A and D (4) A, B, C and D

1491. Socrates says that

A. knowledge virtue already present in man.
B. knowledge of justice already present in man.
C. there is nothing.
D. every judgement is tantology.

Select the correct answer from the codes given below :

(1) A and B (2) B and C
(3) B and D (4) C and D

1492. Gorgias was regarded as

A. master of rhetoric.
B. the art of persuasion developer.
C. conversational philosopher.
D. Homo Mensura doctrine given philosopher.

Select the correct answer from the codes given below :

(1) A and B (2) B and C
(3) A, B, C and D (4) C and D

1493. Anaximenses says that

A. air is the fundamental stuff of the universe.
B. condensation and rarefaction are regarded as two principles.
C. fire is the ultimate stuff of universe.
D. everything is influx.

Select the correct answer from the codes given below :

(1) A and B (2) B and D
(3) B and C (4) A and D

1494. Democritus believes in

A. atoms
B. perception and thought
C. air
D. fire

Select the correct answer from the codes given below :

(1) A and B (2) B and C
(3) B and C (4) All of these

1495. Perception is regarded as

A. knowledge
B. important feature of Protagoras.
C. important feature of Sophist.
D. important feature of Plato.

Select the correct answer from the codes given below :

(1) A, B and C (2) B, C and D
(3) A, B and D (4) A, C and D

1496. Protagoras say that

A. knowledge is perception.
B. perception is knowledge.
C. knowledge cannot be communicated.
D. virtue is knowledge.

Select the correct answer from the codes given below :

(1) A and B (2) B and C
(3) A and C (4) A and D

1497. Thales was regarded as

A. naturalistic.
B. non-naturalistic.
C. hylozistic.
D. non-hylozistic.

Select the correct answer from the codes given below :

(1) A and B (2) A and C
(3) B and D (4) A and D

1498. Socrates says that

A. virtue is knowledge through concepts.
B. vice is ignorance.
C. virtue can be taught.
D. virtue is one.

Select the correct answer from the codes given below :

(1) A, C and D (2) A and C
(3) A, B and C (4) All of these

1499. Aristotle was regarded as

A. logical thinker.
B. philosopher of science.
C. non-logical thinker.
D. non-moral.

Select the correct answer from the codes given below :

(1) A and B (2) A and C
(3) B and C (4) C and D

1500. Aristotle worte

A. Nichomachean ethics.
B. Theatens.
C. Logic as organon.
D. Logical.

Select the correct answer from the codes given below :

(1) A and B (2) B and C
(3) A and C (4) A and D

1501. Which one among the following is real to Plato ?

(1) Objects (2) Ideas
(3) Soul (4) None of these

1502. Plato suggests that ideas are substances and these ideas are

(1) Particulars (2) Generals
(3) Universals (4) None of these

1503. The epistemology of .... and .... became the classical expression of subjective idealism.

(1) Berkeley, Kant (2) Berkeley, Hume
(3) Hume, Spinoza (4) None of these

1504. Founder of scientific logic is
(1) Plato (2) Aristotle
(3) Pythagoras (4) Parmenides

1505. Plato's dialectics come under
(1) Theory of knowledge
(2) Logic
(3) Metaphysics (4) All these

1506. The author of *'Memorabilia'* is
(1) Xenophon (2) Socrates
(3) Plato (4) Aristotle

1507. ....agreed with Plato, that knowledge is of the universal, but held that such universal forms should not be conceived as 'separated' from the matter embodying them.
(1) Augustine (2) Aquinas
(3) Aristotle (4) None of these

1508. A close connection with religious and mythological ideas was typical of Plato's
(1) Realism
(2) Idealism
(3) Objective idealism
(4) None of the above

1509. ....admits a 'two-world' concept, the world of imitations and the world of
(1) Aristotle, perfect entities
(2) Plato, perfect entities
(3) Plato, practical objects
(4) None of the above

1510. In whose philosophy the name of God is demiurge ?
(1) Parmenides (2) Heraclitus
(3) Anaximander (4) Plato

1511. According to Aristotle, we arrive at the concept of universals by a process of
(1) Realization
(2) Abstraction from particulars
(3) Conceptualization
(4) None of the above

1512. To have the concept is to have in mind the...............of the object.
(1) Primary Qualities
(2) Defining characteristics
(3) Real characteristics
(4) None of the above

1513. The problem of universals was first introduced into philosophy by
(1) Aquinas (2) Aristotle
(3) Plato (4) Berkeley

1514. ....is anything that can have instances and has general properties.
(1) Universal
(2) Particular
(3) Empirical object
(4) None of these

1515. The scientific interpretation of the term 'individual' as a member of society rests on the conception of man as a biosocial being whose essence is the aggregate of social relations. This view is given by
(1) Plato (2) Aristotle
(3) Marx (4) Berkeley

1516. Plato's chief concern with universals was in the context of moral properties and
(1) Ideas
(2) General properties
(3) Mathematical entities
(4) None of the above

1517. ....believed we recollect the concepts from a previous existence, prior to our birth in this world, in which we perceived them directly.
(1) Plato (2) Aristotle
(3) Descartes (4) Berkeley

1518. 'Particulars exist in space and time, but universals are neither in space nor in time', this view is given by
(1) Aristotle (2) Hume
(3) Descartes (4) Plato

1519. Plato presented two principal views to explain universal, these are archetype and
(1) Particularity (2) Ideas
(3) Abstract ideas (4) Participation

1520. According to Plato the soul is composed of
(1) reason, faith and appetite
(2) spirit, faith and appetite
(3) reason, faith and spirit
(4) reason, spirit and appetite

1521. By substance, in the primary sense, Aristotle means that which is
(1) predicable of a subject
(2) present in a subject
(3) both predicable of a subject and present in a subject
(4) neither predicable of a subject nor present in a subject

1522. The philosophy of..........was a classical form of objective idealism.
(1) Plato (2) Aristotle
(3) Descartes (4) None of these

1523. Which one of the following statements is closest to Aristotle's view of substance?
(1) Substance is form or universal
(2) Substance is that which exists by itself.
(3) Substance is the concrete individual
(4) Substance is static and eternal.

1524. Which one among the following kinds of substances is not admitted by Aristotle?
(1) Sensible and perishable
(2) Sensible and eternal
(3) Non-sensible and eternal
(4) Non-sensible and perishable

1525. Plato was primarily concerned to do two things at once, a two-world theory and a
(1) Theory of particulars
(2) Theory of ideas
(3) Theory of universals
(4) None of the above

1526. Which one of the following statements is not true according to Aristotle?
(1) Form and matter are relative terms
(2) Matter is potentiality, form is actuality
(3) Formless matter exists.
(4) Matterless form is real

1527. Which one of the following is not consistent with Aristotle's conception of matter and form?
(1) Matter and form are inseparable
(2) Form is universal, matter is particular
(3) Forms has seperate existence out of individuals.
(4) God is matterless form.

1528. Aristotle admits.........kinds of causes.
(1) Two (2) Four
(3) Five (4) Six

1529. Aristotle suggests a substance is an individual in which..........and.............are inseparably blended.
(1) Form, matter
(2) Substantiality, attributes
(3) Matter, qualities
(4) None of the above

1530. Aristotle..........God and soul as substance, though these two are form without matter.
(1) Rejects (2) Accepts
(3) Transforms (4) None of these

1531. ....believes some substances are sensible, some are sensible and eternal, and some are super-sensible and eternal.
(1) Aristotle (2) Plato
(3) Descartes (4) Spinoza

1532. What is the central concept of Aristotle's metaphysics?
(1) The concrete individual things or substance.
(2) There are four kinds of causes
(3) God is the only substance
(4) None of the above

1533. Which one of the following causes does not belong to Aristotle's philosophy?
(1) Necessary cause (2) Formal cause
(3) Material cause (4) Efficient cause

1534. ....is the compound of universal and particular according to Aristotle.
(1) Matter (2) Mind
(3) Substance (4) None of these

1535. ....suggests that substance is the combination of both the universals class and its individuals.
(1) Plato (2) Aristotle
(3) Locke (4) Berkeley

1536. Entire Western Philosophy is the foot note on the Philosophy of
(1) Socrates (2) Aristotle
(3) Plato (4) Parmanides

1537. Which of the following is not advocated by Aristotle ?
(1) Virtue is a state of character
(2) To know what is virtue is to be virtuous
(3) Virtue lies in a mean
(4) Virtue must be combined with practical wisdom.

1538. Plato claims the nature of things exist in the..........of them, an existence more real than that of sensible, individual things.
(1) Ideas (2) Qualities
(3) Attributes (4) None of these

1539. According to Plato, in there is no object in itself to be known at all.
(1) Perception (2) Conception
(3) Ideas (4) None

1540. Which of the following is not derived from Pythagoras in Plato's philosophy.
(1) Belief in the immortality of soul
(2) The doctrine of the transmigration of the soul
(3) Pre-existence of the soul
(4) The doctrine of the eternity and changelessness of idea

1541. Plato accepts the...........view of universals.
(1) Realistic (2) Nominalistic
(3) Conceptualistic (4) None of these

1542. Which of the following does not express Plato's theory?
(1) Ideas as universals are the real originals.
(2) Universal ideas can be copied by the perceptibles.
(3) Some perceptibles are also original ideas
(4) Ideas can be thought but not sensed.

1543. Plato has rejected
(1) Realistic theory of universals.
(2) Nominalistic theory of universals.
(3) Conceptualistic theory of universals.
(4) (2) and (3) both

1544. According to Plato learning of Ideas is really
(1) thought (2) recollection
(3) Experience (4) None of these

1545. According to Plato knowledge is
(1) not opinion (2) right opinion
(3) wrong opinion (4) none of these

1546. According to Plato the highest form of knowledge is
(1) conjectural knowledge
(2) rational insight
(3) Practical knowledge
(4) Hypothetical knowledge

1547. ....gives us the knowledge of forms or ideas.
(1) Conjectural knowledge
(2) Rational insight
(3) Practical knowledge
(4) Hypothetical knowledge

1548. Which of the following is not correct regarding Plato's theory?

(1) Conjectural knowledge is always erroneous.
(2) Practical knowledge is knowledge received through sense-organs.
(3) Hypothetical knowledge is the mediator knowledge and the rational insight.
(4) Right opinion is the real knowledge.

1549. Choose the wrong statement regarding Plato's theory

(1) Plato, has separated the soul from body, but, has not clarified the relationship between them.
(2) The soul is immortal, the body is perishable.
(3) The body is composition of fire, air, earth and water.
(4) The body was three parts of reason, high spirits and appetites.

1550. Which among the following is not correct regarding Plato's theory.

(1) God is eternal and does not change.
(2) God is good but not righteous.
(3) God is not creator.
(4) God is an architect.

1551. According to Aristotle which of the following sciences is concerned with pure, abstract knowledge?

(1) Logic
(2) Practical science
(3) Theoretical science
(4) The productive science

1552. Which knowledge is pursued as a means to conduct rather than as an end in itself.

(1) Logic (2) Theoria
(3) Proxis (4) Techne

1553. Which of the following sciences is a part of esthetics?

(1) Theoria (2) Proxis
(3) Techne (4) Logic

1554. Aristotle's work on logic is known as

(1) Theoria (2) Organon
(3) Proxis (4) Techne

1555. For Aristotle,

(1) Form and things interact each other after some interval.
(2) Form resides in heaven, things on earth.
(3) (1) and (2) both
(4) Forms and things go together

1556. Concept of 'Unmoved Mover' for God was developed by

(1) St. Thomas Acquinas
(2) St. Anselm
(3) Aristotle
(4) Plato

1557. Which one of the following statements is not admit by Plato?

(1) Universals are unchanging and eternal.
(2) Universals are more real than particulars.
(3) Universals have an independent existence while particulars have only a borrowed existence.
(4) Universals can exist only in particulars.

1558. On the question of describing the relation of Forms to particulars, Plato said that

(1) Forms participate in their particulars.
(2) Particulars participate in their Forms.
(3) Forms are abstracted form particulars.
(4) Particulars are caused by Forms.

1559. In the philosophy of Plato, 'ideas' are

(1) real but not existent.
(2) existent but unreal.
(3) neither existent nor real.
(4) both existent and real.

1560. Who believed that spiritual and appetites are two sections of soul ?

(1) Plato (2) Aristotle
(3) Parmenides (4) Anaximander

1561. Which one of the following statements illustrates Platonic theory of universals?
(1) Universals alone are real.
(2) Universals and particulars are equally real.
(3) Universals are copies of particulars.
(4) Universals are not real entities but are only concepts.

1562. 'The third man argument' aims to show that Plato's theme of Ideas involves.
(1) inconsistent assertions
(2) circular reasoning
(3) petitio principilii
(4) infinite regress

1563. Plato's ethics is
(1) teleological
(2) deontological
(3) partly deontological and partly imperatival
(4) neither teleological nor deontological.

1564. ....points out that substance is a self-existent permanent reality and the qualities are phenomenal in character.
(1) Aristotle (2) Plato
(3) Descartes (4) Spinoza

1565. Plato thinks that substance is a............ and...........idea.
(1) Unknown, fictitious
(2) Known, imaginary
(3) Universal, general
(4) None of the above

1566. According to...........individual horses are not substances, they are mere copies of substance 'horseness'.
(1) Plato (2) Aristotle
(3) Spinoza (4) Berkeley

1567. According to Plato, the.............is eternal, unchangeable and imperishable.
(1) God (2) Idea
(3) Soul (4) None of these

1568. ....thinks, universals are particulars and are logically dependent on one another.
(1) Plato (2) Aristotle
(3) Descartes (4) Spinoza

1569. Aristotle claims, universals, exists........not as in Plato,............
(1) Independently, dependently
(2) In object, in minds
(3) Only in things, prior to things
(4) None of the above

1570. A universal is........in each of the particulars in which it occurs.
(1) Identical
(2) Superior
(3) Different
(4) None of these

1571. A universal is a property that is...........in all the particulars that....................it.
(1) Logically present, reject
(2) Identically present, instantiate
(3) Really present, negate
(4) None of the above

1572. ....suggests that only individual things with their individual properties really exist.
(1) Realism (2) Idealism
(3) Nominalism (4) None of these

1573. ....suggests that only particulars exist and we give a name when a class of things have a common property.
(1) Extreme nominalism
(2) Naive realism
(3) Representative realism
(4) Subjective idealism

1574. A universal is a name and what it names is only a.............., according to extreme nominalism.

(1) Collection of particulars
(2) Representation
(3) Understanding of particulars
(4) None of the above

1575. The nominalists did not understand the general concepts reflect the .... existing things.
(1) Real nature of
(2) Real existence of
(3) Real qualities of objectively
(4) None of the above

1576. Aristotle's theory of universal is called
(1) Realism
(2) Nominalism
(3) Nominalistic Realism
(4) Realistic Nominalism

1577. According to Plato
(1) God is the cause of the ideas
(2) Ideas are the cause of God
(3) Ideas are equal to God
(4) Ideas are material

1578. 'The objects dealt with by the dialectician namely, abstract concepts, must also be things in the real world, though in this case their real world is a transcendent world of timeless and purely intelligible entities'. This view is expressed by
(1) Aristotle (2) Descartes
(3) Leibnitz (4) Plato

1579. On which of the following statements does Aristotle differ from Plato regarding the nature of universals?
(1) Universals are real
(2) Universals are inherent in particulars.
(3) Universals are not mental constructions
(4) Universals are real in themselves.

1580. 'God is pure form, pure actuality, absolutely perfect and intelligent and the first and final cause of the world.' This is the view of
(1) Aristotle (2) Aquinas
(3) Leibniz (4) Spinoza

1581. With the help of predicables, Aristotle gives
(1) An exposition of definitions, divisions etc.
(2) the way to unreality of ideas.
(3) (1) and (2) both
(4) Neither (1) nor (2)

1582. In the..........Plato expounded a theory of innate ideas.
(1) Republic (2) Phaedo
(3) The Laws (4) Meno

1583. Which among the following is correct according to Aristotle?
(1) God is supreme form with matter
(2) God cannot exist apart from matter
(3) God is matterless form
(4) God's palace is known as 'the lost heaven.'

1584. Who accepts that the agreement or disagreement of ideas is knowledge ?
(1) Plato (2) Aristotle
(3) Heraclitus (4) Pythagoras

1585. Plato did not propose that
(1) Ideas have independent existence.
(2) Ideas are real.
(3) Ideas are the copies of things.
(4) Ideas are numberless.

1586. For Plato, Dialectics
(1) is based on reason
(2) gives us mere appearances
(3) rests on personal feelings
(4) is the art of thinking in concepts.

1587. According to Aristotle, God is the
(1) material cause of the Universe
(2) efficient cause of the Universe
(3) instrumental cause of the Universe
(4) final cause of the Universe

1588. Plato proposed
(1) Idealistic Philosophy
(2) Materialistic Philosophy
(3) Dualism
(4) Monism

1589. In so far as the substance resembles the idea, they are...........and in so far as they differ from it, they are.............., according to Plato.
(1) Empirical, spiritual
(2) Real, unreal
(3) Empirical, unnatural
(4) None of the above

1590. Being a realist,..........believes that universals as well as particulars really exist and their existence is in no way dependent on mind.
(1) Plato (2) Aristotle
(3) Zeno (4) Kant

1591. Reason, high sprits and .... are regarded as the parts of the emobodied soul.
(1) appetities (2) informal
(3) general (4) normal

1592. Match list I with list II and select the correct answer by using the codes given below the lists :

List-I	List-II
(a) Aristotle	(i) Mind the matter are relative substances
(b) Descartes	(ii) Substance is a universal and general idea
(c) Plato	(iii) In substance form and matter are inseparably blended.

Codes :

	(a)	(b)	(c)
(1)	(iii)	(ii)	(i)
(2)	(iii)	(i)	(ii)
(3)	(i)	(ii)	(iii)
(4)	(ii)	(iii)	(i)

1593. Match the following

List-I	List-II
(a) Republic	(i) Positive
(b) Threatetus	(ii) Negative
(c) Plato	(iii) Phaedo
(d) Aristotle	(iv) Nichomachean ethics

Codes :

	(a)	(b)	(c)	(d)
(1)	(i)	(ii)	(iii)	(iv)
(2)	(iv)	(iii)	(ii)	(i)
(3)	(ii)	(iii)	(iv)	(i)
(4)	(i)	(iv)	(iii)	(ii)

1594. Match the following

List-I	List-II
(a) Aristotle	(i) Logical thinker
(b) Plato	(ii) Republic
(c) Formal cause	(iii) Shape
(d) Material cause	(iv) Wood

Codes :

	(a)	(b)	(c)	(d)
(1)	(i)	(ii)	(iii)	(iv)
(2)	(iv)	(ii)	(iii)	(i)
(3)	(ii)	(iii)	(iv)	(i)
(4)	(i)	(iv)	(iii)	(ii)

1595. Match list I with list II and select the correct answer by using the codes given below the lists :

List-I	List-II
(a) Plato	(i) Substance is the compound of universal and particular
(b) Aristotle	(ii) Substance is a self-existent permanent reality
(c) Descartes	(iii) God is an absolute substance

Codes :

	(a)	(b)	(c)
(1)	(ii)	(i)	(iii)
(2)	(i)	(ii)	(iii)
(3)	(ii)	(iii)	(i)
(4)	(iii)	(ii)	(i)

1596. Match the following

List-I	List-II
(a) Aristotle	(i) Theory of causation
(b) Plato	(ii) Rational knowledge
(c) Opinion	(iii) False
(d) Soul	(iv) Immortal

Codes :

	(a)	(b)	(c)	(d)
(1)	(i)	(ii)	(iii)	(iv)
(2)	(iv)	(ii)	(iii)	(i)
(3)	(iv)	(iii)	(ii)	(i)
(4)	(ii)	(i)	(iii)	(iv)

1597. Match the following

List-I	List-II
(a) Plato	(i) Knowledge and opinion
(b) Aristotle	(ii) Classification of sciences
(c) Theory of Ideas	(iii) Third man fallacy
(d) Hypothetical	(iv) Numbers

Codes :

	(a)	(b)	(c)	(d)
(1)	(i)	(ii)	(iii)	(iv)
(2)	(ii)	(iii)	(iv)	(i)
(3)	(ii)	(iv)	(iii)	(i)
(4)	(iv)	(i)	(ii)	(iii)

1598. Match list I with list II and select the correct answer using the codes give below the lists :

List-I (Universals)	List-II (Philosophers)
(a) Thought deals only with particular ideas	(i) Plato
(b) Thought is concerned essentially with the universal and cannot deal directly with anything individual	(ii) Aristotle
(c) Universal (Form) runs through particulars	(iii) Berkeley
(d) Universals inhere in particular	(iv) Nyāya Vaiśeṣika
	(v) Buddhists

Codes :

	(a)	(b)	(c)	(d)
(1)	(i)	(iv)	(ii)	(iii)
(2)	(iii)	(i)	(ii)	(iv)
(3)	(ii)	(i)	(v)	(iv)
(4)	(iii)	(ii)	(iv)	(v)

1599. Match the following

List-I	List-II
(a) Rational knowledge	(i) Highest
(b) Conjectural knowledge	(ii) Lowest
(c) Practical knowledge	(iii) Knowledge of world
(d) Hypothetical	(iv) Mathematics

Codes :

	(a)	(b)	(c)	(d)
(1)	(i)	(ii)	(iii)	(iv)
(2)	(ii)	(iii)	(iv)	(i)
(3)	(iv)	(iii)	(ii)	(i)
(4)	(i)	(iv)	(iii)	(ii)

1600. Match List-I (Philosophers) with List-II (Works) and select the correct answer using the codes given below the lists :

List-I	List-II
(a) Plato	I Parmenides
(b) Aristotle	II Discourse on Method
(c) Berkeley	III Nicomechian Ethics
(d) Descartes	IV Principles of Human Knowledge

Codes :

	(a)	(b)	(c)	(d)
(1)	I	II	III	IV
(2)	I	IV	II	III
(3)	I	III	II	IV
(4)	I	III	IV	II

1601. Match the following

List-I	List-II
(a) Aristotle	(i) Biologist
(b) Plato	(ii) Theory of ideas
(c) Descartes	(iii) Mind and matter
(d) Leibniz	(iv) Monadology

Codes :

	(a)	(b)	(c)	(d)
(1)	(i)	(ii)	(iii)	(iv)
(2)	(ii)	(iii)	(iv)	(i)
(3)	(i)	(iv)	(iii)	(ii)
(4)	(ii)	(iv)	(iii)	(i)

1602. Match the following

List-I	List-II
(a) Aristotle	(i) Soul and God
(b) Plato	(ii) Ideas are universal
(c) Substance	(iii) Exist in itself
(d) Descartes	(iv) Cartesian doubt

Codes :

	(a)	(b)	(c)	(d)
(1)	(i)	(ii)	(iii)	(iv)
(2)	(iv)	(iii)	(ii)	(i)
(3)	(iii)	(iv)	(ii)	(i)
(4)	(i)	(iv)	(iii)	(ii)

1603. Match the following

List-I	List-II
(a) Plato	(i) Rational knowledge
(b) Aristotle	(ii) Form and matter
(c) Potentiality	(iii) Matter
(d) Actuality	(iv) Form

Codes :

	(a)	(b)	(c)	(d)
(1)	(i)	(ii)	(iii)	(iv)
(2)	(iv)	(ii)	(iii)	(i)
(3)	(iv)	(iii)	(ii)	(i)
(4)	(i)	(iv)	(iii)	(ii)

1604. Match list I with list II

List-I	List-II
(a) Logic	(i) Organon
(b) Theoria	(ii) Poetics
(c) Praxis	(iii) Ethics
(d) Techne	(iv) Philosophy

Codes :

	(a)	(b)	(c)	(d)
(1)	(iii)	(i)	(ii)	(iv)
(2)	(ii)	(iii)	(iv)	(i)
(3)	(i)	(iv)	(iii)	(ii)
(4)	(iv)	(iii)	(ii)	(i)

1605. Match list I with list II and select the correct answer from the codes given below:

List-I	List-II
(a) Material cause	(i) Skill
(b) Efficient cause	(ii) Wood
(c) Formal cause	(iii) Shape
(d) Final cause	(iv) Arm-chair

Codes :

	(a)	(b)	(c)	(d)
(1)	(i)	(ii)	(iii)	(iv)
(2)	(ii)	(iii)	(iv)	(i)
(3)	(ii)	(i)	(iii)	(iv)
(4)	(i)	(iii)	(ii)	(iv)

Directions. The following items consist of two statements, one labelled the 'Assertion A' and the other labelled the 'Reason R'. You are to examine these two statements carefully and decide if the Assertion A and the reason R individually true and if so, whether the reason is a correct explanation of the assertion. Select your answers to these items using the codes given below

Codes :

(1) Both A and R are true and R is the correct explanation of A.

(2) Both A and R are true but R is not the correct explanation of A.

(3) A is true but R is flase.

(4) A is false but R is true.

1606. **Assertion (A).** According to Aristotle, neither universals nor particulars are substances.

Reason (R). Substance is not a compound of universal and particular.

1607. **Assertion (A).** Aristotle is dissatisfied with Plato's 'two-world theory.

Reason (R). Aristotle thinks that there is no second realm apart from particulars inhabited wholly by universals.

1608. **Assertion (A).** According to Plato nobody knows what the perceived object is in itself.

Reason (R). Perception is a joint product of the perceived object and percipient.

1609. **Assertion (A).** According to Plato soul can recall the knowledge of virtue or anything else which it once possessed.

Reason (R). The soul is immortal and has been born many times, and has seen all thins both here and in other world.

1610. **Assertion (A).** According to Plato rational insight is highest form of knowledge.

Reason (R). Rational insight gives the knowledge of ideas of universals.

1611. **Assertion (A).** Conjectural knowledge is the lowest type of knowledge.

Reason (R). According to Plato it includes illusions, hallucinations, dreams and pathological experience etc.

1612. **Assertion (A).** According to Plato, God is an architect but not a creator God.

Reason (R). God created the world not out of himself, but according to the original pattern in heaven.

1613. **Assertion (A).** According to Aristotle universals cannot exist apart from individuals.

Reason (R). The independent existence of universals will land us into regresses ad infinitum.

1614. **Assertion (A).** Aristotle believes in the classification of the sciences.

Reason (R). He gave four sciences as the classification.

1615. **Assertion (A).** God is regarded as matterless form.

Reason (R). God is regarded as a supreme form with matter.

1616. **Assertion (A).** Actuality is prior to potency, according to Aristotle.

Reason (R). Actuality is regarded as the end.

1617. **Assertion (A).** God is not a creator God, according to Plato.

Reason (R). God created the world, according to the original pattern.

1618. **Assertion (A).** God is regarded as an architects, according to Plato.

Reason (R). Plato believes in universal ideas only.

1619. **Assertion (A).** Plato's theory of reminiscence criticised Aristotle.

Reason (R). Without are knowing this knowledge we have this supreme science.

1620. **Assertion (A).** Aristotle causation view is metaphysical.

Reason (R). He believes in all the causes.

1621. **Assertion (A).** Conjectural knowledge is regarded as the lowest type of knowledge.

Reason (R). It includes illusionary world.

1622. **Assertion (A).** Aristotle says the idea of Plato is not a substance.

Reason (R). Plato's idea exists apart from individuals.

1623. **Assertion (A).** The Aristotaleon concept of causation is not scientific in modern sense.

Reason (R). The very meaning of material cause is not same as the physical matter.

1624. Assertion (A). Aristotle's concept of cause is not scientific.

Reason (R). For Aristotle all the four kinds of causes are simultaneously present together.

1625. Assertion (A). Aristotle's view of causation is metaphysical.

Reason (R). He is in search of the first and final cause of the universe.

1626. Assertion (A). According to Aristotle matter and form are inseperable.

Reason (R). Both of them do not have their own independent existence apart from each other.

1627. Assertion (A). Actuality is prior to potency.

Reason (R). Actuality is the end.

1628. Assertion (A). Aristotle criticises. Plato's theory of reminiscence.

Reason (R). When we are told that all embracing knowledge is innate, it seems incredible that we should have this supreme science all along without our knowing it.

1629. Consider the following statements :
According to Aristotle,

A. Universals do not exist separately from individual things.
B. Without the theory of Universals there could be scientific knowledge.
C. As Universals are motionless, they could help understand things as we know them

Of these statements
(1) A and B are correct
(2) A and C are correct
(3) B and C are correct
(4) A, B and C are correct

1630. Consider the following statements about Aristotle doctrines :

A. Every individual is a compound of 'matter' and 'form'.
B. 'Matter' means the physical substance, and 'form' means the shape.
C. 'Matter' and 'form' are relative terms in the real world.
D. 'Matter' and 'form' are separable in thought, but they are not separable in fact.

(1) A, B and C (2) B, C and D
(3) A, B and D (4) A, C and D

1631. Consider the following statements :

A. Human reason does not have the power of discern the forms in their particular exemplifications.
B. Forms constitute the essences of things.
C. Universals are the last things we reach in our thinking but are first in nature.
D. Categories are the most fundamental and universe predicates, which can be affirmed of anything.

Which of the above statements are accepted by Aristotle?
(1) A and B (2) B and D
(3) B, C and D (4) A, C and D

1632. Aristotle believes in

A. logic.
B. practical science.
C. non-logic.
D. non-practical science.

Select the correct answer from the codes given below :
(1) A and B (2) B and C
(3) B and D (4) A and D

1633. Plato wrote

A. Republic.
B. Apology of Socrates.
C. Nichomachean ethics.
D. Ethics.

Select the correct answer from the codes given below :

(1) A and B (2) B and C
(3) A and C
(4) A, B, C and D

1634. Regarding universals which of the following views are held by Plato?

A. Universal is a one beyond the many
B. Universal is a none in many.
C. Universal is a timeless entity.

Select the correct answer using the codes given below :

(1) A and C (2) A and B
(3) B and C (4) A, B and C

1635. Aristotle was regarded as

A. biologist.
B. non-biologist.
C. eudaemonist.
D. non-endaemonist.

Select the correct answer from the codes given below :

(1) A and B (2) B and C
(3) A and C (4) C and D

1636. Plato regards

A. soul as simple.
B. soul as complex.
C. body as composite of the four elements of Earth.
D. boyd as not composite of the four elements of Earth.

Select the correct answer from the codes given below :

(1) A and B (2) B and C
(3) B and D (4) A and C

1637. Which of the following statements about Plato's doctrines show that he is a realist about Universals?

A. Whenever a number of objects have a common name, they also have a common form.
B. Particular ideas are imperfect copies of ideas.
C. The word 'cat' means the ideal cat, unique and eternal.
D. Particular objects are not objects of knowledge.

Select the correct answer from the codes given below :

Codes :

(1) A and B (2) A, B and C
(3) B and C (4) B, C and D

1638. Practical sciences means

A. Ethics
B. Commercial
C. Politics
D. Mathematical

Select the correct answer from the codes given below :

(1) A and B (2) B and C
(3) A and C (4) C and D

1639. Plato says that the three parts of the embodied soul are

A. reason.
B. high spirits.
C. appetities.
D. non-appetities.

Select the correct answer from the codes given below :

(1) A, B and C (2) A, C and D
(3) B, C and D (4) All of these

1640. Consider the following statement :

A. Universals are absolute and ultimate realities.
B. Each universal is a unity.
C. Universals are immutable and imperishable.
D. Universals cannot exist without particulars.

Which of these statements have been attributed to Plato?

(1) A, B and D (2) B, C and D
(3) A, C and D (4) A, B and C

1641. Ontological argument was presented systematically by St. Anselm is
(1) Monologion (2) Proslogium
(3) (1) and (2) both
(4) None of these

1642. Which kind of argument to prove the existence of God shows that the very essence of the idea of perfect God implies his existence?
(1) Ontological argument
(2) Cosmological argument
(3) Causal argument
(4) Teleological argument

1643. Which kind of following arguments says that the non-existence of God can not be entertained even in thought if one understands the meaning of 'God'?
(1) Cosmological (2) Teleological
(3) Ontological (4) Causal

1644. According to Anselm, an idea of a perfect being not existing is
(1) God (2) inferior
(3) superior (4) None of these

1645. Which of the following is not consistent with Anselm's Ontological argument?
(1) A 'perfect' being is meant a being which has a number of excellent attributes each in perfection.
(2) 'Existence' is also an attribute.
(3) A perfect being should be non-existent.
(4) Everything depends on regarding 'existence' as an attribute.

1646. The whole proof of Anselm depends on the reality of............idea.
(1) Aristotalian (2) Pythagorean
(3) Socrates' (4) Platonic

1647. The Ontological argument of St. Anselm was rephrased by
(1) Descartes (2) Leibnitz
(3) (1) and (2) both
(4) Kant

1648. The Ontological argument was criticized by
(1) Descartes (2) Leibnitz
(3) Spinoza (4) Kant

1649. Which one of the following is not St. Augustine view?
(1) Evil is privation of good.
(2) Soul is a trinity of existence, knowledge and will.
(3) Our knowledge of the world is more reliable than our knowledge of the soul.
(4) The highest knowledge of reason is an insight into the creative principle.

1650. According to St. Augustine, the origin of the world is from
(1) divine miracle (2) emanation
(3) the material principle
(4) matter and form

1651. St. Augustine argues that when a will chooses evil, the cause of the choice is
(1) God (2) Satan
(3) Lack of knowledge
(4) Nature

1652. Which one of the following is not the view of St. Augustine?
(1) The only knowledge worth having is knowledge of God.
(2) Reason is opposed to faith and irrelevant to it.
(3) Logic, metaphysics and ethics are valuable only if they contribute to the knowledge of God.
(4) My knowledge that I exist is an indubitable only if they contribute to the knowledge that I exist is an indubitable certainty.

1653. Who acclaimed that man is the highest creature in the world ?

(1) St. Anselm
(2) St. Augustine
(3) St. Thomas Acquinas
(4) All the above

1654. Stage of moral conversion as per Saint Augustine is

(1) Faith (2) Hope
(3) Clarity (4) All the three

1655. St. Augustine characterises the human soul as

(1) an individual substance.
(2) a rational substance suited for ruling the body.
(3) an eternal substance identical with the cosmos.
(4) a material substance characterized by conscious.

1656. Which one of the following statements is true according to St. Augustine?

(1) Man has a measure of freedom to respond to or reject, the offer of grace from God.
(2) Man has absolutely no freedom.
(3) A rational man with reason as his unfailing guide is absolutely free.
(4) Man becomes free only when he realises that he is identical with God.

1657. .... is a distinctive feature of Christian philosophy since the thirteenth century.

(1) Religion (2) Theology
(3) Moral values (4) Scholasticism

1658. Unlike Aquinas, ...strove to separate philosophy, and theology, arguing that it is impossible to find rational grounds for the idea of creation from nothing and admitting that reason is dependent on the will.

(1) Occam (2) Duns Scotus
(3) Berkeley (4) None of these

1659. Anselm says that the general concepts affirmed by.......are only 'vibrations of the air'.

(1) Descartes (2) Roscelin
(3) Hume (4) Kant

1660. Ontological argument for the existence of God given by Anselm suggests

(1) The existence of God derives from the concept of God.
(2) God can be thought without his existence.
(3) Both (1) and (2)
(4) Neither (1) nor (2)

1661. While giving the proof for the existence of God, Descartes imagined that he was saying the same things as

(1) Plato (2) Aquinas
(3) Aristotle (4) Anselm

1662. 'There is nothing in the intellect that was not previously in the senses', besides Locke, this view is also accepted by

(1) Berkeley (2) Plato
(3) Thomas Aquinas (4) None of these

1663. Who is the 'Father of Deism'?

(1) Descartes (2) Spinoza
(3) Rousseau
(4) Herbert of Cherbury

1664. The proof of God's existence is

(1) Existence of Divine utterances
(2) Only God can create organic objects
(3) Both of the above
(4) None of the above

1665. Which one of the following statements supports the privation theory of evil in Augustine's philosophy?

(1) Evil has no place in God's creation
(2) Evil is the creation of mortal beings
(3) Evil is mere denial of good
(4) Evil is essential for the elevation of the value of good

1666. According to St. Augustine, the supreme end of moral life is
(1) No pleasure no pain
(2) An Ascetic life
(3) Happiness
(4) Devotion

1667. Which one of the following arguments for the existence of God is not accepted by St. Aquinas?
(1) The argument from motion
(2) The argument from the governance of the world
(3) The argument from the gradation to be found in things
(4) The ontological argument

1668. Which one of the following principles is used in each of the first three of the 'five ways' of Aquinas?
(1) God's essence involves existence.
(2) The perfections found in the world must have their source in a perfect being
(3) Contingent things must have a necessary being as their first cause.
(4) An infinite causal regress is impossible.

1669. Which one of the following reasons is given by Aquinas to prove the immortality of the soul?
(1) People have memories of past lives.
(2) The human soul faith in God.
(3) The human soul is pure immaterial substance.
(4) The human soul has knowledge of Universals.

1670. According to Aquinas, the view that the world has no beginning in time.
(1) is contradicted by revelation
(2) would imply that God is not the creator of the world
(3) would contradict the doctrine of 'creation from nothing.
(4) is a philosophical absurdity

1671. Which one of the following pairs of powers, according to Aquinas, is associated with the soul?
(1) Feeling and emotion
(2) Intellect and will
(3) Desires and appetites
(4) Opinions and beliefs

1672. Which one of the following is not accepted by Thomas Aquinas?
(1) The cause must be prior of the effect
(2) The casual regress cannot be infinite.
(3) No contingent thing would exist now unless there is a necessary first cause.
(4) The existence of God can be inferred from the very idea of god.

1673. Who proved the existence of God through arguments based on Ontology ?
(1) St. Thomas Acquinas
(2) St. Anselm
(3) St. Augustine
(4) All the these

1674. 'God chooses to create the best of all possible worlds' is stated by
(1) Leibniz and Descartes
(2) Leibniz and St. Augustine
(3) Leibniz and Locke
(4) Leibniz and Thomas Aquinas

1675. ....are always perceived by God, thus they must be ideas in the divine mind.
(1) Sensible things (2) Minds
(3) Real facts (4) None of these

1676. Predicates are applied to the Creator and the creature neither univocally nor equivocally but analogically. This theory maintained by
(1) Naiyāyikas
(2) Descartes
(3) St. Augustine
(4) St. Thomas Aquinas

1677. Creation of the world in time is a sacrament. It can not be demonstrated by reason. It is an inner instinct which God endows us with. It comes from without as a result of miracles. This view is held by

(1) Thomas Aquinas
(2) St. Augustine
(3) Descartes
(4) Spinoza

1678. Who among the following objected the Ontological argument of Anselm?

(1) Descartes (2) Gaunilo
(3) Augustine (4) Aquinas

1679. Which of the following is not a work of Anselm?

(1) Monologian
(2) Proslogium
(3) Summa Contra Gentiles
(4) None of the above

1680. Who among the following is known as an angelic doctor?

(1) Augustine (2) Anselm
(3) Aquinas (4) Peter Abelard

1681. Which of the following argument is not given by Aquinas to prove the existence of God?

(1) Ontological argument
(2) Teleological argument
(3) From graded excellence
(4) From contingency

1682. Who first propounded the ontological argument for the existence of God ?

(1) St. Augustine (2) St. Anselm
(3) Thomas Aquinas
(4) Rene Descartes

1683. According to Aquinas, without the starting point of.............no knowledge is possible.

(1) Sensation (2) Reason
(3) Intuition (4) Perception

1684. Which among the following owing statement is associated with St. Thomas Aquinas.

(1) There can be nothing in intellect which was not previously given in the senses.
(2) Universals do not inhere in particulars
(3) There can be some imageless thinkings
(4) None of the above

1685. Which among the following is the correct interpretation of Aquinas regarding universals?

(1) Universals are matterless forms existing in heaven.
(2) Universals are material entities existing outside the particulars
(3) No universal is possible without being instantiated in particulars
(4) None of the above

1686. For Aquinas, which among the following is not correct.

(1) Sensation is only the starting point of knowledge.
(2) Sensation is possible only in a soul without body-soul complex
(3) Sensation, itself, is no knowledge at all.
(4) No particular things are possible without being universalised.

1687. According to Augustine, the knowledge of God is known as

(1) Intellectual (2) Reasonal
(3) Sensual (4) Analogical

1688. Neoplatonism had reinforced the............ principle that the way of return to God must be through escape from the body.

(1) Scholastic (2) Manichaean
(3) Rationalistic (4) None of these

1689. Augustine insisted that a true knowledge of the................nature can be based only on the immediate awareness of self-conscious-ness.

(1) God's (2) Individual's
(3) Soul's (4) None of these

1690. Augustine claims that there is an/a............ that exists, knows and wills.
(1) Ego (2) Spirit
(3) Soul (4) None of these

1691. Augustine suggests...........is 'the will of a good God that good things should be'
(1) Imagination (2) Creation
(3) Belief (4) None of these

1692. 'The City of God' is written by
(1) Aquinas (2) Aristotle
(3) Augustine (4) Plato

1693. Like............, Augustine believes that the intuitive judgements like the propositions of mathematics are not the construction of the individual mind.
(1) Aquinas (2) Plato
(3) Descartes (4) Locke

1694. ....philosophy is a religious philosophy of predestination.
(1) Aquinas (2) Augustine's
(3) Plato's (4) Democritus'

1695. Neoplatonism is a theory which claims that there is only one reality.
(1) Spiritual dualism
(2) Spiritual monism
(3) Monism
(4) Stoicism

1696. The universe exists as a series of............. from absolute unity according to the Neoplatonism.
(1) Being (2) Degenerations
(3) Contradiction (4) None of these

1697. ....is the intermediary between the spheres of spirit and of sense, according to Neoplatonism.
(1) Human being (2) God
(3) Soul (4) None of these

1698. "Evil is not good, but it is good that there is evil" is said by
(1) Aquinas (2) Augustine
(3) Anselm (4) Aristotle

1699. 'Confessions' is written by
(1) Aquinas (2) Augustine
(3) Anselm (4) None of these

1700. Christ's human life is man's example of the ascetic victory over
(1) The pains and pleasures of the flesh
(2) Ignorance of ordinary people
(3) The pains of the body
(4) None of the above

1701. In 1879, the views of Thomas Aquinas were officially proclaimed as the philosophy of
(1) Scholasticism (2) Catholicism
(3) Rationalism (4) None of these

1702. Saint Augustine was greatly influenced by
(1) Cicero (2) Plato
(3) Aristotle (4) None of these

1703. ....is a materialistic dualism which suggests the creation of the world as the product of a conflict between light and dark substances.
(1) Aristotleianism (2) Catholicism
(3) Manichaeism (4) None of these

1704. Augustine has taken................, in which he found solutions about the being of God and the nature, origin of evil.
(1) Neoplatonism (2) Rationalism
(3) Scholasticism (4) None of these

1705. ....is the lowest and last product of the supreme unity.
(1) Matter (2) Mind
(3) Atom (4) None of these

1706. ....is the least real of all things, being simply the absence of Good.
(1) Matter (2) God
(3) Evil (4) None of these

1707. ....is the 'changeless light', the source of every intuitive recognition of truth and goodness.

(1) God (2) Soul
(3) Intellect (4) None of these

1708. ....is light and...............is darkness.

(1) God, evil
(2) God, falsity
(3) Good, bad
(4) God, false knowledge

1709. The first man Adam had free will, but with his fall by disobedience to God, Adam lost his free will. This condemnation of Adam being a sinner is known as

(1) The doctrine of original sin
(2) Accidental sin
(3) Virtual sin
(4) Moral sin

1710. Which one of the following is not acceptable to Thomas Aquinas ?

(1) Causal regress cannot be infinite.
(2) A perfect being is the source of various perfections in the world.
(3) The existence of God is a self-evident truth for man.
(4) The source of contingent things must lie in a necessary being.

1711. Saint Augustine's influential work, The City of God was considered as the first book on

(1) Comparative Philosophy
(2) Philosophy of Religion
(3) Philosophy of History
(4) Philosophy of Christianity

1712. Summa Theologica was written by

(1) Saint Augustine
(2) Saint Anselm
(3) St. Thomas Aquinas
(4) None of the above

1713. 'Ontological Argument' of Saint Anselm was adopted by

(1) Descartes (2) Spinoza
(3) Leibnitz (4) Locke

1714. Who said that "our earthly life is a pilgrimage to God" ?

(1) St. Paul
(2) St. Augustine
(3) St. Anselm
(4) St. Thomas Aquinas

1715. ....believes reason and faith cannot contradict each other, because they come from the same divine source.

(1) Aristotle (2) Plato
(3) Aquinas (4) Augustine

1716. 'Summa theologica' is written by

(1) Augustine (2) Aquinas
(3) Zeno (4) Heraclitus

1717. Aquinas claims,.............is capable of proving rationally the existence of God and refuting objections to the truth of faith.

(1) Reason (2) Belief
(3) Judgment (4) Final Cause

1718. Saint Augustine was .... influenced by Plato.

(1) externally (2) internally
(3) greatly (4) ordinary

1719. Who was the great medieval Catholic theologian.

(1) Descartes
(2) Spinoza
(3) Thomas Aquinas
(4) Leibnitz

1720. Aquinas has developed his idealist philosophy from a theological interpretation of whose teachings and its adaptation to Christian dogma.

(1) Aristotle's (2) Plato's
(3) Zeno's (4) None of these

1721. Aquinas claims, everything existing is created by..................in the hierarchic order.
(1) Individual (2) Soul
(3) God (4) None of these

1722. God is pure being or.............according to Aquinas.
(1) Creator
(2) The act of existing
(3) Supreme soul
(4) None of the above

1723. Augustine suggests.........is the better part of human being and the body is a prison for it.
(1) Soul (2) Knowledge
(3) Wisdom (4) Intellect

1724. ....regarded man as acting in the image of God to the extent that he exercises and seeks to fulfil his intelligent nature.
(1) St. Augustine (2) Thomas Aquinas
(3) Plato (4) Aristotle

1725. Plato and Aristotle were not satisfied with the................solution of the problems of change as a general solution.
(1) Atomistic (2) Rationalistic
(3) Sceptic (4) None of these

1726. Aristotle thought God as pure form, as ....cause and as prime mover.
(1) Formal (2) Efficient
(3) Final (4) None of these

1727. 'Harmony of faith and reason is the basic principle of philosophy' is associated with.....
(1) Augustine (2) St. Anselm
(3) Thomas Aquinas
(4) None of these

1728. According to Aquinas we obtain knowledge when..............
(1) Intuition arises
(2) Reason works
(3) Sensation arises
(4) Sensation becomes thought

1729. Who has said, "Faith seeks, understanding finds."
(1) Augustine (2) Anselm
(3) Aquinas (4) Plato

1730. According to St. Augustine, human soul is
(1) an eternal substance identical with the Cosmos
(2) a material substance characterised by consciousness
(3) an individual substance
(4) a rational substance suited for ruling the body

1731. According to St. Aquinas as the view that the world has 20 beginning in time
(1) is contradicted by revelation
(2) would imply that God is not the creator of the world
(3) world contradict the Doctrine of 'Creation from nothing'
(4) is a philosophical absurdity

1732. Match list I (Philosophers) with list II (Tenets) and select the correct answer using the codes given below the lists:

List-I	List-II
(a) Aristotle	(i) Analogical predication
(b) Saṅkara	(ii) Apṛthaksiddhi
(c) Rāmānuja	(iii) Pañcikaraṇa
(d) Thomas Aquinas	(iv) Pure Form

Codes :

	(a)	(b)	(c)	(d)
(1)	(iv)	(ii)	(iii)	(i)
(2)	(iv)	(iii)	(ii)	(i)
(3)	(i)	(iii)	(ii)	(iv)
(4)	(i)	(ii)	(iii)	(iv)

1733. Match list I (Doctrines) with list II (Philosophers) and select the correct answer using the codes given below the lists :

List-I	List-II
(a) Intellectual love of God	(i) St. Augustine
(b) Identity of indiscernibles	(ii) Spinoza
(c) Evil is privation of Good	(iii) Leibnitz
(d) Analogical prediction	(iv) Thomas Aquinas

Codes :

	(a)	(b)	(c)	(d)
(1)	(iii)	(ii)	(i)	(iv)
(2)	(ii)	(iii)	(i)	(iv)
(3)	(iii)	(ii)	(iv)	(i)
(4)	(ii)	(iii)	(iv)	(i)

1734. Match list I with list II and select the correct answer from the codes given below

List-I	List-II
(a) Augustine	(i) Summa Theologiae
(b) Anselm	(ii) Proslogium
(c) Aquinas	(iii) The City of God

Codes :	(a)	(b)	(c)
(1)	(iii)	(ii)	(i)
(2)	(i)	(ii)	(iii)
(3)	(ii)	(i)	(iii)
(4)	(iii)	(i)	(ii)

1735. Match list I with list II and select the correct answer by using the codes given below the lists :

List-I	List-II
(a) Summa Theological	(i) Spinoza
(b) Confessions	(ii) Rene Descartes
(c) The Discourse on method	(iii) St. Augustine
(d) Tractatus Theologico Politicus	(iv) Thomas Aquinas

Codes :

	(a)	(b)	(c)	(d)
(1)	(iv)	(iii)	(i)	(ii)
(2)	(ii)	(iii)	(i)	(iv)
(3)	(iii)	(iv)	(i)	(ii)
(4)	(iv)	(iii)	(ii)	(i)

1736. Match list I with list II and select the correct answer by using the codes given below the lists :

List-I	List-II
(a) The way of return to God must be through escape from the body	(i) Solipsism
(b) A materialistic dualism suggests the creation of the world as the product of a conflict between light and dark.	(ii) Neoplatonism
(c) Subjective idealist theory claims only man and his consciousness exist.	(iii) Manichaeism

Codes :

	(a)	(b)	(c)
(1)	(i)	(ii)	(iii)
(2)	(i)	(iii)	(ii)
(3)	(ii)	(i)	(iii)
(4)	(ii)	(iii)	(i)

1737. Match list I with list II and select the correct answer by using the codes given below the lists :

List-I	List-II
(a) The City of God	(i) Descartes
(b) The Ethics	(ii) Berkeley
(c) The Meditations	(iii) St. Augustine
(d) A treatise concerning the Principles of Human Knowledge	(iv) Spinoza

Codes :

	(a)	(b)	(c)	(d)
(1)	(iii)	(iv)	(ii)	(i)
(2)	(iii)	(iv)	(i)	(ii)
(3)	(iv)	(iii)	(i)	(ii)
(4)	(i)	(iv)	(iii)	(ii)

1738. Match list I with list II and select the correct answer by using the codes given below the lists :

List-I	List-II
(a) God is pure form final cause, prime mover	(i) St. Augustine
(b) Harmony of faith and reason is the basic principle of philosophy	(ii) Aristotle
(c) God as the 'Changeless light' is the source of every intuitive recognition of truth and goodness.	(iii) Thomas Aquinas

Codes :

	(a)	(b)	(c)
(1)	(i)	(iii)	(ii)
(2)	(ii)	(iii)	(i)
(3)	(ii)	(i)	(iii)
(4)	(iii)	(ii)	(i)

1739. Match list I with list II and select the correct answer by using the codes given below the lists :

List-I	List-II
(a) Augustine	(i) Moral evil
(b) Anselm	(ii) Ontological argument
(c) Aquinas	(iii) Harmony of faith and reason

Codes :

	(a)	(b)	(c)
(1)	(i)	(iii)	(ii)
(2)	(iii)	(ii)	(i)
(3)	(i)	(ii)	(iii)
(4)	(ii)	(i)	(iii)

1740. Match the following

List-I	List-II
(a) Augustine	(i) City of God
(b) Anselm	(ii) Ontological argument
(c) Aquinas	(iii) Rejection of innate ideas
(d) Aristotle	(iv) God as final cause

Codes :

	(a)	(b)	(c)	(d)
(1)	(i)	(ii)	(iii)	(iv)
(2)	(ii)	(iii)	(iv)	(i)
(3)	(iv)	(iii)	(ii)	(i)
(4)	(i)	(iv)	(iii)	(ii)

1741. Match the following

List-I	List-II
(a) Augustine	(i) Confessions
(b) Anselm	(ii) Monologion
(c) Aquinas	(iii) Reflection of ontological argument
(d) Plato	(iv) Idealistic

Codes :

	(a)	(b)	(c)	(d)
(1)	(i)	(ii)	(iii)	(iv)
(2)	(iv)	(iii)	(ii)	(i)
(3)	(i)	(iv)	(iii)	(ii)
(4)	(iv)	(ii)	(iii)	(i)

1742. Match the following

List-I	List-II
(a) Augustine	(i) Moral evil
(b) Anselm	(ii) Proslogium
(c) Aquinas	(iii) Posterior
(d) Hocke	(iv) Empiricism

Codes :

	(a)	(b)	(c)	(d)
(1)	(i)	(ii)	(iii)	(iv)
(2)	(ii)	(iii)	(iv)	(i)
(3)	(i)	(iv)	(iii)	(ii)
(4)	(ii)	(iv)	(iii)	(i)

1743. Match the following

List-I	List-II
(a) Motion argument	(i) God as first mover

(b) Efficient argument	(ii) God as first efficient cause
(c) Contingency	(iii) Necessary being
(d) Teleological	(iv) End is pursued by God

Codes :

	(a)	(b)	(c)	(d)
(1)	(i)	(ii)	(iii)	(iv)
(2)	(ii)	(iii)	(iv)	(i)
(3)	(i)	(iv)	(iii)	(ii)
(4)	(iv)	(iii)	(ii)	(i)

1744. Match the following

List-I	List-II
(a) Augustine	(i) Problem of evil
(b) Anselm	(ii) Idea of perfect being
(c) Aquinas	(iii) Essences and existence
(d) Graded exce-llence	(iv) God is the ground of all perfections

Codes :

	(a)	(b)	(c)	(d)
(1)	(i)	(ii)	(iii)	(iv)
(2)	(ii)	(iii)	(iv)	(i)
(3)	(iv)	(iii)	(ii)	(i)
(4)	(i)	(iv)	(iii)	(ii)

1745. Match the following

List-I	List-II
(a) Augustine	(i) The Doctrine of Original Sin
(b) Descartes	(ii) The discourse
(c) Anselm	(iii) Ontological argument
(d) Aquinas	(iv) Summa theological

Codes :

	(a)	(b)	(c)	(d)
(1)	(i)	(ii)	(iii)	(iv)
(2)	(ii)	(iii)	(iv)	(i)
(3)	(i)	(iv)	(iii)	(ii)
(4)	(ii)	(iv)	(iii)	(i)

1746. Match the following

List-I	List-II
(a) The Ethics	(i) Spinoza
(b) The Meditations	(ii) Descartes
(c) The City of God	(iii) St. Augustine
(d) Essence and Existence	(iv) St. Aquinas

Codes :

	(a)	(b)	(c)	(d)
(1)	(i)	(ii)	(iii)	(iv)
(2)	(iv)	(iii)	(ii)	(i)
(3)	(i)	(iv)	(iii)	(ii)
(4)	(ii)	(iii)	(iv)	(i)

1747. Match the following

List-I	List-II
(a) Augustine	(i) Platonian
(b) Aquinas	(ii) Aristotlian
(c) Hocke	(iii) Ideas
(d) Hume	(iv) Sceptic

Codes :

	(a)	(b)	(c)	(d)
(1)	(i)	(ii)	(iii)	(iv)
(2)	(iv)	(iii)	(ii)	(i)
(3)	(iii)	(iv)	(ii)	(i)
(4)	(iv)	(ii)	(iii)	(i)

Directions. The following items consist of two statements, one labelled as the 'Assertion A' and the other labelled as 'Reason R'. You are to examine these two statements carefully and decide if the Assertion 'A' and the Reason 'R' are individually true and if so, whether the Reason is a correct explanation of the Assertion. Select your answer to these items using the codes given below and mark your answer sheet accordingly :

Codes:

(1) Both A and R are true and R is the correct explanation of A.

(2) Both A and R are true but R is not the correct explanation of A.

(3) A is true but R is false.

(4) A is false but R is true

1748. **Assertion (A).** Aquinas adopted Aristotle's teaching that the soul is man's form and the body is his matter.

Reason (R). For Aquinas, God is a pure being.

1749. **Assertion (A).** Augustine claims, the individual thinker does not make the truth.

Reason (R). Individual finds the truth from his 'inward teacher', Christ.

1750. **Assertion (A).** Aquinas established harmony between Aristotleianism and Christianity.

Reason (R). The harmony is not forced but achieved by a new understanding of philosophical principles.

1751. **Assertion (A).** According to Augustine God is light and evil is darkness.

Reason (R). The 'Changeless light' of God is spiritual being and the evil is non-entity.

1752. **Assertion (A).** Augustine turned to Neoplatonism after disillusioned with Manichaeism.

Reason (R). Augustine was not satisfied with Manichaean notion of ultimate reality.

1753. **Assertion (A).** Augustine claims that the soul is the better part of human being.

Reason (R). There is an ego, that exists, knows and wills.

1754. **Assertion (A).** Now, one can entertain the idea of a perfect being without any actual entity corresponding to it.

Reason (R). Since the time of Kant, existence is not regarded as an attribute.

1755. **Assertion (A).** Anselm says that God exists.

Reason (R). According to Anselm, the non-existence of God cannot be entertained even in thought if one understands the meaning of 'God'.

1756. **Assertion (A).** Gaunilo, a monk, objected to the ontological argument of Anselm.

Reason (R). According to Gaunilo, in this argument the idea of God and the idea of existence have been put together.

1757. **Assertion (A).** God cannot be an object of knowledge.

Reason (R). God is non-sensible.

1758. **Assertion (A).** St. Augustine favours the transmission theory of soul from parents to son.

Reason (R). He believes in the original sin of man and accepts the theory of predestination.

1759. Which of the following statements are associated with St. Augustine?

A. The only knowledge worth having is the knowledge of God and self.

B. Believe in order that you may understand.

C. Knowledge is power.

Select the correct answer from the codes given below :

Codes :

(1) A and C (2) B alone

(3) A and B (4) B and C

1760. St. Anselm believes in

(A) ontological argument

(B) idea of perfect being.

(C) idea of non-perfect being.

(D) non-ontological argument.

Codes:

(1) A and B (2) B and C

(3) A and C (4) B and D

1761. 'Meditations on First Philosophy" was written by

(1) Descartes (2) Spinoza

(3) Leibnitz (4) Locke

1762. Which is the independent monad according to Leibniz ?

(1) Soul (2) Universe
(3) Space (4) Time

1763. Who was the Philosopher invited by the Queen of Sweden ?
(1) Descartes (2) Spinoza
(3) Leibniz (4) Locke

1764. 'Descartes' method if doubt is centrally aimed at
(1) methodological scepticism
(2) self knowledge
(3) systematic discovery of truth
(4) rejection of empiricism

1765. Find out the odd :
(1) Descartes was a monist.
(2) Hume was a sceptic.
(3) Leibnitz was a pluralist.
(4) Locke was an empiricist.

1766. Descartes says that he can be confident of the existence of the external objects because
(1) he directly sees his own body and external objects.
(2) hc cannot doubt his own existence.
(3) God is not a deceiver.
(4) innate ideas exist in every human-being.

1767. Which one of the following types of substances is not admitted by Descartes?
(1) Infinite and uncreated
(2) Perpetually changing
(3) Finite and spiritual
(4) Finite and material

1768. According to Descartes, the idea of God is
(1) adventitious (2) fictitious
(3) demonstrative (4) innate

1769. According to Descartes, deduction differs from intuition, since
(1) intuition is unreliable, while deduction is reliable.
(2) intuition is sensory, while deducted is not so.
(3) intuition does not yield any new truth, while deduction does.
(4) a certain movement or succession belongs to deduction, and not to intuition.

1770. Man may often choose that which is wrong and even rather than good. This happens, according to Descartes, because
(1) the power that God has given man to distinguish the true from the false is not complete.
(2) man can realise the greatness of God only because of realising his own perfections.
(3) Nothing is perfect, everything can be doubted.
(4) God is omnipotent but not perfectly benevolent.

1771. Descartes' theory about the relation between the body and the mind asserts that
(1) all mental states are epiphenomena accompanying physical changes.
(2) all mental states are caused by physical states.
(3) all physical states are caused by mental states.
(4) physical states and mental states both affect each other.

1772. The most fundamental character of matter, according to Descartes, is that it is
(1) coloured (2) temporary
(3) extended (4) an idea

1773. Which one of the following is not asserted by Descartes?
(1) Matter has two kinds of qualities— primary and secondary.
(2) Matter has two states, one of motion and another of rest.
(3) The animals are devoid of soul.
(4) There is purpose in the world.

1774. Which one of the following distinctions is not found in Descartes' account of matter and mind?

(1) Intuition and deduction
(2) Ultimate and relative substance
(3) Primary and secondary qualities
(4) Real and nominal essence

1775. According to Descartes, our knowledge of the existence of the external world is a/an

(1) self-evident truth
(2) inferred knowledge
(3) innate principle
(4) perceptual knowledge

1776. Who has said that two kinds of substances are attributes?

(1) Plato (2) Locke
(3) Descartes (4) Hume

1777. Which one of the following is *not* accepted by Descartes?

(1) 'Substance' means that which requires nothing in order to exist.
(2) The world 'substance' cannot be predicated of God and other beings in strictly the same sense.
(3) The world 'substance' applies primarily to God and relatively to creatures.
(4) The word 'substance' has totally different meanings when predicated of minds and materials bodies.

1778. Descartes' one of the arguments to prove God's existence is that every effect must have an adequate cause. This argument is based on the principle of

(1) Sufficient reason
(2) nihil ex nihilo fit
(3) Continuity
(4) Modus ponens

1779. Which one of the following principles is not used by Descartes in his proofs for the existence of God?

(1) I could not understand my imperfections unless have the idea of a perfect being.
(2) Only a perfect being can be the cause of the idea of a perfect being.
(3) If I were my creator. I could have given myself at the perfections I know of.
(4) The existence of the world cannot be explained without accepting a perfect being as its first cause.

1780. The principle that a cause must be as great as the effect, is used by Descartes to Demonstrate.

(1) the veracity of clear and distinct ideas.
(2) the existence of God.
(3) the existence of the external world.
(4) the existence of the soul.

1781. In which one of the following orders did Descartes prove the existence of God?

(1) God, Matter, Self
(2) Self, Matter, God
(3) God, Self, Matter
(4) Self, God, Matter

1782. The idea of God, according to Descartes, is

(1) natural and received from tradition.
(2) innate and received from God.
(3) innate but not received from God.
(4) gained from experience.

1783. According to descartes man falls in to error essentially because

(1) reason leads to error
(2) experience leads to error
(3) the will leads to error
(4) passions leads to error

1784. Which one of the following is a correct definition of 'substance' according to Descartes in the strict sense of the term?

(1) Substance is a principle of spiritual force.

(2) The idea of substance is a logical category through.
(3) Substance is that which requires nothing other in order to exist.
(4) Substance is a room for attributes.

1785. Who has said that mind has innate ideas?
(1) Plato (2) Locke
(3) Descartes (4) Moore

1786. In the order of existence, God is........, he creates the reason together with its criterion.
(1) Ultimate (2) First
(3) Superior (4) None of these

1787. Descartes thinks the only thing which raises man above the brute is his..........., which is a creation of God.
(1) Power of imagination
(2) Rational soul
(3) Intellect
(4) None of the above

1788. Descartes thinks the soul or mind is.........with the body.
(1) Intimately united
(2) Not connected
(3) Not co-existent
(4) None of the above

1789. An especially active interaction between the soul and body is developed in
(1) Mind (2) Pineal gland
(3) Pituitary gland (4) None of these

1790. Pineal gland is the.............of the soul.
(1) Seat (2) Subject
(3) Controller (4) None of these

1791. Descartes thinks there is.............world/s and this/these is/are...............
(1) One, limited
(2) Two, limited
(3) Only one, illimitable
(4) None of the above

1792. Descartes, doctrine of man is
(1) Monistic (2) Dualistic
(3) Spiritualistic (4) Mechanistic

1793. According to Descartes, ...created matter together with motion and rest, and maintains the same quantity of motions and rest in matter.
(1) Mind (2) Atom
(3) God (4) Soul

1794. No idea is higher or clearer than the idea of God or the most perfect being is suggested by
(1) Descartes (2) Kant
(3) Patañjali (4) Śridhara

1795. ....does not mean for Spinoza, a transcendent, personal spirit, but only the essential heart of things.
(1) Soul (2) God
(3) Spirit (4) None of these

1796. God is..............., in the sense that, he does nothing except that towards which his own nature impels him, that he acts in accordance with the laws of his being.
(1) Final cause (2) Superior cause
(3) Free cause (4) None of these

1797. The ground of God's action is the same as the ground of his
(1) Existence (2) Permanence
(3) Non-existence (4) None of these

1798. God's power and his............coincide.
(1) Essence (2) Existence
(3) Superiority (4) None of these

1799. The infinite substance stands related to finite substance as..............to the.........
(1) Many, one
(2) Universal, particular
(3) One, particular
(4) None of these above

1800. Spinoza claims, ultimately, the wisdom, that philosophy seeks is achieved when one perceives the universe in its wholeness, through the

(1) Intellect (2) Ideas

(3) Intellectual love of God

(4) None of the above

1801. Spinoza viewed the universe............as a single infinite substance, God.

(1) Elaborately (2) Pantheistically

(3) Really (4) None of these

1802. The order of the actions and passions of our body is simultaneous in nature with the order of the actions and passions of the

(1) God (2) Spirit

(3) Substance (4) Mind

1803. Spinoza treats the soul as

(1) God

(2) A sum of ideas

(3) Infinite attributes

(4) None of these

1804. The rationalism of............is heightened by Spinoza.

(1) Plato (2) Descartes

(3) Aristotle (4) None of these

1805. Spinoza suggests, if everything is to be cognizable through mathematics then everything

(1) Can be explained by it

(2) Must take place necessarily

(3) Can be replaced by it

(4) None of the above

1806. According to........, substance does not affect us by its mere existence, but through an attribute.

(1) Descartes (2) Spinoza

(3) Kant (4) Locke

1807. Among the innumerable divine attributes the human mind knows only......... and........

(1) Thought, motion

(2) Though, extension

(3) Belief, motion

(4) None of the above

1808. Spinoza asserts mind is the............of the infinite consciousness of God the matter is the........of God's unlimited extension.

(1) Picture, substance

(2) Expression, limitation

(3) Expression, appearance

(4) None of the above

1809. God is free from every negation and limitation and is to be conceived as the absolutely

(1) Determinate (2) Indeterminate

(3) Dependent (4) None of these

1810. Spinoza equates substance with..........and ....

(1) Qualities, God (2) Nature, God

(3) Nature, Soul (4) None of these

1811. The attribute of mind and matter, i.e., thought and extension are two .... attributes of God.

(1) Special (2) Parallel

(3) Empirical (4) None of these

1812. By admitting only God, Spinoza fails to explain plurality, diversity, motion and change of the

(1) Individual souls

(2) Objects of the world

(3) Empirical world

(4) None of the above

1813. The idea of a perfect being is necessarily the idea of an existent being, since a being that lacked existence would not be perfect. God as a perfect being, therefore, must exist. This argument for the existence of God is

(1) causal argument

(2) moral argument

(3) ontological argument

(4) teleological argument

1814. The proposition "I think", according to Descartes, is self-verifying because

(1) Thinking is my essence

(2) It is a logical truth

(3) Doubting it, confirms it

(4) It is a necessary truth

1815. Which one of the following statements adequately sums up Descartes' philosophy?

(1) Mind and matter are two aspects of the same reality.

(2) The world is made of two radically different kinds of substance, mind and matter.

(3) Matter alone is real and mind is only an illusion

(4) Mind creates matter.

1816. Which one of the following views is held by Descartes?

(1) Mind and body are the two substances which exist independently of each other.

(2) God is the only substance and mind and matter are its attributes.

(3) Mind is the only substance and matter is only a fiction.

(4) Matter is the only substance and mind is one of its modes of existence.

1817. Which one of the following principles is used by Descartes to prove the existence of God?

(1) A perfect being must be the cause of contingent as beings.

(2) A perfect being must be the cause of the world as a whole.

(3) A perfect being must be the cause of the idea of perfect being.

(4) A perfect being must be the cause of the harmony in world.

1818. Which one of the following statements is true, according to Spinoza?

(1) Substance can exist outside of God.

(2) Substance and God are independent reals.

(3) There can be no substance outside of God.

(4) Substance and God are imaginary.

1819. By 'mode' Spinoza means that which

(1) is in itself and is conceived through itself.

(2) exists in itself

(3) is a being that is absolutely infinite.

(4) exists through something other than itself.

1820. There are two kinds of substances, of which one is known intuitively, and the other is known demonstratively.' This is the view of

(1) Nyāya-Vais'eṣika

(2) Aristotle

(3) Descartes (4) Spinoza

1821. What is true of Spinoza's parallelism?

(1) It explains the mental by the physical

(2) It explains the physical by the mental

(3) It is double aspect theory accepting both the mental and physical realms as manifestations of the same substance.

(4) It accepts the mental and the physical as two stages of evolution.

1822. According to Spinoza, God is free because

(1) God is a substance.

(2) God is infinite

(3) God acts according to inner necessity

(4) God is omnipresent

1823. By the expression "the face of entire universe" Spinoza means

(1) the infinite collection of particular extended object in nature

(2) the universe conceived as a single indivisible nature

(3) the way the universe appears to God

(4) the way the universe appears to us

1824. Which one of the following statements is not correct according to Spinoza?

(1) The mind exists as a finite temporal mode consisting of its thoughts, feelings and volitions.

(2) The human mind is 'the idea of the body'.

(3) The states of mind are effects of bodily processes.

(4) Every mind is a part of the infinite intellect.

1825. Which one of the following is the Spinozistic account on the issue of matter and mind?

(1) Mind and matter are two independent substances.

(2) Mind and matter are two attributes (thought and extension) of the substance which men can conceive as the essence of the substance.

(3) Mind and Matter interact.

(4) None

1826. Spinoza claims substance is............and ....

(1) Many, finite (2) One, infinite

(3) Many, limited (4) One, limited

1827. What is the essence of substantiality according to Spinoza?

(1) Dependence (2) Independence

(3) Completeness (4) None of these

1828. By................Spinoza understands that which is in itself and which is conceived by means of itself.

(1) Matter (2) Body

(3) Substance (4) None of these

1829. Accepting............definition of substance, Spinoza points out that if this definition is strictly adhered to, there can be only one substance, God.

(1) Descartes' (2) Leibnitz's

(3) Kant's (4) Hume's

1830. Mind and matter......................regarded as substance, since they are dependent on God for their existence, Spinoza claims.

(1) Must be (2) Can never be

(3) is always (4) None of these

1831. The idea of God is an original endowment, it is as..................as the idea of myself, according to Descartes.

(1) Innate (2) Empirical

(3) Mental (4) None of these

1832. In order to escape................., Descartes has introduced the idea of God.

(1) Spiritualism (2) Solipsism

(3) Empiricism (4) Dualism

1833. Granting everything as a mistake, Descartes points out that the............is not a mistake.

(1) Belief (2) Thinking

(3) Judgement (4) None of these

1834. God cannot be thought apart from existence, he has the ground of his existence, he has the ground of his existence in himself, he is

(1) Omnipotent (2) Universal

(3) Supreme soul (4) Causa sui

1835. Anselm's argument suggests the existence of God from the...............itself.

(1) Nature of God

(2) Concept of God

(3) Presence of God

(4) None of the above

1836. Among the attributes of God his is of special importance.

(1) Nature (2) Perfection

(3) Existence (4) Veracity

1837. The monads which constitute the body are the first and............object of the............

(1) Indirect, individual

(2) Indirect, soul

(3) Direct, soul

(4) None of the above

1838. The rationalist philosopher.............wants to give philosophy a stable character like mathematics.

(1) Descartes (2) Kant
(3) Spinoza (4) Leibnitz

1839. ....defines substance as "an existent thing which requires nothing but itself in order to exist."

(1) Spinoza (2) Locke
(3) Descartes (4) Hume

1840. According to Descartes the idea of God is infinite, independent and

(1) Universal having particular qualities
(2) Omnipotent
(3) Particular
(4) None of the above

1841. Descartes claims God as the............ substance, and mind and matter as.............

(1) Absolute, created
(2) Absolute, finite
(3) Only, created
(4) None of the above

1842. Descartes suggests................as absolute substance.

(1) God (2) Mind
(3) Soul (4) None of these

1843. Descartes claims that we cannot accept anything as true without

(1) Reasoning
(2) Critical examination
(3) Deduction
(4) None of the above

1844. Which one of the following pairs is not correct?

(1) Immaterialism............Berkeley
(2) Representative Realism.........Locke
(3) Pantheism............Spinoza
(4) Atheism.............Descartes

1845. There must be an unknown and unknowable substratum which supports the existence of.............qualities.

(1) Primary (2) Secondary
(3) Basic (4) None of these

1846. ....points out that if Descartes, definition of substance is to be strictly adhered to, there can be only one substance, i.e. God.

(1) Spinoza (2) Hume
(3) Locke (4) Berkeley

1847. The secondary properties of substance are known as

(1) Modes (2) Attribute
(3) Relative property
(4) None of these

1848. Regarding the relation between matter and mind, which one of the following statements is not supported by Descartes?

(1) They are independent substances.
(2) They are two separate substances alongside God.
(3) They are inter-related to one another
(4) They are both identical

1849. According to Spinoza, body and mind

(1) Are causally independent
(2) Interact with each other
(3) Are parallel to each other
(4) Are providentially synchronized by God

1850. Descartes explains body-mind relation through

(1) Psycho-Physical Parallelism.
(2) Interactionism.
(3) Pre-established harmony.
(4) Epiphenomenalism.

1851. The view that one may consider God both as Natura naturans and Natura naturata is maintained by

(1) Thomas Aquinas

(2) Spinoza
(3) Descartes
(4) St. Augustine

1852. Who among the following was obsessed with the intellectual love of God?
(1) Sankara (2) Descartes
(3) Spinoza (4) St. Augustine

1853. Ideas of colour, taste, extension, motion, thinking, doubting are...............qualities which actually exist in things.
(1) Primary (2) Secondary
(3) Basic (4) None of these

1854. Which one of the following is not included in Leibnitz' principle of identity of indiscernibles?
(1) That two things in the universe can be exactly alike in all respects.
(2) No two things can be exactly alike in every respect except numerically.
(3) No two things are identical since each possesses something which no other possesses.
(4) All things that differ numerically are spatially separated and have discernible difference.

1855. According to Spinoza, substance and modes are related in such a way that
(1) substance is the most basic
(2) modes are more basic to substance
(3) substance and modes are two independent things
(4) they are mutually dependent

1856. Regarding the problem of mind-body relation which one of the following solutions on the analogy of two clocks keeping time together perfectly is acceptable to Leibnitz?
(1) They are mechanically connected with each other
(2) They are placed in charge of a skilled workman who regulates them from moment to moment
(3) God has so synchronized them from the beginning
(4) They are part and parcel of the larger whole.

1857. The principle of sufficient reason was propounded by
(1) Locke (2) Berkeley
(3) Leibnitz (4) Plato

1858. Who among the following advocates that in every true proposition the predicate is contained in the subject ?
(1) Descartes (2) Kant
(3) Hume (4) Leibnitz

1859. According to Leibnitz, soul is
(1) not a monad
(2) an independent monad
(3) supreme monad
(4) in the 'pineal gland'

1860. The perception of external objects is termed ...., that of internal phenomena is..............
(1) Sensation, thinking
(2) Sensation, reflection
(3) Representation, reflection
(4) None of the above

1861. ....declares that there are no substances other than God.
(1) Spinoza (2) Kant
(3) Hume (4) Locke

1862. Mind is the expression of the infinite .... of God and matter is the appearance of God's............
(1) Characteristic, nature
(2) Consciousness, nature
(3) Characteristic, unlimited extension
(4) Consciousness, unlimited extension

1863. Which one of the following statement is true?
(1) Descartes' method is a procedure to arrive at certainty.

(2) Descartes' method is an expression of wavering condition of mind.
(3) Descartes' method is a mechanical procedure.
(4) Descartes' method is the method of scepticism.

1864. Which one of the following statements is entitled by Descartes' cogito ergo sum?
(1) Only I exist
(2) Only God exists
(3) I exist while I think
(4) Only matter exists

1865. Descartes recognises mind and matter as............substances which are created by God.
(1) Absolute (2) Relative
(3) Neutral (4) Real

1866. Descartes classifies created substances under two heads,............and spiritual.
(1) Objective (2) Relative
(3) Independent (4) Corporeal

1867. Descartes suggests mind and matter are
(1) Opposed to each other
(2) Dependent on each other
(3) Independent of each other
(4) None of the above

1868. Descartes advocates.............by admitting mind and matter as two substances.
(1) Dualism (2) Individualism
(3) Rationalism (4) None of these

1869. To solve mind and body problem, descartes has introduced
(1) Dualism
(2) Psycho-physical interactionism
(3) Psycho-physiological theory
(4) None of the above

1870. Descartes distinguished between three kinds of ideas, the one of the following is not included in those three, which is
(1) Innate ideas
(2) Complex ideas
(3) Factitious ideas
(4) Adventitious ideas

1871. Who among the following thinkers makes use of the principle 'there must be at least as much reality in the efficient and total cause as in the effect of that cause,' in his proofs for the existence of God ?
(1) Leibnitz (2) Spinoza
(3) Aquinas (4) Descartes

1872. Which one of the following principles is *not true* of Leibnitz ?
(1) The principle of sufficient reason
(2) The law of non-contradiction
(3) The indiscernibility of identicals
(4) The identity of indiscernibles

1873. Consider the following statement :
The union of soul and body............ consists only in the perfect mutual agreement, purposely established by the order of the first creation, in virtue of which each substance, following its own laws, agrees with what the other demands; and the operation of the one thus follow or accompany the operation or the change of the other.'
This is the view of
(1) Descartes (2) Spinoza
(3) Berkeley (4) Leibnitz

1874. The two attributes, i.e., thought and extension correspond to two classes of
(1) Qualities (2) Substances
(3) Modes (4) None of these

1875. The most important modifications of extension are............and.............
(1) Attributes, motion
(2) Shape, rest
(3) Speed, motion
(4) Rest, motion

1876. In the phenomenal world, there is no............ or..............cause, because of the endlessness in the series of causes.
(1) First, ultimate
(2) First, superior
(3) Primary, ultimate
(4) None of the above

1877. Spinoza says, the..............is nothing but the idea of an actual body.
(1) God (2) Soul
(3) Spirit (4) None of these

1878. God cannot be thought otherwise than existing as his................include his............
(1) Concepts, existence
(2) Presence, infinity
(3) Concepts, infinity
(4) None of the above

1879. Spinoza claims that the things which make up the world are related to God as the properties of................to its concepts.
(1) Theorem
(2) Geometrical figure
(3) Quality
(4) None of the above

1880. 'There can be only one substance which is causa sui (cause of itself) and this single substance must be identified with the universe as a whole. This unique all inclusive totality is, therefore, God or Nature'. In the above statement Spinoza speaks of 'the unique all inclusive totality' to establish.
(1) Naturalism (2) Theism
(3) Pantheism (4) Monotheism

1881. God is regarded as the only cause and bearer of all qualities, is said by
(1) Berkeley (2) Hume
(3) Spinoza (4) G.E. Moore

1882. Instead of learning from mathematics, ...theory became subservient to it.
(1) Descartes' (2) Spinoza's
(3) Hume's (4) Kant's

1883. The attribute of mind is...............and the attribute of matter is.................
(1) Thought, size
(2) Thought, extension
(3) Infinity, extension
(4) None of the above

1884. According to Spinoza man is not free because
(1) Man is made in the image of God.
(2) World is mechanistic.
(3) Everything in the universe necessarily follows from Nature of God.
(4) Man is sinful.

1885. Descartes admitted three main types of particles, viz., the splinter particles,......... and the biggest particles.
(1) Spatial particles
(2) Spherical particles
(3) Medium particles
(4) None of the above

1886. Which one of the following is *not true* of Spinoza ?
(1) The physical can have no effect on the mental.
(2) Psycho-physical interactionism.
(3) God is at once both mental and material.
(4) The mental can have no effect on the physical.

1887. Descartes says that ultimately there are ....main types of particles.
(1) Four (2) Six
(3) Three (4) None of these

1888. Descartes constructed an/a...........theory without atoms in the classifical sense.
(1) Materialistic (2) Realistic
(3) Atomic (4) None of these

1889. 'By substance I understand that which is in itself and is conceived by means of itself, i.e., that the conception of which can be formed without the aid of the conception of any other thing'—who is the speaker?

(1) Descartes (2) Spinoza
(3) Hume (4) Kant

1890. Which of the following is supported by Leibnitz?

(1) Monads differ from God both in degree and kind.
(2) Force is an ontological reality.
(3) The doctrine of pre-established harmony necessarily implies existence of God.
(4) God chooses the best of the possible worlds.

1891. Which theory is propounded by Spinoza regarding the relation between Mind and Body?

(1) Occasionalism
(2) Parallelism
(3) Pre-established harmony
(4) None of the above

1892. According to Leibnitz.

(1) the soul is conscious while the body is extended.
(2) the soul is active, while the body is passive.
(3) the soul is self-conscious, while the body is unconscious.
(4) both soul and body are conscious, though in different degrees.

1893. Which one of the following terms is not used by Leibnitz in his theory of monads?

(1) Entelechy (2) City of God
(3) Possible worlds (4) Vital impulse

1894. For Leibnitz, monad is windowless because

(1) it is absolutely free from external influence
(2) it is extended
(3) it is a composite body
(4) it is something material

1895. According to Leibnitz natural changes of monads come from an internal principle, since an external cause cannot influence their inner being. The action of this inner principle is called

(1) appetite (2) appetition
(3) petit perception (4) apperception

1896. ....admits innumerable monads or spiritual atoms.

(1) Leibnitz (2) Hume
(3) Berkeley (4) Locke

1897. The monads are..............and everything is potential or implicit in it.

(1) Very strong (2) Active
(3) Windowless (4) None of these

1898. Leibnitz takes............as the monad of all monads who is the creator of all monads.

(1) Soul (2) Spirit
(3) God (4) None of these

1899. Every monad is a mirror of the...........and it is a living mirror, which generates the images of things by its own activity.

(1) Empirical world
(2) Substance
(3) Thing-in-itself (4) Universe

1990. In Leibnitz's view, there is nothing truly real in the world except the.............and their representation.

(1) Substance (2) Real substance
(3) Infinite substance
(4) Monads

1901. ....thinks that substance is to be defined by active force

(1) Spinoza (2) Leibnitz
(3) Descartes (4) Hume

1902. There are infinite number of substances which are called as monads according to

(1) Spinoza (2) Hume
(3) Descartes (4) Leibnitz

1903. The primary aim of Descartes is
(1) to explain the relation between body and mind.
(2) to prove the existence of God.
(3) to refute the reality of the external world.
(4) to reach clear and certain knowledge.

1904. Modes are variable..............of created substances.
(1) Representation (2) Modifications
(3) Destruction (4) None of these

1905. ....pre-establishes the unity and harmony among the monads at the time of creating them.
(1) Spirit (2) God
(3) Soul (4) None of these

1906. Everything in nature is so organized that there is no............bodies, no dead matter.
(1) Physical (2) External
(3) Soulless (4) None of these

1907. Leibnitz suggests that to have clear and distinct perceptions only is the prerogative of
(1) Soul (2) God
(3) Spirit (4) None of these

1908. Leibnitz suggests that God alone is..........but all finite beings are passive.
(1) Pure (2) Pure activity
(3) Pure self (4) None of these

1909. Leibnitz gives three principal grades of monads, viz., the simple or naked monad, the soul and
(1) God (2) Continuousness
(3) Spirit (4) None of these

1910. Leibnitz gives us the general idea of a........which finds special application in the problem of the interaction between body and soul.
(1) God
(2) Pre-established harmony
(3) Pure self (4) None of these

1911. Which of the following statements is not true ?
(1) According to Descartes, there is pre-established harmony.
(2) Berkeley advocates immaterialism.
(3) According to Hume, impressions are atomic.
(4) Kant was roused from his dogmatic slumber by Hume.

1912. Leibnitz defines substance or 'monad' as
(1) Active force (2) Physical object
(3) Mental object (4) None of these

1913. Leibnitz asserts that every monad represents all others in itself, is a concentrated all,
(1) The whole world
(2) The universe in miniature
(3) The practical world
(4) None of the above

1914. Every monad is a............of the universe which generates the images of things by its own activity.
(1) Clear aspect
(2) Definite explanation
(3) Living mirror
(4) None of the above

1915. Leibnitz believes that the history of the universe is a single
(1) Method
(2) Great process in numberless reflection
(3) Consistent process
(4) None of the above

1916. Leibnitz asserts that the pre-established harmony does not interfere with..........but yields them.

(1) General laws (2) Empirical laws
(3) Natural laws (4) None of these

1917. According to Leibnitz, organisms are........... of which the soul is supreme and the rest is its body.
(1) Existent being
(2) Complex of monads
(3) Both physical and mental
(4) None of the above

1918. Leibnitz claims that there is only a .... between soul and body, instituted by God.
(1) Complete substance
(2) Complete correspondence
(3) Indistinct correspondence
(4) None of the above

1919. Spinoza's monistic pluralism reduces individuals to the following :
(1) Idea (1) Attribute
(3) Substance (4) Mode

1920. According to Descartes, to attain certainity, false opinions and traditional views are to be replaced with
(1) Scholarly opinion
(2) Faculty of reason
(3) Sense perception
(4) Scriptures

1921. According to Spinoza intellectual love of God is
(1) loving God like an intellectual devotee.
(2) realising rationally that we are modes of God and that by loving ourselves we actually love God
(3) Having rational faith in God and avoiding blind faith.
(4) proving with arguments the modes and attributes of his all-loving character.

1922. When Spinoza says that God is free, it implies that
(1) God could have chosen not to create the world
(2) God could have chosen to create a world different from the existing one.
(3) God freely exercises his will to promote human welfare
(4) God is determined in his actions by himself alone.

1923. Which one of the following statements is associated with Spinoza?
(1) Mind and body are two independent entities in perfect harmony with each other
(2) Mind and body interact and there is a causal relation between the two.
(3) Mind and body are not two independent substances but are two parallel manifestations of the same reality.
(4) Mind is an epiphenomenon of the body

1924. Regarding the problem of mind-body interaction, which one of the following solutions is suggested by Spinoza?
(1) God miraculously intervenes so as to make mental-physical interaction possible.
(2) There is a perfect co-ordination between mind and body in accordance with some pre-established harmony.
(3) The so-called mental is actually physical, hence there is only physical-physical interaction.
(4) The mind and the body are one and the same substance conceived under two attributes.

1925. Match the following

List-I	List-II
(a) Descartes	(i) Dualist
(b) Spinoza	(ii) Monistheistic
(c) Leibniz	(iii) Pluralist
(d) Pre-established harmony	(iv) God

Codes : (a) (b) (c) (d)
(1) (iv) (iii) (ii) (i)
(2) (ii) (iv) (iii) (i)
(3) (iv) (ii) (iii) (i)
(4) (i) (ii) (iii) (iv)

1926. Match list I with list II and select the correct answer by using the codes given below the lists :

List-I	List-II
(a) Aristotle	(i) Transcendental unity of Apperception
(b) Spinoza	(ii) Pre-established Harmony
(c) Leibnitz	(iii) Unmoved Mover
(d) Kant	(iv) Intellectual love of God

Codes : (a) (b) (c) (d)
(1) (iii) (iv) (i) (ii)
(2) (iii) (iv) (ii) (i)
(3) (ii) (i) (iv) (iii)
(4) (iv) (iii) (ii) (i)

1927. Match list I with list II and select the correct answer by using the codes given below the lists :

List-I	List-II
(a) Substance is an existent thing which requires nothing but itself in order to exist.	(i) Spinoza
(b) Substance is in itself and is conceived by means of itself.	(ii) Leibnitz
(c) Substance acts through itself or contains in itself the ground of its changing states.	(iii) Descartes

Codes : (a) (b) (c)
(1) (ii) (iii) (i)
(2) (iii) (i) (ii)
(3) (iii) (ii) (i)
(4) (i) (ii) (iii)

1928. Match the following

List-I	List-II
(a) Leibniz	(i) Identity of indescernibles
(b) Descartes	(ii) Discourse on method
(c) Spinoza	(iii) Pantheist
(d) God	(iv) Supreme Monad

Codes :
(a) (b) (c) (d)
(1) (i) (ii) (iii) (iv)
(2) (iv) (iii) (ii) (i)
(3) (ii) (iv) (iii) (i)
(4) (i) (iv) (iii) (ii)

1929. Match list I with list II and select the correct answer by using the codes given below the lists :

List-I	List-II
(a) Descartes	(i) A true knowledge of soul's nature can be based on the immediate awareness
(b) Spinoza	(ii) No idea is higher or clearer than the idea of God or the most perfect being
(c) St. Augustine	(iii) Substance is one and infinite

Codes :
(a) (b) (c)
(1) (ii) (i) (iii)
(2) (ii) (iii) (i)
(3) (iii) (ii) (i)
(4) (i) (iii) (ii)

1930. Match list I with list II and select the correct answer by using the codes given below the lists :

List-I (Mind-body Theories)	List-II (Philosophers)
(a) Dualism	(i) Spinoza
(b) Parallelism	(ii) Descartes

(c) Pre-established harmony (iii) Leibnitz

(d) Occasionalism (iv) Malebranche

(v) J.J.C. Smart

Codes :

	(a)	(b)	(c)	(d)
(1)	(i)	(ii)	(v)	(iv)
(2)	(ii)	(i)	(iii)	(iv)
(3)	(ii)	(i)	(iv)	(v)
(4)	(iv)	(v)	(iii)	(ii)

1931. Match the following

List-I	List-II
(a) Descartes	(i) Need for method
(b) Spinoza	(ii) Substance is one
(c) Leibniz	(iii) Appetition in Monads
(d) Hume	(iv) Empiricism

Codes :

	(a)	(b)	(c)	(d)
(1)	(i)	(ii)	(iii)	(iv)
(2)	(iv)	(iii)	(ii)	(i)
(3)	(ii)	(iii)	(iv)	(i)
(4)	(i)	(iv)	(iii)	(ii)

1932. Match list I with list II and select the correct answer by using the codes given below the lists :

List-I	List-II
(a) Attribute	(i) The attribute of mind
(b) Thought	(ii) The fundamental property of substance
(c) Extension	(iii) The attribute of matter

Codes :

	(a)	(b)	(c)
(1)	(i)	(iii)	(ii)
(2)	(ii)	(i)	(iii)
(3)	(iii)	(ii)	(i)
(4)	(ii)	(iii)	(i)

1933. Match list I with list II and select the correct answer by using the codes given below the lists :

List-I	List-II
(a) Cogito Argument	(i) The existence of God
(b) Arguments from opposites	(ii) The Falsity of Plato's theory of ideas
(c) Aristotle's Third Non-Argument	(iii) The immortality of soul
(4) Ontological Argument	(iv) The existence of self

Codes :

	(a)	(b)	(c)	(d)
(1)	(iv)	(iii)	(i)	(ii)
(2)	(iv)	(iii)	(ii)	(i)
(3)	(ii)	(iv)	(i)	(iii)
(4)	(iii)	(iv)	(ii)	(i)

1934. Match the following

List-I	List-II
(a) Descartes	(i) Dualist
(b) Spinoza	(ii) Monistheistic
(c) Leibniz	(iii) Pluralist
(d) Pre-established harmony	(iv) God

Codes :

	(a)	(b)	(c)	(d)
(1)	(i)	(ii)	(iii)	(iv)
(2)	(ii)	(iii)	(iv)	(ii)
(3)	(iv)	(iii)	(ii)	(i)
(4)	(iii)	(ii)	(iv)	(i)

1935. Match list I with list II and select the correct answer by using codes given below the lists:

List-I	List-II
(a) Descartes	(i) There is only one substance, God
(b) Locke	(ii) The secondary properties are modes
(c) Spinoza	(iii) Idea of substance is a complex idea

Codes :

	(a)	(b)	(c)
(1)	(ii)	(iii)	(i)
(2)	(i)	(ii)	(iii)
(3)	(iii)	(i)	(ii)
(4)	(iii)	(ii)	(i)

1936. Match list-I (Concept) with list II (Thinker) and select the correct answer using the codes given below the lists :

List-I	List-II
(a) Monad has consciousness	(i) Descartes
(b) Matter does not have consciousness	(ii) Spinoza
(c) Mind and matter are attributes of substance	(iii) Leibnitz

Codes :

	(a)	(b)	(c)
(1)	(i)	(ii)	(iii)
(2)	(i)	(iii)	(ii)
(3)	(iii)	(ii)	(i)
(4)	(iii)	(i)	(ii)

1937. Match the following

List-I	List-II
(a) Monad	(i) Descartes
(b) Matter does not have consciousness	(ii) Spinoza
(c) Mind and matter are regarded as attributes of substances	(iii) Leibniz
(d) Occasionalism	(iv) Melecbranche

Codes :

	(a)	(b)	(c)	(d)
(1)	(i)	(ii)	(iii)	(iv)
(2)	(iii)	(i)	(ii)	(iv)
(3)	(i)	(iv)	(iii)	(ii)
(4)	(ii)	(iii)	(iv)	(i)

1938. Match the following by using the code below :

List-I (Thinker)	List-II (Doctrine)
(a) Descartes	(i) Doctrine of modes
(b) Berkeley	(ii) Doctrine of monads
(c) Leibnitz	(iii) Esse est percipi
(d) Spinoza	(iv) Doctrine of Innate Ideas.

Codes :

	(a)	(b)	(c)	(d)
(A)	(iv)	(i)	(ii)	(iii)
(B)	(iv)	(iii)	(ii)	(i)
(C)	(ii)	(iii)	(iv)	(i)
(D)	(iii)	(iv)	(ii)	(i)

Direction. Following questions will follow the same rule as given in chapter one for Assertion-Reason Problems.

Codes:

(1) Both A and R are true and R is the correct explanation of A.

(2) Both A and R are true but R is not correct explanation of A.

(3) A is true but R is false.

(4) A is false but R is true.

1939. **Assertion (A).** God is self-caused and it does not depend on anything else to exist according to Descartes.

Reason (R). Descartes does not recognise mind and matter as separate substances.

1940. **Assertion (A).** Spinoza thinks, substance does not affect us by its mere existence, but through an attribute.

Reason (R). There is only one substance, i.e., God.

1941. **Assertion (A).** The idea of the infinite has not been derived from the idea of the finite by abstraction and negation.

Reason (R). The infinite contains more reality than the finite.

1942. **Assertion (A).** Body or motion is nothing but the object or event in the sphere of extended actuality corresponding to an idea.

Reason (R). Everything is both body and spirit.

1943. **Assertion (A).** Instead of learning from mathematics Spinoza's theory became subservient to it.

Reason (R). According to Spinoza, the things which make up the world are related to God as the properties of geometrical figure.

1944. **Assertion (A).** Spinoza declares God as the essence of all things.

Reason (R). God is both the cause and effect.

1945. **Assertion (A).** Spinoza thinks substance is one and infinite.

Reason (R). An absolutely self-dependent being can neither be limited, nor occur more than once in the world.

1946. **Assertion (A).** Substance is the being which is dependent on nothing but on which everything depends.

Reason (R). Spinoza thinks substance itself is uncaused, affects all else, it presupposes nothing, but itself constitutes the presupposition of all.

1947. **Assertion (A).** Descartes' doctrine of man is dualistic.

Reason (R). Descartes has rejected the atomistic theory of the world.

1948. **Assertion (A).** Descartes has rejected the atomic theory of the world.

Reason (R). Descartes has suggested matter, as well as space, has no smallest, indivisible parts and the extension of the world has no end.

1949. **Assertion (A).** Spinoza has failed to explain the plurality, diversity, motion and change of the objects in the world.

Reason (R). Spinoza admits only one substance, i.e., God.

1950. **Assertion (A).** Spinoza believes the things which make up the world are related to God as the properties of geometrical figure to its concepts.

Reason (R). Spinoza depends on mathematics while establishing his theory.

1951. **Assertion (A).** Descartes believed that persons are essentially nonphysical.

Reason (R). According to Descartes the persons is composed of two distinct substances, mind and matter, the former being essential to persons while the latter is contingent.

1952. **Assertion (A).** Spinoza believed that there is only one substance.

Reason (R). Substance, according to Spinoza, is that which exists in itself and is conceived by itself independent of anything else.

1953. **Assertion (A).** Leibnitz principle of the identity of the indiscernibles states that all substances (monads) are identical which have the same complete concept.

Reason (R). For every substance, there is a 'complete' concept which contains within it the concept of everything that may be truly predicated of that substance.

1954. **Assertion (A).** Leibnitz suggests that every monad is a mirror of the universe.

Reason (R). The monad has no windows through which anything could pass in or out.

1955. Regarding doctrine or substance which of the following views are held by Descartes?

A. Substance is an existent thing which requires nothing but itself in order to exist.

B. Strictly speaking, God alone can be said to be a substance.

C. Substance is that whose existence cannot be doubted.

Select the correct answer using the codes given below :

Codes :

(1) A and B (2) A, B and C
(3) B and C (4) A and C

1956. Leibniz gives

A. identity of indiscernibles.
B. pre-established harmony.
C. attributes.
D. modes.

Select the correct answer from the codes given below :

(1) Only A (2) B and C
(3) C and D (4) A and B

1957. Descartes wrote a book on

A. Regulae.
B. Discourse on Method.
C. Treatise on Human Nature.
D. Monadology.

Select the correct answer from the codes given below :

(1) A and B (2) A and C
(3) B and C (4) C and D

1958. Which of the following statements can be attributed to Spinoza?

A. God possesses an infinity of attributes.
B. All determination is negation.
C. God is the creator of the world.

Select the correct answer from the codes given below :

Codes :

(1) A and B (2) B and C
(3) A and C (4) A, B and C

1959. Descartes gives

A. causal proof.
B. cosmological proof.
C. non-causai proof.
D. non-cosmological proof.

Select the correct answer from the codes given below :

(1) B and C (2) A and C
(3) A and B (4) C and D

1960. Which of the following views are held by Spinoza?

A. The mind's highest virtues is to know God.
B. Conceived under the from of eternity. God literally is his infinite attributes.
C. Conceived under the from of time, God is the world.
D. Our highest good consists in the emotional love of God.

Select the correct answer from the codes given below :

Codes :

(1) A, B and D (2) B, C and D
(3) A, B and C (4) A, C and D

1961. Descartes believes in

A. concept of method.
B. need for method.
C. no need for method.
D. monadology.

Select the correct answer from the codes given below :

(1) A and B (2) A and C
(3) B and C (4) C and D

1962. Leibniz gives

A. truth of reason.
B. truth of fact.
C. truth of falsity.
D. truth of logic.

Select the correct answer from the codes given below :

(1) A and B (2) A and C
(3) B and C (4) C and D

1963. Consider the following statements

A. When we consider Nature under the attribute of extension of under the attribute of thought.........we shall find one and the same order, and one and the same connections of causes.'

B. 'The mind has no knowledge of itself save in so far as it perceives the ideas of the modifications of the body.'

These statements express the doctrine of

(1) Interactionism
(2) Parallelism
(3) Occasionalism
(4) Pre-established harmony

1964. Leibniz wrote a book on

A. Monadology.
B. Discourse on Metaphysics.
C. Regulae.
D. Treatise on God.

Select the correct answer from the codes given below :

(1) A and B (2) A and C
(3) B and C (4) C and D

1965. Spinoza gives

A. three orders of knowing.
B. attributes.
C. non-attributes.
D. four orders of knowing.

Select the correct answer from the codes given below :

(1) A and B (2) A and C
(3) B and C (4) C and D

1966. Consider the following terms :

A. Petit perception.
B. Appetition
C. Entelechy
D. Apperception.

The terms which occur in the writings of Leibnitz include

(1) A and B
(2) A, C and D
(3) B, C and D
(4) A, B, C and D

1967. The monads of Leibnitz may be characterised as follows :

A. Monads are windowless
B. Monads are spiritual
C. Monads perceive each other

Select the correct answer from the codes given below :

Codes :

(1) A, B and C (2) A and B
(3) B and C (4) A and C

1968. Descartes introduced

I. Mathematical Method
II. Advanced Proofs for the existence of God.
III. Explained body-mind relation.
IV. Introduced the distinction between primary and secondary qualities.

Find the correct answer by using the code below :

(1) only I and II are correct.
(2) only II and III are correct.
(3) only III and IV are correct.
(4) only I, II & III are correct.

1969. Spinoza was regarded as

A. rationalist. B. empiricist.
C. monotheist. D. dualist.

Select the correct answer from the codes given below :

(1) A and B (2) A and C
(3) B and C (4) C and D

1970. David Hume's philosophical standpoint is :

A. Empirical
B. Positivistic
C. Agnostic
D. All the above

Find the correct answer by using the code below :

(1) A and B are only correct.
(2) B and C are only correct.
(3) A and C are only correct.
(4) D is correct.

1971. Locke suggests that the idea of substance is a.............idea.
(1) Simple (2) Complex
(3) Particular (4) None of these

1972. Locke believes that there ....innate principles in the mind.
(1) Are (2) Are no
(3) Must be (4) None of these

1973. Which one of the following according to Locke is correct description of substance?
(1) Substance is spiritual in nature
(2) Substance has both real and nominal essences
(3) Substance is a known locus of qualities
(4) Substance is the cause of the world

1974. Which one of the following according to Locke justifies the distinction between primary and secondary qualities?
(1) God has created primary qualities
(2) Secondary qualities are given in experience
(3) Primary qualities and secondary qualities are logically different
(4) Primary qualities are objective while secondary qualities are subjective

1975. Berkeley rejects Locke's distinction between primary and secondary qualities because
(1) All qualities are subjective
(2) Only secondary qualities are subjective
(3) Qualities are created by God
(4) Qualities inhere in substances

1976. Locke admits of material and mental substances as unknown support of...........and respectively.
(1) Perception, thinking
(2) Sensible qualities, mental states
(3) Perception, mental states
(4) None of the above

1977. Locke suggests that mind knows directly the...........and not the objects themselves.
(1) Sensation
(2) Ideas of the object
(3) Qualities
(4) None of the above

1978. ....suggests ideas are of two types, simple and complex.
(1) Descartes (2) Spinoza
(3) Locke (4) Berkeley

1979. Locke suggests that the understanding is like a piece of............on which perception inscribes its character.
(1) White paper (2) Stone
(3) Metal (4) None of these

1980. Locke recommends...........and............ substances.
(1) Primary, secondary
(2) Empirical, experimental
(3) Cogitative, incogitative
(4) None of the above

1981. Locke asserts we get...........knowledge of our own mind or soul and..........knowledge of the existence of God.
(1) Real, demonstrative
(2) Intuitive, demonstrative
(3) Empirical, demonstrative
(4) Spiritual, intuitive

1982. According to Locke, knowledge is the perception of..........or..........between ideas.
(1) Similarity, difference
(2) Agreement, disagreement
(3) Real, infinite knowledge
(4) None of the above

1983. As an empiricist, Locke claims that all our knowledge is derived either through sensation or

(1) Perception (2) Reflection
(3) Thinking (4) None of these

1984. Both..........and............agree with Berkeley that spiritual beings alone are active, and active beings alone real, and that the being of the inactive consists in their being perceived.

(1) Descartes, Spinoza
(2) Leibnitz, Fichte
(3) Descartes, Fichte
(4) None of the above

1985. Berkeley thinks the objective ideas are impressed upon finite spirits by the.......... from without.

(1) Infinite Spirit (2) Mind
(3) Physical objects
(4) None of the above

1986. Classical subjective idealism is represented by Berkeley, Hume and

(1) Kant (2) Spinoza
(3) Fichte (4) Augustine

1987. The philosopher that distinguishes between 'matters of fact' and 'association of ideas' is

(1) Descartes (2) Hume
(3) Leibnitz (4) Spinoza

1988. Who said that the relation between cause and effect is not logical, but only psychological?

(1) Hume (2) Kant
(3) Russell (4) Heidegger

1989. According to whom 'to start with, mind is a clean state' ?

(1) Plato (2) Descartes
(3) Spinoza (4) Locke

1990. 'We never have an idea of 'Space' or bare 'extension' which is neither solid, nor line, nor surface.'

The claim leads to the view that

(1) it is possible for the mind to construct abstract ideas.
(2) universals exist apart from the particulars.
(3) any word that we use to designate the common feature of a class of things is a mere name.
(4) all ideas are derived either from sensation or from reflection.

1991. Which one of the following pairs is correctly matched

(1) Locke : Substance constitutes the object of sensitive knowledge
(2) Leibnitz : Substances can be of two types, extended and non-extended
(3) Spinoza : Substance is the primary essence of things
(4) Descartes : Substance must contain a dynamic force.

1992. Which one of the following views truly explains the status of matter in the light of Berkeley's thesis 'esse est percipii'?

(1) Whatever is known is only substance or concrete things.
(2) Whatever is known is only ideas.
(3) We experience in perception only objects with qualities
(4) Apart from ideas, matter exists.

1993. It being impossible to recall the past impressions, in order to compare them with our present ideas, and see whether their arrangement be exactly similar." Expresses the view of

(1) Plato (2) Locke
(3) Hume (4) Russell

1994. Which of the following is not acceptable to Berkeley ?

(1) We have an idea of self.
(2) We have an idea of God.
(3) We have ideas of sensible qualities.
(4) We have ideas of pain and pleasure.

1995. According to Hume, the belief that similar causes must give rise to similar effects is based on
(1) Reason (2) Intuition
(3) Induction (4) Custom

1996. Mind is never found without thought, so there is no............mind.
(1) Empirical (2) Unconscious
(3) Super (4) None of these

1997. Our sensations of qualities are ideas and ....is a simple, indivisible reality which perceives and produces the idea.
(1) Mind (2) God
(3) Sense-experience
(4) None of these

1998. The sensation of one colour differs from another colour due to the.........if it.
(1) Difference (2) Opposition
(3) Objective nature
(4) None of these

1999. Berkeley is
(1) Idealist (2) Realist
(3) Pagmatist (4) None

2000. Monadology is the work of
(1) Locke (2) Leibnitz
(3) Bacon (4) Berkeley

2001. ....claims only minds and their ideas exist.
(1) Berkeley (2) Hume
(3) Locke (4) Spinoza

2002. Berkeley claims that, all things of the world are the ideas of the
(1) Mind (2) Divine mind
(3) Soul (4) None of these

2003. In the philosophy of nature.............. prefers the teleological to the mechanical view.
(1) Locke (2) Berkeley
(3) Spinoza (4) Hume

2004. Berkeley understands by the term............. that which the soul perceives, but the popular mind thinks that through which the soul perceives an object.
(1) Mind (2) god
(3) Idea (4) None of these

2005. ....claims that everything exists only in virtue of its participation in the one, permanent and all comprehensive spirit.
(1) Locke (2) Berkeley
(3) Hume (4) Kant

2006. John Locke claims that all reality is.........., and that universals exist only in the.............
(1) General, particular
(2) Individual, abstract understanding
(3) General, objects of the empirical world
(4) None of the above

2007. Berkeley suggests, as all beings are particular, so all ideas are
(1) Universal ideas
(2) Particular ideas
(3) Empirical ideas
(4) None of the above

2008. Berkeley.............the assumption of general ideas in the mind and the belief in the existence of a material world outside it.
(1) Accepts (2) Rejects
(3) Transforms
(4) None of the above

2009. Which one of the following statements is correct?
(1) Realism is opposite of utopianism
(2) Realism is a mixture of utopianism and idealism
(3) Realism is another name of utopianism
(4) None of the above

2010. Which among the following is not true for Berkeley.
(1) Matter is not perceived
(2) The existence of matter is not based on inference.
(3) The existence of matter serves no useful purpose.
(4) External objects are real and exist outside our mind.

2011. ....says that our sense-experiences (ideas) of primary qualities are...........of the same qualities, as they really do characterize the object in the outside world.
(1) Locke, qualities
(2) Locke, resemblance
(3) Locke, similar
(4) None of the above

2012. According to................, the ideas of imagination are produced by ourselves and real perceptions are produced by God.
(1) Locke (2) Berkeley
(3) Descartes (4) Hume

2013. ....believed that there are physical objects existing independently of perception, but that the way these objects appear to us is in many ways different from the way they really are
(1) Descartes (2) Locke
(3) Berkeley (4) Hume

2014. John Locke has divided the qualities of things into..........and...........
(1) A priori, a posteriori
(2) Empirical, intuitive
(3) Primary, Secondary
(4) None of the above

2015. Which of the following is not acceptable to Locke ?
(1) Self is known through intuition.
(2) God's existence is a case of demonstrative knowledge.
(3) Objects in the external world have independent existence.
(4) In perception mind has direct access to the objects in the external world.

2016. The ideas of nominalism were developed on an idealist basis in the doctrine of Berkeley and
(1) Kant (2) Leibnitz
(3) Hume (4) Spinoza

2017. Who is the principal exponent of representative realism?
(1) Locke (2) Berkeley
(3) Russell (4) None of these

2018. Which one of the following is true of Berkeley?
(1) There is a material substratum underlying qualities.
(2) There is no material substratum underlying qualities.
(3) There is no material substratum underlying qualities but there is a material world independent of ideas.
(4) Primary qualities alone are objectively real and matter is the same as these primary qualities.

2019. Which one of the following these is the most fundamental to Berkeley's world-view?
(1) All qualities are ideas and so any object consisting of qualities is an idea.
(2) Qualities of an object do not inhere in a material substratum
(3) Secondary qualities are the powers to produce sensations in us by their primary qualities.
(4) Primary qualities are produced by our minds.

2020. Which one of the following is the view of Berkeley?
(1) The nature of body consists not in weight, hardness, colour and the like, but in extension alone.

(2) Bodies are mere appearances of our outer sense, and not things-in-themselves.

(3) Body is only a system of floating ideas without any substance to support them.

(4) Body is composed of centres of force that are in a constant process of development.

2021. Who says that mind in the beginning is a 'tabula rasa', a 'dark chamber', or an 'empty cabinet' ?

(1) Locke (2) Berkeley
(3) Hume (4) Russell

2022. Which one of the following statements is not implied by Berkeley's view that 'to be is to be perceived'?

(1) Ideas can exist only as long as they are being perceived.

(2) Qualities cannot exist independently of the perceiving mind.

(3) Objects cannot exist when they are not perceived by any mind.

(4) Objects cannot exist when they are not perceived by human beings.

2023. Which one of the following does not figure in Berkeley's rejection of abstract ideas?

(1) There is no such thing in any mind as an abstract idea.

(2) Knowledge of external worlds is possible without the abstract idea 'Matter'.

(3) Acceptance of abstract ideas leads to atheism and materialism.

(4) A particular idea can be made to represent all other particular ideas of the same sort.

2024. According to Berkeley, it is possible for us to

(1) have some notion of spirit.

(2) perceive spirit

(3) have an idea of spirit

(4) doubt the existence of spirit.

2025. Who, among the following western philosophers attempted to refute 'Matter'?

(1) Kant (2) Berkeley
(3) Locke (4) Hume

2026. Berkeley's view that we cannot have an idea of the soul is based upon.

(1) rejection of innate ideas.

(2) rejection of abstract ideas.

(3) passivity of ideas

(4) distinction between simple and complex ideas

2027. According to Berkeley we do not have an idea of the soul because

(1) there is nothing like substratum

(2) we have no awareness of the soul

(3) self is active

(4) self is non spatial

2028. Berkeley says, 'we perceive a continual succession of ideas, some are a new excited, others are changed or totally disappear. There is, therefore, some cause of these ideas.' This cause according to him is

(1) sensible qualities of objects

(2) thought and imagination

(3) spirit (4) God

2029. Which one of the following views statements is acceptable to Berkeley?

(1) Everything that is real is an idea or a collection of ideas.

(2) Everything that is real depends for its existence on being perceived.

(3) There is no difference between a real and an imaginary object

(4) From the point of view of an individual perceiver, there exist ideas other than his own.

2030. Berkeley had to invoke the notion of an infinite spirit to give sanctity to the external world because

(1) his position on esse est percipi would have otherwise led him to solipsism.

(2) since God exists, he is by definition the creator of the world
(3) since he is an empiricist, he could not have posited ontological categories without God.
(4) perception was only a criterion, and not a proof of the external world.

2031. Which one of the following statements not accepted by Berkeley?
(1) Conception of a general idea is absurd
(2) There is no soul
(3) There is no matter
(4) Conception of spirit is absurd

2032. According to Berkeley, which one of the following is not a correct explanation of the term 'exist' in the statement 'The table exists'?
(1) The table is being perceived at present
(2) Given the right conditions the table would have been perceived
(3) The table is there though no spirit is perceiving it.
(4) The table is being thought of or conceived.

2033. Which one of the following is true of Locke's view of substance?
(1) Substance is the sum of qualities
(2) Substance is the substratum of qualities
(3) Substance is the some of ideas
(4) Substance is the logical construction of sense data

2034. Which one of the following arguments is advanced by Locke for the rejection of innate ideas?
(1) If there were innate ideas, then all human beings would be identical.
(2) If there were innate ideas then we should find them expressed in infants and untutored savages.
(3) If there were innate ideas then there must be a God who generates them
(4) If there were innate ideas than human beings should be eternal

2035. According to Locke the spirit and the body are
(1) identical
(2) very similar though not identical
(3) different but with the same properties
(4) different with different properties

2036. Which one of the following is not accepted by Locke
(1) There are no innate ideas is the mind
(2) There are innate powers in the mind
(3) All ideas of sensible qualities correctly represent the qualities of objects
(4) There are abstract ideas in the mind.

2037. Which one of the following is the correct definition of secondary qualities, according to Locke?
(1) Secondary qualities are nothing in the objects themselves but powers to produce sensations in us by their primary qualities.
(2) Secondary qualities are those which arc imposed on the external objects by human mind
(3) Secondary qualities are those that vary according to variations in conditions of perception
(4) Secondary qualities are those whose ideas are not exact resemblances of qualities of objects.

2038. Locke states that motion of substance is of an.................substratum.
(1) known (2) unknown
(3) qualityless (4) divine

2039. With regard to natural phenomena Berkeley............ causality.
(1) did not accept (2) accept
(3) confuses (4) None of these

2040. 'Matter is an abstract idea, for it means something which is moving and stationary, hard and soft etc. all and yet none of these.' This view is maintained by

(1) Locke (2) Hume
(3) Berkeley (4) Kant

2041. Which one of the following statement is not correct according to Locke?

(1) Substance is the permanent substratum of qualities.
(2) Substance is a complex idea made up of simple ideas put together by the mind.
(3) Material substance is directly known by us in sense perception.
(4) Substance is of two kinds, material and conscious.

2042. Which among the following is not included under the Berkeley's classification of spirit.

(1) Myself
(2) Others similar to myself
(3) Animal spirit
(4) God

2043. 'By attribute I mean that which the intellect perceives as constituting the essence of substance.' This statement is made by

(1) Descartes (2) Leibnitz
(3) Locke (4) Spinoza

2044. ....claims a material world which exists apart from perceiving mind, is unnecessary and false.

(1) Locke (2) Berkeley
(3) Descartes (4) Hume

2045. A thing in order to exist must be perceived by the......according to Berkely

(1) Subject (2) Mind
(3) Knower (4) None of these

2046. ....claims God as a creator who sustain the world as a system of ideas within his own mind.

(1) Locke (2) Berkeley
(3) Kant (4) Spinoza

2047. Which of the following books is not written by David Hume?

(1) A Treatise of Human Nature.
(2) An Enquiry Concerning Human Understanding
(3) Epistolae
(4) Of the immortality of the soul

2048. According to Hume there are two kinds of contents of the mind, namely, ...

(1) sensations and impressions.
(2) knowledge and ignorance.
(3) subjective and objective ideas.
(4) Impressions and their ideas.

2049. Which of the following does not match with Hume's view?

(1) Reflection is the copy of sensation
(2) Reflection is not the copy of sensation
(3) What is distinguishable is separable
(4) Impressions are always simple

2050. ....are always simple but the ideas can be both...........and complex.

(1) Sensation, simple
(2) Impressions, simple
(3) Imaginations, simple
(4) None of the above

2051. Hume's theory, that all impressions as such are distinct and separate with no logically connection between them, is known as

(1) Humean atomism
(2) Humean scepticism
(3) Humean agnosticism
(4) Humean idealism

2052. Hume does not believe in

(1) Causal relation exists
(2) External world is unreal
(3) Certainty of knowledge
(4) Moral principles and God are man-made entities

2053. For Hume..............consideration is relevant for epistemological analysis of causation.
(1) Mental (2) Physical
(3) Genetic (4) Specific

2054. 'Substance is a product of human imagination' is said by
(1) Descartes (2) Spinoza
(3) Locke (4) Hume

2055. ....believes that repeated experience and association lie at the root of our belief in a permanent material substance, underlying the collection of some qualities always found together.
(1) Hume (2) Spinoza
(3) Kant (4) Berkeley

2056. According to Berkeley, 'esse est percipi' means
(1) Existence is one of the basic qualities of perception.
(2) Existence is an inference from the fact of perception.
(3) Existence is different from perception.
(4) Existence consists in perception.

2057. Locke says intuitive knowledge is that which
(1) is self-evident and certain
(2) is gained through comparison
(3) we have in experience
(4) can be proved

2058. An Essay Concerning Human Understanding was written by
(1) Descartes (2) Spinoza
(3) Leibnitz (4) Locke

2059. According to Empiricists, all knowledge springs from
(1) Experience (2) Understanding
(3) God (4) Reason

2060. According to whom 'we know only what we experience in sensation and reflection'?
(1) Locke (2) Berkeley
(3) Hume (4) Descartes

2061. According to Berkeley esse est percipi means
(1) 'I think Therefore I am.'
(2) 'To be is to be perceived.'
(3) 'Doubt implies doubter.'
(4) 'Analysis of perceived things.'

2062. All knowledge, according to Locke, comes through two avenues ?
(1) Reason and Ideas
(2) Sensation and Reflection
(3) Ideas and Experience
(4) Experience and Reason

2063. 'The True Knowledge of External World is impossible' – is the view held by
(1) Spinoza (2) Leibnitz
(3) Locke (4) Berkeley

2064. The main aim of Berkeley in refuting *abstract* idea was
(1) to criticize Rationalism
(2) to criticize Locke
(3) to refute Matter
(4) to refute Idealism

2065. According to Hume, the contrary of every matter of fact is possible because
(1) it can never imply a contradiction
(2) the contrary is never a contradictory
(3) matters of fact are merely historically true
(4) we do imagine contrary to fact situations

2066. Which of the following is not a primary quality according to Locke?
(1) Extension (2) Hardness
(3) Motion (4) Solidity

2067. Match list I (Philosophers) with list II (Statements) and select the correct answer using the codes given below the lists :

List-I (Philosophers)	List-II (Statements)
(a) Berkeley and	(i) Body is the matter and soul is its form
(b) Aristotle	(ii) The soul is a distinct immaterial being or essence, imprisoned in the body.
(c) Plato	(iii) The soul is a spiritual substance.
(d) Locke	(iv) Mind alone is real and not matter.

Codes :	(a)	(b)	(c)	(d)
(1)	(iv)	(i)	(ii)	(iii)
(2)	(ii)	(iii)	(iv)	(i)
(3)	(i)	(iv)	(ii)	(iii)
(4)	(iv)	(i)	(iii)	(ii)

2068. Match list I (Idea) with list II (Thinkers) and select the correct answer using the codes given below the lists :

List-I	List-II
(a) Mind is indivisible unextended and consequently incorruptible	(i) Leibnitz
(b) Mind-body relationship is established on a causal basis	(ii) Spinoza
(c) Mind and body are the two aspects of a single substance	(iii) Berkeley
(d) Mind-body relation is explained in terms of a divine force.	(iv) Descartes

Codes :	(a)	(b)	(c)	(d)
(1)	(ii)	(iii)	(iv)	(i)
(2)	(iii)	(i)	(iv)	(ii)
(3)	(iii)	(iv)	(ii)	(i)
(4)	(i)	(iv)	(ii)	(iii)

2069. Match list I with list II and select the correct answer using the codes given below the lists :

List-I (Philosophers)	List-II (Theories)
(a) Locke	(i) Subjective Idealism
(b) Vaibhāṣikas	(ii) Objective Idealism
(c) Berkeley	(iii) Epistemological dualism
(d) Saṁkara	(iv) Naive Realism

Codes :	(a)	(b)	(c)	(d)
(1)	(iv)	(iii)	(ii)	(i)
(2)	(iii)	(iv)	(i)	(ii)
(3)	(iii)	(iv)	(ii)	(i)
(4)	(iv)	(iii)	(ii)	(i)

2070. Match list I with list II and select the correct answer using the codes given below the lists :

List-I (Philosophers)	List-II (Theories)
(a) Descartes	(i) Parallelism
(b) Spinoza	(ii) Interactionism
(c) Leibnitz	(iii) Mentalism
(d) Berkeley	(iv) Reestablished harmony

Codes :	(a)	(b)	(c)	(d)
(1)	(i)	(ii)	(iii)	(iv)
(2)	(ii)	(i)	(iv)	(iii)
(3)	(iii)	(ii)	(i)	(iv)
(4)	(i)	(ii)	(iv)	(iii)

2071. Match list I (Philosophers) with list II (Works) and select the correct answer using the codes given below the lists :

List-I	List-II
(a) Spinoza	(i) Principles of Human knowledge
(b) Plato	(ii) Ethics
(c) Descartes	(iii) Parmenides
(d) Berkeley	(iv) Discourse on Method

Codes :	(a)	(b)	(c)	(d)
(1)	(ii)	(iii)	(iv)	(i)
(2)	(i)	(ii)	(iii)	(iv)
(3)	(iii)	(ii)	(iv)	(i)
(4)	(ii)	(iii)	(i)	(iv)

2072. Match list I with list II and select the correct answer from the codes given below:

List-I	List-II
(a) Leibnitz	(i) An Enquiry concerning Human understanding
(b) Locke	(ii) La Monadologie
(c) Berkeley	(iii) Essay concerning Human understanding
(d) Hume	(iv) New Theory of vision

Codes :	(a)	(b)	(c)	(d)
(1)	(i)	(ii)	(iii)	(iv)
(2)	(ii)	(iii)	(iv)	(i)
(3)	(iii)	(iv)	(i)	(ii)
(4)	(iv)	(i)	(ii)	(iii)

2073. Match list I with list II and select the correct answer by using the codes given below the list

List-I	List-II
(a) Leibnitz	(i) France
(b) Descartes	(ii) England
(c) John Locke	(iii) Rome
(d) Cicero	(iv) Germany

Codes :	(a)	(b)	(c)	(d)
(1)	(iv)	(i)	(ii)	(iii)
(2)	(iv)	(ii)	(i)	(iii)
(3)	(iii)	(iv)	(i)	(ii)
(4)	(iii)	(ii)	(i)	(iv)

2074. Match list I with list II and select the correct answer by using the codes given below the lists :

List-I	List-II
(a) Substance must be known by the mind	(i) Kaṇāda
(b) Sensations convince us that there are solid extended substances, and reflection convinces that there is thinking substance.	(ii) Descartes
(c) Substance exists in itself and is conceived by itself.	(iii) Locke
(d) Substance is a category which is the substratum of qualities and actions.	(iv) Berkeley
	(v) Aristotle

Codes :	(a)	(b)	(c)	(d)
(1)	(iv)	(iii)	(ii)	(i)
(2)	(i)	(v)	(iv)	(iii)
(3)	(ii)	(iv)	(iii)	(i)
(4)	(iv)	(iii)	(ii)	(v)

2075. Match list I with list II and select the correct answer by using the codes given below the lists :

List-I	List-II
(a) Locke	(i) God is the absolute and matter and mind are the created substances
(b) Berkeley	(ii) There is only one substance, i.e., God
(c) Descartes	(iii) God, mind and matter are three kinds of substance
(d) Spinoza	(iv) Only mind and their ideas exist.

Codes :	(a)	(b)	(c)	(d)
(1)	(iii)	(iv)	(ii)	(i)
(2)	(iii)	(iv)	(i)	(ii)
(3)	(iv)	(iii)	(i)	(ii)
(4)	(ii)	(i)	(iii)	(iv)

2076. Match list I with list II and select the correct answer by using the codes given below the list :

List-I	List-II
(a) Descartes	(i) Mind and matter are not substances
(b) Spinoza	(ii) Ideas are of two types, simple and complex
(c) Locke	(iii) Substantiality of mind exists as the bearer of ideas
(d) Berkeley	(iv) Created substances are of two kinds, corporeal and spiritual.

Codes :	(a)	(b)	(c)	(d)
(1)	(iv)	(ii)	(iii)	(i)
(2)	(iv)	(i)	(ii)	(iii)
(3)	(iii)	(iv)	(i)	(ii)
(4)	(iii)	(i)	(ii)	(iv)

2077. Match list I with list II and select the correct answer by using the codes given below the lists :

List-I	List-II
(a) Locke	(i) Matter is corporeal and mind is spiritual
(b) Descartes	(ii) Material world exists apart from perceiving mind is false
(c) Berkeley	(iii) There are no innate principles in this mind.

Codes :	(a)	(b)	(c)
(1)	(i)	(ii)	(iii)
(2)	(iii)	(ii)	(i)
(3)	(iii)	(i)	(ii)
(4)	(i)	(iii)	(ii)

2078. Match list I with list II and select the correct answer by using the codes given below the lists :

List-I	List-II
(a) Locke	(i) Mind and matter depend upon God.
(b) Berkeley	(ii) Understanding is like a piece of white paper on which perception inscribes.
(c) Descartes	(iii) Sensible things are always perceived by God.

Codes :	(a)	(b)	(c)
(1)	(ii)	(iii)	(i)
(2)	(ii)	(i)	(iii)
(3)	(iii)	(ii)	(i)
(4)	(i)	(iii)	(ii)

2079. Match list I with list II and select the correct answer by using the codes given below the lists :

List I	List II
(a) Locke	(i) Sensible things have no absolute existence independent of mind.
(b) Hume	(ii) Ideas first known are particular impressions of the senses.
(c) Berkeley	(iii) The notion of substance is a fiction of the mind.

Codes :	(a)	(b)	(c)
(1)	(ii)	(iii)	(i)
(2)	(ii)	(i)	(iii)
(3)	(i)	(ii)	(iii)
(4)	(i)	(iii)	(ii)

2080. Match the following

List-I	List-II
(a) Locke	(i) Rational
(b) Berkeley	(ii) Bundle theorist
(c) Hume	(iii) Rejection of material
(d) Descartes	(iv) Idea of substance

Codes :	(a)	(b)	(c)	(d)
(1)	(i)	(ii)	(iii)	(iv)
(2)	(iv)	(iii)	(ii)	(i)
(3)	(iv)	(ii)	(iii)	(i)
(4)	(ii)	(iv)	(iii)	(i)

2081. Match the following

List-I	List-II
(a) Problem of induction	(i) Attributes
(b) Immaterialism	(ii) Berkeley
(c) Idea of modes	(iii) Hume
(d) Spinoza	(iv) Locke

Codes :	(a)	(b)	(c)	(d)
(1)	(i)	(ii)	(iii)	(iv)
(2)	(ii)	(iii)	(iv)	(i)
(3)	(iv)	(iii)	(ii)	(i)
(4)	(iii)	(ii)	(iv)	(i)

2082. Match the following

List-I	List-II
(a) Locke	(i) Sensations convince us

(b) Berkeley (ii) Subjective idealist
(c) Descartes (iii) Substance exist in itself
(d) Hume (iv) Sceptic

Codes : (a) (b) (c) (d)
(1) (i) (ii) (iii) (iv)
(2) (iv) (iii) (ii) (i)
(3) (iv) (ii) (iii) (i)
(4) (i) (iv) (iii) (ii)

2083. Match the following

List-I	List-II
(a) Locke	(i) Matters of fact
(b) Berkeley	(ii) Tabula rasa
(c) Descartes	(iii) God perceived sensible things
(d) Hume	(iv) Regulae

Codes : (a) (b) (c) (d)
(1) (i) (ii) (iii) (iv)
(2) (ii) (iii) (iv) (i)
(3) (iv) (iii) (ii) (i)
(4) (iii) (ii) (iv) (i)

2084. Match the following

List-I	List-II
(a) Descartes	(i) Sceptic
(b) Berkeley	(ii) Non-sceptic
(c) Locke	(iii) Critique of abstract ideas
(d) Hume	(iv) Metaphysics

Codes : (a) (b) (c) (d)
(1) (i) (ii) (iii) (iv)
(2) (iv) (ii) (iii) (i)
(3) (ii) (iii) (iv) (i)
(4) (i) (iv) (iii) (ii)

2085. Match the following

List-I	List-II
(a) Locke	(i) Simple
(b) Berkeley	(ii) Of the immortiality of the soul
(c) Hume	(iii) New theory of vision
(d) Ideas of modes	(iv) Rejection of innate ideas

Codes : (a) (b) (c) (d)
(1) (i) (ii) (iii) (iv)
(2) (ii) (iii) (iv) (i)
(3) (iv) (iii) (ii) (i)
(4) (ii) (iv) (iii) (i)

2086. Match the following

List-I	List-II
(a) Locke	(i) Theory of knowledge
(b) Ideas	(ii) Idealist
(c) Hume	(iii) Impressions
(d) Berkeley	(iv) Simple

Codes : (a) (b) (c) (d)
(1) (i) (ii) (iii) (iv)
(2) (iv) (iii) (ii) (i)
(3) (ii) (iv) (iii) (i)
(4) (i) (iv) (iii) (ii)

2087. Match the following

List-I	List-II
(a) Locke	(i) Idea of substance
(b) Berkeley	(ii) Esse est percipi
(c) Hume	(iii) Agnostic
(d) Spinoza	(iv) Rationalist

Codes : (a) (b) (c) (d)
(1) (i) (ii) (iii) (iv)
(2) (iv) (ii) (iii) (i)
(3) (ii) (iv) (iii) (i)
(4) (i) (iv) (iii) (ii)

Directions : The following items consist of two statements, one labelled as the 'Assertion A' and the other labelled as 'Reason R'. You are to examine these two statements carefully and decide if the Assertion 'A' and the Reason 'R' are individually true and if so, whether the Reason is a correct explanation of the Assertion. Select your answer to these items using the codes given below and mark your answer sheet accordingly :

Codes :

(1) Both A and R are true and R is the correct explanation of A.
(2) Both A and R are true but R is not the correct explanation of A.
(3) A is true but R is false.
(4) A is false but R is true

2088. **Assertion (A).** Locke says, 'the real nature of mind is unknown.'

Reason (R). We get the knowledge of mind through reflection.

2089. **Assertion (A).** Locke was compelled to say, 'Substance is something I know not what.'

Reason (R). Locke draws a distinction between intuitive, demonstrative and 'sensitive' knowledge.

2090. **Assertion (A).** Locke made a distinction between primary and secondary qualities.

Reason (R). Locke sought to distinguish between appearance and reality.

2091. **Assertion (A).** Locke believed that there are physical objects existing independently of our perception.

Reason (R). A counterpart of the external object is sometimes regarded as a representation of it.

2092. **Assertion (A).** The ideas of imagination are produced by ourselves, real perceptions are produced by God.

Reason (R). Things do not exist independently of perception according to Berkeley.

2093. **Assertion (A).** If nominalism says that what occurs in our minds is only images, then it is wrong.

Reason (R). There are concepts, over and above any images we may have.

2094. **Assertion (A).** Sensible things are ideas in finite mind given by God, suggested by Berkeley.

Reason (R). Sensible things are imprinted on or presented to finite minds by the unceasing divine activity.

2095. **Assertion (A).** Material objects have no reality independent of our sense-experience according to Berkeley.

Reason (R). God as a creator, sustains the world as a system of ideas within his own mind.

2096. **Assertion (A).** The idea of substance cannot be called innate idea.

Reason (R). The empiricist philosophers believe that the idea of substance is not derived from experience.

2097. **Assertion (A).** Idea is eternal and unchangeable reality beyond space and time.

Reason (R). Substance is a universal and general idea.

2098. **Assertion (A).** Locke thinks that there are no innate principles in the mind.

Reason (R). Ideas are not present in the understanding from the beginning, but received through sensation.

2099. **Assertion (A).** Locke admit both the primary and secondary qualities.

Reason (R). Some of the simple ideas represent the properties of things are they really are.

2100. **Assertion (A).** Hume says that the certainty of mathematical reasoning cannot be ultimately guaranteed.

Reason (R). Hume believes in the frailty of the judging powers of man.

2101. **Assertion (A).** According to Hume knowledge is only probable.

Reason (R). He maintains that the rules of the demonstrative sciences are 'certain and infallible' but due to our frail faculties our application of them is notoriously fallible.

2102. **Assertion (A).** Hume shows that in causation there is no logical but psychological necessity.

Reason (R). Hume accepts the law of association.

2103. **Assertion (A).** Locke says, that innate ideas don't exist.

Reason (R). Mind is a blank slate.

2104. **Assertion (A).** The real nature of mind is regarded as unknown according to Locke.

Reason (R). The knowledge of mind is known through reflection.

2105. **Assertion (A).** According to Locke, a distinction between primary and secondary quality exist.

Reason (R). Locke also made a distinction between appearance and reality.

2106. **Assertion (A).** According to Berkeley, external or material things don't exist.

Reason (R). He was against abstract ideas.

2107. **Assertion (A).** Berkeley was regarded as subjective idealist.

Reason (R). His subjective idealist was reduced to solipsist.

2108. **Assertion (A).** Berkeley believes in immaterialism.

Reason (R). He believes in the rejection of the distinction between primary and secondary quality.

2109. **Assertion (A).** Hume was regarded as sceptic.

Reason (R). He believes in the rejection of mctaphysics.

2110. **Assertion (A).** Locke says, that idea of modes comes under the domain of complex ideas.

Reason (R). He believes in natural ideas.

2111. **Assertion (A)** : According to Locke, to start with mind is a tabula rasa.

Reason (R) : Locke rejects Innate Ideas.

2112. **Assertion (A).** Locke made a distinction between primary and secondary qualities.

Reason (R). Locke sought to distinguish between appearance and reality.

2113. Berkeley rejected abstract ideas on one or more of the following grounds.

A. Abstract ideas represent universals which exist

B. Abstract ideas represent universals which cannot exist.

C. Abstract ideas are mere general names of particular objects.

Which of the above is/are correct?

Codes:

(1) A alone (2) A and B

(3) A and C (4) B and C

2114. According to Berkeley, which of the following statements are correct?

A. The abstract general ideas are rejected.

B. It is not possible to frame an idea of a triangle which includes all the characteristics of different types.

C. The general ideas, too, have no function to perform.

Select the correct answer using the codes given below :

(1) A and B (2) B and C

(3) A and C (4) A, B and C

2115. If A and B is causally related, then which among the following is not the necessary and sufficient condition of A becoming the cause of B according to Hume.

A. A be precedent and contiguous to B.

B. Events resembling A be precedent and contiguous to events resembling B.

C. The idea of A be associated with the idea of B.

D. The idea of A be followed by the idea of B.

E. B must be present in A.

(1) A and B (2) B and D

(3) Only E (4) D and E

2116. Locke talks about

A. primary qualities

B. secondary qualities

C. empirical qualities

D. external qualities

Codes:

(1) B and C (2) A and B

(3) All of the above (4) None of these

2117. Hume was regarded as

A. empiricist B. positivist

C. rationalist D. negativist

Codes:

(1) A and B (2) B and C

(3) C and D (4) A and D

2118. Berkeley regarded as

A. immaterialism B. subjective idealist

C. rationalist D. materialist

Codes:

(1) A and B (2) B and C

(3) B and D (4) A and D

2119. Berkeley rejects

A. abstract ideas

B. materialism

C. non-abstract ideas

D. empiricism

Codes:

(1) A and B (2) B and C

(3) A and C (4) A and D

2120. For Locke, knowledge means

A. agreement B. disagreement

C. similarity D. dissimilarity

Codes:

(1) A and B (2) B and C

(3) B and D (4) A and D

2121. Which one of the following statements is not associated with kantian ethics?

(1) Reason is the regulative principle in the life of a person.

(2) The moral law is made for the sake of man and not man for the sake of law.

(3) The complete good is virtue and happiness in harmony with each other.

(4) Prudence has nothing to do with virtue.

2122. In Kant's view imperfect duties are imperfect because

(1) their maxims cannot be willed so as to become universal law of nature.

(2) they are only self-regarding

(3) they can overridden by perfect duties.

(4) they are not determinate.

2123. The meaning of a categorical imperative, as defined by Kant, can be elucidated as

(1) you must do X because X is good in itself.

(2) you must do X because X is good for attaining happiness.

(3) you must do X because there is nothing better than X.

(4) You must do X because the divine will so commands.

2124. According to Kant, moral duty is

(1) the command of God

(2) given by one's intuition

(3) the imperative of pure reason

(4) determined by majority

2125. In Kantian ethics, 'an objective principle of action' is called

(1) a maxim (2) a rule

(3) a practical law (4) an imperative

2126. As per Kantian ethics, saving the life of person at the risk of his own life is

(1) determinate duty

(2) indeterminate duty

(3) divine duty

(4) human obligation

2127. The formula of the end-in-itself in Kantian ethics enjoins us to treat a person

(1) always only as an end

(2) sometimes as an end

(3) never simply as a means

(4) always as a means

2128. According to Kant, a person becomes aware of the freedom of his will because

(1) it is an a priori condition of the experience of obligation

(2) he has empirical experience of it

(3) it is an a priori condition of experience of senses
(4) it can be demonstrated by science

2129. According to Kant, we ought to treat humanity
(1) Always only as an end
(2) Sometimes as an end
(3) Always only as means
(4) Never only as a means

2130. For Kant, the notion of 'ought' is applicable to
(1) Animals
(2) Fully rational creatures
(3) 'A Holy will'
(4) man who is rational and yet has inclinations

2131. According to Kant, abstract from the personal differences and the content of personal differences is required in the categorical imperative in the context of the formula of
(1) Universal law
(2) Universal law of nature
(3) End in itself
(4) Kingdom of ends

2132. According to Kant, moral law is
(1) a priori, and based on reason.
(2) *a priori,* and not based on reason.
(3) *a posteriori,* and not based on reason.
(4) *a posteriori,* and based on reason.

2133. Kant's Copernican revolution in philosophy is
(1) The mind must approach the objects to be known at all.
(2) The objects must approach the mind to be known at all.
(3) Mind obtained reason because of sun.
(4) None of the above

2134. 'Reason must approach the nature not as a pupil but as a judge' is
(1) Descartes' view (2) Augustine's view
(3) Kant's view (4) Locke's view

2135. The evolution of idealism after the disintegration of the Hegelian school was the result of the..............its progressive social role and fighting against dialectical materialism.
(1) Capitalists reforming
(2) Bourgeoisie abandoning
(3) Bourgeoisie presenting
(4) None of the above

2136. ....is the author of an all-embracing system of dialectical idealism.
(1) Hegel (2) Kant
(3) Hume (4) None of these

2137. According to Hegel
(1) The personal God of Christianity is the Absolute Reality.
(2) The world spirit is some sort of personal mind
(3) (1) and (2) both
(4) None of the above

2138. According to whom, "Punishment is the negative reward of the criminals"?
(1) Kant (2) Bradley
(3) Both (1) and (2)
(4) None of the above

2139. 'A system of categories arranged dialectically in triads' is the description of
(1) Substance (2) Spirit
(3) Hegelean Method (4) The Absolute

2140. According to Hegel, there are three stages in the logical development of spirit : subjective mind, objective mind and
(1) Absolute God (2) Absolute mind
(3) Absolute spirit (4) Absolute idea

2141. The spirit posits its other, in the form of Nature and life. In Hegelean words this movement is

(1) Thesis (2) Anti-thesis
(3) Synthesis (4) None of these

2142. ....method, which is the proper method of philosophy, according to Hegel, is determined by the subject matter of philosophy itself.

(1) The synthetical
(2) The analytical
(3) The dialectical
(4) The geometrical

2143. In Transcendental Aesthetic, Kant discusses the theory of

(1) Knowledge (2) Space and time
(3) Existence of God
(4) Morality

2144. The spirit-in-itself is undisturbed identity or unity within itself, which as yet is obvious of its object. This movement is known as (in Hegel's words)

(1) Thesis (2) Anti-thesis
(3) Synthesis (4) None of these

2145. Kant's conception of the 'Kingdom of ends' approximates to the Gitā's conception of

(1) Asceticism
(2) Solidarity of humanity
(3) Humanism
(4) None of the above

2146. ....ethics is formalistic, but the ethics of............is teleological.

(1) Kant's, the Hindus
(2) Ross, the West
(3) Kant's, the Gitā
(4) None of the above

2147. There is the final movement in which the spirit reduces Nature to the inwardness, which the spirit itself is. Only at this stage the spirit rises to self consciousness in man. According to Hegel this stage is

(1) Thesis (2) Antithesis
(3) Synthesis (4) None of these

2148. Kant believes that the will is................ when it is a law unto itself, when it acts solely from a sense of duty.

(1) Compulsory (2) Autonomous
(3) Independent (4) None of these

2149. Kant suggests that a will is..........when it is guided by some end or moved by desire.

(1) Autonomous (2) Heternomous
(3) Dependent (4) None of these

2150. Kant's rationalism is akin to philosophical

(1) Rigorism
(2) Refined hedonism
(3) intuitionism
(4) None of the above

2151. Which is regarded as practical reason in Kant's view?

(1) Conscience
(2) Sense-experience
(3) True belief
(4) None of the above

2152. Kant's rationalism is opposed to

(1) Empiricism (2) Hedonism
(3) Neo-Plantonism (4) None of these

2153. Who among following philosophers maintains the view that 'nothing can possibly be conceived in the world, or even out of it, which can be called good without qualification except a good will"?

(1) Plato (2) Kant
(3) Hegel (4) G.E. Moore

2154. The key motion of Hegel is

(1) The world (2) Idea
(3) Geist (4) None of these

2155. ....agrees that rightness of actions is objective and apprehended only by reason.

(1) Bentham (2) Kant
(3) Ross (4) None of these

2156. In the physical world we connect the determination of events by............with the ability to predict events.

(1) A posteriori causes
(2) Antecedent causes
(3) Ultimate causes
(4) None of the above

2157. For Kant, freedom of will is

(1) An impossibility
(2) A vague concept
(3) One of the postulates of morality
(4) An a posteriori truth

2158. Kant's rationalism is a kind of

(1) Rigorism
(2) Categorical imperative
(3) Rational intuitionism
(4) None of the above

2159. God is moral posture has been defined by

(1) Bradley (2) Immanuel Kant
(3) William James (4) None of these

2160. Duties ought to be performed for the sake of duty, this standpoint of Gitā resembles with that of

(1) Kant (2) Frankena
(3) Ross (4) None of these

2161. ....argues that the demand of the conscience for justice and equity points to the existence of a future life.

(1) Kant (2) Martineau
(3) Hoffding (4) None of these

2162. Kant, after speaking of truth and goodness, sets out to discuss the nature of beauty in his critique of

(1) Practical reason
(2) Pure reason
(3) Judgement
(4) None of the above

2163. The knowledge which is constructed by the understanding, by means of its categories, is the knowledge of the phenomena, and as regards noumena, which Kant, by preference, calls things-in-themselves, they lie entirely beyond the application of categories. So we cannot have any knowledge of noumenal world at all. This is what is proved by Kant in the

(1) Transcendental Analytic
(2) Transcendental Dialectic
(3) Transcendental Synthetic
(4) None of the above

2164. According to Kant, the transcendental illusion arise out of the very nature of reason because of its irresistible temptation to regard the ideas of the soul, the world as a totality and

(1) Knowledge (2) Substance
(3) God (4) None of these

2165. Who has called spinozism as a black night in which all cows are equally black.

(1) Kant (2) Bradeley
(3) Hume (4) Hegel

2166. The Absolute for Hegel is

(1) Substance (2) Soul
(3) God (4) Idea

2167. 'The real is the rational, and the rational is the real' is the doctrine of

(1) Fichte (2) Schelling
(3) Kant (4) Hegel

2168. Who said 'History is general is the development of spirit in time, as nature is the development of the idea in space?"

(1) Fichte (2) Schelling
(3) Kant (4) Hegel

2169. According to Hegel, in moral evolution there is transition from goodness, as the outward submission to an external law, to goodness, as inward submission to the internal law of conscience, both being reconciled in a social morality which is their

(1) Thesis (2) Anti-thesis
(3) Synthesis (4) None of these

2170. Criminology regards every crime as a..............phenomenon, a mild form of insanity, an innate or acquired physiological defect

(1) Psychological
(2) Sociological
(3) Pathlogical
(4) None of these

2171. According to the Absolute Idealism of Hegel

(1) There is only one reality
(2) Reality is relative
(3) There are many realities
(4) None of the above

2172. According to Kant, knowledge begins with sense, proceeds thence to..........and ends in...........

(1) Understanding, reason
(2) Reason, understanding
(3) Noumena, phenomena
(4) None of the above

2173. Kant has called his epistemological enquiry

(1) Critical (2) Agnostic
(3) Transcendental (4) Rational

2174. According to Kant the ideas of reason are not.........but.........pinciples of knowledge.

(1) Regulative, constitutive
(2) Affirmative, negative
(3) Negative, affirmative
(4) Constitutive, regulative

2175. According to Kant the mode of our knowledge of objects is to be possible

(1) A posteriori (2) A priori
(3) (1) and (2) both
(4) None of the above

2176. A further process of synthesis is effected a priori by the three ideas of reason, namely, ...

(1) Sense, object, knowledge
(2) Intellect, intuition, cognition
(3) World, soul, God
(4) Mind, body, absolute

2177. For Hegel, Idea means

(1) Concrete particular
(2) Concrete universal
(3) Abstract particular
(4) Abstract universal

2178. That branch of philosophy according to which it is claimed that human beings have no faculty for knowing certain ultimate realities, is known as

(1) Scepticism (2) Agnosticism
(3) Idealism (4) Realism

2179. Kant's philosophy is known as

(1) Criticism (2) Rationalism
(3) Empiricism (4) Dogmatism

2180. A proposition in which the predicate does not belong to the subject, is known as

(1) Synthetic (2) Analytic
(3) Simple (4) Complex

2181. Who has stated 'knowledge by Acquaintance' and 'knowledge by Description' ?

(1) Ayer (2) Moore
(3) Russell (4) Ryle

2182. Logical Atomism is the doctrine propounded by

(1) Wittgenstein (2) Russell
(3) Quine (4) Ryle

2183. Who propounded the theory of 'Language Game'?
(1) Whitehead (2) G.E. Moore
(3) Wittgenstein (4) A.J. Ayer

2184. The Philosopher who defended common sense philosophy is
(1) Berkeley (2) Hegel
(3) Moore (4) Green

2185. Nietzsche's ethics may be considered
(1) Naturalistic (2) Hedonistic
(3) Realistic (4) None of these

2186. What man desire most, according to Nietzsche, is
(1) Money (2) Liberation
(3) Love (4) Power

2187. Suffering as an ingredient of the creative life and also as a means to the requisite self control, is condemned by
(1) Russell (2) Moore
(3) Nietzsche (4) None of these

2188. Who says that "Philosophy is a battle against the betwitchment of intelligence by language."
(1) Russell (2) Moore
(3) Wittgentein (4) Heidegger

2189. Nietzsche thinks that life is ever risked willingly for a change of
(1) more money (2) greater power
(3) peacefull life (4) None of these

2190. Who among the following accepts the possession and creative exercise of power as happiness?
(1) Sartre (2) Goethe
(3) Nietzsche (4) Moore

2191. 'Ubermenschen' (superman) is considered by
(1) Sartre (2) Goethe
(3) Nietzsche (4) Moore

2192. The superiority of superman, according to Nietzsche, is a function of
(1) race (2) caste
(3) culture (4) none of these

2193. Man can attain the state of superman by
(1) sublimating his impulses
(2) employing impulses creatively
(3) forcefully acting on impulses
(4) (1) and (2) together

2194. According to Nietzsche, we lack great power as long as we are dominated by
(1) animal passions (2) a penchant
(3) love (4) weakness

2195. Those who attain, according to Nietzsche, the state of great power are
(1) Ubermenschen (2) Gods
(3) Demons (4) None of these

2196. According to Moore, Berkeley is guilty of a confusion between the sensation as a conscious act of sensing and
(1) perception of external objects
(2) sensation as the object sensed
(3) (1) and (2) both
(4) None of the above

2197. Nietzsche, Spengler, Bergson are the exponents of
(1) Nominalism (2) Pragmatism
(3) Realism (4) None of these

2198. According to.................., in order to comprehend the 'essence of existence' man must deny himself any considerations of aim or practicality, realise his morality, frailty.
(1) Kierkegaard (2) Sartre
(3) Heidegger (4) None of these

2199. Sartre, Heidegger are the .... philosophers.
(1) Existentialist (2) Nominalist
(3) Idealist (4) Realist

2200. 'Universal is an eternal timeless entity which may be shared by many particulars'—this view is also accepted by the modern realists like

(1) A.J. Ayer (2) Bertrand Russell
(3) G.E. Moore (4) B.R. Gross

2201. 'World is ultimately meaningless and it is necessary to struggle with it' is suggested by

(1) Kant (2) Hume
(3) F.H. Bradley (4) Nietzsche

2202. *The Consolation of Philosophy* is written by

(1) Boethius (2) Kant
(3) Aquinas (4) Leibnitz

2203. The true founder of modern phenomenology is

(1) Heidegger (2) Russell
(3) Sartre (4) Husserl

2204. Phenomenology is subjectivistic in that its investigations are initially directed, in ...., towards the ego and its presentations.

(1) Conversational fashion
(2) Cartesian fashion
(3) Mautic fashion (4) None of these

2205. ...., according to Husserl, is an intrinsic trait of the subjective process of consciousness whereby they refer to objects.

(1) Sensationality (2) Philosophy
(3) Intentionality (4) Metaphysics

2206. Husserl frequently uses the expression .... to refer to the purification of experience of its factuality.

(1) Intentionality (2) Meditation
(3) Rationality (4) Epoche

2207. Who among the following criticized Christianity as 'slaves' revolt and as 'slave morality'?

(1) Sartre (2) Russell
(3) Nietzsche (4) Moore

2208. Nietzsche has given one word for the sentence 'the secret hatred and envy of all those more favoured than oneself'.

(1) Ressentiment (2) Renunciation
(3) Sublimation (4) Denunciation

2209. The dominant strain in.............thinking is to examine and discuss an idea in exclusion from other ideas and scrupulous avoidance of mixing up and merging of Ideas.

(1) G.E. Moore (2) Nietzsche
(3) Berkeley (4) None

2210. The procedure given in question no. 2209 is known as

(1) Synthesis (2) Analysis
(3) Dialectic (4) None of these

2211. Moore was an analyst of

(1) Idealism (2) Immaterialism
(3) Ideas per excellence
(4) None of the above

2212. Moore is

(1) Idealist (2) Immaterialist
(3) Subjective Idealist
(4) Realist

2213. The statement, 'Logic is a mirror image of the world', is made by

(1) Wittgenstein (2) Russell
(3) Quine (4) Ryle

2214. The article, Refutation of Idealism, appeared in MIND, London in 1903, was written by

(1) Bertrand Russell (2) Whitehead
(3) J.S. Mill (4) G.E. Moore

2215. How many meanings, according to Moore, does the conjoining word 'est' in Esse est percipi' has?

(1) 1 (2) 3
(3) 5 (4) 7

2216. 'Treating equals equally and unequals unequally' is the view of :
(1) Socrates (2) Bentham
(3) Aristotle (4) Mill

2217. How many kinds of propositions are there?
(1) 5 (2) 4
(3) 3 (4) 3

2218. Which kinds of propositions are said to be tautologies?
(1) Analytic (2) Synthetic
(3) (1) and (2) both
(4) Neither (1) nor (2)

2219. Nietzche's 'Ressentiment' is associated with
(1) the state of public
(2) the state of mind
(3) the state of life
(4) Neitzsche's critique of Christian Morals

2220. Nietzsche's 'revaluation of all values' consists in an internal criticism of
(1) Modernity (2) traditionality
(3) Christian ethics
(4) None of the above

2221. For Peirce, the habit which any idea establishes is
(1) the meaning of that idea
(2) the tendency of that idea
(3) Only appearance of that idea
(4) None of the above

2222. According to Peirce A belief affects
(1) Our action (2) Our habits
(3) Our body (4) None of these

2223. The conception of soul in Buddhism as an unbrokwn stream of consciousness is also in the philosophy of
(1) C.S. Peirce (2) William James
(3) John Dewey (4) Bertrand Russell

2224. The philosophy of Nietzsche inspired the political ideology of
(1) Natzism (2) Fascism
(3) Socialism (4) Marxism

2225. "Dead are all Gods". Who said this?
(1) Schopenhauer (2) Nietzsche
(3) Darwin (4) Herbert Spencer

2226. Nietzsche's conception of superman may be contrasted with.......conception of superman.
(1) Gandhi's (2) Sri Aurobindo's
(3) Swami Vivekananda's
(4) Raja Ram Mohan Roy's

2227. The Refutation of Idealism is an article of Moore, which is based on the criticism of one ultimate premiss
(1) Cogito ergo sum
(2) Esse est percipii
(3) Causa sui (4) Natura naturans

2228. 'Semiotic' or theory of signs was developed by
(1) C.S. Peirce (2) William James
(3) Johns Dewey (4) None of these

2229. According to Berkeley esse est percipi means
(1) 'I think Therefore I am.'
(2) 'To be is to be perceived.'
(3) 'Doubt implies doubter.'
(4) 'Analysis of perceived things.'

2230. Russell's theory of propositional functions is a theory about
(1) Absolute (2) Universal
(3) Substance (4) Particular

2231. Who among the following has strongly rejected the Descartes theory of dualism between matter and mind?
(1) Moore (2) C.S. Peirce
(3) Russell (4) All of these

2232. Select the logical positivist among the following :
(1) Husserl (2) Heidegger
(3) A.J. Ayer (4) C.S. Pierce

2233. Who utilitarianism don't believe in what?
(1) J.S. Mill (2) Bentham
(3) Aristotle (4) Kant

2234. The doctrine of the stream of thoughts is given by
(1) C.S. Peirce (2) Moore
(3) James (4) Russell

2235. Nietzsche has not written the following book
(1) Beyond Good and Evil
(2) Thus Spake Zarathustra
(3) Will to Power
(4) The World as Will and Idea

2236. Concept of 'Category mistake' is advocated by
(1) William James (2) Heidegger
(3) Gilbert Ryle (4) G.E. Moore

2237. Who among the following thinkers maintains that the truth of an idea is not a stagnant property inherent in it ?
(1) Russell (2) William James
(3) Ayer (4) Moore

2238. According to Kant knowledge consists of
(1) synthetic a priori judgements
(2) synthetic a posteriori judgements
(3) analytic judgements
(4) none of the above

2239. G. E. Moore refutes the following doctrine of the idealists
(1) Time is unreal
(2) To be is to be perceived
(3) Reality is spiritual
(4) All relations are internal

2240. Which one of the following is NOT the work of Bertrand Russell ?
(1) Discourse on method
(2) Our knowledge of the external world
(3) An inquiry into meaning and truth
(4) Human knowledge : Its scope and limits

2241. Pragmatism is characterised by.............as "a new name for same old ways of thinking."
(1) C.S. Peirce (2) William James
(3) John Dewey (4) C.I. Lewis

2242. Pragmatism is a method of inquiry and a theory of meaning and truth derived from .... and applicable to philosophy.
(1) Mathematics (2) Natural sciences
(3) Logic (4) Psychology

2243. Who enunciated the pragmatic principle in an epoch-making article entitled "How to make our idea clear"?
(1) C.S. Peirce (2) James
(3) Dewey (4) C.I. Lewis

2244. ....is an attempt to constitute a precise logical theory of concepts, of judgements and inferences in their various forms by considering primarily how thought functions in the experimental determination of future consequence
(1) Pragmatism (2) Existentialism
(3) Instrumentalism (4) Positivism

2245. Phenomenology is an investigation of phenomena and it deals with...........only but not the...............
(1) Universals, Particulars
(2) Particulars, Universals
(3) Quality, Quantity
(4) Quantity, Quality

2246. ....was the official founder of existentialism and believed that existence precedes essence.
(1) Karl Jaspers (2) Martin Heidegger
(3) Soren Kierkegaard
(4) Jean Paul Sartre

2247. The proposition, basic to Idealism, which Moore rejects is
(1) Ideas are no less real than matter
(2) *Esse est percipii* (To be, is to be perceived)

(3) The thing-in- itself is non-empirical
(4) *Cogito, ergo Sum* (I think therefore I am)

2248. ....as a constructive epistemological position asserts that the object of knowledge is distinct from an independent of the act of awareness.
(1) Idealism (2) Rationalism
(3) Empiricism (4) Realism

2249. ....maintains that there are no universal moral rules which apply to all persons.
(1) Subjectivism
(2) Objectivism
(3) Ethical relativism
(4) Naturalism

2250. Willium James favours
(1) Objective life (2) Moral life
(3) Useless life (4) Subjective life

2251. According to James, which of the following has to steer us practically as their most important function.
(1) Percepts (2) Thoughts
(3) Concepts (4) None of these

2252. James distinguished.............ends or parts served by concepts.
(1) 2 (2) 3
(3) 4 (4) 5

2253. According to James if two concepts lead us to identical consequences, what do they mean?
(1) They mean two different things
(2) They mean the two absurd things
(3) They mean nothing
(4) They mean the two same things

2254. Heidegger espoused
(1) Pragmatism (2) Evolutionism
(3) Existentialism (4) None of these

2255. Heidegger believes that science investigates the................., whereas philosophy studies the................
(1) Being-there, being-per se
(2) Being-per se, being-there
(3) Subjective, objective
(4) Matter, God

2256. According to Heidegger man finds himself in a world, which is
(1) Being per se (2) Dasein
(3) Illusory (4) None of these

2257. Dasein means
(1) Being-per se (2) Nothing
(3) Being-there (4) Demon

2258. According to Heidegger the inner principle which organizes is relations to the world is
(1) Dasein (2) Being-per se
(3) Being there (4) Care or concern

2259. "Nothing nothings itself" is saying of
(1) Sartre (2) Heidegger
(3) Russell (4) Moore

2260. According to Heidegger
(1) The negative judgement is based upon nothingness
(2) Nothingness is the source of negation.
(3) Negation is not the source of nothingness
(4) All of the above

2261. Which of the following theories works to make the foundations of the science to rid it of the pseudo concepts of metaphysics.
(1) Pragmatism (2) Idealism
(3) Logical positivism
(4) None of the above

2262. 'The meaning of a proposition lies in the method of its verification' is advocated by
(1) Existentialism (2) Pragmatism
(3) Logical atomism
(4) Logical positivism

2263. 'The existence of an object is not dependent on the experience of it' is said by

(1) Hume (2) Berkeley
(3) G.E. Moore (4) None of these

2264. The famous book, 'The Refutation of Idealism' is written by

(1) Russell (2) G.E. Moore
(3) Hume (4) Locke

2265. ....attempt at thorough-going empiricism and his rejection of metaphysics is regarded as the characteristic of the logical positivists.

(1) Kant's (2) Hume's
(3) Wittgenstein's (4) None of these

2266. David Hume is an advocate of

(1) Empiricism (2) Psychologism
(3) Determinism (4) None of these

2267. Moore claims, a proposition is composed neither of words nor thoughts nor any mental entities, but of...............related in a certain way.

(1) Judgements (2) Words
(3) Concepts (4) None of these

2268. Moore calls a proposition a.............which can stand to each other in an infinite number of relations.

(1) Judgement (2) Complex concept
(3) Real concept (4) None of these

2269. Meinong's views bear a striking resemblance to early views of

(1) Russell (2) Moore
(3) Schlick (4) None of these

2270. ....claimed that Meinong's theory lacked a feeling for reality

(1) Russell (2) Wittgenstein
(3) Moore (4) None of these

2271. 'Logic, I should maintain, must no more admit a unicorn than zoology can, for logic is concerned with the real world just as truly as zoology, though with its more abstract and general features'.—Who is the speaker?

(1) Kant (2) Schlick
(3) Russell (4) None of these

2272. 'The faculty which God has given man to supply the want of clear and certain knowledge, in cases where that cannot be had, is judgement; whereby the mind takes its ideas to agree or disagree, or which is the same, any proposition to be true of false'. —who is the speaker?

(1) Russell (2) Moore
(3) Locke (4) None of these

2273. ....holds that judgement is at least in part about our ideas as mental entities, and whether they do in fact correspond with what is the case or reality.

(1) Russell (2) Moore
(3) Frege (4) None of these

2274. ....introduces the word 'concept' by which he means Bradley's 'universal meaning'.

(1) Moore (2) Russell
(3) Frege (4) None of these

2275. ....is ascribed to propositions in virtue of the relations among the concepts of which they are composed

(1) Truth (2) Falsity
(3) Truth or falsity (4) None of these

2276. Moore holds that the relation of a..........to the fact to which it refers is this : that the proposition which is the object of the belief has both being and also another simple unanalyzable property-truth

(1) True belief (2) Concept
(3) Judgement (4) None of these

2277. By 'proposition'..................means any symbolic form—words, thoughts, symbols or gestures, which can express what may be said to be true or false.

(1) Carnap (2) Frege
(3) Russell (4) None of these

2278. A.................is an expression with a blank space or a variable in it, such that when the blank space is filled in with, or the variable substituted for, with the right sort of thing, the result is a true proposition.
(1) Truth function (2) Concept
(3) Proposition function (4) None of these

2279. A...........is a letter, usually x, y, z used in such a way in a propositional function that by substituting certain expressions for it we get a proposition.
(1) Copula (2) Word
(3) Variable (4) None of these

2280. ....states 'every proposition in which a description which describes nothing has a primary occurrence is false.'
(1) Moore (2) Russell
(3) Frege (4) None of these

2281. According to Wittgenstein
(1) Philosophy is nothing but analysis and discussion of language.
(2) Philosophy contains discussions only of metaphysics.
(3) Philosophy is useless.
(4) Philosophy is the best science.

2282. 'Philosophical Investigations' is a work of
(1) Russell (2) Heidegger
(3) Wittgenstein (4) Sartre

2283. According to Wittgenstein Metaphysical language is
(1) Confusing (2) Related to facts
(3) Related to religion (4) Full of reality

2284. Husserl's 'phenomenological reduction' is concerned with
(1) reduction of material objects of sense-data
(2) reduction of noumeno to phenomena
(3) isolating the content of experience from any reference to existence
(4) reducing the ending self to discrete mental states

2285. For James pragmatism points towards ....rather than...........or...............
(1) Pluralism, Monism, Absolutism
(2) Monism, Pluralism, Absolutism
(3) Absolutism, Monism, Pluralism
(4) None of the above

2286. "....universe unfinished with doors and windows open to possibilities uncontrollable in advance." Above statement is of
(1) Peirce (2) James
(3) Russell (4) Whitehead

2287. James treatment of the stream of consciousness emphasizes his relations to a
(1) Noumenological approach
(2) Mechanical approach
(3) Phenomenological approach
(4) None of the above

2288. Russell's original contributions to philosophy are in...............and Russell has given realism a...............foundation.
(1) Mathematics, Mathematical
(2) Physics, Physical
(3) Logic, Logical
(4) Geometry, Geometrical

2289. Match the following

List-I	List-II
(a) G Ryle	(i) Critique of cartesian
(b) Wittgenstein	(ii) Seven propositions
(c) William James	(iii) Meaning theory
(d) Husserl	(iv) Phenomenologist

Codes :

	(a)	(b)	(c)	(d)
(1)	(i)	(iii)	(ii)	(iv)
(2)	(ii)	(iii)	(iv)	(i)
(3)	(i)	(ii)	(iii)	(iv)
(4)	(iv)	(iii)	(ii)	(i)

2290. Match the following

List-I	List-II
(a) Phenomenologist	(i) Husserl
(b) Pragmatist	(ii) Peirce
(c) Descriptivist	(iii) Russerl
(d) Non-naturalist	(iv) Moore

Codes :

	(a)	(b)	(c)	(d)
(1)	(i)	(ii)	(iii)	(iv)
(2)	(ii)	(iii)	(iv)	(i)
(3)	(iv)	(iii)	(ii)	(i)
(4)	(iv)	(ii)	(iii)	(i)

2291. Match list I with list II and select the correct answer by using the codes given below the lists :

List-I	List-II
(a) A refutation of Idealism	(i) Mortiz Schlick
(b) The Phenomenological method	(ii) Jean-Paul Sartre
(c) Existence precedes essence	(iii) Edmund Husserl
(d) The Vienna Circle	(iv) G.E. Moore

Codes :

	(a)	(b)	(c)	(d)
(1)	(i)	(ii)	(iv)	(iii)
(2)	(iv)	(iii)	(ii)	(i)
(3)	(i)	(iii)	(ii)	(iv)
(4)	(iv)	(ii)	(iii)	(i)

2292. Match the following

List-I	List-II
(a) Wittgenstein	(i) Tractatus
(b) Moore	(ii) Refutation of idealism
(c) A.J. Ayer	(iii) Critique metaphysics
(d) Husserl	(iv) Ideem

Codes :

	(a)	(b)	(c)	(d)
(1)	(i)	(ii)	(iii)	(iv)
(2)	(iv)	(iii)	(ii)	(i)
(3)	(iii)	(ii)	(iv)	(i)
(4)	(i)	(iv)	(iii)	(ii)

2293. Match the following

List-I	List-II
(a) Heidegger	(i) Dread
(b) Husserl	(ii) Intentionality
(c) Carnap	(iii) Logical positivist
(d) William James	(iv) Truth theory

Codes :	(a)	(b)	(c)	(d)
(1)	(iii)	(iv)	(ii)	(i)
(2)	(i)	(ii)	(iii)	(iv)
(3)	(iv)	(ii)	(iii)	(i)
(4)	(iv)	(iii)	(ii)	(i)

2294. Match list I with list II and select the correct answer by using the codes given below the lists :

List-I	List-II
(a) G.E. Moore	(i) Theory of definite description
(b) L. Wittgenstein	(ii) Category mistake
(c) G. Ryle	(iii) Impossibility of private language
(d) B. Russell	(iv) Naturalistic fallacy

Codes :	(a)	(b)	(c)	(d)
(1)	(iii)	(iii)	(ii)	(i)
(2)	(iii)	(i)	(ii)	(iv)
(3)	(ii)	(iii)	(i)	(iv)
(4)	(iv)	(ii)	(iii)	(i)

2295. Match the following

List-I	List-II
(a) Kant	(i) Schematism
(b) Hegel	(ii) Concrete monism
(c) Husserl	(iii) Critique of psychology
(d) Heidegger	(iv) Ontology metaphysics

Codes :

	(a)	(b)	(c)	(d)
(1)	(i)	(ii)	(iii)	(iv)
(2)	(iv)	(iii)	(ii)	(i)
(3)	(iv)	(ii)	(iii)	(i)
(4)	(ii)	(iii)	(iv)	(ii)

2296. Match list I with list II and select the correct answer from the codes given below the lists:

List-I	List-II
(a) Formalism	(i) A pragmatic view of reality and knowledge as suited to the fulfillment of practical needs.
(b) Mechanism	(ii) The theory that the world should be viewed as an organism
(c) Contextualism	(iii) Theory of fixed essences and universal
(d) Organicism	(iv) Mechanical models of the world process

Codes :	(a)	(b)	(c)	(d)
(1)	(iii)	(iv)	(i)	(ii)
(2)	(iv)	(iii)	(ii)	(i)
(3)	(i)	(ii)	(iii)	(iv)
(4)	(ii)	(i)	(iv)	(iii)

2297. Match the following

List-I	List-II
(a) G. Ryle	(i) Concept of Mind
(b) Hegel	(ii) Absolute Idealist
(c) A.J. Ayer	(iii) Emotivist
(d) Wittgenstein	(iv) Blue book

Codes :	(a)	(b)	(c)	(d)
(1)	(i)	(ii)	(iii)	(iv)
(2)	(iv)	(iii)	(ii)	(i)
(3)	(ii)	(iv)	(iii)	(i)
(4)	(i)	(iv)	(iii)	(ii)

2298. Match list I with list II and select the correct answer by using the codes given below the lists :

List-I	List-II
(a) Metaphysical theory of space and time of Samuel Alexander	(i) Absolute idealism of Bradley and Bosanquet
(b) A doctrine of emergent evolution of Samuel Alexander	(ii) Direct realism of Moore, Russell
(c) A perspectivism of Samuel Alexander	(iii) Bergson's creative evolutionism
(d) Theory of value of human freedom dom and of deity of Samuel Alexander.	(iv) Physical theory of relativity

Codes :

	(a)	(b)	(c)	(d)
(1)	(ii)	(iii)	(iv)	(i)
(2)	(iii)	(iv)	(i)	(ii)
(3)	(iv)	(iii)	(ii)	(i)
(4)	(i)	(ii)	(iii)	(iv)

2299. Match the following

List-I	List-II
(a) William James	(i) Instrumental truth
(b) Ryle	(ii) British philosopher
(c) Pragmatism	(iii) Practical consequences
(d) Russerl	(iv) Acquaintance

Codes :

	(a)	(b)	(c)	(d)
(1)	(ii)	(i)	(iv)	(iii)
(2)	(i)	(ii)	(iii)	(iv)
(3)	(iii)	(i)	(ii)	(iv)
(4)	(iii)	(iv)	(ii)	(i)

2300. Match list I with list II and select the correct answer from the codes given below the lists:

List-I	List-II
(a) William James	(i) Conceptual pragmatism
(b) John Dewey	(ii) Radical Empiricism
(c) C.I. Lewis	(iii) Contextualism
(d) Stephen Pepper	(iv) Instrumentalism

Codes :

	(a)	(b)	(c)	(d)
(1)	(iii)	(ii)	(iv)	(i)
(2)	(ii)	(iv)	(i)	(iii)
(3)	(iv)	(i)	(iii)	(ii)
(4)	(i)	(iii)	(ii)	(iv)

2301. Match the following

List-I	List-II
(a) C.S. Peirce	(i) Pragmatic
(b) Heidegger	(ii) Hermenentic
(c) Husserl	(iii) Logical investigations
(d) G. Ryle	(iv) Category mistake

Codes :

	(a)	(b)	(c)	(d)
(1)	(i)	(ii)	(iii)	(iv)
(2)	(i)	(iv)	(iii)	(ii)
(3)	(iv)	(iii)	(ii)	(i)
(4)	(iv)	(ii)	(iii)	(i)

2302. Match the following by using the code below and select the correct answer using the code given below :

List – I (Author)	List – II (Texts)
(a) Gilbert Ryle	(i) Philosophical Studies
(b) Bertrand Russell	(ii) Either/or
(c) Heidegger	(iii) The Concept of Mind
(d) G.E. Moore	(iv) An inquiry into meaning and truth

Codes :

	(a)	(b)	(c)	(d)
(1)	(iv)	(iii)	(ii)	(i)
(2)	(ii)	(i)	(iv)	(iii)
(3)	(iii)	(iv)	(ii)	(i)
(4)	(iii)	(ii)	(iv)	(i)

2303. Match list I with list II and select the correct answer from the codes given below the lists:

List-I	List-II
(a) Thomas Hobbes	(i) Creative morality
(b) David Hume	(ii) Naturalistic fallacy
(c) G.E. Moore	(iii) General subjectivism
(d) Henri Bergson	(iv) Ego-centric subjectivism

Codes :

	(a)	(b)	(c)	(d)
(1)	(iv)	(iii)	(ii)	(i)
(2)	(i)	(ii)	(iii)	(iv)
(3)	(ii)	(iii)	(iv)	(i)
(4)	(iii)	(ii)	(i)	(iv)

2304. Match the following

List-I	List-II
(a) Gilbert Ryle	(i) Utilitarianism
(b) J. Kant	(ii) Category mistake
(c) Jormy Bentham	(iii) Picture theory of meaning
(d) Ludving Wittgenstein	(iv) Categorical imperative

Codes :

	(a)	(b)	(c)	(d)
(1)	(iv)	(ii)	(ii)	(iii)
(2)	(i)	(iii)	(ii)	(iv)
(3)	(iii)	(ii)	(i)	(iv)
(4)	(ii)	(iv)	(i)	(iii)

Directions. The following items consist of two statements, one labelled the 'Assertion A' and the other labelled the 'Reason R'. You are to examine these two statements carefully and decide if the Assertion A and the reason R individually true and if so, whether the reason is a correct explanation of the assertion. Select your answers to these items using the codes given below.

Codes:

(1) Both A and R are true and R is the correct explanation of A

(2) Both A and R are true but R is not a correct explanation of A

(3) A is true but R is false

(4) A is false but R is true.

2305. **Assertion (A).** In Moore's view the statement "This circle is square" is an analytic and not a synthetic proposition.
Reason (R). Given proposition do not refer to any actual state of affairs and are merely elucidatory or definitional.

2306. **Assertion (A).** For James Pragmatism points towards pluralism rather than monism or absolutism.
Reason (R). He was convinced that reality as perceptually experienced shows us a world of change

2307. **Assertion (A).** According to Heidegger nothingness is experienced.
Reason (R). Dread reveals nothing.

2308. **Assertion (A).** Logical positivists have restricted philosophy to a narrow and technical function of evaluating the scientific assertion.
Reason (R). According to logical positivists philosophy is to science what grammar is to language.

2309. **Assertion (A).** According to Wittgenstein language is nothing but "the totality of propositions."
Reason (R). The entire fabric of language is, as Wittgenstein holds, analyzable in compound statements, which in turn, are analyzable in simple statements.

2310. **Assertion (A).** According to Wittgenstein, "A proposition is a picture of reality."
Reason (R). Language represents the facts of experience.

2311. **Assertion (A).** Ethical thought of Bertrand Russell resembles the emotive theory of the logical positivists.
Reason (R). Russell regards value judgements as expression of our emotions and not as assertion of facts which are truly independent of our emotions.

2312. **Assertion (A).** According to Moore Mill has committed a naturalistic fallacy.
Reason (R). Mill has defined a natural property 'goodness' in terms of another natural property called pleasure.

2313. **Assertion (A).** Rudolf carnap rejects metaphysics.
Reason (R). The linguistic analysis of metaphysical statements shows them to be devoid of any meaning.

2314. **Assertion (A).** Peirce urged that Descartes universal doubt was a fake.
Reason (R). According to Peirce we do not doubt in general or wholesale fashion. It is only when we have some question about a specific item that doubt occurs.

2315. **Assertion (A).** Carnap was against metaphysics.
Reason (R). Metaphysics shows no meaning.

2316. **Assertion (A).** Pure phenomenology was important for Husserl.
Reason (R). Pure phenomenology signifies preparatory science.

2317. **Assertion (A).** Moore says that Mill committed a naturalistic fallacy.
Reason (R). Mill defines goodness in terms of another natural property.

2318. **Assertion (A).** For Hegel, there is only one reality.

Reason (R). More than one reality will be regarded as limited.

2319. **Assertion (A).** Nothingness is experience according to Heidegger.

Reason (R). Dread reveals nothing, according to Heidegger.

2320. **Assertion (A).** According to Moore, Mill has committed a naturalistic fallacy.

Reason (R). Mill has defined a natural property 'goodness' in terms of another natural property pleasure.

2321. **Assertion (A).** Phenomenology means description of phenomena.

Reason (R). Husseri was regarded as a phenomenologist.

Direction. There are six questions given. Each question contains two statements, you have to find out whether these statements are true or false.

Codes :

(1) A and B both are true.

(2) A is true but B is false.

(3) A is false but B is true

(4) A and B both are false.

2322. **Statement (A).** Husserl conceived pure phenomenology as a necessary preparatory science.

Statement (B). Phenomenology, says Husserl, is the science of pure possibilities which must everywhere precede the science of real facts.

2323. **Statement (A).** Husserl invokes the theory of intentional reference in his interpretation of the objects of phenomenological study.

Statement (B). Husserl was a phenomenologist.

2324. **Statement (A).** Russell describes sense data as public objects capable of existing unsensed.

Statement (B). Moore describes sense data as private objects, since there is only one person to whom they can be immediately present and regarded them as capable of being existing only when sensed.

2325. **Statement (A).** Realism is based upon the reality of relations, and asserts that all relations are external.

Statement (B). Rationalism denies the reality of relations and asserts that all relations are internal.

2326. **Statement (A).** The world offers itself to us to be put to use with no permanent staticity but with change, novelty and spontaneity as the constituents of its structure. This is what Peirce called tychism.

Statement (B). The world is neither good nor bad in term of value but has to be dealt with in order to the good or bad by the response of the will. This is what Peirce called meliorism.

2327. **Statement (A).** Epistemological monism of neo realism is the doctrine that knowledge is presentational, that the object of knowledge is directly given to consciousness.

Statement (B). Epistemological dualism of new realism is the doctrine that knowledge is representational, that 'object' of knowledge is known only through the mediation of 'ideas' or 'contents' of knowledge, the content and object of knowledge are numerically distinct elements in the knowledge situation.

2328. William James says that

A. truth is applicable to concepts.

B. false is applicable to concepts.

C. belief is regarded as true.

D. belief is regarded as false.

Select the correct answer from the codes given below :

(1) A and B (2) B and C
(3) A and C (4) C and D

2329. We should show our love of our fellows, as Nietzsche thinks, by
A. commiserating with them
B. aiding them to attain power
C. sometimes being hard with them
D. vying with them in a competitive effort
Codes :
(1) A and B (2) A, B and C
(3) B, C and D (4) A, B, C and D

2330. Which among the following theories are related to William James?
A. Stream of Consciousness
B. Voluntarism
C. Pluralism
D. Pragmatism
Codes :
(1) A and B (2) A, B and C
(3) B, C and D (4) A, B, C and D

2331. Pragmatism means
A. practical consequences.
B. relevant theory.
C. meaning theory.
D. acceptance theory.
Select the correct answer from the codes given below :
(1) A and B (2) A and C
(3) B and C (4) C and D

2332. Which of the following statements express correctly the Moore's view?
Choose your answer from the codes given below :
A. Knowledge is a complex whole.
B. Knowledge is a relation of independent elements
C. Content of consciousness is always something external.
D. Ideas are the basis of external objects.
Codes :
(1) A and D (2) B and C
(3) C and D (4) B and D

2333. Peirce says that
A. truth is regarded as public.
B. truth is regarded as private.
C. object in true opinion is regarded as real.
D. object in false opinion is regarded as real.
Select the correct answer from the codes given below :
(1) A and B (2) A and C
(3) B and C (4) C and D

2334. Peirce was regarded as
A. pragmatist. B. non-pragmatist.
C. public truth believer.
D. non-public truth believer.
Select the correct answer from the codes given below :
(1) A and B (2) A and C
(3) B and C (4) C and D

2335. Read the following arguments :
(i) If I am the President of India, then I am famous. I am not the President of India. Therefore, I am not famous.
(ii) If the weather is fine, the match will be played. The weather is not fine. Therefore, the match will not be played.
Find out the 'Argument Form' of the above arguments, using the code below :

(1) $p \supset q$
$\sim p$
$\therefore q$

(2) $p \cdot q$
p
$\therefore q$

(3) $p \supset q$
$\sim p$
$\therefore \sim p$

(4) $p \wedge q$
$\sim \sim q$
$\therefore p$

2336. If A and B are true statements and X and Y are false statements, the compound statement $\sim (A \vee X)$ is

(1) True (2) False
(3) Doubtful (4) None of these

2337. The scheme of the FIRST figure of the syllogism is

(1) P – M
S – M
———
S – P

(2) M – P
S – M
———
S – P

(3) P – M
M – S
———
S – P

(4) M – P
M – S
———
S – P

2338. Read the following syllogism and point out the fallacy in it :

"All graduates are voters
John is not a graduate
John is not a voter."

(1) The fallacy of Four Terms.
(2) The fallacy of undistributed middle.
(3) Illicit Major
(4) Illicit Minor

2339. In categorical syllogism, the middle term is the term that occurs in

(1) Major premise only
(2) Minor premise only
(3) Both major and minor premises
(4) Conclusion only

2340. Wittgenstein authored :

I. Tractatus Logico Philosophicus
II. Philosophical Investigations
III. On certainty
IV. Zettle

Select the correct answer by using the code:

(1) I and II are only correct.
(2) II and III are only correct.
(3) I and IV are only correct.
(4) I, II, III and IV are correct.

2341. $p \supset q$ is false when

(1) p is true and q is true.
(2) p is true and q is false.
(3) p is false and q is true.
(4) p is false and q is false.

2342. A statement form that has only FALSE substitution instances is called

(1) Tautology (2) Contradiction
(3) Contingent (4) Implication

2343. Which one of the following is a tautology?

(1) $p \supset \sim p$
(2) $(p \supset \sim p) . (\sim p \supset p)$
(3) $p \supset (p \supset p)$
(4) $(p \supset p) \supset p$

2344. Match List I (Symbolic Forms) with List–II (Rules) and select the correct answer :

List – I (Symbolic Form)	List – II (Rule of Inference)
a. $p \supset q$, p, $\therefore q$	(i) Disjunctive syllogism
b. $p \supset q$, $\sim q$, $\therefore \sim p$	(ii) Hypothetical syllogism
c. $p \supset q$, $q \supset r$, $\therefore p \supset r$	(iii) Modus Tollens
d. $p \vee q$, $\sim p$, $\therefore q$	(iv) Modus Ponens

Codes :

	a	b	c	d
(1)	(iv)	(i)	(ii)	(iii)
(2)	(ii)	(i)	(iv)	(iii)
(3)	(iii)	(iv)	(i)	(ii)
(4)	(iv)	(iii)	(ii)	(i)

2345. Match List – I with List – II and select the correct answer from given code :

List – I	List – II
(a) (p ⊃ q). (r ⊃ S) / ∴ −p v − r − q v	(i) De M.
(b) −(p.q)/−p v − q	(ii) Disjunctive syllogism
(c) p v q /∴ q − p	(iii) Transportation

(d) $(p \supset q) / \therefore (-q \supset -p)$ (iv) Destructive Dilemma

Codes :

	(a)	(b)	(c)	(d)
(1)	(iv)	(ii)	(i)	(iii)
(2)	(i)	(iii)	(iv)	(ii)
(3)	(iv)	(ii)	(iii)	(i)
(4)	(iv)	(i)	(ii)	(iii)

2346. Select the correct option from given below :

$(\exists x)$ [Kx . (y) (Ly $\supset$ My)]
(x) Kx $\supset$ [$(\exists y)$ (Ny . My) $\supset$ Ox]
$\therefore$ $(\exists y)$ (Ny . Ly) $\supset$ $(\exists x)$
is

(1) Valid (2) Invalid
(3) True (4) False

2347. In the traditional square of opposition if 'I' proposition is false, which one of the following can be determined ?

(1) A, E and O are undetermined.
(2) A, E and O are false.
(3) A is true, E is true and O is false.
(4) A is false, E is true and O is true.

2348. Which one of the following is the equivalent of $\sim p \supset q$?

(1) $p \supset \sim q$ (2) $q \vee p$
(3) $q \supset \sim p$ (4) $\sim q \supset \sim p$

2349. 'p.q', 'p v q', 'p $\supset$ q' and 'p $\equiv$ q' are all true only when

(1) p is true and q is false.
(2) p is false and q is true.
(3) p and q are both false.
(4) p and q are both true.

2350. If 'O' is false, find out the true option as given below :

(1) I and E are true and A is false.
(2) I and A are true and E is false.
(3) A and I are false and E is true.
(4) O is true but E and I are false.

2351. Find out the false statement as given below : Statements :

(1) Converse of 'A' is 'I'.
(2) If 'A' is false, then 'O' is true.
(3) Obverse of 'O' is 'I'.
(4) Obverse of 'E' is 'I'.

2352. Mark the correct symbolization (as given below) for given statement :

Statement :

Bees and wasps sting if they are either angry or frightened. (Bx, Wx, Sx, Ax, Fx)
Symbolization

(1) $(\exists x)$ {(Bx · Wx) $\supset$ [(Ax $\vee$ Fx) $\supset$ Sx]}
(2) (x) {(Bx $\vee$ Wx) $\supset$ [(Ax $\vee$ Fx) $\supset$ Sx]}
(3) (x) {(Bx $\vee$ Wx) $\supset$ Ax $\vee$ Fx $\supset$ Sx
(4) (x) (Bx $\vee$ Wx) $\supset$ (Ax $\vee$ Fx) $\supset$ Sx

2353. Match List – I with List – II and mark the correct option :

List – I	List – II
a. $p \equiv p \vee q$	(i) Material implication
b. $(p \supset q) \equiv (-q \supset -p)$	(ii) Tautology
c. $(p \supset q) \equiv (-p \vee -q)$	(iii) Commutation
d. $(p \vee q) \equiv (q \vee p)$	(iv) Transportation

Codes :

	(a)	(b)	(c)	(d)
(1)	(i)	(ii)	(iv)	(iii)
(2)	(ii)	(iv)	(i)	(iii)
(3)	(iii)	(iv)	(ii)	(i)
(4)	(iv)	(ii)	(iii)	(i)

2354. Examine the following argument and spot the right option :

Argument :

$P \supset (Q \vee R)$
$S \supset (T \cdot U)$
$-T$
$\therefore P \supset U$

Options :

(1) Valid (2) Invalid
(3) Both of these (4) None of these

2355. Mark the correct symbolization for given statement :

Statement :

If anything is damaged, someone will be blamed.

Symbolization :

(1) (∃x) Dx ⊃ (∃y) (Py · By)

(2) (∃x) Dx ⊃ (Py · By)

(3) (∃x) – Dx ⊃ – (∃y) (Py · By)

(4) None of these

2356. Match List – I with List – II and mark the correct option :

	List – I	List – II
a.	– (p∨q) ≡ (–p · – q)	(i) Distribution
b.	[p · (q ∨ r)] ≡ [(p · q) ∨ (p · r)]	(ii) Double Negation
c.	p ≡ – –p	(iii) Exportation
d.	[(p · q) ⊃ r] ≡ [p ⊃ (q ⊃ r)]	(iv) De Morgan's theorem

Codes :

	a	b	c	d
(1)	(iv)	(i)	(ii)	(iii)
(2)	(i)	(iii)	(ii)	(iv)
(3)	(ii)	(iv)	(i)	(iii)
(4)	(iv)	(iii)	(ii)	(i)

2357. Evaluate the given argument and mark the correct option :

Argument :

(V ⊃ –W) · (X ⊃ Y)

(–W ⊃ Z) · (Y ⊃ –A)

(Z ⊃ –B) · (–A ⊃ C)

V · X

∴ –B · C

Options :

(1) Valid (2) Invalid

(3) Both of these (4) None of these

2358. A compound proposition truth or falsity is unequivocally determined by whom?

(1) Truth or falsity of its components of all cases

(2) Proposition with no define truth value

(3) Truth of its consequent

(4) None of the above

2359. Whether construction of formula are essential for truth functional.

(1) Yes (2) No

(3) Can't say (4) Don't know

2360. What are the inputs of Boolean functions.

(1) P (2) Q

(3) R (4) S

2361. The inputs P and Q is associated with how many digit binary outputs?

(1) 6 (2) 5

(3) 4 (4) 8

2362. What is the symbol of disjunctive?

(1) • (2) ∨

(3) ⊃ (4) >

2363. What is the symbol of hypothetical?

(1) > (2) ⊃

(3) ≡ (4) ∨

2364. Truth-function forms which sentence out of constituent sentences?

(1) Complex (2) Compound

(3) Regulate (4) None of these

2365. A basic conjunction is true on how many assignment of truth values of its atoms?

(1) 1 (2) 4

(3) 2 (4) 3

2366. ¬ A is truth-functionally equivalent to what?

(1) A ↓ A (2) A ↑ A

(3) B ↓ B (4) B ↑ B

2367. AVB is truth functionally equivalent to what?

(1) (A ↓ A) ↓ (B ↓ B)

(2) C ↓ C

(3) B ↓ B (4) A ↓ A

2368. What do you mean by connective?

(1) Sheffer stroke

(2) William Jones stroke

(3) Plato stroke (4) None of these

2369. > A is truth-functionally equivalent to what?

(1) C ↓ A (2) A ↓ A
(3) C ↓ B (4) B ↓ C

2370. (AVB) is truth-functionally equivalent to what?

(1) C ↓ A (2) B ↓ B
(3) (A ↓ A) ↓ (B ↓ B)
(4) B ↓ C

2371. What is the symbol of equivalence?

(1) ↔ (2) ↓
(3) < (4) >

2372. What is the task of a logical operator?

(1) To modify one statement of make a different statement
(2) To modify five statement
(3) To modify four statement
(4) All of the above

2373. What do you mean by inclusive sense?

(1) One is false
(2) Both disjuncts are true
(3) One or the other is true
(4) All of the above

2374. Another name of material equivalence is what?

(1) Biconditional proportion
(2) Conditional concept
(3) Complex proportion
(4) All of the above

2375. $a \to b$

$\frac{a}{b}$ is referred as what?

(1) Modus ponens (2) Modus tautology
(3) Negative (4) None of these

2376. $a \to b$

$\frac{\neg a}{\neg b}$ is referred as what?

(1) Modus tollens (2) Modus strong
(3) Intention (4) None of these

2377. Another name of modus tollens is what?

(1) E-introduction
(2) P-elimination
(3) q-introduction
(4) Modus tollendo tollens

2378. $\frac{a \to b}{a \to (a \,\&\, b)}$ is known as what?

(1) Absorption (2) Conjuction
(3) Consequent (4) None of these

2379. A inter-replaceable with what?

(1) $a \wedge b$ (2) $a \vee b$
(3) $a \to b$ (4) $\sim a$

2380. $a \to b$ is inter-replaceable with what?

(1) $\neg a \vee b$ (2) $a \vee b$
(3) $a < b$ (4) $\equiv a$

2381. Quantification helps in what?

(1) To interpret non-compound premises as compound statements
(2) All possible truth function
(3) Existential
(4) None of the above

2382. Logical constant is interpreted as what?

(1) Nothing (2) For all
(3) For two (4) For three

2383. Rule of contradiction is referred as what?

(1) $\sim p \to c \therefore p$
(2) p or q p $\sim$ r, $q \wedge r \therefore r$
(3) $p \therefore q$ (4) $p \to q$

2384. Consistency and completeness comes under the domain of what?

(1) Classical deductive logic
(2) General proposition
(3) Logical concept
(4) None of the above

2385. Consistency can be proved by means of which domain of what?

(1) Arithmetic (2) Fat
(3) Mathematics (4) Ethics

2386. An axiomatic system is called complete when?

(1) Every statement is derivable
(2) Every statement is negative
(3) Lower order versions of quantities them
(4) None of the above

2387. An argument is logically valid when?

(1) If and only, if its conclusion is a logical consequence of its premises
(2) If and only, if its conclusion is a logical antecedent of its premises
(3) If and only if negative
(4) If and only conclusion

2388. There are how many approaches through which we can show that an argument is valid?

(1) 2 (2) 5
(3) 3 (4) 4

2389. In which argument, the premises provide a guarantee for the truth of the conclusion?

(1) Deductive (2) Reflective
(3) Notion (4) None of these

2390. Consistency and completeness comes under the .... system in logic.

(1) axiomatic
(2) begging of the dream
(3) awareness (4) formal logic

2391. Match the following

List-I	List-II
(a) Negation	(i) If and then
(b) Disjunctive	(ii) And
(c) Conjunction	(iii) Or
(d) Hypothetical	(iv) Not

Codes :	(a)	(b)	(c)	(d)
(1)	(i)	(ii)	(iii)	(iv)
(3)	(iv)	(ii)	(iii)	(i)
(3)	(ii)	(iii)	(iv)	(i)
(4)	(iv)	(iii)	(ii)	(i)

2392. Match the following

List-I	List-II
(a) •	(i) And
(b) v	(ii) Equivalence
(c) ⊃	(iii) Implication
(d) ≡	(iv) Either .... or ....

Codes :	(a)	(b)	(c)	(d)
(1)	(i)	(ii)	(iii)	(iv)
(2)	(iv)	(iii)	(ii)	(i)
(2)	(ii)	(iv)	(iii)	(i)
(4)	(i)	(iv)	(iii)	(ii)

2393. Match the following

List-I	List-II
(a) Universal quantifier	(i) ∀
(b) Existential quantifier	(ii) ∍
(c) Rule of inference	(iii) Modus Ponens
(d) Rue of replacement	(iv) Tantology

Codes :	(a)	(b)	(c)	(d)
(1)	(i)	(ii)	(iii)	(iv)
(2)	(iv)	(iii)	(ii)	(i)
(3)	(i)	(iv)	(iii)	(ii)
(4)	(iv)	(ii)	(i)	(iii)

2394. Match the following

List-I	List-II
(a) Modus Ponens	(i) $\dfrac{a \to b \quad \neg a}{\neg b}$
(b) Modus tollens	(ii) $\dfrac{a \to b}{a \to (a \,\&\, b)}$
(c) Absorption	(iii) $\dfrac{a \quad b}{a \,\&\, b}$
(d) Conjunction	(iv) $\dfrac{a \to b \quad a}{b}$

Codes :	(a)	(b)	(c)	(d)
(1)	(i)	(ii)	(iii)	(iv)
(2)	(iv)	(iii)	(ii)	(i)
(3)	(i)	(iv)	(iii)	(ii)
(4)	(iv)	(ii)	(i)	(iii)

2395. Match the following

List-I	List-II
(a) Axiomatic system	(i) Ten
(b) Universal quantifier	(ii) Nine
(c) Inference rule	(iii) Completeness
(d) Replacement rule	(iv) Quantification

Codes :	(a)	(b)	(c)	(d)
(1)	(i)	(ii)	(iii)	(iv)
(2)	(iii)	(ii)	(iv)	(i)
(3)	(iv)	(iii)	(ii)	(i)
(4)	(iii)	(iv)	(ii)	(i)

2396. Match the following

List-I	List-II
(a) Universal instantiation	(i) (x) (Qx) ∴ (Qv)
(b) Universal generalisation	(ii) Qy ∴ (x) (Qx)
(c) Existential instantiation	(iii) (∃x) (Qx) ∴ Qu
(d) Existential generalisation	(iv) Qv ∴ (∃x) (Qx)

Codes :

	(a)	(b)	(c)	(d)
(1)	(i)	(ii)	(iii)	(iv)
(2)	(ii)	(iii)	(i)	(iv)
(3)	(iv)	(iii)	(ii)	(i)
(4)	(i)	(iv)	(iii)	(ii)

2397. Match the following

List-I	List-II
(a) Inclusive sense	(i) v
(b) Exclusive sense	(ii) Weak
(c) Disjunction	(iii) Strong
(d) Negation	(iv) Not

Codes :

	(a)	(b)	(c)	(d)
(1)	(i)	(ii)	(iii)	(iv)
(2)	(ii)	(iii)	(iv)	(i)
(3)	(iv)	(iii)	(ii)	(i)
(4)	(iv)	(ii)	(iii)	(i)

2398. Match the following

List-I	List-II
(a) Universal instantiation	(i) Consistency
(b) Universal generalisation	(ii) P(c)→∀×Σ×P(x)
(c) Existential generalisation	(iii) ∀×Σ×P(x)
(d) Axiomatic system	(iv) ∀×Σ×P(x)→P(c)

Codes :

	(a)	(b)	(c)	(d)
(1)	(i)	(iv)	(iii)	(ii)
(2)	(iv)	(iii)	(ii)	(i)
(3)	(iv)	(ii)	(iii)	(i)
(4)	(i)	(ii)	(iii)	(iv)

2399. A truth function is referred as

A. set of truth values.

B. infinite number of truth values.

C. finite number of truth values.

Select the correct answer using the codes given below

(1) A and C (2) B and C

(3) A and B (4) All of the above

2400. Proportional logic is referred as

A. statements logic.

B. proposition which join entire proposition.

C. argument logic.

Select the correct answer using the codes given below

(1) A and C (2) B and C

(3) A, B and C (4) A and B

2401. Material implication is referred as

A. ⊃ B. →

C. ∨ D. •

Select the correct answer using the codes given below

(1) A and B (2) B and C

(3) A and D (4) A, B and C

2402. Proposition logic involves
A. logical connectives
B. non-logical connectives
C. words like and
D. words like of
Select the correct answer using the codes given below
(1) A, B and C (2) B, C and D
(3) A, C and D (4) All of these

2403. Disjunctive is referred as
A. ∧ B. ⊃
C. or
Select the correct answer using the codes given below
(1) A and B (2) B and C
(3) A and C (4) A and D

2404. Inclusive sense means
A. One disjunct are true.
B. Other disjunct are false.
C. Both disjunct are true.
D. Both disjunct are false.
Select the correct answer using the codes given below
(1) A and C (2) B and C
(3) A and B (4) A, B and C

2405. Rules of inference are
A. applied when the main operators are in use.
B. nine in number.
C. applied only to entire statements.
D. not applied to entire statements.
Select the correct answer using the codes given below
(1) A, B and C (2) B, C and D
(3) A, C and D (4) All of these

2406. Rules of replacement are
A. ten
B. eleven
C. taken as primitive
D. taken as non-primitive
Select the correct answer using the codes given below
(1) A and B (2) B and C
(3) B and D (4) A and C

2407. Match List – I with List – II and select the right answer using the code, given below:

List-I	List-II
(a) AAA	(i) Ferio
(b) AII	(ii) Celarent
(c) EAE	(iii) Darii
(d) EIO	(iv) Barbara
	(v) Baroco

Codes :

	(a)	(b)	(c)	(d)
(1)	(iii)	(v)	(iv)	(i)
(2)	(iii)	(iv)	(i)	(ii)
(3)	(iv)	(iii)	(ii)	(i)
(4)	(v)	(iv)	(i)	(iii)

2408. Proportional logic is used to join what?
(1) Entire proposition
(2) Whole proposition
(3) Triple proposition
(4) Dual proposition

2409. In which argument, the premises only support the conclusion?
(1) Deductive (2) Inductive
(3) Invalid (4) None of these

2410. Which arithmetic shows an intricate relationship between the consistency and its completeness?
(1) Peano (2) Plato
(3) Russell (4) Socrates

Answers

1. (1) 2. (1) 3. (2) 4. (3) 5. (1) 6. (4) 7. (4) 8. (4) 9. (3) 10. (1)
11. (1) 12. (4) 13. (4) 14. (3) 15. (2) 16. (4) 17. (4) 18. (1) 19. (1) 20. (1)
21. (2) 22. (3) 23. (1) 24. (1) 25. (4) 26. (1) 27. (3) 28. (1) 29. (1) 30. (4)
31. (1) 32. (3) 33. (2) 34. (4) 35. (2) 36. (2) 37. (2) 38. (1) 39. (1) 40. (1)
41. (1) 42. (3) 43. (3) 44. (1) 45. (3) 46. (4) 47. (2) 48. (4) 49. (3) 50. (4)
51. (1) 52. (4) 53. (4) 54. (4) 55. (1) 56. (2) 57. (2) 58. (4) 59. (4) 60. (3)
61. (1) 62. (2) 63. (2) 64. (2) 65. (3) 66. (2) 67. (1) 68. (1) 69. (4) 70. (3)
71. (1) 72. (3) 73. (4) 74. (1) 75. (1) 76. (2) 77. (1) 78. (2) 79. (3) 80. (2)
81. (3) 82. (1) 83. (3) 84. (1) 85. (3) 86. (1) 87. (1) 88. (4) 89. (1) 90. (1)
91. (1) 92. (1) 93. (4) 94. (1) 95. (2) 96. (2) 97. (4) 98. (2) 99. (4) 100. (3)
101. (3) 102. (3) 103. (4) 104. (3) 105. (2) 106. (2) 107. (4) 108. (4) 109. (4) 110. (2)
111. (3) 112. (4) 113. (3) 114. (1) 115. (4) 116. (3) 117. (1) 118. (1) 119. (1) 120. (2)
121. (1) 122. (1) 123. (1) 124. (1) 125. (3) 126. (1) 127. (1) 128. (1) 129. (1) 130. (1)
131. (1) 132. (1) 133. (1) 134. (1) 135. (1) 136. (1) 137. (1) 138. (1) 139. (1) 140. (1)
141. (4) 142. (4) 143. (2) 144. (2) 145. (3) 146. (1) 147. (3) 148. (1) 149. (1) 150. (4)
151. (3) 152. (2) 153. (1) 154. (4) 155. (3) 156. (2) 157. (3) 158. (4) 159.(1) 160. (3)
161. (1) 162. (2) 163. (3) 164. (3) 165. (3) 166. (4) 167. (1) 168. (2) 169.(1) 170. (4)
171. (2) 172. (3) 173. (1) 174. (1) 175. (3) 176. (4) 177. (4) 178. (3) 179. (2) 180. (2)
181. (4) 182. (1) 183. (3) 184. (3) 185. (4) 186. (4) 187. (2) 188. (1) 189. (1) 190. (3)
191. (4) 192. (4) 193. (1) 194. (3) 195. (2) 196. (4) 197. (1) 198. (4) 199. (4) 200. (3)
201. (2) 202. (3) 203. (1) 204. (3) 205. (2) 206. (4) 207. (1) 208. (3) 209. (1) 210. (2)
211. (3) 212. (4) 213. (1) 214. (1) 215. (3) 216. (1) 217. (4) 218. (2) 219. (2) 220. (3)
221. (4) 222. (1) 223. (3) 224. (1) 225. (2) 226. (1) 227. (3) 228. (2) 229. (1) 230. (4)
231. (1) 232. (3) 233. (1) 234. (3) 235. (2) 236. (4) 237. (1) 238. (3) 239. (2) 240. (3)
241. (4) 242. (3) 243. (2) 244. (3) 245. (1) 246. (1) 247. (2) 248. (3) 249. (1) 250. (1)
251. (2) 252. (3) 253. (4) 254. (1) 255. (4) 256. (2) 257. (3) 258. (4) 259. (4) 260. (3)
261. (4) 262. (1) 263. (2) 264. (3) 265. (3) 266. (4) 267. (1) 268. (2) 269. (3) 270. (3)
271. (4) 272. (1) 273. (2) 274. (1) 275. (3) 276. (2) 277. (4) 278. (4) 279. (2) 280. (1)
281. (3) 282. (1) 283. (3) 284. (4) 285. (4) 286. (3) 287. (3) 288. (2) 289. (2) 290. (4)
291. (2) 292. (2) 293. (3) 294. (1) 295. (2) 296. (3) 297. (1) 298. (4) 299. (4) 300. (3)
301. (2) 302. (3) 303. (3) 304. (3) 305. (4) 306. (1) 307. (2) 308. (3) 309. (2) 310. (3)
311. (4) 312. (1) 313. (3) 314. (1) 315. (1) 316. (1) 317. (1) 318. (1) 319. (1) 320. (1)
321. (1) 322. (1) 323. (2) 324. (1) 325. (1) 326. (1) 327. (1) 328. (1) 329. (1) 330. (1)
331. (1) 332. (1) 333. (2) 334. (1) 335. (1) 336. (1) 337. (1) 338. (1) 339. (1) 340. (1)
341. (1) 342. (1) 343. (3) 344. (1) 345. (1) 346. (1) 347. (1) 348. (1) 349. (4) 350. (4)
351. (1) 352. (1) 353. (2) 354. (1) 355. (3) 356. (4) 357. (1) 358. (1) 359. (2) 360. (1)
361. (3) 362. (1) 363. (1) 364. (2) 365. (1) 366. (1) 367. (1) 368. (3) 369. (1) 370. (1)
371. (2) 372. (2) 373. (1) 374. (1) 375. (1) 376. (1) 377. (4) 378. (1) 379. (1) 380. (2)

381. (4) **382.** (3) **383.** (2) **384.** (1) **385.** (3) **386.** (2) **387.** (1) **388.** (4) **389.** (3) **390.** (2)
391. (4) **392.** (3) **393.** (4) **394.** (2) **395.** (3) **396.** (2) **397.** (1) **398.** (3) **399.** (1) **400.** (3)
401. (2) **402.** (3) **403.** (2) **404.** (3) **405.** (4) **406.** (1) **407.** (4) **408.** (4) **409.** (2) **410.** (4)
411. (4) **412.** (3) **413.** (3) **414.** (1) **415.** (4) **416.** (2) **417.** (1) **418.** (1) **419.** (1) **420.** (4)
421. (3) **422.** (4) **423.** (3) **424.** (2) **425.** (2) **426.** (3) **427.** (4) **428.** (3) **429.** (1) **430.** (2)
431. (3) **432.** (3) **433.** (3) **434.** (4) **435.** (2) **436.** (4) **437.** (2) **438.** (3) **439.** (1) **440.** (2)
441. (4) **442.** (1) **443.** (4) **444.** (2) **445.** (2) **446.** (1) **447.** (3) **448.** (3) **449.** (3) **450.** (1)
451. (1) **452.** (2) **453.** (1) **454.** (1) **455.** (3) **456.** (1) **457.** (1) **458.** (1) **459.** (1) **460.** (1)
461. (1) **462.** (2) **463.** (1) **464.** (3) **465.** (2) **466.** (3) **467.** (4) **468.** (3) **469.** (1) **470.** (3)
471. (2) **472.** (2) **473.** (4) **474.** (3) **475.** (3) **476.** (2) **477.** (2) **478.** (4) **479.** (4) **480.** (3)
481. (3) **482.** (4) **483.** (1) **484.** (2) **485.** (2) **486.** (4) **487.** (2) **488.** (4) **489.** (3) **490.** (4)
491. (2) **492.** (4) **493.** (1) **494.** (1) **495.** (4) **496.** (4) **497.** (4) **498.** (4) **499.** (4) **500.** (1)
501. (2) **502.** (3) **503.** (2) **504.** (1) **505.** (2) **506.** (4) **507.** (1) **508.** (2) **509.** (4) **510.** (3)
511. (4) **512.** (3) **513.** (4) **514.** (4) **515.** (2) **516.** (3) **517.** (3) **518.** (1) **519.** (1) **520.** (2)
521. (1) **522.** (3) **523.** (1) **524.** (2) **525.** (1) **526.** (2) **527.** (1) **528.** (1) **529.** (3) **530.** (1)
531. (1) **532.** (2) **533.** (1) **534.** (1) **535.** (4) **536.** (1) **537.** (1) **538.** (1) **539.** (1) **540.** (2)
541. (3) **542.** (2) **543.** (3) **544.** (3) **545.** (2) **546.** (1) **547.** (1) **548.** (1) **549.** (3) **550.** (2)
551. (2) **552.** (1) **553.** (1) **554.** (1) **555.** (1) **556.** (4) **557.** (4) **558.** (3) **559.** (4) **560.** (1)
561. (2) **562.** (1) **563.** (3) **564.** (3) **565.** (1) **566.** (3) **567.** (2) **568.** (3) **569.** (1) **570.** (1)
571. (3) **572.** (1) **573.** (2) **574.** (1) **575.** (2) **576.** (2) **577.** (2) **578.** (3) **579.** (4) **580.** (3)
581. (2) **582.** (4) **583.** (2) **584.** (3) **585.** (1) **586.** (2) **587.** (1) **588.** (1) **589.** (1) **590.** (1)
591. (1) **592.** (1) **593.** (1) **594.** (1) **595.** (1) **596.** (2) **597.** (1) **598.** (4) **599.** (1) **600.** (1)
601. (1) **602.** (1) **603.** (4) **604.** (1) **605.** (2) **606.** (2) **607.** (2) **608.** (2) **609.** (1) **610.** (2)
611. (1) **612.** (1) **613.** (1) **614.** (1) **615.** (1) **616.** (1) **617.** (1) **618.** (2) **619.** (1) **620.** (2)
621. (4) **622.** (1) **623.** (1) **624.** (1) **625.** (1) **626.** (1) **627.** (1) **628.** (1) **629.** (1) **630.** (2)
631. (3) **632.** (2) **633.** (1) **634.** (3) **635.** (1) **636.** (2) **637.** (1) **638.** (1) **639.** (3) **640.** (1)
641. (1) **642.** (1) **643.** (1) **644.** (3) **645.** (1) **646.** (2) **647.** (1) **648.** (3) **649.** (1) **650.** (1)
651. (1) **652.** (4) **653.** (2) **654.** (3) **655.** (3) **656.** (4) **657.** (3) **658.** (4) **659.** (2) **660.** (1)
661. (1) **662.** (1) **663.** (1) **664.** (3) **665.** (1) **666.** (1) **667.** (1) **668.** (4) **669.** (1) **670.** (3)
671. (1) **672.** (1) **673.** (1) **674.** (1) **675.** (1) **676.** (2) **677.** (1) **678.** (3) **679.** (3) **680.** (4)
681. (2) **682.** (3) **683.** (1) **684.** (3) **685.** (1) **686.** (4) **687.** (1) **688.** (2) **689.** (2) **690.** (2)
691. (4) **692.** (1) **693.** (1) **694.** (2) **695.** (2) **696.** (1) **697.** (1) **698.** (2) **699.** (2) **700.** (3)
701. (1) **702.** (3) **703.** (2) **704.** (2) **705.** (1) **706.** (2) **707.** (1) **708.** (3) **709.** (3) **710.** (1)
711. (3) **712.** (3) **713.** (3) **714.** (2) **715.** (3) **716.** (1) **717.** (2) **718.** (2) **719.** (1) **720.** (4)
721. (2) **722.** (1) **723.** (3) **724.** (3) **725.** (3) **726.** (1) **727.** (2) **728.** (1) **729.** (1) **730.** (1)
731. (1) **732.** (1) **733.** (1) **734.** (1) **735.** (2) **736.** (1) **737.** (1) **738.** (1) **739.** (1) **740.** (1)
741. (1) **742.** (1) **743.** (3) **744.** (2) **745.** (1) **746.** (4) **747.** (3) **748.** (4) **749.** (4) **750.** (4)
751. (1) **752.** (2) **753.** (1) **754.** (2) **755.** (1) **756.** (1) **757.** (2) **758.** (3) **759.** (3) **760.** (1)
761. (1) **762.** (4) **763.** (1) **764.** (2) **765.** (4) **766.** (2) **767.** (1) **768.** (3) **769.** (3) **770.** (1)
771. (2) **772.** (2) **773.** (1) **774.** (2) **775.** (3) **776.** (2) **777.** (3) **778.** (1) **779.** (2) **780.** (2)
781. (2) **782.** (2) **783.** (1) **784.** (2) **785.** (2) **786.** (3) **787.** (2) **788.** (4) **789.** (1) **790.** (2)
791. (1) **792.** (2) **793.** (1) **794.** (3) **795.** (2) **796.** (2) **797.** (2) **798.** (2) **799.** (1) **800.** (2)

801. (3)	**802.** (3)	**803.** (4)	**804.** (2)	**805.** (1)	**806.** (1)	**807.** (4)	**808.** (1)	**809.** (4)	**810.** (2)
811. (2)	**812.** (3)	**813.** (4)	**814.** (1)	**815.** (2)	**816.** (2)	**817.** (4)	**818.** (3)	**819.** (1)	**820.** (2)
821. (3)	**822.** (2)	**823.** (2)	**824.** (1)	**825.** (2)	**826.** (1)	**827.** (3)	**828.** (2)	**829.** (3)	**830.** (2)
831. (3)	**832.** (1)	**833.** (1)	**834.** (1)	**835.** (1)	**836.** (1)	**837.** (1)	**838.** (3)	**839.** (2)	**840.** (1)
841. (1)	**842.** (1)	**843.** (1)	**844.** (1)	**845.** (1)	**846.** (1)	**847.** (4)	**848.** (3)	**849.** (2)	**850.** (3)
851. (2)	**852.** (3)	**853.** (4)	**854.** (3)	**855.** (2)	**856.** (3)	**857.** (2)	**858.** (3)	**859.** (4)	**860.** (2)
861. (2)	**862.** (2)	**863.** (2)	**864.** (1)	**865.** (2)	**866.** (1)	**867.** (2)	**868.** (2)	**869.** (3)	**870.** (2)
871. (2)	**872.** (3)	**873.** (1)	**874.** (1)	**875.** (2)	**876.** (3)	**877.** (1)	**878.** (2)	**879.** (3)	**880.** (1)
881. (2)	**882.** (3)	**883.** (2)	**884.** (1)	**885.** (1)	**886.** (2)	**887.** (1)	**888.** (3)	**889.** (1)	**890.** (2)
891. (1)	**892.** (2)	**893.** (1)	**894.** (4)	**895.** (3)	**896.** (2)	**897.** (1)	**898.** (1)	**899.** (3)	**900.** (1)
901. (3)	**902.** (3)	**903.** (1)	**904.** (1)	**905.** (2)	**906.** (1)	**907.** (2)	**908.** (2)	**909.** (3)	**910.** (1)
911. (3)	**912.** (1)	**913.** (1)	**914.** (2)	**915.** (3)	**916.** (2)	**917.** (2)	**918.** (1)	**919.** (1)	**920.** (1)
921. (2)	**922.** (1)	**923.** (1)	**924.** (2)	**925.** (1)	**926.** (1)	**927.** (1)	**928.** (4)	**929.** (3)	**930.** (3)
931. (2)	**932.** (2)	**933.** (2)	**934.** (2)	**935.** (3)	**936.** (2)	**937.** (3)	**938.** (3)	**939.** (2)	**940.** (2)
941. (1)	**942.** (1)	**943.** (1)	**944.** (1)	**945.** (3)	**946.** (1)	**947.** (2)	**948.** (3)	**949.** (2)	**950.** (1)
951. (2)	**952.** (4)	**953.** (1)	**954.** (2)	**955.** (2)	**956.** (3)	**957.** (3)	**958.** (4)	**959.** (1)	**960.** (1)
961. (4)	**962.** (2)	**963.** (3)	**964.** (2)	**965.** (3)	**966.** (4)	**967.** (2)	**968.** (4)	**969.** (1)	**970.** (3)
971. (1)	**972.** (3)	**973.** (1)	**974.** (2)	**975.** (1)	**976.** (1)	**977.** (4)	**978.** (3)	**979.** (3)	**980.** (3)
981. (3)	**982.** (2)	**983.** (2)	**984.** (4)	**985.** (2)	**986.** (1)	**987.** (1)	**988.** (3)	**989.** (4)	**990.** (3)
991. (2)	**992.** (2)	**993.** (2)	**994.** (1)	**995.** (3)	**996.** (3)	**997.** (1)	**998.** (1)	**999.** (1)	**1000.** (1)
1001. (3)	**1002.** (1)	**1003.** (3)	**1004.** (1)	**1005.** (1)	**1006.** (1)	**1007.** (4)	**1008.** (1)	**1009.** (3)	**1010.** (1)
1011. (1)	**1012.** (1)	**1013.** (1)	**1014.** (2)	**1015.** (2)	**1016.** (1)	**1017.** (3)	**1018.** (3)	**1019.** (2)	**1020.** (2)
1021. (3)	**1022.** (1)	**1023.** (1)	**1024.** (1)	**1025.** (2)	**1026.** (3)	**1027.** (1)	**1028.** (3)	**1029.** (1)	**1030.** (2)
1031. (1)	**1032.** (2)	**1033.** (2)	**1034.** (1)	**1035.** (2)	**1036.**(4)	**1037.** (4)	**1038.** (2)	**1039.** (2)	**1040.** (2)
1041. (2)	**1042.** (1)	**1043.** (2)	**1044.** (3)	**1045.** (2)	**1046.** (2)	**1047.** (2)	**1048.** (1)	**1049.** (2)	**1050.** (1)
1051. (2)	**1052.** (3)	**1053.** (3)	**1054.** (1)	**1055.** (3)	**1056.** (3)	**1057.** (1)	**1058.** (4)	**1059.** (4)	**1060.** (1)
1061. (3)	**1062.** (2)	**1063.** (3)	**1064.** (3)	**1065.** (1)	**1066.** (2)	**1067.** (3)	**1068.** (2)	**1069.** (3)	**1070.** (1)
1071. (3)	**1072.** (4)	**1073.** (1)	**1074.** (2)	**1075.** (1)	**1076.** (4)	**1077.** (2)	**1078.** (3)	**1079.** (2)	**1080.** (4)
1081. (2)	**1082.** (4)	**1083.** (1)	**1084.** (1)	**1085.** (2)	**1086.** (1)	**1087.** (1)	**1088.** (4)	**1089.** (4)	**1090.** (2)
1091. (3)	**1092.** (1)	**1093.** (2)	**1094.** (3)	**1095.** (3)	**1096.** (1)	**1097.** (4)	**1098.** (2)	**1099.** (4)	**1100.** (1)
1101. (3)	**1102.** (2)	**1103.** (4)	**1104.** (1)	**1105.** (1)	**1106.** (1)	**1107.** (1)	**1108.** (2)	**1109.** (3)	**1110.** (4)
1111. (1)	**1112.** (2)	**1113.** (2)	**1114.** (2)	**1115.** (2)	**1116.** (2)	**1117.** (3)	**1118.** (3)	**1119.** (1)	**1120.** (2)
1121. (2)	**1122.** (2)	**1123.** (2)	**1124.** (3)	**1125.** (3)	**1126.** (1)	**1127.** (2)	**1128.** (3)	**1129.** (2)	**1130.** (3)
1131. (1)	**1132.** (1)	**1133.** (2)	**1134.** (3)	**1135.** (1)	**1136.** (4)	**1137.** (2)	**1138.** (3)	**1139.** (2)	**1140.** (4)
1141. (2)	**1142.** (3)	**1143.** (3)	**1144.** (3)	**1145.** (4)	**1146.** (2)	**1147.** (1)	**1148.** (3)	**1149.** (1)	**1150.** (3)
1151. (3)	**1152.** (1)	**1153.** (2)	**1154.** (2)	**1155.** (2)	**1156.** (2)	**1157.** (1)	**1158.** (1)	**1159.** (2)	**1160.** (1)
1161. (3)	**1162.** (3)	**1163.** (1)	**1164.** (3)	**1165.** (1)	**1166.** (2)	**1167.** (4)	**1168.** (1)	**1169.** (3)	**1170.** (4)
1171. (1)	**1172.** (3)	**1173.** (1)	**1174.** (1)	**1175.** (4)	**1176.** (3)	**1177.** (4)	**1178.** (2)	**1179.** (1)	**1180.** (1)
1181. (1)	**1182.** (1)	**1183.** (1)	**1184.** (3)	**1185.** (1)	**1186.** (2)	**1187.** (2)	**1188.** (3)	**1189.** (4)	**1190.** (2)
1191. (1)	**1192.** (1)	**1193.** (1)	**1194.** (1)	**1195.** (1)	**1196.** (1)	**1197.** (1)	**1198.** (1)	**1199.** (2)	**1200.** (1)
1201. (1)	**1202.** (2)	**1203.** (1)	**1204.** (1)	**1205.** (1)	**1206.** (1)	**1207.** (1)	**1208.** (2)	**1209.** (2)	**1210.** (2)
1211. (1)	**1212.** (1)	**1213.** (4)	**1214.** (4)	**1215.** (3)	**1216.** (1)	**1217.** (4)	**1218.** (4)	**1219.** (4)	**1220.** (3)

1221. (3) 1222. (3) 1223. (1) 1224. (2) 1225. (4) 1226. (3) 1227. (3) 1228. (2) 1229. (4) 1230. (3)
1231. (4) 1232. (2) 1233. (2) 1234. (4) 1235. (2) 1236. (1) 1237. (2) 1238. (2) 1239. (4) 1240. (3)
1241. (3) 1242. (1) 1243. (4) 1244. (4) 1245. (4) 1246. (2) 1247. (1) 1248. (2) 1249. (1) 1250. (1)
1251. (1) 1252. (1) 1253. (1) 1254. (1) 1255. (1) 1256. (1) 1257. (1) 1258. (1) 1259. (1) 1260. (1)
1261. (3) 1262. (1) 1263. (1) 1264. (1) 1265. (3) 1266. (1) 1267. (2) 1268. (1) 1269. (1) 1270. (1)
1271. (1) 1272. (1) 1273. (1) 1274. (1) 1275. (1) 1276. (1) 1277. (2) 1278. (2) 1279. (1) 1280. (2)
1281. (1) 1282. (1) 1283. (1) 1284. (1) 1285. (1) 1286. (1) 1287. (2) 1288. (1) 1289. (2) 1290. (2)
1291. (1) 1292. (4) 1293. (1) 1294. (1) 1295. (1) 1296. (3) 1297. (1) 1298. (1) 1299. (1) 1300. (1)
1301. (3) 1302. (1) 1303. (1) 1304. (3) 1305. (2) 1306. (2) 1307. (1) 1308. (4) 1309. (2) 1310. (2)
1311. (1) 1312. (4) 1313. (4) 1314. (4) 1315. (1) 1316. (2) 1317. (3) 1318. (1) 1319. (1) 1320. (4)
1321. (1) 1322. (4) 1323. (4) 1324. (4) 1325. (2) 1326. (4) 1327. (1) 1328. (3) 1329. (2) 1330. (1)
1331. (3) 1332. (2) 1333. (1) 1334. (4) 1335. (3) 1336. (2) 1337. (1) 1338. (3) 1339. (4) 1340. (3)
1341. (2) 1342. (2) 1343. (2) 1344. (4) 1345. (1) 1346. (3) 1347. (3) 1348. (4) 1349. (2) 1350. (2)
1351. (1) 1352. (1) 1353. (2) 1354. (2) 1355. (3) 1356. (3) 1357. (4) 1358. (4) 1359. (1) 1360. (1)
1361. (2) 1362. (3) 1363. (2) 1364. (1) 1365. (3) 1366. (2) 1367. (3) 1368. (1) 1369. (2) 1370. (3)
1371. (3) 1372. (4) 1373. (3) 1374. (2) 1375. (3) 1376. (3) 1377. (3) 1378. (1) 1379. (3) 1380. (2)
1381. (4) 1382. (1) 1383. (1) 1384. (2) 1385. (3) 1386. (3) 1387. (3) 1388. (1) 1389. (4) 1390. (4)
1391. (1) 1392. (2) 1393. (3) 1394. (3) 1395. (4) 1396. (2) 1397. (2) 1398. (4) 1399. (3) 1400. (4)
1401. (4) 1402. (3) 1403. (4) 1404. (1) 1405. (4) 1406. (1) 1407. (3) 1408. (3) 1409. (2) 1410. (1)
1411. (1) 1412. (1) 1413. (2) 1414. (2) 1415. (3) 1416. ( ) 1417. (1) 1418. (4) 1419. (2) 1420. (3)
1421. (1) 1422. (1) 1423. (1) 1424. (1) 1425. (1) 1426. (1) 1427. (1) 1428. (3) 1429. (1) 1430. (3)
1431. (3) 1432. (2) 1433. (3) 1434. (1) 1435. (1) 1436. (1) 1437. (1) 1438. (1) 1439. (1) 1440. (1)
1441. (1) 1442. (3) 1443. (1) 1444. (4) 1445. (1) 1446. (2) 1447. (1) 1448. (1) 1449. (1) 1450. (1)
1451. (1) 1452. (1) 1453. (1) 1454. (1) 1455. (1) 1456. (1) 1457. (1) 1458. (1) 1459. (1) 1460. (1)
1461. (1) 1462. (1) 1463. (1) 1464. (1) 1465. (1) 1466. (1) 1467. (1) 1468. (1) 1469. (1) 1470. ( )
1471. (1) 1472. (1) 1473. (1) 1474. (1) 1475. (2) 1476. (1) 1477. (1) 1473. (1) 1479. (1) 1480. (1)
1481. (1) 1482. (1) 1483. (1) 1484. (4) 1485. (2) 1486. (1) 1487. (1) 1488. (1) 1489. (1) 1490. (3)
1491. (1) 1492. (1) 1493. (1) 1494. (1) 1495. (1) 1496. (1) 1497. (2) 1498. (4) 1499. (1) 1500. (3)
1501. (1) 1502. (3) 1503. (2) 1504. (3) 1505. (1) 1506. (2) 1507. (3) 1508. (3) 1509. (2) 1510. (2)
1511. (2) 1512. (2) 1513. (3) 1514. (1) 1515. (3) 1516. (3) 1517. (1) 1518. (4) 1519. (4) 1520. (2)
1521. (1) 1522. (1) 1523. (3) 1524. (4) 1525. (3) 1526. (3) 1527. (3) 1528. (2) 1529. (1) 1530. (2)
1531. (1) 1532. (1) 1533. (1) 1534. (3) 1535. (2) 1536. (4) 1537. (2) 1538. (4) 1539. (1) 1540. (4)
1541. (1) 1542. (3) 1543. (4) 1544. (2) 1545. (1) 1546. (2) 1547. (2) 1548. (4) 1549. (4) 1550. (2)
1551. (3) 1552. (3) 1553. (3) 1554. (2) 1555. (4) 1556. (1) 1557. (4) 1558. (4) 1559. (4) 1560. (4)
1561. (1) 1562. (4) 1563. (1) 1564. (2) 1565. (3) 1566. (1) 1567. (2) 1568. (2) 1569. (3) 1570. (1)
1571. (2) 1572. (3) 1573. (1) 1574. (1) 1575. (3) 1576. (1) 1577. (2) 1578. (4) 1579. (3) 1580. (1)
1581. (1) 1582. (2) 1583. (3) 1584. (1) 1585. (1) 1586. (1) 1587. (1) 1588. (1) 1589. (1) 1590. (1)
1591. (1) 1592. (2) 1593. (2) 1594. (1) 1595. (1) 1596. (1) 1597. (1) 1598. (3) 1599. (1) 1600. (1)
1601. (1) 1602. (1) 1603. (2) 1604. (1) 1605. (3) 1606. (3) 1607. (1) 1608. (1) 1609. (1) 1610. (1)
1611. (1) 1612. (1) 1613. (1) 1614. (1) 1615. (1) 1616. (2) 1617. (1) 1618. (1) 1619. (1) 1620. (1)
1621. (1) 1622. (1) 1623. (1) 1624. (1) 1625. (1) 1626. (1) 1627. (1) 1628. (1) 1629. (2) 1630. (4)
1631. (3) 1632. (4) 1633. (1) 1634. (3) 1635. (3) 1636. (4) 1637. (2) 1638. (3) 1639. (1) 1640. (4)

1641. (2) **1642.** (1) **1643.** (2) **1644.** (2) **1645.** (2) **1646.** (4) **1647.** (3) **1648.** (4) **1649.** (2) **1650.** (1)
1651. (4) **1652.** (2) **1653.** (2) **1654.** (4) **1655.** (2) **1656.** (1) **1657.** (4) **1658.** (2) **1659.** (2) **1660.** (1)
1661. (4) **1662.** (3) **1663.** (4) **1664.** (3) **1665.** (4) **1666.** (3) **1667.** (4) **1668.** (4) **1669.** (1) **1670.** (1)
1671. (2) **1672.** (4) **1673.** (2) **1674.** (2) **1675.** (1) **1676.** (4) **1677.** (1) **1678.** (2) **1679.** (3) **1680.** (3)
1681. (1) **1682.** (2) **1683.** (1) **1684.** (1) **1685.** (3) **1686.** (2) **1687.** (4) **1688.** (2) **1689.** (3) **1690.** (1)
1691. (2) **1692.** (3) **1693.** (2) **1694.** (2) **1695.** (2) **1696.** (2) **1697.** (2) **1698.** (2) **1699.** (2) **1700.** (1)
1701. (2) **1702.** (1) **1703.** (3) **1704.** (1) **1705.** (1) **1706.** (3) **1707.** (1) **1708.** (1) **1709.** (1) **1410.** (3)
1711. (2) **1712.** (3) **1713.** (1) **1714.** (2) **1715.** (3) **1716.** (2) **1717.** (1) **1718.** (3) **1719.** (3) **1720.** (1)
1721. (3) **1722.** (2) **1723.** (1) **1724.** (2) **1725.** (1) **1726.** (3) **1727.** (3) **1728.** (4) **1729.** (1) **1730.** (4)
1731. (4) **1732.** (2) **1733.** (2) **1734.** (1) **1735.** (4) **1736.** (4) **1737.** (2) **1738.** (2) **1739.** (3) **1740.** (1)
1741. (1) **1742.** (1) **1743.** (1) **1744.** (1) **1745.** (1) **1746.** (1) **1747.** (1) **1748.** (2) **1749.** (1) **1750.** (1)
1751. (1) **1752.** (1) **1753.** (1) **1754.** (1) **1755.** (1) **1756.** (1) **1757.** (1) **1758.** (1) **1759.** (2) **1760.** (3)
1761. (1) **1762.** (1) **1763.** (1) **1764.** (1) **1765.** (1) **1766.** (2) **1767.** (2) **1768.** (4) **1769.** (4) **1770.** (2)
1771. (4) **1772.** (3) **1773.** (1) **1774.** (4) **1775.** (4) **1776.** (3) **1777.** (1) **1778.** (2) **1779.** (3) **1780.** (1)
1781. (4) **1782.** (2) **1783.** (1) **1784.** (3) **1785.** (3) **1786.** (2) **1787.** (2) **1788.** (1) **1789.** (2) **1790.** (1)
1791. (3) **1792.** (2) **1793.** (3) **1794.** (1) **1795.** (2) **1796.** (3) **1797.** (1) **1798.** (1) **1799.** (2) **1800.** (3)
1801. (2) **1802.** (4) **1803.** (2) **1804.** (2) **1805.** (2) **1806.** (2) **1807.** (2) **1808.** (3) **1809.** (2) **1810.** (2)
1811. (2) **1812.** (2) **1813.** (3) **1814.** (3) **1815.** (1) **1816.** (1) **1817.** (3) **1818.** (3) **1819.** (4) **1820.** (3)
1821. (3) **1822.** (2) **1823.** (3) **1824.** (3) **1825.** (2) **1826.** (2) **1827.** (2) **1828.** (3) **1829.** (1) **1830.** (2)
1831. (1) **1832.** (2) **1833.** (2) **1834.** (4) **1835.** (2) **1836.** (4) **1837.** (3) **1838.** (1) **1839.** (3) **1840.** (2)
1841. (1) **1842.** (1) **1843.** (2) **1844.** (1) **1845.** (1) **1846.** (1) **1847.** (1) **1848.** (4) **1849.** (3) **1850.** (2)
1851. (2) **1852.** (3) **1853.** (1) **1854.** (3) **1855.** (1) **1856.** (3) **1857.** (3) **1858.** (4) **1859.** (3) **1860.** (2)
1861. (1) **1862.** (4) **1863.** (1) **1864.** (3) **1865.** (2) **1866.** (4) **1867.** (1) **1868.** (1) **1869.** (2) **1870.** (2)
1871. (1) **1872.** (3) **1873.** (1) **1874.** (3) **1875.** (4) **1876.** (1) **1877.** (2) **1878.** (1) **1879.** (2) **1880.** (3)
1881. (3) **1882.** (2) **1883.** (2) **1884.** (3) **1885.** (2) **1886.** (2) **1887.** (3) **1888.** (3) **1889.** (2) **1890.** (3)
1891. (2) **1892.** (4) **1893.** (2) **1894.** (1) **1895.** (3) **1896.** (1) **1897.** (3) **1898.** (3) **1899.** (4) **1900.** (4)
1901. (2) **1902.** (4) **1903.** (4) **1904.** (2) **1905.** (2) **1906.** (3) **1907.** (2) **1908.** (2) **1909.** (3) **1910.** (2)
1911. (1) **1912.** (1) **1913.** (2) **1914.** (3) **1915.** (2) **1916.** (3) **1917.** (2) **1918.** (2) **1919.** (4) **1920.** (2)
1921. (2) **1922.** (4) **1923.** (3) **1924.** (4) **1925.** (2) **1926.** (2) **1927.** (2) **1928.** (2) **1929.** (1) **1930.** (2)
1931. (1) **1932.** (2) **1933.** (2) **1934.** (1) **1935.** (1) **1936.** (4) **1937.** (4) **1938.** (2) **1939.** (3) **1940.** (3)
1941. (2) **1942.** (1) **1943.** (2) **1944.** (1) **1945.** (2) **1946.** (1) **1947.** (1) **1948.** (2) **1949.** (1) **1950.** (1)
1951. (1) **1952.** (2) **1953.** (1) **1954.** (1) **1955.** (2) **1956.** (1) **1957.** (1) **1958.** (1) **1959.** (1) **1960.** (2)
1961. (1) **1962.** (1) **1963.** (2) **1964.** (1) **1965.** (1) **1966.** (4) **1967.** (4) **1968.** (2) **1969.** (4) **1970.** (4)
1971. (2) **1972.** (2) **1973.** (3) **1974.** (4) **1975.** (1) **1976.** (2) **1977.** (2) **1978.** (3) **1979.** (1) **1980.** (3)
1981. (2) **1982.** (2) **1983.** (2) **1984.** (2) **1985.** (1) **1986.** (3) **1987.** (2) **1988.** (1) **1989.** (4) **1990.** (4)
1991. (1) **1992.** (2) **1993.** (3) **1994.** (4) **1995.** (4) **1996.** (2) **1997.** (1) **1998.** (3) **1999.** (1) **2000.** (2)
2001. (1) **2002.** (2) **2003.** (2) **2004.** (3) **2005.** (2) **2006.** (2) **2007.** (2) **2008.** (2) **2009.** (1) **2010.** (4)
2011. (2) **2012.** (2) **2013.** (2) **2014.** (3) **2015.** (4) **2016.** (3) **2017.** (1) **2018.** (2) **2019.** (3) **2020.** (2)
2021. (1) **2022.** (1) **2023.** (4) **2024.** (1) **2025.** (2) **2026.** (2) **2027.** (1) **2028.** (2) **2029.** (1) **2030.** (3)
2031. (4) **2032.** (3) **2033.** (1) **2034.** (2) **2035.** (4) **2036.** (3) **2037.** (1) **2038.** (2) **2039.** (1) **2040.** (1)
2041. (4) **2042.** (3) **2043.** (4) **2044.** (2) **2045.** (2) **2046.** (2) **2047.** (3) **2048.** (4) **2049.** (2) **2050.** (2)
2051. (2) **2052.** (2) **2053.** (3) **2054.** (4) **2055.** (1) **2056.** (4) **2057.** (1) **2058.** (4) **2059.** (1) **2060.** (1)

2061. (2) **2062.** (3) **2063.** (3) **2064.** (3) **2065.** (4) **2066.** (4) **2067.** (2) **2068.** (1) **2069.** (3) **2070.** (2)

2071. (1) **2072.** (1) **2073.** (1) **2074.** (1) **2075.** (2) **2076.** (2) **2077.** (3) **2078.** (1) **2079.** (1) **2080.** (2)

2081. (4) **2082.** (1) **2083.** (2) **2084.** (3) **2085.** (3) **2086.** (4) **2087.** (1) **2088.** (1) **2089.** (1) **2090.** (1)

2091. (1) **2092.** (2) **2093.** (1) **2094.** (1) **2095.** (1) **2096.** (3) **2097.** (2) **2098.** (1) **2099.** (1) **2100.** (1)

2101. (1) **2102.** (1) **2103.** (1) **2104.** (1) **2105.** (1) **2106.** (1) **2107.** (1) **2108.** (2) **2109.** (1) **2110.** (4)

2111. (1) **2112.** (3) **2113.** (4) **2114.** (1) **2115.** (3) **2116.** (2) **2117.** (1) **2118.** (1) **2119.** (1) **2120.** (1)

2121. (4) **2122.** (1) **2123.** (1) **2124.** (3) **2125.** (1) **2126.** (4) **2127.** (1) **2128.** (1) **2129.** (1) **2130.** (4)

2131. (4) **2132.** (1) **2133.** (2) **2134.** (3) **2135.** (2) **2136.** (1) **2137.** (2) **2138.** (1) **2139.** (4) **2140.** (3)

2141. (2) **2142.** (3) **2143.** (2) **2144.** (1) **2145.** (2) **2146.** (3) **2147.** (3) **2148.** (2) **2149.** (2) **2150.** (3)

2151. (1) **2152.** (2) **2153.** (2) **2154.** (3) **2155.** (2) **2156.** (2) **2157.** (3) **2158.** (3) **2159.** (2) **2160.** (1)

2161. (1) **2162.** (3) **2163.** (2) **2164.** (3) **2165.** (4) **2166.** (3) **2167.** (4) **2168.** (4) **2169.** (3) **2170.** (3)

2171. (1) **2172.** (1) **2173.** (3) **2174.** (4) **2175.** (2) **2176.** (3) **2177.** (2) **2178.** (2) **2179.** (1) **2180.** (1)

2181. (2) **2182.** (3) **2183.** (1) **2184.** (3) **2185.** (1) **2186.** (4) **2187.** (3) **2188.** (3) **2189.** (2) **2190.** (3)

2191. (3) **2192.** (4) **2193.** (1) **2194.** (1) **2195.** (1) **2196.** (2) **2197.** (2) **2198.** (3) **2199.** (1) **2200.** (2)

2201. (4) **2202.** (1) **2203.** (1) **2204.** (2) **2205.** (3) **2206.** (4) **2207.** (3) **2208.** (1) **2209.** (1) **2210.** (2)

2211. (3) **2212.** (4) **2213.** (2) **2214.** (4) **2215.** (2) **2216.** (3) **2217.** (4) **2218.** (4) **2219.** (3) **2220.** (3)

2221. (1) **2222.** (1) **2223.** (2) **2224.** (2) **2225.** (2) **2226.** (2) **2227.** (2) **2228.** (1) **2229.** (1) **2230.** (2)

2231. (3) **2232.** (2) **2233.** (1) **2234.** (3) **2235.** (4) **2236.** (2) **2237.** (3) **2238.** (1) **2239.** (2) **2240.** (3)

2241. (2) **2242.** (2) **2243.** (1) **2244.** (3) **2245.** (1) **2246.** (3) **2247.** (3) **2248.** (4) **2249.** (3) **2250.** (1)

2251. (3) **2252.** (2) **2253.** (4) **2254.** (3) **2255.** (1) **2256.** (2) **2257.** (3) **2258.** (4) **2259.** (2) **2260.** (4)

2261. (3) **2262.** (2) **2263.** (3) **2264.** (2) **2265.** (2) **2266.** (3) **2267.** (3) **2268.** (2) **2269.** (2) **2270.** (1)

2271. (3) **2272.** (3) **2273.** (2) **2274.** (1) **2275.** (3) **2276.** (1) **2277.** (3) **2278.** (3) **2279.** (3) **2280.** (2)

2281. (1) **2282.** (3) **2283.** (1) **2284.** (3) **2285.** (1) **2286.** (2) **2287.** (3) **2288.** (3) **2289.** (3) **2290.** (1)

2291. (2) **2292.** (1) **2293.** (2) **2294.** (1) **2295.** (1) **2296.** (1) **2297.** (1) **2298.** (3) **2299.** (2) **2300.** (2)

2301. (1) **2302.** (4) **2303.** (1) **2304.** (2) **2305.** (1) **2306.** (1) **2307.** (1) **2308.** (1) **2309.** (1) **2310.** (1)

2311. (1) **2312.** (1) **2313.** (1) **2314.** (1) **2315.** (1) **2316.** (1) **2317.** (1) **2318.** (1) **2319.** (1) **2320.** (4)

2321. (1) **2322.** (1) **2323.** (1) **2324.** (4) **2325.** (2) **2326.** (1) **2327.** (1) **2328.** (3) **2329.** (3) **2330.** (4)

2331. (2) **2332.** (2) **2333.** (2) **2334.** (2) **2335.** (1) **2336.** (2) **2337.** (2) **2338.** (3) **3399.** (3) **2340.** (1)

2341. (4) **2342.** (2) **2343.** (2) **2344.** (1) **2345.** (4) **2346.** (3) **2347.** (2) **2348.** (3) **2349.** (2) **2350.** (4)

2351. (3) **2352.** (1) **2353.** (2) **2354.** (2) **2355.** (1) **2356.** (1) **2357.** (3) **2358.** (1) **2359.** (1) **2360.** (2)

2361. (3) **2362.** (1) **2363.** (1) **2364.** (1) **2365.** (1) **2366.** (1) **2367.** (1) **2368.** (3) **2369.** (1) **2370.** (2)

2371. (3) **2372.** (1) **2373.** (1) **2374.** (2) **2375.** (1) **2376.** (1) **2377.** (1) **2378.** (4) **2379.** (2) **2380.** (2)

2381. (1) **2382.** (2) **2383.** (1) **2384.** (1) **2385.** (1) **2386.** (1) **2387.** (1) **2388.** (1) **2389.** (1) **2390.** (1)

2391. (3) **2392.** (4) **2393.** (1) **2394.** (2) **2395.** (4) **2396.** (1) **2397.** (2) **2398.** (3) **2399.** (3) **2400.** (4)

2401. (3) **2402.** (4) **2403.** (3) **2404.** (1) **2405.** (1) **2406.** (1) **2407.** (4) **2408.** (1) **2409.** (2) **2410.** (1)

(Revised Pattern)

MODEL PAPER-1

Note : This paper contains **hundred** (100) Objective type questions, each question carrying **two** (2) marks. Attempt all of them.

1. Vyavaharika Satta refutes
   (1) Pāramārthika Sattā
   (2) Pratibhāsika Sattā
   (3) Both Pāramarthika and Pratibhāsika Sattā
   (4) Neither Pāramarthika nor Pratibhāsika Sattā

2. The view that *cit* and *acit* are two parts of Brahman is upheld by
   (1) Saṅnkara (2) Maddhva
   (3) Rāmānuja (4) Jaimini

3. Empirical, objective, subjective and transcendental are four grades of
   (1) Pure consciousness
   (2) Theoretic consciousness
   (3) Pure Reason
   (4) Practical Reason

4. Ambedkar distinguishes between
   (1) Need to kill and drive to kill
   (2) Need to kill and love to kill
   (3) Need to kill and will to kill
   (4) Will to kill and refusal to kill

5. According to whom 'Yoga is the cessation of the modification of Citta'.
   (1) Vasubandhu
   (2) Patanjali
   (3) Isvarakrisna
   (4) Vijnahbhikhsu

6. "Continuity feigns identity" is the position maintained by
   (1) Locke
   (2) Berkeley
   (3) Hume
   (4) Davidson

7. Protagoras propounded
   (1) Man is measure of all things
   (2) Man is mortal
   (3) Man is immortal
   (4) Man is divine

8. "A great many expressions of everyday life are systematically misleading." This is the argument by
   (1) Wittgenstein (2) Ayer
   (3) Ryle (4) Moore

9. Which is *not* a school of Buddhism ?
   (1) Madhyamika
   (2) Puranika
   (3) Vaibhasika
   (4) Sautrantika

10. Identify the correct pair
    (1) Kierkegaard — Epoche
    (2) Nietzsche — Existence
    (3) Jaspers — Boundary situations
    (4) Heidegger — God is dead

11. The argument for existence of God that is based on the concept of 'Existence' is called
    (1) Moral (2) Teleological
    (3) Ontological (4) Cosmological

12. Aristotle's work on logic is known as
    (1) Theoria
    (2) Organon

(3) Techne
(4) Proxis

13. The mind without fear, without belief is silent. J. Krishnamurti calls it
(1) Religious mind
(2) Spiritual mind
(3) Devotional mind
(4) Developed mind

14. Absolute is conceived by Rādhākrishnan as Pure Consciousness, Freedom and
(1) Pure Bliss
(2) Infinite Possibility
(3) Pure Existence
(4) Infinite Bliss

15. "The truth of any hypothesis is measured by the success in resolving the problem which occasioned it." This view is held by
(1) William James
(2) C.I. Lewis
(3) John Dewey
(4) Charles Peirce

16. Which of the following represent the right chronological order ?
(1) Brāimanas, Aranyakas, Samhitas and Upanisads
(2) Samhitas, Brahmanas, Áranyakas and Upanisads
(3) Samhitas, Aranyakas, Brāimanas and Upanisads
(4) Brahmanas, Samhitas, Aranyakas and Upanisads

17. The four causes, given by Aristotle, can be arranged in the correct order as
(1) Formal, Material, Efficient and Final
(2) Material, Efficient, Final and Formal
(3) Material, Formal, Efficient and Final
(4) Material, Efficient, Formal and Final

18. Which of the following is defined by Patanjali as 'one who is free from the effects of afflicted actions' ?
(1) Citta (2) Kaivalya
(3) Para-Brahma (4) God

19. Which is not in the triple transformation according to Sri Aurobindo ?
(1) Psychic transformation
(2) Material transformation
(3) Spiritual transformation
(4) Supermental transformation

20. Logical positivists eliminate metaphysics because metaphysical statements are
(1) Incorrect
(2) Non-sensical
(3) Inconsistent
(4) Ineffable

21. Cartesian doubt implies the existence of
(1) thinker (2) doubter
(3) self (4) myself

22. Which source of knowledge is acceptable to Carvakas?
(1) Inference (2) Comparison
(3) Testimony (4) Perception

23. The hierarchy of existence is topped according to Leibnitz by
(1) Monads
(2) God
(3) Sleeping monads
(4) Windowless monads

24. According to later Wittgenstein, universals can be understood as
(1) Names
(2) Concepts
(3) Resemblances
(4) Entities

25. The non-existence of milk in oil is an example of
(1) Atyantabhava
(2) Pradhvansabhava
(3) Anyonyabhava
(4) Pragabhava

26. According to Tagore, man has yearning for Mukti because of
(1) Finite aspect (2) Infinite aspect
(3) Jivandevata (4) God

27. Cessation of suffering in Buddhism is described in the
(1) Third noble truth
(2) First noble truth
(3) Second noble truth
(4) Fourth noble truth

28. According to Hegel, which of the following holds true ?
(1) Real is rational but rational is not real
(2) Rational is real but real is not rational
(3) Neither real is rational nor rational is real
(4) Real is rational and rational is real

29. The two modes of existence in Heidegger's philosophy are
(1) real and unreal existence
(2) free and enslaved existence
(3) authentic and inauthentic existence
(4) ethical and unethical existence

30. In order to avoid the dogma of the ghost in the machine, mental phenomena have to be understood as
(1) Acquisitions (2) Properties
(3) Dispositions (4) Entitiesz

31. For Ryle, knowing how to do things
(1) is dependent on mental theorizing
(2) is independent of mental theorizing
(3) neither independent nor dependent on mental theorizing
(4) both independent and dependent on mental theorizing

32. "Truth has no path" is maintained by
(1) J. Krishnamurti
(2) K.C. Bhattacharya
(3) Mahatma Gandhi
(4) Swami Vivekananda

33. In defense of commonsense, Moore refutes
(1) Spinoza's Pantheism
(2) Russell's Logical Atomism
(3) Berkeley's Subjective Idealism
(4) Leibnitz's Monodaism

34. Russell upheld the
(1) Ordinary Language Approach
(2) Logical Language Approach
(3) Ideal Language Approach
(4) Pragmatic Language Approach

35. St. Augustine's influential work The City of God' was considered as the first book on
(1) Comparative Philosophy
(2) Philosophy of Religion
(3) Philosophy of History
(4) Philosophy of Christianity

36. According to St. Aquinas theology presupposes faith in
(1) Devotion of God
(2) Divine revelation
(3) Authority of Scriptures
(4) Intuition

37. According to Wittgenstein's Tractatus, the world, thought and proposition share the same
(1) Logical form (2) Dialectical form
(3) Spiritual form (4) Empirical form

38. The following view not held by Aristotle is
(1) Four causes work simultaneously
(2) God is unmoved mover
(3) Four causes do not work simultaneously
(4) Prime matter is featureless

39. According to Ramanuja, which of the following cannot be in Vaikuntha?
(1) God
(2) Eternal selves
(3) Liberated selves
(4) Spirit and matter

40. Which is not accepted by K.C. Bhattacharya?
(1) Philosophy of Science
(2) Philosophy of the object
(3) Philosophy of the subject
(4) Philosophy of truth

41. Which statement is not true of Sophists ?
(1) They were skilled rhetoricians
(2) They charged fees for imparting their skills
(3) According to them 'man is the measure of all the things'
(4) According to them Virtue is knowledge'

42. What is the ultimate goal of Indian Ethics ?
(1) Liberation (Moksha)
(2) Duty
(3) Obey the ethics
(4) Social harmony

43. Spinoza's solution to mind-body problem is called
(1) Causal Interactionism
(2) Psycho-physical parallelism
(3) Epiphenomenalism
(4) Biological naturalism

44. Match List I with List II and choose correct answer from the codes given below

List-I	List-II
(a) Air	(i) Thales
(b) Limitless	(ii) Heraclitus
(c) Change	(iii) Anaximenes
(d) Water	(iv) Anaximander

Codes :

	(a)	(b)	(c)	(d)
(1)	(iii)	(iv)	(ii)	(i)
(2)	(iii)	(iv)	(i)	(ii)
(3)	(iv)	(ii)	(iii)	(i)
(4)	(iv)	(ii)	(i)	(iii)

45. Match List I with List II and select the correct answer from the codes given below:

List-I	List-II
(a) Russell	(i) Language game theory
(b) William James	(ii) Picture theory of meaning
(c) Early Wittgenstein	(iii) Logical atomism
(d) Later Wittgenstein	(iv) Pragmatic theory of truth

Codes :

	(a)	(b)	(c)	(d)
(1)	(i)	(ii)	(iii)	(iv)
(2)	(iv)	(iii)	(ii)	(i)
(3)	(ii)	(iii)	(iv)	(i)
(4)	(iii)	(iv)	(ii)	(i)

46. Plato has rejected :
A. Realists theory of universals
B. Nominalistic theory of universals
C. Conceptualistic theory of universals
D. Comparative theory of universals

Select the correct answer from the codes given below :
(1) A and B
(2) A, B and C
(3) B and C
(4) A, C and D

47. The theories that are not advocated by Plato are :

A. theory of ideas
B. theory of recognition
C. theory of recollection
D. theory of categories

Select the correct answer from the codes given below :

Codes :

(1) A and B (2) B and D
(3) A and C (4) C and B

48. Which of the following statements is/are not true for Heraclitus ?

A. Fire is the basic world stuff
B. To men all things are fair and good
C. To God all things are fair and good
D. One cannot step into the same river twice

Select the correct answer from the codes given below :

(1) B and C (2) A and B
(3) B only (4) C and D

49. The pair of opposites which are not mentioned by Pythagoras are :

A. Straight and crooked
B. Light and heavy
C. Right and wrong
D. Square and oblong

Select the correct answer from the codes given below :

(1) A and B (2) C and D
(3) B, C and D (4) A, B and D

50. **Assertion (A).** The Alayavijnana is immanent in all beings.

Reason (R). Six perfections are emphasized.

Select the correct answer from the codes given below :

(1) Both (A) and (R) are individually true
(2) (A) is true but (R) is false
(3) Both (A) and (R) are individually false
(4) (A) is false but (R) is true

51. The relation of contradiction exists between

(1) 'I' and 'O' propositions
(2) 'A' and 'E' propositions
(3) 'A' and 'I' propositions
(4) 'E' and 'I' propositions

52. According to Jainism, Jīva is

(1) only eternal
(2) only non-eternal
(3) both eternal and non-eternal
(4) non-existent

53. A proposition is

(1) Neither true nor false
(2) Either true or false
(3) Both true and false
(4) Valid and invalid

54. The validity of a deductive argument is determined by its

(1) Truth of its premises
(2) Truth of its conclusion
(3) Form
(4) Content

55. The number of Pramāṇas accepted by Saṁkhya is

(1) Two (2) Three
(3) Four (4) Five

56. According to Hume, cause and effect are not related through

(1) Logical necessity
(2) Constant conjunction
(3) Association of ideas
(4) Antecedence of events

57. Vallabhācarya's path towards liberation is called

(1) Karmamārga
(2) Puṣtimārga
(3) Bhaktimārga
(4) Prapattimārga

58. Who rejects the Enlightenment prejudice against prejudice?
(1) Gadamer
(2) Habermas
(3) Ricoeur
(4) Husserl

59. For Aristotle, form or structure is determined by
(1) Composition
(2) Quality
(3) Function
(4) Quantity

60. Prapatti as the path to liberation was advocated by
(1) Madhvācārya
(2) Nimbārkācārya
(3) Vallabhācārya
(4) Ramānujācārya

61. According to Hinduism the ultimate goal of human life is
(1) Dharma (2) Artha
(3) Kama (4) Moksa

62. According to 'Quran' the total number of Nabis is
(1) 26 (2) 28
(3) 27 (4) 25

63. According to Sankarācārya, God is
(1) Only a material cause of the world
(2) Only an efficient cause of the world
(3) Both material and efficient cause of the world
(4) a samavāyi cause of the world

64. The view that memory is central to personal identity was upheld by
(1) Hobbes (2) Locke
(3) Hume (4) Kant

65. According to Zarathushtra, God has these many sacred powers
(1) Two (2) Seven
(3) Eight (4) Six

66. Phenomenalism is the view that physical objects are
(1) Metaphysical constructions of sense data
(2) Spiritual constructions of sense data
(3) Logical constructions of sense data
(4) Physical constructions of sense data

67. Pramana is defined by Buddhism as
(1) Karaṇa of Pramā
(2) Yathārtha anubhava
(3) Sva-para- vyavasāyi-jñāna
(4) Avisaṁvādījñāna

68. Which of the following is a formulation of Kant's categorical imperative ?
(1) Mean between extremes
(2) Humanity as an end-in-itself
(3) The highest good
(4) Divine good

69. Which of the following is not correct with reference to Gandhiji ?
(1) In its negative form Ahiṁsā means physical and mental noninjury to any being
(2) In its positive form, it means largest love, love for enemy
(3) The follower of Ahiṁsā should be neutral towards his enemy
(4) Ahiṁsā consists of truth and fearlessness

70. Scepticism about whether the future resembles the past is a part of
(1) The hypothetico-deductive method
(2) The problem of induction
(3) Cartesian scepticism
(4) Pyrrohnian scepticism

71. Bhāṭṭa mīmamsā accepts the following theory of error
(1) Asatkhyāti
(2) Viparitakhyāti
(3) Anyathākhyāti
(4) Akhyāti

72. Like the deterrence theory, the rehabilitative approach to punishment is
(1) Oriented to the past
(2) Oriented to the present
(3) Oriented to the future
(4) Oriented to decent

73. The category of Sāmānya resides in
(1) Dravya, Karma and Vis'eṣa
(2) Dravya, Guṇa and Abhāva
(3) Dravya, Guṇa and Samavāya
(4) Dravya, Guṇa and Karma

74. According to Abhihitānvayavāda
(1) First sentence meaning is grasped, then word meaning
(2) First word meaning is grasped, then sentence meaning
(3) Both are grasped simultaneously
(4) Both are grasped in an irregular sequence

75. According to Naiyāyikas word meaning relation is determined
(1) only by divine convention
(2) only by human convention
(3) in some cases by divine convention, in some cases by human convention
(4) by no conventions, as the relation is eternal

76. According to christianity, love of God is
(1) Agape
(2) Eros
(3) Motherly love
(4) Fatherly love

77. For Gadamer, the fusion of horizons of interpretation and object is
(1) reference (2) meaning
(3) cognition (4) method

78. The notion of intentionality was propounded by
(1) Sartre (2) Schütz
(3) Heidegger (4) Brentano

79. According to Austin, performatives can be judged as
(1) Valid and invalid
(2) True and false
(3) Possible and impossible
(4) Happy and unhappy

80. When one perceives a table and has cognition of the form, "This is a table", it is according to Buddhists a case of
(1) Pratyakṣa Pramāṇa
(2) Anumāna Pramāṇa
(3) Sabda Pramāṇa
(4) Vikalp

81. According to the Ṛna theory we are indebted by birth, to the following
(1) God, parents and neighbours
(2) Gods, ancestors and teachers
(3) God, parents and society
(4) Gods, nature and living beings

82. At practical level, Advaita-Vedāntia ns accept the following number of pramāṇas
(1) Three (2) Four
(3) Five (4) Six

83. How many truth-possibilities/rows will be there in the truth table of
$[(p \supset q) \cdot (q \supset r)]\ (p \supset r)$
(1) 4 (2) 6
(3) 12 (4) 8

84. The best ās'rama for pursuing all the three purusarthas viz., Artha, Kāma and Dharma, was supposed to be
(1) Brahmacharya
(2) Gṛhastha
(3) Vānaprastha
(4) Saṁnyāsa

85. Identify the form of the following argument
$(E \supset N) \cdot (\sim L \supset \sim K)$
$\sim N \vee K \,/\, \therefore \sim E \vee L$
(1) Modus Tollens (M.T.)
(2) Constructive Dilemma (C.D.)
(3) Destructive Dilemma (D.D.)
(4) Disjunctive Syllogism (D.S.)

86. According to Russell
(1) All relations are external
(2) All relations are internal
(3) Internal-external division is not applicable to relations
(4) Relations are both, internal and external

87. Indubitable knowledge of Vyāpti is questioned by the following system
(1) Cārvāka
(2) Buddhism
(3) Jainism
(4) Saṁkhya

88. Existence of Dik can be established according to Nyāya -Vaiśeṣikas on the basis of
(1) Perception of things in space
(2) Intuition of spatial distances
(3) Linguistic usages such as 'to the east'.
(4) Reference in the Vedas

89. The attributes of validity and invalidity can belong only to
(1) deductive arguments
(2) inductive arguments
(3) deductive and inductive arguments both
(4) propositions

90. The subject term of the conclusion of a categorical syllogism is called
(1) Middle term
(2) Major term
(3) Minor term
(4) Negative term

91. The relation between two separables and that between two inseparables respectively are called in Nyaya -Vaisesikas as
(1) Tadutpatti and Tādātmya
(2) Saṁyoga and Samavāya
(3) Pṛthaksiddhi and Apṛthaksiddhi
(4) Bheda and Abheda

92. Samavāya relation does not subsist between
(1) Anuyogin-Pratiyogin
(2) Dravya-Guna
(3) Jāti and Vyakti
(4) Avayava and Avayavi

93. Total number of Tirthankaras in Jainism are
(1) 21 (2) 20
(3) 24 (4) 18

94. "We may understand by metaphysics........the effect to comprehend the universe, not simply piecemeal or by fragments but somehow as a whole." This statement can be attributed to
(1) Bradley
(2) Aristotle
(3) Aquinas
(4) Schopenhauer

95. "Women must always be honoured and respected by father, brothers, husband and brother-in-law. Who desire their welfare." This statement is made by

(1) Manu (2) Gandhi
(3) Tilak (4) Vivekananda

96. For Aristotle, a Universal is

(1) a property (2) an entity
(3) a concept (4) a name

97. According to Rāmānuja Brahman has

(1) No qualities
(2) Human-like qualities
(3) All and only good qualities
(4) Mostly good qualities but a few bad qualities

98. For Husserl the constitution of an intentional object as an object across different perceptual acts requires the following form of consciousness

(1) Cognitive (2) Subjective
(3) Temporal (4) Spatial

99. The prasthānatrayī of vedānta-system consists of

(1) Upaniṣadas, Smṛtis and Purāṇas
(2) Saṁhita, Āraṇyaka and Upaniṣadas
(3) Upanisadas, Brahmasutra and the Gītā
(4) Brahmasūtra, the Gītā and Bhāgvat apurana

100. Utilitarianism has another distinguishing character besides hedonism, namely

(1) Teleology (2) Deontology
(3) Biologism (4) Altruism

Answers

1. (2)	**2.** (3)	**3.** (2)	**4.** (2)	**5.** (3)	**6.** (1)	**7.** (2)	**8.** (4)	**9.** (2)	**10.** (1)
11. (2)	**12.** (4)	**13.** (2)	**14.** (3)	**15.** (3)	**16.** (3)	**17.** (4)	**18.** (2)	**19.** (3)	**20.** (2)
21. (2)	**22.** (1)	**23.** (3)	**24.** (4)	**25.** (2)	**26.** (4)	**27.** (4)	**28.** (4)	**29.** (4)	**30.** (4)
31. (4)	**32.** (1)	**33.** (3)	**34.** (4)	**35.** (2)	**36.** (2)	**37.** (4)	**38.** (2)	**39.** (1)	**40.** (2)
41. (3)	**42.** (2)	**43.** (4)	**44.** (3)	**45.** (2)	**46.** (1)	**47.** (4)	**48.** (2)	**49.** (3)	**50.** (4)
51. (4)	**52.** (3)	**53.** (2)	**54.** (3)	**55.** (2)	**56.** (1)	**57.** (2)	**58.** (1)	**59.** (3)	**60.** (4)
61. (4)	**62.** (2)	**63.** (3)	**64.** (2)	**65.** (4)	**66.** (3)	**67.** (4)	**68.** (2)	**69.** (3)	**70.** (2)
71. (2)	**72.** (3)	**73.** (4)	**74.** (2)	**75.** (3)	**76.** (1)	**77.** (2)	**78.** (4)	**79.** (4)	**80.** (4)
81. (2)	**82.** (4)	**83.** (4)	**84.** (2)	**85.** (3)	**86.** (1)	**87.** (1)	**88.** (3)	**89.** (1)	**90.** (3)
91. (2)	**92.** (1)	**93.** (3)	**94.** (1)	**95.** (2)	**96.** (1)	**97.** (3)	**98.** (3)	**99.** (3)	**100.** (1)

MODEL PAPER-2

Note : This paper contains **hundred** (100) Objective type questions, each question carrying **two** (2) marks. Attempt all of them.

1. Who says that there are a semantic difference between imperative and declarative sentences?
   (1) Consequentialist theory
   (2) Cognitivism
   (3) Relativity view
   (4) None of the above

2. Which one of the following is not true according to Gandhi ?
   (1) Ahiṁsā is a practical expression of Satya.
   (2) Man can know the absolute truth.
   (3) There is a chain of ends and means of values.
   (4) Satya and Ahiṁsā are inseparable

3. Nietzsche begins with the presumption
   (1) How can I become a Christian ?
   (2) Know yourself
   (3) God is dead
   (4) Man is the measure of all things

4. Yoga is defined by Patañjali as
   (1) Yogah Karmasu Kausalam
   (2) Yogah Cittavrttinirodhah
   (3) Samatvam Yogah Ucyate
   (4) Dhyanayoga

5. Plato's hierarchy is topped by
   (1) Idea of God
   (2) Idea of Good
   (3) God
   (4) Goodness

6. Surrendering oneself to God is called, in Yoga
   (1) Bhakti (2) Prapatti
   (3) Kriyayoga (4) Isvarapranidhana

7. Kumbhaka is a step in
   (1) Niyama
   (2) Asana
   (3) Yama
   (4) Pranayama

8. In the philosophy of Plato's 'Ideas' are
   (1) real but non-existent
   (2) existent but unreal
   (3) neither real nor non-existent
   (4) both real and existent

9. The philosopher who is associated with stoicism is
   (1) Thales (2) Plato
   (3) Heraclitus (4) Zeno

10. Which of the following is not mentioned in the concept of 'Tri-rna' ?
    (1) Rsi-rna
    (2) Deva-rna
    (3) Nisarga-rna
    (4) Pitru-rna

11. According to Aristotle, the science that is concerned with pure abstract knowledge is
    (1) Logic
    (2) Practical science
    (3) Theoretical science
    (4) The productive science

12. According to Tagore the finite form of Human tells about the characteristics of man such as
(1) Universality and Ego
(2) Individuality and Ego
(3) Creativity and Ego
(4) Creativity and Individuality

13. The ultimate human destiny, according to Radhakrishnan, is not individual but universal redemption called
(1) Sarvodaya
(2) Sarvamukti
(3) Bodhisattva
(4) Mahaparinirvana

14. "Jñana, Karma, Bhakti and Yoga are the means to Liberation" is maintained by
(1) K.C. Bhattacharya
(2) J. Krishnamurti
(3) Swami Vivekananda
(4) B.R. Ambedkar

15. "The movement from certainty to uncertainty is what I call fear" is said by
(1) K.C. Bhattacharya (2) Iqbal
(3) J. Krishnamurti
(4) S. Radhakrishnan

16. The dialectical method of Hegel consists of
(1) thesis and hypothesis
(2) thesis, synthesis and hypothesis
(3) antithesis and hypothesis
(4) thesis, antithesis and synthesis

17. According to Russell, language has a/an
(1) representative function
(2) empirical function
(3) pragmatic function
(4) expressive function

18. The strong verification principle was upheld by
(1) Schlick (2) Moore
(3) Carnap (4) Ayer

19. Point out from the following reason why Dr. B. R. Ambedkar opposes the caste system prevalent in India ?
(1) as it is suggested by smritis
(2) as it is Vedic heritage
(3) as it creates discrimination, social injustice and inequality within the Indian Nation
(4) as it is suggested by karma

20. Which of the following is not characteristic of Modern Indian Philosophy ?
(1) Belief in liberation
(2) Belief in reality of world
(3) No belief in superstition and dogmatism
(4) No belief in human existence and freedom of man

21. St. Augustine argues that when a will chooses evil, the cause of the choice is
(1) God
(2) Satan
(3) Lack of Knowledge
(4) Nature

22. The concept of Apurva is propounded by
(1) Vedanta
(2) Samkhya
(3) Mimansa
(4) Nyaya

23. In his 'Philosophical Investigations', Wittgenstein regards traditional philosophical problems as
(1) Complex
(2) Pseudo
(3) Genuine
(4) Simple

24. According to Gandhi, Ahimsa means
(1) not only non-violence but love

(2) not only non-violence but also love, service and sacrifice

(3) not only non-violence but also love and service

(4) not only non-violence but also service

25. In his refutation of idealism, Moore criticizes

(1) Spinoza's Natura Naturans

(2) Locke's Tabula Rasa

(3) Descartes' Cogito ergo sum

(4) Berkeley's Esse Est Percipi

26. Who refuted the Manuvada ?

(1) B. R. Ambedkar

(2) B. G. Tilak

(3) Sri Aurobindo

(4) M. N. Roy

27. The study of mathematics is the key to understand the structure and order of universe is the opinion of

(1) Aristotle

(2) Pythagoras

(3) Empedocles

(4) Democritus

28. In their unity of science project, the logical positivists gave the highest position to

(1) History and Physics

(2) Sociology and Physics

(3) Economics and Physics

(4) Physics

29. According to Hegel, the goal of the development of Absolute is

(1) Redemption

(2) Self-consciousness

(3) Cipher

(4) God

30. Heidegger's fundamental ontology is about

(1) Interpretation of Being

(2) Philosophy of Language

(3) Interpretation of Religion

(4) Interpretation of Dasein

31. 'All knowable objects are nameable the pot is knowable object, therefore the pot is nameable'. It is an example of the inference called

(1) Kevalanvayi

(2) Kevala Vyatireki

(3) Seshavat

(4) Anvaya-Vyatireki

32. Wittgenstein distinguished between 'sense' and 'non-sense' by

(1) analyzing the value-judgments which represent the world of facts

(2) refuting philosophy of language

(3) drawing a limit to the expression of thoughts but not to thinking

(4) describing the contents of judgements

33. Hume's account of causation is

(1) Epistemological

(2) Psychological

(3) Logical

(4) Historical

34. The prominent sophists were

(1) Socrates and Plato

(2) Protagoras and Gorgias

(3) Anaxagoras and Democritus

(4) Democritus and Protagoras

35. Berkeley regards God as

(1) Monad of all monads

(2) Eternal perceiver

(3) The Highest Reality

(4) All-embracing Truth

36. According to Vaisesika consciousness is

(1) Permanent property of soul

(2) Accidental property of soul

(3) Nature of soul

(4) Pure consciousness

37. According to Vivekananda, Absolute has become the universe by passing through

(1) Matter, Life, Mind

(2) Space, Time, Causation

(3) Jiva, Mind, Soul

(4) Matter, Spirit, God

38. Tagore's philosophy is based on

(1) Contemplation

(2) Personal Realization

(3) Argumentation

(4) Discussion

39. According to Ramanuja, the relation between matter, spirit and God is called

(1) Samavaya

(2) Samyoga

(3) Ayutasiddhi

(4) Aprthaksiddhi

40. St. Anselm's ontological argument for the existence of God is criticized by

(1) Leibnitz

(2) Descartes

(3) Bradley

(4) Kant

41. The problem of universals was first introduced into philosophy by

(1) Aristotle

(2) Aquinas

(3) Berkeley

(4) Plato

42. "A clear idea is one which is so apprehended that it will be recognized wherever it is met with, so that no other will be mistaken for it." This is held by

(1) William James

(2) C.S. Pierce

(3) John Dewey

(4) Wittgenstein

43. Which one of the following is not correctly matched ?

(1) Tripitaka — A Buddhist text

(2) Tattvacintamani — Nyaya text

(3) Tattvarthadhigamasutra — A Mimamsa text

(4) Kiranavali — A Vaisesika text

44. Match the pair and choose the correct alternative from the codes given below :

List-I	List-II
(a) Ramanuja	(i) Dvaita
(b Vallabha	(ii) Visistadvaita
(c) Nimbarka	(iii) Suddhadvaita
(d) Madhva	(iv) Dvaitadvaita

Codes :

	(a)	(b)	(c)	(d)
(1)	(ii)	(iv)	(iii)	(i)
(2)	(ii)	(iii)	(iv)	(i)
(3)	(i)	(iii)	(iv)	(ii)
(4)	(i)	(iv)	(iii)	(ii)

45. Which one of the following pairs is correctly matched ?

List-I	List-II
(1) Svatantra-Vijnanavada	— Dinnaga
(2) Shunyavada	— Dharmakirti
(3) Vijnanavada	— Nagarjuna
(4) Pratityasamutpada	— Vatsyayana

46. Consider the List I and the List II and select the code correctly matched :

List I	List II
(a) Thales	(i) Ideas
(b) Plato	(ii) Change
(c) Pythagoras	(iii) Numbers
(d) Heraclitus	(iv) Water

Codes :

	(a)	(b)	(c)	(d)
(1)	(i)	(iii)	(iv)	(ii)
(2)	(iv)	(i)	(iii)	(ii)
(3)	(iii)	(ii)	(iv)	(i)
(4)	(ii)	(iv)	(i)	(iii)

47. Which one of the following pairs is correctly matched ?

List-I		List-II
(1) Iqbal	—	Self is immortal
(2) Vivekananda	—	integral yoga
(3) Radhakrishnan	—	Rejection of Nirguna brahman
(4) K.C. Bhattacharya	—	Critique of modern civilization

48. Which of the following is an incorrect match?

(1) Ryle — Category mistake
(2) Heidegger — Meta-ethics
(3) Husserl — Phenomenology
(4) Nietzsche — Existentialism

49. **Assertion (A).** Logical positivists reject the metaphysical propositions.

Reason (R). Truth of the proposition depends upon the method of its verification.

(1) Both (A) and (R) are individually true
(2) (A) is true but (R) is false
(3) (A) is false but (R) is true
(4) Both (A) and (R) are individually false

50. Which of the philosophers noted below belong to Milesian school ?

The correct code is :

A. Thales
B. Anaximander
C. Parmenides
D. Anaximanes

Codes :

(1) B and C
(2) A, B and D
(3) B and D
(4) A, B, C and D

51. The principle of act utilitarianism is concerned with

(1) The motive of an action
(2) Consequences of similar actions
(3) The character of the agent
(4) The consequence of actions

52. The view that 'Jati' is as much as real as the Vyakti is held by :

(1) Carvakas
(2) Naiyayikas
(3) Buddhists
(4) Samkhya

53. Which of the following is not a postulate of morality ?

(1) Uniformity of nature
(2) Free-will
(3) Immortality of soul
(4) Existence of God

54. Facticity and Transcendence are regarded as the criteria of personal identity by :

(1) Nietzsche
(2) Heidegger
(3) Sartre
(4) Jaspers

55. Which among the following is not the Hetvābhāsa ?

(1) Bādhita
(2) Vyabhichāribhāva
(3) Asiddha
(4) Virudha

56. The view that language has one to one correspondence with reality is related to :

(1) Pragmatic theory of meaning
(2) Behaviourist theory of meaning
(3) Picture theory of meaning
(4) Use theory of meaning

57. Which of the following pairs is consistent ?
(1) Badhita — Anupasamhari
(2) Savyabhichara — Anaikantika
(3) Satpratipaksa — Svarupasiddha
(4) Viruddha — Sadharana

58. Prabhakara and Bhatta differ on the following
(1) Pramana, Prameya, Dharma
(2) Pramana, Prameya, Khyati
(3) Pramana, Khyati, Dharma
(4) Prameya, Dharma, Khyati

59. Which of the following indicate the theories of Punishment ?
(1) Preventive and Reactionary
(2) Reactionary and Reassuring
(3) Retributive and Reformative
(4) Reassuring and Retributive

60. The most notable intuitionist of twentieth century is :
(1) Thomas Reid
(2) G.E. Moore
(3) A.J. Ayer
(4) Stevenson

61. If the statement 'q' is true, the truth values of '$p \supset q$' and '$p \cdot q$' are :
(1) both '$p \supset q$' and '$p \cdot q$' are true
(2) both '$p \supset q$' and '$p \cdot q$' are false
(3) '$p \supset q$' is false and '$p \cdot q$' is true
(4) '$p \supset q$' is true and '$p \cdot q$' is false

62. The view that Isvara is only nimitta karana of the world is upheld by :
(1) Nyaya system
(2) Vedanta system
(3) Jainism
(4) Mimamsa system

63. Which of the following view is not correct according to Vaisesika ?
(1) Atoms are eternal
(2) Compounds made of atoms are not eternal
(3) All atoms are of the same kind
(4) Atoms are known by inference

64. "Fire is cold, because it has fireness." The inference commits the fallacy of:
(1) Viruddha
(2) Satpratipaksa
(3) Badhita
(4) Sadharana

65. The problem of induction is mainly about :
(1) Accepting induction
(2) Defining induction
(3) Justifying induction
(4) Falsifying induction

66. The statement form which is not a contingent is :
(1) $p \supset p$ (2) $\sim(p \cdot q)$
(3) $p \supset q$ (4) $p \vee p$

67. Which one of the following is not a component of pararthanumana according to Nyāya?
(1) Upanaya
(2) Udāharaṇa
(3) Tarka
(4) Hetu

68. According to Zarathushtra, God has these many powers
(1) Two (2) Seven
(3) Eight (4) Six

69. According to Jainism real (sat) is
(1) Permanent and unchangeable

(2) Impermanent
(3) Origination, decay and permanance
(4) Origination and decay

70. The chief exponent of representative realism is
(1) Locke (2) Berkeley
(3) Spinoza (4) Russell

71. Habermas characterises the social sciences as :
(1) Non-hermeneutic
(2) Hermeneutic
(3) Double hermeneutic
(4) Quasi hermeneutic

72. According to Gandhi 'Sarvadharma Samabhava' means :
(1) All religions teach moral values
(2) All religions should be synthesised
(3) There isn't unity of all religions
(4) All religions should be treated equally

73. Which of the following proposition is true ?
(1) Rāmānuja propounds Brahmaparinamavāda
(2) Saṁkāra propounds asatkāryavāda
(3) Madhva is a non-dualist
(4) Nimbārka is a dualist

74. The world of experience is the product of maya which possesses the powers of
(1) Vikalpa and Dharana
(2) Avarana and Viksepa
(3) Vikalpa and Viksepa
(4) Avarana and Vikalpa

75. Which of the following is a prophetic religion ?
(1) iiinduism
(2) Buddhism
(3) Islam
(4) Vedic

76. According to Asatkaryavāda, the effect comes into being on the destruction of
(1) Anyonyābhāva
(2) Prāgabhāva
(3) Pradhvaṁsābhāva
(4) Atyantābhāva

77. This is not a duo related to statements
(1) A priori — A posteriori
(2) Analytic — Synthetic
(3) Simple — Complex
(4) Empirical — Rational

78. Which of the following proposition is true ?
The idea of spiritual substance
(1) is maintained by Berkeley but repudiated by Hume
(2) is maintained by Locke but repudiated by Berkeley
(3) is maintained by both Berkeley and Hume
(4) is maintained by neither Locke nor Berkeley

79. Abhihitanvayavada is the view held by
(1) Prasastapāda
(2) Kumārila Bhatta
(3) Prabhākara Bhatta
(4) Sabara

80. Testimony as a source of validk nowledge (Pramana) is rejected by
(1) Sankaracarya
(2) Mimarhsaka
(3) Nyaya
(4) Bauddha

81. According to Nyāya, Substance Akasa is known by
(1) Verbal testimony
(2) Perception
(3) Intuition
(4) Inference

82. Who was the chief exponent of dvaitādvaitavāda ?
(1) Nimbārka
(2) Sankar
(3) Madhva
(4) Ramānuja

83. According to A.J. Ayer ethical statements are
(1) Expressions of approval
(2) Assertions
(3) Expressions of emotions
(4) Expressions of truth value

84. Which of the following schools does not accept inference and testimony as the valid sources of knowledge ?
(1) Buddhism
(2) Nyaya
(3) Carvaka
(4) Samkhya

85. The proposition in which the subject is distributed but the predicate not distributed is
(1) I proposition
(2) A proposition
(3) E proposition
(4) O proposition

86. The main objective of Mimamsa system is to establish the authority of the
(1) Vedas
(2) Tripitakas
(3) Upanisadas
(4) Bhagwadgita

87. Which theory of punishment presumes the goodness of human beings ?
(1) Reformative theory of punishment
(2) Deterrent theory of punishment
(3) Retributive theory of punishment
(4) Preventive theory of punishment

88. The figure of a syllogism is determined by the position of in the premises.
(1) Major Term
(2) Minor Term
(3) Middle Term
(4) Quantifier

89. If the statement 'p' is false, the truth values of '$p \supset q$' and '$p \cdot q$' are
(1) both '$p \supset q$' and '$p \cdot q$' are true
(2) both '$p \supset q$' and '$p \cdot q$' are false
(3) '$p \supset q$' is true and '$p \cdot q$' is false
(4) '$p \supset q$' is false and '$p \cdot q$' is true

90. The total number of vows prescribed by Gandhiji for Satyagrahi are
(1) Five
(2) Nine
(3) Eleven
(4) Twenty one

91. Name the philosopher who is not phenomenologist
(1) Brentano
(2) Meinong
(3) Husserl
(4) Quine

92. Which of the following pairs of religion could be considered as 'non-theistic' ?
(1) Judaism—Christianity
(2) Islam—Zoraastrianism
(3) Jainism—Buddhism
(4) iiinduism—Sikhism

93. According to Islam, 'Zakat' means Muslim has to
(1) pay 10% of his wealth
(2) pay 2½ to 5% of his income for poor and needy
(3) pay 3% of his income
(4) pay 7% of his income

94. Naiyayikas accept the following theory of error
(1) Asat-khyāti
(2) Sat-khyāti
(3) Ātma-khyāti
(4) Anyathā-khyāti

95. Identify the pair of sceptics
(1) Ayer and Descartes
(2) Hume and Ayer
(3) Plato and Descartes
(4) Hume and Descartes

96. According to Nyāya, substance is
(1) the collection of qualities
(2) unintelligible without the qualities
(3) dependent upon the qualities
(4) substratum of the qualities and actions

97. Rights are intimately related to
(1) Constitution
(2) Thinking
(3) State
(4) Duties

98. The standard definition of knowledge explores the following conditions
(1) belief, certainty, verification
(2) belief, truth, verification
(3) cognition, certainty, verification
(4) belief, truth, justification

99. Which of the following statements is incorrect ?
(1) Karl Popper mentions intuition as a way of knowing
(2) Ayer accepts memory as a source of knowledge
(3) Hume ascribes the highest importance to rational knowledge
(4) Ryle distinguishes between knowing-how and knowing-that

100. The view that all types of Pratyaksa are nirvikalpaka is upheld by
(1) Bauddha
(2) Nyāya
(3) Vaiseṣika
(4) Visistādvaita

Answers

1. (2)	**2.** (2)	**3.** (3)	**4.** (2)	**5.** (2)	**6.** (4)	**7.** (4)	**8.** (4)	**9.** (4)	**10.** (3)
11. (3)	**12.** (4)	**13.** (2)	**14.** (3)	**15.** (4)	**16.** (1)	**17.** (1)	**18.** (3)	**19.** (3)	**20.** (4)
21. (4)	**22.** (3)	**23.** (2)	**24.** (2)	**25.** (4)	**26.** (1)	**27.** (2)	**28.** (4)	**29.** (2)	**30.** (4)
31. (1)	**32.** (3)	**33.** (2)	**34.** (2)	**35.** (2)	**36.** (2)	**37.** (2)	**38.** (2)	**39.** (4)	**40.** (4)
41. (4)	**42.** (1)	**43.** (4)	**44.** (2)	**45.** (1)	**46.** (2)	**47.** (1)	**48.** (2)	**49.** (2)	**50.** (3)
51. (4)	**52.** (2)	**53.** (3)	**54.** (2)	**55.** (2)	**56.** (3)	**57.** (2)	**58.** (4)	**59.** (3)	**60.** (2)
61. (1)	**62.** (2)	**63.** (3)	**64.** (3)	**65.** (3)	**66.** (1)	**67.** (3)	**68.** (4)	**69.** (3)	**70.** (1)
71. (2)	**72.** (4)	**73.** (1)	**74.** (2)	**75.** (4)	**76.** (2)	**77.** (4)	**78.** (1)	**79.** (2)	**80.** (4)
81. (4)	**82.** (1)	**83.** (3)	**84.** (3)	**85.** (3)	**86.** (3)	**87.** (1)	**88.** (3)	**89.** (3)	**90.** (2)
91. (4)	**92.** (3)	**93.** (2)	**94.** (4)	**95.** (4)	**96.** (4)	**97.** (4)	**98.** (4)	**99.** (3)	**100.** (1)

PREVIOUS YEARS' PAPERS

June, 2015

PHILOSOPHY

PAPER-II

Note : This paper contains **fifty (50)** objectives type questions, each question carrying **two (2)** marks. Attempt **all** the questions.

1. Given below are two statements, one labelled as Assertion (A) and the other labelled as Reason (R) Considering (A) and (R) select the correct code :

Assertion (A) : In Taijas the self enjoys subtle objects.

Reason (R) : In a dreaming State the self creates its own imaginary objects.

Codes :

(1) Both (A) and (R) are true and (R) is the correct explanation of (A).

(2) Both (A) and (R) are true but (R) is not the correct explanation of (A).

(3) (A) is true but (R) is false.

(4) (A) is false but (R) is true.

2. Hiranyagarbha in Upanisad is also known as

(1) *Viśvakarmā*

(2) *Prajāpati*

(3) *Sahasrākṣa*

(4) *Sahasraśirsa*

3. Select the correct Sequence

(1) *Artha, Kāma, Dharma, Mokṣa*

(2) *Artha, Dharma, Kāma, Moksa*

(3) *Moksa, Dharma, Artha, Kāma*

(4) *Dharma, Artha, Kāma, Moksa*

4. Match the List - I with List - II and select the correct answer by using the codes given below :

List - I	List - II
(a) Naigam naya	(i) Whereby the universal qualities are treated as absolutely real and particulars are rejected as unreal.
(b) Saṅgraha naya	(ii) Whereby a thing is perceived to be having both universal and particular qualities and we fail to distinguish between them.
(c) Vyavhāra naya	(iii) Whereby the real is identified with the momentary,
(d) Rjusutra naya	(iv) Whereby things are taken as concrete particulars.

Codes :

	(a)	(b)	(c)	(d)
(1)	(i)	(ii)	(iii)	(iv)
(2)	(iv)	(iii)	(ii)	(i)
(3)	(ii)	(i)	(iv)	(iii)
(4)	(iii)	(ii)	(iv)	(i)

5. Match the List - I with List - II and select the correct answer by using the codes given below :

List - I	List - II
(a) Vasubandhu	(i) Mahāyāna sūtralaṁkāra
(b) Asaṅga	(ii) Vigraha Vyāvārtinī
(c) Nāgārjuna	(iii) Mahāyāna Shraddhotpāda Shāstra
(d) Aśvaghosa	(iv) Vijñapti - Mātratā Siddhi

Codes :

	(a)	(b)	(c)	(d)
(1)	(iv)	(i)	(ii)	(iii)
(2)	(ii)	(iii)	(i)	(iv)
(3)	(iii)	(iv)	(ii)	(i)
(4)	(i)	(ii)	(iii)	(iv)

6. The concept of *Anyonya abhāva* (mutual negation) is propounded by :

(1) Sāṁkhya
(2) Nyāya
(3) Visiṣṭadvaita
(4) Advaita

7. Consider given Assertion (A) and Reason (R) and then mark the correct option as given below :

Assertion (A) : The soul is neither produced nor destroyed.

Reason (R) : It is devoid of origin and end.

Codes :

(1) (A) and (R) are both true and (R) provides correct explanation of (A).
(2) (A) and (R) are both false and (R) provides correct explanation of (A).
(3) (A) and (R) are both true but (R) does not provide correct explanation of (A).
(4) (A) is false and (R) is true, but (R) provides correct explanation of (A).

8. Match the List - I with List - II and select the correct answer by using the codes given below :

List--I	List - II
(a) A pot does not exist before destruction	(i) Anyonyabhāva
(b) after destruction	(ii) Atyantābhāva
(c) nor as a cloth	(iii) Prāgabhāva
(d) nor as a liquid pot	(iv) Pradhvamsābhāva

Codes :

	(a)	(b)	(c)	(d)
(1)	(i)	(ii)	(iii)	(iv)
(2)	(ii)	(iii)	(iv)	(i)
(3)	(iv)	(iii)	(ii)	(i)
(4)	(iii)	(iv)	(i)	(ii)

9. Ākriti according to Pūrva-Mīmāṁsa is also known as

(1) Viśeṣa
(2) Saṁasthāna
(3) Samvāya
(4) Guna

10. According to Ramanuja, the word *nirguna* means

(1) Without auspicious qualities
(2) Without inauspicious qualities
(3) Without any Characteristics
(4) None of the above

11. *Sapta anupapatti* (Seven classical objections) against the doctrine of *Māyā* was levelled by

(1) Vallabha
(2) Madhva
(3) Rāmanuja
(4) Niṁbārka

12. Śaṁkaraś philosophy is designated as

(1) Monism
(2) Integral Nondualism
(3) Non-dualism
(4) All the above

13. *Viśiṣṭādvaita* philosophy approves only :

(1) Jivanmukti
(2) Videha mukti
(3) Both
(4) None of the above

14. Which statement is not correct ?
(1) Madhva advocates Radical Pluralism
(2) Madhva is a Strong Realist
(3) Madhva is a grand theist
(4) Madhva advocates Brahma-Jīva-abheda-vāda

15. As per Nyāya the effect is known as
(1) Kāraṇa
(2) Prāgabhāva Pratiyogi
(3) Asamvāyikāraṇa
(4) Kāraka

16. All cognitions must be true in themselves, is the view propounded by :
(1) Nyāya
(2) Vedānta
(3) Mīmāṁsa
(4) Jaina

17. Consciousness is an adventitious quality of self is accepted by
(1) Vedānta
(2) Pūrva-Mimāmsā
(3) Nyāya
(4) Sāṁkhya

18. Which one of the following statements is correct ?
(1) *Apṛthak Siddhi* is the relation of Brahman with *Jīva* only
(2) *Apṛthak Siddhi* is the relation of Brahman with *Jīva* and *jagat*
(3) *Apṛthak Siddhi* is the relation of Brahman with *jagat* only
(4) *Apṛthak Siddhi* is no relation at all

19. The Nyāya theory of causation is called
(1) *Vivartavāda*
(2) *Asatkāryavāda*
(3) *Satkāryavāda*
(4) *Yadṛcchāvāda*

20. Given below are two statements, one labelled as Assertion (A), and the other labelled as Reason (R) Choose the correct answer from the code given below.

Assertion (A) : "Abhyāsa Vairāgyābhyām Tannirodhah.

Reason (R) : Suppression of citta vṛttis is brought about by persistent practice and non-attachment.

Codes :
(1) (R) is the correct explanation of (A).
(2) (A) and (R) are incorrect.
(3) (A) and (R) contradict each other.
(4) (A) is true but (R) is false.

21. By conceiving God as the Supreme Ego, Iqbal means
(1) God as light
(2) A dynamic and creative life
(3) Infinite creative possibilities
(4) A creative progress of the world

22. Which one of the following pairs is correctly matched ?
(1) Personality, Hind swaraj - Gandhi
(2) The life Divine, East and West - Sri Aurobindo
(3) Sadhana, Personality - Tagore
(4) East and West in Religion, the Human Cycle - Radhakrishnan

23. Match the List - I with List - II and choose the correct answer from the code given below

List - I (Authors)	List - II (Texts)
(a) K.C. Bhattacharya	(i) The ideal of human unity
(b) Radhakrishnan	(ii) The secrets of self
(c) Iqbal	(iii) Studies in Vedantism
(d) Sri Aurobindo	(iv) The Recovery of faith

Codes :

	(a)	(b)	(c)	(d)
(1)	(iii)	(iv)	(ii)	(i)
(2)	(i)	(ii)	(iii)	(iv)
(3)	(ii)	(iv)	(i)	(iii)
(4)	(iv)	(i)	(ii)	(iii)

24. Intuition and intellect are complementary to each other according to
(1) Bergson
(2) Kant
(3) Radhakrishnan
(4) Ambedkar

25. According to whom 'Mumukṣutva' is an evidence in the favour of immortality ?
(1) Shankara
(2) Ramanuja
(3) Radhakrishnan
(4) Vivekananda

26. Match Set - I with Set - II and findout the **correct** option using the following codes :

Set - I	Set - II
(a) Leibnitz	(i) World is bundle of monads
(b) Wittgenstein	(ii) World is bundle of atoms
(c) Hume	(iii) World is bundle of impressions
(d) Berkeley	(iv) World is bundle of perceptions

Codes :
(1) (a) and (iv)
(2) (d) and (i)
(3) (c) and (iii)
(4) (b) and (ii)

27. Match Set - I with Set - II and find out the incorrect option from following codes

Set-I	Set - II
(a) Locke	(i) Interactionism
(b) Leibnitz	(ii) Pantheism
(c) Spinoza	(iii) Pluralism
(d) Descartes	(iv) Idealism

Codes :
(1) (c) and (ii)
(2) (d) and (i)
(3) (a) and (iv)
(4) (b) and (iii)

28. Select the correct option
Innate ideas for Rationalists are :
(1) Eternal
(2) Contingent
(3) Both eternal and contingent
(4) Neither eterna

29. Select the correct option
The principle of interactionism was propounded by
(1) Leibnitz
(2) Descartes
(3) Berkeley
(4) Spinoza

30. Select the correct option :
Who accepts that the existence of an object depends upon its experience ?
(1) Plato (2) Hume
(3) Berkeley (4) Locke

31. Match Set - I with Set - II and find out the correct answer from the given codes :

Set - I	Set - II
(a) Locke	(i) Synthetic Apriori judgment
(b) Berkeley	(ii) Synthetic Aposteriori Judgment
(c) Hume	(iii) Knowledge of Ideas
(d) Kant	(iv) Knowledge of sensations

Codes :
(1) (a) and (iii)
(2) (d) and (i)
(3) (c) and (ii)
(4) (b) and (iv)

32. Select the correct option :
Pre-established harmony is relation :
(1) between mind and body
(2) between God and nature
(3) between attribute and modes
(4) among monads

33. Match the List - I with List - II and mark the correct code as given below :

List - I	List - II
(a) Speech Act	(i) Wittgenstein
(b) Language Game	(ii) Ayer
(c) Verification Theory of Meaning	(iii) Peirce
(d) Operational Theory of Meaning	(iv) Ryle

Codes :

	(a)	(b)	(c)	(d)
(1)	(i)	(ii)	(iii)	(iv)
(2)	(iv)	(iii)	(ii)	(i)
(3)	(iii)	(ii)	(iv)	(i)
(4)	(ii)	(iii)	(iv)	(i)

34. Mark the correct option :
(1) Hegel is an absolute idealist and Husserl supports transcendental idealism.
(2) Hegel is a rationalist and Spinoza is a realist.
(3) Husserl supports transcendental idealism and Kant is an empiricist.
(4) Hegel is an absolute idealist but Husserl rejects transcendental idealism.

35. According to G.E. Moore whenever there is a conflict between a philosophical doctrine and common sense it was more likely that :
(1) Common sense has gone astray rather than the philosophical doctrine.
(2) The argument has gone astray rather than the common sense.
(3) Both argument and common sense have gone astray.
(4) Neither the argument nor common sense had gone astray.

36. In the context of Russell's Philosophy, consider the given Assertion (A) and Reason (R) then mark the correct option as given below :

Assertion (A) : General Propositions are not existential.

Reason (R) : Atoms are neither mental nor physical.

Options :
(1) (A) and (R) both are true but (R) does not provide direct explanation of (A).
(2) (A) and (R) are both false but (R) provides direct explanation of (A).
(3) (A) is true, (R) is false and (R) provides direct explanation of (A).
(4) (A) is false and (R) is true, but (A) does not provide direct explanation of (R).

37. Which of the following statements are true according to Existentialism and Gītā ?
(1) We are doers and sufferers not spectators only.
(2) We are spectators only, neither doers nor sufferers.
(3) We are doers, sufferers and spectators as well.
(4) None of the options given above are acceptable.

38. Which one of the following is called as "radical empiricist' ?
(1) Ayer (2) Locke
(3) James (4) Moore

39. In a restricted sense "Epoche" means :
(1) to believe in the existence of objects.
(2) to disbelieve in the existence of object.
(3) to obtain a categorical judgement regarding the existence of outer world.
(4) suspension of judgements regarding existence of objects.

40. What are the three aspects of 'Care' according to Heidegger ?
(1) facticity, possibility, fallenness
(2) facticity, attention, discipline
(3) attention, discipline, service
(4) service, attention, facticity

41. Moore analyses :
(1) Language
(2) Linguistic facts

(3) Extra linguistic entity
(4) All of these

42. Which one of the following pairs in not correctly matched ?
(1) Psychologism – Husserl
(2) Ghost in Machine – Descartes
(3) Dasein – Heidegger
(4) Rationalism – Hegel

43. Match List-I with List-II with reference to the works of Plato and mark the correct code

List-I	List-II
(a) Meno	(i) Life and death of Socrates
(b) Gorgias	(ii) Nature of knowledge and instruction
(c) Apology and Crito	(iii) Virtue of self-control
(d) Charmides	(iv) Deals with study of rhetoric

Codes :

	(a)	(b)	(c)	(d)
(1)	(ii)	(iv)	(iii)	(i)
(2)	(iv)	(ii)	(i)	(iii)
(3)	(ii)	(iv)	(i)	(iii)
(4)	(iii)	(i)	(iv)	(ii)

44. Consider the following statements with reference to Thomas Aquinas and mark the correct code :
(i) Aquinas rejected doctrines of universal hylomorphism and plurality of forms,
(ii) Human being has a single rational soul, which acts as the one substantial form.
(iii) Only in God there is no composition at all, his essence is purely and simply his act of existing.

Codes :
(1) Only (ii) and (iii) are true
(2) Only (i) and (ii) are true
(3) Only (i) and (iii) are true
(4) All (i), (ii) and (iii) are true

45. Consider the following Assertion (A) and Reason (R) in the light of St. Augustine's philosophy and mark the correct code :
Assertion (A) : Degrees of goodness are identified with degrees of being.
Reason (R) : If there is no goodness at all in a particular thing, then there is no reality in it either.

Codes :
(1) Both (A) and (R) are true and (R) is the correct explanation of (A)
(2) Both (A) and (R) are true, but (R) is not the correct explanation of (A)
(3) (A) is true and (R) is false
(4) Both (A) and (R) are false

46. The doctrine of the three classes of men as - lovers of wisdom, lovers of honour and lovers of gain - was brought out by :
(1) Pythagoras
(2) Heraclitus
(3) Aristotle
(4) Leucippus

47. Which of the following words are authored by Plato ?
(i) Republic (ii) Laws
(iii) Politics (iv) Crito

Codes :
(1) Only (i) and (iv)
(2) Only (ii), (iii) and (iv)
(3) Only (ii) and (iv)
(4) Only (i), (ii) and (iv)

48. Read carefully following statements and mark the correct option in the context of pragmatism.
Statements :
(i) The meaning of 'Meaning' is the clarity of apprehension,
(ii) Meaning emerges out of experimental phenomenon,
(iii) Mind is an ontological entity,
(iv) Knowledge is an activity.

Options:
(1) All the statements written above are true
(2) Only (i), (ii) and (iii) are true but (iv) is false
(3) Only (i), (ii) and (iv) are true but (iii) is false
(4) Only (ii), (iii) and (iv) are true but (i) is false

49. Match the Set-I with Set-II and find out the correct option from the codes given below

Set-I	Set-II
(a) Spinoza	(i) Representationalism
(b) Descartes	(ii) Parallelism
(c) Locke	(iii) Scepticism
(d) Hume	(iv) Pantheism

Codes:
(1) (c) and (i)
(2) (b) and (iv)
(3) (a) and (iii)
(4) (d) and (ii)

50. Match the Set-I with Set-II and find out the correct answer from the codes given below

Set-I	Set-II
(a) Descartes	(i) Dualist
(b) Spinoza	(ii) Pluralist
(c) Leibnitz	(iii) Pantheist
(d) Locke	(iv) Idealist

Codes:
(1) (d) and (iv) (2) (b) and (iii)
(3) (a) and (ii) (4) (c) and (i)

Answers

1. (1)	**2.** (2)	**3.** (4)	**4.** (3)	**5.** (1)	**6.** (2)	**7.** (1)	**8.** (4)	**9.** (2)	**10.** (2)
11. (3)	**12.** (3)	**13.** (2)	**14.** (4)	**15.** (2)	**16.** (3)	**17.** (3)	**18.** (2)	**19.** (2)	**20.** (1)
21. (1)	**22.** (3)	**23.** (1)	**24.** (3)	**25.** (4)	**26.** (3)	**27.** (3)	**28.** (1)	**29.** (2)	**30.** (3)
31. (2)	**32.** (4)	**33.** (4)	**34.** (1)	**35.** (3)	**36.** (1)	**37.** (4)	**38.** (3)	**39.** (4)	**40.** (3)
41. (3)	**42.** (2)	**43.** (3)	**44.** (4)	**45.** (2)	**46.** (1)	**47.** (4)	**48.** (3)	**49.** (1)	**50.** (2)

June, 2015

PHILOSOPHY

PAPER-III

Note : This paper contains **seventy five (75)** objective type questions of **two (2)** marks each. **All** questions are compulsory.

1. 'Names give us universals which are purely imaginary, illusory and negative'. The view is propounded by :
(1) Dharmakīrti
(2) Dinnāga
(3) Prabhākara
(4) Kamalśīla

2. 'When substance does not exist, the qualities which depend on it also do not exist' - is the view held by :
(1) Jainas
(2) Naiyāyikās
(3) Mīmānisakās
(4) Buddhists

3. Accepted and confirmed by the Jaina school of thought which of the following does not belong to the category of *Triratna* :
(1) Samyak Jnāna
(2) Samyak Cārītraya
(3) Samyak Prayās
(4) Samyak Darśana

4. *Khyāti* is not a unitary knowledge but is a composite of two unrelated cognitions is the view propounded by :
(1) Prabhākara
(2) Kumārila
(3) Rāmānuja
(4) Udyotkara

5. Which one of the following represents Novelty as the feature of knowledge according to Pūrva-Mīmānisā ?
(1) Yathārtha
(2) Bādhaka Jñanarahita
(3) Agrhitagrahi
(4) Karanadosarahita

6. Match List-I with List-II and choose the correct answer with the help of codes given below :

List-I	List-II
(a) Paksadharmata	(i) fire is cool
(b) Vi-paksasattva	(ii) sound is eternal as it is caused
(c) Bādhita	(iii) smoke is present in the hill
(d) Viruddha	(iv) fire in the lake

Codes :

	(a)	(b)	(c)	(d)
(1)	(iv)	(i)	(iii)	(ii)
(2)	(i)	(ii)	(iii)	(iv)
(3)	(ii)	(iii)	(i)	(iv)
(4)	(iii)	(iv)	(i)	(ii)

7. Which of the following is an equivalent of Ṛta ?
(1) Aditi
(2) Indra
(3) Soma
(4) Uṣas

8. The term Yoga in Bhagvadgītā has not been used in the sense of
(1) Samatva (2) Kausala
(3) Karma (4) Kriya

9. The respective stages of self evolution in Jainism are known as
(1) *Apramattasṁayat*
(2) *Avirat*
(3) *Upaśāntakaṣāya*
(4) *Guṇasthāna*

10. Which of the following pair aptly depicts the verse 'Bhūta' as Kṣara' and Kūtastha' as 'Akṣara':
(1) *Prakṛti-Puruṣa*
(2) *JīvaMāyā*
(3) *BrahmaJīva*
(4) *Māyā-Jīva*

11. Which of the following texts assumes the process of creation in the form of 'Yajña'?
(1) *Puruṣa Sūkta*
(2) *Nāsadīya Sūkta*
(3) *Hiraṇyagarbha Sūkta*
(4) *Taittirya Brāhmana*

12. According to Bhagvadgītā which of the following is authentic authority in deciding between 'kartavya' and 'Akartavya'?
(1) *Āptavākya*
(2) *Paramparā*
(3) *Śāstra*
(4) *Svātma*

13. Which one of the following does not refer to 'Prakrti' according to Bhagvadgītā?
(1) *Mahat*
(2) *Caitanya*
(3) *Kartṛ*
(4) *Buddhi*

14. According Vaiśeṣikato *Nitya drayya* is:
(1) *Tryanuka*
(2) *Atman*
(3) *Dvyanuka*
(4) *Karma*

15. Which one of the following is not a relation?
(1) *Svarūpa* (2) *Apṛthaksiddhi*
(3) *Guṇa* (4) *Samavāya*

16. 'Religion is a Home Sickness', stated by
(1) Radhakrishnan
(2) Vivekananda
(3) Tagore
(4) Gandhi

17. *Dik, Ātman* and *Manas* according to the Naiyāyikās are:
(1) *Bhautika*
(2) *Murta*
(3) *Both bhautika and murta*
(4) *Neither bhautika nor murta*

18. Match the following lists and choose the correct code:

List-I	List-II
(a) *Brahman*	(i) *Vyāvahārika Sattā*
(b) *Svapna*	(ii) *Pāramārthika Sattā*
(c) *Jagat*	(iii) *Prātibhāsika Sattā*
(d) *Turīya*	(iv) *Tādātmya*

Codes:

	(a)	(b)	(c)	(d)
(1)	(iii)	(ii)	(iv)	(i)
(2)	(i)	(iv)	(ii)	(iii)
(3)	(ii)	(iii)	(i)	(iv)
(4)	(i)	(ii)	(iv)	(iii)

19. In Kantian ethics 'an objective principle of action' is called
(1) a maxim
(2) a rule
(3) a practical law
(4) an imperative

20. Which one of the followings has recommended internal sanctions:
(1) Bentham
(2) Spencer
(3) Mill
(4) Epicuras

21. 'Either freedom of will is a fact or moral judgement a delusion' this statement is of:
(1) Martineau (2) Hobbes
(3) Kant (4) Mill

22. 'Divine law is the ultimate moral law'. Which one of the following holds this view?
(1) Hobbes
(2) Desecrates
(3) Bain
(4) Spencer

23. Mark the correct alternative from the following
According to Perfectionism :
(1) Pleasure alone is the standard of morality.
(2) Reason alone is the standard of morality.
(3) Intuition is the standard of morality.
(4) Utility is the index of morality.

24. Match List-I with List-II and choose the correct answer with the help of code given below

List-I (Authors)	List-II (Texts)
(a) Ross	(i) Prolegomena to Ethics
(b) Moore	(ii) Foundations of Ethics
(c) Kant	(iii) Ethics
(d) Green	(iv) Metaphysics of Morals

Codes :

	(a)	(b)	(c)	(d)
(1)	(ii)	(iii)	(iv)	(i)
(2)	(i)	(iv)	(ii)	(iii)
(3)	(ii)	(iii)	(i)	(iv)
(4)	(iv)	(ii)	(i)	(iii)

25. Who among the following has said 'Nothing is unconditionally good save the good will' ?
(1) Clark
(2) Martineau
(3) Sidgwick
(4) Kant

26. Only the motive of an action is the basis of its moral Judgement. Which one of the following holds this view ?
(1) Hedonist
(2) Rationalist
(3) Intuitionist
(4) Rigorist

27. Which one of the following thinkers has regarded A-words, D-words and G-words as belonging to one family ?
(1) Moore
(2) Ross
(3) Spencer
(4) Nowell-smith

28. Which one of the following has stated that there is emotive factor in moral judgement ?
(1) Moore
(2) Ross
(3) Ayer
(4) Stevenson

29. Galloway does not accept one of the following as a form of Religion ?
(1) Tribal Religion
(2) National Religion
(3) Universal Religion
(4) Primitive Religion

30. Which of the following is the source of 'Tao'?
(1) Primitive Religion
(2) Naturalistic Religion
(3) Humanistic Religion
(4) None of the above

31. Which one of the following is true about the position of Gandhi ?
(1) God and truth are universal concepts.
(2) God is absolute and truth is relative.
(3) God and truth are interchangeable.
(4) God is truth and truth is god.

32. The principle of 'Bread labour' for Gandhi essentially consists of
(1) Mental work (2) Physical work
(3) Social work (4) Political work

33. Non-violence according to Gandhi is not
(1) The law of the human species
(2) The Gospel of human action
(3) Goodwill towards all life
(4) Passive resistance

34. Gandhian economic programmes were based on :
(1) Ideal principles of economic grasping
(2) By producing all wants of the people
(3) The ideal of self sufficiency
(4) Sharing all economic productions

35. Brahman according to vallabha is :
(1) *Nirguna* only
(2) *Saguna* only
(3) Both *Nirguna and Saguna*
(4) Neither

36. The relation between *Brahman* and *Jivatma* according to Madhva is :
(1) *Abheda*
(2) *Bheda*
(3) *Bhedābheda*
(4) All the above

37. 'Samvrti' is distinguished as Tathyasamvrti' and TVlithyasamvrti' by :
(1) Āryadeva
(2) Diṅnāga
(3) Nāgārjuna
(4) Chandrakirti

38. Match the following using the proper code :

List-I	List-II
(a) Śaṁkara	(i) Viṣṇutattvavinirṇaya
(b) Vallabha	(ii) Drgdrsya viveka
(c) Madhva	(iii) Prasthānaratnākara
(d) Niṁbārka	(iv) Vedānta Pārijāta Kusuma

Codes :

	(a)	(b)	(c)	(d)
(1)	(iii)	(i)	(iv)	(ii)
(2)	(iii)	(iv)	(ii)	(i)
(3)	(ii)	(iii)	(i)	(iv)
(4)	(iv)	(i)	(iii)	(ii)

39. "Words are relational and thus state only about the universal (Jati) not the Real (Svalaksna).
(1) Āryadeva
(2) Chandrakīrti
(3) Nāgārjuna
(4) Dinnāga

40. The view that - hermeneutics should confine itself to the epistemological problems of interpretation and not try to engage with the deepest conditions of human existence - held by
(1) Paul Ricoeur
(2) Emilio Betti
(3) Habermors
(4) Derrida

41. Who among the following has maintained a distinction between grammatical interpretation and psychological interpretation ?
(1) Wilhelm Dilthey
(2) Friedrich Schleiermacher
(3) Gadamer
(4) Heidegger

42. Truth is a necessary constituent of a systematically coherent whole - can be ascribed to
(1) Pragmatic theory of truth
(2) Correspondence theory of truth
(3) Coherence theory of truth
(4) Relational theory of truth

43. Who among the following philosophers held that the correspondence theory of truth is of an identity between constituents of the fact and that of the proposition ?
(1) Frege (2) Russell
(3) Carnap
(4) Quine

44. Which one of the following correctly depicts the concept of '*Atyantābhāva*' ?
(a) total absence of colour in air.
(b) the absence of a relation between two things in the past, present and future.

(c) this absence has a beginning but does not have an end.

Codes :

(1) Only (a) and (c) are true.
(2) Only (a) and (b) are true.
(3) Only (a) is true.
(4) Only (b) is true.

45. Which one of the following is the stand point of anti-realism ?

(1) There is no guarantee that every declarative sentence is determinately true or false.
(2) Every declarative sentence is determinately true or false.
(3) Every declarative sentence is always true.
(4) Every declarative sentence is always false.

46. Consider the following statements with reference to Frege and mark the correct code is

(a) Frege introduces a distinction between the reference and the sense of an expression.
(b) Objects are what proper names stand for.
(c) He invented the theory of quantification.

Codes :

(1) Only (a) and (b) are true.
(2) Only (a) and (c) are true.
(3) Only (c) is true.
(4) All (a), (b) and (c) are true.

47. Who among the following philosophers criticised the concept of human rights by saying - "there are no such rights and belief in them is one with belief in witches and in unicorns".

(1) Jeremy Bentham
(2) Alasdair MacIntyre
(3) Edmand Burke
(4) John Locke

48. Atoms according to Naiyāyikās are inactive and motionless, this leads to conclude that

(a) Motion is imparted to them by unseen power (Adṛṣta) of Dharma and Adharma residing in individual soul.
(b) Atoms combine in geometrical progression and not in arithmetical way.
(c) Physical order presupposes the moral order.

Codes :

(1) (a) is a valid inference.
(2) (b) is an invalid inference.
(3) (a), (c) are valid inferences.
(4) (a), (b), (c) are valid inferences.

49. Mark the code which does not consist a true statement

(1) A conjunction is true if all of its components are true but false otherwise.
(2) Every compound statement is a truth functional statement.
(3) In two valued logic every statement is either true or false.
(4) A simple statement is a statement that does not contain any other statement as its component part.

50. Who one of the following held that space and time are a priori percepts ?

(1) Hume (2) Kant
(3) Leibnitz (4) Einstein

51. Consider the following statements with reference to *Upamāna* (Comparison) and mark the correct code.

(a) Vedantins argue that *Upamāna* can be derived syllogistically from the premises.
(b) Sāmkhya school of thinkers hold that *Upamāna* can be shown to be a case of perception.
(c) According to *Nyāya*, comparison is the knowledge of the relation between a word and the object denoted by that word.

Codes :
(1) Only (a) and (b) are true.
(2) Only (b) and (c) are true.
(3) Only (c) is true.
(4) All (a), (b) and (c) are true.

52. Consider the given Assertion (A) and Reason (R) with reference to inductive inference and mark the correct code from below.

Assertion (A) : Inductive inference proceeds from known to the unknown.

Reason (R) : Inductive inference attempts to reach a conclusion concerning all the members of a class from observation of all of them.

Codes :
(1) Both (A) and (R) are true and (R) is the correct explanation of (A).
(2) Both (A) and (R) are true and (R) is not the correct explanation of (A).
(3) (A) is true and (R) is false.
(4) (R) is true and (A) is false.

53. Who holds that matter, motion, space and time are relativities ?
(1) Newton
(2) Einstein
(3) Hume
(4) Leibnitz

54. Which one of the following is not a kind of 'uniformity' according to Mill ? Mark the correct option.
(1) Uniformity of succession
(2) Uniformity of science
(3) Uniformity of coexistence
(4) Uniformity of similarity

55. Consequence of action is the basis of moral Judgement. Which one of the following holds this view ?
(1) Hedonist
(2) Intuitionist
(3) Rigorist
(4) Idealist

56. Austin while giving an account of correspondence makes a distinction between :
(1) Descriptive and Demonstrative conventions
(2) Descriptive and correlative conventions
(3) Demonstrative and locutionary conventions
(4) Locutionary and perlocutionary conventions

57. Who among the following philosophers criticised Frege's method of building up the series of natural numbers out of merely logical notions ?
(1) Wittgenstein
(2) Austin
(3) Bertrand Russell
(4) Strawson

58. According to Rusell, denoting phrases are phrases which :
(1) have a complete meaning
(2) never have any meaning in themselves
(3) have meaning independent of a proposition
(4) contain meanings in themselves

59. Protocol statements according to logical positivism refer to
(1) Complex empirical statements
(2) Simple relational statements
(3) Elementary statements
(4) Metaphorical statements

60. Consider the following statements with reference to induction and mark the correct code.
(a) J.S. Mill conceived induction as essentially an evidencing process.
(b) Whewell conceives it as essentially discovery.
(c) Charles peirce views induction as generalisation and contrasts it with inference.

Codes :
(1) Only (a) and (b) are true.
(2) Only (a) and (c) are true.
(3) All (a), (b) and (c) are true.
(4) Only (a) is true.

61. Which of the following statements is not acceptable to a sceptic ?

(1) No absolute, unquestionable, complete knowledge is possible.

(2) Evidence is indecisive, judgement should be suspended.

(3) There are fixed and eternal values which stand irrespective of time and place.

(4) Questioning or doubting as a means to gaining knowledge.

62. Which of the following statement/s is/are true with reference to Plato ? Mark the correct code.

(a) Justice is a quality of the soul.

(b) Spirit of collectivism should permeate the individual.

(c) The eternal laws of morality are not mere conventions.

Codes :

(1) Only (a) is true.

(2) Only (b) is true.

(3) Only (a) and (c) are true.

(4) (a), (b) and (c) are true.

63. Match **List-I** with **List-II** with reference to idealism and mark the correct code.

List-I	List-II
(a) Personalistic idealism	(i) Finite self is a part, mode or appearance of the one
(b) Monistic idealism	(ii) Concrete reality is personal selfhood
(c) Subjective idealism	(iii) Recognises the reality of non-ideal types
(d) Realistic idealism	(iv) Nature is merely the projection of the finite mind

Codes :

	(a)	(b)	(c)	(d)
(A)	(iv)	(iii)	(ii)	(i)
(B)	(ii)	(iv)	(i)	(iii)
(C)	(ii)	(i)	(iv)	(iii)
(D)	(i)	(ii)	(iii)	(iv)

64. Perception is an unerring knowledge of the unique particular ______ is the view of.

(1) Buddhists (2) Prabhākara

(3) Naiyāyikas (4) Vedāntins

65. Who propounded the 'law of sufficient reason' ?

(1) Aristotle (2) Plato

(3) Leibnitz (4) Kant

66. Examine given argument and choose the correct name of the fallacy out of codes given below.

Argument :

All horses are four footed animals.

No oxen are horse.

∴ No oxen are four footed animal.

Codes :

(1) Fallacy of illicit major

(2) Fallacy of illicit middle

(3) Fallacy of illicit minor

(4) None of these

67. According to 'opposition of propositions' if "summer days are generally hot" is true the propositions "All summer days are hot" will be

(1) True (2) False

(3) Doubtful (4) None of these

68. An argument has essentially :

(1) Form and proposition

(2) Truth and form

(3) Truth and fallacity

(4) Form, proposition and truth

69. Which one of the following is the right symbolization of statement "Bees and wasps sting if they are either angry or frightened" (Bx, Wx, Sx, Ax, Fx)

(1) $(\exists x)\{(Bx.Wx) \supset [(Ax \vee Fx) \supset Sx]\}$

(2) $(x)\{(Bx \vee Wx) \supset [(Ax \vee Fx) \supset Sx]\}$

(3) $(x)(Bx \vee Wx) \supset Ax \vee Fx \supset Sx$

(4) $(x)(Bx \vee Wx) \supset (Ax \vee Fx) \supset Sx$

70. Examine following argument and spot the correct code.

$P \supset (Q \vee R)$

$S \supset (T.U)$

$-T$

$\therefore\ P \supset U$

Codes :

(1) Valid (2) Invalid

(3) True (4) False

71. Read carefully argument I and II the mark the correct code :

Argument I : If there is smoke then there is fire. There is no smoke. Therefore there is no fire.

Argument II : Death is the end of life. The end of life is perfection. Therefore death is perfection.

Codes :

(1) Argument I has the fallacy of denying the antecedent and II is a valid argument.

(2) I is valid and II has fallacy of excluded middle.

(3) Both I and II are valid arguments.

(4) Argument I has fallacy of denying the antecedent and II has fallacy of four terms.

72. Which one of the following is not a valid mood of first figure ?

(1) Barbara (2) Darii

(3) Celarent (4) Baroco

73. Match List I with List II and mark the correct code as given below :

List I	List II
(a) $p . q$ $\therefore P$	(i) Modus Ponens
(b) $p > q$ p $\therefore q$	(ii) Constructive Dilemma
(c) p $\therefore p \vee q$	(iii) Simplification
(d) $(p > q) . (r > s)$ $p \vee r$ $\therefore q \vee s$	(iv) Addition

Codes :

	(a)	(b)	(c)	(d)
(1)	(iii)	(ii)	(iv)	(i)
(2)	(iii)	(i)	(iv)	(ii)
(3)	(iv)	(ii)	(iii)	(i)
(4)	(iii)	(ii)	(i)	(iv)

74. Mark the code which does not show a rule of inference

(1) Hypothetical syllogism

(2) Disjunctive syllogism

(3) Categorical syllogism

(4) Simplification

75. Which pair supports Ecofeminism ?

(1) Vandana Shiva and Maria Mies

(2) Vandana Shiva and Simon De Beauvoir

(3) Maria Mies and Simon De Beauvoir

(4) Simon De Beauvoir and Mahasheveta Devi

Answers

1. (2)	2. (4)	3. (3)	4. (1)	5. (3)	6. (4)	7. (1)	8. (4)	9. (4)	10. (1)
11. (1)	12. (3)	13. (2)	14. (2)	15. (1)	16. (3)	17. (4)	18. (3)	19. (4)	20. (3)
21. (1)	22. (2)	23. (3)	24. (1)	25. (4)	26. (3)	27. (4)	28. (3)	29. (4)	30. (3)
31. (4)	32. (2)	33. (4)	34. (2)	35. (2)	36. (2)	37. (4)	38. (3)	39. (4)	40. (2)
41. (2)	42. (3)	43. (2)	44. (2)	45. (1)	46. (4)	47. (2)	48. (4)	49. (2)	50. (2)
51. (4)	52. (3)	53. (2)	54. (2)	55. (1)	56. (1)	57. (3)	58. (2)	59. (3)	60. (3)
61. (3)	62. (4)	63. (3)	64. (1)	65. (3)	66. (1)	67. (3)	68. (1)	69. (2)	70. (2)
71. (4)	72. (4)	73. (2)	74. (3)	75. (1)					

December, 2015

PHILOSOPHY

PAPER-II

Note : This paper contains **fifty (50)** objectives type questions, each question carrying **two (2)** marks. Attempt **all** the questions.

1. *Ṛta* in its moral sense may be equated with :
(1) *Artha* (2) *Mokṣa*
(3) *Satya* (4) *Niṣedha*

2. Which of the following is indicative of *Ārthibhāvanā* ?
(1) *The YajDhātu* (2) *Liṅga*
(3) *Nipāta* (4) *Ākhyāta*

3. Which of the following theory accepts *Khyāti* as *Smṛtipramoṣa* ?
(1) *Asat Khyāti*
(2) *Akhyati*
(3) *Anirvacanīya Khyāti*
(4) *Sat Khyāti*

4. The kind of knowledge that reveals the mental states of others is known in Jaina Philosophy as :
(1) *Avadhi* (2) *Kevala*
(3) *Mad* (4) *Manaḥparyāya*

5. According to the Naiyāyikas we can perceive all cases of smoke only by :
(1) *Yogaja pratyāṣatti*
(2) *Sāmānyalakṣaṇa pratyāṣatti*
(3) *Jñāalakṣaṇa pratyasatti*
(4) *Śamavāya sannikarṣa*

6. By what type of perception, according to Nyaya one can perceive the objects of past, present and future ?
(1) *Sāmānyalakṣaṇa*
(2) *Yogaja*
(3) *Śrāvaṇa*
(4) *Jñānalakṣaṇa*

7. 'Fire is cold because it is a substance'. What type of fallacy is committed by the above argument according to the Nyaya ?
(1) *Viruddha* (2) *Asiddha*
(3) *Bādha* (4) *Satpratipakṣa*

8. Match Set - I with Set - II and select the code which is correctly matched

Set - I	Set - II
(a) *Prāgābhāva*	(i) Nyāya
(b) *Pramāṇābhāva*	(ii) Mīmāṁsā
(c) *Prājña*	(iii) Vaiśeṣika
(d) *Pramānasaṁplava*	(iv) Vedānta

Codes :

	(a)	(b)	(c)	(d)
(1)	(i)	(ii)	(iii)	(iv)
(2)	(ii)	(i)	(iv)	(iii)
(3)	(iii)	(ii)	(iv)	(i)
(4)	(iii)	(i)	(ii)	(iv)

9. In the context of *Abhāva*, what does *'Jala'* in the statement *'Jale Gandho Nāsti'* stands for :
(1) *Pratiyogī* (2) *Anuyogī*
(3) *Anuyogitā*
(4) *Pratiyogitāvachedakdharma*

10. *'Ākāśatva* inneres in *Ākāśa* as :
(1) *Guṇa - Guṇībhāva*
(2) *Avayavī - Avayavī bhāva*
(3) *Jāti - Vyakti bhāva*
(4) *Viśeṣa - Nityadravya bhāva*

11. "The total energy remains the same while the world is constantly evolving, cause and effect are only more or less evolved forms of

the same ultimate energy" is the view upheld by :

(1) *Vedānta* (2) *Sāṁkhya*
(3) *Nyāya* (4) *Buddhism*

12. According to Cārvāka the so called self is nothing but the :
(1) Body itself
(2) Consciousness itself
(3) Body with Consciousness
(4) Body without Consciousness

13. What type of *Kāraṇa* of *Jñāna* the self is according to the Nyāya ?
(1) *Samavāyī* (2) *Asamavāyī*
(3) *Nimitta* (4) *Upādāna*

14. 'The hill is fiery because it possesses blue smoke'. This inference according to Nyāya commits the fallacy of :
(1) *Anaikāntika*
(2) *Āśrayāsiddha*
(3) *Vyāpyatvāsiddha*
(4) *Bādhita*

15. The status of *Jagat* according to Śaṁkara is :
(1) *Sat* (2) *Asat*
(3) *Sadasadvilakṣaṇa* (4) *Sadāsat*

16. *Īśvara* according to Rāmānuja is :
(1) Only *Nimittakāraṇa* of the world.
(2) Only *Upādānakāraṇa* of the world.
(3) *Abhinnanimittopādāna kāraṇa* of the world
(4) Akāraṇa

17. Madhva's interpretation of the *mahāvākya* : '*ahaṁbrahmāsmi*' means :
(1) *Tādātmya* of *Jīva* and *Brahman*
(2) *Sādṛsya* of *Jīva* and *Brahman*
(3) *Jīva* as *Viśeṣaṇa* of *Brahman*
(4) *Prakāra - Prakāri* of *Jīva* and *Brahman*

18. Match List - I with List - II and choose the correct answer with the help of codes given below :

List - I	List - II
(a) Vidyāraṇya	(i) *Tattvaprakāsikā*
(b) Sriniwās	(ii) *Vedantaparijata*
(c) Jayatīrtha	(iii) *Pañcadaśī*
(d) Niṁbārka	(iv) *Yatmdramatadīpikā*

Codes :

	(a)	(b)	(c)	(d)
(1)	(i)	(iii)	(iv)	(ii)
(2)	(iii)	(iv)	(i)	(ii)
(3)	(ii)	(iii)	(iv)	(i)
(4)	(i)	(ii)	(iii)	(iv)

19. Which one of the following is not accepted by Ambedkar ?
(1) Liberty, Equality, Fraternity
(2) Education, Organisation, Agitation
(3) Caste, Varna, Karma
(4) Buddha, Dhamma, Sangha

20. Which one of the following is admitted by Tagore to be the essential aspect of human being ?
(1) Physical and Mental
(2) Vital and Mental
(3) Physical and Spiritual
(4) Mental and Spiritual

21. Match List - I with List - II and choose the correct answer with the help of codes given below

List - I	List - II
(a) Gandhi	(i) Life Ahead
(b) Tagore	(ii) The Recovery of Faith
(c) Radhakrishnan	(iii) Crisis in Civilization
(d) J. Krishnamurti	(iv) The Art of Living

Codes :

	(a)	(b)	(c)	(d)
(1)	(i)	(iii)	(ii)	(iv)
(2)	(iv)	(iii)	(ii)	(i)
(3)	(iii)	(ii)	(iv)	(i)
(4)	(ii)	(i)	(iii)	(iv)

22. What is the correct sequence of the following in the evolutionary process, according to Sri Aurobindo ?
(1) Overmind, Higher mind, Illumined mind, Intuitive mind
(2) Higher mind, Illumined mind, Intuitive mind, Overmind

(3) Illumined mind, Higher mind, Intuitive mind, Overmind
(4) Intuitive mind, Higher mind, Illumined mind, Overmind

23. The creation according to the Vaiśeṣikas starts with the conjunction of atoms by
(1) The *svabhāva* of the atoms
(2) The will of God
(3) Productive mechanism
(4) Accident

24. *Pratityasamutpāda* in Buddhist Philosophy means :
(1) The effect pre - exists in its cause
(2) The existence of everything is momentary
(3) The existence of everything is conditional
(4) Whatever is, is eternal

25. Which one among the following according to the Sāṁkhya cannot be the reason for the existence of *Prakṛti*?
(1) *Bhedānām parimāṇāt*
(2) *Samanvayāt*
(3) *Bhoktṛbhāvāt*
(4) *Kāraṇa-kārya vibhāgāt*

26. Consider the following statements in the light of philosophy of St. Thomas Aquinas and mark the correct code :
(a) Philosophy passes from facts to God and theology from God to facts.
(b) He made a distinction between reason and faith and argued that matters of faith such as revealed truths are beyond reason, but not contrary to reason.
(c) Faith is a matter of will and the will commands acceptance.

Codes :
(1) Only (a) is true
(2) Only (b) is true
(3) Only (a) and (c) are true
(4) (a), (b) and (c) are true

27. Match List - I with List - II and choose the correct answer with the help of code given below :

List - I	List - II
(a) Protagoras	(i) Whatever is 'is', we cannot know 'is not'
(b) Gorgias	(ii) Man is the measure of all things
(c) Thrasymachus	(iii) Nothing exists, even if it exists it cannot be known
(d) Parmenides	(iv) Justice is the interest of the strong

Codes :

	(a)	(b)	(c)	(d)
(1)	(iv)	(iii)	(ii)	(i)
(2)	(ii)	(iii)	(iv)	(i)
(3)	(ii)	(iv)	(iii)	(i)
(4)	(iii)	(i)	(ii)	(iv)

28. Which one of the following philosophers of Medieval period stated : 'Understand in order that you may believe, believe in order that you may understand. Some-things we do not believe unless we understand them; others we do not understand unless we believe."
(1) St. Anselm (3) St. Augustine
(2) St. Aquinas (4) William Occam

29. Consider the following statements in the light of Pythagoras and mark the correct code :
(a) Pythagoreans believed in the Idea of eternal recurrence.
(b) Pythagoreans held that the soul was immortal and it undergoes a sequence of re-birth.
(c) Pythagoreans rejected the view that the process of the world is endless and unchanging.

Codes :
(1) Only (a) is true
(2) Only (b) is true
(3) Only (a) and (c) are true
(4) Only (a) and (b) are true

30. Choose the correct order from lowest to the highest with reference to Plato's theory of knowledge.

(1) Knowledge derived from senses, conjectural knowledge, discursive intellect, rational insight.
(2) Conjectural knowledge, knowledge derived from senses, discursive intellect, rational insight.
(3) Knowledge derived from senses, conjectural knowledge, rational insight, discursive intellect.
(4) Discursive intellect, conjectural knowledge, knowledge derived from senses, rational insight.

31. Given below are two statements, one labelled as Assertion (A) and the other labelled as Reason (R). Considering (A) and (R) in the light of Aristotelian Theory of Categories mark the correct code.

Assertion (A): Substance is pre-eminent among categories.

Reason (R): Substance is that which is predicable of a subject and present in a subject.

Codes :
(1) Both (A) and (R) are true and (R) is the correct explanation of (A).
(2) Both (A) and (R) are true, but (R) is not the correct explanation of (A).
(3) (A) is true but (R) is false.
(4) (A) is false but (R) is true.

32. The Doctrine of 'innate ideas' is acceptable to :
(1) Descartes and Spinoza
(2) Descartes and Berkeley
(3) Descartes and Hume
(4) Locke and Fitche

33. 'Ontological Argument' in favour of the existence of God was popularized by :
(1) Descartes
(2) Descartes and St. Anselm
(3) Hume
(4) Berkeley

34. Which one of the following correctly depicts Locke's conception of 'Idea' ?
(1) Whatsoever the mind indirectly apprehends; which is the immediate object of perception, thought or understanding.
(2) Whatsoever the mind directly apprehends; which is the immediate object of perception, thought or understanding.
(3) Whatsoever the mind indirectly apprehends; which is the mediate object of perception, thought or understanding.
(4) Whatsoever the mind directly apprehends; which is the mediate object of perception, thought or understanding.

35. Which one of the following modern philosophers conceptualised - "philosophy as a whole is like a tree whose roots are metaphysics, whose trunk is physics and whose branches, which issue from this trunk, are all the other sciences" ?
(1) Spinoza (2) Berkeley
(3) Descartes (4) Leibnitz

36. Consider the following statements in the light of Spinozas' theory of knowledge and mark the correct code.
(a) Obscure and inadequate ideas have their source in sensation and the imagination.
(b) Reason comprehends the Universal essences of things and understands these in their relation to God.
(c) Intuitive knowledge advances from an adequate idea of the objective essence of certain attributes of God to the adequate essence of things.

Codes :
(1) Only (a) and (c) are true
(3) Only (c) is true
(2) Only (b) and (c) are true
(4) (a), (b) and (c) are true

37. Which one of the following statements is true with reference to the doctrine of Force of Leibnitz ?
(1) Force persists when motion ceases, as it is the ground of motion.
(2) Extension is the essential attribute of body.
(3) There is no substance that is an expression of force.
(4) What is active is Unreal.

38. Which one of the following statements is true with reference to Berkeley ?

(1) Berkeley makes use of the basal empiricism of Locke to establish idealism and thereby endorses materialism and atheism.

(2) Berkeley makes use of the basal empiricism of Locke to establish idealism and thereby refutes materialism and atheism.

(3) Mind has the capacity to frame abstract ideas.

(4) Existence of an object does not depend on being perceived or known by the mind.

39. The so called relation between cause and effect according to Hume is

(1) inferred prior to experience

(2) based on observation and experience

(3) effect is immanent in the cause

(4) both are necessarily connected

40. Antinomy of Pure Reason is dealt with by Kant in his doctrine of :

(1) Transcendental Theology

(2) Transcendental Cosmology

(3) Transcendental Psychology

(4) All the above

41. 'Elementary propositions depict the picture of Reality' is formulated by :

(1) Moore

(2) Russell

(3) Wittgenstein

(4) Husserl

42. Match the List - I with List - II and choose the correct answer from the code given hereunder

List - I	**List - II**
(a) Husserl	(i) Verification theory
(b) A.J. Yer	(ii) Category mistake
(c) William James	(iii) Epoche
(d) G. Ryle	(iv) Pragmatic theory

Codes :

	(a)	**(b)**	**(c)**	**(d)**
(1)	(iii)	(i)	(iv)	(ii)
(2)	(iii)	(iv)	(i)	(ii)
(3)	(iii)	(i)	(ii)	(iv)
(4)	(i)	(ii)	(iii)	(iv)

43. Which of the following book is authored by Heidegger ?

(1) *Lebenswelt*

(2) *Being and Time*

(3) *Pragmatism*

(4) *Phenomenology*

44. Logical positivism rejects the metaphysics on the following grounds :

(1) Metaphysical questions are beyond the limit of the categories of Human understanding.

(2) Metaphysical questions are doubtful.

(3) Metaphysical questions are nonsensical as they are non-verifiable.

(4) Metaphysical questions are beyond space and time.

45. According to G. Ryle which one of the following is correct ?

(1) All the physical events are reducible to the mental events.

(2) All the mental events are reducible to the physical events.

(3) Both kinds of events are inter reducible to each other.

(4) None of the above

46. Moore's atomistic analysis is supposed to be the reaction against:

(1) Kantian dichotomy between Epistemology and Ontology.

(2) Hegelian identity between thought and being.

(3) Bradleian Absolutism.

(4) All the above.

47. Consider the Assertion (A) and Reason (R) and mark the correct option in the light of Kant's view of knowledge.

Assertion (A): Universality, Necessity and Novelty are the criteria of knowledge.
Reason (R): Synthetic a priori judgement fulfils all the required criteria of knowledge.
Codes :
(1) (A) and (R) both are true and (R) is the correct explanation of (A).
(2) (A) and (R) both are false and (R) does not provide the correct explanation of (A).
(3) (A) is true and (R) is false and (R) does not provide correct explanation of (A).
(4) (A) is false and (R) is true, and (R) does not provide the correct explanation of (A).

48. Which one of the following is a correct sequence of the existential structures according to Heidegger ?
(1) Existenz, Fallenness, Facticity
(2) Existenz, Facticity, Fallenness
(3) Facticity, Fallenness, Existenz
(4) Fallenness, Facticity, Existenz

49. Husserl has borrowed the concept of intentionality from the following philosophers :
(1) Kant (2) Hegel
(3) Brentano (4) Descartes

50. Consider the Assertion (A) and Reason (R) and mark the correct option in the light of Wittgenstein's views :
Assertion (A): Every proposition has a clear and definite sense.
Reason (R): Propositions of everyday life contain complex expressions which are logically proper names.
Codes :
(1) (A) and (R) both are true and (R) is the correct explanation of (A).
(2) (A) and (R) both are false and (R) is not the correct explanation of (A).
(3) (A) is true and (R) is false and (R) is not the correct explanation of (A).
(4) (A) is false and (R) is true and (R) is not the correct explanation of (A).

Answers

1. (3)	**2.** (4)	**3.** (2)	**4.** (4)	**5.** (2)	**6.** (2)	**7.** (3)	**8.** (*)	**9.** (2)	**10.** (4)
11. (2)	**12.** (3)	**13.** (1)	**14.** (3)	**15.** (3)	**16.** (3)	**17.** (2)	**18.** (2)	**19.** (3)	**20.** (3)
21. (2)	**22.** (2)	**23.** (2)	**24.** (3)	**25.** (3)	**26.** (4)	**27.** (2)	**28.** (3)	**29.** (4)	**30.** (2)
31. (3)	**32.** (1)	**33.** (2)	**34.** (2)	**35.** (3)	**36.** (4)	**37.** (1)	**38.** (2)	**39.** (2)	**40.** (2)
41. (3)	**42.** (1)	**43.** (2)	**44.** (3)	**45.** (2)	**46.** (3)	**47.** (1)	**48.** (2)	**49.** (3)	**50.** (3)

* No option is correct.

December, 2015

PHILOSOPHY

PAPER-III

Note : This paper contains **seventy five (75)** objective type questions of **two (2)** marks each. **All** questions are compulsory.

1. Recognise the *Hetvabhasa* in,
All smoky objects are fiery.
The hill is smoky.
Therefore, the hill is fiery.
Codes :
(1) *Viruddha*
(2) *Prakaraṇasama*
(3) *Asiddha*
(4) *Savyabhicāra*

2. Who among the following denies that perceptual experiences can be expressed in words :
(1) Jayrāśibhaṭṭa alone
(2) Dharmakirti alone
(3) Mahavira alone
(4) Dharmakirti and Viśvanātha

3. According to which of the following schools Abhava is perceived through Viśeṣaṇatā Sannikarṣa ?
(1) Sāṁkhya
(2) Bauddha
(3) Nyāya
(4) Jaina

4. If two propositions with the same subject and predicate can both be true but cannot both be false then the relation between them is :
(1) Contradiction
(2) Contrary
(3) Sub-contrary
(4) Sub-Altern

5. Knowing the meaning of a *pada* by observing the behaviour of others is known as :
(1) *Āptavākya*
(2) *Prasiddhapadasānnidhya*
(3) *Vṛddhavyavahāra*
(4) *Vivaraṇa*

6. Match Set - I with Set - II and select the code correctly matched

Set- I	Set - II
(a) *Asatkhyātivāda*	(i) Yogācāra Bauddha
(b) *Ātmakhyātivāda*	(ii) Prabhākara Mīmāṁsā
(c) *Anyathākhyātivāda*	(iii) Mādhyamika Bauddha
(d) *Akhyātivāda*	(iv) Nyāya

Codes :

	(a)	(b)	(c)	(d)
(1)	(i)	(ii)	(iii)	(iv)
(2)	(i)	(ii)	(iv)	(iii)
(3)	(iii)	(i)	(iv)	(ii)
(4)	(iii)	(ii)	(i)	(iv)

7. In case of pot, the father of the potter is treated as :
(1) *Samavāyikāraṇa*
(2) *Asamavāyikārana*
(3) *Anyāthasiddha*
(4) *Nimittākaraṇa*

8. The *kāraṇatā* of *paramāṇu saṁyoga* in the production of *dvyaṇuka* is :
(1) *Samavāyikāraṇatā*

(2) *Asamavāyikāraṇatā*
(3) *Nimittakāraṇatā*
(4) *Sāmagnkāraṇatā*

9. According to Śaṅkara the *Jagat* looses its *vyāvahārikasattā* when we have the realisation of :
(1) *Pāramārthikasatta* of Brahman only
(2) *Prātibhāsikasattā of* dream - objects
(3) Both *Pāramārthika sāttā of* Brahman and Pratibhasika satta of dream-objects
(4) Temporal state of worldly objects

10. Which *bhūtadravyas* are *nitya* ?
(1) *Ākāśa* only
(2) *Mārut* only
(3) The *Paramāṇus* of *Kṣiti, Apa, Teja, Māruta* only
(4) *Ākāśa* and the *Paramāṇus* of *Kṣiti, Apa, Teja* and *Maruta*

11. According to whom the liberated self is a *bhaktā* ?
(1) Śaṅkara
(2) Rāmānuja
(3) Madhva
(4) Nimbārka

12. Among the following, which one is not correct according to Madhva?
(1) The *jagat* is real
(2) The *Brahman* is Supreme
(3) *Mokṣa* consists in the realisation of the inherent bliss of the *Jīva*
(4) *Brahman* is *nirguṇa*

13. Among the following which one is correct according to Rāmānuja ?
(1) In essence *the jiva* is the same as *Brahman.*
(2) *Pratyakṣa* is always *nirvikalpaka*
(3) *Prapattih* the royal road to *Mokṣa*
(4) *Brahman* is the seat of *A vidyā*

14. The doctrine of 'four gradations in *Mokṣā is* advocated by :
(1) Śaṁkara
(2) Rāmānuja
(3) Nimbārka
(4) Madhva

15. *Jivanmukti*though desirable is logically untenable – this view is held by :
(1) Śaṁkara and Madhva
(2) Rāmānuja and Śaṁkara
(3) Rāmānuja and Madhva
(4) Vallabha and Vācaspati

16. The ultimate means to *Moksa* according to Samkara is :
(1) *Karma*
(2) *Jñana Karma Samucchaya*
(3) *Jñana* and *Jñana* alone
(4) All the above

17. Performance of *Karma* induces in the *Sādhaka* the desire to have *mokṣa* - this view is propounded by :
(1) Prakāśātman
(2) Vācaspati Miśra
(3) Padmapāda
(4) Ānandagiri

18. Match the following and choose the correct answer by using the codes :

List - I	List - II
(a) Rāmānuja	(i) *Sāṁkhya Kārikā*
(b) Madhva	(ii) *Tattva Vaiśardi*
(c) Vācaspati Miśra	(iii) *Śrībhāṣya*
(d) Iśwara Krisṇa	(iv) *Mahābhārata tātparya nirṇaya*

Codes :

	(a)	(b)	(c)	(d)
(1)	(iii)	(iv)	(ii)	(i)
(2)	(ii)	(i)	(iv)	(iii)
(3)	(iv)	(iii)	(i)	(ii)
(4)	(ii)	(iii)	(i)	(iv)

19. The meaning of a word is '*Jativiśiṣta Vyakti*' is the view given by :
(1) Viśvanātha
(2) Jagdisha
(3) Udayanācārya
(4) Rāmākṛṣṇa

20. *'Saṁskārajanya Jñānam'* refers to :

(1) *Pratyakṣa*

(2) *Anumāna*

(3) *Viparyaya*

(4) *Smṛti*

21. Given below are the two statements, one labelled as Assertion (A) and the other labelled as Reason (R). Considering (A) and (R) in the context of Vedanta, select the correct code :

Assertion (A): *"Vyāpāravad asādhāraṇam Kāraṇam Karaṇani"*

Reason (R): Mind, being a common factor to all sorts of knowledge is to be regarded as an *asādhāraṇa Kāraṇa*

Codes :

(1) Both (A) and (R) are true and (R) is the correct explanation of (A).

(2) Both (A) and (R) are true but (R) is not the correct explanation of (A).

(3) (A) is true but (R) is false.

(4) (A) is false but (R) is true.

22. The relation between *Kriyātva* and *Kārakatva* is known by :

(1) *Ākānkshā*

(2) *Yogyatā*

(3) *Sannidhi*

(4) *Tātparya*

23. Which system of Indian Philosophy holds the view that *Prāmāṇya* and *aprāmāṇya* of cognition is *parataḥ* ?

(1) Buddhism

(2) Purva Mimāṁsā

(3) Vedānta

(4) Nyāya

24. According to which system of Indian Philosophy *Pramanya* of cognition is *Svatah* and *apramanya* is *paratah* ?

(1) Nyāya

(2) Bauddha

(3) Vedānta

(4) Pūrva-mimamsa

25. Given below are two statements, one labelled as Assertion (A) and the other labelled as Reason (R). Considering (A) and (R) in the context of Advaitins select the correct code.

Assertion (A): All cases of smoke are cases of fire.

Reason (R): Universal proposition is really inferred from the universal concomitance between smokeness and fireness.

Codes :

(1) Both (A) and (R) are true and (R) is the correct explanation of (A).

(2) Both (A) and (R) are true but (R) is not the correct explanation of (A).

(3) (A) is true but (R) is false.

(4) (A) is false but (R) is true.

26. Given below are two statements, one labelled Assertion (A) and the other labelled as Reason (R). Considering (A) and (R) select the correct code.

Assertion (A): Kant argues that space and time are the subjective forms of perceiving any object for all human beings.

Reason (R): Kant believes that since space and time are subjective in the same way for all human beings, they are truly objective.

Codes :

(1) Both (A) and (R) are true and (R) is the correct explanation of (A).

(2) Both (A) and (R) are true and (R) is not the correct explanation of (A).

(3) (A) is true, but (R) is false.

(4) (A) is false, but (R) is true.

27. Which one of the following groups, correctly depicts Hume's conception of relations dependent on ideas alone ?

(1) Resemblance, Contrariety, Identity, Time and Place.

(2) Resemblance, Contrariety, Degrees in quality and Degrees in quantity.

(3) Resemblance, Contrariety, Time and Space, Cause and effect.

(4) Resemblance, Identity, Degrees in quality and Degrees in quantity.

28. Consider the following statements in the light of Bradley's theory of Appearence and Reality and mark the correct code.
   (a) We apprehend the nature of reality through its appearances, which are things of everyday life.
   (b) Reality is related to appearances, and appearances are appearences of Reality.
   (c) Reality is found in all appearances, but not in the same degree.

   Codes :
   (1) Only (b) is false
   (2) Only (b) and (c) are false
   (3) Only (a) and (b) are false
   (4) (a), (b) and (c) are true

29. Heidegger's concept of anxiety is the state of being into which individual falls :
   (1) When he sees that he alone has the question of being and the responsibility to answer it.
   (2) When he sees that he alone has the answer to all questions.
   (3) When he sees everyone endowed with the question of being.
   (4) When he rejects the question of being and responsibility to answer it.

30. Reality, according to Leibnitz is :
   (1) Cannot be one but many and each is eternal and real.
   (2) Cannot be one but many and each is temporal and unreal.
   (3) Cannot be many but one and is eternal and real.
   (4) Cannot be many but one and is temporal and unreal.

31. Who among the following authored the work ''Gender trouble'' ?
   (1) Simon de Bouvour
   (2) Luce Irigary
   (3) Judith Butler
   (4) Allen Showalter

32. Who among the following philosophers coined the concept' 'group-differentiated rights'' ?
   (1) Thomas Hobbes
   (2) Amartya Sen
   (3) Will Kymlicka
   (4) Mac Intyre

33. Who among the following introduced the concept of 'Annadayee Shrama Siddhanta'?
   (1) Gandhi
   (2) Vinobabhave
   (3) Tilaka
   (4) J.B. Kripalani

34. Match List - I with List - II and choose the correct answer from the codes given below :

List - I (Author)	List - II (Text)
(a) Gandhi	(i) Rastriyata Aur Samajvada
(b) J.B. Kripalani	(ii) Gandhiji in Indian Villages
(c) Mahadev Desai	(iii) Politics of Charakha
(d) Narendra Dev	(iv) Ethical Religion (Niti Dharma)

Codes :

	(a)	(b)	(c)	(d)
(1)	(i)	(ii)	(iii)	(iv)
(2)	(iv)	(iii)	(ii)	(i)
(3)	(ii)	(iii)	(iv)	(i)
(4)	(iii)	(ii)	(i)	(iv)

35. Which one of the following statements is not true with respect to Gandhi ?
   (1) Non-violence is a law of human species.
   (2) Means justify the end.
   (3) End justify the means.
   (4) All lands belongs to Gopal.

36. Who among the following uphold 'Village Republic' ?
   (1) Tagore
   (2) Gandhi

(3) Vivekananda
(4) Radhakrishṇan

37. Which one of the following statements is true regarding Gandhi's goal of 'Constructive Programme'?
(1) Only providing economic relief to unemployed
(2) Only distributing some wages to spinners and weavers
(3) Only creating non-violent order of society
(4) All the above

38. Which of the following is the correct pair of prophetic religion?
(1) Jainism and Buddhism
(2) Christianity and Islam
(3) Sikhism and Islam
(4) Hinduism and Zoroastrianism

39. Match List - I with List - II and select the correct answer from codes given below :

List - I (Religion)	**List - II (Aspiring Process)**
(a) Buddhism	(i) Guṇasthānaka
(b) Islam	(ii) Nāmasmaraṇa
(c) Sikhism	(iii) Aṣṭāṅgikamārga
(d) Jainism	(iv) Praying five times a day

Codes :

	(a)	(b)	(c)	(d)
(1)	(iii)	(iv)	(ii)	(i)
(2)	(iii)	(i)	(ii)	(iv)
(3)	(i)	(iii)	(iv)	(ii)
(4)	(iv)	(ii)	(i)	(iii)

40. Which one of the following philosophers believed that 'intuition is the essential element in Induction, the process in which thought rises from sense perception to the knowledge of Universals"?
(1) Aristotle
(2) Pythagoras
(3) Democritus
(4) Protagoras

41. Given below are two statements, one labelled as Assertion (A) and the other labelled as Reason (R). Considering (A) and (R) select the correct code.
Assertion (A): Spinoza conceives error not as defect of knowledge.
Reason (R): No idea is either true or false as such; what makes an idea true is the presence of an appropriate object.
Codes :
(1) Both (A) and (R) are true and (R) is the correct explanation of (A).
(2) Both (A) and (R) are true but (R) is not the correct explanation of (A).
(3) (A) is true but (R) is false.
(4) (A) is false but (R) is true.

42. Which one of the following philosophers argued that two mutually contradictory statements might be equally true, but one might be ' 'better" than the other?
(1) Aristotle
(2) Protagoras
(3) Parmenides
(4) Democritus

43. Which one of the following statements is false with reference to Leibnitz's theory of knowledge?
(1) All knowledge lies implicit in the mind
(2) Experience does not create knowledge
(3) Universal and necessary propositions can only be derived from the senses
(4) Leibnitz asserts the existence of 'minute' perceptions - perceptions of which the mind is unconscious

44. The view that 'Beliefs are the most natural and most metaphysical of all things; knowledge is the practical outgrowth of beliefs and beliefs modify and shape reality' is held by which one of the following philosophers?
(1) JohnDewey
(2) Kant
(3) Descartes
(4) Aristotle

45. Match the List - I with List - II and choose the correct answer from the codes given below :

List - I	List - II
(a) Rationalism	(i) Ayer
(b) Emotivism	(ii) Hare
(c) Utilitarianism	(iii) Kant
(d) Prescriptivism	(iv) Mill

Codes :

	(a)	(b)	(c)	(d)
(1)	(i)	(ii)	(iii)	(iv)
(2)	(iii)	(i)	(iv)	(ii)
(3)	(iv)	(ii)	(iii)	(i)
(4)	(iv)	(iii)	(ii)	(i)

46. 'The political laws are the highest court of appeal in the matters of morality'. Which one of the following persons hold this view?
(1) Spencer
(2) Mill
(3) Kant
(4) Hobbes

47. Match List - I with List - II and choose the correct answer with the help of codes given below :

List - I (Authors)	List - II (Texts)
(a) Hare	(i) Metaphysics of morals
(b) Stephen	(ii) The Right and the good
(c) Ross	(iii) Science of Ethics
(d) Kant	(iv) Freedom and Reason

Codes :

	(a)	(b)	(c)	(d)
(1)	(i)	(ii)	(iii)	(iv)
(2)	(ii)	(iii)	(i)	(iv)
(3)	(iii)	(ii)	(iv)	(i)
(4)	(iv)	(iii)	(ii)	(i)

48. Which one of the following theory holds the view : 'Eye for an eye' ?
(1) Preventive theory
(2) Reformative theory
(3) Retributive theory
(4) All the above

49. Who among the following has said that' 'pleasure if ever good must be good in a different sense from that in which good activities are so" ?
(1) Moore
(2) Ross
(3) Ayer
(4) Hare

50. Who among the following has said that 'Autonomy is the basis of the dignity of human and of every rational being' ?
(1) Hobbes
(2) Kant
(3) Stevenson
(4) Bentham

51. Who among the following has given this statement ?
'Act only on the maxim which thou canst at the same time will to become a universal law.'
(1) Kant
(2) Hegel
(3) Hobbes
(4) Mill

52. Consider the following argument and argument form and choose the correct answer from options given below :

(a) $\dfrac{(A \cdot B) \supset C \qquad (A \cdot B)}{\therefore C}$ (b) $\dfrac{p \supset q \qquad p}{\therefore q}$

(1) (a) is the argument form of (b).
(2) (b) is the specific argument form of (a).
(3) (b) is the argument form of (a).
(4) (a) is the specific argument form of (b).

53. Which one of the following options is correct regarding the weak and strong sense of disjunction ?
(1) In a weak sense (inclusive) of disjunction only one disjunct is true whereas

in a strong sense (exclusive) both the disjuncts are true.

(2) In a weak (inclusive) and strong (exclusive) both senses of disjunction both the disjuncts are true.

(3) In a weak and strong both senses of disjunction only one disjunct is true.

(4) In a weak sense of disjunction both the disjuncts are true whereas in a strong sense of disjunction only one disjunct is true.

54. Match the List - I with List - II and select the correct answer by using the codes given below :

List - I	**List - II**
(a) DIMARIS	(i) I[st] figure
(b) FELAPTON	(ii) IInd figure
(c) BAROCO	(iii) IIIrd figure
(d) DARII	(iv) IVth figure

Codes :

	(a)	**(b)**	**(c)**	**(d)**
(1)	(i)	(ii)	(iii)	(iv)
(2)	(ii)	(iii)	(i)	(iv)
(3)	(iii)	(iv)	(ii)	(i)
(4)	(iv)	(iii)	(ii)	(i)

55. Mark the correct answer out of the following statements.

(a) Contradiction is a relation between propositions that differ both in their quality and quantity.

(b) Contrary is a relation between universal propositions.

(c) Sub-contrary is a relation between particular propositions.

(d) Universal propositions are the principal or super - altern to particular propositions.

Codes :

(1) (a) and (c) are correct

(2) (b) and (c) are incorrect

(3) (c) and (d) are incorrect

(4) All of the above statements are correct

56. Two statements are said to be logically equivalent in which one of the following cases ?

(1) Their biconditional is tautologous

(2) Their biconditional is contradictory

(3) Their biconditional is contingent

(4) Both have the same truth value

57. Which one of the following expression is the correct form of Demorgan theorem ?

(1) $[(p \equiv q) \equiv (p > q) \cdot (q > p)]$ and $[(p \equiv q) \equiv (p \cdot q) \vee (\sim p \cdot \sim q)]$

(2) $[\sim(p.q) \equiv (\sim p \vee \sim q)]$ and $[\sim(p \vee q)] \equiv [(\sim p \cdot \sim q)]$

(3) $[(p \equiv (p \cdot p)]$ and $[p \equiv (p \vee p)]$

(4) $[(p \cdot q) \equiv (q \cdot p)]$ and $[(p \vee q) \equiv (q \vee p)]$

58. The Invalidity of an argument can be proved through the shorter truth table technique in which of the following ways ?

(1) By assigning the 'True' truth value to both the premises and the conclusion.

(2) By assigning the 'False' truth value to both the premises and the conclusion.

(3) By assigning the 'False' truth value to the premises and 'True' truth value to the conclusion.

(4) By assigning the 'True' truth value to the premises and 'False' truth value to the conclusion.

59. The obversion of the proposition "All leaves are green" is :

(1) No non-leaves are non-green

(2) All leaves are non-green

(3) Some leaves are non-green

(4) No leaves are non-green

60. The common and essential teaching of all religions is :

(1) Morality is the cream of life

(2) Upgradation of social values

(3) Establishment of *manava dharma* of mutual love and respect

(4) All the above

61. Strawson explains in his book 'Logical Theory' that the 'formal systems' are useful in appraising one of the following :
(1) 'Context-free' discourse
(2) 'Context-bound' discourse
(3) 'Context-neutral' discourse
(4) All the above

62. Consider the given Assertion (A) and Reason (R) in the light of elementary propositions, verification and metaphysical statements and mark the correct code from given below :

Assertion (A): If all statements are truth-functions of elementary propositions which report observations then they will all be either empirical in themselves or else tautologies or contradictions.

Reason (R): Metaphysical statements do not seem to be classifiable under any of these heads as above.

Codes :
(1) Both (A) and (R) are true and (R) is the correct explanation of (A).
(2) Both (A) and (R) are true and (R) is not the correct explanation of (A).
(3) (A) is true and (R) is false.
(4) (A) is false and (R) is true.

63. In Investigations Wittgenstein holds the theory of meaning known as :
(1) Picture theory of meaning
(2) Use theory of meaning
(3) Language - game theory of meaning
(4) Speech act theory of meaning

64. According to Russell's theory of the definite description the proposition 'the author of Waverley is Scotch' is analysed as the following :
(a) At least one person wrote waverley.
(b) At most one person wrote waverley.
(c) Whoever wrote waverley is scotch.

Which one of the given below is correct code according to Russell ?
(1) Conjunction of (a) and (b)
(2) Conjunction of (b) and (c)
(3) Conjunction of (a) and (c)
(4) Conjunction of (a), (b) and (c)

65. Match List - I with List - II and choose the correct code given below in the light of Peirce's classification of 'Semiotics' done in his book 'Foundations of the theory of signs':

List - I	List - II
(a) Syntactics	(i) Describes the relation between signs and their interpreters
(b) Semantics	(ii) Describes the relations of signs one to another
(c) Pragmatics	(iii) Describes the manner in which they designate

Codes :

	(a)	(b)	(c)
(1)	(ii)	(iii)	(i)
(2)	(iii)	(ii)	(i)
(3)	(i)	(ii)	(iii)
(4)	(i)	(iii)	(ii)

66. Consider the given Assertion (A) and Reason (R) in the light of Wittgenstein's view of proposition and mark the correct code given below :

Assertion (A): A proposition's range is identical with its 'truth ground'.

Reason (R): A proposition's range is a conjunction of atomic propositions.

Codes :
(1) Both (A) and (R) are true and (R) is the correct explanation of (A).
(2) Both (A) and (R) are true and (R) is not the correct explanation of (A).
(3) (A) is true and (R) is false.
(4) (A) is false and (R) is true.

67. "Language is our second nature; it is through language that the world is opened

up for us" - is the philosophical position of which one of the following Hermeneutic thinkers ?

(1) Schleiermacher (2) Dilthey
(3) Gadamer (4) Heidegger

68. 'Ontological turn' is Hermeneutics is contributed by which one of the following philosophers ?

(1) Martin Heidegger
(2) Ricoeur
(3) Derrida
(4) Habermas

69. Which one of the following Hermeneutic thinkers attempted to reconcile ontological hermeneutics with critical hermeneutics ?

(1) Gadamer
(2) Derrida
(3) Ricoeur
(4) Habermas

70. The phenomenological analysis of 'consciousness of has two sides as : (i) noematic and (ii) noetic.

Choose the correct option from the given below regarding their relationship :

(1) Separable
(2) Non-separable
(3) Inseparable
(4) Conjoined

71. The goal of the study of Comparative Religions is the need to :

(1) Understand inter - religious dialogues
(2) Understand commonality and differences amongst religions
(3) To get at the core and harmony of plurality of religions
(4) All the above

72. '*Pratyakṣaṁ Kalpanāpoḍam nāmajātyadya - 'saṁyutam'*. This definition of *Pratyaksa* was upheld by :

(1) Dharmakirti (2) Dharmottara
(3) Vatsyayana (4) Dinnaga

73. *Jñānākaraṇakam Jñānaṁ Pratyakṣaṁ.* This definition of *Pratyaksa* was formulated first by :

(1) Diṅnāga (2) Gautama
(3) Gaṅgeśa (4) Vācaspati Miśra

74. Which one of the following philosophers has said that 'each one for himself to each one for others no road' ?

(1) Mill (2) Bentham
(3) Kant (4) Martineau

75. Which one of the following provides the metaphysical ground of morality ?

(1) Cordinal virtue
(2) Freedom and Responsibility
(3) Immortality of soul
(4) Growth of character

Answers

1. (4)	**2.** (4)	**3.** (3)	**4.** (3)	**5.** (3)	**6.** (3)	**7.** (3)	**8.** (2)	**9.** (1)	**10.** (4)
11. (3)	**12.** (4)	**13.** (3)	**14.** (4)	**15.** (3)	**16.** (3)	**17.** (2)	**18.** (1)	**19.** (*)	**20.** (4)
21. (3)	**22.** (1)	**23.** (4)	**24.** (4)	**25.** (1)	**26.** (2)	**27.** (2)	**28.** (4)	**29.** (1)	**30.** (1)
31. (3)	**32.** (3)	**33.** (1)	**34.** (2)	**35.** (3)	**36.** (2)	**37.** (4)	**38.** (2)	**39.** (1)	**40.** (1)
41. (4)	**42.** (2)	**43.** (3)	**44.** (1)	**45.** (*)	**46.** (4)	**47.** (4)	**48.** (3)	**49.** (2)	**50.** (2)
51. (1)	**52.** (3)	**53.** (4)	**54.** (4)	**55.** (4)	**56.** (1)	**57.** (2)	**58.** (4)	**59.** (4)	**60.** (4)
61. (1)	**62.** (2)	**63.** (2)	**64.** (4)	**65.** (1)	**66.** (2)	**67.** (3)	**68.** (1)	**69.** (3)	**70.** (3)
71. (4)	**72.** (*)	**73.** (3)	**74.** (4)	**75.** (3)					

* No option is correct.

July, 2016

PHILOSOPHY

PAPER-II

Note : This paper contains **fifty (50)** objectives type questions, each question carrying **two (2)** marks. Attempt **all** the questions.

1. The asamāyikraaṇa of an earthen pot according to the Vaiśeṣikas is
   (1) Earth itself
   (2) Pot itself
   (3) Parts of the pot
   (4) The conjunction of the parts of the pot

2. Parvatḥ vahnimān dhumāt
   What type of hetvābhāsa is committed by the above anumāna ?
   (1) Asādhārana Savyabhicāra
   (2) Anupasamhāri
   (3) Bādhita
   (4) Vyāpytvāsiddha

3. According to which school a thing may be 'is' and 'is not' at the same time ?
   (1) Cārāvka (2) Vedānta
   (3) Jaina (4) Bauddha

4. According to Cārvākas anumāna cannot be a pramāṇa because
   (1) It cannot prove God.
   (2) It is not infallible.
   (3) Its vyāpti cannot be established.
   (4) It is self-contradictory.

5. In Vedic tradition yajña is performed under the direction of
   (1) Yajmna (2) Ṛtvika
   (3) Gṛhakarta (4) Isvara

6. Select the code that states the correct sequence :
   (1) Brāhmaṇa, Saṁhitā, Āraṇyaka, Upaniṣad
   (2) Upaniṣad, Saṁhitā, Āraṇyaka, Brāhmaṇa
   (3) Saṁhitā, Brhma a, Āraṇyaka, Upaniṣad
   (4) Saṁhitā, Upaniṣad, Brāhmaṇa, Āraṇyaka

7. Which of the following school holds that the magnitude of the body (dehaporimāa) is the magnitude of the ātmā ?
   (1) Cārvāka (2) Vaiśeṣika
   (3) Yoga (4) Jaina

8. Given below one Assertion (A) and a Reason (R). Consider them in the light of Nyāya Philosophy and select the correct code given below :
   Assertion (A) : Lakṣnā cannot be a Vṛtti .
   Reason (R) : Śakti is a Vṛtti and Śakti is not Lakṣaṇā.
   Codes :
   (1) (A) and (R) both are true and (R) is the correct explanation of (A).
   (2) (A) and (R) both are true and (R) is not the correct explanation of (A).
   (3) (A) is true, but (R) is false.
   (4) (A) is false and (R) is true.

9. Ṛṣirṇa can be repaid by
   (1) Brahmacarya
   (2) Performing yajña
   (3) Giving birth to a son
   (4) Helping the poor

10. Given below one Assertion (A) and one Reason (R). Consider them in the light of Nyàya-Vai[e ika Philosophy and select the correct code from given below :

Assertion (A) : The liberated soul must be Jaḍa (matter).

Reason (R) : The liberated soul looses even its consciousness.

Codes :

(1) (A) and (R) both are true and (R) provides the correct explanation of (A).
(2) (A) and (R) both are true and (R) does not provide correct explanation of (A).
(3) (A) is true and (R) is false.
(4) (A) is false and (R) is true.

11. Which one among the following is the cause of the magnitude (Parimāṇa) of trasareṇu according to the Vaiśeṣikas ?
(1) Number of the Paramāṇus
(2) Number of the dryaṇukas
(3) Number of the trasarenus
(4) Trasareṇu themselves

12. Match the List – I with List – II and select the correct code from given below :

List – I	**List - II**
a. Brahmasūktras	i. Kaṇāda
b. Mimāṁsāsūktras	ii. Jaimini
c. Vaiśeṣikasūtras	iii. Patañjali
d. Yogasūtras	iv. Bādarāyaṇa

Codes :

	(a)	**(b)**	**(c)**	**(d)**
(1)	i	ii	iii	iv
(2)	i	iii	ii	iv
(3)	iv	ii	i	iii
(4)	iv	i	ii	iii

13. Who holds the view that 'Religion is acceptance, not tolerance' ?
(1) Sri Aurobindo
(2) Vivekananda
(3) J. Krishnamurti
(4) Radhakrishnan

14. Who holds the view that world is 'Cradle of Human Spirit' ?
(1) J. Krishnamurti
(2) K.C. Bhattacharya
(3) Vivekananda
(4) Tagore

15. Which one of the following philosophers propounds that rebirth is essential for individual evolution ?
(1) Radhakrishnan
(2) Gandhi
(3) Sri Aurobindo
(4) Tagore

16. Which one of the following holds that 'The region of Negation is the region of the Indefinite' ?
(1) K.C. Bhattacharya
(2) Vivekananda
(3) Tagore
(4) Radhakrishnan

17. Who among the following maintains 'By education I mean an all-round drawing out of the best in child and man – body, mind and spirit' ?
(1) Tagore
(2) Vivekanand
(3) Sri Aurobindo
(4) Gandhi

18. Which one of the following is correct ?

	(Books)	**(Authors)**
(1)	Philosophy of Hinduism, On Fear	– Ambedkar
(2)	You are the World, The limits of Thought	– J. Krishnamurti
(3)	Fruit Gathering, Total Freedom	– Tagore
(4)	The Human Cycle, The Recovery of Faith	– Sri Aurobindo

19. Consider given Assertion (A) and Reason (R) and then mark the correct option as given below :

Assertion (A) : Śūnya in the sense of mere negation is pure nihilism.

Reason (R) : Śūnya is contradicted by all valid means of knowledge.

Codes :

(1) (A) and (R) are both true and (R) does not provide correct explanation of (A).

(2) (A) is false and (R) is true and (R) provides correct explanation of (A).
(3) (A) and (R) are both true and (R) provides correct explanation of (A).
(4) (A) is true and (R) is false and (R) provides the incorrect explanation of (A).

20. In Rāmānuja-Vednta all the following propositions are true except :
(1) Jīva is in organic relation with Brahman.
(2) Jīva is existentially one with Brahman.
(3) Jīva is the Viśeṣaṇa of Brahman.
(4) Jīva is entirely dependent on Brahman.

21. "The silver that appears in a shell cannot be unreal because it appears; that silver cannot also be real because it is found to be not there when we see the shell proerly." This is the view of the
(1) Viśiṣdāvaitins
(2) Śūnyavādins
(3) Sāṁkhyans
(4) Advaitins

22. "Brahman is truly independent among the reals; there is nothing equal or superior to it" – this view is upheld by
(1) Śaṁkara
(2) Iśwara Krişṇa
(3) Madhva
(4) Prabhākara

23. Match List – I with List – II and select the correct answer by using the codes given below:

List – I	**List – II**
i. Śāṁkhya	a. Prasthānatraya
ii. Yoga	b. Svarga prāpti
iii. Pūrva-Mimāṁsa	c. Asaṁprajñāta samādhi
iv. Vedānta	d. Puruṣa-prakṛti-viveka jñāna

Codes :

	(a)	**(b)**	**(c)**	**(d)**
(1)	ii	i	iv	iii
(2)	iv	iii	ii	i
(3)	iii	iv	i	ii
(4)	iii	iv	ii	i

24. According to Śākhya-yoga Puru a is
(1) Conscious and active
(2) Conscious and inactive
(3) Unconscious and active
(4) Unconscious and inactive

25. Select the code which presents the Skandhas in correct sequence :
(1) Vijñna, rūpa, vedanā, saṁjñā and saṁskāra
(2) Sa jñ, vijñna, rūpa, vedanā, and saṁskāra
(3) Rūpa, vedanā, saṁjñā, saṁskāra and vijñna
(4) Rūpa, saṁjñā, vedanā, saṁskāra and vijñna

26. "Forms are not apart from things, but inherent in them; they are not transcendent but immanent" is the view that can be ascribed to which one of the following Greek philosophers ?
(1) Socrates (2) Plato
(3) Aristotle (4) Democritus

27. Given below are two statements, one labelled as Assertion(A) and the other labelled as Reason(R). Considering (A) and (R) in the light of Plato's epistemology. Mark the correct code :

Assertion (A) : Conceptual knowledge is the only genuine knowledge.

Reason (R) : Conceptual knowledge does not presuppose the reality of corresponding ideal or abstract objects.

Codes :
(1) Both (A) and (R) are true and (R) is the correct explanation of (A).
(2) Both (A) and (R) are true but (R) is not the correct explanation of (A).
(3) (A) is true, but (R) is false.
(4) (A) is false, but (R) is true.

28. Consider the following statements with reference to St. Anselm and mark the correct code :
(i) He attempted to find necessary reasons for the truths of the faith.
(ii) 'I believe in order to understand'.

(iii) By God we mean 'that than which no greater can be thought'.

Codes :

(1) Only (i) is true.
(2) Only (i) and (ii) is true.
(3) Only (iii) is true.
(4) All (i), (ii) and (iii) are true.

29. Given below are two statements, one labelled as Assertion (A) and the other labelled as Reason (R). Considering (A) and (R) in the light of Thales. Select the correct code :

Assertion (A) : Magnet has a soul.

Reason (R) : Magnet possesses a power to move other things.

Codes :

(1) Both (A) and (R) are true and (R) is the correct explanation of (A).
(2) Both (A) and (R) are true, but (R) is not the correct explanation of (A).
(3) (A) is true, but (R) is false.
(4) (A) is false, but (R) is true.

30. Consider the following statements in the light of Heraclitus and mark the correct code:

(i) Heraclitus held that the world had always existed and thus rejected cosmogony.
(ii) The world and its constituents are in a state of perpetual flux.
(iii) He argued that 'The path up is the same as path down'.

Codes :

(1) Only (i) is true.
(2) Only (i) and (ii) are true.
(3) All (i), (ii) and (iii) are true.
(4) Only (i) and (iii) are true.

31. Consider the following statements in the light of St. Augustine and mark the correct code :

(i) Mutability is a mark of every creature.
(ii) God is strictly immutable.
(iii) Changeable things are not fully but only "partially" real.
(iv) All creatures are absolutely real.

Codes :

(1) Only (i) and (ii) are true.
(2) Only (ii) and (iv) are true.
(3) Only (iii) and (iv) are true.
(4) Only (i), (ii) and (iii) are true.

32. Match List – I with List – II and select the correct answer by using the codes given below:

List – I	List – II
i. Locke	a. 'I think therefore I am'
ii. Descartes	b. God is immanent in the world
iii. Spinoza	c. Pre-established harmony
iv. Leibnitz	d. Secondary qualities are subjective

Codes :

	(a)	(b)	(c)	(d)
(1)	iii	ii	i	iv
(2)	ii	iii	iv	i
(3)	i	iv	ii	iii
(4)	iv	i	iii	ii

33. Consider given Assertion (A) and Reason (R) and then mark the correct option as given below :

Assertion (A) : According to Leibnitz there is a necessary relation between the gushing wind and the shutting of the door.

Reason (R) : There is pre-established harmony.

Codes :

(1) (A) is true and (R) is false and (R) provides the incorrect explanation of (A).
(2) Both (A) and (R) are true and (R) provides the correct explanation of (A).
(3) (A) is false and (R) is true and (R) provides the correct explanation of (A).
(4) Both (A) and (R) are true and (R) provides incorrect explanation of (A).

34. All the following statements are inconsistent with Spinoza except :

(1) Mind and Body are two unlike substances.

(2) Doubting implies the existence of the doubter.
(3) God is ontologically different from the world.
(4) The world and its changes are but modes of God.

35. 'The entire universe is mirrored in each unit of the substance except for the difference that it is mirrored only slightly differently from unit to unit.' This position is acceptable to
(1) Spinoza (2) Leibnitz
(3) Descartes
(4) St. Thomas Aquinas

36. G.E. Moore's refutation of idealism is based on which one of the following ?
(1) Distinction between act of awareness and object of awareness.
(2) Distinction between knower and the act of knowing.
(3) Distinction between mind and matter.
(4) Distinction between sense and reference.

37. Which one of the following statements are true with reference to Russell's "problems of philosophy" ?
(1) Universals are real entities which exist neither in the mental nor in the physical worlds, and yet have a subsistent or logical status.
(2) Universals are unreal, that exist only in imagination.
(3) Universals are real entities, that exist in both mental and physical worlds.
(4) Universals are real entities that exist only in the mental world.

38. Consider the following statements with reference to logical positivism and mark the correct code :
(i) Strong verification requires that to be meaningful a statement should be verifiable or falsifiable by direct confrontation with experience.
(ii) Logical positivism employs verifiability as the criterion of meaning.
(iii) Strong verification requires both direct and indirect methods of verifiability.

Codes :
(1) Only (i) is true.
(2) Only (i) and (ii) are true.
(3) Only (iii) is true.
(4) Only (i) and (iii) are true.

39. The view that "Happiness does not consist of a preponderance of pleasurable moments which are free from pain but in the possession and creative exercise of power." – Can be attributed to which one of the following philosophers ?
(1) Hegel (2) Moore
(3) Nietzsche (4) Heidegger

40. Consider the following statements with reference to pragmatism of C.S. Peirce, and mark the correct code.
(i) Pragmatism is not a method of reflection.
(ii) Pragmatism is a method of reflection having for its purpose to render ideas clear.
(iii) It is merely a technique for ascertaining the meaning of conceptions.

Codes :
(1) Only (i) is true.
(2) Only (i) and (ii) are true.
(3) Only (ii) is true.
(4) Only (ii) and (iii) are true.

41. Consider the following statements with reference to Hegel and mark the correct code :
(i) The evolution is a logical, not a temporal process.
(ii) There must be both unity and opposition in the absolute.
(iii) Being is a rational process, an orderly evolution.

Codes :
(1) Only (i) is true.
(2) Only (i) and (ii) are true.
(3) Only (i) and (iii) are true.
(4) All (i), (ii) and (iii) are true.

42. Match the List – I with List – II and select the correct answer by using the codes given below :

List – I	List – II
a. Highest certainty; our assent to it is faith.	i. Hegel
b. Although all our knowledge begins with experience it does not follow that it arises out of experience .	ii. Hume
c. Thought proceeds from the most simple, abstract and empty concepts to the more complex, concrete and richer 'notions'.	iii. Kant
d. The mind is a bundle or collection of different perceptions.	iv. Locke

Codes :

	(a)	(b)	(c)	(d)
(1)	iv	ii	i	iii
(2)	ii	iv	iii	i
(3)	iv	i	ii	iii
(4)	iii	ii	i	iv

43. When the mind perceives the agreement or disagreement of two ideas by direct inspection without intervention of any other ideas is known as :

(1) Intuitive knowledge
(2) Demonstrative knowledge
(3) Sensitive knowledge
(4) None of the above

44. Which of the following is the Apodictic form of judgement according to Kant ?

(1) Every effect must have a cause
(2) This may be poison
(3) The substance is either solid or fluid
(4) All of the above

45. Consider given Assertion (A) and Reason (R) and then mark the correct option given below :

Assertion (A) : For Hume, we have no idea of a substance.

Reason (R) : We have no idea of anything but a perception whereas substance is entirely different from a perception.

Codes :

(1) Both (A) and (R) are true and (R) provides a correct explanation of (A).
(2) Both (A) and (R) are false and (R) provides an incorrect explanation of (A).
(3) (A) is true and (R) is false and (R) is an incorrect explanation of (A).
(4) (A) is false and (R) is true and (R) is a correct explanation of (A).

46. Consider the following assertions :

(i) Agreement or disagreement of ideas is knowledge.
(ii) There is distinction between primary and secondary qualities.
(iii) Objects are represented through their qualities.
(iv) Knowledge of the object is pre-established in the mind.

Select the correct code in the light of John Locke's philosophy.

Codes :

(1) (i) and (ii) are true.
(2) (i), (ii) and (iii) are true.
(3) (ii), (iii) and (iv) are true.
(4) (i), (ii), (iii) and (iv) are true.

47. Consider following assertions :

(i) Synthetic Apriori Judgement is the standard of knowledge.
(ii) Synthetic Aposteriori Judgement is the standard of knowledge.
(iii) Analytic Apriori Judgment is the standard of knowledge.
(iv) Analytic Aposteriori Judgement is the standard of knowledge.

Select the correct code in the light of Kant's view-point :

Codes :

(1) Only (i) is correct.
(2) Only (ii) is correct.

(3) Only (i) and (iv) are correct.
(4) Only (iii) is correct.

48. Consider following assertions :
If sugar has sweetness today, it does not mean that it will remain sweet tomorrow also because –
(i) Sweetness is not inherent in the sugar.
(ii) There is only circumstantial relation between sugar and the sweetness.
(iii) There is no necessary causal relation between sugar and the sweetness.
(iv) There is only conjunction between sugar and the sweetness.

Select the correct code in the light of David Hume's view-point :

Codes :
(1) Only (i) is correct.
(2) Only (ii) is correct.
(3) Only (iii) and (iv) are correct.
(4) Only (ii) and (iv) are correct.

49. Consider the following assertion :
To be is to be perceived – this view is held by
(i) Locke
(ii) Berkeley
(iii) Locke and Berkeley
(iv) Locke, Berkeley and Hume

Select the correct code :

Codes :
(1) Only (i) is correct.
(2) Only (ii) is correct.
(3) Only (i) and (ii) are correct.
(4) Only (iv) is correct.

50. Match the List – I with List – II and select the correct answer by using the codes given below :

List – I	List – II
a. I could not have been the cause of my own existence for I have an idea of perfection.	i. Hume
b. If a principle can be imprinted on the soul without being known, it is impossible to distinguish between what is nature and what not.	ii. Berkeley
c. Mind is incapable of framing abstract ideas.	iii. Descartes
d. Objects are not necessarily but the ideas are connected in our mind by association.	iv. Locke

Codes :

	(a)	(b)	(c)	(d)
(1)	ii	i	iii	iv
(2)	iv	ii	i	iii
(3)	i	ii	iv	iii
(4)	iii	iv	ii	i

Answers

1. (4)	2. (4)	3. (3)	4. (3)	5. (2)	6. (3)	7. (4)	8. (4)	9. (1)	10. (4)
11. (3)	12. (3)	13. (2)	14. (4)	15. (3)	16. (1)	17. (4)	18. (2)	19. (3)	20. (2)
21. (4)	22. (3)	23. (2)	24. (2)	25. (3)	26. (3)	27. (3)	28. (4)	29. (1)	30. (3)
31. (4)	32. (2)	33. (2)	34. (4)	35. (2)	36. (1)	37. (1)	38. (2)	39. (3)	40. (4)
41. (4)	42. (*)	43. (1)	44. (1)	45. (1)	46. (2)	47. (1)	48. (3)	49. (2)	50. (4)

* All options are correct.

July, 2016

PHILOSOPHY

PAPER-III

Note : This paper contains **seventy five (75)** objective type questions of **two (2)** marks each. **All** questions are compulsory.

1. The self is related to the body according to the Vaiśeṣikas by the relation

(1) Svarkūpa (2) Samavāya
(3) Saṁyoga (4) Viseṣaṇatā

2. According to the Vaiśeṣikas the absence of knowledge resides in human self by the relation of

(1) Samavāya (2) Svarkūpa
(3) Saṁyoga (4) Vaiśiṣṭya

3. Which one among the following is the Samavāyikāraṇa of the world in Vaiśeṣika philosophy ?

(1) Trasareṇu (2) Dvyaṇuka
(3) Parmāṇu (4) Iśvara

4. Ākāśa, Kāla and Dik all these three dravyas have some common characteristics. Select which one correctly states those characteristics :

(1) one, physical (bhuta) and eternal
(2) one, eternal and composite
(3) one, all-pervading and eternal
(4) many, all-pervading and eternal

5. Which one among the following is not a nitya dravya ?

(1) Ātman (2) Ākāśa
(3) Viśeṣa (4) Kāla

6. Consider the Assertion (A) and Reason (R) and select the correct code given below :

Assertion (A) : Ākāśatva must be a jātī.

Reason (R) : It is an essential characteristic of ākāśa.

Codes :

(1) (A) and (R) both are true and (R) is the correct explanation of (A).
(2) (A) and (R) both are true and (R) is not the correct explanation of (A).
(3) (A) is false and (R) is true.
(4) Both (A) and (R) are false.

7. "Self-identity does not belong to various perceptions by uniting them together, rather it is merely a quality which we attribute to these perceptions because of the Union of their ideas in the imagination" is the view of which one of the following philosophers?

(1) Hume (2) Spinoza
(3) Kant (4) Kierkegaard

8. "Bodies have no existence without a mind; and it is a contradiction in terms to say those matter exists unperceived by any mind" is the view held by

(1) Berkeley (2) Leibnitz
(3) Spinoza (4) Hume

9. Consider the following statements with reference to Kant and select the correct code :

(i) Kant rejects the notion the space and time are concepts which have been derived from our experience of relations between things.
(ii) Kant accepts the notion the space and time are concepts which have been derived from our experience of relations between things.
(iii) Kant rejects the notion that space and time are concepts which are not derived from our experience of relations between things.

Codes :

(1) Only (i) is true.
(2) Only (i) and (ii) are true.

(3) Only (ii) is true.
(4) Only (ii) and (iii) are true.

10. Given below are two statements, one labelled Assertion (A) and the other labelled as Reason (R). Considering (A) and (R) with reference to Descartes' concept of substance, select the correct code :

Assertion (A) : Mind and Body are two relative substances.

Reason (R) : Mind and Body are dependent on each other.

Codes :

(1) Both (A) and (R) are true and (R) is the correct explanation of (A).
(2) Both (A) and (R) are true but (R) is not the correct explanation of (A).
(3) (A) is true but (R) is false.
(4) (A) is false but (R) is true.

11. Which one of the following statements is true with reference to Locke's theory of causality ?

(1) The idea of causality is not derived from voluntary action.
(2) The idea of causality is necessarily connected with uniformity.
(3) The idea of causality is derived from voluntary action and is not necessarily connected with uniformity.
(4) The connections and dependencies of cause and effect on each other can be discovered in our ideas.

12. In Smṛti there is a mental creation of world under the influence of Avidyā as aided by the impressions of waking experiences is the view upheld by

(1) Mīmāṁsā (2) Vedānta
(3) Nyāya (4) Buddhism

13. 'Doṣa is the cause of apramā and Guṇa is the cause of Pramā' is upheld by

(1) Viśvanātha (2) Gautama
(3) Kumārila (4) Abhinavgupta

14. 'The verbal suffix is the sentence', is the view held by

(1) Vedānta (2) Buddhism
(3) Mīmāṁsā (4) Nyāya

15. According to which of the following schools the meaning of words can be learned only from their use in sentences ?

(1) Navya-Nyāya (2) Nyāya
(3) Mīmāṁsā (4) Vedānta

16. Match the List – I with List – II and select the correct answer by using the codes given below :

	List – I	List – II
a.	Attention which fixes anything in the mind	i. Nibandha
b.	Association which connects different experiences	ii. Parigraha
c.	Characteristics mark that recalls to which an object belongs.	iii. Praṇidhāna
d.	Ownership which is suggestive of the owner	iv. Lakṣaṇa

Codes :

	(a)	(b)	(c)	(d)		(a)	(b)	(c)	(d)
(1)	ii	i	iii	iv	(2)	i	iv	iii	ii
(3)	iv	i	ii	iii	(4)	iii	i	iv	ii

17. While propagating the theory of illusion, which one of the following philosophers argued that 'the world of sense is an illusion'?

(1) Francis Bacon (2) Parmenides
(3) Protagoras (4) William James

18. Which one of the following philosophers argued that the source of error is the disparity between the finitude of the human intellect and the infinitude of the human will ?

(1) Descartes (2) Locke
(3) Bradley (4) Kierkegaard

19. The distinction between 'propositions of matters of fact' and 'propositions of relations of ideas' was made by

(1) Locke and Berkeley (2) Berkeley only
(3) Hume and Locke (4) Hume only

20. Write the correct sequence of the following concepts according to Hegel :

(1) Thesis, synthesis and antithesis
(2) Thesis, antithesis and synthesis
(3) Synthesis, thesis and antithesis
(4) Antithesis, thesis and synthesis

21. Which pair of philosophers holds the view that 'I can be aware of myself without being aware of an object'?
(1) Locke and Hume
(2) Berkeley and Locke
(3) Hume and Spinoza
(4) Hume and Berkeley

22. Manas is the Saṁkalpātmikā Vṛtti of Antaḥkaraṇa, is the position held by
(1) Nyāya (2) Mīmāṁsā
(3) Advaita Vedānta (4) Buddhism

23. The cognition of silver in the shell is erroneous because it manifests the non-existent silver as existent and we become conscious of this when our first cognition of silver is contradicted by the subsequent cognition of shell, is an example of
(1) Akhyāti (2) Anyathākhyāti
(3) Asatkhyāti (4) Ātmakhyāti

24. According to Nyāya, which of the following requires conscious reference to a past and a present state of the same object?
(1) Smṛti
(2) Anandhyavasāya
(3) Pratyabhijñā
(4) Nirvikalpaka Pratyakṣa

25. Which of the following statement is not acceptable to Nyāya?
(1) Indriyārthasannikaṣra janyaṁ jñānaṁ pratyakṣam
(2) Dravyāśritā jāeyā nirguṇā niṣkriy guṇāḥ
(3) Saṁdigdhasādhyavān pakṣah
(4) Arthakriyāsmarthya is the criterion of existence

26. Match the List – I with List – II and select the correct answer by using the codes given below

List – I	List – II
a. Presence of middle term in all positive instances	i. Vipakṣāsatva
b. Absence of middle term in all negative instances	ii. Asatpratipakṣa
c. Middle term must not aim at contradictory objects	iii. Sapakṣasatva
d. Absence of contradicting reasons leading to contradictory conclusion	iv. Abādhitviṣayatva

Codes :

	(a)	(b)	(c)	(d)		(a)	(b)	(c)	(d)
(1)	iii	iv	i	ii	(2)	ii	iii	iv	i
(3)	iii	i	iv	ii	(4)	i	iii	iv	ii

27. Which type of hetvbhsa is committed by the following annumna?
Select the correct code.
'Maṇimayaḥ parvataḥ vahnimān dhūkmāt'
(1) Anupasaṁhāri Savyabhicāra
(2) Āśrayāsiddha
(3) Svarūpāsiddha
(4) Bādhita

28. Select the correct sequence :
(1) Kāma, artha, dharma, mokṣa
(2) Mokṣa dharma, artha, kāma
(3) Dharma, artha, kāma, mokṣa
(4) Dharma, kāma, artha, mokṣa

29. According to Sri Kṛṣṇa Varṇa is divided on the basis of
(1) Jāti and Karma (2) Guṇa and Karma
(3) Jāti and Guṇa
(4) Svadharma and Jāti

30. Which of the following is needed by an aspirant of Samyak cāritra?
(1) Siddhaśīlā (2) Guṇasthāna
(3) Sadasadviveka (4) Pancavṛata

31. Which of the following is not a Triratna?
(1) Saṁyak Darśana (2) Saṁyak Jñāna
(3) Saṁyak Cāritra (4) Saṁyak Samādhi

32. Match the List – I with List – II and select the correct answer by using the codes given below :

List – I	List – II
a. Sukhānuśayī	i. abhiniveṣa
b. Dṛg-darśana-śaktyor-ekātmeva	ii. dueṣah
c. Duḥkhānuśayī	iii. asmitā
d. Svarasvāhī vidhuso'pi tathārākdhah	iv. rga

Codes :

	(a)	(b)	(c)	(d)		(a)	(b)	(c)	(d)
(1)	iii	ii	i	iv	(2)	iv	iii	ii	i
(3)	ii	iv	i	iii	(4)	i	iii	ii	iv

33. Which one of the following has advocated 'Either freedom of will is a fact or moral judgement a delusion' ?

(1) Martineau (2) Bentham
(3) Kant (4) Spencer

34. Match the List – I with List – II and select the correct answer by using the codes given below :

List – I (Authors)	List – II (Text)
a. Urban	i. *The Language of Morals*
b. Broad	ii. *Five Types of Ethical Theories*
c. R.M. Hare	iii. *The Place of Reason in Ethics*
d. Toulmin	iv. *Fundamentals of Ethics*

Codes :

	(a)	(b)	(c)	(d)		(a)	(b)	(c)	(d)
(1)	i	iii	iv	ii	(2)	iv	ii	i	iii
(3)	iii	iv	ii	i	(4)	i	ii	iii	iv

35. Which one of the following is inconsistent pair ?

(1) Emotivism – A.J. Ayer
(2) Intuitionism – Martineau
(3) Naturalism – S.E. Toulmin
(4) Rationalism – Kant

36. Which one of the following is a statement of naturalistic Ethical theory ?

(1) A good is what a rational person desires.
(2) The good is desirable.
(3) A right action is one that is approved by God.
(4) A right action is one that is approved by my conscience.

37. Who among the following has said 'Autonomy is the basis of the dignity of human and of every rational being' ?

(1) Ross (2) Hegel
(3) Kant (4) Green

38. 'John is punished not because he has stolen the sheep but for others may not steal it'. This statement belongs to which theory of punishment ?

(1) Retributive (2) Preventive
(3) Reformative (4) Sadistic

39. Which of the following statements is/are true with reference to Bentham and Mill ? Mark the correct code :

(a) Both believe that man is essentially happiness seeking.
(b) Both believe that 'Ought' can be derived from 'is'.
(c) Both justify the ideal of greatest happiness of the greatest number on the ground of self interest.

Codes :

(1) (a) and (c) (2) (a) and (b)
(3) (b) and (c) (4) (a), (b) and (c)

40. 'Ought' originates from external commands. Which one of the following maintains it ?

(1) Jural theory (2) Intuitionism
(3) Hedonism (4) Idealism

41. Truth is the attribute of

(1) Term (2) Proposition
(3) Syllogism
(4) Both proposition and syllogism

42. If two propositions having the same subject and predicate cannot both be true but can both the false, their relation is called

(1) Sub-alternation (2) Contradictory
(3) Contrary (4) Subcontrary

43. If O proposition is given as false the corresponding A, E and I, will be

(1) A is true, E is false and I is false.
(2) A is true, E is false and I is true.

(3) E is false and both A and I are undetermined.

(4) A is false and E and I are undetermined

44. Which one among the following is not a law of thought ?

(1) Principle of identity

(2) Principle of sufficient reason

(3) The principle of excluded middle

(4) The principle of non-contradiction

45. Which one among the following is a tautology ?

(1) $P \vee P$ (2) $P \cdot P$

(3) $P \cdot {\sim}P$ (4) $P \supset P$

46. Consider the following argument (a) and argument form (b) and answer by marking the correct code given below :

(a) $(A \supset B) \cdot (C \supset D)$

$\therefore A \supset B$

(b) $(p \supset q) \cdot (r \supset s)$

$\therefore p \supset q$

(1) (a) is the argument form of (b).

(2) (b) is the argument form of (a).

(3) (a) is the specific argument form of (b).

(4) (b) is the specific argument form of (a).

47. Match the List – I and List – II and select the correct answer by using the codes given below

	List – I	List – II
a.	FERIO	i. 4th figure
b.	CAMESTRES	ii. 3rd figure
c.	DATISI	iii. 2nd figure
d.	DIMARIS	iv. 1st figure

Codes :

	(a)	(b)	(c)	(d)		(a)	(b)	(c)	(d)
(1)	i	ii	iii	iv	(2)	iv	iii	ii	i
(3)	ii	i	iii	iv	(4)	iv	iii	i	ii

48. The obversion of 'No men are perfect' is

(1) All men are imperfect.

(2) All perfect beings are men.

(3) No perfect beings are man.

(4) Some perfect beings are men.

49. Which one of the following is equivalent to ${\sim} p \supset {\sim}{\sim} q$?

(1) $q \supset {\sim} p$ (2) $p \supset q$

(3) $p \supset q$ (4) ${\sim} p \supset {\sim} q$

50. Match List – I with List – II and select the correct code given below :

	List – I	List – II
a.	Exportation	i. $(p \supset q) \equiv ({\sim}q \supset {\sim} p)$
b.	Tautology	ii. $(p \supset q) \equiv ({\sim}p \supset q)$
c.	Transposition	iii. $p \equiv (p \vee p)$
d.	Material implication	iv. $[(p \vee q) \supset r] \equiv [p \supset (q \supset r)]$

Codes :

	(a)	(b)	(c)	(d)		(a)	(b)	(c)	(d)
(1)	i	ii	iii	iv	(2)	iv	ii	iii	i
(3)	iv	iii	i	ii	(4)	iii	iv	i	ii

51. Match List – I with List – II and choose the correct answer by using the codes given blow

	List – I	List – II
a.	Hinduism	i. Five main pillars
b.	Buddhism	ii. Saptabhaginaya
c.	Jainism	iii. Pratītyasamutpāda
d.	Islam	iv. Varṇāśrama

Codes :

	(a)	(b)	(c)	(d)		(a)	(b)	(c)	(d)
(1)	iii	iv	i	ii	(2)	iv	iii	ii	i
(3)	ii	i	iv	iii	(4)	i	ii	iv	iii

52. Match List – I with List – II and choose the correct answer by using codes given below:

	List – I	List – II
a.	The Holy Ghost	i. Zoroastrianism
b.	Ahramazda	ii. Christianity
c.	Talmud	iii. Sikhism
d.	Gurubani	iv. Judaism

Codes :

	(a)	(b)	(c)	(d)		(a)	(b)	(c)	(d)
(1)	i	ii	iii	iv	(2)	ii	i	iv	iii
(3)	iii	iv	i	ii	(4)	iv	iii	ii	i

53. Karma siddhānta in Hinduism means

(1) Fatalism

(2) The doctrine of Moral causation

(3) Doing Karma expecting the result

(4) Performing sacrificial rites

54. "All aspects of a thing are real, whereas the thing is a mere logical construction" is the view of

(1) Frege (2) Russell
(3) Wittgenstein (4) Austin

55. Theoretical reasons for a distinction between "there is" and "exists" has been accepted by Frege in order to explain
(1) Identity
(2) Negative existential
(3) Indirect speech
(4) Propositional attitudes

56. Consider given Assertion (A) and Reason (R) and then mark the correct option as given below:
Assertion (A) : "The test of truth is its practical consequences."
Reason (R) : Pragmatism determines the truth or falsity of propositions according as they do or do not fulfil our purpose.
Codes :
(1) Both (A) and (R) are correct and (R) provides a correct explanation of (A).
(2) Both (A) and (R) are false.
(3) (A) is true and (R) is false and (R) does not provide correct explanation of (A).
(4) (A) is false and (R) is true and (R) provides incorrect explanation of (A).

57. Which of the following condition is unacceptable to Donald Davidson with regard to two people having benefits about the same external object ?
(1) Belief about oneself
(2) Belief about other people
(3) Belief about language rules.
(4) Belief about the world come into existence jointly

58. Consider the following pairs with reference to Hermeneutics and mark the correct code;
(i) Friedrich Schleiermacher – Romantic Hermeneutics
(ii) Heidegger – Radical Hermeneutics
(iii) Derrida – Hermeneutics phenomenology
Codes :
(1) Only (i) is correctly matched.
(2) Only (i) and (ii) are correctly matched.
(3) Only (iii) is correctly matched.
(4) Only (ii) and (iii) are correctly matched.

59. Noesis in Husserl's phenomenology refers to
(1) Real content of an intentional act
(2) Ideal content of an intentional act
(3) Real content of an unintentional act
(4) Ideal content of an unintentional act

60. Who among the following philosophers is responsible for shifting the centre from consciousness to existence in phenomenological studies ?
(1) Husserl (2) Heidegger
(3) Hegel (4) Kierkegaard

61. Match List – I with List – II and choose the correct answer by using codes given below:

	List – I	List – II
a.	Śuddha Advaita	i. Nimbarka
b.	Dvaitdvaita	ii. Vallabha
c.	Advaita	iii. Madhva
d.	Dvaita	iv. Śaṁkara

Codes :

	(a)	(b)	(c)	(d)		(a)	(b)	(c)	(d)
(1)	ii	i	iv	iii	(2)	i	ii	iii	iv
(3)	iii	iv	i	ii	(4)	iv	iii	ii	i

62. Consider given Assertion (A) and Reason (R) in Sāmkara's view and then mark the correct option from given below :
Assertion (A) : Brahman is abhinnanimittopādanakāraṇa of the world.
Reason (R) : There is nothing else other than Brahman.
Codes :
(1) (A) is false and (R) is true and (R) provides the correct explanation of (A).
(2) (A) and (R) are both true and (R) provides the correct explanation of (A).
(3) (A) is true and (R) is false and (R) does not provide correct explanation of (A).
(4) (A) and (R) are both true and (R) does not provide correct explanation of (A).

63. Match the Status of Jagat with the view of the following Vedntjns of List – I and List – II and choose the correct answer by using the codes :

List – I	List – II
a. Sat	i. Mādhyamika Buddhism
b. Asat	ii. Madhva
c. Sadasat	iii. Bhart prapañca
d. Sadasadvilakṣana	iv. Śaṁkara

Codes :

	a	b	c	d
(1)	i	ii	iv	iii
(2)	ii	i	iii	iv
(3)	iv	iii	i	ii
(4)	iii	iv	ii	i

64. Mokṣa in Vedānta means
(1) Freedom to be free from gross body (Sthula Śarīra)
(2) Freedom from all empirical limitations.
(3) Permanent stay in Svarga
(4) Occasional visit to heaven

65. The meaning of the word Mithā according to Advaita is
(1) The world is not at all empirically real.
(2) The world is absolutely non-existent.
(3) The world is not transcendentally real.
(4) The world is mistaken for Brahman.

66. All the following propositions are false, except :
(1) Karma-yoga is advocated by Śaṁkara as a primary means to Mukti.
(2) Karma-yoga is advocated by Śaṁkara as a primary means to Videha Mukti.
(3) Jñāna-yoga is advocated by Śaṁkara as a primary means to Jīvan Mukti.
(4) Jñāna-yoga is advocated by Śaṁkara as a primary means to Videha Mukti.

67. Match List – I with List – II and choose the correct answer by using the codes given below :

List – I	List – II
a. Tādātmya of Jīva and Brahman	i. Madhva
b. Sādṛṣya of Jiva and Brahman	ii. Śaṁkara
c. Jiva as Visèṣana of Brahman	iii. Nimbarka
d. Jiva as having bhedābheda Saṁbandha with brahman	iv. Rāmānuja

Codes :

	(a)	(b)	(c)	(d)		(a)	(b)	(c)	(d)
(1)	iii	iv	ii	i	(2)	ii	i	iv	iii
(3)	iv	iii	i	ii	(4)	iii	ii	i	iv

68. Match List – I with List – II and choose the correct answer by using the codes given below :

List – I (Authors)	List – II (Texts)
a. Mahadev Desai	i. Gandhi Ki Shava Parikṣsa
b. Gandhi	ii. The Annihilation of Caste and a Reply to Mahatma Gandhi
c. Yashpal	iii. Women and Social Justice
d. Ambedkar	iv. The Story of Bardoli

Codes :

	a	b	c	d
(1)	iv	iii	i	ii
(2)	i	ii	iv	iii
(3)	ii	iv	i	iii
(4)	iv	iii	ii	i

69. Match the following and choose the correct answer by using the codes :

List – I	List – II
a. Gandhi	i. Maya is simply a statement of facts, as they exist.
b. Tagore	ii. Evolution is preconditioned by involution.
c. Sri Aurobindo	iii. As soon as we lose the moral basis we cease to be religious.
d. Vivekananda	iv. He (man) is earth's child but heaven's heir.

Codes :

	a	b	c	d
(1)	i	iv	ii	iii
(2)	ii	iv	i	iii
(3)	iii	iv	ii	i
(4)	iv	i	iii	ii

70. Which one of the following is not true according to Gandhi ?

(1) Ahimsā is a practical expression of Satya.
(2) Man can know the absolute truth.
(3) There is a chain of ends and means of values.
(4) Satya and Ahimsā are inseparable.

71. Anti-Untouchability fasting was started by Gandhiji against

(1) British Government
(2) Savarṇa Hindu
(3) Christian
(4) Sanatani Hindus

72. Match the List – I with List – II and choose the correct code :

List – I (Authors)	List – II (Texts)
a. Gandhi	i. Gandhiji in Indian Villages
b. J.B. Kriplani	ii. Ethical Religion
c. Mahadev Desai	iii. The Philosophy of Mahatma Gandhi
d. Datta D.M.	iv. The Gandhian Way

Codes :

	a	b	c	d
(1)	ii	iv	i	iii
(2)	i	ii	iv	iii
(3)	iii	ii	i	iv
(4)	iv	i	iii	ii

73. "Natural Right is one of self-preservation" is the view held by

(1) Hobbes (2) Paine
(3) Kant (4) Aquinas

74. Hermeneutic circle, according to Gadamer, refers to

(1) Co-determination of text and reader
(2) Co-determination of text and author
(3) Co-determination of text and context
(4) Co-determination of author and reader

75. Consider the following statements in the light of Schleiermacher's theory of Hermeneutics and mark the correct code :

(i) Problem of interpretation is the problem of understanding.
(ii) Hermeneutics is an art of avoiding misunderstanding.
(iii) Extended the domain of hermeneutics from deciphering sacred texts to all human texts and modes communication.

Codes :

(1) Only (i) is true.
(2) Only (i) and (ii) are true.
(3) Only (i) and (iii) are true.
(4) All (i), (ii) and (iii) are true.

Answers

1. (3)	**2.** (2)	**3.** (3)	**4.** (3)	**5.** (3)	**6.** (3)	**7.** (1)	**8.** (1)	**9.** (1)	**10.** (3)
11. (3)	**12.** (2)	**13.** (1)	**14.** (3)	**15.** (3)	**16.** (4)	**17.** (2)	**18.** (1)	**19.** (4)	**20.** (2)
21. (4)	**22.** (3)	**23.** (3)	**24.** (3)	**25.** (4)	**26.** (3)	**27.** (2)	**28.** (3)	**29.** (2)	**30.** (4)
31. (4)	**32.** (2)	**33.** (1)	**34.** (2)	**35.** (3)	**36.** (2)	**37.** (3)	**38.** (2)	**39.** (2)	**40.** (1)
41. (2)	**42.** (3)	**43.** (2)	**44.** (*)	**45.** (4)	**46.** (*)	**47.** (2)	**48.** (1)	**49.** (2)	**50.** (3)
51. (2)	**52.** (2)	**53.** (2)	**54.** (2)	**55.** (2)	**56.** (1)	**57.** (3)	**58.** (1)	**59.** (1)	**60.** (2)
61. (1)	**62.** (2)	**63.** (2)	**64.** (2)	**65.** (3)	**66.** (3)	**67.** (2)	**68.** (1)	**69.** (3)	**70.** (2)
71. (2)	**72.** (1)	**73.** (1)	**74.** (1)	**75.** (4)					

* All options are correct.

January, 2017

PHILOSOPHY

PAPER-II

Note : This paper contains **fifty (50)** objectives type questions, each question carrying **two (2)** marks. Attempt all the questions.

1. In vedic tradition the movement of earth was regulated by

(1) Brahman (2) Iśvara

(3) Ṛta (4) Sūrya

2. Which type of ṛna in Vedic tradition can be repaid by performing Yajna ?

(1) Ṛsiṛṇa (2) Devaṛṇa

(3) Pitṛṛṇa (4) Pṛthviṛṇa

3. The term 'Paryāya' in Jaina thought refers to

(1) Āgantuka Dharma

(2) Nitya Dharma

(3) Manah Parvāya

(4) Naya

4. Given below are an Assertion (A) and a Reason (R). Consider them and select the correct code given below in the context of C.rv.ka Philosophy.

Assertion (A) : The dead body must be conscious.

Reason (R) : Consciousness is an attribute of body.

Codes :

(1) (A) and (R) both are true and (R) is the correct explanation of (A).

(2) (A) and (R) both are true and (R) is not the correct explanation of (A).

(3) (A) is true and (R) is false.

(4) (A) is false and (R) is true.

5. Who among the following holds that blue colour and the knowledge of the blue colour are one and the same ?

(1) Bhaspati (2) Vasubandhu

(3) Bh.sarvanjna (4) Prabh.kara

6. Consider Set – I and Set – II and select the code correctly matched given below :

Set – I	**Set – II**
a. Pañcaśila	i. Nyāya
b. Pañcāvayava	ii. Bauddha
c. Pañca parameṣṭi	iii. Jaina
d. Pañcaklesha	iv. Yoga

Codes :

	a	b	c	d
(1)	i	ii	iii	iv
(2)	ii	iii	iv	i
(3)	ii	i	iii	iv
(4)	iii	i	ii	iv

7. According to the Naiyāyikas Samavāya is perceived by the Sannikarṣa known as

(1) Samavāya

(2) Samaveta samāvya

(3) Sayukta samavāya

(4) Viśeṣaṇatā

8. In Nyāya Philosophy of language Iśvarecchā is :

(1) The cause of sákti

(2) The cause of Lakṣanā

(3) Zakti itself

(4) The cause of Śbdabodha

9. Which system takes the help of adṛṣta to prove the existence of god ?

(1) Nyāya only

(2) Nyāya and Vaiśeṣika

(3) Nyāya, Vaiśeṣika and Yoga

(4) Yoga and Vaiśeṣika

10. Select the code that states the correct sequence :

(1) kṣipta, mūḍha, vikṣipta, ekāgra, niruddha
(2) kṣipta, mūḍha, vikṣipta, ekāgra, niruddha
(3) kṣipta, vikṣipta, mūḍha, ekāgra, niruddha
(4) niruddham, ekāgra, mūḍha, kṣipta, vikṣipta,

11. Match List – I with List – II and choose the correct answer with the help of codes given below :

List – I	List – II
a. Abhihitānvaya vāda	i. Man ana
b. Anvitābhidhāna vāda	ii. Kumārila
c. Sphotavāda	iii. Prabhākara
d. Apoha vāda	iv. Di naga

Codes :

	a	b	c	d
(1)	iii	ii	iv	i
(2)	ii	iii	i	iv
(3)	i	ii	iii	iv
(4)	iii	i	iv	ii

12. Match List – I with List – II and choose the correct answer with the help of codes given below :

List – I	List – II
a. Saṁkhya Darśana	i. Asatkārya vāda
b. Dvaita Vedānta	ii. Vivartavāda
c. Advaita Vedānta	iii. Sadasatakārya vāda
d. Nyāya Darśana	iv. Satkārya vāda

Codes :

	a	b	c	d
(1)	iii	iv	i	ii
(2)	iv	iii	ii	i
(3)	i	ii	iii	iv
(4)	ii	i	iv	iii

13. Given below are an Assertion (A) and a Reason (R). Consider them and select the correct code given below in the context of Śaṇkara's Philosophy.

Assertion (A) : Brahman is abhinna nimitto pādāna Kārana of jagat.

Reason (R) : There is nothing other than Brahman.

Codes :
(1) Both (A) and (R) are true and (R) is the correct explanation of (A).
(2) Both (A) and (R) are true and (R) is not the correct explanation of (A).
(3) (A) is false and (R) is true.
(4) Both (A) and (R) are false.

14. Select the correct sequence of the gradations of Mokṣa in Madhva Vedānta
(1) Sāyujya, Sārūpya, Sāmipya, Sālokya
(2) Sālokya, Sāmipya, Sārūpya, Sāyujya
(3) Sārūpya, Sāmipya, Sālokya, Sāyujya
(4) Sālokya, Sāyujya, Sārūpya, Sāmipya,

15. In the view of Śaṇkara, the only pramānā that imparts knowledge of Brahman is
(1) Arthāpatti (2) Pratyakṣa
(3) Anumāna (4) Śabda

16. The Indian philosopher who makes a distinction between Anupramāṇa and Kevala pramāṇa is
(1) Patañjali (2) Śankara
(3) Madhva (4) Iśwarakṛṣna

17. One of the steps in Sādhana Catuṣṭaya according to Sakara is
(1) Prakrti – purusa jñna
(2) Mumuksuttva
(3) Nityavibhkti jñna
(4) Anumna jñna

18. The teaching common to all the vedātins is that Brahman is
(1) Nirguṇa (2) Saguṇa
(3) Saguṇa–nirguṇa (4) Ananta

19. Given below are some modes of subjectivity :
i. Bodily Subjectivity
ii. Psychic Subjectivity
iii. Spiritual Subjectivity
iv. Religious Subjectivity

Which three modes of Subjectivity are accepted by K.C. Bhattacharya ? Select the correct answer from the codes given below :

Codes :

(1) i iii iv

(2) ii iii iv

(3) i ii iii

(4) i ii iv

20. Which one of the following holds the view that 'when you deprive truth of its appearance, it loses the best part of reality' ?

(1) Sri Aurobindo

(2) Tagore

(3) J. Krishnamurti

(4) Vivekananda

21. Who among the following holds the view that 'space, time and causation are not metaphysical realities, they are mere forms' ?

(1) Tagore

(2) Vivekananda

(3) Radha Krishnan

(4) J. Krishnamurti

22. Who among the following holds the view that 'creation is plunge of the spirit into ignorance' ?

(1) Tagore (2) Gandhi

(3) Vive Kanandan (4) Sri Aurobindo

23. Match List – I with List – II and select the correct answer from the code given below :

List – I (Thinker)	List – II (Thinking)
a. Radha Krishnan	i. God as the Supreme ego
b. Tagore	ii. Village Republic
c. Gandhi	iii. Doctrine, Devotion, Worship
d. Iqbal	iv. Religion is home sickness

Codes :

	a	b	c	d
(1)	i	ii	iii	iv
(2)	iv	ii	i	iii
(3)	iii	iv	ii	i
(4)	iii	iv	i	ii

24. Match List – I with List – II and choose the correct answer with the help of codes given below :

List – I	List – II
a. Prājña	i. jāgṛta
b. Taijasa	ii. suṣupti
c. Vaiśvānava	iii. Svapna
d. Advaya	iv. Turīya

Codes :

	a	b	c	d
(1)	iii	ii	i	iv
(2)	ii	iii	i	iv
(3)	ii	i	iii	iv
(4)	iv	iii	ii	i

25. Match List – I with List – II and choose the correct answer with the help of codes given below :

List – I	List – II
a. Prakṛti	i. Passive
b. Puruṣa	ii. Active
c. Mahat	iii. Second evolute
d. Ahaṁkāra	iv. First evolute

Codes :

	a	b	c	d
(1)	i	ii	iii	iv
(2)	ii	i	iv	iii
(3)	iii	iv	ii	i
(4)	iv	iii	i	ii

26. In the context of Locke's philosophy, consider the given Assertion (A) and Reason (R) and then mark the correct option as given below :

Assertion (A) : All our knowledge is A posteriori.

Reason (R) : Knowledge is received through sensation and reflection.

Options :

(1) Both (A) and (R) are true and (R) does not provide the correct explanation of (A).

(2) (A) is true and (R) is false but (R) does not provide the correct explanation of (A).

(3) (A) is true and (R) is false but (R) provides the correct explanation of (A).

(4) Both (A) and (R) are true and (R) provides the correct explanation of (A).

27. Match List – I with List – II and mark the correct code :

List – I	List – II
a. Hume	i. Parallelism
b. Locke	ii. Scepticism
c. Berkeley	iii. Empiricism
d. Spinoza	iv. Idealism

Codes :

	a	b	c	d
(1)	i	ii	iii	iv
(2)	ii	i	iv	iii
(3)	ii	iii	iv	i
(4)	iv	iii	i	ii

28. Sensationism, Empiricism and Representationism are altogether attributed to
(1) Hume (2) Locke
(3) Kant (4) Berkeley

29. Match List – I with List – II and mark the correct code from given below :

List – I (Thinkers)	List – II (Books)
a. Locke	i. Principles of Human Knowledge
b. Hume	ii. Principia Philosophia
c. Descartes	iii. Essay concerning Human Understanding
d. Berkeley	iv. Enquiry concerning Human Understanding

Codes :

	a	b	c	d
(1)	i	ii	iii	iv
(2)	ii	iv	iii	i
(3)	iii	i	ii	iv
(4)	iii	iv	ii	i

30. The distinction between impression and idea was made by
(1) Kant (2) Locke
(3) Hume (4) Berkeley

31. Given below are two statements, one labelled as Assertion (A) and the other labelled as Reason (R). Considering (A) and (R) in the light of logical positivism select the correct code :

Assertion (A) : According to the principle of verification 'meaning of a proposition is the mode of its verification'.

Reason (R) : All the statements which could neither be verified nor falsified by experience are meaningful.

Codes :

(1) Both (A) and (R) are true and (R) is the correct explanation of (A).
(2) Both (A) and (R) are true and (R) is not the correct explanation of (A).
(3) (A) is true, but (R) is false.
(4) (A) is false, but (R) is true.

32. Which one of the following statements is true with reference to St. Thomas Aquinas ?
(1) God's essence is identified with Reason.
(2) God's essence is identified with his existence, as pure actuality.
(3) God's essence is identified with his potentiality.
(4) God has only existence, but no essence.

33. As per Aristotle's distinction between various sciences, "the pure and abstract knowledge" is dealt by
(1) Theoretical sciences such as Politics and Ethics
(2) Practical sciences such as Theology and Metaphysics.
(3) Theoretical sciences such as Mathematics and Physics.
(4) Practical Sciences such as politics and Ethics

34. Given below are two statements, one labelled as Assertion (A) and the other labelled as Reason (R). Considering (A) and (R), mark the correct code.

Assertion (A) : Plato rejected the view that "knowledge is opinion" in his theatetus.

Reason (R) : Knowledge must be grounded on faith, and not on Reason.

Codes :

(1) Both (A) and (R) are true and (R) is the correct explanation of (A).

(2) Both (A) and (R) are true and (R) is not the correct explanation of (A).
(3) (A) is true, but (R) is false.
(4) (A) is false, but (R) is true.

35. "Atoms exist – they are the existent. Empty space exists – even if it is paradoxically called the non-existent. And nothing else exists." is the philosophical position of –
(1) Heraclitus (2) Democritus
(3) Anaxagoras (4) Parmenides

36. Who among the following believed that "All things are full of Souls and Spirits"?
(1) Democritus (2) Heraclitus
(3) Parmenides (4) Pythagoras

37. Which of the following statements are true with reference to Protagoras. Mark the correct code :
(i) Man is the measure of all things.
(ii) Truth is objective.
(iii) What is true to one person need not be so to the other.

Codes :
(1) only (i) is true.
(2) only (i) and (ii) are true.
(3) only (i) and (iii) are true.
(4) only (ii) and (iii) are true.

38. Gilbert Ryle's theory of "Ghost in the Machine" rejects
(1) Descarte's Body-Mind Dualism
(2) Berkeley's Idealism
(3) Spinoza's Pantheism
(4) Rational capacity of the mind as such

39. Match the List – I with List – II and select the correct answer by using the codes below :

List – I	List – II
a. There must be both unity and opposition in the Absolute	i. Locke
b. The forms of sensibility are intuitional, the understanding is conceptual	ii. Hume
c. Ideas of substances are inadequate	iii. Kant
d. Ideas are not entirely loose or joined by chance, they introduce each other with a certain degree of method and regularity	iv. Hegel

Codes :

	a	b	c	d
(1)	i	iv	ii	iii
(2)	iii	ii	iv	i
(3)	iv	iii	i	ii
(4)	ii	i	iii	iv

40. According to Hegel, the absolute mind expresses its essence of truth in the form of Intuition in
(1) Morality (2) Art
(3) Religion (4) Philosophy

41. 'Being-towards-death is a constant fleeing in the face of death' expresses the philosophy of
(1) Russell (2) Husserl
(3) Heidegger (4) Moore

42. Match the List – I with List – II and select the correct answer by using the codes below :

List – I	List – II
a. The set of all 'givens' which I encounter in my existence	i. Care
b. The experience which discloses concrete beings over all to us	ii. Dasmann
c. Everyone is the other and no one is himself	iii. Facticity
d. Unity of Existenz, facticity, fallenness	iv. Mood

Codes :

	a	b	c	d
(1)	iv	i	iii	ii
(2)	i	iv	ii	iii
(3)	ii	iii	i	iv
(4)	iii	iv	ii	i

43. Match the List – I with List – II and select the correct answer. For Descartes, the human body is like a machine.

List – I	List – II
a. The moving principle of body is	i. The heat in the heart
b. The organs of motion	ii. Nerves
c. The organs of sensations	iii. Muscles

Codes :

	a	b	c
(1)	i	iii	ii
(2)	iii	i	ii
(3)	ii	i	iii
(4)	ii	iii	i

44. The 'Predicate-in subject' principle is propounded by

(1) Descartes (2) Leibnitz

(3) Spinoza (4) Locke

45. The essence of the 'new man' is joyful wisdom according to

(1) Husserl (2) Moore

(3) Nietzsche (4) Frege

46. Consider the Assertion (A) and Reason (R) and select the correct code from given below :

Assertion (A) : According to Russell, 'Denoting phrases never have any meaning in themselves'.

Reason (R) : I. In, 'the brother of Charles II was deposed', 'Charles II was deposed is a denoting phrase', and thus, has no meaning.

II. In, 'the brother of Charles II was deposed', the brother of Charles II is a denoting phrase and thus, has no meaning.

Codes :

(1) (A) is true and (R) I, II correctly explain (A).

(2) (A) is true and (R) I is correct explanation of (A) and (R) II is false.

(3) (A) is true and (R) II is a correct explanation of (A) and (R) I is false.

(4) (A) is true but neither (R) I nor (R) II correctly explains (A).

47. Consider the Assertion (A) and Reason (R) & select the correct code given below :

Assertion (A) : Monads have no windows.

Reason (R) : I. Nothing is passed to them from outside.

II. Each of their state is generated from their own nature.

III. Monads do not interact.

Codes :

(1) (A) is true and (R) I, II, III are correct explanations of (A).

(2) (A) is true and (R) I is the only correct explanation of (A).

(3) (A) is true and (R) I, II are correct explanations of (A).

(4) (A) is true and (R) II, III are the correct explanations of (A).

48. Consider the following statements in the light of Russell's logical Atomism and mark the correct code :

(i) Corresponding to individual variables and propositional functions of logic, the world contains particulars and universals.

(ii) Corresponding to the particulars and universals of the logic, the world contains variables and propositional functions.

(iii) The world contains independent atomic facts corresponding to the simple propositions.

Codes :

(1) only (i) is true.

(2) only (i) and (ii) are true.

(3) only (i) and (iii) are true

(4) only (ii) and (iii) are true.

49. Consider the following statements in the light of pragmatism and mark the correct code :

(i) Both William James and C.S. Peirce agree completely on the method of pragmatism.

(ii) William James went beyond Peirce in presenting a moral theory on pragmatic grounds.

(iii) C.S. Peirce called his own theory as pragmaticism.

Codes :

(1) only (i) is true.
(2) only (i) and (ii) are true.
(3) only (ii) and (iii) are true.
(4) only (i) and (iii) are true.

50. Who among the following philosophers advocated "Pragmaticism" ?

(1) William James
(2) C.S. Peirce
(3) G. Ryle
(4) A.J. Ayer

Answers

1. (3)	**2.** (2)	**3.** (1)	**4.** (4)	**5.** (2)	**6.** (3)	**7.** (4)	**8.** (3)	**9.** (2)	**10.** (1)
11. (2)	**12.** (2)	**13.** (1)	**14.** (2)	**15.** (4)	**16.** (3)	**17.** (2)	**18.** (4)	**19.** (3)	**20.** (2)
21. (2)	**22.** (4)	**23.** (3)	**24.** (2)	**25.** (2)	**26.** (4)	**27.** (3)	**28.** (2)	**29.** (4)	**30.** (3)
31. (3)	**32.** (2)	**33.** (3)	**34.** (3)	**35.** (2)	**36.** (2)	**37.** (3)	**38.** (1)	**39.** (3)	**40.** (2)
41. (3)	**42.** (4)	**43.** (1)	**44.** (2)	**45.** (3)	**46.** (3)	**47.** (1)	**48.** (3)	**49.** (3)	**50.** (2)

January, 2017

PHILOSOPHY

PAPER-III

Note : This paper contains **seventy five (75)** objective type questions of **two (2)** marks each. All questions are compulsory.

1. The pen I am writing with according to Advaita is
   (1) Sat (2) Asat
   (3) Both Sat and Asat
   (4) Neither Sat nor Asat

2. Which one according to the Vaiśesikas is the asamavayikarana of a pot ?
   (1) Kapāla (2) Kapāla-saṁyoga
   (3) Upādāna (4) Danda-saṁyoga

3. Select the code that states nitya mūrta-dravyas only
   (1) Ksiti, manas, ākāśā
   (2) Dik, Kāta, atmā
   (3) Paramāus of Kṣiti, teja and maruta
   (4) Kāla, ātma and manas.

4. The absence (abhāva) of bitterness resides in sugar _____ by the relation of
   (1) Samavāya (2) Saṁyoga
   (3) Viśesanatā (4) Svarūpa

5. In case of a pot the stick of the potter is according to the Vaiśsikas :
   (1) Samavāyikāraṇa
   (2) Asamavayikāraṇa
   (3) Nimittakāraṇa
   (4) Anyathāsiddha

6. The relation between jāti and vyakti according to Kumārila is
   (1) Śamavāya (2) Tādātmya
   (3) Svarūpa (4) Saṁyoga

7. Which one of the following is true with reference to Leibnitz's doctrine of pre-established Harmony ?
   (1) Bodies and Souls work inconsonance with each other and become one.
   (2) Bodies act as if there were no souls, and souls act as if there were no bodies, but both act as if one influenced the other.
   (3) Bodies act on souls and souls act on bodies.
   (4) Both bodies and souls are one and the same.

8. Consider the following statements with reference to Kant and mark the correct code :
   (i) Space and Time are objective and exist in their own right.
   (ii) Space and Time are not objective but only appearances and are relative.
   (iii) Space and Time are a priori.
   Codes :
   (1) Only (ii) is true
   (2) Only (i) and (ii) are true
   (3) Only (iii) is true
   (4) Only (i) and (iii) are true

9. Consider the following statements with reference to Descartes and mark the correct code :
   (i) All Mental states are reducible to Physical states.
   (ii) All Physical states are reducible to Mental states.
   (iii) Body-Mind relation is not similar to that of Car and Driver.
   (iv) There is no Corporeal and non-corporeal distinction with respect to human beings.

Codes :
(1) Only (iii) is true.
(2) Only (i) and (iv) are true
(3) Only (ii) and (iii) are true
(4) Only (ii), (iii) and (iv) are true

10. 'It is impossible to realize perfect truth so long as we are imprisoned in the mortal frame' is the view of
(1) K.C. Bhattacharya
(2) Radhakrishnan
(3) J. Krishnamurti
(4) Gandhi

11. Consider given Assertion (A) and Reason (R) in the light of Hume and mark the correct code.

Assertion (A) : Personal identity is the work of imagination.

Reason (R) : The succession of pleasure-pain, sensations and images are connected together by resemblance, contiguity and causation.

Codes :
(1) Both (A) and (R) are true and (R) is the correct explanation of (A).
(2) Both (A) and (R) are true, but (R) is not the correct explanation of (A).
(3) (A) is true, but (R) is the false.
(4) (A) is false, but (R) is true.

12. Relation between word and its' meaning is not natural is the view upheld by
(1) Bauddhas (2) Vedāntins
(3) Mimāmsākas (4) Naiyāyikās

13. Which of the following pair supports the view that Truth of Cognition has not to be verified by any other cognition ?
(1) Vedanta and Mimāṁsa
(2) Mimāṁsa and Sāṁkhya
(3) Mimāṁsa and Nyāya
(4) Vedānta and Nyāya

14. When the i plied meaning of a word or an expression excludes the primary meaning partially, then it is the case of
(1) Abhidhā
(2) Ajahat lakṣaṇā
(3) Jahat – Ajahat lakṣaṇā
(4) Vyañjanœ

15. Match List-I with List-II and select the correct answer by using the codes below :

List – I	List – II
a. The capacity of the meanings of the words to become objects of enquiry regarding each other.	i. Tātparya
b. Non-contradiction of the relation between meanings of the words.	ii. Āsatti
c. The apprehension without an interval of the meanings of words that is produced by those words.	iii. Ākānksā
d. The capacity of a sentence to convey a particular meaning.	iv. Yogyatā

Codes :

	a	b	c	d
(1)	ii	i	iii	iv
(2)	i	iii	iv	ii
(3)	iv	iii	ii	i
(4)	iii	iv	ii	i

16. The negation of the non-cow is a positive entity and is different from the non-cow is the view appropriated by :
(1) Naigama Naya
(2) Apohavāda
(3) Pratibiṁbavāda
(4) Saptabhanginaya

17. 'Pratyakṣam Kalpanāpodaṁ' this definition of pratyakṣa was given by :
(1) Dinnāga (2) Dharmakirti
(3) Gaṅgeśa (4) Iśvarakṛṣṇa

18. The nirvikalpaka state of pratyak a is proved by the Naiyyikas by
(1) Pratyakṣa (2) Anumāna
(3) Upamāna (4) Sábda

19. 'Yāga na svargahetuh kriyatrāt' which type of hetvābhāsa is committed by the above anumāna ?
(1) Bādhita (2) Satpratipakṣa
(3) Viruddha (4) Savyabhichāri

20. Self according to the Vaiśesikas cannot be the serlestratum of knowledge when it becomes
(1) Knower (2) Known
(3) In bondage (4) Liberated

21. It is through the mind that one sees, that one hears. Indeed, everything is perceived on being invested with the light of Buddhi like an object in the dark illumined by a lamp located in front of it, in the view of
(1) Gangeśa (2) Śanikara
(3) Vallabha (4) Kapila

22. Which list of puru œrthas is acceptable to the Cœrvœkas ? Select the code given below :
(1) Artha and Kāma
(2) Artha, Kāma and Dharma
(3) Mokṣa and Kāma
(4) Kāma and Dharma

23. Which of the following is not a teaching of 'Bhagvad gitā?
(1) Renunciation of fruits of actions.
(2) Performance of ones natural and appointed duties.
(3) Elevation at good fortune and depression at loss should be conquered.
(4) All egoistic desires should not be directed to God.

24. Which of the following does not belong to the group of Brahmavihāra ?
(1) Muditā (2) Karuṇā
(3) Ekāgratā (4) Maitri

25. Which of the following is not a Tri-ratna according to Jainism ?
(1) Samyak Bhāvanā
(2) Samyak Cāritra
(3) Samyak Darśana
(4) Samyak Jñāna

26. 'Śabda nitya śabdatvāt', which type of hetvābhāsa is committed by the above anumāna ?
(1) Sādhārana savyabhichāra
(2) Anupasaṁhāri
(3) Satpratipk a
(4) Asādhāra a savyabhichāra

27. Find the equivalence by matching List-I with List-II and select the correct answer by using codes below :

List – I	List – II
a. $[(p.q) \supset r] \equiv$	i. $[(p \supset q) . (q \supset p)]$
b. $[p \vee (q.r)] \equiv$	ii. $\sim p \vee q$
c. $[p \equiv q] \equiv$	iii. $[p \supset (q \supset r)]$
d. $[p \supset q] \equiv$	iv. $[(p \vee q) . (p \vee r)]$

Codes :

	a	b	c	d
(1)	i	iii	iv	ii
(2)	ii	iv	iii	i
(3)	iv	ii	i	ii
(4)	iii	iv	i	ii

28. In the context of Traditional square of opposition of proposition, Match list-I with list-II and select the correct answer by choosing the codes given below :

List – I	List – II
a. If 'I' is false	i. E is undetermined
b. If 'O' is true	ii. 'I' is undetermined
c. If 'I' is true	iii. 'O' is undetermined
d. If 'A' is false	iv. 'A' is false

Codes :

	a	b	c	d
(1)	iv	i	iii	ii
(2)	iii	ii	iv	i
(3)	ii	iii	i	iv
(4)	i	iv	ii	iii

29. Match the List-I with List-II and select the correct answer by using the codes below :

List – I	List – II
a. Fallacy committed in directing an emotional appeal 'to the people' to win their	i. Petitio Principii

assent to a conclusion unsupported by good evidence.	
b. The method is not always fallacious for the reference to an admitted authority in the special field of his competence may carry weight.	ii. Ignoratio Elenchi
c. In establishing the truth of a proposition, one often casts about for acceptable premises from which the proposition in question can be deduced as conclusion.	iii. Argumentum ad populum
d. Fallacy committed when an argument purporting to establish a particular conclusion is directed to proving a different conclusion.	iv. Argumentum ad verecundiam

Codes :

	a	b	c	d
(1)	i	iii	ii	iv
(2)	ii	i	iv	iii
(3)	iii	iv	i	ii
(4)	iv	iii	ii	i

30. Set down the relation between universal and existential quantification by matching the List-I with List-II and select the appropriate code for your answer :

List – I	List – II
a. $[(x)\ \phi x]$	i. $\equiv [\sim (x)\ \phi x]$
b. $[(\exists x)\ \phi x]$	ii. $\equiv [\sim (\exists x)\ \phi x]$
c. $[(x) \sim \phi x]$	iii. $\equiv [\sim (x) \sim \phi x]$
d. $[(\exists x) \sim \phi x]$	iv. $\equiv [\sim (\exists x) \sim \phi x]$

Codes :

	a	b	c	d
(1)	i	ii	iii	iv
(2)	iv	iii	ii	i
(3)	ii	iv	i	iii
(4)	iii	i	iv	ii

31. Which of the following abbreviated forms of, 'Neither fill more nor Harding was the greatest President', is correct ?

(1) $(\sim f) . (\sim H)$ (2) $(\sim F \vee \sim H)$
(3) $F \vee H$ (4) $\sim (F . H)$

32. Match the List-I with List-II and select the correct answer by using the code given below :

List – I (Obvertend)	List – II (Obverse)
a. Some S is not-P	i. Some S is not-non-P
b. No S is P	ii. No S is non-P
c. Some S is P	iii. Some S is non-P
d. All S is P	iv. All S is non-P

Codes :

	a	b	c	d
(1)	i	iv	ii	iii
(2)	ii	iii	iv	i
(3)	iv	i	ii	iii
(4)	iii	iv	i	ii

33. Consider the Assertion (A) and Reason (R) and select the correct code given below :

Assertion (A) : The number of distributed terms in the conclusion must be at least one less than the total number of distributed terms in the premises.

Reason (R) : The middle term does not appear in the conclusion.

Select the correct answer from the codes given below :

Codes :

(1) (A) and (R) both are true and (R) is the correct explanation of (A).
(2) (A) and (R) both are true, but (R) is not the correct explanation of (A).
(3) (A) is false and (R) is the true.
(4) Both (A) and (R) are false.

34. Consider the Assertion (A) and Reason (R) and select the correct code given below :

Assertion (A) : If one Premise is particular, the conclusion must be particular.

Reason (R) : (i) An affirmative particular has no distributed terms, and a negative particular has only one.

(ii) The premises cannot both be particular and thus must differ in quantity.

Codes :

(1) (A) and (R) both are true and (R) (i), (ii) correctly explain of (A).

(2) (A) and (R) both are true, but (R) (i) is a correct explanation of (A).

(3) (A) and (R) both are true and (R) (ii) is a correct explanation of (A).

(4) (A) is true, but (R) (i) and (ii) are incorrect explanations of (A).

35. "If a language is provided with a truth definition, that is sufficient condition of its concept of truth" – is advocated by

(1) Correspondence theory of truth

(2) Redundance theory of truth

(3) Semantic theory of truth

(4) Pragmatic theory of truth

36. Who among the following is not a sceptic ?

(1) Hume (2) Pyrrho

(3) Bayle (4) Descartes

37. What is the criterion of truth according to Descartes ?

(1) Clearness and uniformity

(2) Clearness and distinctness

(3) Clearness and completeness

(4) Clearness and directness

38. Which one of the following pair does not match correctly with reference to Leibnitz ?

(1) Truths of Reason – necessarily true

(2) Truths of Fact – based on principle of sufficient reason.

(3) Truths of Reason – based on Law of Contraction.

(4) Truths of Fact – cannot be denied without contradiction.

39. "Ideas are of two kinds; ideas imprinted on the senses and ideas formed by memory and imagination." ____ is the view advocated by;

(1) Locke (2) Berkeley

(3) Hume (4) Leibnitz

40. Consider the following statements with reference to Locke's theory of knowledge and mark the correct code :

(i) knowledge depends on the mental power to perceive or apprehend ideas.

(ii) knowledge is not rational.

(iii) knowledge consists in seeing the agreement or disagreement between ideas.

Codes :

(1) Only (i) is true.

(2) Only (ii) is true

(3) Only (i) and (iii) are true.

(4) Only (i) and (ii) are true

41. Which one of the following is not correct about 'Sthitaprajña' of Bhagavadg ta ?

(1) A 'Sthitaprajña'discards are desires from his mind.

(2) A 'Sthitaprajña'is not disturbed in suffering.

(3) 'Sthitaprajña'is not desirous of pleasure.

(4) 'Sthitaprajña' always thinks to do good for others.

42. Given below are two statements, one labelled as Assertion (A) and the other labelled as Reason (R). Considering (A) and (R), select the correct code :

Assertion (A) : Kant's ethics of categorical imperative is formal and regoristic.

Reason (R) : It disparages the role of sensibility.

Codes :

(1) Both (A) and (R) are true and (R) is the correct explanation of (A).

(2) Both (A) and (R) are true, but (R) is not the correct explanation of (A).

(3) (A) is true, but (R) is the false.

(4) (A) is false, but (R) is true.

43. Match List-I with List-II and select the correct answer by using codes given below :

List – I (Writer)	List – II (Writings)
a. G.E. Moore	i. Freedom and Reason
b. R.M. Hare	ii. Ethics
c. T.H. Green	iii. The Logic of Moral Discourse
d. Paul Edward	iv. Prolegomene to Ethics

Codes :

	a	b	c	d
(1)	iv	i	ii	iii
(2)	i	iii	iv	ii
(3)	ii	i	iv	iii
(4)	i	ii	iii	iv

44. It has been pointed out that the Mill's argument for Refined altruistic Hedonism suffers from the fallacy. Select the correct answer from the given below :

(1) Illicit major
(2) Illicit minor
(3) Undistributed middle
(4) Fallacy of figure of speech

45. The aim of deterrent theory of punishment is

(1) To take revenge from the crime done
(2) To prevent future act of crime
(3) To reform the criminal
(4) To assert the autonomy of individual

46. How would a normative ethicist explain the statement 'This is good' ?

(1) 'This' is the end of life
(2) 'This' is approved by people in General
(3) I approve 'this'
(4) do 'this'

47. Which one of the following expresses the basis tenet of hedonism ?

(1) Honesty is good in itself.
(2) Honesty is good because it promotes happiness.
(3) Honesty is good because it is a natural capacity of man.
(4) Honesty is good because it distinguishes man from beast.

48. Match List-I with List-II and select the correct answer by using codes given below :

List – I (Thinker)	List – II (Thinking)
a. Kant	i. Prima Facie obligation
b. Hegel	ii. My station and its duties
c. Bradley	iii. Be a Person
d. Ross	iv. Act as a member of kingdom of end

Codes :

	a	b	c	d
(1)	i	ii	iii	iv
(2)	iv	iii	ii	i
(3)	ii	iii	i	iv
(4)	iii	i	iv	ii

49. Match List-I with List-II and select the correct answer by using codes given below :

List – I (Theory)	List – II (Thinker)
a. Prescriptivism	i. Rudolf Carnap
b. Descriptivism	ii. Butler
c. Non Naturalism	iii. R.M. Hare
d. Emotivism	iv. P.T. Geach

Codes :

	a	b	c	d
(1)	iii	iv	ii	i
(2)	i	ii	iv	iii
(3)	ii	i	iii	iv
(4)	iv	ii	i	iii

50. 'Good' according to Moore is indefinable because

(1) It has innumerable qualities
(2) It is a simple term
(3) It is a super sensible thing
(4) It is a meaningless term

51. Who among the following pairs of Vedāntins, do not justify the concept of Jivanmukti ?

(1) Saṅkara and Rāmānuja
(2) Rāmānuja and Madhva
(3) Saṅkara and Madhva
(4) Vācaspati and Prakāśātman

52. Who among the Pūdrva-mīmāsins hold the view that Dharma is only an intrinsic value and not instrumental ?
(1) Kumārila
(2) Prabhākara
(3) Śabara
(4) Murāri Miśra

53. With reference to Patanjali's Yogadarśana, select the correct sequence.
(1) Niyama, yama, prāṇāyāma, āsana, pratyāhāra
(2) Yama, niyama, prāṇāyāma, āsana, pratyāhāra
(3) Yama, niyama, āsana, prāṇāyāma, pratyāhāra
(4) āsana, prāṇāyāma, pratyāhāra, yama, niyama

54. Match List-I with List-II and select the correct with the help of the codes given below :

List – I	List – II
a. Yadcchavda	i. Vedntins
b. Pratītya Samutpāda	ii. Carwka
c. Iśvaravāda	iii. Bauddhas
d. Paramānuvāda	iv. Jainas

Codes :

	a	b	c	d
(1)	iii	iv	ii	i
(2)	ii	iii	i	iv
(3)	iii	ii	iv	i
(4)	iv	ii	iii	i

55. Match List-I with List-II and select the correct answer with the help of codes given below :

List – I	List – II
a. Cārvāka	i. Pratyak a, Anumana, Upamāna, Śabda only
b. Bauddhas	ii. Pratyaksa only
c. Sāṁkhyans	iii. Pratyaksa Anumāna only
d. Naiyāyikas	iv. Pratyaksa, Anumāna, Śabda only

Codes :

	a	b	c	d
(1)	ii	iii	iv	i
(2)	iii	ii	i	iv
(3)	i	iii	ii	iv
(4)	iv	ii	iii	i

56. Who among the Indian Philosophers makes a distinction between Dharmabhūtajñāna and Dharm bhūtajñāna ?
(1) Vasubandhu (2) Madhva
(3) Rmnuja (4) Vallabha

57. "Whose among the following is the philosophy of bhedābheda ?
(1) Citsukha (2) Kundakunda
(3) Jaimini (4) Nimbārka

58. Who among the following philosophers advocate Avikṛta pariṇāmavāda ?
(1) Nimbārka (2) Saṅkara
(3) Vallabha (4) Madhva

59. Match List-I with List-II and choose the correct answer with the help of codes given below :

List – I	List – II
a. Talmud	i. Zorastrianism
b. Tripitaka	ii. Sikhism
c. Granthsaheb	iii. Judaism
d. Zenda Avastha	iv. Buddhism

Codes :

	a	b	c	d
(1)	iii	iv	ii	i
(2)	iv	iii	i	ii
(3)	ii	i	iv	iii
(4)	i	ii	iii	iv

60. Which religion amongst the following advocates fire worship ?
(1) Judaism (2) Christianity
(3) Islam (4) Zorastrianism

61. Consider given Assertion (A) and Reason (R) and then mark the correct option as given below.
Assertion (A) : Gandhi accepted 'Satyāgraha' as a weapon to fight the British Empire.

Reason (R) : He was afraid of British rulers.

Codes :

(1) (A) and (R) both are true and (R) is the correct explanation of (A).

(2) (A) and (R) both are true, but (R) is not the correct explanation of (A).

(3) (A) is true, but (R) is false.

(4) (A) is false, but (R) is true.

62. Which one of the following statements is true with reference to Eco-feminism ?

(1) It identifies culture with female and nature with male and questions the dominance of female.

(2) It identifies culture with male and nature with female and questions the dominance of male.

(3) It identifies culture with male and nature with female and questions the dominance of female.

(4) It identifies culture with female and nature with male and questions the dominance of male.

63. Who among the following philosophers held the view that "A natural right is a son that never had a father'?

(1) Edmurd Burke

(2) Bentham

(3) Nietzsche

(4) Mac Intyre

64. Which one of the following is not correct about Gandhian ethics ?

(1) Truth as the end

(2) Non-Violence as the means

(3) Both the end means should be just

(4) A Just end justifies the bad means

65. Match List-I with List-II and select the correct answer by using codes given below :

List – I (Writer)	**List – II (Writing)**
a. Desai Mahadev	i. Religion and Society
b. Gandhi	ii. The story of Bardoli
c. Radhakrishnan	iii. Why Socialism ?
d. Narayan Jaya Prakash	iv. The Wheel of Fortune

Codes :

	a	b	c	d
(1)	i	ii	iii	iv
(2)	ii	iv	iii	i
(3)	ii	iv	i	iii
(4)	iii	ii	iv	i

66. "I will kill you" is an example of which one of the following speech Acts according to Austin ?

(1) Locutionary (2) Illocutionary

(3) Perlocutionary (4) Non-locutionary

67. Which one of the following lists correctly depicts Austin's division of verbs that differ in their illocutionary force ?

(1) Verdictives exercitives commissives, behavitives and expositives.

(2) Verdictives, exercitives, commissives, syntactical and expositives.

(3) Verdictives, exercitives, commissives, semantical and behavitives.

(4) Verdictives, exercitives, semantical, syntactical and commissives.

68. "To be is to be the value of a variable" is the standpoint advocated by

(1) Quine (2) Frege

(3) Russell (4) Strawson

69. Which one of the following cannot be considered as indefinite description as per Russell ?

(1) Present king of Ayodhya

(2) Present President of India

(3) Present Governor of Reserve Bank of India

(4) Present Prime Minister of India.

70. "There is no one standard meaning of a given word, it has as many meanings as it has uses, and that these are countless." – is the view held by :

(1) Russell (2) Frege

(3) Wittgenstein (4) Dammett

71. "Death destroys all our possibilities" is the statement of

(1) Heideggar (2) Husserl

(3) Sartre (4) Jaspers

72. According to which one of the following 'essences' can be 'seen' just as 'tones' can be 'heard'.
(1) Heideggar (2) Marcel
(3) Husserl (4) Satre

73. Which one of the following is not the aim of Husserl's phenomenology ?
(1) To discover the foundations of knowledge and experience.
(2) To lay bare the structure which constitutes the essences of logical concepts.
(3) To take neutral position with respect to the states of consciousness.
(4) To accept the presuppositions of a given systems.

74. Match List-I with List-II and mark the correct code :

List – I	List – II
a. Schleiermacher	i. Phenomenological Hermeneutics
b. Heidegger	ii. Radical Hermeneutics
c. Derrida	iii. Marxist Hermeneutics
d. Fredric Jameson	iv. Romantic Hermeneutics

Codes :

	a	b	c	d
(1)	i	ii	iii	iv
(2)	iv	i	iii	ii
(3)	iv	ii	i	iii
(4)	iv	i	ii	iii

75. Which one of the following philosophers Contributed 'Ontological turn' to Hermeneutics.
(1) Paul Ricoeur (2) Derrida
(3) Habermas (4) Heidegger

Answers

1. (4)	**2.** (2)	**3.** (3)	**4.** (4)	**5.** (3)	**6.** (2)	**7.** (2)	**8.** (3)	**9.** (1)	**10.** (4)
11. (1)	**12.** (4)	**13.** (1)	**14.** (3)	**15.** (4)	**16.** (2)	**17.** (1)	**18.** (2)	**19.** (1)	**20.** (4)
21. (2)	**22.** (1)	**23.** (4)	**24.** (3)	**25.** (1)	**26.** (4)	**27.** (4)	**28.** (1)	**29.** (3)	**30.** (2)
31. (1)	**32.** (4)	**33.** (1)	**34.** (3)	**35.** (3)	**36.** (4)	**37.** (2)	**38.** (4)	**39.** (2)	**40.** (3)
41. (4)	**42.** (1)	**43.** (3)	**44.** (4)	**45.** (2)	**46.** (4)	**47.** (2)	**48.** (2)	**49.** (1)	**50.** (2)
51. (2)	**52.** (2)	**53.** (3)	**54.** (2)	**55.** (1)	**56.** (3)	**57.** (4)	**58.** (3)	**59.** (1)	**60.** (4)
61. (3)	**62.** (2)	**63.** (2)	**64.** (4)	**65.** (3)	**66.** (2)	**67.** (1)	**68.** (1)	**69.** (1)	**70.** (3)
71. (3)	**72.** (3)	**73.** (4)	**74.** (4)	**75.** (4)					

November, 2017

PHILOSOPHY

PAPER-II

Note : This paper contains **fifty (50)** objectives type questions, each question carrying **two (2)** marks. Attempt all the questions.

1. One may be free from devarṇa by :
   (1) Observing brahmac'arya
   (2) Performing yajṅa
   (3) Uttering mantras
   (4) Giving birth to a child

2. The movement of the heavenly bodies according to the vedic tradition is guided by :
   (1) The will of the gods
   (2) Ṛta, the cosmic law
   (3) The moral virtues of the people
   (4) Prajāpati

3. Match the Set-I with Set-II and select the correct code :

Set - I	Set - II
(a) Ṛk	(i) Udgātā
(b) Sāma	(ii) Hota
(c) Yajuḥ	(iii) Adhvaryu
(d) Atharva	(iv) Brahmā

Codes :

	(a)	(b)	(c)	(d)
(1)	(i)	(ii)	(iii)	(iv)
(2)	(ii)	(i)	(iii)	(iv)
(3)	(i)	(iii)	(ii)	(iv)
(4)	(iv)	(iii)	(ii)	(i)

4. The absence of horseness in cow according to the Vaiśeṣikas is known as :
   (1) Anyonyābhāva (2) Prāgabhāva
   (3) Dhvaṁsābhāva (4) Atyantābhāva

5. There are two types of Bandhana of the soul : Bhāvabandhana and dravyabandhana. This view is held by :
   (1) Cārvāka (2) Jaina
   (3) Sāṁkhya (4) Mīmāṁsā

6. Which one among the following is not acceptable to the Vaiṣeṣikas ?
   (1) Veda is created by none
   (2) Tattvajñāna is not the sufficient condition for niḥśreyasa
   (3) Abhāva can be perceived
   (4) Īśvara is a type of ātmā

7. Which one among the following codes is acceptable to the cārvākas ? Answer considering (a), (b), (c), (d) ?
   (a) Kṣti and Kāma
   (b) Artha and Puṇya
   (c) Sukha and Artha
   (d) Marut and Vyoma

   Code :
   (1) (a) and (b) (2) (a) and (c)
   (3) (a) and (d) (4) (b) and (c)

8. Select the correct sequence with reference to apavarga in Nyāya :
   (1) duḥkha, pravṛtti, doṣa, janma, mithyājṅāna
   (2) mithyājṅāna, doṣa, pravṛtti, janma, duḥkha
   (3) janma, duḥkha, pravṛtti, doṣa, mithyājñāna
   (4) janma, duḥkha, mithyājñāna, pravṛtti, doṣa

9. Which one among the following is not an avayava of pañcāvayavinyāya according to the Naiyāyikas ?
   (1) Udāharaṇa (2) Upanaya
   (3) Upamāna (4) Nigamana

10. Which one among the following is not a condition of Vākyārtha (sentential meaning) jñāna according to the Naiyāyikas ?
(1) Vyākaraña (2) Tātparya
(3) Ākāṅkṣa (4) Āsatti

11. Which type of hetvābhāsa is committed by the following anumāna ? Select the correct code :
'Parvataḥ vahnimān nīladhūmāt'
(1) Sādhāraṇa Savyabhicāra
(2) Svarūpāsiddha
(3) Vyāpyatvāsiddha
(4) Bādhita

12. According to the Naiyāyikas 'padaśákti' is :
(1) An additional padārtha
(2) An eternal padārtha
(3) A relation between two *padas*
(4) A relation between a pada and a padārtha that stands for it

13. Which of the following statements is not true with regard to Pātanjala Yoga ?
(1) God is one among Puruṣas
(2) Pātanjala Yoga admits three pramāṇas
(3) Pātanjala Yoga advocates Monism
(4) Pātanjala Yoga admits prior moral training

14. "The silver that appears in a shell cannot be unreal because it appears ; that silver cannot also be real because it is found to be not there when we see the shell properly". This is the view of :
(1) Rāmānuja (2) Īśwarakāisṇa
(3) Śaṁkara (4) Nāgārjuna

15. Match List-I and List-II and choose the correct answer with the help of the code given below :

List - I	List - II
(a) Jivanmukti	(i) Nyāya-Vaiśeṣikas
(b) Videhamukti	(ii) Early Mīmāṁsakas
(c) Niḥīreyasah	(iii) Śaṁkara
(d) Svarga	(iv) Madhva

Codes :

	(a)	(b)	(c)	(d)
(1)	(iv)	(iii)	(ii)	(i)
(2)	(iii)	(iv)	(i)	(ii)
(3)	(ii)	(i)	(iii)	(iv)
(4)	(i)	(ii)	(iv)	(iii)

16. Given below are Assertion (A) and Reason (R). Consider them and select the correct code given below, in the context of Śaṁkara's Philosophy :
Assertion (A) : Śaṁkara's philosophy denies the world outright.
Reason (R) : The fact is that there is a real external world
Code :
(1) (A) and (R) are both true and (R) is the correct explanation of (A)
(2) (A) and (R) are both true and (R) is not the correct explanation of (A)
(3) (A) is false and (R) is true
(4) (A) is true and (R) is false

17. The correct sequence of evolution according to Sāṁkhya is :
(1) Ahaṁkāra, manas, karmendriyas, Jñānendriyas, mahat
(2) Jñānendriyas, manas, karmendriyas, ahaṁkāra, mahat
(3) Karmendriyas, Jñānendriyas, manas, mahat, ahaṁkāra
(4) Mahat, ahaṁkāra, manas, Jñānendriyas, karmendriyas

18. Prakṛti in Sāṁkhya philosophy is :
(1) Unconscious and dependent
(2) Conscious and passive
(3) Unconscious and active
(4) Conscious and independent

19. In Mīmāṁsā philosophy, all the following propositions are true except :
(1) Mīmāṁsā upholds the theory of Svataḥ prāmāṇyavāda
(2) Self is considered as active
(3) Vedas are apauruṣeya
(4) The perceptual error in case of shell-silver illusion is because of adhyāsa

20. Given below are Assertion (A) and a Reason (R). Consider them and select the correct code in the context of Buddhism :

Assertion (A) : Nirvāṇa is momentary

Reason (R) : Sarvam Kṣaṇikaṁ Kṣaṇikaṁ

Code :

(1) Both (A) and (R) are true and (R) is the correct explanation of (A)
(2) Both (A) and (R) are true and (R) is not the correct explanation of (A)
(3) (A) is true and (R) is false
(4) (A) is false and (R) is true

21. Match List-I with List - II and choose the correct answer with the help of code given below :

List - I (Writer)	List - II (Writing)
(a) Sri Aurobindo	(i) Freedom from the known
(b) J. Krishnamurti	(ii) The Recovery of Faith
(c) K.C. Bhattacharya	(iii) Studies in Vedantism
(d) S. Radhakrishnan	(iv) Savitri, a Legend and a symbol

Codes :

	(a)	(b)	(c)	(d)
(1)	(i)	(ii)	(iv)	(iii)
(2)	(iv)	(i)	(iii)	(ii)
(3)	(ii)	(iv)	(i)	(iii)
(4)	(iii)	(i)	(ii)	(iv)

22. Which among the following is not correctly matched with Sri Aurobindo's concept of three poises of Supermental consciousness ?

(1) Comprehending consciousness
(2) Apprehending consciousness
(3) Analytical consciousness
(4) Projecting consciousness

23. Who among the following has addressed supreme reality as 'Jeevana Devatā' ?

(1) Sri Aurobindo
(2) S. Radhakrishnan
(3) B.R. Ambedkar
(4) R.N. Tagore

24. Who among the following has said that 'It is better that mankind should become atheist by following reason than blindly believe in two million of gods' ?

(1) Gandhi (2) Tagore
(3) Vivekananda (4) Ambedkar

25. Given below are an Assertion (A) and a Reason (R). Consider them and select the correct code given below in the context of K.C. Bhattacharya :

Assertion (A) : Judgements of Philosophy are Pseudo Judgements.

Reason (R) : In all Judgements Predicate is Contained in the Subject

Code :

(1) Both (A) and (R) are true and (R) is the correct explanation of (A)
(2) Both (A) and (R) are true but (R) is not the correct explanation of (A)
(3) (A) is true but (R) is false
(4) (A) is false but (R) is true

26. Who among the following holds the view that : 'Divine knowledge is creational, and as there is nothing outside God. He himself is the object of his knowledge. He creates as he knows, and knows as he creates.

(1) Tagore
(2) Vivekananda
(3) K.C. Bhattacharya
(4) Iqbal

27. Match List - I with List - II and choose the correct answer with the help of code given below :

List - I (Thinker)	List - II (Thought)
(a) S. Radhakrishnan	(i) What is spoken must be in the first instance believed
(b) Vivekananda	(ii) The destiny of the human soul is to realise its oneness with the Supreme

(c) K.C. Bhattacharya	(iii) The infinite and finite are one as song and singing are one
(d) Tagore	(iv) Immortality is the realisation of oneness with everything

Codes :

	(a)	(b)	(c)	(d)
(1)	(i)	(ii)	(iv)	(iii)
(2)	(ii)	(iv)	(iii)	(i)
(3)	(iv)	(ii)	(i)	(iii)
(4)	(ii)	(iv)	(i)	(iii)

28. According to the ex nihilo theory of St. Augustine ;

(1) God created the world out of the existent
(2) God created the world out of nothing
(3) God created the evil out of something
(4) God created himself out of nothing

29. "If there are no individual circular things ; there would be no such thing as the form called circularity", can be attributed to ;

(1) Socrates (2) Plato
(3) Aristotle (4) St. Augustine

30. Consider the following statements in the light of Plato's metaphysics and mark the correct code :

(a) What is truly real is not the objects we encounter in sensory experience
(b) Forms can only be grasped intellectually
(c) Forms are just ideas or concepts in the mind of some one

Code :

(1) Only (a) is true
(2) Only (a) and (b) are true
(3) Only (a) and (c) are true
(4) All (a), (b) and (c) are true

31. Who among the following holds the view that "Things are things because they can be ennumerated" ?

(1) Pythagoras (2) Anaximander
(3) Heraclitus (4) Parmenides

32. Given below are Assertion (A) and Reason (R). Consider them in the light of Thomas Aquinas and mark the correct code :

Assertion (A) : God is the uncaused cause of the world.

Reason (R) : Anything that begins to exist has to be caused to exist by something that already exists.

Code :

(1) Both (A) and (R) are true and (R) is the correct explanation of (A).
(2) Both (A) and (R) are true and (R) is not the correct explanation of (A).
(3) (A) is true and (R) is false.
(4) (A) is false and (R) is true.

33. Which one of the following early Greek Philosophers held that ;

"You can not know what is not, nor can you express it. What can be thought of and what can be - they are the same".

(1) Parmenides (2) Heraclitus
(3) Empedocles (4) Democritus

34. Match List - I with List - II and choose the correct answer with the help of code given below :

List - I	**List - II**
(a) Anaximenes	(i) Nous
(b) Anaximander	(ii) Air
(c) Thales	(iii) Apeiron
(d) Anaxagoras	(iv) Water

Codes :

	(a)	(b)	(c)	(d)
(1)	(iii)	(ii)	(i)	(iv)
(2)	(ii)	(iii)	(iv)	(i)
(3)	(i)	(iv)	(iii)	(ii)
(4)	(iv)	(i)	(ii)	(iii)

35. Which of the following sequence correctly represent the successive stages of the Absolute mind according to Hegel ?

(1) imagination, intuition, conception
(2) religion, psychology, philosophy
(3) art, religion, philosophy
(4) religion, art, philosophy

36. In the light of Kant's philosophy, match List - I with List - II and choose the correct answer with the help of code given below:

List - I	List - II
(a) The Problematical Judgement	(i) Heat is a form of motion
(b) The Infinite Judgement	(ii) This may be poison
(c) The Apodictic Judgement	(iii) Mind is unextended
(d) The Affirmative Judgement	(iv) Every effect must have a cause

Codes:

	(a)	(b)	(c)	(d)
(1)	(i)	(ii)	(iii)	(iv)
(2)	(ii)	(iii)	(iv)	(i)
(3)	(iii)	(iv)	(i)	(ii)
(4)	(iv)	(iii)	(ii)	(i)

37. In the light of Heidegger's thought match the following List - I with List - II and choose the correct answer with the help of code given below:

List - I	List - II
(a) Phenomenon	(i) Possibility
(b) Fear	(ii) That which reveals itself
(c) Ready-to-hand	(iii) A mode of man's being
(d) Existenz	(iv) Circumspection

Codes:

	(a)	(b)	(c)	(d)
(1)	(iv)	(iii)	(ii)	(i)
(2)	(iii)	(ii)	(i)	(iv)
(3)	(ii)	(iii)	(iv)	(i)
(4)	(i)	(iv)	(iii)	(ii)

38. Given below are Assertion (A) and Reason (R). Consider them and select the correct code:

Assertion (A) : According to Gilbert Ryle, to say of someone that 'x' is intelligent implies

Reason (R) : (i) It is an assertion about x's mind (ii) It is our knowledge of x's public performance

Code :

(1) Both (A) and (R) (i), (ii) are true and (R) (i), (ii) both are correct explanations of (A)
(2) (A) and (R) are true but (R) (i) only is the correct explanation of (A)
(3) (A) and (R) are true but (R) (ii) only is the correct explanation of (A)
(4) Both (A) and (R) are false and (R) (i), (ii) is not a correct explanation of (A)

39. Which of the following statement is incorrect in the context of Nietzsche :

(1) Slave morality settles for the imaginary revenge of the after life
(2) Slave morality is inauthentic because it is always a reaction, never originating impulse
(3) Slave morality immediately says yes to what comes from outside, to what is different, to what is not oneself
(4) Slave morality is a morality of resignation, deferment and prohibition

40. In the light of William James, which of the following is not a correct statement ?

(1) Life demands a response -"forced options"
(2) False ideas are those that we cannot verify
(3) Theories are only man - made language, in which we write our reports of nature
(4) True ideas cannot be validated

41. Phenomenology, according to Husserl, rests upon which of the following radical conviction ?

(1) Meaning is in the mind alone
(2) Meaning is in the world alone
(3) Meaning is neither in the mind nor in the world
(4) Meaning is in the intentional relationship between the mind and the world

42. Given below are Assertion (A) and Reason (R). Consider them and select the correct code:

Assertion (A) : According to Kant, though we cannot directly experience Noumena, a special class of Transcendental Ideas bridges the gap between the Phenomenal and Noumenal Worlds

Reason (R) : (i) Ideas are called Transcendental because they are products of reason alone and not the result of the mind's interaction with sensation (ii) They 'Unify' or 'make possible' having experience in the first place.

Code :

(1) Both (A) and (R) (i), (ii) are true and (R) is the correct explanation of (A)
(2) (A) and (R) (i) are true and (R) (i) is the only correct explanation of (A)
(3) (A) and (R) (ii) are true and (R) (ii) alone is the correct explanation of (A)
(4) Both (A) and (R) (i), (ii) are false and (R) does not provide a correct explanation of (A)

43. Match List - I with List - II and mark the correct code from given below :

List - I	List - II
(a) Epoche	(i) The intending consciousness
(b) Eidos	(ii) Suspension of the empirical and metaphysical presupposition
(c) Intuition	(iii) The invariant structure
(d) Noesis	(iv) An active repossession of the passive play of possibilities, reuniting them in a single grasp

Codes :

	(a)	(b)	(c)	(d)
(1)	(iv)	(i)	(ii)	(iii)
(2)	(iii)	(ii)	(iv)	(i)
(3)	(i)	(iv)	(iii)	(ii)
(4)	(ii)	(iii)	(iv)	(i)

44. Which one of the following code is correct with reference to the thought given below ? Answer considering (a), (b), (c) and (d) :

Thought : ".... mind and body, extension and thought as two of the many inseparable aspects of a single, all - inclusive reality. Being co - existent attributes of the substance, thought and extension cannot interact".

(a) Descartes (b) Leibnitz
(c) Spinoza (d) Berkeley

Code :

(1) Spinoza
(2) Both Berkeley and Descartes
(3) Leibnitz
(4) Both Spinoza and Berkeley

45. For Leibnitz, monads are :

(1) Indivisible and Spiritual only
(2) Indivisible and Self - active only
(3) Self-active and material only
(4) Indivisible, Self - active and Spiritual

46. Match List - I with List - II and choose the correct answer by using code given below :

List - I	List - II
(a) Hume	(i) The idea of causality is not necessarily connected with uniformity
(b) Locke	(ii) God is the real cause of spirits and things
(c) Berkeley	(iii) The relation of the soul to the body is of the nature of the pilot and his machine
(d) Descartes	(iv) Past experience of constant conjunction.

Codes :

	(a)	(b)	(c)	(d)
(1)	(i)	(iii)	(ii)	(iv)
(2)	(iv)	(i)	(ii)	(iii)
(3)	(ii)	(i)	(iii)	(iv)
(4)	(iv)	(i)	(iii)	(ii)

47. Which one among the following code is acceptable to John Locke ? Answer considering (a), (b), (c) and (d) :

(a) Only Agreement of Ideas is Knowledge

(b) Only Agreement of Sensations is Knowledge
(c) Agreement or Disagreement of Ideas is Knowledge
(d) Agreement or Disagreement of Sensations is Knowledge

Code :

(1) (d) and (c) (2) (d) and (a)
(3) (c) and (a) (4) (a) and (b)

48. Which one among the following code is acceptable to Spinoza ? Answer considering (a), (b), (c), (d) :

(a) Nature as a self-creating reality is known as Natura Naturans.
(b) Nature as a self-creating reality is known as Natura Naturata.
(c) In its aspect of a creative product, Nature is known as Natura Naturata.
(d) In its static aspect, Nature is known as Natura Naturans.

Code :

(1) (a) and (b) (2) (a) and (c)
(3) (a) and (d) (4) (b) and (d)

49. In the philosophy of Berkeley, all the following statements are true except :

(1) There are no physical objects
(2) What we call objects are only ideas
(3) God creates ideas in us
(4) There are ideas of flying horses

50. Select the correct sequence of process of evolution regarding Sri Aurobindo's philosophy :

(1) Widening, Heightening, Integration
(2) Heightening, Widening, Integration
(3) Heightening, Integration, Widening
(4) Integration, Heightening, Widening

Answers

1. (2)	**2.** (2)	**3.** (2)	**4.** (1)	**5.** (2)	**6.** (1)	**7.** (2)	**8.** (2)	**9.** (3)	**10.** (1)
11. (3)	**12.** (4)	**13.** (3)	**14.** (3)	**15.** (2)	**16.** (3)	**17.** (4)	**18.** (3)	**19.** (4)	**20.** (4)
21. (2)	**22.** (3)	**23.** (4)	**24.** (3)	**25.** (3)	**26.** (4)	**27.** (4)	**28.** (2)	**29.** (3)	**30.** (2)
31. (1)	**32.** (1)	**33.** (1)	**34.** (2)	**35.** (3)	**36.** (2)	**37.** (3)	**38.** (1)	**39.** (3)	**40.** (4)
41. (4)	**42.** (1)	**43.** (4)	**44.** (1)	**45.** (4)	**46.** (2)	**47.** (3)	**48.** (2)	**49.** (4)	**50.** (1)

November, 2017

PHILOSOPHY

PAPER-III

Note : This paper contains **seventy five (75)** objective type questions of **two (2)** marks each. All questions are compulsory.

1. The cause of the apprehension of past and present according to the Vaiśeṣikas is :
   (1) Akāśa (2) Dik
   (3) Kāla (4) Manas

2. According to Rāmānuja, apṛthaksiddhi is a relation between :
   (1) Jiva and Jagat only
   (2) Jiva and Brahman only
   (3) Jagat and Brahman only
   (4) Between Brahman and Jiva on the one hand and between Brahman and Jagat on the other.

3. What is the asamavāyikāraṇa of a dvyaṇuka according to the Vaiśeṣikas ?
   (1) Paramāṇu
   (2) Parimāṇa of the paramāṇu
   (3) Paramāṇu saṁyoga
   (4) Īśvara

4. According to the Vaiśeṣikas sattā sāmānya exists in :
   (1) Dravya, Guṇa and Karma only
   (2) Dravya, Guṇa, Karma and Sāmānya only
   (3) Guṇa and Karma only
   (4) Dravya and Guṇa only

5. Which one among the following is not a mūrtadravya ?
   (1) Marut (2) Manas
   (3) Ātman (4) Kṣiti

6. Who among the following Early Greek Philosophers distinguished between appearance and reality as a contrast between apparent permanence and hidden reality of continuous change ?
   (1) Heraclitus (2) Anaxagoras
   (3) Empedocles (4) Democritus

7. Consider the following statements in the light of the philosophy of Locke and mark the correct code :
   (a) Primary qualities are sensible qualities that depend on the perceiver.
   (b) Primary qualities are Color, Sound, Taste and Texture.
   (c) Secondary qualities are those whose existence is independent of any perceiver.
   (d) Primary qualities are objective properties of things whereas secondary qualities are subjective properties.

   Code :
   (1) Only (a) and (b) are true
   (2) Only (b) and (c) are true
   (3) Only (c) and (d) are true
   (4) Only (d) is true

8. According to Cartesian dualism human beings are a combination of :
   (1) Incorporeal and corporeal substances each operating according to separate sets of laws.
   (2) Corporeal substances operating according to the same set of laws.
   (3) Incorporeal substances each operating according to separate sets of rules.
   (4) Incorporeal and corporeal substances both operating to the same set of laws.

9. An individual for Plato can be :
   (1) Sensible object that can be known by perception.
   (2) Image that can be known by perception.

(3) Sensible object that can be known by reason.

(4) Sensible object that can be known by imagination.

10. Which one of the following can be placed under "Opinion", according to Plato ?

(1) Belief of Chair
(2) Chairness
(3) Blackness of Chair
(4) Whiteness of Chair

11. According to Nichomachean Ethics phronesis refers to :

(1) Practical Wisdom
(2) Cardinal Virtue
(3) Natural Excellence
(4) Happiness

12. "The mind creates the ideas of causality and necessity ; we do not observe them." This statement can be attributed to which one of the following modern western philosophers ?

(1) Mill (2) Hume
(3) Descartes (4) Locke

13. Consider the following statements in the context of William James' pragmatism and mark the correct code :

(a) Universalist notion of truth is rejected
(b) Truth is contextless
(c) Truth happens to an idea

Code :

(1) Only (a) is true
(2) Only (a) and (c) are true
(3) Only (b) is true
(4) Only (b) and (c) are true

14. According to which one of the following Western Philosophers "Truth is a subjective condition, not an objective one."

(1) Kierkegaard (2) Hume
(3) Kant (4) William James

15. 'Self' according to Hume is :

(1) a static subject
(2) a static physical entity
(3) without a persistent identity
(4) with a persistent identity

16. Which of the following is not a correct statement ?

(1) Sāṁkhya holds that a word signifies a particular.
(2) Kumārila holds that word cannot mean particular.
(3) Early Mimāṁsakās hold that word means Ākṛti.
(4) Naiyāyikās hold that word does not mean Jāti

17. In Indian logic vācyārtha does not mean :

(1) Abhidheyārtha
(2) Mukhyārtha
(3) Vyangyārtha
(4) Śakyārtha

18. According to which one of the following schools, Truth of Pramā is considered to be 'Abādhitārtha - Viṣayakatva" ?

(1) Cārvāka (2) Jaina
(3) Advaita (4) Sāṁkhya

19. 'The name and the universal concept are supplied by our imagination' is the view of :

(1) Advaitins (2) Buddhists
(3) Naiyāyikās (4) Vaiśeṣikas

20. Which one of the following theory of Khyāti illustrates that "Khyāti is non-apprehension' of the distinction between two cognitions which are partial and imperfect" ?

(1) Viparīta khyāti (2) Akhyāti
(3) Yathārtha khyāti (4) Anyāthā khyāti

21. Upamāna is considered as a case of Pratyabhijñā by :

(1) Jainas (2) Sāṁkhya
(3) Vaiśeṣikas (4) Naiyāyikās

22. Consider the Assertion (A) and Reason (R) and select the correct code given below :

Assertion (A) : Advaitins accept only 'Anvayī' but not 'Kevalānvyī' Anumāna.

Reason (R) : The thing to be inferred must not be the counter positive of non-existence.

Code :

(1) Both (A) and (R) are true and (R) is the correct explanation of (A).
(2) Both (A) and (R) are true but (R) is not a correct explanation of (A).
(3) (A) is false and (R) is true.
(4) Both (A) and (R) are false.

23. According to Advaita Vedānta, the term Antaḥ-Karaṇa-Vṛtti refers to :
(1) Cognitive mode of mind
(2) Affective mode of mind
(3) Conative mode of mind
(4) All of the above

24. Consider the Assertion (A) and Reason (R) and select the correct code given below :

Assertion (A) : According to Advaita, anything perceived is not revealed by Pramātṛ-Caitanya.

Reason (R) : Anything Unperceived is veiled by Ajñāna .

Code :
(1) Both (A) and (R) are true and (R) is the correct explanation of (A).
(2) (A) is true but (R) is false and (R) is not the correct explanation of (A).
(3) (A) is false and (R) is true.
(4) Both (A) and (R) are false.

25. Match List-I with List-II and choose the correct answer by using code given below :

List-I	List-II
(a) Sākṣātpratitīh Pratyakṣaṁ	(i) Dingnāga
(b) Viśeṣāvadhāraṇa-Pradhāna Pratyakṣaṁ	(ii) Gangeśa
(c) Pratyakṣaṁ kalpana-podhaṁ jñānaṁ	(iii) Prabhākara
(d) Jñānākarñakaṁ jñānaṁ Pratyakṣaṁ	(iv) Yoga

Codes :

	(a)	(b)	(c)	(d)
(1)	(i)	(ii)	(iii)	(iv)
(2)	(ii)	(i)	(iv)	(iii)
(3)	(iii)	(iv)	(i)	(ii)
(4)	(iv)	(iii)	(ii)	(i)

26. Lokasaṁgraha is meant for :
(1) The benefit of the Victims
(2) The benefit of the Ancestors
(3) The benefit of the Masses
(4) The benefit of selected few

27. Which one does not represent triratna ?
(1) Samyak jñāna (2) Samyak karmānta
(3) Samyak darśana (4) Samyak Cāritra

28. Select the correct sequence :
(1) Artha, Kāma, Dharma, Mokṣa
(2) Mokṣa, Kāma, Dharma, Artha
(3) Dharma, Kāma, Artha, Mokṣa
(4) Dharma, Artha, Kāma, Mokṣa

29. Observation of brahmacarya is a means of meeting :
(1) Pitṛ-ṛña only (2) Ṛśi-ṛña only
(3) Deva-ṛña only
(4) Pitṛ-ṛña and Deva-ṛña only

30. Match List-I with List-II and choose the correct answer from the code given below :

List-I (Writer)	List-II (Writing)
(a) Broad	(i) Language of Morals
(b) Urban	(ii) Five types of Ethical Theory
(c) Hare	(iii) Metaphysics of Morals
(d) Kant	(iv) Fundamentals of Ethics

Codes :

	(a)	(b)	(c)	(d)
(1)	(i)	(iii)	(ii)	(iv)
(2)	(iv)	(ii)	(i)	(iii)
(3)	(ii)	(iv)	(iii)	(i)
(4)	(ii)	(iv)	(i)	(iii)

31. Match List-I with List-II and choose the correct answer with the help of code given below :

List-I (Philosopher)	List-II (View)
(a) Zeno	(i) Sense of dignity
(b) Hegel	(ii) Social equilibrium
(c) J.S. Mill	(iii) Be a person
(d) Samuel Alexander	(iv) Life according to nature

Codes : (a) (b) (c) (d)
(1) (iv) (iii) (i) (ii)
(2) (iv) (ii) (i) (iii)
(3) (iii) (ii) (i) (iv)
(4) (ii) (i) (iii) (iv)

32. According to Ayer, when you say 'This is good' you are :
(1) Communicating your feelings
(2) Expressing your feelings
(3) Describing a particular things
(4) Influencing others feelings

33. Match List-I with List-II and choose the correct answer with the help of code given below :

List-I	List-II
(a) Legal theory	(i) Practical Reason is the true source of moral obligation
(b) Kant's view	(ii) The state is the source of moral obligation
(c) Intentionist view	(iii) The self is the source of moral obligation
(d) Eudaemonist view	(iv) Moral obligation is imposed by conscience, which is the supreme authority

Codes :
(a) (b) (c) (d)
(1) (ii) (i) (iv) (iii)
(2) (i) (iii) (ii) (iv)
(3) (iii) (iv) (ii) (i)
(4) (iv) (iii) (ii) (i)

34. Who among the following has said that 'Punishment brings wisdom. It is the healing art of Wickedness' ?
(1) Socrates (2) Plato
(3) Aristotle (4) Nietzsche

35. Who among the following has said that "True law is the rightÿ reason in agreement with nature; it is of universal application, unchanging and everlastingÿ ?
(1) Kant (2) Cicero
(3) Hegel (4) Darwin

36. Definition of 'good' in terms of self realisation according to Moore would be :
(1) Naturalistic fallacy
(2) Metaphysical fallacy
(3) Both Naturalistic and Metaphysical fallacy
(4) Neither Naturalistic nor Metaphysical

37. Which philosopher among the following has classified 'Adjectives' in three categories (A - words, D - words, G - words) as per their functions ?
(1) Ayer (2) Hare
(3) Nowell Smith (4) Stevenson

38. Which one of the following is consistent regarding moral Judgement ?
(1) It is an 'Is' Judgement
(2) It is a Logical Judgement
(3) It is a Natural Judgement
(4) It is a Normative Judgement

39. According to which one of the following views value-judgements are essentially imperative ?
(1) Descriptivism (2) Emotivism
(3) Prescriptivism (4) Intuitionism

40. Find out the fallacy committed in the syllogistic form : AAI-1
(1) Undistributed middle term
(2) Illicit Major
(3) Illicit Minor (4) Existential Fallacy

41. Given below are an Assertion (A) and a Reason (R), consider them and select the correct answer from code given here under :
Assertion (A) : A Categorical syllogism commits a fallacy of four terms if more than three terms are used.
Reason (R) : In a standard form of categorical syllogism, there are three and only three terms occurring twice each in the same meaning.
Code :
(1) (A) and (R) both are true and (R) is not the correct explanation of (A).

(2) (A) and (R) both are true and (R) is the correct explanation of (A).
(3) (A) is true and (R) is false.
(4) (A) and (R) both are false.

42. The difference between Aristotlean and Boolean interpretation of categorical propositions is as follows :
(1) Aristotlean accepts contrary, sub - contrary, sub-alternation and contradictory relations whereas Boolean accepts only contradictory relations.
(2) Aristotlean accepts contrary, sub - contrary and Boolean accepts only contradictory relations.
(3) Aristotlean and Boolean both accepts all the above relations.
(4) Aristotlean and Boolean both accept none of the above relations.

43. If 'A' proposition is converted to 'A' and 'E' proposition is contraposited to E, what kind of fallacy is commited according to Boole ?
(1) Undistributed Middle term
(2) Existential Fallacy
(3) Illicit Major (4) Illicit Minor

44. Which of the following is a correct statement in the light of truth and validity ?
(1) The truth or falsity of an argument's conclusion does by itself determine the validity or invalidity of that argument.
(2) The validity of an argument does guarantee the truth of its conclusion.
(3) Truth and falsity are attributed to the arguments while validity and invalidity are attributed to the propositions.
(4) The truth or falsity of an argument's conclusion does not by itself determine the validity or invalidity of that argument and the fact that an argument is valid does not guarantee the truth of its conclusion.

45. Which one of the following is not the correct formulation of De morgan theorems ?
(1) $\sim(p \vee q) \equiv (\sim p . \sim q)$
(2) $\sim(p . q) \equiv (\sim p \vee \sim q)$
(3) $\sim(p . q) \equiv \sim(p \vee q)$
(4) $(\sim p \vee \sim q) \equiv \sim(p . q)$

46. Match the List-I with List-II and select the correct answer from the code given here under in the argument and argument form :

List-I (Arguments)	**List-II (Argument form)**
(a) A $\therefore A \vee B$	(i) $(p \supset q).(r \supset s)$ $p \vee r$ $\therefore q \vee s$
(b) C.D $\therefore C$	(ii) p $\therefore p \vee q$
(c) H I $\therefore H.I$	(iii) p.q $\therefore p$
(d) $(A \supset B).(C \supset D)$ $A \vee C$ $\therefore B \vee D$	(iv) p q $\therefore p.q$

Codes :

	(a)	(b)	(c)	(d)
(1)	(i)	(ii)	(iii)	(iv)
(2)	(ii)	(iii)	(iv)	(i)
(3)	(iii)	(ii)	(i)	(iv)
(4)	(iv)	(iii)	(ii)	(i)

47. What are the correct symbolization of the paradoxes of material implication ?
(1) $\sim p \supset (q \supset p)$ and $p \supset (q \supset p)$
(2) $p \supset (q \supset p)$ and $\sim p \supset (p \supset q)$
(3) $\sim p \supset (q \supset p)$ and U $\sim p \supset (p \supset q)$
(4) $p \supset (q \supset p)$ and $p \supset (p \supset q)$

48. A statement form is said to be tautologous :
(1) If all of its substitution instances are false.
(2) If its substitution instances are admixture of true and false.
(3) If all of its substitution instances are true.
(4) If its substitution instances are neither true nor false.

49. Two statements are said to materially equivalent if :
(1) Both are true and both are false.
(2) One is true and another is false.
(3) One is false and another is true.
(4) There is no question, of truth and falsity is involved.

50. Who among the following has not criticised Human Rights ?
(1) Bentham (2) Alian Pellet
(3) Locke (4) Nietzsche

51. Which one of the following feminist activists gave the slogan 'The personal is political' ?
(1) Carol Harisch
(2) Simon de Beauvoir
(3) Mary R. Beard (4) Kate Millet

52. Which one of the following philosophers celebrates the free play of language as an endless difference of meaning ?
(1) Derrida (2) Russell
(3) Wittgenstein (4) Husserl

53. Which one of the following lists correctly depicts Heidegger's four modes of language ?
(1) Assertion, Discourse, Idle talk and Saying
(2) Assertion, Reason, Emotion and Idle talk
(3) Assertion, Understanding, Discourse and talking
(4) Assertion, Reason, Understanding and Idle talk

54. Who among the following mentioned a distinction between authentic and inauthentic forms of existential discourse ?
(1) Heidegger (2) Husserl
(3) Sartre (4) Derrida

55. Three major modes of intentionality, according to Husserl are :
(1) Perception, Inference and Opinion.
(2) Perception, Imagination and Understanding.
(3) Perception, Imagination and Signification.
(4) Perception, Inference and Signification.

56. Which one of the following lists of phenomena of consciousness in-itself is listed by Sartre under the ontological category of 'being' ?
(1) Necessity, Essentiality, Objectivity and Fame
(2) Necessity, Facticity, Objectivity and Shame
(3) Necessity, Essentiality, Facticity and Shame
(4) Essentiality, Facticity, Objectivity and Fame

57. Consider the following Assertion (A) and Reason (R) in the light of Gandhian view and select the correct code :
Assertion (A) : Non - Violence presupposes the capacity to strike.
Reason (R) : Strike is a passive resistance.
Code :
(1) Both (A) and (R) are true and (R) is the correct explanation of (A).
(2) Both (A) and (R) are true but (R) is not the correct explanation of (A).
(3) (A) is true but (R) is false.
(4) (A) is false but (R) is true.

58. Match List-I with List-II and select the code from the given below :

List-I (Author)	List-II (Writing)
(a) Tagore	(i) Foundations of Indian Culture
(b) Gandhi	(ii) Search for the absolute in Neo - Vedanta
(c) K.C. Bhattacharya	(iii) My Religion
(d) Sri Aurobindo	(iv) Thought Relics

Codes :

	(a)	(b)	(c)	(d)
(1)	(i)	(ii)	(iv)	(iii)
(2)	(iv)	(iii)	(ii)	(i)
(3)	(ii)	(iv)	(i)	(iii)
(4)	(iii)	(i)	(ii)	(iv)

59. Who among the following upholds the view that 'The principle of demand and supply can not be the basis of any Science' ?
(1) Ambedkar (2) Gandhi
(3) Vivekananda (4) Marx

60. Which among the following is not true about the Gandhian principle of 'Bread Labour' ?
(1) It was designed to promote simple living among all citizens.

(2) It was designed to promote dignity of labour.

(3) It was designed to promote reaction against capitalists.

(4) It was designed to promote a sense of equality transcending the prevailing division of labour.

61. Who among the following has said that, 'If we want to Cultivate true spirit of democracy, we can not afford to be intolerant. Intolerance betrays want of faith in one's cause' ?

(1) Vivekananda (2) Ambedkar
(3) Tilak (4) Gandhi

62. Match the List-I with List-II and choose the correct answer by selecting one of the code given below :

List-I	List-II
(a) 'On Referring'	(i) Donald Davidson
(b) Theory of Description	(ii) J.L. Austin
(c) T - Sentences	(iii) P.F. Strawson
(d) Speech - Act	(iv) Bertrand Russell

Codes :	(a)	(b)	(c)	(d)
(1)	(iv)	(ii)	(i)	(iii)
(2)	(iii)	(ii)	(iv)	(i)
(3)	(iv)	(iii)	(ii)	(i)
(4)	(iii)	(iv)	(i)	(ii)

63. In the light of Frege's view which of the following is incorrect ?

(1) Definite descriptions with proper names have both sense and reference, and their reference is determined by their sense

(2) Sense, is the mode of presentation of object which is the reference of the expression whose sense it is

(3) The reference of the predicate is concept

(4) The reference is the mode of presentation

64. The meaning, is the useÿ does not imply that :

(1) Useless discourse is gibberish

(2) Language games vary from one form of life to another

(3) If the linguistic expression turns out to be an apt tool within the context of it's language game, it is meaningful

(4) Analysis of language cannot eliminate puzzlements

65. When 'Callingÿ something good is characteristically praising or commending or recommending; it refers to :

(1) Descriptive fallacy

(2) Assertion fallacy

(3) Speech Act fallacy

(4) Naturalistic fallacy

66. Consider the Assertion (A) and Reason (R) given below and choose the correct code as your answer :

Assertion (A) : 'We can and must conceive that blue might exist and yet the sensation of blue not existÿ.

Reason (R) : Sensation, according to Moore, has two elements, consciousness and the other, object of consciousness.

Code :

(1) Both (A) and (R) are true and (R) correctly explains (A)

(2) Both (A) and (R) are true but (R) is not a correct explanation of (A)

(3) (A) is true, (R) is false

(4) Both (A) and (R) are false

67. In Madhva's philosophy all the following propositions are true except :

(1) Brahman rules every jīva from within

(2) Every jīva is dependent on Brahman

(3) jīva is not free

(4) Every jīva is organically related to Brahman

68. Buddhism advocates the following except :

(1) Nairātmya vāda

(2) Syādavāda

(3) Pratītyasamutpāda

(4) Kṣañabhangura vāda

69. The Mahāvākyā ,'Tattvamasi' occurs in :
(1) Bṛhadārṇyaka Upaniṣad
(2) Māndūkya Upaniṣad
(3) Chāndogya Upaniṣad
(4) Taiṭṭirīya Upaniṣad

70. Match List-I and List-II and choose the correct answer with the help of code given below :

List-I	**List-II**
(a) Satakhyāti	(i) Yogacāra Buddhists
(b) Abhinavaanyathā khyāti	(ii) Mādhyāmika Buddhists
(c) Ātmakhyāti	(iii) Sāṁkhya
(d) Asatakhyāti	(iv) Madhva

Codes :

	(a)	**(b)**	**(c)**	**(d)**
(1)	(iv)	(iii)	(ii)	(i)
(2)	(iii)	(iv)	(i)	(ii)
(3)	(i)	(ii)	(iii)	(iv)
(4)	(ii)	(i)	(iv)	(iii)

71. The 'Pradhāna malla' of 'Advaitin's' is :
(1) The Naiyāyikas
(2) The Bauddhas
(3) The Sāṁkhyans
(4) The Vaiśeṣikas

72. All the following propositions according to RÂmÂnuja are false except :
(1) Rāmānuja advocates Karma - Yoga as the principal means to Jīvanmukti
(2) Rāmānuja advocates Jñāna - Yoga as the principal means to Videhamukti
(3) Rāmānuja advocates Karma - Yoga as the principal means to Videhamukti
(4) Rāmānuja advocates Bhakti - Yoga as the principal means to Videhamukti

73. According to Islam, all the following propositions are true except :
(1) Prime of place is given to prayer and fasting
(2) Charity is the greatest virtue
(3) Pilgrimage is a sacred undertaking to gain the grace of God
(4) Failing to surrender to the will of God

74. The sequence of the process of bondage and release of jīva, according to Jainism is :
(1) Bandha, saṁvara, nirjarā, mokṣa, āśrava.
(2) Āśrava, bandha, saṁvara, nirjarā, mokṣa
(3) Saṁvara, nirjarā, mokṣa, Āśrava, bandha.
(4) Nirjarā, mokṣa, Āśrava, bandha, saṁvara.

75. According to Zoroastrianism, all the following propositions are true except :
(1) Zoroastrianism advocates fire - worship.
(2) In Zoroastrianism, Ahramazda is recognised as the God for the good.
(3) In Zoroastrianism, Ahriman is recognised as the God for the evil.
(4) Zoroastrianism advocates Varnāṣrama Vyavasthā .

Answers

1. (3) **2.** (4) **3.** (3) **4.** (1) **5.** (3) **6.** (1) **7.** (4) **8.** (1) **9.** (1) **10.** (1)
11. (1) **12.** (2) **13.** (2) **14.** (1) **15.** (3) **16.** (4) **17.** (3) **18.** (3) **19.** (2) **20.** (2)
21. (1) **22.** (1) **23.** (1) **24.** (3) **25.** (3) **26.** (3) **27.** (2) **28.** (4) **29.** (2) **30.** (4)
31. (1) **32.** (2) **33.** (1) **34.** (2) **35.** (2) **36.** (1) **37.** (3) **38.** (4) **39.** (3) **40.** (4)
41. (2) **42.** (1) **43.** (2) **44.** (4) **45.** (3) **46.** (2) **47.** (2) **48.** (3) **49.** (1) **50.** (3)
51. (1) **52.** (1) **53.** (1) **54.** (1) **55.** (3) **56.** (2) **57.** (3) **58.** (2) **59.** (2) **60.** (3)
61. (4) **62.** (4) **63.** (4) **64.** (4) **65.** (3) **66.** (1) **67.** (4) **68.** (2) **69.** (3) **70.** (2)
71. (3) **72.** (4) **73.** (4) **74.** (2) **75.** (4)

July, 2018

PHILOSOPHY

PAPER-II

Note : This paper contains **hundred (100)** objective type questions of **two (2)** marks each. **All** questions are **compulsory.**

1. *Vṛtti* according to Nyāya is a relation between :
   (1) Two *Padas*
   (2) Two *Padārthas*
   (3) *Pada* and *Padārtha*
   (4) *Pada* and *Vākya*

2. According to Nyāya the objects of visual sense-organ are also the objects of tactual sense - organ except :
   (1) *Rūpa* only
   (2) *Rūpatva* only
   (3) *Both rūpa* and *rūpatva*
   (4) Both *Rūpa* and *sparśa*

3. Which type of *hetvābhāsa* is committed by the following *anumāna* ? Select the correct code given below :
   marinmayaḥ parvataḥ vahnimān
   (1) *Asādhāraṇa savyabhicāra*
   (2) *Svarūpāsiddha hetvābhāsa*
   (3) *Āśryāsiddha hetvābhāsa*
   (4) *Viruddha*

4. By what type of *sannikarṣa* do we perceive patābhāva in *ghata* according to the Nyāya ?
   (1) *Saṁyoga*
   (2) *Saṁyukta Samavāya*
   (3) *Samavāya*
   (4) *Viśeṣaṇata*

5. Which type of *kāraṇa* of the world *God* is in Vaiśeṣika philosophy ?
   (1) *Samavāyikāraṇa*
   (2) *Asamavāyikāraṇa*
   (3) *Upādānakāraṇa*
   (4) *Nimittakāraṇa*

6. Which among the following is **not** compatible to the vaiśeṣikas ?
   (1) *Pratyakṣa is pramāṇa*
   (2) *Anumāna is pramāṇa*
   (3) *Śabda is pramāṇa*
   (4) *Śabda is svatantra* (independent) *pramāṇa*

7. Given below are one **Assertion (A)** and a **Reason (R)**. Consider them and select the correct code in the context of *Cārvāka* philosophy.
   (A) *Pratyakṣa* is the only *pramāṇa*
   (R) *Anumāna* is not a *pramāṇa*
   Code :
   (1) Both (A) and (R) are true and (R) is the correct explanation of (A).
   (2) Both (A) and (R) are true and (R) is not the correct explanation of (A).
   (3) (A) is true and (R) is false.
   (4) (A) is false and (R) is true.

8. The view that *Iśvara* is a kind of *ātmā* is upheld by :
   (1) Cārvāka only
   (2) Vaiśeṣika only
   (3) Nyāya only
   (4) Nyāya and Vaiśeṣika

9. When the *lakṣaṇā* of a word excludes *Śakyārtha* completely then that *lakṣaṇā* is called in Nyāyaepistemology:
   (1) *Jahat lakṣaṇā*
   (2) *Vyañjanā*
   (3) *Ajahadlakṣaṇā*
   (4) *Jahadajahadlakṣaṇā*

10. Given below an **Assertion (A)** and one **Reason (R)**. Consider them and select the correct code given below :

(A) The existence of *paramāṇu* must be admitted.

(R) *Dvyaṇuka* is *sāvayava.*

Code :

(1) (A) and (R) both are true and (R) is the correct ground for (A).
(2) (A) and (R) both are true and (R) is not the correct ground for (A).
(3) (A) is true and (R) is false.
(4) (A) is false and (R) is true.

11. Match Set - I and Set - II and select the correct code given below :

Set - I	Set - II
(a) *Pratyakṣaṁ kalpanā-poḍaṁ nāmajātyādy-asaṁyutaṁ*	(i) Dharmakīrti
(b) *Jñānākaraṇakaṁ jñānaṁ pratyakṣaṁ*	(ii) Diṅnāga
(c) *Indriyārthasannik-arṣotpannaṁ jñānaṁ avyapadeśyaṁ avyabhicāri vyāvasāyātmikaṁ pratyakṣaā*	(iii) Gaṅgeśa
(d) *Pratyakṣaṁ kalpanā-poḍaṁ abhrāntaṁ*	(iv) Gautama

Codes :

	(a)	(b)	(c)	(d)
(1)	(i)	(ii)	(iii)	(iv)
(2)	(ii)	(iv)	(iii)	(i)
(3)	(ii)	(iii)	(iv)	(i)
(4)	(iii)	(ii)	(iv)	(i)

12. *Ākāśa* according to the vaiśeṣikas is :

(1) One only
(2) *Bibhu* only
(3) *Nitya* only
(4) *One, bibhu* and *nitya*

13. At liberated state *ātmā* according to the Nyāya school is devoid of :

(1) *Duḥkha* only
(2) *Sukha* only
(3) *Caitanya* only
(4) *Duḥkha, Sukha* and *Caitanya*

14. Ātmā, according to the Naiyāyikas can be :

(1) *knower* only
(2) *known* only
(3) *knowledge* only
(4) *knower* and *known*

15. What type of *kāraṇa* the colour of the threads is in respect of the colour of the cloth according to the vaiśeṣikas ?

(1) *Samavāyi*
(2) *Asamavāyī*
(3) *Nimitta*
(4) *Upādāna*

16. Which type of hetvābhāsa is committed by the following *anumāna* ? Select the correct code :

vahni, anuṣṇa, dravyatvāt

(1) *Aśrayāsiddha*
(2) *Bādhita*
(3) *Viruddha*
(4) *Satpratipakṣa*

17. Match List - I and List - II and choose the correct code :

List - I	List - II
(a) *Pūrva-mīmāṁsa*	(i) *Sadasadvilakṣaṇa*
(b) *Advaita Vedānta*	(ii) *Apṛthak siddhi*
(c) *Dvaita Vedūnta*	(iii) *Parūdhīna viśeṣāpti*
(d) *Viśiṣṭādvaita Vedānta*	(iv) *Jātiśaktivāda*

Codes :

	(a)	(b)	(c)	(d)
(1)	(ii)	(iii)	(i)	(iv)
(2)	(iv)	(i)	(iii)	(ii)
(3)	(iii)	(ii)	(i)	(iv)
(4)	(iii)	(iv)	(ii)	(i)

18. Which one of the following propositions is not compatible with Kumārila School of Pūrva-mimāṁsa ?

(1) Advocacy of *abhihitānvayavāda*
(2) Perceptual error consists in mutual superimposition of shell and silver

(3) Knowledge is constituted of *tripuṭi*
(4) Perceptual error is an act of commission

19. Which one of the following is incompatible to Dvaita Vedānta ?
(1) The concepts of *bheda* and *Viśeṣa* are basic and central to Dvaita Vedānta
(2) *Jagat* is an appearance
(3) *Brahman* is *ananthakalyana-guṇa paripūrṇa*
(4) *Jīva* is ontologically different from *Brahman*

20. Write the correct sequence according to the Upaniṣads :
(1) *nididhyāsana, manana, śravaṇa*
(2) *manana, śravaṇa, nididhyāsana*
(3) *śravaṇa, manana, nididhyāsana*
(4) *śravaṇa, nididhyāsana, manana*

21. Mark the incompatible of the following with reference to Kumarila's epistemology :
(1) *Svataḥ prāmāṇya vāda*
(2) *Viparītakhyāti vāda*
(3) *Parataḥ prāmāṇya vada*
(4) *Abhihitānvaya vāda*

22. *Anvitabhidhānavāda* is supported by the following pair of philosophers :
(1) Prabhākara and Manḍana
(2) Kumārila and Vācaspati
(3) Gotama and Praśastapāda
(4) Nāgārjuna and Diṅnāga

23. Among the following, what is acceptable to Śamkara ?
(1) *Brahman* and *Jīva* are different from and identical with each other
(2) *Brahman* is *nirguṇa*
(3) Proponent of Sanaka *Saṁpradāya* of Vaiṣṇavism
(4) *Mokṣa* is obtainable by *jñāna* through *Iśwara prasāda* (God's grace) generated by *Bhakti*

24. The Direct knowledge of the thoughts of other, according to Jain Philosophy is :
(1) *Avadhi* (2) *Manahparyāya*
(3) *Mati* (4) *Kevala*

25. What are the trinity principles espoused by Dr. Ambedkar ?
(1) Non-violence, Truth and Peace
(2) Non-Cooperation, Non-stealing and Non-equalization
(3) Revolution, Historical Materialism and Dialectical materialism
(4) Liberty, Equality and Fraternity

26. Which hetvābhāsa is committed by the following anumāna ? Select the correct code :
Sabda anitya cākṣuṣatvāt
(1) *Svarūpāsiddha hetvābhāsa*
(2) *Bādhita hetvābhāsa*
(3) *Viruddha hetvābhāsa*
(4) *Savyabhicāra hetvābhāsa*

27. Given below are the statements about a *Karmayogin*. Select the correct code given below :
(a) A *Karmayogi* works for attaining liberation
(b) A *Karmayogi* works for heaven
(c) A *Karmayogi* works for the renunciation of all the *karma*
(d) A *Karmayogi* works for *lokasaṁgraḥ*

Code :
(1) (a) and (b) (2) (b) and (c)
(3) (a) and (d) (4) (b) and (d)

28. The basis of division of four types of *varṇa* according to the Gītā is :
(1) *Guṇa* only
(2) *Karma* only
(3) *Both guṇa* and *karma*
(4) *Lokaprasiddhi* only

29. Match List - I with List - II and choose the correct answer regarding *Khyātivāda* by using the code given below :

List - I	List - II
(a) *Akhyāti*	(i) *Vijñānavāda*
(b) *Ātmakhyāti*	(ii) *Prabhākara Mīmāṁsā*
(c) *Anyathākhyāti*	(iii) *Nyāya*
(d) *Anirvacanīyakhyāti*	(iv) *Advaita vedānta*

Codes :

	(a)	(b)	(c)	(d)
(1)	(ii)	(i)	(iii)	(iv)
(2)	(i)	(iii)	(ii)	(iv)
(3)	(i)	(ii)	(iii)	(iv)
(4)	(ii)	(iii)	(i)	(iv)

30. Match List - I with List - II and choose the correct answer regarding Prāmāṇya by using code below :

List - I	List - II
(a) Buddhism	(i) *Paratah Prāmāṇya, aprāmāṇya*
(b) Sāṅkhya	(ii) *Svatah Prāmāṇya, Paratah aprāmāṇya*
(c) Mīmāṁsā	(iii) *Svatah Prāmāṇya, Paratah aprāmāṇya*
(d) Nyāya-Vaiśeṣika	(iv) *Svatah Prāmāṇya, aprāmāṇya*

Codes :

	(a)	(b)	(c)	(d)
(1)	(ii)	(iii)	(i)	(iv)
(2)	(ii)	(iv)	(iii)	(i)
(3)	(iii)	(ii)	(iv)	(i)
(4)	(i)	(iii)	(iv)	(ii)

31. 'Treating equals equally and unequals unequally' is the view of :

(1) Socrates (2) Bentham
(3) Aristotle (4) Mill

32. Who among the following has said that "Personality and property go together" ?

(1) Kant (2) Hegel
(3) Ross (4) Rawls

33. Who among the following has identified three types of Justice - Distributive, Retributive, Commutative ?

(1) Plato (2) Aristotle
(3) Hobbes (4) Locke

34. 'Men are not hanged for stealing horse so that horse may not be stolen by others' can be attributed to :

(1) Retributive theory of punishment
(2) Reformative theory of punishment
(3) Theory of capital punishment
(4) Deterrent theory of punishment

35. 'Either freedom of will is a fact or moral judgement a delusion' is a statement of :

(1) Hobbes (2) Martinue
(3) Kant (4) Hegel

36. Match List - I with List - II and choose the correct answer with the help of the code given below :

List - I (Thinking)	List - II (Statement)
(a) *Radical Feminism*	(i) The struggle for women's liberation is essentially bound up with the struggle against capitalism.
(b) *Liberal Feminism*	(ii) Men and Women should be treated equal.
(c) *Socialist Feminism*	(iii) A Women is not born but made.
(d) *Marxist Feminism*	(iv) Both Men and Women are essentially rational creatures.

Codes :

	(a)	(b)	(c)	(d)
(1)	(iii)	(iv)	(ii)	(i)
(2)	(i)	(iii)	(ii)	(iv)
(3)	(ii)	(i)	(iv)	(iii)
(4)	(iv)	(iii)	(i)	(ii)

37. Which among the following is the distinctive feature of ethical judgements, according to Stevenson ?

(1) Statement of Command
(2) Approval of the Consequence of an act
(3) Statement of Fact
(4) Disagreement in Attitude

38. It has been pointed out that Mill's arguments for *Utilitarianism* Suffer from the fallacy of :

(1) *Illicit major*
(2) *Illicit Minor*

(3) *Undistributed Middle term*
(4) *Figure of Speech*

39. 'The goodness of an action is determined by its consequence' is the theory attributed to :
(1) Descriptive
(2) Deontological
(3) Prescriptive
(4) Teleological

40. According to Kant, Moral Laws are :
(1) *Apriori* based on reason
(2) *Apriori not* based on reason
(3) *Aposteriori* not based on reason
(4) *Aposteriori* based on reason

41. Consider the Syllogism below and identify the fallacy involved in it.
All pets are domestic animals.
No lions are domestic animals.
Therefore, some lions are not pets.
Code :
(1) *Fallacy of Exclusive terms*
(2) *Fallacy of Illicit minor*
(3) *Existential fallacy*
(4) *Fallacy of undistributed middle*

42. Which combination of fallacies occur if the rule "Any term distributed in the conclusion must be distributed in the premises" is not followed :
(1) Undistributed middle and Illicit major
(2) Undistributed middle and fallacy of Exclusive premises
(3) Illicit major and Illicit minor
(4) Fallacy of exclusive premises and Illicit major

43. To obvert a proposition in an immediate inference :
(1) Only quality of the proposition is to be changed
(2) Only quantity of the proposition is to be changed.
(3) Quality is to be changed and the predicate term is to be replaced with its complement.
(4) Quantity is to be changed and the predicate term is to be replaced with its complement.

44. In the traditional square of opposition, if 'O' is true, then :
(1) 'A' is true; 'E' is false; 'I' is undetermined.
(2) 'A' is true; 'E' and 'I' are undetermined.
(3) 'A' is false; 'E' and 'I' are undetermined.
(4) 'A' is false; 'E' and 'I' are true.

45. Match List - I (Figures) with List - II (Moods) and choose the correct answer with the help of code given below :

List - I (Figures)	**List - II (Moods)**
(a) *First figure*	(i) Fresison
(b) *Second figure*	(ii) Ferio
(c) *Third figure*	(iii) Festino
(d) *Fourth figure*	(iv) Ferison

Codes :

	(a)	(b)	(c)	(d)
(1)	(ii)	(iii)	(i)	(iv)
(2)	(ii)	(i)	(iii)	(iv)
(3)	(ii)	(iii)	(iv)	(i)
(4)	(ii)	(iv)	(i)	(iii)

46. In which one of the following cases an argument can be invalid ?
(1) Premises are True and Conclusion is True
(2) Premises are True and Conclusion is False
(3) Premises are False and Conclusion is False
(4) Premises are False and Conclusion is True

47. Consider the following propositions and choose the correct answer :
"All judges are lawyers".
"Some judges are not lawyers".
Code :
(1) Both the statements are opposed in Quality only.
(2) Both the statements are opposed in Quantity only.

(3) The statements are opposed both in Quality and Quantity.
(4) The statements are opposed in Quality and not in Quantity.

48. If two propositions can both be true, but can not both be false together, their relation is :
(1) Contrary (2) Contradictory
(3) Sub-Contrary (4) Sub-altern

49. Which one of the following rules of inference is employed in the argument :
$[N \supset (O.P)] \bullet [Q \supset (O.R)]$
$N \vee Q$
$\therefore (O.P) \vee (O.R)$
(1) Hypothetical Syllogism
(2) Disjunctive Syllogism
(3) Constructive Dilemma
(4) Modus Ponens

50. Which one of the following forms represents 'Modus Tollens' ?
(1) $p \supset q$
$\sim q$
$\therefore \sim p$
(2) $p \vee q$
$\sim p$
$\therefore q$
(3) $p \supset q$
$\therefore p \supset (p.q)$
(4) $p \supset q$
p
$\therefore q$

51. Consider the following statements in the light of Plato's metaphysics and select the correct code :
(a) What is truly real is objects that we encounter in sensory experience.
(b) What is truly real is forms that can only be grasped intellectually.
(c) Forms are eternal and changing.

Code :
(1) Only (a) is true
(2) Only (a) and (c) are true
(3) Only (b) is true
(4) Only (b) and (c) are true

52. Which one of the following opined that "Philosophy is based on precepts of reason; theology on truths of revelation held on faith and philosophy serves as a handmaiden for theology."
(1) Augustine (2) Anselm
(3) Aquinas (4) Aristotle

53. Given below are Assertion (A) and Reason (R). Consider them in the light of Plato's Theory of Forms and select the correct code.

Assertion (A) : Circularity does not exist in the physical world.

Reason (R) : Circularity is not an example of form.

Code :
(1) Both (A) and (R) are true and (R) is the correct explanation of (A).
(2) Both (A) and (R) are true, but (R) is not the correct explanation of (A).
(3) (A) is true and (R) is false.
(4) (R) is true and (A) is false.

54. Which one of the following statements appropriately represents the position of Nietzsche ?
(a) He equates the will to truth with the will to power.
(b) The distinction between good and evil is based on the will to power.
(c) The distinction between good and evil is rooted in objectivity.
(d) All life and all happiness are governed by the will to power.

Code :
(1) Only (a) and (b) are true
(2) Only (c) and (d) are true
(3) Only (a), (b) and (d) are true
(4) Only (b) and (d) are true

55. Match List - I with List - II and mark the correct code :

List - I	List - II
(a) Friedrich Nietzsche	(i) How to make our ideas clear
(b) William James	(ii) The will to power

(c) C.S. Peirce (iii) Logical Investigations

(d) Edmund Husserl (iv) The Meaning of Truth

Codes :

	(a)	(b)	(c)	(d)
(1)	(i)	(iii)	(ii)	(iv)
(2)	(ii)	(i)	(iii)	(iv)
(3)	(ii)	(iv)	(i)	(iii)
(4)	(ii)	(iv)	(iii)	(i)

56. Idealism is refuted by which of the following philosophers ? Select the correct code :

(a) Moore (b) Russell

(c) Berkeley

Code :

(1) Only (a) and (c) are true

(2) Only (a) is true

(3) Only (a) and (b) are true

(4) Only (b) and (c) are true

57. Which one of the following Logical positivists replaced 'Verification' with 'Confirmation' on the basis that although Universal laws cannot be verified, they can be confirmed ?

(1) Carnap (2) Ayer

(3) Schlock (4) W.V.O. Quine

58. 'Reality which is Absolute is a Coherent thought system with logical connectivity' is the view that can be ascribed to :

(1) Hegel (2) Berkeley

(3) Moore (4) Spinoza

59. Which one of the following statements represents the philosophical position of Anaximander correctly ?

(1) The 'Limitless' is the principle of the things that exist.

(2) It is from the principle of 'Limitless air' that everything that exists comes into being.

(3) "Limitless number" is the principle of things that exist.

(4) 'Limitless earth' is the basic principle of everything that exists.

60. The theory of metempsychosis or the theory of transmigration of soul - is ascribed to which one of the following Pre-socratic philosophers ?

(1) Pythagoras (2) Anaximander

(3) Parmenides (4) Democritus

61. The purpose of Phenomenological reduction of Husserl is to :

(1) examine the meanings produced by pure impersonal consciousness.

(2) examine the meanings of objects of the world.

(3) examine meanings of objects of personal consciousness.

(4) reject the meanings produced by pure impersonal consciousness.

62. Match List - I and List - II and choose the correct code :

List - I	List - II
(a) Locke	(i) *An Enquiry Concerning Human Understanding*
(b) Berkeley	(ii) *Critique of Practical Reason*
(c) Hume	(iii) *Three Dialogues between Hylas and Philonous*
(d) Kant	(iv) *An Essay Concerning Human Understanding*

Codes :

	(a)	(b)	(c)	(d)
(1)	(i)	(ii)	(iii)	(iv)
(2)	(i)	(iv)	(ii)	(iii)
(3)	(iv)	(iii)	(i)	(ii)
(4)	(iii)	(iv)	(ii)	(i)

63. Given below are Assertion (A) and Reason (R). Consider them and select the correct code :

Assertion (A) : In the context of Descarte's philosophy whatever is clear and distinct must necessarily be true.

Reason (R) : Knowledge is constituted of clear and distinct ideas.

Code :

(1) Both (A) and (R) are true and (R) is not the correct explanation of (A).

(2) (A) is true and (R) is false.
(3) (A) is false and (R) is true and (R) is the correct explanation of (A).
(4) Both (A) and (R) are true and (R) is the correct explanation of (A).

64. "Matter is the permanent possibility of sensation". This famous statement is from :
(1) James Mill
(2) John Stuart Mill
(3) Locke
(4) Hume

65. All the following propositions except one are compatible with Leibnitz's Philosophy :
(1) *Monads* are infinitesimal Spiritual entities.
(2) *Monads* are windowless
(3) There is no hierarchy among the *monads*
(4) *Monads* are indiscernible

66. Descartes advocacy of *Interactionism* and Spinoza's *parallelism* undermine :
(1) Monism and dualism
(2) Dualism and pluralism
(3) Dualism and naturalism
(4) Dualism and Pantheism

67. Mark the incompatible with Hume's philosophy :
(1) There is no such thing as causal relation.
(2) The so called self is only an aggregate of mental states
(3) The world and its changes are because of God's supremacy
(4) All that can be known could be divided into *'matters of fact'* and *'relations of ideas'*

68. Match List - I and List - II and choose the correct code :

List - I	List-II
(a) *'Matter is something I know not what'*	(i) Berkeley
(b) *Matter as such does not exist*	(ii) Locke
(c) *What we can know is only the phenomenon*	(iii) Hegel
(d) *'The real is the rational'*	(iv) Kant

Codes :

	(a)	(b)	(c)	(d)
(1)	(i)	(ii)	(iii)	(iv)
(2)	(ii)	(i)	(iv)	(iii)
(3)	(iv)	(iii)	(ii)	(i)
(4)	(iv)	(ii)	(iii)	(i)

69. Consider (a), (b), (c) and (d) and then select the correct answer with reference to Descartes :
(a) Truths of sciences can be doubted.
(b) Sense - testimony can be doubted.
(c) Nothing except the self can be doubted.
(d) Act of doubting cannot be doubted.

Code :
(1) (a) and (b) are only correct.
(2) (a), (b) and (c) are only correct
(3) (a), (b) and (d) are only correct
(4) (b), (c) and (d) are only correct

70. Match List - I with List - II and choose the correct answer with the help of code given below :

List - I	List - II
(a) Berkeley	(i) Interactionism
(b) Spinoza	(ii) Constant Conjunction
(c) Descartes	(iii) Parallelism
(d) Hume	(iv) Subjective Idealism

Codes :

	(a)	(b)	(c)	(d)
(1)	(i)	(iv)	(iii)	(ii)
(2)	(iv)	(iii)	(i)	(ii)
(3)	(iv)	(i)	(iii)	(ii)
(4)	(iv)	(iii)	(ii)	(i)

71. Given below are an Assertion (A) and a Reason (R). Consider them and select the correct code with reference to Locke :

Assertion (A) : According to Locke knowledge depends on the mental power to perceive or apprehend ideas and not in the more receptivity of ideas.

Reason (R) : Knowledge is rational for it consists in seeing the agreement or disagreement between ideas.

Code:

(1) Both (A) and (R) are true and (R) is the correct explanation of (A).
(2) Both (A) and (R) are true and (R) is not the correct explanation of (A).
(3) Both (A) and (R) are false.
(4) (A) is true and (R) is false.

72. Given below are Assertion (A) and Reason (R). Consider them and select the correct code:

Assertion (A) : Hume regards impressions to be the basic touch stone of knowledge.

Reason (R) : With the help of the law of association Hume shows that in causation there is no logical but psychological necessity.

Code:

(1) Both (A) and (R) are false.
(2) Both (A) and (R) are true and (R) gives the correct explanation of (A).
(3) Both (A) and (R) are true and (R) does not give correct explanation of (A).
(4) (A) is true and (R) is false.

73. Given below are Assertion (A) and Reason (R). Consider them and select the correct code with reference to Berkeley:

Assertion (A) : Berkeley, instead of subjectifying things tries to objectify ideas. "I am not for changing things into ideas but rather ideas into things."

Reason (R) : External things are caused by the Supreme Spirit or God who is external to any finite spirits.

Code:

(1) Both (A) and (R) are true and (R) is the correct explanation of (A).
(2) Both (A) and (R) are true and (R) is not the correct explanation of (A).
(3) Both (A) and (R) are false.
(4) (A) is true and (R) is false.

74. Match List - I with List - II and choose the correct answer with the help of code given below:

List - I	List - II
(a) Pantheism	(i) Kant
(b) Dualism	(ii) Spinoza
(c) Transcendental Illusion	(iii) Descartes
(d) Pluralism	(iv) Leibnitz

Codes:

	(a)	(b)	(c)	(d)
(1)	(i)	(ii)	(iv)	(iii)
(2)	(ii)	(i)	(iii)	(iv)
(3)	(ii)	(iii)	(i)	(iv)
(4)	(iii)	(ii)	(iv)	(i)

75. Select the correct option.

The standard of Scientific Knowledge for Kant is:

(1) *Synthetic aposteriori judgement*
(2) *Analytic apriori judgement*
(3) *Synthetic apriori judgement*
(4) *Analytic aposteriori judgement*

76. ăta in Vedic tradition was identified with:

(1) *Satya* only
(2) *Dharma* only
(3) *Karma* only
(4) *Satya* and *Dharma*

77. Select the correct sequence of the states of upanişadic self:

(1) *Suşupti, svapna, Jāgrat, turīya*
(2) *Jāgrat, svapna, suşupti, turīya*
(3) *Jāgrat, suşupti, svapna, turīya*
(4) *turīya, svapna, suşupti, Jāgrat*

78. By what *sannikarşa* do we perceive the relation between a flower and its red colour according to the Nyāya?

(1) *Saṁyoga*
(2) *Samavāya*
(3) *Viśeşanatā*
(4) *Samaveta Samavāya*

79. Which among the following statements is not acceptable to the Cārvāka?

(1) Consciousness is something produced
(2) Consciousness is not real
(3) Consciousness is produced by physical entities
(4) Consciousness must go with the body

80. What type of abhāva of *jñāna* is admitted by the vaiśeşikas in liberated self?

(1) Prāgabhāva
(2) Dhvaṁsābhāva
(3) Atyantābhāva
(4) Anyonyābhāva

81. What is the cause of the knowledge of nearness and farness according to the vaiśeṣikas ?

(1) *Kāla* (2) *Ākāśa*
(3) *Dik* (4) *Manas*

82. By which *pramāṇa* does the Nyāya school prove a state of *nirvikalpaka pratyakṣa* ?

(1) Pratyakṣa (2) Anumāna
(3) Upamāna (4) ìabda

83. Consider the following Assertion (A) and Reason (R) and select the correct code from Vaiśeṣika Standpoint :

Assertion (A) : *Paramāṇu* is not divisible.

Reason (R) : Whatever is not visible is not divisible.

Code :

(1) Both (A) and (R) are true and (R) is the correct explanation of (A).
(2) Both (A) and (R) are true and (R) is not the correct explanation of (A).
(3) (A) is true and (R) is false.
(4) (A) is false and (R) is true.

84. Which among the following is not a means of *vyāptigraha* ?

(1) *Tarka*
(2) *Sāmānyalakṣaṇa pratyakṣa*
(3) *Āptavākya*
(4) *Upādhinirāsa*

85. Which type of *hetvābhāsa* is committed by the following *anumāna* ? Select the correct code :

This animal must be a cow because it possesses horseness.

(1) *Satpratipakṣa*
(2) *Savyabhicāra*
(3) *Viruddha*
(4) *Bādhita*

86. Which one among the following is not a *nityadravya* according to the Vaiśeṣikas ?

(1) *Paramāṇu*
(2) *Dvyaṇuka*
(3) *Manas*
(4) *Dik*

87. Match List - I with List - II and choose the correct answer from the code given below :

List - I	List - II
(a) *Savitarka*	(i) When the *Citta* is concentrated on a subtler object of meditation like the tanmātrās.
(b) *Savicāra*	(ii) When the *Citta* is concentrated on a still subtler object of meditation which produces Joy, like the senses.
(c) *Sānanda*	(iii) When the *Citta* is concentrated on a grass object of meditation.
(d) *Sāsmita*	(iv) When the *Citta* is concentrated on the ego substence with which the self is generally identified.

Codes :

	(a)	(b)	(c)	(d)
(1)	(iii)	(i)	(ii)	(iv)
(2)	(i)	(ii)	(iii)	(iv)
(3)	(ii)	(i)	(iv)	(iii)
(4)	(iv)	(iii)	(ii)	(i)

88. Given below are Assertion (A) and Reason (R). Consider them and select the correct code given below, in the context of Buddhism :

Assertion (A) : *Nirvāṇa* cannot be sufferingless.

Reason (R) : *Sarvaṁ Duhkhaṁ Duhkhaṁ.*

Code :

(1) (A) and (R) both are true and (R) is the correct explanation of (A).
(2) (A) and (R) both are true and (R) is not the correct explanation of (A).
(3) (A) is true and (R) is false
(4) (A) is false and (R) is true

89. Given below are Assertion (A) and Reason (R). Consider them and select the correct code given below, in the context of Buddhism :

Assertion (A) : There is suffering in the world.

Reason (R) : It is not created by us.

Code :

(1) (A) and (R) both are true and (R) is the correct explanation of (A).

(2) (A) and (R) both are true and (R) is not the correct explanation of (A).

(3) (A) is false and (R) is true.

(4) (A) is true and (R) is false.

90. All the following propositions except one are compatible with Prabhākara school of *Pūrva -mīmāmsa* :

(1) Knowledge consists of *triputi*

(2) Advocacy of *Anvitābhidhānavāda*

(3) Advocacy of *Anupalabdhi* as an independent *pramāṇa*

(4) Perceptual error is an act of omission

91. Given below are Assertion (A) and Reason (R). Consider them and select the correct code :

Assertion (A) : In the view of Madhva, Brahman the *mahāvastu* is *ananta-kalyaṇa-guṇaparipūrna.*

Reason (R) : Even an ordinary thing *Sādhāraṇa Vastu* Cannot be without *guṇas*.

Code :

(1) Both (A) and (R) are true but (R) is not the correct explanation of (A).

(2) (A) is true and (R) is false but (R) is not the correct explanation of (A).

(3) (A) is true and (R) is false, but (R) is the correct explanation of (A).

(4) Both (A) and (R) are true and (R) is the correct explanation of (A).

92. Mark the incompatible in view of *Viśiṣòādvaita Vedānta* :

(1) The Means to Mokṣa is *jñāna-karma-Samuchhaya*

(2) *Jīvātmā* is one with Brahman

(3) *Satkhyāti* satisfactorily explains the perceptual error.

(4) *Saptavidha anupapattis* are aimed at the refutation of *Māyā*.

93. Match List - I and List - II and choose the correct code :

List - I	**List - II**
(a) Śaṁkara	(i) *Nityavibhūti*
(b) Rāmānuja	(ii) *Viśeṣa*
(c) Madhva	(iii) *Puṣtimārga*
(d) Vallabha	(iv) *Adhyāsa*

Codes :

	(a)	**(b)**	**(c)**	**(d)**
(1)	(ii)	(iv)	(iii)	(i)
(2)	(iii)	(ii)	(i)	(iv)
(3)	(iv)	(i)	(ii)	(iii)
(4)	(ii)	(iii)	(iv)	(i)

94. Anupalabdhi is an independent *pramāṇa* according to :

(1) Rāmānuja (2) Madhva

(3) Kumārila (4) Prabhākara

95. Which one of the following is not acceptable to *Jain* Philosophy ?

(1) Realistic and relativistic pluralism.

(2) *'Dravya'* and *'Guṇa'* are inseparable.

(3) We can know an object in all its aspects.

(4) *Keval-Jñāna* is unlimited and absolute knowledge.

96. Ambedkar's theory of relation is essentially :

(1) Spiritual (2) Metaphysical

(3) Naturalistic (4) Hermeneutical

97. Which among the following is true regarding K.C. Bhattacharya's two branches of Philosophy of object ?

(1) Ethics and Logic

(2) Religion and Ethics

(3) Logic and Metaphysics

(4) Physics and Metaphysics

98. Given below are the four principles of Existence.

(a) The Super - Cosmic theory

(b) The Cosmic or the Terrestrial

(c) The Supraterrestrial or the other worldly

(d) The integral or the synthetic

Which one of the following philosopher has mentioned in his philosophy ?

(1) Vivekanand

(2) K.C. Bhattacharya

(3) Iqbal

(4) Sri Aurobindo

99. Gandhian View of trusteeship was not designed to :

(1) evolve a new social order

(2) promote love and sacrifice among people

(3) give every opportunity to an individual to rise

(4) apply force to deprive the priviledged class of their wealth

100. Which one of the following pair is correctly matched ?

(Thinkers)	**(Works)**
(1) Sri Aurobindo	- *The Human cycle, Freedom's battle*
(2) Tagore	- *Lover's gift and crossing, My Soul's Agony*
(3) Gandhi	- *The wheel of fortune, Delhi Diary*
(4) Radhakrishnan	- *Religion and Society, Massege From the East*

Answers

1. (3)	**2.** (3)	**3.** (3)	**4.** (4)	**5.** (4)	**6.** (4)	**7.** (2)	**8.** (4)	**9.** (1)	**10.** (1)
11. (3)	**12.** (4)	**13.** (4)	**14.** (4)	**15.** (2)	**16.** (2)	**17.** (2)	**18.** (*)	**19.** (2)	**20.** (3)
21. (3)	**22.** (1)	**23.** (2)	**24.** (2)	**25.** (4)	**26.** (1)	**27.** (3)	**28.** (3)	**29.** (1)	**30.** (2)
31. (3)	**32.** (2)	**33.** (2)	**34.** (4)	**35.** (2)	**36.** (1)	**37.** (4)	**38.** (4)	**39.** (4)	**40.** (1)
41. (3)	**42.** (3)	**43.** (3)	**44.** (3)	**45.** (3)	**46.** (2)	**47.** (3)	**48.** (3)	**49.** (3)	**50.** (1)
51. (3)	**52.** (3)	**53.** (3)	**54.** (3)	**55.** (3)	**56.** (3)	**57.** (1)	**58.** (1)	**59.** (1)	**60.** (1)
61. (1)	**62.** (3)	**63.** (4)	**64.** (3)	**65.** (3)	**66.** (*)	**67.** (3)	**68.** (2)	**69.** (3)	**70.** (2)
71. (*)	**72.** (3)	**73.** (2)	**74.** (3)	**75.** (3)	**76.** (4)	**77.** (2)	**78.** (3)	**79.** (2)	**80.** (2)
81. (3)	**82.** (2)	**83.** (3)	**84.** (3)	**85.** (3)	**86.** (2)	**87.** (1)	**88.** (4)	**89.** (4)	**90.** (3)
91. (4)	**92.** (2)	**93.** (3)	**94.** (3)	**95.** (3)	**96.** (3)	**97.** (3)	**98.** (4)	**99.** (4)	**100.** (3)

* The marks have been awarded to all the Candidates against the question(s)

December, 2019

PHILOSOPHY

PAPER-II

Note : This paper contains **hundred (100)** objective type questions of **two (2)** marks each. **All questions are compulsory**.

1. In vedic tradition Brahmā would be the *Ṛtuika* of
(1) *Ṛtuika* only
(2) *Sāmaveda* only
(3) *Yajurveda* only
(4) *Ṛk. Sāma* and *Yajurveda*

2. In Jaina epistemology the knowledge of past, subtle and distant objects is called:
(1) *Mati* (2) *Manaḥparyāya*
(3) *Avadhi* (4) *Kevala*

3. *Anumāna* according to the Cārvāka CANNOT be a *pramāṇa* because:
(1) *Anumāna* is always incorrect
(2) *Anumāna* is sometimes incorrect
(3) *Anumāna* is dependent on pratyaksa
(4) *Vyāpti* cannot be established

4. Select the correct sequence:
(1) *Tṛṣṇā, upādāna, bhava, jāti*
(2) *Tṛṣṇā, jāti, upādāna, bhava*
(3) *Upādāna, jāti, bhava, tṛṣṇā*
(4) *Tṛṣṇā, upādāna, jāti, bhava*

5. Who holds that colour and the knowledge of it are the same thing?
(1) Vasubhandhu (2) Nāgārjuna
(3) Kumārila (4) Praśastapāda

6. Given below are the four lists of sense organs. Select the option that states the sense organs by all of which we can perceive substances in Nyāya epistemology
(1) Visual sense organ and auditory sense organ
(2) Auditory and tactual sense organ
(3) Visual, auditory and olfactory
(4) Visual, tectual and internal sense-organs

7. In Nyaya epistemology, we perceive a snake in place of a rope by:
(1) *Saṁyoga sannikarṣa*
(2) *Sāmānya lakṣaṇa sannikarṣa*
(3) *Jñānalakṣaṇa sannikarṣa*
(4) *Yogaja sannikarṣa*

8. In Nyāya epistemology which one among the following can be the objects of *sāmānyalakṣaṇa pratyakaṣa* only?
(1) A particular case of smoke
(2) Smokeness
(3) Some cases of smoke
(4) All cases of smoke

9. Which one among the following is NOT a mark of Sathetu in Nyaya epistemology
(1) *Pakṣasattva* (2) *Vipakṣasattva*
(3) *Sapakṣasattva*
(4) *Abādhita Viṣayatva*

10. Given below are some states of affairs. Which one indicates the state of affairs where *anumiti* is not possible according to Nyāya epislomology?
(1) The absence of the will the infer accompanied by the absence of *siddhi*
(2) The absence of the will the infer accompanied by the presence of *siddhi*
(3) The absence of the will the infer accompanied by the *siddhi*
(4) The absence of the will the infer accompanied by the presence of *siddhi*

11. Match List – I with List – II and select the correct answer by using the code given below :

List – I	List – II
a. *Akhyātivāda*	i. Nāgārjuna
b. *Asathyātivāda*	ii. Vasubandhu
c. *Ātmakhyātivāda*	iii. Kumārila
d. *Viparītakhyātivāda*	iv. Prabhākara

Codes :

	(a)	(b)	(c)	(d)		(a)	(b)	(c)	(d)
(1)	i	ii	iii	iv	(2)	ii	i	iii	iv
(3)	iv	i	ii	iii	(4)	iv	ii	i	iii

12. Given below are two statements, one is labelled as **Assertion (A)** and the other is labelled as **Reason (R)**.

(A) *Duyaṇuka* must be eternal

(R) *Duyaṇuka* is made of eternal atoms

Code :

(1) Both (A) and (R) are true and (R) is the correct explanation of (A).

(2) Both (A) and (R) are true and (R) is not the correct explanation of (A).

(3) (A) is true and (R) is false.

(4) (A) is false and (R) is true.

13. Match List – I with List – II and select the correct answer by using the code given below :

List – I	List – II
a. *Pramāṇavyavasthā*	i. Mīmāmsā
b. *Pramāṇasaṁplava*	ii. Cārvāka
c. *Svataphramāṇyavāda*	iii. Bauddha
d. *Svabhāvavāda*	iv. Nyāya

Codes :

	(a)	(b)	(c)	(d)		(a)	(b)	(c)	(d)
(1)	i	ii	iii	iv	(2)	iii	iv	i	ii
(3)	iii	ii	iv	i	(4)	ii	iii	iv	i

14. Match List – I with List – II and select the correct answer by using the code given below :

List – I	List – II
a. *Dehatmavāda*	i. Vaiśeṣika
b. *Ātmadehaprimāṇavāda*	ii. Jain
c. *Nairātmyavāda*	iii. Bauddha
d. *Nitya – ātmāvāda*	iv. Cārvāka

Codes :

	(a)	(b)	(c)	(d)		(a)	(b)	(c)	(d)
(1)	i	ii	iii	iv	(2)	iv	ii	iii	i
(3)	iv	i	ii	iii	(4)	ii	iii	iv	i

15. Given below are some characteristics of God in Vaiśeṣika school.

(a) *Samavāyakaraṇa* of the world

(b) *Nimittakāraṇa* of the world

(c) *Paramātman*

(d) *Nimittakāraṇa* of the Vedas

Choose the correct option:

(1) (a), (b), (c) and (d)

(2) (b), (c) and (d)

(3) (c) and (d)

(4) (a) and (b)

16. "Śabda nitya Cākṣu ṣatvāt". Which type of *hetvābhāsa* is committed by the above inference:

(1) *Sadhāraṇa Savyābhicāra*

(2) *Viruddha*

(3) *Svarūpāsiddha*

(4) *Satpratipakṣa*

17. By which sannikarṣa according to Nyaya do we perceive the relation between a cow and cowness?

(1) *Samavāya*

(2) *Saṁyukta samavāya*

(3) *Saṁyoga*

(4) *Viśeṣaṇata*

18. The view that knowledge lights up the object of knowledge, the subject of knowledge and knowledge itself is supported by the school of:

(1) Bhatta Mīmāmsā

(2) Prabhākara Mīmāmsā

(3) Sāmkhya

(4) Buddhism

19. Arthāpatti is an independent parmāṇa according to:

(1) Ramanuja (2) Śamkara

(3) Madhva

(4) Udayana

20. Which one among the following is not Citta Bhumi as per Yoga philosophy?
(1) Kṣipta (2) Vikṣipta
(3) Niruddha (4) Rāga

21. According to Samkara which one of the following is unacceptable?
(1) The perceptual error is *anirvacaniya*
(2) Brahman is *ananta kalyāna guṇa paripūrṇa*
(3) The means to Mokṣa is jñāna and jñāna alone
(4) The satta of *Jagat* is vyavahārika

22. Select the option having the correct sequence of Aśtanga – mārga.
(1) Samyak *dṛsti*, Samyak samkalpa, Samyak *vāc*, Samayk Karmāntra
(2) Samyak *dṛsti*, Samyak *vāc*, Samyak samkalpa, Samayk Karmāntra
(3) Samyak *dṛsti*, Samyak samkalpa, Samayk Karmāntra, Samyak *vāc*
(4) Samyak samkalpa, Samyak *dṛsti*, Samyak *vāc*, Samayk Karmāntra

23. Which one of the following is NOT acceptable to Aristotle?
(1) Every empirical object is a compound of Form and Matter
(2) Logic consists of syllogism
(3) The doctrine of a causation is a illusion
(4) Oil is potentially present in the oil-seed

24. The doctrine of immortality of soul is upheld by which pair of the following:
(1) Plato and Gorgias
(2) Plato and Socrates
(3) Plato and Protegoras
(4) Plato and AlFarabi

25. Which one of the following philosophical standpoints is acceptable to Plato?
(1) Ideas are illusory
(2) Ideas are perfect and eternal
(3) Ideas change from moment to moment
(4) Ideas are contingent

26. "All knowledge is knowledge through concepts". This is a contention of which of the following philosophers?
(1) Anaximenes
(2) Socrates
(3) Protogoras
(4) Gorgias

27. Match List – I with List – II and select the correct answer by using the code given below :

List – I	List – II
a. Apeiron	i. Thales
b. Water	ii. Anaximander
c. Air	iii. Democritus
d. Atoms	iv. Anaximenes

Codes :

	(a)	(b)	(c)	(d)		(a)	(b)	(c)	(d)
(1)	i	ii	iii	iv	(2)	ii	i	iv	iii
(3)	iii	iv	i	ii	(4)	iv	iii	ii	i

28. Which among the following is acceptable to The Sophists?
(1) Knowledge is objective
(2) Truth is subjective
(3) The good is objective
(4) The beauty is in the object

29. "That is fundamental stuff, which through the process of rarefaction and condensation brings into existence this universe". Whose philosophic conjecture is this?
(1) Socrates
(2) Anaximenes
(3) Pythagoras
(4) Anaxagoras

30. Which on of the following is incompatible with Hegel?
(1) Hegel advocated absolute idealism
(2) Hegel endorsed Kant's agnosticism
(3) Hegel adovated dialectical method
(4) Hegel synthesised the contradictory concepts of being and non-being

31. Given below are two statements, one is labelled as **Assertion (A)** and the other is labelled as **Reason (R)**.
(A) God as world, for Spinoza, is *Natura Naturata*
(R) God is *Natura Naturans*

Code :

(1) Both (A) and (R) are true and (R) is the correct explanation of (A).
(2) Both (A) and (R) are true and (R) is not the correct explanation of (A).
(3) (A) is true and (R) is false.
(4) (A) is false and (R) is true.

32. Which one of the following is NOT a category of Understanding as per Kant?
(1) Unity
(2) Limitation
(3) Affirmation
(4) Cause and Effect

33. Match List – I with List – II and select the correct answer by using the code given below :

List – I	List – II
a. Rejection of Metaphysics	i. Leibnitz
b. Esse Est Percipii	ii. Locke
c. Three Grade of Knowledge	iii. Berkeley
d. Problem of Freedom	iv. Hume

Codes :

	(a)	(b)	(c)	(d)		(a)	(b)	(c)	(d)
(1)	i	iii	iv	ii	(2)	iv	iii	i	ii
(3)	iv	iii	ii	i	(4)	ii	iii	iv	i

34. Match List – I with List – II and select the correct answer by using the code given below :

List – I	List – II
a. Determinatio Nagatio Est	i. Leibnitz
b. Law of Sufficient Reason	ii. Spinoza
c. Subjective Idealism	iii. Kant
d. Transcendental Illusion	iv. Berkeley

Codes :

	(a)	(b)	(c)	(d)		(a)	(b)	(c)	(d)
(1)	i	ii	iv	iii	(2)	ii	i	iii	iv
(3)	ii	i	iv	iii	(4)	i	ii	iii	iv

35. Given below are two statements, one is labelled as **Assertion (A)** and the other is labelled as **Reason (R)**.

(A) Hume is a sceptic
(R) Law of causation is the backbone of Empiricism

Code :

(1) Both (A) and (R) are true and (R) is the correct explanation of (A).
(2) Both (A) and (R) are true and (R) is not the correct explanation of (A).
(3) (A) is true and (R) is false.
(4) (A) is false and (R) is true.

36. Given below are two statements, one is labelled as **Assertion (A)** and the other is labelled as **Reason (R)**.

(A) Monads are windowless
(R) There is pre-established harmony among Monads

Code :

(1) Both (A) and (R) are true and (R) is the correct explanation of (A).
(2) Both (A) and (R) are true and (R) is not the correct explanation of (A).
(3) (A) is true and (R) is false.
(4) (A) is false and (R) is true.

37. Consider the following with reference to Kantian model of scientific judgment

(a) Analytic (b) Apriori
(c) Synthetic (d) Aposteriori

Choose the correct option:
(1) (a) and (b) (2) (c) and (b)
(3) (a) and (d) (4) (c) and (d)

38. The statement , ~ (P ⊃ Q) is equivalent to
(1) P . Q (2) P ∨ Q
(3) P. ~ Q (4) Q ⊃ P

39. Match List – I with List – II and select the correct answer by using the code given below :

List – I	List – II
a. Hume	i. Impression
b. Descrates	ii. Subjective Idealism
c. Berkeley	iii. Representationist
d. Locke	iv. Dualism

Codes :

	(a)	(b)	(c)	(d)		(a)	(b)	(c)	(d)
(1)	i	iv	iii	ii	(2)	i	iv	ii	iii
(3)	i	iii	iv	ii	(4)	i	ii	iii	iv

40. Which one of the following book is authored by Berkeley?

(1) Enquiry concerning Human Understanding
(2) Principle of Human Knowledge
(3) Essay concerning Human Understanding
(4) Phenomenology of Spirit

41. 'Agreement or disagreement of ideas is knowledge' is held by:

(1) Aristotle (2) Locke
(3) Plato (4) Berkeley

42. Which of the following is associated with Spinoza?

(a) Parallelism
(b) Interactionism
(c) Pantheism
(d) Occasionalism

Choose the correct option:

(1) (a) and (b) (2) (d) and (c)
(3) (b) and (c) (4) (a) and (c)

43. Who among the following has said that "the infinite and finite are one as song and singing are one"?

(1) Vivekananad (2) Tagore
(3) Sri Aurobindo (4) Gandhi

44. Match List – I with List – II and select the correct answer by using the code given below :

List – I (Vedic priest)	**List – II (Function)**
a. Hotā	i. Who sings the hymns in sweet musical tones
b. Udgātā	ii. Who addresses hymns in praise of the gods
c. Adhvarya	iii. Who is the general supervisor, well versed in all the vedas
d. Brahma	iv. Who performs the sacrifice according to the strict ritualistic codes

Codes :

	(a)	(b)	(c)	(d)		(a)	(b)	(c)	(d)
(1)	ii	i	iv	iii	(2)	i	ii	iii	iv
(3)	ii	iv	i	iii	(4)	iv	iii	ii	i

45. "The states withers away in the end." Who among the following advocates this?

(1) Isaiah Berlin
(2) Bernard Williams
(3) Rawls
(4) Marx

46. Which one of the following has maintained that moral language is prescriptive?

(1) Ross (2) Moore
(3) Hare (4) Ayer

47. Which one of the following is upheld by Śa ṁ kara?

(1) *Nityānitya vastuviveka*
(2) *Jñānā – karma – samuccaya vāda*
(3) *Bheduvāda*
(4) *Prapañca – nityatavavāda*

48. In which of the following dialogues Plato writes about the Ring of Gyges?

(1) Phaedo
(2) Republic
(3) Crito
(4) Apology

49. Which school/schools among the following upheld the reality of external object in Buddhism?

(1) Mādhyamika only
(2) Yogācāra only
(3) Sautrāntika only
(4) Both Sautrāntika and Vaibhhāṣika

50. Which one of the following is not consistent with 'adṛṣṭ a' according to Nyāya?

(1) The stock of merit and demerit
(2) Unseen power
(3) Unintelligent
(4) Moral governor

51. Which one of the following theories maintains the principles that the severity of punishment should be directly proportional to the seriousness of crime?
(a) Deterrent theory
(b) Retributive theory
(c) Reformative theory
Choose the correct option:
(1) (a) and (b) (2) (c) only
(3) (a) only (4) (b) only

52. Which of the following statements match with emotive theory of ethics?
(a) The function of ethical language is to express feelings
(b) If statements is not verifiable by observation, it is not tautologous
(c) Ethical predicates are factual
Choose the correct option:
(1) (a) only
(2) (b) and (c)
(3) (a) and (c)
(4) (a), (b) and (c)

53. Match List – I with List – II and select the correct answer by using the code given below:

List – I (Author)	List – II (Writings)
a. Spencer	i. Data of Ethics
b. Mackenzie	ii. Metaphysics of Morals
c. Sidgwick	iii. A Manual of Ethics
d. Kant	iv. Methods of Ethics

Codes:

	(a)	(b)	(c)	(d)		(a)	(b)	(c)	(d)
(1)	ii	i	iv	iii	(2)	iii	ii	i	iv
(3)	i	iii	iv	ii	(4)	i	ii	iii	iv

54. Given below are one **Assertion (A)** and a **Reason (R)**. Consider them and select the correct code in the context of *Cārvāka* philosophy.
(A) Reason must be taken as moral standard
(R) Happiness cannot be taken as moral standard
Code:
(1) Both (A) and (R) are true and (R) is the correct explanation of (A).
(2) Both (A) and (R) are true and (R) is not the correct explanation of (A).
(3) (A) is true and (R) is false.
(4) (A) is false and (R) is true.

55. Match List – I with List – II and select the correct answer by using the code given below:

List – I (Author)	List – II (Writing)
a. Sri Aurobindo	i. India Wins Freedom
b. J. Krishnamurti	ii. Hindu View of Life
c. Radhakrishnan	iii. From Darkness to Light
d. Maulana Azad	iv. The Problem of Rebirth

Codes:

	(a)	(b)	(c)	(d)		(a)	(b)	(c)	(d)
(1)	iv	iii	ii	i	(2)	i	iv	iii	ii
(3)	ii	i	iv	iii	(4)	iii	ii	i	iv

56. Match List – I with List – II and select the correct answer by using the code given below:

List – I (Thinker)	List – II (View)
a. K.C. Bhattacharya	i. Māyā is simply a statement of facts
b. Tagore	ii. The region of negation is the region of the Indefinite
c. Vivekananda	iii. World is an ordered whole

d. Radhakrishna	iv. When you deprive truth of its appearances it loses the best part of reality		

Codes :

	(a)	(b)	(c)	(d)		(a)	(b)	(c)	(d)
(1)	i	iii	ii	iv	(2)	iv	i	ii	iii
(3)	iii	i	ii	iv	(4)	ii	iv	i	iii

57. Write correct sequence regarding Sri Aurobindo's concept of triple transformation
(1) Spiritual transformation, Psychic transformation, supramental transformation
(2) Psychic transformation, supramental transformation, Spiritual transformation
(3) Supramental transformation, Psychic transformation, Spiritual transformation
(4) Psychic transformation, supramental transformation, Spiritual transformation

58. Who among the following upholds the concepts of "Gnostic Being"?
(1) J. Krishnamurti
(2) Narayana Guru
(3) D.D. Upadhyaya
(4) Sri Aurobindo

59. Given below are two statements, one is labelled as **Assertion (A)** and the other is labelled as **Reason (R)**.
(A) If one takes care of the means, the end will take care of itself
(R) Ends justify the means
Code :
(1) Both (A) and (R) are true and (R) is the correct explanation of (A).
(2) Both (A) and (R) are true and (R) is not the correct explanation of (A).
(3) (A) is true and (R) is false.
(4) (A) is false and (R) is true.

60. According to K.C. Bhattacharya which one of the following pairs is the branch of philosophy of object?
(1) Logic and Epistemology
(2) Logic and Metaphysics
(3) Logic and Mathematics
(4) Logic and Science

61. Which one of the following is NOT included in 'Vedtrayi'?
(1) Rgveda
(2) Yajurveda
(3) Atharvaveda
(4) Sāmaveda

62. Which one of the following holds the view that "The Civil law alone is the Supreme Court of Appeal in all cases of 'Right' and 'Wrong'?
(1) Mill (2) Hobbes
(3) Descartes (4) Locke

63. The view that "The law is made for the sake of man and not for the sake of the law' represent the criticism of which of the following thinkers?
(1) Moore (2) Hegel
(3) Kant (4) Spencer

64. Who among the following has said that "My religion teaches me that whenever there is distress which cannot be removed one must fast and pray"?
(1) Vivekananda
(2) Gandhi
(3) Tagore (4) Radharkrishnan

65. $P \supset q, q \supset r$ therefore, $p \supset r$ is of the form of:
(1) Modus Tollens
(2) Hypothetical Syllogism
(3) Modus Ponens
(4) Disjunctive Syllogism

66. When a conclusion is drawn from only one premise it is called:
(1) Induction
(2) Immediate Inference
(3) Mediate Inference
(4) Inductive Mediate Inference

67. Which type of argument makes the claim that its conclusion is supported by its premises conclusively?

(1) Inductive
(2) Deductive
(3) Hypothetical Argument
(4) Indirect Proof

68. The characteristic of any deductive argument whose premises if true would provide conclusive grounds for the truth of its conclusion is called:
(1) Implication (2) Truth Value
(3) Validity (4) Modus Ponens

69. (x) (φx): φv (Where v is any individual symbol) is form of:
(1) Universal Generalization
(2) Universal Instantiation
(3) Existential Instantiation
(4) Existential Generalisation

70. Type of immediate inference in which subject and predicate terms are simply interchanged is called:
(1) Conversion (2) Obversion
(3) Contraposition (4) Inversion

71. Choose the correct option for the symbolisation of the following:
All women are brave. Some humans are women. Therefore some humans are brave.

(1) (x) (Wx ⊃ Bx)
(∃x) (Hx . Wx)
∴ (∃x) (Hx . Bx)

(2) (x) (Bx ⊃ Wx)
(∃) (Wx . Hx)
∴ (∃x) (Wx ⊃ Hx)

(3) (x) (Wx ⊃ Bx)
(∃)(Hx ⊃ Wx)
∴ (∃x)(Hx . Bx)

(4) (x) (Wx ⊃ Bx)
(∃x) (Wx ⊃ Hx)
∴ (∃x)(Bx . Hx)

73. According to traditional square of opposition if E is given as false then:
(1) 'I' is false 'A' is undetermined, 'O' is false
(2) 'I' is false, 'A' is undetermined, 'O' is undetermined
(3) 'I' is false, 'A' is true, 'O' is undetermined
(4) 'I' is true, 'A' is undetermined, 'O' is undetermined

73. The law of thought that asserts 'if any statements is true then it is true' is
(1) Principle of Identity
(2) Principle of Non-contradiction
(3) Principle of Excluded middle
(4) Principle of Material Implication

74. Proofs in propositional logic using rules of inference are called
(1) Natural deduction
(2) Rules of Inference
(3) Elementary valid argument
(4) Laws of thought

75. The statement –"war and courage have done greater things than charity" can be attributed to:
(1) Nietzsche (2) John Deway
(3) Sartre (4) Heidegger

76. 'Beetle in the box' analogy/example presented by Wittgenstein in his Philosophical Investigations pertains to:
(1) Fideism
(2) Notion of Philosophy
(3) The picture theory
(4) Critique of Private Language

77. For Sartre treating oneself as a part of facticity alone amounts to:
(1) Being-for-others
(2) Being-for-itself
(3) Bad Faith (4) Humanism

78. The idea of "transvaluation of Values" is propounded by:
(1) Moore (2) Nietzsche
(3) Kierkegaard (4) Sartre

79. Match List – I with List – II and select the correct answer by using the code given below :

List – I	List – II
a. Sartre	i. Fear and Trembling
b. Nietzsche	ii. Being and Nothingness
c. Kierkegaard	iii. Varieties of Religious Experiences
d. William James	iv. Geneology of Morals

Codes :

	(a)	(b)	(c)	(d)		(a)	(b)	(c)	(d)
(1)	ii	i	iv	iii	(2)	ii	iv	i	iii
(3)	iv	ii	i	iii	(4)	iii	ii	i	iv

80. According to Kāmandakīya Nītisāra the term 'trayi' refers to

(1) Bhagvadgīta, Upaniṣadas, Brahmasutras
(2) ṚK, Yajur, Sāma
(3) Smṛtis, Śruti, Upaniṣads
(4) Āraṇyakas, Smṛtis and Upaniṣads

81. According to Kautilya's Arthaśāstra, the authority vested in the King to make law is derived from which of the following sources?

(1) Dharma, Vyavahāra, Charita, Rājaśāsana
(2) Dharma, Vyavastha, Charita, Rājaśāsana
(3) Iśvara, Janaśāsana, Charita, Rājaśāsana
(4) Iśvara, Janapada, Charita, Trayi

82. Which of the following is not enumerated by Kautilya as an essential organ of the State?

(1) Daṇḍa (2) Mitra
(3) Durga (4) Jñānapada

83. To create doubt in the mind of the enemy amounts to which of the following Upayas as mentioned in Arthaśāstra?

(1) Sāma (2) Dāma
(3) Daṇḍa (4) Bheda

84. Which of the following is NOT true of Will Kymlicka's views regarding multiculturalism?

(1) He advances a theory of 'mirror representation'
(2) He seeks to replace the individualistic model of representation by model of group representation
(3) A group should be represented in proportion to its numbers in the population at large
(4) The groups cannot refuse the provision of their separate representation

85. Who among the following feminist thinkers argues that women have been given dependent derivative status as 'the other of man' as the product of her upbringing in society and challenges Freud's dictum 'anatomy is destiny'?

(1) Mary Wollstonecraft
(2) Simone de Beauvoir
(3) Carole Pateman
(4) Betty Friedan

86. Who among the following can be said to have discovered a method of making procedural justice an instrument of meeting the requirement of substantive justice?

(1) Bernard Williams
(2) John Rawls
(3) Robert Nozick
(4) Dworkin

87. Isaiah Berlin associated the idea of negative liberty chiefly with which of the following?

(1) Classical Marxism
(2) Later Marxism
(3) Classical Liberal Tradition
(4) Communitarianism

88. Which of the following ethical principles forms the underlying assumption of Peter Singer's views in Applied Ethics?

(1) Duty for Duty's sake
(2) Golden Mean
(3) Maximum amount of happiness for maximum number of people
(4) Intrinsic value of all objects

89. Which one of the following issues comes under the purview of Business Ethics?

(a) Corporate Moral Agency
(b) Corporate Moral Responsibility
(c) Corporate Social Responsibility
(d) Advertising

Choose the correct option:

(1) Only (b), (c) and (d)
(2) Only (b) and (c)
(3) Only (a), (c) and (d)
(4) All (a), (b), (c) and (d)

90. Which of the following is not true of 'Land Ethic' as propounded by Aldo Leopold?

(1) A Land Ethic can prevent the alteration, management and use of nature and its resources

(2) Land Ethic affirms the right of nature and its resource to continued existence

(3) Land Ethic can changes the role of Homo Sapiens from the conqueror of the land community to plain member and citizen of it

(4) It implies respect for his fellow-members and also respect for the community as such

Question Numbers : (91 to 95)

Question Label: Comprehension

Read the passage below and answer the questions which follow.

The word 'analysis' from the ancient Greek term 'analusis'. The prefix 'ana' means 'up', and 'lusis' means 'loosing', 'release' or 'separation', so that 'analusis' means 'loosening up' or 'dissolution'. The term was readily extended to the solving or dissolving of a problem, and it was in this sense that it was employed is ancient Greek geometry and philosophy. The method of analysis that was developed in ancient Greek geometry had an influence on both Plato and Aristotle. Also important, however, was the influence of Socrates's concern with definition, in which the roots of modern conceptual analysis can be found. What we have in ancient Greek thought, then, is a complex web of methodologies, of which the most important are Socratic definition, which Plato elaborated into his method of division, his related method of hypothesis, which drew on geometrical analysis, and the method(s) that Aristotle developed in his Analytics. Far from a consensus having established itself over the last two millennia, the relationship between these methodologies are the subject of increasing debate today. At the heart of all of them, too, lie the philosophical problems raised by Meno's paradox, which anticipates what we now know as the paradox of analysis, concerning how an theory of recollection, which has spawned a vast literature on its own.

91. Plato's method of hypothesis draws on:

(1) philosophical analysis

(2) ethical analysis

(3) geometrical analysis

(4) physical analysis

92. Socrates' concern with definition led to:

(1) physical analysis

(2) geometrical analysis

(3) mathematical analysis

(4) conceptual analysis

93. Socrates' definition was extended by Plato into:

(1) Meno's paradox

(2) Geometrical analysis

(3) Method of division

(4) Method of science

94. Paradox of analysis relates to

(1) how a line can be extended

(2) how any analysis can be informative

(3) how physics is a science

(4) how recollection is possible

95. Greek thought contains:

(1) A single method of analysis

(2) a complex network of methods

(3) a simple web of methodologies

(4) a rejection of all methods

Question Numbers : (96 to 100)

Question Label: Comprehension

Read the passage below and answer the questions which follow.

One of the philosophic problem that Nāgārjuna raised for epistemology has to do with an alleged regress of justification on the assumption that a pramāna is required in order to know and that to identify the source of a bit of knowledge is to certify the proposition embedded. Nāgārjuna claims that is absurd in that it would require an infinite series of pramāna, of identification of a more fundamental pramāna for every pramāna, relied on, Mimāmasā and Vedānta philosophers argue that such a threat of regress shows that knowledge is self-certifying, svatah prāmāna. Vedāntins connect the Upanishadic teaching of a truest or deepest self (*ātman*) as having "self-illumining awareness" (*sva-prakāśa*) with a Mimamāsā epistemological theory of self-certification: at least in the case of spiritual knowledge (*vidyā*) awareness is self-aware. From this it follows that only awareness is right concerning all questions about awareness, since only awareness itself has, so to say, access to itself. Awareness itself is the only consideration relevant to any question about awareness itself, its existence or its nature.

96. The paragraph above could be considered as a good argument against
   (a) The possibility of cognition
   (b) Possibilities of justification of a piece of cognition
   (c) Illuminative character of knowledge
   (d) Possibilities of absolute foundations of knowledge
   Choose the correct option:
   (1) (a) and (d) (2) (a) and (c)
   (3) (b) and (d) (4) (b) and (c)

97. The difficulty pointed out by the mimāsakas with reference to pratah pramanyavāda is:
   (1) *Anavastha* (2) *Cakraka*
   (3) *Kūtabhāsa* (4) *Savyabhicāra*

98. Which of the following is the counterpart of infinite regress in Indian Philosophy?
   (1) Cakraka doṣa
   (2) Anavasthā doṣa
   (3) Anyonya asraya doṣa
   (4) Atmāṣraya doṣa

99. What following from svatha pramāṇ yatā of knowledge
   (1) Cognition turns into awareness through another act of awareness
   (2) Awareness of cognition is a matter of inference
   (3) Cognition comes along with the awareness by the very nature of its being
   (4) Awareness of cognition is always a second order activity

100. What CANNOT be reasonably taken to follow from the given passage?
   (1) All awareness is self-awareness according to Mimāmsā and Vedānta
   (2) Things are devoid of existence
   (3) There can be no ultimate justification for any knowledge claim
   (4) Reflexivity is an ineluctable part of any awareness

Answers

1. (4)	2. (3)	3. (4)	4. (1)	5. (1)	6. (4)	7. (3)	8. (4)	9. (2)	10. (2)
11. (3)	12. (4)	13. (2)	14. (2)	15. (2)	16. (3)	17. (4)	18. (2)	19. (2)	20. (4)
21. (2)	22. (1)	23. (3)	24. (2)	25. (2)	26. (2)	27. (2)	28. (2)	29. (2)	30. (2)
31. (2)	32. (3)	33. (3)	34. (3)	35. (3)	36. (2)	37. (2)	38. (3)	39. (2)	40. (2)
41. (2)	42. (4)	43. (2)	44. (1)	45. (4)	46. (3)	47. (1)	48. (2)	49. (4)	50. (4)
51. (4)	52. (1)	53. (3)	54. (2)	55. (1)	56. (4)	57. (4)	58. (4)	59. (2)	60. (2)
61. (3)	62. (2)	63. (3)	64. (2)	65. (2)	66. (2)	67. (2)	68. (3)	69. (2)	70. (1)
71. (1)	72. (4)	73. (1)	74. (1)	75. (1)	76. (4)	77. (3)	78. (2)	79. (2)	80. (2)
81. (1)	82. (4)	83. (4)	84. (4)	85. (2)	86. (2)	87. (3)	88. (3)	89. (4)	90. (1)
91. (3)	92. (4)	93. (3)	94. (2)	95. (2)	96. (3)	97. (1)	98. (2)	99. (3)	100. (2)

September, 2020

PHILOSOPHY

PAPER-II

Note : This paper contains **hundred (100)** objective type questions of **two (2)** marks each. **All** questions are **compulsory**.

1. In Vedic tradition, the controlling power of the cosmos is:
   (1) *Iṣvara* (2) *Brahman*
   (3) *Ṛta* (4) *Brahmā*
2. Which one among the following is NOT a mark of a *sat hetu* in Nyāya epistemology?
   (1) *Paksasattva* (2) *Sapakṣa Sattva*
   (3) *Vipakṣa Sattva* (4) *Abādhita viṣayatva*
3. In Nyāya epistemology, we perceive by *sāmānyalakṣaṇa sannikarṣa*:
   (1) A particular instance of fire
   (2) Some instances of fire
   (3) Fireness
   (4) All the instances of fire
4. Select the code correctly matched in terms of magnitude *(Parimāṇa)* of *dravyas* in Vaiśeṣika metaphysics:
   (1) *Ākaśa, kāla, ātmā*
   (2) *Ākaśa, kāla, manas*
   (3) *Kāla, parmāṇu, dik*
   (4) *Manas, ātmā, dik*
5. In Vedic tradition, *yajña* is performed for the benefit of:
   (1) *Devatā* (2) *Ṛṣis*
   (3) *Ṛtvika* (4) *Yajmāna*
6. Which one in jaina metaphysics is NOT an *ajiva dravya?*
   (1) *Ākaśa* (2) *Sthāvara*
   (3) *Pudgala* (4) *Dharma*
7. Given below are two statements, one is labelled as **Assertion (A)** and the other is labelled as **Reason (R)**.
   (A) God does not suffer
   (R) God lacks body
   Code:
   (1) Both (A) and (R) are true and (R) is the correct explanation of (A).
   (2) Both (A) and (R) are true and (R) is not the correct explanation of (A).
   (3) (A) is true and (R) is false.
   (4) (A) is false and (R) is true.
8. Who hold's that, a shade of blue colour and the knowledge of it is one and same thing?
   (1) Vasubandhu (2) Nagarjuna
   (3) *Kumārila* (4) *Praśastapāda*
9. Dialogue regarding 'Sreyas and Preyas' was held between
   (1) Prajapati and Indra
   (2) Virochan and Prajāpati
   (3) Yama and Nachiketā
   (4) Yājñavalkya and Maitreyi
10. Which one of the following is false regarding 'Apūrva'?
    (1) *Apūrva* can sustain the world
    (2) *Apūrva* is the link between the act and its fruit
    (3) *Apūrva* is the casual potency in the act
    (4) *Apūrva* is produced in the soul of the agent
11. Fire is cold because it is a substance. Which type of fallacy is committed by the above inference?
    (1) *Savyabhicāra* (2) *Visuddha*
    (3) *Asiddha* (4) *Bādhita*

12. Who among the following upheld the view that a smaller present-good is not to be preferred to a greater future good?
(1) Sidgwik (2) Hobbes
(3) Spencer (4) Kant

13. The view that the law is made for the sake of man not for the sake of law, is upheld by:
(1) Kant (2) Mackenzie
(3) Jacobi (4) Spencer

14. Who among the following holds the view that Science is literal thought, but Philosophy is symbolic thinking?
(1) J. Krishnamurti
(2) M.N. Roy
(3) K.C. Bhattacharya
(4) Maulana Azad

15. Which one of the following codes states the virtues which are not consistent with *Brahmāṇa Varṇa*?
(1) Tranquillity, Austerities
(2) Purity, Forgiveness
(3) Sense control, Wisdom
(4) Heroism, Sovereignity

16. Which one of the following assertions is **false**?
(1) A false proposition implies any proposition whatsoever
(2) A true proposition is implied by any proposition whatsoever
(3) A propositional function is either true or false
(4) Singular proposition does not require instantiation

17. Which one of the following assertions is false?
(1) '~' (negation) is a binary truth-functional operator
(2) 'Inductive leap' makes the conclusion of an inductive argument probable
(3) Boolean interpretation accepts only the contradictory square of opposition of propositions
(4) Truth-table is a decision procedure.

18. Which one of the following is the correct symbolic representation of the sentence below:
We shall swim even if it rains
[where W = We shall swim and R = it rains]
(1) $R \supset S$ (2) $S \supset (R \vee \sim R)$
(3) $(R \vee \sim R) \supset S$ (4) $(R . \sim R) \supset S$

19. Which one of the following issues do not directly pertain to the domain of Medical ethics?
(a) Consent to treatment and duty to treat
(b) Truth-telling
(c) Paternalism
(d) Confidentiality
(e) Advertising of medical drugs and other medical products
Choose the correct option:
(1) (a), (b), (d) and (e)
(2) (a), (c) and (e)
(3) (a), (b), (c), (d) and (e)
(4) (a), (b), (c) and (d)

20. Which one of the following statements is true according to Hume?
(1) A statement is true if it is verifiable
(2) Only knowledge concerning the matters of fact is impossible
(3) Metaphysical statements are meaningless
(4) Casual relation is based on constant conjunction

21. Who holds the view that 'all knowledge is, knowledge through concepts'?
(1) Anaximander (2) Anaximenes
(3) Protagoras (4) Socrates

22. 'Matter is something, I know not what'
This view is attributed to which one of the following?
(1) Berkeley and Descartes
(2) Spinoza and David Hume
(3) Locke only
(4) Descartes and Locke

23. What is Aristotle's correct description of God?

(1) Pure matter and pure potentiality
(2) Pure matter and pure actuality
(3) Pure form and pure actuality
(4) Pure form and pure potentiality

24. Which one of the following is acceptable to David Hume?
(1) Causality is a category of human understanding
(2) Causality is a form of uniformity of nature
(3) Causality is necessary relation between cause and effect
(4) Causality is merely a habit of mind

25. Which one of the followings is compatible with Spinoza's philosophy
(1) Agnosticism
(2) Atheism
(3) Pantheism
(4) Theism

26. Those philosophers who subscribe to the view that the silver that appears in a shell is neither real nor unreal?
(1) Viśiṣṭādvaitins
(2) Śunyavādins
(3) Sāṁkhyas
(4) Advaitins

27. Who are the philosophers who hold that cloth is something new, created out of threads?
(1) Advaitinīs (2) Mīmāṁsakas
(3) Naiyāyikas (4) Sāṁkhyans

28. The philosophical phrase: 'Identity of indiscernibles' is associated with
(1) Locke (2) Leibnitz
(3) Descartes (4) David Hume

29. According to which system, the right way to kaivalya is Puruṣa-prakṛti viveka jñāna?
(1) Pūrva-Mīmamsa
(2) Nyāya
(3) Sāṁkhya
(4) Vaiśesika

30. In Jaina epistemology, the knowledge of past, subtle and distant object is called:
(1) Mati (2) Kevala
(3) Sruta (4) Avadhi

31. Which one of the following is incompatible with the views of Sartre?
(1) Morality is objective
(2) The meaning of life depends on the life we build up
(3) Reflective consciousness can be treated as moral consciousness
(4) Man is responsible for his actions

32. Which one of the following is incorrect with reference to Wittgenstein?
(1) Private language is not possible
(2) Don't ask for the meaning, but better to ask for the use language
(3) Just like there are different language games; there are different forms of life
(4) Religion is a faith based on the existence of God

33. Which one of the following is incompatible with the views of Quine?
(1) Ontology is relative
(2) There is no role of dogmas in philosophy
(3) Traditional epistemology is the foundation of naturalized epistemology
(4) Translation is always indeterminate

34. Which one of the following involves Category mistake according to G.Ryle?
(1) The cat is on the chair
(2) The child of a barren woman
(3) The University of Delhi contains various departments
(4) Saturday is on the bed

35. Identify which one of the following goes against Frege?
(1) The term 'sense' means 'mode of presentation'.
(2) Thought is neither physical, nor mental; it is something else
(3) Frege's semantics is based on concept-notation
(4) Thought is at par with Idea.

36. The Bhātta Mīmāmsakas advocate which one of the following theories?
(1) *Anvitābhidhāna vāda*
(2) *Abhihitānvaya vāda*
(3) *Apohavāda*
(4) *Sphoṭavāda*

37. Which one of the following statements refers to the coherence theory of truth?
(1) A proposition is true if it conforms to fact
(2) A proposition is true if it results in success
(3) A proposition is true if it does not contradict the accepted proposition
(4) A proposition is true or false by virtue of its own structure

38. Who holds the view that 'Man without society is either a beast or a god'?
(1) Russell (2) Marx
(3) John Locke (4) Aristotle

39. Which one of the following is acceptable to David Hume?
(1) Sensationalism
(2) Parallelism of Mind and Matter
(3) Materialism
(4) Spiritualism

40. Which one of the following doctrines is incompatible with Spinoza?
(1) Parallelism of attributes
(2) Pre-established harmony
(3) Determinism
(4) Natura – *Naturans*

41. According to Nyāya epistemology, we perceive by tectual sense-organ all the objects which we perceive by the visual sense-organ, except;
(a) Sparśatva
(b) Rūpatva
(c) Rūpa
(d) Sparśa
Choose the correct option:
(1) (a) only (2) (b) and (a)
(3) (c) only (4) (b) and (c)

42. According to the Nyāya epistemology, we can perceive external substances by:
(a) Visual sense-organ
(b) Tectual sense-organ
(c) Internal sense-organ
(d) Gustatory sense-organ
Choose the correct option:
(1) (a) only
(2) (b) only
(3) (a) and (b) only
(4) (b) and (c) only

43. Given below are some conditions of anumiti in accordance with the Nyāya epistemology. Select the code which states the conditions where anumiti (inference) is NOT possible?
(a) The absence of will to infer accompanied by siddhi
(b) The absence of will to infer accompanied by he absence of siddhi
(c) The presence of will to infer accompanied by siddhi
(d) The presence of will to infer accompanied by absence of siddhi
Choose the correct option:
(1) (a) only
(2) (a) and (b) only
(3) (a) and (c) only
(4) (b) and (c) only

44. Śakti according to Nyāya is:
(a) *Iśvarecchā*
(b) *Icchāmātra*
(c) *A Vṛitti*
(d) *A separate padārtha*
Choose the correct option:
(1) (a) only
(2) (a) and (b) only
(3) (a), (b) and (c)
(4) (a), (b), (c) and (d)

45. Who among the following admits both *jāvanmukti* and *videhamukti*?
(a) Buddha (b) *Śaṅkara*
(c) *Rāmānuja* (d) Madhava

Choose the correct option:
(1) (a) only
(2) (a) and (b) only
(3) (a), (b) and (c)
(4) (a), (b), (c) and (d)

46. Which of the following combinations are the trinity principles espoused by Dr. Ambedkar?
(a) Liberty, Equality and Truth
(b) Liberty, Fraternity and Peace
(c) Liberty, Equality, and Fraternity
(d) Liberty, Fraternity and Solidarity
Choose the correct option:
(1) (a) only (2) (d) only
(3) (b) only (4) (c) only

47. Which of the following propositions are compatible with Thales?
(a) Air is the fundamental source of the universe
(b) Number is the fundamental source of the Universe
(c) Water is the fundamental source of the Universe
(d) Earth is a flat disc that floats on water
Choose the correct option:
(1) (a) only (2) (b) only
(3) (b) and (d) (4) (c) and (d)

48. Which of the following propositions are acceptable to Berkeley?
(a) Perceived entities exist
(b) Unperceived entities exist
(c) Self is but the substratum of a bundle of sensations
(d) matter invariably exists
Choose the correct option:
(1) (b) only
(2) (d) only
(3) (b) and (c) only
(4) (a) and (c) only

49. Which of following propositions are NOT acceptable to Haraclitus?
(a) Being consists of nothing but Being
(b) One cannot step into the river twice
(c) Being passes into Not-Being and Not-Being into Being
(d) Apeiron is the fundamental stuff of the universe
Choose the correct option:
(1) (a) and (b) (2) (b) and (b)
(3) (a) and (c) (4) (a) and (d)

50. Which of the following are the stages of subjectivity according to K.C. Bhattacharya?
(a) Bodily
(b) Psychic
(c) Spiritual
(d) Biological
Choose the correct option:
(1) (a) and (b)
(2) (b) and (c)
(3) (a), (b) and (c)
(4) (b), (c) and (d)

51. Which one of the following is correct?
(a) Gandhi is the author of *Sādhanā*
(b) Sri Aurobindo is the author of *Personality*
(c) Radhakrishnan is the author of *Freedom and Culture*
(d) Tagore is the author or *Dhammapada*
Choose the correct option:
(1) (a) only (2) (b) only
(3) (c) only (4) (d) only

52. *Anupalabdhi* is an independent *Pramāna* that is advocated by which philosopher?
(a) Prabhākara
(b) Śaṁkara
(c) Rāmānuja and Madhva
(d) Kumārila
Choose the correct option:
(1) (a) only (2) (c) only
(3) (a) and (c) (4) (b) and (d)

53. 'Reason grows into revelation and the two are not opposed to each other'
Who among the following totally rejects this view?
(a) F.H. Bradley
(b) St Thomas Aquinas

(c) St Augustine
(d) Henri Bergson
Choose the correct option:
(1) (a) and (d) (2) (a) and (b)
(3) (b) and (c) (4) (d) only

54. A real proper name is singular, placed only in the subject position of a subject-predicate proposition and it stands for an object. Who holds this view?
(a) Mill
(b) Russell
(c) Frege
(d) Wittgentein
Choose the correct option:
(1) (a) only (2) (b) only
(3) (a) and (b) (4) (b) and (c)

55. According to whom since ordinary language is ambiguous, ideal, or artificial, language needs to be formulated for showing the relationship between language and reality?
(a) Russell (b) Frege
(c) Austin (d) Ryle
Choose the correct option:
(1) (a) only (2) (a) and (d)
(3) (a) and (c) (4) (a) and (b)

56. Which of the following statements is NOT true according to Aristotle?
(1) Form and matter are relative in terms
(2) Matter is potentiality, form is actuality
(3) Formless matter exists
(4) Matterless form is real

57. Which one of the following is compatible with Plato's views?
(1) Ideas are not real but existent
(2) Ideas are real but existent
(3) Ideas are doubtful but existent
(4) Ideas are doubtful but no-existent

58. According to Mohammad Iqbal, which of the following are true of humans?
(a) Humans are instantiated from a universal super-ego.
(b) Humans have evolved from a Universal intellect
(c) Humans are divinely created
(d) Humans have evolved from Spirit
(e) Humans have evolved from matter
Choose the correct option:
(1) (a) and (b) (2) (b), (c) and (d)
(3) (c) and (e) (4) (a) and (d)

59. Which one of the following thinkers maintains that freedom lies in pure observation?
(1) Jiddu Krishnamurty
(2) Sri Aurbindo
(3) Narayan Guru
(4) Radhakrishna

60. J L Austin makes a distinction between which of the following speech acts?
(a) Protocutionary
(b) Locutionary
(c) Illocutionary
(d) Mislocutionary
(e) Perlocutionary
Choose the correct option:
(1) (c), (d) and (e) (2) (b), (c) and (e)
(3) (a), (b) and (d) (4) (a), (c) and (d)

61. The field of Applied Ethics concerning the conflict between the interest of stakeholders and the interest of stockholder most appropriately pertains to:
(1) Business Ethics
(2) Bio-ethics
(3) Media-ethics
(4) Ethics of Technology

62. Charles Taylor makes a distinction between which of the following?
(a) Politics of dignity
(b) Politics of difference
(c) Politics of gender
(d) Politics of entitlement
(e) Politics of distribution
Choose the correct option:
(1) (d) and (e) only (2) (a) and (b) only
(3) (c) and (e) only (4) (a) and (d) only

63. The ethical claim in business ethics that deceptive advertising is wrong because deceiving others is disrespectful to them and uses them as mere means, pertains to:

(1) Kant's deotological ethics
(2) Virtue ethics
(3) Rule-utilitarianism
(4) Act-utilitarianism

64. The question regarding what might constitute criteria necessary for personhood is most central with reference to:

(1) Abortion
(2) Active Euthanasia
(3) Passive Euthanasia
(4) Eugenics

65. In the ethics of Technology, the notion that technology is only instrument, the good or bad use of which depends on its users and technology is not good or bad in itself, is known as:

(1) User's dilemma
(2) Dichotomy of the doer and deed
(3) Neutrality thesis
(4) Ethics of instrumentality

66. Match List – I with List – II and select the correct answer by using the code given below :

List – I	List – II
a. *Veda*	i. Fire burns out of its own nature
b. *Cārvāka*	ii. Fire burns because of ṛta
c. *Mīmāṁsaka*	iii. Fire burns because of its burning power (*dāhikā śakti*) which is a separate padartha
d. *Vaiśeṣika*	iv. Fire is a physical substance

Codes :

	(a)	(b)	(c)	(d)		(a)	(b)	(c)	(d)
(1)	iii	iv	ii	i	(2)	ii	i	iii	iv
(3)	i	ii	iv	iii	(4)	iv	iii	ii	i

67. Match List – I with List – II and select the correct answer by using the code given below :

List – I	List – II
a. Jnatatavada	i. Prabhakara
b. Triputipratayksavada	ii. Kumarila
c. Dvaitavada	iii. Madhva
d. Bhedanbhedavada	iv. Nimbarka

Codes :

	(a)	(b)	(c)	(d)		(a)	(b)	(c)	(d)
(1)	ii	i	iii	iv	(2)	i	ii	iii	iv
(3)	ii	iii	i	iv	(4)	iii	ii	i	iv

68. Match List – I with List – II and select the correct answer by using the code given below :

List – I	List – II
a. The state of nature was one in which there were no enforceable criteria of right and wrong	i. Locke
b. The state of nature was one in which the right of life and property were generally recognized under natural law	ii. Rousseau
c. In the state of nature, humans were unwarlike and somewhat undeveloped in their reasoning, morality and responsibility	iii. Hobbes
d. Justice consists of the basic principle of government that free and rational individuals would agree to in a hypothetical situation perfect equality	iv. John Rawls

Codes :

	(a)	(b)	(c)	(d)		(a)	(b)	(c)	(d)
(1)	ii	iii	i	iv	(2)	iii	ii	i	iv
(3)	i	iii	ii	iv	(4)	iii	i	ii	iv

69. Match List – I with List – II and select the correct answer by using the code given below :

List – I	List – II
a. Bheda dhikkāra	i. Madhva
b. Bhedā satākra	ii. Sankara
c. Acintyabhedābheda	iii. Rāmānuja
d. Apṛthak Siddhi	iv. Chaitanya-Baladeva

Codes :

	(a)	(b)	(c)	(d)		(a)	(b)	(c)	(d)
(1)	i	ii	iii	iv	(2)	ii	i	iv	iii
(3)	iv	iii	i	ii	(4)	iii	iv	ii	i

70. Match List – I with List – II and select the correct answer by using the code given below :

List – I	List – II
a. *Śamkara*	i. *Jñāna - karma - Samuççhayavāda*
b. *Rāmānuja*	ii. *Jnāña and jñāna alone*
c. Madhva	iii. *Puṣti mārga*
d. Vallabha	iv. *Nirmala Bhakti*

Codes :

	(a)	(b)	(c)	(d)		(a)	(b)	(c)	(d)
(1)	i	ii	iii	iv	(2)	ii	i	iv	iii
(3)	iv	iii	ii	i	(4)	iii	iv	i	ii

71. Match List – I with List – II and select the correct answer by using the code given below :

List – I	List – II
a. Subjective idealism	i. Bosanquet
b. Realism	ii. Berkeley
c. Objective Idealism	iii. Kant
d. Critical philosophy	iv. Locke

Codes :

	(a)	(b)	(c)	(d)		(a)	(b)	(c)	(d)
(1)	ii	iv	i	iii	(2)	iv	ii	iii	i
(3)	i	ii	iv	iii	(4)	iii	ii	i	iv

72. Match List – I with List – II and select the correct answer by using the code given below :

List – I	List – II
a. Leucippus and Democritus	i. The *City of God*
b. St. Augustine	ii. Five proofs for the existence of god
c. St. Thomas Aquinas	iii. Ontological Argument
d. St. Anselm	iv. Atomic theory

Codes :

	(a)	(b)	(c)	(d)		(a)	(b)	(c)	(d)
(1)	ii	iii	iv	i	(2)	iv	i	ii	iii
(3)	ii	iii	i	iv	(4)	i	ii	iii	iv

73. Match List – I with List – II and select the correct answer by using the code given below :

List – I	List – II
a. Tagore	i. One must work like master and not like slave
b. Iqbal	ii. What is spoken must be in the first instance believed
c. Vivekananda	iii. The world for me is both individual and universal
d. K.C. Bhattacharya	iv. Body is accumulated action or habit of the self

Codes :

	(a)	(b)	(c)	(d)		(a)	(b)	(c)	(d)
(1)	ii	iii	i	iv	(2)	iii	iv	i	ii
(3)	iv	i	iii	ii	(4)	i	ii	iv	iii

74. Match List – I with List – II and select the correct answer by using the code given below :

List – I	List – II
a. $P \equiv q$	i. $(p \cdot q) \cdot r$
b. $\sim(p \supset q)$	ii. $(p \supset r) \cdot (q \supset r)$
c. $p \cdot (q \cdot r)$	iii. $(p \cdot q) \vee (\sim p \cdot \sim q)$
d. $(p \vee q) \supset r$	iv. $p \cdot \sim q$

Codes :

	(a)	(b)	(c)	(d)		(a)	(b)	(c)	(d)
(1)	iii	ii	i	iv	(2)	ii	iv	i	iii
(3)	i	iii	iv	ii	(4)	iii	iv	i	ii

75. Match List – I with List – II and select the correct answer by using the code given below :

List – I	List – II
a. Vivekananda	i. Creations is the 'Lila' of the creator
b. K.C. Bhattacharya	ii. Reality is one but not a 'whole'
c. Tagore	iii. Philosophy is the self-evident elaboration of the self-evident
d. Iqbal	iv. Intuitive experience is knowing by being

Codes :

	(a)	(b)	(c)	(d)		(a)	(b)	(c)	(d)
(1)	i	ii	iv	iii	(2)	iv	i	iii	ii
(3)	ii	iii	i	iv	(4)	iii	i	iv	ii

76. Arrange the following in the correct sequence for yoga *Samadhi*

(a) *Sānanda* (b) *Sāsmita*
(c) *Savitārka* (d) *Savicāra*

Choose the correct option:
(1) (a), (b), (c), (d)
(2) (c), (d), (b), (a)
(3) (c), (d), (a), (b)
(4) (b), (c), (d), (a)

77. Arrange the following in the correct sequence with reference to Buddhism

(a) *Nāma-rūpa* (b) *Shadayatana*
(c) *Vijñāna* (d) *Vedanā*
(e) *Sparś*

Choose the correct option:
(1) (a), (b), (d), (c), (e)
(2) (c), (a), (b), (e), (d)
(3) (c), (b), (d), (e), (a)
(4) (a), (d), (c), (b), (e)

78. Select the correct sequence with reference to yoga system

(a) *Niyama* (b) *Prāṇāyāma*
(c) *Yama* (d) *Āsana*
(e) *Pratyāhāra*

Choose the correct option:
(1) (a), (b), (d), (e), (c)
(2) (c), (d), (e), (a), (b)
(3) (c), (a), (d), (b), (e)
(4) (c), (a), (e), (b), (d)

79. Select the correct sequence according to jainism

(a) *Syadnāsti*
(b) *Syādāsti nāstica*
(c) *Syādavaklāvyam*
(d) *Syādāsti ca avaklāyam ca*
(e) *Syādāsti*

Choose the correct option:
(1) (a), (b), (c), (d), (e)
(2) (e), (a), (b), (d), (c)
(3) (e), (a), (b), (c), (d)
(4) (e), (c), (d), (a), (b)

80. Arrange the following processes in sequence as per Sri Aurobindo's Theory of Evolution

(a) Heightening
(b) Widening
(c) Integration

Choose the correct option:
(1) (a), (b), (c) (2) (c), (b), (a)
(3) (b), (c), (a) (4) (b), (a), (c)

81. Which of the following expresses a correct sequence with reference to Buddhism?

(a) Animilta-samādhi, Apraṇihita-samādhi, Shūnyalā-samādhi
(b) Apraṇihita-samādhi, Shūnyalā-samādhi, Animilta-samādhi
(c) Shūnyalā-samādhi, Animilta-samādhi, Apraṇihita-samādhi

(d) Shūnyalā-samādhi, Apraṇihita-samādhi, Animilta-samādhi

Choose the correct option:

(1) (a) only (2) (d) only
(3) (b) only (4) (c) only

82. Arrange the following stages of acquiring Moksha as per Dvaita Vedanta in the correct sequence

(a) Sārūpya, Sārūpya, Sāmīpya, Sālokya
(b) Sālokya, Sāmīpya, Sārūpya, Sārūpya
(c) Sāmeepya, Sālokya, Sārūpya, Sārūpya
(d) Sālokya, Sārūpya, Sārūpya, Sāmīpya

Choose the correct option:

(1) (a) only (2) (b) only
(3) (c) only (4) (d) only

83. In the practical teaching of the Upaniṣads, what is the correct sequence of the three orders of knowing?

(a) *Manana, Śravaṇa, nididhyāsana*
(b) *Śravaṇa, Manana, nididhyāsana*
(c) *Manana, nididhyāsana, Śravaṇa*
(d) *Śravaṇa, nididhyāsana, Manana*

Choose the correct option:

(1) (a) only (2) (b) only
(3) (c) only (4) (d) only

84. Arrange the following types of ignorances, as per Sri Aurbindo, in the correct sequence

(a) Original Ignorance, Cosmic ignorance, Egoistic ignorance, Temporal ignorance
(b) Original Ignorance, Egoistic ignorance, Cosmic ignorance, Temporal ignorance
(c) Original Ignorance, Temporal ignorance, Cosmic ignorance, Egoistic ignorance
(d) Egoistic ignorance, Cosmic ignorance, Original Ignorance, Temporal ignorance,

Choose the correct option:

(1) (a) only (2) (b) only
(3) (c) only (4) (d) only

85. The problem of Universals was first introduced into Philosophy by

(1) Acquinas (2) Aristotle
(3) Plato (4) Berkeley

86. Given below are two statements, one is labelled as **Assertion (A)** and the other is labelled as **Reason (R)**.

In the light of Bhagvadgītā

(A) True renunciation is the renunciation of fruits of all actions
(R) Fruits of actions stand in the way to renunciation

Code:

(1) Both (A) and (R) are true and (R) is the correct explanation of (A).
(2) Both (A) and (R) are true and (R) is not the correct explanation of (A).
(3) (A) is true and (R) is false.
(4) (A) is false and (R) is true.

87. Given below are two statements, one is labelled as **Assertion (A)** and the other is labelled as **Reason (R)**.

(A) In case of a valid deductive argument, the conclusion is logically deduced from the given premise(s)
(R) The conclusion is not formally contained in the premise(s)

Code:

(1) Both (A) and (R) are true and (R) is the correct explanation of (A).
(2) Both (A) and (R) are true and (R) is not the correct explanation of (A).
(3) (A) is true and (R) is false.
(4) (A) is false and (R) is true.

88. Given below are two statements, one is labelled as **Assertion (A)** and the other is labelled as **Reason (R)**.

(A) According to Advaita Vedanta, Brahman is indeterminate
(R) The intellect cannot possibly grasp it, but only point to it

Code:

(1) Both (A) and (R) are true and (R) is the correct explanation of (A).
(2) Both (A) and (R) are true and (R) is not the correct explanation of (A).

(3) (A) is true and (R) is false.
(4) (A) is false and (R) is true.

89. Given below are two statements, one is labelled as **Assertion (A)** and the other is labelled as **Reason (R)**.

(A) In Rāmānuja, monism and theism are succinctly harmonized

(R) Harmonisation is not at the cost of philosophical argumentation

Code:

(1) Both (A) and (R) are true and (R) is the correct explanation of (A).
(2) Both (A) and (R) are true and (R) is not the correct explanation of (A).
(3) (A) is true and (R) is false.
(4) (A) is false and (R) is true.

90. Given below are two statements, one is labelled as **Assertion (A)** and the other is labelled as **Reason (R)**.

(A) The concept of Nirguna Brahman seems to be neutral to the demands of religious feeling

(R) Religious feelings and logical thinking cannot go together

Code:

(1) Both (A) and (R) are true and (R) is the correct explanation of (A).
(2) Both (A) and (R) are true and (R) is not the correct explanation of (A).
(3) (A) is true and (R) is false.
(4) (A) is false and (R) is true.

Question Numbers: (91 to 95)

Question Label: Comprehension

Read the given passage carefully and answer the questions that follow

...although different people may see the table slightly differently, still they all see more or less similar things when they look at the table, and the variations in what they see follow the laws of perspective and reflection of light, so that it is easy to arrive at a permanent object underlying all the different people's sense-data...Thus it is the fact that different people have similar sense-data, which makes us suppose that over and above the sense-data there is a permanent public object which underlies or causes the sense-data of various people at various times.

Now in so far as the above considerations depend upon supposing that there are other people besides ourselves, they beg the very question at issue. Other people are represented to me by certain sense-data, such as the sight of them or the sound of their voices, and if I had no reason to believe that there were physical objects independent of my sense-data, I should have no reason to believe that other people exist except as part of my dream. Thus, we are trying to show that there must be objects independent of our own sense-data, we cannot appeal to the testimony of other people, since this testimony itself consists of sense-data.

91. The second paragraph of the above passage draws upon:

(1) Idealism (2) Realism
(3) Solipsism (4) Relativism

92. First paragraph of the above passage makes a case for which of the following?

(1) Idealism (2) Realism
(3) Solipsism (4) Relativism

93. Which of the following is/are included in the reason offered to prove the existence of the external world in the given passage?

(a) Testimony of other people
(b) The similarity in sense data in similar conditions
(c) The variations in our sense data can be explained through the laws of perspective and reflection of light
(d) The fallibility of sense experience.

Choose the correct option:

(1) (a) and (b) (2) (a), (b) and (c)
(3) (a), (b) and (d) (4) (d) only

94. I Should have no reason to believe that other people exist, except as part of my dream because:

(a) I have no way to ascertain that the other person could be lying
(b) Existence of other people could also be reduced to sense-data

(c) Things that I see in a dream do not exist in the real world

(d) I can only be sure of my own experience

Choose the correct option:

(1) (a) only (2) (b) only

(3) (b) and (c) only (4) (a) and (b) only

95. The philosophical position which is contrary to the position that 'there are other people in the world apart from ourselves' is termed as:

(1) Solipsism

(2) Subjective Idealism

(3) Transcendental Idealism

(4) Scepticism

Question Numbers : (96 to 100)

Question Label: Comprehension

Read the given passage carefully and answer the questions that follow.

If you think that such and such objects of true cognition are established through the instruments of true cognition (*pramāṇas*). We ask: how are those 'instruments of cognition' established? If you think that the 'objects of true cognition' *(prameya)* are established through the 'means of true cognition and those 'means of true cognition' are established through other 'means of true cognition' then there is....

Now if you think that those *pramānas* are established without *pramāṇas*, then your philosophical position is abandoned.

The view that *pramāṇas* establish themselves as well as other things, is called *svataḥpramānyavāda* that was advocated by prabhākara and Sankara.

Now if you think that through the establishment of *pramāṇas* are established the *prameyas*, and that through the establishment of *premeyas* are established the *pramāṇas*, then there will be *anyanayāsraya* dosa.

96. Which of the following schools of Indian Philosophy believe that 'the *pramāṇas* establish themselves'?

(a) *Nyāya*

(b) Buddhism

(c) *Prabhākara*

(d) Saṃkara's Advaita

Choose the correct option:

(1) (a) and (b) only (2) (b), (c) and (d)

(3) (c) and (d) (4) (b) and (c)

97. Which fallacy would occur if one believes that through the establishment of *pramāṇas* are the established *prameyas* and that through the establishment of *prameyas* are established the *pramāṇas*?

(1) *Anavasthā doṣa* (infinite regress)

(2) *Cakraka doṣa* (fallacy of circularity)

(3) *Anyanāśrya* (Interdependece)

(4) *Gaurana doṣa* (Redundant)

98. The kind of reasoning used in the given passage is:

(1) Dilemma (2) Paradox

(3) Puzzle (4) Strawman

99. If one believes that instruments of true cognition are themselves established without any instruments of true cognition, then which philosophical position is abandoned?

(1) Objects of true cognition *(prameyas)* are established through the instruments of true cognition *(pramaṇas)*

(2) *Pramāṇas* are self-established

(3) *Prameyas* are self-established

(4) Both *pramāṇas and premeyas* are self-established

100. The statement that '*pramāṇas* established themselves as well as other things' represents the doctrine of:

(1) *Parataḥprāmāṇyavāda*

(2) *Swataḥprāmāṇyavāda*

(3) *Swataḥaprāmāṇyavāda*

(4) *Parataḥaprāmāṇyavāda*

Answers

1. (3)	2. (3)	3. (4)	4. (1)	5. (4)	6. (2)	7. (1)	8. (1)	9. (3)	10. (1)
11. (4)	12. (1)	13. (3)	14. (3)	15. (4)	16. (3)	17. (1)	18. (3)	19. (*)	20. (4)
21. (4)	22. (3)	23. (3)	24. (4)	25. (3)	26. (4)	27. (3)	28. (2)	29. (3)	30. (4)
31. (1)	32. (4)	33. (3)	34. (4)	35. (4)	36. (2)	37. (3)	38. (4)	39. (1)	40. (2)
41. (4)	42. (3)	43. (1)	44. (3)	45. (2)	46. (4)	47. (4)	48. (4)	49. (4)	50. (3)
51. (3)	52. (4)	53. (4)	54. (3)	55. (4)	56. (3)	57. (2)	58. (3)	59. (1)	60. (2)
61. (1)	62. (2)	63. (1)	64. (1)	65. (3)	66. (2)	67. (1)	68. (4)	69. (2)	70. (2)
71. (1)	72. (2)	73. (2)	74. (4)	75. (3)	76. (3)	77. (2)	78. (3)	79. (3)	80. (4)
81. (4)	82. (2)	83. (2)	84. (1)	85. (3)	86. (1)	87. (3)	88. (1)	89. (1)	90. (1)
91. (1)	92. (2)	93. (2)	94. (2)	95. (1)	96. (3)	97. (3)	98. (1)	99. (1)	100. (2)

❖❖❖

November, 2021

PHILOSOPHY

PAPER-II

Note : This paper contains **hundred (100)** objective type questions of **two (2)** marks each. **All** questions are **compulsory.**

Question Numbers : (1 to 5)

Read the passage and answer the following questions:

In one sense it must be admitted that we can never prove the existence of things other than ourselves and our experiences. No logical absurdity results from the hypothesis that the world consists of myself and my thoughts and feelings and sensations, and that everything else is mere fancy. In dreams a very complicated world may seem to be present, and yet on waking we find it was a delusion; that is to say, we find that the sense-data in the dream do not appear to have corresponded with such physical objects as we should naturally infer from our sense-data. (It is true that, when the physical world is assumed, it is possible to find physical causes for the sense-data in dreams: a doorbanging, for instance, may cause us to dream of a naval engagement. But although, in this case, there is a physical cause for the sense-data, there is not a physical object corresponding to the sense-data in the way in which an actual naval battle would correspond.) There is no logical impossibility in the supposition that the whole of life is a dream, in which we ourselves create all the objects that come before us. But although this is not logically impossible, there is no reason whatever to suppose that it is true; and it is, in fact, a less simple hypothesis, viewed as a means of accounting for the facts of our own life, than the common-sense hypothesis that there really are objects independent of us, whose action on us causes our sensations.

1. The view that "the hypothesis that the world consists of myself and my thoughts and feelings and sensations, and that everything else is mere fancy." is compatible with which of the following doctrine/s?

A. Solipsism B. Idealism

C. Phenomenalism D. Naïve Realism

(1) A, B and D only (2) A, B and C only

(3) B, C and D only (4) A, C and D only

2. Which of the following philosopher/s could possibly be attributed with the view – "In one sense it must be admitted that we can never prove the existence of things other than ourselves and our experiences."? Consider the following options and choose the most appropriate option given thereafter.

A. Berkley B. Descartes

C. Hume D. Locke

Choose the most appropriate answer from the options given below:

(1) A, B and D only (2) A, B and C only

(3) B, C and D only (4) A, C and D only

3. From the last sentence of the paragraph what could be possibly inferred about the overall philosophical position of the author?

(1) The author is arguing against scepticism in favour of possibility of knowledge

(2) The author is arguing against realism in favor of idealism

(3) The author is arguing in favor of scepticism

(4) The author is merely suggesting that skeptic's position is insurmountable

4. The argument –"There is no logical impossibility in the supposition that the whole of life is a dream, in which we ourselves create all the objects that come before us." is also presented in which of the following text of Philosophy?
   (1) Discourse on Method
   (2) An Essay Concerning Human Understanding
   (3) A Treatise of Human Nature
   (4) A Critique of Pure Reason

5. The statement – "there is a physical cause for the sense-data" is compatible with which of the following philosophical position/s?
   A. Naïve Realism
   B. Representative Realism
   C. Idealism D. Solipsism
   Choose the correct answer from the options given below:
   (1) A and C only (2) A and B only
   (3) B and D only (4) C and D only

Question Numbers : (6 to 10)

Read the passage and answer the following questions:

All the objects of human reason or enquiry may naturally be divided into two kinds, which are Relations of Ideas, and Matters of Fact. Of the first kind are the sciences of Geometry, Algebra, and Arithmetic; and in short, every affirmation which is either intuitively or demonstratively certain. That the square of hypotenuse is equal to the squares of the two sides is a proposition which expresses a relation between these figures. That three times five is equal to the half of thirty, expresses a relation between these numbers. Propositions of this kind are discoverable by the mere operation of thought, without dependence on what is anywhere existent in the universe. Though there never was a circle or triangle in nature, the truths demonstrated by Euclid would forever retain their certainty and evidence. Matters of fact, which are the second objects of human reason, are not ascertained in the same manner; nor is our evidence of their truth, however great, of a like nature with the foregoing. The contrary of every matter of fact is still possible; because it can never imply a contradiction, and is conceived by the mind with the same facility and distinctness, as if ever so conformable to reality.

That the sun will not rise tomorrow is no less intelligible a proposition, and implies no more contradiction than the affirmation, that it will rise. We should in vain, therefore, attempt to demonstrate its falsehood.

6. Given below are two statements, one is labelled as Assertion A and the other is labelled as Reason R

   Assertion A : Though there never was a circle or triangle in nature, the truths demonstrated by Euclid would forever retain their certainty and evidence.

   Reason R : Propositions of this kind are discoverable by the mere operation of thought, without dependence on what is anywhere existent in the universe.

   In light of the above statements, choose the correct answer from the options given below
   (1) Both A and R are true and R is the correct explanation of A
   (2) Both A and R are true but R is NOT the correct explanation of A
   (3) A is true but R is false
   (4) A is false but R is true

7. As per the perspective of the passage, Knowledge in empirical sciences would fall under which of the following kinds?
   (1) Matters of fact
   (2) relations of ideas
   (3) Transcendental knowledge
   (4) Pure speculation

8. According to the given passage Geometry is concerned with
   (1) Matters of fact (2) Relations of Ideas
   (3) Both matters of fact and relations of ideas
   (4) Relations between facts

9. As per the perspective of the passage, the nature of reasoning concerning matters of fact are based on

(1) Perception only (2) Inference only
(3) Both perception and inference
(4) Relation of cause and effect only

10. "That the sun will not rise tomorrow is no less intelligible a proposition, and implies no more contradiction than the affirmation, that it will rise." According to the passage which of the following could be most appropriate reasons for this statement?
A. That both the statements namely 'sun will not rise tomorrow' and 'that it will rise' are matters of fact.
B. The statements 'sun will not rise tomorrow' and 'that it will rise' do not imply any contradiction.
C. Both the statements are conceived by the mind with the same facility and distinctness
D. Propositions of this kind are discoverable by the mere operation of thought.
Choose the correct answer from the options given below:
(1) A, B and D only (2) A, B and C only
(3) B and C only (4) A and D only

11. In Vedic tradition fire burns because
(1) It is the will of God
(2) It is a natural law
(3) There is a cosmic order
(4) There is a physical order

12. Which one among the following is Not a means of *vyaptigrāha*?
(1) *Anvaya* (2) *Vyatireka*
(3) *Sāmānyalakṣṇa pratyakṣa*
(4) *Upamāna*

13. By what relation the absence of *duḥkha* exists in liberated self, according to the Vaiśeṣikas
(1) *Samavāya* (2) *Saṁyoga*
(3) *Svarūapa* (4) *Tādātmya*

14. By which sannikarṣa do we perceive the absence of a pot on the ground according to Nyāya?
(1) *Saṁyoga* (2) *Viśeṣaṇat*
(3) *Samavāya*
(4) *Samaveta Samavāya*

15. In vedic tradition, *Ṛtvika* of sāmveda is called
(1) *Brahmā* (2) *Hotā*
(3) *Adhvūrya* (4) *Udgātā*

16. According to the Nyāya epistemology, we perceive a snake on a rope by
(1) *Yogaja sannikarṣa*
(2) *Sāmānyalakṣaṇa sannikarṣa*
(3) *Jñānalakṣaṇa sannikarṣa*
(4) *Saṁyoga sannikarṣa*

17. Which one among the following is Not a *cittavṛtti* according to Pātañjala-yoga?
(1) *Pramāṇa* (2) *Vikalpa*
(3) *Nidrā* (4) *Avidyā*

18. *Īsvarapraṇidhāna*, according to Yoga philosophy, is a kind of:
(1) *Yama* (2) *Niyama*
(3) *Āsana* (4) *Dhyāna*

19. What type of absence (abhāva) is the absence of cowness in horseness according to the *Vaiśeṣikas*?
(1) *Anyonyābhāva* (2) *Prāgabhāva*
(3) *Atyantābhāva* (4) *Dhvaṁsābhāva*

20. Which one of the following is an *asamavāyikāraṇa* of a pot according to the *Vaśeṣikas*?
(1) *Kapāla* (2) *Daṇḍa*
(3) *Kapāla-daṇḍa Saṁyoga*
(4) *Kapālasaṁyoga*

21. In Jaina Philosophy intuitive, complete and absolute knowledge is called
(1) *Avadhi* (2) *Mati*
(3) *Kevela* (4) *Śruta*

22. "When shell is perceived as silver, some real silver is actually present in that shell". Who holds this view?
(1) Śaṅkara (2) Prabhākar
(3) Kumārila (4) Rāmānuja

23. Who advocates the view that Brahman is *abhinnanimittopādāna kāraṇa* of jagat?
(1) Śaṅkara and Madhva
(2) Śaṅkara and Rāmānuja
(3) Śaṅkara and Kapila
(4) Madhva and Kaṇāda

24. When Advaita Vedanta says that the world is *mithyā*, what is its implication?

(1) World is absolutely non-existent
(2) World is absolutely existent
(3) World is both existent and non-existent
(4) World is neither existent nor non-existent, but different from both

25. Ātmā according to Nyāya can be:

(1) Knower only (2) Known only
(3) Knowledge only
(4) Both knower and known

26. Which dravyas according to the Vaiśeṣikas are sometimes *nitya* and sometimes *anitya*. Select the correct code.

(1) Earth, water, fire, air and ether only
(2) Earth, water, fire and air only
(3) Earth, water and fire only
(4) Earth and water only

27. Given below are two statements, one is labelled as Assertion A and the other is labelled as Reason R

Consider them and select the correct code in the context of Cārvāka Philosophy:

Assertion A : The dead body must be as much conscious as the living body is.

Reason R : Consciousness is an attribute of body.

In light of the above statements, choose the correct answer from the options given below

(1) Both A and R are true and R is the correct explanation of A/(A)
(2) Both A and R are true but R is NOT the correct explanation of A
(3) A is true but R is false
(4) A is false but R is true

28. Select the code that states the correct sequence of the following:

A. *Ahiṁsā* B. *Satya*
C. *Brahmacarya* D. *Asteya*
E. *Aprigraha*

Choose the correct answer from the options given below

(1) A, B, C, D, E (2) A, B, D, C, E
(3) A, B, E, C, D (4) A, C, B, D, E

29. Select the code that states the correct sequence of the following:

A. *Upādāna* B. *Tṛṣṇa*
C. *Bhava* D. *Jāti*

Choose the correct answer from the options given below

(1) A, B, C, D (2) A, C, B, D
(3) B, A, C, D (4) B, C, A, D

30. Consider the following and select the code acceptable to the Cārvākas:

A. *Karmavāda* B. *Bhūtacaitanyavāda*
C. *Dehātmavāda* D. *Sukhavāda*

Choose the correct answer from the options given below:

(1) A and B only (2) A, B and C only
(3) B and C only (4) B, C and D only

31. *Svalakṣaṇa* according to the Buddhists is:

A. Eternal B. Real
C. Momentary D. Unreal

Choose the correct answer from the options given below:

(1) A and B only (2) B and C only
(3) C and D only (4) A and D only

32. Consider the following in the context of Vedic philosophy and select the code indicating the correct assertions.

A. The *Ṛtvika* of *Ṛkveda* is called hotā
B. *Ṛsiṛṇa* can be paid off by *brahmacarya*
C. *Ṛta* regulates not only natural phenomena but also heavenly bodies
D. *Ṛta* is identified with truth

Choose the correct answer from the options given below:

(1) A only (2) A and B only
(3) A, B and C only (4) A, B, C and D

33. Match List I with List II

List I	List II
A. Vedānta	i. Knowledge is a quality of *ātmā*
B. Jaina	ii. Knowledge is the essence of *ātmā*
C. Mimaṁsā	iii. Knowledge is an act of *ātmā*
D. Nyāya	iv. Knowledge is *ātmā* itself

Choose the correct answer from the options given below:

(1) A - i, B - ii, C - iii, D - iv
(2) A - ii, B - i, C - iii, D - iv
(3) A - iv, B - ii, C - iii, D - i
(4) A - ii, B - i, C - iv, D - iii

34. Match List I with List II

List I	List II
A. Viparitakhyāti	i. Prabhakāra
B. Akhyāti	ii. Kumārila
C. Anyathākhyāti	iii. Madhva
D. Abhinavaanya-thākhyāti	iv. Gautama

Choose the correct answer from the options given below:

(1) A - ii, B - i, C - iv, D - iii
(2) A - i, B - ii, C - iii, D - iv
(3) A - iii, B - ii, C - i, D - iv
(4) A - ii, B - iii, C - i, D - iv

35. Match List I with List II

List I	List II
A. Veda	i. *Ṛta* is a cosmic order.
B. Cārvāka	ii. Fire burns out of its own nature.
C. Vaiśeṣika	iii. Śabda is not a separate pramāna
D. Mimāṁsā	iv. Śnupalabdhi is a separate pramāna

Choose the correct answer from the options given below:

(1) A - i, B - ii, C - iii, D - iv
(2) A - ii, B - i, C - iii, D - iv
(3) A - i, B - ii, C - iv, D - iii
(4) A - ii, B - i, C - iv, D - iii

36. Which one of the following is the view of Vivekananda with regard to the origin of religion?

(1) Only in Ancestor worship
(2) Only in nature worship
(3) The struggle to transcend the limitations of the senses
(4) In the conceptualization of evil

37. Which of the following forms of satyagraha are advocated by Gandhi?

(1) Disobedience, indirect action and non-cooperation
(2) Disobedience, direct cooperation and direct action
(3) Disobedience, direct action and noncooperation
(4) Disobedience, indirect action and fasting

38. Which of the following represents the correct ordering of ascent from mind to supermind as per Aurobindo?

(1) Higher mind, Illumined mind, intuition and overmind.
(2) Higher mind, overmind, Illumined mind and intuition.
(3) Illumined mind, intuition, overmind and higher mind.
(4) Higher mind, intuition, overmind and illumined mind.

39. According to K C Bhattacharya Philosophy is concerned with:

A. Transcendental consciousness
B. Objective consciousness
C. Spiritual consciousness
D. Empirical consciousness

Choose the correct answer from the options given below:

(1) A and B only (2) B and C only
(3) A, B and C only (4) D only

40. Given below are two statements, one is labelled as Assertion A and the other is labelled as Reason R. Consider them in the context of Philosophy of Iqbal.

Assertion A : Intuition is an unanalyzable unity.

Reason R : In intuition, the knower becomes one with the known and thereby realizes it.

In light of the above statements, choose the correct answer from the options given below

(1) Both A and R are true and R is the correct explanation of A
(2) Both A and R are true but R is NOT the correct explanation of A
(3) A is true but R is false
(4) A is false but R is true

41. Given below are two statements, one is labelled as Assertion A and the other is labelled as Reason R. Consider them with reference to Kierkegaard.

Assertion A : Truth is subjective.

Reason R : Truth is not in what you believe, but in how you live.

In light of the above statements, choose the correct answer from the options given below

(1) Both A and R are true and R is the correct explanation of A
(2) Both A and R are true but R is NOT the correct explanation of A
(3) A is true but R is false
(4) A is false but R is true

42. To live authentically, for Sartre, means,

(1) To make choices unintentionally about one's life and one's future
(2) To make choices intentionally about one's death
(3) To make choices intentionally about one's life and one's future
(4) To make choices unintentionally about one's life and other's future

43. Consider the following statements with reference to Heidegger.

A. Innermost nature of human being is caring.
B. Human beings are essentially temporal beings.
C. The temporality of human thinking is 'ecstatic.'

Choose the correct answer from the options given below:

(1) A only (2) A and C only
(3) C only (4) A, B and C only

44. Who among the following advocated the view that "If you withhold your assent to religious beliefs, then you will lose the benefits that come from accepting those beliefs. And it is worse to lose the benefits than to gain the protection from erring."

(1) William James (2) Kierkegaard
(3) Sartre (4) Nietzsche

45. "Our responsibility for the other is not a derivative feature of our subjectivity, rather it founds our subjective being in the world by giving it a meaningful direction and orientation." – is the perspective of which one of the following philosophers?

(1) Immanuel Levinas
(2) MorleauPonty
(3) Rorty (4) Nietzsche

46. Consider the following statements with reference to Kautilya.

A. The aim of the polity is the yogakshema of the subjects.
B. Curbing of the mastyanyaya within the State is advocated.
C. Yogakshema is not the responsibility of the state.

Choose the correct answer from the options given below:

(1) A only (2) A and B only
(3) C only (4) A, B and C only

47. Upeksha, according to Kamandaka is;

(1) Deliberate neglect of the situation
(2) Abandoning the decision
(3) Diplomatic indifference
(4) Diplomatic impatience

48. Which one of the following is not correct with reference to Affirmative action?

(1) It is intended to promote opportunities to the defined disadvantaged groups.
(2) It provides equal access to disadvantaged minorities.
(3) It justifies the compensation for the past discrimination.
(4) It does not support opportunities on the basis of race, gender and caste.

49. Which one of the following feminist theories argue for working within the structure of mainstream society to integrate women into that structure?

(1) Liberal feminism
(2) Socialist feminism
(3) Radical Feminism
(4) Ecofeminism

50. As per the politics of recognition of Charles Taylor, which one of the following it true.
(1) It advocated politics of difference that emphasized that everyone owed recognition of the unique identity.
(2) It advocated politics of indifference that emphasized that everyone owed recognition of the unique identity.
(3) It advocated politics of difference that emphasized that everyone owed recognition of the universal shared identity.
(4) It emphasized a move from recognition to nonrecognition

51. As per the axioms of quality of a categorical syllogism ;
(1) Both the premises can be negative.
(2) If one premise is positive, the conclusion must be positive.
(3) If one premise is negative, the conclusion must be negative.
(4) If one premise is negative, the conclusion can be either positive or negative.

52. Which one of the following is the correct combination of moods of the third figure?
(1) Darapti, Datisi, Felapton, Ferison, Disamis and Bocardo
(2) Darapti, Datisi, Felapton, Fesapo, Disamis and Bocardo
(3) Darapti, Darii, Felapaton, Ferison, Disamis and Bocardo
(4) Darapti, Datisi, Felapton, Ferison, Dimaris and Bocardo

53. Which one of the following represents the relation between the following propositions?
All students are young.
Some students are not young.
(1) Subcontrary (2) Contradictory
(3) Subaltern (4) contrary

54. Which one of the following is an invalid inference?
(1) If p then q, not p, therefore q.
(2) If p then q, not q, therefore not p.
(3) If p then q, p, therefore q.
(4) Either p or q, not p, therefore q.

55. "Students are never foolish" is a proposition of the form of;
(1) A proposition (2) I proposition
(3) O proposition (4) E proposition

56. Consider the following statements with reference to the distribution of the terms of the Categorical propositions?
A. Predicate term of the Negative propositions is distributed.
B. Predicate term of the afirmative propositions is undistributed.
C. Subject term of the universal propositions is distributed.
Choose the correct answer from the options given below:
(1) A only (2) A and B only
(3) B only (4) A, B and C only

57. Consider the following syllogism and mark the correct code.
Some snakes are friendly
No friendly beings bite
Therefore, no Snakes bite.
(1) It is a valid syllogism
(2) Commits the fallacy of illicit major
(3) Commits the fallacy of four terms
(4) Commits the fallacy of illicit minor

58. Which one is the contrapositive of the proposition "All members are voters?"
(1) All nonvoters are members.
(2) All voters are nonmembers.
(3) All nonvoters are nonmembers.
(4) No nonvoters are members.

59. Select the code which is not correct in the context of deductive argument with two premises
(1) An argument with two true premises and a true conclusion is valid
(2) An argument with one true and one false premises and a false conclusion is valid
(3) An argument with two false premises and a false conclusion is valid
(4) An argument with two true premises and a false conclusion is valid

"The buddhi obtains an intention when it thinks that the soul has a desire for experience, and because it has that experience the sense organs [too obtain an intention]. This is incorrect; because [they are] unconscious. For the buddhi is unconscious, and so are the sense organs. If they do not experience intention, how can their modification into the shape of the objects be decided upon?"

Above statement represents the criticism of:

(1) Sāṁkhya by the Nyāya school
(2) Nyāya by the Sāṁkhya school
(3) Advaita by the Sāṁkhya school
(4) Advaita by the Viśiṣṭādvaita school

87. Given below are two statements

Statement I: The deterministic doctrine states roughly that human actions like all other natural events are determined by preceding conditions, by the immutable laws of nature.

Statement II: The karma doctrine endorsed by most the Classical Indian Schools of Philosophy leads to determinism since a person's present actions are a product of his past actions.

In light of the above statements, choose the most appropriate answer from the options given below

(1) Both Statement I and Statement II are correct
(2) Both Statement I and Statement II are incorrect
(3) Statement I is correct but Statement II is incorrect
(4) Statement I is incorrect but Statement II is correct

88. Which of the following statements is true of Karma theory as advocated in Classical Indian notions of ethics and morality?

A. The karma theory in its simplest form means that every act, whether good or bad, produces a certain result or consequence which can be escaped or overcome by the perpetrator of the act.
B. The doctrine of karma is posited in a religious context as a moral necessity.
C. It is an attempt to answer the question of moral responsibility in man.
D. Metaphysically, it is based upon the doctrine of physical causation, according to which each effect has to be accounted for by its causal precedents.
E. It is a kind of extrapolation or extension of the doctrine of causation from the physical realm to the moral realm.

Choose the correct answer from the options given below:

(1) A, B and D only
(2) A, B, C and D only
(3) B,C,D and E only
(4) A and C only

89. According to Vaiśeṣika philosophy which of the following are included among qualities of the soul?

A. Effort
B. Subliminal impressions
C. Desire
D. Indifference

Choose the correct answer from the options given below:

(1) A, B and C only
(2) C and D only
(3) A, B and D only
(4) A, C and D only

90. Read the following statements carefully.

A. Mechanistic view of creation is premised on the idea that matter formed itself unaided into organisms of an almost incredible complexity.
B. Teleological view of creation is premised on the idea that order and efficacy apparent in the things created have been imposed from outside by a rational agent working on plan.
C. Nyāya view of creation is mechanistic
D. Nyāya view of creation is teleological

Choose the most appropriate answer from the options given below:

(1) A and B only (2) A, B and D only
(3) A and C only (4) B and C only

91. Read the following sentences with reference to ethics of Vaiśeṣika philosophy:

Statement I: Correct knowledge enables people to see that all activity leads to suffering.

Statement II: One should abstain from all activity and obtain liberation.

In light of the above statements, choose the most appropriate answer from the options given below

(1) Both Statement I and Statement II are correct

(2) Both Statement I and Statement II are incorrect

(3) Statement I is correct but Statement II is incorrect

(4) Statement I is incorrect but Statement II is correct

92. According to Sāṁkhya system *dharma* and *adharma* are

(1) Qualities of the soul

(2) Qualities of Buddhi

(3) Modifications of the soul

(4) Modifications of Buddhi

93. Given below are two statements

Statement I: Emotivism as a metaethical theory holds that the action-guiding force of morality could be explained only with reference to the special "evaluative element" in moral judgment.

Statement II: Prescriptivism as a metaethical theory held that the action-guiding force of morality could be explained only with reference to the special "evaluative element" in moral judgment.

In light of the above statements, choose the most appropriate answer from the options given below

(1) Both Statement I and Statement II are correct

(2) Both Statement I and Statement II are incorrect

(3) Statement I is correct but Statement II is incorrect

(4) Statement I is incorrect but Statement II is correct

94. Which of the following is true regarding R.M. Hare's views on moral judgments?

A. They are prescriptive in character.

B. To assent to them is to assent to the imperatives that they entail.

C. To assent to an imperative involves doing something or making something the case.

D. They are a kind of fact-stating, truth-functional discourse.

Choose the correct answer from the options given below:

(1) A, B and D only (2) B, C and D only

(3) A, C and D only (4) A, B and C only

95. "Moral words like "good" and "wrong" resemble ordinary descriptive words like "red" and "rectangular" in that their meaning and their application-conditions are firmly linked, so that to change either is to change the other." Which of the following metaethical theories is best represented by this statement?

(1) Descriptivism (2) Emotivism

(3) Prescriptivism (4) Cognitivism

96. Which of the following are Kant's postulates of morality?

A. Freedom of the will

B. Immortality of the soul

C. The existence of God

D. Kingdom of Ends

Choose the correct answer from the options given below:

(1) A, B and D only (2) A, B and C only

(3) B, C and D only (4) A, C and D only

97. Who among the following ethicists argues that the hedonist definition implies that the question "is anything which is pleasant good?" means the same as the question "is anything which is pleasant pleasant?"

(1) Kant (2) G E Moore

(3) C L Stevenson (4) R M Hare

98. Which of the following theory of morality advocates the view that basic moral propositions are self-evident, and that moral properties are non-natural properties?

(1) Intuitionism (2) Prescriptivism

(3) Supernaturalism (4) Emotivism

99. Match List I with List II

List I	List II
A. Biocentrism	I. The ethical belief that some animals warrant moral consideration as ends in themselves, rather than means to human ends.
B. Ecocentricism	II. The ethical belief that all living individual beings have moral value as ends in themselves, rather than as means to human ends.
C. Anthropocentrism	III. The ethical belief that both individuals and whole ecosystems, watersheds, species, the biotic community have inherent value as ends in themselves.
D. Zoocentricism	IV. The view that human beings are the only, or the primary, bearers of moral rights.

Choose the correct answer from the options given below:

(1) A - II, B - IV, C - I, D - III
(2) A - III, B - I, C - II, D - IV
(3) A - II, B - I, C - IV, D - III
(4) A - II, B - III, C - IV, D - I

100. Given below are two statements, one is labelled as Assertion A and the other is labelled as Reason R

Assertion A : According to advocates of animal killing the argument that to kill an animal is objectionable because it is contrary to its will is not acceptable.

Reason R : Animals lack the degree of self-consciousness necessary to conceive of, deliberate about, and plan for their own future lives.

In light of the above statements, choose the correct answer from the options given below

(1) Both A and R are true and R is the correct explanation of A
(2) Both A and R are true but R is NOT the correct explanation of A
(3) A is true but R is false
(4) A is false but R is true

Answers

1. (2)	**2.** (2)	**3.** (1)	**4.** (1)	**5.** (2)	**6.** (1)	**7.** (1)	**8.** (2)	**9.** (3)	**10.** (2)
11. (3)	**12.** (4)	**13.** (3)	**14.** (2)	**15.** (4)	**16.** (3)	**17.** (4)	**18.** (2)	**19.** (1)	**20.** (4)
21. (3)	**22.** (4)	**23.** (2)	**24.** (4)	**25.** (4)	**26.** (2)	**27.** (4)	**28.** (2)	**29.** (3)	**30.** (4)
31. (2)	**32.** (4)	**33.** (3)	**34.** (1)	**35.** (1)	**36.** (3)	**37.** (3)	**38.** (1)	**39.** (3)	**40.** (1)
41. (2)	**42.** (3)	**43.** (4)	**44.** (1)	**45.** (1)	**46.** (2)	**47.** (3)	**48.** (4)	**49.** (1)	**50.** (1)
51. (3)	**52.** (1)	**53.** (2)	**54.** (1)	**55.** (4)	**56.** (4)	**57.** (4)	**58.** (3)	**59.** (4)	**60.** (2)
61. (4)	**62.** (3)	**63.** (2)	**64.** (4)	**65.** (2)	**66.** (3)	**67.** (1)	**68.** (3)	**69.** (4)	**70.** (3)
71. (2)	**72.** (2)	**73.** (4)	**74.** (2)	**75.** (4)	**76.** (2)	**77.** (2)	**78.** (2)	**79.** (2)	**80.** (3)
81. (4)	**82.** (4)	**83.** (4)	**84.** (1)	**85.** (2)	**86.** (1)	**87.** (2)	**88.** (3)	**89.** (1)	**90.** (1)
91. (2)	**92.** (4)	**93.** (1)	**94.** (4)	**95.** (1)	**96.** (2)	**97.** (2)	**98.** (1)	**99.** (4)	**100.** (1)

October, 2022

PHILOSOPHY

PAPER-II

Note : This paper contains **hundred (100)** objective type questions of **two (2)** marks each. **All** questions are **compulsory**.

1. According to Merleau Ponty, perception is
   (1) science of the world
   (2) A conscious act
   (3) Not embodied
   (4) Not perspectival
2. Which one of the following presents Kierkegaard's philosophy appropriately?
   (1) Subjectivity is truth
   (2) Hegelianism and Rationalism
   (3) Being of the human being
   (4) Reality of the Universal
3. Wittgenstein is convinced that the particular employment of words are deemed to be one of the following :
   (1) An ontological use of language
   (2) Metaphysical use of language
   (3) Axiological use of language
   (4) An ethical use of language
4. According to P. F. Strawson, the concept of a person that is embodied mind is a primitive concept and through this argument, Strawson rejected one of the following
   (1) Psychological behaviourism and Cartesian dualism
   (2) Empiricism and Rationalism
   (3) Transendental Idealism
   (4) Idealism
5. What is multiculturalism?
   (1) It is the existence of cultural diversity within a given society.
   (2) It is the existence of minority groups in a society.
   (3) It is the existence of political diversity in a society.
   (4) It is the existence of ethnic minority groups in a society.
6. Who propounded the ethics of ambiguity?
   (1) Martin Heidegger
   (2) Karl Jaspers
   (3) Simon De Beauvoir
   (4) Jean Paul Sartre
7. What is the concern of the ethics of Levinas?
   (1) Responsibility towards other
   (2) Regulation with oneself
   (3) Charity to the other
   (4) Unconditional faith to the other
8. Dworkin proposed that rights should be thought of as
   (1) "Triumphs" which reveal their distinctive power
   (2) "Privileges" which reveal their unique power
   (3) "Opportunities" which reveal their capacities
   (4) "Wealth" which discloses the inner power
9. Which one of the following is consistent with Spinoza?
   (1) *Mind* and *Matter* are the parallel attributes of substance
   (2) *Mind* and *Matter* are two distinct substances
   (3) *Mind* is derived from *Matter*
   (4) *Matter* is derived from *Mind*
10. The division of qualities into primary and secondary is unphilosophical. Who held this view?
    (1) Locke

(2) Berkeley
(3) Locke and Berkeley
(4) Locke and Descartes

11. Which of the following is not acceptable to Kant?
(1) Knowledge consists of synthetic *apriori* judgements
(2) Analytic judgements are always *apriori*
(3) Analytic judgements do not add to our knowledge
(4) Synthetic judgements give cent percent sure knowledge

12. According to whom –'One idea cannot perceive another idea. Therefore there should exist a soul which perceives ideas".
(1) Locke (2) Hume
(3) Berkeley (4) Leibniz

13. Which of the following statement is incompatible with Hegel's view?
(1) Contradiction is the root of all life and movement
(2) Everything tends to change into its opposite
(3) The seed for example contradicts itself and transcends itself
(4) The Absolute is a myth

14. In Vaiśeṣika metaphysics, which *dravyas* can be both *nirāvayuva* and *sāvayavu*?
(1) *Kṣiti, ap, teju, and marut* only
(2) *Ap, teja, marut and vyoma* only
(3) *Kṣiti, ap, teja, marut and vyoma* only
(4) *Kṣiri, manas, marut, ap and vyoma* only

15. Which one among the following is NOT a means of *Saktigraha*?
(1) *Āptavākya*
(2) *Sāmānyalaksaṇa pratyakṣa*
(3) *Vyākaraṇa*
(4) *Vṛddhavyavahāra*

16. Which system of Vedanta, postulates the conception of three grades of *Sattā* (*Sattātraya*)?
(1) *Viśiṣṭāvaita Vedānta*
(2) *Dvaita Vedānta*
(3) *Advaita Vedānta*
(4) *Dvaitddvaita Vedānta*

17. By which relation, the relation between a pot and its colour is related with the pot according to the Vaiśeṣikas?
(1) *Samavāya* (2) *Saṁyoga*
(3) *Tādātmya* (4) *Svarūpa*

18. Which one among the following is the direct knowledge of the thoughts of others in Jaina epistemology?
(1) *Pratyakṣa* (2) *Avadhi*
(3) *Manaḥparyāya* (4) *Kevala*

19. In Vedic literature *Ṛta* is equated with
(1) *Satya* only
(2) *Dharma* only
(3) Both *Satya* and *Dharma*
(4) Neither *Surya* nor *Dharma*

20. By begetting off-spring one can repay :
(1) *Pitṛṇa* only (2) *Pitṛṇa and ṛṣirṇa*
(3) *Ṛṣirṇa* only (4) *Devarna* only

21. According to the *Cārvākas* fire burns because
(1) It is divine will
(2) It is a cosmic order
(3) It is the nature of fire
(4) The burning power is the essence of fire

22. Which school is of the opinion that there is no contradiction in holding the judgement that a *ghataḥ* is and is not at the same time?
(1) Nyāya (2) Bauddha
(3) Jaina (4) Advaita Vedānta

23. In Nyāya epistemology, by which *sannikarṣa* do we perceive the relation between my hand and the pen I am writing with?
(1) *Saṁyoga*
(2) *Saṁyukta samavāya*
(3) *Samavāya*
(4) *Viśeṣanatā*

24. Which of the following philosophers advocate a distinction between *Anumāna* and *Arthāpatti pramāṇa*?
(1) Rāmānuja and Madhva
(2) Śamkara and Kumārila
(3) Madhva and Nimbārka
(4) Kumārila and Rāmānuja

25. In Nyāya philosophy of language *Iśvarecchā* is
(1) The cause of śabda
(2) The cause of śakti
(3) Śabda itself
(4) Śakti itself

26. Which type of *hetvābhāsa* is committed by the *anumāna: Śabah nityaḥ śabdatvāt?*
(1) *Sādhārarṇa savyabhicāra*
(2) *Asādhāraṇa savyabhicāra*
(3) *Svarūpāsiddha*
(4) *Viruddha*

27. Which one among the following is NOT a characteristic of *sat hetu*?
(1) *Pakṣasattva*
(2) *Vipaksasattva*
(3) *Sapaksasattva*
(4) *Abādhita viṣyatva*

28. Which type of cause is *Kapālasaṁyoga* in the production of *ghatah*?
(1) *Samavāyi* (2) *Asamavāyi*
(3) *Nimitta* (4) *Nimitta - Upādāna*

29. What is the nature of *jīva* (individual self) according to Ramanuja?
(1) *Jīva* is fundamentally non dual with Brahman.
(2) *Jīva* is absolutely different from Brahman.
(3) *Jīva* is both fundamentally non dual and absolutely different from Brahman.
(4) *Jīva* is existentially different but inseparably connected with Brahman.

30. Kumarila's advocacy of *pramāṇas* was endorsed by which of the following systems
(1) *Nyāya* (2) *Sāṁkhya*
(3) *Advaita* (4) *Śuddha Advaita*

31. Figures of categorical syllogism are determined on the basis of
(1) Position of the major term in the premises.
(2) Position of the minor term in the premises.
(3) Position of the middle term in the premises.
(4) Position of the major term in the conclusion.

32. Which one of the following is the obversion of the proposition "All residents are voters"?
(1) All voters are residents
(2) No voters are residents
(3) No residents are voters
(4) No residents are non-voters

33. Which one of the following does not fall under the category of Fallacies of Relevance
(1) The Red Herring
(2) The Straw Man
(3) The appeal to emotion
(4) Begging the question

34. If A and B are true statements and X, Y and Z are false statements, determine which one of the following is true.
(1) $[A \supset (X \cdot Y)] \supset [(A \supset X) v (A \supset Y)]$
(2) $[(A \cdot X) \supset B] \supset [(A \supset X)$
(3) $(A \supset Z) \supset B] \supset Y$
(4) $[(A \cdot X) \supset Y] \supset [(A \supset X)$

35. Which one of the following is the correct combination of moods in the fourth figure?
(1) Datisi, Disamis and Ferison
(2) Camenes, Dimaris and Festino
(3) Datisi, Disamis and Ferio
(4) Camenes, Dimaris and Fresison

36. Which one of the following represents the relation between propositions provided below?
Some pens are red.
Some pens are not red.
(1) Contrary (2) Contradictory
(3) Sub-Altern (4) Sub-Contrary

37. Consider the following syllogism and identify the fallacy involved in it:
– Some friends are rich.
– No rich persons are helpful.
∴ No helpful persons are friends.
(1) Illicit major
(2) Illicit minor
(3) Undistributed middle
(4) Fallacy of four terms

38. Consider the following syllogism and identify the fallacy in it.

. No dogs are bipeds.
. No cats are bipeds.
∴ No cats are dogs.

(1) Illicit minor
(2) Fallacy of ambiguity
(3) Fallacy of two negative premises
(4) Undistributed middle

39. Identify the contraposition of the proposition

"Some philosophers are not-scientists"

(1) Some non-scientists are not non-philosophers
(2) Some non-philosophers are non-scientists
(3) No non-scientists are non-philosophers
(4) All scientists are non-philosophers

40. Who said that "I don't care of God, if he is anything but truth"?

(1) K. C. Bhattacharya
(2) Iqbal
(3) Vivekananda
(4) M. K. Gandhi

41. Which of the following philosophers conceptualized God as "personal being" or "supreme person".

(1) Iqbal (2) Radhakrishnan
(3) Ambedkar (4) Tagore

42. Who among the following Contemporary Indian Thinkers expresses the view that self knowledge is equivalent to knowing oneself in relation?

(1) M. N. Roy
(2) K. C. Bhattacharya
(3) Jiddu Krishnamurthy
(4) Jyotiba Phule

43. Who among the following is the ancient Greek pluralist?

(1) Permenides (2) Zeno
(3) Empedocles (4) Anaximander

44. Which of the following is philosophically unacceptable to St Anselm?

(1) Faith
(2) Understanding faith
(3) Understanding why revelation is true
(4) Giving up reason

45. "The so called cause is nothing but one event immediately succeeded by another event, the succeeded event may be called effect. That is all" Who among the following holds this view?

(1) Locke (2) Kant
(3) Hume (4) Descartes

46. Which of the following statement is incompatible with Descartes?

(1) Taking mathematics as the model of philosophical method
(2) Setting the face against old authorities
(3) Viewing sense-experience as a gateway to all knowledge
(4) Reconciliation of mechanism and the notions of God, Soul and Freedom

47. What of the following is incorrect as far as Rationalism is concerned (as a Philosophical theory)?

(1) Reason and Reason alone is the source of all philosophical knowledge
(2) Reason is permanent and unchanged
(3) Sense experience is deceptive and therefore cannot act as a source of philosophical knowledge
(4) Reason limits itself and is defective

48. Berkeley is called as Idealist because

(1) He was a bishop.
(2) There is no knowledge which is not in the form of ideas.
(3) Matter matters least to him.
(4) He postulated the principle : Think with the learned and speak with the vulgar.

49. "Men may come and men may go, but the man-type, the human race goes on forever". Whose view is this?

(1) Aristotle (2) Plato
(3) Protogoras (4) Gorgias

50. Who held the view that 'God is the Unmoved Mover'?

(1) Socrates (2) Plato
(3) Thales (4) Aristotle

51. Which of the following is the correct view of Anaxagoras?
(1) Elements are without qualities.
(2) Elements are only four in number.
(3) Change is impossible.
(4) Mind initiates motion in the elements.

52. "Knowledge is possible : It is concerned with the general and typical, not the particular and accidental". Who among the following holds this view?
(1) Sophists (2) Atomists
(3) Socrates (4) Empedocles

53. "The impulse towards pleasure, if too predominant, defeats its own aim". Who among the following holds this view?
(1) Bentham (2) J. S. Mill
(3) Sidgwick (4) Kant

54. Who amongst the following criticized Cartesian Rationalism?
(1) St. Augustine (2) Spinoza
(3) Leibnitz (4) Hume

55. Which of the following aim is NOT conducive to Immanuel Kant?
(1) To limit Hume's skepticism
(2) To limit dogmatism
(3) To prove that reason was all in all
(4) To show the possibility of synthetic apriori propositions

56. Who among the following is inclined to accept Transcendental Idealism?
(1) Hegel (2) Kant
(3) Descartes (4) Hume

57. Who is the chief architect for the reconciliation between Rationalism and Empiricism?
(1) Locke (2) Spinoza
(3) Hume (4) Kant

58. For Kant, what is the faculty that coordinates sensations and perception?
(1) Time
(2) Transcendental unity of apperception
(3) Space
(4) Category

59. Which of the following position is incompatible with the view of Berkeley?
(1) Acceptance of ideas
(2) Acceptance of the existence of soul
(3) Acceptance of abstract ideas
(4) Acceptance of nominalism

60. What is the place of God in Plato's philosophy?
(1) God is the cause of Idea
(2) God is different from Idea
(3) God is the same as Idea
(4) Idea is the cause of God

61. Which one of the following is unacceptable to David Hume?
(1) Knowledge as relation of ideas
(2) Knowledge as matters of fact
(3) Refutation of the causal relation
(4) Knowledge of Soul. World and God is possible

62. Who holds the following view about emotive theory?
"Only the propositions of the mathematics and empirical sciences have sense, and all other propositions are without senses".
A. A. J. Ayer B. R. Carnap
C. G. E. Moore D. B. Russell
Choose the correct answer from the options given below:
(1) A only (2) A and B only
(3) B only (4) C and D only

63. "Self-realization is the highest good". This view is maintained by:
A. Rigorism B. Eudaemonism
C. Emotivism D. Egoism
Choose the correct answer from the options given below:
(1) B only (2) A and B only
(3) B and D only (4) C and D only

64. Consider the following and select the code stating Bahiranga Limbs of *Aṣṭānga yoga*:
A. *Yuma, Niyama, Āsana*
B. *Dhyāna, Dhāraṇā*
C. *Prāṇāyāma, Pratyāhāra*
D. *Dhāraṇā, Dhyāna, Somādhi*
Choose the correct answer from the options given below:

(1) A and B only (2) A and C only
(3) A and D only (4) C and D only

65. *Lokasaṁgraha* stands for:
A. Fruitless activities
B. Moral activities
C. Religious activities
D. Public welfare activities
Choose the correct answer from the options given below.
(1) A only (2) A and B only
(3) C and D only (4) D only

66. We can perceive, according to Nyāya, the external substances by:
A. Visual sense organ
B. Tactual sense organ
C. Gustatory sense organ
D. Internal sense organ
Choose the correct answer from the options given below:
(1) A only (2) A and B only
(3) A and C only (4) A, B and C only

67. Who among the following admits both Jīvanrnukti and Videhamukti
A. Śankara B. Buddha
C. Rāmānuja D. Madhva
Choose the correct answer from the options given below.
(1) A only (2) B only
(3) A and B only (4) A, B and C only

68. Which of the following text is composed by Maulana Azad?
A. *Ghubur-e-Khatir*
B. *Education and Religious Identity*
C. *India Wins Freedom*
D. *Tarjumanul Qurun*
E. *Tarjurnanul Geeta*
Choose the correct answer from the options given below:
(1) A and D only (2) A, C and D only
(3) A, B, C, D and E (4) A, D and E only

69. Who among the following are votaries of caturvarnya system?
A. M. K Gandhi
B. Sarvepalli Radhakrishnan
C. Narayana Guru
D. Deendayal Upadhyaya
Choose the correct answer from the options given below.
(1) A and B only (2) A, B and C only
(3) A, B and D only (4) A, B, C and D

70. Consider the following statements with reference to conjunction and choose the correct combination:
A. If 'p' is true and 'q' is true, then 'p-q' is true
B. If 'p' is false and 'q' is true, then 'p-q' is false
C. If 'p' is true and 'q' is false, then 'p-q' is true
D. If 'p' is false and 'q' is false, then 'piq' is true
Choose the correct answer from the options given below:
(1) A only (2) A and C only
(3) A and B only (4) C only

71. Consider the following with reference to distribution of terms in categorical propositions :
A. A proposition distributes only its predicate term.
B. E proposition distributes both its subject and predicate terms.
C. I proposition distributes its only subject term.
D. O proposition distributes only its predicate term.
Choose the correct answer from the options given below.
(1) A and B only (2) B and C only
(3) A and D only (4) B and D only

72. Match List I with List II

List I	List II
A. Advaita Vedanta	I. Egoistic Hedonism
B. Buddhism	II. Performance of Duties
C. Gita	III. Self-realization
D. Cārvaka	IV. Noble Truth

Choose the correct answer from the options given below:

(1) A - I, B - II, C - III, D - IV
(2) A - III, B - IV, C - II, D - I
(3) A - IV, B - III, C - I, D - II
(4) A - I, B - III, C - IV, D - II

73. Match List I with List II

List I	List II
A. Buddhism	I. *Sādhana Catuṣṭāya*
B. Yoga	II. *Pancha Mahāvrata*
C. Jainism	III. *Dwādasanidāna*
D. Advāita Vedanta	IV. *Pancaklesha*

Choose the correct answer from the options given below:
(1) A - IV, B - I, C - III, D - I
(2) A - I, B - III, C - II, D - IV
(3) A - III, B - IV, C - II, D - I
(4) A - II, B - III, C - I, D - IV

74. Match List I with List II

List I	List II
A. Bhāsarvañja	I. Tattopaplavasingha
B. Jayrāśibhaṭṭa	II. Nyāyasāra
C. Hemachandra	III. Vijñptimātratāsiddhi
D. Vasubandhu	IV. Pramāṇamimāṁsā

Choose the correct answer from the options given below:
(1) A - I, B - II, C - III, D - IV
(2) A - II, B - I, C - IV, D - III
(3) A - I, B - III, C - II, D - IV
(4) A - II, B - III, C - I, D - IV

75. Match List I with List II

List I	List II
A. Empedocles	I. Atomic Theory
B. Anaxagoras	II. The doctrine of elements
C. Pythagoras	III. The doctrine of *nous*
D. Leuicippus and Democritus	IV. The doctrine of numbers

Choose the correct answer from the options given below:
(1) A - III, B - IV, C - I, D - II
(2) A - II, B - III, C - IV, D - I
(3) A - III, B - II, C - I, D - IV
(4) A - IV, B - II, C - I, D - III

76. Match List I with List II

List I	List II
A. Interactionism	I. Hume
B. Parallelism	II. Descartes
C. Pre-established harmony	III. Spinoza
D. Scepticism	IV. Leibnitz

Choose the correct answer from the options given below:
(1) A - III, B - II, C - I, D - IV
(2) A - II, B - III, C - IV, D - I
(3) A - III, B - I, C - II, D - IV
(4) A - I, B - II, C - III, D - IV

77. Match List I with List II

List I	List II
A. Self is active and conscious	I. Advaita Vedānta
B. Self is inactive conscious	II. Sāṁkhya
C. Self is the body itself	III. Vaiśeṣika
D. Self is knowledge itself	IV. Cārvāka

Choose the correct answer from the options given below:
(1) A - I, B - II, C - III, D - IV
(2) A - I, B - II, C - IV, D - III
(3) A - III, B - II, C - IV, D - I
(4) A - III, B - IV, C - I, D - II

78. Match List I with List II

List I	List II
A. The effect is produced in the presence of its cause	I. Vaiśeṣika
B. The effect is produced in the absence of its cause	II. Advaita Vedānta
C. The effect preexists in its cause before its production	III. Buddha
D. The effect is not real but the cause is real	IV. Sāṁkhya

Choose the correct answer from the options given below:
(1) A - I, B - II, C - III, D - IV
(2) A - I, B - III, C - IV, D - II
(3) A - II, B - III, C - IV, D - I
(4) A - I, B - II, C - IV, D - III

79. Match List I with List II

List I	List II
A. Constructive Dilemma	I. pvq, ~p, ∴ q
B. Addition	II. p⊃q, p, ∴ q
C. Modus Ponens	III. p ∴ p, v q
D. Disjunctive Syllogism	IV. (p⊃q), (r⊃s), pvr, ∴ qvs

Choose the correct answer from the options given below:

(1) A - I, B - III, C - II, D - IV
(2) A - II, B - I, C - IV, D - III
(3) A - IV, B - III, C - II, D - I
(4) A - III, B - II, C - I, D - IV

80. Match List I with List II

List I	List II
A. Hobbes	I. Absolute Idealism
B. Amartya Sen	II. The Second Sex
C. Hengel	III. Social Contract
D. Simone D. Beauvoir	IV. The idea of Justice

Choose the correct answer from the options given below:

(1) A - IV, B - II, C - III, D - I
(2) A - II, B - IV, C - III, D - I
(3) A - III, B - IV, C - I, D - II
(4) A - I, B - IV, C - III, D - II

81. Consider the following and select the code consistent with Kant's Categorical Imperative:

A. Internal law of conscience
B. Apriori
C. Moral law
D. Natural law

Choose the correct answer from the options given below:

(1) A only (2) A and B only
(3) A, B and C only (4) B, C and D only

82. Consider the following and select the correct sequence from the codes given below

(A) Artha (B) Dharma
(C) Mokṣa (D) Kāma

Choose the correct answer from the options given below

(1) A, B, C and D
(2) B, A, D and C
(3) B, A, C and D
(4) D, A, B and C

83. Select the correct sequence :

A. Avagraha B. Dhāraṇā
C. Ihā D. Avāya

Choose the correct answer from the options given below

(1) A, C, D and B
(2) A, B, C and D
(3) A, D, C and B
(4) C, A, B and D

84. Consider the following explanation of the fallacies:

Statement I: The deliberate misrepresentation of opponent's position is the fallacy of straw man

Statement II: An attack upon the character or special circumstances of the opponent involves fallacy of Ad hominem

In light of the above statements, choose the most appropriate answer from the options given below

(1) Both Statement I and Statement II are correct
(2) Both Statement I and Statement II are incorrect
(3) Statement I is correct but Statement II is incorrect
(4) Statement I is incorrect but Statement II is correct

85. Given below are two statements :

Statement I: Radhakrishnan rejects naturalistic explanation of the world as it fails to appreciate the nature of the ultimate reality.

Statement II: The absolute is conceived by Radhakrishnan as pure consciousness, pure freedom and infinite possibility.

In light of the above statements, choose the correct answer from the options given below

(1) Both Statement I and Statement II are true

(2) Both Statement I and Statement II are false
(3) Statement I is true but Statement II is false
(4) Statement I is false but Statement II is true

86. Consider the following statements with reference to Iqbal's intuition.
Statement I: Intuition is an immediate knowledge of reality.
Statement II: Intuition is the property of heart.
In light of the above statements, choose the correct answer from the options given below
(1) Both Statement I and Statement II are true
(2) Both Statement I and Statement II are false
(3) Statement I is true but Statement II is false
(4) Statement I is false but Statement II is true

87. Given below are two statements:
Statement I: Gandhian trinity of development consists in *Sarvodaya, Swadeshi* and *Swaraj*.
Statement II: Gandhian trinity of development consists in *Swadeshi, Swaraj* and *Asteya*.
In light of the above statements, choose the most appropriate answer from the options given below
(1) Both Statement I and Statement II are true
(2) Both Statement I and Statement II are false
(3) Statement I is true but Statement II is false
(4) Statement I is false but Statement II is true

88. Given below are two statements, one is labelled as Assertion A and the other is labelled as Reason R
Assertion A: According to Madhva, *Jīva* (individual self) is not the same as *Brahman*.
Reason R: *Jīva* (individual self) entirely depends on *Brahman* for its existence (*sattā*), Knowledge (*pramiti*) and action (*kriyā*).
In light of the above statements, choose the correct answer from the options given below
(1) Both A and R are true and R is the correct explanation of A
(2) Both A and R are true but R is NOT the correct explanation of A
(3) A is true but R is false
(4) A is false but R is true

89. Given below are two statements, one is labelled as Assertion A and the other is labelled as Reason R
Assertion A: *Vedas* cannot be a ground for God's existence.
Reason R: God is the author of the Vedas.
In light of the above statements, choose the correct answer from the options given below
(1) Both A and R are true and R is the correct explanation of A
(2) Both A and R are true but R is NOT the correct explanation of A
(3) A is true but R is false
(4) A is false but R is true

90. Given below are two statements, one is labelled as Assertion A and the other is labelled as Reason R
Answer with reference to Mills, Utilitarianism
Assertion A: The general happiness is good to the aggregate of all persons.
Reason R: Each persons happiness is good to the person concerned.
In light of the above statements, choose the correct answer from the options given below
(1) Both A and R are true and R is the correct explanation of A
(2) Both A and R are true but R is NOT the correct explanation of A
(3) A is true but R is false
(4) A is false but R is true

Read the below passage and answer the five questions that follow:

There are several reasons why "Know yourself" has obscured "Take care of yourself". We are more inclined to see taking care of ourselves as an immorality, as a means of escape from all possible rules. We inherit the tradition of Christian morality which makes self-renunciation the condition for salvation. To know oneself was, paradoxically, a means of self-renunciation. We also inherit a secular tradition that sees in external law the basis for morality. How then can respect for the self be the basis for morality? We are the inheritors of a social morality that seeks the rules for acceptable behavior in relations with others. Since the 16th century, criticism of established morality has been undertaken in the name of the importance of recognizing and knowing the self. Therefore, it is difficult to see the care of the self as compatible with morality. "Know thyself" has obscured "Take care of yourself" because our morality, a morality of asceticism, insist that the self is that which one can reject.

...To summarize: There has been an inversion in the hierarchy of the two principles of antiquity, "Take care of yourself" and "Know yourself". In Greco-Roman culture, knowledge of oneself appeared as the consequence of the care of the self. In the modern world, knowledge of oneself constitutes the fundamental principle".

91. What do you understand as the import of this paragraph?
(1) Greece-Roman understanding of Self
(2) Compatibility of the care of the self with morality
(3) Development of the understanding of Self
(4) Self as the ultimate moral principle

92. "Know yourself" has obscured "Take care of yourself" because
(1) Our morality is able to appropriate the Self
(2) A morality of asceticism rejects the Self
(3) We inherited the tradition of Christian morality
(4) Morality is recognized in terms of knowing the Self

93. Select tradition advocates one of the following :
(1) External circumstances as the basis for morality.
(2) Internal circumstances as the basis for morality.
(3) Respect for law as the basis for morality.
(4) External law as the basis for morality.

94. According to Michel Foucault:
(1) Renouncing the world is a path towards salvation.
(2) Self-realization and self-renunciation are same.
(3) Self-renunciation is the condition to salvation.
(4) Self-knowledge is the condition for salvation.

95. According to Foucault, social morality implies one of the following :
(1) Importance of recognizing and knowing the Self
(2) Impotence of external law
(3) Seeks rules for acceptable behaviour in realtion with others
(4) Importance of the knowledge of oneself

Read the below passage and answer the following five questions.

Summing up, then, it should first of all, be borne in mind that the norms and tendencies of the Deep Ecology movement are not derived from ecology or logic or induction. Ecological knowledge and the life style of the ecological field worker have suggested, inspired and fortified the perspectives of Deep Ecology movements. Secondly, it should be fully appreciated that the significant tenets of the Deep Ecology movement are clearly and forcefully non-native. They express a value priority system only in part based on result (or law of results) of scientific research. Today, ecologists try to influence policy-making bodies largely through threats, through predictions concerning pollutants and resource depletion, knowing that policy makers accept at least certain minimum norms concerning health and just distribution. There are political potentials in this movement which have little to do with pollution and resource depletion. Thirdly, in so far as ecology movements deserve our attention, they are eco-philosophical rather than ecological. Ecology is a limited science which makes use of scientific methods. Philosophy is the most general forum of debate on fundamentals, descriptive as well as prescriptive, and political philosophy one of its subsections. By an ecosophy, I mean a philosophy of ecological harmony or equilibrium. A philosophy as a kind of Sofia wisdom, is openly normative; it contains" both norms, rules, postulates, value priority announcements and hypotheses concerning the state of affairs in our universe... An ecosophy is more like a system of the kind constructed by Aristotle or Spinoza... The basic relation is that between subsets of premises and subsets of conclusions, that is, the relation of derivability. At the moment, ecosophy might profitably use models of systems, rough approximations of global systemizationsm, under the name of ecologism, various deviations from the deep movement have been championed - primarily with a one sided stress on pollution and resource depletion..."

96. In the name of ecologism, deep movement has various deviations which are one sided and laid emphasis on:
(1) Ecological harmony
(2) Pollution and resource depletion
(3) Ecological knowledge
(4) A theory of ecologism

97. What does Arne Naess intend to convey in this paragraph?
(1) Advocating a theory of ecologism.
(2) Advocating a philosophy of ecological harmony.
(3) Advocating the limitation of ecology as a science.
(4) Advocating the perspective of Deep Ecology movement that has normative and ecophilosophical dimensions.

98. Deep Ecology movement is fortified by one of the following:
(1) Policy-making bodies by ecologists.
(2) A movement that culminated in ecosophy.
(3) Ecological knowledge and the life style of the ecological field workers.
(4) A policy that emphasizes ecological harmony.

99. According to Naess, Deep Ecology movement involves:
(1) Value priority system based on results of scientific research.
(2) Scientific potentials based on scientific research.
(3) Policy-making bodies of ecologists.
(4) A philosophical outlook that implies ecological harmony.

100. According to Naess, ecosophy is
(1) A theory of ecologism.
(2) A philosophy of ecological harmony.
(3) A limited science based on scientific methods.
(4) A normative theory on ecology.

Answers

1. (*)	**2.** (1)	**3.** (*)	**4.** (1)	**5.** (1)	**6.** (3)	**7.** (1)	**8.** (1)	**9.** (1)	**10.** (2)
11. (4)	**12.** (3)	**13.** (4)	**14.** (1)	**15.** (2)	**16.** (3)	**17.** (4)	**18.** (3)	**19.** (3)	**20.** (1)
21. (3)	**22.** (3)	**23.** (2)	**24.** (2)	**25.** (4)	**26.** (2)	**27.** (2)	**28.** (2)	**29.** (4)	**30.** (3)
31. (3)	**32.** (4)	**33.** (4)	**34.** (1)	**35.** (4)	**36.** (4)	**37.** (1)	**38.** (3)	**39.** (1)	**40.** (4)
41. (4)	**42.** (3)	**43.** (3)	**44.** (4)	**45.** (3)	**46.** (3)	**47.** (4)	**48.** (2)	**49.** (2)	**50.** (4)
51. (4)	**52.** (3)	**53.** (3)	**54.** (4)	**55.** (3)	**56.** (2)	**57.** (4)	**58.** (2)	**59.** (3)	**60.** (3)
61. (4)	**62.** (3)	**63.** (2)	**64.** (2)	**65.** (4)	**66.** (2)	**67.** (3)	**68.** (2)	**69.** (3)	**70.** (3)
71. (4)	**72.** (2)	**73.** (3)	**74.** (2)	**75.** (2)	**76.** (2)	**77.** (3)	**78.** (2)	**79.** (3)	**80.** (3)
81. (3)	**82.** (2)	**83.** (1)	**84.** (1)	**85.** (1)	**86.** (1)	**87.** (3)	**88.** (1)	**89.** (4)	**90.** (1)
91. (3)	**92.** (2)	**93.** (4)	**94.** (3)	**95.** (3)	**96.** (2)	**97.** (4)	**98.** (3)	**99.** (1)	**100.** (2)

December, 2023

PHILOSOPHY

PAPER-II

Note : This paper contains **hundred (100)** objective type questions of **two (2)** marks each. **All** questions are **compulsory**.

1. Which one among the following is accepted by Immanuel Kant as moral imperative?
(1) Hypothetical Imperative
(2) Categorical Imperative
(3) Scientific imperative
(4) Assertorial Imperative

2. Kant claims that the moral law is given to each person by
(1) Law of state
(2) Constitution of the state
(3) One's own will
(4) Will of the other

3. In Kant's epistemology, the concept of the thing-in-itself is something not knowable by the senses, but at least thinkable, is a
(1) Limiting concept
(2) Liberating concept
(3) Paradoxical concept
(4) Logical concept

4. The objects of mathematical knowledge for Plato are
(1) Sensible particulars
(2) Real universals
(3) Intelligible particulars
(4) Addable numbers

5. Which one of the following statements is not true according to the Philosophy of Vivekananda?
(1) There is identical relationship between soul and God.
(2) Vivekananda's Philosophy is called Neo-Vedanta.
(3) The world is totally different from God.
(4) Maya is ground of the creation of the world.

6. Which one of the following statements regarding Shankara's concept of Maya is not true?
(1) It is inherent power of potency of Brahman.
(2) It is Spiritual and self-conscious.
(3) It is beginningless
(4) It is indescribable and indefinable

7. "Being is what it is not and is not what it is"- this statement is associated with the philosophy of
(1) Beauvoir (2) Kierkegaard
(3) Sartre (4) Nietzche

8. The claim that philosophy is a rigorours a science from its earliest beginnings is a position that is denied by
(1) Descrates (2) Husserl
(3) Heideggar (4) Merieu-Ponty

9. Humans for Sartre are free because their being is based on.
(1) A living body
(2) Annihilation of being in itself
(3) Surrender before being in itself
(4) Its relation to itself is primitive

10. Which one of the following schools of Indian philosophy does not support Parinam vada?
(1) Samkhya (2) Yoga
(3) Ramanuja (4) Nyaya

11. Which one of the following statements is not true according to Samkhya philosophy?

(1) Purusa is itself pure and transcendental consciousness
(2) Purusa is principle of pure consciousness
(3) Purusa is The ultimate knower
(4) Purusa is a by-product of matter.

12. Which one of the following views is acceptable to Chārvāka regarding Vyāpti?
(1) 'Vyapti' is universal and invariable relationship between middle term and major term
(2) 'Vyapti' cannot be proved by perception or inference or testimony
(3) 'Vyapti' is universal and invariable relationship between major term and middle term.
(4) 'Vyapt' is universal and invariable relationship between major term and minor term.

13. Which one of the following views regarding Samavāya has been propounded by Vaiśeṣika?
(1) Samavāya is separable and transient relation.
(2) Samavāya is separable and inseparable relation
(3) Samavāya is inseparable relation
(4) Samavāya is accidental relation.

14. According to whom Truth is Human truth.
(1) Jyotiba Phule
(2) Mahatma Gandhi
(3) J. Krishnamurti
(4) Rabindra Nath Tagore

15. Moral evils cannot mar the beauty of universal creation, since it springs from the will of man or of fallen angels; it merely represents a privation of good (Privation boni). Who says so?
(1) Marcus Aurelieus
(2) St. Augustine
(3) St. Anselm
(4) St. Thomas Aqvinas

16. The term 'Infosphere' is an idea associated with:
(1) Herman T. Tavani
(2) David F. Noble
(3) Luciano Floridi
(4) Martin Heideggar

17. "Women are not born, but made," The above mentioned statement has been asserted by:
(1) Mary Wolstencraft
(2) Simone De Beauvoir
(3) Mary Fleming
(4) John Stuart Mill

18. Which method of causal analysis is NOT eliminative in nature?
(1) Method of Agreement
(2) Method of Difference
(3) Method of Residues
(4) Method of Concomitant Variation

19. Which one of the following statements is not correct according to Iqbal:
(1) Creation and God are Ego-nature
(2) Reconstruction of Islamic Truth
(3) Introspection is immediacy
(4) Islam believers in polytheism

20. Some German Shepherds are not good hunters.
All German Shepherds are gentle dogs
Therefore, no gentle dogs are good hunters.
Identify the fallacy that is committed in the above invalid syllogism.
(1) Fallacy of the undistributed middle
(2) Fallacy of the Illicit Major
(3) Fallacy of the Illicit Minor
(4) Fallacy of Exclusive Premises

21. In traditional square of opposition, the superaltern of the proposition, 'Some scientists are Mathematicians'- are as follows-
(1) Some Scientists are not Mathematicians
(2) All Scientists are Mathematicians
(3) No Scientists are Mathematician
(4) Some Scientists are Mathematician

22. Which one of the following is a believer in Law as command'
(1) H.L.A. Hart (2) Thomas Aquinas
(3) J.L. Austin (4) Jeremy Bentham

23. Which one of the following is not true according to Kamandaka?

(1) Mantra Shakti (2) Prabhav Shakti
(3) Utsah Shakti (4) Daivi Shakti

24. The political ideology known as liberalism is Characterised by:
(1) Individuality and freedom
(2) Collectivism and equality
(3) Individuality and equality
(4) Equality and freedom.

25. Who has asserted that reason dictates that there should be a state of peace and that every man should seek after peace?
(1) Locke (2) Rousseau
(3) Hobbes (4) Kant

26. Who maintains that the nature of social contract indicates that absolute monarchy is inconsistent with civil society?
(1) Hobbes (2) Rousseau
(3) Locke (4) David Hume

27. Individual can not attain the good in isolation, but only in society, the mission of the state is to promote virtue and happiness' is the statement of:
(1) Aristotle (2) Plato
(3) Socrates (4) Protagoras

28. From any true substitution instance of a propositional function, we may validly infer the existential quantification of that propositional function.
This effect comes from which quantification Rule:
(1) Universal Instantiation
(2) Universal Generalization
(3) Existential Instantiation
(4) Existential Generalization

29. "The architype of extension and colour can exist only in some other mind, and the objects of senses are nothing but sensations combined blended together in a concrete nexus." This view is adhered to:
(1) Descartes (2) Berkeley
(3) Leibnitz (4) Hume

30. Which of the following is the correct conversion of the proposition, "No politicians are Idealists"
(1) All idealists are politicians
(2) No Idealists are politicians
(3) Some Idealists are politicians
(4) Some idealists are not politicians

31. Which one of the following statements is NOT true according to S. Radhakrishnan?
(1) Ultimate reality is Absolute
(2) Absolute reality is pure-consciousness.
(3) Absolute is Pure-freedom
(4) Absolute is personal God.

32. According to Kant which of the following is accompanied by an appropriate degree of happiness for perfectly good universe?
(1) Moral will (2) Political will
(3) Goodwill (4) Human will

33. Who said that Maya is Principle of Cosmic Error'?
(1) Vivekanand
(2) Rabindra Nath Tagore
(3) S. Radha Krishnan
(4) Mahatma Gandhi

34. Ludwig Wittgenstein terms philosophy as " a battle against the bewitchment of our intelligence by means of language" in his book.
(1) Tractatus -Iogico-Philosophicus
(2) Philosophical Investigation
(3) On certainty
(4) The blue and Brown Books

35. That the world history is in the process of working out the knowledge of that which it is potentially is a view held by
(1) Aristotle
(2) Friedrich Schiller
(3) G.W.D. Hegel
(4) Arthur Schopenhauer

36. According to Jainism Aprigrah means?
(1) To lead a celibate life
(2) Not to injure only living beings
(3) Renunciation by thoughts words and deeds,
(4) Not to steal

37. Who among the following propounds accidentalism (yadrcchavada)?
(1) Mimamsa (2) Vaisesika
(3) Charvaka (4) Nyaya

38. "All the waters of all the seas are not to be compared with the flood of tears which has flowed since the universe first was", this is related to the idea of:
(1) Astāng Yoga (2) Sarvam Dukham
(3) Law of Karma
(4) Charvaka's Hedonism

39. David Hume agrees that genuine knowledge must be self-evident, but he finds no such knowledge anywhere except in which merely analyses its own concepts.
(1) Theology (2) Mathematics
(3) Metaphysics (4) Epistemology

40. St. Anselm offers his ontological proof for the existence of God in his work:
(1) Monologium (2) Proslogium
(3) Summa Theologca
(4) Cur Deus Homo

41. Who among the following philosophers are proponents of Sunyvada?
A. Sri Harsha B. Nagarjuna
C. Brhaspati D. Chandrakirti
Choose the correct answer from the options given below:
(1) A and C only (2) B and D only
(3) B, C and D only (4) A, B and C only

42. Who among the following thinkers are considered rationalists?
A. Berkley B. Descartes
C. Liebniz D. Spinoza
Choose the correct answer from the options given below:
(1) A and C only (2) A, C and D only
(3) B, C and D only (4) B and C only

43. Which of the following arguments is correct according to Samkhya philosophy given for exsistence of pursuit
(A) Sanght parathatvat
(B) Trigunadi Viparyayat
(C) Bhedanam Pravirmanat
(D) Kaivalyartha Pravirteh
Choose the correct answer from the options given below:
(1) (A) and (D) only
(2) (A) and (C) only
(3) (B) and (C) only
(4) (A), (B) and (D) only.

44. Which of the following are included as the central tenets of Budhisism
(A) Sanghatvada
(B) Prartiyā Samutpada
(C) Anekatmavād
(D) Anitytavād
(E) Astāngyoga
Choose the correct answer from the options given below:
(1) (A), (B) and (E) only
(2) (A), (B) and (C) only
(3) (A), (B), and (D) only
(4) (C), (E) and (B) only

45. Substance Dualism, also referred to as Cartesian/Classical dualism, asserts that there are two kinds of things 'Descartes' main arguments in favour of dualism are
A. The argument from doubt
B. The argument from indivisibility
C. The argument from irreducibility
D. The argument from category error
E. The argument from scientific evidence
Choose the correct answer from the options given below:
(1) A, B and C only
(2) B, C and D only
(3) D, C and E only
(4) A, D and E only

46. Which of the following purusharthas are included in Tri- Varg
A. Moksha B. Dharma
C. Kaam D. Arth
Choose the correct answer from the options given below:
(1) A, B and C only
(2) B, C and D only
(3) A, C and D only
(4) B, A and D only

47. Which of the following are included in Ekadash-vrata (Eleven vratas) of Mahatma Gandhi-
A. Education B. Fearlessness
C. Non-Stealing D. Physical Labour

Choose the correct answer from the options given below:
(1) A, B and C only (2) A, C and D only
(3) A, B and D only (4) B, C and D only

48. Arrange the following in chronological order in accordance with Jain Philosophy
A. Asrava B. Nirjara
C. Bandh D. Samvara
Choose the correct answer from the options given below:
(1) A, C, D, B (2) A, B, C, D
(3) B, C, A, D (4) A, D, B, C

49. Which of the following statements are true with reference to Samkhya Philosophy?
A. Prakriti is root cause of the world.
B. Prakriti is intelligent and conscious principle
C. Prakriti is the first principle of the universe.
D. Prakriti is manifested state of all effects
Choose the correct answer from the options given below:
(1) A and C only (2) A and B only
(3) B and D only (4) B and C only

50. According to the Gandhi, which of the following is the supreme end?
A. Morality B. Aparigrah
C. Truth D. Non-violence
E. Self- Purification
Choose the correct answer from the options given below:
(1) A and E only (2) C only
(3) E only (4) B and D only

51. If A. B and C are true attachments and X, Y and Z are false statements^ which of the following is true?
A. (A.X) ∨ (B.Y)
B. (X∨Z).(~X∨Z)
C. ~[(A.B) ∨ ~(B.A)]
D. {~[(B.~C) ∨ (Y.~Z)].[(B∨X) ∨ (B∨~Y)}
E. [(A∨B).~(B∨A)]
Choose the correct answer from the options given below:
(1) A and C only (2) B only
(3) A and D only (4) C and D only

52. Which of the following are included among the central tenets of John Rawl's Theory of justice?
A. The Fairness principle
B. Retributive justice
C. The difference Principle
D. The veil of ignorance
Choose the correct answer from the options given below:
(1) A and B only (2) B and C only
(3) A, B and C only (4) A, B, C and D

53. The opponents of verificationism place these objections to refute this principle
A. It is not a tautology.
B. It is not contingent
C. It is not empirically verifiable
D. It is not theoretically verifiable
E. It is intuitive
Choose the correct answer from the options given below:
(1) A and E only (2) B and C only
(3) A and C only (4) D and E only

54. For Spinoza everything is substance or requires substance as its basis because it has attributes of
A. Only Extension
B. Only Thought
C. Neither Thought nor extension
D. Both thought and extension
E. Attributes are infinite but only two are knowable by us humans
Choose the correct answer from the options given below:
(1) A and E only (2) B and C only
(3) D and B only (4) D and E only

55. Who among the following has supported social contract Theory?
A. John Locke B. Berkeley
C. Hobbes D. Rousseau
Choose the correct answer from the options given below:
(1) A and B only (2) B and C only
(3) A, C and D only (4) B and D only

56. Which of the following statements is not true according to Plato's Philosophy?

A. The ideal society forms a complete unity.
B. Plato supports right to private property.
C. The state is an educational institution as the instrument of civilization.
D. Laws are necessary to the realization of our true good.

Choose the correct answer from the options given below:
(1) A and E only (2) A, C and D only
(3) B and C only (4) B and D only

57. According to Hume, the association of ideas is a :
A. Logical Necessity
B. Psychological Necessity
C. Sociological Necessity
D. Mathematical Necessity
E. Emotioal Necessity

Choose the correct answer from the options given below:
(1) C and D only (2) B only
(3) E only (4) A and E only

58. Identify the fallacy in the given statement that is–"You must agree that Times of India is best daily newspaper in the city because seventy percent people read it.
A. Argumentum ad misericordiam
B. Argumentum ad Populum
C. Argumentum ad Baculum
D. Argumentum ad Hominem
E. Argumentum ad Verecandium

Choose the correct answer from the options given below:
(1) A and C only (2) B only
(3) A and D only (4) C and E only

59. The categorical syllogism having major terms distributed in the conclusion but undistributed in the major premises is invalid and having the fallacy known as:
A. Fallacy of Illicit Major
B. Fallacy of Exclusive premises
C. Fallacy of illicit minor
D. Fallacy of undistributed middle
E. Fallacy of Four terms

Choose the correct answer from the options given below:
(1) A only (2) A and B only
(3) B and C only (4) A and D only

60. In Kant's transcendental procedure, the unity of self- consciousness is presupposed by the categories, as the categories are presupposed by:
A. Intuition B. Experience
C. Understanding D. Reason
E. Holy will

Choose the correct answer from the options given below:
(1) D only (2) B only
(3) A and C only (4) A and B only

61. A pattern of inductive inference in which it is concluded that, when one phenomenon varies consistently with some other phenomenon in some manner, there is some causal relation between the two phenomena, is called
A. Joint Method
B. Concomitant Variation
C. Method of Residues
D. Method of Difference
E. Method of Doubt

Choose the correct answer from the options given below:
(1) A and E only (2) B only
(3) C only (4) D and B only

62. Who among the following classical Indian thinkers belong to Nyaya School?
A. Jayant Bhatt
B. Dharamaraja Adhvarin
C. Gangesa
D. Vimal Kirti

Choose the correct answer from the options given below:
(1) A, B and C only
(2) A and C only
(3) B and D only
(4) A, C and D only

63. Which of the following means of knowledge are accepted by Nyaya school?
A. Perception (Pratyaksh)

B. Inference (Anuman)
C. Comparison (Upmān)
D. Postulation (Arthapatti)

Choose the correct answer from the options given below:
(1) A, B and D only
(2) A and B only
(3) A, B, C and D
(4) A, B and C only

64. Which of the following schools of thought maintain that absence (abhava) is known through anuplabdhi?
A. Mimasa B. Nyaya
C. Advaita Vedanta D. Vaisesika

Choose the correct answer from the options given below:
(1) B and C only (2) A, B and C only
(3) A and C only (4) B, C and D only

65. Which of the following classical Indian texts belong is Nyaya school?
A. Mandukyakarika
B. Bhasa Pariccheda
C. Nyayamanjari
D. Nyaya bindu

Choose the correct answer from the options given below:
(1) A, C and D only (2) B and C only
(3) B, C and D only (4) C and D only

66. Match List I with List II

List I Theory	List II School of Philosphy
A. Prakrti Parinamvada	I. Buddhism
B. Brahma Parinamvada	II. Samikhya
C. Arambhavada	III. Nayaya
D. Anitya Parmanu Karanavada	IV. Ramanuja

Choose the correct answer from the options given below:
(1) A-II, B-IV, C-III, D-I
(2) A-III, B-I, C-II, D-IV
(3) A-IV, B-III, C-II, D-I
(4) A-I, B-II, C-III, D-IV

67. Match List I with List II

List I Theory	List II School
A. Anyattiakhyativada	I. Prabhakar
B. Vipant Khyativada	II. Kumarila
C. Anirvachniya Khyativada	III. Shankara
D. Akhyativad	IV. Nyaya

Choose the correct answer from the options given below:
(1) A-I, B-II, C-III, D-IV
(2) A-IV, B-III, C-II, D-I
(3) A-IV, B-II, C-III, D-I
(4) A-I, B-IV, C-II, D-III

68. Match List I with List II

List I Theory	List II Philosophy School
A. Theory of Relativity of Knowledge	I. Charvaka
B. Materialism	II. Nyaya
C. Logical Realism	III. Jainism
D. Triputi-pratyakshvada	IV. Prabhakar

Choose the correct answer from the options given below:
(1) A-I, B-II, C-III, D-IV
(2) A-II, B-I, C-III, D-IV
(3) A-IV, B-III, C-II, D-I
(4) A-III, B-II, C-I, D-IV

69. Match List I with List II

List I	List II
A. Charvaka	I. Apurva
B. Jainism	II. Astāngikmarga
C. Buddhism	III. Hedonism
D. Mimansa	IV. Tri-ratna

Choose the correct answer from the options given below:
(1) A-II, B-IV, C-III, D-I
(2) A-III, B-I, C-II, D-IV
(3) A-IV B-III, C-II, D-I
(4) A-I, B-II, C-III, D-IV

70. Match List I with List II

List I Book	List II Author
A. The Republic	I. Aristotle
E. Fragment on Government	II. Robert Nozick
C. Politics	III. Plato
D. Anarchy, State and utopia	IV. J. Bentham

Choose the correct answer from the options given below:

(1) A-III, B-II, C-I, D-IV
(2) A-I, B-II, C-III, D-IV
(3) A-III, B-IV, C-I, D-II
(4) A-IV, B-I, C-III, D-II

71. Match List I with List II

List I Philosopher	List II Theory
A. Pythagoras	I. Plenum & Vacuum
B. Anaximander	II. flux
C. Heracleitus	III. Apeiron
D. Democritus	IV. Numbers

Choose the correct answer from the options given below:

(1) A-IV, B-III, C-I, D-II
(2) A-IV, B-III, C-II, D-I
(3) A-III, B-I, C-IV, D-II
(4) A-IV, B-II, C-I, D-III

72. Match List I with List II

List I View	List II Thinker
A. Critique of Enlightenment	I. Merle an-Porty
B. Embodied Consciousness	II. Rorty
C. Philosophy of 'Other'	III. Nietzsche
D. Critique of reprentationatism	IV. Levinas

Choose the correct answer from the options given below:

(1) A-III, B-II, C-I, D-IV
(2) A-IV, B-I, C-III, D-II
(3) A-III, B-I, C-IV, D-II
(4) A-II, B-III, C-IV, D-I

73. Match List I with List II

List I Book	List II Author
A. Leviathan	I. John Locke
B. A theory of Justice	II. H.L.A Hart
C. Two Treatises on Government	III. John Rawls
D. The Concept of Law	IV. Hobbes

Choose the correct answer from the options given below:

(1) A-IV, B-III, C-I, D-II
(2) A-I, B-II, C-III, D-IV
(3) A-II, B-III, C-IV, D-I
(4) A-I, B-IV, C-III, D-II

74. Match List I with List II

List I Theory	List II Concept
A. Active Voluntary Euthanasia	I. Directly causing death without the consent of the patient
B. Active Non voluntary Euthanasia	II. Directly causing death with the consent of the patient
C. Passive voluntary Euthanasia	III. Withdrawing life-sustaining measures with the consent of the patient
D. Passive Non-voluntary Euthanasia	IV. Withdrawing life-sustaining measures without the consent of the patient.

Choose the correct answer from the options given below:

(1) A-I, B-II, C-III, D-IV
(2) A-II, B-I, C-III, D-IV
(3) A-II, B-I, C-IV, D-III
(4) A-I, B-IV, C-III, D-II

75. Match List I with List II

List I Author/Thinker	List II Theory
A. D.P. Chattopadhyaya	I. Humanism

B. Narayan Guru II. Marxist Aproach
C. Maulana Azad III. Mahima Dharma
D. Sant Kabi Shima Bhai IV. One caste, one religion, one god.

Choose the correct answer from the options given below:
(1) A-I, B-II, C-III, D-IV
(2) A-II, B-IV, C-I, D-III
(3) A-IV, B-II, C-III, D-I
(4) A-II, B-IV, C-III, D-I

76. As per Samkhya view of evolution, arrange the following in sequential order.
A. Prakriti in Homogenous state
B. Manas
C. Mahat
D. Ahankara

Choose the correct answer from the options given below:
(1) A, C, D, B (2) A, D, C, B
(3) D, C, B, A (4) C, D, B, A

77. Arrange the following in accordance with Plato's affirmation of hierarchy of knowledge starting from the lowest level to the highest level.
A. Conjecture as a kind of sensuous knowledge
B. Belief as the knowledge of sensible objects
C. Discursive intellect the knowledge of hypothetical nature
D. Dialectical knowledge as achieved in dialectic.

Choose the correct answer from the options given below:
(1) A, C, B, D (2) D, C, B, A
(3) A, B, C, D (4) B, A, C, D

78. Arrange the names of following medieval thinkers in chronological order starting with the latest.
A. Augustine B. Anselm
C. Aquinas D. Duns Scotus

Choose the correct answer from the options given below:
(1) D, C, A, B (2) D, C, B, A
(3) C, D, B, A (4) A, B, C, D

79. As per Locke's philosophy, arrange the following operations of mind in sequential order beginning from the last up to the first.
A. Perception
B. Discerning comparing and compounding
C. Abstraction
D. Retention and recalling
E. Naming

Choose the correct answer from the options given below:
(1) B, C, E, D, A (2) A, B, D, C, E
(3) C, E, B, D, A (4) A, D, B, E, C

80. As per Chanakyas view of seven organs of the State arrange the following starting with the one lowermost in hierarchy up to the supreme.
A. Swami B. Amatya
C. Janpad D. Durga

Choose the correct answer from the options given below:
(1) A, C, B, D (2) D, C, B, A
(3) A, B, C, D (4) D, B, C, A

81. Arrange the following in sequential order in accordance with Buddhist notion of twelve links of the causal wheel of dependent origination.
A. Jāti B. Tṛṣṇā
C. Bhava D. Upādāna
E. Vedanā

Choose the correct answer from the options given below:
(1) B, C, D, A, E (2) A, C, D, B, E
(3) E, B, D, C, A (4) B, D, C, A, E

82. Arrange the following statements in sequential order in accordance with Buddhist notion of noble truths.
A. There is a way of suffering
B. There is cause of suffering
C. There is cessation of suffering
D. There is suffering

Choose the correct answer from the options given below:
(1) A, B, C, D (2) B, D, C, A
(3) D, B, C, A (4) D, C, B, A

83. As per Nyaya's philosophy, arrange the following steps of inference in sequential order.

A. Wherever there is smoke, there is fire, as in the kitchen
B. The mountain has fire.
C. Because mountain has smoke.
D. Therefore, the mountain has fire
E. The mountain also has smoke accompanied by fire, like the kitchen.

Choose the correct answer from the options given below:

(1) B, C, E, A, D (2) B, E, A, C, D
(3) B, C, A, E, D (4) B, A, E, C, D

84. Arrange the following in sequential order in accordance with eight-fold Yoga

A. Samadhi
B. Meditation
C. Sense-withdrawal
D. Concentration

Choose the correct answer from the options given below:

(1) D, C, B, A (2) C, D, B, A
(3) A, B, D, C (4) C, B, D, A

85. As per Nyaya definition of perception, arrange the following in sequential order

A Sense-object contact (indriyārtha sannikarṣa)
B. Indeterminate (Avyapadeśyam)
C. Determinate (vyavsāyātmakam)
D. Non-erroneous (avyābhichari)

Choose the correct answer from the options given below:

(1) B, C, A, D (2) A, B, D, C
(3) A, D, B, C (4) C, B, D, A

86. Given below are two statements: one is labelled as Assertion A and the other is labelled as Reason R

Assertion A: According to M.N. Roy Philosophy is materialistic.

Reason R: Materialism is the only possible philosophy.

In the light of the above statements, choose the most appropriate answer from the option given below

(1) Both A and R are correct and R is correct explanation of A.
(2) Both A and R are correct but R is not the correct explanation of A.
(3) A is correct but R is not correct
(4) A is not correct but R is correct

87. Given below are two statements: one is labelled as Assertion A and the other is labelled as Reason R

Assertion A: According to Gandhi Truth is God

Reason R: He believed that non-violence is the means to realize God

In the light of the above statements, choose the most appropriate answer from the option given below

(1) Both A and R are correct and R is correct explanation of A.
(2) Both A and R are correct but R is not the correct explanation of A.
(3) A is correct but R is not correct
(4) A is not correct but R is correct

88. Given below are two statements: one is labelled as Assertion A and the other is labelled as Reason R

According to Radhakrishanan

Assertion A: The idea of welfare and public service have been quite active in Hinduism.

Reason R: Hindu Religion has accepted life in its entirety.

In the light of the above statements, choose the most appropriate answer from the option given below

(1) Both A and R are correct and R is correct explanation of A.
(2) Both A and R are correct but R is not the correct explanation of A.
(3) A is correct but R is not correct
(4) A is not correct but R is correct

89. Given below are two statements: one is labelled as Assertion A and the other is labelled as Reason R

Assertion A: According to Buddhism in empirical world dominated by the intellect, everything is relative conditional, dependent and impermanent.

Reason R: According to Buddhism, depending on the cause the effect arises. Thus every object of thought is necessarily relative.

In the light of the above statements, choose the most appropriate answer from the option given below:

(1) Both A and R are correct and R is correct explanation of A.
(2) Both A and R are correct but R is not the correct explanation of A.
(3) A is correct but R is not correct
(4) A is not correct but R is correct

90. Given below are two statements: one is labelled as Assertion A and the other is labelled as Reason R

Assertion A: According to Shankara Brahman associated with its potency, Maya is Saguna Brahman and is creator, preserver and destroyer of the world.

Reason R: Maya is indescribable, neither existent nor non-existent nor both.

In the light of the above statements, choose the most appropriate answer from the option given below:

(1) Both A and R are correct and R is correct explanation of A.
(2) Both A and R are correct but R is not the correct explanation of A.
(3) A is correct but R is not correct
(4) A is not correct but R is correct

Read the following Passage and answer the questions

They say 'means are after all means' I would say means are after all everything: as the means so the end. There is no wall of separation between means and end. Indeed, the Creator, has given us control (and that too very limited) over means, but none over the end. Realization of the goal is in exact proportion to that of the means. This is a proportion that admits of no exception.

–Mahatma Gandhi

91. The above mentioned paragraph is stated by Mahatma Gandhi in the following book:

(1) Young India
(2) Hind Swaraj
(3) My Experiments with Truth
(4) Mooknayak

92. The given paragraph seems to advocate which particular model of ethics?

(1) Virtue Ethics
(2) Consequential Ethics
(3) Deontological Ethics
(4) Intuitionalistic Ethics

93. In the Gandhian philosophy, the attainment of 'Truth-as-end' depends on:

(1) Truth also as means.
(2) Non-violence as end
(3) Non-violence as means
(4) Decentralization as end

94. In Gandhian ethics, the influence of disinterested action (Niskama Karma) is clearly visible in:

(1) Realization of Truth
(2) Purity of means
(3) Attainment of liberation
(4) Acquisition of knowledge.

95. Gandhiji strongly recommends that "As soon as we lose the moral basis, we cease to be ______."

(1) Political (2) Religious
(3) Social (4) Democratic

Raed the following passage and answer the question

Contemporary defenders of the traditional natural Law approach might seek to mount a secular defense of Aquinas's notion that the purpose of law is to promote the common good. They may point out that what we understand as oppression and exploitation was understood by those who enacted slave laws as just and right. Their point is not to endorse the relativist notion that something is made right by the simple fact that people think it is right. The traditional natural law view clearly rejects any such relativism in favor of the idea that there are objective moral truths. Rather, their point is to suggest that in enacting laws people are trying to do what is right, however flawed their notions of right and wrong may be if this is what people are trying to do, then we can still say that the purpose of law is to promote morality and justice. This is the human aim of law, regardless of whether it is God's aim as well.

96. What is the subject matter discussed in the passage. Given above?
(1) Traditional Natural Law
(2) Divine Law
(3) Constitutional Law
(4) Statutory Law

97. According to Aquinas, the purpose of law is
(1) To promote common good
(2) To promote common will
(3) To promote common right
(4) To promote common divinity

98. Which one of the following is a supporter of traditional natural law theory?
(1) Immanuel Kant (2) H.L.A. Hart
(3) J.L. Austin (4) T. Aquinas

99. What is the relation between morality and justice in Law?
(1) Constituent components of law
(2) Constituent connections of law
(3) Constituent components of reason
(4) Constituent connections of reason

100. Traditional natural law clearly rejects relativism in favor of the idea that
(1) There are subjective moral truth
(2) There are objective moral truth
(3) There are objective legal truth
(4) There are subjective legal truth

Answers

1. (2)	**2.** (3)	**3.** (1)	**4.** (3)	**5.** (3)	**6.** (2)	**7.** (3)	**8.** (2)	**9.** (2)	**10.** (4)
11. (4)	**12.** (2)	**13.** (3)	**14.** (4)	**15.** (2)	**16.** (3)	**17.** (2)	**18.** (4)	**19.** (4)	**20.** (3)
21. (2)	**22.** (3)	**23.** (4)	**24.** (1)	**25.** (3)	**26.** (3)	**27.** (2)	**28.** (4)	**29.** (2)	**30.** (2)
31. (4)	**32.** (3)	**33.** (1)	**34.** (2)	**35.** (3)	**36.** (3)	**37.** (3)	**38.** (2)	**39.** (2)	**40.** (2)
41. (2)	**42.** (3)	**43.** (*)	**44.** (3)	**45.** (1)	**46.** (2)	**47.** (4)	**48.** (1)	**49.** (1)	**50.** (2)
51. (2)	**52.** (4)	**53.** (3)	**54.** (4)	**55.** (3)	**56.** (*)	**57.** (2)	**58.** (2)	**59.** (1)	**60.** (2)
61. (2)	**62.** (2)	**63.** (4)	**64.** (3)	**65.** (2)	**66.** (1)	**67.** (3)	**68.** (*)	**69.** (*)	**70.** (3)
71. (2)	**72.** (3)	**73.** (1)	**74.** (2)	**75.** (2)	**76.** (1)	**77.** (3)	**78.** (2)	**79.** (3)	**80.** (2)
81. (2)	**82.** (3)	**83.** (3)	**84.** (2)	**85.** (2)	**86.** (1)	**87.** (1)	**88.** (1)	**89.** (1)	**90.** (2)
91. (1)	**92.** (3)	**93.** (3)	**94.** (2)	**95.** (2)	**96.** (1)	**97.** (1)	**98.** (4)	**99.** (1)	**100.** (2)

Choose the *correct* answer from the options given below:

(1) A, B Only (2) C, D Only
(3) B, D Only (4) D, E Only

11. Consider the following about texts of Indian-Philosophy and identify the correct items:

A. "Laukiko- mārgo- anusartavyaḥ" is the view seconded by Jayarāśi

B. 'Tttvopplavasiṁha' is a Vaitandika text

C. Vaidalya- sūtra supports the assertion of Nyāya- Sutra

Choose the *correct* answer from the options given below:

(1) A and C Only
(2) A, B and C Only
(3) B and C Only
(4) A and B Only

12. Which of the following is incorrect?

(1) Vijñānvādin Buddhism believes in Sva-prakāśavāda
(2) Buddhists reject Pramāṇa- Samplava
(3) Nyāya adheres to Para-Prakāśavāda
(4) For Vaibhāṣika, perception as a source of external world's knowledge cannot be conciliated with kṣaṇikavāda

13. Identify the consistent items with the vedāntic- view of perception

A. Kedārī- kulyā- Nyāya

B. Transcendental knowledge is related to Vrtti Caitanya

C. Pramātṛ- Caitanya is related to subject

D. Pramātṛ- Caitanya is related to object

Choose the *correct* answer from the options given below:

(1) A and B Only
(2) A, B and D Only
(3) B and C Only
(4) A and C Only

14. You explain the meaning of the term hyena to your friend by giving its description since you are quite familiar with hyenas. Two of you go to a jungle and see a creature, your friend recalls your description and compares it to the creature and knows, "this is 'hyena'," in that situation your knowledge, "this is hyena" is through (as per nyāya) :-

(1) Pratyakṣa (2) Anumāna
(3) Upamāna (4) Śabda

15. Which among the following are incorrect

A. For Leibniz, our ideas of space, figure, motion have their origin, in the common sense, in the mind itself

B. For Spinoza, thought and extension are separate substances

C. According to Hegel, concrete universal notion is the synthesis of opposites

D. According to Kant, all synthetic judgements give us genuine knowledge

E. According to Berkeley, the idea of soul can be formed on the basis of its acts,

Choose the *correct* answer from the options given below:

(1) A, C and D Only
(2) C, D and E Only
(3) A, B and D Only
(4) B, D and E Only

16. Match the **List-I** with **List-II**

LIST I (Humean View)	**LIST II (Its justification)**
A. Empirical	I. Our knowledge is limited to the world of phenomena
B. Positivistic	II. Our knowledge has its source in experience
C. Agnostic	III. We know nothing of the ultimates
D. Humanistic	IV. The human mental world is the only legitimate sphere of science and enquiry

Choose the *correct* answer from the options given below:

(1) A-I, B-II, C-III, D-IV
(2) A-III, B-II, C-I, D-IV
(3) A-IV, B-I, C-II, D-III
(4) A-II, B-I, C-III, D-IV

17. Match the **List-I** with **List-II**

LIST I (Kant's Judgment)	**LIST II (Example)**
A. The Particular Judgment	I. Every effect must have a cause.
B. The Infinite Judgment	II. If the air is warm, the thermometer rises.
C. The Hypothetical Judgment	III. Mind is unextended.
D. The Apodictic Judgment	IV. Some animals are herbivores.

Choose the *correct* answer from the options given below:

(1) A-I, B-II, C-III, D-IV
(2) A-I, B-IV, C-II, D-III
(3) A-III, B-IV, C-II, D-I
(4) A-IV, B-III, C-II, D-I

18. The crux of Kant's Transcendental Method lies in the argument that it leads:

(1) From the presuppositions to their logical outcomes
(2) From experience to its necessary presuppositions
(3) From individual experiences to general experiences
(4) From one postulate to several other leading postulates

19. The following assertions are attributed to Rene Descartes:

(A) I know that I perceive the truth clearly and distinctly, because God exists and is not a deceiver.
(B) I know that God exists and is not a deceiver because I perceive this truth clearly and distinctly.

In the logical terms, the above mentioned assertions commit the informal fallacy called as ________

(1) Appeal to Authority
(2) Complex Question
(3) Circular Reasoning
(4) Appeal to Ignorance

20. According to John Locke, sometimes the mind perceives the agreement or disagreement of two ideas by direct inspection, without the intervention of any other ideas. Such knowledge is called

(1) Hypothetical Knowledge
(2) Sensitive Knowledge
(3) Intuitive Knowledge
(4) Demonstrative Knowledge

21. Rene Descartes defends the external world by posing following arguments:

A. Belief in an external world is not natural.
B. The mind is primarily its conceptions.
C. Imagination and perception do not depend just on conception.
D. Belief in an external world is required to explain the phenomena of imagination and perception.
E. The existence of an all-perfect God is the surest guarantee of the external world.

Choose the *correct* answer from the options given below:

(1) A, B, C, D Only
(2) B, C, D, E Only
(3) A, C, D, E Only
(4) A, B, D, E Only

22. Match the **List-I** with **List-II**

LIST I (Thinkers)	**LIST II (Ancient School of Philosophy)**
A. Hippo, Idaeus, Diogenes	I. The Stoics
B. Xenophanes, Parmenides, Zeno	II. The Atomists
C. Leucippus and Democritus	III. The Ionic School
D. Zeno, Cleanthes, Chrysippus	IV. The Eleatic School

Choose the *correct* answer from the options given below:

(1) A-I, B-III, C-IV, D-II
(2) A-III, B-IV, C-II, D-I

(3) A-IV, B-I, C-II, D-III
(4) A-II, B-III, C-I, D-IV

23. The philosophic knowledge that stands as the preserve of 'philosopher- tillers' is expressed in:
A. The Simile of the Sun
B. The Divided Line
C. The Story of the Flying arrow
D. The Simile of the Cave
E. The Parable of the Beast
Choose the *correct* answer from the options given below:
(1) A, B, C Only
(2) A, B, D Only
(3) B, C, D Only
(4) D, C, E Only

24. Modem 'Brain in a Vat' arguments are direct descendants of:
(1) Aristotle's Akrasia
(2) Cartesian Doubt
(3) Humean Doubt
(4) Hegclian Geist

25. Match the **List-I** with **List-II**

LIST I (Aristotelian Terms)	**LIST II (Meaning of the Term)**
A. Phronesis	I. Flourishing
B. Arete	II. Weakness of the will
C. Akrasia	III. Virtue or Excellence
D. Eudaimonia	IV. Practical Wisdom

Choose the *correct* answer from the options given below:
(1) A-I, B-II, C-III, D-IV
(2) A-II, B-I, C-IV, D-III
(3) A-III, B-IV, C-I, D-II
(4) A-IV, B-II, C-II, D-I

26. Which of the following is not in line with the philosophical thought of St. Thomas Aquinas
(1) Faith is a gift from the creator
(2) It is better to know an object of greatest magnitude imperfectly than to love it
(3) Indetermination is c[illegible] istics of the will
(4) Grace is a bridge betwee[illegible] creator and a finite creation

27. "Credent Intelligas" (Believe in order that you may understand) is a dictum of
(1) St. Augustine
(2) St. Anslem
(3) St. Thomas Aquinas
(4) Protagoras

28. What among the following can not be attributed to Leibniz
(1) The source of mechanics lies in metaphysics
(2) Bodies act according to the laws of final causes, by means of desire, ends and means
(3) Monads are spiritual
(4) Every Monad is 'charged with the past' and 'big with the future.

29. Match the **List-I** with **List-II**
Match the definition of happiness with the system of philosophies

LIST I	**LIST II**
A. Psychophysical happiness	I. Nyāya
B. Absolute absence of misery	II. Vedānta
C. Absolute separation of soul from Body	III. Cārvāka
D. Blissfulness	IV. Jainism

Choose the *correct* answer from the options given below:
(1) A-III, B-I, C-IV, D-II
(2) A-II, B-II, C-I, D-IV
(3) A III, B-II, C-IV, D-I
(4) A-II, B-IV, C-III, D-I

30. Which among the following Āśrama is also known as "Vaikhānasa"?
(1) Gṛhastha
(2) Brahmacarya
(3) Sannyāsa
(4) Vānaprastha

...nation among the following ...the meaning of 'Karma"?

...reap what you sow.

...ne present life is a by chance occurrence.

C. You don't get the result of an unperformed Karma.

D. All our decisions are entirely determined by previous Karma.

E. The law of causation is compatible with the theory of Karma.

Choose the *correct* answer from the options given below:

(1) B, C, D Only
(2) A, B, C Only
(3) A, C, E Only
(4) B, D, E Only

32. Match the **List-I** with **List-II**

LIST I	LIST II
A. Nitya Karma	I. We should take bath daily,
B. Naimittika Kanna	II. If we want to clean ourselves, we should take bath daily
C. Kāmya Karma	III. We should take bath after eclipse
D. Niṣiddha Karma	IV. We should avoid stale food,

Choose the *correct* answer from the options given below:

(1) A-I, B-II, C-III, D-IV
(2) A-I, B-III, C-IV, D-II
(3) A-I, B-III, C-II, D-IV
(4) A-IV, B-II, C-I, D-III

33. What are the factors of Cikīrṣā, according to Nyāya philosophy, among the following?

A. Balavad aniṣta asambhāvyatā jñāna
B. Prārabdha phala jñāna
C. Krtisādhyata jñāna
D. Iṣtasādhanatā jñāna
E. Akarmasādhyatā jñāna

Choose the *correct* answer from the options given below:

(1) C, D, E Only
(2) A, C, D Only
(3) B, C, D Only
(4) A, B, C Only

34. In which, among the following sense Apūrva is not considered

(1) Karma
(2) Relation between Karma and its result
(3) Sanskāra
(4) Sādhana / Kārya / Linga

35. Arrange the following elements of Pratityasamutpada in correct cause- effect order:

A. Nāma- rūpa B. Vedana
C. Ṣadāvatana D. Tṛṣṇā
E. Sparśa

Choose the *correct* answer from the options given below:

(1) A-E-D-B-C
(2) A-C-E-B-D
(3) A-B-C-D-E
(4) A-C-B-E-D

36. No one can stay without action even for a moment due to .... according to the Bhagavadgītā.

(1) Guṇa of Prakṛti
(2) Divine Will
(3) Compassion
(4) Cowardice

37. Match the **List-I** with **List-II**

LIST I (Authors)	LIST II (Books)
A. Henery Sidgwick	I. Data of Ethics
B. Herbert Spencer	II. Ethics
C. J.S. Mill	III. Outlines of the History of Ethics
D. G.E. Moore	IV. Utilitarianism

Choose the *correct* answer from the options given below:

(1) A-I, B-III, C-IV, D-II
(2) A-III, B-IV, C-I, D-II
(3) A-III, B-I, C-IV D-II
(4) A-I, B-II, C-III, D-IV

38. What is the "naturalistic fallacy"?
(1) A problem created by the Nature
(2) Human being is by nature problematic
(3) Mistaking an ethical judgement with a factual one
(4) Focusing on the good of nature

39. What is not true to Utilitarianism?
(1) An action is good if it produces useful things.
(2) An action is intrinsically good or bad.
(3) The merit of Law is due to its effect.
(4) Good is equivalent to pleasurable

40. Match the **List-I** with **List-II**

LIST I (Thinkers)	**LIST II (Thoughts)**
A. Jeremy Bentham	I. Good means I approve it,
B. J.S. Mill	II. Quantitative distinction of pleasure,
C. C.L. Stevenson	III. Good means I prescribe it,
D. R.M. Hare	IV. Quantitative distinction of pleasure

Choose the *correct* answer from the options given below:
(1) A-II, B-IV, C-I, D-III
(2) A-I, B-IV, C-II, D-III
(3) A-II, B-II, C-I, D-IV
(4) A-II, B-IV, C-III, D-I

41. Match the **List-I** with **List-II**

LIST I (Thinkers)	**LIST II (Thoughts)**
A. Henry Davie Thoreau	I. Be a member of a kingdom of ends.
B. G.E. Moore	II. That government is best which governs the least.
C. Immanuel Kant	III. My station and its duties.
D. F.H. Bradley	IV. Good is simple and indefinable.

Choose the *correct* answer from the options given below:
(1) A-I, B-II, C-III, D-IV
(2) A-II, B-IV, C-I, D-III
(3) A-II, B-IV, C-III, D-I
(4) A-IV, B-II, C-I, D-III

42. Which of the following statements are correct?
A. Highest good in Kant is goodwill.
B. Henry Sidswick's view of utilitarianism is Rational Utilitarianism.
C. J.S. Mill does not accept quantitative differences in pleasures.
D. The number of virtues in socrates is 'one'.

Choose the *correct* answer from the options given below:
(1) A, B, C Only
(2) A, B, C, D Only
(3) B, D Only
(4) A, C Only

43. Which theory among the following is not compatible with capital punishment?
(1) Deterrent Theory
(2) Reformative Theory
(3) Retributive Theory
(4) Preventive Theory

44. Which one among the following is not a Metaethical question?
(1) What is the meaning of a moral judgement?
(2) What is the meaning of 'Good'?
(3) What is the right thing to do?
(4) Can moral judgements be proved

45. Which among the following is not a true statement with reference to Metaethics?
(1) Some non-cognitivists are intuitionists.
(2) For an emotivist, "Killing is bad" means "Killing, boo!"
(3) C.L. Stevenson is not an emotivist.
(4) According to G.E. Moore, the meaning of an ethical term can be intuited.

46. Which among the following are true to Intuitionism?

A. Conscience is a universal faculty of all persons.
B. Rightness and wrongness are inherent qualities of actions.
C. Actions are intrinsically right or wrong.
D. The moral merit of an action is dependent on its result.
E. Co nscience reveals the rightness of an action by way of perceiving its consequence.

Choose the *correct* answer from the options given below:
(1) A, B, C Only
(2) C, D, E Only
(3) B, D, E Only
(4) B, C, D Only

47. Which among the following is an inconsistent thought in the light of Swami Vivekananda?
(1) Monistic Idealism
(2) Reality is determinate
(3) No distinction of qualifications can be ascribed to Reality
(4) As a pantheist, he holds God to be personal

48. Which among the following is incorrect in the light of Sarvepalli Radhakrishnan
(1) Man is a combination of egoism and self-transcendence,
(2) Universe is a planned activity
(3) The created world is not an illusion
(4) World is an ordered whole

49. Annihilation of Caste of Ambedkar has a detailed response to
(1) Gandhi
(2) M.N. Roy
(3) Nehru
(4) D.P. Chattopadhyaya

50. The following from Upanisad-s encapsulates the entire message of Hindu religion as per Gandhi:-
(1) Bhṛgu- Varuṇa dialogue in Taittirīya
(2) Yama- Naciektā samvāda in Kāṭha
(3) Satyameva Jayate from Muṇḍaka
(4) The first verse from Īṣa

51. The following is not a feature of Gnostic Being in Sri Aurobindo:-
(1) He has undergone supramental transformation
(2) He relentlessly works for materializing the divine life
(3) There are types of Gnostic Beings, such as intuitional, overmental, etc
(4) He is same as Jīvanmukta of Vedānta

52. The following is not true about Radical Humanism of MN Roy:
(1) It is basically a type of speculative ontology
(2) The ethical norms are this- worldly
(3) To be moral one needs to be only human
(4) Freedom is the highest value

53. Which among the following can be claimed in the context of Neitzche's moral thought
A. The idea of superman is an attempt to restore the ideals of master morality.
B. Master morality asks the man to be empathetic.
C. The values of the master are expressions of the will to power.
D. Master-morality creates its own values.
E. The slave can one day become the master.

Choose the *correct* answer from the options given below:
(1) B, C and E Only
(2) C, D and E Only
(3) B, D and E Only
(4) A, C and D Only

54. Which of the following is incorrectly matched
(1) 'Here is a Hand' argument- G.E. Moore
(2) Systematically Misleading Expression- Gilbert Ryle
(3) Virtue Epistemology- A.J. Ayer
(4) Naturalized Epistemology- Quine

55. The idea through which Husserl dispels solipsism is
(1) Transcendental Monadology
(2) Lenbenswelt
(3) Phenomenological Reduction
(4) Ego, Cogito, Cogitata

56. In the context of 'Phenomenological Reduction' what can not be claimed
A. The act by which bracketing is made possible is called 'epoche'
B. According to Husserl, there is only one type of reduction i.e. Phenomenological
C. 'Epoche' is going to be a position of the origin of our knowledge
D. 'Cartesian doubt' and 'Epoche' are essentially same for Husserl,
E. 'Epoche' eliminates all elements which make doubt possible,

Choose the *correct* answer from the options given below:
(1) A and C Only
(2) B and E Only
(3) C and E Only
(4) B and D Only

57. Which among the following cannot be claimed in the light of Heidegger's thought
A. Philosophy committed a mistake by dissociating itself from the notion of Being since the tune of Plato.
B. The real self is ethical not cognitive.
C. Being must be approached through an investigation into Dasein.
D. Being is God.
E. The world can be bracketed or doubted.

Choose the *correct* answer from the options given below:
(1) D and E Only
(2) C and E Only
(3) B and C Only
(4) A and C Only

58. Which is not correct about Sartre:-
(1) "Being and nothingness" demolishes the spirit of seriousness.
(2) The aim of "Transcendence of Ego" is to respond to the misgivings about Existentialism.
(3) A comrade believing in 'all is well' owing to his egalitarian dream is a case of bad faith owing to denial of facticity.
(4) My body is my facticity.

59. The central conception in Kierkegaard's "Sickness unto Death" is:
(1) Dread
(2) Three Spheres of Being
(3) Freedom
(4) Despair

60. Which of the following is incorrect about Wittgenstein's philosophy:
(1) There is no example of object in the text of tractatus
(2) There is no example of name in the text of tractatus
(3) Resolute and Irresolute readings are methods to read "Philosophical Investigation"
(4) "New Wittgenstein" is a book by group of Wittgensteinian scholars

61. A. J. Ayer's approach regarding 'non-sensical nature of certain observations' was shaped by Willgenstein's famous remark at the end of:
(1) Tractatus- Logico- Philosophions
(2) Philosophical Investigations
(3) On Certainty
(4) Blue Book

62. Doing anything with language- whether making statements or promising, commanding, asking and so forth are all:
(1) Perlocutionary act
(2) Locutionary act
(3) Illocutionary act
(4) Nonsensical act

63. Which of the following statements can be credited to Ayer's Emotivism?
A. Ethical statements are neither laute logics nor empirically verifiable.

B. Ethical statements are unsayable 'pseudo concepts'.
C. Ethical statements simply evince i.e. indicate approval or disapproval.
D. Ethical statements express feeling, but cannot arouse feeling in others.

Choose the *correct* answer from the options given below:
(1) A, B, C Only
(2) B, C, D Only
(3) A, B, D Only
(4) A, B, C, D Only

64. Put the following analytical philosophers in the correct chronological order:
A. Carnap B. Quine
C. Ryle D. Moore
E. Frege

Choose the *correct* answer from the options given below:
(1) E, A, B, C, D
(2) E, C, D, B, A
(3) E, D, A, C, B
(4) E, A, C, D, B

65. Which among the following is incorrect in the context of Tagore's philosophy
(1) The reason for creation is joy
(2) Metaphysically, man in many respects is God- like
(3) The 'Surplus' in man indicates the finite aspect of man's nature
(4) The infinite nature of man's personality is dynamic

66. Match the **List-I** with **List-II**

LIST I	LIST II
A. Sādharaṇa Dharma	I. Telling lie to save the life of an innocent
B. Rājadharma	II. The nature of a person should be determined by the proportion of Sattva, Rajas and Tamas guna
C. Āpaddharma	III. Every person must practice non-violence
D. Varṇāśrama Dharma	IV. The behaviour of a king should be guided by moral excellence

Choose the *correct* answer from the options given below:
(1) A-III, B-IV, C-I, D-II
(2) A-I, B-IV, C-III, D-II
(3) A-I, B-III, C-IV, D-II
(4) A-I, B-II, C-III, D-IV

67. Match the **List-I** with **List-II**

LIST I (Article)	LIST II (Subject matter)
A. Art. 21A	I. Right to Equality
B. Art.14	II. Right to Life
C. Art. 21	III. Abolition of Untouchability
D. Art. 17	IV. Right to Education

Choose the *correct* answer from the options given below:
(1) A-I, B-II, C-III, D-IV
(2) A-IV, B-I, C-II, D-III
(3) A-IV, B-I, C-III, D-II
(4) A-I, B-IV, C-II, D-III

68. Which one among the following is not included as the parts (limbs) of State, according to Kautilva
(1) Society (Janapada)
(2) Economy (Koṣa)
(3) Fort (Durga)
(4) Constitution (Samvidhāna)

69. The correct sequence in Gandhian scheme of social change in the order of succession is
A. Swadeshi B. Swarājya
C. Sarvodaya

Choose the *correct* answer from the options given below:
(1) A, C, B (2) A, B, C
(3) B, A, C (4) B, C, A

70. According to the Mahābhārata, which of the following four are included in the means to achieve the end of the State
A. Truth (Satya)
B. Reasoning (Upapatti)
C. Expediency (Upāya)
D. Good conduct (Sadāchāra)
E. Punishment (Danda)
Choose the *correct* answer from the options given below:
(1) B, C, D, E Only
(2) C, D, E, A Only
(3) A, B, C, D Only
(4) A, B, C, E Only

71. Match the **List-I** with **List-II**

LIST I **Political Ideology)**	**LIST II** **(Nature of the State)**
A. Liberalism	I. Denial
B. Conservatism	II. Common Good
C. Socialism	III. Coercion
D. Anarchism	IV. Weak paternalism

Choose the *correct* answer from the options given below:
(1) A-I, B-II, C-III, D-IV
(2) A-II, B-I, C-IV, D-III
(3) A-III, B-IV C-I, D-II
(4) A-IV, B-III, C-II, D-I

72. Consider the following statements about Judith Butler
A. There is an unchallenged distinction between sex and gender
B. Gender may be seen as a cultural interpretation of sex
C. Gender is not to culture as sex is to nature
D. "Gender Trouble" is one of the masterpiece works by Butler
Choose the *correct* answer from the options given below:
(1) A, B and D Only
(2) A, C and D Only
(3) B, C and D Only
(4) C and D Only

73. Consider the following statements and identify the correct ones:
A. In Hobbes, the contract leads to both society and state.
B. In Joint Locke, there are two contracts - one gives rise to the state, the other to the government.
C. In Locke as well as Rousseau, state is an organism.
D. Hobbes belongs to rational natural traditions of political philosophy.
Choose the *correct* answer from the options given below:
(1) A and B Only
(2) A, B and C Only
(3) B and D Only
(4) A Only

74. Consider the following statements about Miranda Fricker's conception of Epistemic Injustice
A. The conception could be a way to understand epistemic ideas through the feminist lens.
B. There are two types of epistemic injustice hermeneutic and testimonial.
C. In order to ensure epistemic justice, one must be a virtuous hearer.
D. The concept of testimony is revisited from a virtue epistemological perspective by Fricker.
Choose the *correct* answer from the options given below:
(1) A and C Only
(2) B, C and D Only
(3) A, B and D Only
(4) A, B, C and D Only

75. The correct sequence of imperfect societies, as per Plato, in the progression of imperfection is
A. Oligarchy
B. Timocracy
C. Tyranny
D. Democracy
Choose the *correct* answer from the options given below:

(1) D, C, A, B
(2) D, A, B, C
(3) A, B, D, C
(4) A, D, B, C

76. What is not true of a valid argument among the following?
(1) If its conclusion is false, then all the premises cannot be true together
(2) If all its propositions are true, then it is a sound argument
(3) If any of the premises is true, then its conclusion is necessarily true
(4) It's conclusion necessarily follows from its premises

77. Name the fallacy committed in the following argument
No poets are accountants
Some artists are poets
Therefore, some artists are accountants
(1) Existential fallacy
(2) Fallacy of Illicit Process
(3) Fallacy of Exclusive Premises
(4) Fallacy of four terms

78. What can be correctly said for argument from "some reformers are fanatics, so some idealists are fanatics, because all reformers are idealists".
(1) AII - III figure; Valid
(2) IAI - III figure; Invalid
(3) IAI - III figure; Valid
(4) AII - III figure; Invalid

79. Match the **List-I** with **List-II**

LIST I (Definition)	LIST II (Description)
A. Stipulative	I. A definition devised to eliminate ambiguity or vagueness by delineating a concept more sharply
B. Lexical	II. A definition that encapsulates an understanding of the theory in which the definiendum term is a key element
C. Precising	III. A definition that reports the meaning that the definiendum already has
D. Theoretical	IV. A definition in which a new symbol is introduced to which some meaning is arbitrarily assigned

Choose the *correct* answer from the options given below:
(1) A-III, B-IV, C-II, D-I
(2) A-I, B-II, C-III, D-IV
(3) A-II, B-I, C-IV, D-III
(4) A-IV, B-III, C-I, D-II

80. Match the **List-I** with **List-II**

LIST I (Fallacy)	LIST II Description)
A. Accident	I. When correct reasoning is undermined by the deliberate misrepresentation of the opponent's position
B. Equivocation	II. When a shift of meaning arises within an argument as a consequence of changes in the emphasis given to its words or parts,
C. The Strawman	III. When one mistakenly applies a generalization to an indindual case that it does not properly govern
D. Accent	IV. When the same word/phrase is

used with two or more meanings in formulating an argument.

Choose the *correct* answer from the options given below:

(1) A-I, B-IV, C-III, D-II
(2) A-IV, B-III, C-II, D-I
(3) A-III, B-IV, C-I, D-II
(4) A-III, B-I, C-II, D-IV

81. Match the **List-I** with **List-II**

LIST I (Proposition)	**LIST II (Example)**
A. Contrary	I. If 'E' is false: 'O' is undetermined
B. Sub-Contrary	II. If 'I' is true: 'A' is undetermined
C. Sub-Altern	III. If 'A' is true: 'E' is false
D. Super-Altern	IV. If 'O' is false: 'I' true

Choose the *correct* answer from the options given below:

(1) A-II, B-I, C-III, D-IV
(2) A-III, B-IV C-II, D-I
(3) A-I, B-III, C-IV D-II
(4) A-IV, B-II, C-III, D-I

82. $(P \vee Q) \supset (R . S)$, $\sim P \supset (T \supset \sim T)$, $\sim R$

Given the above three are consistent what all is entailed bv these

A. ~P B. ~Q
C. ~S D. ~T

Choose the *correct* answer from the options given below:

(1) A, B, C Only
(2) A, C, D Only
(3) A, B, D Only
(4) B, C, D Only

83. If a valid argument form is converted into a Statement form, then

A. Such a statement form must be a conditional statement
B. Such a statement form is always a tautology
C. The truth value of such statement form is indeterminate
D. In forming such a statement form conjunction must be used

Choose the *correct* answer from the options given below:

(1) A, B, D Only (2) A and B Only
(3) A, C, D Only
(4) A and C Only

84. Consider the following statements about Deductive systems

A. The method of 19 rules in Copi's method of deduction is incomplete minus the rule of Absorption.
B. 'Post Criterion' is criterion for consistency.
C. If an axiom is derivable as a theorem from some other axioms outside the given axiomatic system, such an axiom is definitely 'independent'.
D. All logistic systems are types of deductive system.

Choose the *correct* answer from the options given below:

(1) A, B, C Only
(2) B, C, D Only
(3) A, B, C, D Only
(4) A, B, D Only

85. The following is incorrect about Quantification Theory

(1) A proposition can be obtained from a propositional function by two processes- Instantiation and Generalization
(2) A singular proposition is a substitution instance of propositional functions
(3) Propositional functions are neither true nor false
(4) $(x)(\phi x) \neq \sim(\exists x) \sim(\phi x)$

86. Which of the following is correct regarding the methods of proving validity in Propositional Logic

A. The Rule of I.P. (Indirect Proof) could be used to prove the validity of argument form.

B. Reductio-Ad-Absurduni could be used to prove the inconsistency of premises.

C. The Rule of conditional proof could be used for only such Argument forms whose conclusion is a conditional statement.

D. The strengthened Rule of conditional proof permits any assumption of limited scope.

Choose the *correct* answer from the options given below:

(1) A, B, C only
(2) A, B, C and D
(3) B, C, D only
(4) A, C, D only

87. Which among the following is not an implication of the statement $\sim[(P \supset Q) \supset P]$

(1) $P \supset Q$ (2) P
(3) $Q \vee \sim P$ (4) ~P

88. According to Kate Millett's Sexual Politics, 'Patriarchy' has the following markers:

A. An Hierarchy Society
B. Sexual Oppression
C. Generational Oppression
D. Acceptance of Queer theory

Choose the *correct* answer from the options given below:

(1) A and B Only
(2) A and C Only
(3) B and D Only
(4) A, B and C Only

89. According to Peter Raabe, what is the key benefit of Philosophical Counseling?

(1) It provides quick solutions to mental health crisis
(2) It employs religious doctrines to guide individuals
(3) It enhances critical thinking and self-awareness
(4) It uses medication to treat psychological issue

90. The most-important distinction in the environmental movement is that of 'Shallow Ecology' and 'Deep Ecology' introduced by:

(1) David Ehrenfield
(2) Arne Naess
(3) William Morris
(4) Rachel Carson

The society of future falls less within the province of a Newtonian anthropology than a pragmatics of language particles. There are many different language games- a heterogeneity of elements. They only give rise to institutions in patches- local determinism. The decision makers, however, attempt to manage these clouds of sociality according to input' output matrices, following a logic which implies that their elements are commensurable and that the whole is determinable. They allocate our lives for the growth of power. In matters of social justice and of scientific truths alike, the legitimation of that power is based on its optimizing the system's performance-efficiency. The application of this criterion to all of our games necessarily entails a certain level of terror, whether soft or hard: be operational (i.e., commensurable) or disappear........ The operativity criterion is technological, it has no relevance for judging what is true or just. Is legitimacy to be found in consensus obtained through discussion..............? Such consensus does violence to the heterogeneity of language games. And invention is always born of dissension.

91. The passage seems to suggest that Newtonian anthropology is not

(1) Essentialist in character
(2) Structuralist in its analysis
(3) Holistic in its analysis
(4) Destabilizing in its analysis

92. The author seems not to be in opposition to:-

(1) Homogeneity of language games
(2) Universal Determinism
(3) Heterogeneity of language games
(4) Logic of maximum performance

93. The operativity criterion cannot be applied to:

A. Questions of Justice
B. Questions of Truth

C. Questions of Information Technology
D. Questions of Natural Science

Choose the *correct* answer from the options given below:

(1) A and B Only
(2) A, B and C Only
(3) A and C Only
(4) B and D Only

94. Consensus is deplorable because it:

A. involves violence
B. involves a neglect of actual language situation
C. is essential for creativity dissension
D. does not involve discussion

Choose the *correct* answer from the options given below:

(1) Only B and D
(2) A and B only
(3) B, C and D only
(4) A, B and C only

95. The passage seems to suggest that:

A. One should learn to celebrate incommensurability
B. One should be sensitive towards differences
C. A power structure undermines our systems
D. Consensus is necessary for creativity and invention

Choose the *correct* answer from the options given below:

(1) A, C and D only
(2) A, B and C only
(3) B, C and D only
(4) C Only

The philosophy of technology is a branch of philosophy that examines the nature, development and impacts of technology on society and human life, This field explores the ethical, social and existential questions raised by technological advancements and seeks to understand how technology shapes and is shaped by human values and practices.

One of the central themes in the philosophy of technology is the relationship between humans and technology. Philosophers debate whether technology' is a neutral tool that humans use to achieve their goals or it actively shapes human behavior and society. The instrumentalist view considers technology as a means to an end, emphasizing human control over technological tools. In contrast, the determinist perspective argues that technology has its own logic and momentum, significantly influencing human actions and social structures. Another critical aspect of the philosophy of technology is the ethical implications of technological innovation. For instance, the rise of Artificial Intelligence (AI) and Machine-learning raises questions about autonomy, responsibility and the potential for biased decision-making. The concept of technological mediation is also significant here, which refers to the ways in which technology influences human perception and interactions with the world. For instance, smartphone and social media platforms alter how people communicate, form relationships and perceive reality.

The philosophy of technology also addresses the notion of: technological utopianism and dystopianism. Utopian-views see technology as a force for positive charge. Dystopian perspectives, on the other hand, warn of potential dangers and negative consequences of unchecked technological advancements, such as loss of privacy, dehumanization and environmental degradation.

96. What is the central theme in the philosophy' of technology?

(1) The economic benefits of technological advancements
(2) The relationship between humans and technology
(3) The technical specifications of new technologies
(4) The market potential of emerging technologies

97. Which view considers technology as a neutral tool used to achieve human goals?

(1) Determinist view

(2) Instrumentalist view
(3) Utopian view
(4) Dystopian view

98. What ethical issues are raised by the rise of artificial intelligence (AI) and machine learning?
(1) The efficiency of production process
(2) The technological complexity of algorithms
(3) The potential for biased decision-making
(4) The cost of implementing AI systems

99. What does the concept of technological mediation refer to?
(1) The economic impact of technology on market
(2) The way technology influences human perception and interaction
(3) The process of developing new technological devices
(4) The technical specifications of communication networks

100. What do dystopian perspectives on technology warn about?
(1) The high cost of technological innovation.
(2) The potential dangers and negative consequences of unchecked technological advancement.
(3) The lack of technological progress in developing nations.
(4) The technical challenges of creating new technologies.

Answers

1. (1)	**2.** (2)	**3.** (2)	**4.** (1)	**5.** (2)	**6.** (1)	**7.** (4)	**8.** (3)	**9.** (4)	**10.** (4)
11. (4)	**12.** (4)	**13.** (4)	**14.** (1)	**15.** (4)	**16.** (4)	**17.** (4)	**18.** (2)	**19.** (3)	**20.** (3)
21. (2)	**22.** (2)	**23.** (2)	**24.** (2)	**25.** (4)	**26.** (2)	**27.** (1)	**28.** (2)	**29.** (1)	**30.** (4)
31. (3)	**32.** (3)	**33.** (2)	**34.** (1)	**35.** (2)	**36.** (1)	**37.** (3)	**38.** (3)	**39.** (2)	**40.** (1)
41. (2)	**42.** (3)	**43.** (2)	**44.** (3)	**45.** (3)	**46.** (1)	**47.** (2)	**48.** (2)	**49.** (1)	**50.** (4)
51. (4)	**52.** (1)	**53.** (4)	**54.** (3)	**55.** (1)	**56.** (4)	**57.** (1)	**58.** (2)	**59.** (4)	**60.** (3)
61. (1)	**62.** (2)	**63.** (1)	**64.** (3)	**65.** (3)	**66.** (1)	**67.** (2)	**68.** (4)	**69.** (2)	**70.** (3)
71. (4)	**72.** (4)	**73.** (4)	**74.** (4)	**75.** (4)	**76.** (3)	**77.** (3)	**78.** (3)	**79.** (4)	**80.** (3)
81. (2)	**82.** (3)	**83.** (2)	**84.** (4)	**85.** (4)	**86.** (2)	**87.** (2)	**88.** (4)	**89.** (3)	**90.** (2)
91. (4)	**92.** (3)	**93.** (1)	**94.** (2)	**95.** (2)	**96.** (2)	**97.** (2)	**98.** (3)	**99.** (2)	**100.** (2)